WHO'S WHO

IN PROPERTY

2004

Estates gazette

WHO'S WHO

IN PROPERTY

2004

Compiled by Estates Gazette Interactive (EG*i*)
Published by *Estates Gazette*
Divisions of Reed Business Information Ltd

Content: Debra Morgan, Anthony Denny
Production: Kate Ahira, Rozynna Fielding, Alison Henry
Design: Rebecca Hapted

First published 2002
This edition 2004

ISBN 0 7282 0430 4

Disclaimer
The information contained in this publication has been compiled by the EG*i* database team. While every effort has been made to avoid errors, such information is subject to continuous change. The publisher is therefore unable to guarantee the accuracy or completeness of the data provided, and cannot be held responsible for any errors or omissions.

Printed and bound by
Short Run Press Limited,
Bittern Road, Sowton Industrial Estates,
Exeter, Devon EX2 7LW

Foreword

Welcome to the third edition of a greatly expanded *Who's Who in Property*. This year, the now invaluable guide to senior individuals involved in commercial property in the UK has grown by 20% in size.

This is testimony to the usefulness of the book as a quick and handy way to discover the career details, contact information and interests of more than 3,400 men and women who work in the sector.

The 426 pages contain, once again, an A-Z of key directors and staff among property owners, developers and agents, along with investment fund managers and property finance house directors. Barristers from leading property chambers and solicitors from the major firms that specialise in the sector are, again, included too. There is also an index at the rear that allows readers to locate entries by company or partnership.

Those selected were drawn from the Who's Who database on EG*i*. This was supplemented by requesting lists of key personnel from a wide range of owners, agents and lawyers. Thanks, again, to all those who contributed. Your help is very much appreciated.

Much effort has gone into achieving accuracy. But if entrants find an error, please, let us know. If non-entrants feel that they should be included in the 2005 edition, also let us know. But, please, by email only, at whoswho@egi.co.uk.

Peter Bill
Editor, *Estates Gazette*

ABBOTTS, Timothy
CIT Group

Position
Asset management director
Qualifications
BSc Hons, Est Man; MRICS
Career history
1998 Joined Capital & Income Trust Group.
1994-98 Property director, Markborough Properties.
1989-94 Development surveyor, Rosehaugh
Professional memberships
RICS
Interests
Golf; sailing; skiing; sport
Contact details
CIT Group plc, 8-10 Bourdon Street, London W1K 3PD
Tel 020 7667 7766
Fax 020 7667 7770
Web www.cit.co.uk
Direct fax 020 7667 7763
Mobile 07775 944 853
Email ta@cit.co.uk

ABEL, John
Capital Shopping Centres

Position
Managing director
Qualifications
FRICS
Professional memberships
RICS
Contact details
Capital Shopping Centres plc, 40 Broadway, London SW1H 0BU
Tel 020 7887 4220
Fax 020 7887 4225
Web www.capital-shopping-centres.co.uk
Direct tel 020 7887 7057
Email john-abel@capshop.co.uk

ADAIR, Murray
Heron International

Position
Development director
Qualifications
BArch; BSc, Arch; MBA
Career history
2001 Joined Heron International.
1995-2001 Village Roadshow.
1993-95 Geoff Malone International
Professional memberships
Royal Incorporation of Architects in Scotland
Interests
Design; family; running
Contact details
Heron International, Heron House, 19 Marylebone Road, London NW1 5JP
Tel 020 7486 4477
Fax 020 7486 3349
Web www.heron-international.com
Direct fax 020 7299 9771
Email madair@heron.co.uk

ADAM, Robert
Robert Adam Architects

Position
Director
Qualifications
Dip Arch (PCL); RIBA; FRSA
Career history
1986 Founded Winchester Design (now Robert Adam Architects)
Other roles
Honorary secretary, RIBA (2001-03); councillor, RIBA; chairman, Design for Homes; founder/chairman, International Network of Traditional Building, Architecture & Urbanism
Professional memberships
Art Workers Guild; Royal Society of Arts
Contact details
Robert Adam Architects Ltd, 9 Upper High Street, Winchester SO23 8UT
Tel 0196 284 3843
Fax 0196 284 3303
Web www.robertadamarchitects.com
Email robert.adam@robertadamarchitects.com

ADAMS, Aubrey
FPDSavills

Position
Group chief executive
Qualifications
MA (Cantab); FRICS
Career history
1990 Joined Savills as finance director. Prior to that time spent at PWC and Peachey Property
Other roles
Non-executive director, Associated British Ports Holdings and Grosvenor Waterside; member, policy committee of BPF
Professional memberships
BPF; RICS
Interests
Opera
Contact details
FPDSavills Ltd, 20 Grosvenor Hill, London W1K 3HQ
Tel 020 7499 8644
Fax 020 7495 3773
Web www.fpdsavills.co.uk
Direct tel 020 7409 9921
Direct fax 020 7491 0505
Mobile 07870 555 858
Email aadams@fpdsavills.co.uk

ADAMS, Geoffrey
Rolfe Judd

Position
Managing director
Qualifications
Dip Arch; ARIBA
Career history
Since 1976 Architect, Rolfe Judd
Professional memberships
Architects Registration Board; Association of Consultant Architects; Europa Nostra; Institute of Directors; RIBA
Contact details
Rolfe Judd Ltd, Old Church Court, Claylands Road, London SW8 1NZ
Tel 020 7556 1500
Fax 020 7556 1501
Web www.rolfe-judd.co.uk
Email geoffa@rolfe-judd.co.uk

ADAMS, John
Drivers Jonas

Position
Partner – Manchester planning
Qualifications
BSc Hons; MRICS
Career history
1985 Joined Drivers Jonas
Professional memberships
RICS
Contact details
Drivers Jonas, 60 Fountain Street, Manchester M2 2FE
Tel 0161 839 9731
Fax 0161 834 3690
Web www.driversjonas.com
Direct tel 0161 827 7302
Email johnadams@driversjonas.com

A

ADAMS, Keith
Matthews & Goodman

Position
Partner
Qualifications
BSc; FRICS
Career history
Since 1982 Partner (valuation department), Matthews & Goodman
Professional memberships
Property Valuation Forum; RICS
Interests
Skiing; windsurfing
Contact details
Matthews & Goodman Ltd, Dorland House, 14-16 Regent Street, London SW1Y 4PH
Tel 020 7747 8847
Fax 020 7747 8848
Web www.matthews-goodman.co.uk
Email kadams@matthews-goodman.co.uk

ADAMS, Roy
Building Design Partnership

Position
Chief executive
Qualifications
BA; Dip TP
Career history
1984 Joined Building Design Partnership as Belfast office chairman; became London office chairman in 1990, then managing director of Paris office in 1993; chief executive since 1995
Professional memberships
RTPI
Interests
Art; football; rugby; running
Contact details
Building Design Partnership Ltd, 16 Brewhouse Yard, London EC1V 4LJ
Tel 020 7812 8000
Fax 020 7812 8399
Web www.bdp.co.uk
Email RA-Adams@bdp.co.uk

AGNEW, Julian
LaSalle Investment Management

Position
Senior director
Qualifications
MRICS
Career history
1987 Joined Jones Lang LaSalle; previously with Henry Butcher and Hall Pain & Foster
Interests
Beer; football; music
Contact details
LaSalle Investment Management, 33 Cavendish Square, London W1A 2NF
Tel 020 7852 4000
Fax 020 7852 4374
Web www.lasalle.com
Direct tel 020 7852 4383
Direct fax 020 7852 4416
Email julian.agnew@lasalle.com

AINSCOUGH, Bill
Langtree Group

Position
Chairman
Contact details
Langtree Group plc, Millfield Business Park, Millfield Lane, St Helens WA11 9UT
Tel 01942 717273
Fax 01942 721303
Web www.langtreegroup.co.uk
Email dswift@langtreegroupplc.co.uk

AITCHISON, Jeremy
Parlison Properties

Position
Director
Qualifications
BSc; MRICS
Career history
1993 Joined Parlison Properties.
1980-93 Director, Savills
Other roles
Director, Helvellyn Properties
Professional memberships
RICS
Interests
Fishing; motor sports; sailing; shooting; sport
Contact details
Parlison Properties Ltd, 94 Mount Street, London W1K 2SZ
Tel 020 7629 0586
Fax 020 7629 1713
Direct tel 020 7355 0134
Mobile 07774 264 855
Email jda@parlisonproperties.co.uk

AITCHISON, Neil
Aitchison Raffety

Position
Commercial managing director
Qualifications
BSc; FRICS
Career history
Since 1989 Commercial director/commercial managing director, Aitchison Raffety.
1974-89 Partner then managing partner, Aitchisons.
1972-74 Investment surveyor, Airways Pension Fund.
1970-72 Weatherall Green & Smith
Other roles
Vice-chairman, Sigma 38 Class Association
Professional memberships
Industrial Agents Society; Office Agents Society; Reading Real Estate Foundation; RICS
Interests
Golf; skiing; yachting
Contact details
Aitchison Raffety Ltd, 63-65 Marlowes, Hemel Hempstead HP1 1LE
Tel 01442 220800
Fax 01442 230114
Web www.argroup.co.uk
Email neil.aitchison@argroup.co.uk

AITKEN, Keith
CB Richard Ellis

Position
Senior director – head of Edinburgh office
Qualifications
BSc; MRICS
Career history
2002 Rejoined CB Hillier Parker (now CB Richard Ellis) as director.
2001-02 Development director, CALA Properties.
1994-2001 Director, CB Hillier Parker.
1991-94 Partner, Knight Frank
Professional memberships
RICS
Contact details
CB Richard Ellis, 7 Castle Street, Edinburgh EH2 3AH
Tel 0131 469 7666
Fax 0131 469 0131
Web www.cbre.com
Email keith.aitken@cbre.com

AKENHEAD, Robert
Atkin Chambers

Position
Barrister
Qualifications
LLB; QC
Career history
1973 Joined Atkin Chambers.
1972 Called to Bar
Other roles
Editor, *Building Law Reports*; contributor to *Building* magazine
Interests
Cricket; skiing; theatre
Contact details
Atkin Chambers (Chambers of John Blackburn QC), Atkin Buildings, 1 Gray's Inn, London WC1R 5AT
Tel 020 7404 0102

Fax 020 7405 7456
Web www.atkinchambers.com
Email clerks@atkinchambers.law.co.uk

AKERS, Richard
Land Securities Properties

Position
Head of retail portfolio management
Qualifications
MA; MRICS
Career history
1995 Joined Land Securities.
1989-95 Development surveyor, AMEC Developments.
1985-89 Development surveyor, ARC Properties
Professional memberships
RICS; British Council of Shopping Centres (affiliate member)
Interests
Golf; tennis
Contact details
Land Securities Properties Ltd, 5 Strand, London WC2N 5AF
Tel 020 7413 9000
Fax 020 7925 0202
Web www.landsecurities.com
Direct tel 020 7024 5438
Direct fax 020 7024 5006
Email richard.akers@landsecurities.com

AKSELSON, Daniel
International Real Estate

Position
Chief executive
Career history
2001 Joined International Real Estate as chief executive
Contact details
International Real Estate plc, 34 St James's Street, London SW1A 1HD
Tel 020 7839 8686
Fax 020 7839 7474
Web www.ireplc.com
Email Daniel@ireplc.com

ALDOUS, Grahame
9 Gough Square

Position
Barrister
Qualifications
LLB
Career history
1979 Called to Bar
Professional memberships
Administrative Law Bar Association; London Common Law & Commercial Bar Association; Professional Negligence Bar Association
Contact details
9 Gough Square (Chambers of John Foy QC), London EC4A 3DE
Tel 020 7832 0500
Fax 020 7353 1344
Web www.9goughsquare.co.uk
Email galdous@9goughsq.co.uk

ALDRICH, Phillippa
Fox Williams

Position
Partner – head of property
Qualifications
Solicitor
Career history
1989 Joined Fox Williams after training at Oppenheimers and Denton Hall; became partner in 2001.
1989 Admitted to Roll of Solicitors
Other roles
Member, City of London Law Society land law subcommittee
Contact details
Fox Williams, 10-14 Dominion Street, London EC2M 2RL
Tel 020 7628 2000
Fax 020 7628 2100
Web www.foxwilliams.com
Direct tel 020 7614 2513
Direct fax 020 7614 1413
Email phaldrich@foxwilliams.com

ALESBURY, Alun
2 Mitre Court Buildings

Position
Barrister
Qualifications
MA, Law
Career history
1974 Called to Bar
Professional memberships
Administrative Law Bar Association; Parliamentary Bar Mess; Planning & Environment Bar Association
Contact details
2 Mitre Court Buildings (Chambers of Guy Roots QC), 2nd Floor, London EC4Y 7BX
Tel 020 7583 1380
Fax 020 7353 7772
Web www.2mcb.co.uk
Email alun.alesbury@2mcb.co.uk

ALEXANDER, Richard
Dunphys

Position
Director – property development
Contact details
Dunphys, York House, Montague Road, London TW3 1JZ
Tel 020 8577 5172
Fax 020 8577 2219
Web www.dunphys.cpd.co.uk
Email richard.alexander@dunphys.co.uk

ALFRED, Fiona
Women in Property

Position
National administrator
Contact details
Women in Property, 24 St Anns Villas, London W11 4RS
Tel 020 7603 4746
Fax 020 7603 2818
Web www.wipnet.org
Email f.alfred@btinternet.com

ALLAN, Mark
UNITE Group

Position
Group finance director
Career history
1999 Joined UNITE after qualifying as chartered accountant with KPMG
Contact details
UNITE Group plc, The Tower Building, 11 York Road, London SE1 7NQ
Tel 020 7902 5050
Fax 020 7902 5051
Web www.unite-group.com
Email mark.allan@unite-group.co.uk

ALLAN, Simon
Berwin Leighton Paisner

Position
Departmental managing partner – head of finance
Career history
1988 Joined Berwin Leighton (now Berwin Leighton Paisner) as partner.
1981-88 Ashurst Morris Crisp.
1979-81 Kenneth Turner Brown.
1979 Admitted to Roll of Solicitors
Other roles
Writes and lectures widely on PFI
Interests
Ballet; music; opera; reading; languages (fluent in French, Spanish and Italian)
Contact details
Berwin Leighton Paisner Ltd, Adelaide House, London Bridge, London EC4R 9HA
Tel 020 7760 1000
Fax 020 7760 1111
Web www.berwinleighton.com
Email simon.allan@blplaw.com

A

ALLEN, Barry
FPDSavills

Position
Director – head of office, Birmingham
Qualifications
MA (Cantab); MRICS
Career history
Since 1998 Director, FPDSavills.
1993-98 Director, DTZ Debenham Thorpe.
1989-93 Director, Debenham Tewson Chesshire.
1980-88 Chesshire Gibson
Other roles
Member, Birmingham City 2000; advisory board member, Locate in Birmingham
Professional memberships
RICS
Interests
Cricket; golf; music; rugby; theatre
Contact details
FPDSavills Ltd, Caxton House, 1 Fore Street, Birmingham B2 5ER
Tel 0121 633 3733
Fax 0121 633 3666
Web www.fpdsavills.co.uk
Direct tel 0121 634 8411
Mobile 07870 555 702
Email ballen@fpdsavills.co.uk

ALLEN, Josephine
Frogmore Developments

Position
Director – leasing
Qualifications
BSc, Val & Est Man; MRICS
Career history
1994 Joined Frogmore.
1988-94 Richard Ellis
Professional memberships
RICS
Interests
Diving/scuba diving; DIY; food; keep fit; theatre
Contact details
Frogmore Developments Ltd, 11-15 Wigmore Street, London W1A 2JZ
Tel 020 7016 6000
Fax 020 7495 5321
Web www.frogmore.co.uk
Email heatherbest@frogmore.co.uk

ALLEN, Martin
DMH

Position
Senior property litigation partner
Career history
1972 Admitted to Roll of Solicitors.
1970 Joined DMH; appointed head of litigation department in 1982, was then head of commercial property 1992-2001; now senior property litigation partner
Other roles
Director, Gardner Arts Centre (theatre and gallery); member, University of Sussex career development forum; regular speaker on property-related subjects
Professional memberships
Property Litigation Association
Contact details
DMH, 100 Queens Road, Brighton BN1 3YB
Tel 01273 329833
Fax 01273 747500
Web www.dmh.co.uk
Direct tel 01273 744324
Direct fax 01273 729599
Email martin.allen@dmh.co.uk

ALLEN, Peter
Westfield Shoppingtowns

Position
Director – Europe
Professional memberships
British Council of Shopping Centres; BPF; British Retail Consortium; International Council of Shopping Centers; Urban Land Institute
Contact details
Westfield Shoppingtowns Ltd, MidCity Place, 58-71 High Holborn, London WC1R 4DP
Tel 020 7734 2121
Fax 020 7734 6545
Web www.westfield.com
Direct fax 020 7292 3148
Email peter.allen@westfield-uk.com

ALLIES, Bob
Allies & Morrison

Position
Partner
Qualifications
MA; Dip Arch (Edinburgh)
Career history
1983 Formed partnership with Graham Morrison
Other roles
Lecturer, University of Cambridge (1989-92); visiting professor, University of Edinburgh (1995); Kea distinguished professor, University of Maryland (1999); visiting professor, University of Bath (1996-99)
Professional memberships
RIBA; Royal Society of Arts
Contact details
Allies & Morrison, 85 Southwark Street, London SE1 0HX
Tel 020 7921 0100
Fax 020 7921 0101
Web www.alliesandmorrison.co.uk
Direct tel 020 7921 0241
Email boballies@alliesandmorrison.co.uk

ALLISON, Charles
Nelson Bakewell

Position
Director – investment consulting
Qualifications
BSc; MRICS
Career history
Since 1983 Director, Nelson Bakewell.
1977-83 Jones Lang Wootton
Professional memberships
RICS
Contact details
Nelson Bakewell Ltd, 25 Sackville Street, London W1S 3HQ
Tel 020 7544 2000
Fax 020 7544 2222
Web www.nelson-bakewell.com
Direct tel 020 7544 2255
Email callison@nelson-bakewell.com

ALLSOP, Christopher
Helaba (Landesbank Hessen-Thüringen)

Position
Deputy director – property finance
Qualifications
MBA; FRICS
Career history
1998-2000 Senior manager (commercial property finance), Halifax.
1990-98 Manager (property finance), Hongkong & Shanghai Banking Corp.
1989-90 Associate director, Electra Property Finance.
1982-89 Vice-president, Manufacturers Hanover Trust (became Chase Manhattan).
1980-82 Controller, ICFC (became 3i)
Professional memberships
RICS
Interests
Sailing (Little Ship Club); skiing (Kandahar Ski Club)
Contact details
Helaba (Landesbank Hessen-Thüringen), 11 Ironmonger Lane, London EC2V 8JN
Tel 020 7334 4500
Fax 020 7334 4534
Web www.helaba.de
Direct tel 020 7334 4539
Direct fax 020 7334 4502
Mobile 07798 666 702
Email christopher.allsop@helaba.de

ALSTON, Stephen
Ahli United Bank (UK)

Position
Head of property finance
Qualifications
BA Hons, Business Studies
Career history
1991 Joined United Bank of Kuwait (now Ahli United Bank (UK)); appointed head of property finance in 1994.
1984-90 Security Pacific/Bank America and First Interstate Bank of California
Professional memberships
Investment Property Forum
Contact details
Ahli United Bank (UK) plc, 7 Baker Street, London W1U 8EG
Tel 020 7487 6500
Fax 020 7487 6402
Web www.ahliunited.com
Direct tel 020 7487 6933
Mobile 07887 830 606
Email stephen.alston@ahliunited.com

AMEY, Julian
Chartered Institution of Building Services Engineers

Position
Chief executive
Qualifications
BA; MA
Career history
1996-2001 Director-general, Canning House.
1994-96 International adviser, DTI.
1989-94 Executive director, BBC World Service.
1972-89 International marketing director, Longman Group
Interests
Music; tennis
Contact details
Chartered Institution of Building Services Engineers, Delta House, 222 Balham High Street, London SW12 9BS
Tel 020 8675 5211
Fax 020 8675 5449
Web www.cibse.org
Email jamey@cibse.org

AMOS, Gideon
Town & Country Planning Association

Position
Director
Qualifications
MA; RIBA
Career history
2000 Joined TCPA as director
Professional memberships
RIBA
Contact details
Town & Country Planning Association, 17 Carlton House Terrace, London SW1Y 5AH
Tel 020 7930 8903
Fax 020 7930 3280
Email tcpa@tcpa.org.uk

AMOS, Terry
Barwood Developments

Position
Director and company secretary
Contact details
Barwood Developments Ltd, The Grange, Warren Office Village, Milton Keynes MK12 5NE
Tel 01908 577600
Fax 01908 312017
Web www.barwood.co.uk
Direct tel 01908 577602
Mobile 07715 577602
Email terry.amos@barwood.co.uk

ANDERSON, John
Burford Group

Position
Chief executive
Contact details
Burford Group Ltd, 20 Thayer Street, London W1U 2DD
Tel 020 7224 2240
Fax 020 7224 1710
Email john.anderson@burfordgroup.com

ANDERSON, John
Chelsfield

Position
Director
Qualifications
FCIOB
Career history
2003 Joined Chelsfield as director.
2000-03 Director, Land Securities Properties.
1993-2000 Managing director, Bovis Construction; also managing director of Bovis Europe 1996-2000 and joint managing director of Bovis Construction Group 1997-2000.
1991-93 Managing director, Property Services Agency, on secondment to government.
1984-99 P&O: managing director of P&O Developments and director of Chelsea Harbour 1984-92; director, P&O Property Holdings from 1985
Other roles
Director, British Council for Offices (since 1996); non-executive director, Maxxiom (since 1997)
Professional memberships
British Council for Offices
Interests
Ballet; gardening; golf (West Surrey Golf Club); opera; RAC; rugby; skiing; socialising; theatre
Contact details
Chelsfield plc, 67 Brook Street, London W1K 4NJ
Tel 020 7493 3977
Fax 020 7493 1444
Web www.chelsfield.com
Mobile 07885 270 098
Email johnanderson@chelsfield.com

ANDERSON, Mark
Hamptons International

Position
Regional director
Contact details
Hamptons International, West Lodge, Station Approach, West Byfleet KT14 6NZ
Tel 01932 353077
Fax 01932 353369
Web www.hamptons.co.uk
Email andersonm@hamptons-int.com

ANDERSON, Miles
English Partnerships

Position
Director – asset transfer
Qualifications
FRICS
Contact details
English Partnerships, Arpley House, 110 Birchwood Boulevard, Warrington WA3 7QH
Tel 01925 651144
Fax 01925 411493
Web www.englishpartnerships.co.uk
Direct tel 01925 644616
Direct fax 01925 644627
Email milesanderson@englishpartnerships.co.uk

ANDERSON, Stuart
Marks & Spencer Group

Position
Head of property acquisition
Contact details
Marks & Spencer Group plc, Michael House, 37-67 Baker Street, London W1U 8EP
Tel 020 7935 4422
Fax 020 7268 2941
Web www.marksandspencer.com
Direct tel 020 7268 3409
Mobile 07879 432307
Email stuart.anderson@marks-and-spencer.com

A

ANDREW, Anthony
Scottish Executive

Position
Chief estates adviser
Qualifications
MA, Land Econ; FRICS
Career history
Since 1999 Head of land and property/chief estates adviser, Scottish Executive.
1989-99 Scottish Office: principal estates officer, then branch head in land use and conservation division; chief estates officer from 1996.
1981-89 Valuation Office.
1978-81 Lecturer, Aberdeen University
Other roles
RICS Scottish council member; RICS Scottish valuation faculty board member; surveying education forum member, RICS in Scotland; Scottish Funding Councils for Further & Higher Education property and capital investment committee member (2003); management committee member, Castle Rock Housing Association; editorial advisory board member, *Journal of Facilities Management*; external examiner (estate management), Heriot-Watt University (1999-2003) and Napier University (2003); editor of planning and valuation sections, *Greens Scottish Surveyors Factbook*
Professional memberships
RICS
Interests
Art; fishing; reading
Contact details
Scottish Executive, Saughton House, Broomhouse Drive, Edinburgh EH11 3XD
Tel 0131 556 8400
Direct tel 0131 244 4521
Direct fax 0131 244 4529
Email anthony.andrew@scotland.gsi.gov.uk

ANDREW, James
Cannons Group

Position
Group property director
Qualifications
MRICS
Career history
1997-2000 Head of acquisition and development, Pizza Hut UK.
1995-97 Partner (out-of-town retail and leisure), Donaldsons.
1990-95 Surveyor (consultancy/out-of-town retail), Angermann Goddard & Loyd
Other roles
Director, Economic Properties; director, Investra; director, DTEC
Professional memberships
ISVA; RICS
Contact details
Cannons Group Ltd, Cannons House, 40-44 Coombe Road, New Malden KT3 4QF
Tel 020 8336 2288
Fax 020 8336 1638
Direct tel 020 8336 8317
Direct fax 020 8336 8300
Email james.andrew@cannons.co.uk

ANDREWS, Donald
Degussa UK Holdings

Position
Managing director
Qualifications
MBA; MPhil; BSc; MRICS
Career history
1987 Joined Degussa UK Holdings (formerly Laporte)
Professional memberships
RICS
Contact details
Degussa UK Holdings Ltd, 42 Brook Street, London W1K 5DB
Tel 020 7958 9089
Web www.degussa.com/en
Email donald.andrews@degussa.com

ANDREWS, Jamie
Threadneedle Property Investments

Position
Portfolio asset manager
Qualifications
Dip Prop Inv; FRICS
Professional memberships
Investment Property Forum; RICS
Interests
Cricket; golf; rugby; sailing
Contact details
Threadneedle Property Investments, 9-15 Sackville Street, London W1A 2JP
Tel 020 7437 8000
Fax 020 7464 5811
Direct tel 020 7464 5889
Direct fax 020 7464 5811
Mobile 0777 417 8432
Email jamie.andrews@threadneedle.co.uk

ANDREWS, John
Edinburgh House Estates

Position
Finance director
Career history
2000-03 Financial controller, BAA Lynton.
1994-99 Deputy finance director, BAA McArthur Glen.
1990-94 Financial accountant, Lynton.
1984-90 Balfour Beatty: including chief accountant for three years on Crystal Palace Hotel project in Nassau, Bahamas
Interests
Food; golf; rugby; sailing; wine
Contact details
Edinburgh House Estates Ltd, 25 Gosfield Street, London W1W 6HQ
Tel 020 7307 9635
Fax 020 7307 9631
Direct tel 020 7291 3465
Mobile 07771 513019
Email john@ehel.co.uk

ANDREWS, Mike
Brixton Investments

Position
Senior director – joint ventures
Qualifications
MRICS
Contact details
Brixton Investments Ltd, 50 Berkeley Street, London W1J 8BX
Tel 020 7399 4500
Fax 020 7399 4550
Web www.brixton.plc.uk
Direct tel 020 7399 4518
Email mikeandrews@brixton.plc.uk

ANDREWS, Will
King Sturge

Position
Partner – investment
Qualifications
BSc; MRICS
Career history
1993 Joined King Sturge
Professional memberships
RICS
Contact details
King Sturge, 7 Stratford Place, London W1C 1ST
Tel 020 7493 4933
Fax 020 7409 0469
Web www.kingsturge.com
Direct tel 020 7318 4226
Email will.andrews@kingsturge.co.uk

ANGEL, Martin
Allsop & Co

Position
Partner – head of residential valuations
Qualifications
FRICS
Career history
1985 Joined Allsop & Co; appointed associate partner in 1987 and equity partner in 1989.

1979-85 Residential valuer, Chestertons
Other roles
Director, Allsop Investments; member, RICS appraisal and valuation standards board
Interests
Boating; cars; music; swimming
Contact details
Allsop & Co, 100 Knightsbridge, London SW1X 7LB
Tel 020 7437 6977
Fax 020 7344 2640
Web www.allsop.co.uk
Direct tel 020 7344 2606
Mobile 07768 152 380
Email martin.angel@allsop.co.uk

ANGELL-JAMES, Henry
FPDSavills
Position
Director
Qualifications
MA; MRICS
Career history
1984 Joined FPDSavills
Professional memberships
RICS
Interests
Art; farming; outdoor pursuits; rugby
Contact details
FPDSavills Ltd, 20 Grosvenor Hill, London W1K 3HQ
Tel 020 7499 8644
Fax 020 7495 3773
Web www.fpdsavills.co.uk
Direct tel 020 7409 8846
Mobile 07870 555 700
Email hangell-james@fpdsavills.co.uk

ANKERS, Neil
Hampton Trust
Position
Managing director
Contact details
Hampton Trust plc, 121 Mount Street, London W1K 3NW
Tel 020 7499 4994
Fax 020 7629 6996
Email nankers@hamptontrust.co.uk

APPLETON, Mark
Boyes Turner
Position
Partner – head of property group
Qualifications
Dip Landlord & Tenant; BA, Law
Career history
1997 Joined Boyes Turner as associate; made partner in 1999.
1993-97 Speechly Bircham.
1992-93 Dibb Lupton Broomhead.
1987-92 Speechly Bircham/Woodham Smith.
1985-87 Jaques & Lewis.
1985 Admitted to Roll of Solicitors
Professional memberships
Law Society
Interests
DIY; family; gardening; skiing
Contact details
Boyes Turner, Abbots House, Abbey Street, Reading RG1 3BD
Tel 0118 959 7711
Fax 0118 957 3257
Web www.boyesturnerlegal.co.uk
Direct tel 0118 952 7246
Direct fax 0118 952 7272
Email mappleton@boyesturner.com

APPLETON, Mike
English Partnerships
Position
Regeneration and planning director
Qualifications
BA Hons; FRSA
Career history
1990 Rejoined English Partnerships.
1996-2000 Director, AMEC Developments.
1993-96 Development director, English Partnerships.
1990-93 Director, English Estates
Other roles
Board member, Liverpool Vision, Sheffield One and New East Manchester
Interests
Family; socialising; travel; walking; RAC; Royal Society of Arts
Contact details
English Partnerships, 110 Buckingham Palace Road, London SW1W 9SA
Tel 020 7881 1600
Fax 020 7730 9162
Web www.englishpartnerships.co.uk
Direct tel 01925 644718
Direct fax 01925 644792
Email mikeappleton@englishpartnerships.co.uk

ARCHER, Ian
Aitchison Raffety
Position
Associate
Qualifications
MRICS
Career history
1988 Joined Aitchison Raffety. Previously at Valuation Office
Professional memberships
RICS
Interests
Golf; sailing
Contact details
Aitchison Raffety Ltd, 63-65 Marlowes, Hemel Hempstead HP1 1LE
Tel 01442 220800
Fax 01442 230114
Web www.argroup.co.uk
Email ian.archer@argroup.co.uk

ARDING, Clive
CB Richard Ellis
Position
Chairman – City business
Qualifications
FRICS
Career history
1964 Joined Insignia Richard Ellis (now CB Richard Ellis)
Professional memberships
British Council for Offices; City Architects Forum; RICS; Worshipful Company of Chartered Surveyors
Contact details
CB Richard Ellis, St Martin's Court, 10 Paternoster Row, London EC4M 7HP
Tel 020 7182 2000
Fax 020 7182 2001
Web www.cbre.com
Email clive.arding@cbre.com

ARDLEY, Philip
GVA Grimley
Position
Partner
Qualifications
FRICS
Career history
1991 Joined GVA Grimley.
1965-91 Vigers
Professional memberships
British Council of Shopping Centres; RICS
Interests
Architecture; golf; skiing
Contact details
GVA Grimley, University Gate, Park Row, Bristol BS1 5UB
Tel 0870 900 8990
Fax 0117 926 0607
Web www.gvagrimley.co.uk
Direct tel 0117 988 5316
Mobile 07771 553 977
Email philip.ardley@gvagrimley.co.uk

A

ARKLEY, Ken
Hand Picked Hotels

Position
Asset management director
Qualifications
BSc Hons; FHCIMA
Career history
2001 Joined Hand Picked Hotels.
1989-2001 Property director, Thistle Hotels.
1979-89 Development director (hotels), Scottish & Newcastle
Professional memberships
Hotel & Catering International Management
Interests
Gardening; rugby; walking
Contact details
Hand Picked Hotels Ltd, The Old Library, The Drive, Sevenoaks TN13 3AB
Tel 0173 247 1000
Fax 0173 247 1001
Web www.handpicked.co.uk
Direct tel 0173 247 1034
Email karkley@handpicked.co.uk

ARKUSH, Jonathan
11 Stone Buildings

Position
Barrister
Qualifications
MA (Oxon)
Career history
1977 Called to Bar
Other roles
Qualified mediator and member of mediation panels of Property Bar Association, Association of Contentious Trust & Probate and Dispute Mediation; author of landlord and tenant disputes chapter in *ADR & Commercial Disputes* (Sweet & Maxwell); deputy master, Chancery Division
Professional memberships
Association of Contentious Trust & Probate Specialists; Chancery Bar Association; Property Bar Association; Commercial Bar Association
Interests
Travel; walking
Contact details
11 Stone Buildings, Lincoln's Inn, London WC2A 3TG
Tel 020 7831 6381
Fax 020 7831 2575
Web www.11stonebuildings.com
Email arkush@11stonebuildings.com

ARMITAGE, Stephen
Dunlop Heywood Lorenz

Position
Director
Qualifications
FRICS
Career history
Since 1982 Director, Dunlop Heywood (now Dunlop Heywood Lorenz).
1978-82 Negotiator, Edward Rushton Son & Kenyon.
1976-78 Valuer, Greater Manchester Council
Other roles
Governor, Micklefield School, Reigate
Professional memberships
RICS
Contact details
Dunlop Heywood Lorenz Ltd, 10 Queen Anne Street, London W1G 9LH
Tel 020 7636 7000
Fax 020 7636 7002
Web www.dhlproperty.co.uk
Mobile 07970 225 042
Email sha@dhlproperty.co.uk

ARMON-JONES, Christopher
Drivers Jonas

Position
Chairman
Qualifications
FRICS
Career history
1971 Joined Drivers Jonas; appointed partner in 1980, group head (agency, development and investment) in 1987, managing partner in 1991, deputy chairman in 1999 and chairman in 2001.
1969-71 Prudential Assurance Co
Other roles
Chairman, Drivers Jonas Financial Services; council member, BPF; non-executive director, Economics Research Associates (US associate company of Drivers Jonas in leisure sector)
Professional memberships
RICS
Contact details
Drivers Jonas, 54-56 avenue Hoche, Paris
Tel +33 1 56 60 58 33
Fax +33 1 56 60 55 35
Web www.driversjonas.com
Direct tel +33 1 56 60 51 81
Mobile 07785 398 718
Email chrisarmon-jones@driversjonas.com

ARMSTRONG, John 'Louis'
Royal Institution of Chartered Surveyors

Position
Chief executive
Qualifications
CBE; MA; Barrister; FCMI; FRSA
Career history
1964-98 Royal Navy
Professional memberships
Honourable Society of the Middle Temple; Institute of Directors; Institute of Management Consultants; Royal Society of Arts
Interests
Art; music; opera; tennis
Contact details
Royal Institution of Chartered Surveyors, 12 Great George Street, London SW1P 3AE
Tel 020 7222 7000
Fax 020 7222 5074
Web www.rics.org
Direct tel 020 7334 3707
Direct fax 020 7222 5074
Email chiefexec@rics.org

ARNOLD, Mike
PricewaterhouseCoopers

Position
Partner – tax
Qualifications
CTA (Fellow)
Career history
1994 Joined Price Waterhouse (specialising in real estate and financial services) from HM Customs & Excise (specialising in VAT and property and insurance, responsible for the affairs of major property groups)
Other roles
Indirect taxes subcommittee member, Chartered Institute of Taxation; national chairman, VAT Practitioners Group; adviser to VAT committee of BPF; member of land and property liaison group (with HM Customs & Excise) representing Chartered Institute of Taxation
Professional memberships
Chartered Institute of Taxation
Interests
Gardening; photography; railways
Contact details
PricewaterhouseCoopers, Southwark Towers, 32 London Bridge Street, London SE1 9AE
Tel 020 7583 5000
Web www.pwc.com
Direct tel 020 7804 2115
Direct fax 020 7804 2888
Mobile 07808 323094
Email mike.arnold@uk.pwc.com

ARROWSMITH, Simon
Martineau Johnson

Position
Head of property department
Contact details
Martineau Johnson Ltd, St Philips House, St Philips Place, Birmingham B3 2PP
Tel 0121 200 3300

A

Fax 0121 200 3330
Web www.martineau-johnson.co.uk
Direct tel 0121 678 1313
Direct fax 0121 625 2661
Email simon.arrowsmith@martjohn.com

ASH, Brian
4-5 Gray's Inn Square

Position
Barrister
Qualifications
QC
Professional memberships
Planning & Environment Bar Association
Contact details
4-5 Gray's Inn Square (Chambers of Elizabeth Appleby QC & Timothy Straker QC), London WC1R 5AH
Tel 020 7404 5252
Fax 020 7242 7803
Web www.4-5graysinnsquare.co.uk
Email clerks@4-5graysinnsquare.co.uk

ASHBY, Jane
Aitchison Raffety

Position
Associate director
Qualifications
BSc Hons; MRICS
Contact details
Aitchison Raffety Ltd, Clifford House, 15 Clifford Street, London W1S 4JY
Tel 020 7851 6950
Fax 020 7851 6953
Web www.argroup.co.uk
Email jane.ashby@argroup.co.uk

ASHBY, Richard
Warnford Investments

Position
Managing director
Qualifications
MSc; BSc, Eng; ARSM; FRICS
Career history
1988-96 Director of estates, Reed Elsevier (UK).
1983-88 Property manager, British Alcan Aluminium.
1978-83 Estates surveyor, Marley Tile Co.
1973-78 Deputy group estates manager, Tarmac
Professional memberships
RICS
Contact details
Warnford Investments Ltd, Salisbury House, London Wall, London EC2M 5RQ
Tel 020 7588 6856
Fax 020 7638 2381
Email administrator@warnford.co.uk

ASHCROFT, Jonathan
Morley Fund Management

Position
Fund manager – South East regional offices
Contact details
Morley Fund Management Ltd, 34-36 Lime Street, London EC3M 7JE
Tel 020 7809 6000
Fax 020 7489 7940
Web www.morleyfm.com
Email jonathan.ashcroft@morleyfm.com

ASHENDEN, Andrew
Howard De Walden Estates

Position
Chief executive
Qualifications
BSc; FRICS
Professional memberships
RICS
Contact details
Howard De Walden Estates Ltd, 23 Queen Anne Street, London W1G 9DL
Tel 020 7580 3163
Fax 020 7436 8152
Web www.hdwe.co.uk
Email brenda.levey@hdwe.co.uk

ASHLEY-BROWN, Michael
Canary Wharf Group

Position
Group legal counsel
Qualifications
Solicitor
Career history
Since 1993 Group legal counsel, Canary Wharf Group
Other roles
Policy committee member and general council member, BPF
Interests
Motor sports; skiing; Oriental Club
Contact details
Canary Wharf Group plc, One Canada Square, London E14 5AB
Tel 020 7418 2000
Fax 020 7418 2222
Web www.canarywharf.com
Direct tel 020 7418 2367
Direct fax 020 7418 2195
Email michael.ashley-brown@canarywharf.com

ASHMEAD, Robert
House Builders Federation

Position
Chief executive
Qualifications
LLB; MBA
Professional memberships
Institute of Directors
Interests
Motorcycling; sailing
Contact details
House Builders Federation Ltd, 56-64 Leonard Street, London EC2A 4JX
Tel 020 7608 5100
Fax 020 7608 5101
Web www.new-homes.co.uk
Email hbf@hbf.co.uk

ASHTON, Mark
ISIS Property Asset Management

Position
Director – property funds
Qualifications
Dip TP; BSc Hons; Dip Prop Inv; MRICS
Career history
1990 Joined ISIS Property Asset Management (formerly property division of Royal SunAlliance).
1987-90 GVA Grimley.
1985-86 Valuation Office
Professional memberships
British Council of Shopping Centres; Investment Property Forum; RICS
Contact details
ISIS Property Asset Management plc, 100 Wood Street, London EC2V 7AN
Tel 020 7506 1100
Fax 020 7600 4180
Web www.isisam.com
Direct tel 020 7506 1249
Email mark.ashton@isisam.com

ASHWORTH, Robert
Pannone & Partners

Position
Partner
Career history
1989 Joined Pannone & Partners.
1984-89 Joynson-Hicks.
1984 Admitted to Roll of Solicitors
Other roles
Independent member of standards committee, Peak District National Park Authority
Interests
Golf; sailing; walking
Contact details
Pannone & Partners, 123 Deansgate, Manchester M3 2BU
Tel 0161 909 3000
Fax 0161 909 4444
Web www.pannone.com
Email robert.ashworth@pannone.co.uk

A

ASLIN, Nigel
Strutt & Parker

Position
Head of corporate real estate consultancy
Qualifications
FRICS
Career history
1971 Joined Strutt & Parker
Professional memberships
CoreNet Global UK; RICS
Interests
Marathon running; skiing; travel
Contact details
Strutt & Parker, 100 Longwater Avenue, Reading RG2 6GP
Tel 0118 945 0333
Fax 0118 945 0492
Web www.struttandparker.com
Direct tel 0118 945 0485
Mobile 07831 317 469
Email naslin@struttandparker.com

ASPLAND-ROBINSON, Richard
Marylebone Warwick Balfour Group

Position
Group acquisitions director
Qualifications
BSc Hons; MRICS
Career history
1998-2001 Director, Prestbury.
1996-98 Director, Marylebone Warwick Balfour Group.
1994-96 Partner, Richard Ellis.
1991-94 Director, Aspland Boyer
Other roles
Development director, MWB Business Exchange
Professional memberships
RICS
Contact details
Marylebone Warwick Balfour Group plc, 1 West Garden Place, London W2 2AQ
Tel 020 7706 2121
Fax 020 7706 8181
Web www.mwb.co.uk
Email rarobinson@mwb.co.uk

ASSON, Tim
Nelson Bakewell

Position
Director – head of corporate real estate
Qualifications
BSc; MRICS
Career history
1988 Joined Nelson Bakewell as associate; became director in 1993.
1984-88 Associate, J Trevor & Son.
1981-84 Gerald Eve
Other roles
Contributor to Henry Stewart, RICS and SMI conferences
Professional memberships
CoreNet Global UK; RICS
Interests
Jazz
Contact details
Nelson Bakewell Ltd, 25 Sackville Street, London W1S 3HQ
Tel 020 7544 2000
Fax 020 7544 2222
Web www.nelson-bakewell.com
Direct tel 020 7544 2288
Direct fax 020 7544 2125
Mobile 07768 104161
Email tasson@nelson-bakewell.com

AUTERAC, Richard
Jones Lang LaSalle

Position
European director – investment
Qualifications
BSc; FRICS
Career history
1980 Joined Jones Lang LaSalle as auctioneer and European director (capital markets)
Other roles
Chairman, RICS real estate auction group
Professional memberships
Investment Property Forum
Contact details
Jones Lang LaSalle Ltd, 22 Hanover Square, London W1A 2BN
Tel 020 7493 6040
Fax 020 7408 0220
Web www.joneslanglasalle.com
Direct tel 020 7399 5300
Direct fax 020 7399 5637
Mobile 07836 742833
Email richard.auterac@eu.joneslanglasalle.com

AVERY, Suzanne
Royal Bank of Scotland

Position
Head of property – corporate banking, London
Qualifications
BA Hons; ACIB
Professional memberships
Association of Property Bankers
Contact details
Royal Bank of Scotland, 280 Bishopsgate, London EC2M 4RB
Tel 020 7833 2121
Web www.rbs.co.uk
Direct tel 020 7672 0960
Email suzanne.avery@rbs.co.uk

AXFORD, Dr Nicholas
CB Richard Ellis

Position
Senior director – EMEA research and consulting
Qualifications
BSc; PhD; Dip Surv
Career history
1994 Joined CB Hillier Parker (now CB Richard Ellis); appointed director in 1998, head of research in 1999 and senior director (EMEA research and consulting) in 2003.
1990-94 Senior research analyst, Gerald Eve
Contact details
CB Richard Ellis, Kingsley House, 1a Wimpole Street, London W1G 0RE
Tel 020 7182 2000
Fax 020 7182 7001
Web www.cbre.com
Direct tel 020 7882 8307
Direct fax 020 7409 3016
Email nick.axford@cbre.com

AYRE, Tim
White Rock Properties

Position
Director
Qualifications
BSc Hons; MRICS
Career history
1987-2002 Investment director, Chartwell Land.
1984-87 Senior regional surveyor, Royal Insurance.
1982-84 Development surveyor, Abacus Developments
Professional memberships
Investment Property Forum; RICS
Contact details
White Rock Properties, Grafton House, 2-3 Golden Square, London W1F 9HR
Tel 020 7439 4438
Fax 020 7439 4483
Web www.whiterockproperties.co.uk
Direct tel 020 7439 4452
Mobile 07836 744 181
Email ta@whiterockproperties.co.uk

BABB, Peter
Manchester City Council

Position
Head of planning

Qualifications
BA Hons; MRTPI

Career history
1993 Joined Manchester City Council.
1983-93 Salford City Council.
1981-83 Cumbernauld New Town Development Corp

Contact details
Manchester City Council, Town Hall Extension, Lloyd Street, Manchester M60 2LA
Tel 0161 234 5000
Web www.manchester.gov.uk
Direct tel 0161 234 4501
Direct fax 0161 234 4508
Email p.babb@notes.manchester.gov.uk

BACKLUND, Rickard
Aberdeen Property Investors Nordic

Position
Chief executive officer

Qualifications
MSc, Eng

Career history
1998 Joined Aberdeen Property Investors Nordic.
1994-98 Head, Finans Fastigheter Skandinavien, Försäkringsbolaget.
1992-94 Head of building and construction, Trygg-Hansa

Other roles
Board chairman, Skandinavian International Property Association; board member, Svensk Fastighetsindex

Interests
Boating; golf; outdoor pursuits

Contact details
Aberdeen Property Investors Nordic AB, Box 3039, Luntmakarg 34, Stockholm
Tel +46 0 8412 8000
Fax +46 0 8412 8004
Direct tel +46 0 8412 8061
Email
rickard.backlund@aberdeenpropertyinvestors.com

BADCOCK, Peter
Capital Shopping Centres

Position
Director – finance and operations

Qualifications
FCCA

Career history
1985-94 Finance and administration director, Bredero Properties.
1970-85 Financial and planning executive, Guinness Breweries Group

Other roles
Director, Liberty International

Professional memberships
Institute of Chartered Accountants in England & Wales

Contact details
Capital Shopping Centres plc, 40 Broadway, London SW1H 0BU
Tel 020 7887 4220
Fax 020 7887 4225
Web www.capital-shopping-centres.co.uk
Email peter-badcock@capshop.co.uk

BAILEY, Andrew
Addleshaw Goddard

Position
Partner – head of property group

Qualifications
LLB (Soton)

Contact details
Addleshaw Goddard, 150 Aldersgate Street, London EC1A 4EJ
Tel 020 7606 8855
Fax 020 7606 4390
Web www.addleshawgoddard.com
Direct tel 020 7880 5625
Email andrew.bailey@addleshawgoddard.com

BAILEY, Jeffrey
Paul Hastings Janofsky & Walker

Position
Partner – real estate

Contact details
Paul Hastings Janofsky & Walker LLP, 88 Wood Street, London EC2V 7AJ
Tel 020 7710 2000
Fax 020 7796 2233
Web www.paulhastings.com
Email jeffreybailey@paulhastings.com

BAILEY, Justyn
Montagu Evans

Position
Partner/head of department – agency

Career history
1991-96 Partner, Bailey Posner.
1987-91 Director, Baker Harris Saunders.
1983-87 Co-founder, Bailey Posner & Partners.
1976-83 Partner, Anthony Lipton.
1974-76 Hillier Parker

Interests
Cricket; golf; sport

Contact details
Montagu Evans, 44-48 Dover Street, London W1S 4AZ
Tel 020 7493 4002
Fax 020 7312 7547
Web www.montagu-evans.co.uk
Email justyn.bailey@montagu-evans.co.uk

BAILEY, Robert
Cable & Wireless

Position
Group property director

Qualifications
BSc Hons, Est Man; MBA; MIMgt; MCRE; MBIFM

Career history
Since 2003 Group property director, Cable & Wireless.
1999-2003 Global head of property, Caradon (now Novar).
1996-99 Director, DTZ Debenham Thorpe.
1983-96 Partner, Colliers Erdman Lewis

Other roles
Former chairman of property in business group, Strategic Planning Society; Prince's Trust adviser

Professional memberships
British Institute of Facilities Management; CoreNet Global UK; Institute of Management Consultants

Interests
Cricket; golf; rugby; running

Contact details
Cable & Wireless plc, 124 Theobalds Road, London WC1X 8RX
Tel 020 7315 4000
Fax 020 7315 5000
Web www.cw.com
Direct tel 020 7315 4732
Email robert.bailey@cw.com

BAILEY, Stuart
Blackfriars Investments

Position
Director

Qualifications

BA Hons
Career history
1995 Joined Blackfriars Investments as director.
1988-95 Acquisitions director, Manywell Heights.
1986-88 Marketing director, Berkeley House
Interests
Art; cosmology; literature; motor sports; opera; theatre
Contact details
Blackfriars Investments Ltd, Suite 4, 32 Lawn Road, London NW3 2XU
Tel 020 7483 0007
Fax 020 7483 2007
Web www.blackfriars-uk.com
Mobile 07770 977483
Email bailey@blackfriars-uk.com

BAILEY-KING, Robert
Landmark Chambers
Position
Barrister
Professional memberships
Chancery Bar Association
Contact details
Landmark Chambers, 4 Breams Buildings, London EC4A 1AQ
Tel 020 7430 1221
Fax 020 7421 1399
Web www.landmarkchambers.co.uk
Email clerks@landmarkchambers.co.uk

BAILLARGEON, Pierre
HOK international
Position
Senior vice-president/director – commercial group
Qualifications
AIA
Career history
1984 Joined HOK as project designer with Dallas office; later spent a year with HOK St Louis before joining London office in 1988
Professional memberships
American Institute of Architects
Contact details
HOK International Ltd, 216 Oxford Street, London W1C 1DB
Tel 020 7636 2006
Fax 020 7636 1987
Web www.hok.com
Email pierre.baillargeon@hok.com

BAIN, Colin
Kier Property
Position
Director
Career history
1999-2000 Project manager, Salmon Developments.
1998-99 Development executive, Crest Homes.
1993-98 Associate director, Mace.
1990-93 Project manager, Tarmac Properties.
1988-90 Project manager, EC Harris Project Services
Professional memberships
Association for Project Management; Chartered Institute of Building; Institute of Management Consultants
Interests
Football
Contact details
Kier Property Ltd, Berkeley Square House, Berkeley Square, London W1J 6BD
Tel 020 7887 6200
Fax 020 7887 6299
Web www.kier.co.uk
Direct tel 020 7887 6295
Direct fax 020 7887 6299
Mobile 07930 547 666
Email colin.bain@kier.co.uk

BAINES, Jonathan
Stephenson & Alexander
Position
Consultant
Qualifications
BSc; FRICS
Career history
2003 Joined Stephenson & Alexander as consultant, setting up new UK commercial fund.
2001-03 Director, Slade & Co, London.
1998-2000 Investment manager (Europe) for Government of Singapore Investment Corp.
1982-97 H&B Spain: including responsibility for Barcelona office
Contact details
Stephenson & Alexander, 16 Hanover Square, London W1S 1HT
Tel 020 7408 9463
Fax 020 7408 9456
Mobile 07768 475 967
Email jonbaines@sanda.uk.com

BAINES, Toby
Citygrove Securities
Position
Chairman and chief executive
Qualifications
BSc; MRICS
Career history
Since 2003 Chairman and chief executive, Citygrove Securities.
1990-2003 Group managing director, Citygrove Leisure.
1988-90 Development director, Citygrove.
1985-88 Jones Lang LaSalle
Professional memberships
RICS
Interests
Harbour Club; Royal Opera House, Covent Garden; sailing; skiing; tennis
Contact details
Citygrove Securities plc, Mill House, 216 Chiswick High Road, London W4 1PD
Tel 08700 601 123
Fax 08700 601 124
Web www.citygrove.com
Email tobybaines@uk.citygrove.com

BAIRSTOW, Malcolm
Ernst & Young
Position
Partner – real estate advisory services
Contact details
Ernst & Young LLP, 1 More London Place, London SE1 2AF
Tel 020 7951 2000
Fax 020 7951 1345
Web www.ey.com/uk
Direct tel 020 7951 3685
Direct fax 020 7951 3411
Email malcolm.bairstow@uk.ey.com

BAKER, Bradley
Knight Frank
Position
Partner – head of City agency
Qualifications
BSc; MRICS
Career history
1989 Joined Knight Frank; become partner in 1990 and equity partner in 1999.
1986-89 Jones Lang Wootton
Professional memberships
RICS
Interests
Chess; motor sports; mountaineering; wine
Contact details
Knight Frank LLP, Kings House, 36 King Street, London EC2V 8QQ
Tel 020 7606 0606
Fax 020 7606 5502
Web www.knightfrank.com
Direct tel 020 7861 1306
Mobile 07831 559 201
Email bradley.baker@knightfrank.com

BAKER, Michael
BH2
Position
Partner

Qualifications
FRICS
Career history
1992-94 Director, Herring Baker Harris.
1976-92 Managing director, Baker Harris Saunders.
1969-76 Partner, Richard Saunders & Partners
Other roles
Director, Halladale; master (2001-02) and member of the court, Chartered Surveyors Company
Professional memberships
RICS
Interests
Entomology; fishing; ornithology
Contact details
BH2, 15-16 Basinghall Street, London EC2V 5BR
Tel 020 7600 5000
Fax 020 7600 5006
Web www.bh2.co.uk
Direct tel 020 7710 7951
Email michaelb@bh2.co.uk

BAKER, Michael
Hammerson
Position
Director – UK offices
Qualifications
BSc Hons; MRICS; MCR
Career history
Since 1994 Director (UK offices), Hammerson.
1991-94 Taylor Woodrow Property Co.
1988-91 Hillier Parker
Other roles
Director, Hammerson UK subsidiaries
Professional memberships
British Council for Offices; CoreNet Global UK; RICS; Westminster Property Owners Association; Worshipful Company of Chartered Surveyors
Interests
Aviation; golf; squash; windsurfing
Contact details
Hammerson plc, 100 Park Lane, London W1K 7AR
Tel 020 7887 1000
Fax 020 7887 1010
Web www.hammerson.co.uk
Direct tel 020 7887 1079
Direct fax 020 7887 1107
Mobile 07768 884 791
Email mbaker@hammerson.co.uk

BAKER, Nick
Legal & General Property
Position
Fund manager
Qualifications
BSc; FRICS
Professional memberships
RICS
Contact details
Legal & General Property Ltd, Bucklersbury House, 3 Queen Victoria Street, London EC4N 8NH
Tel 020 7528 6500
Fax 020 7528 6848
Web www.legal-and-general.co.uk
Direct tel 020 7528 6909
Mobile 07771 731 084
Email nick.baker@lgim.co.uk

BAKER, Nigel
EDS International
Position
EMEA real estate director
Contact details
EDS International, 4 Roundwood Avenue, Stockley Park, Uxbridge UB11 1BQ
Tel 020 8848 8989
Fax 020 8756 0130
Web www.eds.com/emea
Direct tel 020 8754 5861
Direct fax 020 8754 5612
Email nigel.j.baker@eds.com

BAKEWELL, Simon
Nelson Bakewell
Position
Director
Qualifications
BSc; MRICS
Career history
1982 Co-founded Nelson Bakewell.
1977-82 Chesterton
Other roles
Director, Quester VCT; director, City of London Sinfonia
Professional memberships
RICS
Contact details
Nelson Bakewell Ltd, 25 Sackville Street, London W1S 3HQ
Tel 020 7544 2000
Fax 020 7544 2222
Web www.nelson-bakewell.com
Email sbakewell@nelson-bakewell.com

BALCH, Charles
Hypo Real Estate Capital
Position
Director – real estate finance
Qualifications
BSc Hons
Career history
2004 Joined Hypo Real Estate Capital as real estate finance director.
1995-2003 DePfa Bank (now Aareal Bank): joined as head of marketing; head of global clients and European property finance from 2000.
1994-95 Head of marketing, Hypo Bank.
1986-94 Credit Lyonnais
Contact details
Hypo Real Estate Capital Ltd, 110 Cannon Street, London EC4N 6EW
Tel 020 7743 7743
Fax 020 7743 7700
Web www.hypointernational.com
Email charles.balch@hypointernational.com

BALCOMBE, Andrew
Dunlop Heywood Lorenz
Position
Director – professional
Qualifications
FRICS; FCIArb
Career history
1987-2000 Partner in charge (landlord and tenant), Matthews & Goodman.
1987-97 Director, Fletcher King.
1986-87 JR Eve
Professional memberships
Chartered Institute of Arbitrators; RICS
Interests
Cricket; golf
Contact details
Dunlop Heywood Lorenz Ltd, 10 Queen Anne Street, London W1G 9LH
Tel 020 7636 7000
Fax 020 7636 7002
Web www.dhlproperty.co.uk
Direct tel 020 7299 7232
Mobile 07900 221 372
Email ab@dhlproperty.co.uk

BALDWIN, Tony
GVA Grimley
Position
Partner in charge, Manchester
Contact details
GVA Grimley, 81 Fountain Street, Manchester M2 2EE
Tel 0870 900 8990
Fax 0161 956 4009
Web www.gvagrimley.co.uk
Email tony.baldwin@gvagrimley.co.uk

BALES, Craig
Lambert Smith Hampton
Position
Chief executive – Birmingham

B

Qualifications
BSc; MRICS
Career history
1993-98 Principal, Craig Bales & Co.
1984-93 Partner, Johnson Fellows
Professional memberships
RICS
Interests
Football; golf; keep fit; running
Contact details
Lambert Smith Hampton Ltd, 35 Newhall Street, Birmingham B3 3PU
Tel 0121 236 2066
Fax 0121 233 1623
Web www.lsh.co.uk
Direct tel 0121 237 2363
Mobile 07770 756 056
Email cbales@lsh.co.uk

BALFOUR-LYNN, Richard
Marylebone Warwick Balfour Group
Position
Chief executive
Qualifications
BA Hons
Contact details
Marylebone Warwick Balfour Group plc, 1 West Garden Place, London W2 2AQ
Tel 020 7706 2121
Fax 020 7706 8181
Web www.mwb.co.uk
Email rbl@mwb.co.uk

BALL, Nigel
NAI Fuller Peiser
Position
Partner
Contact details
NAI Fuller Peiser, 16 St George Street, London W1S 1LX
Tel 0870 700 2233
Fax 020 7491 1961
Web www.nai-fullerpeiser.com
Email nball@nai-fullerpeiser.com

BALLIN, Giles
Strutt & Parker
Position
Investment partner, London
Qualifications
FRICS
Career history
1976 Joined Strutt & Parker.
1974-76 Premises surveyor, Lloyds Bank.
1972-74 Clive Lewis & Partners
Professional memberships
RICS
Contact details
Strutt & Parker, 13 Hill Street, London W1J 5LQ
Tel 020 7629 7282
Fax 020 7629 0387
Web www.struttandparker.com
Direct tel 020 7318 5008
Direct fax 020 7355 1385
Email gballin@struttandparker.com

BALMOND, Cecil
Arup Group
Position
Director and chairman – operations division
Qualifications
BSc, Eng; MSc; DIC; MIStructE
Interests
Guitar; IT
Contact details
Arup Group Ltd, 13-17 Fitzroy Street, London W1T 4BS
Tel 020 7636 1531
Web www.arup.com
Direct tel 020 7465 3592
Email cecil.balmond@arup.com

BANHAM, Russell
CB Richard Ellis
Position
Senior director – shopping centre development
Contact details
CB Richard Ellis, Kingsley House, 1a Wimpole Street, London W1G 0RE
Tel 020 7182 2000
Fax 020 7182 7001
Web www.cbre.com
Email russell.banham@cbre.com

BANKS, James
Rapleys
Position
Senior partner – development/special projects
Qualifications
FRICS
Career history
1975 Joined Rapleys; elected partner in 1977 and senior partner in 1989
Professional memberships
RICS
Contact details
Rapleys, Maddox House, 1 Maddox Street, London W1S 2PZ
Tel 0870 777 6292
Fax 020 7439 7678
Web www.rapleys.co.uk
Direct tel 020 7255 8050
Email jcb@rapleys.co.uk

BANKS, Peter
Strutt & Parker
Position
Professional department partner, London
Qualifications
FRICS; ACIArb; IRRV
Career history
1965 Joined Strutt & Parker; helped grow commercial division.
1963-65 Montagu Evans
1959-63 Weatherall Green & Smith
Other roles
Private executorships and trusteeships; director, In & Out naval and military club
Professional memberships
Chartered Institute of Arbitrators; Institute of Revenues Rating & Valuation; RICS
Interests
Family; fishing; skiing; travel; wine
Contact details
Strutt & Parker, 13 Hill Street, London W1J 5LQ
Tel 020 7629 7282
Fax 020 7629 0387
Web www.struttandparker.com
Direct tel 020 7318 5080
Direct fax 020 7408 0734
Email pbanks@struttandparker.com

BARBER, Amanda
GVA Grimley
Position
Partner – national head of automotive and roadside
Qualifications
BSc Hons; FRICS; MInstPet; MCIArb
Career history
1985 Joined GVA Grimley
Other roles
Chairman, RICS working party on valuation of petrol filling stations; member, RICS trading-related property panel; member of RICS panel of independent experts and arbitrators
Professional memberships
Arbrix; Index; Institute of Arbitrators; RICS
Interests
Gardening; motor sports
Contact details
GVA Grimley, 3 Brindleyplace, Birmingham B1 2JB
Tel 0870 900 8990
Fax 0121 609 8314
Web www.gvagrimley.co.uk
Direct tel 0121 609 8261
Mobile 07831 820 613
Email amanda.barber@gvagrimley.co.uk

BARBER, Martin
Capital & Regional

Position
Chief executive
Other roles
Chairman, CenterPoint Properties Trust, USA
Contact details
Capital & Regional plc, 10 Lower Grosvenor Place, London SW1W 0EN
Tel 020 7932 8000
Fax 020 7802 5600
Web www.capreg.com
Email martin.barber@capreg.com

BARBOUR, Ian
Markham Vaughan Gillingham

Position
Director – development
Qualifications
FRICS
Professional memberships
RICS
Contact details
Markham Vaughan Gillingham, Clifton Heights, Bristol BS8 1EJ
Tel 0117 909 9000
Fax 0117 915 9764
Web www.mvgretail.com
Email ibarbour@mvgretail.com

BARBY, Peter
Castlemore Securities

Position
Technical director
Contact details
Castlemore Securities Ltd, Cedar Court, 221 Hagley Road, Halesowen B63 1ED
Tel 0121 585 4444
Fax 0121 585 4441
Web www.castlemore.co.uk
Email peter@castlemore.co.uk

BARCLAY, Kenneth
James Barr

Position
Chairman
Qualifications
FRICS
Professional memberships
RICS
Contact details
James Barr, 226 West George Street, Glasgow G2 2LN
Tel 0141 300 8000
Fax 0141 300 8001
Web www.jamesbarr.co.uk
Email kbarclay@jamesbarr.co.uk

BARDEN, Mark
Gerald Eve

Position
Partner – head of industrial team
Qualifications
BSc; FRICS
Career history
1977 Joined Gerald Eve; now partner and head of industrial team
Other roles
Rating revaluation steering group member, British Ceramic Confederation
Professional memberships
British Ceramic Confederation; RICS
Interests
Photography; sailing
Contact details
Gerald Eve, 7 Vere Street, London W1G 0JB
Tel 020 7493 3338
Fax 020 7491 1825
Web www.geraldeve.com
Direct tel 020 7333 6266
Email mbarden@geraldeve.com

BAREFOOT, Peter
Alder King

Position
Partner
Contact details
Alder King, 5 Little London Court, Swindon SN1 3HY
Tel 01793 615477
Fax 01793 610385
Web www.alderking.com
Email pbarefoot@alderking.com

BARK, Nick
Hodnett Martin Smith

Position
Partner
Contact details
Hodnett Martin Smith Ltd, Charles House, 5-11 Regent Street, London SW1Y 4LR
Tel 020 7839 8181
Fax 020 7839 8069
Web www.hodnettmartinsmith.com
Email nickbark@hodms.co.uk

BARKHAM, Dr Richard
Grosvenor

Position
Head of UK research
Qualifications
BA Hons, Economics & Geography; PhD, Economics
Career history
1998-2000 Head of projects and consultancy, CB Hillier Parker.
1987-98 University of Reading: lecturer in land management, then reader in finance from 1995
Other roles
Continuing professional development committee member, Investment Property Forum; board member, National Retail Planning Forum
Professional memberships
American Real Estate Society; Society of Property Researchers
Interests
Football; history; literature; sailing; windsurfing
Contact details
Grosvenor Ltd, 70 Grosvenor Street, London W1K 3JP
Tel 020 7408 0988
Fax 020 7629 9115
Web www.grosvenor.com
Direct tel 020 7312 6388
Direct fax 020 7873 1388
Mobile 07884 115860
Email richard.barkham@grosvenor.com

BARLOW, Adrian
Pinsents

Position
Partner – head of property group, Leeds
Qualifications
MA; BA
Career history
1987 Joined Simpson Curtis (now Pinsents)
Interests
Art; cinema; mountaineering; skiing; theatre
Contact details
Pinsents, 3 Colmore Circus, Birmingham B4 6BH
Tel 0121 200 1050
Fax 0121 626 1040
Web www.pinsents.com
Direct tel 0113 294 5220
Direct fax 0113 244 8000
Mobile 07767 224090
Email adrian.barlow@pinsents.com

BARNARD, Anthony
DTZ Debenham Tie Leung

Position
Director
Qualifications
BA Hons; Dip LE; MRICS
Career history
Since 2000 Head of West End investment team, DTZ Debenham Tie Leung
1996-2000 Director (West End investment), Jones Lang LaSalle.
1991-96 Associate director (central London investment), Chesterton

Professional memberships
RICS
Interests
Golf; motorcycling; rugby
Contact details
DTZ Debenham Tie Leung, One Curzon Street, London W1A 5PZ
Tel 020 7408 1161
Fax 020 7643 6000
Web www.dtz.com
Email anthony.barnard@dtz.com

BARNDEN, Derek
Westminster City Council
Position
Corporate property controller
Qualifications
MRICS
Professional memberships
RICS
Contact details
Westminster City Council, City Hall, 64-77 Victoria Street, London SW1E 6QP
Tel 020 7641 6000
Fax 020 7798 3438
Web www.westminster.gov.uk
Direct tel 020 7641 2694
Direct fax 020 7641 2532
Email dbarnden@westminster.gov.uk

BARNES, James
Herbert Smith
Position
Partner – head of real estate department, London
Qualifications
LLB (Belfast)
Career history
1987 Joined Herbert Smith; partner since 1989.
1980 Admitted to Roll of Solicitors
Professional memberships
Law Society
Interests
Motoring; sailing; skiing; sport
Contact details
Herbert Smith, Exchange House, 10 Primrose Street, London EC2A 2NY
Tel 020 7374 8000
Fax 020 7374 0888
Web www.herbertsmith.com
Direct tel 020 7466 2156
Mobile 07785 254969
Email james.barnes@herbertsmith.com

BARNES, Mark
King Sturge
Position
Partner – development, Leeds
Qualifications
MRICS
Professional memberships
RICS
Contact details
King Sturge, Capitol House, Russell Street, Leeds LS1 5SP
Tel 0113 244 1441
Fax 0113 242 1404
Web www.kingsturge.com
Direct tel 0113 235 5245
Email mark.barnes@kingsturge.co.uk

BARNES, Michael
Wilberforce Chambers
Position
Barrister
Qualifications
QC
Professional memberships
Administrative Law Bar Association; Chancery Bar Association; Planning and Environment Bar Association
Contact details
Wilberforce Chambers, 8 New Square, London WC2A 3QP
Tel 020 7306 0102
Fax 020 7306 0095
Web www.wilberforce.co.uk
Email mbarnes@wilberforce.co.uk

BARNES-BATTY, Nick
Lewis Ellis
Position
Partner
Contact details
Lewis Ellis, St Andrew's House, 62 Bridge Street, Manchester M3 3BW
Tel 0161 832 1615
Fax 0161 832 9561
Email lewisellis@btinternet.com

BARNETT, Bob
GVA Grimley
Position
Partner
Qualifications
MRICS
Career history
1972 Joined GVA Grimley
Professional memberships
RICS
Contact details
GVA Grimley, Three Brindleyplace, Birmingham B1 2JB
Tel 0870 900 8990
Fax 0121 609 8314
Web www.gvagrimley.co.uk
Direct tel 0121 609 8305
Direct fax 0121 609 8007
Email Bob.Barnett@gvagrimley.co.uk

BARNETT, Ian
Hewitsons
Position
Senior partner
Contact details
Hewitsons, 7 Spencer Parade, Northampton NN1 5AB
Tel 01604 233233
Fax 01604 627941
Web www.hewitsons.com
Email ianbarnett@hewitsons.com

BARNETT, Keith
Taylor Wessing
Position
Partner
Career history
2002 Joined Taylor Wessing as consultant; now partner.
1993-2002 Garretts (became Andersen Legal Garretts). Previously with DJ Freeman.
1985 Admitted to Roll of Solicitors
Professional memberships
BPF; Law Society; Property Valuation Forum
Interests
Art; family; football
Contact details
Taylor Wessing, Carmelite, 50 Victoria Embankment, London EC4Y 0DX
Tel 020 7300 7000
Fax 020 7300 7100
Web www.taylorwessing.com
Email k.barnett@taylorwessing.com

BARNWELL, Mark
Carisbrooke Alliance
Position
Director
Professional memberships
Investment Property Forum; RICS
Contact details
Carisbrooke Alliance Ltd, 22 Grosvenor Square, London W1K 6DT
Tel 020 7493 6774
Fax 020 7493 2454
Email mbarnwell@carisbrookealliance.co.uk

BARRACLOUGH, Andrew
HOK International
Position
Senior vice-president, director – public and institutional architecture

Qualifications
BA Hons, Arch; Dip Arch (Dist); MSc, Proj Man (Dist)
Other roles
Also leads HOK public and institutional group and specialist historic building conservation group
Professional memberships
Association for Project Management; RIBA
Interests
Sailing
Contact details
HOK International Ltd, 216 Oxford Street, London W1C 1DB
Tel 020 7636 2006
Fax 020 7636 1987
Web www.hok.com
Direct tel 020 7898 5149
Mobile 07774 236 366
Email andrew.barraclough@hok.com

BARRAS, Richard
Property Market Analysis
Position
Senior partner
Qualifications
MA (Cantab); MSc, Econ; PhD
Contact details
Property Market Analysis LLP, 2 Lygon Place, London SW1W 0JR
Tel 020 7881 0300
Fax 020 7881 0400
Web www.pma.co.uk
Email richard.barras@pma.co.uk

BARRETT, Christopher
Allsop & Co
Position
Partner – City agency
Career history
1975 Joined Allsop & Co.
1971-75 Newton Perkins
Interests
Cricket; rugby
Contact details
Allsop & Co, 2 London Wall Buildings, London EC2M 5PP
Tel 020 7588 4433
Fax 020 7374 8212
Web www.allsop.co.uk
Mobile 07973 793516
Email christopher.barrett@allsop.co.uk

BARRETT, John
Kings Chambers
Position
Barrister
Qualifications
BA Hons; Barrister
Career history
1982 Called to Bar
Other roles
Former editor, *Encyclopaedia of Environmental Health* (Sweet & Maxwell); occasional lecturer in environmental law at University of Newcastle upon Tyne; prosecutor for Health & Safety Executive
Professional memberships
Administrative Law Bar Association; Planning & Environment Bar Association
Contact details
Kings Chambers, 40 King Street, Manchester M2 6BA
Tel 0161 832 9082
Fax 0161 835 2139
Web www.kingschambers.com
Mobile 07966 217466
Email jbarrett@kingschambers.com

BARRIE, Michael
ISIS Property Investments
Position
Director – property funds
Contact details
ISIS Property Investments Ltd, 100 Wood Street, London EC2V 7AN
Tel 020 7506 1100
Fax 020 7600 4180
Web www.isisam.com
Direct tel 020 7506 3534
Email michael.barrie@isisam.com

BARROLL BROWN, John
CIT Group
Position
Chairman and chief executive
Qualifications
BA Hons, Law (Lond)
Career history
1993-95 Consultant, Reynolds Porter Chamberlain.
1992-93 Partner, Davenport Lyons
Interests
Flying (helicopter pilot); golf; reading; tennis; travel
Contact details
CIT Group plc, 8-10 Bourdon Street, London W1K 3PD
Tel 020 7667 7766
Fax 020 7667 7770
Web www.cit.co.uk
Direct fax 020 7667 7761
Email jbb@cit.co.uk

BARROTT, Ronald
Stannifer Group Holdings
Position
Chairman and chief executive
Career history
1991 Founded Stannifer
Other roles
Board member and media committee member, British Council of Shopping Centres
Professional memberships
British Council of Shopping Centres; Institute of Directors
Interests
Farming; golf; sailing
Contact details
Stannifer Group Holdings Ltd, Ryon Hill House, Ryon Hill Park, Stratford-upon-Avon CV37 0UX
Tel 01789 415565
Fax 01789 415262
Web www.stannifer.co.uk
Direct tel 01789 207000
Direct fax 01789 207025
Email ronbarrott@stannifer.co.uk

BARRY, Roun
Dunedin Property Asset Management
Position
Managing director
Qualifications
BComm; LLB
Career history
Since 1996 Dunedin Property/Dunedin Property Asset Management.
1992-96 General manager, ING Real Estate.
1987-92 Jones Lang Wootton: became partner in 1990
Contact details
Dunedin Property Ltd, 27 Dover Street, London W1S 4DY
Tel 020 7495 1011
Fax 020 7495 1044
Web www.dunedinproperty.co.uk
Mobile 07768 740598
Email rbarry@dunedinproperty.co.uk

BARTER, Stephen
Grosvenor Group Holdings
Position
Group projects director
Qualifications
MA (Cantab); FRICS; FRSA
Career history
2003 Joined Grosvenor Group Holdings.
2000-03 Head of European real estate, Babcock & Brown.
1979-2000 Richard Ellis: appointed partner in 1987 and equity partner in 1993, then

B

became director of Richard Ellis Financial Services in 1984; became head of Richard Ellis Consulting in 1990

Other roles

External member, MOD defence estates committee; member, ODPM property advisory group; member, Bank of England property forum; member, CBI property group; governor, London Institute; member, London Symphony Orchestra advisory council; SFA registered representative

Professional memberships

Investment Property Forum; RICS; Royal Society of Arts

Interests

Art; music

Contact details

Grosvenor Group Holdings Ltd, 70 Grosvenor Street, London W1K 3JP

Tel 020 7408 0988

Fax 020 7491 2970

Web www.grosvenor.com

Email stephen.barter@grosvenor.com

BARTHOLOMEW, Richard
Boots Properties

Position

Director of property

Qualifications

BSc; Dip Prop Inv; FRICS

Career history

Since 1989 Boots Properties.
1981-89 Boots the Chemists.
1976-81 Estates manager, Errill Properties

Professional memberships

Investment Property Forum; RICS

Interests

Running; sailing; windsurfing

Contact details

Boots Properties plc, 1 Thane Road, Nottingham NG90 5GT

Tel 0115 950 6111

Direct tel 0115 949 5937

Direct fax 0115 949 2896

Email richard.bartholomew@boots.co.uk

BARTLETT, Andrew
Crown Office Chambers

Position

Barrister

Qualifications

QC; FCIArb

Career history

1974 Called to Bar

Professional memberships

Chartered Institute of Arbitrators; Commercial Bar Association; London Common Law & Commercial Bar Association; Professional Negligence Bar Association; Society of Construction Law; Technology & Construction Bar Association

Contact details

Crown Office Chambers, 2 Crown Office Row, London EC4Y 7HJ

Tel 020 7797 8100

Fax 020 7797 8101

Web www.crownofficechambers.com

Email bartlett@crownofficechambers.com

BARTON, Nicholas
Tops Estates

Position

Head of new development

Contact details

Tops Estates plc, 77 South Audley Street, London W1K 1EE

Tel 020 7355 3000

Fax 020 7355 2222

Email ncsptfr@aol.com

BARWICK, Julian
Development Securities

Position

Joint managing director

Qualifications

MA; FRICS

Career history

1998 Joined Development Securities.
1978-98 MEPC.
1976-78 Daniel Smith

Other roles

Chairman, Paddington Regeneration Partnership; property adviser to Bedford Estate

Professional memberships

British Council for Offices; RICS

Interests

Golf; real tennis; tennis

Contact details

Development Securities plc, Portland House, Stag Place, London SW1E 5DS

Tel 020 7828 4777

Fax 020 7828 4999

Web www.developmentsecurities.com

Email julian.barwick@devsecs.co.uk

BARZYCKI, Sarah
British Land Corp

Position

Corporate services executive

Qualifications

MA

Career history

1998 Joined British Land

Contact details

British Land Corp Ltd, 10 Cornwall Terrace, London NW1 4QP

Tel 020 7486 4466

Web www.britishland.com

Email sarah.barzycki@britishland.com

BASTOW, Gillian
Lewis Silkin

Position

Partner – head of social housing group

Qualifications

LLM; MA, Jurisprudence

Career history

1981 Admitted to Roll of Solicitors.
1979 Joined Lewis Silkin; became partner in 1984

Other roles

Member, National Housing Federation lawyers subgroup; writes for Lewis Silkin's *Social Housing Newsnotes*

Professional memberships

City of Westminster & Holborn Law Society; Law Society

Interests

Opera; skiing; theatre; travel

Contact details

Lewis Silkin, 12 Gough Square, London EC4A 3DW

Tel 020 7074 8000

Fax 020 7832 1200

Direct fax 020 7832 1713

Email gillian.bastow@lewissilkin.com

BATCHELOR, Andrew
Hartnell Taylor Cook

Position

Partner

Qualifications

BSc; MRICS

Professional memberships

RICS

Contact details

Hartnell Taylor Cook, Somerset House, 18 Canynge Road, Bristol BS8 3JX

Tel 0117 923 9234

Fax 0117 923 9237

Web www.htc.uk.com

Direct tel 0117 946 4510

Mobile 07836 744015

Email andrew.batchelor@htc.uk.com

BATE, Richard
Wragge & Co

Position

Partner – head of residential development

Career history

1997 Joined Wragge & Co; partner since 1998.
1990 Admitted to Roll of Solicitors.
1988-97 Eversheds, Birmingham

Professional memberships
Law Society
Interests
DIY; music; squash
Contact details
Wragge & Co LLP, 55-73 Colmore Row, Birmingham B3 2AS
Tel 0870 903 1000
Fax 0870 904 1099
Web www.wragge.com
Direct tel 0121 685 2796
Email richard_bate@wragge.com

BATE, Sarah
Knight Frank
Position
Partner – head of central London research
Qualifications
BSc Hons
Career history
1998 Joined Knight Frank as analyst; appointed associate in 2000 and partner in 2002.
1996-98 Analyst, Jones Lang LaSalle
Professional memberships
Society of Property Researchers
Contact details
Knight Frank LLP, 20 Hanover Square, London W1S 1HZ
Tel 020 7629 8171
Fax 020 7493 4114
Web www.knightfrank.com
Direct tel 020 7861 1239
Direct fax 020 7629 1610
Email sarah.bate@knightfrank.com

BATEMAN, Mark
GVA Grimley
Position
Partner – global corporate services
Qualifications
BSc; MRICS
Career history
1990 Joined GVA Grimley.
1983-90 Vigers
Other roles
APC assessor for RICS
Contact details
GVA Grimley, 10 Stratton Street, London W1J 8JR
Tel 0870 900 8990
Fax 020 7911 2560
Web www.gvagrimley.co.uk
Direct tel 020 7911 2524
Email mark.bateman@gvagrimley.co.uk

BATES, Graham
Gerald Eve
Position
Partner – head of planning and development
Qualifications
BSc; FRICS
Professional memberships
Institute of Directors; RICS
Contact details
Gerald Eve, 7 Vere Street, London W1G 0JB
Tel 020 7493 3338
Fax 020 7491 1825
Web www.geraldeve.com
Direct tel 020 7333 6262
Direct fax 020 7333 6402
Email gbates@geraldeve.com

BATES, Jeremy
FPDSavills
Position
Director – head of business space
Contact details
FPDSavills Ltd, 20 Grosvenor Hill, London W1K 3HQ
Tel 020 7499 8644
Fax 020 7495 3773
Web www.fpdsavills.co.uk
Direct tel 020 7409 8813
Mobile 07968 550349
Email jbates@fpdsavills.co.uk

BATES, John
Old Square Chambers
Position
Barrister
Career history
1973 Called to Bar
Other roles
Author, *Water & Drainage Law, Marine Environment Law, UK Waste Law* (2nd edition, 1997)
Professional memberships
Environmental Law Foundation; International Bar Association; Planning & Environment Bar Association; UK Environmental Law Association
Contact details
Old Square Chambers (Chambers of John Hendy QC), 1 Verulam Buildings, London WC1R 5LQ
Tel 020 7269 0300
Fax 020 7405 1387
Web www.oldsquarechambers.co.uk
Email bates@oldsquarechambers.co.uk

BATES, John
Vets4Pets
Position
Property director
Qualifications
FRICS
Career history
2003 Joined Vets4Pets.
1998-2003 Granada/Compass Roadside
Interests
Cricket; football; golf; sport; travel
Contact details
Vets4Pets, PO Box 11556, Solihull B93 8ZR
Tel 01564 732356
Fax 01564 732357
Web www.vets4pets.eu.com
Mobile 07870 554607
Email john.bates@vets4pets.eu.com

BATES, Nicholas
British Land Properties
Position
Director
Qualifications
BSc; MRICS
Career history
1990-96 Asset manager, Broadgate Properties.
1988-90 Development surveyor, Burton Property Trust.
1984-88 Development surveyor, Standard Life
Professional memberships
RICS
Interests
Running; sailing; skiing; tennis
Contact details
British Land Properties Ltd, 10 Cornwall Terrace, London NW1 4QP
Tel 020 7486 4466
Fax 020 7935 5552
Web www.britishland.com
Direct tel 020 7467 2844
Direct fax 020 7935 8413
Email nick.bates@britishland.com

BATLEY, Steve
IKEA
Position
Project manager
Career history
1995 Joined IKEA
Contact details
IKEA, 255 North Circular Road, London NW10 0JQ
Tel 020 8233 2300
Web www.ikea.com
Email steve.batley@memo.IKEA.com

BATTEN, Richard
King Sturge
Position
Partner and national head of valuation

Qualifications
BA; MRICS; SIOR
Career history
1982 Joined King Sturge
Professional memberships
Non-Administrative Receivers Association; RICS; Society of Industrial & Office Realtors (international affiliate)
Interests
Ballet; cricket; golf; opera; rugby; singing
Contact details
King Sturge, 7 Stratford Place, London W1C 1ST
Tel 020 7493 4933
Fax 020 7409 0469
Web www.kingsturge.com
Direct tel 020 7318 4220
Mobile 07802 665752
Email richard.batten@kingsturge.co.uk

BATTERSBY, Stephen
Underwoods
Position
Partner – industrial
Qualifications
BSc Hons; MRICS
Professional memberships
RICS
Contact details
Underwoods, Shire House, Pyramid Close, Northampton NN3 8PH
Tel 01604 404060
Fax 01604 404099
Web www.underwoods.co.uk
Email sb@underwoods.co.uk

BATTISCOMBE, David
Berwin Leighton Paisner
Position
Partner
Career history
2004 Joined Berwin Leighton Paisner.
1998-2004 Finers Stephens Innocent.
1997-98 Speechly Bircham.
1986-86 Baileys & Shaw Gillett.
1983-86 Monro Pennefather.
1983 Admitted to Roll of Solicitors
Interests
Music (plays bass in band $100 Bills); travel
Contact details
Berwin Leighton Paisner Ltd, Adelaide House, London Bridge, London EC4R 9HA
Tel 020 7760 1000
Fax 020 7760 1111
Email david.battiscombe@blplaw.com

BATTLE, Ian
storeys:ssp
Position
Director
Qualifications
FRICS; MCIArb; BA
Career history
1978 Joined Storey Sons & Parker (became storeys:ssp); director of Black Horse Agencies during brief interregnum; founder director of management buyout in 1991.
1976-78 Development surveyor, Milton Keynes Development Corp.
1974-76 Management surveyor, MEPC.
1972-74 Barclays Bank
Professional memberships
Chartered Institute of Arbitrators; RICS
Interests
Golf; travel; walking
Contact details
storeys:ssp, St James House, 139 Albert Road, Middlesbrough TS1 2PP
Tel 01642 230800
Fax 01642 241994
Web www.storeys-ssp.com
Direct tel 01642 803281
Mobile 07957 823207
Email ian.battle@storeys-ssp.co.uk

BAUCHER, Nicholas
CB Richard Ellis
Position
Chairman – central London
Qualifications
FRICS
Career history
1993 Joined Hillier Parker (now CB Richard Ellis) as partner; became senior executive director in 1998; chairman (central London) since 2003.
1977-93 Partner, Baker Harris Saunders.
1974-77 Richard Saunders & Partners
Other roles
Surveyor, Leathersellers' Company
Contact details
CB Richard Ellis, Kingsley House, 1a Wimpole Street, London W1G 0RE
Tel 020 7182 2000
Fax 020 7182 7001
Web www.cbre.com
Direct tel 020 7182 2729
Direct fax 020 7182 2060
Email nick.baucher@cbre.com

BAUM, Dr Andrew
Oxford Property Consultants
Position
Managing director
Qualifications
BSc; MPhil; PhD; FRICS; ASIP
Career history
2000 Joined Oxford Property Consultants.
1993-2000 Chief investment officer (international property), Henderson Investors.
1991-93 Chairman, Real Estate Strategy.
1987-89 Divisional director for property research, Prudential.
1975-83 Lecturer, University of Reading
Other roles
Professor of land management, University of Reading; editorial board member, *Journal of Property Valuation & Investment*; editorial board member, *Real Estate Finance* (US); member of supervisory board, Schroder Exempt Property Unit Trust; author, *Commercial Property Investment* (Estates Gazette, 2002); non-executive director, Grosvenor
Professional memberships
American Real Estate Society; European Real Estate Society; Investment Property Forum; RICS; Society of Investment Professionals; Society of Property Researchers; Urban Land Institute
Contact details
Oxford Property Consultants, 6 St Giles Court, Southampton Street, Reading RG1 2QL
Tel 0118 958 5848
Fax 0118 958 5849
Web www.opconsultants.com
Mobile 07909 521690
Email ab@opconsultants.com

BAX, Peter
Citigroup
Position
Vice-president – European real estate
Contact details
Citigroup Ltd, 41 Berkeley Square, London W1J 5AN
Tel 020 7508 8000
Fax 020 7508 8989
Web www.citigroup.com
Email peter.bax@citigroup.com

BAYLEY, Daniel
ATIS REAL Weatheralls
Position
Director – City office agency
Qualifications
MRICS
Career history
1991 Joined ATIS REAL Weatheralls; now based in City office, specialising in City, Midtown and Docklands offices
Professional memberships
RICS

Interests
Cricket; golf; wine
Contact details
ATIS REAL Weatheralls Ltd, City Tower, 40 Basinghall Street, London EC2V 5DE
Tel 020 7338 4400
Fax 020 7588 4542
Web www.atisrealweatheralls.com
Direct tel 020 7338 4444
Mobile 07879 421192
Email daniel.bayley@atisrealweatheralls.com

BAYLIS, Simon
Wragge & Co
Position
Partner – head of construction
Career history
1999 Joined Wragge & Co.
1992-99 Partner, Neil F Jones & Co
Professional memberships
Chartered Institute of Arbitrators; RICS; Technology & Construction Solicitors Association
Contact details
Wragge & Co LLP, 55-73 Colmore Row, Birmingham B3 2AS
Tel 0870 903 1000
Fax 0870 904 1099
Web www.wragge.com
Direct tel 0121 629 1841
Email simon_baylis@wragge.com

BAYNHAM, Simon
Howard De Walden Estates
Position
Director of estate management
Qualifications
BSc, Est Man; FRICS
Career history
1995 Joined Howard De Walden Estates.
1984-95 Associate, Weatherall Green & Smith.
1979-84 Surveyor, London Merchant Securities
Other roles
Managing director, Howard De Walden Management
Professional memberships
RICS
Interests
Art; cricket; rugby
Contact details
Howard De Walden Estates Ltd, 23 Queen Anne Street, London W1G 9DL
Tel 020 7580 3163
Fax 020 7436 8152
Web www.hdwe.co.uk
Email simon.baynham@hdwe.co.uk

BEACHAM, Justin
Vail Williams
Position
Associate partner – investment
Qualifications
BSc Hons; MRICS
Contact details
Vail Williams, Thames Valley Office, 130 Wharfedale Road, Winnersh RG41 5RB
Tel 0118 933 5600
Fax 0118 933 5634
Web www.vailwilliams.com
Email jbeacham@vailwilliams.com

BEARDMORE, David
GL Hearn
Position
Director – landscape and urban design
Qualifications
FRICS; FRTPI; MLI; FCMI; MSc; Dip LD; Dip LA; Dip UD; Dip Bldg Cons; FIM
Career history
1980-99 Director, Planning Practice.
1976-80 Liaison officer, Wiltshire County Council.
1974-76 Principal planning officer, Avon County Council
Professional memberships
RICS; RTPI
Interests
Music
Contact details
GL Hearn Ltd, Leonard House, 5-7 Marshalsea Road, London SE1 1EP
Tel 020 7450 4000
Fax 020 7450 4010
Web www.glhearn.com
Email david_beardmore@glhearn.com

BEARDSLEY, Duncan
Hammerson
Position
Group treasurer
Qualifications
MA; MCT; MIMgt
Other roles
Non-executive director, Stonemartin
Contact details
Hammerson plc, 100 Park Lane, London W1K 7AR
Tel 020 7887 1000
Fax 020 7887 1010
Web www.hammerson.co.uk
Direct tel 020 7887 1013
Direct fax 020 7887 1020
Email dbeardsley@hammerson.co.uk

BEARDWOOD, Mark
DLA
Position
Location head, real estate, Liverpool
Qualifications
BA, Jurisprudence
Career history
1988 Joined DLA.
1983-88 Linklaters & Paines
Professional memberships
Law Society
Contact details
DLA, India Buildings, Water Street, Liverpool L2 0NH
Tel 0870 011 1111
Web www.dla.com
Direct tel 0151 237 4711
Direct fax 0151 237 4891
Email mark.beardwood@dla.com

BEASTALL, Richard
Bennett Interior Design
Position
Partner
Qualifications
BA Hons; BArch Hons; RIBA
Contact details
Bennett Interior Design Ltd, One America Street, London SE1 0NE
Tel 020 7208 2000
Fax 020 7208 2021
Web www.bennettinteriordesign.co.uk
Email richardb@tpbennett.co.uk

BEATON, Andrew
ING Real Estate Investment Management (UK)
Position
Director – client operations
Qualifications
FRICS
Career history
Since 1997 Director (client operations), ING Real Estate Investment Management (UK).
1977-97 Assistant director, Rothschild Asset Management.
1972-77 Hillier Parker
Professional memberships
Investment Property Forum; RICS
Contact details
ING Real Estate Investment Management (UK) Ltd, 9 Devonshire Square, London EC2M 4WX
Tel 020 7398 4310
Fax 020 7398 4311
Web www.ingrealestate.co.uk
Direct tel 020 7398 5528
Direct fax 020 7398 5504

Mobile 07775 750603
Email andrew.beaton@ingrealestate.co.uk

BEATTIE, Trevor
English Partnerships

Position
Corporate strategy director
Other roles
Board member, Catalyst Corby; board member, Hull Citybuild; board member, Association of Town Centre Management
Contact details
English Partnerships, 110 Buckingham Palace Road, London SW1W 9SA
Tel 020 7881 1600
Fax 020 7730 9162
Web www.englishpartnerships.co.uk
Email trevorbeattie@englishpartnerships.co.uk

BEAUMONT, Mark
GVA Grimley

Position
Partner – head of national investment business
Qualifications
BSc Hons; MRICS
Career history
1986 Joined GVA Grimley
Other roles
Member, J Sainsbury Developments retail warehouse forum
Professional memberships
Investment Property Forum
Interests
Current affairs; entertaining; food and drink; football; golf; rugby; skiing
Contact details
GVA Grimley, 10 Stratton Street, London W1J 8JR
Tel 0870 900 8990
Fax 020 7911 2560
Web www.gvagrimley.co.uk
Direct tel 020 7911 2183
Direct fax 020 7911 2221
Mobile 07831 451685
Email mark.beaumont@gvagrimley.co.uk

BECKETT, Roy
DLA

Position
Managing partner – Manchester office
Qualifications
LLB Hons
Career history
1989 Joined DLA as property partner; appointed managing partner of Manchester office in 1998.
1983 Admitted to Roll of Solicitors
Professional memberships
Interact; Law Society; Manchester Financial & Professional Forum; Manchester Law Society
Interests
Diving/scuba diving; family; football; local history; racquet sports; sailing; skiing; squash; tennis
Contact details
DLA, 101 Barbirolli Square, Manchester M2 3DL
Tel 08700 111111
Web www.dla.com
Direct tel 0161 235 4020
Direct fax 0161 235 4129
Mobile 07971 142149
Email roy.beckett@dla.com

BECKETT, Simon
King Sturge

Position
Partner – West End investment
Qualifications
BSc; MRICS
Professional memberships
RICS
Contact details
King Sturge, 7 Stratford Place, London W1C 1ST
Tel 020 7493 4933
Fax 020 7409 0469
Web www.kingsturge.com
Direct tel 020 7318 4389
Email simon.beckett@kingsturge.co.uk

BECKHAM, James
King Sturge

Position
Partner – head of City investment
Qualifications
BA; FRICS
Professional memberships
RICS
Contact details
King Sturge, Princes Court, 7 Princes Street, London EC2R 8AQ
Tel 020 7796 5454
Fax 020 7796 5450
Web www.kingsturge.com
Direct tel 020 7796 5471
Email james.beckham@kingsturge.co.uk

BECKLEY, Robin
Rickerbys

Position
Partner – head of commercial property
Career history
1984 Joined Rickerby Watterson (became Rickerbys); partner since 1987.
1982-84 Herbert Smith.
1982 Admitted to Roll of Solicitors.
1980-82 Slaughter & May
Professional memberships
Country Land & Business Association
Interests
Shooting
Contact details
Rickerbys, Ellenborough House, Wellington Street, Cheltenham GL50 1YD
Tel 01242 224422
Fax 01242 518428
Web www.rickerbys.com
Direct tel 01242 246482
Mobile 07801 446350
Email robin.beckley@rickerbys.com

BECKWITH, Sir John
Pacific Investments

Position
Chairman
Qualifications
CBE
Contact details
Pacific Investments plc, 124 Sloane Street, London SW1X 9BW
Tel 020 7225 2250
Email jlb@beckwithlondon.com

BECKWITH, Peter
PMB Holdings

Position
Chairman
Qualifications
Hon LLD (Cantab)
Career history
1992 Joined PMB Holdings.
1972-92 Deputy chairman, London & Edinburgh Trust.
1970-72 Norton Rose.
1968-70 Herbert Smith
Other roles
Executive chairman, Harbour Club Milano and Aspria; deputy chairman, Ambassador Theatre Group; vice-patron, Cambridge University (since 1992); governor, Harrow School (since 1992); founder donor, Royal Opera House Trust; friend of Diva Opera; founder trustee, Peter Beckwith Harrow School Trust, Richmond Park Charitable Trust, Tennis First Charitable Trust
Professional memberships
Law Society
Interests
Football; opera; skiing; tennis; theatre; travel
Contact details
PMB Holdings Ltd, Hill Place House, 55a High Street, London SW19 5BA
Tel 020 8944 1288
Fax 020 8944 1054
Email pbeckwith@aspria.com

BEDFORD, Andrew
Denton Wilde Sapte

Position
Partner – real estate
Qualifications
BA Hons, Law
Career history
2003 Joined Denton Wilde Sapte.
2001-03 Partner, Osborne Clark.
1994-2001 Partner, McGuinness Finch.
1989-94 Denton Hall.
1988-89 Oppenheimers
Professional memberships
Law Society
Interests
Football; horse racing
Contact details
Denton Wilde Sapte, One Fleet Place, London EC4M 7WS
Tel 020 7246 7000
Fax 020 7246 7777
Web www.dentonwildesapte.com
Direct tel 020 7246 7488
Mobile 07733 307 302
Email ajb@dentonwildesapte.com

BEER, Charles
KPMG

Position
Tax partner and head of property tax
Career history
1981 Joined KPMG tax department; partner since 1989; head of property tax since 1993.
1978 Called to Bar
Contact details
KPMG LLP, One Canada Square, London E14 5AB
Tel 020 7311 1000
Web www.kpmg.co.uk
Direct tel 020 7311 4193
Direct fax 020 7311 4088
Mobile 07802 615194
Email charles.beer@kpmg.co.uk

BEESE, Mike
GL Hearn

Position
Planning director
Career history
1991-99 Director, Planning Practice.
1981-91 Senior planner/director, MWT Planning.
1974-81 Senior planning officer, Avon County Council
Professional memberships
RTPI
Interests
Golf; rugby; tennis
Contact details
GL Hearn Ltd, The Malt House, Sydney Buildings, Bath BA2 6BZ
Tel 0122 544 6525
Fax 0122 548 2899
Web www.glhearn.com
Email mike_beese@glhearn.com

BEESTON, James
Invigour

Position
Chairman and director
Qualifications
Dip TP; MRTPI
Career history
2001 Appointed chairman, Invigour. Previous roles include: chief executive, Millennium Point Trust; chief executive, Birmingham Heartlands Development Corp; assistant director, Birmingham City Council
Other roles
Director, Beeston Associates; Midlands regional chapter committee member, British Council for Offices; consultant, Hammond; school governor
Professional memberships
RTPI
Interests
Lunar Society
Contact details
Invigour Ltd, 23 Colmore Row, Birmingham B3 2BP
Tel 0121 200 1891
Fax 0121 233 0883
Web www.invigour.com
Mobile 07815 143817
Email jim.beeston@invigour.com

BEEVOR, Stuart
Grosvenor

Position
Group fund management director
Other roles
Board member, Grosvenor Group Holdings
Contact details
Grosvenor Ltd, 70 Grosvenor Street, London W1K 3JP
Tel 020 7408 0988
Fax 020 7629 9115
Web www.grosvenor.com
Email stuart.beevor@grosvenor.com

BELCHER, Anthony
Mellersh & Harding

Position
Partner – project management
Qualifications
BSc; Dip Arb; FRICS; FCIArb; MAPM; FBEng
Career history
1975 Joined Mellersh & Harding; became equity partner in 1990
Professional memberships
Association for Project Management; Association of Building Engineers; Chartered Institute of Arbitrators; RICS
Interests
Badminton; fishing; golf; skiing
Contact details
Mellersh & Harding, 6 Duke Street, London SW1Y 6BN
Tel 020 7499 0866
Fax 020 7522 8503
Web www.mellersh.co.uk
Direct tel 020 7522 8530
Mobile 07880 740501
Email abelcher@mellersh.co.uk

BELL, Chris
Thomas Eggar

Position
Partner – commercial property
Qualifications
LLB
Career history
1970 Joined Church Adams Tatham (became Thomas Eggar Church Adams, then Thomas Eggar); head of property division 1998-2002
Professional memberships
Academy of Experts
Interests
Canal boating; skiing
Contact details
Thomas Eggar, Chatham Court, Lesbourne Road, Reigate RH2 7FN
Tel 01737 240111
Fax 01737 248249
Web www.thomaseggar.com
Email chris.bell@thomaseggar.com

BELL, Christopher
Knight Frank

Position
Partner – managing director (Europe)
Qualifications
MA; BSc; MRICS
Career history
1988 Joined City Agency at Knight Frank; became managing partner of Spain office in 1990, returned to London in 1994 as partner in business space developments; now managing director (Europe)
Professional memberships
RICS
Interests

B

Cricket; poetry; rugby
Contact details
Knight Frank LLP, 20 Hanover Square, London W1S 1HZ
Tel 020 7629 8171
Fax 020 7493 4114
Web www.knightfrank.com
Direct tel 020 7861 1145
Direct fax 020 7495 0925
Email chris.bell@knightfrank.com

BELL, Colin
Chesterton International
Position
Director – central London rent reviews
Interests
Golf; music
Contact details
Chesterton International, 30-34 Moorgate, London EC2R 6DN
Tel 020 7248 5022
Fax 020 7606 0649
Web www.chesterton.co.uk
Direct tel 020 7651 0919
Direct fax 020 7606 0649
Mobile 07712 868872
Email colin.bell@chesterton.co.uk

BELL, Colin
GVA Grimley
Position
Partner – planning, development and regeneration
Qualifications
BA Hons, Town & Country Planning; MSocSc, Urban Regional Studies
Career history
1984 Joined GVA Grimley.
1978-84 Dudley Metropolitan Borough Council
Other roles
Corporate member, RTPI
Contact details
GVA Grimley, 3 Brindleyplace, Birmingham B1 2JB
Tel 0870 900 8990
Fax 0121 609 8314
Web www.gvagrimley.co.uk
Direct tel 0121 609 8442
Mobile 07831 820615
Email colin.bell@gvagrimley.co.uk

BELL, John
Glenny
Position
Partner – head of business space agency division
Qualifications
MRICS
Career history
1995-2002 Edwin Hill: promoted to partner and head of north M25 office.
1994-95 Associate director/head of Docklands business space agency, Grant & Partners.
1992-94 Consultant to KPMG: corporate recovery assisting with Rosehaugh receivership.
1987-92 Rosehaugh
Professional memberships
RICS
Interests
Football; tennis
Contact details
Glenny, Crossfield Chambers, 1 Gladbeck Way, London EN2 7HR
Tel 020 8367 2334
Fax 020 8367 2336
Web www.glenny.co.uk
Direct tel 020 8370 4087
Mobile 07766 225489
Email j.bell@glenny.co.uk

BELL, Lucinda
British Land Co
Position
Head of tax and accounting
Qualifications
MA; FCA
Career history
1992 Appointed corporate finance director, British Land Corp; became head of tax administration in 1999; head of tax since 2001
Contact details
British Land Co plc, 10 Cornwall Terrace, London NW1 4QP
Tel 020 7486 4466
Fax 020 7935 5552
Web www.britishland.com
Direct tel 020 7467 2888
Direct fax 020 7467 2988
Email lucinda.bell@britishland.com

BELL, Tim
F&C Property Investment Management
Position
Managing director
Qualifications
FRICS
Career history
1996 Joined F&C Property Investment Management as managing director.
1982-96 ESN Property Investments: became property investment director in 1989.
1979-82 Sun Life Properties.
1975-79 Jones Lang Wootton
Professional memberships
Investment Property Forum; RICS
Interests
Cricket; fishing; golf
Contact details
F&C Property Investment Management Ltd, Exchange House, 10 Primrose Street, London EC2A 2NY
Tel 020 7628 8000
Fax 020 7825 2291
Direct tel 020 7825 2128
Direct fax 020 7917 9028
Email tbell@fandc.co.uk

BELLERBY, Richard
Jewson
Position
Property director
Other roles
Property director, Saint-Gobain in UK and Ireland (SG owns Jewson)
Contact details
Jewson Ltd, 96 Leeds Road, Huddersfield HD1 4RH
Tel 01484 412500
Fax 01484 411327
Web www.jewson.co.uk
Email richard.bellerby@jewson.co.uk

BELLHOUSE, Joe
Wedlake Bell
Position
Partner
Qualifications
BA Hons, Law; MSc, Construction & Arbitration Law
Career history
2002 Joined Wedlake Bell as partner
Professional memberships
Chartered Institute of Arbitrators
Interests
Golf; rugby
Contact details
Wedlake Bell, 16 Bedford Street, London WC2E 9HF
Tel 020 7395 3000
Fax 020 7836 9966
Web www.wedlakebell.co.uk
Direct tel 020 7395 3073
Direct fax 020 7395 3004
Mobile 07734 556627
Email jbellhouse@wedlakebell.com

BELLMAN, Peter
CBGA
Position
Partner
Qualifications
FRICS
Career history

1989 Established CBGA (formerly Crowson Bellman Gill)
Other roles
Non-executive director, Property Investment Exchange
Professional memberships
Investment Property Forum
Interests
Cycling; skiing; walking
Contact details
CBGA, 43 Dover Street, London W1S 4NU
Tel 020 7495 6838
Fax 020 7495 3056
Web www.cbga.co.uk
Email pbellman@cbga.co.uk

BENHAM, Amanda
Landwell & Partners
Position
Consultant
Qualifications
LLB (Lond); LLM (Cantab)
Career history
2000 Joined Landwell as partner; became consultant in 2001.
1994-2000 Partner, Wilde Sapte (became Denton Wilde Sapte).
1988-94 Stephenson Harwood.
1987 Admitted to Roll of Solicitors
Professional memberships
Law Society
Interests
Gardening; motor sports
Contact details
Landwell & Partners, 1 Embankment Place, London WC2N 6DX
Tel 020 7212 1616
Fax 020 7212 1570
Web www.landwellglobal.com
Email amanda.benham@uk.landwellglobal.com

BENNETT, Alex
Grosvenor
Position
Service development director
Qualifications
MRICS
Career history
1997-2000 Retail fund manager, Guardian Properties.
1989-97 Investment surveyor, Jones Lang LaSalle.
1980-88 Helicopter pilot, Royal Navy
Professional memberships
Investment Property Forum; RICS
Interests
Current affairs; history; music; sport
Contact details
Grosvenor Ltd, 70 Grosvenor Street, London W1K 3JP
Tel 020 7408 0988
Fax 020 7629 9115
Web www.grosvenor.com
Direct tel 020 7312 6294
Direct fax 020 7312 6242
Mobile 07867 552694
Email alex.bennett@grosvenor.com

BENNETT, Matthew
Citigroup
Position
Vice-president – European real estate
Qualifications
BSc Hons; MRICS
Career history
1998-2001 Ardwood Property Holdings.
1995-98 Chesterfield Properties.
1990-94 Warner Estate Holdings
Contact details
Citigroup Ltd, 41 Berkeley Square, London W1J 5AN
Tel 020 7508 8000
Fax 020 7508 8989
Web www.citigroup.com
Email matthew.bennett@citigroup.com

BENNETT, Michael
Charles Russell
Position
Deputy senior partner
Qualifications
LLB
Contact details
Charles Russell, 8-10 New Fetter Lane, London EC4A 1RS
Tel 020 7203 5000
Fax 020 7203 0200
Web www.cr-law.co.uk
Direct tel 020 7203 5021
Direct fax 020 7203 5398
Email michaelb@cr-law.co.uk

BENNETT, Paul
TM Retail
Position
General manager – property
Qualifications
BSc; FRICS
Career history
1982-88 Property manager, Pickfords Travel.
1978-82 Charles Hawkins & Sons
Professional memberships
Property Managers Association; RICS
Interests
Architecture; history; IT; literature; poetry; rugby; theatre
Contact details
TM Retail Ltd, TM House, Ashwells Road, Brentwood CM15 9ST
Tel 01277 372916
Fax 01277 372151
Direct tel 0127 737 6314
Mobile 07970 136753
Email hpbennett@compuserve.com

BENNETT, Peter
Corporation of London
Position
Deputy City surveyor
Qualifications
MA (Cantab); FRICS
Career history
1985-90 City estate agent and valuer, City of Swansea.
1977-85 Bradford Metropolitan District Council.
1972-77 Valuation officer, District Valuer's Office and Inland Revenue
Other roles
Chairman, RICS London regional board (since 2000)
Professional memberships
Cambridge University Land Society; RICS
Interests
Gardening; opera
Contact details
Corporation of London, PO Box 270, Guildhall, London EC2P 2EJ
Tel 020 7606 3030
Fax 020 7332 1536
Web www.cityoflondon.gov.uk
Direct tel 020 7332 1502
Direct fax 020 7332 3955
Mobile 07785 301612
Email peter.bennett@corpoflondon.gov.uk

BENSON, John
Alder King
Position
Senior partner
Contact details
Alder King, Pembroke House, 15 Pembroke Road, Bristol BS8 3BA
Tel 0117 317 1000
Fax 0117 317 1001
Web www.alderking.com
Email jbenson@alderking.com

BENSON, Roger
Lawrence Graham
Position
Partner

B

Qualifications
LLB Hons
Career history
1981 Joined Lawrence Graham; became partner in 1986.
1981 Admitted to Roll of Solicitors.
1979-81 Turner Peacock
Other roles
External tutor to University of Reading
Professional memberships
British Council of Shopping Centres; City of Westminster & Holborn Law Society; Law Society
Interests
Golf; sailing; skiing
Contact details
Lawrence Graham, 190 Strand, London WC2R 1JN
Tel 020 7379 0000
Fax 020 7379 6854
Web www3.lawgram.com
Direct tel 020 7395 4502
Mobile 07770 742953
Email roger.benson@lawgram.com

BENSON, Stephen
Cobbetts
Position
Client services partner
Qualifications
LLB Hons
Career history
1981 Joined Cobbetts as retail property lawyer; head of property 1999-2003; also member of executive and management board.
1981 Admitted to Roll of Solicitors
Professional memberships
American Bar Association; International Bar Association
Interests
Art; cars; walking
Contact details
Cobbetts, Ship Canal House, King Street, Manchester M2 4WB
Tel 0161 833 3333
Fax 0161 833 3030
Web www.cobbetts.co.uk
Direct tel 0161 833 5232
Direct fax 0161 830 2704
Email stephen.benson@cobbetts.co.uk

BENZECRY, Edward
CMS Cameron McKenna
Position
Partner – head of real estate
Qualifications
LLB Hons
Career history
1988 Admitted to Roll of Solicitors
Interests
Golf; tennis
Contact details
CMS Cameron McKenna, Mitre House, 160 Aldersgate Street, London EC1A 4DD
Tel 020 7367 3000
Fax 020 7367 2000
Web www.cmck.com
Email edward.benzecry@cmck.com

BENZECRY, Toby
Modus Group
Position
Director
Qualifications
MBA; MA; MEng
Career history
Since 1990 Director, Modus Group.
1986-90 Management consultant, Orr & Boss.
1982-86 Industrial engineer, Racal
Contact details
Modus Group Ltd, Greencoat House, Francis Street, London SW1P 1DH
Tel 020 7828 9009
Fax 020 7828 0009
Web www.modusgroup.com
Email toby@modusgroup.com

BERESFORD, Amanda
Addleshaw Goddard
Position
Head of environmental law
Contact details
Addleshaw Goddard, Sovereign House, Sovereign Street, Leeds LS1 1HQ
Tel 0113 209 2000
Fax 0113 209 2060
Web www.addleshawgoddard.com
Email
amanda.beresford@addleshawgoddard.com

BERESFORD, Valentine
Pillar Property Group
Position
Director – head of acquisitions and disposals
Career history
Since 1991 Divisional acquisition manager, Pillar Property.
1989-91 Assistant to chief executive, Bellhouse & Joseph
Other roles
Acquisition director, Pillar Retail Parks; director, Pillar Developments; director, Canning Street Property Co
Contact details
Pillar Property Group Ltd, Lansdowne House, 57 Berkeley Square, London W1J 6HQ
Tel 020 7915 8000
Fax 020 7915 8001
Web www.pillarproperty.com
Direct fax 020 7915 8033
Mobile 07860 211378
Email valentine.beresford@pillarproperty.com

BERGIN, Terence
Henderson Chambers
Position
Barrister
Contact details
Henderson Chambers, Ground Floor, 2 Harcourt Buildings, London EC4Y 9DB
Tel 020 7583 9020
Fax 020 7583 2686
Web www.hendersonchambers.co.uk
Email tbergin@hendersonchambers.co.uk

BERNERD, Elliott
Chelsfield
Position
Chairman
Other roles
Chairman, Global Switch
Contact details
Chelsfield plc, 67 Brook Street, London W1K 4NJ
Tel 020 7493 3977
Fax 020 7493 1444
Web www.chelsfield.com
Direct fax 020 7499 5639
Email ebernerd@chelsfield.com

BERNSTEIN, Simon
UNITE Group
Position
Chief financial officer
Qualifications
BA Hons; ACCA
Career history
2001 Joined UNITE Group.
1996-2001 UBS Warburg.
1991-96 Price Waterhouse.
1989-91 Department of Energy.
1985-89 Price Waterhouse
Interests
Opera; theatre; wine
Contact details
UNITE Group plc, The Tower Building, 11 York Road, London SE1 7NQ
Tel 020 7902 5050
Fax 020 7902 5051
Web www.unite-group.com
Email simon.bernstein@unite-group.co.uk

BERRILL, Simon
DTZ Corporate Finance

Position
Chief executive – head of corporate finance
Qualifications
MA, Jurisprudence; MBA
Career history
1995-2002 Principal, SP Berrill & Co.
1990-95 Managing director (Europe), O'Connor Group.
1988-90 Chief executive, Benlox.
1985-88 Director, Morgan Grenfell Laurie.
1980-85 Director, Michael Laurie & Partners
Contact details
DTZ Corporate Finance Ltd, One Curzon Street, London W1A 5PZ
Tel 020 7408 1161
Fax 020 7643 6000
Web www.dtz.com
Direct tel 020 7643 6462
Mobile 07785 908510
Email simon.berrill@dtz.com

BERRIMAN, Christopher
Allsop & Co

Position
Partner – residential auctions
Qualifications
BA Hons; Dip Surv (CEM); MRICS
Career history
1987 Joined Allsop & Co as residential auctioneer and surveyor; appointed partner in 1995 and equity partner in 1999
Other roles
Member, RICS auction committee; chairman, RICS auction competition committee
Professional memberships
RICS
Interests
Cricket; football; golf; music
Contact details
Allsop & Co, 100 Knightsbridge, London SW1X 7LB
Tel 020 7437 6977
Fax 020 7344 2640
Web www.allsop.co.uk
Direct tel 020 7494 3686
Direct fax 020 7581 3058
Email christopher.berriman@allsop.co.uk

BERRY, Nic
Masons

Position
Partner – property, planning and environment
Qualifications
LLB Hons; LLM
Career history
1992 Joined Masons; appointed partner in 1994.
1988 Admitted to Roll of Solicitors.
1985-92 Freshfields.
1983 Called to Bar
Professional memberships
Law Society
Interests
Guitar; IT; photography; tennis
Contact details
Masons, Woodbridge House, 30 Aylesbury Street, London EC1R 0ER
Tel 020 7329 2288
Fax 020 7490 2545
Web www.masons.com
Direct tel 020 7490 6285
Mobile 07901 715830
Email nic.berry@masons.com

BERRY, Nicholas
Southernhay Chambers

Position
Barrister
Qualifications
BA Hons
Career history
1988 Called to Bar
Other roles
Lectures on landlord and tenant law for Law Society
Professional memberships
Housing Law Practitioners Association
Contact details
Southernhay Chambers (Chambers of David Tyzack), 33 Southernhay East, Exeter EX1 1NX
Tel 01392 255777
Fax 01392 412021
Mobile 07971 054482
Email nmdberry@aol.com

BERRY, Simon
9 Old Square

Position
QC
Qualifications
QC; LLB
Career history
1977 Called to Bar
Other roles
Bencher of Lincoln's Inn; recorder; deputy High Court judge for chancery division; theatre panel judge for 1999 Olivier Awards
Professional memberships
Anglo-American Real Property Institute; Chancery Bar Association; Professional Negligence Bar Association; Property Bar Association
Interests
Family; skiing
Contact details
9 Old Square (Chambers of Michael Driscoll QC), Ground Floor, London WC2A 3SR
Tel 020 7405 4682
Fax 020 7831 7107
Web www.9oldsquare.co.uk
Email simon.berry@9oldSquare.co.uk

BERRY, Stephen
ING Real Estate Investment Management (UK)

Position
Development director
Qualifications
MA (Oxon); CEng; MICE
Career history
Since 2003 Development director, ING Real Estate.
1997-2003 Director, London & Amsterdam Developments (subsidiary of ING Real Estate)
Other roles
Chairman of trustees, ChildSmile children's charity
Contact details
ING Real Estate Investment Management (UK) Ltd, 33 Cavendish Square, London W1G 0BQ
Tel 020 7659 9620
Fax 020 7659 9621
Web www.ingrealestate.co.uk
Mobile 07774 151395
Email stephen.berry@ingrealestate.com

BEST, Craig
Bee Bee Developments

Position
Managing director
Contact details
Bee Bee Developments Ltd, Berry House, 4 Berry Street, London EC1V 0AA
Tel 020 7336 0202
Fax 020 7336 0220
Email craig@beebee.co.uk

BEST, Peter
Prudential Property Investment Managers

Position
Investment management director
Qualifications
BSc; MRICS
Contact details
Prudential Property Investment Managers Ltd, Princeton House, 271-273 High Holborn, London WC1V 7NE
Tel 020 7548 6600
Fax 020 7548 6999
Web www.prupim.com

B

Direct tel 020 7548 6878
Direct fax 020 7548 6661
Email peter.best@prupim.com

BEVAN, Simon
BDO Stoy Hayward

Position
Business assurance and advisory partner
Qualifications
FCA
Career history
1981 Joined BDO Stoy Hayward; qualified as chartered accountant in 1984; became partner in 1988; managing partner 2000-01
Other roles
Committee member, Association of Partnership Practitioners; director, BDO Stoy Hayward Public Sector Consulting Services (1996-2000)
Professional memberships
CBI; FIABCI; Institute Of Chartered Accountants in England & Wales; Investment Property Forum
Interests
Football; motor sports; rowing; rugby; sport; squash; travel
Contact details
BDO Stoy Hayward, 8 Baker Street, London W1U 3LL
Tel 020 7486 5888
Fax 020 7487 3686
Web www.bdo.co.uk
Direct tel 020 7893 2574
Mobile 07831 455268
Email simon.bevan@bdo.co.uk

BEWICK, Robert
GVA Grimley

Position
Partner
Contact details
GVA Grimley, 10 Stratton Street, London W1J 8JR
Tel 0870 900 8990
Fax 020 7911 2560
Web www.gvagrimley.co.uk
Email robert.bewick@gvagrimley.co.uk

BHALOO, Zia
Enterprise Chambers

Position
Barrister
Qualifications
LLB (Lond); LLM (Lond)
Career history
1990 Called to Bar
Professional memberships
Chancery Bar Association
Contact details
Enterprise Chambers (Chambers of Anthony Mann QC), 9 Old Square, London WC2A 3SR
Tel 020 7405 9471
Fax 020 7242 1447
Web www.enterprisechambers.com
Email ziabhaloo@enterprisechambers.com

BHANDARI, Nitin
Bear, Stearns International

Position
Managing director – principal and real estate finance
Qualifications
ACA
Contact details
Bear, Stearns International Ltd, One Canada Square, London E14 5AB
Tel 020 7516 6000
Fax 020 7516 6030
Web www.bearstearns.com
Direct tel 020 7516 5259
Direct fax 020 7516 6556
Email nbhandari@bear.com

BIBBY, Howard
Arlington Business Services

Position
Managing director
Qualifications
BSc Hons; FRICS; CIM
Career history
1997 Joined Arlington.
1996-97 Director, Johnson Controls.
1969-94 Partner, St Quintin
Professional memberships
Chartered Institute of Marketing; RICS
Interests
IT
Contact details
Arlington Business Services Ltd, Arlington House, 1025 Arlington Business Park, Reading RG7 4SA
Tel 0118 930 4141
Fax 0118 930 4383
Web www.arlington.co.uk
Direct tel 0118 930 3211
Mobile 07973 147807
Email howard.bibby@arlington.co.uk

BIBRING, Michael
Marylebone Warwick Balfour Group

Position
Director – commercial
Contact details
Marylebone Warwick Balfour Group plc, 1 West Garden Place, London W2 2AQ
Tel 020 7706 2121
Fax 020 7706 8181
Web www.mwb.co.uk
Email mbibring@mwb.co.uk

BICKELL, Brian
Shaftesbury

Position
Finance director/company secretary
Qualifications
FCA
Professional memberships
Institute of Chartered Accountants in England & Wales
Contact details
Shaftesbury plc, Pegasus House, 37-43 Sackville Street, London W1S 3DL
Tel 020 7333 8118
Fax 020 7333 0660
Web www.shaftesbury.co.uk
Email brian.bickell@shaftesbury.co.uk

BICKFORD-SMITH, Stephen
Landmark Chambers

Position
Barrister
Career history
1972 Called to Bar
Other roles
Member, Chartered Institute of Arbitrators panel of construction adjudicators; author of publications including *Butterworths' Construction Law Manual*, *Party Walls: the New Law* (Jordans) and *Rights of Light: the Modern Law* (Jordans), as well as various articles; an editor of *Emden's Construction Law*; contributor to the Civil Court Service
Professional memberships
Chancery Bar Association; Chartered Institute of Arbitrators; Planning & Environment Bar Association; Technology & Construction Bar Association
Contact details
Landmark Chambers, 4 Breams Buildings, London EC4A 1AQ
Tel 020 7430 1221
Fax 020 7421 1399
Web www.landmarkchambers.co.uk
Email clerks@landmarkchambers.co.uk

BICKMORE, Anthony
Crown Estate

Position
Director of urban estates
Qualifications
FRICS
Career history

B

1973-94 Hillier Parker

Other roles

Honorary treasurer, British Council for Offices

Professional memberships

RICS

Interests

IT; outdoor pursuits

Contact details

Crown Estate, 16 Carlton House Terrace, London SW1Y 5AH

Tel 020 7210 4377

Fax 020 7210 4236

Web www.crownestate.co.uk

Direct tel 020 7210 4208

Direct fax 020 7930 8202

Email tony.bickmore@crownestate.co.uk

BIDDLE, Michael
Angermann Goddard & Loyd

Position

Managing director

Contact details

Angermann Goddard & Loyd Ltd, 26 Mount Row, London W1K 3SQ

Tel 020 7409 7303

Fax 020 7493 1029

Direct tel 020 7465 5103

Email mike.biddle@agl-london.co.uk

BIGGS, Kevin
Royal Bank of Scotland

Position

Director – property finance group

Qualifications

MRICS

Professional memberships

RICS

Contact details

Royal Bank of Scotland, 280 Bishopsgate, London EC2M 4RB

Tel 020 7833 2121

Web www.rbs.co.uk

Direct tel 020 7672 1169

Direct fax 020 7672 1709

Email kevin.biggs@rbs.co.uk

BIGNELL, Janet
Falcon Chambers

Position

Barrister

Qualifications

MA (Cantab); BCL (Oxon)

Career history

Since 1993 Member of Falcon Chambers.
1992 Called to Bar

Other roles

Contributor to *Encyclopaedia of Forms & Precedents vol 3 (1): Auctioneers, Estate Agents & Valuers*; co-author, *Registered Land – the New Law* (2002); contributor to *Fisher & Lightwood's Law of Mortgage* (2001); executive editor, landlord and tenant section of *Lawyers Factbook*; editorial board member, *Landlord & Tenant Review*

Professional memberships

Chancery Bar Association; London Common Law & Commercial Bar Association; Property Bar Association

Contact details

Falcon Chambers, Falcon Court, London EC4Y 1AA

Tel 020 7353 2484

Fax 020 7353 1261

Web www.falcon-chambers.com

Email bignell@falcon-chambers.com

BILES, Peter
BOC Group

Position

Group surveyor

Qualifications

BSc Hons, Est Man; FRICS

Career history

1972-82 Gerald Eve

Professional memberships

RICS

Contact details

BOC Group plc, The Priestly Centre, 10 Priestley Road, Guildford GU2 7XY

Tel 01483 579857

Fax 01483 505211

Direct tel 01483 244396

Direct fax 01483 244173

Email peter.biles@boc.com

BILL, Peter
Estates Gazette

Position

Editor

Career history

1997 Joined *Estates Gazette* as editor.
1996-97 Research manager, Robert Fleming.
1990-96 Editor, *Building* magazine

Interests

Reform Club

Contact details

Estates Gazette, 151 Wardour Street, London W1F 8BN

Tel 020 7411 2540

Fax 020 7411 2518

Web www.estatesgazettegroup.com

Email peter.bill@rbi.co.uk

BILTON, Anton
Raven Group

Position

Chief executive

Qualifications

BSc, Econ

Career history

Since 1992 Chief executive, Raven Group

Other roles

Executive director, Avanti Capital; executive director, Raven Mount

Interests

Architecture; deer farming

Contact details

The Raven Group, 21 Knightsbridge, London SW1X 7LY

Tel 020 7235 0422

Fax 020 7235 0455

Mobile 07767 486786

Email abilton@ravenproperties.co.uk

BINGHAM, David
Hartnell Taylor Cook

Position

Partner – hotel agency

Qualifications

MA; FRICS

Career history

1979 Joined Hartnell Taylor Cook.
1973-79 Debenham Tewson & Chinnocks

Other roles

Director, HTC Project Management; director, HTC International

Professional memberships

Non-Administrative Receivers Association; RICS

Contact details

Hartnell Taylor Cook, 12-13 Conduit Street, London W1S 2XH

Tel 020 7491 7323

Fax 020 7491 3032

Web www.htc.uk.com

Direct tel 020 7409 3701

Mobile 07785 114500

Email david.bingham@htc.uk.com

BINKS, Charles
C2G Property Solutions

Position

Director

Qualifications

BSc Hons; MRICS

Other roles

Chairman, Industrial Agents Society

Professional memberships

Industrial Agents Society; RICS

Interests

Cricket; rugby; sport

Contact details
C2G Property Solutions Ltd, 58 Queen Anne Street, London W1G 8HW
Tel 0845 230 6700
Web www.c2gworld.com
Direct tel 020 7935 7536
Direct fax 01473 289009
Mobile 07793 441911
Email charlesbinks@c2gworld.com

BINNIE, Bill
GVA Grimley
Position
Partner
Career history
1991 Opened Grimley JR Eve commercial office in Glasgow
Interests
Golf (Pollok Golf Club)
Contact details
GVA Grimley, Sutherland House, 149 St Vincent Street, Glasgow G2 5NW
Tel 0870 900 8990
Fax 0141 204 1986
Web www.gvagrimley.co.uk
Direct tel 0141 305 6314
Email bill.binnie@gvagrimley.co.uk

BIRCH, Michael
Rock Capital Group
Position
Director
Contact details
Rock Capital Group, 14 Half Moon Street, London W1J 7BD
Tel 020 7409 2400
Direct tel 020 7318 9753
Mobile 07887 720620
Email m.birch@rockcapitalgroup.com

BIRCHENALL, David
Dawnay, Day Property Finance
Position
Chief executive
Qualifications
ACIB
Career history
1994 Co-founded Dawnay, Day Property Finance.
1977-93 Banking
Professional memberships
Chartered Institute of Bankers
Interests
Cricket; golf (Northwood Golf Club); music; rugby
Contact details
Dawnay, Day Property Finance Ltd, 7 Beeston Place, London SW1W 0JJ
Tel 020 7828 8344
Fax 020 7630 0122
Web www.dawnayday.co.uk
Mobile 07818 061488
Email dbirchenall@dawnayday.co.uk

BIRCHMORE, Trevor
Frogmore Estates
Position
Company secretary
Qualifications
FCCA
Other roles
Director, Frogmore Developments; director, Frogmore Investments
Contact details
Frogmore Estates Ltd, 11-15 Wigmore Street, London W1A 2JZ
Tel 020 7016 6000
Fax 020 7495 5321
Web www.frogmore.co.uk
Email trevorbirchmore@frogmore.co.uk

BIRD, Andrew
Barlows
Position
Property director
Qualifications
BSc Hons; MRICS
Career history
1991 Joined Barlows; on main board since 1994.
1986-90 Development surveyor, Sibec Developments.
1983-86 Dunlop Heywood & Co
Professional memberships
RICS
Interests
Sailing; shooting
Contact details
Barlows plc, Chepstow House, Dee Hills Park, Chester CH3 5AR
Tel 0124 435 0202
Fax 0124 431 1522
Web www.barlowsplc.co.uk
Email andrew.bird@barlowsplc.co.uk

BIRD, Ciaran
Dalgleish
Position
Retail director
Career history
1991 Joined Dalgleish.
1989-91 Clive Lewis & Partners.
1988-89 Fletcher King
Interests
Football (Arsenal Football Club); rugby (Esher Rugby Club); socialising; travel
Contact details
Dalgleish, 80 New Bond Street, London W1S 1DD
Tel 020 7663 5555
Fax 020 7491 0098
Web www.dalgleish.co.uk
Direct tel 020 7663 5514
Mobile 07967 697 908
Email cbird@dalgleish.co.uk

BIRD, Michael
Land Securities Properties
Position
Portfolio director
Qualifications
FRICS
Career history
1974 Joined Land Securities; with subsidiary City of London Real Property Co until 1978, then again, as director, from 1986; director of Land Securities Properties since 1990
Other roles
Board member, Bankside Business Partnership; board member, Better Bankside
Professional memberships
RICS
Interests
Motor sports; rugby; sailing; theatre; travel
Contact details
Land Securities Properties Ltd, 5 Strand, London WC2N 5AF
Tel 020 7413 9000
Fax 020 7925 0202
Web www.landsecurities.com
Direct tel 020 7024 5244
Direct fax 020 7024 5003
Mobile 07768 598060
Email mike.bird@landsecurities.com

BIRKETT, Anthony
Edwin Hill
Position
Partner
Qualifications
BSc, Est Man; FRICS
Career history
1978 Joined Edwin Hill; now partner.
1976-78 King & Co.
1972-76 Gerald Eve & Co
Professional memberships
RICS
Contact details
Edwin Hill, 18 Savile Row, London W1S 3PW
Tel 020 7287 2020
Fax 020 7734 1255
Web www.edwinhill.co.uk
Email ajb@edwinhill.co.uk

BISHOP, Jeremy
Citigroup

Position
Vice-president – European real estate
Contact details
Citigroup Ltd, 41 Berkeley Square, London W1J 5AN
Tel 020 7508 8000
Fax 020 7508 8989
Web www.citigroup.com
Email jeremy.bishop@citigroup.com

BISHOP, John
Masons

Position
Senior resident partner, Asia Pacific
Qualifications
LLB Hons
Career history
1983 Qualified as solicitor in Hong Kong.
1971 Admitted to Roll of Solicitors (England & Wales).
1969 Joined Masons; made partner in 1972; managing partner 1986-90; appointed senior partner in 1990
Other roles
President, Technology & Construction Solicitors Association; dean of Faculty of Mediation & ADR; vice-chairman, Academy of Experts
Professional memberships
Chartered Institute of Arbitrators; Faculty of Building
Contact details
Masons, Central Plaza, 18 Harbour Road, Hong Kong
Tel +852 2521 5621
Fax +852 2845 2956
Web www.masons.com
Direct tel +852 2294 3338
Mobile +852 9106 6646
Email john.bishop@masons.com

BISHOP, Paul
Gap

Position
Head of UK real estate
Qualifications
BSc Hons; MRICS
Professional memberships
RICS
Contact details
Gap, Castle Mound Way, Rugby CV23 0WA
Tel 01788 818300
Web www.gap.com
Direct tel 01788 866335
Mobile 07710 108276
Email paul_bishop@gap.com

BISMUTH, Claude
Morgan

Position
Head of real estate
Contact details
Morgan, 36-38 avenue Paul Vaillant Couturier, 93120 La Courneuve, Paris, France
Tel +33 1 43 11 42 42
Fax +33 1 43 11 42 00
Web www.morgandetoi.com
Email info@morgan.fr

BISONI, David
Warner Bros Theatres (UK)

Position
Vice-president, business affairs and general counsel
Contact details
Warner Bros Theatres (UK) Ltd, Warner House, 98 Theobalds Road, London WC1X 8WB
Tel 020 7984 5000
Direct tel 020 7984 6000
Email david.bisoni@warnerbros.com

BLACK, Alan
Donaldsons

Position
Manchester office partner
Qualifications
BSc; FRICS
Career history
1988 Joined Donaldsons as partner.
1983-88 Head of property services, Leeds City Council.
1971-83 Chief valuer, Sheffield City Council
Professional memberships
RICS
Interests
Sport; travel
Contact details
Donaldsons, Century House, 8-11 St Peters Square, Manchester M2 3DN
Tel 0161 237 9977
Fax 0161 237 3311
Web www.donaldsons.co.uk
Mobile 07808 479206
Email alan.black@donaldsons.co.uk

BLACK, Bill
Capital & Counties

Position
Director
Qualifications
BSc; FRICS
Career history
1984 Joined Capital & Counties; became director in 1994.
1972-84 James Abbott Partnership
Other roles
Chairman, Capital Enterprise Centres (Jersey); founder and formerly chairman, Qudos Broadband; member of board of management and executive committee as well as chairman of membership committee, British Council for Offices
Professional memberships
British Council For Offices; Investment Property Forum; RICS
Interests
Cricket; football; travel
Contact details
Capital & Counties, 40 Broadway, London SW1H 0BU
Tel 020 7887 7000
Fax 020 7887 0003
Web www.capitalandcounties.com
Direct tel 020 7887 7009
Direct fax 020 7887 0005
Mobile 07977 222198
Email bill-black@capcount.com

BLACK, Bruce
Homes For Scotland

Position
Executive director
Contact details
Homes For Scotland Ltd, Forsyth House, 93 George Street, Edinburgh EH2 3ES
Tel 0131 243 2595
Fax 0131 243 2596
Email b.black@homesforscotland.com

BLACK, Ian
Cuff Roberts Solicitors

Position
Partner – head of commercial property
Career history
1986 Joined Cuff Roberts; appointed partner in 1993; member of executive board since 1997
Professional memberships
Law Society; Liverpool Law Society
Contact details
Cuff Roberts Solicitors, 100 Old Hall Street, Liverpool L3 9TD
Tel 0151 237 7777
Fax 0151 237 7676
Web www.cuffroberts.co.uk
Email ian.black@cuffroberts.co.uk

BLACK, Robert
Academy Land

Position
Managing director
Qualifications

BSc, Eng; ACGI
Career history
2002 Joined Academy Land as director; now managing director.
1987-2002 Baltic: appointed main board director in 1995; head of property from 1992
Professional memberships
Association of Property Bankers
Interests
Family; sport
Contact details
Academy Land Ltd, 2 Hinde Street, London W1U 2AZ
Tel 020 7935 2330
Fax 020 7935 1175
Email rb@academyland.co.uk

BLAIR, Christopher
Blair Kirkman

Position
Senior partner
Qualifications
BSc; FRICS
Career history
Since 1984 Blair Kirkman.
1981-84 Leavers.
1977-81 Edward Erdman
Professional memberships
Arbrix; British Council of Shopping Centres; RICS; Shop Agents Society
Contact details
Blair Kirkman, St Georges House, 12a St George Street, London W1S 1FQ
Tel 020 7409 0899
Fax 020 7629 8022
Web www.blairkirkman.com
Mobile 07977 998835
Email chrisb@blairkirkman.com

BLAIR, James
Stannifer Group Holdings

Position
Company secretary
Contact details
Stannifer Group Holdings Ltd, Ryon Hill House, Ryon Hill Park, Stratford-upon-Avon CV37 0UX
Tel 01789 415565
Fax 01789 415262
Web www.stannifer.co.uk
Direct tel 01789 207036
Direct fax 01789 207038
Email jamesblair@stannifer.co.uk

BLAKE, Ian
Matrix Securities

Position
Property director
Contact details
Matrix Securities Ltd, Gossard House, 7-8 Savile Row, London W1S 3PE
Tel 020 7292 0800
Fax 020 7287 9228
Web www.matrixgroup.co.uk
Email iblake@matrix-securities.co.uk

BLAKE, Keith
NAI Fuller Peiser

Position
International partner – head of investment
Qualifications
FRICS
Career history
1984 Joined Fuller Peiser
Professional memberships
CoreNet Global UK; Investment Property Forum; RICS
Interests
Family; sport; travel
Contact details
NAI Fuller Peiser, 16 St George Street, London W1S 1LX
Tel 0870 700 2233
Fax 020 7491 1961
Web www.nai-fullerpeiser.com
Direct tel 020 7647 1374
Mobile 07836 261917
Email kblake@nai-fullerpeiser.com

BLAKE, Simon
Holley Blake

Position
Partner
Qualifications
MA; MRICS
Professional memberships
RICS
Contact details
Holley Blake Ltd, 1 Mount Street, London W1K 3LE
Tel 020 7629 4171
Fax 020 7493 2267
Web www.holleyblake.com
Email jo@holleyblake.co.uk

BLAKER, Gary
Lamb Chambers

Position
Barrister
Qualifications
MA (Cantab)
Career history
1993 Called to Bar
Other roles
Management committee member, Planning Aid for London; writes extensively on property-related issues in *Journal of Planning & Environment Law* and *Solicitors Journal*; lectures on property, planning and administrative law
Professional memberships
Chancery Bar Association; Property Bar Association
Interests
Football; opera; theatre; travel
Contact details
Lamb Chambers, Lamb Building, London EC4Y 7AS
Tel 020 7797 8300
Fax 020 7797 8308
Web www.lambchambers.co.uk
Email garyblaker@lambchambers.co.uk

BLAKEY, Michael
Hill Dickinson

Position
Partner – head of commercial property, Manchester
Career history
Since 2002 Hill Dickinson; partner at Gorna & Co prior to merger with Hill Dickinson
Interests
Football; golf; theatre
Contact details
Hill Dickinson, 50 Fountain Street, Manchester M2 2AS
Tel 0161 817 7200
Fax 0161 817 7201
Web www.hilldickinson.com
Email michael.blakey@hilldickinson.com

BLAND, Simon
Mason Owen & Partners

Position
Partner – investment and development
Qualifications
BA Hons
Career history
1995 Joined Mason Owen.
1992-95 Sedgwick Energy.
1988-92 British Army: 14th/20th King's Hussars
Contact details
Mason Owen & Partners Ltd, Gladstone House, 11 Union Court, Liverpool L2 4UQ
Tel 0151 242 3000
Fax 0151 236 2569
Web www.masonowen.com
Direct tel 0151 242 3041
Mobile 07770 855803
Email simon.bland@masonowen.com

BLAND, Simon
Strutt & Parker

Position
Investment partner, London
Qualifications
BSc Hons; MRICS
Career history
1981 Joined Strutt & Parker.
1979-80 Norwich Union
Professional memberships
Investment Property Forum; RICS
Interests
Sport
Contact details
Strutt & Parker, 13 Hill Street, London W1J 5LQ
Tel 020 7629 7282
Fax 020 7629 0387
Web www.struttandparker.com
Direct tel 020 7318 5012
Direct fax 020 7355 1385
Email sbland@struttandparker.com

BLANEY, Trevor
Lawrence Graham

Position
Partner – head of planning team
Qualifications
MSc, Econ
Career history
1992 Joined Lawrence Graham.
1978-92 Solicitor, BT.
1977-78 Greater London Council.
1977 Admitted to Roll of Solicitors.
1975-77 East Sussex County Council
Other roles
Member, Law Society specialist planning panel; regular contributor to planning publications and lectures widely on planning issues
Professional memberships
Law Society; RTPI; UK Environmental Law Association
Contact details
Lawrence Graham, 190 Strand, London WC2R 1JN
Tel 020 7379 0000
Fax 020 7379 6854
Web www3.lawgram.com
Direct tel 020 7759 6503
Email trevor.blaney@lawgram.com

BLASCHKE, Georg
Helaba (Landesbank Hessen-Thüringen)

Position
Senior marketing officer – international real estate finance
Qualifications
Dipl-Kfm
Career history
1998 Joined Helaba as marketing officer (property finance); now senior marketing officer (international real estate finance)
Contact details
Helaba (Landesbank Hessen-Thüringen), Main Tower, Neue Mainzer Strasse 52-58, Frankfurt
Tel +49 69 91 32 01
Fax +49 69 29 15 17
Web www.helaba.de
Direct tel +49 69 9132 2109
Direct fax +49 69 9132 82109
Email Georg.Blaschke@Helaba.de

BLOOD, Edward
King Sturge

Position
Partner – investment
Qualifications
BSc; MRICS
Contact details
King Sturge, 81 Fountain Street, Manchester M2 2EE
Tel 0161 236 8793
Fax 0161 228 7972
Web www.kingsturge.com
Direct tel 0161 238 6212
Email edward.blood@kingsturge.co.uk

BLOXHAM, Tom
Urban Splash

Position
Chairman
Qualifications
MBE; Hon FRIBA; FRSA
Career history
1993 Co-founded Urban Splash Group
Other roles
Chairman, Baa Baa; chair, North West Arts Board; chair, Galaxy 102; director of Liverpool's City of Culture bid; member, Urban Sounding Board; member, ODPM property advisory group
Professional memberships
RIBA; Royal Society of Arts
Contact details
Urban Splash Ltd, Timber Wharf, 32 Worsley Street, Manchester M15 4NX
Tel 0161 839 2999
Fax 0161 839 8999
Web www.urbansplash.co.uk
Email tombloxham@urbansplash.co.uk

BLUNDELL, Gerald
LaSalle Investment Management

Position
Head – research and strategy
Contact details
LaSalle Investment Management, 33 Cavendish Square, London W1A 2NF
Tel 020 7852 4000
Fax 020 7852 4374
Web www.lasalle.com
Email gerald.blundell@lasalle.com

BLURTON, Andrew
Marylebone Warwick Balfour Group

Position
Group finance director – main board director
Qualifications
FCA
Career history
1997 Joined Marylebone Warwick Balfour Group as finance director.
1990-97 Finance director, Ex-lands.
1986-90 Managing director, Local London Group.
1984-86 Corporate finance, W Greenwell.
1977-84 Tax and corporate planning with Deloitte Haskins & Sells, Australia, and NatWest Bank, London.
1975 Qualified as chartered accountant with Deloitte Haskins & Sells
Contact details
Marylebone Warwick Balfour Group plc, 1 West Garden Place, London W2 2AQ
Tel 020 7706 2121
Fax 020 7706 8181
Web www.mwb.co.uk
Direct tel 020 7479 2929
Direct fax 020 7262 7192
Email ablurton@mwb.co.uk

BLYTH, Paul
Stannifer Corovest Fund Management

Position
Director
Contact details
Stannifer Corovest Fund Management Ltd, Ryon Hill House, Ryon Hill Park, Stratford-upon-Avon CV37 0UX
Tel 01789 415565
Fax 01789 415262
Web www.stannifer.co.uk
Direct tel 01789 207028
Email paulblyth@stannifer.co.uk

BLYTHE, Chris
Chartered Institute of Building

Position
Chief executive
Qualifications
BA; FCMA
Other roles

B?

Former director of Halton, Vale Royal and Warrington Business Links

Professional memberships

Chartered Institute of Management Accountants; Royal Society of Arts; Worshipful Company of Constructors

Interests

Flying (holder of private pilot's licence); rugby union (refereed for 25 years)

Contact details

Chartered Institute of Building, Englemere, Kings Ride, Ascot SL5 7TB

Tel 01344 630700

Fax 01344 630777

Web www.ciob.uk

Direct fax 01344 630794

Email recept@ciob.org.uk

BLYTHEN, Bob
Alfred McAlpine Special Projects

Position

Managing director

Contact details

Alfred McAlpine Special Projects, Somerfield House, Whitchurch Lane, Bristol BS14 0TJ

Tel 01565 756800

Fax 01565 756850

Web www.amsprojects.com

Direct tel 01565 756800

Direct fax 01565 756850

Email bob.blythen@alfred-mcalpine.com

BOADLE, Simon
PricewaterhouseCoopers

Position

Partner – corporate finance

Career history

1998 Joined PricewaterhouseCoopers.
1986-97 County NatWest/NatWest Markets corporate finance, London, Tokyo, Hong Kong.
1983-86 KPMG, Hong Kong.
1979-83 Binder Hamlyn

Interests

Sailing (Itchenor Sailing Club; Royal Hong Kong Yacht Club); shooting; tennis; wine; Hurlingham Club

Contact details

PricewaterhouseCoopers, 1 Embankment Place, London WC2N 6RH

Tel 020 7583 5000

Fax 020 7882 4652

Web www.pwc.com

Direct tel 020 7212 4118

Direct fax 020 7213 1055

Mobile 07711 898548

Email simon.h.boadle@uk.pwc.com

BOAG, Robert
Haslemere Estates Management

Position

Senior portfolio manager

Qualifications

BSc, Land Econ; MRICS

Career history

2000 Joined Haslemere Estates Management.
1986-2000 Property investment manager, Scottish Metropolitan Property

Professional memberships

RICS

Contact details

Haslemere Estates Management Ltd, Hobart House, 80 Hanover Street, Edinburgh EH2 1EL

Tel 0131 718 4600

Fax 0131 717 4606

Mobile 07740 444870

Email rboag@haslemerenv.com

BODEN, Paul
Jones Lang LaSalle

Position

European director – development and project management

Qualifications

FRICS; MAPM; BSc; MSc

Career history

1983 Joined Jones Lang LaSalle as building surveyor; appointed development manager in 1987; now responsible for development and project management team and lead director for professional services

Other roles

Visiting lecturer, College of Estate Management and Reading University

Professional memberships

Association for Project Management; RICS

Interests

Diving/scuba diving; DIY; reading; travel

Contact details

Jones Lang LaSalle Ltd, 22 Hanover Square, London W1A 2BN

Tel 020 7493 6040

Fax 020 7408 0220

Web www.joneslanglasalle.com

Direct tel 020 7399 5887

Direct fax 020 7399 5784

Mobile 07778 353722

Email paul.boden@eu.joneslanglasalle.com

BODHANI, Jitu
Chesterton International

Position

National director – rating

Qualifications

BSc MRICS

Career history

1974-2001 Director, Chesterton

Professional memberships

Institute of Revenues Rating & Valuation; Rating Surveyors Association

Interests

Community work; socialising

Contact details

Chesterton International, 30-34 Moorgate, London EC2R 6DN

Tel 020 7248 5022

Fax 020 7606 0649

Web www.chesterton.co.uk

Direct tel 020 7651 0914

Email jitu.bodhani@chesterton.co.uk

BOLTON, Keith
Delma Developments

Position

Managing director

Qualifications

FRICS

Career history

1987-98 Development director, Amec Developments.
1980-87 Associate partner, Dunlop Heywood

Professional memberships

RICS

Interests

Cycling; mountaineering

Contact details

Delma Developments Ltd, Lynton House, Ackhurst Park, Chorley PR7 1NY

Tel 01257 238600

Fax 01257 238601

Email kbolton@lyntonhouse.com

BOLTON, William
Harvey Spack Field

Position

Partner – major retail park lettings

Qualifications

BA Hons; MRICS

Professional memberships

RICS

Contact details

Harvey Spack Field, 33 Bruton Street, London W1J 6QU

Tel 020 7629 9663

Fax 020 7491 1964

Web www.harveyspackfield.co.uk

Direct tel 020 7518 0463

Mobile 07771 662 593

Email bolton@harveyspackfield.co.uk

B

BOND, Alistair
Hartnell Taylor Cook

Position
Senior partner
Qualifications
FRICS
Career history
1972 Joined Hartnell Taylor Cook.
1972 Goadsby & Harding.
1970-72 Clive Lewis & Partners.
1962-70 Harvey & Wheeler
Other roles
South West regional committee member, Office Agents Society
Interests
Country pursuits; sailing; shooting
Contact details
Hartnell Taylor Cook, Somerset House, 18 Canynge Road, Bristol BS8 3JX
Tel 0117 923 9234
Fax 0117 923 9237
Web www.htc.uk.com
Direct tel 0117 946 4505
Mobile 07836 599903
Email alistair.bond@htc.uk.com

BOND, Gary
McArthurGlen European Development

Position
Chief executive
Qualifications
MRICS; BSc Hons; QS
Career history
1996-2001 Group development director, BAA McArthurGlen UK.
1989-96 Development manager, Tarmac Properties.
1985-89 Senior surveyor, John Laing Construction
Professional memberships
RICS
Interests
Golf; squash; tennis
Contact details
McArthurglen European Development Ltd, Seymour Mews House, 26-37 Seymour Mews, London W1H 6BN
Tel 020 7535 2515
Fax 020 7535 2512
Web www.mcarthurglen.com
Direct tel 020 7535 2506
Direct fax 020 7535 2512
Email gary.bond@mgedevco.com

BONWELL, Robert
Jones Lang LaSalle

Position
European director – corporate solutions
Qualifications
BSc; FRICS; MBA
Other roles
Member of occupiers committee, British Council for Offices
Professional memberships
British Council for Offices; CoreNet Global UK; International Association of Corporate Real Estate Executives
Contact details
Jones Lang LaSalle Ltd, 22 Hanover Square, London W1A 2BN
Tel 020 7493 6040
Fax 020 7408 0220
Web www.joneslanglasalle.com
Direct tel 020 7399 5872
Direct fax 020 7493 5536
Mobile 07970 884752
Email robert.bonwell@eu.joneslanglasalle.com

BORE, Malcolm
LCC UK

Position
Chairman – UK
Qualifications
MRICS
Career history
1972-2001 Smith-Woolley/Smith Woolley Telecom: partner, then managing director
Professional memberships
RICS
Interests
Cricket; golf; sailing
Contact details
LCC UK Ltd, Capital Park, Fulbourn, Cambridge CB1 5XE
Tel 0122 388 3999
Fax 0122 388 3998
Web www.lcc.com
Direct tel 0122 388 3920
Mobile 07770 975651
Email malcolm_bore@lcc.com

BORET, Marcus
Akeler Developments

Position
Director
Qualifications
MCIOB
Contact details
Akeler Developments Ltd, 7 Clifford Street, London W1S 2WE
Tel 020 7864 1800
Fax 020 7864 1801
Web www.akeler.com
Mobile 07768 057057
Email marcusb@akeler.com

BORLAND, Matt
Dresdner Kleinwort Wasserstein

Position
Director – real estate and projects
Qualifications
BSc; FRICS
Career history
2001 Joined Dresdner Kleinwort Wasserstein as global head of real estate; appointed director of real estate and projects in 2003.
1997-2001 Property director, Tyco Fire & Security
Professional memberships
RICS
Contact details
Dresdner Kleinwort Wasserstein, Box 560, 20 Fenchurch Street, London EC3P 3DB
Tel 020 7623 8000
Fax 020 7623 4069
Web www.drkw.com
Direct tel 020 7475 7025
Direct fax 020 7475 5203
Mobile 07813 196355
Email matt.borland@drkw.com

BORTOLOZZO, Mario
Donaldsons

Position
Partner – head of London retail
Qualifications
MRICS
Interests
Golf; motor sports; travel
Contact details
Donaldsons, 48 Warwick Street, London W1B 5NL
Tel 020 7534 5000
Fax 020 7434 0045
Web www.donaldsons.co.uk
Direct tel 020 7534 8437
Direct fax 020 7434 0045
Email mario.bortolozzo@donaldsons.co.uk

BORTON, Christopher
Nelson Bakewell

Position
Director – retail management
Qualifications
BSc; MRICS
Career history
1995 Joined Nelson Bakewell as director.
1989-95 Partner, Antill Cowper Reeves.
1985-89 Debenham Tewson & Chinnocks
Other roles
Director, Sackville Resource Management
Professional memberships
British Council of Shopping Centres; RICS

Interests
Golf; rowing; rugby
Contact details
Nelson Bakewell Ltd, 25 Sackville Street, London W1S 3HQ
Tel 020 7544 2000
Fax 020 7544 2222
Web www.nelson-bakewell.com
Direct tel 020 7544 2115
Mobile 07887 631226
Email cborton@nelson-bakewell.com

BOSSOM, Bruce
Orion Capital Managers (UK)
Position
Managing director
Qualifications
FRICS; FRSA
Career history
1999 Joined Orion Capital Managers (UK) as managing director.
1993-99 Managing director, Jones Lang LaSalle.
1988-93 Property director, Mountleigh Group.
1985-88 Property director, Phoenix Finance & Investments.
1972-85 Partner, Jones Lang Wootton
Professional memberships
RICS
Contact details
Orion Capital Managers (UK) Ltd, 7 Cavendish Square, London W1G 0PE
Tel 020 7612 9399
Fax 020 7612 9398
Web www.orioncapman.com
Direct tel 020 7612 9360
Email bbossom@orioncapman.com

BOSWORTH, John
Bevan Ashford
Position
Partner – head of regulatory department
Qualifications
LLB Hons
Career history
Since 1995 Bevan Ashford.
1990-95 Ashurst Morris Crisp
Other roles
Member of Law Society's planning panel
Professional memberships
RTPI (legal associate)
Interests
Boating; entertaining; music; walking
Contact details
Bevan Ashford, 35 Colston Avenue, Bristol BS1 4TT
Tel 0117 923 0111
Fax 0117 929 1865
Web www.bevanashford.co.uk
Direct tel 0117 975 1731
Mobile 07775 928165
Email john.bosworth@bevanashford.co.uk

BOTHAMLEY, Michael
Beachcroft Wansbroughs
Position
Regional senior partner, Bristol
Career history
1982 Admitted to Roll of Solicitors.
1980 Joined Beachcroft Wansbroughs; appointed partner in 1986 and became regional senior partner of Bristol office in 2001
Professional memberships
Law Society
Contact details
Beachcroft Wansbroughs, 10-22 Victoria Street, Bristol BS99 7UD
Tel 0117 918 2000
Fax 0117 918 2100
Web www.bwlaw.co.uk
Email mbothamley@bwlaw.co.uk

BOTT, Bruce
Mason Owen & Partners
Position
Partner – business space
Qualifications
MRICS
Professional memberships
RICS
Contact details
Mason Owen & Partners Ltd, Gladstone House, 11 Union Court, Liverpool L2 4UQ
Tel 0151 242 3000
Fax 0151 236 2569
Web www.masonowen.com
Direct tel 0151 242 3025
Mobile 07741 052522
Email bruce.bott@masonowen.com

BOTTOMLEY, Andrew
Stylo Barratt Properties
Position
Managing director
Qualifications
FRICS
Professional memberships
RICS
Contact details
Stylo Barratt Properties Ltd, Stylo House, Harrogate Road, Bradford BD10 0NW
Tel 0127 461 7761
Direct tel 0127 489 3327
Direct fax 0127 762 1746
Mobile 07885 654155
Email Andrew.Bottomley@stylo.co.uk

BOULD, Robert
GVA Grimley
Position
Investment partner
Qualifications
FRICS
Career history
1976 Joined Grimley as associate; became divisional head of investment management in 1981.
1972-76 Edwards Bigwood & Bewlay
Other roles
Past chairman, Investment Property Forum; director, Grimley Financial Services; member, Grimley Group Executive; non-executive director, Property Fund Management, Trinity Tower Property Co and Marktune
Professional memberships
FIABCI; Institute of Continuing Professional Development; RICS; Worshipful Company of Chartered Surveyors
Interests
Golf; shooting; skiing
Contact details
GVA Grimley, 10 Stratton Street, London W1J 8JR
Tel 0870 900 8990
Fax 020 7911 2560
Web www.gvagrimley.co.uk
Direct tel 020 7911 2170
Direct fax 020 7911 2221
Mobile 07836 767029
Email rob.bould@gvagrimley.co.uk

BOURCHIER, Christopher
Crown Estate
Position
Head of rural estates
Qualifications
BSc Hons, Agriculture
Career history
1990-96 ADAS/MAFF: national dairy industry specialist and head of marketing; head of agriculture from 1993
Other roles
Member of Country Landowners Association executive and chairman of CLA institutional landowners group; chairman, Oxford Farming Conference 2000; trustee, Nuffield Trust; trustee, Frank Parkinson Trust
Professional memberships
British Society of Animal Science
Interests
Football; golf; rugby; running

Contact details
Crown Estate, 16 Carlton House Terrace, London SW1Y 5AH
Tel 020 7210 4377
Fax 020 7210 4236
Web www.crownestate.co.uk
Direct tel 020 7210 4325
Email chris.bourchier@crownestate.co.uk

BOURGEOIS, Mark
Mall Corp
Position
Director – asset management
Qualifications
BA Hons; Dip Surv; MRICS
Career history
1998 Joined Capital & Regional Properties as group asset manager; appointed director of Capital & Regional company Mall Corp when brand launched in 2002.
1991-98 Partner (shopping centre management), Donaldsons.
1990-91 KPMG
Other roles
Advisory board, CEM/BCSC diploma in shopping centre management
Professional memberships
British Council of Shopping Centres; RICS
Contact details
Mall Corp Ltd, 10 Lower Grosvenor Place, London SW1W 0EN
Tel 020 7592 9000
Fax 020 7802 5600
Mobile 07771 941779
Email mark.bourgeois@themall.co.uk

BOURNE, Mark
King Sturge
Position
Partner – head of City agency
Contact details
King Sturge, Princes Court, 7 Princes Street, London EC2R 8AQ
Tel 020 7796 5454
Fax 020 7796 5450
Web www.kingsturge.com
Direct tel 020 7796 5461
Email mark.bourne@kingsturge.co.uk

BOWDEN, Robert
British Land Co
Position
Property investment director
Qualifications
BSc; FRICS
Other roles
Chairman, British Land Properties
Professional memberships
RICS
Contact details
British Land Co plc, 10 Cornwall Terrace, London NW1 4QP
Tel 020 7486 4466
Fax 020 7935 5552
Web www.britishland.com
Direct tel 020 7467 2892
Email bob.bowden@britishland.com

BOWEN, Richard
Barwood Developments
Position
Managing director
Contact details
Barwood Developments Ltd, The Grange, Warren Office Village, Milton Keynes MK12 5NE
Tel 01908 577600
Fax 01908 312017
Web www.barwood.co.uk
Direct tel 01908 577603
Mobile 07715 577603
Email richard.bowen@barwood.co.uk

BOWER, Robert
Montagu Evans
Position
Partner – professional services
Qualifications
BSc Hons; MRICS
Professional memberships
RICS
Contact details
Montagu Evans, 44-48 Dover Street, London W1S 4AZ
Tel 020 7493 4002
Fax 020 7312 7547
Web www.montagu-evans.co.uk
Direct fax 020 7312 7536
Email rob.bower@montagu-evans.co.uk

BOWLES, John
NAI Fuller Peiser
Position
Partner – head of planning services
Qualifications
BSc Hons; Dip TP; Dip Surv; MRTPI
Career history
1993 Joined NAI Fuller Peiser. Previously held directorship and management roles in two town planning and architectural practices; before that, worked in office of London Regional Transport
Professional memberships
RTPI
Interests
Cricket; family; golf; rugby
Contact details
NAI Fuller Peiser, 16 St George Street, London W1S 1LX
Tel 0870 700 2233
Fax 020 7491 1961
Web www.nai-fullerpeiser.com
Direct tel 020 7399 3580
Direct fax 020 7399 3595
Mobile 07768 142903
Email jbowles@nai-fullerpeiser.com

BOWLES, Mark
HMV UK
Position
Head of property – HMV Europe and Waterstone's
Contact details
HMV UK Ltd, Film House, 142 Wardour Street, London W1F 8DD
Tel 020 7432 2008
Fax 020 7432 2099
Web www.hmv.co.uk
Email mark.bowles@hmv.co.uk

BOYD, Nick
Edward Symmons & Partners
Position
Partner – head of hospitality and leisure
Qualifications
FRICS
Career history
1996 Joined Edward Symmons & Partners as partner.
1986-96 Associate, Richard Ellis
Professional memberships
RICS
Interests
Motor sports; sailing
Contact details
Edward Symmons & Partners, Nuffield House, 41-46 Piccadilly, London W1J 0DS
Tel 020 7344 4500
Fax 020 7344 4555
Web www.edwardsymmons.com
Email nick.boyd@edwardsymmons.com

BOYES, Jeremy
BAA Lynton
Position
Investment director
Qualifications
BSc, Est Man; FRICS
Other roles
Chairman, Reigate & Banstead Housing Trust
Professional memberships
RICS

B

Contact details
BAA Lynton plc, 67-69 New Bond Street, London W1S 1DF
Tel 020 7907 9200
Fax 020 7907 9299
Web www.baa.com
Direct tel 020 7907 9203
Email jeremy_boyes@baa.com

BRADBEER, Nick
Stiles Harold Williams

Position
Director
Qualifications
FRICS
Career history
1988 Joined Stiles Harold Williams (Brighton office); has run south coast offices since 1995, specialising in investment agency.
1980-88 Copping Joyce: in charge of commercial property agency department
Professional memberships
RICS
Interests
Sailing; skiing
Contact details
Stiles Harold Williams Ltd, Castle Square House, 9 Castle Square, Brighton BN1 1DZ
Tel 01273 321200
Fax 01273 202436
Web www.shw.co.uk
Direct tel 01273 231220
Mobile 07850 605770
Email nbradbeer@shw.co.uk

BRADBURY, Jimmi
Cyril Sweett

Position
International director
Qualifications
BSc; Dip Proj Man; FRICS
Career history
Since 2001 International director, Cyril Sweett.
1999-2001 Director, Davis Langdon Adamson, New York.
1996-98 Director, Davis Langdon & Seah, Philippines.
1985-96 Senior associate, Cyril Sweett & Partners
Professional memberships
RICS
Contact details
Cyril Sweett Ltd, 60 Gray's Inn Road, London WC1X 8AQ
Tel 020 7061 9000
Fax 020 7430 0603
Web www.cyrilsweett.co.uk
Direct tel 020 7061 9017
Email Jimmi.Bradbury@cyrilsweett.com

BRADFORD, Douglas
Hermes Property Asset Management

Position
Portfolio manager
Contact details
Hermes Property Asset Management Ltd, Lloyds Chambers, 1 Portsoken Street, London E1 8HZ
Tel 020 7702 0888
Fax 020 7702 9453
Web www.hermes.co.uk
Email d.bradford@hermes.co.uk

BRADFORD, Katie
Linklaters

Position
Head of property and finance litigation
Qualifications
LLM; LLB Hons
Career history
Since 1992 Head of property litigation, Linklaters.
1984-91 Lovell White Durrant.
1980-84 Osmond Gaunt & Rose
Other roles
Honorary member, American Bar Association; PACT arbitrator; CEDR accredited mediator; arbitrator and independent expert,
Law Society panel and RICS panel; founding member of Property Litigation Association and Women's Property Litigation Group
Professional memberships
Chartered Institute of Arbitrators; Royal Society of Arts
Interests
Cricket; opera; theatre
Contact details
Linklaters, 1 Silk Street, London EC2Y 8HQ
Tel 020 7456 2000
Fax 020 7456 2222
Web www.linklaters.com
Direct tel 020 7456 4234
Direct fax 020 7456 3929
Email katie.bradford@linklaters.com

BRADLEY, Andrew
Hartnell Taylor Cook

Position
Partner
Qualifications
BSc; MRICS
Career history
1996 Joined Hartnell Taylor Cook.
1988-96 Partner, Donaldsons.
1985-88 Hillier Parker
Professional memberships
RICS; Shop Agents Society
Interests
Football; sailing
Contact details
Hartnell Taylor Cook, 12-13 Conduit Street, London W1S 2XH
Tel 020 7491 7323
Fax 020 7491 3032
Web www.htc.uk.com
Direct tel 020 7409 3709
Mobile 07768 058070
Email andrew.bradley@htc.uk.com

BRADLEY, Graeme
DLA

Position
Head of construction and engineering
Career history
1997 Joined DLA as partner; appointed head of construction and engineering in 2000.
1994-97 Head of construction, Eversheds.
1993-94 Advocate (international arbitration group) SG Archibald.
1985-93 Masons: moved from London to Hong Kong in 1989
Other roles
Accredited mediator since 1997; member of Centre for Effective Dispute Resolution
Professional memberships
Society of Construction Law; Technology & Construction Solicitors Association
Interests
Film-making; psychology
Contact details
DLA, Victoria Square House, Victoria Square, Birmingham B2 4DL
Tel 08700 111 111
Fax 0121 262 5795
Web www.dla.com
Direct tel 0121 262 5880
Mobile 07971 142157
Email graeme.bradley@dla.com

BRADMAN, Godfrey
European Land Group of Companies

Position
Chairman
Contact details
European Land Group of Companies, 22 Old Bond Street, London W1S 4PZ
Tel 020 7706 0189
Fax 020 7723 5341
Email gb@godfreybradman.com

BRADSHAW, Andrew
Ford Motor Co

Position
Manager, European real estate services, Ford Land
Professional memberships
CoreNet Global UK; RICS
Contact details
Ford Motor Co Ltd, Eagle Way, Brentwood CM13 3BW
Tel 01277 253000
Fax 01277 211285
Web www.ford.com
Direct tel 01277 253009
Direct fax 01277 251388
Email abradsha@ford.com

BRAIM, Edwin
Mason Philips

Position
Director
Qualifications
MA; MRICS; FSI
Other roles
Consultant, Velleman & Co
Professional memberships
RICS
Contact details
Mason Philips Ltd, 33 Great Portland Street, London W1W 8QG
Tel 020 7436 1212
Fax 020 7436 1350
Email ebraim@masonphilips.co.uk

BRAITHWAITE, Mark
Easter Development Group

Position
Director
Contact details
Easter Development Group Ltd, PO Box 802, Manchester M60 2XN
Tel 0161 834 9474
Email markabraithwaite@hotmail.com

BRAITHWAITE, Peter
DTZ Residential

Position
Managing director
Qualifications
FRICS
Career history
1971 Joined DTZ Debenham Tie Leung; chairman/managing director of DTZ Debenham Thorpe (Southern) residential division 1994-99; managing director of DTZ Residential and director of DTZ Debenham Tie Leung since 2000
Professional memberships
RICS
Contact details
DTZ Residential, One Curzon Street, London W1A 5PZ
Tel 020 7408 1161
Fax 020 7643 6000
Web www.dtzresidential.co.uk
Direct tel 020 7643 6310
Email peter.braithwaite@dtz.com

BRAMLEY, Kevin
CB Richard Ellis

Position
Chairman – North East division
Qualifications
BSc; MRICS
Career history
1977-79 Weatherall Holice & Gale.
1975-76 Valuation Office, Sheffield
Professional memberships
RICS
Interests
Sport
Contact details
CB Richard Ellis, Bank House, King Street, Leeds LS1 2HL
Tel 0113 233 7666
Fax 0113 233 7660
Web www.cbre.com
Mobile 07778 354740
Email kevin.bramley@cbre.com

BRASIER, Michael
Brasier Harris

Position
Partner
Qualifications
FRICS
Career history
1984 Co-founded Brasier Harris.
1979-84 Walker Son & Packman.
1969-79 Richard Ellis
Other roles
Director, Callcott Holdings; director, Rayner Estates & Investments; director, Pyramid Estates; governor, St Clement Danes School, Chorleywood
Interests
Cinema; family; France; golf; rugby; sailing; walking
Contact details
Brasier Harris, Victoria House, 49 Clarendon Road, Watford WD17 1HP
Tel 01923 210810
Fax 01923 236605
Web www.brasierharris.co.uk
Direct tel 01923 205504
Email mab@brasierharris.co.uk

BRATT, Andrew
FurnitureLand

Position
Property director
Qualifications
BSc; MRICS
Career history
1993-99 Associate director, Gooch Webster
Professional memberships
Accessible Retail; RICS
Interests
Mountaineering
Contact details
FurnitureLand Ltd, 9th Floor, Yeoman House, 57-63 Croydon Road, London SE20 7TP
Tel 020 8768 7100
Fax 020 8768 7130
Web www.furnitureland.co.uk
Direct tel 020 8768 7135
Mobile 07970 124 841
Email abratt@furnitureland.co.uk

BRAY, Tony
Dunlop Heywood Lorenz

Position
Director
Qualifications
BSc Hons; MRICS
Career history
1998-2001 Director, Weatherall Green & Smith.
1992-98 Associate, Edwin Hill
Professional memberships
RICS
Interests
Cinema; cooking; entertaining; football; golf; racquet sports; sailing; travel; walking; yachting
Contact details
Dunlop Heywood Lorenz Ltd, Abbey House, 32 Booth Street, Manchester M2 4QP
Tel 0161 237 7777
Fax 0161 237 7778
Web www.dhlproperty.co.uk
Direct tel 0161 237 7306
Mobile 07970 225006
Email ajb@dhlproperty.co.uk

BRAYSON, Richard
White Young Green

Position
Chief executive
Contact details
White Young Green, Arndale Court, Arndale Centre, Leeds LS6 2UJ
Tel 0113 278 7111
Fax 0113 278 3487
Web www.wyg.com
Email richard.brayson@wyg.com

B

BREESE, Richard
Stannifer Group Holdings

Position
Finance director
Qualifications
ACA; ACIB; MBA
Contact details
Stannifer Group Holdings Ltd, Ryon Hill House, Ryon Hill Park, Stratford-upon-Avon CV37 0UX
Tel 01789 415565
Fax 01789 415262
Web www.stannifer.co.uk
Direct tel 01789 207019
Direct fax 01789 415230
Email richardbreese@stannifer.co.uk

BRETHERTON, Philip
Berwin Leighton Paisner

Position
Partner – real estate
Qualifications
MA
Career history
1994 Joined Berwin Leighton (now Berwin Leighton Paisner) as partner.
1981 Qualified as solicitor in Hong Kong.
1978-94 Simmons & Simmons: became property partner in 1979.
1974-78 Slaughter & May.
1974 Admitted to Roll of Solicitors
Professional memberships
City Livery Club; East India Club; Law Society; Worshipful Company of Poulters
Interests
Music; opera; reading; squash; tennis
Contact details
Berwin Leighton Paisner Ltd, Adelaide House, London Bridge, London EC4R 9HA
Tel 020 7760 1000
Fax 020 7760 1111
Web www.berwinleighton.com
Email philip.bretherton@blplaw.com

BRETT, Alan
Hewitsons

Position
Managing partner
Qualifications
LLM (Dist); MBA; LLB Hons; Dip Int'l Law (Cantab)
Career history
1977 Joined Hewitson Becke + Shaw as partner in commercial property department; became head of property in 1991 and managing partner in 1994.
1972 Admitted to Roll of Solicitors
Other roles
Director, CAC (Holdings); lectures in property law for London University LLB; governor, Perse School for Girls, Cambridge; chairman, Cambridge Interact; Centre for Law Firms Management (Nottingham Law School)
Professional memberships
Institute of Directors; Law Society
Interests
Cinema; family; theatre; travel
Contact details
Hewitsons, Shakespeare House, 42 Newmarket Road, Cambridge CB5 8EP
Tel 01223 461155
Fax 01223 316511
Web www.hewitsons.com
Direct tel 01223 532735
Email alanbrett@hewitsons.com

BRETT, Guy
PricewaterhouseCoopers

Position
Senior manager – real estate advisory
Qualifications
BA Hons; MA; MPhil (Cantab)
Career history
2000 Joined PricewaterhouseCoopers; previously with GVA and DTZ Pieda Consulting
Contact details
PricewaterhouseCoopers, Southwark Towers, 32 London Bridge Street, London SE1 9AE
Tel 020 7583 5000
Web www.pwc.com
Direct tel 020 7212 6171
Email guy.brett@uk.pwcglobal.com

BREWSTER, David
Fortis Bank

Position
Deputy director – construction and real estate
Qualifications
BSc Hons; ACIB
Other roles
Ward of Cordwainer Club
Professional memberships
Association of Property Bankers; Chartered Institute of Bankers; Investment Property Forum
Interests
Cricket; sailing; travel
Contact details
Fortis Bank, Camomile Court, 23 Camomile Street, London EC3A 7PP
Tel 020 7444 8000
Fax 020 7444 8810
Web www.fortisbank.com
Direct tel 020 7444 8744
Direct fax 020 7444 8710
Mobile 07771 816736
Email david.brewster@fortisbank.com

BRIAM, Tony
Clifford Chance

Position
Partner
Qualifications
MA (Cantab)
Career history
Since 1981 Partner, Clifford Turner/Clifford Chance.
1974-81 Boodle Hatfield and Allen & Overy.
1974 Admitted to Roll of Solicitors
Contact details
Clifford Chance, 10 Upper Bank Street, London E14 5JJ
Tel 020 7600 1000
Fax 020 7600 5555
Web www.cliffordchance.com
Direct tel 020 7006 4004
Email tony.briam@cliffordchance.com

BRIANT, Julian
Cluttons

Position
Partner – London estate management
Qualifications
BA; MRICS
Career history
1984 Joined Daniel Smith (merged with Cluttons in 1997).
1983-84 Debenham Tewson & Chinnocks
Other roles
Member, BPF working party on leasehold enfranchisement
Professional memberships
BPF; RICS
Contact details
Cluttons, Meridien House, 42 Upper Berkeley Street, London W1H 5EP
Tel 020 7724 4545
Fax 020 7723 7277
Web www.cluttons.com
Direct tel 020 7408 1010
Email jbriant@cluttons.com

BRIDLE, Elizabeth
Grenville Smith & Duncan

Position
Finance director and company secretary
Qualifications
ACMA
Career history
1999-2001 Company secretary, Remote Management & Security.

Since 1998 Financial director/company secretary, Grenville Smith & Duncan.
1995-98 European accountant, Alpnet.
1993-94 Treasury supervisor, TSB Bank
Professional memberships
Chartered Institute of Management Accountants; Institute of Directors
Interests
Athletics; gardening; rugby
Contact details
Grenville Smith & Duncan Ltd, Waterloo House, 20 Waterloo Street, Birmingham B2 5TB
Tel 0121 631 2277
Fax 0121 665 6565
Web www.g-s-d.co.uk
Mobile 07799 837211
Email Liz.Bridle@g-s-d.co.uk

BRIGDEN, David
CB Richard Ellis
Position
Senior director – head of retail professional team
Qualifications
TD; MA; FRICS; MCIArb
Career history
1984 Joined Hillier Parker; became partner in 1993 and director of CB Hillier Parker (now CB Richard Ellis) in 1998.
1982-84 Debenham Tewson & Chinnocks
Contact details
CB Richard Ellis, Kingsley House, 1a Wimpole Street, London W1G 0RE
Tel 020 7182 2000
Fax 020 7182 7001
Web www.cbre.com
Direct tel 020 7182 2042
Direct fax 020 7182 2980
Mobile 07966 153347
Email david.brigden@cbre.com

BRIGGS, Michael
Serle Court
Position
Barrister
Qualifications
QC
Other roles
Chairman, Bar Council law reform committee
Professional memberships
Chancery Bar Association; Commercial Bar Association
Contact details
Serle Court, 6 New Square, London WC2A 3QS
Tel 020 7242 6105
Fax 020 7405 4004
Web www.serlecourt.co.uk
Email mbriggs@serlecourt.co.uk

BRIGGS, Philip
Chesterton International
Position
Group financial controller
Qualifications
BA; ACA
Career history
1994 Joined Chesterton International.
1990-94 Bear Stearns.
1985-90 British & Commonwealth.
1982-85 Spicer & Pegler
Contact details
Chesterton International, Embassy House, Queens Avenue, Bristol BS8 1SB
Tel 0117 920 9000
Fax 0117 920 9001
Web www.chesterton.co.uk
Email philip.briggs@chesterton.co.uk

BRIGHT, Roger
Crown Estate
Position
Chief executive
Qualifications
MA (Cantab)
Career history
Since 1999 Crown Estate: joined as director of finance and administration; became commissioner in 2000; chief executive since 2001.
1973–99 Principal private secretary and press secretary to DOE secretary of state; deputy chief executive of the Housing Corporation; head of finance and operations, then chief executive, Personal Investment Authority; head of investment business department (PIA firms), Financial Services Authority
Interests
Music; reading; sailing; shooting; walking
Contact details
Crown Estate, 16 Carlton House Terrace, London SW1Y 5AH
Tel 020 7210 4377
Fax 020 7210 4236
Web www.crownestate.co.uk
Direct tel 020 7210 4280
Email lucia.corrigan@crownestate.co.uk

BRILLIANT, Simon
Lamb Chambers
Position
Barrister
Career history
1976 Called to Bar
Professional memberships
Honourable Society of Middle Temple; Professional Negligence Bar Association; Property Bar Association
Interests
Cricket; reading
Contact details
Lamb Chambers, Lamb Building, London EC4Y 7AS
Tel 020 7797 8300
Fax 020 7797 8308
Web www.lambchambers.co.uk
Email simonbrilliant@lambchambers.co.uk

BRINDLEY, Ian
Haslams
Position
Partner – business space
Qualifications
MRICS
Career history
1996-99 Associate/head of industrial agency, Matthews & Goodman.
1994-96 Associate, Oliver Liggins.
1989-94 Colliers Stewarts Newiss
Professional memberships
RICS
Interests
Golf; motor sports
Contact details
Haslams, 156 Friar Street, Reading RG1 1HH
Tel 0118 960 1010
Fax 0118 960 1022
Web www.haslams-online.co.uk
Direct tel 0118 960 1015
Mobile 07879 600066
Email ib@haslams-surveyors.co.uk

BRINSMEAD, Keith
Parsons Son & Basley
Position
Partner
Qualifications
BSc Hons; MRICS
Contact details
Parsons Son & Basley, 32 Queens Road, Brighton BN1 3YE
Tel 01273 326171
Fax 01273 821224
Web www.psandb.co.uk
Direct tel 01273 274003
Mobile 07703 346446
Email keithbrinsmead@psandb.co.uk

BRISTOL, Jeremy
Birketts
Position
Partner – head of commercial property

B

Career history
1972 Joined Birketts; appointed partner same year; head of property department since 1997
Professional memberships
Law Society
Interests
Classical music; family; gardening; reading; theatre
Contact details
Birketts, 24-26 Museum Street, Ipswich IP1 1HZ
Tel 0147 323 2300
Fax 0147 323 0524
Web www.birketts.co.uk
Direct tel 0147 340 6221
Direct fax 0147 340 6385
Email jeremy-bristol@birketts.co.uk

BRITTAIN, Anthony
British Property Federation
Position
Director (tax and accounting) and company secretary
Career history
1986 Company secretary, British Property Federation.
1967-86 Company secretary, Cable Television Association.
1960-67 Low Moor Alloy Steelworks
Professional memberships
Chartered Institute of Secretaries & Administrators
Interests
Cooking; reading; travel
Contact details
British Property Federation, 1 Warwick Row, London SW1E 5ER
Tel 020 7828 0111
Fax 020 7834 3442
Web www.bpf.org.uk
Direct tel 020 7802 0113
Email abrittain@bpf.org.uk

BRITTEN, Nigel
NAI Fuller Peiser
Position
Partner
Qualifications
FRICS; HND Bldg; BSc, Est Man
Career history
1996 Joined Fuller Peiser.
1984-95 Director, Chesterton.
1983-84 Own practice
Professional memberships
RICS
Interests
Cooking; cycling; DIY; gardening; IT; keep fit; mountain biking; shooting; travel
Contact details
NAI Fuller Peiser, Waterloo House, 20 Waterloo Street, Birmingham B2 5TB
Tel 0870 700 2233
Fax 0121 605 2244
Web www.nai-fullerpeiser.com
Direct tel 0121 243 2060
Mobile 07768 143108
Email Nbritten@nai-fullerpeiser.com

BROADBENT, Bill
Marylebone Warwick Balfour Group
Position
Director – design
Contact details
Marylebone Warwick Balfour Group plc, 1 West Garden Place, London W2 2AQ
Tel 020 7706 2121
Fax 020 7706 8181
Web www.mwb.co.uk
Email bbroadbent@mwb.co.uk

BROADHURST, Marisa
Beachcroft Wansbroughs
Position
Regional senior partner – London
Career history
1989 Joined Beachcroft Wansbroughs; now regional senior partner for London and also head of commercial property department in London.
1988-89 Solicitor, London Residuary Body.
1971-76 Solicitor, Greater London Council.
1970-71 Partner, Max Bitel Greene & Co.
1970 Admitted to Roll of Solicitors
Interests
Family; theatre
Contact details
Beachcroft Wansbroughs, 100 Fetter Lane, London EC4A 1BN
Tel 020 7242 1011
Fax 020 7831 6630
Web www.bwlaw.co.uk
Direct tel 020 7894 6521
Direct fax 020 7894 6768
Email mbroadhurst@bwlaw.co.uk

BROCK, Jonathan
Falcon Chambers
Position
QC
Qualifications
QC; MA; FCIArb
Career history
1977 Called to Bar
Other roles
Elected member of Bar Council; chairman, London Common Law & Commercial Bar Association; recorder; church commissioner
Professional memberships
Chancery Bar Association; Chartered Institute of Arbitrators; Commonwealth Law Society; London Common Law & Commercial Bar Association; Property Bar Association
Interests
Cricket; football; shooting; skiing
Contact details
Falcon Chambers, Falcon Court, London EC4Y 1AA
Tel 020 7353 2484
Fax 020 7353 1261
Web www.falcon-chambers.com
Email brock@falcon-chambers.com

BROCKLEHURST, Clive
Aitchison Raffety
Position
Associate director
Qualifications
BSc Hons; MRICS
Professional memberships
RICS
Contact details
Aitchison Raffety Ltd, 8 High Street, High Wycombe HP11 2AZ
Tel 01494 538800
Fax 01494 436362
Web www.argroup.co.uk
Email clive.brocklehurst@argroup.co.uk

BRODTMAN, Michael
CB Richard Ellis
Position
Executive director – valuation and investment
Qualifications
MA; Dip TP; FRICS
Professional memberships
RICS; RTPI
Contact details
CB Richard Ellis, St Martin's Court, 10 Paternoster Row, London EC4M 7HP
Tel 020 7182 2000
Fax 020 7182 2001
Web www.cbre.com
Direct tel 020 7182 3084
Email michael.brodtman@cbre.com

BROKENSHIRE, David
FPDSavills
Position
Director – head of rating
Contact details
FPDSavills Ltd, 25 Finsbury Circus, London EC2M 7EE
Tel 020 7499 8644

B

Fax 020 7588 7323
Web www.fpdsavills.co.uk
Direct tel 020 7409 8906
Email dbrokenshire@fpdsavills.co.uk

BROOKE, Jennifer
Business Centre Association

Position
Executive director
Contact details
Business Centre Association Ltd, Kinetic Business Centre, Theobald Street, Borehamwood WD6 4PJ
Tel 020 8387 1444
Fax 020 8387 1454
Web www.bca.uk.com
Email info@bca.uk.com

BROOKE-WEBB, James
UK & European Investments

Position
Director – UK property
Qualifications
BSc Hons; MRICS
Career history
2000 Joined UK & European Investments as director; appointed director of UK property in 2002.
1994-2000 Development executive, Chelsfield.
1990-94 Richard Ellis
Professional memberships
RICS
Interests
Cricket; diving/scuba diving; fishing; tennis
Contact details
UK & European Investments Ltd, West World, West Gate, London W5 1DT
Tel 020 8991 4660
Fax 020 8991 5955
Web www.ukandeuropean.com
Direct tel 020 8991 4624
Mobile 07711 894531
Email james.brooke-webb@ukandeuropean.com

BROOKS, Colin
REALM

Position
Managing director
Contact details
REALM Ltd, The Farmhouse, Farm Road, Street BA16 0FB
Tel 01458 840222
Fax 01458 446780
Web www.realm-ocm.com
Email cbrooks@realm-ocm.com

BROOKS, David
King Sturge

Position
Partner and national head of industrial agency and development
Qualifications
BSc Hons, Est Man; MRICS
Career history
Since 1993 Equity partner, King Sturge.
1988-93 Equity partner, Chesterton.
1987-88 Equity partner, Colin Brooks & Partners.
1977-87 Associate, Dunlop Heywood & Co
Professional memberships
RICS
Contact details
King Sturge, 81 Fountain Street, Manchester M2 2EE
Tel 0161 236 8793
Fax 0161 228 7972
Web www.kingsturge.com
Direct tel 0161 238 6239
Email david.brooks@kingsturge.co.uk

BROTHWELL, Tony
DTZ Debenham Tie Leung

Position
Director – fund management
Qualifications
BSc Hons, Est Man; MRICS
Career history
1984-99 Fund manager, Imperial Tobacco Pension Fund.
1981-84 Surveyor, Standard Life
Professional memberships
RICS
Contact details
DTZ Debenham Tie Leung, One Curzon Street, London W1A 5PZ
Tel 020 7408 1161
Fax 020 7643 6000
Web www.dtz.com
Direct tel 020 7643 6378
Direct fax 020 7643 6433
Mobile 07887 755878
Email tony.brothwell@dtz.com

BROUGHTON, Steve
District Surveyors Association

Position
President
Qualifications
MRICS
Career history
1998-2002 Head of building control, Kennet District Council.
1987-98 Principal building surveyor, Swale Borough Council.
1977-87 Building control surveyor, Newcastle City Council
Other roles
Building control manager, West Berkshire Council (since 2002); company director, LABC Services (2000); former chairman, Local Authority National Type Approval Confederation; former chairman, Wessex Building Control Consortium; former chairman, Local Authority Building Control West
Professional memberships
RICS
Interests
Cycling; music; weight training (NABBA qualified weight-training instructor)
Contact details
District Surveyors Association, 137 Lupus Street, London SW1V 3HE
Tel 020 7641 8737
Fax 020 7641 8739
Web www.labc-services.co.uk
Direct tel 01635 519694
Direct fax 01635 519408
Mobile 07769 643422
Email info@labc-services.co.uk

BROUNGER, James
CB Richard Ellis

Position
Director – national office agency and leasing
Qualifications
BSc
Career history
1987 Joined CB Richard Ellis
Interests
Cricket; food; rugby; sailing; wine
Contact details
CB Richard Ellis, Kingsley House, 1a Wimpole Street, London W1G 0RE
Tel 020 7182 2000
Fax 020 7182 7001
Web www.cbre.com
Direct tel 020 7304 7226
Mobile 07860 618231
Email james.brounger@cbre.com

BROWN, Andrew
Church Commissioners for England

Position
Secretary and chief executive
Qualifications
BSc; FRICS
Career history
2003 Joined Church Commissioners for England as chief surveyor; became secretary and chief executive in 2003.
1984-94 Partner, St Quintin.

B

1981-84 Healey & Baker

Professional memberships

RICS

Interests

Church; family; golf; skiing

Contact details

Church Commissioners for England, 1 Millbank, London SW1P 3JZ

Tel 020 7898 1000

Web www.churchcommissioners.org

Direct fax 020 7898 1131

Email andrew.brown@c-of-e.org.uk

BROWN, Bruce
Lambert Smith Hampton

Position

Chairman

Qualifications

BSC; FRICS

Other roles

Non-executive chairman, TE Portfolios (EIS Investment Fund)

Contact details

Lambert Smith Hampton Ltd, Mimosa House, Princes Street, London W1B 2LL

Tel 020 7494 4000

Fax 020 7495 4207

Web www.lsh.co.uk

Direct tel 01295 760734

Direct fax 01295 760427

Mobile 07711 595151

Email bbrown@lsh.co.uk

BROWN, Charles
Dechert

Position

Partner – head of construction unit

Qualifications

LLB Hons

Career history

1996 Joined Dechert; now partner and head of construction unit.

1980 Admitted to Roll of Solicitors.

1974-95 Freedman & Co: appointed partner in 1980

Other roles

Accredited arbitrator in the Gulf Co-operation Council states; Technology & Construction Solicitors Association accredited adjudicator in the UK

Professional memberships

International Bar Association; London Solicitors Litigation Association; Society of Construction Law; Technology & Construction Solicitors Association

Interests

Cricket; football; golf; opera; rugby

Contact details

Dechert LLP, 2 Serjeants' Inn, London EC4Y 1LT

Tel 020 7583 5353

Fax 020 7353 3683

Web www.dechert.com

Direct tel 020 7775 7574

Email charles.brown@dechert.com

BROWN, David
Deloitte

Position

Lead partner – real estate funds

Qualifications

ACA

Career history

1990-2002 Arthur Andersen

Other roles

Member of tax committee, Inland Revenue

Contact details

Deloitte, 180 Strand, London WC2R 1BL

Tel 020 7936 3000

Fax 020 7583 1198

Web www.deloitte.co.uk

Direct tel 020 7007 2954

Direct fax 020 7007 2293

Email debrown@deloitte.co.uk

BROWN, Duncan
Tuckerman

Position

Director

Qualifications

MRICS

Contact details

Tuckerman, 40 Great Smith Street, London SW1P 3BU

Tel 020 7222 5511

Fax 020 7222 0558

Web www.tuckerman.co.uk

Email dbrown@tuckerman.co.uk

BROWN, John
DTZ Debenham Tie Leung

Position

Director – residential in Scotland

Qualifications

FRICS; MRTPI; Dip LE; FSA

Career history

1976 Joined DTZ. Previously at Knight Frank and Ryden

Professional memberships

RICS; RTPI

Interests

Family; gardening; rugby; sailing; swimming

Contact details

DTZ Debenham Tie Leung, 14 Queensferry Street, Edinburgh EH2 4PG

Tel 0131 459 2222

Fax 0131 226 3739

Web www.dtz.com

Direct tel 0131 535 1260

Direct fax 0131 459 1973

Email john.brown@dtz.com

BROWN, Louise
Laytons

Position

Managing partner, Bristol

Qualifications

LLB Hons

Career history

1995 Admitted to Roll of Solicitors.

1993 Joined Laytons; appointed partner in 2001 and managing partner of Bristol office in 2003

Other roles

National chairman, Association of Women in Property

Professional memberships

Faculty of Building

Interests

Horse riding; photography

Contact details

Laytons, St Bartholomews, Lewins Mead, Bristol BS1 2NH

Tel 0117 930 9500

Fax 0117 929 3369

Web www.laytons.com

Email louise.brown@laytons.com

BROWN, Michael
Helical Bar

Position

Investment director

Career history

1997 Joined Helical Bar.

1992-97 Director, Threadneedle

Other roles

Management board member, Investment Property Forum

Professional memberships

RICS

Interests

Cycling; music; ornithology; tennis; travel

Contact details

Helical Bar plc, 11-15 Farm Street, London W1J 5RS

Tel 020 7629 0113

Fax 020 7408 1666

Web www.helical.co.uk

Mobile 07799 621238

Email pmb@helical.co.uk

BROWN, Nicholas
CMS Cameron McKenna

Position
Partner – real estate
Career history
1974 Admitted to Roll of Solicitors
Other roles
Land law subcommittee member, City of London Law Society
Professional memberships
Investment Property Forum
Contact details
CMS Cameron McKenna, Mitre House, 160 Aldersgate Street, London EC1A 4DD
Tel 020 7367 3000
Fax 020 7367 2000
Web www.cmck.com
Direct tel 020 7367 2103
Email nick.brown@cmck.com

BROWN, Peter
Brasier Harris

Position
Partner – head of business space agency
Qualifications
BSc Hons; MRICS
Career history
1991-2000 Aitchison Raffety Buckland: became associate director in 1994 and director in 1997.
1987-91 Associate partner, Freeth Melhuish.
1985-87 Aitchisons
Professional memberships
Industrial Agents Society; Office Agents Society; RICS
Interests
Cycling; skiing; tennis; walking
Contact details
Brasier Harris, Victoria House, 49 Clarendon Road, Watford WD17 1HP
Tel 01923 210810
Fax 01923 236605
Web www.brasierharris.co.uk
Direct tel 01923 205521
Mobile 07740 170458
Email pb@brasierharris.co.uk

BROWN, Peter
Gerald Eve

Position
Partner – asset management
Qualifications
FRICS
Career history
1984-2001 Whitbread: joined as estates manager in retail division; appointed acquisition director for Whitbread Property in 1987 and estates director in 1990
Professional memberships
RICS
Contact details
Gerald Eve, Avebury House, Avebury Boulevard, Milton Keynes MK9 1AU
Tel 01908 685950
Fax 01908 685951
Web www.geraldeve.com
Direct tel 01908 685952
Mobile 07836 688470
Email pbrown@geraldeve.com

BROWN, Richard
Churston Heard

Position
Director – investment department
Qualifications
BSc Hons; MRICS
Career history
1992 Joined Churston Heard.
1988-92 Investment surveyor, Edward Erdman
Professional memberships
RICS
Interests
Football; hockey; squash
Contact details
Churston Heard Ltd, 7 Hanover Square, London W1S 1HQ
Tel 020 7409 2199
Fax 020 7495 1339
Web www.churstonheard.co.uk
Direct tel 020 7318 7818
Email rbrown@churstonheard.co.uk

BROWN, Richard
Thomas Eggar

Position
Partner
Qualifications
MA, Jurisprudence (Oxon)
Career history
1978 Admitted to Roll of Solicitors.
1976 Joined Thomas Eggar; became partner in 1983 and deputy managing partner in 1999
Other roles
CEDR accredited commercial mediator; committee member and past chairman of litigation subcommittee, City of Westminster & Holborn Law Society
Professional memberships
Law Society; London Solicitors Litigation Association; Property Litigation Association
Interests
Rugby; sailing; tennis
Contact details
Thomas Eggar, 76 Shoe Lane, London EC4A 3JB
Tel 020 7842 0000
Fax 020 7842 3900
Web www.thomaseggar.com
Direct fax 020 7842 3902
Email richard.brown@thomaseggar.com

BROWN, Rod
Allen & Overy

Position
Partner – real estate
Qualifications
BA (Oxon)
Career history
1975 Joined Allen & Overy; partner since 1981; head of real estate department 1995-2000
Professional memberships
Anglo-American Real Property Institute; City of London Law Society; Law Society
Interests
Cycling
Contact details
Allen & Overy, One New Change, London EC4M 9QQ
Tel 020 7330 3000
Fax 020 7330 9999
Web www.allenovery.com
Email rod.brown@allenovery.com

BROWN, Stephen
GVA Grimley

Position
Partner – head of planning and regeneration
Career history
1988 Joined GVA Grimley
Professional memberships
RTPI
Contact details
GVA Grimley, 10 Stratton Street, London W1J 8JR
Tel 0870 900 8990
Fax 020 7911 2560
Web www.gvagrimley.co.uk
Direct tel 020 7911 2335
Mobile 07831 451684
Email stephen.brown@gvagrimley.co.uk

BROWN, Stephen
RICS Foundation

Position
Director of research
Other roles
Committee member, Society of Property Researchers; property subcommittee member, Chartered Institute of Actuaries; research committee member, National Retail Planning Forum
Professional memberships

African Real Estate Society; Asian Real Estate Society; International Real Estate Society

Contact details

RICS Foundation, 12 Great George Street, London SW1P 3AD
Tel 020 7695 1568
Fax 020 7334 3894
Web www.rics-foundation.org
Direct tel 020 7334 3725
Email stephen@rics-foundation.org

BROWN, Ted
Ford & Warren

Position
Head of commercial property
Qualifications
LLB Hons
Other roles
School governor; trustee to several charities
Interests
Football; hockey
Contact details
Ford & Warren, Westgate Point, 30 Westgate, Leeds LS1 2AX
Tel 0113 243 6601
Fax 0113 242 0905
Direct fax 0113 234 5249
Email clientmail@forwarn.com

BROWNE, Peter
Lisney

Position
Director
Qualifications
FSCS; FRICS; FIAVI
Professional memberships
RICS
Contact details
Lisney, 24 St Stephen's Green, Dublin
Tel 353 1 638 2700
Fax 353 1 638 2706
Web www.lisney.com
Email pbrowne@lisney.com

BROWNHILL, Joanna
5 Paper Buildings

Position
Barrister
Qualifications
MA, Jurisprudence (Oxon)
Career history
1997 Called to Bar
Contact details
5 Paper Buildings (Chambers of Richard King QC), Ground Floor, London EC4Y 7HB
Tel 020 7815 3200
Fax 020 7815 3201
Web www.5paper.com
Email joannabrownhill@5paper.com

BROWNING, Georgina
Citigroup Smith Barney

Position
Equities analyst
Qualifications
BSc Hons; MRICS
Other roles
Hotels, leisure travel, gambling and pub equities analyst
Contact details
Citigroup Smith Barney, 33 Canada Square, London E14 5LB
Tel 020 7986 4000
Web www.citigroup.com
Direct tel 020 7986 4455
Email georgina.browning@citigroup.com

BROWNLOW, Marcus
Coffee Republic

Position
Property director
Qualifications
BSc; MRICS
Career history
1999 Joined Coffee Republic.
1995-99 City Centre Restaurants
Professional memberships
RICS
Interests
Sport
Contact details
Coffee Republic plc, Zetland House, 5-25 Scrutton Street, London EC2A 4HJ
Tel 020 7033 0600
Direct fax 020 7407 6329
Email marcusbrownlow@coffeerepublic.co.uk

BRUCE-WATT, Hugh
Masons

Position
Partner
Career history
Since 1999 Partner, Masons.
1997 Admitted to Roll of Solicitors (England and Wales).
1984 Admitted to Roll of Solicitors (Scotland)
Professional memberships
Law Society of Scotland; Law Society
Contact details
Masons, Woodbridge House, 30 Aylesbury Street, London EC1R 0ER
Tel 020 7329 2288
Fax 020 7490 2545
Web www.masons.com
Direct tel 020 7490 6423
Email hugh.bruce-watt@masons.com

BRUMMER, Malcolm
Tesco

Position
Property legal director
Qualifications
MA Hons (Cantab)
Career history
1999 Joined Tesco as property legal director.
1972 Admitted to Roll of Solicitors.
1970-99 Berwin Leighton: partner 1975-99; chairman 1990-94
Other roles
Consultant, Berwin Leighton Paisner
Professional memberships
Law Society
Interests
Opera
Contact details
Tesco plc, Tesco House, Delamere Road, Cheshunt EN8 9SL
Tel 01992 632222
Web www.tesco.com
Direct tel 01992 644231
Email malcolm.brummer@uk.tesco.com

BRUNSDON, Mark
GVA Grimley

Position
Partner
Qualifications
BSc Hons; FRICS
Career history
1987 Joined GVA Grimley
Other roles
External tutor (applied valuation) for College of Estate Management
Professional memberships
RICS
Interests
Family; tennis; walking
Contact details
GVA Grimley, University Gate, Park Row, Bristol BS1 5UB
Tel 0870 900 8990
Fax 0117 926 0607
Web www.gvagrimley.co.uk
Direct tel 0117 988 5300
Mobile 07768 448392
Email mark.brunsdon@gvagrimley.co.uk

BRUNSKILL, Julie
Argos

Position
Property director

Qualifications
BSc; MRICS
Career history
1994-2000 Property director, Budgens
Other roles
Property director, Homebase
Professional memberships
RICS
Interests
Horse riding; tennis; theatre
Contact details
Argos Ltd, 489-499 Avebury Boulevard, Milton Keynes MK9 2NW
Tel 01908 690333
Fax 01908 692301
Web www.argos.co.uk
Direct tel 01908 600112
Direct fax 01908 204040
Email julie.brunskill@argos.co.uk

BRUSH, David
Deutsche Bank
Position
Managing director – global head of real estate private equity
Contact details
Deutsche Bank AG, Winchester House, 1 Great Winchester Street, London EC2N 2DB
Tel 020 7545 8000
Fax 020 7545 6155
Web www.db.com
Direct tel 020 7547 5300
Direct fax 020 7547 5444
Mobile 07802 941593
Email david.m.brush@db.com

BRUSHFIELD, Joss
Royal Bank of Scotland
Position
Director – structured property finance group
Qualifications
BSc Hons; MRICS
Career history
2000 Joined Royal Bank of Scotland as property analyst in European Real Estate Capital group; now director.
1992-2000 Associate (investments), Chesterton
Professional memberships
RICS
Contact details
Royal Bank of Scotland, 5th Floor, 135 Bishopsgate, London EC2M 3UR
Tel 020 7375 5000
Web www.rbs.co.uk
Direct tel 020 7375 6052
Direct fax 020 7375 6054
Mobile 07747 768887
Email Joss.brushfield@rbos.com

BRYANT, Mike
GE Capital
Position
Director – business development team
Qualifications
MA (Cantab); MRICS
Career history
Since 2003 Director (business development team), GE Capital.
2000-03 Real estate finance director, HVB Real Estate Capital.
1996-2000 Head of commercial property finance, Erste Bank.
1993-96 Senior manager (management consultancy services), Coopers & Lybrand.
1988-93 Healey & Baker
Professional memberships
RICS
Contact details
GE Capital Ltd, Clarges House, 6-12 Clarges Street, London W1J 8DH
Tel 020 7302 6000
Fax 020 7302 6830
Web www.gecapital.com
Email michael.bryant@ge.com

BUCHANAN, Stuart
Haslemere Estates Management
Position
Senior portfolio manager
Qualifications
BSc Land Econ; MRICS
Career history
1987-2000 Acquisition and development manager, Scottish Metropolitan Property
Professional memberships
RICS
Contact details
Haslemere Estates Management Ltd, Hobart House, 80 Hanover Street, Edinburgh
Tel 0131 718 4600
Fax 0131 717 4606
Email sbuchanan@haslemerenv.com

BUCKEY, Robert
Castlemore Securities
Position
Construction director
Qualifications
MRICS
Contact details
Castlemore Securities Ltd, Cedar Court, 221 Hagley Road, Halesowen B63 1ED
Tel 0121 585 4444
Fax 0121 585 4441
Web www.castlemore.co.uk
Email rob@castlemore.co.uk

BUCKLEY, Tim
Stannifer Developments
Position
Group leasing director
Contact details
Stannifer Developments Ltd, Ryon Hill House, Ryon Hill Park, Stratford-upon-Avon CV37 0UX
Tel 01789 415565
Fax 01789 415262
Web www.stannifer.co.uk
Direct tel 01789 207012
Email timbuckley@stannifer.co.uk

BUDDEN, Mark
Austin Adams
Position
Director – planning and development
Qualifications
BA Hons; MRTPI
Professional memberships
RTPI
Contact details
Austin Adams, 10 Cumberland Place, Southampton SO15 2BH
Tel 023 8033 8811
Fax 023 8023 6588
Web www.austinadams.co.uk
Email MB@austinadams.co.uk

BUDGE, Richard
Denton Wilde Sapte
Position
Partner – head of real estate department
Career history
1985 Joined Denton Wilde Sapte.
1985 Admitted to Roll of Solicitors
Interests
Sailing; skiing
Contact details
Denton Wilde Sapte, One Fleet Place, London EC4M 7WS
Tel 020 7246 7000
Fax 020 7246 7777
Web www.dentonwildesapte.com
Direct tel 020 7320 6262
Mobile 07771 842827
Email rgb@dentonwildesapte.com

BUKOWSKA, Monika
Cushman & Wakefield Healey & Baker
Position
Investment research consultant
Qualifications

B

LLB; LLM

Career history

1999 Joined Cushman & Wakefield Healey & Baker as investment research consultant

Professional memberships

Society of Property Researchers

Interests

Current affairs; hockey; netball

Contact details

Cushman & Wakefield Healey & Baker, 43-45 Portman Square, London W1A 3BG

Tel 020 7935 5000

Fax 020 7152 5360

Web www.cushwake.com

Direct tel 020 7152 5764

Direct fax 020 7152 5366

Mobile 07967 568190

Email monika.bukowska@eur.cushwake.com

BULL, Andrew
LaSalle Investment Management

Position

European director

Qualifications

FRICS

Career history

1979-2000 Jones Lang LaSalle: became partner in 1987.

1972-79 Equity & Law

Professional memberships

RICS

Contact details

LaSalle Investment Management, 33 Cavendish Square, London W1A 2NF

Tel 020 7852 4000

Fax 020 7852 4374

Web www.lasalle.com

Direct tel 020 7852 4514

Direct fax 020 7852 4416

Mobile 07836 647064

Email andrew.bull@lasalle.com

BULL, Clive
Cushman & Wakefield Healey & Baker

Position

Partner – head of central London investment

Qualifications

BSc Hons; MRICS

Professional memberships

RICS

Contact details

Cushman & Wakefield Healey & Baker, 43-45 Portman Square, London W1A 3BG

Tel 020 7935 5000

Fax 020 7152 5360

Web www.cushwake.com

Direct tel 020 7152 5179

Direct fax 020 7152 5382

Mobile 07764 398179

Email clive.bull@eur.cushwake.com

BULL-DIAMOND, Christopher
FPDSavills

Position

Managing director, Frankfurt

Qualifications

FRICS

Career history

1998 Joined FPDSavills.

1968-98 Partner, Weatherall Green & Smith

Professional memberships

RICS

Interests

Golf

Contact details

FPDSavills Ltd, Untermainkai 30, Frankfurt, Germany

Tel +49 69 273 0000

Fax +49 69 25 25 38

Web www.fpdsavills.co.uk

Direct tel +49 69 273 00011

Mobile +49 172 7730792

Email cbull-diamond@fpdsavills.de

BULLER, Alfred
Bee Bee Developments

Position

Chairman

Contact details

Bee Bee Developments Ltd, Berry House, 4 Berry Street, London EC1V 0AA

Tel 020 7336 0202

Fax 020 7336 0220

Email alfie@beebee.co.uk

BULLER, Chris
Edward Symmons & Partners

Position

Partner

Contact details

Edward Symmons & Partners, 2 Southwark Street, London SE1 1RQ

Tel 020 7955 8454

Fax 020 7407 6423

Web www.edwardsymmons.com

Direct fax 020 7407 6364

Email christopher.buller@edwardsymmons.com

BULLOUGH, John
Grosvenor

Position

Retail director

Qualifications

MRICS

Career history

1989 Joined Grosvenor.

1979-89 Principal property surveyor, Legal & General Property.

1973-79 Estates surveyor, Pearl Assurance

Other roles

Member, British Council of Shopping Centres urban task force; member of Association of Town Centre Management's business improvement districts steering group; member, DTI retail strategy group project team

Professional memberships

British Council of Shopping Centres; International Council of Shopping Centers; RICS

Interests

Art; cycling; history; music; walking

Contact details

Grosvenor Ltd, 70 Grosvenor Street, London W1K 3JP

Tel 020 7408 0988

Fax 020 7629 9115

Web www.grosvenor.com

Direct tel 020 7312 6358

Mobile 07768 480146

Email john.bullough@grosvenor.com

BUNCH, Anthony
Masons

Position

International managing partner

Qualifications

BA

Career history

1980 Joined Masons as partner; senior resident partner in Hong Kong 1985-90; managing partner 1991-96; worldwide managing partner since 1996.

1978 Admitted to Roll of Solicitors

Other roles

Member, Masons partnership board; former council member, Chartered Institute of Arbitrators; CEDR accredited mediator; member, departmental advisory committee responsible for Arbitration Act 1996; member, international advisory board to Arbitration Institute of Stockholm Chamber of Commerce

Professional memberships

Chartered Institute of Arbitrators

Interests

Cycling; music; theatre

Contact details

Masons, Woodbridge House, 30 Aylesbury Street, London EC1R 0ER

Tel 020 7329 2288

Fax 020 7490 2545

Web www.masons.com

Email tony.bunch@masons.com

B

BUNGE, Wenceslao
Credit Suisse First Boston

Position
Director – investment banking, real estate group

Career history
1993 Joined Credit Suisse First Boston.
1988-93 Financial analyst, Bunge & Born

Interests
Motoring; rugby; tennis

Contact details
Credit Suisse First Boston, One Cabot Square, London E14 4QJ
Tel 020 7888 8888
Fax 020 7883 5819
Web www.csfb.com
Direct tel 020 7883 8729
Mobile 07769 885910
Email wenceslao.bunge@csfb.com

BUNKER, Tim
Ryden

Position
Partner – professional group

Qualifications
FRICS; IRRV

Career history
1979 Joined Ryden; now partner in professional group

Professional memberships
Institute of Revenues Rating & Valuation; RICS

Interests
Cricket; golf; hockey

Contact details
Ryden, 46 Castle Street, Edinburgh EH2 3BN
Tel 0131 225 6612
Fax 0131 225 5766
Web www.ryden.co.uk
Direct tel 0131 473 3215
Mobile 07721 763971
Email tim.bunker@ryden.co.uk

BUNTING, Mark
Aitchison Raffety

Position
Group director – commercial agency

Qualifications
MRICS; IRRV; ACIArb

Career history
1986 Joined Aitchisons Raffety Buckland (now Aitchison Raffety).
1985-86 Valuation Office

Professional memberships
Institute of Revenues Rating & Valuation; RICS

Interests
Football; karting; running; skiing

Contact details
Aitchison Raffety Ltd, 2 Holywell Hill, St Albans AL1 1BZ
Tel 01727 843232
Fax 01727 843098
Web www.argroup.co.uk
Email mark.bunting@argroup.co.uk

BURBAGE, John
Burbage Realty

Position
Director

Qualifications
BSc; FRICS; MILT

Career history
2003 Founded Burbage Realty.
1979-2003 National industrial director and eastern area chief executive, Lambert Smith Hampton and acquired companies.
1978-79 Valuer, District Valuer's Office

Professional memberships
Institute of Logistics & Transport; RICS

Interests
Football; rugby; snooker; squash

Contact details
Burbage Realty, Conduit House, 65 St Giles Street, Northampton NN1 1JF
Tel 01604 232555
Fax 01604 232999
Web www.burbagerealty.com
Mobile 07769 670231
Email john.burbage@burbagerealty.com

BURDETT, Geoff
McAlpines Business Services

Position
Director

Qualifications
MSc

Professional memberships
British Institute of Facilities Management

Interests
Family; golf; rugby; travel

Contact details
McAlpines Business Services, City House, 36 City Road, Chester CH88 3AN
Tel 01244 693508
Mobile 07715 159225
Email geoff.burdett@mcalpineplc.com

BURDETT, Stephen
Lambert Smith Hampton

Position
Director – management accountant

Contact details
Lambert Smith Hampton Ltd, Saddlers House, Gutter Lane, London EC2V 6HS
Tel 020 7796 4000
Fax 020 7600 1398
Web www.lsh.co.uk
Direct tel 020 7601 1845
Direct fax 020 7601 1857
Email sburdett@lsh.co.uk

BURGER, Alec
GE Capital

Position
Managing director – UK

Contact details
GE Capital Ltd, Clarges House, 6-12 Clarges Street, London W1J 8DH
Tel 020 7302 6000
Fax 020 7302 6830
Web www.gecapital.com
Email alec.burger@gecapital.com

BURGESS, Nicholas
London & Cambridge Properties

Position
Director

Qualifications
Dip Rural Est Man

Career history
1991 Joined London & Cambridge Properties.
1988-91 Management surveyor, Conway Relf.
1978-87 Self-employed

Other roles
Director of LCP Management and other subsidiary companies

Interests
Golf; IT; rugby; sailing

Contact details
London & Cambridge Properties Ltd, 20th Floor, Millbank Tower, Millbank, London SW1P 4QP
Tel 020 7233 5255
Fax 020 7233 5266
Web www.lcp-properties.co.uk
Mobile 07831 093621
Email nburgess@lcpproperties.co.uk

BURGESS, Paul
British Land Developments

Position
Director

Contact details
British Land Developments Ltd, 10 Cornwall Terrace, London NW1 4QP
Tel 020 7486 4466
Fax 020 7935 5552
Web www.britishland.com
Email paul.burgess@britishland.com

BURGESS, Quentin
Hermes Property Asset Management

Position
Director – commercial

B?

Contact details
Hermes Property Asset Management Ltd, Lloyds Chambers, 1 Portsoken Street, London E1 8HZ
Tel 020 7702 0888
Fax 020 7702 9453
Web www.hermes.co.uk
Email q.burgess@hermes.co.uk

BURGESS, Simon
Daniel Watney
Position
Partner
Qualifications
BSc; MRICS; ACIArb
Career history
2000 Joined Daniel Watney as head of management department.
1990-2000 National estates surveyor, Youth Hostels Association (England and Wales)
Contact details
Daniel Watney, 25 Hosier Lane, London EC1A 9DW
Tel 020 7246 5000
Fax 020 7248 7001
Web www.danwat.com
Email sburgess@danwat.com

BURKE, Sean
Shoosmiths
Position
Partner – head of commercial property
Contact details
Shoosmiths, Lock House, Castle Meadow Road, Nottingham NG2 1AG
Tel 0115 906 5000
Fax 0115 906 5001
Web www.shoosmiths.co.uk
Direct tel 0115 906 5030
Email sean.burke@shoosmiths.co.uk

BURKS, Philip
Big Yellow Group
Position
Joint chief executive
Qualifications
BSc; MRICS
Career history
1989-98 Edge Properties: joined as director; appointed joint chief executive in 1996.
1986-89 Director, Citygrove
Professional memberships
RICS
Contact details
Big Yellow Group plc, 2 The Deans, Bridge Road, Bagshot GU19 5AT
Tel 01276 470190
Fax 01276 470191
Web www.bigyellow.co.uk
Email pburks@thebigyellow.co.uk

BURNIE, Andrew
Heron International
Position
Operations director
Qualifications
MRICS
Career history
1981 Joined Heron International
Other roles
Asset management director, UK Portfolio
Contact details
Heron International, Heron House, 19 Marylebone Road, London NW1 5JP
Tel 020 7486 4477
Fax 020 7486 3349
Web www.heron-international.com
Direct fax 020 7487 3190
Email aburnie@heron.co.uk

BURNS, John
Derwent Valley Holdings
Position
Managing director
Contact details
Derwent Valley Holdings plc, 25 Savile Row, London W1S
Tel 020 7659 3000
Fax 020 7659 3100
Web www.derwentvalley.co.uk
Email john.burns@derwentvalley.co.uk

BURRELL, Simon
9 Old Square
Position
Barrister
Qualifications
MA (Oxon)
Career history
1988 Called to Bar
Professional memberships
Chancery Bar Association
Contact details
9 Old Square (Chambers of Michael Driscoll QC), Ground Floor, London WC2A 3SR
Tel 020 7405 4682
Fax 020 7831 7107
Web www.9oldsquare.co.uk
Email simon.burrell@9oldsquare.co.uk

BURROUGHS, Jonathan
Bidwells Property Consultants
Position
Partner – commercial department
Qualifications
BSc; FRICS
Career history
1986 Joined Bidwells.
1982-86 Healey & Baker
Contact details
Bidwells Property Consultants, Trumpington Road, Cambridge CB2 2LD
Tel 01223 841841
Fax 01223 845150
Web www.bidwells.co.uk
Direct tel 01223 559347
Direct fax 01223 840294
Mobile 07836 220811
Email jburroughs@bidwells.co.uk

BURROUGHS, Philip
McGrigors
Position
Head of real estate group
Qualifications
LLB Hons
Career history
1993-2000 Coudert Brothers: joined as partner; appointed managing partner in 1997.
1983-93 Lawrence Graham: partner on leaving.
1980-83 Freshfields.
1980 Admitted to Roll of Solicitors.
1978-80 Sedgwick Turner Sworder & Wilson
Professional memberships
Anglo-American Chamber of Commerce; City of London Law Society
Interests
Cars; gardening; sport; travel; wine
Contact details
McGrigors Ltd, 1-2 Dorset Rise, London EC4Y 8AE
Tel 020 7694 2500
Fax 020 7694 2501
Web www.mcgrigors.com
Direct tel 020 7694 2691
Mobile 07748 321743
Email philip.burroughs@mcgrigors.com

BURROWS, Christopher
Hodnett Martin Smith
Position
Consultant
Qualifications
BSc; FRICS
Interests
Cricket (MCC); golf (Bramley Golf Club); RAC; rugby; running; squash; tennis
Contact details
Hodnett Martin Smith Ltd, Charles House, 5-11 Regent Street, London SW1Y 4LR
Tel 020 7839 8181
Fax 020 7839 8069

Web www.hodnettmartinsmith.com
Direct tel 020 7747 1519
Email christopherburrows@hodms.co.uk

BURTON, Jeremy
Osmond Tricks

Position
Director
Qualifications
FRICS; FCIArb
Career history
1992 Joined Osmond Tricks.
1987-92 Associate and director, Pepper Fox.
1983-87 C&J Clark Retail Properties.
1974-83 Bristol City Council
Professional memberships
Chartered Institute of Arbitrators; RICS
Interests
Motorcycling; rugby; walking; wine
Contact details
Osmond Tricks Ltd, 40 Queen Square, Bristol BS1 4QP
Tel 0117 929 3171
Fax 0117 929 4508
Web www.osmond-tricks.co.uk
Mobile 07774 172605
Email jburton@osmond-tricks.co.uk

BURTON, Nigel
Waitrose

Position
Director of development and services
Qualifications
FRICS
Professional memberships
British Council of Shopping Centres; Property Managers Association; RICS
Contact details
Waitrose Ltd, 171 Victoria Street, London SW1E 5NA
Tel 01344 424680
Fax 01344 824488
Web www.waitrose.com
Email nigel_burton@waitrose.co.uk

BUSH, Clive
Exemplar Properties

Position
Director
Qualifications
MA (Cantab); MRICS
Career history
2003 Joined Exemplar Properties.
1999-2003 Development director, Development Securities.
1997-99 Development manager, City & West End Developments.
1995-97 Development manager, MEPC.
1991-95 CB Hillier Parker
Professional memberships
RICS
Interests
Sailing; shooting; skiing
Contact details
Exemplar Properties Ltd, 1 Berkeley Street, London W1J 8DJ
Tel 0870 606 1066
Fax 020 7016 9117
Web www.exemplarproperties.com
Mobile 07767 783737
Email cb@exemplarproperties.com

BUSH, Clive
Topland Group of Companies

Position
Property director
Qualifications
FRICS
Career history
1997 Joined Topland Group as group surveyor; appointed property director in 1999.
1988-97 Property director, Chaucer Estates.
1980-88 Legal & General
Professional memberships
RICS
Interests
Motor sports; shooting
Contact details
Topland Group of Companies, Nations House, 103 Wigmore Street, London W1U 1QS
Tel 020 7493 3373
Fax 020 7493 4055
Web www.topland.co.uk
Email cliveb@topland.co.uk

BUSHNELL, Patrick
Henderson Global Investors

Position
Director of property – Europe
Contact details
Henderson Global Investors Ltd, 4 Broadgate, London EC2M 2DA
Tel 020 7818 1818
Fax 020 7818 1819
Web www.henderson.com
Email patrick.bushnell@henderson.com

BUSSY, Anthony
Penningtons

Position
Partner – head of property, Basingstoke
Career history
1966 Joined Ward Bowie & Co (became Penningtons Ward Bowie; now Penningtons).
1966 Admitted to Roll of Solicitors
Other roles
Council member, Hampshire Law Society
Interests
Golf
Contact details
Penningtons, Da Vinci House, Basing View, Basingstoke RG21 4EQ
Tel 01256 407100
Fax 01256 479425
Web www.penningtons.co.uk
Email bussyap@penningtons.co.uk

BUTLER, Alan
Simmons & Simmons

Position
Senior property partner
Qualifications
BA Hons, Jurisprudence
Career history
1973 Joined Simmons & Simmons; became partner in 1976.
1973 Admitted to Roll of Solicitors
Professional memberships
City of London Solicitors Company; Law Society
Contact details
Simmons & Simmons, Citypoint, 1 Ropemaker Street, London EC2Y 9SS
Tel 020 7628 2020
Fax 020 7628 2070
Web www.simmons-simmons.com
Direct tel 020 7825 3584
Email alan.butler@simmons-simmons.com

BUTLER, Robin
Chelsfield

Position
Director
Qualifications
MA (Cantab); MRICS
Career history
1987 Founder director, Chelsfield
Professional memberships
RICS
Contact details
Chelsfield plc, 67 Brook Street, London W1K 4NJ
Tel 020 7493 3977
Fax 020 7493 1444
Web www.chelsfield.com
Direct fax 020 7629 0971
Email rbutler@chelsfield.co.uk

BUTT, Avril
King Sturge

Position
Partner – residential development

Career history
Since 2003 Partner, King Sturge
1992-2003 Principal director, De Groot Collis (which then merged with Chesterton).
1973-92 Negotiator/equity partner, De Groot Collis.
1972-73 Knight Frank
Interests
Art; bridge; IT; keep fit; skiing; tennis; travel
Contact details
King Sturge, 7 Stratford Place, London W1C 1ST
Tel 020 7493 4933
Fax 020 7409 0469
Web www.kingsturge.com
Direct tel 020 7318 4279
Direct fax 020 7493 3226
Email avril.butt@kingsturge.co.uk

BUTTERS, David
Gerald Eve
Position
Senior partner – head of leisure team
Qualifications
BSc; FRICS
Career history
1972 Joined Gerald Eve; appointed partner in 1982 and senior partner in 2001
Professional memberships
Entertainment & Leisure Forum; RICS
Contact details
Gerald Eve, 7 Vere Street, London W1G 0JB
Tel 020 7493 3338
Fax 020 7491 1825
Web www.geraldeve.com
Direct tel 020 7333 6237
Direct fax 020 7333 6407
Email dbutters@geraldeve.com

BUTTERWORTH, Paul
TLT Solicitors
Position
Partner – social housing
Career history
Since 2003 Partner, TLT Solicitors.
2000-03 Manches: head of social housing, then partner from 2001.
1997-2000 Burges Salmon.
1995-97 Kingfisher Housing Association.
1992-95 West Wiltshire District Council
Other roles
Member, Law Society subcommittee on housing law (1998-2000); board member, Westlea Housing Association (2000-02)
Professional memberships
Law Society
Interests
Cricket; family; photography; rugby
Contact details
TLT Solicitors, 1 Redcliffe Street, Bristol BS99 7JZ
Tel 0117 917 7777
Fax 0117 917 7779
Web www.tltsolicitors.com
Direct tel 0117 917 7575
Email pbutterworth@tltsolicitors.com

BUXTON, James
Bidwells Property Consultants
Position
Senior partner
Qualifications
FRICS
Career history
1978 Joined Bidwells; appointed managing partner in 1994 and senior partner in 2000
Other roles
Vice-chairman, CBI council, East of England
Professional memberships
CBI; RICS
Contact details
Bidwells Property Consultants, Trumpington Road, Cambridge CB2 2LD
Tel 01223 841841
Fax 01223 845150
Web www.bidwells.co.uk
Direct tel 01223 559520
Direct fax 01223 559194
Mobile 07836 706568
Email jbuxton@bidwells.co.uk

BYRON, Annette
Freshfields Bruckhaus Deringer
Position
Partner – real estate
Career history
1996 Joined Freshfields Bruckhaus Deringer; now partner
1989 Admitted to Roll of Solicitors
Contact details
Freshfields Bruckhaus Deringer, 65 Fleet Street, London EC4Y 1HT
Tel 020 7936 4000
Fax 020 7832 7001
Web www.freshfields.com
Direct tel 020 7832 7064
Email annette.byron@freshfields.com

BYWATER, John
Hammerson
Position
Managing director – UK
Qualifications
FRICS
Career history
1998 Joined Hammerson.
1992-98 Partner, Donaldsons.
1973-92 Managing director, Burton Property Trust, Burton Group
Professional memberships
RICS
Interests
Golf; music; opera; tennis
Contact details
Hammerson plc, 100 Park Lane, London W1K 7AR
Tel 020 7887 1000
Fax 020 7887 1010
Web www.hammerson.co.uk
Email jbywater@hammerson.co.uk

CABLE, Neil
Standard Life Investments

Position
Investment director – business development
Qualifications
MA Hons; Dip Prop Inv; RICS
Career history
1990 Joined Standard Life; various positions in research and European fund management; appointed business development manager in 2000.
1989-90 Lecturer in economics, Cardonald College, Glasgow
Professional memberships
Investment Property Forum
Interests
Fishing; music; rugby; travel
Contact details
Standard Life Investments Ltd, 1 George Street, Edinburgh EH2 2LL
Tel 0131 245 2700
Fax 0131 245 2710
Web www.standardlife.com
Direct tel 0131 245 2735
Direct fax 0131 240 0333
Email neil_cable@standardlife.com

CABLE, Richard
Capital Shopping Centres

Position
Director
Qualifications
BSc Hons; MRICS
Other roles
Co-opted board member, British Council of Shopping Centres
Professional memberships
RICS
Contact details
Capital Shopping Centres plc, 40 Broadway, London SW1H 0BU
Tel 020 7887 4220
Fax 020 7887 4225
Web www.capital-shopping-centres.co.uk
Direct tel 020 7887 7103
Email richard-cable@capshop.co.uk

CADMAN, Prof David
Environmental Governance

Position
Founder
Qualifications
BSc; MA (Cantab); FRICS
Other roles
Visiting professor, University College London (planning, environment and public policy, School of Public Policy); visiting professor, Bartlett School of Architecture, Planning & the Built Environment; chairman of Prince's Foundation; adviser, Coal Management Trustees; non-executive director, TransEuropean (PRICOA); adviser to main board, Bidwells; member, Carillion (environment panel)
Professional memberships
RICS
Contact details
Environmental Governance Ltd, 70 Cowcross Street, London EC1M 6EJ
Tel 020 7250 3900
Fax 020 7250 3580
Web www.pegonline.net
Email d.cadman@environgov.co.uk

CADWALLADER, Neil
Exchange Chambers

Position
Barrister
Qualifications
MA (Cantab); Dip Law; FSALS
Career history
1997 Joined Exchange Chambers.
1985-97 Chancery barrister, Chambers of William George, Liverpool.
1984 Called to Bar
Other roles
Mediator; councillor, St Gregory's Society
Professional memberships
Bar European Group; Centre for Effective Dispute Resolution; Chancery Bar Association; Honourable Society of the Inner Temple; Northern Chancery Bar Association; Northern Circuit Commercial Bar Association; Professional Negligence Bar Association; Society For Advanced Legal Studies
Interests
Art; church; classical music; hill walking; martial arts; painting; philosophy; poetry
Contact details
Exchange Chambers, 7 Ralli Court, West Riverside, Manchester M3 5FT
Tel 0161 833 2722
Fax 0161 833 2789
Web www.exchangechambers.co.uk
Mobile 07764 510986
Email cadwallader@exchangechambers.co.uk

CAIGER, Tim
Oracle Corporation UK

Position
Vice-president – real estate and facilities, EMEA
Qualifications
FBIFM
Career history
1988 Joined Oracle Corp.
1987-88 Construction manager, Digital Corp.
1981-87 Facilities manager (UK), Hewlett Packard
Other roles
Director, Thames Valley Park Management Co; director, Total Corporate FM; chairman, Thames Valley chapter of CoreNet Global UK
Professional memberships
British Institute of Facilities Management; CoreNet Global
Interests
Sailing; skiing; walking
Contact details
Oracle Corporation UK Ltd, Oracle Parkway, Thames Valley Park, Reading RG6 1RA
Tel 0118 924 0000
Web www.oracle.com
Direct tel 0118 924 6906
Direct fax 0118 924 8522
Mobile 07836 747812
Email tim.caiger@oracle.com

CAIRNEY, Mike
EC Harris Solutions

Position
Chief operating officer
Qualifications
BSc; FAPM; AMICE
Career history
1995-2002 Managing director, Axima FM.
1986-95 Director, EC Harris Project Management.
1983-86 Project manager, Beard Dove Project Management.
1980-83 Senior engineer, Trollope & Colls.
1977-80 Engineer, Norwest Holst
Other roles
Partner, EC Harris
Professional memberships
Association for Project Management; British Institute of Management; Institute of Chartered

C

Engineers; Institute of Directors

Interests

Golf; rugby

Contact details

EC Harris Solutions Ltd, Lynton House, 7-12 Tavistock Square, London WC1H 9LX

Tel 020 7387 8431

Direct tel 020 7391 4166

Direct fax 020 7388 8489

Mobile 07768 463278

Email mike.cairney@echarris.com

CALDER, Stuart

Helios Properties

Position

Director

Qualifications

BArch; MBA

Contact details

Helios Properties plc, 2 Berkeley Square, London W1J 6EB

Tel 020 7629 6452

Fax 020 7629 6453

Web www.heliosproperties.com

Email calder@heliosproperties.com

CALLANDER, John

King Sturge

Position

Partner – residential development

Career history

1995-2003 Director (residential development and investment), Chesterton.

1982-95 Director of own practice specialising in residential development, supported by general practice agency Callender Wright.

1976-82 Residential development department, Hampton & Sons

Interests

Golf; snowboarding; tennis; tobogganing; wine

Contact details

King Sturge, 7 Stratford Place, London W1C 1ST

Tel 020 7493 4933

Fax 020 7409 0469

Web www.kingsturge.com

Direct tel 020 7529 6546

Direct fax 020 7493 3226

Mobile 07977 460062

Email john.callander@kingsturge.co.uk

CALNAN, Robert

Jones Lang LaSalle

Position

Director in charge – office and industrial agency

Qualifications

MRICS

Professional memberships

RICS

Contact details

Jones Lang LaSalle Ltd, 9 Queen Victoria Street, London EC4N 4YY

Tel 020 7248 6040

Fax 020 7248 0088

Web www.joneslanglasalle.com

Direct tel 020 7399 5862

Direct fax 020 7399 5500

Email robert.calnan@eu.joneslanglasalle.com

CALVERLEY, David

Galliford Try

Position

Chief executive

Contact details

Galliford Try plc, 2 High Street, Uxbridge UB8 2AL

Tel 01895 855001

Fax 01895 855098

Web www.gallifordtry.plc.uk

Email david.calverley@gallifordtry.co.uk

CAMAMILE, Simon

Jones Lang LaSalle

Position

European director – national investment

Qualifications

MRICS

Career history

1976 Joined Jones Lang LaSalle; now European director responsible for UK industrial business and Middle East business focus

Other roles

Chairman, London ProHelp (providing free advice to community projects)

Professional memberships

RICS

Interests

Golf; shooting

Contact details

Jones Lang LaSalle Ltd, 22 Hanover Square, London W1A 2BN

Tel 020 7493 6040

Fax 020 7408 0220

Web www.joneslanglasalle.com

Direct tel 020 7399 5311

Direct fax 020 7399 5110

Mobile 07770 847429

Email simon.camamile@eu.joneslanglasalle.com

CAMERON, Ewan

Ryden

Position

Partner – head of office agency, Glasgow

Qualifications

FRICS

Other roles

Regional managing partner, Ryden, Glasgow; council member, Glasgow Chamber of Commerce; active in Wooden Spoon charity

Professional memberships

RICS

Interests

Golf; rugby; sailing

Contact details

Ryden, 130 St Vincent Street, Glasgow G2 5HF

Tel 0141 204 3838

Fax 0141 204 3554

Web www.ryden.co.uk

Direct tel 0141 270 3132

Email ewan.cameron@ryden.co.uk

CAMERON, Neil

Landmark Chambers

Position

Barrister

Qualifications

BA Hons

Career history

1982 Called to Bar

Other roles

Recorder (2002)

Professional memberships

Parliamentary Bar Mess; Planning & Environment Bar Association

Contact details

Landmark Chambers, 4 Breams Buildings, London EC4A 1AQ

Tel 020 7430 1221

Fax 020 7421 1399

Web www.landmarkchambers.co.uk

Email clerks@landmarkchambers.co.uk

CAMP, David

Stanhope

Position

Chief executive

Contact details

Stanhope plc, Norfolk House, 31 St James's Square, London SW1Y 4JJ

Tel 020 7170 1700

Fax 020 7170 1701

Web www.stanhopeplc.com

Email david.camp@stanhopeplc.com

CAMP, Simon

Grosvenor

Position

Commercial projects director

Contact details

Grosvenor Ltd, 70 Grosvenor Street, London W1K 3JP

Tel 020 7408 0988

Fax 020 7629 9115
Web www.grosvenor.com
Email simon.camp@grosvenor.com

CAMPBELL, Adrian
French Connection Group

Position
Acquisitions manager
Contact details
French Connection Group plc, 66 Great Portland Street, London W1W 7NF
Tel 020 7399 7300
Web www.frenchconnection.com
Email adrian.campbell@frenchconnection.com

CAMPBELL, Casandra
EuroPlex Cinemas

Position
Executive vice-president – real estate
Career history
1998-2000 European development director, Chelverton Properties.
1995-98 European property director, Warner Bros International Theatres.
1992-95 Manager, Hillier Parker May & Rowden, Italy.
1991-92 New business director, Retail Strategems.
1988-91 Property services director, Small Back Room
Professional memberships
British Council of Shopping Centres; International Council of Shopping Centers
Contact details
EuroPlex Cinemas, Haymarket House, 28 Haymarket, London SW1Y 4SP
Tel 020 7321 5550
Fax 020 7321 5599
Email ccampbell@europlexcinemas.com

CAMPBELL-HORNE, Iain
Arrowcroft Group

Position
Construction director
Qualifications
FRICS
Career history
1973 Joined Arrowcroft.
1966-73 Jones Lang Wootton
Professional memberships
RICS
Interests
Food; golf; travel
Contact details
Arrowcroft Group plc, 110 Park Street, London W1K 6AD
Tel 020 7499 5432
Fax 020 7493 0323
Web www.arrowcroft.com
Email campho@arrowcroft.com

CANE, Marion
KPMG

Position
Property tax director, KPMG Real Estate Advisors
Other roles
Regular speaker at seminars and conferences on property tax issues
Professional memberships
Institute of Chartered Accountants in England & Wales
Contact details
KPMG LLP, One Canada Square, London E14 5AB
Tel 020 7311 1000
Web www.kpmg.co.uk
Direct tel 020 7311 6521
Direct fax 020 7311 4088
Mobile 07748 181490
Email marion.cane@kpmg.co.uk

CANN, Philip
Dalgleish

Position
Investment director
Career history
1991 Joined Dalgleish.
1988-91 Daniel Smith
Interests
Golf (Wimbledon RFC); rugby
Contact details
Dalgleish, 80 New Bond Street, London W1S 1DD
Tel 020 7663 5555
Fax 020 7491 0098
Web www.dalgleish.co.uk
Direct tel 020 7663 5595
Direct fax 020 7663 5502
Email pcann@dalgleish.co.uk

CANNON, David
Phoenix Beard

Position
Director – asset management
Contact details
Phoenix Beard, The Exchange, 19 Newhall Street, Birmingham B3 3PJ
Tel 0121 200 4500
Fax 0121 200 4599
Web www.phoenix-beard.co.uk
Email david.cannon@phoenix-beard.co.uk

CANNON, James
Nelson Bakewell

Position
Director – investment consulting
Qualifications
BSc; MRICS
Career history
1997 Joined Nelson Bakewell; appointed director in 1999.
1990-96 Jones Lang Wootton.
1979-90 Army
Other roles
Auctioneer
Professional memberships
RICS
Interests
History; rowing; shooting
Contact details
Nelson Bakewell Ltd, 25 Sackville Street, London W1S 3HQ
Tel 020 7544 2000
Fax 020 7544 2222
Web www.nelson-bakewell.com
Direct tel 020 7544 2241
Direct fax 020 7544 2005
Mobile 07900 408360
Email jcannon@nelson-bakewell.com

CANNON, Patrick
Tax Chambers

Position
Barrister
Qualifications
LLB; BCL; CTA (Fellow)
Career history
2003 Called to Bar. Formerly head of stamp taxes at PricewaterhouseCoopers
Other roles
Stamp duty columnist, *Property Week*; author of *Tolley's Stamp Taxes* and *Butterworths' Stamp Duty Tax Cases*; council member, Chartered Institute of Taxation
Contact details
Tax Chambers (Rex Bretten, QC), 24 Old Buildings, London WC2A 3UP
Tel 020 7242 2744
Fax 020 7831 8095
Web www.taxchambers.co.uk
Email patrick@patrickcannon.net

CAPNER, Gareth
Barton Willmore

Position
Senior partner
Qualifications
MA; FRTPI; MIMgt
Career history

C

1979 Joined Barton Willmore as associate; became partner in 1981, senior planning partner in 1985 and senior partner in 1996.
1973-79 Principal planning officer, Berkshire County Council.
1970-73 Development control officer, Kent County Council.
1969-70 Planner, Ministry of Housing & Local Government

Professional memberships
RTPI
Interests
Boating; rugby
Contact details
Barton Willmore, Beansheaf Farmhouse, Bourne Close, Reading RG31 7BW
Tel 0118 943 0000
Fax 0118 943 0003
Web www.bartonwillmore.co.uk
Mobile 07850 491320
Email gareth.capner@bartonwillmore.co.uk

CAPSTICK, Charlotte
Berrymans Lace Mawer
Position
Senior partner – London office
Qualifications
LLB
Career history
1984 Joined Berrymans (now Berrymans Lace Mawer); became partner 1988 and senior partner of London office in 2002.
1984 Admitted to Roll of Solicitors
Interests
Family; France; horse riding; reading
Contact details
Berrymans Lace Mawer, Salisbury House, London Wall, London EC2M 5QN
Tel 020 7638 2811
Fax 020 7920 0361
Web www.blm-law.com
Email charlotte.capstick@blm-law.com

CARDIN, Gary
Drivers Jonas
Position
Partner – head of Birmingham office
Qualifications
BA Hons; MRTPI
Career history
1984-99 Principal associate, GVA Grimley.
1983-84 Planning assistant, Bromsgrove District Council
Professional memberships
RTPI
Contact details
Drivers Jonas, Somerset House, 37 Temple Street, Birmingham B2 5DP
Tel 0121 236 8777
Fax 0121 236 8799
Web www.driversjonas.com
Direct tel 0121 237 4404
Mobile 07775 858895
Email garycardin@driversjonas.com

CAREY, Roger
Industrious Asset Management
Position
Chairman
Qualifications
FRICS
Career history
1996-97 Joint chief executive, Rutland Group.
1983-96 Group managing director, Slough Estates.
1969-83 Senior executive, MEPC
Other roles
Non-executive director, Bassett Trust; past president and member of general council, BPF
Professional memberships
RICS
Interests
Bridge; golf; tennis
Contact details
Industrious Asset Management Ltd, Cranford House, Kenilworth Road, Leamington Spa CV32 6RQ
Tel 01926 426526
Fax 01926 426026
Web www.industrious.co.uk
Direct tel 01926 455701
Direct fax 01926 832623
Mobile 07767 270605
Email rogerc@industrious.co.uk

CARLIN, Steve
London & Cambridge Properties
Position
Retail director
Qualifications
MRICS
Career history
1992 Joined London & Cambridge Properties after 19 years with MEPC
Other roles
Various public/private partnership initiatives
Contact details
London & Cambridge Properties Ltd, Building 23, First Avenue, Kingswinford DY6 7NA
Tel 01384 400123
Fax 01384 400862
Web www.lcp-properties.co.uk
Mobile 07831 338014
Email scarlin@lcpproperties.co.uk

CARNEIRO, Ray
ABN AMRO Bank
Position
Global head of property services
Contact details
ABN AMRO Bank, 250 Bishopsgate, London EC2M 4AA
Tel 020 7678 8000
Fax 020 7678 9000
Web www.abnamro.com
Email ray.carneiro@uk.abnamro.com

CAROE, Peter
Knight Frank
Position
Senior agricultural partner
Qualifications
FRICS
Other roles
Chairman, Knight Frank Africa
Professional memberships
RICS
Contact details
Knight Frank LLP, 20 Hanover Square, London W1S 1HZ
Tel 020 7629 8171
Fax 020 7493 4114
Web www.knightfrank.com
Direct tel 020 7861 1063
Direct fax 020 7409 7819
Mobile 07836 599492
Email peter.caroe@knightfrank.com

CARPENTER, Mark
Henderson Global Investors
Position
Director – portfolio management
Qualifications
BSc; FRICS
Career history
1983-90 Partner (investment), Rohleder Lumby.
1975-83 Conrad Ritblat.
1973-75 Bernard Thorpe & Partners
Professional memberships
RICS
Interests
Golf; sport; tennis; wine
Contact details
Henderson Global Investors Ltd, 4 Broadgate, London EC2M 2DA
Tel 020 7818 1818
Fax 020 7818 1819
Web www.henderson.com
Direct tel 020 7818 4496
Email mark.carpenter@henderson.com

C

CARR, James
Barton Willmore

Position
Partner
Qualifications
RIBA
Career history
1987 Joined Barton Willmore as associate; became director and then partner.
1980-87 Architect, Solon South East Housing Association.
1978-80 Junior architect, Haringey Borough Council Architects
Interests
Climbing
Contact details
Barton Willmore, Venture House, 27-29 Glasshouse Street, London W1B 5BW
Tel 020 7446 6888
Fax 020 7446 6889
Web www.bartonwillmore.co.uk
Email architects.london@bartonwillmore.co.uk

CARRAFIELL, John
Morgan Stanley

Position
Managing director – head of European real estate
Contact details
Morgan Stanley, 25 Cabot Square, London E14 4QA
Tel 020 7513 8000
Fax 020 7513 8990
Web www.morganstanley.com
Direct tel 020 7425 5654
Direct fax 020 7425 3099
Mobile 07770 934641
Email John.Carrafiell@morganstanley.com

CARRAGHER, Madeleine
Workspace Group

Position
Operations director
Qualifications
FRICS
Career history
Since 1987 Operations director, Workspace Group.
1977-87 Management surveyor, DE&J Levy.
1976-77 Stock Conversion & Investment Trust
Professional memberships
RICS
Interests
Diving/scuba diving; reading; sailing; theatre
Contact details
Workspace Group plc, Magenta House, 85 Whitechapel Road, London E1 1DU
Tel 020 7247 7614
Fax 020 7247 0157
Web www.workspacegroup.co.uk
Email maddy.carragher@workspacegroup.co.uk

CARRICK, Kevan
storeys:ssp

Position
Director – company secretary
Qualifications
BSc, Est Man; FRICS; MCIArb
Career history
1968 Joined Storey Sons & Parker (now storeys:ssp).
1964-68 Goddard & Smith
Other roles
Accredited mediator; vice-chairman, Northern Dispute Resolutions; director, Arbrix; director, Sunderland Urban Regeneration Co; past chairman, RICS North East region; chairman, Northern Counties School (special needs, non-maintained school and registered charity); chairman, Knowledge Foundation; immediate past chairman, Northumbria branch of Chartered Institute of Arbitrators; RICS regeneration policy panel member; RICS public policy panel member; promoter, Regional Centre of Excellence in Regeneration for North East region
Professional memberships
Chartered Institute of Arbitrators; RICS
Interests
Family; gardening; keep fit; walking
Contact details
storeys:ssp, Higham House, New Bridge Street West, Newcastle upon Tyne NE1 8AU
Tel 0191 232 6291
Fax 0191 232 4610
Web www.storeys-ssp.com
Direct tel 0191 206 8702
Mobile 07957 811824
Email kevan.carrick@storeys-ssp.co.uk

CARRICK, Steve
FPDSavills

Position
Director – head of marketing
Contact details
FPDSavills Ltd, 20 Grosvenor Hill, London W1K 3HQ
Tel 020 7499 8644
Fax 020 7495 3773
Web www.fpdsavills.co.uk
Direct tel 020 7409 8834
Mobile 07931 783267
Email scarrick@fpdsavills.co.uk

CARSON, Elspeth
Semple Fraser

Position
Partner – head of group
Qualifications
LLB (Hons); Dip LP
Career history
1993 Joined Semple Fraser; appointed associate in 1995 and partner in 1997.
1991 Admitted to Roll of Solicitors.
1990-93 Tods Murray
Professional memberships
Law Society of Scotland; WS Society
Interests
Skiing; travel; walking
Contact details
Semple Fraser, 130 St Vincent Street, Glasgow G2 5HF
Tel 0141 221 3771
Fax 0141 221 3776
Web www.semplefraser.co.uk
Direct tel 0141 270 2269
Email elspeth.carson@semplefraser.co.uk

CARSWELL, Alan
Black & Decker

Position
Director – European real estate
Qualifications
BSc; MRICS; MCR
Career history
Since 1999 Director of European real estate, Black & Decker; also director of corporate services, Colliers CRE.
1993-99 Director, DTZ.
1980-93 Associate in 1987 and partner 1990, Bernard Thorpe & Partners
Professional memberships
CoreNet Global UK; RICS
Contact details
Black & Decker, 210 Bath Road, Slough SL1 3YD
Tel 01753 511234
Fax 01753 551155
Web www.blackanddecker.com
Direct tel 01753 500836
Direct fax 01753 573939
Mobile 07788 568646
Email alan.carswell@blackdecker.com

CARSWELL, Andrew
GVA Grimley

Position
Regional senior partner – Scotland
Qualifications
FRICS
Career history

C?

1987 Joined McEvoy Vigers (merged with GVA Grimley in 1989).
1967-87 Valuation office: promoted to deputy director of economic development and estates in 1979

Professional memberships
RICS

Interests
Golf

Contact details
GVA Grimley, 34 Melville Street, Edinburgh EH3 7HA
Tel 0870 900 8990
Fax 0131 220 1798
Web www.gvagrimley.co.uk
Email andy.carswell@gvagrimley.co.uk

CARTER, Colin
Woolworths

Position
Property director

Contact details
Woolworths plc, Woolworth House, 242-246 Marylebone Road, London NW1 6JL
Tel 020 7262 1222
Fax 020 7706 5416
Web www.woolworths.co.uk
Email colin.carter@woolworths.co.uk

CARTER, Daniel
Arrowcroft Group

Position
Director

Qualifications
BSc Hons; FRICS

Career history
1987 Joined Arrowcroft Group; became director in 1990; appointed to main board in 1994.
1982-87 Retail development surveyor, Donaldsons

Professional memberships
RICS; Worshipful Company of Chartered Surveyors

Contact details
Arrowcroft Group plc, 110 Park Street, London W1K 6AD
Tel 020 7499 5432
Fax 020 7493 0323
Web www.arrowcroft.com
Email dcarter@arrowcroft.com

CARTER, David
Diageo

Position
Corporate property director

Qualifications
FRICS; Dip Land Use Control

Career history
1985 Joined Grand Metropolitan (now Diageo): various property director roles.
1982-85 Estates manager, Whitbread

Professional memberships
RICS

Contact details
Diageo plc, Lakeside Drive, London NW10 7HQ
Tel 020 8978 6000
Web www.diageo.com
Direct tel 020 8978 8621
Direct fax 020 8978 8536
Mobile 07803 854580
Email david.carter@diageo.com

CARTER, Simon
Aaron & Partners

Position
Managing partner – head of property planning

Qualifications
LLB; MCIArb; MInstD

Career history
1986 Joined Aaron & Partners.
1983-86 Chief assistant solicitor, Wigan Metropolitan Borough Council.
1980-83 Principal solicitor, West Yorkshire Metropolitan County Council.
1978-80 Senior solicitor, Maidstone Borough Council.
1976 Admitted to Roll of Solicitors.
1975-78 East Hertfordshire District Council.
1973-75 Pinsent Curtis

Other roles
Trustee, Barrowmore; director, ADWaste; director, Flintshire Community Trust; director, SQ Environmental Trust

Professional memberships
Chartered Institute of Arbitrators; Environmental Law Foundation; Law Society; UK Environmental Law Association

Interests
Gardening; golf; singing; sport

Contact details
Aaron & Partners, Grosvenor Court, Foregate Street, Chester CH1 1HG
Tel 01244 405555
Fax 01244 405566
Web www.aaronandpartners.com
Email simoncarter@aaronandpartners.com

CARTLEDGE, Graham
Benoy

Position
Chairman and managing director

Qualifications
Dip Arch (Leics); RIBA; FCSD

Career history
Since 1992 Sole owner, Benoy.
1987-92 Managing director, Fitch Benoy.
1974-87 Partner, Gordon Benoy & Partners

Professional memberships
British Council of Shopping Centres; Chartered Society of Designers; RIBA

Interests
Football; golf

Contact details
Benoy Ltd, 210 High Holborn, London WC1V 7DL
Tel 020 7404 7666
Fax 020 7404 7980
Web www.benoy.com
Email graham.cartledge@benoy.com

CARTLIDGE, Denise
Acacia Group

Position
Chief executive

Contact details
Acacia Group Ltd, 58 Acacia Road, London NW8 6AG
Tel 020 7483 2281
Fax 020 7483 2258
Web www.acaciagroup.co.uk
Email offices@acaciagroup.co.uk

CARVALHO, Ciaran
Dechert

Position
Partner – head of real estate group, London

Qualifications
BA Hons, Law

Career history
1986 Joined Dechert; became partner in real estate group in 1990.
1983-86 Assistant solicitor, Arnold Fooks & Chadwick

Other roles
Education committee member and Advanced Education Faculty board member, Investment Property Forum; writes for industry and legal press; regular conference speaker

Professional memberships
British Council of Shopping Centres; Investment Property Forum

Interests
Golf; squash; tennis

Contact details
Dechert LLP, 2 Serjeants' Inn, London EC4Y 1LT
Tel 020 7583 5353
Fax 020 7353 3683
Web www.dechert.com
Direct tel 020 7775 7473
Email ciaran.carvalho@dechert.com

CARY-ELWES, Gerald
British Urban Regeneration Association

Position
Business development director
Qualifications
MA Hons; FRSA
Professional memberships
Royal Society of Arts
Interests
Cricket
Contact details
British Urban Regeneration Association, 63-66 Hatton Garden, London EC1N 8LE
Tel 020 7539 4030
Fax 020 7404 9614
Web www.bura.org.uk
Mobile 07714 265680
Email gerald@bura.org.uk

CASEY, Stephen
Fairview New Homes

Position
Managing director
Contact details
Fairview New Homes Ltd, 50 Lancaster Road, Enfield EN2 0BY
Tel 020 8366 1271
Fax 020 8366 0189
Web www.fairview.co.uk
Email stephen.casey@fnhltd.co.uk

CASH, David
Building Design Partnership

Position
Chairman, Manchester office
Contact details
Building Design Partnership Ltd, Sunlight House, Quay Street, Manchester M60 3JA
Tel 0161 834 8441
Fax 0161 832 4280
Web www.bdp.co.uk
Email DC-Cash@bdp.co.uk

CASS, Robert
Nelson Bakewell

Position
Director – business space
Qualifications
BSc; MRICS
Career history
1996-99 Acquisition surveyor, Baring, Houston & Saunders.
1994-96 Investment surveyor, Healey & Baker
Professional memberships
RICS
Interests
Golf; skiing
Contact details
Nelson Bakewell Ltd, 25 Sackville Street, London W1S 3HQ
Tel 020 7544 2000
Fax 020 7544 2222
Web www.nelson-bakewell.com
Direct tel 020 7544 2256
Direct fax 020 7544 2005
Mobile 07901 518752
Email rcass@nelson-bakewell.com

CASSIDY, Ian
FPDSavills

Position
Director – head of office, Barcelona
Contact details
FPDSavills Ltd, Rambla Catalunya 86 – 5º, Barcelona, Spain
Tel +34 93 272 4100
Fax +34 93 272 4101
Web www.fpdsavills.co.uk
Direct tel +34 93 272 4100
Mobile +34 609 60 08 94
Email icassidy@fpdsavills.es

CASSIDY, Michael
Hammonds

Position
Partner
Qualifications
BA; MBA
Career history
Since 2003 Partner, Hammonds.
2003 Consultant, Olswang.
2002-03 Partner, DJ Freeman.
1971 Admitted to Roll of Solicitors.
1969-2002 Maxwell Batley: solicitor and partner 1971-91; senior partner from 1991.
Other roles
Non-executive director, British Land; non-executive director, UBS; chairman, Hemingway Property Group; chairman, Eagle Strategic Land; chairman, Askonas Holt
Professional memberships
Architecture Club; Association of MBAs; City Architects Forum; City of London Law Society; City of London Solicitors Company; Fletchers Livery Company; Freeman of City of London; Institute of Management Consultants; Law Society; RIBA; Royal Society of Arts
Interests
Boating
Contact details
Hammonds, 7 Devonshire Square, London EC2M 4YH
Tel 0870 839 0000
Fax 0870 839 1001
Web www.hammonds.com
Mobile 07710 014810
Email michael.cassidy@hammonds.com

CATTERALL, Tim
Sanderson Weatherall

Position
Director
Qualifications
FRICS; ACIArb
Career history
1976 Rejoined Sanderson Townend and Gilbert (now Sanderson Weatherall); became partner in 1981; now director, since firm's incorporation.
1973-76 Healey & Baker.
1971-73 Sanderson Townend & Gilbert
Other roles
Member of RICS president's panel of independent experts
Professional memberships
Chartered Institute of Arbitrators; RICS
Interests
Cricket; fly fishing; music; Army & Navy Club
Contact details
Sanderson Weatherall, Robert House, Westpoint Road, Stockton-on-Tees TS17 6BA
Tel 01642 870870
Fax 01642 870877
Web www.sandersons.com
Direct tel 01642 808610
Mobile 07831 777447
Email tim.catterall@sandersonweatherall.com

CATTERMOLE, Richard
Elizabeth Holdings

Position
Chief executive
Other roles
His Lordship of Furneaux in Whatfield; president, Great Yarmouth, Lowestoft & District Licensed Victuallers Association
Interests
Antiques; art; theatre
Contact details
Elizabeth Holdings Ltd, 33 Fore Street, Ipswich IP4 1JL
Tel 0147 321 7458
Fax 0147 325 8237
Web www.elizabethhotels.co.uk
Email beverley.heffer@elizabethholdings.co.uk

CAVE, Chris
Vail Williams

Position
Partner – site assembly and development
Career history
1980 Joined Vail Williams.

1971-80 Goadsby & Harding

Interests

Cricket; DIY; fishing; gardening

Contact details

Vail Williams, Thames Valley Office, 130 Wharfedale Road, Winnersh RG41 5RB

Tel 0118 933 5600

Fax 0118 933 5634

Web www.vailwilliams.com

Mobile 07836 687644

Email ccave@vailwilliams.com

CAVEN, Robin
Lend Lease UK

Position

Chief commercial officer

Contact details

Lend Lease UK Ltd, 10 Maltravers Street, London WC2R 3BX

Tel 020 7395 7315

Fax 020 7395 7496

Web www.lendlease.com.au

Direct tel 020 7395 7302

Email robin_caven@lendlease.co.uk

CAWS, Eian
Landmark Chambers

Position

Barrister

Qualifications

BA (Oxon)

Career history

1974 Called to Bar

Other roles

Contributor to *Halsbury's Laws of England* on compulsory acquisition; has sat as an inspector and chairman of a structure plan

Professional memberships

Planning & Environment Bar Association

Contact details

Landmark Chambers, 4 Breams Buildings, London EC4A 1AQ

Tel 020 7430 1221

Fax 020 7421 1399

Web www.landmarkchambers.co.uk

Email clerks@landmarkchambers.co.uk

CHAGGAR, Rabinder
Lawrence Graham

Position

Partner – commercial property

Qualifications

LLB Hons

Career history

1987-98 Partner, Forsyte Kerman.

1985-87 Philip Hodges & Co.

1985 Admitted to Roll of Solicitors.

1983-85 Muscatt Walker & Co

Professional memberships

British Council of Shopping Centres; Law Society

Interests

Reading; theatre

Contact details

Lawrence Graham, 190 Strand, London WC2R 1JN

Tel 020 7379 0000

Fax 020 7379 6854

Web www3.lawgram.com

Direct tel 020 7759 6700

Email rabinder.chaggar@lawgram.com

CHALDECOTT, Kay
Capital Shopping Centres

Position

Director

Qualifications

BSc; MRICS

Professional memberships

RICS

Contact details

Capital Shopping Centres plc, 40 Broadway, London SW1H 0BU

Tel 020 7887 4220

Fax 020 7887 4225

Web www.capital-shopping-centres.co.uk

Direct tel 020 7887 7103

Email kay-chaldecott@capshop.co.uk

CHALMERS, David
GL Hearn

Position

Consultant

Qualifications

FRICS

Career history

1972 Joined GL Hearn; became an associate partner in 1981, director (Scotland) in 1986 and consultant in 2002.

1966-72 Associate partner, Henry J Crone & Partners

Interests

Golf

Professional memberships

RICS

Contact details

GL Hearn Ltd, 241 St Vincent Street, Glasgow G2 5QY

Tel 0141 248 4007

Fax 0141 221 7703

Web www.glhearn.com

Email david_chalmers@glhearn.com

CHALWIN, Simon
Gerald Eve

Position

Partner

Qualifications

BSc; FRICS; IRRV

Career history

1978 Joined Gerald Eve; partner since 1988

Other roles

Adviser, Universities UK

Professional memberships

Institute of Revenues Rating & Valuation; Rating Surveyors Association; RICS

Contact details

Gerald Eve, 7 Vere Street, London W1G 0JB

Tel 020 7493 3338

Fax 020 7491 1825

Web www.geraldeve.com

Direct tel 020 7333 6314

Direct fax 020 7333 6401

Email schalwin@geraldeve.com

CHAMBERLAIN, Adrian
Lend Lease Corp

Position

Chief executive – EMEA region

Contact details

Lend Lease Corp, York House, 23 Kingsway, London WC2B 6UJ

Tel 020 7379 0222

Fax 020 7379 0213

Web www.lendlease.com.au

Email danielle_yalden@lendlease.co.uk

CHAMBERLAIN, John
Chamberlain Holdings

Position

Chief executive

Career history

Since 1960 Chamberlain Holdings

Interests

Classic cars; motor racing; photography

Contact details

Chamberlain Holdings plc, Houghton Hall, The Green, Dunstable LU5 5DY

Tel 01582 845555

Fax 01582 845577

Web www.chamberlaingroup.co.uk

Email

john.chamberlain@chamberlaingroup.co.uk

CHAMBERS, Tony
Aquila House Developments

Position

Managing director

Qualifications

MSc; Dip Building Economics

Career history
Since 2002 Aquila, since company's inception.
1992-2002 Founder and managing director, Bermac Properties.
1991-92 Managing director (homes division), Rialto Group.
1985-91 Director (commercial division), Countryside Properties.
1978-85 EC Harris & Partners
Other roles
Director, Monument Group
Professional memberships
RICS
Interests
Fishing; sailing
Contact details
Aquila House Developments Ltd, 86a Broomfield Road, Chelmsford CM1 1SS
Tel 01245 292150
Fax 01245 491606
Email tonychambers@aquilaholdings.co.uk

CHAMIEH, Mark
UBS Global Asset Management (UK)
Position
Head of business development
Career history
2000-03 Managing director (marketing), Lend Lease Real Estate Investments.
1999-2000 Vice-president (business development), Putnam Investments.
1996-99 Vice-president (sales and marketing), Chase Asset Management.
1990-96 Vice-president, Chase Manhattan Bank
Contact details
UBS Global Asset Management (UK) Ltd, 21 Lombard Street, London EC3V 9AH
Tel 020 7901 5050
Fax 020 7929 0487
Web www.ubs.com
Direct tel 020 7901 5676
Direct fax 020 7901 5528
Email mark.chamieh@ubs.com

CHANDE, Manish
Mountgrange Capital
Position
Chief executive
Qualifications
ACA
Career history
1998-2002 Chief executive, Land Securities Trillium.
1985-98 Imry Holdings: finance director, then chief executive from 1996.
1981-85 Deloitte Haskins & Sells.
1975-81 Midgley Snelling & Co
Other roles
Commissioner of English Heritage (since 2003); non-executive chairman, NCP Group; non-executive director, Mitie Group; director, Property Fund Management
Professional memberships
Institute of Chartered Accountants in England & Wales
Interests
Cricket; rugby
Contact details
Mountgrange Capital plc, Arcade House, 13 Albemarle Street, London W1S 4HJ
Tel 020 7297 4960
Fax 020 7297 4969
Email manish@mountgrange.net

CHANNING, Michael
Hill Samuel Asset Management International
Position
Investment manager
Contact details
Hill Samuel Asset Management International Ltd, PO Box 909, 15 Dalkeith Road, Edinburgh EH16 5BU
Tel 0131 655 8500
Fax 0131 662 0293
Email michael.channing@swipartnership.com

CHAPLIN, Russell
Henderson Global Investors
Position
Director of property research (Europe)
Qualifications
BSc Hons, Est Man; MPhil, Land Econ (Cantab); PhD, Land Econ (Cantab)
Professional memberships
American Real Estate Society; European Real Estate Society; Society of Property Researchers
Contact details
Henderson Global Investors Ltd, 4 Broadgate, London EC2M 2DA
Tel 020 7818 1818
Fax 020 7818 1819
Web www.henderson.com
Direct tel 020 7818 5646
Email russell.chaplin@henderson.com

CHAPMAN, Kevin
CLS Holdings
Position
UK property director
Qualifications
BSc; MRICS
Career history
1986-2003 Nelson Bakewell: became associate in 1988 and director in 1991.
1984-86 Healey & Baker
Professional memberships
Investment Property Forum; RICS
Contact details
CLS Holdings plc, One Citadel Place, Tinworth Street, London SE11 5EF
Tel 020 7582 7766
Fax 020 7582 2363
Direct tel 020 7840 7727
Email kchapman@clsholdings.com

CHAPMAN, Robert
King Sturge
Position
Partner in charge, Bath
Qualifications
FRICS
Professional memberships
RICS
Contact details
King Sturge, 2 Wood Street, Bath BA1 2JG
Tel 01225 319300
Fax 01225 337053
Web www.kingsturge.com
Direct tel 01225 324105
Email robert.chapman@kingsturge.co.uk

CHAPPELL, Keith
BAA Lynton
Position
Development director
Qualifications
BSc Hons; MRICS
Career history
1987-94 Associate director, Neale House Investments.
1984-87 Senior development surveyor, Henry Boot Developments
Professional memberships
RICS
Contact details
BAA Lynton plc, 67-69 New Bond Street, London W1S 1DF
Tel 020 7907 9200
Fax 020 7907 9299
Web www.baa.com
Direct tel 020 7907 9234
Direct fax 020 7907 9328
Mobile 07785 392996
Email Keith_Chappell@baa.co.uk

CHAPPLE GILL, Sandy
Brabners Chaffe Street
Position
Partner – head of department, Liverpool
Qualifications

LLB Hons

Career history

1984-2000 Lace Mawer/Berrymans Lace Mawer.

1982 Admitted to Roll of Solicitors.

1980-84 Laces & Co

Other roles

Committee member, Liverpool Merchants' Guild; honorary treasurer, Old Swan Youth Club

Professional memberships

Law Society

Interests

Cricket; food; football; gardening; wine

Contact details

Brabners Chaffe Street, 1 Dale Street, Liverpool L2 2ET

Tel 0151 600 3000

Fax 0151 600 3300

Web www.brabnerschaffestreet.com

Email sandy.gill@brabnerscs.com

CHARKHAM, Sam
Finers Stephens Innocent

Position

Partner – head of property dealing

Career history

1987 Joined Gershon Young Finer & Green (became Finers Stephens Innocent).

1983-87 Partner, Wurzel Singleton & Charkham.

1977 Admitted to Roll of Solicitors

Interests

Diving/scuba diving; football

Contact details

Finers Stephens Innocent, 179 Great Portland Street, London W1W 5LS

Tel 020 7323 4000

Fax 020 7344 5600

Web www.finersstephensinnocent.com

Email scharkham@fsilaw.co.uk

CHARLTON, Mark
PricewaterhouseCoopers

Position

Head of European real estate research

Qualifications

BSc Hons, Management Science

Career history

1994-2000 Head of research, Lambert Smith Hampton.

1990-94 Strategic planning manager, Eagle Star Properties.

1987-90 Senior research analyst, Prudential Portfolio Managers.

1980-87 J Sainsbury

Other roles

Chairman, Society of Property Researchers

Professional memberships

American Real Estate Society; European Real Estate Society; Investment Property Forum; Society of Property Researchers; Urban Land Institute

Interests

Classic cars; rugby; skiing; squash; travel

Contact details

PricewaterhouseCoopers, Plumtree Court, London EC4A 4HT

Tel 020 7583 5000

Fax 020 7862 4652

Web www.pwc.com

Direct tel 020 7212 6263

Direct fax 020 7212 6666

Mobile 07740 639894

Email mark.charlton@uk.pwc.com

CHARLTON, Michael
London First Centre

Position

Chief executive

Qualifications

BSc; ACA

Career history

1996 Joined London First Centre.

1985-96 KPMG

Professional memberships

Institute of Chartered Accountants in England & Wales

Contact details

London First Centre, 1 Hobhouse Court, Suffolk Street, London SW1Y 4HH

Tel 020 7925 2000

Fax 020 7925 2022

Web www.LFC.co.uk

Email mcharlton@lfc.co.uk

CHASE, Graham
Chase & Partners

Position

Chairman

Qualifications

Dip, Est Man; FRICS; FCIArb; FICPD

Career history

1995 Founded Chase & Partners.

1993-95 Director/chairman of retail group, Colliers Erdman Lewis.

1980-92 Clive Lewis & Partners: became partner in 1986.

1978-79 Estates surveyor, Ladbroke Racing.

1975-78 Estates and planning department, BBC

Other roles

Director, Property Advertising Marketing & Design Awards; non-executive director, Medical Property Investment Fund; director, Liberty Regent; director, Regent Properties; chairman, RICS commercial faculty board; member, RICS president's panels of arbitrators and independent experts; court member, Chartered Surveyors Livery Company; member, HM Treasury modernising stamp duty review consultation group (2002); past president, RICS general practice division; past chairman, RICS Oxford CPD Weekend; trustee/governor, Alford House; governor, Mill Hill School

Professional memberships

Accessible Retail; British Council of Shopping Centres; Chartered Institute of Arbitrators; Freeman of the City of London; Institute of Continuing Professional Development; RICS; Shop Agents Society

Interests

Current affairs; cycling; food; golf; hockey; reading; rugby; sailing; squash; walking; wine

Contact details

Chase & Partners Ltd, 20 Regent Street, London SW1Y 4PH

Tel 020 7389 9494

Fax 020 7389 9456

Web www.chaseandpartners.com

Mobile 07971 687638

Email graham.chase@chaseandpartners.co.uk

CHASE, Martyn
Donaldsons

Position

Chairman

Qualifications

BSc; FRICS

Career history

1976 Joined Donaldsons; became equity partner in 1989

Other roles

Board member, British Council of Shopping Centres

Professional memberships

Association of Town Centre Management; British Council of Shopping Centres; RICS; Royal Society of Arts

Contact details

Donaldsons, 48 Warwick Street, London W1B 5NL

Tel 020 7534 5000

Fax 020 7434 0045

Web www.donaldsons.co.uk

Direct tel 020 7534 5001

Direct fax 020 7434 0045

Mobile 07808 479279

Email martyn.chase@donaldsons.co.uk

CHATFIELD, Leslie
Bovis Lend Lease

Position

Divisional managing director

Contact details

Bovis Lend Lease Ltd, Bovis House,
142 Northolt Road, Harrow HA2 0EE
Tel 020 8271 8000
Fax 020 8271 8018
Web www.bovislendlease.com
Email les.chatfield@eu.bovislendlease.com

CHATHAM, Mark
Countryside Properties (Commercial)

Position
Director
Qualifications
BSc Hons; FRICS
Career history
Since 1988 Director, Countryside Properties (Commercial).
1984-88 Senior development surveyor, Benson Kayley.
1980-84 Weatherall Green & Smith
Professional memberships
RICS
Interests
Cricket; golf; hockey; photography; rugby; sailing; skiing; sport; squash; tennis
Contact details
Countryside Properties (Commercial) plc,
20 Berkeley Square, London W1J 6EQ
Tel 020 7408 0099
Fax 020 7408 0772
Web www.countryside-properties.com
Direct tel 020 7399 1202
Mobile 07801 980930
Email mark.chatham@cpplc.com

CHATTERTON, Neil
Corus Group

Position
Manager – property and valuation
Qualifications
BSc; FRICS
Career history
1984 Rejoined British Steel (became Corus Group).
1974-83 District Valuer's Office.
1973-74 British Steel
Professional memberships
RICS
Contact details
Corus Group plc, PO Box 101, Weldon Road,
Corby NN17 5UA
Tel 01536 402121
Fax 01536 404699
Web www.corusgroup.com
Direct tel 01536 404696
Email neil.chatterton@corusgroup.com

CHEETHAM, David
Cheetham & Mortimer

Position
Joint senior partner
Qualifications
FRICS; Dip Est Man
Career history
Since 1978 Founder and joint senior partner, Cheetham & Mortimer.
1976-78 Dunlop Heywood.
1974-76 Woods & Partners.
1970-74 John Postlethwaite & Co
Professional memberships
Accessible Retail; Arbrix; Manchester Society of Land Agents & Surveyors; North West Estate Management Club; RICS
Interests
Cricket; football; golf; hockey; skiing; sport
Contact details
Cheetham & Mortimer, 17 St Ann's Square,
Manchester M2 7PW
Tel 0161 832 3375
Fax 0161 832 0453
Mobile 07770 774773
Email dcheetham@cheetham-mortimer.com

CHEFFINGS, Nicholas
Lovells

Position
Partner – head of property litigation
Qualifications
LLB Hons; FCIArb
Career history
1990-99 Property litigation partner, Nabarro Nathanson.
1983-90 Assistant solicitor, British Coal Corp.
1983 Admitted to Roll of Solicitors
Other roles
Member, CoreNet real estate partnerships special interest group committee; member, Forum for Dispute Resolution
Professional memberships
Arbrix; Chartered Institute of Arbitrators; CoreNet Global UK; Law Society
Interests
Sport; travel
Contact details
Lovells, Atlantic House, 50 Holborn Viaduct,
London EC1A 2FG
Tel 020 7296 2000
Fax 020 7296 2001
Web www.lovells.com
Direct tel 020 7296 2459
Email nicholas.cheffings@lovells.com

CHEGWIDDEN, Neil
Cluttons

Position
Partner – head of research
Qualifications
BSc Hons
Career history
1997 Joined Cluttons as head of research.
1990-97 Senior lecturer (property investment analysis), Sheffield Hallam University.
1989-90 Senior investment analyst, Chesterton International.
1987-89 Research analyst, Hillier Parker May & Rowden
Professional memberships
Society of Property Researchers
Contact details
Cluttons, Portman House, 2 Portman Street,
London W1H 6DU
Tel 020 7408 1010
Fax 020 7629 3263
Web www.cluttons.com
Direct fax 020 7495 4146
Email nchegwidden@cluttons.com

CHERRINGTON, John
WS Atkins

Position
Managing director – architects
Contact details
WS Atkins plc, Woodcote Grove, Ashley Road,
Epsom KT18 5BW
Tel 01372 726140
Fax 01372 740055
Web www.wsatkins.com
Email john.cherrington@atkinsglobal.com

CHERRY, Alan
Countryside Properties

Position
Chairman
Qualifications
CBE; DL; FRICS Hon; MRTPI
Career history
1971 Joined Countryside Properties as managing director; now chairman.
1951-71 Founder partner, Bairstow Eves.
Other roles
Deputy chairman, Workspace Group; vice-president, Essex Community Foundation; recent member of government's urban task force; past board member, NatWest Bank's City & West End advisory board; past chairman, New Homes Marketing Board; member, Joseph Rowntree Foundation inquiry into planning for housing; past national president, House Builders Federation; past board member, Teeside

C

Development Corp; past member, CBI national council; past chairman, CBI East of England regional council

Professional memberships

Freeman of the City of London; RICS; Royal Society of Arts

Interests

Music; reading; skiing; walking

Contact details

Countryside Properties plc, Countryside House, The Drive, Brentwood CM13 3AT

Tel 01277 260000

Fax 01277 690690

Web www.countryside-properties.com

Email alan.cherry@cpplc.com

CHERRY, Graham
Countryside Properties

Position

Chief executive

Qualifications

BSc Hons; MCIOB

Career history

1980 Joined Countryside Properties; appointed to board in 1984; now chief executive

Professional memberships

Chartered Institute of Building; Worshipful Company of Blacksmiths

Interests

Sailing; shooting; singing; skiing

Contact details

Countryside Properties plc, Countryside House, The Drive, Brentwood CM13 3AT

Tel 01277 260000

Fax 01277 690690

Web www.countryside-properties.com

Direct tel 01277 690516

Direct fax 01277 690659

Email graham.cherry@cpplc.com

CHERRY, Mark
Allders Department Stores

Position

Head of property

Qualifications

RICS; BSc Hons

Career history

1994-2003 Burford Group.

1991-94 Postel Investment Management.

1989-91 Nelson Bakewell

Contact details

Allders Department Stores Ltd, Centre Tower, The Whitgift Centre, London CR9

Tel 020 8681 5232

Web www.allders.com

Direct tel 020 8256 7728

Email mark.cherry@allders.com

CHERRY, Mark
Green Property

Position

Director – UK operations

Qualifications

BSc; MRICS

Career history

1986-89 Director, Surelodge.

1985-86 Investment surveyor, Peter Taylor & Co.

1982-85 Estates surveyor, Target Life

Professional memberships

RICS

Interests

Cooking; hockey; rugby

Contact details

Green Property Ltd, Liberty House, 222 Regent Street, London W1B 5TR

Tel 020 7499 6494

Fax 020 7629 0296

Email mcherry@greenpropertyltd.com

CHERRY, Richard
Countryside Properties

Position

Group new business director

Contact details

Countryside Properties plc, Countryside House, The Drive, Brentwood CM13 3AT

Tel 01277 260000

Fax 01277 690690

Web www.countryside-properties.com

Email richard.cherry@cpplc.com

CHERRYMAN, John
Landmark Chambers

Position

Barrister

Qualifications

QC

Professional memberships

Chancery Bar Association

Contact details

Landmark Chambers, 4 Breams Buildings, London EC4A 1AQ

Tel 020 7430 1221

Fax 020 7421 1399

Web www.landmarkchambers.co.uk

Email clerks@landmarkchambers.co.uk

CHERRYMAN, Rupert
Chesterton International

Position

Director in charge, Docklands office

Contact details

Chesterton International, Harbour Island, 28 Harbour Exchange Square, London E14 9GE

Tel 020 7538 3575

Fax 020 7538 1458

Web www.chesterton.co.uk

Email rupert.cherryman@chesterton.co.uk

CHERVAK, Dmytro
High Point Estates

Position

Managing director

Contact details

High Point Estates, High Point House, 7 Victoria Avenue, Harrogate HG1 1EQ

Tel 01423 504808

Email demi@highpointestates.co.uk

CHESS, Robert
Fleurets

Position

Director

Career history

2004 Joined Fleurets.

1987-2004 Director, Chesterton.

1985-87 Estate manager, Grand Metropolitan.

1983-85 Assistant estates manager, Imperial Group.

1981-83 Area valuer, Greater London Council

Professional memberships

Arbrix; Association of Valuers of Licensed Property; Entertainment & Leisure Forum; RICS

Interests

Cinema; food; football; theatre

Contact details

Fleurets Ltd, 18 Bloomsbury Square, London WC1A 2NS

Tel 020 7636 8992

Fax 020 7636 7490

Email robert.chess@fleurets.com

CHESSER, Andrew
Beachcroft Wansbroughs

Position

Partner – head of London property litigation

Career history

1990 Joined Beachcroft Stanleys (now Beachcroft Wansbroughs); appointed partner in 1998 and head of London property litigation and planning in 2003.

1987-90 Stafford Clark & Co.

1987 Admitted to Roll of Solicitors

Contact details

Beachcroft Wansbroughs, 100 Fetter Lane, London EC4A 1BN

Tel 020 7242 1011

Fax 020 7831 6630

Web www.bwlaw.co.uk

Direct tel 020 7894 6527

Direct fax 020 7894 6660

Email achesser@bwlaw.co.uk

CHESTER, Mark
Wragge & Co

Position
Partner – real estate and development
Qualifications
LLB Hons
Career history
2000 Joined Wragge & Co as associate; became partner in 2003.
1995-2000 Linklaters.
1992-95 Berwin Leighton
Other roles
Chairman, NSPCC Birmingham business group
Professional memberships
Law Society
Contact details
Wragge & Co LLP, 55-73 Colmore Row, Birmingham B3 2AS
Tel 0870 903 1000
Fax 0870 904 1099
Web www.wragge.com
Direct tel 0121 629 1869
Mobile 07717 335956
Email mark_chester@wragge.com

CHETWOOD, Laurie
Chetwood Associates

Position
Chairman
Contact details
Chetwood Associates Ltd, 12-13 Clerkenwell Green, London EC1R 0QJ
Tel 020 7490 2400
Fax 020 7250 1916
Web www.chetwood-associates.com
Email
laurie.chetwood@chetwood-associates.com

CHILDS, Alan
McKay Securities

Position
Finance director
Other roles
Company secretary
Contact details
McKay Securities plc, 20-30 Greyfriars Road, Reading RG1 1PE
Tel 0118 950 2333
Fax 0118 939 1393
Email info@mckaysecurities.plc.uk

CHILTON, Paul
Cluttons

Position
Partner – project and building consultancy
Qualifications
BSc Hons; FRICS; MCIArb
Career history
1989-2001 Partner, Knight Frank.
1987-89 Building surveyor, Clifford Tee & Gale.
1984-87 Wilks Head & Eve
Professional memberships
Chartered Institute of Arbitrators; RICS
Interests
Architecture; football; IT; music
Contact details
Cluttons, Portman House, 2 Portman Street, London W1H 6DU
Tel 020 7408 1010
Fax 020 7629 3263
Web www.cluttons.com
Direct tel 020 7647 7203
Direct fax 020 7647 7177
Mobile 07909 924558
Email pj.chilton@cluttons.com

CHILVER, Graham
Barclays Bank

Position
Head of sales and marketing – property finance
Qualifications
ACIB
Interests
Family; football (Crystal Palace FC); golf
Contact details
Barclays Bank plc, 54 Lombard Street, London EC3P 3AH
Tel 020 7699 5000
Web www.barclays.com
Direct tel 020 7699 4857
Mobile 07775 544290
Email graham.a.chilver@barclayscorporate.com

CHING, Derek
Clarks Solicitors

Position
Partner – head of commercial property
Contact details
Clarks Solicitors, 1 Forbury Square, Reading RG1 3EB
Tel 0118 958 5321
Fax 0118 960 4611
Web www.clarkslegal.com
Email derekching@clarks-solicitors.co.uk

CHRISP, Stewart
British Airways Pension Fund

Position
Property manager
Qualifications
FRICS
Professional memberships
RICS
Contact details
British Airways Pension Fund, Alton House, 177 High Holborn, London WC1V 7AA
Tel 020 7845 4900
Web www.britishairways.com
Email stewart.chrisp@bapensions.com

CHUBB, Roger
Hartnell Taylor Cook

Position
Partner – investment
Qualifications
BSc; FRICS
Career history
1992 Joined Hartnell Taylor Cook.
1981-92 Jones Lang Wootton.
1979-81 Osmond Tricks, Bristol.
1976-79 District Valuer's Office, Bath
Professional memberships
RICS
Interests
Cycling; diving/scuba diving; running; swimming
Contact details
Hartnell Taylor Cook, Somerset House, 18 Canynge Road, Bristol BS8 3JX
Tel 0117 923 9234
Fax 0117 923 9237
Web www.htc.uk.com
Direct tel 0117 946 4517
Mobile 07775 534044
Email roger.chubb@htc.uk.com

CHUMBLEY, Malcolm
Cluttons

Position
Partner – head of development agency
Qualifications
FRICS; Dip TP; MRTPI
Career history
1986 Joined Cluttons
Professional memberships
RICS; RTPI
Interests
Sailing; skiing; travel
Contact details
Cluttons, Portman House, 2 Portman Street, London W1H 6DU
Tel 020 7408 1010
Fax 020 7629 3263
Web www.cluttons.com
Direct tel 020 7647 7143
Mobile 07767 637282
Email mchumbley@cluttons.com

CHURCH, David
Deutsche Bank

Position
Managing director – UK real estate investment

Qualifications
BSc; MRICS
Professional memberships
RICS
Contact details
Deutsche Bank AG, Winchester House, 1 Great Winchester Street, London EC2N 2DB
Tel 020 7545 8000
Fax 020 7545 6155
Web www.db.com
Direct tel 020 7547 5328
Email david.church@db.com

CHURCH, Trevor
Freeth Melhuish

Position
Partner – head of business space agency
Qualifications
MRICS
Career history
1990 Joined Freeth Melhuish.
1981-90 Associate partner, Aitchisons
Professional memberships
RICS
Interests
Football; golf; music; skiing; sport
Contact details
Freeth Melhuish, The Courtyard, 77–79 Marlowes, Hemel Hempstead HP1 1LF
Tel 01442 263033
Fax 01442 260628
Direct tel 01442 298808
Mobile 07831 619734
Email tdc@freethmelhuish.co.uk

CLARK, Charles
ATIS REAL Weatheralls

Position
Director – head of UK investment
Qualifications
BSc; FRICS
Career history
1973 Joined ATIS REAL Weatheralls; appointed partner in 1983; now director and head of UK investment.
1971-72 Conway Relf & Sabey
Other roles
Regulated by FSA to advise on property-related collective investment schemes
Professional memberships
Investment Property Forum; RICS
Interests
Sailing
Contact details
ATIS Real Weatheralls Ltd, Norfolk House, 31 St James's Square, London SW1Y 4JR
Tel 020 7338 4200
Fax 020 7493 0746
Web www.atisrealweatheralls.com
Direct tel 020 7338 4210
Email charles.clark@atisrealweatheralls.com

CLARK, David
Dunphys

Position
Director – commercial property
Contact details
Dunphys, 162 Goldhawk Road, London W12 8HL
Tel 020 8743 1105
Fax 020 8743 3442
Web www.dunphys.cpd.co.uk
Email david.clark@dunphys.co.uk

CLARK, George
Aberdeen Property Investors UK

Position
Associate director
Qualifications
MRICS
Professional memberships
RICS
Interests
Sailing; skiing
Contact details
Aberdeen Property Investors UK Ltd, 123 St Vincent Street, Glasgow G2 5EA
Tel 0141 306 7600
Fax 0141 306 7706
Web www.aberdeenpropertyinvestors.com
Email
george.clark@aberdeenpropertyinvestors.com

CLARK, John
DLA

Position
Partner
Qualifications
LLB Hons
Career history
1998-2003 Partner, DJ Freeman.
1995-98 Partner, Stones Porter.
1984-95 Stoneham Langton & Passmore: became partner in 1986.
1983 Admitted to Roll of Solicitors
Contact details
DLA, 3 Noble Street, London EC2V 7EE
Tel 08700 111111
Fax 020 7796 6666
Web www.dla.com
Email john.clark@dla.com

CLARK, Martin
Stiles Harold Williams

Position
Director
Qualifications
MRICS
Contact details
Stiles Harold Williams Ltd, Castle Square House, 9 Castle Square, Brighton BN1 1DZ
Tel 01273 321200
Fax 01273 202436
Web www.shw.co.uk
Email mclark@shw.co.uk

CLARK, Paul
Church Commissioners for England

Position
Chief surveyor
Qualifications
MPhil; MRICS
Contact details
Church Commissioners for England, 1 Millbank, London SW1P 3JZ
Tel 020 7898 1000
Web www.churchcommissioners.org
Email paul.clark@c-of-e.org.uk

CLARK, Paul
Property Market Analysis

Position
Partner – investment
Qualifications
BSc; MRICS
Career history
1989 Joined Property Market Analysis.
1987-89 Researcher, College of Estate Management.
1986-87 Hillier Parker
Professional memberships
Investment Property Forum; RICS; Society of Property Researchers
Contact details
Property Market Analysis LLP, 2 Lygon Place, London SW1W 0JR
Tel 020 7881 0300
Fax 020 7881 0400
Web www.pma.co.uk
Direct tel 020 7881 0337
Email paul.clark@pma.co.uk

CLARK, Philip
Morley Fund Management

Position
Head – specialist fund
Qualifications
BSc; MA; MRICS
Career history

1998 Joined Norwich Union

Other roles

Member, Investment Property Forum education committee; chairman, RICS finance and funding panel

Professional memberships

Investment Property Forum; RICS

Contact details

Morley Fund Management Ltd, 34-36 Lime Street, London EC3M 7JE
Tel 020 7809 6000
Fax 020 7489 7940
Web www.morleyfm.com
Direct tel 020 7809 6873
Direct fax 020 7332 9122
Mobile 07713 146707
Email phil.clark@morleyfm.com

CLARK, Robin
Taylor Clark

Position

Chairman

Contact details

Taylor Clark plc, 30-34 Haymarket, London SW1Y 4TP
Tel 020 7930 8494
Fax 020 7930 5575
Email mail@taylorclark.co.uk

CLARK, Simon
Linklaters

Position

Head of European real estate

Qualifications

BA Hons, Law

Career history

1979 Joined Linklaters; made partner in 1988 and head of real estate department in 1999

Other roles

Specialist in UK taxation of real estate transactions and investment structuring; European council member, Urban Land Institute; member, Investment Property Forum working party on securitisation of property

Professional memberships

Anglo-American Real Property Institute; Association of Foreign Investors in Real Estate; Investment Property Forum; National Association of Real Estate Investment Trusts (US); Urban Land Institute

Contact details

Linklaters, 1 Silk Street, London EC2Y 8HQ
Tel 020 7456 2000
Fax 020 7456 2222
Web www.linklaters.com
Direct tel 020 7456 4902
Email simon.clark@linklaters.com

CLARK, Stephen
ASDA Stores

Position

Director of property

Qualifications

MA; FRICS

Professional memberships

RICS

Contact details

ASDA Stores Ltd, Asda House, Great Wilson Street, Leeds LS11 5AD
Tel 0113 243 5435
Fax 0113 241 8835
Web www.asda.co.uk
Direct tel 0113 241 8702
Email sgclark@asda.co.uk

CLARK, Vanessa
Stiles Harold Williams

Position

Director

Qualifications

MA; BSc Hons

Career history

1993 Joined Stiles Harold Williams

Interests

Art; cinema; skiing; theatre; travel

Contact details

Stiles Harold Williams Ltd, 6 Babmaes Street, London SW1Y 6HD
Tel 020 7389 1500
Fax 020 7389 1515
Web www.shw.co.uk
Direct tel 020 7389 1505
Direct fax 020 7389 1529
Mobile 07889 164772
Email vclark@shw.co.uk

CLARK, Wayne
Falcon Chambers

Position

Barrister

Contact details

Falcon Chambers, Falcon Court, London EC4Y 1AA
Tel 020 7353 2484
Fax 020 7353 1261
Web www.falcon-chambers.com
Email clark@falcon-chambers.com

CLARKE, Bob
Cluttons

Position

Partner – fund management

Qualifications

FRICS

Career history

1989 Joined Cluttons.
1970-89 Richard Ellis.
1961-69 George Belbin & Co

Other roles

Managing agent to Crown Estate and Church Commissioners for England; trustee, Investment Property Forum Educational Trust

Professional memberships

Investment Property Forum; RICS

Interests

Family; golf

Contact details

Cluttons, Portman House, 2 Portman Street, London W1H 6DU
Tel 020 7408 1010
Fax 020 7629 3263
Web www.cluttons.com
Direct tel 020 7647 7110
Direct fax 020 7647 7067
Mobile 07768 608527
Email rgcclarke@cluttons.com

CLARKE, Giles
Crown Estate

Position

Head of residential estates

Qualifications

MRICS

Career history

1997-2003 Cluttons.
1989-96 Associate, Strutt & Parker.
1988-89 Countryside Properties

Professional memberships

RICS

Interests

Golf

Contact details

Crown Estate, 16 Carlton House Terrace, London SW1Y 5AH
Tel 020 7210 4377
Fax 020 7210 4236
Web www.crownestate.co.uk
Direct tel 020 7210 4393
Email giles.clarke@crownestate.co.uk

CLARKE, Graham
T&S Stores

Position

Estates and legal compliance director

Qualifications

BSc; MRICS

Contact details

T&S Stores plc, Apex Road, Walsall WS8 7TS
Tel 01543 363000
Fax 01543 363628
Direct tel 01543 363089
Email graham_clarke@tands.co.uk

CLARKE, Greg
Lend Lease Corp

Position
Chief executive
Career history
Since 2002 Chief executive, Lend Lease. Previous roles include: vice-president (cellular), Nortel Communications; chief executive, Cable & Wireless Mobile; chief operating officer and then chief executive, Cable & Wireless Communications
Contact details
Lend Lease Corp, York House, 23 Kingsway, London WC2B 6UJ
Tel 020 7379 0222
Fax 020 7379 0213
Web www.lendlease.com.au
Email jacinta_mcallister@lendlease.co.uk

CLARKE, Julian
FPDSavills

Position
Director – head of land development
Contact details
FPDSavills Ltd, 20 Grosvenor Hill, London W1K 3HQ
Tel 020 7499 8644
Fax 020 7495 3773
Web www.fpdsavills.co.uk
Direct tel 020 7409 8743
Mobile 07870 555705
Email jclarke@fpdsavills.co.uk

CLARKE, Keith
WS Atkins

Position
Chief executive
Career history
2003 Joined WS Atkins. Previously executive vice-president, Skanska, responsible for UK, Poland and Czech Republic. Has also worked for Olympia & York, Trafalgar House and Kvaerner
Contact details
WS Atkins plc, Woodcote Grove, Ashley Road, Epsom KT18 5BW
Tel 01372 726140
Fax 01372 740055
Web www.wsatkins.com
Email cathie.hill@atkinsglobal.com

CLARKE, Paul
Duchy of Lancaster Office

Position
Clerk of the council and chief executive
Qualifications
FRICS
Career history
1996-2000 Property investment manager, Wellcome Trust.
1981-96 Partner, Clarke & Green.
1974-81 Management surveyor, Grosvenor Estate
Other roles
Property adviser, Greenwich Hospital
Professional memberships
Country Land & Business Association; Investment Property Forum; RICS; Worshipful Company of Chartered Surveyors
Interests
Cinema; horse riding; skiing; travel; walking
Contact details
Duchy of Lancaster Office, 1 Lancaster Place, London WC2E 7ED
Tel 020 7836 8277
Fax 020 7379 5743
Email pclarke@duchyoflancaster.com

CLARKE, Peter
British Land Corp

Position
Director
Qualifications
FCIS; ACIArb
Other roles
Joint head of asset management, British Land; vice-chairman, British Ski & Snowboarding Federation
Contact details
British Land Corp Ltd, 10 Cornwall Terrace, London NW1 4QP
Tel 020 7486 4466
Web www.britishland.com
Email peter.clarke@britishland.com

CLARKE, Peter
King Sturge

Position
Partner – valuation, Birmingham
Qualifications
FRICS
Professional memberships
RICS
Contact details
King Sturge, 1 Cornwall Street, Birmingham B3 2DT
Tel 0121 233 2898
Fax 0121 236 2563
Web www.kingsturge.com
Direct tel 0121 200 7122
Email peter.clarke@kingsturge.co.uk

CLARKE, Rupert
Hermes Pensions Management

Position
Head of property
Qualifications
BSc Hons, Eng & Man
Career history
1991-2003 Jones Lang LaSalle Corporate Finance.
1985-91 Managing director, Woolgate Property Finance.
1981-85 Second vice-president, Chase Manhattan Bank
Other roles
Board member and past chairman (1999–2000), Investment Property Forum
Professional memberships
Investment Property Forum
Interests
Golf; skiing; tennis; wine
Contact details
Hermes Pensions Management Ltd, Lloyds Chambers, 1 Portsoken Street, London E1 8HZ
Tel 020 7702 0888
Fax 020 7702 9453
Web www.hermes.co.uk
Email r.clarke@hermes.co.uk

CLARKE, Sir Stanley
St Modwen Properties

Position
Chairman
Qualifications
CBE; DL
Other roles
Chairman of Bath, Brighton, Chepstow, Fontwell Park, Hereford, Great Yarmouth, Newcastle, Sedgefield and Uttoxeter racecourses; director, Branston Properties; director, Widnes Regeneration; trustee, Clarke Charitable Settlement; president, Needwood Singers; president, Barton-under-Needwood Ladies Hockey Club; vice-president of local sports clubs; member, Jockey Club; Deputy Lieutenant of Staffordshire; High Sheriff of Staffordshire; honorary doctorate from Staffordshire University
Contact details
St Modwen Properties plc, Lyndon House, 62 Hagley Road, Birmingham B16 8PE
Tel 0121 456 2800
Fax 0121 456 1829
Web www.stmodwen.co.uk
Email sclarke@stmodwen.co.uk

CLARKE, Stephen
Russell-Cooke

Position
Partner – head of commercial property
Qualifications
BA; LLB

Career history
1973 Admitted to Roll of Solicitors.
1971 Joined Russell-Cooke
Professional memberships
South London Law Society
Contact details
Russell-Cooke, 2 Putney Hill, London SW15 6AB
Tel 020 8789 9111
Fax 020 8780 1194
Web www.russell-cooke.co.uk
Direct tel 020 8788 7887
Direct fax 020 8780 9004
Email clarkes@russell-cooke.co.uk

CLARKSON, Patrick
Landmark Chambers

Position
Barrister
Qualifications
QC
Career history
1992 Appointed QC.
1972 Called to Bar
Other roles
Crown Court recorder
Professional memberships
Parliamentary Bar Association; Planning & Environment Bar Association
Contact details
Landmark Chambers, 4 Breams Buildings, London EC4A 1AQ
Tel 020 7430 1221
Fax 020 7421 1399
Web www.landmarkchambers.co.uk
Email clerks@landmarkchambers.co.uk

CLARKSON, Philip
storeys:ssp

Position
Director – head of Leeds rating division
Qualifications
BA; FRICS; IRRV
Career history
1989 Joined Storey Sons & Parker (now storeys:ssp) rating division
Other roles
Corporate member, Institute of Revenues Rating & Valuation
Interests
Church; classical music; cricket; football
Contact details
storeys:ssp, Leigh House, 28-32 St Pauls Street, Leeds LS1 2PX
Tel 0113 242 8999
Fax 0113 242 8944
Web www.storeys-ssp.com
Direct tel 0113 237 6903
Mobile 07786 262722
Email philip.clarkson@storeys-ssp.co.uk

CLAY, Jeremy
Mayer, Brown, Rowe & Maw

Position
Partner – head of property group
Qualifications
MA (Oxon)
Professional memberships
Law Society
Interests
Golf; tennis
Contact details
Mayer, Brown, Rowe & Maw LLP, 11 Pilgrim Street, London EC4V 6RW
Tel 020 7248 4282
Fax 020 7248 2009
Web www.mayerbrownrowe.com
Direct tel 020 7782 8988
Email jclay@mayerbrownrowe.com

CLAYTON, Richard
ISG Occupancy

Position
Director – agency
Qualifications
BSc; MRICS
Contact details
ISG Occupancy Ltd, 17-19 Maddox Street, London W1S 1QG
Tel 020 7290 3333
Fax 020 7290 3334
Web www.isgplc.com
Email richard.clayton@isgplc.com

CLAYTON, Rob
CIT Group

Position
Treasury director
Qualifications
BA Hons, Economic & Social Studies
Career history
1997-99 Industrial Bank of Japan: senior manager of Shanghai branch, then head of corporate banking (London) from 1999
Contact details
CIT Group plc, 8-10 Bourdon Street, London W1K 3PD
Tel 020 7667 7766
Fax 020 7667 7770
Web www.cit.co.uk
Direct fax 020 7667 7759
Email rc@cit.co.uk

CLAYTON, Sue
CB Richard Ellis

Position
Director – capital markets, investment
Qualifications
BSc, Est Man; FRICS
Career history
1979 Joined Richard Ellis; appointed partner in 1987; now director
Other roles
Practising tutor in department of property valuation and management, City University business school; member, 2003 advisory board for *Property Week*
Professional memberships
Investment Property Forum; RICS
Interests
Sport
Contact details
CB Richard Ellis, Kingsley House, 1a Wimpole Street, London W1G 0RE
Tel 020 7182 2000
Fax 020 7182 7001
Web www.cbre.com
Direct tel 020 7304 7387
Email sue.clayton@cbre.com

CLEAL, Adam
Allen & Overy

Position
Head of London real estate
Qualifications
LLB
Career history
1990 Joined Allen & Overy; appointed partner in 1991 and head of London real estate in 2000.
1982 Admitted to Roll of Solicitors
Other roles
Freeman of the City of London
Professional memberships
Law Society
Interests
Art; cycling; diving/scuba diving; Reform Club
Contact details
Allen & Overy, One New Change, London EC4M 9QQ
Tel 020 7330 3000
Fax 020 7330 9999
Web www.allenovery.com
Email adam.cleal@allenovery.com

CLEAVER, Robert
Basepoint

Position
Chief executive
Qualifications

C?

FRICS; IRRV

Professional memberships

Institute of Revenues Rating & Valuation; RICS

Interests

Cinema; cycling; skiing; squash; theatre

Contact details

Basepoint plc, Charlecote Mews, Staple Gardens, Winchester SO23 8SR

Tel 01962 842244

Fax 01962 867037

Email robcleaver@basepoint.co.uk

CLEGG, Barry
Estates & General

Position

Property director

Contact details

Estates & General plc, Penn House, 30 High Street, Rickmansworth WD3 1EP

Tel 01923 285999

Fax 01923 770547

Email barry.clegg@estates-general.com

CLIFFORD, Malory
Blackfriars Investments

Position

Managing director

Interests

Architecture; cooking; golf; travel

Contact details

Blackfriars Investments Ltd, Suite 4, 32 Lawn Road, London NW3 2XU

Tel 020 7483 0007

Fax 020 7483 2007

Web www.blackfriars-uk.com

Email clifford@blackfriars-uk.com

CLIFTON-BROWN, James
CB Richard Ellis Investors

Position

Senior executive director

Qualifications

BSc; MRICS

Career history

1982-84 Investment surveyor, Richard Ellis.

1980-82 Residential negotiator, Pearsons

Contact details

CB Richard Ellis Investors Ltd, 64 North Row, London W1K 7DA

Tel 020 7399 9600

Fax 020 7399 9601

Web www.cbreinvestors.com

Direct tel 020 7399 9622

Email jclifton-brown@cbreinvestors.com

CLISSITT, Phil
Wragge & Co

Position

Partner – head of property corporate support

Career history

1990 Admitted to Roll of Solicitors.

1986 Joined Wragge & Co, partner from 1998

Professional memberships

Law Society

Interests

Cricket; football

Contact details

Wragge & Co LLP, 55-73 Colmore Row, Birmingham B3 2AS

Tel 0870 903 1000

Fax 0870 904 1099

Web www.wragge.com

Direct tel 0121 685 2709

Email phil_clissitt@wragge.com

CLOSE, Richard
Daniel Watney

Position

Partner – professional department

Qualifications

Bsc Hons; MRICS; Dip Prop Inv

Contact details

Daniel Watney, 25 Hosier Lane, London EC1A 9DW

Tel 020 7246 5000

Fax 020 7248 7001

Web www.danwat.com

Direct tel 020 7246 5016

Email rclose@danwat.com

CLOTHIER, Roger
TLT Solicitors

Position

Partner – commercial property

Qualifications

LLB

Career history

Since 1997 Partner, Lawrence Tucketts (merged with Trumps to form TLT).

1986 Admitted to Roll of Solicitors.

1984-97 Lawrence & Co

Other roles

Author of landlord and tenant articles for relevant press and publications; regular speaker at seminars and conferences on landlord and tenant issues

Interests

Football; golf

Contact details

TLT Solicitors, 1 Redcliffe Street, Bristol BS99 7JZ

Tel 0117 917 7777

Fax 0117 917 7779

Web www.tltsolicitors.com

Direct tel 0117 917 7988

Email rclothier@TLTsolicitors.com

CLUFF, Peter
Europa Capital Partners

Position

Finance director

Qualifications

ACA

Career history

1990-99 Finance director, Morgan Grenfell Equity Partners.

1986-90 BDO Binder Hamlyn

Other roles

Founder member, British Venture Capital Association regulatory committee; founder member, Venture Capital Finance Directors Forum

Professional memberships

Institute of Chartered Accountants in England & Wales

Interests

Golf; piano; renovation

Contact details

Europa Capital Partners Ltd, 136 Sloane Street, London SW1X 9AY

Tel 020 7881 6800

Fax 020 7881 0501

Web www.europafund.com

Email peter.cluff@europacapitalpartners.com

CLUTTON, Gareth
Cluttons

Position

Managing partner

Qualifications

BA; FRICS

Career history

1983 Joined Cluttons; appointed partner in 1990; became full partner in 1995 and managing partner in 2003

Other roles

Crown steward of the island and the royal manor of Portland; managing agent to Crown Estate Commissioners

Professional memberships

RICS

Interests

Motorbikes; rugby; walking

Contact details

Cluttons, Portman House, 2 Portman Street, London W1H 6DU

Tel 020 7408 1010

Fax 020 7629 3263

Web www.cluttons.com

Email gclutton@cluttons.com

COBB, Richard
GL Hearn

Position
Chairman
Qualifications
FRICS
Career history
1973 Joined GL Hearn as partner; became chairman in 2002.
1969-73 Valuation Office, Inland Revenue
Professional memberships
RICS
Interests
Boating; outdoor pursuits; theatre
Contact details
GL Hearn Ltd, Leonard House, 5-7 Marshalsea Road, London SE1 1EP
Tel 020 7450 4000
Fax 020 7450 4010
Web www.glhearn.com
Email richard_cobb@glhearn.com

COBB, Robert
Cluttons

Position
Partner – commercial asset management
Qualifications
FRICS
Professional memberships
RICS
Contact details
Cluttons, Portman House, 2 Portman Street, London W1H 6DU
Tel 020 7408 1010
Fax 020 7629 3263
Web www.cluttons.com
Email rcobb@cluttons.com

COCHRANE, Luther
Bovis Lend Lease

Position
Chairman
Contact details
Bovis Lend Lease Ltd, 31 Lovat Lane, London EC3R 8EB
Web www.bovislendlease.com
Email luther.cochrane@bovislendlease.com

COCKBURN, Ian
Lend Lease Real Estate Investments

Position
Chairman – Europe
Qualifications
MRICS
Career history
Since 1998 Chairman (Europe), Lend Lease Real Estate Investments.
1990-98 Investment director, Grosvenor Estate.
1986-90 Property director, ESN.
1980-86 Head of property, British Steel Pension Fund
Professional memberships
British Council of Shopping Centres; RICS
Interests
Football; golf; squash
Contact details
Lend Lease Real Estate Investments Ltd, York House, 23 Kingsway, London WC2B 6UJ
Tel 020 7379 0222
Fax 020 7379 0213
Web www.lendlease.com.au
Direct tel 020 7395 7445
Mobile 07801 621709
Email ian_cockburn@lendlease.co.uk

COCKBURN, Miranda
Credit Suisse First Boston

Position
Director – pan-European real estate
Contact details
Credit Suisse First Boston, One Cabot Square, London E14 4QJ
Tel 020 7888 8888
Fax 020 7883 5819
Web www.csfb.com
Email miranda.cockburn@csfb.com

COCKBURN, Paul
FPDSavills

Position
Director – investment, central London
Qualifications
MA; MRICS
Career history
1992 Joined FPDSavills as director (central London investment)
Professional memberships
R3
Contact details
FPDSavills Ltd, 20 Grosvenor Hill, London W1K 3HQ
Tel 020 7499 8644
Fax 020 7495 3773
Web www.fpdsavills.co.uk
Direct tel 020 7409 8788
Direct fax 020 7409 2635
Mobile 07870 555706
Email pcockburn@fpdsavills.co.uk

COCKERTON, David
Royal Bank of Scotland

Position
Head of asset management
Qualifications
BSc; MBA; FRICS
Contact details
Royal Bank of Scotland, Drummond House, PO Box 1727, 1 Redheughs Avenue, Edinburgh
Tel 0131 556 8555
Web www.rbs.co.uk
Direct tel 0131 523 7335
Direct fax 0131 317 7964
Mobile 07836 756793
Email david.cockerton@rbs.co.uk

COFFELL, Howard
Field Fisher Waterhouse

Position
Partner – head of industrial property
Contact details
Field Fisher Waterhouse, 35 Vine Street, London EC3N 2AA
Tel 020 7861 4000
Fax 020 7488 0084
Web www.ffwlaw.com
Email Howard.Coffell@ffw.com

COFFER, David
Davis Coffer Lyons

Position
Chairman
Qualifications
FRICS; PRPAS
Career history
Since 1972 Chairman, Davis Coffer Lyons.
1967-72 De Groot Collis.
1965-67 Dudley Samuel & Harrison.
1964-65 Druce & Co
Other roles
Contributing author on restaurant valuation in *The Law & Valuation of Leisure Premises* (Estates Gazette); chairman, GN9 preparation committee for the Red Book in connection with restaurant valuation; committee founder and chairman, annual RICS property quiz; founder and president, Restaurant Property Advisors Society (responsible for Restaurant 2002 conference)
Professional memberships
RICS
Contact details
Davis Coffer Lyons Ltd, 52 Portland Place, London W1B 1NH
Tel 020 7299 0700
Fax 020 7299 0710
Web www.daviscofferlyons.co.uk
Email dcoffer@daviscofferlyons.co.uk

COFFIN, Ben
Matthews & Goodman

Position
Partner – head of landlord and tenant, London

C

Qualifications
Dip VEM; BSc Hons; MRICS; ACIArb
Career history
1998-2001 Nelson Bakewell.
1995-98 Rogers Chapman.
1994-95 King Sturge
Contact details
Matthews & Goodman, Dorland House, 14-16 Regent Street, London SW1Y 4PH
Tel 020 7747 8847
Fax 020 7747 8848
Web www.matthews-goodman.co.uk
Email bcoffin@matthews-goodman.co.uk

COGGAN, Peter
Phoenix Beard
Position
Director
Contact details
Phoenix Beard, The Exchange, 19 Newhall Street, Birmingham B3 3PJ
Tel 0121 200 4500
Fax 0121 200 4599
Web www.phoenix-beard.co.uk
Email peter.coggan@phoenix-beard.co.uk

COHEN, Adam
Tops Estates
Position
Operations finance director
Professional memberships
Institute of Chartered Accountants in England & Wales
Contact details
Tops Estates plc, 77 South Audley Street, London W1K 1EE
Tel 020 7355 3000
Fax 020 7355 2222
Mobile 07836 734567
Email adam.cohen@topsestates.co.uk

COHEN, Allen
Fladgate Fielder
Position
Partner – head of commercial property
Professional memberships
Law Society
Contact details
Fladgate Fielder, 25 North Row, London W1K 6DJ
Tel 020 7323 4747
Fax 020 7629 4414
Web www.fladgate.com
Direct tel 020 7462 2200
Email acohen@fladgate.com

COHEN, Edward
11 Stone Buildings
Position
Barrister
Qualifications
MA (Cantab)
Career history
1972 Called to Bar
Other roles
Recorder
Contact details
11 Stone Buildings, London WC2A 3TG
Tel 020 7831 6381
Fax 020 7831 2575
Web www.11stonebuildings.com
Email cohen@11stonebuildings.com

COHEN, Roger
Berwin Leighton Paisner
Position
Partner and head of real estate disputes
Qualifications
Solicitor; FCIArb
Career history
1984 Joined Berwin Leighton (now Berwin Leighton Paisner); became partner in 1989.
1982-84 Matthew Arnold & Baldwin.
1982 Admitted to Roll of Solicitors
Other roles
Lecturer and author of articles on property law and general litigation; senior CEDR-registered mediator; part-time chairman of appeals panel of Specialist Training Authority of the Medical Royal Colleges; professional member of Law Society's civil/commercial mediation panel
Professional memberships
Administrative Law Bar Association; Arbrix; City of London Solicitors Company; Law Society; Property Litigation Association; Society for Advanced Legal Studies
Interests
Football; music; reading
Contact details
Berwin Leighton Paisner Ltd, Adelaide House, London Bridge, London EC4R 9HA
Tel 020 7760 1000
Fax 020 7760 1111
Web www.berwinleighton.com
Direct tel 020 7760 4346
Mobile 07770 638260
Email roger.cohen@blplaw.com

COKE, Richard
Lambert Smith Hampton
Position
Regional chief executive – eastern region
Qualifications
FRICS
Career history
1989-92 Partner, Coke Wipperman.
1982-89 Sweby Cowan: joined as partner; became managing partner in 1988.
1976-82 Surveyor estate department, Prudential Corp
Professional memberships
RICS
Interests
Sailing; shooting; sport
Contact details
Lambert Smith Hampton Ltd, Wellbrook Court, 6 Girton Road, Cambridge CB3 0NA
Tel 01223 814111
Fax 01223 276226
Web www.lsh.co.uk
Email rcoke@lsh.co.uk

COLDERICK, Stewart
Dalgleish
Position
Director – head of investment
Contact details
Dalgleish, 80 New Bond Street, London W1S 1DD
Tel 020 7663 5555
Fax 020 7491 0098
Web www.dalgleish.co.uk
Direct tel 020 7663 5502
Email scolderick@dalgleish.co.uk

COLE, Andrew
Edwin Hill
Position
Partner – agency/investment agency
Qualifications
MSc; MRICS
Professional memberships
RICS
Interests
Cricket; football; golf
Contact details
Edwin Hill, Highbridge House, Padbury Oaks, London UB7 0EH
Tel 01753 689000
Fax 01753 689191
Web www.edwinhill.co.uk
Mobile 07767 816143
Email ac@edwinhill.co.uk

COLE, Edward
Falcon Chambers
Position
Barrister
Qualifications
MA (Oxon); Dip Law

Career history
1980 Called to Bar
Other roles
Contributing editor, *Hill & Redman's Law of Landlord & Tenant*; contributor, *Halsbury's Laws of England* (4th edition) (vol 27) (landlord and tenant); contributor to *Megarry on the Rent Acts* (11th edition)
Contact details
Falcon Chambers, Falcon Court, London EC4Y 1AA
Tel 020 7353 2484
Fax 020 7353 1261
Web www.falcon-chambers.com
Email cole@falcon-chambers.com

COLE, Graham
Ashcroft Estates
Position
Director
Contact details
Ashcroft Estates plc, Ashcroft House, 162-166 Fulham Palace Road, London W6 9PA
Tel 020 8741 7411
Fax 020 8741 7758
Email cole@ashcroft.co.uk

COLE, Harry
Electrolux Holdings
Position
Group property and European real estate manager
Qualifications
BA, Accountancy; MRICS; MCR
Career history
1998 Joined Electrolux.
1996-98 Group property manager, APV.
1993-96 Surveyor, GEC
Other roles
Member, RICS corporate occupiers group; editorial board member, *Journal of Corporate Real Estate*
Professional memberships
RICS
Interests
Cricket; fishing; wine
Contact details
Electrolux Holdings Ltd, Oakley Road, Luton LU4 9QQ
Tel 01582 491234
Web www.electrolux.com
Direct tel 01582 588244
Direct fax 01582 588585
Mobile 07710 301559
Email harry.cole@electrolux.co.uk

COLE, Lawrence
Royal Bank of Scotland
Position
Director – European real estate
Contact details
Royal Bank of Scotland, Waterhouse Square, 138-142 Holborn, London EC1N 2TH
Tel 020 7427 8000
Web www.rbs.co.uk
Email laurence.cole@rbos.com

COLE, Peter
Hammerson
Position
Director – development and acquisitions
Qualifications
BSc; MRICS
Career history
1989 Joined Hammerson.
1980-89 Abbey Life Property Fund
Professional memberships
RICS
Contact details
Hammerson plc, 100 Park Lane, London W1K 7AR
Tel 020 7887 1000
Fax 020 7887 1010
Web www.hammerson.co.uk
Email pcole@hammerson.co.uk

COLEMAN, Ben
Lambert Smith Hampton
Position
Director – head of Northampton office
Qualifications
BSc; FRICS
Professional memberships
Non-Administrative Receivers Association; RICS
Contact details
Lambert Smith Hampton Ltd, St Giles House, 76 St Giles Street, Northampton NN1 1BG
Tel 01604 233123
Fax 01604 250590
Web www.lsh.co.uk
Mobile 07802 564637
Email bcoleman@lsh.co.uk

COLEMAN, Piers
Nicholson Graham & Jones
Position
Partner and head of property
Qualifications
LLB Hons
Career history
1993 Joined Nicholson Graham & Jones as partner.
1980-92 Partner, Sebastian Coleman & Co.
1978 Admitted to Roll of Solicitors
Other roles
Appointed to Civic Trust board of trustees (2001)
Professional memberships
Law Society
Interests
Cricket; tennis
Contact details
Nicholson Graham & Jones, 110 Cannon Street, London EC4N 6AR
Tel 020 7648 9000
Fax 020 7648 9001
Web www.ngj.co.uk
Direct tel 020 7360 8206
Email piers.coleman@ngj.co.uk

COLES, Martin
NAI Fuller Peiser
Position
Managing partner
Qualifications
BSc; FRICS; ACIArb
Career history
Since 1982 Fuller Peiser (now NAI Fuller Peiser)
Professional memberships
RICS
Contact details
NAI Fuller Peiser, Waterloo House, 20 Waterloo Street, Birmingham B2 5TB
Tel 0870 700 2233
Fax 0121 605 2244
Web www.nai-fullerpeiser.com
Mobile 07778 542139
Email mcoles@nai-fullerpeiser.com

COLGAN, Liam
Crown Estate
Position
Head of special projects
Qualifications
FRICS; MBA
Career history
1998 Joined Crown Estate.
1995-98 Property Holdings (PACE from 1996): head of planning (London and South East), then director (London and South East) from 1995
Professional memberships
RICS
Interests
Bridge; farming; sailing
Contact details
Crown Estate, 16 Carlton House Terrace, London SW1Y 5AH
Tel 020 7210 4377
Fax 020 7210 4236
Web www.crownestate.co.uk

C

Direct tel 020 7210 4839
Email liam.colgan@crownestate.co.uk

COLLAR, Neil
Brodies

Position
Partner – head of planning law department
Qualifications
LLB Hons; LLM; Dip LP
Career history
1993 Admitted to Roll of Solicitors.
1992 Joined Brodies; appointed partner (head of planning law department) in 1998
Professional memberships
Law Society of Scotland; RTPI; Scottish Planning & Environmental Law
Contact details
Brodies LLP, 15 Atholl Crescent, Edinburgh EH3 8HA
Tel 0131 228 3777
Fax 0131 228 3878
Web www.brodies.co.uk
Email neil.collar@brodies.co.uk

COLLEDGE, Julian
GL Hearn

Position
Director – property management
Qualifications
FRICS
Career history
1988-2000 Managing director, H&C Management.
1984-87 Head of property management, Leavers.
1982-83 Colliers Bigwood & Bewlay
Professional memberships
RICS
Interests
Gardening
Contact details
GL Hearn Ltd, Leonard House, 5-7 Marshalsea Road, London SE1 1EP
Tel 020 7450 4000
Fax 020 7450 4010
Web www.glhearn.com
Email julian_colledge@glhearn.com

COLLETT, Alan
Allsop & Co

Position
Senior partner
Qualifications
BSc; FRICS
Career history
1972 Joined Allsop & Co
Other roles
Member, RICS marketing policy committee; member, BPF working party on developing private rented sector; chairman, BPF working party on space over shops; honorary fellow, College of Estate Management; management board member, Empty Homes Agency; member, Joseph Rowntree Foundation (policy and practice development programme)
Professional memberships
RICS
Interests
Cars; motor sports; shooting; skiing
Contact details
Allsop & Co, 27 Soho Square, London W1D 3AY
Tel 020 7437 6977
Fax 020 7437 8984
Web www.allsop.co.uk
Email alan.collett@allsop.co.uk

COLLIDGE, Sean
Freeport

Position
Chief executive
Contact details
Freeport plc, 9-13 George Street, London W1U 3FL
Tel 020 7299 9360
Fax 020 7299 9388
Web www.freeportplc.com
Email seancollidge@freeportleisure.com

COLLIER, Richard
Carphone Warehouse Group

Position
Group property director
Qualifications
BSc Hons, Est Man; FRICS
Career history
1988-99 Property services director, Sears Group Properties.
1986-88 Acquisition surveyor, Dixons.
1985-86 Portfolio management surveyor, Land Securities.
1984-85 Estates surveyor, Thorn EMI
Professional memberships
RICS
Interests
Cricket; football; golf; music; reading; tennis
Contact details
Carphone Warehouse Group plc, North Acton Business Park, Wales Farm Road, London W3 6RS
Tel 020 8896 5000
Fax 020 8896 5005
Web www.carphonewarehouse.com
Direct tel 020 8753 8477
Direct fax 020 8753 8177
Mobile 07715 170070
Email collierr@cpw.co.uk

COLLINS, Mark
Land Securities Group

Position
Chief executive – portfolio management
Qualifications
BSc; FRICS
Career history
1996-2002 Senior managing director, GE Capital Real Estate.
1990-96 Assistant general manager, Sumitomo Bank.
1988-90 Commercial development director, Freemantle Properties.
1984-88 Associate partner, Richard Ellis.
1980-83 Development manager, Hong Kong Land
Other roles
Executive director, Land Securities
Professional memberships
Investment Property Forum; Property & Finance Club; RICS
Contact details
Land Securities Group plc, 5 Strand, London WC2N 5AF
Tel 020 7413 9000
Fax 020 7024 5007
Web www.landsecurities.com
Direct tel 020 7024 5427
Direct fax 020 7024 5012
Email mark.collins@landsecurities.com

COLLINS, Nicholas
GVA Grimley

Position
National head of industrial
Qualifications
BSc; MRICS
Career history
1986-2001 ATIS REAL Weatheralls (formerly Weatherall Green & Smith).
1983-85 Landmark Real Estate
1980-82 CB Hillier Parker
Professional memberships
RICS
Interests
Fishing; rugby; wine
Contact details
GVA Grimley, 10 Stratton Street, London W1J 8JR
Tel 0870 900 8990
Fax 020 7911 2560
Web www.gvagrimley.co.uk
Direct tel 020 7911 2112

Mobile 07771 943970
Email nicholas.collins@gvagrimley.co.uk

COLLINS, Nick
Nabarro Nathanson

Position
Partner – real estate
Qualifications
LLB
Career history
Since 1999 Nabarro Nathanson
Other roles
Business development partner (real estate)
Professional memberships
BPF
Interests
Rugby; sailing
Contact details
Nabarro Nathanson, Lacon House, Theobald's Road, London WC1X 8RW
Tel 020 7524 6000
Fax 020 7524 6524
Web www.nabarro.com
Direct tel 020 7524 6290
Email n.collins@nabarro.com

COLLINS, Peter
DTZ EuroInvest

Position
Chairman
Qualifications
BSc; FRICS
Career history
2000 Joined DTZ EuroInvest as managing director, and global head for investment services; also director of DTZ International since 2002.
1997-2000 Regional managing director and managing director of Singapore, Colliers Jardine.
1985-97 Richard Ellis: became deputy managing director (Spain) in 1988 and managing director (Indonesia) in 1994.
1980-82 Vigers
Professional memberships
RICS
Contact details
DTZ EuroInvest, One Curzon Street, London W1A 5PZ
Tel 020 7408 1161
Fax 020 7643 6000
Web www.dtz.com
Direct tel 020 7643 6495
Email peter.collins@dtz.com

COLLINS, Peter
Warner Estate Holdings

Position
Finance director
Qualifications
MBA; BSc; FCA
Career history
1998 Joined Warner Estate Holdings as finance director.
1994-98 Group finance director, Jourdan.
1987-94 Group finance director positions at three quoted groups
Professional memberships
Institute of Chartered Accountants in England & Wales; Institute of Directors
Interests
Bridge; hockey
Contact details
Warner Estate Holdings plc, Nations House, 103 Wigmore Street, London W1U 1AE
Tel 020 7907 5100
Fax 020 7907 5102
Web www.warnerestate.co.uk
Direct tel 020 7535 1901
Mobile 07771 575525
Email petercollins@weh-plc.co.uk

COLLINS, Tracy
Nelson Bakewell

Position
Director – West End agency
Qualifications
BSc; MRICS
Career history
1986 Joined Nelson Bakewell; became associate in 1988 and director in 1991.
1984-86 Richard Ellis
Professional memberships
RICS
Interests
Football; golf; rugby
Contact details
Nelson Bakewell Ltd, 25 Sackville Street, London W1S 3HQ
Tel 020 7544 2000
Fax 020 7544 2222
Web www.nelson-bakewell.com
Direct tel 020 7544 2200
Mobile 07831 420528
Email tcollins@nelson-bakewell.com

COLLISON, Ralph
Alder King

Position
Partner
Career history
1982 Joined Alder King
Other roles
Director, Devon Historic Building Trust; RICS registered property receiver
Professional memberships
Non-Administrative Receivers Association; RICS
Interests
Kite boading; motor racing; mountain biking; windsurfing
Contact details
Alder King, 19 Southernhay West, Exeter EX1 1PJ
Tel 01392 413300
Fax 01392 413537
Web www.alderking.com
Mobile 07990 891029
Email rcollison@alderking.com

COLLYER, Richard
Allen Hodkinson

Position
Consultant
Qualifications
MRICS
Career history
1995-2003 Collyer Coxhead/GVA Collyer Coxhead.
1994-95 King Sturge.
1989-94 Donaldsons
Professional memberships
RICS
Interests
Motor sports; skiing; tennis; travel
Contact details
Allen Hodkinson, 39 Thurloe Street, London SW7 2LQ
Tel 020 7761 6402
Fax 020 7761 6405
Mobile 07973 908250
Email richard@allenhodkinson.com

COLVILLE, Bill
DTZ Debenham Tie Leung

Position
Director and regional chairman
Qualifications
BSc, Land Econ; MRICS
Career history
1989 Joined DTZ Debenham Tie Leung.
1980-89 Jones Lang Wootton
Professional memberships
British Council for Offices
Interests
Football; golf (Pollok Golf Club); sport
Contact details
DTZ Debenham Tie Leung, 199 St Vincent Street, Glasgow G2 5QD
Tel 0141 226 5241
Fax 0141 221 0910
Web www.dtz.com
Direct tel 0141 304 3230

C

Mobile 07768 580819
Email bill.colville@dtz.com

COLVIN, William
NHP
Position
Chief executive
Career history
1992-99 Finance director, British-Borneo Oil & Gas
Contact details
NHP plc, Dukes Court, Duke Street, Woking GU21 5BH
Tel 01483 754760
Fax 01483 727509
Email info@nhprops.co.uk

COMYN, David
FPDSavills
Position
Director – investment, central London
Contact details
FPDSavills Ltd, 25 Finsbury Circus, London EC2M 7EE
Tel 020 7499 8644
Fax 020 7588 7323
Web www.fpdsavills.co.uk
Direct tel 020 7409 8903
Mobile 07879 640580
Email dcomyn@fpdsavills.co.uk

CONNELLAN, Paul
Benchmark Group
Position
Head of property
Qualifications
BSc; FRICS
Career history
1998-2001 Chief surveyor, Equitable Life Assurance Society; then head of equitable property investments, Clerical Medical Investment Management, from 2001.
1986-98 Director, Haslemere Estates.
1980-86 Valuation surveyor, Stock Conversion.
1978-80 District Valuer's Office
Professional memberships
RICS
Contact details
Benchmark Group plc, 11-14 Grafton Street, London W1S 4EW
Tel 020 7659 0500
Fax 020 7659 0501
Web www.benchmarkgroup.plc.uk
Direct tel 020 7629 0542
Mobile 07900 190935
Email pconnellan@benchmarkgroup.plc.uk

CONNOLLY, Eileen
Donaldsons
Position
Partner – retail marketing
Career history
1982 Joined Donaldsons; became director of shopping centre marketing in 1986, director of communications in 1991 and director of retail marketing in 1999
Other roles
Board member, British Council of Shopping Centres; Purple Apple Marketing Awards task force member; International Council of Shopping Centers/Solal Marketing Awards jury chair and judge; ICSC marketing faculty member
Professional memberships
British Council of Shopping Centres; International Council of Shopping Centers
Contact details
Donaldsons, 48 Warwick Street, London W1B 5NL
Tel 020 7534 5000
Fax 020 7434 0045
Web www.donaldsons.co.uk
Direct tel 020 7534 8514
Direct fax 020 7434 0045
Mobile 07808 479236
Email eileen.connolly@donaldsons.co.uk

CONRADI, Dr Johannes
Freshfields Bruckhaus Deringer
Position
Co-head – global real estate practice
Career history
1998 Joined Bruckhaus Westrick Heller Lober (now Freshfields Bruckhaus Deringer).
1997 Admitted to Roll of Solicitors (England and Wales).
1996-97 Foreign associate, SJ Berwin & Co, London.
1993 Admitted to German Bar.
1992-93 Foreign associate, Milbank, Tweed, Hadley & McCloy, New York
Contact details
Freshfields Bruckhaus Deringer, Alsterarkaden 27, Hamburg, Germany
Tel +49 40 3 69 06 0
Fax +49 40 3 69 06 15 5
Web www.freshfields.com
Direct tel +49 40 3 69 06 168
Email
johannes.conradi@freshfieldsbruckhaus.com

CONSTANTINE, Clem
Arcadia Group
Position
Property and store development director
Contact details
Arcadia Group Ltd, Colegrave House, 68-70 Berners Street, London W1T 3NL
Tel 020 7636 8040
Web www.arcadia.co.uk
Direct tel 020 7927 1969
Direct fax 020 7291 2170
Email clem.constantine@arcadiagroup.co.uk

CONWAY, Jonathan
Arrowcroft Northwest
Position
Director
Qualifications
BA Hons; MRICS
Contact details
Arrowcroft Northwest Ltd, Stock Exchange, 4 Norfolk Street, Manchester M2 1DW
Tel 0161 834 8881
Fax 0161 834 8885
Mobile 07775 635484
Email jconway@arrowcroft-nw.co.uk

CONWAY-HUGHES, Christopher
Hemingway Properties
Position
Director and company secretary
Contact details
Hemingway Properties Ltd, 21 Devonshire Street, London W1G 6EP
Tel 020 7487 3737
Fax 020 7935 1460
Web www.hemingway.co.uk
Email cch@hemingway.co.uk

COOK, Nicholas
Bellway Homes
Position
Managing director – planning and development division
Qualifications
BA Hons; MRTPI
Professional memberships
RTPI
Contact details
Bellway Homes Ltd, Seaton Burn House, Dudley Lane, Newcastle upon Tyne NE13 6BE
Tel 0191 217 0717
Fax 0191 236 6230
Web www.bellway.co.uk
Email nick.cook@bellway.co.uk

COOK, Paul
DHL International (UK)
Position
Property services manager

Contact details
DHL International (UK) Ltd, Orbital Park, 178-188 Great South West Road, London
Tel 020 8818 8000
Web www.dhl.com
Direct fax 020 8818 8228
Email pcook@gb.dhl.com

COOK, Stephen
DS Smith

Position
Group property manager
Contact details
DS Smith plc, 4-16 Artillery Row, London SW1P 1RZ
Tel 020 7932 5000
Fax 020 7932 5003
Web www.dssmith.uk.com
Email stephen.cook@dssmith.co.uk

COOK, Stuart
Chesterton International

Position
Director in charge, Southampton office
Contact details
Chesterton International, Alleyn House, 23-27 Carlton Crescent, Southampton SO1 2ES
Tel 023 8023 3303
Fax 023 8038 5033
Web www.chesterton.co.uk
Email stuart.cook@chesterton.co.uk

COOKE, Andrew
London First Centre

Position
Director of strategy and marketing
Qualifications
BA; MCIM
Contact details
London First Centre, 1 Hobhouse Court, Suffolk Street, London SW1Y 4HH
Tel 020 7925 2000
Fax 020 7925 2022
Web www.lfc.co.uk
Direct tel 020 7665 1508
Email acooke@lfc.co.uk

COOKE, Gregory
ATIS REAL Weatheralls

Position
Chairman
Qualifications
BSc; MRICS
Career history
1974 Joined ATIS REAL Weatheralls; became senior partner in 1998 and chairman in 2001.
1971-73 Capital & Counties
Other roles
Non-executive director, Warner Estate Holdings
Professional memberships
British Council for Offices; Office Agents Society; RICS
Contact details
ATIS REAL Weatheralls Ltd, Norfolk House, 31 St James's Square, London SW1Y 4JR
Tel 020 7338 4200
Fax 020 7493 0746
Web www.atisrealweatheralls.com
Direct tel 020 7338 4202
Direct fax 020 7839 3721
Mobile 07770 686921
Email greg.cooke@atisrealweatheralls.com

COOKSLEY, Karen
Masons

Position
Partner – head of public law
Qualifications
LLB Hons; AKC; LLM, Env Law
Career history
1989 Admitted to Roll of Solicitors
Professional memberships
Law Society
Interests
Ballet; food; keep fit; literature; music; wine
Contact details
Masons, Woodbridge House, 30 Aylesbury Street, London EC1R 0ER
Tel 020 7329 2288
Fax 020 7490 2545
Web www.masons.com
Direct tel 020 7490 6320
Direct fax 020 7490 6448
Mobile 07979 516844
Email karen.cooksley@masons.com

COOKSON, Simon
Ashurst

Position
Partner – head of real estate
Qualifications
BA, Jurisprudence; MA (Oxon)
Career history
1984 Admitted to Roll of Solicitors.
1982 Joined Ashurst Morris Crisp; appointed partner in 1991 and head of real estate in 1998
Contact details
Ashurst, Broadwalk House, 5 Appold Street, London EC2A 2AG
Tel 020 7638 1111
Fax 020 7638 1112
Web www.ashursts.com
Direct tel 020 7859 1441
Email simon.cookson@ashursts.com

COOMBE, Christopher
Linklaters

Position
Partner
Qualifications
MA, Law
Career history
1975 Joined Linklaters; became partner in 1983
Other roles
Council member, Toynbee Hall
Professional memberships
British Council for Offices; Lambda Alpha; Law Society
Contact details
Linklaters, 1 Silk Street, London EC2Y 8HQ
Tel 020 7456 2000
Fax 020 7456 2222
Web www.linklaters.com
Direct tel 020 7456 4810
Email cristopher.coombe@linklaters.com

COOMBS, Richard
Chesterton International

Position
Director in charge, Bristol office
Qualifications
MRICS
Career history
2000 Joined Chesterton.
1997-2000 Partner (investment agency), Donaldsons.
1995-97 Associate (investment agency), Fuller Peiser.
1994-95 Associate, Pepper Angliss & Yarwood.
1988-94 CB Hillier Parker.
1984-85 Healey & Baker
Professional memberships
Investment Property Forum; RICS
Interests
Golf; sailing; walking
Contact details
Chesterton International, Embassy House, Queens Avenue, Bristol BS8 1SB
Tel 0117 920 9000
Fax 0117 920 9001
Web www.chesterton.co.uk
Direct tel 0117 920 9081
Direct fax 0117 920 9002
Email richard.coombs@chesterton.co.uk

COONEY, Chris
GCL Solicitors

Position
Managing partner

Interests
Rugby (London Wasps Rugby Club); skiing
Contact details
GCL Solicitors, Connaught House, Alexandra Terrace, Guildford GU1 3DA
Tel 0148 357 7091
Fax 0148 357 9252
Web www.gcl-solicitors.co.uk
Direct tel 0148 323 0126
Direct fax 0148 323 0152
Mobile 07803 199816
Email chris.cooney@gcl-solicitors.co.uk

COONEY, Keith
Knight Frank

Position
Deputy head – rating department
Qualifications
MRICS; IRRV; BSc; Dip Env Econ
Career history
1994 Joined Knight Frank.
1986-92 Senior valuation officer, Valuation Office
Professional memberships
Institute of Revenues Rating & Valuation; RICS; Royal Society of Arts
Interests
Art; diving/scuba diving; horse riding; sailing; skiing; tennis
Contact details
Knight Frank LLP, 20 Hanover Square, London W1S 1HZ
Tel 020 7629 8171
Fax 020 7493 4114
Web www.knightfrank.com
Direct tel 020 7861 1111
Direct fax 020 7629 7239
Mobile 07771 594875
Email keith.cooney@knightfrank.com

COOPER, Chris
Land Securities Trillium

Position
Account director (PRIME)
Career history
1997 Joined Land Securities Trillium as regional director (services) for Midlands and Wales; became account director in 2000. Previously national estates manager for Benefits Agency (DSS)
Professional memberships
British Institute of Facilities Management; Institute of Directors
Interests
Cinema; football; literature; travel
Contact details
Land Securities Trillium Ltd, 140 London Wall, London EC2Y 5DN
Tel 020 7796 5500
Fax 020 7796 5501
Web www.landsecurities.co.uk
Direct tel 0121 452 7504
Direct fax 0121 452 7584
Mobile 07711 732671
Email chris.cooper@lstrillium.com

COOPER, Nicholas
ING Real Estate Investment Management (UK)

Position
Managing director – head of indirect investment and Europe
Qualifications
BSc; FRICS
Career history
1981-90 Partner, Cluttons.
1979-81 Valuer, London Borough of Ealing
Other roles
Managment committee member, Association of Property Unit Trusts
Professional memberships
RICS; Worshipful Company of Chartered Surveyors
Interests
Cricket; rugby; wine
Contact details
ING Real Estate Investment Management (UK) Ltd, 9 Devonshire Square, London EC2M 4WX
Tel 020 7398 4310
Fax 020 7398 4311
Web www.ingrealestate.co.uk
Direct tel 020 7398 5541
Mobile 07770 658082
Email nicholas.cooper@ingrealestate.co.uk

COOTE, Nick
Lambert Smith Hampton

Position
Regional director – head of Reading office
Qualifications
MRICS
Career history
1995 Joined Lambert Smith Hampton.
1989-95 Associate, Campbell Gordon
Other roles
Board member, LSH National Office Division; Southern region chairman, Office Agents Society
Professional memberships
Office Agents Society; RICS
Interests
Cinema; cricket; fishing; football; reading; sport; theatre
Contact details
Lambert Smith Hampton Ltd, Holybrook House, 63 Castle Street, Reading RG1 7SN
Tel 0118 959 8855
Fax 0118 950 3363
Web www.lsh.co.uk
Direct tel 0118 960 6912
Mobile 07831 353870
Email ncoote@lsh.co.uk

COPE, Christopher
Benchmark Group

Position
Development director
Qualifications
BSc; MBA; MRICS
Career history
1994-96 Property director, BAA USA.
1988-94 BAA Lynton; appointed assistant director in 1993
Professional memberships
RICS
Contact details
Benchmark Group plc, 11-14 Grafton Street, London W1S 4EW
Tel 020 7659 0500
Fax 020 7659 0501
Web www.benchmarkgroup.plc.uk
Email cdcope@benchmarkgroup.plc.uk

COPE, Dennis
Frogmore Estates

Position
Chairman
Other roles
Director, Frogmore Developments; director, Frogmore Investments
Contact details
Frogmore Estates Ltd, 11-15 Wigmore Street, London W1A 2JZ
Tel 020 7016 6000
Fax 020 7495 5321
Web www.frogmore.co.uk
Email denniscope@frogmore.co.uk

COPE, Mark
Harvey Spack Field

Position
Partner
Contact details
Harvey Spack Field, 33 Bruton Street, London W1J 6QU
Tel 020 7629 9663
Fax 020 7491 1964
Web www.harveyspackfield.co.uk
Direct tel 020 7518 0457
Mobile 07836 227523
Email cope@harveyspackfield.co.uk

COPLEY, Peter
Reuters Group

Position
Group property director
Career history
1999-2001 Property director, AWG.
1992-99 Property director, Emap
Professional memberships
RICS
Contact details
Reuters Group plc, Reuters Building, 85 Fleet Street, London EC4Y 1DY
Tel 020 7250 1122
Web www.reuters.com
Direct tel 020 7542 0938
Direct fax 020 7542 7236
Email peter.copley@reuters.com

CORAL, Lynda
Capital & Regional

Position
Director of funds development
Qualifications
BSc; FCA
Career history
1988 Joined Capital & Regional Properties, now director of funds development.
1982-88 Chartered accountant, Stoy Hayward
Professional memberships
Institute of Chartered Accountants in England & Wales
Contact details
Capital & Regional plc, 10 Lower Grosvenor Place, London SW1W 0EN
Tel 020 7932 8000
Fax 020 7802 5600
Web www.capreg.com
Email lynda.coral@capreg.com

CORBETT, Michael
GVA Grimley

Position
Chief executive
Qualifications
FRICS
Career history
1966 Joined Grimley & Son; head of GVA Grimley's agency division from 1985; elected group managing partner in London in 1993; elected chief executive of GVA Grimley in 1999
Other roles
Chairman, GVA Worldwide
Professional memberships
RICS; Society of Industrial & Office Realtors (international affiliate)
Interests
Tennis
Contact details
GVA Grimley, 10 Stratton Street, London W1J 8JR
Tel 0870 900 8990
Fax 020 7911 2560
Web www.gvagrimley.co.uk
Direct tel 020 7911 2114
Email michael.corbett@gvagrimley.co.uk

CORBYN, Stuart
Cadogan Estates

Position
Chief executive
Qualifications
FRICS
Other roles
Past president, BPF; member of BPF general council; church commissioner; finance committee member of Royal Commission for the Exhibition of 1851; trustee of Royal Parks Foundation; trustee, Chelsea Festival; council member, Chelsea Society
Contact details
Cadogan Estates Ltd, 18 Cadogan Gardens, London SW3 2RP
Tel 020 7730 4567
Fax 020 7730 5239
Web www.cadogan.co.uk
Email stuart.corbyn@cadogan.co.uk

CORDINGLEY, Emma
Taylor Woodrow Developments

Position
Regional director – North West
Qualifications
BSc; MRICS
Contact details
Taylor Woodrow Developments Ltd, Genesis Centre, Science Park South, Warrington WA1 7SP
Tel 01925 250250
Fax 01925 250251
Web www.taylorwoodrow.com
Mobile 07816 517033
Email emma.cordingley@uk.taylorwoodrow.com

CORNICK, Nigel
Christian Salvesen

Position
Group property manager
Qualifications
MRICS
Career history
Since 1997 Group property manager, Christian Salvesen
Professional memberships
RICS
Contact details
Christian Salvesen plc, Unit 3, 500 Pavilion Drive, Northampton Business Park, Northampton NN4 7YS
Tel 01604 662600
Fax 01604 662601
Web www.salvesen.com
Email nigel.cornick@salvesen.com

CORRY, Robert
London & Associated Properties

Position
Finance director
Qualifications
BA; FCA
Career history
Since 1992 Finance director, London & Associated Properties.
1990-92 Finance director, Nelson Bakewell.
1987-90 Group financial controller, Speyhawk.
1985-87 Financial controller, Wootton Jeffreys
Other roles
Chairman, Black Wattle Colliery; director, Bisichi Coal Mining
Professional memberships
Institute of Chartered Accountants in England & Wales
Interests
Golf; music; sport
Contact details
London & Associated Properties plc, 8-10 New Fetter Lane, London EC4A 1NQ
Tel 020 7415 5000
Fax 020 7353 3500
Web www.laprops.co.uk
Email r.corry@laprops.co.uk

CORSER, Graham
P&O Developments

Position
Senior development surveyor
Qualifications
FRICS; MCIOB
Career history
Since 1991 Senior development surveyor, P&O Developments.
1983-91 Development manager, Crowngap Developments.
1980-83 Contracts surveyor, JM Jones & Sons
Professional memberships
Chartered Institute of Building; RICS
Contact details
P&O Developments Ltd, 4 Carlton Gardens, London SW1Y 5AB
Tel 020 7839 5611
Fax 020 7930 2098
Direct tel 020 7321 4616

Mobile 07768 670690
Email graham.corser@podevelopments.com

COSNETT, Andrew
Cosnett Price

Position
Partner
Qualifications
BSc; FRICS
Professional memberships
RICS
Interests
Motor sports; skiing
Contact details
Cosnett Price, Kings Court, 17 School Road, Birmingham B28 8JG
Tel 0121 244 1804
Fax 0121 244 1801
Mobile 07973 632353
Email acosnett@cosnettprice.co.uk

COSSEY, Brian
Society of Investment Professionals

Position
Chairman
Contact details
Society of Investment Professionals, 21 Ironmonger Lane, London EC2V 8EY
Tel 020 7796 3000
Fax 020 7796 3333
Web www.uksip.org
Email uksipstaff@uksip.org.uk

COSSONS, Sir Neil
English Heritage

Position
Chairman
Career history
Since 2000 Chairman, English Heritage
Interests
Industrial archaeology
Contact details
English Heritage, Fortress House, 23 Savile Row, London W1S 2ET
Tel 020 7973 3000
Fax 020 7973 3001
Web www.english-heritage.org.uk
Direct tel 020 7973 3334
Email june.prunty@english-heritage.org.uk

COSTER, Paul
Minerva

Position
Property director
Contact details
Minerva plc, 42 Wigmore Street, London W1U 2RY
Tel 020 7535 1000
Fax 020 7535 1001
Email pcoster@minervaplc.co.uk

COTTERELL, Gill
Marks & Spencer Group

Position
Head of development
Contact details
Marks & Spencer Group plc, Michael House, 37-67 Baker Street, London W1U 8EP
Tel 020 7268 8070
Fax 020 7268 2652
Web www.marksandspencer.com
Direct tel 020 7268 8199
Email gill.cotterell@marks-and-spencer.com

COTTON, Richard
Cluttons

Position
Senior partner
Qualifications
BSc, Est Man; FRICS
Professional memberships
RICS; Worshipful Company of Chartered Surveyors
Contact details
Cluttons, Portman House, 2 Portman Street, London W1H 6DU
Tel 020 7408 1010
Fax 020 7629 3263
Web www.cluttons.com
Direct tel 020 7647 7266
Direct fax 020 7647 7076
Mobile 07775 618523
Email rcotton@cluttons.com

COUCH, Phil
Aberdeen Property Investors UK

Position
Director – development management
Professional memberships
Chartered Institute of Building; Chartered Management Institute
Contact details
Aberdeen Property Investors UK Ltd, 123 St Vincent Street, Glasgow G2 5EA
Tel 0141 306 7600
Fax 0141 306 7706
Web www.aberdeenpropertyinvestors.com
Email
phil.couch@aberdeenpropertyinvestors.com

COULL, Ian
Slough Estates

Position
Chief executive
Qualifications
FRICS
Career history
1988-2002 Director, J Sainsbury.
1983-88 Director, Ladbrokes and Texas Homecare.
1975-82 Cavenham Foods.
1971-75 Bell-Ingram
Other roles
Non-executive director, House of Fraser; regional board member, Royal & SunAlliance; co-chairman, London Sustainable Development Commission; member, 2003 advisory board for *Property Week*
Interests
Family; golf (Temple Golf Club); reading; sport; travel
Contact details
Slough Estates plc, 234 Bath Road, Slough SL1 4EE
Tel 01753 537171
Fax 01753 820585
Web www.sloughestates.com
Direct tel 01753 213342
Direct fax 01753 219342
Email ian.coull@sloughestates.co.uk

COURT, Dr Yvonne
Cushman & Wakefield Healey & Baker

Position
Partner – head of retail and consultancy
Qualifications
BA; MA; PhD
Career history
Since 1989 Partner, Cushman & Wakefield Healey & Baker.
1987-89 Consultant, CACI.
1985-87 Research analyst, Knight Frank
Other roles
Advisory board member and chair of European research group, International Council of Shopping Centers Europe; visiting research fellow, University of Reading
Professional memberships
International Council of Shopping Centers; Market Research Society; Royal Geographical Society
Contact details
Cushman & Wakefield Healey & Baker, 43-45 Portman Square, London W1A 3BG
Tel 020 7935 5000
Fax 020 7152 5360
Web www.cushwake.com
Direct tel 020 7152 5028
Direct fax 020 7152 5366
Mobile 07793 808028
Email yvonne.court@eur.cushwake.com

COURTAULD, Toby
Great Portland Estates

Position
Chief executive
Career history
1990-2002 Various positions, MEPC
Other roles
Member of policy committee, BPF; member, 2003 advisory board, *Property Week*
Professional memberships
Investment Property Forum; RICS
Interests
Art; sailing
Contact details
Great Portland Estates plc, 56 Mortimer Street, London W1W 7RT
Tel 020 7580 3040
Fax 020 7631 5169
Web www.gpe.co.uk
Direct tel 020 7612 1442
Direct fax 020 7612 1492
Mobile 07775 564812
Email toby.courtauld@gpe.co.uk

COURTENAY, Ralph
HOK International

Position
Senior vice-president, director – corporate architecture
Qualifications
RIBA; MSAI; FCSD
Professional memberships
Chartered Society of Designers; RIBA; Society of Architectural Illustrators
Contact details
HOK International Ltd, 216 Oxford Street, London W1C 1DB
Tel 020 7636 2006
Fax 020 7636 1987
Web www.hok.com
Email ralph.courtenay@hok.com

COUSE, James
Edward Symmons & Partners

Position
Partner in charge – City agency and investment
Career history
1994 Joined Edward Symmons; promoted to partner in 1999
Professional memberships
Bankside Traders Association
Interests
Fly fishing; golf; rugby
Contact details
Edward Symmons & Partners, 2 Southwark Street, London SE1 1RQ
Tel 020 7955 8454
Fax 020 7407 6423
Web www.edwardsymmons.com
Email james.couse@edwardsymmons.com

COUSINS, Julian
AIG Global Investment Corp (Europe)

Position
Vice-president – asset management
Qualifications
BSc, Est Man; FRICS; MBIFM
Professional memberships
British Institute of Facilities Management; RICS
Contact details
AIG Global Investment Corp (Europe) Ltd, Birchin Court, 20 Birchin Lane, London
Tel 020 7335 8100
Fax 020 7335 0000
Direct tel 020 7335 8180
Direct fax 020 7220 7519
Mobile 07802 224520
Email julian.cousins@aig.com

COWAN, Archie
Lambert Smith Hampton

Position
Director
Qualifications
BSc; MRICS
Career history
1992-2003 Knight Frank
Professional memberships
RICS
Contact details
Lambert Smith Hampton Ltd, Regent Arcade House, 19-25 Argyll Street, London W1F 7TS
Tel 020 7494 4000
Fax 020 7414 0866
Web www.lsh.co.uk
Email acowan@lsh.co.uk

COWEN, Gary
Falcon Chambers

Position
Barrister
Contact details
Falcon Chambers, Falcon Court, London EC4Y 1AA
Tel 020 7353 2484
Fax 020 7353 1261
Web www.falcon-chambers.com
Email cowen@falcon-chambers.com

COWEN, Tim
11 Stone Buildings

Position
Barrister
Qualifications
LLB (Liverpool)
Career history
1993 Called to Bar
Other roles
Regularly contributes to chambers' property bulletin; lectures on commercial property topics
Professional memberships
Chancery Bar Association; Property Bar Association
Interests
Cycling; family
Contact details
11 Stone Buildings, London WC2A 3TG
Tel 020 7831 6381
Fax 020 7831 2575
Web www.11stonebuildings.com
Email cowen@11stonebuildings.com

COWLISHAW, John
Wedlake Bell

Position
Partner – head of commercial property
Qualifications
LLB Hons
Career history
1975 Joined Wedlake Bell; partner from 1982. 1975 Admitted to Roll of Solicitors
Contact details
Wedlake Bell, 16 Bedford Street, London WC2E 9HF
Tel 020 7395 3000
Fax 020 7836 9966
Web www.wedlakebell.co.uk
Direct tel 020 7395 3095
Email jcowlishaw@wedlakebell.com

COX, Andrew
Mitchells & Butlers

Position
Director – property
Qualifications
BSc Hons; MRICS
Professional memberships
RICS
Contact details
Mitchells & Butlers plc, 27 Fleet Street, Birmingham B3 1JP
Tel 0870 609 3000
Fax 0121 233 2267
Web www.mbplc.com
Email andrew.cox@mbplc.com

COX, Ian
Herbert Smith

Position
Partner – real estate

Qualifications
LLB
Career history
1989 Admitted to Roll of Solicitors.
1987 Joined Herbert Smith
Professional memberships
Law Society
Interests
Cricket; rugby
Contact details
Herbert Smith, Exchange House,
10 Primrose Street, London EC2A 2NY
Tel 020 7374 8000
Fax 020 7374 0888
Web www.herbertsmith.com
Email ian.cox@herbertsmith.com

COX, John
Domino's Pizza Group
Position
Head of property
Contact details
Domino's Pizza Group Ltd, Lasborough Road,
Milton Keynes MK10 0AB
Tel 01908 580000
Web www.dominos.com
Email johnc@dominos.co.uk

COXON, Iain
Dalgleish
Position
Professional director
Contact details
Dalgleish, 80 New Bond Street, London
W1S 1DD
Tel 020 7663 5555
Fax 020 7491 0098
Web www.dalgleish.co.uk
Email icoxon@dalgleish.co.uk

CRAIG, Elizabeth
Bidwells Property Consultants
Position
Partner – head of landlord and tenant
Qualifications
BSc Hons; MRICS; MCIArb
Contact details
Bidwells Property Consultants, Trumpington
Road, Cambridge CB2 2LD
Tel 01223 841841
Fax 01223 845150
Web www.bidwells.co.uk
Direct tel 01223 559326
Direct fax 01223 840294
Mobile 07771 933217
Email ecraig@bidwells.co.uk

CRAIG, Gregory
EPR Architects
Position
Managing director
Contact details
EPR Architects Ltd, 21 Douglas Street, London
SW1P 4PA
Tel 020 7834 4411
Fax 020 7932 0130
Web www.epr.co.uk
Email greg.craig@epr.co.uk

CRAIG, John
Sanderson Weatherall
Position
Director
Qualifications
FRICS; IRRV
Career history
1982 Joined Sanderson Townend & Gilbert (now
Sanderson Weatherall); became partner in 1989
Interests
Antiques; architecture; art; fishing; yachting
Contact details
Sanderson Weatherall, 22-24 Grey Street,
Newcastle upon Tyne NE1 6AD
Tel 0191 261 2681
Fax 0191 261 4761
Web www.sandersons.com
Direct tel 0191 269 0100
Mobile 07901 710666
Email john.craig@sandersonweatherall.com

CRASTON, Edmund
UBS Investment Bank
Position
Head of European real estate investment banking
Career history
Since 1987 Head of European real estate
investment banking, UBS Investment Bank
Other roles
Member of management board, EPRA
Contact details
UBS Investment Bank, 2 Finsbury Avenue,
London EC2M 2PG
Tel 020 7567 8000
Fax 020 7568 4800
Direct tel 020 7568 2341
Direct fax 020 7568 2808
Mobile 07785 904729
Email edmund.craston@ubs.com

CRAVEN, Andrew
Greycoat Estates
Position
Property director
Qualifications
MA; MRICS
Career history
1986 Joined Greycoat (now Greycoat Estates,
since 1999 management buyout).
1985-86 Haslemere Estates.
1981-85 Collier & Madge
Professional memberships
British Council for Offices; BPF; RICS
Contact details
Greycoat Estates Ltd, Brettenham House,
9 Savoy Street, London WC2E 7EG
Tel 020 7379 1000
Fax 020 7379 8744
Email acraven@greycoat.co.uk

CRAWFORD, James
FPDSavills
Position
Director – investment (central London)
Contact details
FPDSavills Ltd, 25 Finsbury Circus, London
EC2M 7EE
Tel 020 7499 8644
Fax 020 7588 7323
Web www.fpdsavills.co.uk
Direct tel 020 7409 8927
Mobile 07870 555707
Email jcrawford@fpdsavills.co.uk

CRAWFORD, James
Town Centre Securities
Position
Property investment director
Qualifications
MRICS
Career history
1992-94 Teesland Group.
1988-92 De Morgan Group.
1986-88 Richard Ellis
Contact details
Town Centre Securities plc, Town Centre House,
Merrion Centre, Leeds LS2 8LY
Tel 0113 222 1234
Fax 0113 242 1026
Direct tel 0113 222 1266
Direct fax 0113 234 0442
Mobile 07976 566651
Email james.crawford@tcs-plc.co.uk

CRAWFORD-INGLE, Angela
PricewaterhouseCoopers
Position
Partner – Europe assurance and advisory real
estate leader
Contact details
PricewaterhouseCoopers, Southwark Towers,
32 London Bridge Street, London SE1 9AE

Tel 020 7583 5000
Web www.pwc.com
Direct tel 020 7212 5225
Email angela.crawford-ingle@uk.pwc.com

CREAMER, Mark
CB Richard Ellis

Position
Joint UK managing director
Qualifications
MA; MRICS
Career history
1985 Joined CB Richard Ellis (formerly CB Hillier Parker).
1980-85 Gerald Eve
Contact details
CB Richard Ellis, St Martin's Court, 10 Paternoster Row, London EC4M 7HP
Tel 020 7182 2000
Fax 020 7182 2001
Web www.cbre.com
Direct tel 020 7182 3010
Email mark.creamer@cbre.com

CREAMER, Michael
Cushman & Wakefield Healey & Baker

Position
Managing director – global corporate services
Qualifications
FRICS; MA; BA
Career history
Since 2000 Cushman & Wakefield Healey & Baker, London.
1998-2000 Cushman & Wakefield, Hong Kong.
1985-98 Healey & Baker, New York.
1983-85 Savills, London
Other roles
Education committee member, CoreNet Global UK
Professional memberships
CoreNet Global UK; RICS
Contact details
Cushman & Wakefield Healey & Baker, 43-45 Portman Square, London W1A 3BG
Tel 020 7935 5000
Fax 020 7152 5360
Web www.cushwake.com
Direct tel 020 7152 5080
Direct fax 020 7152 5365
Mobile 07788 914876
Email michael.creamer@eur.cushwake.com

CREANER, Paul
Chancery House Chambers

Position
Barrister
Qualifications
BSc; LLB; MRICS
Contact details
Chancery House Chambers, 7 Lisbon Square, Leeds LS1 4LY
Tel 0113 244 6691
Fax 0113 244 6766
Web www.chanceryhouse.co.uk
Email paul.creaner@chanceryhouse.co.uk

CREEDY, Mark
Legal & General Property

Position
Managing director
Qualifications
BSc, Est Man; MSc, Urban Land Appraisal; FRICS
Career history
1991-2002 Chartwell Land: investment director, then managing director from 1994.
1987-91 Joint managing director, B&C Properties
Other roles
Former member of management board, Investment Property Forum
Professional memberships
Accessible Retail; Investment Property Forum; RICS
Interests
Cricket; golf; squash; theatre; walking
Contact details
Legal & General Property Ltd, Bucklersbury House, 3 Queen Victoria Street, London EC4N 8NH
Tel 020 7528 6500
Fax 020 7528 6848
Web www.legal-and-general.co.uk
Direct tel 020 7528 6996
Email mark.creedy@lgim.co.uk

CREEDY SMITH, Mark
Ingleby Trice Kennard

Position
Partner – investment
Qualifications
BSc; MRICS
Career history
2003 Joined Ingleby Trice Kennard as partner.
1978-2002 CB Hillier Parker; in 1990 made equity partner and head of City investment team
Professional memberships
RICS
Interests
Family; France; golf; sailing
Contact details
Ingleby Trice Kennard, 11 Old Jewry, London EC2R 8DU
Tel 020 7606 7461
Fax 020 7726 2578
Mobile 07966 406766
Email m.creedysmith@inglebytk.co.uk

CRERAR, Prof Lorne
Harper Macleod

Position
Managing partner
Qualifications
LLB Hons; NP
Career history
1985 Joined Harper Macleod.
1974-84 Partner, Mckenzie Roberton
Other roles
Part-time chair of banking law, Universities of Glasgow and Strathclyde; convener, Standards Commission for Scotland under Ethics in Public Life (Scotland) Act
Professional memberships
Chartered Institute of Bankers
Interests
Art; fishing; golf; rugby (discipline chairman for Scottish Rugby Union, European Rugby Cup and Six Nations); walking
Contact details
Harper Macleod, The Ca'd'Oro, 45 Gordon Street, Glasgow G1 3PE
Tel 0141 221 8888
Fax 0141 226 4198
Web www.harpermacleod.co.uk
Email lorne.crerar@harpermacleod.co.uk

CRICHTON, Rodger
Scottish & Newcastle Retail

Position
Property director
Qualifications
FRICS
Professional memberships
RICS
Contact details
Scottish & Newcastle Retail Ltd, Lakeside House, The Lakes, Northampton NN4 7SN
Tel 01604 239000
Fax 01604 612145
Direct tel 01604 612782
Email rodger.crichton@snr.co.uk

CRICKMORE, Nicola
Newport Holdings

Position
Finance director
Contact details
Newport Holdings plc, 11a Home Farm, Wantage OX12 8PN
Tel 01235 861994
Fax 01235 861805

Web www.newportholdings.com
Email invest@newportholdings.com

CRIPPS, David
Strutt & Parker

Position
Head of commercial division and investment partner
Qualifications
BSc, Est Man; FRICS
Career history
1971 Joined Strutt & Parker.
1965-68 Jones Lang
Other roles
Board member, European Property Association
Professional memberships
RICS
Contact details
Strutt & Parker, 13 Hill Street, London W1J 5LQ
Tel 020 7629 7282
Fax 020 7629 0387
Web www.struttandparker.com
Direct tel 020 7318 5007
Direct fax 020 7491 3178
Email dcripps@struttandparker.com

CRITCHER, Brad
Castlemore Securities

Position
Development director
Qualifications
BSc Hons; MRICS
Career history
Since 1998 Development director, Castlemore Securities.
1988-98 Development surveyor, Homebase/ J Sainsbury
Professional memberships
Accessible Retail; Investment Property Forum
Contact details
Castlemore Securities Ltd, Cedar Court, 221 Hagley Road, Halesowen B63 1ED
Tel 0121 585 4444
Fax 0121 585 4441
Web www.castlemore.co.uk
Mobile 0788 7658471
Email brad@castlemore.co.uk

CROCOMBE, Keith
Bidwells Property Consultants

Position
Partner
Qualifications
BSc; MRICS
Contact details
Bidwells Property Consultants, Trumpington Road, Cambridge CB2 2LD
Tel 01223 841841
Fax 01223 845150
Web www.bidwells.co.uk
Direct tel 01223 559336
Direct fax 01223 559335
Mobile 07768 142705
Email kcrocombe@bidwells.co.uk

CROFTS, Max
King Sturge

Position
Partner – landlord and tenant
Qualifications
BSc; FRICS
Career history
1970 Joined JP Sturge & Sons (now King Sturge); appointed partner in 1982
Other roles
Chairman, RICS public affairs policy committee; past chairman, RICS junior organisation; past chairman, Chartered Surveyors (1913) Club; RICS general council member
Professional memberships
Arbrix; RICS; Society of Industrial & Office Realtors (international affiliate); Worshipful Company of Chartered Surveyors
Interests
Music; rugby; theatre
Contact details
King Sturge, 40 Berkeley Square, Bristol BS8 1HU
Tel 0117 927 6691
Fax 0117 929 9669
Web www.kingsturge.com
Direct tel 0117 930 5811
Direct fax 0117 925 3587
Mobile 07831 370353
Email max.crofts@kingsturge.co.uk

CROMPTON, Matt
AMEC Developments

Position
Director
Contact details
AMEC Developments Ltd, Anchorage 1, Anchorage Quay, Salford M50 2YJ
Tel 0161 877 3400
Fax 0161 877 5480
Web www.amec.com
Email matt.crompton@amec.com

CROOK, Michael
Cushman & Wakefield Healey & Baker

Position
Partner – planning and environment department
Qualifications
MA (Cantab); FRICS; Dip Proj Man
Career history
1969 Joined Healey & Baker (now Cushman & Wakefield Healey & Baker)
Professional memberships
RICS
Interests
Bridge; golf; historical buildings
Contact details
Cushman & Wakefield Healey & Baker, 43-45 Portman Square, London W1A 3BG
Tel 020 7935 5000
Fax 020 7152 5360
Web www.cushwake.com
Direct tel 020 7152 5164
Direct fax 020 7152 5392
Mobile 07764 398164
Email michael.crook@eur.cushwake.com

CROPPER, Philip
CB Richard Ellis

Position
Managing director – investment consulting
Career history
1996 Joined CB Hillier Parker (now CB Richard Ellis) as senior director (investment consulting); now managing director – investment consulting
Contact details
CB Richard Ellis, Kingsley House, 1a Wimpole Street, London W1G 0RE
Tel 020 7182 2000
Fax 020 7182 7001
Web www.cbre.com
Email philip.cropper@cbre.com

CROSS, Richer
BC Asset Management

Position
Director – property
Qualifications
BSc; FRICS
Career history
1999-2000 Property investment director, Hill Samuel Asset Management.
1984-99 Abbey Life Investment Services: appointed head of property investment in 1995.
1979-84 Investment surveyor, Edward Erdman.
1977-79 Collier & Madge
Other roles
Director, Canford Property Management
Professional memberships
RICS
Interests
Sailing; walking
Contact details
BC Asset Management Ltd, BC House, Ling Road, Poole BH12 4NZ
Tel 01202 305900

Fax 01202 305905
Web www.bcam.co.uk
Direct tel 01202 305908
Mobile 07753 822038
Email richer.cross@bcam.co.uk

CROSS, Siobhan
Masons

Position
Partner – property litigation
Qualifications
BA Hons
Career history
1988 Joined Masons; partner since 1993.
1987-88 Russell-Cooke.
1987 Admitted to Roll of Solicitors.
1985-87 Lawrence Messer
Professional memberships
Law Society; Property Litigation Association
Contact details
Masons, Woodbridge House, 30 Aylesbury Street, London EC1R 0ER
Tel 020 7329 2288
Fax 020 7490 2545
Web www.masons.com
Direct tel 020 7490 6277
Mobile 07771 808143
Email siobhan.cross@masons.com

CROSSFIELD, Jon
FPDSavills

Position
Director – international investment
Contact details
FPDSavills Ltd, 20 Grosvenor Hill, London W1K 3HQ
Tel 020 7499 8644
Fax 020 7495 3773
Web www.fpdsavills.co.uk
Direct tel 020 7409 8886
Mobile 07870 555786
Email jcrossfield@fpdsavills.co.uk

CROSSFIELD, Richard
DLA

Position
Location head, real estate, London
Qualifications
LLB
Contact details
DLA, 3 Noble Street, London EC2V 7EE
Tel 08700 111111
Fax 020 7796 6666
Web www.dla.com
Direct tel 020 7796 6147
Mobile 07971 142345
Email richard.crossfield@dla.com

CROSSLAND, David
Crossland Otter Hunt

Position
Partner
Qualifications
BSc; MRICS
Professional memberships
RICS
Contact details
Crossland Otter Hunt, President Buildings, 17 Savile Street East, Sheffield S4 7UQ
Tel 0114 296 0099
Fax 0114 249 0700
Web www.c-o-h.com
Email david@c-o-h.com

CROSSLEY, John
Association of Residential Lettings Agents

Position
Chairman
Qualifications
FRICS
Professional memberships
RICS
Contact details
Association of Residential Lettings Agents, Maple House, 53-55 Woodside Road, Amersham HP6 6AA
Tel 01494 431680
Fax 01494 431530
Web www.arla.co.uk
Email info@arla.co.uk

CROSSLEY, Peter
Broadway Malyan

Position
Managing director
Contact details
Broadway Malyan Ltd, Weybridge Business Park, Addlestone KT15 2BW
Tel 01932 845599
Fax 01932 856206
Web www.broadwaymalyan.com
Email p.crossley@broadwaymalyan.com

CROSSMAN, Howard
Maxwell Batley

Position
Partner – head of construction team
Qualifications
BA, Law
Career history
1990-2002 Masons: equity partner from 1999.
1989-90 Hamlin Slowe
Other roles
Links with and writes for Institute of Lighting Engineers, County Surveyors Society and Quarry Products Association; has written widely as legal reporter for *Construction News*
Professional memberships
Law Society; Society of Construction Law; Technology & Construction Solicitors Association
Interests
Cinema; reading; squash
Contact details
Maxwell Batley, 27 Chancery Lane, London WC2A 1PA
Tel 020 7440 4400
Fax 020 7440 4444
Web www.maxwellbatley.com
Direct tel 020 7440 4479
Email hcrossman@maxwellbatley.com

CROWLEY, David
B-Serv

Position
Director – asset management
Qualifications
MRICS; MCIArb
Career history
1998-2000 Senior associate, King Sturge.
1995-98 Senior surveyor, Hill Samuel.
1992-95 Associate, DTZ
Professional memberships
Chartered Institute of Arbitrators; RICS
Interests
Cricket; golf; rugby; travel
Contact details
B-Serv Ltd, 50 Berkeley Street, London W1J 8BX
Tel 020 7399 4500
Fax 020 7399 4550
Web www.b-serv.ltd.uk
Direct tel 020 7399 4517
Mobile 07909 926420
Email davidcrowley@b-serv.ltd.uk

CROWTHER, Andrew
Frontier Estates

Position
Joint managing director
Qualifications
BSc Hons; MRICS
Career history
1993-96 Senior project manager, Redborn Group.
1989-93 Development and investment surveyor, Morgan Grenfell Laurie
Professional memberships
RICS; Worshipful Company of Chartered Surveyors
Interests
IT; skiing
Contact details
Frontier Estates Ltd, Acorn House, Midsummer

C

Boulevard, Milton Keynes MK9 3HP
Tel 01908 238888
Fax 01908 241111
Web www.frontier-estates.com
Email andrewcrowther@frontier-estates.com

CROYDON, Robert
King Sturge

Position
Partner in charge, Cardiff
Qualifications
MSc; FRICS
Career history
1989 Joined JP Sturge (now King Sturge) as partner.
1986-89 Partner, Powell & Powell.
1976-85 RH Seel & Co; partner from 1979
Professional memberships
Academy for Design in Wales; Arbrix; Institute of Welsh Affairs; RICS; Royal Society of Architects in Wales; Royal Society of Arts; Urban Regeneration Forum; Urban Villages Forum
Interests
Art; music
Contact details
King Sturge, Haywood House, Dumfries Place, Cardiff CF10 3GA
Tel 029 2022 7666
Fax 029 2037 3196
Web www.kingsturge.com
Direct tel 029 2072 6003
Email robert.croydon@kingsturge.co.uk

CRUICKSHANK, Peter
Biggart Baillie

Position
Head of property
Qualifications
LLB; NP
Career history
1988 Joined Biggart Baillie; appointed partner in 1989 and head of property in 1999
Professional memberships
British Council of Shopping Centres; BPF; Law Society of Scotland; Scottish Law Agents' Society
Interests
Motor racing; sailing
Contact details
Biggart Baillie, Dalmore House, 310 St Vincent Street, Glasgow G2 5QR
Tel 0141 228 8000
Fax 0141 228 8310
Web www.biggartbaillie.co.uk
Direct tel 0141 228 8058
Mobile 07788 923140
Email pcruickshank@biggartbaillie.co.uk

CUCKSON, David
Stephenson Harwood

Position
Consultant – environmental law
Qualifications
Solicitor
Career history
1989 Joined Stephenson Harwood. Previously worked in local government, including Test Valley Borough Council
Other roles
Has participated as lead legal speaker at several conferences and seminars; co-author, *Conveying Contaminated Land* (CLTPP); member of UK Environmental Law Association's contaminated land working party and waste working party; past chairman, UKELA (1999-2001)
Professional memberships
UK Environmental Law Association
Contact details
Stephenson Harwood, One St Paul's Churchyard, London EC4M 8SH
Tel 020 7329 4422
Fax 020 7606 0822
Web www.shlegal.com
Direct tel 020 7809 2505
Email david.cuckson@shlegal.com

CUCKSON, Neil
ep2

Position
Managing partner – head of building surveying
Qualifications
BSc; MRICS
Career history
1986 Joined ep2 (formerly ep2 Elliott Partnership).
1983-86 Povall Worthington Associates
Professional memberships
RICS
Contact details
ep2, Brazennose House West, Brazennose Street, Manchester M2 5EP
Tel 0161 834 0011
Fax 0161 834 0146
Web www.ep2.co.uk
Direct tel 0161 934 2130
Mobile 07768 531404
Email neil.cuckson@ep2.co.uk

CULLEN, Dr Ian
Investment Property Databank

Position
Director – head of systems and information standards
Qualifications
BA; MPhil; PhD
Contact details
Investment Property Databank, 7-9 Greenland Place, London NW1 0AP
Tel 020 7482 5149
Fax 020 7267 0208
Web www.ipdindex.co.uk
Email ian.cullen@ipdindex.co.uk

CULLINGFORD, David
Frogmore Developments

Position
Director
Qualifications
BSc Hons, Urban Est Surv; MRICS
Career history
1986-96 Trafalgar House Business Parks
Professional memberships
RICS
Contact details
Frogmore Developments Ltd, 11-15 Wigmore Street, London W1A 2JZ
Tel 020 7016 6000
Fax 020 7495 5321
Direct tel 020 7016 6018
Direct fax 020 7016 6061
Email davidcullingford@frogmore.co.uk

CUMMING-BRUCE, Roualeyn
Jones Lang LaSalle

Position
International director – head of national investment
Qualifications
MRICS
Career history
1972 Joined Jones Lang LaSalle; became partner in 1983, appointed head of national investment team in 1991 and international director in 1999
Professional memberships
RICS
Contact details
Jones Lang LaSalle Ltd, 22 Hanover Square, London W1A 2BN
Tel 020 7493 6040
Fax 020 7408 0220
Web www.joneslanglasalle.com
Direct tel 020 7399 5544
Direct fax 020 7399 5299
Mobile 07836 653494
Email
roualeyn.cumming-bruce@eu.joneslanglasalle.com

CUMMINGS, Mike
B-Serv

Position
Director – asset management

Contact details

B-Serv Ltd, 50 Berkeley Street, London W1J 8BX

Tel 020 7399 4500

Fax 020 7399 4550

Web www.b-serv.ltd.uk

Direct tel 020 7399 4511

Mobile 07768 827568

Email mikecummings@b-serv.ltd.uk

CUMPSON, John
Nabarro Nathanson

Position

Partner – real estate

Qualifications

LLB

Career history

1991 Nabarro Nathanson

Other roles

Firm relationship manager, Land Securities Group

Professional memberships

British Council of Shopping Centres; British Council for Offices; BPF

Interests

Family; golf; reading

Contact details

Nabarro Nathanson, Lacon House, Theobald's Road, London WC1X 8RW

Tel 020 7524 6000

Fax 020 7524 6524

Web www.nabarro.com

Direct tel 020 7524 6125

Email j.cumpson@nabarro.com

CUNNINGHAM, Andrew
Grainger Trust

Position

Deputy chief executive – finance director

Qualifications

MA; FCA

Career history

1978-96 Deloitte Haskins & Sells/Coopers & Lybrand: became partner in 1989

Professional memberships

Institute of Chartered Accountants in England & Wales

Interests

Family; golf; sport

Contact details

Grainger Trust plc, Citygate, St James Boulevard, Newcastle upon Tyne NE1 4JE

Tel 0191 261 1819

Fax 0191 269 5901

Web www.graingertrust.co.uk

Email rr@graingertrust.co.uk

CURIEL, Raul
Fitzroy Robinson

Position

Chairman

Qualifications

MArch; RIBA

Career history

1978 Joined Fitzroy Robinson; founded and heads masterplanning department

Professional memberships

RIBA

Interests

Cycling; theatre

Contact details

Fitzroy Robinson, 14 Devonshire Street, London W1G 7AE

Tel 020 7636 8033

Fax 020 7580 3996

Web www.fitzroyrobinson.com

Email raul.c@fitzroyrobinson.com

CURNOW, Anthony
Ashurst

Position

Partner – head of planning and public sector

Qualifications

LLB; LARTPI

Career history

1988 Joined Ashurst Morris Crisp; became partner in 1996.

1986-88 Assistant clerk/solicitor, Mole Valley District Council.

1979-86 Assistant solicitor, Leicester City Council and South Somerset District Council.

1979 Admitted to Roll of Solicitors

Professional memberships

Law Society

Interests

Family; Italy; tennis

Contact details

Ashurst, Broadwalk House, 5 Appold Street, London EC2A 2AG

Tel 020 7638 1111

Fax 020 7638 1112

Web www.ashursts.com

Direct tel 020 7859 1375

Mobile 07768 121697

Email anthony.curnow@ashursts.com

CURTIS, Alan
ProLogis Developments

Position

UK managing director

Other roles

Founding member, Rail Interchange Investment Group

Contact details

ProLogis Developments Ltd, ProLogis House, 1 Monkspath Hall Road, Solihull B90

Tel 0121 224 8700

Fax 0121 224 8904

Web www.prologis.com

Email acurtis@prologis.com

CURTIS, Christopher
Christopher Curtis & Associates

Position

Director

Qualifications

FRICS

Professional memberships

RICS

Contact details

Christopher Curtis & Associates, 125 avenue des Champs Elysees, Paris 75008, France

Tel +33 1 5689 0550

Fax +33 1 4723 6121

Email cdfc@beckwithparis.com

CURTIS, Sarah-Jane
Grosvenor

Position

London estate director

Qualifications

BSc Hons, Land Mgmt; MRICS

Career history

1986 Joined Grosvenor as valuation surveyor; became associate director (Belgravia south team); director since 1998.

1984-86 Edward Erdman

Other roles

External examiner, Northumbria University

Professional memberships

British Council of Shopping Centres; International Council of Shopping Centers; Investment Property Forum; RICS

Interests

Golf; squash; travel; wine

Contact details

Grosvenor Ltd, 70 Grosvenor Street, London W1K 3JP

Tel 020 7408 0988

Fax 020 7629 9115

Web www.grosvenor.com

Direct tel 020 7312 6234

Direct fax 020 7873 1234

Mobile 07767 638692

Email sarah-jane.curtis@grosvenor.com

CURTIS, Simon
Cushman & Wakefield Healey & Baker

Position

Partner – head of lease advisory services

Qualifications

C

MA; FRICS; MCIArb

Career history

2002 Joined Cushman & Wakefield Healey & Baker.

1988-2002 Partner, Knight Frank.

1981-88 Associate partner, Debenham Tewson & Chinnocks.

1977-81 Jones Lang Wootton

Other roles

Chairman, RICS property measurement panel

Professional memberships

Arbrix; Chartered Institute of Arbitrators; RICS

Interests

Golf

Contact details

Cushman & Wakefield Healey & Baker, 43-45 Portman Square, London W1A 3BG

Tel 020 7935 5000

Fax 020 7152 5360

Web www.cushwake.com

Direct tel 020 7152 5563

Direct fax 020 7152 5396

Mobile 07793 808563

Email simon.curtis@eur.cushwake.com

CUSHING, James
Vail Williams

Position

Partner – head of agency

Career history

1995 Joined Vail Williams.

1981-95 Chilvers/Connell Wilson.

1977-81 Daniel Watney.

1972-77 Savills

Interests

Gardening; reading; shooting

Contact details

Vail Williams, Thames Valley Office, 130 Wharfedale Road, Winnersh RG41 5RB

Tel 0118 933 5600

Fax 0118 933 5634

Web www.vailwilliams.com

Direct tel 0118 933 5608

Direct fax 0118 933 5633

Mobile 07768 724341

Email jcushing@vailwilliams.com

CUSSEN, Edward
King Sturge

Position

Partner – development

Qualifications

BSc; FRICS

Career history

1975 Joined JP Sturge (now King Sturge); partner in charge of Bristol office 1994-99.

1973-75 Montagu Evans & Son.

1972-73 Valuer, Greater London Council

Professional memberships

Bristol Property Agents Association; British Council for Offices; BPF; CBI; Faculty of Building; Industrial Agents Society; RICS

Interests

Art; cricket; gardening; golf; rugby; sport

Contact details

King Sturge, 40 Berkeley Square, Bristol BS8 1HU

Tel 0117 927 6691

Fax 0117 929 9669

Web www.kingsturge.com

Direct tel 0117 930 5730

Email ned.cussen@kingsturge.co.uk

CUTHBERT, David
Hodnett Martin Smith

Position

Partner – decentralised office and industrial agency

Qualifications

BSc; MRICS

Career history

1998 Joined Hodnett Martin Smith.

1993-98 Associate director/director, Conrad Ritblat.

1988-93 Surveyor/associate director, Sinclair Goldsmith

Professional memberships

Office Agents Society; RICS

Contact details

Hodnett Martin Smith Ltd, Charles House, 5-11 Regent Street, London SW1Y 4LR

Tel 020 7839 8181

Fax 020 7839 8069

Web www.hodnettmartinsmith.com

Email davidcuthbert@hodms.co.uk

CUTHBERT, David
Sanderson Weatherall

Position

Director – corporate affairs

Qualifications

BSc; FRICS

Career history

1972 Joined Sanderson Townend & Gilbert; appointed partner in 1983; commercial property managing partner in 1983-97.

1971-72 Assistant surveyor, City of Newcastle upon Tyne

Professional memberships

BSc (Estate Management) Club; RICS; Non-Administrative Receivers Association

Interests

Cinema; football; theatre; travel; wine

Contact details

Sanderson Weatherall, 22-24 Grey Street, Newcastle upon Tyne NE1 6AD

Tel 0191 261 2681

Fax 0191 261 4761

Web www.sandersons.com

Direct tel 0191 269 0101

Mobile 07901 710660

Email davidc@sandersons.com

CUTHBERTSON, Michael
Lamb & Edge

Position

Partner

Qualifications

FRICS

Career history

1988 Joined Lamb & Edge as associate; partner since 1990.

1983-88 Principal valuer, Stockton-on-Tees Borough Council

Professional memberships

RICS

Interests

Cinema; music; sport

Contact details

Lamb & Edge, Yorkshire Chambers, 112-118 Pilgrim Street, Newcastle upon Tyne NE1 6LL

Tel 0191 261 2361

Fax 0191 232 6374

Web www.lambedge.co.uk

Direct tel 0191 269 0507

Mobile 07785 917278

Email michael.c@lambedge.co.uk

CUTLER, Carol
Institute of Revenues Rating & Valuation

Position

President

Contact details

Institute of Revenues Rating & Valuation, 41 Doughty Street, London WC1N 2LF

Tel 020 7831 3505

Web www.irrv.org.uk

Email enquiries@irrv.org.uk

CUTTERIDGE, Michael
DTZ Debenham Tie Leung

Position

Head of investor services and London markets

Qualifications

FRICS

Career history

1979 Joined DTZ Debenham Thorpe; appointed director in 1989, managing director for investment and financial services in 1998 and head of London markets in 2001.

1976-79 Kemsley Whiteley & Ferris (City office).
1974-76 Philip Andrews & Co, Mayfair.
1973-74 Messenger May & Batherstock, Guildford

Professional memberships

Investment Property Forum; RICS

Contact details

DTZ Debenham Tie Leung, One Curzon Street, London W1A 5PZ
Tel 020 7408 1161
Fax 020 7643 6000
Web www.dtz.com
Direct tel 020 7643 6350
Mobile 07771 513212
Email michael.cutteridge@dtz.com

CUTTS, John
Parkridge Holdings

Position

Chairman

Qualifications

BSc; FRICS

Career history

1994-2000 Chief executive, ProLogis.
1989-94 Director, Ashford Developments.
1985-89 Development surveyor, Wilson Bowden

Professional memberships

RICS

Interests

Golf; skiing; squash

Contact details

Parkridge Holdings Ltd, Oracle House, Blythe Valley Park, Solihull B90 8AA
Tel 0121 745 0700
Email parkridge@parkridge.co.uk

D'AMBROSIO, Claudia
Withers

Position
Principal – head of commercial property
Qualifications
BA Hons
Career history
1984 Joined Withers; appointed partner in 1991
Professional memberships
Bond Street Association; Hotel Property Network; Law Society; Mayfair & St James Association; Movers & Shakers
Contact details
Withers LLP, 16 Old Bailey, London EC4M 7EG
Tel 020 7597 6000
Fax 020 7597 6543
Web www.withersworldwide.com
Direct tel 020 7597 6139
Email
claudia.d'ambrosio@withersworldwide.com

DADY, Charles
Cushman & Wakefield Healey & Baker

Position
Partner – head of Thames Valley office
Qualifications
BSc; MRICS
Career history
Since 1998 Partner, Healey & Baker.
1988-98 Associate, Jones Lang Wootton
Professional memberships
Office Agents Society; RICS
Interests
Tennis
Contact details
Cushman & Wakefield Healey & Baker, Lakeside House, 1 Furzeground Way, Uxbridge UB11 1ED
Tel 020 8569 1600
Web www.cushwake.com
Direct tel 020 7152 5273
Direct fax 020 8569 1633
Mobile 07867 790513
Email charles.dady@eur.cushwake.com

DAGGETT, Mike
Cluttons

Position
Partner – investment
Qualifications
BSc; FRICS
Career history
1992-2000 Director, Lambert Smith Hampton.
1989-92 Managing director, De Morgan & Co.
1976-89 Richard Ellis: partner from 1986
Professional memberships
Investment Property Forum; RICS
Interests
Bridge; golf; sailing
Contact details
Cluttons, Portman House, 2 Portman Street, London W1H 6DU
Tel 020 7408 1010
Fax 020 7629 3263
Web www.cluttons.com
Direct tel 020 7647 7139
Email mdaggett@cluttons.com

DAGWELL, Robert
Stiles Harold Williams

Position
Director
Qualifications
BSc; FRICS
Other roles
Registered property receiver
Professional memberships
RICS
Contact details
Stiles Harold Williams Ltd, 6 Babmaes Street, London SW1Y 6HD
Tel 020 7389 1500
Fax 020 7389 1515
Web www.shw.co.uk
Direct tel 020 7389 1520
Email rdagwell@shw.co.uk

DAKIN, Adam
Telereal

Position
Managing director
Contact details
Telereal Ltd, 19 Stratford Place, London W1C 1BQ
Tel 020 7290 4000
Email adam.dakin@telereal.com

DALE, Geoffrey
CB Richard Ellis

Position
Senior director – City professional
Qualifications
MA; FRICS
Career history
1973 Joined Hillier Parker (now CB Richard Ellis)
Professional memberships
RICS
Interests
Family; gardening
Contact details
CB Richard Ellis, St Martin's Court, 10 Paternoster Row, London EC4M 7HP
Tel 020 7182 2000
Fax 020 7182 2001
Web www.cbre.com
Email geoffrey.dale@cbre.com

DALES, Richard
Valuation Office Agency

Position
Director – business development
Qualifications
FRICS
Professional memberships
RICS
Contact details
Valuation Office Agency, New Court, Carey Street, London WC2A 2JE
Tel 020 7506 1700
Fax 020 7506 1998
Web www.voa.gov.uk
Direct tel 020 7506 1814
Direct fax 020 7506 1992
Email richard.a.dales@voa.gsi.gov.uk

DALGARNO, Les
Paull & Williamsons

Position
Partner – head of commercial property
Qualifications
LLB
Career history
1973 Admitted to Roll of Solicitors.
1971 Joined Paull & Williamsons; appointed partner in 1977
Professional memberships
Law Society of Scotland
Interests
Golf; sport
Contact details
Paull & Williamsons, New Investment House, 214 Union Street, Aberdeen AB10 1QY
Tel 01224 621621

Fax 01224 627437
Web www.paull-williamsons.co.uk
Mobile 07710 836030
Email LSDalgarno@paull-williamsons.co.uk

DALGLEISH, Malcolm
Dalgleish

Position
Managing director
Qualifications
FRICS
Career history
1977-79 Head of retail agency, Conway Relf.
1975-77 Head of West End retail agency, Chesterton.
1973-75 Development surveyor, J Lyons & Co
Other roles
Advisory board member, *Property Week* (2003)
Professional memberships
British Council of Shopping Centres; British Retail Consortium; Investment Property Forum; RICS
Contact details
Dalgleish, 80 New Bond Street, London W1S 1DD
Tel 020 7663 5555
Fax 020 7491 0098
Web www.dalgleish.co.uk
Direct tel 020 7663 5599
Direct fax 020 7663 5508
Mobile 07967 697939
Email mdalgleish@dalgleish.co.uk

DALTON, Maurice
ProLogis Developments

Position
First vice-president – commercial
Qualifications
BSc; MRICS
Contact details
ProLogis Developments Ltd, ProLogis House, 1 Monkspath Hall Road, Solihull B90
Tel 0121 224 8700
Fax 0121 224 8904
Web www.prologis.com
Email mdalton@prologis.com

DAMESICK, Dr Peter
CB Richard Ellis

Position
Senior director – head of research and consulting, UK
Qualifications
MA; PhD
Career history
1986-88 Senior consultant, Coopers & Lybrand.
1979-86 Lecturer, Birkbeck College, London
Professional memberships
Investment Property Forum; Society of Property Researchers
Contact details
CB Richard Ellis, St Martin's Court, 10 Paternoster Row, London EC4M 7HP
Tel 020 7182 2000
Fax 020 7182 2001
Web www.cbre.com
Direct tel 020 7182 3163
Email peter.damesick@cbre.com

DANGOOR, David
Monopro

Position
Managing director
Contact details
Monopro Ltd, 10 Fleet Place, London EC4M 7RH
Tel 020 7399 0850
Fax 020 7399 0860
Email david@monopro.com

DANIEL, Peter
Boyes Turner

Position
Partner – property
Qualifications
LLB
Career history
1971 Joined Boyes Turner.
1971 Admitted to Roll of Solicitors
Professional memberships
Environmental Law Foundation; Law Society
Interests
Gardening; keep fit; military history; opera; wine
Contact details
Boyes Turner, Abbots House, Abbey Street, Reading RG1 3BD
Tel 0118 959 7711
Fax 0118 957 3257
Web www.boyesturnerlegal.co.uk
Direct tel 0118 952 7237
Direct fax 0118 952 7272
Email pdaniel@boyesturner.com

DANIELL, Philip
Allied London Properties

Position
Property director
Qualifications
FRICS
Contact details
Allied London Properties Ltd, 40 Portman Square, London W1H 6LT
Tel 020 7486 6080
Fax 020 7299 2611
Web www.allied-london-properties.com
Email philipd@alp.co.uk

DANIELS, Philip
Rogers Chapman

Position
Divisional director – national office agency
Qualifications
MRICS
Contact details
Rogers Chapman plc, Prince Frederick House, 37 Maddox Street, London W1S 2PP
Tel 020 7499 8600
Fax 020 7493 5290
Web www.rogerschapman.co.uk
Direct tel 020 7647 7863
Mobile 07788 188846
Email philip.daniels@rogerschapman.co.uk

DANKS, Paul
NAI Fuller Peiser

Position
Executive partner – markets service
Qualifications
BSc; FRICS
Career history
1982 Joined Fuller Peiser; head of Northern region (Sheffield and Manchester) 1992-98; appointed executive partner (Southern division) in 1998.
1979-82 Inland Revenue Valuation Office
Professional memberships
CoreNet Global UK; Rating Surveyors Association; RICS
Interests
Cycling; football; golf; sailing
Contact details
NAI Fuller Peiser, 16 St George Street, London W1S 1LX
Tel 0870 700 2233
Fax 020 7491 1961
Web www.nai-fullerpeiser.com
Mobile 07836 652369
Email pdanks@nai-fullerpeiser.com

DARKE, Andrew
Barlows

Position
Investment manager
Qualifications
MRICS
Career history
1990-97 Investment director, Rowlinson Securities.
1988-90 Asset manager, Sun Alliance Group Properties
Other roles
North West committee member, Investment Property Forum
Professional memberships

RICS

Interests

Golf; motor sports; shooting

Contact details

Barlows plc, Chepstow House, Dee Hills Park, Chester CH3 5AR

Tel 0124 435 0202

Fax 0124 431 1522

Web www.barlowsplc.co.uk

Email andrew.darke@barlowsplc.co.uk

DARKINS, James
Henderson Global Investors

Position

Managing director – property

Qualifications

BA Hons

Career history

1998 Joined Henderson as head of property in New Zealand; became director of property (Sydney), then managing director of property in 2001. Previous roles in property and development-related industries in New Zealand and UK

Interests

Family; sailing

Contact details

Henderson Global Investors Ltd, 4 Broadgate, London EC2M 2DA

Tel 020 7818 1818

Fax 020 7818 1819

Web www.henderson.com

Direct tel 020 7818 4130

Direct fax 020 7818 3346

Email james.darkins@henderson.com

DARWIN, Andrew
Memery Crystal

Position

Partner – head of property litigation

Career history

1996 Joined Memery Crystal; appointed partner in 1999

Professional memberships

Property Litigation Association

Contact details

Memery Crystal, 31 Southampton Row, London WC1B 5HT

Tel 020 7242 5905

Fax 020 7242 5908

Web www.memerycrystal.com

Email adarwin@memerycrystal.com

DAVEY, Geoffrey
Montagu Evans

Position

Partner – agency

Qualifications

BSc; MRICS

Professional memberships

RICS

Interests

Architecture; IT; music; sailing; travel

Contact details

Montagu Evans, 44-48 Dover Street, London W1S 4AZ

Tel 020 7493 4002

Fax 020 7312 7547

Web www.montagu-evans.co.uk

Direct tel 020 7312 7436

Direct fax 020 7312 7549

Mobile 07818 012436

Email geoff.davey@montagu-evans.co.uk

DAVIDSON, Billy
Vodafone

Position

Head of property strategy

Qualifications

BSc; MBA; MRICS

Career history

2000 Joined Vodafone. Previously with Valuation Office of Inland Revenue and National Westminster Bank

Professional memberships

Association of MBAs; Institute of Professional Managers; RICS

Contact details

Vodafone Ltd, Vodafone House, The Connection, Newbury RG14 2FN

Tel 01635 33251

Web www.vodafone.co.uk

Direct tel 01635 674548

Mobile 07748 328669

Email billy.davidson@vodafone.com

DAVIDSON, David
Cushman & Wakefield Healey & Baker

Position

Partner in charge, Edinburgh office

Qualifications

BSc; MRICS

Career history

1992 Joined Cushman & Wakefield Healey & Baker.

1989-92 Davidson Partners.

1982-89 Gerald Eve

Other roles

Head of investment, Scotland, Cushman & Wakefield Healey & Baker; vice-chairman of commercial faculty board, RICS (Scotland)

Professional memberships

RICS

Interests

Golf; squash

Contact details

Cushman & Wakefield Healey & Baker, 66 Hanover Street, Edinburgh EH2 1EL

Tel 0131 226 8700

Fax 0131 226 8755

Web www.cushwake.com

Direct tel 0131 226 8751

Mobile 07887 795502

Email david.davidson@eur.cushwake.com

DAVIDSON, Gerald
ASDA Property Holdings

Position

Managing director

Contact details

ASDA Property Holdings Ltd, 58 Queen Anne Street, London W1G 8HW

Tel 020 7224 1030

Fax 020 7224 0574

Web www.asda.net

DAVIDSON, Keith
Cobbetts

Position

Head of environment

Qualifications

LLM, Env Law

Career history

1997-2002 Eversheds.

1995-97 Nabarro Nathanson

Other roles

Contaminated land and asbestos specialist; qualified environmental auditor; council member, UK Environmental Law Association environmental industries commission

Professional memberships

Institute of Environmental Management & Assessment

Interests

Piano

Contact details

Cobbetts, Ship Canal House, King Street, Manchester M2 4WB

Tel 0161 833 3333

Fax 0161 833 3030

Web www.cobbetts.co.uk

Direct tel 0161 833 7056

Email keith.davidson@cobbetts.co.uk

DAVIDSON, Manny
Asda Property Holdings

Position

Chairman

Career history

1951 Started Asda Property Holdings

Other roles

Non-executive director, Leopold Joseph; non-executive director, Grainger Trust

Interests

Art; MCC; Savile Club

Contact details

Asda Property Holdings Ltd, 58 Queen Anne Street, London W1G 8HW

Tel 020 7224 1030

Fax 020 7224 0574

Web www.asda.net

Direct tel 020 7009 5908

Direct fax 020 7486 0405

Email edavidson@asda.net

DAVIDSON, Peter
London & Paris Estates

Position

Chairman

Qualifications

FRICS

Career history

Since 1970 Managing director/chairman, Interland Estates/London & Paris.
1965-70 Partner, Sedley & Davidson.
1960-65 Conrad Ritblat

Professional memberships

RICS; Worshipful Company of Chartered Surveyors

Contact details

London & Paris Estates Ltd, 1 Sloane Square, London SW1W 8EE

Tel 020 7730 8484

Fax 020 7730 1811

Web www.londonetparis.com

Email peterdavidson@londonetparis.com

DAVIES, Ashley
Modus Group

Position

Director

Qualifications

Dip Constr Man

Career history

Since 1990 Director, Modus Group.
1987-90 Director, Hanscomb.
1983-87 Senior surveyor, J&P (Oman)

Professional memberships

Association for Project Management

Interests

Aviation; golf; rugby

Contact details

Modus Group Ltd, Greencoat House, Francis Street, London SW1P 1DH

Tel 020 7828 9009

Fax 020 7828 0009

Web www.modusgroup.com

Email ashley@modusgroup.com

DAVIES, Bill
Walton Group

Position

Chairman

Contact details

Walton Group plc, Atlantic Court, Exchange Flags, Liverpool L2 3YL

Tel 0151 236 6915

Email waltonplc@yahoo.co.uk

DAVIES, Christopher
Barclays Group Property Services

Position

Property services director

Qualifications

FRICS

Career history

1973-81 Regional estates manager, Bass.
1967-73 Samuel Day & Son (now James Lister Lea)

Professional memberships

FIABCI; RICS; Westminster Property Owners Association

Contact details

Barclays Group Property Services Ltd, North West House, 119-127 Marylebone Road, London NW1 5PX

Tel 020 7725 3906

Fax 020 7706 7203

Direct tel 020 7725 3541

Direct fax 020 7725 3930

Email chris.davies@barclays.co.uk

DAVIES, Graeme
Lambert Smith Hampton

Position

Director in charge, Edinburgh

Contact details

Lambert Smith Hampton Ltd, 101 George Street, Edinburgh EH2 3ES

Tel 0131 226 0333

Web www.lsh.co.uk

Email gwdavies@lsh.co.uk

DAVIES, Huw
King Sturge

Position

Partner – national head of business recovery

Qualifications

BSc; MRICS

Professional memberships

RICS

Contact details

King Sturge, 7 Stratford Place, London W1C 1ST

Tel 020 7493 4933

Fax 020 7409 0469

Web www.kingsturge.com

Direct tel 020 7318 4254

Email huw.davies@kingsturge.co.uk

DAVIES, Jane
Crown Office Chambers

Position

Barrister

Qualifications

MA (Oxon)

Career history

1981 Called to Bar

Contact details

Crown Office Chambers, 2 Crown Office Row, London EC4Y 7HJ

Tel 020 7797 8100

Fax 020 7797 8101

Web www.crownofficechambers.com

Direct tel 020 7797 6238

Email jdavies@crownofficechambers.com

DAVIES, Paul
Ernst & Young

Position

Partner – real estate, hospitality and construction

Contact details

Ernst & Young LLP, 1 More London Place, London SE1 2AF

Tel 020 7951 2000

Fax 020 7951 1345

Web www.ey.com/uk

Direct tel 020 7951 4050

Email pdavies3@uk.ey.com

DAVIES, Penny
Denton Wilde Sapte

Position

Partner – commercial property

Career history

1978 Admitted to Roll of Solicitors.
1976 Joined Oppenheimers (merged with Denton Hall; now Denton Wilde Sapte); appointed partner in 1982

Professional memberships

Law Society

Contact details

Denton Wilde Sapte, 5 Chancery Lane, London EC4A 1BU

Tel 020 7242 1212

Fax 020 7404 0087

Web www.dentonwildesapte.com

Direct tel 020 7320 6164

Email pad@dentonwildesapte.com

DAVIES, Peter
Gateley Wareing

Position

Partner – head of property

D

Contact details

Gateley Wareing, 11 Edmund Street, Birmingham B3 2HJ
Tel 0121 234 0000
Fax 0121 234 0001
Web www.gateleywareing.com
Email pdavies@gateleywareing.com

DAVIES, Philip
English Heritage

Position
Director – London region

Qualifications
MA; DipTP; MRTPI; RRHistS; IHBC

Career history
1990 Joined English Heritage as assistant regional director; appointed director of London region in 1997.
1978-90 Principal conservation/urban design adviser, Westminster City Council

Other roles
Board member, Central London Partnership; board member, Westminster City Council Public Art advisory panel; adviser to government of West Bengal on conservation-led regeneration in Calcutta

Professional memberships
British Association for Cemeteries in South Asia; Institute of Historic Building Conservation; International Council on Monuments & Sites; Royal Historical Society; Royal Asiatic Society

Contact details
English Heritage, Fortress House, 23 Savile Row, London W1S 2ET
Tel 020 7973 3000
Fax 020 7973 3001
Web www.english-heritage.org.uk
Direct tel 020 7973 3710
Direct fax 020 7973 3792
Email philip.davies@english-heritage.org.uk

DAVIES, Robert
Holmes Place

Position
Group property director

Career history
2000 Joined Holmes Place as European development director. Formerly development director for London & Metropolitan and Disney Developments and principal at Renaissance Developments

Professional memberships
Architects Registration Council of the UK; RIBA

Contact details
Holmes Place plc, 4th Floor, 17a Old Court Place, London W8 4HP
Tel 020 7795 4100
Web www.holmesplace.co.uk
Direct tel 020 7795 4131
Mobile 07785 242844
Email robert.davies@holmesplace.com

DAVIES, Stephen
8 King Street Chambers

Position
Barrister

Qualifications
MA (Cantab)

Career history
1987 Joined 8 King Street Chambers.
1985 Called to Bar

Professional memberships
Northern Circuit Commercial Bar Association; Professional Negligence Bar Association; Technology & Construction Bar Association

Contact details
8 King Street Chambers (Chambers of GF McDermott QC), Manchester M2 6AQ
Tel 0161 834 9560
Fax 0161 834 2733
Email srdavieschambers@aol.com

DAVIES, Stuart
BAA

Position
Senior property manager – Terminals 1 and 2

Qualifications
BSc Hons; MRICS

Career history
1998-2000 Management surveyor, Co-operative Properties (Oxford, Swindon and Gloucester).
1997-98 Smith Price

Professional memberships
RICS

Contact details
BAA plc, Room 2020, Pinnacle Suite, Queens Building, London UB3 5AP
Tel 0870 000 0123
Web www.baa.com
Direct tel 020 8745 0145
Direct fax 020 8745 5142
Mobile 07810 757386
Email stuart_davies@baa.com

DAVIS, Henry
Centreland Investments

Position
Chairman

Qualifications
FRICS

Career history
1967-96 Senior partner, Henry Davis & Co

Professional memberships
BPF; RICS

Contact details
Centreland Investments Ltd, Harcourt House, 19 Cavendish Square, London W1G
Tel 020 7460 5454
Fax 020 7493 0161
Email hdavis@centreland.com

DAVIS, Ian
Federation of Master Builders

Position
Director-general

Contact details
Federation of Master Builders, Gordon Fisher House, 14-15 Great James Street, London WC1N 3DP
Tel 020 7242 7583
Fax 020 7405 0854
Web www.fmb.org.uk
Email ian.davis@fmb.org.uk

DAWBNEY, Martin
Herbert Smith

Position
Partner

Qualifications
LLB (Glasgow)

Career history
1985 Joined Herbert Smith; partner since 1996.
1984 Admitted to Roll of Solicitors (England and Wales).
1982-85 Blake Lapthorn, Portsmouth.
1979-82 Moncrieff Warren Paterson & Co, Glasgow.
1979 Admitted to Roll of Solicitors (Scotland).
1977-79 McClure Naismith Anderson & Gardiner, Glasgow

Professional memberships
Leisure Property Forum

Interests
Family; gardening; photography

Contact details
Herbert Smith, Exchange House, 10 Primrose Street, London EC2A 2NY
Tel 020 7374 8000
Fax 020 7374 0888
Web www.herbertsmith.com
Direct tel 020 7466 2015
Mobile 07785 775044
Email martin.dawbney@herbertsmith.com

DAWSON, Bob
Hermes Property Asset Management

Position
Portfolio manager

Qualifications
BSc; MRICS

Professional memberships

RICS

Contact details

Hermes Property Asset Management Ltd, Lloyds Chambers, 1 Portsoken Street, London E1 8HZ
Tel 020 7702 0888
Fax 020 7702 9453
Web www.hermes.co.uk
Direct tel 020 7680 2142
Email r.dawson@hermes.co.uk

DAWSON, Paul
Glenny

Position

Partner – head of professional division

Qualifications

FRICS; MCIArb

Career history

1974 Joined Glenny; became partner in 1984 and head of professional division in 1988; appointed to manage and expand north London and Hertfordshire office in 1994

Professional memberships

RICS

Interests

Football; golf; tennis

Contact details

Glenny, Crossfield Chambers, 1 Gladbeck Way, London EN2 7HR
Tel 020 8367 2334
Fax 020 8367 2336
Web www.glenny.co.uk
Direct tel 020 8370 4089
Mobile 07771 572834
Email p.dawson@glenny.co.uk

DAWSON, Peter
Brixton Investments

Position

Senior director – investment and asset management

Qualifications

BSc Hons; MRICS

Contact details

Brixton Investments Ltd, 50 Berkeley Street, London W1J 8BX
Tel 020 7399 4500
Fax 020 7399 4550
Web www.brixton.plc.uk
Direct tel 020 7399 4523
Mobile 07768 827566
Email peterdawson@brixton.plc.uk

DAWSON, Peter
Russell-Cooke

Position

Partner – head of commercial property

Qualifications

LLB Hons

Career history

1979 Admitted to Roll of Solicitors.
1977 Joined Russell-Cooke

Interests

Golf; sailing; skiing

Contact details

Russell-Cooke, 8 Bedford Row, London WC1R 4BU
Tel 020 7405 6566
Fax 020 7831 2565
Web www.russell-cooke.co.uk
Direct fax 020 7405 0053
Email dawsonp@russell-cooke.co.uk

DAWSON, Stuart
GVA Grimley

Position

Partner – residential land

Contact details

GVA Grimley, 3 Brindleyplace, Birmingham B1 2JB
Tel 0870 900 8990
Fax 0121 609 8314
Web www.gvagrimley.co.uk
Direct tel 0121 609 8409
Email stuart.dawson@gvagrimley.co.uk

DAY, Alan
Cushman & Wakefield Healey & Baker

Position

Partner – project management

Qualifications

MRICS

Career history

1981 Joined Cushman & Wakefield Healey & Baker

Professional memberships

RICS

Contact details

Cushman & Wakefield Healey & Baker, 43-45 Portman Square, London W1A 3BG
Tel 020 7935 5000
Fax 020 7152 5360
Web www.cushwake.com
Direct tel 020 7152 5146
Direct fax 020 7152 5311
Email alan.day@eur.cushwake.com

DAY, Brian
Marylebone Warwick Balfour Group

Position

Group project director

Qualifications

BSc Hons; BArch; RIBA; ARIAS; MAPM

Career history

1986-94 Director, Trench Farrow & Partners (project management consultancy).
1979-86 Company architect, Coats Viyella.
1975-79 Senior architect, Glasgow District Council

Professional memberships

Association for Project Management; Royal Incorporation of Architects in Scotland; RIBA

Contact details

Marylebone Warwick Balfour Group plc, 1 West Garden Place, London W2 2AQ
Tel 020 7706 2121
Fax 020 7706 8181
Web www.mwb.co.uk
Direct tel 020 7479 2928
Mobile 07711 212363
Email bday@mwb.co.uk

DAY, Christopher
Christie & Co

Position

Managing director

Qualifications

MRICS

Career history

1985 Joined Christie & Co, appointed managing director in 1993.
1983-85 Wrather & Co.
1982-83 Development surveyor, Townson Developments.
1979-82 WT Gunson & Sons

Other roles

Director, Christie Group

Professional memberships

RICS

Interests

Golf

Contact details

Christie & Co, 50 Victoria Street, London SW1H 0NW
Tel 020 7227 0700
Fax 020 7220 0702
Web www.christie.com
Direct tel 020 7227 0777
Direct fax 020 7227 0717
Mobile 07831 263536
Email chris.day@christie.com

DAY, Thomas
Lisney

Position

Director

Qualifications

FIAVI

Contact details

Lisney, 24 St Stephen's Green, Dublin
Tel +353 1 638 2700
Fax +353 1 638 2706

Web www.lisney.com
Email tday@lisney.com

DE BARR, Robert
Land Securities Properties

Position
Director
Qualifications
FRICS
Career history
1977 Joined Land Securities
Other roles
Junior vice-president, British Council of Shopping Centres
Professional memberships
British Council of Shopping Centres; International Council of Shopping Centers; RICS
Interests
Football; golf; sport; tennis
Contact details
Land Securities Properties Ltd, 5 Strand, London WC2N 5AF
Tel 020 7413 9000
Fax 020 7925 0202
Web www.landsecurities.com
Direct tel 020 7024 3744
Direct fax 020 7024 3880
Email bob.debarr@landsecurities.com

DE BEAUFORT-SUCHLICK, Anthony
Ashcroft Estates

Position
Finance director
Professional memberships
Institute of Chartered Accountants in England & Wales
Contact details
Ashcroft Estates plc, Ashcroft House, 162-166 Fulham Palace Road, London W6 9PA
Tel 020 8741 7411
Fax 020 8741 7758
Email suchlick@ashcroft.co.uk

DE BLABY, Rick
Dwyer

Position
Chief executive
Qualifications
BSc, Est Man; MRICS
Career history
1993-2003 Countryside Properties.
1983-93 Trafalgar House Developments.
1982-83 Chestertons.
1980-82 Healey & Baker
Professional memberships
RICS
Interests
Sailing; skiing; windsurfing
Contact details
Dwyer plc, 40 Park Street, London W1K 2JG
Tel 020 7629 6666
Fax 020 7493 5096
Mobile 07867 781234
Email rick.deblaby@dwyer.co.uk

DE BURGH SIDLEY, Elizabeth
Drivers Jonas

Position
Partner – party walls and neighbourly matters
Qualifications
BA Hons; FRICS
Career history
1976 Joined Drivers Jonas.
1974-76 JA Warner & Partners, Rochester
Professional memberships
RICS
Contact details
Drivers Jonas, 6 Grosvenor Street, London W1K 4DJ
Tel 020 7896 8000
Fax 020 7896 8001
Web www.driversjonas.com
Direct tel 020 7896 8340
Email elizabethdeburghsidley@driversjonas.com

DE GREY, Spencer
Foster & Partners

Position
Partner
Qualifications
CBE; MA; Dip Arch (Cantab)
Career history
1973 Joined Foster & Partners
Other roles
Architectural adviser, Royal Botanical Gardens, Kew; governor, Building Centre Trust; teaches at Royal College of Art
Professional memberships
RIBA
Interests
Music; opera; travel
Contact details
Foster & Partners, Riverside Three, 22 Hester Road, London SW11 4AN
Tel 020 7738 0455
Fax 020 7738 1107
Web www.fosterandpartners.com
Email sdegrey@fosterandpartners.com

DE HAAST, Arthur
Jones Lang LaSalle Hotels

Position
Global chief executive officer
Qualifications
BA; FHCIMA
Career history
1987 Joined Jones Lang LaSalle; appointed director in 1992, managing director (Europe) for Jones Lang LaSalle Hotels in 1999, and international director of Jones Lang LaSalle in 2000; became global chief executive officer in 2003.
1984-87 Managing consultant, Stoy Hayward
Professional memberships
Hotel & Catering International Management
Interests
Travel; walking; wine
Contact details
Jones Lang LaSalle Hotels, 22 Hanover Square, London W1A 2BN
Tel 020 7493 6040
Fax 020 7399 5694
Web www.joneslanglasallehotels.com
Direct tel 020 7399 5873
Mobile 07770 304335
Email arthur.dehaast@eu.joneslanglasalle.com

DE LA PIQUERIE, Paul
Falcon Chambers

Position
Barrister
Career history
1966 Called to Bar
Interests
Golf
Contact details
Falcon Chambers, Falcon Court, London EC4Y 1AA
Tel 020 7353 2484
Fax 020 7353 1261
Web www.falcon-chambers.com
Email delapiquerie@falcon-chambers.com

DE PASS, Geoff
Lambert Smith Hampton

Position
Director
Qualifications
BSc Hons; MRICS
Career history
1996 Joined Lambert Smith Hampton.
1995-96 Building surveyor, Herring Baker Harris.
1989-95 Building surveyor, Herring Son & Daw
Professional memberships
RICS
Interests
Art; fishing; walking
Contact details
Lambert Smith Hampton Ltd, 51-55 Whiteladies Road, Bristol BS8 2LY

Tel 0117 926 6666
Fax 0117 925 0527
Web www.lsh.co.uk
Direct tel 0117 914 2020
Mobile 07702 836627
Email gdepass@lsh.co.uk

DE PURY, Christopher
Herbert Smith

Position
Partner
Qualifications
MA (Oxon)
Career history
1992 Admitted to Roll of Solicitors.
1990 Joined Herbert Smith; became partner in 1998
Interests
Theatre; travel
Contact details
Herbert Smith, Exchange House, 10 Primrose Street, London EC2A 2NY
Tel 020 7374 8000
Fax 020 7374 0888
Web www.herbertsmith.com
Email christopher.de-pury@herbertsmith.com

DE ST CROIX, John
Norton Rose

Position
Head of property litigation team
Contact details
Norton Rose, Kempson House, Camomile Street, London EC3A 7AN
Tel 020 7283 6000
Fax 020 7283 6500
Web www.nortonrose.com
Email john.destcroix@nortonrose.com

DE STEFANO, John
London & Henley Property Holdings

Position
Group chairman
Qualifications
BA
Career history
1997 Joined London & Henley
Other roles
Senior partner, John De Stefano & Co (since 1982); chairman, Stratford Investments (since 1994); chairman, Arcadian Estates (since 1994)
Interests
Motor sports; travel
Contact details
London & Henley Property Holdings Ltd, 13 Stratford Place, London W1C 1BD
Tel 020 7493 9999
Fax 020 7493 1200
Email jds@johndestefano.co.uk

DE VINK, Peter
Edinburgh Financial & General Holdings

Position
Managing director
Qualifications
BComm
Career history
Since 1978 Managing director, Edinburgh Financial & General Holdings.
1966-78 Ivory & Sime; appointed partner in 1969 and director in 1975
Professional memberships
Institute of Directors
Interests
Country pursuits; golf
Contact details
Edinburgh Financial & General Holdings Ltd, 7 Howe Street, Edinburgh EH3 6TE
Tel 0131 225 6661
Fax 0131 556 6651
Direct tel 01875 830345
Direct fax 01875 830522
Mobile 07836 702335
Email PdeV@efgh.co.uk

DE WAAL, John
St Philips Chambers

Position
Barrister – head of property team
Career history
1998 Joined St Philips Chambers.
1992 Called to Bar
Other roles
CEDR registered mediator
Professional memberships
Midland Chancery & Commercial Bar Association; Property Bar Association
Contact details
St Philips Chambers (Chambers of John Randall QC), 55 Temple Row, Birmingham B2 5LS
Tel 0121 246 7000
Fax 0121 246 7001
Web www.st-philips.co.uk
Direct tel 0121 246 2147
Email jdewaal@st-philips.co.uk

DE WIT, Elisa
Nicholson Graham & Jones

Position
Partner – head of planning and environment
Career history
Since 2003 Partner, Nicholson Graham & Jones.
2000-03 Berwin Leighton Paisner.
1998-2000 Team leader, BSE Inquiry.
1991-97 Environment and planning lawyer, Australia
Other roles
Member of UK Environmental Law Association working party for waste, contaminated land and IPPC
Professional memberships
Chartered Institute of Waste Management; Environmental Services Association; UK Environmental Law Association
Interests
Food; gardening; renovation; wine
Contact details
Nicholson Graham & Jones, 110 Cannon Street, London EC4N 6AR
Tel 020 7648 9000
Fax 020 7648 9001
Web www.ngj.co.uk
Email elisa.dewit@ngj.co.uk

DEAN, James
FPDSavills

Position
Director – investment, central London
Qualifications
FRICS
Career history
1973 Joined Savills (now FPDSavills)
Professional memberships
RICS
Contact details
FPDSavills Ltd, 20 Grosvenor Hill, London W1K 3HQ
Tel 020 7499 8644
Fax 020 7495 3773
Web www.fpdsavills.co.uk
Direct tel 020 7409 8710
Mobile 07771 772309
Email jdean@fpdsavills.co.uk

DEAN, Robert
FPDSavills

Position
Consultant
Qualifications
BSc; FRICS
Career history
1961 Joined Savills (now FPDSavills)
Other roles
Chairman, Investment Property Databank; management committee chairman, Wilson Centre, Cambridge; chairman, Sackville Property Unit Trust
Professional memberships
RICS
Contact details
FPDSavills Ltd, 25 Finsbury Circus, London

D

EC2M 7EE
Tel 020 7499 8644
Fax 020 7588 7323
Web www.fpdsavills.co.uk
Direct tel 020 7409 8967
Email rdean@fpdsavills.co.uk

DEAN, Roger
Dormon Dean Heaton Associates
Position
Partner
Qualifications
FRICS
Career history
1974 Joined Strutt & Parker; appointed equity partner in 1985; head of central London business team specialising in office, retail and residential development 1991-99.
1973-74 West End agency, Hillier Parker May & Rowden.
1969-73 Central London retail agency, Healey & Baker
Professional memberships
RICS
Contact details
Dormon Dean Heaton Associates, Marble Arch Tower, 55 Bryanston Street, London W1H 7AA
Tel 020 7402 8668
Fax 020 7706 9075

DEANESLY, Clare
Jones Day
Position
Partner – head of environment
Qualifications
LLB Hons (Soton)
Career history
1977 Joined Gouldens (now Jones Day); became partner in 1980.
1977 Admitted to Roll of Solicitors.
1975-77 Field Fisher Martineau
Other roles
Member, UK Environmental Law Association waste working party; member of policy and planning committees, Environmental Services Association; environmental committee member, International Chamber of Commerce
Professional memberships
Energy from Waste Association; Environmental Services Association; Law Society; UK Environmental Law Association
Interests
Opera; skiing; tennis; theatre; travel
Contact details
Jones Day, 21 Tudor Street, London EC4Y 0DJ
Tel 020 7039 5959
Fax 020 7039 5999
Web www.jonesday.com
Direct tel 020 7842 6144
Email cdeanesly@jonesday.com

DEAS, Paula
Coventry Centre for Investment
Position
Inward investment and marketing manager
Qualifications
BA Hons
Career history
1993 Joined Coventry City Council as inward investment officer concentrating on US market
Interests
Interior design; IT
Contact details
Coventry Centre for Investment, John Sinclair House, Coventry Canal Basin, Coventry CV1 4LY
Tel 024 7683 3333
Fax 024 7683 2180
Web www.ccfi.co.uk
Direct tel 024 7683 1391
Mobile 07980 892759
Email Paula.Deas@Coventry.gov.uk

DEBNEY, Richard
Haslemere
Position
Chief executive
Qualifications
BSc; MRICS
Professional memberships
RICS
Contact details
Haslemere NV, 43-45 Portman Square, London W1H 6HE
Tel 020 7467 4500
Fax 020 7467 4505
Email rdebney@haslemerenv.com

DEEBLE-ROGERS, Richard
EA Shaw
Position
Partner
Contact details
EA Shaw, 9-12 Bow Street, London WC2E 7AB
Tel 020 7240 2255
Fax 020 7831 1012
Web www.eashaw.com
Direct tel 020 7420 3007
Email rdr@eashaw.com

DEIGMAN, Patrick
Arlington Securities
Position
Chief executive
Qualifications
HND, Building
Career history
1986 Joined Arlington Business Parks as managing director; became director in 1990; chief executive of Arlington Securities since 1992
Professional memberships
Institute of Directors; Institute of Management Consultants; Royal Society of Arts
Interests
Football; squash; tennis; theatre
Contact details
Arlington Securities plc, Arlington House, 1025 Arlington Business Park, Reading RG7
Tel 0118 930 4141
Fax 0118 930 4383
Web www.arlington.co.uk
Direct fax 0118 930 4535
Email patrick.deigman@arlington.co.uk

DEL BEATO, Ilaria
GE Real Estate
Position
Head of asset management
Qualifications
MRICS
Career history
2001-03 Lend Lease Real Estate Investments: joined as senior vice-president (capital transactions); appointed head of capital transactions (Europe) in 2002.
1996-2001 Head of office investment, MEPC
Professional memberships
RICS
Contact details
GE Real Estate, Clarges House, 6-12 Clarges Street, London W1J 8DH
Tel 020 7302 6000
Fax 020 7302 6830
Direct tel 020 7302 6255
Mobile 07717 517020
Email ilaria.delbeato@ge.com

DELLAL, Guy
Allied Commercial Exporters
Position
Managing director
Interests
Art; football; photography; Queen's Club; Hurlingham Club
Contact details
Allied Commercial Exporters Ltd, Bowater House, 114 Knightsbridge, London SW7
Tel 020 7225 0066
Fax 020 7823 8985
Email guy@alliedcommercial.com

DELLAR, Russell
Landwell & Partners

Position
Head of real estate
Career history
2002 Joined Landwell.
1992-2002 Denton Wilde Sapte
Other roles
Panel member, Prince's Youth Business Trust
Professional memberships
Non-Administrative Receivers Association
Interests
Sport
Contact details
Landwell & Partners, 1 Embankment Place, London WC2N 6DX
Tel 020 7212 1616
Fax 020 7212 1570
Web www.landwellglobal.com
Direct tel 020 7212 1679
Email russell.dellar@uk.landwellglobal.com

DENBY, Nigel
Hamlet Residential

Position
Finance director
Qualifications
ACA
Career history
1993-2001 Finance director, BPT.
1991-93 Group finance director, Illingworth Morris.
1982-91 Divisional finance director, Hickson International
Other roles
Consultant, Town Centre Securities
Professional memberships
Institute of Chartered Accountants in England & Wales
Contact details
Hamlet Residential Ltd, 2 Weirside Court, Dockfield Road, Shipley BD17 7AD
Tel 01274 590655
Fax 01274 590655
Mobile 07711 326115
Email ndenby@hamletresidential.com

DENEHAN, Edward
9 Stone Buildings

Position
Barrister
Qualifications
LLB Hons
Career history
1981 Called to Bar
Other roles
Sometime tutor in property law, University of Warwick; sometime tutor in landlord and tenant law and in planning and local government law at Inns of Court School of Law; lectures to Property Litigation Association; author of Inns of Court School of Law advocacy manual *Guide to Possession Actions* (6th edition, Blackstone Press); joint author of Inns of Court School of Law *Landlord & Tenant Manual* (2nd edition, Blackstone Press); sits as member of Bar disciplinary tribunal and on disciplinary tribunal of Society of Trust & Estate Practitioners
Professional memberships
Chancery Bar Association; Honourable Society of Lincoln's Inn; International Association of Irish Lawyers
Contact details
9 Stone Buildings, London WC2A 3NN
Tel 020 7404 5055
Fax 020 7405 1551
Web www.9stonebuildings.com
Email clerks@9stonebuildings.com

DENNESS, Robin
Churston Heard

Position
Director
Qualifications
FRICS
Career history
1982-2001 Director, Lambert Smith Hampton.
1980-82 Director, Peter Hunter & Co.
1971-80 Associate director, Conrad Ritblat & Co
Professional memberships
RICS
Contact details
Churston Heard Ltd, 7 Hanover Square, London W1S 1HQ
Tel 020 7409 2199
Fax 020 7495 1339
Web www.churstonheard.co.uk
Direct tel 020 7318 7873
Mobile 07810 435913
Email rdenness@churstonheard.co.uk

DENNIS, Cyril
Capital & Provident Management

Position
Chairman
Qualifications
MBE
Contact details
Capital & Provident Management Ltd, 6 Harbour Exchange Square, London E14 9HE
Tel 020 7510 8888
Fax 020 7510 8800
Email cyril.dennis@capitalandprovident.com

DENNY, Chris
Denton Wilde Sapte

Position
Partner – head of retail sector group
Career history
1986 Joined Oppenheimers (merged with Denton Hall; now Denton Wilde Sapte); appointed partner in 1989.
1984-86 Ellis Wood & Co.
1982 Admitted to Roll of Solicitors.
1980-84 Richard Butler
Interests
Food; rugby; travel; wine
Contact details
Denton Wilde Sapte, Regency Court, 206 Upper Fifth Street, Milton Keynes MK9 2HR
Tel 01908 690260
Fax 01908 668535
Web www.dentonwildesapte.com
Direct tel 020 7320 3908
Direct fax 020 7320 3949
Mobile 07887 628098
Email cjd@dentonwildesapte.com

DENT, Graham
Aerion Fund Management

Position
Property manager
Qualifications
BSc; FRICS
Contact details
Aerion Fund Management Ltd, Heron House, 322 High Holborn, London WC1V 7PW
Tel 020 7242 5005
Direct tel 020 7269 4938
Email graham.dent@aerionfm.com

DENT, Jean
Leeds City Council

Position
Director of development
Qualifications
FRICS
Professional memberships
RICS
Contact details
Leeds City Council, Merrion House, 110 Merrion Centre, Leeds LS2 8DR
Tel 0113 247 8000
Web www.leeds.gov.uk
Direct tel 0113 247 7893
Email jean.dent@leeds.gov.uk

DENTON, Peter
Eurohypo

Position
Director

Qualifications
BSc Hons; ACA
Career history
1998-2002 Director (real estate investment banking), Deutsche Bank.
1994-98 Member of real estate business assurance group, Arthur Andersen & Co
Professional memberships
Institute of Chartered Accountants in England & Wales
Contact details
Eurohypo AG, 90 Long Acre, London WC2E 9RA
Tel 020 7759 7600
Fax 020 7759 7672
Web www.eurohypo.com
Direct tel 020 7759 7632
Direct fax 020 7759 7675
Email peter.denton@eurohypo.com

DENYER-GREEN, Barry
Falcon Chambers
Position
Barrister
Qualifications
LLM; PhD; Hon FRICS
Other roles
Author, *Compulsory Purchase & Compensation* (6th edition, 2003); joint author, *Development & Planning Law* (3rd edition, 1999); editor, *Estates Gazette Law Reports*; joint editor, *Planning Law Reports*
Professional memberships
Honourable Society of the Middle Temple; RICS; Central Association of Agricultural Valuers (honorary member)
Contact details
Falcon Chambers, Falcon Court, London EC4Y 1AA
Tel 020 7353 2484
Fax 020 7353 1261
Web www.falcon-chambers.com
Email denyer-green@falcon-chambers.com

DESMOND, Danny
Bride Hall Group
Position
Chairman and chief executive
Career history
1984 Established Bride Hall Group.
1968-83 Managing director, Hunting Gate Group
Interests
Family; golf
Contact details
Bride Hall Group Ltd, 49 Hays Mews, London W1J 5QQ
Tel 020 7493 3996
Fax 020 7499 4388
Direct fax 0158 283 3801
Email daniel.desmond@bride-hall.co.uk

DESMOND, Nigel
Bride Hall Group
Position
Joint managing director
Career history
1989 Joined Bride Hall as development director; appointed joint managing director in 2000.
1987-89 Fairclough/AMEC.
1985-87 Gordon Hudson & Co
Contact details
Bride Hall Group Ltd, 49 Hays Mews, London W1J 5QQ
Tel 020 7493 3996
Fax 020 7499 4388
Mobile 07768 448382
Email nigel.desmond@bride-hall.co.uk

DEVINE, Paul
AWG Asset Managment
Position
Managing director – commercial developments, Scotland and Ireland
Career history
1991 Joined Morrison Developments (now AWG Asset Management); now managing director (commercial developments), Scotland and Ireland.
1984-91 Ryden
Interests
Golf; rugby
Contact details
AWG Asset Management Ltd, Atholl House, 49 Melville Street, Edinburgh EH3 7HL
Tel 0131 226 4666
Fax 0131 226 4166
Email paul.devine@awg.com

DEVLIN, Tony
Dalgleish
Position
Retail director
Contact details
Dalgleish, 80 New Bond Street, London W1S 1DD
Tel 020 7663 5555
Fax 020 7491 0098
Web www.dalgleish.co.uk
Email tdevlin@dalgleish.co.uk

DI MAMBRO, David
Lamb Chambers
Position
Barrister
Qualifications
LLB Hons (Lond); Blackstone scholar, Middle Temple; FSALS; MCIArb
Career history
1973 Called to Bar
Other roles
Member of editorial board of *Butterworths' Civil Court Practice* (the Green Book); general editor of *Butterworths' Law of Limitation*; general editor of *Butterworths' Manual of Civil Appeals*; general editor of *Butterworths' Civil Court Manual 1999*; contributing editor, *Atkins Court Forms: CPR*; contributing editor, *Atkins Court Forms: Appeals (CPR)*; contributing editor, *Atkins Court Forms: Service of Documents out of Jurisdiction*
Professional memberships
Chancery Bar Association; Property Bar Association
Interests
Cricket; military history; rugby; yachting
Contact details
Lamb Chambers, Lamb Building, London EC4Y 7AS
Tel 020 7797 8300
Fax 020 7797 8308
Web www.lambchambers.co.uk
Email daviddimambro@lambchambers.co.uk

DICKENS, Scott
Bear, Stearns International
Position
Managing director – real estate finance
Interests
Golf
Contact details
Bear, Stearns International Ltd, One Canada Square, London E14 5AB
Tel 020 7516 6000
Fax 020 7516 6030
Web www.bearstearns.com
Mobile 07887 987076
Email sdickens@bear.com

DICKINSON, Alan
Royal Bank of Scotland
Position
Head of corporate banking
Contact details
Royal Bank of Scotland, 135 Bishopsgate, London EC2M 3UR
Tel 020 7375 5000
Web www.rbs.co.uk
Email alan.dickinson@rbs.co.uk

DICKINSON, Paul
GL Hearn
Position
Director – rating and valuation

Qualifications
MRICS; BSc Hons, Est Man
Career history
1985 Joined GL Hearn.
1982-85 Valuation Office
Professional memberships
RICS
Interests
Reading
Contact details
GL Hearn Ltd, Leonard House, 5-7 Marshalsea Road, London SE1 1EP
Tel 020 7450 4000
Fax 020 7450 4010
Web www.glhearn.com
Email paul_dickinson@glhearn.com

DICKINSON, Rupert
Grainger Trust
Position
Chief executive
Qualifications
BSc Hons; MRICS
Career history
1991 Joined Grainger Trust.
1987-91 Richard Ellis
Other roles
Chief executive, BPT; director, Northumberland & Durham Property Trust; director, Grainger Investment Properties; director, Grainger (London); director, N&D (London); director, Cross House Buildings
Professional memberships
BPF; RICS
Contact details
Grainger Trust plc, 203 Brompton Road, London SW3 1LA
Tel 020 7795 4700
Fax 020 7795 4701
Web www.graingertrust.co.uk
Direct tel 020 7795 4705
Mobile 07768 392232
Email rjd@graingertrust.co.uk

DICKINSON, Stephen
Grainger Trust
Position
Non-executive deputy chairman
Contact details
Grainger Trust plc, Citygate, St James Boulevard, Newcastle upon Tyne NE1 4JE
Tel 0191 261 1819
Fax 0191 269 5901
Web www.graingertrust.co.uk
Email ceke@graingertrust.co.uk

DICKSON, Steven
Scottish Power
Position
UK group estates director
Contact details
Scottish Power plc, Avondale House, Phoenix Crescent, Bellshill ML4 3NJ
Tel 01698 413000
Web www.scottishpower.com
Direct tel 01698 396236
Direct fax 01698 396192
Email steven.dickson@scottishpower.com

DIGBY-BELL, Christopher
Palmer Capital Partners
Position
Chief executive
Qualifications
Solicitor
Career history
1998 Joined Palmer Capital Partners.
1989-97 Frere Cholmeley Bischoff: became marketing partner in 1992 and international managing partner in 1995.
1972 Admitted to Roll of Solicitors.
1966-89 Managing partner, Taylor Wessing.
1966-82 Taylor & Humbert; partner from 1975
Other roles
Director, Wrenbridge Land; director, Opus Land; director, Danescroft Commercial Developments; director, Frontier Estates; director, Thistle Land; solicitor/consultant, Forsters; honorary legal adviser, Down's Syndrome Association
Professional memberships
Law Society
Interests
Cinema; cricket; golf; music; photography
Contact details
Palmer Capital Partners Ltd, 17 Clifford Street, London W1S 3RQ
Tel 020 7437 9444
Fax 020 7437 9555
Web www.palmercapital.co.uk
Mobile 07770 777399
Email property@palmercapital.co.uk

DIGGLE, Catherine
Lawrence Graham
Position
Partner – commercial property
Qualifications
BA Hons
Interests
Football
Contact details
Lawrence Graham, 190 Strand, London WC2R 1JN
Tel 020 7379 0000
Fax 020 7379 6854
Web www3.lawgram.com
Direct tel 020 7759 6702
Direct fax 020 7173 8702
Email catherine.diggle@lawgram.com

DIGHT, Marc
11 Stone Buildings
Position
Barrister
Qualifications
LLB (Bristol)
Career history
1984 Called to Bar
Other roles
Recorder
Professional memberships
Chancery Bar Association; Property Bar Association
Interests
Foreign culture
Contact details
11 Stone Buildings, London WC2A 3TG
Tel 020 7831 6381
Fax 020 7831 2575
Web www.11stonebuildings.com
Email dight@11stonebuildings.com

DILLON, Mal
Crown Estate
Position
Head of regional estate
Interests
IT; sport
Contact details
Crown Estate, 16 Carlton House Terrace, London SW1Y 5AH
Tel 020 7210 4377
Fax 020 7210 4236
Web www.crownestate.co.uk
Direct tel 020 7210 4264
Mobile 07785 731775
Email mal.dillon@crownestate.co.uk

DILLON, Mark
Sheppard Robson
Position
Partner
Qualifications
BA; Dip Arch; RIBA
Professional memberships
British Council for Offices; RIBA
Interests
Football; gardening; golf
Contact details
Sheppard Robson, 77 Parkway, London

D

NW1 7PU
Tel 020 7504 1700
Fax 020 7504 1701
Web www.sheppardrobson.com
Email mark.dillon@sheppardrobson.com

DINGLE, Stephen
Ernst & Young

Position
Partner – co-head real estate finance
Qualifications
MA; ACIB
Other roles
Honorary treasury and trustee, Shakespeare's Global Trust
Interests
Golf; skiing; theatre; wine
Contact details
Ernst & Young LLP, 1 More London Place, London SE1 2AF
Tel 020 7951 2000
Fax 020 7951 1345
Web www.ey.com/uk
Direct tel 020 7951 3777
Direct fax 020 7951 3411
Mobile 07802 836275
Email sdingle@uk.ey.com

DINSDALE, Michael
Aberdeen Property Investors UK

Position
Director
Contact details
Aberdeen Property Investors UK Ltd, 123 St Vincent Street, Glasgow G2 5EA
Tel 0141 306 7600
Fax 0141 306 7706
Web www.aberdeenpropertyinvestors.com
Email
michael.dinsdale@aberdeenpropertyinvestors.com

DISLEY-TINDELL, Paul
Land Securities Trillium

Position
Director – corporate real estate
Qualifications
BSc Hons; MRICS; PGC Prop Invest
Career history
1991-98 Estate surveyor, Post Office Property Holdings
Professional memberships
RICS
Interests
Architecture; golf; IT; motor sports
Contact details
Land Securities Trillium Ltd, 140 London Wall, London EC2Y 5DN
Tel 020 7796 5500
Fax 020 7796 5501
Web www.landsecurities.co.uk
Direct tel 020 7796 5587
Direct fax 0845 090 2351
Mobile 07802 686565
Email paul.disley-tindell@lstrillium.com

DISNEY, Mark
Dalgleish

Position
Shopping centre director
Qualifications
BSc Hons; MRICS
Career history
1991 Joined Dalgleish; appointed director in 1999.
1988-91 Healey & Baker
Other roles
Former chairman, RICS Hockey Club
Professional memberships
British Council of Shopping Centres
Contact details
Dalgleish, 80 New Bond Street, London W1S 1DD
Tel 020 7663 5555
Fax 020 7491 0098
Web www.dalgleish.co.uk
Direct tel 020 7663 5530
Email mdisney@dalgleish.co.uk

DIX, Michael
Cluttons

Position
Partner – valuation
Contact details
Cluttons, Portman House, 2 Portman Street, London W1H 6DU
Tel 020 7408 1010
Fax 020 7629 3263
Web www.cluttons.com
Email mdix@cluttons.com

DIXON, Alistair
Deutsche Bank

Position
Managing director – real estate opportunities group
Qualifications
BSc Hons; MBA
Career history
1999 Joined Deutsche Bank
Contact details
Deutsche Bank AG, 1 Appold Street, London EC2A 2HE
Tel 020 7545 8000
Fax 020 7545 4444
Web www.db.com
Direct tel 020 7547 5350
Mobile 07802 943714
Email alistair.dixon@db.com

DIXON, Colin
RadcliffesLeBrasseur

Position
Partner – property department
Qualifications
LLB Hons
Career history
2002 Joined RadcliffesLeBrasseur.
1998-2002 CMS Cameron McKenna.
1995-98 Addleshaw Booth & Co.
1993-95 Freshfields
Other roles
Has published articles in Budapest press; speaker at central European conferences
Professional memberships
Law Society
Interests
Cycling; golf; mountain biking; skiing; tennis
Contact details
RadcliffesLeBrasseur, 6-7 Park Place, Leeds LS1 2RU
Tel 0113 234 1220
Fax 0113 234 1573
Web www.rlb-law.com
Direct tel 0113 261 5503
Email colin.dixon@rlb-law.com

DIXON, Mark
Regus

Position
Chief executive
Interests
Chess; squash; windsurfing
Contact details
Regus plc, 3000 Hillswood Drive, Chertsey KT16 0RS
Tel 01932 895000
Fax 01932 895001
Direct tel 01932 895135
Direct fax 01932 895263
Email mark.dixon@regus.com

DOBSON, Keith
FPDSavills

Position
Director – head of office, Edinburgh
Qualifications
BLE; MRICS
Career history
1997 Joined FPDSavills.
1993-97 Associate director, Chesterton.
1990-93 Associate, Conroy Hunter

D

Professional memberships
Investment Property Forum
Interests
Family; fishing; golf; rugby; shooting
Contact details
FPDSavills Ltd, 86 George Street, Edinburgh EH2 3BU
Tel 0131 247 3800
Fax 0131 247 3838
Web www.fpdsavills.co.uk
Direct tel 0131 247 3801
Mobile 07799 418541
Email kdobson@fpdsavills.co.uk

DOBSON, Roger
Hodnett Martin Smith
Position
Partner
Career history
1991 Joined Hodnett Martin Smith.
1988-91 Peachey Property Corp.
1985-88 Schroder Properties.
1980-85 Debenham Tewson & Chinnocks
Contact details
Hodnett Martin Smith Ltd, Charles House, 5-11 Regent Street, London SW1Y 4LR
Tel 020 7839 8181
Fax 020 7839 8069
Web www.hodnettmartinsmith.com
Direct tel 020 7747 1506
Email rogerdobson@hodms.co.uk

DOCHERTY, Kevin
Irwin Mitchell
Position
Head of commercial property
Contact details
Irwin Mitchell Ltd, St Peter's House, Hartshead, Sheffield S1 2EL
Tel 0870 150 0100
Fax 0114 275 3306
Web www.imonline.co.uk
Email dochertyk@irwinmitchell.co.uk

DODGSON, Robert
Davies Lavery
Position
Partner – head of property
Qualifications
LLB
Career history
1997 Joined Davies Lavery as associate; appointed partner and head of property in 1999; also equity partner/management board member.
1994-97 Partner (head of commercial property), Days.
1990-94 Godloves
Professional memberships
Institute of Directors; Locate in Kent
Interests
Cricket; family; football; rugby; travel
Contact details
Davies Lavery, Victoria Court, 17-21 Ashford Road, Maidstone ME14 5FA
Tel 01622 625625
Fax 01622 625600
Web www.davies-lavery.co.uk
Direct tel 01622 625657
Direct fax 01622 625601
Mobile 07786 732622
Email Robert.Dodgson@davies-lavery.co.uk

DODINGTON, Mark
Monsoon Accessorize
Position
Head of property
Career history
2002 Joined Monsoon as head of property.
Formerly with New Look
Contact details
Monsoon Accessorize Ltd, Monsoon Building, 179 Harrow Road, London W2 6NB
Tel 020 7313 4000
Fax 020 7313 4400
Web www.monsoon.co.uk
Direct tel 020 7313 4166
Direct fax 020 7313 4470
Email mdodington@monsoon.co.uk

DODSON, Rupert
Cushman & Wakefield Healey & Baker
Position
Partner – valuation
Qualifications
BSc; FRICS
Professional memberships
RICS
Contact details
Cushman & Wakefield Healey & Baker, 43-45 Portman Square, London W1A 3BG
Tel 020 7935 5000
Fax 020 7152 5360
Web www.cushwake.com
Direct tel 020 7152 5042
Direct fax 020 7152 5390
Email rupert.dodson@eur.cushwake.com

DODSWORTH, Catriona
Masons
Position
Partner – construction and engineering group
Qualifications
BA Hons
Career history
1991 Admitted to Roll of Solicitors.
1989 Joined Masons; appointed senior associate in 1998 and partner in 2000
Professional memberships
Chartered Institute of Arbitrators; Faculty of Building; Society of Construction Law; Technology & Construction Solicitors Association
Interests
Cinema; food; motor sports; rugby; travel
Contact details
Masons, Woodbridge House, 30 Aylesbury Street, London EC1R 0ER
Tel 020 7329 2288
Fax 020 7490 2545
Web www.masons.com
Direct tel 020 7490 6298
Mobile 07768 506495
Email catriona.dodsworth@masons.com

DOLEMAN, Peter
Innes England
Position
Director – agency
Qualifications
MRICS
Career history
1992 Joined Innes England, Leicester.
1988-92 DTZ, London.
1985-88 King Sturge, London
Professional memberships
RICS
Interests
Rugby; sailing
Contact details
Innes England Ltd, 12-16 De Montfort Street, Leicester LE1 7GJ
Tel 0116 255 5455
Fax 0116 255 4924
Web www.innes-england.com
Mobile 07836 692565
Email pdoleman@innes-england.com

DOLLAR, Peta
Denton Wilde Sapte
Position
Partner – real estate and PFI
Qualifications
LLB Hons
Career history
1984 Joined Denton Wilde Sapte; appointed partner in 1988.
1980 Admitted to Roll of Solicitors.
1978-84 Clifford-Turner
Other roles
Author, *Tenants' Pre-emption Rights – A Landlord's Guide to the Landlord & Tenant Act*

D?

1987 (Jordans, 1999); editor of property, planning and construction section, *Corporate Briefing*; editorial board member, *Landlord & Tenant Review*

Professional memberships

BPF; Law Society

Interests

Art; fishing; music; writing

Contact details

Denton Wilde Sapte, One Fleet Place, London EC4M 7WS

Tel 020 7246 7000

Fax 020 7246 7777

Web www.dentonwildesapte.com

Direct tel 020 7320 6241

Email pxd@dentonwildesapte.com

DOLPHIN, Giles
Greater London Authority

Position

Head of planning decisions

Qualifications

Dip TP; MRTPI

Career history

1987-2000 London Planning Advisory Committee.
1980-87 Lambeth Council.
1974-80 Hammersmith & Fulham Council.
1971-74 Croydon Council

Professional memberships

RTPI

Contact details

Greater London Authority, City Hall, 110 The Queens Walk, London SE1 2AA

Tel 020 7983 4000

Fax 020 7983 4057

Direct fax 020 7983 4706

Mobile 07776 165817

Email giles.dolphin@london.gov.uk

DONALD, James
Strutt & Parker

Position

Partner – investment and development

Qualifications

BSc, Est Man; FRICS

Career history

1972 Joined Strutt & Parker.
1967-72 Savills

Professional memberships

Investment Property Forum; RICS

Interests

Golf; rugby; travel

Contact details

Strutt & Parker, 13 Hill Street, London W1J 5LQ

Tel 020 7629 7282

Fax 020 7629 0387

Web www.struttandparker.com

Direct tel 020 7318 5020

Direct fax 020 7491 1160

Mobile 07831 513944

Email jdonald@struttandparker.com

DONNELLY, Tony
AWG Asset Management

Position

Managing director

Qualifications

BA Hons; ACMA

Interests

Family; football; golf; tennis

Contact details

AWG Asset Management Ltd, Atholl House, 49 Melville Street, Edinburgh EH3 7HL

Tel 0131 226 4666

Fax 0131 226 4166

Direct tel 0131 200 4431

Email tony.donnelly@awgdevelopments.com

DOOGAN, Gerry
ISIS Property Asset Management

Position

Director – building services

Contact details

ISIS Property Asset Management plc, Park Lodge, London Road, Dorking RH4 1QP

Tel 01306 651800

Fax 01306 651802

Web www.isisam.com

Direct tel 01306 651851

Email gerry.doogan@isisam.com

DOOLEY, Gary
Rank Group

Position

Director of development

Contact details

Rank Group plc, Stafferton Way, Maidenhead SL6 1AY

Tel 01628 504000

Email gary_dooley@rank.com

DORAN, Iain
Dundas & Wilson

Position

Partner – head of real estate

Contact details

Dundas & Wilson, 181-195 West George Street, Glasgow G2 2LB

Tel 0141 222 2200

Fax 0141 222 2201

Web www.dundas-wilson.com

Email iain.doran@dundas-wilson.com

DORINS, Hugh
Edward Symmons & Partners

Position

Partner – professional services

Qualifications

LLB Hons; Dip Surv; MRICS; MCIArb

Contact details

Edward Symmons & Partners, 39 York Place, Leeds LS1 2ED

Tel 0113 245 8454

Fax 0113 246 8556

Web www.edwardsymmons.com

Email hugh.dorins@edwardsymmons.com

DORNFORD, Alan
Nelson Bakewell

Position

Director – agency and development services

Qualifications

BSc; MRICS

Career history

Since 1992 Main board director, Nelson Bakewell.
1988-92 Bernard Thorpe.
1986-88 Matthews & Goodman

Other roles

Executive director, Nelson Bakewell; managing director, Newmark, Nelson Bakewell (London/New York joint venture)

Professional memberships

CoreNet Global UK; RICS

Interests

Cricket; football; golf; skiing; tennis

Contact details

Nelson Bakewell Ltd, 25 Sackville Street, London W1S 3HQ

Tel 020 7544 2000

Fax 020 7544 2222

Web www.nelson-bakewell.com

Direct tel 020 7544 2211

Direct fax 020 7544 2125

Email adornford@nelson-bakewell.com

DOSSETT, Roger
Estates & General

Position

Managing director

Contact details

Estates & General plc, Penn House, 30 High Street, Rickmansworth WD3 1EP

Tel 01923 285999

Fax 01923 770547

Email roger.dossett@estates-general.com

DOUETIL, Guy
Cushman & Wakefield Healey & Baker

Position

Partner – global corporate services

D

Qualifications
BSc; MRICS
Career history
1986 Joined Cushman & Wakefield Healey & Baker
Professional memberships
CoreNet Global UK; RICS
Interests
IT; sailing; skiing
Contact details
Cushman & Wakefield Healey & Baker, 43-45 Portman Square, London W1A 3BG
Tel 020 7935 5000
Fax 020 7152 5360
Web www.cushwake.com
Direct tel 020 7152 5220
Direct fax 020 7152 5363
Email guy.douetil@eur.cushwake.com

DOUGHERTY, Ian
Ryden
Position
Partner – investment and finance group
Qualifications
MRICS
Career history
1997 Joined Ryden, Glasgow.
1994-97 Richard Ellis, Glasgow.
1986-94 Property Security Investment Trust
Contact details
Ryden, 130 St Vincent Street, Glasgow G2 5HF
Tel 0141 204 3838
Fax 0141 204 3554
Web www.ryden.co.uk
Direct tel 0141 270 3163
Mobile 07831 175710
Email ian.dougherty@ryden.co.uk

DOUGLAS, Carol
Land Securities Trillium
Position
Asset management director
Qualifications
BSc Hons; MRICS
Career history
1998 Joined Land Securities Trillium as asset management director (corporate real estate group). Previously at Prudential
Professional memberships
RICS
Interests
Diving/scuba diving; photography; tennis
Contact details
Land Securities Trillium Ltd, 140 London Wall, London EC2Y 5DN
Tel 020 7796 5500
Fax 020 7796 5501
Web www.landsecurities.co.uk
Direct tel 020 7796 5646
Direct fax 0845 090 2387
Email carol.douglas@lstrillium.com

DOUGRAY, Chris
Donaldsons
Position
Partner – Scotland
Contact details
Donaldsons, 9-11 Hope Street, Edinburgh EH2 4EL
Tel 0131 260 7300
Fax 0131 225 8970
Web www.donaldsons.co.uk
Email chris.dougray@donaldsons.co.uk

DOVE, Michael
Knight Frank
Position
Office head, Leeds
Qualifications
BSc Hons; FRICS
Professional memberships
RICS
Contact details
Knight Frank LLP, 10 Park Place, Leeds LS1 2RU
Tel 0113 246 1533
Fax 0113 244 6654
Web www.knightfrank.com
Mobile 07771 886036
Email mike.dove@knightfrank.com

DOVE, Paul
SJS Property Management
Position
Director – estates and portfolio
Qualifications
BSc, Est Man; MRICS
Career history
Since 2000 Director (estates and portfolio), SJS Property Management (property management operating company for Littlewoods)
Professional memberships
RICS
Interests
Gardening; mountaineering; sailing; swimming; theatre; travel; water sports; windsurfing
Contact details
SJS Property Management Ltd, Sir John Moores Building, 100 Old Hall Street, Liverpool
Tel 0151 235 2456
Fax 0151 235 3453
Email paul.dove@littlewoods.co.uk

DOWDING, Nicholas
Falcon Chambers
Position
Barrister
Qualifications
MA (Cantab); QC
Career history
1979 Called to Bar
Other roles
Past editor, *Handbook of Rent Review*; editor, *Woodfall: Landlord & Tenant;* joint author, *Dilapidations – the Modern Law & Practice* (2nd edition, 2001)
Professional memberships
Chancery Bar Association; London Common Law & Commercial Bar Association
Contact details
Falcon Chambers, Falcon Court, London EC4Y 1AA
Tel 020 7353 2484
Fax 020 7353 1261
Web www.falcon-chambers.com
Direct tel 020 7427 7317
Mobile 07775 721458
Email dowding@falcon-chambers.com

DOWLEY, Keith
Holley Blake
Position
Partner – industrial/development
Career history
1995 Joined Holley Blake.
1987-95 Associate, Brian Cooper & Co.
1985-87 DE&J Levy
Contact details
Holley Blake Ltd, 1 Mount Street, London W1K 3LE
Tel 020 7629 4171
Fax 020 7493 2267
Web www.holleyblake.com
Mobile 07775 745608
Email keith@holleyblake.co.uk

DOWNER, Alan
Chesterton International
Position
Director in charge, Milton Keynes office
Qualifications
FRICS
Contact details
Chesterton International, Chesterton House, 352 Avebury Boulevard, Milton Keynes MK9 2JH
Tel 01908 608866
Fax 01908 609951
Web www.chesterton.co.uk
Email alan.downer@chesterton.co.uk

D

DOWSELL, Graham
NAI Fuller Peiser

Position
Partner
Contact details
NAI Fuller Peiser, 16 St George Street, London W1S 1LX
Tel 0870 700 2233
Fax 020 7491 1961
Web www.nai-fullerpeiser.com
Direct tel 020 7645 1830
Email gdowsell@nai-fullerpeiser.com

DOYLE, Nicholas
St Modwen Properties

Position
Director – London office
Qualifications
BSc; MRICS
Professional memberships
Investment Property Forum; RICS
Interests
Football; golf; rugby
Contact details
St Modwen Properties plc, Hereditable House, 28-29 Dover Street, London W1X 3PA
Tel 020 7499 5666
Fax 020 7629 4262
Web www.stmodwen.co.uk
Email ndoyle@stmodwen.co.uk

DRABBLE, Richard
Landmark Chambers

Position
QC
Qualifications
BA Hons; QC
Career history
1975 Called to Bar
Other roles
Chairman, Administrative Law Bar Association
Professional memberships
Administrative Law Bar Association; Planning & Environment Bar Association; Society for Advanced Legal Studies
Contact details
Landmark Chambers, 4 Breams Buildings, London EC4A 1AQ
Tel 020 7430 1221
Fax 020 7421 1399
Web www.landmarkchambers.co.uk
Email clerks@landmarkchambers.co.uk

DRAY, Martin
Falcon Chambers

Position
Barrister
Qualifications
LLB Hons
Career history
Since 1993 Barrister, Falcon Chambers.
1992 Called to Bar
Professional memberships
Chancery Bar Association; Property Bar Association
Contact details
Falcon Chambers, Falcon Court, London EC4Y 1AA
Tel 020 7353 2484
Fax 020 7353 1261
Web www.falcon-chambers.com
Email dray@falcon-chambers.com

DRISCOLL, Michael
9 Old Square

Position
Barrister – head of chambers
Qualifications
QC
Contact details
9 Old Square (Chambers of Michael Driscoll QC), Ground Floor, London WC2A 3SR
Tel 020 7405 4682
Fax 020 7831 7107
Web www.9oldsquare.co.uk
Email michael.driscoll@9oldsquare.co.uk

DRIVER, Nicholas
London Merchant Securities

Position
Managing director
Qualifications
BSc; FRICS
Career history
1970 Joined London Merchant Securities.
1966-70 Cluttons
Professional memberships
RICS
Contact details
London Merchant Securities plc, Carlton House, 33 Robert Adam Street, London W1U 3HR
Tel 020 7935 3555
Fax 020 7935 3737
Web www.lms-plc.com
Email ndriver@lms-plc.com

DRUMMOND, Bill
Brodies

Position
Managing partner
Qualifications
LLB; WS
Career history
1983 Joined Brodies WS; appointed partner in commercial property in 1986; elected managing partner in 1998 and again in 2001.
1983 Admitted to Roll of Solicitors
Professional memberships
Law Society of Scotland; WS Society
Contact details
Brodies LLP, 15 Atholl Crescent, Edinburgh EH3 8HA
Tel 0131 228 3777
Fax 0131 228 3878
Web www.brodies.co.uk
Email bill.drummond@brodies.co.uk

DRUMMOND, Stewart
Cushman & Wakefield Healey & Baker

Position
Partner – development agency
Qualifications
BSc; FRICS
Professional memberships
RICS
Contact details
Cushman & Wakefield Healey & Baker, 43-45 Portman Square, London W1A 3BG
Tel 020 7935 5000
Fax 020 7152 5360
Web www.cushwake.com
Direct tel 020 7152 5206
Direct fax 020 7152 5392
Email stewart.drummond@eur.cushwake.com

DUCKWORTH, David
Walker Morris

Position
Partner – head of property
Career history
1968 Admitted to Roll of Solicitors
Interests
Sailing; sport
Contact details
Walker Morris Ltd, Kings Court, 12 King Street, Leeds LS1 2HL
Tel 0113 283 2500
Fax 0113 245 9412
Web www.walkermorris.co.uk
Direct tel 0113 283 2574
Email dxd@walkermorris.co.uk

DUDGEON, Peter
Land Securities Group

Position
Company secretary
Contact details
Land Securities Group plc, 5 Strand, London WC2N 5AF
Tel 020 7413 9000
Fax 020 7024 5007

Web www.landsecurities.com
Email peter.dudgeon@landsecurities.com

DUDLEY, Andrew
Brown & Lee
Position
Partner – commercial
Contact details
Brown & Lee, Sovereign Court, 211 Witan Gate East, Milton Keynes MK9 2HP
Tel 01908 690469
Fax 01908 672687
Web www.brownandlee.co.uk
Email andrew.dudley@brownandlee.com

DUDLEY-SMITH, Paul
Aitchison Raffety
Position
Director
Qualifications
BSc Hons; FRICS
Professional memberships
RICS
Interests
Golf; rugby
Contact details
Aitchison Raffety Ltd, 3 Kimbell Mews, Northampton NN1 4HU
Tel 01604 821133
Fax 01604 821144
Web www.argroup.co.uk
Email paul.dudley-smith@argroup.co.uk

DUFFY, Dr Francis
DEGW
Position
Founder
Qualifications
CBE; PhD; MArch; AA Dipl Hons
Career history
1974 Co-founded DEGW with John Worthington and Luigi Giffone.
1971-73 Head of London office, JFN.
1964-67 NBA
Other roles
Chairman of steering group that ran RIBA's strategic study of future of architectural profession; past president, RIBA
Professional memberships
Architects Registration Board; Architectural Association; RIBA; Royal Society of Arts; Urban Land Institute
Contact details
DEGW, 589 Eighth Avenue, New York NY 10018, USA
Tel +1 212 290 1601
Fax +1 212 290 1619
Web www.degw.com
Email fduffy@degw.com

DUGGAN, John
Gazeley Properties
Position
Managing director
Contact details
Gazeley Properties Ltd, Gazeley House, 26 Rockingham Drive, Milton Keynes MK14 6DP
Tel 01908 838100
Fax 01908 838101
Web www.gazeley.com
Email john_duggan@gazeley.co.uk

DUGUID, Andrew
Edwin Hill
Position
Partner – rating
Qualifications
FRICS
Professional memberships
RICS
Contact details
Edwin Hill, Olympic Court, The Village, Manchester M17 1AP
Tel 0161 877 6622
Fax 0161 877 9876
Web www.edwinhill.co.uk
Email andrewd@edwinhill.co.uk

DUGUID, Bill
Ryden
Position
Partner and head of Aberdeen office
Qualifications
FRICS; IRRV
Career history
1986 Joined Ryden as associate; appointed partner in 1992.
1983-85 Principal surveyor (industrial development), Aberdeen City Council.
1978-83 Principal surveyor (industrial development), Irvine Development Corp
Professional memberships
Institute of Revenues Rating & Valuation; RICS
Interests
Football; sport; walking
Contact details
Ryden, 1 Albyn Terrace, Aberdeen AB10 1YP
Tel 01224 637300
Fax 01224 642349
Web www.ryden.co.uk
Mobile 07831 106327
Email bill.duguid@ryden.co.uk

DUKES, Paul
TRI Hospitality Consulting
Position
Chairman
Contact details
TRI Hospitality Consulting Ltd, 88 Baker Street, London W1M 1DA
Tel 020 7486 5191
Fax 020 7486 1189
Email paul.dukes@trihc.com

DUNCAN, Bryan
Donaldsons
Position
Partner – head of retail division
Qualifications
MBA; MRICS
Career history
1996 Joined Donaldsons.
1988-96 Director/head of retail (Scotland), Chesterton.
1985-88 Associate director, Edward Erdman
Professional memberships
British Council of Shopping Centres; International Council of Shopping Centers; RICS
Interests
Church; family; golf; music; rugby; skiing; sport
Contact details
Donaldsons, 48 Warwick Street, London W1B 5NL
Tel 020 7534 5000
Fax 020 7434 0045
Web www.donaldsons.co.uk
Direct tel 020 7534 8543
Mobile 07808 479217
Email bryan.duncan@donaldsons.co.uk

DUNCAN, Ian
Duncan Allison
Position
Director
Qualifications
BSc; MRICS
Career history
2003 Joint founder, Duncan Allison
Professional memberships
RICS
Contact details
Duncan Allison, Warnford Court, 29 Throgmorton Street, London EC2N 2AT
Tel 020 7256 8444
Fax 020 7256 8450
Web www.duncanallison.com
Direct tel 020 7256 8532
Mobile 07740 030227
Email ian@duncanallison.com

D

DUNCAN, Ken
Stephenson Harwood

Position
Partner – head of property litigation and rating group

Career history
1971 Admitted to Roll of Solicitors.
1969 Joined Stephenson Harwood; appointed partner in 1977

Contact details
Stephenson Harwood, One St Paul's Churchyard, London EC4M 8SH
Tel 020 7329 4422
Fax 020 7606 0822
Web www.shlegal.com
Direct tel 020 7809 2313
Email ken.duncan@shlegal.com

DUNCAN, Robert
Donaldsons

Position
Partner – office and industrial agency

Qualifications
FRICS

Career history
1984 Became partner with Bayleys, Cheltenham (now Donaldsons, since 1995 merger)

Professional memberships
RICS

Interests
Sport; theatre

Contact details
Donaldsons, 120 Edmund Street, Birmingham B3 2ED
Tel 0121 212 1090
Fax 0121 212 1099
Web www.donaldsons.co.uk
Direct tel 0121 710 5609
Mobile 07808 479260
Email robert.duncan@donaldsons.co.uk

DUNKERLEY, John
London & Capital Properties

Position
Head of property

Career history
1996-2002 Fletcher King.
1990-96 Jones Lang Wootton

Interests
Cinema; family; rugby; running; skiing; water sports

Contact details
London & Capital Properties Ltd, 10 Maltravers Street, London WC2R 3NL
Tel 020 7396 3200
Fax 020 7396 3201
Web www.londonandcapital.com
Direct tel 020 7396 3248
Direct fax 020 7396 3240
Mobile 07775 580059
Email John.Dunkerley@londonandcapital.com

DUNN, Alistair
Lisney

Position
Consultant

Qualifications
BSc, Econ; FRICS; ACIArb

Career history
1981 Joined Lisney; chairman since 2002.
1978-81 District estates surveyor, Property Services Agency.
1971-78 Valuation Office

Professional memberships
Chartered Institute of Arbitrators; RICS

Interests
Mountaineering; music; tennis

Contact details
Lisney, Lancashire House, 5 Linenhall Street, Belfast BT2 8AA
Tel 02890 501501
Fax 02890 501500
Web www.lisney.com
Email adunn@lisney-belfast.com

DUNN, Barry
JJB Sports

Position
Property director

Career history
1995 Rejoined JJB Sports.
1992-95 Matalan.
1986-92 JJB Sports

Contact details
JJB Sports, Martland Park, Challenge Way, Wigan WN5 OLD
Tel 01942 221400
Fax 01942 629809
Web www.jjb.co.uk
Mobile 07768 253858
Email bdunn@jjbsports.com

DUNNETT, Anthony
International Health Partners

Position
President

Qualifications
CBE; BComm, Econ; MA; FCIOB; FRSA

Career history
1999-2003 Chief executive, South East England Development Agency.
1996-98 Chief executive, English Partnerships.
1994-96 Director of industrial development unit, DTI.
1986-94 Corporate and institutional banking, Midland Bank/HSBC: rose to finance director.
1977-86 Royal Bank of Canada

Professional memberships
Chartered Institute of Bankers; Royal Society of Arts

Interests
Church; gardening; opera; walking; woodwork

Contact details
International Health Partners, The Fold, Beech Hill, Wadhurst TN5 6JR
Tel 0189 278 4117
Fax 0189 278 4696
Mobile 07801 978290
Email internationalhealthpartners@yahoo.co.uk

DURGAN, Martin
FPDSavills

Position
Director – head of landlord and tenant

Contact details
FPDSavills Ltd, 20 Grosvenor Hill, London W1K 3HQ
Tel 020 7499 8644
Fax 020 7495 3773
Web www.fpdsavills.co.uk
Direct tel 020 7409 8893
Mobile 07870 555667
Email mdurgan@fpdsavills.co.uk

DURIE, Robert
Alder King

Position
Partner

Qualifications
FRICS

Other roles
Director, Business West (formerly Bristol Chamber of Commerce & Initiative); vice-patron, National Association of Almshouses; surveyor to a number of trusts and charities (particular interest in charitable housing for the frail)

Interests
Horse riding; sailing; walking

Contact details
Alder King, Pembroke House, 15 Pembroke Road, Bristol BS8 3BA
Tel 0117 317 1000
Fax 0117 317 1001
Web www.alderking.com
Mobile 07990 891034
Email rdurie@alderking.com

DURIE, Roy
Ryden

Position
Senior partner

Qualifications
FRICS; MIMgt
Career history
1973 Joined Ryden.
1972-73 Richard Ellis.
1967-72 Lieutenant, Royal Navy
Other roles
Director, Social Firm Development Trust (Eastern Europe); chairman, Merchants Hall; chairman, Chamber Developments; director, Edinburgh Chamber of Commerce; elder of St Giles Cathedral, Edinburgh; chairman, Merchant Co property and finance committee
Professional memberships
Institute of Management Consultants; RICS
Interests
Golf; rugby; sailing; skiing; walking
Contact details
Ryden, 46 Castle Street, Edinburgh EH2 3BN
Tel 0131 225 6612
Fax 0131 225 5766
Web www.ryden.co.uk
Mobile 07836 347247
Email roy.durie@ryden.co.uk

DUTTON, Timothy
9 Old Square
Position
Barrister
Career history
1985 Called to Bar
Other roles
Treasurer, Property Bar Association
Professional memberships
Chancery Bar Association; Property Bar Association
Contact details
9 Old Square (Chambers of Michael Driscoll QC), Ground Floor, London WC2A 3SR
Tel 020 7405 4682
Fax 020 7831 7107
Web www.9oldsquare.co.uk
Email tim.dutton@9oldsquare.co.uk

DUXBURY, Nigel
Birthdays
Position
Property director
Contact details
Birthdays Ltd, Dumers Lane, Bury BL9 9UR
Tel 0161 763 7353
Fax 0161 763 8375
Web www.birthdays.co.uk
Direct tel 0161 763 8390
Email nigel.duxbury@birthdays.co.uk

DYE, David
Land Securities Group
Position
Development director
Qualifications
BSc; CEng; MICE
Career history
1997-2001 Development director, Whitecliff Properties.
1987-97 Senior development surveyor, Arlington Securities.
1985-87 Development manager, Jones Lang Wootton.
1981-85 Project director, LJH Project Management
Other roles
Chairman, Kent Developers Group; director, Locate in Kent
Professional memberships
British Council for Offices; European Institute of Business Administration; Institution of Civil Engineers
Interests
Family; shooting; socialising
Contact details
Land Securities Group plc, 5 Strand, London WC2N 5AF
Tel 020 7413 9000
Fax 020 7024 5007
Web www.landsecurities.com
Direct tel 020 7024 3755
Direct fax 020 7024 3770
Email david.dye@landsecurities.com

DYMOND, Christopher
London & Paris Estates
Position
Managing director
Qualifications
BSc Hons; MRICS
Career history
1986 Joined London & Paris; appointed director in 1990 and managing director in 1996.
1983-86 Cluttons
Other roles
Liveryman, Worshipful Company of Chartered Surveyors
Professional memberships
RICS
Interests
Cricket; football; rugby; skiing; sport; travel; wine
Contact details
London & Paris Estates Ltd, 1 Sloane Square, London SW1W 8EE
Tel 020 7730 8484
Fax 020 7730 1811
Web www.londonetparis.com
Mobile 07810 300600
Email chrisdymond@londonetparis.com

DYSON, Bob
Dunlop Heywood Lorenz
Position
Executive chairman
Qualifications
MSc; FRICS
Career history
1972 Joined Dunlop Heywood (now Dunlop Heywood Lorenz)
Professional memberships
Investment Property Forum; RICS; Worshipful Company of Chartered Surveyors
Interests
Sailing; skiing; swimming; walking
Contact details
Dunlop Heywood Lorenz Ltd, 10 Queen Anne Street, London W1G 9LH
Tel 020 7636 7000
Fax 020 7636 7002
Web www.dhlproperty.co.uk
Direct tel 020 7299 7236
Mobile 07970 225000
Email rwd@dhlproperty.co.uk

DYTE, John
Hartnell Taylor Cook
Position
Partner
Qualifications
MRICS
Professional memberships
RICS
Contact details
Hartnell Taylor Cook, Somerset House, 18 Canynge Road, Bristol BS8 3JX
Tel 0117 923 9234
Fax 0117 923 9237
Web www.htc.uk.com
Direct tel 0117 946 4511
Mobile 07831 453847
Email john.dyte@htc.uk.com

E

EAGAN, Mark
Paul Hastings Janofsky & Walker

Position
Partner – real estate
Qualifications
Property finance attorney
Career history
1995-99 Partner, Kirkland & Ellis.
1986 Admitted to Roll of Solicitors.
1985-95 Associate, Simpson Thacher & Bartlett
Other roles
Vice-chairman of London office
Professional memberships
Association of the Bar of the City of New York; Law Society; Urban Land Institute
Contact details
Paul Hastings Janofsky & Walker LLP, 88 Wood Street, London EC2V 7AJ
Tel 020 7710 2000
Fax 020 7796 2233
Web www.paulhastings.com
Direct tel 020 7710 2045
Email markeagan@paulhastings.com

EAGLE, Todd
Goldman Sachs International

Position
Executive director – real estate advisory
Contact details
Goldman Sachs International, Peterborough Court, 133 Fleet Street, London EC4A 2PP
Tel 020 7774 1000
Fax 020 7774 4477
Email todd.eagle@gs.com

EASBY, Peter
Cushman & Wakefield Healey & Baker

Position
Managing partner
Qualifications
FCA
Career history
1988 Joined Cushman & Wakefield Healey & Baker.
1975-88 Partner, Ball Baker Leake.
1967-75 Peat Marwick Mitchell, London
Other roles
Director, IHL (IPD holding company)
Professional memberships
Institute of Chartered Accountants in England & Wales
Contact details
Cushman & Wakefield Healey & Baker, 43-45 Portman Square, London W1A 3BG
Tel 020 7935 5000
Fax 020 7152 5360
Web www.cushwake.com
Direct tel 020 7152 5002
Direct fax 020 7152 5350
Email peter.easby@eur.cushwake.com

EASTAUGH, Jamie
Cluttons

Position
Partner – asset management
Qualifications
MRICS
Career history
1995 Joined Cluttons.
1990-94 Caws & Morris.
1987-89 Stratton & Holborow
Contact details
Cluttons, Portman House, 2 Portman Street, London W1H 6DU
Tel 020 7408 1010
Fax 020 7629 3263
Web www.cluttons.com
Direct tel 020 7647 7098
Direct fax 020 7647 7070
Email jeastaugh@cluttons.com

EASTMAN, Eric
Michael Peddar & Co

Position
Managing director
Qualifications
BA; FRICS
Career history
1972 Started acquiring shops
Professional memberships
British council of shopping centres; RICS
Contact details
Michael Peddar & Co, 12 John Princes Street, London W1G 0NY
Tel 020 7629 3004
Fax 020 7491 3314
Web www.michaelpeddar.co.uk
Email eeastman@michaelpeddar.co.uk

EASTON, Ewan
Maclay Murray & Spens

Position
Partner – head of property litigation unit
Qualifications
LLB Hons; WS
Career history
1982 Joined Maclay Murray & Spens; seconded to Herbert Smith 1984-85; partner (commercial litigation), Maclay Murray & Spens since 1985.
1982 Admitted to Roll of Solicitors
Other roles
Chairman, Property Litigation Association (Scotland)
Professional memberships
Property Litigation Association; WS Society
Interests
Architecture
Contact details
Maclay Murray & Spens, 3 Glenfinlas Street, Edinburgh EH3 6AQ
Tel 0131 226 5196
Fax 0131 226 3174
Web www.mms.co.uk
Direct tel 0131 479 2772
Email ewan.easton@mms.co.uk

EASTON, Paul
storeys:ssp

Position
Director – head of rating
Qualifications
MRICS; IRRV
Career history
1977 Joined Storey Sons & Parker (now storeys:ssp)
Professional memberships
Institute of Revenues Rating & Valuation; Rating Surveyors Association; RICS
Interests
Boating; skiing; water sports
Contact details
storeys:ssp, Higham House, New Bridge Street West, Newcastle upon Tyne NE1 8AU
Tel 0191 232 6291
Fax 0191 232 4610
Web www.storeys-ssp.com
Direct tel 0191 206 8709
Mobile 07957 823896
Email paul.easton@storeys-ssp.co.uk

ECKETT, Michael
GL Hearn

Position
Director – valuation and compulsory purchase
Qualifications
MRICS; BSc Hons, Val & Est Man

Career history
1990 Joined GL Hearn; became associate partner in 1994; appointed valuation and compulsory purchase director in 1997
Professional memberships
RICS
Interests
Diving/scuba diving
Contact details
GL Hearn Ltd, Leonard House, 5-7 Marshalsea Road, London SE1 1EP
Tel 020 7450 4000
Fax 020 7450 4010
Web www.glhearn.com
Email michael_eckett@glhearn.com

EDGE, John
Knight Frank
Position
Partner – head of commercial division
Qualifications
FRICS
Career history
1976 Joined Knight Frank; appointed partner in 1980, head of valuations in 1985 and head of commercial division in 2001.
1972-76 Investment surveyor, Strutt & Parker.
1970-72 Development surveyor, Greater London Council
Professional memberships
RICS
Interests
Beer; golf; IT; running; sailing; tennis; theatre; travel
Contact details
Knight Frank LLP, 20 Hanover Square, London W1S 1HZ
Tel 020 7629 8171
Fax 020 7493 4114
Web www.knightfrank.com
Direct tel 020 7861 1280
Direct fax 020 7861 1380
Email john.edge@knightfrank.com

EDGE, Mike
Halliwell Landau
Position
Head of property
Professional memberships
UK Environmental Law Association
Contact details
Halliwell Landau, St James Court, 30 Brown Street, Manchester M2 2LD
Tel 0161 835 3003
Fax 0161 835 2994
Web www.halliwells.co.uk
Email medge@halliwells.co.uk

EDGERLEY, Bill
Edgerley Simpson Howe & Partners
Position
Senior partner
Qualifications
MRICS
Career history
1992 Joined Edgerley Simpson Howe & Partners as senior partner.
1988-92 Director, Lane Fox.
1986-88 Investment surveyor, Gooch & Wagstaff.
1983-86 Assistant property manager, St Martins
Professional memberships
RICS; Worshipful Company of Chartered Surveyors
Interests
Family; golf; rugby; skiing; tennis
Contact details
Edgerley Simpson Howe & Partners, 39 Dover Street, London W1S 4NN
Tel 020 7499 6000
Fax 020 7499 9433
Web www.eshp.com
Email lou@eshp.com

EDGERLEY, William
P&O Developments
Position
Managing director
Qualifications
MA; MSc; MRICS
Career history
Since 1994 Managing director, P&O Developments.
1990-94 Chief executive, Riverbus Partnership (P&O)
Professional memberships
Institution of Civil Engineers; RICS
Interests
Architecture; golf; sailing
Contact details
P&O Developments Ltd, 4 Carlton Gardens, London SW1Y 5AB
Tel 020 7839 5611
Fax 020 7930 2098
Direct tel 020 7321 4627
Email wedgerley.dev@p-and-o.com

EDGLEY, Tony
Jones Lang LaSalle Corporate Finance
Position
Chairman
Qualifications
BSc; MRICS
Professional memberships
RICS
Contact details
Jones Lang LaSalle Corporate Finance Ltd, 22 Hanover Square, London W1A 2BN
Tel 020 7399 5550
Fax 020 7399 5490
Web www.joneslanglasalle.com
Direct tel 020 7399 5944
Direct fax 020 7399 5650
Mobile 07771 635204
Email tony.edgley@eu.joneslanglasalle.com

EDMOND, Catherine
Davis Coffer Lyons
Position
Director – professional department
Contact details
Davis Coffer Lyons Ltd, 52 Portland Place, London W1B 1NH
Tel 020 7299 0700
Fax 020 7299 0710
Web www.daviscofferlyons.co.uk
Email cedmond@dclleisure.com

EDWARDS, Chris
Charles Russell
Position
Partner – head of commercial property department
Qualifications
LLB Hons
Career history
2002 Joined Charles Russell.
1982-2002 Titmuss Sainer & Webb (now Dechert); appointed partner in 1984.
1980-82 Assistant solicitor, City of London Corp.
Previously with Stoneham Langton & Passmore
Professional memberships
City Property Association; Investment Property Forum; Lambda Alpha; Property Valuation Forum
Interests
Cycling; family; football; swimming
Contact details
Charles Russell, 8-10 New Fetter Lane, London EC4A 1RS
Tel 020 7203 5000
Fax 020 7203 0200
Web www.cr-law.co.uk
Direct tel 020 7203 5199
Direct fax 020 7203 0204
Mobile 07775 556664
Email chris.edwards@charlesrussell.co.uk

EDWARDS, Christopher
Phoenix Beard
Position
Consulltant
Qualifications

E

FRICS

Career history

1975 Joined Phoenix Beard; appointed director of asset management department in 1987 and chairman in 1994; now consultant

Other roles

Past president, ISVA (1996-97)

Professional memberships

British Council of Shopping Centres; British Council for Offices; RICS

Contact details

Phoenix Beard, 7-10 Chandos Street, London W1G 9EH

Tel 020 7323 4681

Fax 020 7436 3581

Web www.phoenix-beard.co.uk

Direct tel 020 7544 1952

Mobile 07808 784777

Email christopher.edwards@phoenix-beard.co.uk

EDWARDS, Douglas
AXA Real Estate Investment Managers

Position

Director – private equity

Career history

1998-2000 Director (real estate private equity), Rodamco.

1997-98 Executive director (real estate), UBS Warburg.

1994-97 Executive director, UBS New York.

1985-94 Director (real estate corporate finance), UBS Phillips & Drew.

1981-85 Account manager, NatWest

Interests

Field sports; rugby; sport

Contact details

AXA Real Estate Investment Managers Ltd, 7 Newgate Street, London EC1A 7HD

Tel 020 7003 1000

Fax 020 7575 8585

Web www.axa-im.co.uk

Direct tel 020 7003 1363

Email douglas.edwards@axa-im.com

EDWARDS, Elizabeth
Berlin Hyp

Position

Managing director – head of London representative office

Qualifications

BSc; FRICS

Career history

Since 1997 Managing director and head of London representative office, Berlin Hyp.

1993-96 Director, Westdeutsche Landesbank/ Westdeutsche Immobilienbank.

1988-92 Vice-president (UK real estate), Security Pacific/Bank America.

1987-88 Fund manager, Lazard Brothers.

1984-87 Drivers Jonas.

1983-84 Consultant, Coopers & Lybrand.

1979-83 European surveyor, St Martins Property Corp

Professional memberships

FIABCI; RICS; Worshipful Company of Chartered Surveyors

Interests

Cars; horse riding; opera; skiing

Contact details

Berlin Hyp, 1 Crown Court, London EC2V 6LR

Tel 020 7572 6336

Fax 020 7572 8258

Direct tel 020 7572 6313

Email eedwards@ibuk.bankgesellschaft.de

EDWARDS, Martin
39 Essex Street

Position

Barrister

Qualifications

BA Hons, Law; MA, Environmental Law

Career history

1995 Called to Bar.

1981 Admitted to Roll of Solicitors

Professional memberships

Planning & Environment Bar Association; RTPI

Interests

Cinema; football; keep fit; music; reading; running; sailing

Contact details

39 Essex Street, London WC2R 3AT

Tel 020 7832 1111

Fax 020 7353 3978

Web www.39essex.com

Email martin.edwards@39essex.com

EDWARDS, Matthew
Ryden

Position

Partner

Qualifications

BSc; MRICS

Professional memberships

RICS

Interests

Football; music; travel; wine

Contact details

Ryden, Coronet House, Queen Street, Leeds LS1 2SH

Tel 0113 243 6777

Fax 0113 243 9323

Web www.ryden.co.uk

Mobile 07778 131872

Email matthew.edwards@ryden.co.uk

EDWARDS, Smita
Forsters

Position

Partner

Qualifications

LLB

Career history

Since 1998 Partner, Forsters; head of commercial property group 1998-2003.

1985-98 Frere Cholmeley Bischoff: rose to partner and head of planning and environmental law group.

1985 Admitted to Roll of Solicitors.

1983-85 Cardales

Professional memberships

Law Society

Interests

Cinema; family; singing; theatre

Contact details

Forsters, 67 Grosvenor Street, London W1K 3JN

Tel 020 7863 8333

Fax 020 7863 8444

Web www.forsters.co.uk

Direct tel 020 7863 8470

Mobile 07721 420493

Email SEdwards@forsters.co.uk

EDWARDS-STUART, Antony
Crown Office Chambers

Position

Barrister

Qualifications

QC

Contact details

Crown Office Chambers, 2 Crown Office Row, London EC4Y 7HJ

Tel 020 7797 8100

Fax 020 7797 8101

Web www.crownofficechambers.com

Email edwards-stuart@crownofficechambers.com

EGGS, Tony
Tesco Stores

Position

Property director

Qualifications

LLB; FRICS

Career history

1979 Joined Tesco; various roles in asset and estates and property acquisition; became property acquisition/town planning director in 1991

Contact details

Tesco Stores Ltd, Cirrus B, Shire Park, Welwyn Garden City AL7 1AB

Tel 01992 632222

Fax 01707 634937

Web www.tesco.com

Direct tel 01707 634062
Direct fax 01707 634062
Email tony.eggs@uk.tesco.com

EIDINOW, John
New Square Chambers

Position
Barrister
Qualifications
MA (Oxon); Dip Law
Career history
1992 Called to Bar
Professional memberships
Chancery Bar Association
Interests
History; IT; literature
Contact details
New Square Chambers (Chambers of Charles Purle QC), 12 New Square, London WC2A 3SW
Tel 020 7419 8000
Fax 020 7419 8050
Web www.newsquarechambers.co.uk
Email john.eidinow@newsquarechambers.co.uk

ELDRED, Adam
Frontier Estates

Position
Joint managing director
Qualifications
BSc Hons; MRICS
Career history
1995-96 Director, Lambert Smith Hampton.
1988-95 Director, Connell Wilson
Professional memberships
RICS
Contact details
Frontier Estates Ltd, Acorn House, Midsummer Boulevard, Milton Keynes MK9 3HP
Tel 01908 238888
Fax 01908 241111
Web www.frontier-estates.com
Mobile 07712 000199
Email adameldred@frontier-estates.com

ELLAHI, Ahsan
Eurohypo

Position
Managing director – senior debt origination
Qualifications
BSc, Econ; ACIB
Career history
1998-2003 GE Capital Real Estate.
1986-98 HSBC Investment Bank: became manager in 1990, then director and head of property finance in 1996.
1980-86 Midland Bank
Professional memberships
Association of Property Bankers; Chartered Institute of Bankers
Interests
Cricket; football
Contact details
Eurohypo AG, 90 Long Acre, London WC2E 9RA
Tel 020 7759 7600
Fax 020 7759 7672
Web www.eurohypo.com
Direct tel 020 7759 7606
Mobile 07813 677195
Email ahsan.ellahi@eurohypo.com

ELLERAY, Anthony
Exchange Chambers

Position
Barrister
Qualifications
QC
Other roles
Recorder; deputy High Court judge
Professional memberships
Chancery Bar Association; Northern Chancery Bar Association; Northern Circuit Commercial Bar Association
Contact details
Exchange Chambers, 7 Ralli Court, West Riverside, Manchester M3 5FT
Tel 0161 833 2722
Fax 0161 833 2789
Web www.exchangechambers.co.uk
Email elleraygc@exchangechambers.co.uk

ELLINGHAM, Hugh
CB Richard Ellis Collective Investors

Position
Director
Qualifications
BSc, Est Man; MRICS
Career history
1979 Joined Richard Ellis; became associate partner in 1983; established Richard Ellis Venture Consultants as founder shareholder in 1986, then Richmount Management in 1988; became equity partner of Richard Ellis in 1994, then board director in 1997
Other roles
Member of RICS working parties on financial services (1986-90); member of general practice divisional council (1991)
Professional memberships
RICS
Contact details
CB Richard Ellis Collective Investors Ltd, 64 North Row, London W1K 7DA
Tel 020 7399 9600
Fax 020 7399 9601
Web www.cbreinvestors.com
Direct tel 020 7399 9642
Mobile 07703 117630
Email hellingham@cbreinvestors.com

ELLINTHORPE, Bryan
LaSalle Investment Management

Position
International director
Contact details
LaSalle Investment Management, 33 Cavendish Square, London W1A 2NF
Tel 020 7852 4000
Fax 020 7852 4374
Web www.lasalle.com
Email bryan.ellinthorpe@lasalle.com

ELLIOTT, Alistair
Knight Frank

Position
Partner – head of national offices
Qualifications
BSc; MRICS
Career history
1983 Joined Knight Frank
Professional memberships
Office Agents Society; RICS
Interests
Eating out; running; shooting
Contact details
Knight Frank LLP, 20 Hanover Square, London W1S 1HZ
Tel 020 7629 8171
Fax 020 7493 4114
Web www.knightfrank.com
Direct tel 020 7861 1141
Direct fax 020 7495 0925
Mobile 07836 233756
Email alistair.elliott@knightfrank.com

ELLIOTT, Martin
Linklaters

Position
Partner
Qualifications
BA, Law
Career history
1979 Admitted to Roll of Solicitors.
1977 Joined Linklaters & Paines (now Linklaters); became partner in 1985
Other roles
Land law subcommittee member
Professional memberships
British Council of Shopping Centres; City of London Law Society; Law Society
Interests
Sport

E

Contact details
Linklaters, 1 Silk Street, London EC2Y 8HQ
Tel 020 7456 2000
Fax 020 7456 2222
Web www.linklaters.com
Direct tel 020 7456 4722
Mobile 07768 914518
Email martin.elliott@linklaters.com

ELLIOTT, Matthew
Drivers Jonas

Position
Partner – head of central London agency
Qualifications
BSc Hons; MRICS
Career history
1995 Joined Drivers Jonas.
1987-95 St Quintin
Professional memberships
RICS
Contact details
Drivers Jonas, 78 Cornhill, London EC3V 3QQ
Tel 020 7896 8000
Fax 020 7626 2835
Web www.driversjonas.com
Direct tel 020 7896 8364
Email matthewelliott@driversjonas.com

ELLIOTT, Richard
AMEC Developments

Position
Director
Qualifications
BSc Hons; Dip TP; MRTPI
Career history
Since 2000 Director, AMEC Developments
Professional memberships
RTPI
Interests
Cricket; family; farming; gardening; geography; ornithology; rugby; reading; travel; walking; wine
Contact details
AMEC Developments Ltd, Bank House, 8 Cherry Street, Birmingham B2 5AQ
Tel 0121 632 4000
Fax 0121 632 5579
Web www.amec.com
Email richard.elliott@amec.com

ELLIS, Ian
Land Securities Trillium

Position
Chief executive
Qualifications
FRICS
Career history
1998 Joined Land Securities Trillium.
1983-98 Richard Ellis: joined City office; appointed partner in 1987; became chief executive of Richard Ellis Investment Management in 1995.
1975-83 District Valuer's Office/Valuation Office
Other roles
Board member, Land Securities Group; board member, Land Securities Trillium; board member, Telereal
Professional memberships
Institute of Directors; Investment Property Forum; RICS
Contact details
Land Securities Trillium Ltd, 140 London Wall, London EC2Y 5DN
Tel 020 7796 5500
Fax 020 7796 5501
Web www.landsecurities.co.uk
Direct tel 020 7796 5553
Direct fax 0845 090 2900
Mobile 07711 732708
Email ian.ellis@lstrillium.com

ELLIS, Jeff
Lewis Ellis

Position
Partner
Qualifications
BSc; MRICS
Professional memberships
RICS
Contact details
Lewis Ellis, 11 Albemarle Street, London W1S 4HH
Tel 020 7493 3330
Fax 020 7493 3033
Email jellis@lewisellis.co.uk

ELLIS, Nigel
Quintain Estates & Development

Position
Chairman
Contact details
Quintain Estates & Development plc, 58 Davies Street, London W1K 5JF
Tel 020 7495 8968
Fax 020 7499 5583
Web www.quintain-estates.com
Email kathleen.finnigan@quintain-estates.com

ELLIS, Paul
Donaldsons

Position
Partner – head of London consultancy division
Contact details
Donaldsons, 48 Warwick Street, London W1B 5NL
Tel 020 7534 5000
Fax 020 7434 0045
Web www.donaldsons.co.uk
Direct tel 020 7534 5030
Email paul.ellis@donaldsons.co.uk

ELLIS, Phil
Morley Fund Management

Position
Head of institutional property funds
Qualifications
BSc Hons; MRICS
Career history
Since 1988 Norwich Union/Morley Fund Management.
1983-88 Legal & General
Professional memberships
Investment Property Forum; RICS
Interests
Family; football; history; travel
Contact details
Morley Fund Management Ltd, 34-36 Lime Street, London EC3M 7JE
Tel 020 7809 6000
Fax 020 7489 7940
Web www.morleyfm.com
Direct tel 020 7809 6870
Direct fax 020 7332 9126
Email phil.ellis@morleyfm.com

ELLIS, Tom
Pannone & Partners

Position
Partner
Qualifications
BA Hons, Law; MCIArb
Career history
1984 Admitted to Roll of Solicitors
Professional memberships
Chartered Institute of Arbitrators; Society of Construction Law
Interests
Chess; football
Contact details
Pannone & Partners, 123 Deansgate, Manchester M3 2BU
Tel 0161 909 3000
Fax 0161 909 4444
Web www.pannone.com
Email tom.ellis@pannone.co.uk

ELLISON, Ian
Pets at Home Superstores

Position
Head of property
Qualifications

Dip Val Surv; MRICS

Career history

1998 Joined Pets at Home Superstores.

1990-98 Beesley Thomson

Professional memberships

RICS

Interests

Football; golf; music

Contact details

Pets at Home Superstores Ltd, Epsom Avenue, Stanley Green Trading Estate, Handforth SK9 3RN

Tel 0161 486 6688

Fax 0161 485 4846

Web www.petsathome.com

Direct tel 0161 486 6150

Email ianellison@petsathome.co.uk

ELMER, Simon
Cushman & Wakefield Healey & Baker

Position

Partner, head of asset management

Career history

1996-2001 CB Hillier Parker.

1993-96 Workspace Group

Contact details

Cushman & Wakefield Healey & Baker, 43-45 Portman Square, London W1A 3BG

Tel 020 7935 5000

Fax 020 7152 5360

Web www.cushwake.com

Direct tel 020 7152 5096

Direct fax 020 7152 5352

Email simon.elmer@eur.cushwake.com

ELMON, Brandon
Davis Coffer Lyons

Position

Director – investment and acquisition

Qualifications

BSc Hons, Urban Est Man; MRPAS

Career history

1993 Joined Davis Coffer Lyons

Professional memberships

Restaurant Property Advisors Society; RICS

Contact details

Davis Coffer Lyons Ltd, 52 Portland Place, London W1B 1NH

Tel 020 7299 0700

Fax 020 7299 0710

Web www.daviscofferlyons.co.uk

Email belmon@daviscofferlyons.co.uk

ELPHICK, Hugh
Cushman & Wakefield Healey & Baker

Position

Partner – investment

Qualifications

MA (Oxon); FRICS

Career history

1972 Joined Cushman & Wakefield Healey & Baker

Professional memberships

FIABCI; RICS

Contact details

Cushman & Wakefield Healey & Baker, 43-45 Portman Square, London W1A 3BG

Tel 020 7935 5000

Fax 020 7152 5360

Web www.cushwake.com

Direct tel 020 7152 5003

Direct fax 020 7152 5190

Email hugh.elphick@eur.cushwake.com

ELPHICK, Jeremy
Blair Kirkman

Position

Partner

Contact details

Blair Kirkman, St Georges House, 12a St George Street, London W1S 1FQ

Tel 020 7409 0899

Fax 020 7629 8022

Web www.blairkirkman.com

Email jeremye@blairkirkman.com

ELVIN, David
Landmark Chambers

Position

Barrister

Qualifications

QC; BA; BCL (Oxon)

Career history

2000 Appointed QC.

1983 Called to Bar

Other roles

Co-author, *Unlawful Interference with Land* (2nd edition, 2002); recorder; assistant commissioner, Boundary Commission

Professional memberships

Administrative Law Bar Association; Chancery Bar Association; Planning & Environment Bar Association

Interests

Music

Contact details

Landmark Chambers, 4 Breams Buildings, London EC4A 1AQ

Tel 020 7430 1221

Fax 020 7421 1399

Web www.landmarkchambers.co.uk

Email delvin@landmarkchambers.co.uk

ELWING, Fredrik
Credit Suisse First Boston

Position

Director – real estate private fund group

Qualifications

BA; MBA

Career history

1998-2001 Senior vice-president, Security Capital Group.

1995-98 Senior vice-president, Lehman Brothers.

1987-95 Vice-president, Credit Suisse First Boston

Contact details

Credit Suisse First Boston, One Cabot Square, London E14 4QJ

Tel 020 7888 8888

Fax 020 7883 5819

Web www.csfb.com

Direct tel 020 7883 5492

Mobile 07970 815533

Email fredrik.elwing@csfb.com

EMBLING, Joanna
Cushman & Wakefield Healey & Baker

Position

Partner – development consultancy

Qualifications

MRICS

Professional memberships

RICS

Contact details

Cushman & Wakefield Healey & Baker, 43-45 Portman Square, London W1A 3BG

Tel 020 7935 5000

Fax 020 7152 5360

Web www.cushwake.com

Direct tel 020 7152 5383

Direct fax 020 7152 5224

Email joanna.embling@eur.cushwake.com

EMMENS, Margaret
Knight Frank

Position

Head of corporate communications

Qualifications

BA; ACIB; ACII; Dip M

Contact details

Knight Frank LLP, 20 Hanover Square, London W1S 1HZ

Tel 020 7629 8171

Fax 020 7493 4114

Web www.knightfrank.com

Direct fax 020 7861 1354

Email margaret.emmens@knightfrank.com

E?

EMMERSON, Robert
Arup Group

Position
Chairman
Qualifications
MA (Cantab); FICE; FConsE; MCIBSE; FREng
Career history
1967 Rejoined Ove Arup & Partners.
1965-67 WJ LeMessurier, Boston, US.
1960-65 Structural engineer on projects such as Sydney Opera House, Ove Arup & Partners
Other roles
Member, European Service Leaders Group advising European Commission; member, executive committee of Associate Parliamentary Engineering Group; trustee, Ove Arup Partnership; trustee, Ove Arup Foundation
Professional memberships
Chartered Institution of Building Services Engineers; Institution of Civil Engineers
Interests
Art; golf; history; skiing
Contact details
Arup Group Ltd, 13-17 Fitzroy Street, London W1T 4BS
Tel 020 7636 1531
Web www.arup.com
Direct tel 020 7755 3373
Direct fax 020 7755 3666
Email bob.emmerson@arup.com

EMMETT, Graham
Goldman Sachs International

Position
Executive director
Qualifications
BSc Hons, Banking & Finance
Career history
1999-2003 Finance director, Delancey Estates.
1989-99 Director, Robert Fleming & Co
Contact details
Goldman Sachs International, Peterborough Court, 133 Fleet Street, London EC4A 2PP
Tel 020 7774 1000
Fax 020 7774 4477
Direct tel 020 7774 6629
Direct fax 020 7774 4852
Email graham.emmett@gs.com

ENGERT, Nicholas
Clarke Willmott

Position
Partner – planning
Qualifications
LLB
Career history
1973 Admitted to Roll of Solicitors.
Professional memberships
Law Society; UK Environmental Law Association
Contact details
Clarke Willmott, Blackbrook Gate, Blackbrook Park Avenue, Taunton TA1 2PG
Tel 0182 344 2266
Fax 0182 344 5800
Web www.clarkewillmott.com
Direct tel 01823 445202
Email nengert@cw-c.co.uk

ENGLAND, Mark
ATIS REAL Weatheralls

Position
Director – head of office agency
Qualifications
BSc Hons; MRICS
Professional memberships
RICS
Contact details
ATIS REAL Weatheralls Ltd, Norfolk House, 31 St James's Square, London SW1Y 4JR
Tel 020 7338 4200
Fax 020 7493 0746
Web www.atisrealweatheralls.com
Direct tel 020 7405 4330
Mobile 07958 349263
Email mark.england@atisrealweatheralls.com

ENGLAND, Mike
Barlows Solicitors

Position
Partner – head of commercial property
Qualifications
LLM
Career history
1973 Admitted to Roll of Solicitors.
1971 Joined Barlows; became partner in 1975
Professional memberships
Chertsey Chamber of Commerce
Interests
Sport
Contact details
Barlows Solicitors, Guildford House, 66 Guildford Street, Chertsey KT16 9BB
Tel 01932 568245
Fax 01932 562650
Web www.barlows-legal.co.uk
Email michaelengland@barlows.co.uk

EPPEL, Leonard
Arrowcroft Group

Position
Chairman
Qualifications
CBE; FRICS
Career history
Since 1969 Chairman, Arrowcroft Group.
1954-68 Managing director, Silk Estates Investment
Other roles
Chairman, Albert Dock Co; non-executive director, North West Tourist Board; freeman of the City of London; freeman of the Worshipful Company of Fletchers; fellow, Institute of Directors; fellow, Royal Society of Arts
Professional memberships
Carlton Club; Institute of Directors; RICS; Royal Society of Arts
Interests
Football; swimming
Contact details
Arrowcroft Group plc, 110 Park Street, London W1K 6AD
Tel 020 7499 5432
Fax 020 7493 0323
Web www.arrowcroft.com
Email khenson@arrowcroft.com

ERWIN, Alan
Fladgate Fielder

Position
Partner – head of construction and projects unit
Contact details
Fladgate Fielder, 25 North Row, London W1K 6DJ
Tel 020 7323 4747
Fax 020 7629 4414
Web www.fladgate.com
Direct tel 020 7462 2256
Email aerwin@fladgate.com

ERWIN, David
Cushman & Wakefield Healey & Baker

Position
Partner – head of retail investment
Qualifications
BSc Hons; MRICS
Career history
1986 Joined Cushman & Wakefield Healey & Baker
Professional memberships
RICS
Interests
Golf; sport
Contact details
Cushman & Wakefield Healey & Baker, 43-45 Portman Square, London W1A 3BG
Tel 020 7935 5000
Fax 020 7152 5360
Web www.cushwake.com
Direct tel 020 7152 5016
Direct fax 020 7152 5381

Mobile 07860 258794
Email david.erwin@eur.cushwake.com

ESFANDI, Joey
Dwyer
Position
Chairman
Qualifications
BA
Other roles
Chief executive, Winglaw Group
Interests
Running; sailing; shooting
Contact details
Dwyer plc, 40 Park Street, London W1K 2JG
Tel 020 7629 6666
Fax 020 7493 5096
Email margaret.whelan@dwyer.co.uk

EVANS, David
Dixon Webb
Position
Partner
Qualifications
FRICS
Professional memberships
RICS
Contact details
Dixon Webb, 35 White Friars, Chester CH1 1QF
Tel 01244 310031
Fax 01244 343242
Web www.dixonwebb.com
Direct tel 01244 404142
Direct fax 01244 404141
Email tdevans@dixonwebb.com

EVANS, David
Insight Investment Management
Position
Director – property investment
Contact details
Insight Investment Management, 33 Old Broad Street, London EC2N 1HZ
Tel 020 7930 5474
Fax 020 7321 1423
Web www.insightinvestment.com
Email david.evans@insightinvestment.com

EVANS, Douglas
Addleshaw Goddard
Position
Partner – head of planning and environment
Qualifications
LLB (Soton)
Career history
1978 Admitted to Roll of Solicitors
Other roles
Member, Law Society specialist planning panel; chairman of planning and development committee, Energy from Waste Association
Professional memberships
Institute of Waste Management; Law Society; Town & Country Planning Association; UK Environmental Law Association
Contact details
Addleshaw Goddard, 150 Aldersgate Street, London EC1A 4EJ
Tel 020 7606 8855
Fax 020 7606 4390
Web www.addleshawgoddard.com
Direct tel 020 7808 5789
Email douglas.evans@addleshawgoddard.com

EVANS, Jonathan
DTZ Debenham Tie Leung
Position
Director
Qualifications
BSc; MRICS
Career history
1996 Joined DTZ Debenham Tie Leung as head of West End agency. Previously head of West End agency, Hillier Parker
Professional memberships
RICS
Contact details
DTZ Debenham Tie Leung, One Curzon Street, London W1A 5PZ
Tel 020 7408 1161
Fax 020 7643 6000
Web www.dtz.com
Direct tel 020 7643 6452
Email jonathan.evans@dtz.com

EVANS, Katherine
TLT Solicitors
Position
Partner – planning and environment
Qualifications
BA Hons, Town & Country Planning; LLB; LPC (Merit)
Career history
1998 Joined Lawrence Tucketts (now TLT Solicitors); became partner in 2000.
1997 Admitted to Roll of Solicitors.
1986-96 Employed by national housebuilders to acquire and project manage major development sites.
1987 Qualified as planner
Professional memberships
Law Society; RTPI
Interests
Family; food; travel; wine
Contact details
TLT Solicitors, 1 Redcliffe Street, Bristol BS99 7JZ
Tel 0117 917 7777
Fax 0117 917 7779
Web www.tltsolicitors.com
Direct tel 0117 917 7941
Email kevans@TLTsolicitors.com

EVANS, Nigel
Stiles Harold Williams
Position
Director
Qualifications
BSc Hons; MRICS
Contact details
Stiles Harold Williams Ltd, 6 Babmaes Street, London SW1Y 6HD
Tel 020 7389 1500
Fax 020 7389 1515
Web www.shw.co.uk
Direct tel 020 7389 1504
Mobile 07850 990427
Email nevans@shw.co.uk

EVANS, Philip
Cushman & Wakefield Healey & Baker
Position
Partner – asset management
Career history
Since 2001 Partner (responsible for retail asset management across Europe), Cushman & Wakefield Healey & Baker.
1997-2001 Property investment manager, Bourne End Properties.
1984-97 Associate partner, Healey & Baker
Other roles
Member of security committee, British Council of Shopping Centres
Professional memberships
British Council of Shopping Centres
Interests
Football; golf; rugby
Contact details
Cushman & Wakefield Healey & Baker, 43-45 Portman Square, London W1A 3BG
Tel 020 7935 5000
Fax 020 7152 5360
Web www.cushwake.com
Direct tel 020 7152 5349
Direct fax 020 7152 5352
Mobile 07764 398349
Email philip.evans@eur.cushwake.com

EVANS, Robert
CB Richard Ellis
Position
Managing director – City business

Contact details
CB Richard Ellis, St Martin's Court,
10 Paternoster Row, London EC4M 7HP
Tel 020 7182 2000
Fax 020 7182 2001
Web www.cbre.com
Email robert.evans@cbre.com

EVANS, Robin
British Waterways

Position
Chief executive
Qualifications
FRICS
Career history
1999 Joined British Waterways as commercial director; became chief executive in 2002. Previously palaces director, Historic Royal Palaces, and chief executive, Landmark Trust
Other roles
Director of Euro Waterways, De Nieuwe Voorhaven (UK), Drifter and ISIS Waterside
Contact details
British Waterways, Willow Grange, Church Road, Watford WD17 4QA
Tel 01923 226422
Fax 01923 226081
Web www.britishwaterways.co.uk
Direct tel 01923 201286
Direct fax 01923 201455
Email robin.evans@britishwaterways.co.uk

EVANS, Tim
Knight Frank

Position
Managing partner, Newcastle office
Contact details
Knight Frank LLP, 37-39 Grey Street, Newcastle upon Tyne NE1 6EE
Tel 0191 221 2211
Fax 0191 232 4114
Web www.knightfrank.com
Email tim.evans@knightfrank.com

EVANS, Tim
Sheppard Robson

Position
Partner – creative director
Qualifications
BA; Dip Arch; RIBA
Career history
1991 Joined Sheppard Robson. Formerly with Terry Farrell and Daryl Jackson, Australia
Other roles
Involved in voluntary work, Nicaragua; teaching at Sydney University, Australia
Professional memberships
RIBA
Interests
Design; film-making; snowboarding
Contact details
Sheppard Robson, 77 Parkway, London NW1 7PU
Tel 020 7504 1700
Fax 020 7504 1701
Web www.sheppardrobson.com
Email tim.evans@sheppardrobson.com

EVERETT, Philip
Crown Estate

Position
Deputy ranger
Qualifications
FRICS
Career history
1982-98 Land agent, Smith Gore: at Exbury Estate, Hants, then at Blenheim Estate, Oxon, from 1986.
1975-82 Land agent, Durrington, PSA/DOE
Professional memberships
Country Land & Business Association; Land Surveyors Club; Royal Agricultural Society of England; RICS
Interests
Boating; shooting; walking
Contact details
Crown Estate, The Great Park, Windsor SL4 2HT
Tel 01753 860222
Fax 01753 620548
Web www.crownestate.co.uk
Mobile 07768 814229
Email philip.everett@crownestate.co.uk

EWING, Michael
Scottish Widows Investment Partnership

Position
Fund director
Contact details
Scottish Widows Investment Partnership Ltd, 10 Fleet Place, London EC4M 7RH
Tel 020 7203 3000
Fax 020 7203 3030
Web www.scottishwidows.co.uk
Email michael.ewing@swipartnership.com

FABER, Steve
Deutsche Property Asset Management

Position
Vice-president – investment
Qualifications
MRICS
Professional memberships
RICS
Interests
Beer; cricket; eating out; football; wine
Contact details
Deutsche Property Asset Management Ltd, 1 Appold Street, London EC2A 2HE
Tel 020 7545 6000
Fax 020 7545 7555
Web www.deam-uk.com
Direct tel 020 7545 1922
Mobile 07901 516332
Email steve.faber@db.com

FAGAN, Brian
Ballymore Properties

Position
Group financial director
Contact details
Ballymore Properties Ltd, 3 Greenwich View Place, London E14 9NN
Tel 020 7510 9100
Fax 020 7510 9110
Email bfagan@ballymore.co.uk

FAIRCLOUGH, Jim
Russell-Cooke

Position
Partner – property
Qualifications
LLB Hons
Career history
1969-2000 Partner, Evill & Coleman.
1966 Admitted to Roll of Solicitors
Interests
Badminton; photography; squash; tennis
Contact details
Russell-Cooke, 2 Putney Hill, London SW15 6AB
Tel 020 8789 9111
Fax 020 8780 1194
Web www.russell-cooke.co.uk
Direct tel 020 8394 6501
Direct fax 020 8394 6566
Email faircloughj@russell-cooke.co.uk

FAIRHURST, Graham
GVA Grimley

Position
Partner – head of building national business unit
Qualifications
BSc Hons; FRICS; MBEng
Professional memberships
RICS
Contact details
GVA Grimley, 81 Fountain Street, Manchester M2 2EE
Tel 0870 900 8990
Fax 0161 956 4009
Web www.gvagrimley.co.uk
Direct tel 0161 956 4433
Email graham.fairhurst@gvagrimley.co.uk

FALKINGHAM, Jonathan
Urban Splash

Position
Chief executive
Qualifications
BA Hons; BArch Hons; RIBA; FRSA
Career history
1989-93 Project architect, Ian Darby Partnership.
1984-85 Assistant architect, ARB Arbeitsgruppe, Bern.
1981-89 Student of architecture, Liverpool University
Other roles
Managing director, Shed KM; director, Baa Bar
Professional memberships
RIBA; Royal Society of Arts
Interests
Cycling; squash; tennis
Contact details
Urban Splash Ltd, Timber Wharf, 32 Worsley Street, Manchester M15 4NX
Tel 0161 839 2999
Fax 0161 839 8999
Web www.urbansplash.co.uk
Mobile 07771 782975
Email jonathanfalkingham@urbansplash.co.uk

FALKOWSKI, Damian
4-5 Gray's Inn Square

Position
Barrister
Qualifications
LL Dip
Career history
1994 Called to Bar
Other roles
Former professional violinist playing with orchestras including Academy of St Martin in the Fields and London Symphony Orchestra
Contact details
4-5 Gray's Inn Square (Chambers of Elizabeth Appleby QC & Timothy Straker QC), London WC1R 5AH
Tel 020 7404 5252
Fax 020 7242 7803
Web www.4-5graysinnsquare.co.uk
Email dfalkowski@4-5graysinnsquare.co.uk

FANCOURT, Timothy
Falcon Chambers

Position
Barrister
Qualifications
QC; MA (Cantab)
Career history
2003 Appointed QC.
Since 1989 Barrister, Falcon Chambers.
1987 Called to Bar
Other roles
Bar Council member (1996-2001); editor, cumulative supplements to *Megarry's The Rent Acts* (11th edition) (Sweet & Maxwell, 1989, 1991, 1993); author, *Enforceability of Landlord & Tenant Covenants* and *Megarry's Assured Tenancies*
Professional memberships
Chancery Bar Association; London Common Law & Commercial Bar Association; Property Bar Association
Contact details
Falcon Chambers, Falcon Court, London EC4Y 1AA
Tel 020 7353 2484
Fax 020 7353 1261
Web www.falcon-chambers.com
Email fancourt@falcon-chambers.com

FARINO, Damian
Edwin Hill

Position
Partner
Qualifications
BSc; MRICS
Career history

F

1982 Joined Edwin Hill

Professional memberships

RICS

Contact details

Edwin Hill, Highbridge House, Padbury Oaks, London UB7 0EH

Tel 01753 689000

Fax 01753 689191

Web www.edwinhill.co.uk

Mobile 07767 816144

Email daf@edwinhill.co.uk

FARNFIELD, Peter
Rutland Investment Management

Position

Chief executive

Qualifications

BSc Hons; FRICS

Career history

1999-2000 Director (UK investment), TrizecHahn Europe.

1988-99 Director, PRICOA Property Investment Management.

1986-88 Investment surveyor, Provident Mutual.

1981-86 Investment surveyor, Baring Houston & Saunders.

1980-81 Investment surveyor, King & Co.

1977-80 Management and investment surveyor, Legal & General

Professional memberships

BSc (Estate Management) Club; RICS

Contact details

Rutland Investment Management Ltd, Rutland House, Dunsfold Park, Cranleigh GU6 8TB

Tel 01483 200900

Fax 01483 200555

Direct tel 01483 542224

Mobile 07971 402339

Email pfarnfield@rutland.co.uk

FARQUHAR, Neil
FPDSavills

Position

Director – head of capital allowances

Qualifications

MRICS; BSc Hons

Career history

Since 1996 Director, FPDSavills.

1993-96 Capital allowances consultant, Arthur Andersen.

1989-93 Gleeds

Professional memberships

Association of Taxation Technicians; RICS

Interests

Golf; tennis; theatre

Contact details

FPDSavills Ltd, 25 Finsbury Circus, London EC2M 7EE

Tel 020 7499 8644

Fax 020 7588 7323

Web www.fpdsavills.co.uk

Direct tel 020 7409 8968

Direct fax 020 7330 8601

Mobile 07881 621832

Email nfarquhar@fpdsavills.co.uk

FARR, Martin
GVA Grimley

Position

Partner – valuation

Qualifications

FRICS; FCIArb

Career history

1983 Joined GVA Grimley.

1973-83 Richard Ellis

Other roles

Founding member, Expert Witness Institute; member of Common Council and committee member (planning and transportation, community services), Corporation of London

Professional memberships

Academy of Experts; Arbrix; Chartered Institute of Arbitrators; City Property Association; Institute of Revenues Rating & Valuation; RICS; Society of Expert Witnesses

Interests

Hill walking; mountaineering; music; theatre

Contact details

GVA Grimley, 25 Bucklersbury, London EC4N 8DA

Tel 0870 900 8990

Fax 020 7911 2846

Web www.gvagrimley.co.uk

Direct tel 020 7911 2822

Email martin.farr@gvagrimley.co.uk

FARRANT, Simon
Phoenix Beard

Position

Director – professional

Qualifications

BSc; FRICS; MCIArb

Career history

1987 Joined Phoenix Beard.

1984-87 Conway Relf Stanton

Professional memberships

Accessible Retail; Chartered Institute of Arbitrators; RICS

Interests

Golf; shooting; squash

Contact details

Phoenix Beard, The Exchange, 19 Newhall Street, Birmingham B3 3PJ

Tel 0121 200 4500

Fax 0121 200 4599

Web www.phoenix-beard.co.uk

Direct tel 0121 200 4572

Mobile 07808 784782

Email simon.farrant@phoenix-beard.co.uk

FARRER, Charles
RadcliffesLeBrasseur

Position

Head of property investment and development

Contact details

RadcliffesLeBrasseur, 5 Great College Street, London SW1P 3SJ

Tel 020 7222 7040

Fax 020 7222 6208

Web www.rlb-law.com

Email charles.farrer@rlb-law.com

FARRIES, David
Heron International

Position

UK development director

Qualifications

BSc, Est Man

Career history

2001 Joined Heron International.

1998-2001 MEPC.

1988-98 Trafalgar House Property.

1985-88 St Quintin

Interests

Antiques; art; family

Contact details

Heron International, Heron House, 19 Marylebone Road, London NW1 5JP

Tel 020 7486 4477

Fax 020 7486 3349

Web www.heron-international.com

Email dfarries@heron.co.uk

FARROW, Christopher
Welsh Development Agency

Position

Executive director, North Wales

Qualifications

MRTPI

Career history

1991-98 Chief executive, Merseyside Development Corp.

1981-91 Director, London Docklands Development Corp

Professional memberships

RTPI

Interests

Family; football

Contact details

Welsh Development Agency, North Wales Division, Ffordd Richard Davies, St Asaph

LL17 OLJ
Tel 01745 586204
Fax 01745 586259
Web www.wda.co.uk
Mobile 07899 921750
Email chris.farrow@wda.co.uk

FARROW, Kevin
DTZ Debenham Tie Leung

Position
Director of central London retail agency
Career history
1998-2003 Director, Colliers CRE.
1984-98 Jones Lang Wootton: joined to help set up shopping centre team; moved to retail agency department in 1985
Interests
Golf; opera; shopping; travel
Contact details
DTZ Debenham Tie Leung, One Curzon Street, London W1A 5PZ
Tel 020 7408 1161
Fax 020 7643 6000
Web www.dtz.com
Direct tel 020 7643 6534
Direct fax 020 7643 6431
Mobile 07768 500162
Email kevin.farrow@dtz.com

FAULDS, Ann
Dundas & Wilson

Position
Partner – head of planning
Qualifications
BA; LLB; Dip LP; MIHT
Career history
1993 Joined Dundas & Wilson; became partner in 1995.
1989 Admitted to Roll of Solicitors.
1987-93 Central Regional Council
Professional memberships
Institution of Highways & Transportation; RTPI
Contact details
Dundas & Wilson, Saltire Court, 20 Castle Terrace, Edinburgh EH1 2EN
Tel 0131 228 8000
Fax 0131 228 8888
Web www.dundas-wilson.com
Direct tel 0131 200 7452
Email ann.faulds@dundas-wilson.com

FAYARD, Pierre
Sephora UK

Position
UK managing director
Career history
1998 Sephora: European purchasing director, then European marketing director, Sephora Europe (LVMH); appointed managing director of Sephora UK in 2003.
1986-98 Relay (Lagardere): various positions in marketing; marketing director for Aeroboutique Duty Free (Lagardere) from 1993
Interests
Golf; sailing
Contact details
Sephora UK Ltd, 63 Gee Street, London EC1V 3RS
Tel 020 7253 7790
Fax 020 7253 2179
Web www.sephora.com
Direct tel 020 7253 7792
Mobile 07855 445719
Email pfayard@sephora.fr

FAZAN, Giles
BAA Lynton

Position
Head of project management
Qualifications
MCIOB; MAPM
Career history
1975-77 JL Eve Construction.
1972-75 Gee Walker Slater
Professional memberships
Association for Project Management; Chartered Institute of Building
Interests
Fly fishing; rugby; sport
Contact details
BAA Lynton plc, 67-69 New Bond Street, London W1S 1DF
Tel 020 7907 9200
Fax 020 7907 9299
Web www.baa.com
Email giles_fazan@baa.co.uk

FEENAN, Rosemary
Jones Lang LaSalle

Position
European director – research
Qualifications
BSc; MA
Career history
1988-98 Chesterton.
1983-88 Property group manager, CACI.
1980-83 Manager (site potential statistics), J Sainsbury.
1977-78 Wandsworth Borough Council
Other roles
Board member, Jones Lang LaSalle Global Research; Global Future Forum advisory board member; member, BPF research committee
Professional memberships
Society of Property Researchers
Contact details
Jones Lang LaSalle Ltd, 22 Hanover Square, London W1A 2BN
Tel 020 7493 6040
Fax 020 7408 0220
Web www.joneslanglasalle.com
Direct tel 020 7399 5166
Direct fax 020 7399 5104
Mobile 07771 542536
Email rosemary.feenan@eu.joneslanglasalle.com

FELCE, Gary
Haslemere Estates Management

Position
Director – investment analysis
Interests
Rugby
Contact details
Haslemere Estates Management Ltd, 43-45 Portman Square, London W1H 6AG
Tel 020 7467 4500
Fax 020 7467 4505
Email Gfelce@haslemerenv.com

FELL, Colin
King Sturge

Position
Partner in charge, Leeds
Qualifications
BSc Hons; FRICS
Career history
Since 1994 Partner, King Sturge.
1984-94 Partner/managing partner (Leeds), Bernard Thorpe/DTZ.
1978-84 Edward Erdman (London)
Professional memberships
CBI; RICS
Contact details
King Sturge, Capitol House, Russell Street, Leeds LS1 5SP
Tel 0113 244 1441
Fax 0113 242 1404
Web www.kingsturge.com
Direct tel 0113 235 5213
Mobile 07889 896839
Email colin.fell@kingsturge.co.uk

FELLOWS, Martin
Knight Frank

Position
Partner – joint head of planning
Qualifications
BA Hons; Dip TP; MRTPI
Career history
1988 Joined Knight Frank.
1979-88 Principal planning research officer,

F

Peterborough Development Corp.
1977-79 Harlow Development Corp

Professional memberships
RTPI

Interests
Music; opera

Contact details
Knight Frank LLP, 20 Hanover Square, London W1S 1HZ
Tel 020 7629 8171
Fax 020 7493 4114
Web www.knightfrank.com
Direct tel 020 7861 1300
Direct fax 020 7495 0556
Mobile 07774 125880
Email martin.fellows@knightfrank.com

FELTHAM, Dominic
Estates Gazette Group

Position
Publishing director

Contact details
Estates Gazette Group, 151-153 Wardour Street, London W1F 8BN
Tel 020 7411 2829
Fax 020 7411 2883
Direct tel 020 7411 2679
Email dominic.feltham@egi.co.uk

FELTHAM, Ian
CB Richard Ellis

Position
Senior director – central London professional

Qualifications
FRICS; MCIArb

Career history
Since 2002 Senior director, CB Richard Ellis.
1991-2002 Partner, Healey & Baker.
1978-91 Richard Ellis: partner from 1985.
1975-78 District Valuer's Office

Contact details
CB Richard Ellis, Kingsley House, 1a Wimpole Street, London W1G 0RE
Tel 020 7182 2000
Fax 020 7182 7001
Web www.cbre.com
Direct tel 020 7182 2722
Mobile 07785 280153
Email ian.feltham@cbre.com

FELTHAM, Mark
Dixons Group Retail Properties

Position
Property asset director

Qualifications
BSc; FRICS; MCIArb

Other roles
Member, RICS dispute resolution faculty board

Professional memberships
Chartered Institute of Arbitrators; RICS

Contact details
Dixons Group Retail Properties Ltd, Maylands Avenue, Hemel Hempstead HP2 7TG
Tel 0870 850 3333
Fax 01727 233218
Direct tel 01727 203988
Direct fax 01727 204599
Email mark.feltham@dixons.co.uk

FELTON, Paul
Stimpsons

Position
Director

Qualifications
BA; MRICS

Professional memberships
RICS

Contact details
Stimpsons, 30 The Avenue, Watford WD17 4AE
Tel 01923 252188
Fax 01923 233927
Email pmf@stimpsons.co.uk

FENNELLY, William
Lisney

Position
Director – investment department

Qualifications
BSc Hons; MRICS; ASCS

Professional memberships
RICS; Society of Chartered Surveyors

Interests
Fishing; shooting

Contact details
Lisney, 24 St Stephen's Green, Dublin
Tel +353 1 638 2700
Fax +353 1 638 2706
Web www.lisney.com
Direct tel +353 1 638 2748
Mobile +353 87 274 5068
Email wfennelly@lisney.com

FENNER, John
Maclay Murray & Spens

Position
Partner

Qualifications
OBE

Career history
1994 Founder and senior partner, Fenners; property partner of Maclay Murray & Spens since 2003 merger with Fenners.
1970-94 Founder partner, Berwin Leighton; appointed managing partner in 1980, chairman of partners in 1984 and senior partner in 1990

Other roles
Trustee of British Urban Regeneration Association Charitable Trust; lecturer on property tax and VAT with various organisations including Hawksmere and Henry Stewart Conference Studies; trustee/director, RICS Foundation

Professional memberships
British Urban Regeneration Association; City of London Solicitors Company

Interests
Opera; skiing; tennis; RAC; Carlton Club

Contact details
Maclay Murray & Spens, 10 Foster Lane, London EC2V 6HR
Tel 020 7606 6130
Fax 020 7600 0992
Web www.mms.co.uk
Email john.fenner@mms.co.uk

FERGUSON, George
Acanthus Ferguson Mann

Position
Chairman

Qualifications
BA; BArch; PRIBA; RWA; RSA

Career history
1979 Founded Ferguson Mann; established national network of practices, Acanthus Associated Architectural Practices, in 1986

Other roles
Owner/creator, Tobacco Factory arts centre, Bristol; lectures and broadcasts on architectural and planning matters; RIBA president (elected 2002); president, Avon Youth Association; patron, Bristol Care & Repair

Professional memberships
RIBA; RICS; Royal Society of Arts; Royal West of England Academy; Society of Merchant Venturers of Bristol

Contact details
Acanthus Ferguson Mann, 18 Great George Street, Bristol BS1 5RH
Tel 0117 929 9293
Fax 0117 929 9295
Web www.acanthus.co.uk
Email george@acanthusfm.co.uk

FERGUSON, Gerry
Scottish Widows Investment Partnership

Position
Investment director

Contact details
Scottish Widows Investment Partnership Ltd, Edinburgh One, 60 Morrison Street, Edinburgh EH3 8BE
Tel 0131 655 8500

Fax 0131 655 3890
Web www.scottishwidows.co.uk
Email gerry.ferguson@swipartnership.co.uk

FERGUSSON, Sandy
Building Design Partnership

Position
Chairman, Glasgow office
Contact details
Building Design Partnership Ltd, 5 Blythswood Square, Glasgow G2 4AD
Tel 0141 226 5291
Fax 0141 221 0720
Web www.bdp.co.uk
Email am-fergusson@bdp.co.uk

FERMOR, Andrew
Cripps Harries Hall

Position
Senior partner
Qualifications
LLB
Career history
1976 Joined Cripps Harries Hall; became partner in 1979 and senior partner in 1998.
1974 Admitted to Roll of Solicitors
Interests
Amateur dramatics; gardening; reading
Contact details
Cripps Harries Hall, Seymour House, 11-13 Mount Ephraim Road, Tunbridge Wells TN1 1EG
Tel 01892 515121
Fax 01892 544878
Web www.e-cripps.co.uk
Direct tel 01892 506089
Email aplf@crippslaw.com

FERRARI, Peter
Heron International

Position
Director
Qualifications
BA Hons; MPhil, Land Man; MRICS
Career history
Since 1995 Director, Heron International.
1994-95 Senior investment manager, SPP LET International.
1986-94 Property development executive, London & Edinburgh Trust
Professional memberships
RICS
Contact details
Heron International, Heron House, 19 Marylebone Road, London NW1 5JP
Tel 020 7486 4477
Fax 020 7486 3349
Web www.heron-international.com
Direct fax 020 7872 3804
Email pferrari@heron.co.uk

FERRIER, Tom
McGrigors

Position
Partner – head of UK property
Contact details
McGrigors, Pacific House, 70 Wellington Street, Glasgow G2 6SB
Tel 0141 248 6677
Fax 0141 204 1351
Web www.mcgrigors.com
Email tom.ferrier@mcgrigors.com

FETHERSTONHAUGH, Guy
Falcon Chambers

Position
Barrister
Qualifications
QC
Career history
2003 Appointed QC.
1983 Called to Bar
Other roles
Joint author, *Handbook of Rent Review*; joint author, *Commonhold* (2004); former contributing editor, *The Litigation Practice*; member, Supplementary Panel of Counsel (Common Law) for property law work; standing counsel to Rent Assessment Committee
Professional memberships
Chancery Bar Association; London Common Law & Commercial Bar Association; Property Bar Association
Contact details
Falcon Chambers, Falcon Court, London EC4Y 1AA
Tel 020 7353 2484
Fax 020 7353 1261
Web www.falcon-chambers.com
Email
fetherstonhaugh@falcon-chambers.com

FIDDES, Richard
King Sturge

Position
Partner – building consultancy
Qualifications
BSc; FRICS; ACIArb
Career history
Since 1995 Partner (building consultancy), King Sturge
Professional memberships
Chartered Institute of Arbitrators; RICS
Contact details
King Sturge, 7 Stratford Place, London W1C 1ST
Tel 020 7493 4933
Fax 020 7409 0469
Web www.kingsturge.com
Direct tel 020 7318 4331
Direct fax 020 7491 7264
Email richard.fiddes@kingsturge.co.uk

FIDGEN, Roger
Gardiner & Theobald

Position
Senior partner
Qualifications
FRICS
Career history
1973 Joined Gardiner & Theobald; became partner in 1975
Other roles
Past president, British Council for Offices (2001-02)
Professional memberships
RICS
Contact details
Gardiner & Theobald, 32 Bedford Square, London WC1B 3JT
Tel 020 7209 3000
Fax 020 7209 1840
Web www.gardiner.com
Direct fax 020 7209 1844
Email rsf@gardiner.com

FIELD, Christopher
Macfarlanes

Position
Head of property department
Qualifications
MA (Oxon)
Career history
1975 Joined Macfarlanes
Professional memberships
Law Society
Interests
Golf
Contact details
Macfarlanes, 10 Norwich Street, London EC4A 1BD
Tel 020 7831 9222
Fax 020 7831 9607
Web www.macfarlanes.com
Direct tel 020 7849 2290
Email chris.field@macfarlanes.com

FIELD, Dominic
Credit Suisse First Boston

Position
Director – real estate private fund group
Qualifications

BSc Hons; MPhil

Career history

Since 2003 Director, Credit Suisse First Boston.
1995-99 Director, Johnson Fry Asset Management.
1989-95 Richard Ellis

Professional memberships

Investment Property Forum; RICS

Contact details

Credit Suisse First Boston, One Cabot Square, London E14 4QJ
Tel 020 7888 8888
Fax 020 7883 5819
Web www.csfb.com
Direct tel 020 7883 5811
Mobile 07718 806366
Email dominic.field@csfb.com

FIELD, Jeffrey
Cluttons

Position

Partner

Qualifications

BA Hons; Dip TP; MA; Dip PVL; MRICS; MRTPI

Career history

1992-97 Associate, Daniel Smith.
1991-92 Principal planner, Prudential Property

Professional memberships

RICS; RTPI

Interests

Football; golf; travel

Contact details

Cluttons, Portman House, 2 Portman Street, London W1H 6DU
Tel 020 7408 1010
Fax 020 7629 3263
Web www.cluttons.com
Direct tel 020 7647 7146
Email jfield@cluttons.com

FIELD, Martin
Hampton Trust

Position

Director

Other roles

Managing director, Arena Central

Contact details

Hampton Trust plc, 121 Mount Street, London W1K 3NW
Tel 020 7499 4994
Fax 020 7629 6996
Email mfield@121mountstreet.co.uk

FIELD, Russell
Harvey Spack Field

Position

Managing partner

Contact details

Harvey Spack Field, 33 Bruton Street, London W1J 6QU
Tel 020 7629 9663
Fax 020 7491 1964
Web www.harveyspackfield.co.uk
Direct tel 020 7518 0458
Mobile 07836 618814
Email field@harveyspackfield.co.uk

FILDES, Richard
Barlows

Position

Chairman

Contact details

Barlows plc, Chepstow House, Dee Hills Park, Chester CH3 5AR
Tel 0124 435 0202
Fax 0124 431 1522
Web www.barlowsplc.co.uk
Email richard.fildes@barlowsplc.co.uk

FILOSE, Juliet
BP International

Position

General manager – property performance unit

Qualifications

BSc; MRICS

Career history

1989 Joined BP International

Professional memberships

CoreNet Global UK; RICS

Contact details

BP International Ltd, Building F, Chertsey Road, Sunbury-on-Thames TW16 7LN
Tel 01932 762000
Web www.bp.com
Direct tel 01932 763021
Direct fax 01932 763746
Mobile 07850 378458
Email filosejn@bp.com

FINCH, Robert
Linklaters

Position

Partner

Career history

1969 Joined Linklaters; became partner in 1974 and head of commercial property department in 1996.
1969 Admitted to Roll of Solicitors

Other roles

Blundell memorial lecturer; master of City of London Solicitors Company (2000-01); sheriff of the City of London (1999-2000); non-executive director, Corney & Barrow; member of Court of Aldermen and Common Council; Justice of the Peace (sits on bench in Wimbledon); member of European council, Urban Land Institute; Lord Mayor of the City of London (November 2003)

Contact details

Linklaters, 1 Silk Street, London EC2Y 8HQ
Tel 020 7456 2000
Fax 020 7456 2222
Web www.linklaters.com
Direct tel 020 7456 4768
Email robert.finch@linklaters.com

FINDLAY, David
Chesterton International

Position

Director in charge, Nottingham office

Qualifications

BSc; MRICS

Career history

1993 Joined Chesterton.
1991-93 Professional department manager, William H Brown.
1985-91 Management and investment surveyor, Edward Bailey & Son

Professional memberships

RICS

Interests

Golf; rugby; squash

Contact details

Chesterton International, 22a The Ropewalk, Nottingham NG1 5DT
Tel 0115 924 3434
Fax 0115 941 9940
Web www.chesterton.co.uk
Email david.findlay@chesterton.co.uk

FINDLAY-SHIRRAS, Alasdair
Henderson Global Investors

Position

Director – institutional marketing, Europe

Qualifications

MA; MBA

Career history

1997 Joined Henderson Global Investors.
1994-97 General manager and head of financial institutions group, Bayerische Vereinsbank, Munich.
1981-93 Managing director, Vereinsbank Capital, New York

Professional memberships

Society of Investment Professionals

Interests

Golf; opera; sailing; skiing; tennis; wine

Contact details

Henderson Global Investors Ltd, 4 Broadgate, London EC2M 2DA
Tel 020 7818 1818
Fax 020 7818 1819

Web www.henderson.com
Direct tel 020 7818 4403
Direct fax 020 7818 6402
Mobile 07770 855602
Email a.fs@henderson.com

FINLAN, John
Morbaine

Position
Chairman
Contact details
Morbaine Ltd, The Finlan Centre, Hale Road, Widnes WA8 8PU
Tel 0151 424 4211
Fax 0151 424 3162
Email info@morbaine.co.uk

FINLAY, Mark
Brodies

Position
Partner – head of construction
Qualifications
LLB Hons; Dip LP
Career history
1987-2000 Assistant/partner, Steedman Ramage.
1986-87 Bird Semple.
1986 Admitted to Roll of Solicitors.
1984-86 Fyfe Ireland
Professional memberships
Notaries Society; Society of Construction Law; WS Society
Contact details
Brodies LLP, 15 Atholl Crescent, Edinburgh EH3 8HA
Tel 0131 228 3777
Fax 0131 228 3878
Web www.brodies.co.uk
Direct tel 0131 656 0101
Mobile 07977 182120
Email mark.finlay@brodies.co.uk

FIORDELISI, Giuseppe
Westdeutsche Immobilienbank

Position
Director
Contact details
Westdeutsche Immobilienbank, 42 Moorgate, London EC2R 6EL
Tel 020 7330 0988
Web www.westimmobank.com
Email giuseppe.fiordelisi@westimmobank.com

FIRTH, Beverley
Mills & Reeve

Position
Partner – head of planning and environmental law
Qualifications
LLB; Solicitor
Career history
1988 Joined Mills & Reeve; appointed partner in 1989 and joined executive board in 1996
Professional memberships
Law Society
Interests
Family; travel
Contact details
Mills & Reeve, Francis House, 112 Hills Road, Cambridge CB2 1PH
Tel 01223 364422
Fax 01223 355848
Web www.mills-reeve.com
Direct tel 01223 222235
Direct fax 01223 222258
Mobile 07771 564526
Email beverley.firth@mills-reeve.com

FIRTH, Paul
DLA

Position
Location head (real estate), Sheffield
Qualifications
BA Hons, Law
Career history
1987 Joined DLA; appointed location head of real estate, Sheffield, in 1991; also office managing partner, Sheffield office.
1985-87 Taylor & Emmet
Contact details
DLA, Fountain Precinct, Balm Green, Sheffield S1 1RZ
Tel 08700 111111
Web www.dla.com
Direct tel 0114 283 3333
Direct fax 0114 272 4941
Email paul.firth@dla.com

FISCHEL, David
Liberty International

Position
Chief executive
Career history
1985 Joined Liberty International
Contact details
Liberty International plc, 40 Broadway, London SW1H 0BT
Tel 020 7960 1200
Fax 020 7960 1333
Direct tel 020 7960 1207
Direct fax 020 7960 1424
Email janet-donald@lib-int.com

FISHER, Tony
Chesterton International

Position
Head of provincial offices
Contact details
Chesterton International, 54 Brook Street, London W1A 2BU
Tel 020 7499 0404
Fax 020 7629 7804
Web www.chesterton.co.uk
Email anthony.fisher@chesterton.co.uk

FISON, David
Skanska Construction Group

Position
Chief executive
Qualifications
MA; CEng; FICE
Contact details
Skanska Construction Group Ltd, Maple Cross House, Denham Way, Rickmansworth WD3 9SW
Tel 01923 776666
Fax 01923 777834
Web www.skanska.co.uk
Email skanska.construction@skanska.co.uk

FITZGERALD, David
Payne Hicks Beach

Position
Partner – head of property department
Career history
1969 Admitted to Roll of Solicitors
Professional memberships
Law Society
Contact details
Payne Hicks Beach, 10 New Square, London WC2A 3QD
Tel 020 7465 4300
Fax 020 7465 4400
Web www.paynehicksbeach.co.uk
Direct fax 020 7465 4303
Email dfitzgerald@paynehicksbeach.co.uk

FITZGERALD, Michael
Chesterton Structured Finance

Position
Managing director
Contact details
Chesterton Structured Finance Ltd, 54 Brook Street, London W1A 2BU
Tel 020 7499 0404
Fax 020 7312 5445
Web www.chesterton.co.uk
Direct tel 020 7312 5425
Mobile 07974 915926
Email michael.fitzgerald@chesterton.co.uk

F

FLACK, Richard
Development Planning Partnership

Position
Senior partner
Qualifications
BA; MRTPI
Career history
Since 1991 Senior partner, Development Planning Partnership
Professional memberships
RTPI
Interests
Antiques; travel; walking; wine
Contact details
Development Planning Partnership, 21 The Crescent, Bedford MK40 2RT
Tel 01234 358863
Fax 01234 271210
Web www.dpp.propertymall.com
Direct tel 01234 321107
Mobile 07710 883960
Email richard.flack@devplanning.com

FLATAU, William
Harvey Spack Field

Position
Partner
Qualifications
BSc Hons; MRICS
Career history
1994 Joined Harvey Spack Field.
1989-94 Edward Erdman
Contact details
Harvey Spack Field, 33 Bruton Street, London W1J 6QU
Tel 020 7629 9663
Fax 020 7491 1964
Web www.harveyspackfield.co.uk
Direct tel 020 7518 0466
Mobile 07836 744170
Email flatau@harveyspackfield.co.uk

FLAVELLE, Robert
Threadneedle Property Investments

Position
Director – asset management
Qualifications
BSc Hons (Reading); MPhil, Town Planning (UCL); FRICS
Career history
Since 1994 Director (asset management), Threadneedle.
1988-94 Asset manager, Allied Dunbar Property Funds.
1985-88 Deputy head property management, Corporation of London.
1981-85 Surveyor, Greater London Council
Other roles
Member, BPF working party on standard lease terms/heads of terms
Professional memberships
RICS
Contact details
Threadneedle Property Investments, 9-15 Sackville Street, London W1S 3DJ
Tel 020 7437 8000
Fax 020 7464 5811
Direct tel 020 7464 5818
Mobile 07770 641126
Email rob.flavelle@threadneedle.co.uk

FLEET, Terry
Nabarro Nathanson

Position
Partner – construction
Qualifications
LLB Hons
Career history
Since 2002 Partner, Nabarro Nathanson.
1987-2002 Berwin Leighton; became partner in 1988.
1984-87 Legal adviser, Cementation International (Trafalgar House).
1982-84 Legal adviser, Babcock International.
1980-82 Legal adviser, Costain Group.
1980 Admitted to Roll of Solicitors.
1979-80 Speechly Bircham
Other roles
Has written articles in *Construction Law*, *Building*, *Property Week*, *Estates Gazette* and *Chartered Surveyor Weekly*; co-author of *Tolley's Guide to Construction Contracts*; speaks at conferences on construction law matters
Professional memberships
International Bar Association; Society of Construction Law
Interests
Aviation; motor sports; RAC; sailing; travel
Contact details
Nabarro Nathanson, Lacon House, Theobald's Road, London WC1X 8RW
Tel 020 7524 6000
Fax 020 7524 6524
Web www.nabarro.com
Direct tel 020 7542 6172
Email t.fleet@nabarro.com

FLEMING, Mark
FPDSavills

Position
Director – head of office, Glasgow
Contact details
FPDSavills Ltd, 17a Blythswood Square, Glasgow G2 4AD
Tel 0141 248 7342
Fax 0141 248 7343
Web www.fpdsavills.co.uk
Direct tel 0141 222 5859
Mobile 07815 799638
Email mfleming@fpdsavills.co.uk

FLEMING, Rodger
HBOS

Position
Head of group property
Contact details
HBOS plc, Trinity Road, Halifax HX1 2RG
Tel 01422 333333
Email rodgerfleming@hbosplc.com

FLETCHER, David
Fletcher King

Position
Chairman
Qualifications
FRICS
Professional memberships
RICS
Contact details
Fletcher King plc, Stratton House, 1 Stratton Street, London W1J 8LA
Tel 020 7493 8400
Fax 020 7491 2100
Web www.fletcherking.co.uk
Email djrf@fletcherking.co.uk

FLETCHER, Peter
Royal Bank of Scotland

Position
Director – property finance group
Contact details
Royal Bank of Scotland, 280 Bishopsgate, London EC2M 4RB
Tel 020 7833 2121
Web www.rbs.co.uk
Direct tel 020 7672 1165
Direct fax 020 7672 1709
Email peter.fletcher@rbs.co.uk

FLEXEN, John
Morgan Stanley

Position
Head of corporate real estate – EMEA
Qualifications
BSc Hons; MRICS
Career history
2000-01 Partner (head of corporate real estate), King Sturge.
1985-2000 Booker: appointed property services director of Booker Belmont Wholesale in 1988 and group property director of Booker in 1991.

1982-84 District Valuer/Valuation Office, Kensington & Chelsea
Other roles
Member, CBI property management forum
Professional memberships
CBI; RICS
Interests
Cinema; running; skiing; theatre
Contact details
Morgan Stanley, 25 Cabot Square, London E14 4QA
Tel 020 7513 8000
Fax 020 7513 8990
Web www.morganstanley.com
Direct tel 020 7425 7700
Mobile 07876 217078
Email john.flexen@morganstanley.com

FLINT, Michael
Vision Express (UK)
Position
Property and development director
Qualifications
BSc; MRICS
Career history
1996 Joined Vision Express (UK) as acquisitions surveyor; became property director in 1998, then property and development director in 2001.
1995-96 Disposals surveyor, Sears Group Properties.
1993-95 Retail surveyor, Patrick Punch & Co.
1988-93 William H Brown Commercial
Professional memberships
RICS
Interests
Golf; rugby; tennis
Contact details
Vision Express (UK) Ltd, Abbeyfield Road, Nottingham NG7 2SP
Tel 0115 986 5225
Fax 0115 988 2175
Web www.visionexpress.com
Direct tel 0115 988 2387
Direct fax 0115 986 6420
Mobile 07768 827247
Email michael.flint@visionexpress.com

FLINT, Noel
Knight Frank
Position
Partner – head of Sloane Avenue office
Qualifications
MRICS
Career history
1980 Joined Knight Frank as land agent in Hereford office; moved to residential land sales based in Hanover Square in 1982; moved to the house sales department of Sloane Street in 1985
Professional memberships
RICS
Interests
Golf; IT; tobogganing
Contact details
Knight Frank LLP, 60 Sloane Avenue, London SW3 3DD
Tel 020 7591 8601
Fax 020 7591 0572
Web www.knightfrank.com
Mobile 07836 287828
Email noel.flint@knightfrank.com

FLOUNDERS, Andrew
Cobbetts
Position
Partner – head of property
Career history
1983 Admitted to Roll of Solicitors.
1981-2002 Reads/Read Hind Stewart: partner from 1984; became head of property in 1987, until 2002 merger with Cobbetts
Professional memberships
Law Society
Interests
Football; keep fit; Round Table
Contact details
Cobbetts, Trafalgar House, 29 Park Place, Leeds LS1 2SP
Tel 0113 246 8123
Fax 0113 244 2863
Web www.cobbetts.co.uk
Direct tel 0113 288 5201
Mobile 07771 616944
Email andrew.flounders@cobbetts.co.uk

FLOWER, Digby
CB Richard Ellis
Position
Senior director – City business
Qualifications
BSc; MRICS
Career history
1995 Joined CB Hillier Parker (now CB Richard Ellis) as director; senior director since 2000.
1985-95 Director, Herring Baker Harris
Other roles
Member, court of Worshipful Company of Chartered Surveyors
Professional memberships
RICS
Interests
Sailing; shooting; skiing
Contact details
CB Richard Ellis, St Martin's Court, 10 Paternoster Row, London EC4M 7HP
Tel 020 7182 2000
Fax 020 7182 2001
Web www.cbre.com
Direct tel 020 7182 3216
Mobile 07785 280152
Email digby.flower@cbre.com

FLYNN, Declan
Lisney
Position
Managing director
Qualifications
BSc Hons, Est Man; MRICS
Career history
1992 Joined Lisney; appointed associate director in 1996, director in 1997 and managing director in 2002
Professional memberships
RICS
Interests
Golf; rugby; tennis
Contact details
Lisney, Lancashire House, 5 Linenhall Street, Belfast BT2 8AA
Tel 02890 501501
Fax 02890 501500
Web www.lisney.com
Direct tel 02890 501515
Direct fax 02890 401573
Mobile 07711 307601
Email dflynn@lisney-belfast.com

FOGEL, Steven
Dechert
Position
Managing partner – London office
Qualifications
LLB Hons; LLM; ACIArb
Career history
1974 Joined Dechert.
1973-74 Cohen & Meyohas, Paris
Other roles
Past chairman, Investment Property Forum; co-author of several leading textbooks on UK real estate law
Professional memberships
Anglo-American Real Property Institute; BPF; Chartered Institute of Arbitrators; Investment Property Forum
Interests
Cinema; jazz; skiing; swimming
Contact details
Dechert LLP, 2 Serjeants' Inn, London EC4Y 1LT
Tel 020 7583 5353
Fax 020 7353 3683
Web www.dechert.com
Email steven.fogel@dechert.com

F

FOGG, Derek
United Co-operatives

Position
General manager – property group
Contact details
United Co-operatives Ltd, Wood House, Etruria Road, Stoke-on-Trent ST1 5NW
Tel 01782 279222
Fax 01782 205360
Direct tel 01782 276318
Direct fax 01782 267466
Email dfogg@coop.co.uk

FOGG, Jane
GL Hearn

Position
Managing director – workspace solutions
Career history
Since 1995 GL Hearn; commercial manager until 1997, then became managing director (workspace solutions)
Professional memberships
British Institute of Facilities Management
Interests
Horse racing
Contact details
GL Hearn Ltd, Monachus House, High Street, Hook RG27 8NW
Tel 01252 845678
Fax 01252 845777
Web www.glhearn.com
Email jane_fogg@glhearn.com

FOLKES, Constantine
Folkes Properties

Position
Chairman
Other roles
Chairman and chief executive, Folkes Holdings
Contact details
Folkes Properties Ltd, Forge House, Dudley Road, Lye DY9 8EL
Tel 01384 424242
Fax 01384 424455
Web www.folkesproperties.co.uk
Email c.j.folkes@folkesgroup.plc.uk

FORD, Ken
Mall Corp

Position
Chief executive
Qualifications
BSc; FRICS
Professional memberships
RICS
Contact details
Mall Corp Ltd, 10 Lower Grosvenor Place, London SW1W 0EN
Tel 020 7592 9000
Fax 020 7802 5600
Email ken.ford@themall.co.uk

FORD, Margaret
English Partnerships

Position
Chairman
Career history
Since 2002 Chairman, English Partnerships
Other roles
Chief executive, Good Practice; non-executive director, Gas & Electricity Markets Authority; non-executive director, Thus Group
Contact details
English Partnerships, 110 Buckingham Palace Road, London SW1W 9SA
Tel 020 7881 1600
Fax 020 7730 9162
Web www.englishpartnerships.co.uk
Direct tel 020 7881 1619
Direct fax 020 7881 1642
Email margaretford@englishpartnerships.co.uk

FORD, Richard
Knight Frank

Position
Partner – head of London residential
Qualifications
MA (Oxon); FRICS
Career history
1981 Joined Knight Frank
Professional memberships
RICS
Interests
Sailing
Contact details
Knight Frank LLP, 20 Hanover Square, London W1S 1HZ
Tel 020 7629 8171
Fax 020 7493 4114
Web www.knightfrank.com
Direct tel 020 7861 1099
Direct fax 020 7861 1364
Email dick.ford@knightfrank.com

FORDHAM, John
Freshfields Bruckhaus Deringer

Position
Partner – real estate
Career history
1996 Joined Freshfields Bruckhaus Deringer.
1988 Admitted to Roll of Solicitors
Contact details
Freshfields Bruckhaus Deringer, 65 Fleet Street, London EC4Y 1HT
Tel 020 7936 4000
Fax 020 7832 7001
Web www.freshfields.com
Direct tel 020 7832 7485
Email john.fordham@freshfields.com

FORDYCE, Rory
Charles Russell

Position
Partner – head of commercial property, Guildford
Career history
Since 1996 Partner, Charles Russell (following merger with Fordyce & Co).
1993-96 Senior partner, Fordyce & Co.
1989-93 Senior partner, Fordyce, Bairstow & Co.
1979-89 Partner, Rooks Rider.
1979 Admitted to Roll of Solicitors.
1972-79 Rooks & Co
Contact details
Charles Russell, Buryfields House, Bury Fields, Guildford GU2 4AZ
Tel 0148 325 2593
Fax 0148 325 2552
Web www.cr-law.co.uk
Email roryf@cr-law.co.uk

FORGIE, Eric
James Barr

Position
Director – head of agency and investment department
Qualifications
FRICS
Professional memberships
RICS
Contact details
James Barr, 226 West George Street, Glasgow G2 2LN
Tel 0141 300 8000
Fax 0141 300 8001
Web www.jamesbarr.co.uk
Email ericforgie@jamesbarr.co.uk

FORRESTER, John
DTZ Debenham Tie Leung

Position
Director
Qualifications
BSc Hons; MRICS
Career history
1988 Joined DTZ.
1986-88 Cluttons
Other roles
Board member, British Council for Offices
Professional memberships
RICS
Interests

Golf; rugby

Contact details

DTZ Debenham Tie Leung, 30 Throgmorton Street, London EC2N 2BL
Tel 020 7710 8000
Fax 020 7710 8080
Web www.dtz.com
Direct tel 020 7710 8084
Direct fax 020 7710 8003
Email john.forrester@dtz.com

FORSDICK, David
Landmark Chambers

Position

Barrister

Qualifications

BA Hons

Career history

1993 Called to Bar

Other roles

Member of B panel of junior counsel to the Crown; contributor to *Halsbury's Law of England* on compulsory acquisition; contributor to *The Human Rights Act & Local Authorities*

Professional memberships

Administrative Law Bar Association; Planning & Environment Bar Association

Interests

Sailing; skiing; sport; walking

Contact details

Landmark Chambers, 4 Breams Buildings, London EC4A 1AQ
Tel 020 7430 1221
Fax 020 7421 1399
Web www.landmarkchambers.co.uk
Email clerks@landmarkchambers.co.uk

FORSHAW, Christopher
British Land Corp

Position

Director

Contact details

British Land Corp Ltd, 10 Cornwall Terrace, London NW1 4QP
Tel 020 7486 4466
Web www.britishland.com
Email chris.forshaw@britishland.com

FOSTER, Bob
ATIS REAL Weatheralls

Position

Director

Qualifications

FRICS

Career history

1972 Joined ATIS REAL Weatheralls; appointed partner in 1986; now heads corporate real estate division

Professional memberships

CoreNet Global Uk; Institute of Directors; RICS

Interests

Art; cooking; fishing; music; tennis

Contact details

ATIS REAL Weatheralls Ltd, 22 Chancery Lane, London WC2A 1LT
Tel 020 7338 4000
Fax 020 7430 2628
Web www.atisrealweatheralls.com
Direct tel 020 7338 4081
Email bob.foster@atisrealweatheralls.com

FOSTER, Ian
Exchange Chambers

Position

Barrister

Professional memberships

Chancery Bar Association; Northern Chancery Bar Association; Northern Circuit Commercial Bar Association

Contact details

Exchange Chambers, 7 Ralli Court, West Riverside, Manchester M3 5FT
Tel 0161 833 2722
Fax 0161 833 2789
Web www.exchangechambers.co.uk
Email foster@exchangechambers.co.uk

FOSTER, James
Lawrence Graham

Position

Partner – head of construction

Contact details

Lawrence Graham, 190 Strand, London WC2R 1JN
Tel 020 7379 0000
Fax 020 7379 6854
Web www3.lawgram.com
Email james.foster@lawgram.com

FOSTER, Lord Norman
Foster & Partners

Position

Chairman

Qualifications

Dip Arch (Manc); MArch (Yale)

Career history

Since 1967 Foster & Partners.
1963-67 Team 4 Architects

Other roles

Chairman of Foster & Partners in Berlin and Foster Singapore; external examiner, RIBA (1971-73); IBM Fellow, Aspen; member, department of architecture, Akademie Der Kunste; member of RIBA visiting board of education (1971); trustee, Architecture Foundation; trustee, Weimar 1999; Commanders Cross of the Order of Merit of the Federal Republic of Germany; Gold Medal of the Academie d'Architecture, France; Praemium Imperiale – Japan Art Association; Order Pour le Mérite for Sciences & Arts, Germany; International Union of Architects Auguste Perret Prize; RIBA Royal Gold Medal; Japan Design Foundation Award; Grosse Kunstpreis; Arnold W Brunner Memorial Prize – AAL; Gold Medal of the AIA; Officer of the Order of the Arts & Letters – Ministry of Culture, France; Order of North Rhine Westphalia; Pritzker Prize for Architecture; die Quadriga prize for Vision, Courage & Responsibility, from Werkstatt Deutschland, Germany; Order of Merit; knighthood and life peerage; Royal Designer for Industry

Professional memberships

Academie Royale de Belgique (associate); American Academy of Arts & Science (foreign honorary member); Architectural Association (past member); Bund Deutscher Architekten (honorary member); Chartered Society of Designers; French Order of Architects; International Academy of Architecture (Sofia); Royal Academy of Arts; Royal Academy of Engineering; Royal Academy of Fine Arts, Sweden (foreign member); Royal College of Art; Royal Incorporation of Architects in Scotland; RIBA; Royal Society of Arts

Contact details

Foster & Partners, Riverside Three, 22 Hester Road, London SW11 4AN
Tel 020 7738 0455
Fax 020 7738 1107
Web www.fosterandpartners.com
Email enquiries@fosterandpartners.com

FOSTER, Tim
Association of Chief Estates Surveyors & Property Managers

Position

Company secretary

Contact details

Association of Chief Estates Surveyors & Property Managers (ACES), 23 Athol Road, Stockport
Tel 0161 439 9589
Fax 0161 440 7383
Web www.aces.org.uk
Email secretary@aces.org.uk

FOSTER TAYLOR, Charles
UBS Global Asset Management (UK)

Position

Managing director – head of acquisitions

Qualifications

MA; MRICS; MBA

Career history

2000-03 Lend Lease Real Estate Investments: joined as head of capital transactions; appointed chief executive officer (Europe) in 2001.

1998-2000 Senior vice-president, Parkes & Co.

1989-98 Partner and director (investment), Weatherall Green & Smith, Paris

Professional memberships

RICS

Contact details

UBS Global Asset Management (UK) Ltd, 21 Lombard Street, London EC3V 9AH

Tel 020 7901 5050

Fax 020 7929 0487

Web www.ubs.com

Email charles.foster-taylor@ubs.com

FOUNTAIN, David
Glenny

Position

Partner

Qualifications

BSc Hons; MRICS

Career history

1989 Joined Glenny; became associate partner in 1994 and salaried partner in 1997.

1987-89 Assistant director, Port of London Properties.

1984-87 Valuation and estates department, Greater London Council (latterly London Residuary Body)

Professional memberships

RICS

Interests

Cycling; tennis; travel

Contact details

Glenny, 118-122 Welling High Street, Welling DA16 1TJ

Tel 020 8304 4911

Fax 020 8303 3380

Web www.glenny.co.uk

Mobile 07768 746061

Email d.fountain@glenny.co.uk

FOWLDS, Robert
Merrill Lynch Global Principal Investments

Position

First vice-president/managing director

Qualifications

BSc; MRICS; MBA, Finance

Career history

Since 1997 First vice-president/managing director/joint head of pan-Europe real estate sector research, Merrill Lynch. Previously with Dresdner Kleinwort Benson, Credit Lyonnais, Morgan Grenfell, DTZ and Gooch & Wagstaff

Professional memberships

RICS

Contact details

Merrill Lynch Global Principal Investments, 2 King Edward Street, London EC1A 1HQ

Tel 020 7628 1000

Web www.ml.com

Direct tel 020 7996 4668

Email robert_fowlds@ml.com

FOWLER, John
Lambert Smith Hampton

Position

Director

Qualifications

BSc; FRICS; MCIArb

Career history

1982 Joined Lambert Smith Hampton as director.

1978-81 Joshua Bury Earle & Co

Professional memberships

Chartered Institute of Arbitrators; Expert Witness Institute; RICS

Contact details

Lambert Smith Hampton Ltd, Grant Thornton House, 206 Silbury Boulevard, Milton Keynes MK9 1LU

Tel 01908 604630

Fax 01908 607077

Web www.lsh.co.uk

Mobile 07860 301849

Email jfowler@lsh.co.uk

FOWLES, Peter
NAI Fuller Peiser

Position

Partner – property & corporate asset management

Qualifications

BSc; MRICS; MPhil, Land Man

Career history

2000 Joined Fuller Peiser.

1988-2000 Weatherall Green & Smith

Contact details

NAI Fuller Peiser, Waterloo House, 20 Waterloo Street, Birmingham B2 5TB

Tel 0870 700 2233

Fax 0121 605 2244

Web www.nai-fullerpeiser.com

Email pfowles@nai-fullerpeiser.com

FOX, Christopher
Arrowcroft Northwest

Position

Managing director

Qualifications

FRICS

Other roles

Director, Arrowcroft Group

Professional memberships

RICS

Interests

Horse racing; shooting; travel

Contact details

Arrowcroft Northwest Ltd, Stock Exchange, 4 Norfolk Street, Manchester M2 1DW

Tel 0161 834 8881

Fax 0161 834 8885

Email cfox@arrowcroft-nw.co.uk

FOX, Nigel
Jones Lang LaSalle

Position

International director – City investment

Qualifications

BSc Hons; MRICS

Career history

1989 Joined Jones Lang LaSalle

Other roles

Surveyor, Clothworkers' Company

Professional memberships

RICS

Interests

Family; golf; travel

Contact details

Jones Lang LaSalle Ltd, 9 Queen Victoria Street, London EC4N 4YY

Tel 020 7248 6040

Fax 020 7248 0088

Web www.joneslanglasalle.com

Direct tel 020 7399 5993

Direct fax 020 7399 5676

Email nigel.fox@eu.joneslanglasalle.com

FOX, Ronan
Standard & Poor's

Position

Director – structured finance

Qualifications

BSc; MRICS

Contact details

Standard & Poor's Ltd, Garden House, 18 Finsbury Circus, London EC2M 7BP

Tel 020 7826 3800

Fax 020 7826 3598

Web www.standardpoor.com

Email ronan_fox@standardandpoors.com

FOX-EDWARDS, Jane
Lawrence Graham

Position

Partner – head of property litigation

Qualifications

MA (Cantab)

Career history

1990 Joined Lawrence Graham; became partner in 1996.

1988 Admitted to Roll of Solicitors.

1986-89 Boodle Hatfield

Other roles

Regular speaker at public seminars/tailor-made seminars for clients; contributes to *Estates Gazette* and other property journals; member of contributors board, *Property Law Journal*

Professional memberships

Law Society; Property Litigation Association

Interests

Fly fishing; food; painting

Contact details

Lawrence Graham, 190 Strand, London WC2R 1JN

Tel 020 7379 0000

Fax 020 7379 6854

Web www3.lawgram.com

Direct tel 020 7759 6527

Email jane.fox-edwards@lawgram.com

FOXLEY, Sue
Jones Lang LaSalle

Position

National director – UK head of research

Career history

1996 Joined Jones Lang LaSalle

Contact details

Jones Lang LaSalle Ltd, 22 Hanover Square, London W1A 2BN

Tel 020 7493 6040

Fax 020 7408 0220

Web www.joneslanglasalle.com

Direct tel 020 7399 5402

Direct fax 020 7399 5103

Email sue.foxley@eu.joneslanglasalle.com

FRAMPTON, Guy
CB Richard Ellis

Position

Senior director – industrial and logistics, Europe

Career history

Since 1988 CB Hillier Parker (now CB Richard Ellis).

1984-88 Edward Erdman.

1978-81 Brinsons

Other roles

Past chairman, Industrial Agents Society; European partner, CB Global Logistics Group

Contact details

CB Richard Ellis, Kingsley House, 1a Wimpole Street, London W1G 0RE

Tel 020 7182 2000

Fax 020 7182 7001

Web www.cbre.com

Direct tel 020 7182 2150

Direct fax 020 7182 2050

Mobile 07836 312704

Email guy.frampton@cbre.com

FRANCIS, Andrew
11 New Square

Position

Barrister

Qualifications

MA (Oxon)

Career history

1979 Joined 11 New Square Chambers.

1977 Called to Bar

Other roles

Author, *Restrictive Covenants over Freehold Land – A Practitioners Guide* (Sweet & Maxwell, 1999); joint author, *Rights of Light* (Jordans, 2000)

Professional memberships

Chancery Bar Association; Honourable Society of Lincoln's Inn; UK Environmental Law Association

Contact details

11 New Square (Chambers of Sonia Proudman QC), Ground Floor, London WC2A 3QB

Tel 020 7831 0081

Fax 020 7405 2560

Web www.11newsquare.co.uk

Mobile 07768 057027

Email francis.newsquare@virgin.net

FRANCIS, Daniel
NHP

Position

Finance director

Qualifications

FCA

Other roles

Director of finance and systems

Professional memberships

Institute of Chartered Accountants in England & Wales

Interests

Cricket; golf

Contact details

NHP plc, Dukes Court, Duke Street, Woking GU21 5BH

Tel 01483 754760

Fax 01483 727509

Direct tel 023 8025 2759

Direct fax 023 8027 5380

Mobile 07831 505665

Email dannyf@nhprops.co.uk

FRANCIS, Graham
Sheppard Robson

Position

Chairman

Qualifications

BA; BArch; RIBA

Professional memberships

British Council for Offices; RIBA

Interests

Art; squash; swimming; tennis; travel; walking

Contact details

Sheppard Robson, 77 Parkway, London NW1 7PU

Tel 020 7504 1700

Fax 020 7504 1701

Web www.sheppardrobson.com

Email graham.francis@sheppardrobson.com

FRANCIS, Mike
Donaldsons

Position

Partner – head of in-town retail

Contact details

Donaldsons, St Pauls House, 23 Park Square South, Leeds LS1 2ND

Tel 0113 246 1161

Fax 0113 244 1637

Web www.donaldsons.co.uk

Email mike.francis@donaldsons.co.uk

FRANCIS, Penny
Lawrence Graham

Position

Managing partner

Career history

1989 Joined Lawrence Graham.

1984 Admitted to Roll of Solicitors.

1982-88 Beachcroft Stanleys

Other roles

Member, RICS dispute resolution panel; member, Property Litigation Association law reform subcommittee; lectures at RICS, Arbrix, Henry Stewart and other conferences; member, Centrepoint

Professional memberships

Law Society; Property Litigation Association; Westminster Property Owners Association

Interests

Ballet; travel

Contact details

Lawrence Graham, 190 Strand, London WC2R 1JN

Tel 020 7379 0000

Fax 020 7379 6854

Web www3.lawgram.com

Direct tel 020 7759 6508

Email penny.francis@lawgram.com

F

FRANKLIN, Nigel
AMEC Developments

Position
Director
Contact details
AMEC Developments Ltd, 19th Floor, Tolworth Tower, Ewell Road, Surbiton KT6 7EL
Tel 020 8390 8300
Fax 020 8339 4699
Web www.amec.com
Email nigel.franklin@amec.com

FRANKS, Nigel
Mothercare

Position
Property manager
Qualifications
FRICS
Career history
1994-2000 Property director, Bhs (part of Storehouse).
1988-94 Property director, Texas Homecare (part of Ladbroke Group).
1967-88 Various roles in property, including director of property at J Sainsbury from 1982
Professional memberships
Association of Corporate Real Estate; RICS
Contact details
Mothercare plc, Cherry Tree Road, Watford WD24 6SH
Tel 01923 241000
Fax 01923 240944
Web www.mothercare.com
Direct tel 01923 206498
Direct fax 01923 206307
Email nigel.franks@mothercare.co.uk

FRASER, Moira
Fladgate Fielder

Position
Partner – head of planning
Qualifications
MA Hons (Cantab)
Career history
1999-2001 Partner, McGuiness Finch.
1988-99 DJ Freeman: promoted to partner and head of planning in 1990.
1982-84 Simmons & Simmons.
1979 Admitted to Roll of Solicitors.
1977-82 Norton Rose
Professional memberships
Law Society; Leisure Property Forum; Town & Country Planning Association; Royal Society of Arts
Interests
Cinema; family; golf
Contact details
Fladgate Fielder, 25 North Row, London W1K 6DJ
Tel 020 7323 4747
Fax 020 7629 4414
Web www.fladgate.com
Direct tel 020 7462 2212
Email mfraser@fladgate.com

FREEDMAN, Philip
Mishcon de Reya

Position
Senior property partner
Career history
1972 Admitted to Roll of Solicitors
Other roles
Chairman, Joint Working Group on Commercial Leases
Professional memberships
Law Society
Interests
Music; photography
Contact details
Mishcon de Reya Ltd, 21 Southampton Row, London WC1B 5HS
Tel 020 7440 7000
Fax 020 7404 5982
Web www.mishcon.co.uk
Direct tel 020 7440 7018
Email philip.freedman@mishcon.co.uk

FREEMAN, Ben
Prudential Property Investment Managers

Position
Finance director
Qualifications
ACA
Career history
1993-99 Finance director and company secretary, Cole & Mason.
1986-92 Company secretary, Helical Bar.
1979-84 KPMG
Other roles
Trustee of childcare charity Family Rights Group and of world development charity Find Your Feet
Professional memberships
Institute of Chartered Accountants in England & Wales
Contact details
Prudential Property Investment Managers Ltd, Princeton House, 271-273 High Holborn, London WC1V 7NE
Tel 020 7548 6600
Fax 020 7548 6999
Web www.prupim.com
Direct tel 020 7548 6522
Direct fax 020 7548 6995
Mobile 07958 344436
Email ben.freeman@prupim.com

FREEMAN, Martyn
Artisan (UK)

Position
Chief executive
Qualifications
FCCA
Career history
2000 Joined Artisan. Previously held directorships in Hunting Gate property group
Professional memberships
Association of Chartered Certified Accountants
Contact details
Artisan (UK) plc, Mace House, Lancaster Way, Huntingdon PE29 6XU
Tel 01480 436666
Fax 01480 436231
Web www.artisandevelopments.co.uk
Email m.freeman@artisan-plc.co.uk

FREEMAN, Michael
Argent Group

Position
Non-executive director
Qualifications
MA (Oxon); Solicitor
Career history
1981 Co-founded Argent Group; joint chief executive until 1997; now non-executive director
Contact details
Argent Group plc, 5 Albany Courtyard, London W1J 0HF
Tel 020 7734 3721
Fax 020 7734 4474
Web www.argentgroup.plc.uk
Mobile 07836 219126
Email michaelf@argentgroup.plc.uk

FREEMAN, Peter
Argent Group

Position
Non-executive director
Qualifications
BA; Solicitor
Career history
1999 Co-founded Freeman Publishing (now Freeman Business Information).
1981 Co-founded Argent Group.
1979-81 DJ Freeman
Other roles
Policy committee member, BPF; publisher, Freeman Business Information; non-executive director, Land Securities; board director, Investment Property Forum
Professional memberships
BPF
Contact details
Argent Group plc, 5 Albany Courtyard, London

W1J 0HF
Tel 020 7734 3721
Fax 020 7734 4474
Web www.argentgroup.plc.uk
Email peterf@argentgroup.plc.uk

FREEMAN, Quentin
UBS Investment Bank

Position
Property analyst
Contact details
UBS Investment Bank, 2 Finsbury Avenue, London EC2M 2PG
Tel 020 7567 8000
Fax 020 7568 4800
Email quentin.freeman@ubsw.com

FREETH, Nigel
Freeth Melhuish

Position
Senior partner
Qualifications
FRICS
Career history
1982 Established Freeth & Co in 1982; merged to form Freeth Melhuish in 1990.
1974-82 Estates manager, Commission for New Towns
Professional memberships
Royal Ornithology Society; Royal Yachting Association
Interests
Football; golf; horse racing; rugby; sailing; skiing
Contact details
Freeth Melhuish, The Courtyard, 77-79 Marlowes, Hemel Hempstead HP1 1LF
Tel 01442 263033
Fax 01442 260628
Email nf@freethmelhuish.co.uk

FREYNE, Michele
Mayer, Brown, Rowe & Maw

Position
Partner – real estate litigation
Qualifications
MA; TCD
Career history
1979 Joined Rowe & Maw (now Mayer, Brown, Rowe & Maw).
1978 Admitted to Roll of Solicitors
Professional memberships
Property Litigation Association; Women in Property Litigation
Interests
Tennis
Contact details
Mayer, Brown, Rowe & Maw LLP, 11 Pilgrim Street, London EC4V 6RW
Tel 020 7248 4282
Fax 020 7248 2009
Web www.mayerbrownrowe.com
Email mfreyne@eu.mayerbrownrowe.com

FROGGATT, Alan
CB Richard Ellis

Position
European chief executive
Qualifications
BSc, Est Man; FRICS
Career history
1971 Joined Richards Ellis (now CB Richard Ellis); appointed chief executive in 1996 and European chief executive in 1997
Other roles
Policy committee member, BPF; member of presidents committee, London First; barker, Variety Club of Great Britain; liveryman, Upholders Company
Professional memberships
RICS
Interests
Horse racing; ornithology; walking
Contact details
CB Richard Ellis, St Martin's Court, 10 Paternoster Row, London EC4M 7HP
Tel 020 7182 2000
Fax 020 7182 2001
Web www.cbre.com
Email alan.froggatt@cbre.com

FROGGATT, Richard
St Modwen Properties

Position
Executive director
Qualifications
FRICS
Other roles
Chairman, Key Property Investments; director, St Modwen Developments and all St Modwen subsidiaries
Professional memberships
RICS
Interests
Golf; motor sports; skiing
Contact details
St Modwen Properties plc, Lyndon House, 62 Hagley Road, Birmingham B16 8PE
Tel 0121 456 2800
Fax 0121 456 1829
Web www.stmodwen.co.uk
Mobile 07860 455556
Email rfroggatt@stmodwen.co.uk

FROST, Giles
Babcock & Brown

Position
Principal – real estate
Career history
1994-2000 Partner, Wilde Sapte.
1985-94 Solicitor, Frere Cholmeley
Contact details
Babcock & Brown, 1 Fleet Place, London EC4M 7RA
Tel 020 7203 7300
Fax 020 7203 7301
Web www.babcockbrown.com
Email giles.frost@babcockbrown.com

FRYER, Graham
Drivers Jonas

Position
Partner – head of project management
Qualifications
MRICS
Career history
1980 Joined Drivers Jonas
Professional memberships
RICS
Contact details
Drivers Jonas, 6 Grosvenor Street, London W1K 4DJ
Tel 020 7896 8000
Fax 020 7896 8001
Web www.driversjonas.com
Direct tel 020 7896 8345
Email grahamfryer@driversjonas.com

FULLERTON, Albie
Dunedin Property

Position
Director and company secretary
Contact details
Dunedin Property Ltd, 22 Rutland Street, Edinburgh EH1 2AN
Tel 0131 221 9799
Fax 0131 221 9533
Web www.dunedinproperty.co.uk
Email afullerton@dunedinproperty.co.uk

FURBER, John
Wilberforce Chambers

Position
Barrister
Qualifications
QC; MA (Cantab)
Career history
1974-99 Chambers at 4 Breams Buildings, London (formerly 2 Paper Buildings).
1973 Called to Bar
Other roles

General editor, *Hill & Redman's Law of Landlord & Tenant*; contributor to *Halsbury's Laws of England* on compulsory acquisition; joint author, *Commonhold & Leasehold Reform Act 2002*

Professional memberships

Chancery Bar Association; Planning & Environment Bar Association; Property Bar Association

Contact details

Wilberforce Chambers, 8 New Square, London WC2A 3QP

Tel 020 7306 0102

Fax 020 7306 0095

Web www.wilberforce.co.uk

Email jfurber@wilberforce.co.uk

FURLONG, Anthony
Sheppard Robson

Position

Senior partner

Other roles

Friend of the Royal Academy

Professional memberships

RIBA

Interests

Royal Society for the Protection of Birds

Contact details

Sheppard Robson, 77 Parkway, London NW1 7PU

Tel 020 7504 1700

Fax 020 7504 1701

Web www.sheppardrobson.com

Mobile 07836 541938

Email anthony.furlong@sheppardrobson.com

FYFE, Alison
Royal Bank of Scotland

Position

Senior director – structured property finance

Qualifications

MA; Dip LE; MRICS

Career history

1996 Joined Royal Bank of Scotland property finance group.

1985-96 Knight Frank: London and Edinburgh

Professional memberships

Investment Property Forum; RICS

Interests

Music; swimming; walking

Contact details

Royal Bank of Scotland, 6th Floor, 6-8 George Street, Edinburgh EH2 2SA

Tel 0131 556 8555

Fax 0131 523 5104

Web www.rbs.co.uk

Direct tel 0131 523 5121

Email alison.fyfe@rbos.com

G

GADBURY, Peter
GL Hearn

Position
Director – building consultancy
Qualifications
FRICS; Dip BS; MSc, Building Maintenance Management
Career history
1982 Joined GL Hearn.
1975-82 Vigers.
1970-75 Metropolitan Police
Professional memberships
RICS
Interests
Cycling; music; photography
Contact details
GL Hearn Ltd, Leonard House, 5-7 Marshalsea Road, London SE1 1EP
Tel 020 7450 4000
Fax 020 7450 4010
Web www.glhearn.com
Email peter_gadbury@glhearn.com

GADSDEN, Philip
Insight Investment Management

Position
Head of external funds, property
Qualifications
BSc; FRICS
Career history
2001-03 Founding co-director, Gatehouse Investment Management.
1983-2001 Jones Lang Wootton: appointed partner in 1990, became director of Jones Lang Wootton Finance in 1991 and head of Jones Lang Wootton Fund Management in 1995; appointed international director, LaSalle Investment Management in 2001
Professional memberships
Investment Property Forum; RICS
Contact details
Insight Investment Management, City Place House, 55 Basinghall Street, London EC2V 5DL
Tel 020 7930 5474
Web www.insightinvestment.com
Direct tel 020 7321 1679
Mobile 07764 183320
Email philip.gadsden@insightinvestment.com

GAINS, Sir John
Mowlem

Position
Group chief executive
Qualifications
KBE; FICE
Career history
1966 Joined Mowlem Group; became managing director of construction division in 1992; group chief executive since 1995
Contact details
Mowlem plc, 25 Ely Place, London EC1N 6TD
Tel 020 7440 7700
Fax 020 7242 0319
Web www.mowlem.com
Email jacqui.lally@mowlem.com

GALE, Richard
Aberdeen Property Investors

Position
Fund manager
Contact details
Aberdeen Property Investors, Charles House, 5-11 Regent Street, London SW1Y 4LR
Tel 020 7747 1700
Fax 020 7839 7460
Web www.aberdeenpropertyinvestors.com
Direct tel 020 7747 1775
Email richard.gale@aberdeenpropertyinvestors.com

GALLAGHER, Peter
Dunlop Heywood Lorenz

Position
Director – head of agency, North West
Career history
Since 1972 Dunlop Heywood/Dunlop Heywood Lorenz: began in general practice department; moved to office agency in 1979; became head of agency (North West) in 1990
Other roles
Founding member, Office Agents Society (North West)
Professional memberships
British Council for Offices
Interests
Fishing; shooting
Contact details
Dunlop Heywood Lorenz Ltd, Abbey House, 32 Booth Street, Manchester M2 4QP
Tel 0161 237 7777
Fax 0161 237 7778
Web www.dhlproperty.co.uk
Direct tel 0161 827 7242
Mobile 07970 225005
Email hpdg@dhlproperty.co.uk

GALLEY, Bob
Co-operative Group

Position
Director of property – CG Property
Contact details
Co-operative Group, New Century House, Manchester M60 4ES
Tel 0161 834 1212
Web www.co-op.co.uk
Direct tel 0161 827 6501
Direct fax 0161 832 5283
Email bob.galley@letsco-operate.com

GALLIMORE, Michael
Lovells

Position
Partner
Qualifications
MA Hons (Cantab)
Career history
1983 Admitted to Roll of Solicitors.
1981 Joined Lovells; became partner in 1988
Other roles
Member, Law Society's planning panel and planning and environmental law committee; member, City of London Law Society planning and environmental law subcommittee
Professional memberships
City of London Solicitors Company; Law Society
Contact details
Lovells, Atlantic House, 50 Holborn Viaduct, London EC1A 2FG
Tel 020 7296 2000
Fax 020 7296 2001
Web www.lovells.com
Email michael.gallimore@lovells.com

GAME, Robert
Citigroup

Position
Head of real estate
Contact details
Citigroup Ltd, 41 Berkeley Square, London W1J 5AN
Tel 020 7508 8000
Fax 020 7508 8989
Web www.citigroup.com
Email robert.game@citigroup.com

G

GAMMAGE, Derek
CB Richard Ellis Hotels

Position
Head of hotels – EMEA
Qualifications
EMEA
Career history
Since 2000 Managing director, Insignia Hotels/CB Richard Ellis Hotels.
1990-2000 Partner and head of hotels, Knight Frank.
1987-90 Manager (hotels), Hanover Druce
Contact details
CB Richard Ellis Hotels Ltd, St Martin's Court, 10 Paternoster Row, London EC4M 7HP
Tel 020 7182 2000
Fax 020 7236 7668
Web www.insigniahotels.com
Direct tel 020 7643 3943
Mobile 07818 041671
Email derek.gammage@cbrehotels.com

GAMMON, Alan
Hamptons International

Position
Director – management services
Qualifications
ARLA
Other roles
Director of property, tenancy and asset management
Interests
Food; reading; travel; wine
Contact details
Hamptons International, 5 Jubilee Place, London SW3 3TD
Tel 020 7808 9001
Fax 020 7808 9000
Web www.hamptons.co.uk
Direct tel 020 7808 9008
Direct fax 020 7823 3666
Email gammona@hamptons-int.com

GARBUTT, John
Nicholson Graham & Jones

Position
Partner – planning and environment group
Career history
1990 Joined Nicholson Graham & Jones.
1969-89 Blue Circle Industries: head of environment until 1985; then chief executive of Blue Circle Industrial Minerals 1986-88 and of Blue Circle Waste Management from 1989.
1965-69 Local government.
1963 Admitted to Roll of Solicitors
Other roles
Member, Law Society's planning panel; committee member, Environment Services Association
Professional memberships
Law Society; Mining & Mineral Law Group; UK Environmental Law Association
Interests
Art; golf; sport; travel
Contact details
Nicholson Graham & Jones, 110 Cannon Street, London EC4N 6AR
Tel 020 7648 9000
Fax 020 7648 9001
Web www.ngj.co.uk
Direct tel 020 7360 8208
Email john.garbutt@ngj.co.uk

GARCIA-VALENCIA, Fernando
Safeway

Position
Property and development director
Qualifications
Engineer; MBA
Career history
2002 Joined Safeway as property and development director. Previously project manager, IDOM Engineering Consultancy; director of construction, Riofisa Group (Spanish developer); and real estate projects director, ING Real Estate, Spain
Contact details
Safeway plc, 6 Millington Road, Hayes UB3 4AY
Tel 020 8848 8744
Fax 020 8756 1596
Web www.safeway.co.uk
Email fernando_gvalencia@safeway.co.uk

GARDINER, Neil
Schroder Property Investment Management

Position
Associate director – residential property investment
Qualifications
MSc, Land Man; BA Hons; MRICS
Other roles
Adviser, London First; adviser, BPF; adviser, ODPM
Interests
Rugby; skiing; wine
Contact details
Schroder Property Investment Management Ltd, 31 Gresham Street, London EC2V 7QA
Tel 020 7658 6000
Fax 020 7658 3960
Email neil.gardiner@schroders.com

GARDNER, Charles
Gerald Eve

Position
Partner – head of investment management
Qualifications
BSc; MRICS; MCIArb
Career history
1986 Joined Gerald Eve.
1984-86 Marks & Spencer
Professional memberships
Chartered Institute of Arbitrators; RICS
Interests
Food and drink; football; skiing; triathlon
Contact details
Gerald Eve, 7 Vere Street, London W1G 0JB
Tel 020 7493 3338
Fax 020 7491 1825
Web www.geraldeve.com
Direct tel 020 7333 6353
Direct fax 020 7333 6403
Email cgardner@geraldeve.com

GARLICK, John
Canada Life

Position
Head of property
Qualifications
BSc; MRICS
Professional memberships
RICS
Contact details
Canada Life Ltd, Martin House, 5 Martin Lane, London EC4R 0DP
Tel 020 7955 0155
Fax 020 7955 0150
Web www.canadalife.com
Email john.garlick@canadalife.co.uk

GARNETT, David
J Sainsbury

Position
Programme disposals manager
Qualifications
MRICS
Career history
2001 Joined J Sainsbury
Contact details
J Sainsbury plc, 33 Holborn, London EC1N 2HT
Tel 020 7695 6000
Fax 020 7695 7610
Web www.j-sainsbury.co.uk
Direct tel 020 7695 7511
Direct fax 020 7695 7511
Email david.garnett@sainsburys.co.uk

GARNHAM, Tim
Minerva

Position
Group development director
Contact details
Minerva plc, 42 Wigmore Street, London W1U 2RY
Tel 020 7535 1000
Fax 020 7535 1001
Direct tel 020 7535 1035
Email tgarnham@minervaplc.co.uk

GARRARD, Sir David
Minerva

Position
Chairman
Qualifications
FFS
Career history
Since 1989 Joint founder and chairman, Minerva (taken public in 1996).
1986 Acquired and took private the publicly quoted Land Investors
Other roles
Sponsor and chair of governors, Business Academy, Bexley; trustee of Police Foundation; chairman of trustees, International Centre for Child Studies; councillor, and director of business division, Prince's Trust; patron, Handicapped Children's Aid; patron, Community Service Volunteers; director, BPF; founder and partner, Garrard Smith & Partners
Contact details
Minerva plc, 42 Wigmore Street, London W1U 2RY
Tel 020 7535 1000
Fax 020 7535 1001
Direct fax 020 7535 1004
Email dgarrard@minervaplc.co.uk

GARRETT, Ian
Leeds & Holbeck Building Society

Position
Head of commercial lending
Contact details
Leeds & Holbeck Building Society, Holbeck House, 105 Albion Street, Leeds LS1 5AS
Tel 08450 505 073
Fax 0113 225 7599
Web www.leeds-holbeck.co.uk
Email igarrett@leeds-holbeck.co.uk

GARVEY, Christine
Deutsche Bank

Position
Global head of corporate real estate services
Career history
1999-2001 Head of worldwide real estate and workplace resources, Cisco Systems.
1991-98 Various property-related positions, Bank of America
Other roles
Non-executive director, Catellus
Contact details
Deutsche Bank AG, Winchester House, 1 Great Winchester Street, London EC2N 2DB
Tel 020 7545 8000
Fax 020 7545 6155
Web www.db.com
Email christine.garvey@db.com

GATES, Dave
Blockbuster Entertainment

Position
Development director
Contact details
Blockbuster Entertainment Ltd, Harefield Place, The Drive, Uxbridge UB10 8AQ
Tel 01895 258866
Fax 01895 866275
Web www.blockbuster.com
Email stacey.barber@blockbuster.com

GATLEY, John
Capital & Regional

Position
Development director
Qualifications
MICE
Career history
2003 Joined Capital & Regional. Prior to this, group property director, Focus Wickes
Contact details
Capital & Regional plc, 10 Lower Grosvenor Place, London SW1W 0EN
Tel 020 7932 8000
Fax 020 7802 5600
Web www.capreg.com
Direct tel 020 7932 8095
Mobile 07802 216615
Email john.gatley@thejunction-uk.com

GAUNT, Jonathan
Falcon Chambers

Position
Joint head of chambers
Qualifications
BA (Oxon); QC
Career history
1998 Bencher of Lincoln's Inn.
1991 Appointed QC.
1972 Called to Bar
Other roles
An editor of landlord and tenant volume of *Halsbury's Laws of England* (vol 27) – rewrote sections on repairing covenants, rent and rent review for 1994 reissue; joint editor, *Gale on Easements* (17th edition, 2002)
Professional memberships
Chancery Bar Association; London Common Law & Commercial Bar Association
Contact details
Falcon Chambers, Falcon Court, London EC4Y 1AA
Tel 020 7353 2484
Fax 020 7353 1261
Web www.falcon-chambers.com
Direct tel 020 7427 7307
Email gaunt@falcon-chambers.com

GAWTHORPE, Steve
One NorthEast

Position
Head of subregional partnership (North)
Contact details
One NorthEast, Stella House, Goldcrest Way, Newcastle upon Tyne NE15 8NY
Tel 0191 229 6200
Fax 0191 229 6201
Web www.onenortheast.co.uk
Direct tel 0191 229 6399
Email steve.gawthorpe@onenortheast.co.uk

GEAVES, Christopher
Strutt & Parker

Position
Equity partner – head of retail
Qualifications
BSc; MRICS
Career history
1993 Joined Strutt & Parker.
1981-93 Edward Erdman
Professional memberships
British Council of Shopping Centres; RICS
Interests
Fishing; golf; sailing; tennis
Contact details
Strutt & Parker, 13 Hill Street, London W1J 5LQ
Tel 020 7629 7282
Fax 020 7629 0387
Web www.struttandparker.com
Direct tel 020 7318 5071
Direct fax 020 7493 7031
Mobile 07831 586280
Email cgeaves@struttandparker.com

GEE, Richard
River Island Clothing Co

Position
Property director

G

Contact details
River Island Clothing Co Ltd, Chelsea House, Westgate, London W5 1DR
Tel 020 8998 8822
Fax 020 8991 1678
Web www.riverisland.com
Email richard.gee@ltg-group.co.uk

GELLATLY, John
Credit Suisse First Boston

Position
Director – real estate investment banking
Qualifications
BA Hons; AIIMR
Career history
1999 Joined Credit Suisse First Boston as property equity analyst; became director of CSFB Property Investment Banking in 2003.
1995-99 Head of investment strategy, Savills Fund Management.
1992-95 Property investment strategist, DTZ Debenham Thorpe.
1988-92 Head of research, Knight Frank Rutley.
1984-88 Property analyst, Merton Associates
Other roles
Management board member and chairman of research steering group, Investment Property Forum
Professional memberships
Investment Property Forum; Society of Business Economists; Society of Investment Professionals; Society of Property Researchers; Strategic Planning Institute
Contact details
Credit Suisse First Boston, One Cabot Square, London E14 4QJ
Tel 020 7888 8888
Fax 020 7883 5819
Web www.csfb.com
Direct tel 020 7883 6107
Direct fax 020 7883 7058
Mobile 07786 061337
Email john.gellatly@csfb.com

GEORGE, Christopher
Knight Frank

Position
Partner – joint head of hotels department
Qualifications
FRICS
Contact details
Knight Frank LLP, Hanover Court, 5 Hanover Square, London W1S 1HE
Tel 020 7629 8171
Fax 020 7493 4114
Web www.knightfrank.com
Direct tel 020 7861 1084
Direct fax 020 7409 7338
Email chris.george@knightfrank.com

GEORGE, Nigel
Derwent Valley Holdings

Position
Director
Qualifications
BSc; MRICS
Professional memberships
RICS
Contact details
Derwent Valley Holdings plc, 25 Savile Row, London W1S 2ER
Tel 020 7659 3000
Fax 020 7659 3100
Web www.derwentvalley.co.uk
Email nigel.george@derwentvalley.co.uk

GEORGE, Philip
Birkett Long

Position
Managing partner
Qualifications
MA Hons (Cantab)
Career history
1975 Joined Smith Morton & Long (now Birkett Long); became partner in 1976.
1975 Admitted to Roll of Solicitors.
1973-75 Beachcroft & Co (now Beachcroft Wansbroughs)
Other roles
Vice-chairman of governors, Colchester Royal Grammar School; trustee, Winsleys Almshouse Charity; board member, Colchester Business Enterprise Agency
Professional memberships
Education Law Association; Law Society; Society for Advanced Legal Studies
Interests
Cricket; IT; squash
Contact details
Birkett Long, Essex House, 42 Crouch Street, Colchester CO3 3HH
Tel 01206 217300
Fax 01206 765534
Web www.birkettlong.co.uk
Direct tel 01206 217315
Mobile 07831 504298
Email philipg@birkettlong.co.uk

GERMAN, John
Aberdeen Property Investors

Position
Director – residential asset management
Contact details
Aberdeen Property Investors, Charles House, 5-11 Regent Street, London SW1Y 4LR
Tel 020 7747 1700
Fax 020 7839 7460
Web www.aberdeenpropertyinvestors.com
Email
john.german@aberdeenpropertyinvestors.com

GEROLD, Mark
ATIS REAL Weatheralls

Position
Director – corporate services and valuation
Qualifications
BSc; FRICS
Career history
1972 Joined ATIS REAL Weatheralls; now head of valuation division and director of London corporate valuation services
Other roles
Chairman of RICS appraisal and valuation standards board and of public sector valuation group working party
Professional memberships
Non-Administrative Receivers Association; RICS
Interests
Charity; cycling
Contact details
ATIS REAL Weatheralls Ltd, 22 Chancery Lane, London WC2A 1LT
Tel 020 7338 4000
Fax 020 7430 2628
Web www.atisrealweatheralls.com
Direct tel 020 7338 4101
Direct fax 020 7242 3237
Email mark.gerold@atisrealweatheralls.com

GERSHINSON, Jon
Allsop & Co

Position
Partner – commercial valuations and insolvency
Qualifications
FRICS
Career history
1993 Joined Allsop & Co as associate; appointed partner in 1996.
1986-93 Associate/director, Hirshfields.
1982-86 Davis & Co
Professional memberships
RICS
Contact details
Allsop & Co, 27 Soho Square, London W1D 3AY
Tel 020 7437 6977
Fax 020 7437 8984
Web www.allsop.co.uk
Direct tel 020 7543 6743
Email jon.gershinson@allsop.co.uk

GERSTEIN, Richard
Goodman Derrick

Position
Partner – construction and dispute resolution
Career history
2002 Joined Goodman Derrick.
1987-2001 Finers/Finers Stephens Innocent: head of litigation 1987-97 and 2000-01, managing partner 1997-2000; head of hotel group 2000-01.
1982-87 Lipman Bray; appointed partner in 1984
Professional memberships
Chartered Institute of Arbitrators; Society of Construction Law
Interests
Cricket; football; golf
Contact details
Goodman Derrick, 90 Fetter Lane, London EC4A 1EQ
Tel 020 7404 0606
Fax 020 7831 6407
Web www.gdlaw.co.uk
Direct tel 020 7421 7934
Direct fax 020 7421 7966
Mobile 07788 992521
Email rgerstein@goodmanderrick.co.uk

GIBBON, Michael
Maitland Chambers

Position
Barrister
Qualifications
BA (Oxon); MPhil (Cantab)
Career history
1993 Called to Bar
Professional memberships
Chancery Bar Association; Wales & Chester Circuit
Contact details
Maitland Chambers, 7 Stone Buildings, London WC2A 3SZ
Tel 020 7406 1200
Fax 020 7406 1300
Web www.maitlandchambers.com
Email mgibbon@maitlandchambers.com

GIBBONS, Michael
Cyril Sweett

Position
Chief executive
Qualifications
BSc; FRICS
Career history
1975 Joined Cyril Sweett: became director of Cyril Sweett Project Consultants in 1985, partner of Cyril Sweett & Partners in 1986, managing director of Cyril Sweett Project Consultants in 1987, then managing director of Frank & Vargeson (Hong Kong) in 1994; chief executive of Cyril Sweett since 1998
Other roles
Director, nc sweett; director, Boyd & Creed Cyril Sweett
Professional memberships
RICS
Interests
Golf; sailing; tennis
Contact details
Cyril Sweett Ltd, 60 Gray's Inn Road, London WC1X 8AQ
Tel 020 7061 9000
Fax 020 7430 0603
Web www.cyrilsweett.co.uk
Mobile 07785 725230
Email sue.seamer@cyrilsweett.com

GIBBONS, Nigel
Alder King

Position
Partner
Contact details
Alder King, Pembroke House, 15 Pembroke Road, Bristol BS8 3BA
Tel 0117 317 1000
Fax 0117 317 1001
Web www.alderking.com
Direct tel 0117 317 1088
Email ngibbons@alderking.com

GIBSON, David
Association of Building Engineers

Position
Chief executive
Contact details
Association of Building Engineers, Lutyens House, Billing Brook Road, Northampton NN3 8NW
Tel 01604 404121
Fax 01604 784220
Email building.engineers@abe.org.uk

GIBSON, David
Burness

Position
Partner
Qualifications
LLB Hons; Dip LP; WS
Career history
1986 Admitted to Roll of Solicitors.
1984 Joined W&J Burness WS (now Burness); became partner in 1990
Professional memberships
Royal Faculty of Procurators; WS Society
Interests
Classic cars; golf; walking
Contact details
Burness, 242 West George Street, Glasgow G2 4QY
Tel 0141 248 4933
Fax 0141 204 1601
Web www.burness.co.uk
Email dbg@burness.co.uk

GIBSON, Geoffrey
Lambert Smith Hampton

Position
Director in charge – Leicester office
Qualifications
BSc; FRICS
Career history
Since 1986 Head of Leicester office, Lambert Smith Hampton and predecessors.
1983-86 Valuer, Leicestershire County Council.
1982-83 Surveyor, Britannic Assurance
Other roles
Treasurer, East Midlands Industrial Agents Society
Professional memberships
Industrial Agents Society; RICS
Interests
Football; keep fit; skiing
Contact details
Lambert Smith Hampton Ltd, 9 De Montfort Street, Leicester LE1 7GE
Tel 0116 255 2694
Fax 0116 255 5460
Web www.lsh.co.uk
Mobile 07711 237190
Email ggibson@lsh.co.uk

GIBSON, Scott
Dunedin Property

Position
Director
Qualifications
BSc; MRICS
Professional memberships
RICS
Interests
Football; golf; sailing
Contact details
Dunedin Property Ltd, 22 Rutland Street, Edinburgh EH1 2AN
Tel 0131 221 9799
Fax 0131 221 9533
Web www.dunedinproperty.co.uk
Mobile 07836 705109
Email sgibson@dunedinproperty.co.uk

G

GIDDINGS, Tony
Argent Group

Position
Construction director
Qualifications
BSc; FCIOB
Other roles
Past chairman of Design Build Foundation and responsible for amalgamation with Reading Construction Forum to form Be
Professional memberships
Chartered Institute of Building
Interests
Football; golf; rugby; skiing
Contact details
Argent Group plc, 5 Albany Courtyard, London W1J 0HF
Tel 020 7734 3721
Fax 020 7734 4474
Web www.argentgroup.plc.uk
Mobile 07836 367033
Email tonyg@argentgroup.plc.uk

GILBARD, Marc
Moorfield Group

Position
Managing director
Qualifications
BSc; MRICS
Career history
Since 1996 Managing director, Moorfield Group.
1994-96 Executive director, Goldman Sachs International.
1989-94 Director, NatWest Markets.
1987-89 Analyst/specialist sales, Union Bank of Switzerland.
1984-87 Associate partner, Edward Erdman.
Other roles
General advisory council member, BPF
Professional memberships
BPF; British Venture Capital Association; European Private Equity & Venture Capital Association; Financial Services Authority; Investment Property Forum; RICS
Interests
Martial arts; reading; squash; tennis; travel
Contact details
Moorfield Group Ltd, Premier House, 44-48 Dover Street, London W1S 4NX
Tel 020 7399 1900
Fax 020 7499 2114
Email marc.gilbard@moorfield.com

GILBART, Andrew
Kings Chambers

Position
Barrister – head of chambers
Qualifications
QC
Career history
1991 Appointed QC.
1972 Called to Bar
Other roles
Author of articles in *Journal of Planning & Environmental Law*; recorder of Crown Court; bencher of Middle Temple
Professional memberships
Administrative Law Bar Association; American Bar Association; Northern Circuit Commercial Bar Association; Planning & Environment Bar Association; UK Environmental Law Association
Interests
History; IT; theatre; travel; walking
Contact details
Kings Chambers, 40 King Street, Manchester M2 6BA
Tel 0161 832 9082
Fax 0161 835 2139
Web www.kingschambers.com
Email agilbart@kingschambers.com

GILBERT, David
Lambert Smith Hampton

Position
Director
Qualifications
BSc Hons; Dip Arb; FRICS; FCIArb; IRRV
Career history
1998 Joined Lambert Smith Hampton.
1988-98 Local director, Adkin.
1978-88 Valuation Office
Professional memberships
Centre for Effective Dispute Resolution; Chartered Institute of Arbitrators; RICS
Interests
Diving/scuba diving; fishing; martial arts; shooting
Contact details
Lambert Smith Hampton Ltd, Midland House, West Way, Oxford OX2 0PH
Tel 01865 200244
Fax 01865 204822
Web www.lsh.co.uk
Mobile 07711 484871
Email dgilbert@lsh.co.uk

GILBERT, Lynn
Morgan Stanley

Position
Head of European property lending
Career history
1998 Joined Morgan Stanley.
1990-98 Société Générale.
1988-90 Privatbanken
Interests
Contact details
Morgan Stanley, 25 Cabot Square, London E14 4QA
Tel 020 7513 8000
Fax 020 7513 8990
Web www.morganstanley.com
Direct tel 020 7677 9900
Direct fax 020 7677 4328
Mobile 07889 706993
Email lynn.gilbert@morganstanley.com

GILBERT, Mark
Addleshaw Goddard

Position
Partner
Qualifications
LLB (Lond)
Contact details
Addleshaw Goddard, 150 Aldersgate Street, London EC1A 4EJ
Tel 020 7606 8855
Fax 020 7606 4390
Web www.addleshawgoddard.com
Direct tel 020 7880 5700
Email mark.gilbert@addleshawgoddard.com

GILBERTSON, Barry
PricewaterhouseCoopers

Position
Partner – real estate, hospitality and leisure
Qualifications
FRICS
Career history
1992 Joined PricewaterhouseCoopers.
1987-92 Managing director, Claridge Group.
1980-87 Partner, Butler & Hatch Waterman
Other roles
Senior vice-president, RICS; member, United Nations real estate advisory group; founder chairman, Non-Administrative Receivers Association (1995-96); founder fellow, Institute of Continuing Professional Development; visiting professor of the built environment, Northumbria University; freeman, City of London; regularly publishes articles and speaks on international valuation standards and other topics; monthly opinion column in *Estates Gazette*
Professional memberships
Chartered Institute of Arbitrators; Counselors of Real Estate; Institute of Continuing Professional Development; Institute of Directors; RICS
Interests
Art; family; Rotary; running; sport
Contact details
PricewaterhouseCoopers, Plumtree Court, London EC4A 4HT

Tel 020 7583 5000
Fax 020 7862 4652
Web www.pwc.com
Direct tel 020 7212 3511
Direct fax 020 7213 8975
Mobile 07710 073456
Email barry.gilbertson@uk.pwc.com

GILBEY, Iain
Shoosmiths

Position
Partner – head of planning group
Qualifications
Solicitor
Career history
2000 Joined Shoosmiths.
1997-2000 Ashurst Morris Crisp.
1994 Admitted to Roll of Solicitors.
1992-97 Berwin Leighton
Professional memberships
Law Society; UK Environmental Law Association
Interests
Rugby; sport; travel
Contact details
Shoosmiths, 125 Colmore Row, Birmingham B3 3SH
Tel 0870 086 4000
Fax 0870 086 4001
Web www.shoosmiths.co.uk
Direct tel 0870 086 4110
Mobile 07802 539694
Email iain.gilbey@shoosmiths.co.uk

GILCHRIST, Robert
PRICOA Investment Management

Position
Managing director
Qualifications
MRICS
Career history
1987 Joined PRICOA; appointed director of PRICOA Property Investment Management in 1988; became chief executive of TransEuropean I in 1991; now also chief executive of TransEuropean II.
1983-87 DTZ
Professional memberships
RICS
Contact details
PRICOA Investment Management Ltd, 166 Sloane Street, London SW1X 9QF
Tel 020 7761 3300
Fax 020 7761 3400
Email robert.gilchrist@prudential.com

GILL, Nicholas
ING Real Estate Investment Management (UK)

Position
Director
Qualifications
BSc; FRICS
Career history
1988 Joined Baring, Houston & Saunders (now ING Real Estate Investment Management (UK)).
1984-88 Senior surveyor (investment department), Hillier Parker.
1980-84 St Quintin
Professional memberships
Investment Property Forum; RICS
Interests
Golf; sailing
Contact details
ING Real Estate Investment Management (UK) Ltd, 9 Devonshire Square, London EC2M 4WX
Tel 020 7398 4310
Fax 020 7398 4311
Web www.ingrealestate.co.uk
Direct tel 020 7398 5523
Mobile 07768 775901
Email nicholas.gill@ingrealestate.co.uk

GILLHAM, Barry
Fleurets

Position
Chairman
Qualifications
FRICS; MCIArb
Career history
1964 Joined Fleurets
Other roles
Past president, Association of Valuers of Licensed Property
Professional memberships
Arbrix; Association of Valuers of Licensed Property; Chartered Institute of Arbitrators; RICS
Interests
Hockey
Contact details
Fleurets Ltd, 18 Bloomsbury Square, London WC1A 2NS
Tel 020 7636 8992
Fax 020 7636 7490
Web www.fleurets.com
Email london@fleurets.com

GILLIES, Sean
Dalgleish

Position
Director – retail, Midlands and East Anglia
Contact details
Dalgleish, 80 New Bond Street, London W1S 1DD
Tel 020 7663 5555
Fax 020 7491 0098
Web www.dalgleish.co.uk
Direct tel 020 7663 5531
Mobile 07967 697919
Email sgillies@dalgleish.co.uk

GILLINGHAM, Martyn
Lambert Smith Hampton

Position
Director
Qualifications
FRICS; MIMgt
Professional memberships
RICS
Contact details
Lambert Smith Hampton Ltd, Greenwood House, 91-99 New London Road, Chelmsford CM2 0PP
Tel 01245 215521
Fax 01245 355877
Web www.lsh.co.uk
Email mgillingham@lsh.co.uk

GILLINGHAM, Nigel
Markham Vaughan Gillingham

Position
Director
Career history
1988 Joined Markham Vaughan Gillingham
Professional memberships
Shop Agents Society
Contact details
Markham Vaughan Gillingham, Clifton Heights, Bristol BS8 1EJ
Tel 0117 909 9000
Fax 0117 915 9764
Web www.mvgretail.com
Mobile 07976 645849
Email ngillingham@mvgretail.com

GILLINGWATER, Clive
Gooch Cunliffe Whale

Position
Director
Qualifications
BSc; FRICS; MCIArb
Contact details
Gooch Cunliffe Whale Ltd, Allan House, 10 John Princes Street, London W1G 0JW
Tel 020 7408 0030
Fax 020 7495 4248
Web www.gcw.co.uk
Direct tel 020 7647 4801
Email clive.gillingwater@gcw.co.uk

G

GILLON, George
LSM Partners

Position
Chairman
Qualifications
FRICS
Career history
Since 2002 Chairman, LSM Partners.
1986-2002 Partner, Drivers Jonas.
1965-86 Associate partner, Richard Ellis.
1963-65 Graham & Sibbald
Other roles
Non-executive director, Stewart Milne Group; member, Court of Common Council, City of London (Cordwainer Ward); master, Chartered Surveyors' Company (2002-03); chairman, Caledonian Club (since 2003); director, Caledonian Club Trust; governor, City of London School for Girls
Professional memberships
CBI; Institute of Directors; RICS
Interests
Fly fishing; travel; walking
Contact details
LSM Partners, 25 James Street, London W1U 1DU
Tel 020 7616 0100
Fax 020 7616 0101
Web www.lsmpartners.co.uk
Mobile 07774 409367
Email ggillon@lsmpartners.co.uk

GILMAN, Tom
Kier Property

Position
Director – office development and investment
Qualifications
MRICS
Contact details
Kier Property Ltd, Berkeley Square House, Berkeley Square, London W1J 6BD
Tel 020 7887 6200
Fax 020 7887 6299
Web www.kier.co.uk
Direct tel 020 7887 6285
Mobile 07766 603447
Email tom.gilman@kier.co.uk

GILMOUR, Moira
Field Fisher Waterhouse

Position
Head of property
Qualifications
MA; LLB
Career history
1998 Joined as partner, Field Fisher Waterhouse.
1994-98 Partner, Allison & Humphreys.
1988-94 Partner, Kennedys.
1986-88 Partner, Blyth Dutton.
1985-86 Nabarro Nathanson.
1981-85 McGrigor Donald.
1981 Admitted to Roll of Solicitors
Professional memberships
Law Society of Scotland; Law Society
Interests
Art; history; literature; sailing
Contact details
Field Fisher Waterhouse, 35 Vine Street, London EC3N 2AA
Tel 020 7861 4000
Fax 020 7488 0084
Web www.ffwlaw.com
Direct tel 020 7861 4115
Email Moira.Gilmour@ffw.com

GILROY, Stephen
storeys:ssp

Position
Director
Contact details
storeys:ssp, Higham House, New Bridge Street West, Newcastle upon Tyne NE1 8AU
Tel 0191 232 6291
Fax 0191 232 4610
Web www.storeys-ssp.com
Email stephen.gilroy@storeys-ssp.co.uk

GIRLING, Mark
Montagu Evans

Position
Partner
Qualifications
BSc Hons; MRICS
Career history
2002-03 Director, Insignia Richard Ellis.
1996-2002 Partner (investment), Knight Frank.
1991-96 Director (investment), Herring Baker Harris.
1983-91 Associate partner (investments), Pepper Angliss & Yarwood
Professional memberships
RICS
Contact details
Montagu Evans, 44-48 Dover Street, London W1S 4AZ
Tel 020 7493 4002
Fax 020 7312 7547
Web www.montagu-evans.co.uk
Email mark.girling@montagu-evans.co.uk

GIROLAMI, Paul
Maitland Chambers

Position
Barrister
Qualifications
QC
Contact details
Maitland Chambers, 7 Stone Buildings, London WC2A 3SZ
Tel 020 7406 1200
Fax 020 7406 1300
Web www.maitlandchambers.com
Email clerks@maitlandchambers.com

GLADWYN, John
Transcend Property

Position
Director
Qualifications
MRICS
Career history
1995-2001 FPDSavills
Professional memberships
RICS
Interests
Skiing
Contact details
Transcend Property Ltd, Berkeley Square House, Berkeley Square, London W1J 6BU
Tel 020 7887 6200
Fax 020 7887 6299
Web www.kier.co.uk
Direct tel 020 7887 6282
Mobile 07989 385020
Email john.gladwyn@kier.co.uk

GLANFIELD, Cliff
Etam

Position
Head of property
Qualifications
Bsc Hons; MRICS
Professional memberships
RICS
Interests
Cricket; music; running
Contact details
Etam plc, Jubilee House, 207-213 Oxford Street, London W1D 2LF
Tel 020 7437 5655
Fax 020 7734 0326
Web www.etam.com
Direct tel 020 7494 7323
Direct fax 020 7494 7323
Email c-glanfield@etam.co.uk

GLANVILLE, Kerry
Pemberton Greenish

Position
Partner – head of property litigation
Qualifications

MCIArb
Professional memberships
Chartered Institute of Arbitrators; Property Litigation Association
Interests
Horse riding; orchid growing
Contact details
Pemberton Greenish, 45 Pont Street, London SW1X 0BX
Tel 020 7591 3333
Fax 020 7591 3300
Web www.pglaw.co.uk
Direct tel 020 7591 3394
Email k.glanville@pglaw.co.uk

GLATMAN, Mark
Abstract Securities
Position
Chief executive
Career history
1988-2000 Chief executive, Akeler.
1985-88 Director, Baltic
Other roles
Trustee, Sick Children's Trust; honorary doctorate in business administration, University of Sunderland
Professional memberships
Law Society
Interests
Art; photography; shooting
Contact details
Abstract Securities Ltd, Queens House, 34 Wellington Street, Leeds LS1 2DE
Tel 0113 246 0060
Fax 0113 244 8340
Email mark.glatman@abstractsecurities.com

GLEDHILL, Ken
Henry Boot Developments
Position
Managing director
Qualifications
BSc; CEng; MICE
Career history
1979 Joined Henry Boot Developments as development manager; appointed director in 1983 and managing director in 1986
Other roles
Managing director of Henry Boot Estates, Henry Boot Projects and First National Housing Trust
Professional memberships
Institution of Civil Engineers
Interests
Golf; guitar; music; piano; singing (singing appearances on Granada and Anglia TV); saxophone; after-dinner speaking
Contact details
Henry Boot Developments Ltd, Banner Cross Hall, 55 Ecclesall Road South, Sheffield S11 9PD
Tel 0114 255 5444
Fax 0114 258 5548
Web www.henrybootdevelopments.co.uk
Email kgledhill@henryboot.co.uk

GLEEK, Julian
Burford Group
Position
Finance director
Contact details
Burford Group Ltd, 20 Thayer Street, London W1U 2DD
Tel 020 7224 2240
Fax 020 7224 1710
Email julian.gleek@burfordgroup.com

GLEN, Philip
17 Carlton Crescent
Position
Barrister
Career history
1983 Called to Bar
Other roles
Deputy district judge
Professional memberships
Bar Council
Interests
Sailing
Contact details
17 Carlton Crescent (Chambers of Jeremy Gibbons QC), Southampton SO15 2XR
Tel 023 8032 0320
Fax 023 8032 0321
Email Pglen@17cc.co.uk

GLENNIE, George
Gerald Eve
Position
Partner and head of business space agency, London
Qualifications
BSc; MRICS
Career history
1993 Joined Gerald Eve
Professional memberships
Industrial Agents Society; RICS
Interests
Sailing; shooting; skiing
Contact details
Gerald Eve, 7 Vere Street, London W1G 0JB
Tel 020 7493 3338
Fax 020 7491 1825
Web www.geraldeve.com
Direct tel 020 7333 6323
Direct fax 020 7333 6408
Mobile 07785 950769
Email gglennie@geraldeve.com

GLOSSOP, Anthony
St Modwen Properties
Position
Chairman elect
Career history
1972 Joined St Modwen Properties (formerly Redman Heenan International) as company secretary; appointed executive director in 1975, chief executive in 1982 and deputy chairman in 1998; now chairman elect.
1969-72 Assistant company secretary, Molins.
1967-69 Partner, W&A Glossop Solicitors
Other roles
Non-executive director, Robinson & Sons; chairman, Worcester CAB
Interests
Family; gardening; sport; walking
Contact details
St Modwen Properties plc, Lyndon House, 62 Hagley Road, Birmingham B16 8PE
Tel 0121 456 2800
Fax 0121 456 1829
Web www.stmodwen.co.uk
Email aglossop@stmodwen.co.uk

GLOSTER, Malcolm
GVA Grimley
Position
Partner in charge, Birmingham office
Qualifications
FRICS
Career history
1976 Joined GVA Grimley; resident partner, Grimley & Son (Florida) 1981-82; on secondment to DOE urban development grant appraiser 1984-86; appointed regional senior partner (Midlands) in 1995
Other roles
Board member and chairman elect from 2004, Birmingham Forward; board member, Locate in Birmingham; council member, West Midlands CBI; director, British American Business Council in the Midlands
Professional memberships
RICS
Interests
Golf; hill walking; rugby; skiing; tennis
Contact details
GVA Grimley, 3 Brindleyplace, Birmingham B1 2JB
Tel 0870 900 8990
Fax 0121 609 8314
Web www.gvagrimley.co.uk

Direct tel 0121 609 8417
Direct fax 0121 609 8011
Mobile 07831 820623
Email malcolm.gloster@gvagrimley.co.uk

GLOVER, Edward
HSBC Specialist Investments

Position
Director – head of property
Qualifications
ACIB
Professional memberships
Association of Property Bankers; Chartered Institute of Bankers
Contact details
HSBC Specialist Investments Ltd, 8 Canada Square, London E14 5HQ
Tel 020 7991 8888
Fax 020 7991 4310
Web www.hsbc.com
Email natasha.l.allen@hsbcib.com

GLOVER, Paul
Civil Aviation Authority

Position
Property manager
Contact details
Civil Aviation Authority, CAA House, 45-59 Kingsway, London WC2B 6TE
Tel 020 7379 7311
Web www.caa.co.uk
Email paul.glover@caa.co.uk

GLOVER, Richard
2 Mitre Court Buildings

Position
Barrister
Qualifications
BA Hons (Cantab)
Career history
1984 Called to Bar
Other roles
Committee member, Parliamentary Bar Mess; editor, *Butterworths' Local Government Law*; editor, *Ryde on Rating & the Council Tax*; editor, *Halsbury's Laws* (on rating)
Professional memberships
Planning & Environment Bar Association
Interests
Food; horse racing; opera; reading; wine
Contact details
2 Mitre Court Buildings (Chambers of Guy Roots QC), 2nd Floor, London EC4Y 7BX
Tel 020 7583 1380
Fax 020 7353 7772
Web www.2mcb.co.uk
Email richard.glover@2mcb.co.uk

GLOYENS, Patrick
Dechert

Position
Partner
Qualifications
LLB Hons
Career history
Since 1987 Partner, Dechert.
1983-87 Partner, George Carter & Co.
Other roles
Recommended in *Insider's Guide to Commercial Property*; co-author, *Securitisation – Freedom for Stranded Capital*
Professional memberships
BPF; Leisure Property Forum
Interests
Fly fishing; gardening
Contact details
Dechert LLP, 2 Serjeants' Inn, London EC4Y 1LT
Tel 020 7583 5353
Fax 020 7353 3683
Web www.dechert.com
Email patrick.gloyens@dechert.com

GLOYN, William
AON Risk Services

Position
Chairman – European commercial property group
Career history
1989-92 Vice-president (insurance), Olympia & York Canary Wharf.
1983-89 Managing director (commercial property services), Clarkson.
1969-83 Group insurance manager, English Property Corp
Other roles
Member of BPF general advisory council, chairman of BPF insurance committee, and represents BPF on several external committees; lecturer for master's degree in construction law, Kings College, London; freeman of the City of London
Professional memberships
British Council for Offices; BPF; Chartered Insurance Institute; FIABCI; Society of Construction Law; Worshipful Company of Masons
Interests
Family; music
Contact details
AON Risk Services Ltd, 6 Devonshire Square, London EC2M 4PL
Tel 020 7623 5500
Fax 020 7882 0208
Direct tel 020 7882 0203
Email bill.gloyn@ars.aon.co.uk

GLYNN, Andrew
TLT Solicitors

Position
Partner – head of property group
Qualifications
LLB
Career history
1992 Joined TLT Solicitors, appointed partner in 1994; head of property group since 1999.
1985-92 Worked in London, primarily for Rowe & Maw.
1985 Admitted to Roll of Solicitors
Professional memberships
Non-Administrative Receivers Association; Mining & Mineral Law Group
Contact details
TLT Solicitors, 1 Redcliffe Street, Bristol BS99 7JZ
Tel 0117 917 7777
Fax 0117 917 7779
Web www.tltsolicitors.com
Direct tel 0117 917 7926
Direct fax 0117 917 7781
Mobile 07768 526638
Email aglynn@TLTsolicitors.com

GODDARD, Chris
GVA Grimley

Position
Partner and head of retail and town-centre planning
Qualifications
MRTPI; MRICS
Career history
1989-2003 CB Hillier Parker.
1987-89 Grimleys
Contact details
GVA Grimley, 10 Stratton Street, London W1J 8JR
Tel 0870 900 8990
Fax 020 7911 2560
Web www.gvagrimley.co.uk
Email chris.goddard@gvagrimley.co.uk

GODDARD, John
Early Learning Centre

Position
Property director
Qualifications
BSc, Land Econ; MRICS
Professional memberships
RICS
Interests
Football
Contact details
Early Learning Centre Ltd, South Marston Park, Swindon SN3 4TJ

Tel 01793 831300
Fax 01793 824114
Web www.elc.co.uk
Direct tel 01793 443232
Mobile 07771 805911
Email john.goddard@elc.co.uk

GODDEN, David
Land Securities Trillium

Position
Chief operating officer
Contact details
Land Securities Trillium Ltd, 140 London Wall, London EC2Y 5DN
Tel 020 7796 5500
Fax 020 7796 5501
Web www.landsecurities.co.uk
Email david.godden@lstrillium.com

GODFREY, Adam
Stiles Harold Williams

Position
Director
Qualifications
FRICS
Contact details
Stiles Harold Williams Ltd, Sterling House, High Street, Crawley RH10 1GE
Tel 0129 344 1300
Fax 0129 344 1334
Web www.shw.co.uk
Email agodfrey@shw.co.uk

GODFREY, Nigel
Gazeley Properties

Position
Development director
Qualifications
MRICS
Career history
1988 Joined Gazeley Properties as development manager; development director since 1990.
1977-88 Surveyor/development manager/ development director, Safeway
Professional memberships
RICS
Contact details
Gazeley Properties Ltd, Gazeley House, 26 Rockingham Drive, Milton Keynes MK14 6PD
Tel 01908 838100
Fax 01908 838101
Web www.gazeley.com
Direct tel 01908 838182
Email nigel_godfrey@gazeley.co.uk

GODFREY, Tony
Aberdeen Property Investors

Position
Director – property management
Qualifications
MRICS
Contact details
Aberdeen Property Investors, Charles House, 5-11 Regent Street, London SW1Y 4LR
Tel 020 7747 1700
Fax 020 7839 7460
Web www.aberdeenpropertyinvestors.com
Direct tel 020 7747 1717
Email
tony.godfrey@aberdeenpropertyinvestors.com

GOING, Patrick
Akeler Developments

Position
Director – UK projects
Qualifications
MRICS
Career history
2001 Joined Akeler Developments.
1987-2001 Healey & Baker
Professional memberships
RICS
Interests
Art; golf; rugby
Contact details
Akeler Developments Ltd, 7 Clifford Street, London W1S 2WE
Tel 020 7864 1800
Fax 020 7864 1801
Web www.akeler.com
Direct tel 020 7864 1854
Mobile 07810 158404
Email patrickg@akeler.com

GOLD, Peter
Michael Peddar & Co

Position
Director
Qualifications
MRICS; IRRV; ACIArb
Professional memberships
Chartered Institute of Arbitrators; Institute of Revenues Rating & Valuation; RICS
Contact details
Michael Peddar & Co, 12 John Princes Street, London W1G 0NY
Tel 020 7629 3004
Fax 020 7491 3314
Web www.michaelpeddar.co.uk
Email pgold@michaelpeddar.co.uk

GOLDIE-SCOT, Neil
HSBC Bank

Position
Head of property
Other roles
Managing director, HSBC corporate finance and advisory
Contact details
HSBC Bank plc, 8 Canada Square, London E14 5HQ
Tel 020 7991 8888
Fax 020 7992 4880
Web www.hsbc.com
Direct tel 020 7992 2452
Direct fax 020 7991 4420
Email neil.goldie-scot@hsbcib.com

GOLDSMITH, James
FPDSavills

Position
Director – international investment
Contact details
FPDSavills Ltd, 20 Grosvenor Hill, London W1K 3HQ
Tel 020 7499 8644
Fax 020 7495 3773
Web www.fpdsavills.co.uk
Direct tel 020 7499 9918
Mobile 07870 555747
Email jgoldsmith@fpdsavills.co.uk

GOLDSTEIN, Peter
Michael Elliott

Position
Joint managing director
Contact details
Michael Elliott, 53 Brooks Mews, London W1K 4ED
Tel 020 7493 8184
Fax 020 7409 2985
Email petergoldstein@michaelelliott.co.uk

GOLDSTONE, David
Longford Business Centres

Position
Chairman
Qualifications
LLB Hons
Career history
Since 2001 Chairman, Longford Business Centres.
1967-2001 Founder, Regalian Properties; became chairman in 1971.
1955-66 Legal practice
Other roles
Deputy chairman, University of London council; deputy chairman, University of London estates

advisory committee; council member and member of finance committee, Royal Albert Hall; director, Wales Millennium Centre; chairman, Coram Family; fellow, London School of Economics

Professional memberships
Law Society

Interests
Football; rugby; tennis

Contact details
Longford Business Centres Ltd, 16a Curzon Street, London W1J 5HP
Tel 020 7070 3570
Direct tel 020 7659 0413
Email djg@davstone.co.uk

GOMERSALL, Peter
Gazeley Properties

Position
Development director – Germany

Contact details
Gazeley Properties Ltd, Gazeley House, 26 Rockingham Drive, Milton Keynes MK14 6PD
Tel 01908 838100
Fax 01908 838101
Web www.gazeley.com
Email peter.gomersall@gazeley.com

GOOCH, David
Gooch Cunliffe Whale

Position
Director

Qualifications
BSc; FRICS

Career history
Since 1989 Director, Gooch Cunliffe Whale.
1987-89 Associate partner, Blair Kirkman.
1982-86 Healey & Baker

Professional memberships
RICS; Shop Agents Society

Interests
Hockey; squash

Contact details
Gooch Cunliffe Whale Ltd, Allan House, 10 John Princes Street, London W1G 0JW
Tel 020 7408 0030
Fax 020 7495 4248
Web www.gcw.co.uk
Direct tel 020 7647 4808
Mobile 07971 958626
Email david.gooch@gcw.co.uk

GOOD, James
Brixton Investments

Position
Director – investment and portfolio management

Qualifications
MRICS; BSc Hons

Career history
2000 Joined Brixton Investments as associate director; promoted to director in 2002.
1998-2000 Senior asset manager, Legal & General Property.
1994-98 CB Hillier Parker

Professional memberships
RICS

Interests
Sport; tennis; wine

Contact details
Brixton Investments Ltd, 50 Berkeley Street, London W1J 8BX
Tel 020 7399 4500
Fax 020 7399 4550
Web www.brixton.plc.uk
Direct tel 020 7399 4520
Mobile 07887 545534
Email jamesgood@brixton.plc.uk

GOODCHILD, David
Aitchison Raffety

Position
Group director – head of professional services

Qualifications
MRICS; IRRV

Professional memberships
Institute of Revenues Rating & Valuation; RICS

Contact details
Aitchison Raffety Ltd, 63-65 Marlowes, Hemel Hempstead HP1 1LE
Tel 01442 220800
Fax 01442 230114
Web www.argroup.co.uk
Email david.goodchild@argroup.co.uk

GOODCHILD, Dr Robin
LaSalle Investment Management

Position
Head of European investment strategy

Qualifications
MA; PhD; FRICS

Career history
1997 Joined LaSalle Investment Management.
1995-97 Principal, Property Investment Solutions.
1978-95 Gerald Eve; partner from 1983.
1975-78 Research student, University of Cambridge.
1971-75 Gerald Eve

Other roles
Visiting professor, Nottingham Trent University

Professional memberships
Investment Property Forum; RICS; Society of Property Researchers; Worshipful Company of Chartered Surveyors

Interests
Cricket; real tennis

Contact details
LaSalle Investment Management, 33 Cavendish Square, London W1A 2NF
Tel 020 7852 4000
Fax 020 7852 4374
Web www.lasalle.com
Direct tel 020 7852 4390
Direct fax 020 7852 4447
Email robin.goodchild@lasalle.com

GOODEY, Mark
Deloitte

Position
Lead partner – property companies

Career history
1981 Joined Deloitte

Contact details
Deloitte, Hill House, 1 Little New Street, London EC4A 3TR
Tel 020 7936 3000
Fax 020 7583 8517
Web www.deloitte.co.uk
Direct tel 020 7007 0851
Direct fax 020 7007 0150
Email mgoodey@deloitte.co.uk

GOODFORD-BROER, Emma
Knight Frank

Position
Partner – national offices

Qualifications
BS Hons, Est Man; MRICS

Career history
1987 Joined Knight Frank

Professional memberships
RICS

Interests
Diving/scuba diving

Contact details
Knight Frank LLP, 20 Hanover Square, London W1S 1HZ
Tel 020 7629 8171
Fax 020 7493 4114
Web www.knightfrank.com
Direct tel 020 7861 1144
Direct fax 020 7495 0925
Mobile 07831 581258
Email emma.goodford-broer@knightfrank.com

GOODMAN, Andrew
No 1 Serjeants' Inn

Position
Barrister

Qualifications

LLB Hons; FCIArb

Career history

1978 Called to Bar

Other roles

Registered CEDR mediator since 1993; founder member and secretary, Professional Negligence Bar Association (1990); executive committee member, London Common Law & Commercial Bar Association; author and editor, *The Court Guide* (OUP, 18th edition, 2004) and *The Prison Guide* (Blackstone, 1999); author, *RCJ Guide* (Longman, 1985); produces *The RCJ Plans* (Legastat); contributor to *Commercial Lawyer*; has appeared on Legal Network Television; an editor of *Professional Negligence & Liability Reports* (Sweet & Maxwell), *The Journal of ADR, Mediation & Negotiation* (CLT) and *Advising Business & Law* (Emis)

Professional memberships

Centre for Effective Dispute Resolution; Chancery Bar Association; Chartered Institute of Arbitrators; Honourable Society of the Inner Temple; London Common Law & Commercial Bar Association; Professional Negligence Bar Association

Interests

Music; travel; writing

Contact details

No 1 Serjeants' Inn (Chambers of Edward Faulks QC), Fleet Street, London EC4Y 1LH
Tel 020 7415 6666
Fax 020 7583 2033
Web www.no1serjeantsinn.co.uk
Email agoodman@no1serjeantsinn.com

GOODMAN, Everard
Tops Estates

Position

Executive chairman

Qualifications

FCA

Career history

1982 Founded Tops Estates

Other roles

Liveryman, City of London; founded Trust of Property Shares (an authorised investment trust); winner, British Council of Shopping Centres Refurbishment First Award for UK Shopping Centres (1998); donor to charitable projects (particular interest in health and education)

Professional memberships

Institute of Chartered Accountants in England & Wales

Interests

Opera; theatre

Contact details

Tops Estates plc, 77 South Audley Street, London W1K 1EE
Tel 020 7355 3000
Fax 020 7355 2222
Email everard.goodman@topsestates.co.uk

GOODRICH, Leonard
Lewis Silkin

Position

Partner – head of property department

Qualifications

LLB Hons

Career history

1982 Admitted to Roll of Solicitors.
1980 Joined Lewis Silkin; appointed partner in 1985

Professional memberships

City of Westminster & Holborn Law Society; Law Society

Interests

Family; music

Contact details

Lewis Silkin, 12 Gough Square, London EC4A 3DW
Tel 020 7074 8000
Fax 020 7832 1200
Direct fax 020 7832 1756
Email leonard.goodrich@lewissilkin.com

GOODWIN, Colin
AXA Real Estate Investment Managers

Position

Fund manager

Qualifications

Dip Prop Inv; MRICS

Career history

1988 Joined AXA Real Estate Investment Managers (formerly AXA Equity & Law Investment Managers) as property manager; became fund manager in 2002.
1978-88 Commercial department manager, Levens

Professional memberships

RICS

Contact details

AXA Real Estate Investment Managers Ltd, 7 Newgate Street, London EC1A 7HD
Tel 020 7003 1000
Fax 020 7575 8585
Web www.axa-im.co.uk
Email colin.goodwin@axa-reim.co.uk

GORDON, Donald
Liberty International

Position

Chairman

Career history

1980 Founded Liberty International; chairman since 1986

Other roles

Honorary president for life, Liberty Group (formerly the controlling shareholder of Liberty International); chairman, CSC and Capital & Counties

Contact details

Liberty International plc, 40 Broadway, London SW1H 0BT
Tel 020 7960 1200
Fax 020 7960 1333
Email carolyn-kenyon@lib-int.com

GORDON, Douglas
Dawnay, Day Property Finance

Position

Chairman

Interests

Shooting (Property Gun & Punt Club); Caledonian Society

Contact details

Dawnay, Day Property Finance Ltd, 7 Beeston Place, London SW1W 0JJ
Tel 020 7828 8344
Fax 020 7630 0122
Web www.dawnayday.co.uk
Email dgordon@dawnayday.co.uk

GORE, Richard
Block Holdings

Position

Managing director

Qualifications

BSc Hons; MRICS

Career history

Since 2003 Managing director, Block Holdings.
1997-2003 Director, Capital & Regional Investments.
1992-97 Managing director, Lanham.
1989-92 Director, Lansbury Holdings.
1985-89 Director, Citygrove

Professional memberships

RICS

Contact details

Block Holdings Ltd, Crown House, 72 Hammersmith Road, London W14 8TH
Tel 020 7559 9730
Fax 020 7559 9731
Mobile 07778 052252
Email rgore@blockproperties.co.uk

GORING, Mark
Council for Licensed Conveyancers

Position

Acting director of the council

Qualifications

LLB Hons; Solicitor

Contact details

G

Council for Licensed Conveyancers, 16 Glebe Road, Chelmsford CM1 1QG
Tel 01245 349599
Fax 01245 341300
Web www.theclc.gov.uk
Email CLC@theclc.gov.uk

GOSWELL, Paul
Delancey

Position
Managing director
Qualifications
BSc; MRICS
Career history
1996 Joined Freehold Portfolios (Delancey bought Freehold Portfolios in 1998).
1987-96 Partner, Healey & Baker
Professional memberships
RICS
Contact details
Delancey, 40 Portman Square, London W1H 0AA
Tel 020 7486 6663
Fax 020 7486 6662
Web www.delancey.com
Email paul.goswell@delancey.com

GOUGH, Carl
Credit Suisse First Boston

Position
Director – European real estate
Contact details
Credit Suisse First Boston, One Cabot Square, London E14 4QJ
Tel 020 7888 8888
Fax 020 7883 5819
Web www.csfb.com
Email carl.gough@csfb.com

GOULBORN, Keith
Unilever

Position
Property controller
Qualifications
FRICS
Career history
1976 Joined Unilever.
1963-76 Debenham Nightingale Chancellors: partner on leaving
Professional memberships
Association of Corporate Real Estate; RICS
Interests
Golf; motor sports; running; tennis
Contact details
Unilever plc, Walton Court, Station Avenue, Walton-on-Thames KT12 1UP
Tel 020 7822 5252
Fax 020 7822 5898
Web www.unilever.com
Direct tel 0193 226 1550
Direct fax 0193 226 1555
Mobile 07802 462663
Email keith.goulborn@unilever.com

GOULD, Dr Andrew
Jones Lang LaSalle

Position
International director – strategic consultancy
Contact details
Jones Lang LaSalle Ltd, 22 Hanover Square, London W1A 2BN
Tel 020 7493 6040
Fax 020 7408 0220
Web www.joneslanglasalle.com
Direct tel 020 7399 5877
Direct fax 020 7399 5688
Mobile 07774 483361
Email andrew.gould@eu.joneslanglasalle.com

GOVE, Alastair
FG Burnett

Position
Director
Qualifications
FRICS; FCIArb; IRRV
Contact details
FG Burnett, 33 Albyn Place, Aberdeen AB10 1YL
Tel 01224 572661
Fax 01224 593496
Web www.fgburnett.co.uk
Email ajg@fgburnett.co.uk

GOWMAN, Louise
Tite & Lewis

Position
Partner – head of real estate
Qualifications
BA
Career history
1998-2000 Partner, Landwell.
1997-98 Tite & Lewis.
1991 Admitted to Roll of Solicitors.
1989-97 Stephenson Harwood
Other roles
Solicitor of the Supreme Court
Professional memberships
Law Society
Contact details
Tite & Lewis, Alder Castle, 10 Noble Street, London EC2V 7TL
Tel 020 7606 2211
Fax 020 7606 3311
Web www.titeandlewis.com
Direct tel 020 7785 1201
Email louise.gowman@titeandlewis.com

GRAHAM, Charles
Europa Capital Partners

Position
Chief executive officer
Qualifications
BSc, Est Man
Other roles
Director, Pacific Investments; director, River & Mercantile; director, AIG French Property Fund Management; director, General Property Investment Co; director, Pacific Investments (Asia)
Interests
Ballet; opera; travel; wine
Contact details
Europa Capital Partners Ltd, 136 Sloane Street, London SW1X 9AY
Tel 020 7881 6800
Fax 020 7881 0501
Web www.europafund.com
Direct tel 020 7881 6810
Mobile 07770 915056
Email
charles.graham@europacapitalpartners.com

GRAHAM, Peter
Stephenson & Alexander

Position
Lead partner
Qualifications
BSc; Dip Prop Inv; FRICS
Career history
Since 1995 Partner, Stephenson & Alexander.
1979-95 DTZ (formerly DTC): associate partner and director since mid-1980s
Interests
Sport
Contact details
Stephenson & Alexander, 5 High Street, Cardiff CF10 1PZ
Tel 029 2034 0244
Fax 029 2022 0469
Direct tel 029 2022 0510
Email petergraham@SandA.uk.com

GRAHAM, William
Fleurets

Position
Director
Qualifications
BSc; FRICS
Career history
1984 Joined Fleurets; previously with Watneys London, Manns Northampton Brewery Co and

Berni Inns

Interests

Art; golf (Hanbury Manor Golf Club); skiing; Unity Club

Contact details

Fleurets Ltd, 18 Bloomsbury Square, London WC1A 2NS

Tel 020 7636 8992

Fax 020 7636 7490

Web www.fleurets.com

Mobile 07774 989270

Email bill.graham@fleurets.com

GRAHAM-CAMPBELL, Alastair
Knight Frank

Position

Partner – investment

Qualifications

BSc; MRICS

Career history

1995 Joined Knight Frank.

1991-95 Associate director, Herring Baker Harris

Professional memberships

RICS

Interests

Fishing; sailing; skiing

Contact details

Knight Frank LLP, 20 Hanover Square, London W1S 1HZ

Tel 020 7629 8171

Fax 020 7493 4114

Web www.knightfrank.com

Direct tel 020 7861 1219

Direct fax 020 7861 1371

Mobile 07767 754398

Email

alastair.graham-campbell@knightfrank.com

GRAHAM-WATSON, Freddie
Allied London Properties

Position

Finance director

Qualifications

FCA; ATII

Career history

1986-90 Group financial controller and company secretary, Clayform Properties (now Development Securities).

1979-86 Manager, KPMG

Interests

Classical music; family; sailing; squash; tennis

Contact details

Allied London Properties Ltd, 40 Portman Square, London W1H 6LT

Tel 020 7486 6080

Fax 020 7299 2611

Web www.allied-london-properties.com

Direct tel 020 7299 2640

Direct fax 020 7299 2629

Email freddiegw@alp.co.uk

GRAINGER, Andrew
British Airways

Position

Head of property strategy

Qualifications

BSc; MRICS

Career history

1998 Joined British Airways as chief surveyor; appointed head of property strategy in 2000.

1990-98 London Docklands Development Corp: became head of land development and property marketing in 1997.

1984-90 Regional estate manager (Charrington & Co), Bass

Professional memberships

RICS

Interests

Skiing; travel; walking

Contact details

British Airways plc, West Drayton UB7 0GB

Tel 020 8738 5050

Web www.britishairways.com

Direct tel 020 8738 3261

Mobile 07771 835856

Email jit.1.brar@britishairways.com

GRANT, Anthony
Sutton Park Estates Corp

Position

President

Qualifications

FRICS

Career history

Since 1998 Active as private investor in UK and USA.

1993-98 Chairman and joint chief executive, Olives Property.

1987-93 President and chief executive (based in New York), London & Leeds Development Corp.

1965-87 Founder, Grant & Partners, Mayfair

Other roles

Past world president, FIABCI

Professional memberships

FIABCI; RICS

Contact details

Sutton Park Estates Corp, 5030 Forsythia Circle, Murrells Inlet, South Carolina 29576, USA

Tel +1 843 357 8755

Fax +1 843 357 8787

Email tonygrant@sc.rr.com

GRANT, Ian
Crown Estate

Position

Chairman and commissioner

Qualifications

CBE

Other roles

Chairman, Scottish Exhibition Centre; deputy chairman, NFU Mutual Insurance Society

Contact details

Crown Estate, 16 Carlton House Terrace, London SW1Y 5AH

Tel 020 7210 4377

Fax 020 7210 4236

Web www.crownestate.co.uk

Email ian.grant@crownestate.co.uk

GRANT, Peter
B&Q

Position

Director – estates management

Contact details

B&Q plc, Link House, 2 Stoneycroft Rise, Chandlers Ford S053 3YU

Tel 023 8062 5000

Web www.b-and-qproperty.co.uk

Direct tel 023 8062 5219

Direct fax 023 8062 5299

Mobile 07774 830088

Email peter.grant@b-and-q.co.uk

GRANT, Peter
Montagu Evans

Position

Partner – investment and development

Qualifications

BLE; MRICS

Professional memberships

RICS

Interests

Entertaining; golf; wine

Contact details

Montagu Evans, 37 Melville Street, Edinburgh EH3 7JF

Tel 0131 225 9541

Fax 0131 225 3677

Web www.montagu-evans.co.uk

Direct tel 0131 240 5427

Email peter.grant@montagu-evans.co.uk

GRANT, Richard
Cadogan Estates

Position

Finance director

Qualifications

BA Hons; ACA

Career history

G

1975-93 Partner (corporate finance), Price Waterhouse
Professional memberships
Institute of Chartered Accountants in England & Wales
Contact details
Cadogan Estates Ltd, 18 Cadogan Gardens, London SW3 2RP
Tel 020 7730 4567
Fax 020 7730 5239
Web www.cadogan.co.uk
Direct tel 020 7881 1042
Direct fax 020 7881 2342
Email richard.grant@cadogan.co.uk

GRAY, Nigel
Hays
Position
Group property surveyor
Qualifications
BSc; MRICS
Career history
1999 Joined Hays.
1987-99 Guardian Properties
Professional memberships
RICS
Interests
Football (Millwall Supporters Club); golf; reading; rugby (Old Shootershillians RUFC)
Contact details
Hays plc, Hays House, Millmead, Guildford GU2 4HJ
Tel 01483 302203
Fax 01483 300388
Direct tel 01483 408414
Direct fax 01483 408488
Mobile 07769 672881
Email nigel.gray@hays.plc.uk

GRAYBOW, Sara
Hamptons International
Position
Regional director – London offices
Contact details
Hamptons International, 50 Belgrave Road, London SW1V 1RQ
Tel 020 7808 9025
Fax 020 7828 5701
Web www.hamptons.co.uk
Email graybows@hamptons-int.com

GREACEN, Robert
UK & European Investments
Position
Managing director
Qualifications
MA; MRICS
Career history
1994 Joined UK & European Investments as director; appointed managing director in 2002.
1986-94 Associate partner, Matthews & Goodman
Professional memberships
BPF; RICS
Interests
Motor sports; shooting
Contact details
UK & European Investments Ltd, West World, West Gate, London W5 1DT
Tel 020 8991 4660
Fax 020 8991 5955
Web www.ukandeuropean.com
Direct tel 020 8991 4640
Email robert.greacen@ukandeuropean.com

GREAVES, Guy
Chesterton International
Position
Director – building and development services
Qualifications
BSc; FRICS
Other roles
Chairman of local resident's association
Professional memberships
British Council of Shopping Centres; Charities' Property Association
Interests
Golf; rowing (Tideway Scullers School – only rowing club dedicated to sculling); sailing
Contact details
Chesterton International, 54 Brook Street, London W1A 2BU
Tel 020 7499 0404
Fax 020 7629 7804
Web www.chesterton.co.uk
Direct tel 020 7312 5401
Direct fax 020 7355 1254
Email guy.greaves@chesterton.co.uk

GREAVES, John
Lambert Smith Hampton
Position
Director
Qualifications
MRICS
Career history
1992 Joined Lambert Smith Hampton as director.
1978-92 Berry Bros: director on leaving
Professional memberships
RICS
Interests
Golf; music
Contact details
Lambert Smith Hampton Ltd, Midland House, West Way, Oxford OX2 0PH
Tel 01865 200244
Fax 01865 204822
Web www.lsh.co.uk
Mobile 07802 627185
Email jgreaves@lsh.co.uk

GREEN, Anthony
Anthony Green & Spencer
Position
Partner
Contact details
Anthony Green & Spencer Ltd, 7 Manchester Square, London W1U 3PG
Tel 020 7935 2335
Fax 020 7935 3586
Email info@AGS.uk.com

GREEN, David
CB Richard Ellis
Position
Executive director – West End investment
Contact details
CB Richard Ellis, Kingsley House, 1a Wimpole Street, London W1G 0RE
Tel 020 7182 2000
Fax 020 7182 7001
Web www.cbre.com
Email david.green@cbre.com

GREEN, Julie
Jones Lang LaSalle Corporate Finance
Position
European director
Qualifications
MBA; BSc Hons
Career history
1988-2002 Executive director, Lazard
Other roles
Audit committee member, Reading University; board member, Prince's Trust; south-east London treasurer, UK Chapter of Urban Land Institute
Professional memberships
Financial Services Authority; Securities Institute; Urban Land Institute
Contact details
Jones Lang LaSalle Corporate Finance Ltd, 22 Hanover Square, London W1A 2BN
Tel 020 7399 5550
Fax 020 7399 5490
Web www.joneslanglasalle.com
Direct tel 020 7399 5227
Mobile 0777 0391250
Email julie.green@eu.joneslanglasalle.com

GREEN, Michael
King Sturge

Position
Partner in charge, Southampton
Qualifications
BSc; MBA; MRICS
Career history
1991-94 Director, Hall Pain & Foster.
1985-91 Associate partner, Donaldsons.
1982-85 Hillier Parker
Professional memberships
RICS; Royal Society of Arts
Interests
IT; sailing
Contact details
King Sturge, Latimer House, 5–7 Cumberland Place, Southampton SO15 2BH
Tel 023 8023 2882
Fax 020 8023 2684
Web www.kingsturge.com
Email michael.green@kingsturge.co.uk

GREEN, Tony
Lambert Smith Hampton

Position
Head of national property management
Qualifications
BSc; FRICS
Career history
1984-93 Associate (fund management), Jones Lang Wootton.
1979-84 Senior surveyor (development management), London Borough of Hackney
Other roles
Company director of various management company vehicles
Professional memberships
RICS
Interests
Golf; motor sports
Contact details
Lambert Smith Hampton Ltd, Regent Arcade House, 19-25 Argyll Street, London W1F
Tel 020 7494 4000
Fax 020 7414 0866
Web www.lsh.co.uk
Mobile 07702 176213
Email tgreen@lsh.co.uk

GREENISH, Damian
Pemberton Greenish

Position
Senior partner – head of residential property
Other roles
Chairman, BPF leasehold reform working party; co-author, *Hague on Leasehold Enfranchisement*
Contact details
Pemberton Greenish, 45 Pont Street, London SW1X 0BX
Tel 020 7591 3333
Fax 020 7591 3300
Web www.pglaw.co.uk
Direct tel 020 7591 3350
Mobile 07899 968444
Email d.greenish@pglaw.co.uk

GREENWOOD, Howard
Poundstretcher

Position
Property director
Contact details
Poundstretcher Ltd, Knowsthorpe Gate, Cross Green Industrial Estate, Leeds LS9 0PG
Tel 0113 240 6406
Fax 0113 240 6360
Web www.poundstretcher.co.uk
Email hgreenwood@poundstretcher.co.uk

GREENWOOD, Jenefer
Grosvenor

Position
Retail strategist
Qualifications
BSc; FRICS
Career history
1978-2003 CB Hillier Parker; became equity partner in 1990; senior executive director (head of retail) on leaving
Other roles
Crown Estate commissioner; immediate past president, British Council of Shopping Centres (2002-03); board member, International Council of Shopping Centers, Europe
Contact details
Grosvenor Ltd, 70 Grosvenor Street, London W1K 3JP
Tel 020 7408 0988
Fax 020 7629 9115
Web www.grosvenor.com
Direct tel 020 7312 6335
Direct fax 020 7873 1335
Mobile 07778 175671
Email jenefer.greenwood@grosvenor.com

GREGORY, Angus
City Centre Restaurants

Position
Property director
Contact details
City Centre Restaurants plc, 56-62 Wilton Road, London SW1V 1DE
Tel 020 7630 2800
Fax 020 7630 2806
Direct tel 020 7630 2835
Direct fax 020 7630 2807
Mobile 07768 143642
Email angusg@ccruk.com

GREGORY, Nick
Castlemore Securities

Position
Director
Career history
1996-2002 USB Global Asset Management.
1993-96 Chesterton
Professional memberships
RICS
Contact details
Castlemore Securities Ltd, Morley House, 11-12 Hanover Street, London W1S 1YF
Tel 020 7187 4444
Web www.castlemore.co.uk
Email nickgregory@castlemore.co.uk

GREGORY, Simon
Blockbuster Entertainment

Position
Estates director
Qualifications
BSc Hons; MRICS
Career history
1999-2002 Estate manager, Specsavers Opticians.
1995-99 Regional estates manager, Victoria Wine
Professional memberships
Property Managers Association
Interests
Snowboarding; surfing
Contact details
Blockbuster Entertainment Ltd, Harefield Place, The Drive, Uxbridge UB10 8AQ
Tel 01895 258866
Fax 01895 866275
Web www.blockbuster.com
Email simon.gregory@blockbuster.com

GRICE, Neil
Christie & Co

Position
Director – head of corporate retail
Qualifications
MRICS
Career history
1999-2003 Director, Nelson Bakewell.
1996-99 Head of retail agency, Gooch & Wagstaff (prior to merger with J Trevor & Webster).
1987-96 Associate director, Churston Heard
Professional memberships
RICS; Shop Agents Society

G

Interests
Football; golf; rugby
Contact details
Christie & Co, 50 Victoria Street, London SW1H 0NW
Tel 020 7227 0700
Fax 020 7220 0702
Web www.christie.com
Direct tel 020 7535 1998
Mobile 07768 773892
Email neil.grice@christie.com

GRICE, Nigel
Drivers Jonas

Position
Partner
Qualifications
MA (Oxon); MRICS
Career history
Since 1989 Partner, Drivers Jonas.
1983-88 Agency surveyor, Richard Saunders & Partners
Professional memberships
RICS
Interests
Classical music; cycling; jazz; motor sports; opera; shooting; skiing
Contact details
Drivers Jonas, 6 Grosvenor Street, London W1K 4DJ
Tel 020 7896 8000
Fax 020 7896 8001
Web www.driversjonas.com
Direct tel 020 7896 8365
Direct fax 020 7896 7910
Email nigelgrice@driversjonas.com

GRIFFITHS, Allan
DZ Bank

Position
Head of property lending
Qualifications
BA (Open)
Career history
1997 Joined DG Bank (now DZ Bank, London branch) as head of property lending.
1993-97 Head of property finance, Sanwa Bank (London branch).
1989-93 Head of commercial property lending, Bayerische Vereinsbank.
1986-89 Head of property finance, Sumitomo Trust
Other roles
Past president, Association of Property Bankers (elected 1998)
Professional memberships
Association of Property Bankers
Interests
Football; rugby; walking
Contact details
DZ Bank AG, 10 Aldersgate Street, London EC1A 4HJ
Tel 020 7776 6000
Fax 020 7776 6002
Web www.dzbank.de
Direct tel 020 7776 6172
Direct fax 020 7776 6162
Mobile 07767 327089
Email allan.griffiths@dzbank.de

GRIFFITHS, Andrew
Gazeley Properties

Position
Property development director
Contact details
Gazeley Properties Ltd, Gazeley House, 26 Rockingham Drive, Milton Keynes MK14 6PD
Tel 01908 838100
Fax 01908 838101
Web www.gazeley.com
Email andy_griffiths@gazeley.co.uk

GRIFFITHS, David
Bank Leumi (UK)

Position
Head of property division
Qualifications
LLB; Barrister; MRICS; MCIArb; CDip AF
Professional memberships
Chartered Institute of Arbitrators; RICS
Contact details
Bank Leumi (UK) plc, 20 Stratford Place, London W1C 1BG
Tel 020 7907 8000
Fax 020 7907 8192
Web www.bankleumi.co.uk
Email dgriffiths@bankleumi.co.uk

GRIFFITHS, Ian
Dunlop Heywood Lorenz

Position
Director – investments
Qualifications
FRICS; IRRV
Career history
1987 Set up Featherstone Griffiths; merged practice with Baker Lorenz; now Dunlop Heywood Lorenz.
1982-87 George Trollope & Sons; became partner in office agency department.
1980-82 Norman Hirshfield Ryde.
1976-80 Garrard Smith & Partners: progressed to running office and industrial agency department
Professional memberships
Institute of Revenues Rating & Valuation; RICS
Interests
Fishing; football; golf; rugby; skiing; sport
Contact details
Dunlop Heywood Lorenz Ltd, 10 Queen Anne Street, London W1G 9LH
Tel 020 7636 7000
Fax 020 7636 7002
Web www.dhlproperty.co.uk
Email ig@dhlproperty.co.uk

GRIFFITHS, Paul
Chesterton International

Position
Director – investment
Contact details
Chesterton International, 54 Brook Street, London W1A 2BU
Tel 020 7499 0404
Fax 020 7629 7804
Web www.chesterton.co.uk
Direct tel 020 7312 5418
Mobile 07712 868548
Email paul.griffiths@chesterton.co.uk

GRIFFITHS, Vaughan
GVA Grimley

Position
Partner – retail property investment
Qualifications
BSc; FRICS
Professional memberships
RICS; Shop Agents Society
Contact details
GVA Grimley, 10 Stratton Street, London W1J 8JR
Tel 0870 900 8990
Fax 020 7911 2560
Web www.gvagrimley.co.uk
Direct tel 020 7911 2211
Email vaughan.griffiths@gvagrimley.co.uk

GRIMSHAW, Aidan
Commercial Estates Management

Position
Director
Qualifications
BSc Hons; FRICS
Career history
1998-2000 Commercial board director, FPDSavills.
1988-98 Managing director, de Havillands
Professional memberships
RICS
Interests
Diving/scuba diving; field sports; sport

G

Contact details
Commercial Estates Management Ltd, Central House, Beckwith Knowle, Harrogate HG3 1PS
Tel 01423 875175
Fax 01423 875375
Direct tel 01423 857555
Mobile 07970 204080
Email aidan@c-e-m.co.uk

GRIMSHAW, Chris
Chesterton International

Position
Director in charge, Exeter office
Qualifications
FRICS; IRRV; MCIArb
Career history
1994 Joined Chesterton; appointed director in charge of Chesterton, Exeter in 1996, regional director, Wales and South West 1997-2000; now director in charge, Exeter office.
1991-94 Director in charge (nationally), Hamptons Commercial.
1987-91 Director in charge (nationally), Bristol & West Commercial.
1969-87 Partner, Webbers of Devon
Professional memberships
Chartered Institute of Arbitrators; Institute of Revenues Rating & Valuation; RICS
Interests
Gardening; psychology; walking
Contact details
Chesterton International, Sterling House, Dix's Field, Exeter EX1 1QA
Tel 0139 288 9500
Fax 0139 227 8879
Web www.chesterton.co.uk
Email chris.grimshaw@chesterton.co.uk

GROSE, Jeremy
Dechert

Position
Partner – head of property litigation team
Qualifications
LLB Hons
Career history
1977 Joined Titmuss Sainer & Webb (now Dechert); became partner in 1982
Other roles
Past chairman, Property Litigation Association; committee member, London Solicitors Litigation Association, and editor of *Resolve* newsletter; contributor to *Estates Gazette* and *LNTV*; rated highly in *Legal Experts* (Legal Business); on legal advisory board of *Estates Gazette*
Interests
Reading; sport
Contact details
Dechert LLP, 2 Serjeants' Inn, London EC4Y 1LT
Tel 020 7583 5353
Fax 020 7353 3683
Web www.dechert.com
Direct tel 020 7775 7430
Email jeremy.grose@dechert.com

GRUNNELL, Mark
R20

Position
Director – head of property finance
Qualifications
BA Hons
Career history
2000-03 Director (head of property finance), Rotch Property Group.
1997-2000 Associate director (head of property finance group), Commerzbank.
1990-97 Corporate manager (structured finance), NatWest
Interests
Golf (Hampton Court Palace Golf Club; Princes Golf Club); jazz; music
Contact details
R20 Ltd, Leconfield House, Curzon Street, London W1J 5JA
Tel 020 7550 3860
Fax 020 7491 0410
Web www.R20.co.uk
Direct tel 020 7663 2403
Mobile 07733 103762
Email m.grunnell@rotch.com

GUEST, Charles
Ryden

Position
Partner – head of agency
Qualifications
FRICS
Career history
Since 1977 Partner, Ryden.
1972-77 Weatherall Green & Smith.
1971-72 Richard Ellis, Johannesburg
Professional memberships
British Council for Offices; RICS
Interests
Fishing; golf; shooting; skiing
Contact details
Ryden, 46 Castle Street, Edinburgh EH2 3BN
Tel 0131 225 6612
Fax 0131 225 5766
Web www.ryden.co.uk
Direct tel 0131 473 3229
Mobile 07770 821567
Email charles.guest@ryden.co.uk

GUISE, John
Hodnett Martin Smith

Position
Director
Contact details
Hodnett Martin Smith Ltd, Charles House, 5-11 Regent Street, London SW1Y 4LR
Tel 020 7839 8181
Fax 020 7839 8069
Web www.hodnettmartinsmith.com
Email johnguise@hodms.co.uk

GULLIFORD, Andrew
Cushman & Wakefield Healey & Baker

Position
Deputy senior partner
Qualifications
BSc, Est Man; FRICS
Career history
1972 Joined Cushman & Wakefield Healey & Baker
Other roles
Property Week advisory board member (2003)
Professional memberships
RICS
Contact details
Cushman & Wakefield Healey & Baker, 43-45 Portman Square, London W1A 3BG
Tel 020 7935 5000
Fax 020 7152 5360
Web www.cushwake.com
Direct tel 020 7152 5007
Direct fax 020 7152 5350
Email andrew.gulliford@eur.cushwake.com

GULLIFORD, Andrew
Jones Lang LaSalle

Position
European director
Qualifications
BSc Hons; MRICS
Career history
Since 1985 European director, Jones Lang LaSalle
Professional memberships
RICS
Interests
Football; rugby
Contact details
Jones Lang LaSalle Ltd, 22 Hanover Square, London W1A 2BN
Tel 020 7493 6040
Fax 020 7408 0220
Web www.joneslanglasalle.com
Direct tel 020 7399 5894
Direct fax 020 7399 5060

Mobile 07836 253548
Email andrew.gulliford@eu.joneslanglasalle.com

GUNSTON, Michael
British Land Corp

Position
Director and chief surveyor
Qualifications
FRICS
Career history
1975 Joined British Land: appointed chief surveyor in 1987 and director in 1991
Professional memberships
RICS
Contact details
British Land Corp Ltd, 10 Cornwall Terrace, London NW1 4QP
Tel 020 7486 4466
Web www.britishland.com
Direct tel 020 7467 2811
Direct fax 020 7467 2991
Mobile 07714 222811
Email michael.gunston@britishland.com

GUY, Rupert
Kitchen La Frenais Morgan

Position
Partner
Qualifications
MRICS
Career history
1995 Joined Kitchen La Frenais Morgan
Professional memberships
RICS
Interests
Golf; rugby
Contact details
Kitchen La Frenais Morgan, 1 Tenterden Street, London W1S 1TA
Tel 020 7317 3700
Fax 020 7317 3701
Web www.klmproperty.co.uk
Email rguy@klmproperty.co.uk

HACKING, Philip
Chesterton International

Position
Director in charge, Norwich office

Contact details
Chesterton International, 16 Queen Street, Norwich NR2 4SQ
Tel 0160 321 9719
Fax 0160 363 3433
Web www.chesterton.co.uk
Email philip.hacking@chesterton.co.uk

HADDEN, David
Stiles Harold Williams

Position
Managing director

Qualifications
MSc; FRICS; ACIArb

Career history
Since 1988 Director, Stiles Harold Williams; appointed head of property management in 1991 and managing director in 2000.
1975-88 Cluttons; various positions, including Middle East posting.
1973-75 City offices negotiator, Chestertons

Other roles
Governor, Plumpton College, East Sussex

Professional memberships
Chartered Institute of Arbitrators; RICS

Interests
Country pursuits

Contact details
Stiles Harold Williams Ltd, Sterling House, High Street, Crawley RH10 1GE
Tel 01293 441300
Fax 01293 441334
Web www.shw.co.uk
Direct tel 01293 441322
Direct fax 01293 441336
Mobile 07050 113109
Email dhadden@shw.co.uk

HADEN-SCOTT, Timothy
Delancey

Position
Investment director

Qualifications
BSc, Land Man; MRICS

Career history
Since 1998 Investment director, Delancey.
1986-98 Conrad Ritblat: moved to investment department in 1990; director from 1994 and board director from 1998

Other roles
Director, Box Properties; director, Ardwood Property Holdings; member of property committee, Haberdashers Livery Company

Professional memberships
BSc (Estate Management) Club; Investment Property Forum; RICS; Worshipful Company of Haberdashers

Interests
Cricket; golf; rugby; sailing; tennis

Contact details
Delancey, 40 Portman Square, London W1H 0AA
Tel 020 7486 6663
Fax 020 7486 6662
Web www.delancey.com
Direct tel 020 7467 5560
Mobile 07785 351425
Email tim.haden-scott@delancey.com

HADLEY, Nick
CMS Cameron McKenna

Position
Partner – real estate

Qualifications
LLB; PhD, Law

Career history
1987 Joined CMS Cameron McKenna; appointed partner in 1989. Previously with Evershed & Tomkinson and Wragge & Co.
1979 Admitted to Roll of Solicitors

Professional memberships
Investment Property Forum; Law Society

Contact details
CMS Cameron Mckenna, Mitre House, 160 Aldersgate Street, London EC1A 4DD
Tel 020 7367 3000
Fax 020 7367 2000
Web www.cmck.com
Direct tel 020 7367 2109
Email nick.hadley@cmck.com

HAGGER, Jonathan
Grosvenor Group Holdings

Position
Group finance director

Qualifications
FCA; FCT

Contact details
Grosvenor Group Holdings Ltd, 70 Grosvenor Street, London W1K 3JP
Tel 020 7408 0988
Fax 020 7491 2970
Web www.grosvenor.com
Email jonathan.hagger@grosvenor.com

HAGGERTY, Elizabeth
Lamb Chambers

Position
Barrister

Qualifications
LLB Hons

Career history
1994 Called to Bar

Professional memberships
Chancery Bar Association; Legal Action; Professional Negligence Bar Association; Property Bar Association

Contact details
Lamb Chambers, Lamb Building, London EC4Y 7AS
Tel 020 7797 8300
Fax 020 7797 8308
Web www.lambchambers.co.uk
Email elizabethhaggerty@lambchambers.co.uk

HAI, Nicholas
Arrowcroft Group

Position
Chief executive

Qualifications
FRICS

Career history
1984 Joined Arrowcroft Group

Professional memberships
BPF; RICS

Contact details
Arrowcroft Group plc, 110 Park Street, London W1K 6AD
Tel 020 7499 5432
Fax 020 7493 0323
Web www.arrowcroft.com
Email nhai@arrowcroft.com

HALE, Paul
King Sturge

Position
Partner – head of London valuation

Qualifications
BSc; MRICS

Career history
Since 1991 Partner in charge (London valuation), King Sturge.

H

1985-91 Investment agent, Lambert Smith Hampton

Professional memberships

RICS

Interests

Music; cooking; golf; rugby; skiing; tennis; travel

Contact details

King Sturge, 7 Stratford Place, London W1C 1ST

Tel 020 7493 4933

Fax 020 7409 0469

Web www.kingsturge.com

Direct tel 020 7318 4373

Direct fax 020 7409 7458

Mobile 07710 974211

Email paul.hale@kingsturge.co.uk

HALES, Tony
Workspace Group

Position

Chairman

Qualifications

BSc

Career history

1979-99 Allied Domecq: chief executive from 1991.

1969-79 Cadbury Schweppes

Other roles

Chairman, Navy Army & Air Force Institutes; non-executive director, Reliance Security Group (since 2000); non-executive director, Aston Villa (since 1997)

Professional memberships

Worshipful Company of Brewers

Interests

Football; theatre

Contact details

Workspace Group plc, Magenta House, 85 Whitechapel Road, London E1 1DU

Tel 020 7247 7614

Fax 020 7247 0157

Web www.workspacegroup.co.uk

Direct tel 020 7369 2273

Email tony.hales@workspacegroup.co.uk

HALL, Brian
Clifford Chance

Position

Partner – global head of planning and environment

Qualifications

LLB; DMA; FCIS

Career history

Since 1988 Partner, Clifford Chance.

1980 Admitted to Roll of Solicitors

Other roles

Former chief legal adviser to local government authority; chairman, City of London Law Society planning and environment law subcommittee (1995-98); member, Law Society's planning panel; regular contributor to legal and professional journals and speaker at planning and environmental conferences

Professional memberships

Law Society; UK Environmental Law Association

Contact details

Clifford Chance, 10 Upper Bank Street, London E14 5JJ

Tel 020 7600 1000

Fax 020 7600 5555

Web www.cliffordchance.com

Direct tel 020 7006 4010

Email brian.hall@cliffordchance.com

HALL, Euan
English Partnerships

Position

Divisional director

Qualifications

RD; MRICS

Career history

1991-97 Head of property, Scottish Enterprise.

1989-91 Associate partner, Euan Wallace & Partners.

1987-89 Pepper Fox

Other roles

Director, Priority Sites; director, Priority Sites Investments; director, Network Space; director, English Environment Fund; director, CL:AIRE; member, Environment Agency regional environment protection advisory committee for the North West

Professional memberships

RICS

Interests

Sailing; shooting; walking

Contact details

English Partnerships, Arpley House, 110 Birchwood Boulevard, Warrington WA3 7QH

Tel 01925 651144

Fax 01925 411493

Web www.englishpartnerships.co.uk

Email euanhall@englishpartnerships.co.uk

HALL, Simon
Hodnett Martin Smith

Position

Partner

Qualifications

MRICS; BSc Hons

Interests

Football; hockey; rugby; travel

Contact details

Hodnett Martin Smith Ltd, Charles House, 5-11 Regent Street, London SW1Y 4LR

Tel 020 7839 8181

Fax 020 7839 8069

Web www.hodnettmartinsmith.com

Direct tel 020 7747 1508

Mobile 07715 323553

Email simonhall@hodms.co.uk

HALLAM, Jonathan
British Land Corp

Position

Head of development administration

Qualifications

LLB; MBA

Career history

1997-2000 Commercial director, Annington Homes.

1995-97 Transactions manager, GE Capital (Real Estate).

1988-95 Commercial director, Rosehaugh/ Broadgate Properties.

1983-87 Clifford Chance

Contact details

British Land Corp Ltd, 10 Cornwall Terrace, London NW1 4QP

Tel 020 7486 4466

Web www.britishland.com

Email jonathan.hallam@britishland.com

HALLIDAY, Roger
Duchy of Cornwall

Position

Land steward

Qualifications

FRICS

Professional memberships

RICS

Contact details

Duchy of Cornwall, Station Road, Liskeard PL14 4EE

Tel 01579 343149

Fax 01579 345672

Web www.duchyofcornwall.com

Email ehall@duchyofcornwall.gov.uk

HALPERN, David
4 New Square

Position

Barrister

Qualifications

MA (Oxon)

Career history

1979 Called to Bar

Other roles

Committee member, Chancery Bar Association

Professional memberships

Chancery Bar Association; Professional Negligence Bar Association; Property Bar

Association

Contact details

4 New Square, London WC2A 3RJ
Tel 020 7822 2000
Fax 020 7822 2001
Web www.4newsquare.com
Direct fax 020 7822 2127
Email d.halpern@4newsquare.com

HALSTEAD, Andrew
NAI Fuller Peiser

Position
Partner – Sheffield office

Contact details
NAI Fuller Peiser, Belgrave House, 47 Bank Street, Sheffield S1 2DR
Tel 0870 700 2233
Fax 0114 275 2565
Web www.nai-fullerpeiser.com
Direct tel 0114 241 2205
Email ahalstead@nai-fullerpeiser.com

HAMER, Chris
Druces & Attlee

Position
Partner – head of property

Qualifications
MA (Cantab); Solicitor

Career history
1974 Admitted to Roll of Solicitors.
1972 Joined Druces & Attlee; became partner in 1977

Other roles
Land law subcommittee member, City of London Law Society

Professional memberships
City of London Law Society; Investment Property Forum; Law Society; Royal National Lifeboat Institution; Royal Yachting Association

Interests
Boating; skiing

Contact details
Druces & Attlee, Salisbury House, London Wall, London EC2M 5PS
Tel 020 7638 9271
Fax 020 7628 7525
Web www.druces.com
Direct tel 020 7216 5506
Mobile 07748 805741
Email c.hamer@druces.com

HAMILTON, Fiona
Hamilton Glen

Position
Partner

Contact details
Hamilton Glen, 19 St Vincent Place, Glasgow G1 2DT
Tel 0141 204 4997
Fax 0141 221 9535
Email fiona.hamilton@hamiltonglen.co.uk

HAMILTON, John
Cushman & Wakefield Healey & Baker

Position
Partner – head of Scotland

Qualifications
BSc; FRICS

Professional memberships
Accessible Retail; British Council of Shopping Centres; RICS; Shop Agents Society

Contact details
Cushman & Wakefield Healey & Baker, 223 West George Street, Glasgow G2 2ND
Tel 0141 248 4433
Fax 0141 204 0080
Web www.cushwake.com
Direct tel 0141 223 8765
Mobile 07887 795498
Email john.hamilton@eur.cushwake.com

HAMILTON, Sophie
Forsters

Position
Senior partner

Qualifications
BA (Cantab); LLD Hons (Nottingham Trent)

Career history
Since 1998 Senior partner, Forsters.
1979 Admitted to Roll of Solicitors.
1977-98 Frere Cholmeley Bischoff; became partner in 1985; and head of property department 1991-94

Other roles
Director, Cheek by Jowl Theatre Co; director, Giltwood Properties; member, AARPI; contributory board member, *Property Law Journal*

Professional memberships
Law Society

Interests
Cinema; reading; theatre

Contact details
Forsters, 67 Grosvenor Street, London W1K 3JN
Tel 020 7863 8333
Fax 020 7863 8444
Web www.forsters.co.uk
Direct tel 020 7863 8450
Mobile 07774 746460
Email SCHamilton@forsters.co.uk

HAMILTON, Tim
Hamilton Associates Architects

Position
Executive chairman

Qualifications
Dipl Arch

Career history
1966 Founded Hamilton Associates

Professional memberships
RIBA

Contact details
Hamilton Associates Architects Ltd, 280 Kings Road, London SW3 5AW
Tel 020 7351 5432
Fax 020 7352 7361
Email ha@hamilton-assoc.com

HAMILTON-STUBBER, James
Quintain Estates & Development

Position
Chief operating officer

Contact details
Quintain Estates & Development plc, 58 Davies Street, London W1K 5JF
Tel 020 7495 8968
Fax 020 7499 5583
Web www.quintain-estates.com
Email
james.hamilton-stubber@quintain-estates.com

HAMMOND, Barry
Hammond Phillips Partnership

Position
Managing director

Career history
1975 Joined Hammond Phillips. Previously with Leavers

Contact details
Hammond Phillips Partnership, 5a Portman Square, London W1H 6BX
Tel 020 7487 5678
Fax 020 7935 6632
Direct tel 020 7309 2370
Mobile 07767 817282
Email bhammond@hammondphillips.co.uk

HAMMOND, David
Allsop & Co

Position
Partner – commercial investments

Qualifications
BSc Hons; FRICS

Career history
1986 Joined Allsop & Co; appointed partner in 1989.
1981-86 Agency and development surveyor, Healey & Baker

Professional memberships
Investment Property Forum; RICS

Contact details
Allsop & Co, 27 Soho Square, London W1D 3AY

H

Tel 020 7437 6977
Fax 020 7437 8984
Web www.allsop.co.uk
Direct tel 020 7543 6721
Mobile 07768 152424
Email david.hammond@allsop.co.uk

HAMMOND, John
Stiles Harold Williams

Position
Director
Career history
Since 1986 Industrial agency and development (south London/Surrey), Stiles Harold Williams; now main board director, regional chairman and head of Surrey and south London business space.
1980-86 Commercial agency and development (south-east London/Kent), Baxter Payne & Lepper.
1978-80 Industrial agency (Greater London, north of Thames), Herring Son & Daw.
1976-78 Polytechnic of Central London.
1974-76 Gerald Eve
Professional memberships
100 Property Club
Interests
Croquet; France; gardening; golf; opera; wine
Contact details
Stiles Harold Williams Ltd, 96 Park Lane, London CR9 2NL
Tel 020 8662 2700
Fax 020 8680 3193
Web www.shw.co.uk
Direct tel 020 8662 2706
Mobile 07711 132019
Email jhammond@shw.co.uk

HANCOCK, Bill
Credit Suisse First Boston

Position
Director – real estate
Contact details
Credit Suisse First Boston, One Cabot Square, London E14 4QJ
Tel 020 7888 8888
Fax 020 7883 5819
Web www.csfb.com
Email william.hancock@csfb.com

HANCOCK, Tim
Terence O'Rourke

Position
Managing director
Qualifications
BA Hons; MPhil; DMS; MRTPI
Career history
1992 Joined Terence O'Rourke as director; appointed managing director in 2003.
Previously spent eight years in local government
Professional memberships
RTPI
Interests
Cycling; walking
Contact details
Terence O'Rourke, Everdene House, Deansleigh Road, Bournemouth BH7 7DU
Tel 0120 242 1142
Fax 0120 243 0055
Web www.torltd.co.uk
Email maildesk@torltd.co.uk

HANDLEY, Richard
Grosvenor

Position
Finance director
Qualifications
MA; FCA
Career history
1991 Joined Grosvenor Estate Holdings as group financial controller; became commercial director of Grosvenor's Continental European and asset management businesses in 1997; finance director of the UK business since 2000.
1987-91 Group chief accountant, TSB Group
Professional memberships
Institute of Chartered Accountants in England & Wales
Interests
Cars; IT; theatre
Contact details
Grosvenor Ltd, 70 Grosvenor Street, London W1K 3JP
Tel 020 7408 0988
Fax 020 7629 9115
Web www.grosvenor.com
Direct tel 020 7312 6368
Direct fax 020 7873 1368
Mobile 07767 328686
Email richard.handley@grosvenor.com

HANNAH, Matthew
Innes England

Position
Director – retail and roadside
Qualifications
MRICS
Career history
Since 1993 Director, Innes England.
1986-93 Associate partner, Knight Frank
Professional memberships
RICS
Interests
Family; golf; rugby
Contact details
Innes England Ltd, 54 The Ropewalk, Nottingham NG1 5DW
Tel 0115 924 3243
Fax 0115 924 2310
Web www.innes-england.com
Mobile 07831 319801
Email mhannah@innes-england.com

HANNAM, Paul
CCLA Investment Management

Position
Head of property
Qualifications
Bsc Hons; MRICS
Career history
1988 Joined CCLA as investment surveyor; appointed fund manager for CBF Church of England property fund on its launch in 1999; also appointed fund manager for local authorities' property fund in 2003; head of property at CCLA since 2003
Professional memberships
RICS
Interests
Football; history; travel
Contact details
CCLA Investment Management Ltd, 80 Cheapside, London EC2V 6EE
Tel 020 7489 6000
Fax 020 7489 6127
Web www.ccla.co.uk
Direct tel 020 7489 6031
Email paulhannam@ccla.co.uk

HANNINGTON, Robert
Knight Frank

Position
Partner – joint head of London investment
Qualifications
BSc; FRICS
Career history
1985 Joined Knight Frank.
1983-85 Morgan Grenfell Property Services.
1977-83 King & Co (London and Brussels)
Other roles
Director, Knight Frank Corporate Finance; co-ordinator, Knight Frank graduate scheme
Interests
Fishing; shooting; tennis
Contact details
Knight Frank LLP, 20 Hanover Square, London W1S 1HZ
Tel 020 7629 8171
Fax 020 7493 4114
Web www.knightfrank.com
Direct tel 020 7861 1175

H?

Direct fax 020 7861 1371
Mobile 07768 733680
Email robert.hannington@knightfrank.com

HANNON, Joe
AMEC Group

Position
Head of property
Qualifications
FRICS
Career history
1985-94 Property manager, Lloyds TSB
Professional memberships
RICS
Interests
Golf; tennis
Contact details
AMEC Group Ltd, Anchorage 1, Anchorage Quay, Salford M50 3YJ
Tel 0161 877 3400
Fax 0161 848 8742
Web www.amec.com
Direct tel 0161 888 1650
Mobile 07714 227329
Email joe.hannon@amec.com

HANSON, Christine
CB Richard Ellis

Position
Director – North West
Career history
1982 Joined Richard Ellis after a year in local government; became regional director in 1993 and equity director in 1995; now responsible for North West consultancy team
Contact details
CB Richard Ellis, 55 Spring Gardens, Manchester M2 2BY
Tel 0161 233 5600
Fax 0161 236 6017
Web www.cbre.com
Email christine.hanson@cbre.com

HANWAY, Bill
EDAW

Position
Managing principal
Qualifications
MArch; BS; AIA
Career history
1997 Managing principal, EDAW.
1988-97 Associate partner, Davis Brody Bond, New York
Other roles
Commission for Architecture & the Built Environment enabler; CABE Space corporate member; CABE/English Heritage urban panel member
Professional memberships
American Institute of Architects
Contact details
EDAW plc, 1a Lonsdale Square, London N1 1EN
Tel 020 7700 9500
Fax 020 7700 9599
Web www.edaw.co.uk
Email hanwayb@edaw.co.uk

HARBRIDGE, Christopher
Caxtons

Position
Chairman
Qualifications
FRICS; MCIArb
Other roles
Liveryman, Worshipful Company of Chartered Surveyors
Professional memberships
Institute of Arbitrators; RICS
Interests
Rotarian; golf (Royal Cinque Ports Golf Club)
Contact details
Caxtons, 1 Castle Street, Canterbury CT1 2QF
Tel 01227 788088
Fax 01227 450003
Web www.caxtons.com
Email charbridge@caxtons.com

HARDIE, Robert
House of Fraser

Position
Director of property
Qualifications
FRICS
Professional memberships
RICS
Interests
Cricket; golf; sport
Contact details
House of Fraser plc, 1 Howick Place, London SW1P 1BH
Tel 020 7963 2000
Fax 020 7963 2698
Web www.houseoffraser.co.uk
Direct tel 020 7963 2426
Email rhardie@hof.co.uk

HARDING, John
Daniel Watney

Position
Partner
Contact details
Daniel Watney, 25 Hosier Lane, London EC1A 9DW
Tel 020 7246 5000
Fax 020 7248 7001
Web www.danwat.com
Email jharding@danwat.com

HARDING, Paul
DTZ Debenham Tie Leung

Position
Director – management
Qualifications
MRICS
Career history
1978 Joined DTZ; roles have included chairman of property management division, national co-ordinator for property management, head of European property management and head of global property management at DTZ Debenham Tie Leung
Other roles
Member, RICS commercial property and town-centre management panel; vice-chairman, British Council of Shopping Centres technical affairs committee
Professional memberships
British Council of Shopping Centres; RICS
Contact details
DTZ Debenham Tie Leung, 3-5 Swallow Place, London W1A 4NA
Tel 020 7408 1161
Fax 020 7493 0937
Web www.dtz.com
Direct tel 020 7408 2520
Mobile 07774 786902
Email paul.harding@dtz.com

HARDING, Philip
Boxclever

Position
Estates manager
Contact details
Boxclever Ltd, Technology House, Ampthill Road, Bedford MK42 9QQ
Tel 01234 355233
Web www.boxclever.co.uk
Email phil.harding@boxclever.co.uk

HARDWICK, Simon
Halliwell Landau

Position
Partner – head of commercial property, London
Qualifications
Solicitor
Career history
1998-2002 Managing partner, Hardwick Stallards.
1985-98 Founding partner, then senior partner, Hardwick & Co

H

1981-85 Partner, Tarrant Hardwick.
1980-81 Pellys: partner on leaving.
1980 Admitted to Roll of Solicitors

Professional memberships
Investment Property Forum; Law Society

Interests
Horse riding (British dressage); rugby; swimming; tennis

Contact details
Halliwell Landau, 75 King William Street, London EC4N 7BE
Tel 020 7929 1900
Fax 020 7929 4800
Web www.halliwells.co.uk
Direct tel 020 7256 3650
Direct fax 020 7469 5250
Email shardwick@halliwells.co.uk

HARDY, Ray
Ballymore Properties

Position
Investment director

Contact details
Ballymore Properties Ltd, 3 Greenwich View Place, London E14 9NN
Tel 020 7510 9100
Fax 020 7510 9110
Email rhardy@ballymore.co.uk

HARGADEN, Ann
Lisney

Position
Director

Qualifications
FSCS; FRICS

Professional memberships
RICS

Contact details
Lisney, 24 St Stephen's Green, Dublin
Tel +353 1 638 2700
Fax +353 1 638 2706
Web www.lisney.com
Email ahargaden@lisney.com

HARGREAVES, Fred
ATIS REAL Weatheralls

Position
Director

Career history
1981 Joined ATIS REAL Weatheralls; appointed partner in 1990; now head of City office

Other roles
Member of the board

Professional memberships
British Council for Offices; Worshipful Company of Chartered Surveyors

Interests
Rugby; skiing; tennis

Contact details
ATIS REAL Weatheralls Ltd, City Tower, 40 Basinghall Street, London EC2V 5DE
Tel 020 7338 4400
Fax 020 7588 4542
Web www.atisrealweatheralls.com
Direct tel 020 7338 4431
Email fred.hargreaves@atisrealweatheralls.com

HARGREAVES, Sara
199 Strand

Position
Barrister

Qualifications
LLB Hons

Professional memberships
ACTAPS; Chancery Bar Association; Parliamentary Bar Mess; Property Bar Association

Contact details
199 Strand (Chambers of David Phillips QC), London WC2R 1DR
Tel 020 7520 4000
Fax 020 7379 9481
Web www.199strand.co.uk
Email shargreaves@199strand.co.uk

HARLEY, Graham
Aquila House Developments

Position
Director

Qualifications
MRICS

Contact details
Aquila House Developments Ltd, 86a Broomfield Road, Chelmsford CM1 1SS
Tel 01245 292150
Fax 01245 491606
Email grahamharley@aquilaholdings.co.uk

HARLING, Marcus
Burges Salmon

Position
Partner – head of construction law

Career history
1985 Admitted to Roll of Solicitors

Contact details
Burges Salmon, Narrow Quay House, Narrow Quay, Bristol BS1 4AH
Tel 0117 939 2000
Fax 0117 902 4400
Web www.burges-salmon.com
Direct tel 0117 939 2206
Email marcus.harling@burges-salmon.com

HARLOW, Tim
Chesterton International

Position
Director – business development

Qualifications
MA; BSc; MRICS

Career history
1985 Joined Chesterton International

Other roles
Over 25 years' involvement with charity for disabled children, HCPT The Pilgrimage Trust

Professional memberships
CoreNet Global UK; CoreNet Global; RICS

Interests
Hill walking; theatre; travel

Contact details
Chesterton International, 54 Brook Street, London W1A 2BU
Tel 020 7499 0404
Fax 020 7629 7804
Web www.chesterton.co.uk
Direct tel 020 7312 5430
Direct fax 020 7491 3787
Mobile 07712 868565
Email tim.harlow@chesterton.co.uk

HARMAN, Robert
Travers Smith Braithwaite

Position
Partner – head of property

Qualifications
MA (Cantab)

Career history
1972 Admitted to Roll of Solicitors.
1970 Joined Travers Smith Braithwaite; became partner in 1977; managing partner 1986-94

Professional memberships
Law Society

Interests
Antiques; art; IT; sport

Contact details
Travers Smith Braithwaite Ltd, 10 Snow Hill, London EC1A 2AL
Tel 020 7295 3000
Fax 020 7295 3500
Direct tel 020 7295 3293
Email robert.harman@traverssmith.com

HARMER, Adrian
Harmer Ray Hoffbrand

Position
Partner

Other roles
Chairman, Shop Agents Society (2002-03)

Professional memberships
RICS; Shop Agents Society

Contact details

Harmer Ray Hoffbrand Ltd, 18 Dering Street, London W1S 1AQ
Tel 020 7499 5399
Fax 020 7409 1004
Email adrian@harmerrayhoffbrand.co.uk

HARPER, Joseph
Landmark Chambers

Position
Barrister
Qualifications
BA; LLB; LLM; QC
Career history
1970 Called to Bar
Other roles
Contributes to and responsible for reissue of compulsory acquisition volume of *Halsbury's Laws of England*; an editor of *Hill & Redman's Law of Landlord & Tenant*
Professional memberships
Chancery Bar Association; Planning & Environment Bar Association
Contact details
Landmark Chambers, 4 Breams Buildings, London EC4A 1AQ
Tel 020 7430 1221
Fax 020 7421 1399
Web www.landmarkchambers.co.uk
Email clerks@landmarkchambers.co.uk

HARRIMAN, Kay
Blair Kirkman

Position
Partner – professional department
Qualifications
FRICS; MCIArb
Career history
1987 Joined Blair Kirkman. Previously, Valuation Office, Legal & General and Morgan Grenfell
Other roles
CEDR accredited mediator; RICS arbitrator
Professional memberships
Chartered Institute of Arbitrators; RICS
Interests
Hill walking; sailing; tennis; theatre
Contact details
Blair Kirkman, St Georges House, 12a St George Street, London W1S 1FQ
Tel 020 7409 0899
Fax 020 7629 8022
Web www.blairkirkman.com
Email kayh@blairkirkman.com

HARRINGTON, Paul
PricewaterhouseCoopers

Position
Director – real estate
Qualifications
MRICS
Professional memberships
British Council for Offices; CoreNet Global UK; RICS
Contact details
PricewaterhouseCoopers, Plumtree Court, London EC4A 4HT
Tel 020 7583 5000
Fax 020 7862 4652
Web www.pwc.com
Direct tel 020 7212 2950
Direct fax 020 7212 8394
Email paul.c.harrington@uk.pwcglobal.com

HARRINGTON, Richard
Nightingale Associates

Position
Managing partner
Contact details
Nightingale Associates Ltd, The Cherry Barn, High Street, Harwell OX11 0EY
Tel 01235 820222
Fax 01235 820145
Email harwell@nightingaleassociates.com

HARRIS, Alan
Green Property Management

Position
Director
Contact details
Green Property Management Ltd, Prince Frederick House, 37 Maddox Street, London W1S 2PP
Tel 020 7499 6494
Email aharris@greenpropertyltd.com

HARRIS, Angela
James Barr

Position
Director – investment
Qualifications
BSc; MRICS
Career history
1997 Joined James Barr.
1995-97 King Sturge.
1989-95 Chesterton
Professional memberships
Investment Property Forum; RICS
Contact details
James Barr, 226 West George Street, Glasgow G2 2LN
Tel 0141 300 8000
Fax 0141 300 8001
Web www.jamesbarr.co.uk
Email aharris@jamesbarr.co.uk

HARRIS, Anthony
Cluttons

Position
Partner – landlord and tenant, rating and telecoms
Qualifications
FRICS; FCIArb
Career history
1993-95 Sole principal, Anthony Harris.
1988-93 Director, Berry Commercial, Cambridge.
1977-88 Normans/Folkard & Hayward: rose to partner
Other roles
RICS APC assessor; committee member, Arbrix; secretary, Methodist Church Conexional Manse Trustees
Professional memberships
Arbrix; Chartered Institute of Arbitrators; Non-Administrative Receivers Association; RICS
Interests
Cricket; golf; hockey
Contact details
Cluttons, Portman House, 2 Portman Street, London W1H 6DU
Tel 020 7408 1010
Fax 020 7629 3263
Web www.cluttons.com
Direct fax 020 7409 7710
Email tharris@cluttons.com

HARRIS, Chris
Blockbuster Entertainment

Position
Vice-president – estates department
Contact details
Blockbuster Entertainment Ltd, Harefield Place, The Drive, Uxbridge UB10 8AQ
Tel 01895 258866
Fax 01895 866275
Web www.blockbuster.com
Direct tel 01895 866316
Direct fax 01895 819768
Email chris.harris@blockbuster.com

HARRIS, Farlane
Hammerson UK Properties

Position
UK finance director
Contact details
Hammerson UK Properties plc, 100 Park Lane, London W1K 7AR
Tel 020 7887 1000
Fax 020 7887 1090
Web www.hammerson.co.uk
Email fharris@hammerson.co.uk

H

HARRIS, Graham
Brasier Harris

Position
Partner
Qualifications
FRICS
Career history
Since 1985 Partner, Brasier Harris.
1983-85 Deputy chief surveyor, Trust House Forte.
1979-83 Industrial property manager, Thorn EMI
Other roles
Chairman, Amersham Conservative Association
Professional memberships
Arbrix; Industrial Agents Society
Interests
Fly fishing
Contact details
Brasier Harris, Victoria House, 49 Clarendon Road, Watford WD17 1HP
Tel 01923 210810
Fax 01923 236605
Web www.brasierharris.co.uk
Direct tel 01923 205503
Mobile 07711 131787
Email gkh@brasierharris.co.uk

HARRIS, Malcolm
Bovis Homes Group

Position
Chief executive
Qualifications
FCMA
Career history
1978 Joined Bovis; managing director, then chief executive from 1996
Other roles
Non-executive director, NHBC
Interests
Bridge; sailing
Contact details
Bovis Homes Group plc, The Manor House, North Ash Road, Longfield DA3 8HQ
Tel 01474 872427
Fax 01474 873849
Web www.bovishomes.co.uk
Direct fax 01474 876244
Email malcolm.harris@bovishomes.co.uk

HARRIS, Matt
Maris Interiors

Position
Managing director
Qualifications
BSc Hons; MCIOB
Contact details
Maris Interiors Ltd, The Tower Building, 11 York Road, London SE1 7NQ
Tel 020 7902 1750
Fax 020 7902 1799
Web www.maris-london.co.uk
Mobile 07787 528945
Email matt.harris@maris-westend.co.uk

HARRIS, Richard
Cardinal Lysander

Position
Director
Contact details
Cardinal Lysander Ltd, Birkett House, 27 Albemarle Street, London W1S 4BG
Tel 020 7493 2843
Email rmh@cardinallysander.com

HARRIS, Rob
Dorrington Holdings

Position
Executive director
Qualifications
BSc; MRICS
Professional memberships
RICS
Contact details
Dorrington Holdings plc, 16 Hans Road, London SW3 1RT
Tel 020 7581 1477
Fax 020 7225 0989
Web www.dorrington.co.uk
Email robert.harris@dorrington.co.uk

HARRIS, Robert
Harvey Ingram Owston

Position
Consultant
Qualifications
LLB Hons
Career history
1969 Admitted to Roll of Solicitors.
1965 Joined Owston & Co (now Harvey Ingram Owston)
Other roles
Local director and chairman of Solicitors Benevolent Association
Professional memberships
Law Society
Interests
Cars; music; rugby; skiing
Contact details
Harvey Ingram Owston, 20 New Walk, Leicester LE1 6TX
Tel 0116 254 5454
Fax 0116 255 4559
Web www.hio.co.uk
Direct tel 0116 257 4422
Direct fax 0116 255 3319
Email rph@hio.co.uk

HARRIS, Roy
Royal Bank of Scotland

Position
Managing director, real estate finance group
Qualifications
BSc; ACGI; ACIB
Career history
1995 Joined Royal Bank of Scotland as head of securitisation; appointed managing director (corporate banking) in 1996; became managing director (real estate finance group) in 2000
Interests
Cars; cricket; golf; IT; music; rugby
Contact details
Royal Bank of Scotland, 135 Bishopsgate, London EC2M 3UR
Tel 020 7375 5000
Web www.rbs.co.uk
Direct tel 020 7375 8886
Direct fax 020 7375 8291
Mobile 07956 321300
Email roy.harris@rbs.co.uk

HARRIS, Wendell
HSBC Bank

Position
European head – real estate and construction
Qualifications
BA Hons; FCA
Professional memberships
Association of Property Bankers; Institute of Chartered Accountants in England & Wales
Contact details
HSBC Bank plc, 8 Canada Square, London E14 5HQ
Tel 020 7991 8888
Fax 020 7992 4880
Web www.hsbc.com
Direct tel 020 7991 2932
Direct fax 020 7992 4875
Email wendell.m.harris@hsbc.com

HARRISON, John
Marylebone Warwick Balfour Group

Position
Main board director
Qualifications
FRICS
Contact details
Marylebone Warwick Balfour Group plc, 1 West Garden Place, London W2 2AQ
Tel 020 7706 2121
Fax 020 7706 8181

Web www.mwb.co.uk
Direct tel 020 7479 2902
Email jharrison@mwb.co.uk

HARRISON, Philomena
Maitland Chambers

Position
Barrister
Contact details
Maitland Chambers, 7 Stone Buildings, London WC2A 3SZ
Tel 020 7406 1200
Fax 020 7406 1300
Web www.maitlandchambers.com
Email pharrison@maitlandchambers.com

HARRISON, Susan
Brantano UK

Position
Property manager
Qualifications
BSc, Land Man; Dip MS
Professional memberships
RICS
Interests
Family; keep fit
Contact details
Brantano UK Ltd, Interlink Way West, Bardon, Leicester LE67 1LD
Tel 0870 990 1601
Fax 0870 990 1602
Web www.brantano.com
Direct tel 01530 516150
Direct fax 01530 516152
Email susanh@brantano.co.uk

HARRISS, Ursula
Freshfields Bruckhaus Deringer

Position
Partner – real estate
Career history
Since 2001 Partner, Freshfields Bruckhaus Deringer.
1992 Admitted to Roll of Solicitors
Contact details
Freshfields Bruckhaus Deringer, 65 Fleet Street, London EC4Y 1HT
Tel 020 7936 4000
Fax 020 7832 7001
Web www.freshfields.com
Direct tel 020 7832 7483
Email ursula.harriss@freshfields.com

HARROCKS, James
Tushingham Moore

Position
Partner
Contact details
Tushingham Moore, Acresfield, St Ann's Square, Manchester M2 7HA
Tel 0161 833 1197
Fax 0161 833 1630
Web www.tushinghammoore.co.uk
Email james@tushinghammoore.co.uk

HARROLD, Richard
MEPC

Position
Chief executive
Contact details
MEPC Ltd, 4th Floor, Lloyds Chambers, 1 Portsoken Street, London E1 8LW
Tel 020 7911 5300
Fax 020 7499 0650
Web www.mepc.com
Email rharrold@mepc.co.uk

HARRY, Timothy
9 Old Square

Position
Barrister
Qualifications
MA; BCL (Oxford)
Career history
1983 Called to Bar
Other roles
Contributing editor, *Hill & Redman's Landlord & Tenant* and *Lloyds Professional Negligence Law Reports*; contributor to *Butterworths' Land Registration Act 2002*
Professional memberships
Chancery Bar Association; Professional Negligence Bar Association; Property Bar Association
Contact details
9 Old Square (Chambers of Michael Driscoll QC), Ground Floor, London WC2A 3SR
Tel 020 7405 4682
Fax 020 7831 7107
Web www.9oldsquare.co.uk
Email timothy.harry@9oldsquare.co.uk

HART, David
1 Crown Office Row

Position
Barrister
Qualifications
QC
Career history
2003 Appointed QC.
1982 Called to Bar
Other roles
Has lectured to UK Environmental Law Association, DETR, Justice and British Institute of International Corporation Law on environmental impact of Human Rights Act; has published articles on human rights and environmental law; responsible for chapter on environmental law in *Introduction to Human Rights & the Common Law* (edited by Havers and English)
Professional memberships
Administrative Law Bar Association; UK Environmental Law Association
Contact details
1 Crown Office Row, Ground Floor, London EC4Y 7HH
Tel 020 7797 7500
Fax 020 7797 7550
Web www.onecrownofficerow.com
Email david.hart@1cor.com

HART, David
William Hill Organization

Position
Development director
Career history
Since 1990 Development director, William Hill Organization.
1973-90 Large stores development manager, Ladbroke Racing.
1972-73 Security and development manager, Ken Munden
Professional memberships
Institute of Directors
Interests
Cricket; football; horse racing; rugby; sport
Contact details
William Hill Organization Ltd, Greenside House, 50 Station Road, London N22 7TP
Tel 020 8918 3600
Direct tel 020 8888 8688
Email dhart@williamhill.co.uk

HARTNELL, Steve
Valuation Office Agency

Position
Director – business resources
Contact details
Valuation Office Agency, New Court, Carey Street, London WC2A 2JE
Tel 020 7506 1700
Fax 020 7506 1998
Web www.voa.gov.uk
Email steve.m.hartnell@voa.gsi.gov.uk

HARTWELL, Terry
Kingfisher

Position
Group property director
Qualifications
BSc; FRICS

H

Other roles
Chairman, B&Q (Ireland); property director, B&Q; director, Kingfisher Pension Fund trustee board; committee member, property policy advisory group; committee member, British Retail Consortium
Professional memberships
Accessible Retail; RICS
Contact details
Kingfisher plc, Portswood House, 1 Hampshire Corporate Park, Chandler's Ford SO53 3YX
Tel 023 8025 6256
Fax 023 8025 7480
Web www.diy.co.uk
Direct tel 023 8062 5202
Direct fax 023 8062 5298
Email terry.hartwell@kingfisher.com

HARVEY, James
Finers Stephens Innocent
Position
Partner – head of property construction
Career history
1997 Joined Finers Stephens Innocent.
1990-97 DJ Freeman.
1985-90 Beale & Co.
1985 Admitted to Roll of Solicitors
Professional memberships
Society of Construction Law
Contact details
Finers Stephens Innocent, 179 Great Portland Street, London W1W 5LS
Tel 020 7323 4000
Fax 020 7344 5600
Web www.finersstephensinnocent.com
Direct tel 020 7344 5597
Email jharvey@fsilaw.co.uk

HARVEY, Robert
Montagu Evans
Position
Partner – professional services
Qualifications
MRICS
Career history
Since 1986 Partner, Montagu Evans.
1983-86 Sole proprietor, RD Harvey & Co.
1981-83 Partner, John Germans.
1976-81 Land agent, Strutt & Parker
Professional memberships
RICS
Interests
Gardening; golf; sailing
Contact details
Montagu Evans, 44-48 Dover Street, London W1S 4AZ
Tel 020 7493 4002
Fax 020 7312 7547
Web www.montagu-evans.co.uk
Direct fax 020 7312 7536
Email robert.harvey@montagu-evans.co.uk

HARWOOD, Richard
39 Essex Street
Position
Barrister
Qualifications
MA; LLM (Cantab)
Career history
1993 Called to Bar
Other roles
Case editor, *Journal of Planning & Environment Law*; author or contributor to eight books; committee member, Planning & Environment Bar Association; advisory council member, Society for Advanced Legal Studies
Professional memberships
Administrative Law Bar Association; Environmental Law Foundation; Planning & Environment Bar Association; Society for Advanced Legal Studies; UK Environmental Law Association
Contact details
39 Essex Street, London WC2R 3AT
Tel 020 7832 1111
Fax 020 7353 3978
Web www.39essex.com
Email rjharwood@aol.com

HASAN, Salmaan
ING BHF-Bank
Position
Head of property lending
Contact details
ING BHF-Bank AG, 61 Queen Street, London EC4R 1AF
Tel 020 7634 2300
Email salmaan.hasan@bhf-bank.co.uk

HATCH, Tony
Bhs
Position
Head of estates
Qualifications
MRICS
Contact details
Bhs Ltd, 129-137 Marylebone Road, London NW1 5QD
Tel 020 7339 4013
Fax 020 7339 4169
Web www.bhs.co.uk
Email tony.hatch@bhs.co.uk

HATT, Michael
Nelson Bakewell
Position
Managing director
Qualifications
BSc; MRICS
Career history
1988 Joined Nelson Bakewell; appointed director in 1991 and managing director in 2001.
1985-88 Hampton & Sons/Lambert Smith Hampton
Other roles
Chairman, ONCOR International
Professional memberships
CoreNet Global UK; RICS
Contact details
Nelson Bakewell Ltd, 25 Sackville Street, London W1S 3HQ
Tel 020 7544 2000
Fax 020 7544 2222
Web www.nelson-bakewell.com
Direct tel 020 7544 2007
Mobile 07768 125195
Email mhatt@nelson-bakewell.com

HATTERSLEY, Carl
Lambert Smith Hampton
Position
Director
Qualifications
BSc; MRICS; MCIArb
Career history
1984-94 Grant & Partners.
1983-84 Leslie Lintott & Associates
Professional memberships
Chartered Institute of Arbitrators; RICS
Interests
Golf; skiing
Contact details
Lambert Smith Hampton Ltd, The Embankment, 3 Sovereign Street, Leeds LS1 4BJ
Tel 0113 245 9393
Fax 0113 244 0420
Web www.lsh.co.uk
Mobile 07702 176053
Email chatter@lsh.co.uk

HAVENHAND, Jonathan
La Tasca Restaurants
Position
Property director
Qualifications
BSc Hons; MA; MRICS
Contact details
La Tasca Restaurants Ltd, Huntingdon House, Princess Street, Bolton BL1 1EJ
Tel 01204 400700

H?

Fax 01204 400800
Web www.latasca.co.uk
Direct tel 0114 229 5759
Mobile 07785 708760
Email jonathan@latasca.co.uk

HAWKER, Graham
Welsh Development Agency

Position
Chief executive
Contact details
Welsh Development Agency, Principality House, The Friary, Cardiff CF10 3FA
Tel 08457 775577
Fax 029 2023 8849
Web www.wda.co.uk
Email graham.hawker@wda.co.uk

HAWKES, Nicholas
GVA Grimley

Position
Partner – valuation
Qualifications
BSc; MRICS
Contact details
GVA Grimley, 3 Brindleyplace, Birmingham B1 2JB
Tel 0870 900 8990
Fax 0121 609 8314
Web www.gvagrimley.co.uk
Direct tel 0121 609 8215
Direct fax 0121 609 8007
Mobile 07831 820628
Email nicholas.hawkes@gvagrimley.co.uk

HAWKINS, Cliff
UBS Global Asset Management (UK)

Position
Managing director – head of UK real estate
Qualifications
BSc Hons, Est Man; FRICS
Career history
Since 1991 Managing director, UBS Asset Management (now UBS Global Asset Management (UK)).
1980-91 Partner, Donaldsons.
1978-79 Weatheralls
Professional memberships
Investment Property Forum; RICS
Interests
Cars; golf; hockey; motor sports
Contact details
UBS Global Asset Management (UK) Ltd, 21 Lombard Street, London EC3V 9AH
Tel 020 7901 5050
Fax 020 7929 0487
Web www.ubs.com
Direct tel 020 7901 5377
Direct fax 020 7901 5528
Mobile 07740 095592
Email cliff.hawkins@ubs.com

HAWKINS, Patrick
British Land Co

Position
Deputy group treasurer
Qualifications
BA Hons
Other roles
Assistant treasurer, Anglian Water; assistant director, Sector Treasury Services; dealer, British & Commonwealth Merchant Bank
Interests
Cycling; sailing; skiing
Contact details
British Land Co, 10 Cornwall Terrace, London NW1 4QP
Tel 020 7486 4466
Fax 020 7935 5552
Web www.britishland.com
Direct tel 020 7467 2909
Direct fax 020 7487 4022
Mobile 07739 292909
Email patrick.hawkins@britishland.com

HAWORTH, Christopher
Alder King

Position
Partner
Qualifications
BSc Hons; FRICS
Career history
Since 1991 Partner, Alder King.
1979-91 Lalonde Bros & Parham/Chesterton Lalonde/Chesterton
Professional memberships
Faculty of Building; RICS
Contact details
Alder King, Pembroke House, 15 Pembroke Road, Bristol BS8 3BA
Tel 0117 317 1000
Fax 0117 317 1001
Web www.alderking.com
Mobile 07990 891007
Email chaworth@alderking.com

HAY, Albert
Capital & City

Position
Chairman
Qualifications
FRICS
Career history
Since 1975 Chairman, Capital & City.
1973-75 Director, English & Continental.
1970-73 Partner, Caplan Hay & Co
Professional memberships
RICS
Contact details
Capital & City plc, Davies House, 33 Davies Street, London W1K 4LR
Tel 020 7499 0583
Fax 020 7499 6866
Email albert.hay@capitalcityplc.com

HAY, Andrew
Knight Frank

Position
Partner – head of country department
Qualifications
MRICS
Career history
1983 Joined Knight Frank
Professional memberships
RICS
Interests
Fishing; gardening; sailing; shooting
Contact details
Knight Frank LLP, 20 Hanover Square, London W1S 1HZ
Tel 020 7629 8171
Fax 020 7493 4114
Web www.knightfrank.com
Mobile 07831 808997
Email andrew.hay@knightfrank.com

HAY, Neil
Dalgleish

Position
Director – head of shopping centres
Qualifications
MRICS
Career history
Since 1986 Director (head of shopping centres), Dalgleish.
1979-86 Churston Heard & Co
Professional memberships
RICS
Contact details
Dalgleish, 80 New Bond Street, London W1S 1DD
Tel 020 7663 5555
Fax 020 7491 0098
Web www.dalgleish.co.uk
Direct tel 020 7663 5536
Email nhay@dalgleish.co.uk

HAY, Phil
Jackson Criss

Position
Partner

Qualifications
BSc Hons; MRICS
Interests
Golf (Tyrrells Wood Golf Club)
Contact details
Jackson Criss, 7-8 Market Place, London W1W 8AG
Tel 020 7637 7100
Fax 020 7637 7101
Web www.jacksoncriss.co.uk
Email phay@jacksoncriss.co.uk

HAYCOCKS, Max
GVA Grimley
Position
Partner
Contact details
GVA Grimley, 10 Stratton Street, London W1J 8JR
Tel 0870 900 8990
Fax 020 7911 2560
Web www.gvagrimley.co.uk
Email max.haycocks@gvagrimley.co.uk

HAYDON-WHITE, Graham
Taylor Woodrow Developments
Position
Development director
Qualifications
BSc Hons; MRICS
Professional memberships
RICS
Contact details
Taylor Woodrow Developments Ltd, 2 Princes Way, Solihull B91 3ES
Tel 0121 600 8000
Fax 0121 600 8001
Web www.taylorwoodrow.com
Direct tel 0121 600 8053
Direct fax 0121 600 8090
Email
graham.haydon-white@uk.taylorwoodrow.com

HAYMAN, Graham
Credit Suisse First Boston
Position
Director – corporate services
Career history
1984-2000 Knight Frank: lead partner of corporate real estate department on leaving.
1970-84 Negotiator, John German
Contact details
Credit Suisse First Boston, One Cabot Square, London E14 4QJ
Tel 020 7888 8888
Fax 020 7883 5819
Web www.csfb.com
Direct tel 020 7888 3387
Direct fax 020 7888 3539
Email graham.hayman@csfb.com

HAYNE, Tim
Liverpool Victoria Asset Management
Position
Head of property investment
Qualifications
FRICS
Career history
1993-98 Hillier Parker.
1987-93 Security Pacific Bank.
1980-87 Equitable Life Assurance
Professional memberships
Investment Property Forum; RICS
Contact details
Liverpool Victoria Asset Management Ltd, Birchin Court, 20 Birchin Lane, London EC3V 9DU
Tel 020 7405 4377
Fax 020 7753 0499
Web www.liverpoolvictoria.co.uk
Direct tel 020 7929 9719
Direct fax 020 7283 4353
Mobile 07715 160572
Email tim.hayne@liverpool-victoria.co.uk

HAYNES, Jonathan
Nelson Bakewell
Position
Director – head of building consultancy
Qualifications
BSc; FRICS
Career history
Since 1982 Partner/director, Nelson Bakewell.
1978-81 Weatherall Green & Smith.
1977-78 Keith Cardale Groves.
1974-77 Richard Ellis
Professional memberships
RICS
Interests
Sailing; shooting
Contact details
Nelson Bakewell Ltd, 25 Sackville Street, London W1S 3HQ
Tel 020 7544 2000
Fax 020 7544 2222
Web www.nelson-bakewell.com
Direct tel 020 7544 2020
Email jhaynes@nelson-bakewell.com

HAYNES, Richard
Knight Frank
Position
Partner – head of consultancy and general practice
Qualifications
BSc; MRICS
Career history
1976 Joined Knight Frank
Other roles
Member of national learning and skills council; on capital committee
Professional memberships
RICS
Interests
Skiing; wine
Contact details
Knight Frank LLP, 20 Hanover Square, London W1S 1HZ
Tel 020 7629 8171
Fax 020 7493 4114
Web www.knightfrank.com
Direct fax 020 7499 1493
Email richard.haynes@knightfrank.com

HAYWARD, Sarah
ING Real Estate Investment Management (UK)
Position
Director – development
Qualifications
BSc Hons; MRICS
Career history
1990 Joined ING Real Estate Investment Management (UK) (formerly Baring, Houston & Saunders); responsible for investment in shopping centre development
Contact details
ING Real Estate Investment Management (UK) Ltd, 9 Devonshire Square, London EC2M 4WX
Tel 020 7398 4310
Fax 020 7398 4311
Web www.ingrealestate.co.uk
Direct tel 020 7398 5512
Email sarah.hayward@ingrealestate.co.uk

HAYWOOD, David
Reynolds Porter Chamberlain
Position
Partner – head of property department
Qualifications
LLB (Manch)
Career history
Since 1990 Partner (head of property department), Reynolds Porter Chamberlain.
1989-90 Partner, Malkin Janners.
1976-89 Partner, Janners.
1971 Admitted to Roll of Solicitors
Professional memberships
Law Society
Interests
Bridge; football; golf

Contact details

Reynolds Porter Chamberlain, Chichester House, 278-282 High Holborn, London WC1V
Tel 020 7242 2877
Fax 020 7242 1431
Web www.rpc.co.uk
Direct tel 020 7306 3497
Email dgh@rpc.co.uk

HAZEEL, Francis
Aareal Bank

Position
General manager – London branch
Qualifications
MA (Oxon)
Career history
Since 1993 Head of London office, DePfa Bank (became Aareal Bank in 2002).
1983-93 Manager (property finance, project finance, export credits), Banque Indosuez.
1974-83 Nordic Bank
Other roles
Head of global clients group, Aareal Bank, (London and Wiesbaden); governor, senior fellow and visiting professor, De Montfort University, Leicester; former member of advisory board, Royal Academy of Arts; trustee, Public Arts Development Trust
Contact details
Aareal Bank AG, 38 Lombard Street, London EC3V 9BS
Tel 020 7456 9200
Fax 020 7929 5055
Web www.aareal-bank.com
Direct tel 020 7456 9201
Email francis.hazeel@aareal-bank.com

HAZON, Graham
storeys:ssp

Position
Director
Qualifications
FRICS
Career history
1976 Joined Storey Sons & Parker (now storeys:ssp)
Other roles
Member of RICS building conservation group
Professional memberships
RICS
Contact details
storeys:ssp, Higham House, New Bridge Street West, Newcastle upon Tyne NE1 8AU
Tel 0191 232 6291
Fax 0191 232 4610
Web www.storeys-ssp.com
Direct tel 0191 232 4610
Mobile 07957 823904
Email graham.hazon@storeys-ssp.co.uk

HEAL, Timothy
Alder King

Position
Partner
Contact details
Alder King, Brunswick House, Gloucester Business Park, Gloucester GL3 4AA
Tel 01452 384333
Fax 01452 528680
Web www.alderking.com
Email theal@alderking.com

HEALEY, Edwin
Stadium Welton

Position
Chairman
Contact details
Stadium Welton Ltd, Welton Grange, Welton Brough HU15 1BN
Tel 01482 667149
Fax 01482 666226
Email amanda.standish@stadiumcity.co.uk

HEALEY, Julian
Lambert Smith Hampton

Position
Director
Qualifications
BSc; FRICS
Career history
1979 Joined Hallam Brackett (became Connell Wilson, then Lambert Smith Hampton) as associate; appointed director in 1988
Other roles
RICS registered property receiver
Professional memberships
Non-Administrative Receivers Association; RICS
Interests
Boating; cars; music; wine
Contact details
Lambert Smith Hampton Ltd, 17-21 Hounds Gate, Nottingham NG1 7DR
Tel 0115 950 1414
Fax 0115 941 0316
Web www.lsh.co.uk
Direct tel 0115 976 6606
Email jhealey@lsh.co.uk

HEANEY, Bill
Chesterton International

Position
Director of group services
Qualifications
LLB; MCIPD
Career history
1984-99 Secretary and head of personnel, Hotel & Catering Training Board
Other roles
Director, Exchequer Partnership (HM Treasury PFI)
Contact details
Chesterton International, 54 Brook Street, London W1A 2BU
Tel 020 7499 0404
Fax 020 7629 7804
Web www.chesterton.co.uk
Direct tel 020 7312 5415
Direct fax 020 7499 4643
Email bill.heaney@chesterton.co.uk

HEAP, David
Walker Singleton

Position
Director – head of commercial and industrial
Qualifications
FRICS; MCIArb; IRRV; NARA
Career history
1982 Joined Walker Singleton, Halifax; associate, partner, then director.
1978-82 Henry Spencer & Sons, Leeds.
1975-78 Surveyor, Calderdale Metropolitan Borough Council, Halifax.
1972-75 Stewart Newiss, Bradford
Other roles
Member, RICS president's panel of independent experts; registered property receiver; past chairman of Northern branch, Industrial Agents Society; director, Oldfield Realty; steward of Lionheart (RICS benevolent fund)
Professional memberships
Accessible Retail; Chartered Institute of Arbitrators; Expert Witness Institute; Institute of Revenues Rating & Valuation; Non-Administrative Receivers Association; RICS
Interests
Food and drink; motor sports; travel
Contact details
Walker Singleton, Property House, Lister Lane, Halifax HX1 5AS
Tel 01422 430000
Fax 01422 430010
Web www.walker-singleton.co.uk
Email david.heap@walkersingleton.co.uk

HEARLE, John
Aitchison Raffety

Position
Chairman
Qualifications
FRICS; MCIArb
Professional memberships

Chartered Institute of Arbitrators; RICS

Contact details

Aitchison Raffety Ltd, 2 Holywell Hill, St Albans AL1 1BZ

Tel 01727 843232

Fax 01727 843098

Web www.argroup.co.uk

Direct tel 01727 844555

Direct fax 01727 844472

Email john.hearle@argroup.co.uk

HEARN, Andrew
CB Richard Ellis Investors

Position

Director

Qualifications

MRICS

Career history

1977 Joined Richard Ellis (now CB Richard Ellis); appointed director in 1995

Professional memberships

Investment Property Forum; RICS

Interests

Cricket; skiing

Contact details

CB Richard Ellis Investors Ltd, 64 North Row, London W1K 7DA

Tel 020 7399 9600

Fax 020 7399 9601

Web www.cbreinvestors.com

Email ahearn@cbreinvestors.com

HEARN, Jimmy
GL Hearn

Position

Group chief executive

Qualifications

MRICS

Professional memberships

RICS

Interests

Feng shui

Contact details

GL Hearn Ltd, Leonard House, 5-7 Marshalsea Road, London SE1 1EP

Tel 020 7450 4000

Fax 020 7450 4010

Web www.glhearn.com

Email jimmy_hearn@glhearn.com

HEATH, Jeremy
Matthews & Goodman

Position

Partner

Contact details

Matthews & Goodman, Dorland House, 14-16 Regent Street, London SW1Y 4PH

Tel 020 7747 8847

Fax 020 7747 8848

Web www.matthews-goodman.co.uk

Email jheath@matthews-goodman.co.uk

HEATLEY, Tim
GVA Grimley

Position

Partner

Qualifications

BSc, Est Man; FRICS

Career history

1981 Joined GVA Grimley; partner since 1989.
1979-81 Telford Development Corp.
1977-78 Allsop Sellers

Other roles

Midlands chapter committee member, CoreNet Global UK; past chairman of Midlands chapter, British Council for Offices; past chairman for Midlands region, Industrial Agents Society

Professional memberships

CoreNet Global UK; Industrial Agents Society; RICS

Interests

DIY; gardening; sailing; skiing

Contact details

GVA Grimley, 3 Brindleyplace, Birmingham B1 2JB

Tel 0870 900 8990

Fax 0121 609 8314

Web www.gvagrimley.co.uk

Direct tel 0121 609 8345

Mobile 07831 820631

Email tim.heatley@gvagrimley.co.uk

HEAWOOD, John
Slough Estates

Position

Group executive director

Qualifications

MSc; MRICS

Career history

1996 Joined Slough Estates as group executive director.
1985-96 Director, DTZ Debenham Thorpe.
1979-85 Associate, Fletcher King.
1977-79 Idris Jones & Partners.
1975-77 JR Eve & Son

Other roles

Management board member, British Council for Offices; trustee, Marshall's Charity

Professional memberships

RICS

Interests

Gardening; skiing; tennis

Contact details

Slough Estates plc, 234 Bath Road, Slough SL1 4EE

Tel 01753 537171

Fax 01753 820585

Web www.sloughestates.com

Email john.heawood@sloughestates.co.uk

HEGINBOTHAM, John
Stimpsons

Position

Director

Qualifications

BA; FRICS; IRRV

Professional memberships

Institute of Revenues Rating & Valuation; RICS

Contact details

Stimpsons, 30 The Avenue, Watford WD17 4AE

Tel 01923 252188

Fax 01923 233927

Email jh@stimpsons.co.uk

HEIGHTON, Mark
CMS Cameron McKenna

Position

Partner – real estate

Career history

1988 Admitted to Roll of Solicitors

Other roles

Has published articles on various topics, particularly retail industry and property development in central and eastern Europe, in publications including *Estates Gazette, Property Week* and *Retail Week*

Professional memberships

British Council of Shopping Centres; International Council of Shopping Centers; Law Society; Leisure Property Forum

Interests

Gardening; walking

Contact details

CMS Cameron McKenna, Mitre House, 160 Aldersgate Street, London EC1A 4DD

Tel 020 7367 3000

Fax 020 7367 2000

Web www.cmck.com

Email mark.heighton@cmck.com

HEILPERN, Nigel
Paul Hastings Janofsky & Walker

Position

Partner – real estate

Career history

1986-2001 Property department, Nabarro Nathanson: became partner in 1994.
1986 Admitted to Roll of Solicitors.
1984-86 May May & Merrimans

Other roles

Frequent lecturer for Henry Stewart and others

on property finance topics

Professional memberships

Investment Property Forum

Contact details

Paul Hastings Janofsky & Walker LLP, 88 Wood Street, London EC2V 7AJ

Tel 020 7710 2000

Fax 020 7796 2233

Web www.paulhastings.com

Direct tel 020 7710 2048

Email nigelheilpern@paulhastings.com

HELLER, John
London & Associated Properties

Position

Chief executive

Contact details

London & Associated Properties plc, 8-10 New Fetter Lane, London EC4A 1NQ

Tel 020 7415 5000

Fax 020 7353 3500

Web www.laprops.co.uk

Email j.heller@laprops.co.uk

HELLER, Michael
London & Associated Properties

Position

Chairman

Qualifications

FCA

Other roles

Chairman, Bisichi Mining; non-executive chairman, Electronic Data Processing plc; deputy chairman, Centre for Policy Studies

Professional memberships

Institute of Chartered Accountants in England & Wales

Interests

Art; ballet; opera; walking

Contact details

London & Associated Properties plc, 8-10 New Fetter Lane, London EC4A 1NQ

Tel 020 7415 5000

Fax 020 7353 3500

Web www.laprops.co.uk

Email m.heller@laprops.co.uk

HELLIER, Tim
Berwin Leighton Paisner

Position

Partner – planning and environment

Qualifications

LLB Hons

Career history

Since 1997 Partner, Berwin Leighton (now Berwin Leighton Paisner).

1986 Admitted to Roll of Solicitors

Professional memberships

Society for Advanced Legal Studies; UK Environmental Law Association

Contact details

Berwin Leighton Paisner Ltd, Adelaide House, London Bridge, London EC4R 9HA

Tel 020 7760 1000

Fax 020 7760 1111

Web www.berwinleighton.com

Email tim.hellier@blplaw.com

HELSBY, Jeremy
FPDSavills

Position

Chairman/chief executive of FPDSavills Commercial

Qualifications

FRICS

Career history

1981 Joined FPDSavills; became head of City agency in 1993 and joined Savills plc board in 1999; appointed chairman of FPDSavills Commercial in 2001

Professional memberships

RICS

Interests

Skiing; squash; tennis; water sports

Contact details

FPDSavills Ltd, 20 Grosvenor Hill, London W1K 3HQ

Tel 020 7499 8644

Fax 020 7495 3773

Web www.fpdsavills.co.uk

Direct tel 020 7409 8947

Mobile 07870 555777

Email jhelsby@fpdsavills.co.uk

HEMENS, Peter
Nelson Bakewell

Position

Director – property management, landlord and tenant

Qualifications

MRICS; MCIArb; Dip ARB

Career history

1999 Joined Nelson Bakewell; divisional director from 1999; appointed director in 2000.

1992-99 Associate, Rapleys.

1985-92 Senior valuer, Valuation Office

Professional memberships

Chartered Institute of Arbitrators; RICS

Interests

Diving/scuba diving; racquet sports

Contact details

Nelson Bakewell Ltd, 25 Sackville Street, London W1S 3HQ

Tel 020 7544 2000

Fax 020 7544 2222

Web www.nelson-bakewell.com

Direct tel 020 7544 2059

Mobile 07880 730025

Email phemens@nelson-bakewell.com

HEMMING, Dan
Wragge & Co

Position

Senior planning partner

Qualifications

BA Hons, Law

Career history

1989 Joined Wragge & Co.

1986-88 Senior solicitor, Solihull Metropolitan Borough Council.

1979-85 Junior/senior/principal solicitor, West Midlands County Council.

1979 Admitted to Roll of Solicitors

Other roles

Member, Law Society planning panel

Professional memberships

Law Society

Interests

Cricket

Contact details

Wragge & Co LLP, 55-73 Colmore Row, Birmingham B3 2AS

Tel 0870 903 1000

Fax 0870 904 1099

Web www.wragge.com

Direct tel 0121 214 1082

Email dan_hemming@wragge.com

HEMMINGS, David
Henderson Global Investors

Position

Director – portfolio management

Qualifications

BSc; MRICS; Dip Prop Inv

Career history

1990 Joined Touche Remnant & Co as fund manager; after 1992 merger with Henderson became fund manager of Henderson Property Asset Management; since 1997 director (portfolio management), Henderson Investors (now Henderson Global Investors)

Professional memberships

RICS

Contact details

Henderson Global Investors Ltd, 4 Broadgate, London EC2M 2DA

Tel 020 7818 1818

Fax 020 7818 1819

Web www.henderson.com

Direct tel 020 7818 4497

Email david.hemmings@henderson.com

H

HEMSLEY, Andrew
Cyril Sweett

Position
Managing director – consulting
Qualifications
FRICS
Career history
Since 1980 Managing director (consulting), Cyril Sweett
Other roles
RICS construction administration and management practice panel member; insurance market liaison panel member, RICS professional information team; Construction Industry Council liability task force member
Professional memberships
Chartered Institute of Purchasing & Supply; RICS
Interests
Antarctic memorabilia
Contact details
Cyril Sweett Ltd, 60 Gray's Inn Road, London WC1X 8AQ
Tel 020 7061 9000
Fax 020 7430 0603
Web www.cyrilsweett.co.uk
Direct tel 020 7061 9007
Email andrew.hemsley@cyrilsweett.com

HENDERSON, Ian
Land Securities Group

Position
Group chief executive
Qualifications
CBE; BSc (Lond); CEM; FRICS
Career history
1971 Joined Land Securities; became director of Land Securities Properties in 1979 and managing director in 1990; meanwhile joined Land Securities main board in 1987; appointed deputy managing director of Land Securities in 1996; group chief executive of Land Securities Group since 1997.
1970-71 Hillier Parker May & Rowden
Other roles
Vice-chairman of management board, Central & Cecil Housing Trust; member of president's committee, London First; board member, British Council for Offices; chairman, New West End Co; vice-chairman, Royal & SunAlliance London regional board; past president, BPF; commissioner for Commonwealth War Graves Commission
Professional memberships
RICS
Contact details
Land Securities Group plc, 5 Strand, London WC2N 5AF
Tel 020 7413 9000
Fax 020 7024 5007
Web www.landsecurities.com
Email ian.henderson@landsecurities.com

HENDERSON, James
Taylor Woodrow Developments

Position
National property development director
Qualifications
BSc Hons, Urban Est Surv; MRICS
Career history
1983 Joined Taylor Woodrow Property Co.
1982-83 Assistant estates officer, Basildon Development Corp
Professional memberships
RICS
Interests
Piano; squash; theatre; travel; walking
Contact details
Taylor Woodrow Developments Ltd, 2 Princes Way, Solihull B91 3ES
Tel 0121 600 8000
Fax 0121 600 8001
Web www.taylorwoodrow.com
Direct fax 0121 600 8515
Mobile 0781 6518656
Email james.henderson@uk.taylorwoodrow.com

HENDERSON, Mark
DTZ Debenham Tie Leung

Position
Director – national head of statutory valuations
Qualifications
BSc Hons; MRICS; IRRV
Career history
1983 Joined DTZ; appointed partner in 1985 and director in 1988
Professional memberships
Institute of Revenues Rating & Valuation; Rating Surveyors Association; RICS
Contact details
DTZ Debenham Tie Leung, 30 Throgmorton Street, London EC2N 2BL
Tel 020 7710 8000
Fax 020 7710 8080
Web www.dtz.com
Direct tel 020 7710 8090
Direct fax 020 7710 8005
Email mark.henderson@dtz.com

HENDERSON, Rorie
Salmon Developments

Position
Managing director
Qualifications
BSc Hons; MRICS
Career history
Since 1992 Director, Salmon Developments.
1987-92 Development surveyor, Rosehaugh.
1986-87 De Groot Collis
Professional memberships
RICS
Contact details
Salmon Developments plc, 46 Mount Street, London W1K 2HH
Tel 020 7499 4378
Fax 020 7499 1317
Web www.salmondevelopments.com
Email rhenderson@salmondevelopments.com

HENDERSON, William
Ryden

Position
Partner and head of professional services
Qualifications
MA; FRICS
Other roles
Member, RICS panel of independent experts and auditors; director, EA Sports
Professional memberships
RICS
Interests
Golf; rugby; tennis; walking
Contact details
Ryden, 46 Castle Street, Edinburgh EH2 3BN
Tel 0131 225 6612
Fax 0131 225 5766
Web www.ryden.co.uk
Direct tel 0131 473 3207
Mobile 07831 478851
Email willie.henderson@ryden.co.uk

HENDY, Hilary
Welsh Development Agency

Position
Chief executive – international divison
Contact details
Welsh Development Agency, Principality House, The Friary, Cardiff CF10 3FA
Tel 08457 775577
Fax 029 2023 8849
Web www.wda.co.uk
Email hilary.hendy@wda.co.uk

HENLEY, Marcus
ATIS REAL Weatheralls

Position
Director – property management
Qualifications
BA; MRICS
Career history
1978 Joined ATIS REAL Weatheralls; became head of South East office agency; now heads

property management team
Professional memberships
British Council for Offices; RICS
Interests
Family; sailing; skiing
Contact details
ATIS REAL Weatheralls Ltd, 22 Chancery Lane, London WC2A 1LT
Tel 020 7338 4000
Fax 020 7430 2628
Web www.atisrealweatheralls.com
Direct tel 020 7338 4177
Direct fax 020 7831 2480
Mobile 07799 133720
Email marcus.henley@atisrealweatheralls.com

HENWOOD, Paul
Chesterton International
Position
Director in charge, City office
Career history
1985 Joined Chesterton International; appointed partner in 1988.
1979-85 Weatherall Green & Smith
Interests
Antiques; food; golf; reading; swimming
Contact details
Chesterton International, 30-34 Moorgate, London EC2R 6DN
Tel 020 7248 5022
Fax 020 7606 0649
Web www.chesterton.co.uk
Direct tel 020 7256 8586
Mobile 07712 868550
Email paul.henwood@chesterton.co.uk

HEPHER, Roger
Hepher Dixon
Position
Senior director
Qualifications
BA; MTP; FRICS; MRTPI
Career history
1995 Joined Hepher Dixon.
1988-95 Partner, Grimley.
1985-88 Partner, JR Eve.
1982-85 Planning surveyor, GL Hearn & Partners.
1979-82 Economic planner, Greater Manchester County Council
Other roles
Director, Land & Vision; director, Dialogue 2000; RICS assessor, planning and development division
Professional memberships
RICS; RTPI
Interests
Cycling; history; music; skiing; theatre; walking
Contact details
Hepher Dixon Ltd, Temple Chambers, 3-7 Temple Avenue, London EC4Y 0HP
Tel 020 7353 0202
Fax 020 7353 1818
Web www.hepherdixon.co.uk
Mobile 07802 416175
Email rhepher@hepherdixon.co.uk

HEPPELL, Philip
storeys:ssp
Position
Director
Qualifications
FRICS; IRRV
Career history
1988 Joined Storey Sons & Parker (now storeys:ssp); became director in 1995.
1962-88 General practice (specialising in rating), Lamb & Edge
Other roles
Past president, Rating Surveyors Association
Professional memberships
Institute of Revenues Rating & Valuation
Contact details
storeys:ssp, Higham House, New Bridge Street West, Newcastle upon Tyne NE1 8AU
Tel 0191 232 6291
Fax 0191 232 4610
Web www.storeys-ssp.com
Direct tel 0191 206 8710
Email philip.heppell@storeys-ssp.co.uk

HEPTON, Richard
Alexon Group
Position
Property director
Qualifications
FRICS
Contact details
Alexon Group plc, 40-48 Guildford Street, Luton LU1 2PB
Tel 0158 272 3131
Fax 0158 239 9890

HEPWORTH, John
Mason Owen & Partners
Position
Partner – asset management/rent review
Qualifications
MRICS
Professional memberships
RICS
Contact details
Mason Owen & Partners Ltd, Gladstone House, 11 Union Court, Liverpool L2 4UQ
Tel 0151 242 3000
Fax 0151 236 2569
Web www.masonowen.com
Direct tel 0151 242 3060
Mobile 07770 855802
Email john.hepworth@masonowen.com

HERBERT, Alan
Ward Hadaway
Position
Partner – property litigation
Contact details
Ward Hadaway, Sandgate House, 102 Quayside, Newcastle upon Tyne NE1 3DX
Tel 0191 204 4000
Fax 0191 204 4001
Web www.wardhadaway.com
Email alan.herbert@wardhadaway.com

HERBERT, Claire
Allied Carpets Group
Position
Property controller
Contact details
Allied Carpets Group plc, 76 High Street, Orpington BR6 0JQ
Tel 01689 895000
Fax 01689 895013
Web www.alliedcarpets.com
Email cherbert@alliedcarpets.com

HERBERT, David
Robert Hitchins
Position
Development consultant
Qualifications
BSc; MRICS; MBA
Career history
1998-2002 Grosvenor Waterside. Previously at Arlington Securities and Robert Hitchins Properties as development surveyor
Professional memberships
RICS
Contact details
Robert Hitchins Ltd, The Manor, Boddington Lane, Cheltenham GL51 0TJ
Tel 01242 680694
Fax 01242 680701
Web www.robert-hitchins-properties.co.uk
Mobile 07803 142009
Email david.herbert11@btopenworld.com

HERBERT, Richard
Strutt & Parker
Position
Investment partner, London
Qualifications

H

FRICS
Professional memberships
RICS
Contact details
Strutt & Parker, 13 Hill Street, London W1J 5LQ
Tel 020 7629 7282
Fax 020 7629 0387
Web www.struttandparker.com
Direct tel 020 7318 5009
Direct fax 020 7355 1385
Mobile 07836 258826
Email rherbert@struttandparker.com

HERD, Steven
ATIS REAL Weatheralls

Position
Director for Scotland
Qualifications
BLE Hons; MRICS
Career history
1987 Joined ATIS REAL Weatheralls in London; head of Scottish business since 1996
Professional memberships
RICS
Interests
Family
Contact details
ATIS REAL Weatheralls Ltd, 20 Charlotte Square, Edinburgh EH2 4DF
Tel 0131 220 4455
Fax 0131 220 0001
Web www.atisrealweatheralls.com
Direct tel 0131 220 1108
Mobile 07774 771743
Email steven.herd@atisrealweatheralls.com

HERRINGTON, Paul
ISIS Property Investments

Position
Managing director
Qualifications
BSc; MRICS
Other roles
Member, Association of British Insurers property investment panel
Professional memberships
British Council of Shopping Centres; British Council for Offices; BPF; RICS
Contact details
ISIS Property Investments Ltd, 100 Wood Street, London EC2V 7AN
Tel 020 7506 1100
Fax 020 7600 4180
Web www.isisam.com
Direct tel 020 7506 1109
Email paul.herrington@isisam.com

HERSOM, Simon
Royal Bank of Scotland

Position
Managing director – European real estate
Qualifications
ACIB
Professional memberships
Chartered Institute of Bankers; Investment Property Forum
Interests
Aviation; horse riding; sailing
Contact details
Royal Bank of Scotland, 5th Floor, 135 Bishopsgate, London EC2M 3UR
Tel 020 7375 5000
Web www.rbs.co.uk
Direct tel 020 7375 6040
Direct fax 020 7375 6054
Mobile 07778 536446
Email simon.hersom@rbos.com

HERZBERG, Henry
Chapman Taylor

Position
Main board director
Qualifications
AA Dip; RIBA
Career history
1980 Joined Chapman Taylor.
1977-79 Architect, Colin St John Wilson and YRM.
1975-77 Buildings editor, *Architects' Journal*.
1969-75 Site architect, McAlpines, Wates and Wimpey
Professional memberships
Architectural Association; British Council of Shopping Centres; RIBA; Society for the Protection of Ancient Buildings; Wind & Watermill Society
Interests
Architecture; gardening
Contact details
Chapman Taylor LLP, MacMillan House, 96 Kensington High Street, London W8 4SG
Tel 020 7371 3000
Fax 020 7371 1949
Web www.chapmantaylor.com
Mobile 07802 378480
Email hherzberg@chapmantaylor.com

HESKETT, Robert
Land Securities Properties

Position
London portfolio director
Qualifications
BSc; FRICS
Career history
1978 Joined Land Securities.
1975-78 Montagu Evans
Other roles
Board member, London First; church commissioner (since 1998)
Professional memberships
RICS
Interests
Cinema; family; golf; sailing; skiing; tennis; theatre
Contact details
Land Securities Properties Ltd, 5 Strand, London WC2N 5AF
Tel 020 7413 9000
Fax 020 7925 0202
Web www.landsecurities.com
Direct tel 020 7024 5247
Email robert.heskett@landsecurities.com

HESSEL, Chris
Donaldsons

Position
Partner – head of valuation
Qualifications
FRICS
Career history
1986 Joined Donaldsons. Previously with Fuller Peiser
Contact details
Donaldsons, 48 Warwick Street, London W1B 5NL
Tel 020 7534 5000
Fax 020 7434 0045
Web www.donaldsons.co.uk
Direct tel 020 7534 8526
Mobile 07808 479248
Email chris.hessel@donaldsons.co.uk

HETHERINGTON, Adam
FPDSavills

Position
Director – head of West End office agency
Qualifications
BSc Hons; MRICS
Career history
1987-97 Weatherall Green & Smith
Professional memberships
RICS
Contact details
FPDSavills Ltd, 20 Grosvenor Hill, London W1K 3HQ
Tel 020 7499 8644
Fax 020 7495 3773
Web www.fpdsavills.co.uk
Direct tel 020 7409 8764
Mobile 07870 555716
Email ahetherington@fpdsavills.co.uk

H

HEWETSON, James
Matthews & Goodman

Position
Partner in charge – valuation
Qualifications
MRICS
Career history
Since 1977 Valuation partner with Kemsley Whiteley & Ferris until incorporated with Matthews & Goodman in 1996
Professional memberships
RICS
Interests
Golf; tennis; travel
Contact details
Matthews & Goodman, Dorland House, 14-16 Regent Street, London SW1Y 4PH
Tel 020 7747 8847
Fax 020 7747 8848
Web www.matthews-goodman.co.uk
Mobile 07770 742387
Email jhewetson@matthews-goodman.co.uk

HEWITSON, Charles
Hewitsons

Position
Partner
Qualifications
LLB
Career history
1977 Joined Hewitson Becke + Shaw (now Hewitsons)
Professional memberships
Agricultural Law Association
Interests
Sailing; shooting; skiing; windsurfing
Contact details
Hewitsons, Shakespeare House, 42 Newmarket Road, Cambridge CB5 8EP
Tel 0122 346 1155
Fax 0122 331 6511
Web www.hewitsons.com
Email charleshewitson@hewitsons.com

HEWITT, Elaine
BT Global Services

Position
Vice-president – workplace and environment
Qualifications
BA Hons; MSc
Career history
Since 1995 Vice-president (workplace and environment), BT Global Services
Contact details
BT Global Services Ltd, Delta Point, 31-35 Wellesley Road, London CR9 2YZ
Tel 020 8666 1322
Fax 020 8666 4977
Mobile 07802 224521
Email elaine.hewitt@bt.com

HEWITT, Graham
WH Smith

Position
Head of property management
Other roles
Director, British Council of Shopping Centres; president, Property Managers Association (1999-2000)
Contact details
WH Smith plc, Greenbridge Road, Swindon SN3 3RX
Tel 020 7409 3222
Fax 01793 562590
Web www.whsmith.co.uk
Email graham.hewitt@group-whsmith.co.uk

HEWITT, John
Finers Stephens Innocent

Position
Partner – head of property dispute resolution
Career history
1988 Joined Thornton Lynne & Lawson (merged with Finers in 1991 to become Finers Stephens Innocent); head of property dispute resolution at Finers Stephens Innocent since 1991.
1979-88 In-house lawyer, ICI.
1979 Admitted to Roll of Solicitors
Other roles
Appointed by Lord Chancellor in 2003 to be part-time lawyer chairman of Rent Assessment Committee/Leasehold Valuation Tribunal
Professional memberships
Property Litigation Association
Contact details
Finers Stephens Innocent, 179 Great Portland Street, London W1W 5LS
Tel 020 7323 4000
Fax 020 7344 5600
Web www.finersstephensinnocent.com
Direct tel 020 7344 5554
Mobile 07768 823818
Email jhewitt@fsilaw.co.uk

HIATT, Christopher
Jones Lang LaSalle

Position
European director – national offices group
Qualifications
FRICS
Career history
Since 1986 European director (national offices), Jones Lang LaSalle.
1975-84 Principal surveyor, Milton Keynes Development Corp
Other roles
Chairman, British Council for Offices out-of-town offices group
Professional memberships
British Council for Offices; RICS
Interests
Cars; golf; sport; tennis
Contact details
Jones Lang LaSalle Ltd, 22 Hanover Square, London W1A 2BN
Tel 020 7493 6040
Fax 020 7408 0220
Web www.joneslanglasalle.com
Direct tel 020 7399 5323
Direct fax 020 7399 5403
Mobile 07836 222323
Email chris.hiatt@eu.joneslanglasalle.com

HIBBERT, David
Browne Jacobson

Position
Partner – head of property department
Contact details
Browne Jacobson, 44 Castle Gate, Nottingham NG1 7BJ
Tel 0115 976 6000
Fax 0115 947 5246
Web www.brownejacobson.com
Email dhibbert@brownej.co.uk

HICKMAN, Roger
Thomas Eggar

Position
Partner – head of commercial property department, London
Qualifications
LLB
Career history
1986 Joined Thomas Eggar; partner since 1987.
1984-86 Saunders Sobell Leigh & Dobin.
1977 Admitted to Roll of Solicitors
Professional memberships
Law Society; Solicitors Benevolent Association
Interests
Cricket; sport
Contact details
Thomas Eggar, 76 Shoe Lane, London EC4A 3JB
Tel 020 7842 0000
Fax 020 7842 3900
Web www.thomaseggar.com
Direct fax 020 7842 3901
Email roger.hickman@thomaseggar.com

H

HICKS, John
Lyons Davidson

Position
Partner – head of property
Qualifications
BA Hons, Law
Career history
1981 Admitted to Roll of Solicitors.
1979 Joined Lyons Davidson; became partner in 1988
Professional memberships
Law Society; Solicitors' European Group
Interests
IT; music; sport
Contact details
Lyons Davidson, Bridge House, 48-52 Baldwin Street, Bristol BS1 1QD
Tel 0117 904 6000
Fax 0117 904 6001
Web www.lyonsdavidson.co.uk
Direct tel 0117 904 5851
Mobile 07802 648483
Email jhicks@lyonsdavidson.co.uk

HICKS, William
Landmark Chambers

Position
Barrister
Qualifications
MA, Econ; QC
Career history
1975 Called to Bar
Other roles
Committee member, Parliamentary Bar Association; committee member, Oxford Planning Law Conference
Professional memberships
Administrative Law Bar Association; Parliamentary Bar Mess; Planning & Environment Bar Association; UK Environmental Law Association
Interests
Fishing; real tennis; skiing; walking
Contact details
Landmark Chambers, 4 Breams Buildings, London EC4A 1AQ
Tel 020 7430 1221
Fax 020 7421 1399
Web www.landmarkchambers.co.uk
Email clerks@landmarkchambers.co.uk

HIGGINS, David
English Partnerships

Position
Chief executive
Career history
2003 Joined English Partnerships as chief executive. Prior to this, group chief executive at Lend Lease
Other roles
Property Week advisory board member (2003)
Contact details
English Partnerships, 110 Buckingham Palace Road, London SW1W 9SA
Tel 020 7881 1600
Fax 020 7730 9162
Web www.englishpartnerships.co.uk
Email davidhiggins@englishpartnerships.co.uk

HIGGINS, Rupert
Littman Chambers

Position
Barrister
Career history
1991 Called to Bar
Contact details
Littman Chambers (Chambers of Mark Littman QC), 12 Gray's Inn Square, London WC1R 5JP
Tel 020 7404 4866
Fax 020 7404 4812
Web www.littmanchambers.com
Email rupert.higgins@littmanchambers.com

HIGHMORE, Robert
Charles Russell

Position
Partner – head of property litigation, London
Qualifications
MA, Law
Career history
Since 2001 Partner, Charles Russell.
1982 Admitted to Roll of Solicitors.
1980-2001 Radcliffes: partner from 1987
Professional memberships
British Council for Offices; BPF; Law Society; Property Litigation Association; Westminster Property Owners Association
Interests
Family; squash
Contact details
Charles Russell, 8–10 New Fetter Lane, London EC4A 1RS
Tel 020 7203 5000
Fax 020 7203 0200
Web www.cr-law.co.uk
Direct tel 020 7203 5201
Direct fax 020 7203 5304
Email robert.highmore@charlesrussell.co.uk

HIGNETT, Andrew
Lester Aldridge

Position
Partner – head of property development team
Qualifications
BA Hons
Career history
1999 Joined Lester Aldridge.
1995-99 Head of planning, Osborne Clarke.
1990-95 Partner, Boyce Hatton.
1981-90 Head of legal, local government.
1978 Admitted to Roll of Solicitors
Professional memberships
British Urban Regeneration Association; Law Society; UK Environmental Law Association
Interests
Sailing; Territorial Army
Contact details
Lester Aldridge, Alleyn House, Carlton Crescent, Southampton SO15 2EU
Tel 023 8082 7411
Fax 023 8082 7410
Web www.lesteraldridge.com
Mobile 07974 724054
Email andrew.hignett@la-law.com

HILL, Adrian
Cushman & Wakefield Healey & Baker

Position
Partner – head of office and industrial agency
Qualifications
BSc; FRICS
Career history
1981 Joined Cushman & Wakefield Healey & Baker
Other roles
International managing partner and member of UK management committee
Professional memberships
British Council for Offices; RICS
Interests
Country pursuits; jazz; shooting
Contact details
Cushman & Wakefield Healey & Baker, 110 Cannon Street, London EC4N 6EU
Tel 020 7935 5000
Fax 020 7514 2398
Web www.cushwake.com
Direct tel 020 7152 5074
Direct fax 020 7152 5385
Mobile 07764 398074
Email adrian.hill@eur.cushwake.com

HILL, Barry
Aberdeen Property Investors

Position
Associate director
Qualifications
MRICS
Professional memberships
RICS
Contact details

Aberdeen Property Investors, Charles House, 5-11 Regent Street, London SW1Y 4LR
Tel 020 7747 1700
Fax 020 7839 7460
Web www.aberdeenpropertyinvestors.com
Email barry.hill@aberdeenpropertyinvestors.com

HILL, William
Schroder Property Investment Management

Position
Managing director
Qualifications
BSc; MRICS; CDip AF
Career history
1989 Joined Schroders; became managing director of property division in 1991.
1982-89 Drivers Jonas
Professional memberships
Association of Property Unit Trusts; BPF; Investment Property Forum; Lambda Alpha; RICS; Worshipful Company of Chartered Surveyors
Interests
Family; gardening; golf; IT; politics; sport
Contact details
Schroder Property Investment Management Ltd, 31 Gresham Street, London EC2V 7QA
Tel 020 7658 6000
Fax 020 7658 3960
Direct tel 020 7658 6726
Mobile 07770 496726
Email william.hill@schroders.com

HILLMAN, Ian
Austin Adams

Position
Director
Qualifications
FRICS
Career history
1982-90 Partner/director, Hall Pain & Foster.
1977-82 Associate, Field Palmer Freeston.
1975-77 Principal valuer, Portsmouth City Council.
1973-75 Development surveyor, International Land Investments.
1967-73 Fox & Sons
Professional memberships
RICS
Contact details
Austin Adams, 10 Cumberland Place, Southampton SO15 2BH
Tel 023 8033 8811
Fax 023 8023 6588
Web www.austinadams.co.uk
Email IFH@austinadams.co.uk

HILLMAN, Philip
King Sturge

Position
Partner – valuation, Bristol
Qualifications
BSc; FRICS
Professional memberships
RICS
Contact details
King Sturge, 40 Berkeley Square, Bristol BS8 1HU
Tel 0117 927 6691
Fax 0117 929 9669
Web www.kingsturge.com
Direct tel 0117 930 5831
Email phili.phillman@kingsturge.co.uk

HINCHLEY, Guy
Mills & Reeve

Position
Managing partner, Birmingham
Qualifications
LLB Hons
Career history
1987 Joined Mills & Reeve; appointed partner in 1990 and managing partner (Birmingham office) in 2001.
1985-87 Greene & Greene.
1985 Admitted to Roll of Solicitors.
1982-84 Buss Stone & Co
Other roles
Leader of firm's Birmingham commercial property team
Professional memberships
Investment Property Forum
Interests
Cars; rowing; rugby; sport
Contact details
Mills & Reeve, 54 Hagley Road, Birmingham B16 8PE
Tel 0121 454 4000
Fax 0121 456 3631
Web www.mills-reeve.com
Direct tel 0121 456 8337
Direct fax 0121 456 8477
Mobile 07771 564546
Email guy.hinchley@mills-reeve.com

HINDLE, John
Brookhouse Group

Position
Chairman
Contact details
Brookhouse Group Ltd, Mercury Park, Manchester M41 7LY
Tel 0161 866 8366
Fax 0161 865 7516
Web www.brookhousegroup.co.uk
Email margaret@brookhousegroup.co.uk

HINDMARSH, Julian
Finers Stephens Innocent

Position
Partner – head of property retail and leisure
Career history
1996 Joined Finers Stephens Innocent.
1994-96 Deborah Mills & Associates.
1992-94 Mackenzie Mills.
1987-92 Payne Hicks Beach
Professional memberships
Law Society
Interests
Football; golf; politics; wine
Contact details
Finers Stephens Innocent, 179 Great Portland Street, London W1W 5LS
Tel 020 7323 4000
Fax 020 7344 5600
Web www.finersstephensinnocent.com
Direct tel 020 7344 5312
Email jhindmarsh@fsilaw.co.uk

HINDS, Neil
F Hinds

Position
Property director
Qualifications
MRICS
Contact details
F Hinds Ltd, 24 Park Road, Uxbridge UB8 1NH
Tel 0189 520 1000
Fax 0189 520 1001
Web www.fhinds.co.uk
Email neil@fhinds.co.uk

HINES, Kevin
Grant Thornton

Position
Director – property advisory services
Qualifications
BSc; MRICS
Career history
Since 2002 Director, Grant Thornton.
1996-2002 Director, Andersen.
1993-96 Asset manager, Threadneedle Property Fund Managers
Interests
Cooking; rugby; theatre; water sports
Contact details
Grant Thornton, Grant Thornton House, 22 Melton Street, London NW1 2EP
Tel 0870 733 6700
Web www.grantthornton.com
Direct tel 0870 991 2899

Direct fax 0870 991 2899
Mobile 07768 546438
Email kevin.hines@gtuk.com

HIRST, Karen
Welsh Development Agency

Position
Investment director
Qualifications
BSc Hons; MRICS
Professional memberships
RICS
Interests
Music; skiing; squash; swimming; tennis; theatre
Contact details
Welsh Development Agency, North Wales Division, Ffordd Richard Davies, St Asaph LL17 0LJ
Tel 01745 586204
Fax 01745 586259
Web www.wda.co.uk
Email karen.hirst@wda.co.uk

HISLOP, Eric
Chesterton International

Position
Director in charge, Glasgow office
Qualifications
BSc; MRICS
Career history
1994 Joined Chesterton.
1989-94 Fuller Peiser.
1985-87 Peter Campbell & Co.
1981-85 Gerald Eve
Contact details
Chesterton International, 48 St Vincent Street, Glasgow G2 5TS
Tel 0141 221 2897
Fax 0141 221 1949
Web www.chesterton.co.uk
Direct tel 0141 228 5907
Mobile 07712 868600
Email eric.hislop@chesterton.co.uk

HITCHCOCK, David
CB Richard Ellis

Position
Joint managing director – building consultancy
Qualifications
BSc Hons; MRICS
Career history
1986 Joined Insignia Richard Ellis (now CB Richard Ellis).
1982-86 Surveyor, Prudential Assurance Co
Other roles
Treasurer and commodore, Chartered Surveyors Sailing Association
Professional memberships
RICS
Interests
Sailing
Contact details
CB Richard Ellis, Kingsley House, 1a Wimpole Street, London W1G 0RE
Tel 020 7182 2000
Fax 020 7182 7001
Web www.cbre.com
Direct tel 020 7304 7424
Email david.hitchcock@cbre.com

HITCHCOTT, Paul
New Look

Position
Property director
Qualifications
Dip VEM; MRICS
Career history
Since 2002 Property director, New Look.
1998-2002 Head of property, Superdrug Stores.
1988-98 Acquisitions manager/acquisitions estates controller, Superdrug Stores.
1985-88 Acquisitions manager, Iceland Frozen Foods
Professional memberships
RICS
Interests
Football; horse racing; sport
Contact details
New Look Ltd, New Look House, Mercery Road, Weymouth DT3 5HJ
Tel 01305 765000
Fax 01305 765004
Email paul.hitchcott@newlook.co.uk

HITCHCOX, John
YOO

Position
Chairman
Career history
1999 Formed YOO with designer Philippe Starck as a design-based international developer specialising in tall residential buildings.
1992 Co-founded Manhattan Loft Corp with Harry Handelsman; still actively involved in many MLC projects
Other roles
Member of Prince's Youth Business Trust; supporter of Amnesty International
Interests
Family; sailing; yoga
Contact details
YOO Ltd, 2 Bentinck Street, London W1U 2FA
Tel 020 7009 0100
Fax 020 7009 0200
Web www.yooarehere.com
Email john@yooarehere.com

HOBBY, Jeffrey
Moorevale

Position
Director
Qualifications
BSc Hons, Est Man; MRICS
Professional memberships
RICS
Contact details
Moorevale Ltd, 53-54 Brook's Mews, London W1K 4EF
Tel 020 7399 2300
Fax 020 7399 2309
Web www.moorevale.com
Email jeffhobby@moorevale.com

HOBSON, Jeremy
ep2

Position
Chief executive
Qualifications
MRICS
Career history
Since 1988 Managing partner/chief executive, ep2 (formerly ep2 Elliott Partnership).
1978-88 Partner, Richard Ellis
Other roles
Member, RICS 1938 Club; member, Manchester Interact
Professional memberships
Manchester Society of Land Agents & Surveyors; RICS
Interests
Golf; running
Contact details
ep2, Brazennose House West, Brazennose Street, Manchester M2 5EP
Tel 0161 834 0011
Fax 0161 834 0146
Web www.ep2.co.uk
Direct tel 0161 934 2121
Mobile 07768 531402
Email jeremy.hobson@ep2.co.uk

HODCROFT, Dean
Ernst & Young

Position
Tax partner – real estate, hospitality/construction
Qualifications
LLB Hons; CTA
Career history
1988 Joined Ernst & Young; now head of real estate tax
Other roles

Affiliate member, ICAEW
Professional memberships
Chartered Institute of Taxation
Interests
Cricket; football; skiing; travel
Contact details
Ernst & Young LLP, 1 More London Place, London SE1 2AF
Tel 020 7951 2000
Fax 020 7951 1345
Web www.ey.com/uk
Direct tel 020 7951 4870
Direct fax 020 7951 3411
Mobile 07747 790126
Email dhodcroft@uk.ey.com

HODGE, Christopher
HBSV Chartered Surveyors
Position
Director
Professional memberships
Industrial Agents Society
Contact details
HBSV Chartered Surveyors, Portland House, 4 Great Portland Street, London W1W 8QJ
Tel 020 7907 4500
Fax 020 7907 4501
Mobile 07774 417237
Email chris.hodge@hbsv.com

HODGE, David
9 Old Square
Position
Barrister
Qualifications
QC
Contact details
9 Old Square (Chambers of Michael Driscoll QC), Ground Floor, London WC2A 3SR
Tel 020 7405 4682
Fax 020 7831 7107
Web www.9oldsquare.co.uk
Email david.hodge@9oldSquare.co.uk

HODGE, John
Balfour & Manson
Position
Head of commercial department
Qualifications
LLB; WS; NP
Career history
1999 Accredited as commercial leasing law specialist.
1975 Joined Balfour & Manson; became partner in 1977.
1973 Admitted to Roll of Solicitors.
1971-75 Tods Murray WS
Professional memberships
Society for Computers & Law; WS Society
Interests
IT; walking
Contact details
Balfour & Manson, 54-66 Frederick Street, Edinburgh EH2 1LS
Tel 0131 200 1200
Fax 0131 200 1366
Web www.balfour-manson.co.uk
Direct tel 0131 200 1260
Direct fax 0131 200 1360
Email john.hodge@balfour-manson.co.uk

HODGKINSON, Aldous
Stanhope
Position
New business director
Contact details
Stanhope plc, Norfolk House, 31 St James's Square, London SW1Y 4JJ
Tel 020 7170 1700
Fax 020 7170 1701
Web www.stanhopeplc.com
Email aldous.hodgkinson@stanhopeplc.com

HODGSON, Stephen
Knight Frank
Position
Partner – head of Yorkshire
Qualifications
BSc, Est Man; FRICS
Career history
Since 1988 Partner, Knight Frank.
1978-88 Associate partner, Henry Spencer & Sons.
1976-78 Valuer, Sheffield City Council
Professional memberships
RICS
Interests
Football; IT; keep fit; sailing; squash; travel
Contact details
Knight Frank LLP, Princess House, 122 Queen Street, Sheffield S1 2DW
Tel 0114 272 9750
Fax 0114 272 9772
Web www.knightfrank.com
Direct tel 0114 252 5727
Mobile 07836 538383
Email stephen.hodgson@knightfrank.com

HODGSON, Tim
DTZ Holdings
Position
Chief operating officer UK
Career history
Since 1993 DTZ: regional managing director (London and South East), then managing director (from 1997), Debenham Tie Leung; became managing director of DTZ Pieda Consulting in 2000; chief operating officer (UK) of DTZ Holdings since 2003.
1977-93 Bernard Thorpe: appointed partner in charge of property management in 1981 and managing partner (London) in 1989.
1970-77 Deputy valuer and estate officer, Stockton-on-Tees Borough Council
Contact details
DTZ Holdings plc, One Curzon Street, London W1A 5PZ
Tel 020 7408 1161
Fax 020 7643 6000
Web www.dtz.com
Direct fax 020 7643 6062
Email tim.hodgson@dtz.com

HODNETT, Julian
Hodnett Martin Smith
Position
Senior partner
Contact details
Hodnett Martin Smith Ltd, Charles House, 5-11 Regent Street, London SW1Y 4LR
Tel 020 7839 8181
Fax 020 7839 8069
Web www.hodnettmartinsmith.com
Email julianhodnett@hodms.co.uk

HOEKSMA, Siep
ING Real Estate Development UK
Position
Joint managing director
Contact details
ING Real Estate Development UK Ltd, 33 Cavendish Square, London W1G 0BQ
Tel 020 7659 9620
Fax 020 7659 9621
Email siep.hoeksma@ingrealestate.com

HOGG, Stuart
Chesterton International
Position
Director in charge, Cardiff office
Career history
Since 2002 Director, Chesterton.
1999-2002 Partner, Alder King.
1992-99 Associate, Henry Butcher
Professional memberships
Non-Administrative Receivers Association; RICS
Interests
Family; golf; music; squash
Contact details
Chesterton International, 12-13 Windsor Place, Cardiff CF10 3BY

H

Tel 029 2064 0111
Fax 029 2064 0225
Web www.chesterton.co.uk
Email stuart.hogg@chesterton.co.uk

HOGGETT, John
Kings Chambers

Position
Barrister
Qualifications
QC
Contact details
Kings Chambers, 40 King Street, Manchester M2 6BA
Tel 0161 832 9082
Fax 0161 835 2139
Web www.kingschambers.com
Email jhoggett@kingschambers.com

HOGGETT, Jonathan
Stephens & Scown

Position
Partner – head of property department
Qualifications
BA, Law
Career history
Since 1994 Partner, Stephens & Scown.
1988-94 Partner, Turner Kenneth Brown.
1985-88 Partner, Jeffrey Green Russell.
1982-85 Nabarro Nathanson.
1979-82 Macfarlanes.
1978 Admitted to Roll of Solicitors.
1976-79 Meade-King & Co, Bristol
Other roles
Member, Exeter Business Leaders Forum; member, Exeter Initiative
Interests
Fishing; horse riding; sailing; shooting; walking
Contact details
Stephens & Scown Ltd, 25-28 Southernhay East, Exeter EX1 1RS
Tel 0139 221 0700
Fax 0139 227 4010
Web www.stephens-scown.co.uk
Direct fax 0139 242 9202
Mobile 07967 220543
Email property.exeter@stephens-scown.co.uk

HOLBECH, Charles
11 Stone Buildings

Position
Barrister
Qualifications
BA (Oxon)
Career history
1988 Called to Bar
Interests
Cricket; golf; rugby
Contact details
11 Stone Buildings, London WC2A 3TG
Tel 020 7831 6381
Fax 020 7831 2575
Web www.11stonebuildings.com
Email holbech@11stonebuildings.com

HOLDEN, Geoff
Parsons Son & Basley

Position
Senior partner
Qualifications
FRICS
Other roles
RICS residential faculty board member; RICS residential valuation and survey group member
Contact details
Parsons Son & Basley, 32 Queens Road, Brighton BN1 3YE
Tel 01273 326171
Fax 01273 821224
Web www.psandb.co.uk
Email geoffholden@psandb.co.uk

HOLDER, Graham
CB Richard Ellis

Position
Managing director – building consultancy
Contact details
CB Richard Ellis, St Martin's Court, 10 Paternoster Row, London EC4M 7HP
Tel 020 7182 2000
Fax 020 7182 2001
Web www.cbre.com
Direct tel 020 7182 3349
Mobile 07774 824688
Email graham.holder@cbre.com

HOLDER, Paul
Parsons Son & Basley

Position
Partner
Qualifications
MRICS
Career history
1991 Joined Parsons Son & Basley.
1987-91 Stiles Harold Williams.
1987 Estates department, Brighton Borough Council
Contact details
Parsons Son & Basley, 32 Queens Road, Brighton BN1 3YE
Tel 01273 326171
Fax 01273 821224
Web www.psandb.co.uk
Direct tel 01273 274018
Email paulholder@psandb.co.uk

HOLGATE, David
Landmark Chambers

Position
Barrister
Qualifications
QC
Career history
1978 Called to Bar
Professional memberships
Administrative Law Bar Association; Planning & Environment Bar Association
Contact details
Landmark Chambers, 4 Breams Buildings, London EC4A 1AQ
Tel 020 7430 1221
Fax 020 7421 1399
Web www.landmarkchambers.co.uk
Email clerks@landmarkchambers.co.uk

HOLLAND, Katharine
9 Old Square

Position
Barrister
Contact details
9 Old Square (Chambers of Michael Driscoll QC), Ground Floor, London WC2A 3SR
Tel 020 7405 4682
Fax 020 7831 7107
Web www.9oldsquare.co.uk
Email katharine.holland@9oldsquare.co.uk

HOLLAND, Philip
Estates & General

Position
Finance director
Contact details
Estates & General plc, Penn House, 30 High Street, Rickmansworth WD3 1EP
Tel 01923 285999
Fax 01923 770547
Email phil.holland@estates-general.com

HOLLANDS, Lisa
EA Shaw

Position
Partner
Contact details
EA Shaw, 9-12 Bow Street, London WC2E 7AB
Tel 020 7240 2255
Fax 020 7831 1012
Web www.eashaw.com
Direct tel 020 7420 3036
Email lh@eashaw.com

HOLLEY, Simon
Holley Blake

Position
Senior partner
Qualifications
BSc Hons; MRICS
Career history
Since 1995 Founder/senior partner, Holley Blake & Cooper (became Holley Blake in 1996).
1991-95 Partner, Brian Cooper & Co.
1980-91 Director, DTZ Debenham Thorpe
Professional memberships
RICS
Contact details
Holley Blake Ltd, 1 Mount Street, London W1K 3LE
Tel 020 7629 4171
Fax 020 7493 2267
Web www.holleyblake.com
Mobile 07747 013196
Email jo@holleyblake.co.uk

HOLLINS, Christopher
Lamberts

Position
Head – landlord and tenant division
Qualifications
FRICS
Professional memberships
RICS
Contact details
Lamberts Ltd, 387 City Road, London EC1V 1NA
Tel 020 7278 8191
Fax 020 7837 5790
Web www.lambertsurv.co.uk
Direct tel 020 7520 2302
Email chrish@lambertsurv.co.uk

HOLLOWOOD, Stephen
GVA Grimley

Position
Partner
Qualifications
BSc Hons; Dip TP; MRTPI; MBEng; Chartered Town Planner
Career history
1988 Joined Grimley (now GVA Grimley).
1975-88 Birmingham City Council
Professional memberships
Association of Building Engineers; RTPI
Contact details
GVA Grimley, 3 Brindleyplace, Birmingham B1 2JB
Tel 0870 900 8990
Fax 0121 609 8314
Web www.gvagrimley.co.uk
Direct tel 0121 609 8318
Mobile 07831 820632
Email stephen.hollowood@gvagrimley.co.uk

HOLMES, Andrew
Edinburgh City Council

Position
Director – city development
Qualifications
BSc, Civil Eng (Leeds); MSc, Transport (Newcastle)
Career history
1973 Joined Edinburgh Corp (Lothian region).
1968-73 Durham City Council
Professional memberships
Scottish Society of Directors of Planning; Society of Chief Officers of Transportation
Interests
Art; canoeing; gardening; hill walking
Contact details
Edinburgh City Council, 1 Cockburn Street, Edinburgh EH1 1BJ
Tel 0131 529 3524
Fax 0131 529 3498
Web www.edinburgh.gov.uk
Email andrew.holmes@edinburgh.gov.uk

HOLMES, Jonathan
FPDSavills

Position
Director – out-of-house investment
Qualifications
BSc Hons; MRICS
Career history
1997 Joined FPDSavills as associate director (fund management); appointed director (national investment) in 2000.
1990-97 Insignia Richard Ellis
Professional memberships
RICS
Interests
Horse riding; keep fit; rugby
Contact details
FPDSavills Ltd, 20 Grosvenor Hill, London W1K 3HQ
Tel 020 7499 8644
Fax 020 7495 3773
Web www.fpdsavills.co.uk
Direct tel 020 7409 8754
Direct fax 020 7409 2635
Mobile 07870 555738
Email jholmes@fpdsavills.co.uk

HOLMES, Rodney
Grosvenor

Position
Retail projects director
Qualifications
BSc; MSc, Arch
Contact details
Grosvenor Ltd, 70 Grosvenor Street, London W1K 3JP
Tel 020 7408 0988
Fax 020 7629 9115
Web www.grosvenor.com
Direct tel 020 7312 6247
Direct fax 020 7312 6242
Mobile 07909 996148
Email rod.holmes@grosvenor.com

HOLT, David
Vail Williams

Position
Consultant – asset management
Qualifications
MRICS
Professional memberships
RICS
Interests
Football; golf
Contact details
Vail Williams, Thames Valley Office, 130 Wharfedale Road, Winnersh RG41 5RB
Tel 0118 933 5600
Fax 0118 933 5634
Web www.vailwilliams.com
Email dholt@vailwilliams.com

HOMER, Stephen
Big Yellow Group

Position
Director
Qualifications
BSc Hons; MRICS
Career history
Since 1999 Director, Big Yellow Group.
1996-99 Senior executive, Edge Properties.
1993-96 Acquisitions manager, Dixons Stores Group.
1989-93 Grant & Partners
Professional memberships
Institute of Directors; RICS
Contact details
Big Yellow Group plc, 2 The Deans, Bridge Road, Bagshot GU19 5AT
Tel 01276 470190
Fax 01276 470191
Web www.bigyellow.co.uk
Mobile 07768 877380
Email shomer@thebigyellow.co.uk

HONE, Dennis
English Partnerships

Position
Regional director – Eastern England and Milton

Keynes
Qualifications
MA, Finance & Accounting
Career history
Since 1999 Corporate services director, English Partnerships; now regional director.
1992-99 Finance director, Commission for the New Towns.
1987-92 Financial controller, London Docklands Development Corp
Other roles
CIPFA Honours (5th prize winner)
Professional memberships
Chartered Institute of Public Finance & Accountancy
Contact details
English Partnerships, Central Business Exchange, 414-428 Midsummer Boulevard, Milton Keynes MK9 2EA
Tel 01908 692692
Fax 01908 691333
Web www.englishpartnerships.co.uk
Direct tel 01908 353732
Direct fax 01908 353647
Mobile 07771 813959
Email dennishone@englishpartnerships.co.uk

HONEY, Malcolm
Edward Symmons & Partners
Position
Partner
Qualifications
FRICS
Contact details
Edward Symmons & Partners, 2 Southwark Street, London SE1 1RQ
Tel 020 7955 8454
Fax 020 7407 6423
Web www.edwardsymmons.com
Email Malcolm.honey@edwardsymmons.com

HONEYWILL, Christopher
Edward Symmons & Partners
Position
Partner
Contact details
Edward Symmons & Partners, Nuffield House, 41-46 Piccadilly, London W1J 0DS
Tel 020 7344 4500
Fax 020 7344 4555
Web www.edwardsymmons.com
Email chris.honeywill@edwardsymmons.com

HOPE, Simon
FPDSavills
Position
Executive director – head of out-of-house investment
Qualifications
MRICS
Career history
1986 Joined FPDSavills; appointed director in 1995 and joined board in 1999
Professional memberships
RICS
Interests
Farming; golf; horse racing; shooting; squash; tennis
Contact details
FPDSavills Ltd, 20 Grosvenor Hill, London W1K 3HQ
Tel 020 7499 8644
Fax 020 7495 3773
Web www.fpdsavills.co.uk
Direct tel 020 7409 8725
Mobile 07740 404003
Email shope@fpdsavills.co.uk

HOPKINS, James
Annington Holdings
Position
Chief executive
Qualifications
MA
Career history
Since 1998 Chief executive, Annington Holdings.
1987-98 Hanson: property manager, then senior property manager, Hanson Properties; managing director of Hanson Land from 1993.
1981-87 Military service, Life Guards
Professional memberships
Institute of Directors
Contact details
Annington Holdings plc, 1 James Street, London W1U 1DR
Tel 020 7960 7500
Fax 020 7960 7501
Web www.annington.co.uk
Direct tel 020 7960 7549
Direct fax 020 7960 7548
Email jamesh@annington.co.uk

HOPKINS, Jameson
Mapeley
Position
Chief executive
Qualifications
MRICS
Career history
1998 Joined Delancey Estates as director; now chief executive of Mapeley.
1990-98 Investment director, FPDSavills
Professional memberships
Business Management Property Forum; RICS
Interests
Horse riding; motorcycling
Contact details
Mapeley Ltd, Euston Tower, 286 Euston Road, London NW1 3UQ
Tel 020 7788 1700
Fax 020 7788 1801
Direct tel 020 7788 1811
Mobile 07775 950045
Email jamie.hopkins@mapeley.com

HOPKINS, Margaret
London & Cambridge Properties
Position
Marketing director
Career history
1972 Joined Joined London & Cambridge group; now marketing director
Other roles
Director of all other London & Cambridge Properties subsidiaries
Interests
Piano; reading
Contact details
London & Cambridge Properties Ltd, Building 23, First Avenue, Kingswinford DY6 7NA
Tel 01384 400123
Fax 01384 400862
Web www.lcp-properties.co.uk
Mobile 07771 554566
Email mhopkins@lcpproperties.co.uk

HOPKINSON, Sonia
Cobbetts
Position
Partner – head of property investment team
Qualifications
MA (Oxon)
Career history
Since 1991 Partner, Cobbetts.
1988-91 Aaron & Partners; partner on leaving.
1987 Admitted to Roll of Solicitors.
1985-88 Biddle & Co
Interests
Food; horse riding; opera; pets; singing; travel; wine
Contact details
Cobbetts, Ship Canal House, King Street, Manchester M2 4WB
Tel 0161 833 3333
Fax 0161 833 3030
Web www.cobbetts.co.uk
Direct fax 0161 830 2645
Mobile 07712 661909
Email sonia.hopkinson@cobbetts.co.uk

H

HOPPER, Carol
Allen & Overy

Position
Partner – real estate
Qualifications
BA (Oxon)
Career history
1989 Joined Allen & Overy; became partner in 1996
Professional memberships
Law Society
Interests
Art; diving/scuba diving; walking
Contact details
Allen & Overy, One New Change, London EC4M 9QQ
Tel 020 7330 3000
Fax 020 7330 9999
Web www.allenovery.com
Direct tel 020 7330 4915
Email carol.hopper@allenovery.com

HORGAN, Matt
CIT Group

Position
Investment director
Qualifications
BA (Yale); JD (Harvard Law School)
Career history
1997-2002 Executive director, Morgan Stanley Real Estate Funds, London.
1992-97 Managing director, Dean Witter Discover & Co, New York
Contact details
CIT Group plc, 8-10 Bourdon Street, London W1K 3PD
Tel 020 7667 7766
Fax 020 7667 7770
Web www.cit.co.uk
Direct fax 020 7667 7763
Email mh@cit.co.uk

HORLER, Christopher
Royal Bank of Scotland

Position
Head of European real estate group
Contact details
Bank of Scotland, 155 Bishopsgate, London EC2M 3YB
Tel 020 7012 9400
Direct tel 020 7012 9368
Email chris.horler@bankofscotland.co.uk

HORNE, Wilson
Kings Chambers

Position
Barrister
Qualifications
LLB Hons (Leeds)
Career history
Since 1992 Barrister, 40 King Street Chambers, Manchester.
1992 Called to Bar
Other roles
Involved in management of chambers and handles accommodation issues; involved in Manchester University's pro bono legal advice unit
Professional memberships
Northern Chancery Bar Association
Interests
Hill walking; marathon running; rugby
Contact details
Kings Chambers, 40 King Street, Manchester M2 6BA
Tel 0161 832 9082
Fax 0161 835 2139
Web www.kingschambers.com
Mobile 07789 934341
Email whorne@kingschambers.com

HORNER, David
Charles Russell

Position
Partner
Career history
Since 1989 Partner, Charles Russell.
1975-89 Assistant solicitor/partner, Braby & Waller Solicitors.
1975 Admitted to Roll of Solicitors.
1971-74 Westminster City Council
Professional memberships
Association of European Lawyers; City of Westminster & Holborn Law Society; Law Society
Interests
Family; IT; jazz; music; piano; running
Contact details
Charles Russell, 8-10 New Fetter Lane, London EC4A 1RS
Tel 020 7203 5000
Fax 020 7203 0200
Web www.cr-law.co.uk
Direct tel 020 7203 5132
Direct fax 020 7203 0204
Mobile 07768 105387
Email david.horner@charlesrussell.co.uk

HORNUNG, Chris
Edward Symmons & Partners

Position
Partner – real estate
Contact details
Edward Symmons & Partners, 2 Southwark Street, London SE1 1RQ
Tel 020 7955 8454
Fax 020 7407 6423
Web www.edwardsymmons.com
Email chris.hornung@edwardsymmons.com

HORRELL, Barry
J Sainsbury

Position
Head of capital projects
Qualifications
FCIOB; MAPM
Career history
1990-2002 Construction director, BAA Lynton
Professional memberships
Association for Project Management; Chartered Institute of Building
Interests
Golf; rugby; sailing; shooting
Contact details
J Sainsbury plc, 33 Holborn, London EC1N 2HT
Tel 020 7695 6000
Fax 020 7695 7610
Web www.j-sainsbury.co.uk
Direct tel 020 7695 0052
Direct fax 020 7695 0052
Mobile 07831 527642
Email barry.horrell@sainsburys.co.uk

HORRELL, Tony
Jones Lang LaSalle

Position
Chief executive – European capital markets
Qualifications
MBA; BSc; MRICS
Career history
1982 Jones Lang LaSalle; appointed partner in 1989, European partner in 1993, international director in 1996 and chief executive (capital markets) in 2000
Professional memberships
Investment Property Forum; RICS
Contact details
Jones Lang LaSalle Ltd, 22 Hanover Square, London W1A 2BN
Tel 020 7493 6040
Fax 020 7408 0220
Web www.joneslanglasalle.com
Direct tel 020 7399 5866
Direct fax 020 7399 5470
Mobile 07774 995542
Email tony.horrell@eu.joneslanglasalle.com

HORRIDGE, Matt
HBS Facilities Management

Position
Managing director

H

Qualifications
BSc Hons; MRICS
Career history
Since 1999 Managing director, HBS Facilities Management.
1996-99 Director of facilities management, Servus.
1990-96 Joined Turner & Townsend before becoming a founding member of Turner & Townsend Facilities Management; became director in 1996
Professional memberships
RICS
Interests
Motor sports
Contact details
HBS Facilities Management Ltd, Ireland House, 150 New Bond Street, London W1S
Tel 020 7317 4800
Fax 020 7317 4801
Web www.HBSFM.com
Direct tel 020 7317 4854
Mobile 07778 792113
Email matt.horridge@HBSFM.com

HORRIX, Peter
House of Fraser
Position
Director – store development
Contact details
House of Fraser plc, 1 Howick Place, London SW1P 1BH
Tel 020 7963 2000
Fax 020 7963 2698
Web www.houseoffraser.co.uk
Email phorrix@hof.co.uk

HORSBURGH, Adrian
King Sturge
Position
Partner – investment
Qualifications
MRICS
Professional memberships
RICS
Contact details
King Sturge, 7 Stratford Place, London W1C 1ST
Tel 020 7493 4933
Fax 020 7409 0469
Web www.kingsturge.com
Direct tel 020 7318 4212
Email adrian.horsburgh@kingsturge.co.uk

HORTON, Matthew
2 Mitre Court Buildings
Position
Barrister
Qualifications
QC
Career history
1989 Appointed QC.
1969 Called to Bar
Professional memberships
Administrative Law Bar Association; Planning & Environment Bar Association
Contact details
2 Mitre Court Buildings (Chambers of Guy Roots QC), 2nd Floor, London EC4Y 7BX
Tel 020 7583 1380
Fax 020 7353 7772
Web www.2mcb.co.uk
Email matthew.horton@2mcb.co.uk

HORTON, Michael
Hortons' Estate
Position
Chairman
Contact details
Hortons' Estate Ltd, 31a Colmore Row, Birmingham B3 2BU
Tel 0121 236 6481
Fax 0121 236 6548
Web www.hortons.co.uk
Email draffan@hortons.co.uk

HOUGH, Robert
Peel Holdings
Position
Non-executive deputy chairman
Qualifications
DL; LLB Hons; Hon DBA; Hon DLitt
Career history
Since 1989 Deputy chairman, Peel Holdings; non-executive deputy chairman from 2002.
1974-89 Partner, Slater Heelis.
1970 Admitted to Roll of Solicitors
Other roles
Chairman, Peel Airports; chairman, Liverpool Airport; deputy chairman, Brammer; chairman, Zero Waste Holdings; chairman, North West Business Leadership Team; deputy chairman, QA; chairman, Century Radio 105.4; non-executive director, Shiloh; non-executive director, Cheshire Building Society; non-executive director, Robert Turley Associates
Professional memberships
Law Society; Notaries' Society
Interests
Gardening; golf; sport
Contact details
Peel Holdings plc, Peel Dome, The Trafford Centre, Manchester M17 8PL
Tel 0161 629 8200
Fax 0161 629 8333
Web www.peel.co.uk
Email rhough@peelholdings.co.uk

HOUGHTON, David
Shops etc
Position
Chairman
Qualifications
FRICS
Other roles
Chairman, St Pancras Street Properties; member of steering committee, Chartered Surveyors Voluntary Service; trustee, New Lease Trust; director, and; director, xyz
Professional memberships
British Council of Shopping Centres; BPF; FIABCI; International Council of Shopping Centers; RICS
Contact details
Shops etc, 1 Tenterden Street, London W1S 1TA
Tel 020 7317 3737
Fax 020 7317 3740
Web www.shopsetc.co.uk
Email dhoughton@shopsetc.co.uk

HOULIHAN, Amanda
Hammerson
Position
Human resources director
Contact details
Hammerson plc, 100 Park Lane, London W1K 7AR
Tel 020 7887 1000
Fax 020 7887 1010
Web www.hammerson.co.uk
Direct fax 020 7887 1050
Email ahoulihan@hammerson.co.uk

HOULSTON, Stuart
Clinton Cards
Position
Property director
Contact details
Clinton Cards plc, The Crystal Building, Langston Road, Loughton IG10 3TH
Tel 020 8502 3711
Fax 020 8502 0295
Web www.clintoncards.co.uk
Direct tel 020 8502 8270
Email stuart.houlston@clintoncards.co.uk

HOUSLEY, Keith
Brabners Chaffe Street
Position
Partner – head of development teams
Contact details
Brabners Chaffe Street, 1 Dale Street, Liverpool

L2 2ET
Tel 0151 600 3000
Fax 0151 600 3300
Web www.brabnerschaffestreet.com
Email keith.housley@brabnerscs.com

HOUSLOP, Mark
DTZ Debenham Tie Leung

Position
Director – head of international investments
Qualifications
FRICS
Career history
1979 Appointed partner, DTZ; has worked in UK and US; set up and ran New York office for five years
Professional memberships
RICS
Contact details
DTZ Debenham Tie Leung, One Curzon Street, London W1A 5PZ
Tel 020 7408 1161
Fax 020 7643 6000
Web www.dtz.com
Direct tel 020 7643 6414
Email mark.houslop@dtz.com

HOUSTON, Paul
Field Fisher Waterhouse

Position
Partner – property
Career history
1991 Admitted to Roll of Solicitors (England and Wales).
1989 Joined Field Fisher Waterhouse; became partner in 1995.
1989 Admitted to Roll of Solicitors (Scotland).
1987-89 Ross Harper & Murphy, Glasgow
Contact details
Field Fisher Waterhouse, 35 Vine Street, London EC3N 2AA
Tel 020 7861 4000
Fax 020 7488 0084
Web www.ffwlaw.com
Direct tel 020 7861 4078
Email Paul.Houston@ffw.com

HOUSTON, Robert
ING Real Estate Investment Management (UK)

Position
Chairman and chief executive
Qualifications
BSc; FRICS
Career history
1980 Joined Baring, Houston & Saunders (now ING Real Estate Investment Management (UK)).
1973-80 Richard Ellis
Other roles
FSA approved
Professional memberships
Academy for Chief Executives; RICS
Contact details
ING Real Estate Investment Management (UK), 9 Devonshire Square, London EC2M 4WX
Tel 020 7398 4310
Fax 020 7398 4311
Web www.ingrealestate.co.uk
Direct tel 020 7398 5559
Email robert.houston@ingrealestate.co.uk

HOWARD, Amanda
Nabarro Nathanson

Position
Partner – real estate finance
Qualifications
LLB
Other roles
Head of property finance team
Contact details
Nabarro Nathanson, Lacon House, Theobald's Road, London WC1X 8RW
Tel 020 7524 6000
Fax 020 7524 6524
Web www.nabarro.com
Direct tel 020 7524 6342
Email a.howard@nabarro.com

HOWARD, Karen
Olswang

Position
Partner – head of planning
Qualifications
Solicitor
Career history
Since 2003 Partner/head of planning, Olswang.
2001-03 Head of planning, DJ Freeman.
2000-01 Legal manager, Ashurst Morris Crisp.
1988-2000 Senior manager, Berwin Leighton Paisner.
1985-88 London Borough of Newham
Professional memberships
ILEX
Interests
Keep fit; motorcycling; music; travel; writing
Contact details
Olswang, 90 High Holborn, London WC1V 6XX
Tel 020 7067 3000
Fax 020 7067 3999
Web www.olswang.com
Direct tel 020 7067 3586
Email karen.howard@olswang.com

HOWARD, Mervyn
Grosvenor

Position
Fund management director
Career history
Since 2001 Fund management director, Grosvenor.
1998-2001 Executive vice-president, TrizecHahn.
1992-98 Director, GE Capital Real Estate
Other roles
Grosvenor's UK and Ireland statutory board member
Contact details
Grosvenor Ltd, 70 Grosvenor Street, London W1K 3JP
Tel 020 7408 0988
Fax 020 7629 9115
Web www.grosvenor.com
Direct tel 020 7312 6181
Direct fax 020 7873 1181
Email mervyn.howard@grosvenor.com

HOWARTH, James
Frontier Estates

Position
Associate director
Qualifications
BSc Hons; MRICS
Career history
1996-99 Associate partner, Matthews & Goodman.
1993-96 King Sturge & Co
Professional memberships
RICS
Interests
IT; sailing; tennis; walking
Contact details
Frontier Estates Ltd, Acorn House, Midsummer Boulevard, Milton Keynes MK9 3HP
Tel 01908 238888
Fax 01908 241111
Web www.frontier-estates.com
Mobile 07714 288317
Email jameshowarth@frontier-estates.com

HOWE, Nick
Edgerley Simpson Howe & Partners

Position
Partner
Career history
Since 1994 Partner, Edgerley Simpson Howe & Partners.
1986-94 Partner/director, Bernard Thorpe/DTZ.
1985-86 St Quintin
Professional memberships
RICS

H

Interests
Food; golf; rugby
Contact details
Edgerley Simpson Howe & Partners, 39 Dover Street, London W1S 4NN
Tel 020 7499 6000
Fax 020 7499 9433
Web www.eshp.com
Mobile 07710 353017
Email nick@eshp.com

HOWE, Robert
Green Property

Position
Director – Northern operations
Qualifications
MRICS; CIMA
Career history
Since 1994 Director, Green Property.
1989-94 Richard Brudenell
Professional memberships
RICS
Interests
Family; golf; rugby
Contact details
Green Property Ltd, 8 Exchange Quay, Salford M5 3EJ
Tel 0161 872 5426
Fax 0161 877 1633
Email rhowe@greenpropertyplc.com

HOWELL, Simon
Rogers Chapman

Position
Divisional director – national office agency
Contact details
Rogers Chapman plc, Prince Frederick House, 37 Maddox Street, London W1S 2PP
Tel 020 7499 8600
Fax 020 7493 5290
Web www.rogerschapman.co.uk
Email simon.howell@rogerschapman.co.uk

HOWELL, Stuart
Hartnell Taylor Cook

Position
Partner
Qualifications
BSc; MRICS
Professional memberships
RICS
Contact details
Hartnell Taylor Cook, 12-13 Conduit Street, London W1S 2XH
Tel 020 7491 7323
Fax 020 7491 3032
Web www.htc.uk.com
Direct tel 020 7409 3702
Mobile 07831 350900
Email stuart.howell@htc.uk.com

HOWELLS, Phillip
Jones Lang LaSalle

Position
European director
Contact details
Jones Lang LaSalle Ltd, 22 Hanover Square, London W1A 2BN
Tel 020 7493 6040
Fax 020 7408 0220
Web www.joneslanglasalle.com
Direct tel 020 7399 5950
Direct fax 020 7499 4815
Email phillip.howells@eu.joneslanglasalle.com

HOWES, Sir Christopher
Sir Christopher Howes

Position
Consultant
Qualifications
KCVO; CB; BSc; MPhil; FRICS; Hon DLitt; Hon FRIBA
Career history
1989-2001 Chief executive/second commissioner, Crown Estate.
1979-89 Director of land and property, HM Government.
1967-79 Partner/senior partner, Percy Howes & Co.
1966-67 Greater London Council
Other roles
Advisory board member, Barclays Private Banking; non-executive director, Norwich & Peterborough Building Society; non-executive director, Howard De Walden Estates; council member, Duchy of Lancaster; BPF council member; member, court of the University of East Anglia; member, court of advisers for St Paul's Cathedral; member, HRH Prince of Wales's Council (since 1990); visiting professor, Bartlett School of Architecture & Planning at London University (since 1985); council member, Norfolk Archaeological Trust; trustee, British Architectural Library
Professional memberships
RIBA; RICS
Interests
Art; music; sailing
Contact details
Sir Christopher Howes' office, Millennium House, 132 Grosvenor Road, London SW1V 3JY
Tel 020 7828 9920
Fax 020 7821 5813
Email christopher@howesuk.com

HOWGATE, Lyn
Matthews & Goodman

Position
Head of marketing
Qualifications
BA Hons; Dip M; MCIM
Career history
1986 Joined Matthews & Goodman as town planner; head of marketing since 1998
Professional memberships
Chartered Institute of Marketing; RTPI
Interests
Art; wine
Contact details
Matthews & Goodman, Dorland House, 14-16 Regent Street, London SW1Y 4PH
Tel 020 7747 8847
Fax 020 7747 8848
Web www.matthews-goodman.co.uk
Direct tel 020 7747 3199
Mobile 07778 899159
Email lhowgate@matthews-goodman.co.uk

HOWIE, Alan
Aberdeen Property Investors

Position
Director – fund management
Contact details
Aberdeen Property Investors, Charles House, 5-11 Regent Street, London SW1Y 4LR
Tel 020 7747 1700
Fax 020 7839 7460
Web www.aberdeenpropertyinvestors.com
Email
alan.howie@aberdeenpropertyinvestors.com

HOWIE, Michelle
Herbert Smith

Position
Partner – real estate
Qualifications
BA Law
Career history
1993 Admitted to Roll of Solicitors
Professional memberships
Law Society
Interests
Sailing; squash; tennis
Contact details
Herbert Smith, Exchange House, 10 Primrose Street, London EC2A 2NY
Tel 020 7374 8000
Fax 020 7374 0888
Web www.herbertsmith.com
Direct tel 020 7466 2104
Email michelle.howie@herbertsmith.com

HOWITT, Nick
Insight Investment Management

Position
Director – property investment
Qualifications
MRICS; BSc
Career history
1994-2002 CMIG.
1988-94 Donaldsons
Other roles
Asset manager, HBOS Group
Professional memberships
Investment Property Forum; RICS
Interests
Golf; tennis
Contact details
Insight Investment Management, City Place House, 55 Basinghall Street, London EC2V 5DL
Tel 020 7930 5474
Web www.insightinvestment.com
Direct tel 020 7321 1256
Direct fax 020 7321 1434
Email nick.howitt@insightinvestment.com

HOYLE, Roger
Veale Wasbrough

Position
Partner – head of construction
Career history
1972 Joined Stanley Wasbrough (now Veale Wasbrough); became partner in 1973
Other roles
Committee member, Technology & Construction Court Solicitors Association (since 1990)
Interests
Photography; walking
Contact details
Veale Wasbrough, Orchard Court, Orchard Lane, Bristol BS1 5DS
Tel 0117 925 2020
Fax 0117 925 2025
Web www.vwl.co.uk
Email rhoyle@vwl.co.uk

HUBBARD, Charles
Edmund Kirby

Position
Managing partner
Qualifications
BSc; FRICS; FICPD
Career history
Since 1988 Partner, Edmund Kirby; managing partner from 2000
Other roles
Board member of Liverpool Housing Action Trust (1994); treasurer, Wilton Trust; president, Property Agents International (2003-05); chairman, RICS education and membership committee (1997-2000); member of general council (1997-2000); chairman, RICS presidents' task force on education (1999-2000)
Professional memberships
Atheneum Club; Institute of Continuing Professional Development; Liverpool Racquets Club; RICS
Interests
Art; opera; sailing; skiing; theatre; walking
Contact details
Edmund Kirby, India Buildings, Water Street, Liverpool L2 0TZ
Tel 0151 236 4552
Fax 0151 236 4024
Web www.edmundkirby.co.uk
Mobile 07802 213946
Email charleshubbard@edmundkirby.co.uk

HUBBARD, Stephen
CB Richard Ellis

Position
Deputy chairman – Europe
Qualifications
MRICS
Career history
1976 Joined Richard Ellis (now CB Richard Ellis)
Professional memberships
RICS
Interests
Sailing; skiing
Contact details
CB Richard Ellis, Kingsley House, 1a Wimpole Street, London W1G 0RE
Tel 020 7182 2000
Fax 020 7182 7001
Web www.cbre.com
Direct fax 020 7182 2060
Email stephen.hubbard@cbre.com

HUBBLE, Geoff
Cluttons

Position
Partner – rating
Contact details
Cluttons, Portman House, 2 Portman Street, London W1H 6DU
Tel 020 7408 1010
Fax 020 7629 3263
Web www.cluttons.com
Direct fax 020 7409 7710
Email ghubble@cluttons.com

HUCKERBY, Bryan
Lambert Smith Hampton

Position
Director
Qualifications
BSc; FRICS
Career history
Since 1995 Director (business space/industrial), Lambert Smith Hampton.
1987-95 Director, Hallam Brackett/Connell Wilson (Derby office).
1978-87 Derby City Council
Professional memberships
RICS
Interests
Football; golf
Contact details
Lambert Smith Hampton Ltd, 17-21 Hounds Gate, Nottingham NG1 7DR
Tel 0115 950 1414
Fax 0115 941 0316
Web www.lsh.co.uk
Email bhuckerby@lsh.co.uk

HUDSON, Mark
Country Land & Business Association

Position
President
Qualifications
MA (Cantab)
Other roles
Vice-chairman, NWF Group
Contact details
Country Land & Business Association, 16 Belgrave Square, London SW1X 8PG
Tel 020 7235 0511
Fax 020 7235 4696
Web www.cla.org.uk
Email mark.hudson@cla.org.uk

HUDSON, Paul
South East England Development Agency

Position
Director – development and infrastructure
Qualifications
BA, Geography; MA, Management; MSc, Town Planning
Career history
1998-99 Chief executive, Locate in Kent.
1981-98 City technical manager, Rochester upon Medway City Council.
1979-81 Director, Travers Morgan
Professional memberships
RTPI
Contact details
South East England Development Agency, SEEDA Headquarters, Cross Lanes, Guildford GU1 1YA
Tel 01483 484200
Fax 01483 484247
Web www.seeda.co.uk
Email paulhudson@seeda.co.uk

H

HUGHES, Alastair
Jones Lang LaSalle

Position
Managing director – England
Qualifications
BA; Dip LE; MRICS
Career history
1988 Joined Jones Lang LaSalle
Professional memberships
RICS
Contact details
Jones Lang LaSalle Ltd, 22 Hanover Square, London W1A 2BN
Tel 020 7493 6040
Fax 020 7408 0220
Web www.joneslanglasalle.com
Direct tel 020 7399 5932
Direct fax 020 7399 5299
Mobile 07771 542541
Email alastair.hughes@eu.joneslanglasalle.com

HUGHES, Andrew
Alder King

Position
Managing partner
Contact details
Alder King, Pembroke House, 15 Pembroke Road, Bristol BS8 3BA
Tel 0117 317 1000
Fax 0117 317 1001
Web www.alderking.com
Email ahughes@alderking.com

HUGHES, Bill
Deutsche Property Asset Management

Position
Chief executive
Qualifications
MA; MSc
Career history
1997-2003 Schroder Property Investment Management: rose to deputy managing director.
1993-97 Associate, Jones Lang Wootton Fund Management.
1991-93 Research analyst, DTZ Debenham Thorpe.
1989-91 Consultant, DP3
Other roles
Committee member, Society of Property Researchers
Professional memberships
Institute of Directors; Investment Property Forum; Society of Business Economists; Society of Investment Professionals; Society of Property Researchers
Contact details
Deutsche Property Asset Management Ltd, 1 Appold Street, London EC2A 2HE
Tel 020 7545 6000
Fax 020 7545 7555
Web www.deam-uk.com
Email bill.hughes@db.com

HUGHES, David
DTZ International

Position
Director
Qualifications
BSc (Hons); CDip AF; MRICS
Career history
1989 Joined DTZ; appointed associate director in 1994 and director in 1999
Other roles
DTZ representative for Business in the Community (ProHelp) in London
Professional memberships
CoreNet Global UK; RICS
Interests
Golf; rugby; wine
Contact details
DTZ International Ltd, One Curzon Street, London W1A 5PZ
Tel 020 7408 1161
Fax 020 7643 6062
Web www.dtz.com
Direct tel 020 7408 2801
Direct fax 020 7408 2857
Mobile 07767 615062
Email david.hughes@dtz.com

HUGHES, David
Swanke Hayden Connell International

Position
Managing director – principal
Qualifications
BA, Arch; Dip Arch; RIBA
Career history
1988 Joined Swanke Hayden Connell International.
1987-88 Skidmore Owings & Merrill
Professional memberships
American Institute of Architects (international associate); Architects Registration Board; British Council for Offices; Institute of Directors; Ordre des Architectes Conseil Régional D'Ile de France; RIBA
Interests
Art; football; golf; jazz; music; rugby; travel
Contact details
Swanke Hayden Connell International Ltd, 25 Christopher Street, London EC2A 2BS
Tel 020 7454 8200
Fax 020 7454 8400
Web www.shca.com
Direct tel 020 7454 8201
Mobile 07798 842116
Email hughes.d@london.SHCA.com

HUGHES, Gerry
GVA Grimley

Position
Partner – head of urban regeneration
Qualifications
MRTPI
Professional memberships
RTPI
Interests
Football; reading; skiing
Contact details
GVA Grimley, 81 Fountain Street, Manchester M2 2EE
Tel 0870 900 8990
Fax 0161 956 4009
Web www.gvagrimley.co.uk
Direct tel 0161 956 4222
Mobile 07831 277672
Email gerry.hughes@gvagrimley.co.uk

HUGHES, Ian
Phoenix Beard

Position
Director – retail
Qualifications
FRICS
Contact details
Phoenix Beard, 7-10 Chandos Street, London W1G 9EH
Tel 020 7323 4681
Fax 020 7436 3581
Web www.phoenix-beard.co.uk
Direct tel 020 7544 1953
Mobile 07808 784781
Email ian.hughes@phoenix-beard.co.uk

HUGHES, Martin
Lambert Smith Hampton

Position
Director – professional
Qualifications
BA; MRICS
Professional memberships
RICS
Contact details
Lambert Smith Hampton Ltd, Holybrook House, 63 Castle Street, Reading RG1 7SN
Tel 0118 959 8855
Fax 0118 950 3363
Web www.lsh.co.uk
Email mhughes@lsh.co.uk

HUGHES, Michael
Helios Properties

Position
Director
Qualifications
BA Hons; MRICS
Career history
1996 Formed Helios Properties; main board director.
1990-96 Senior development surveyor, Hyperion Properties.
1988-90 Vail Williams
Other roles
Founding member, Rail Interchange Investment Group; chairman, Railfreight Interchange Investment Group
Professional memberships
RICS
Contact details
Helios Properties plc, 2 Berkeley Square, London W1J 6EB
Tel 020 7629 6452
Fax 020 7629 6453
Web www.heliosproperties.com
Email hughes@heliosproperties.com

HUGHES, William
Cluttons

Position
Partner – head of rural asset management
Qualifications
FRICS
Professional memberships
Country Land & Business Association
Contact details
Cluttons, 1 Eastwood Court, Broadwater Road, Romsey SO51 8JJ
Tel 01794 522670
Fax 01794 523142
Web www.cluttons.com
Email bhughes@cluttons.com

HUGILL, Nigel
Chelsfield

Position
Managing director
Other roles
Member, advisory group to Bartlett School of Planning, University College London; trustee, Architecture Foundation
Contact details
Chelsfield plc, 67 Brook Street, London W1K 4NJ
Tel 020 7493 3977
Fax 020 7493 1444
Web www.chelsfield.com
Email nhugill@chelsfield.co.uk

HUME, Robert
Bride Hall Developments

Position
Development director
Qualifications
BA Hons; BTP; MRTPI
Career history
1988 Joined Bride Hall.
1986-88 Development executive, Pelham Homes/Rosehaugh
Professional memberships
RTPI
Interests
Cinema; family; football; music
Contact details
Bride Hall Developments Ltd, 49 Hays Mews, London W1J 5QQ
Tel 020 7493 3996
Fax 020 7499 4388
Mobile 07768 125057
Email robert.hume@bride-hall.co.uk

HUMPHRIES, Colin
Global Servicing Solutions Europe

Position
Asset manager
Qualifications
MRICS
Career history
1993-2003 DePfa Bank (now Aareal): became head of property services in 1999; transferred to Amsterdam in 2000; on leaving, director of structured finance.
1985-92 Valuer (City of London)/investment agent (Belgium), St Quintin
Professional memberships
RICS
Interests
Golf; sailing; windsurfing
Contact details
Global Servicing Solutions Europe Ltd, 2 King Edward Street, London EC1A 1HQ
Tel 020 7628 1000
Direct tel 020 7996 3763
Direct fax 020 7995 0537
Mobile 07789 746357
Email colin_humphries@ml.com

HUNT, Nigel
Crossland Otter Hunt

Position
Partner
Qualifications
Dip Est Man; FRICS
Career history
Since 1988 Partner, Crossland Otter Hunt.
1976-88 Healey & Baker
Other roles
Committee member, Arbrix; co-founder of Office Agents Society; secretary, Index
Professional memberships
RICS
Interests
Art; beer; cricket; golf; rugby; skiing; wine
Contact details
Crossland Otter Hunt, Greybrook House, 28 Brook Street, London W1K 5DH
Tel 020 7408 1114
Fax 020 7499 8436
Web www.c-o-h.com
Mobile 07801 928666
Email nigel@cohlondon.com

HUNT, Peter
Strutt & Parker

Position
City office partner, London
Contact details
Strutt & Parker, 1 Angel Court, London EC2R 7EQ
Tel 020 7600 3456
Fax 020 7600 3330
Web www.struttandparker.com
Email phunt@struttandparker.com

HUNT, Stephen
Goldsmiths Group

Position
Head of property
Contact details
Goldsmiths Group plc, Goldsmiths House, 2 Elland Road, Leicester LE3 1TT
Tel 0116 232 2000
Fax 0116 231 1686
Web www.goldsmiths.co.uk
Email s_hunt@goldsmiths.co.uk

HUNTER, Charles
Insight Investment Management

Position
Head of property investment
Qualifications
FRICS
Career history
1975-95 National Mutual of Australia: property manager, then property director of NM Investment Management.
1970-74 Gerald Eve & Co/Jones Lang Wootton
Professional memberships
Investment Property Forum; RICS
Interests
Sailing; singing; skiing
Contact details
Insight Investment Management, 33 Old Broad

H

Street, London EC2N 1HZ
Tel 020 7930 5474
Fax 020 7321 1423
Web www.insightinvestment.com
Direct tel 020 7321 1020
Direct fax 020 7321 1434
Email charles.hunter@insightinvestment.com

HUNTER, David
Aberdeen Property Investors

Position
Chief executive
Qualifications
FRICS
Career history
1996 Formed Argyll (became RREEF in 2000, then acquired by Aberdeen Property Investors in 2001).
1978-96 Scottish Amicable Group.
1973-78 James Barr & Son
Other roles
President, BPF; honorary Swedish consul to Glasgow
Professional memberships
BPF; Investment Property Forum; RICS
Interests
Fishing; golf; music; walking
Contact details
Aberdeen Property Investors, Charles House, 5-11 Regent Street, London SW1Y 4LR
Tel 020 7747 1700
Fax 020 7839 7460
Web www.aberdeenpropertyinvestors.com
Email
david.hunter@aberdeenpropertyinvestors.com

HUNTER, Jason
Russell-Cooke

Position
Partner – head of contentious property
Qualifications
LLB
Career history
1992 Admitted to Roll of Solicitors.
1989 Joined Russell-Cooke
Other roles
Chairman, Property Litigation Association (2003/04)
Professional memberships
Property Litigation Association
Contact details
Russell-Cooke, 8 Bedford Row, London WC1R 4BU
Tel 020 7405 6566
Fax 020 7831 2565
Web www.russell-cooke.co.uk
Email hunterj@russell-cooke.co.uk

HUNTER JONES, Nicholas
BNP Paribas

Position
Head of property
Qualifications
BSc, Est Man
Career history
Since 1986 Head of property, BNP Paribas.
1982-86 Property share analyst, Quilter Goodison Co.
1976-82 Research, Jones Lang Wootton
Other roles
Non-executive director, Warnford investments
Interests
Cricket; golf; music
Contact details
BNP Paribas, 10 Harewood Avenue, London NW1 6AA
Tel 020 7595 2000
Fax 020 7595 2555
Web www.bnpparibas.com
Direct tel 020 7595 2331
Direct fax 020 7595 3355
Email nick.hunter-jones@bnpparibas.com

HUNTING, Jeremy
Freeth Melhuish

Position
Partner
Qualifications
FRICS; IRRV; MCIArb
Career history
1984 Joined Freeth & Co (now Freeth Melhuish) as associate; became partner in 1990.
1980-84 Group estates surveyor, Express Dairy
Professional memberships
Chartered Institute of Arbitrators; Institute of Revenues Rating & Valuation; RICS
Interests
Cricket; golf
Contact details
Freeth Melhuish, The Courtyard, 77-79 Marlowes, Hemel Hempstead HP1 1LF
Tel 01442 263033
Fax 01442 260628
Direct tel 01442 298803
Mobile 07836 796707
Email jmh@freethmelhuish.co.uk

HURT, Colin
Wragge & Co

Position
Partner – head of property finance
Qualifications
MA (Cantab), Law
Career history
1994 Joined Wragge & Co; partner since 1997.
1988-94 Freshfields.
1986-88 Fox & Gibbons.
1986 Admitted to Roll of Solicitors
Professional memberships
Birmingham Law Society
Interests
Gardening; horse riding; tennis
Contact details
Wragge & Co LLP, 55-73 Colmore Row, Birmingham B3 2AS
Tel 0870 903 1000
Fax 0870 904 1099
Web www.wragge.com
Direct tel 0121 214 1063
Email colin_hurt@wragge.com

HUSSEY, Michael
Land Securities Development

Position
Director
Career history
1997-2002 Head of leasing and marketing, Canary Wharf
Contact details
Land Securities Development Ltd, 5 Strand, London WC2N 5AF
Tel 020 7413 9000
Web www.landsecurities.com
Email mike.hussey@landsecurities.com

HUTCHINGS, David
Cushman & Wakefield Healey & Baker

Position
Head of European research
Qualifications
BSc Hons, Geography
Career history
1988 Joined research department, Cushman & Wakefield Healey & Baker.
1986-88 Research assistant, University of West of England.
1984-85 Assistant scientific officer, Institute of Hydrology
Other roles
Lead partner in research into investment; forecasting in UK and throughout Europe; blue sky research committee member, British Council for Offices
Professional memberships
British Council for Offices; Society of Property Researchers
Contact details
Cushman & Wakefield Healey & Baker, 43-45 Portman Square, London W1A 3BG
Tel 020 7935 5000
Fax 020 7152 5360
Web www.cushwake.com

H

Direct tel 020 7152 5029
Direct fax 020 7152 5366
Email david.hutchings@eur.cushwake.com

HUTCHINGS, Martin
199 Strand

Position
Barrister
Qualifications
MA (Oxon)
Professional memberships
Chancery Bar Association; Professional Negligence Bar Association
Contact details
199 Strand (Chambers of David Phillips QC), London WC2R 1DR
Tel 020 7520 4000
Fax 020 7379 9481
Web www.199strand.co.uk
Email mhutchings@199strand.co.uk

HUTCHINSON, Andrew
Dechert

Position
Partner – head of property investment
Qualifications
BA Hons, Law
Career history
1986 Joined Titmuss Sainer & Webb (became Titmus Sainer Dechert, then Dechert) as assistant solicitor; partner since 1990
Other roles
Contributor to *Landlord & Tenant Factbook* (Franey & Co, 1992)
Contact details
Dechert LLP, 2 Serjeants' Inn, London EC4Y 1LT
Tel 020 7583 5353
Fax 020 7353 3683
Web www.dechert.com
Direct tel 020 7775 7428
Email andrew.hutchinson@dechert.com

HUTCHINSON, Phil
BDG McColl

Position
Joint managing director
Qualifications
BA Hons, 3D Design (Interiors)
Contact details
BDG McColl Ltd, 33 St John Street, London EC1M 4PJ
Tel 020 7559 7400
Fax 020 7559 7401
Web www.bdg-workfutures.com
Email philhutchinson@bdgworkfutures.com

HUTTON, Caroline
Enterprise Chambers

Position
Barrister
Qualifications
MA (Cantab); FCIArb
Career history
1979 Called to Bar
Other roles
Founder and first secretary, Property Bar Association; joint editor, *Commercial Property Disputes, Practice & Precedents* (Sweet & Maxwell, 1999)
Professional memberships
Bar European Group; Chancery Bar Association; Chartered Institute of Arbitrators; Justice
Contact details
Enterprise Chambers (Chambers of Anthony Mann QC), 9 Old Square, London WC2A 3SR
Tel 020 7405 9471
Fax 020 7242 1447
Web www.enterprisechambers.com
Email carolinehutton@enterprisechambers.com

HUTTON, David
Lend Lease Europe

Position
Director – Europe
Qualifications
BA, Business
Other roles
Board member, Investment Property Forum; licensed real estate agent
Contact details
Lend Lease Europe Ltd, York House, 23 Kingsway, London WC2B 6UJ
Tel 020 7379 0222
Fax 020 7379 0213
Web www.lendlease.com.au
Direct tel 020 7395 7306
Direct fax 020 7395 7353
Email david_hutton@lendlease.co.uk

HYETT, Paul
RyderHKS

Position
Chairman
Qualifications
AA Dipl; MPhil; RIBA; MEWI; AABC
Career history
Since 2000 Chairman, RyderHKS; previously principal in Paul Hyett Architects and Hyett Salisbury Whiteley Architects before merger with Ryder
Other roles
Immediate past president, RIBA; international vice-president, RIBA; council member, Architectural Association; trustee, British Architectural Library Trust; trustee, Architectural Education Trust
Professional memberships
Architectural Association; RIBA
Interests
Hill walking; sailing
Contact details
RyderHKS, 36-37 Featherstone Street, London EC1Y 8QZ
Tel 020 7553 9712
Fax 020 7251 1691
Web www.ryderhks.com
Mobile 07775 787700
Email phyett@ryderhks.com

HYNARD, Andrew
Jones Lang LaSalle

Position
International director – capital markets
Qualifications
BSc; MRICS
Career history
1984 Joined Jones Lang LaSalle
Professional memberships
Investment Property Forum; RICS
Interests
Family; golf; sailing; squash; theatre
Contact details
Jones Lang LaSalle Ltd, 22 Hanover Square, London W1A 2BN
Tel 020 7493 6040
Fax 020 7408 0220
Web www.joneslanglasalle.com
Direct tel 020 7399 5370
Direct fax 020 7399 5653
Mobile 07831 427345
Email andrew.hynard@eu.joneslanglasalle.com

IACOBESCU, George
Canary Wharf Group

Position
Chief executive
Qualifications
CBE
Career history
1987 Joined Canary Wharf Group as vice-president (construction); appointed director in 1993, deputy chief executive in 1995 and chief executive in 1997.
1984-87 Vice-president (development and construction), World Financial Centre, Olympia & York. Previously project director for Olympia Centre and Neiman Marcus Buildings, Chicago, Olympia & York
Other roles
Board member, London First; co-chairman, Teach First; Board member, UK Career Academy Foundation
Professional memberships
Institute of Directors
Interests
Antiques; football; jazz; opera; tennis
Contact details
Canary Wharf Group plc, 1 Canada Square, London E14 5AB
Tel 020 7418 2000
Fax 020 7418 2222
Web www.canarywharf.com
Direct tel 020 7418 2209
Direct fax 020 7418 2082
Email george.iacobescu@canarywharf.com

IDDIOLS, John
British Land Corp

Position
Director
Qualifications
BSc, Est Man; FRICS
Career history
1984 Joined British Land; currently responsible for shopping centres.
1971-84 Rank Organisation.
1966-71 J Sainsbury
Professional memberships
Christians in Property; RICS
Contact details
British Land Corp Ltd, 10 Cornwall Terrace, London NW1 4QP
Tel 020 7486 4466
Web www.britishland.com
Direct tel 020 7467 2813
Direct fax 020 7467 2835
Mobile 07714 222813
Email john.iddiols@britishland.com

ILLINGWORTH, Martin
Selfridges

Position
Head of store design and development
Qualifications
BA Hons; BArch Hons; RIBA
Other roles
Responsibility for ongoing refurbishments in Selfridges Oxford Street, Trafford Centre and Exchange Square
Professional memberships
RIBA
Contact details
Selfridges, 400 Oxford Street, London W1A 1AB
Tel 08708 377377
Fax 020 7495 8321
Web www.selfridges.co.uk
Direct tel 020 7318 3579
Direct fax 020 7499 2608
Email martin.illingworth@selfridges.co.uk

INGALL, Michael
Allied London Properties

Position
Chief executive
Qualifications
FRICS; BSc Hons, Est Man
Career history
1990-90 Property director, Raglan Properties.
1984-90 Director, Molyneux Rose.
1981-84 Portfolio manager, Drivers Jonas
Professional memberships
RICS; Royal Society of Arts
Contact details
Allied London Properties Ltd, 40 Portman Square, London W1H 6LT
Tel 020 7486 6080
Fax 020 7299 2611
Web www.allied-london-properties.com
Direct tel 020 7299 2610
Email mikei@alp.co.uk

INGHAM, Michael
R20

Position
Finance director
Contact details
R20 Ltd, Leconfield House, Curzon Street, London W1J 5JA
Tel 020 7550 3860
Fax 020 7491 0410
Web www.R20.co.uk
Email m.ingham@rotch.com

INKIN, Tony
GCL Solicitors

Position
Partner
Contact details
GCL Solicitors, Connaught House, Alexandra Terrace, Guildford GU1 3DA
Tel 0148 357 7091
Fax 0148 357 9252
Web www.gcl-solicitors.co.uk
Direct tel 0148 323 0129
Direct fax 0148 323 0159
Mobile 07710 116449
Email tony.inkin@gcl-solicitors.co.uk

INNES, Colin
Shepherd + Wedderburn

Position
Partner – head of planning and environmental law group
Qualifications
LLB Hons; LLM, Environmental Law
Career history
1994 Admitted to Roll of Solicitors (England and Wales).
1994 Admitted to Roll of Solicitors (Scotland).
1992 Joined Shepherd & Wedderburn; became partner in 1998
Interests
Architecture; fishing
Contact details
Shepherd + Wedderburn, Saltire Court, 20 Castle Terrace, Edinburgh EH1 2ET
Tel 0131 228 9900
Fax 0131 228 1222
Web www.shepwedd.co.uk
Direct tel 0131 473 5167
Email colin.innes@shepwedd.co.uk

INNES, Duncan
English Partnerships

Position
Regional director – Southern England
Qualifications
MA

I

Career history
1997 Joined English Partnerships. Prior to this, Strutt & Parker, London Borough of Bromley, London Docklands Development Corp, Countryside Properties, Millennium Commission
Other roles
Director of various public/private sector regeneration bodies
Interests
Cricket; rugby
Contact details
English Partnerships, 110 Buckingham Palace Road, London SW1W 9SA
Tel 020 7881 1600
Fax 020 7730 9162
Web www.englishpartnerships.co.uk
Direct tel 020 7881 1603
Direct fax 020 7730 4979
Email duncaninnes@englishpartnerships.co.uk

INNES-TAYLOR, Julian
Linklaters
Position
Partner – real estate
Qualifications
LLB Hons
Career history
1986 Joined Linklaters; worked in London, Hong Kong and Paris; partner since 1995.
1984-86 Isadore Goldman & Son
Professional memberships
CoreNet Global UK; Franco-British Lawyers' Association
Contact details
Linklaters, 1 Silk Street, London EC2Y 8HQ
Tel 020 7456 2000
Fax 020 7456 2222
Web www.linklaters.com
Direct tel 020 7456 4732
Email julian.innes-taylor@linklaters.com

IRELAND, Christopher
King Sturge
Position
Joint managing partner
Qualifications
MRICS
Career history
1980 Joined King & Co (now King Sturge); now partner
Professional memberships
Investment Property Forum; RICS
Contact details
King Sturge, 7 Stratford Place, London W1C 1ST
Tel 020 7493 4933
Fax 020 7409 0469
Web www.kingsturge.com
Direct tel 020 7318 4211
Email christopher.ireland@kingsturge.co.uk

IRVINE, Andrew
Jones Lang LaSalle
Position
Managing director – Scotland
Qualifications
MBE; BSc; FRICS
Career history
1978 Joined Jones Lang LaSalle; appointed partner in 1982.
1975-78 Richard Ellis.
1973-75 Ryden
Other roles
Various non-executive directorships
Professional memberships
RICS
Interests
Football; golf; rugby; walking
Contact details
Jones Lang LaSalle Ltd, Lismore House, 127 George Street, Edinburgh EH2 4JN
Tel 0131 225 8344
Fax 0131 225 2147
Web www.joneslanglasalle.com
Direct tel 0131 473 6724
Mobile 07785 290744
Email andy.irvine@eu.joneslanglasalle.com

IRVINE, John
Grosvenor
Position
Director – Scotland and Ireland
Qualifications
BSc; FRICS
Career history
Since 1989 Director, Grosvenor.
1986-89 Ian Kennard & Co.
1982-86 Hammerson Group.
1981-82 Sun Alliance.
1978-81 Greater London Council
Professional memberships
British Council for Offices; RICS
Contact details
Grosvenor Ltd, 22 Alva Street, Edinburgh EH2 4PY
Tel 0131 225 5775
Fax 0131 225 1955
Web www.grosvenor.com
Email john.irvine@grosvenor.com

IRWIN, John
storeys:ssp
Position
Director
Contact details
storeys:ssp, St James House, 139 Albert Road, Middlesbrough TS1 2PP
Tel 01642 230800
Fax 01642 241994
Web www.storeys-ssp.com
Email john.irwin@storeys-ssp.co.uk

ISAAC, Nicholas
199 Strand
Position
Barrister
Qualifications
BA Hons
Career history
1993 Called to Bar
Professional memberships
Chancery Bar Association; Property Bar Association
Interests
Mountaineering; skiing; walking
Contact details
199 Strand (Chambers of David Phillips QC), London WC2R 1DR
Tel 020 7520 4000
Fax 020 7379 9481
Web www.199strand.co.uk
Direct tel 0121 246 1100
Direct fax 0121 247 0757
Mobile 07711 017379
Email nisaac@199strand.co.uk

ISAAC, Roger
Electra Partners Europe
Position
Director
Qualifications
BA Hons, Econ
Career history
1986 Joined Electra Group as property investment specialist.
1978-86 Vice-president (UK real estate group), Manufacturers Hanover Trust Co of New York.
1972-78 Property finance specialist, Old Broad Street Securities
Other roles
Non-executive director, Welbeck Land; Electra Partners nominee on boards of all investee property companies; founder participant in Property Mezzanine Partners
Professional memberships
Investment Property Forum
Interests
Food; sport; travel; wine
Contact details
Electra Partners Europe Ltd, 65 Kingsway, London WC2B 6QT
Tel 020 7831 6464

I

Fax 020 7831 6142
Web www.electraeurope.com
Direct tel 020 7306 3975
Mobile 07711 593069
Email risaac@electraproperty.com

ISAACS, Paul
Cathedral Group

Position
Managing director
Career history
1997-2002 Director, Frogmore Developments.
1989-97 Hill Samuel Bank/Lloyds TSB Group.
1981-89 National Westminster Bank
Interests
Shooting; skiing; water sports
Contact details
Cathedral Group plc, Foxbury Manor, Kemnal Road, Chislehurst BR7 6LY
Tel 020 8295 8660
Fax 020 8467 9838
Web www.cathedralgroup.com
Direct tel 020 8295 8665
Mobile 07831 527624
Email paulisaacs@cathedral-plc.com

ISHERWOOD, Simon
Redrow Commercial Developments

Position
Managing director
Qualifications
BSc, Est Man; MRICS
Career history
Since 2000 Managing director, Redrow Commercial Developments.
1990-2000 Development director, AMEC Developments.
1981-90 Partner, HH&J Robinson
Professional memberships
RICS
Interests
Golf; hockey; sport
Contact details
Redrow Commercial Developments Ltd, 60 Oxford Street, Manchester M1 5EE
Tel 0161 234 6800
Email simon.isherwood@redrow.co.uk

IZATT, Gordon
Scottish & Newcastle

Position
Group property director
Contact details
Scottish & Newcastle plc, 33 Ellersly Road, Edinburgh EH12 6HX
Tel 0131 528 2000
Email gordon.izatt@scottish-newcastle.co.uk

IZETT, John
Rogers Chapman

Position
Managing director
Qualifications
MA; MRICS
Career history
1985 Joined Rogers Chapman; became director in 1989 and managing director in 2003
Other roles
Adviser on key development projects including World Business Centre (for BAA), Heathrow House (for Threadneedle) and Heathrow Gateway (for British Land); adviser on corporate relocation projects including BMRB, British Airways, Vodafone, SITA, Thomson-Thorn and Amadeus
Interests
Gardening; politics (Conservative Party); travel
Contact details
Rogers Chapman plc, Grantley House, 9 Park Lane, Cranford, Heathrow TW5 9RW
Tel 020 8759 4141
Fax 020 8759 5367
Web www.rogerschapman.co.uk
Email john.izett@rogerschapman.co.uk

JACKSON, Andrew
North Rae Sanders

Position
Partner
Qualifications
FRICS
Career history
Since 2003 Partner, North Rae Sanders.
1996-2003 Partner, Holley Blake.
1980-96 Partner, Weatherall Green & Smith
Other roles
National committee member and treasurer, Industrial Agents Society; out-of-town offices committee member, British Council for Offices
Professional memberships
British Council for Offices; Industrial Agents Society; RICS
Interests
Sailing; shooting; walking
Contact details
North Rae Sanders, 66 New Bond Street, London W1S 1RW
Tel 020 7493 2180
Fax 020 7493 2176
Web www.northraesanders.co.uk
Mobile 07747 774201
Email ajackson@northraesanders.co.uk

JACKSON, Andrew
Standard Life Investments

Position
Investment director
Career history
1991 Joined Standard Life; appointed head of property research team in 1999 and investment director in 2002
Other roles
Board member, Investment Property Forum (Scotland); speaker at numerous conferences; author of several articles published in newspapers and journals
Contact details
Standard Life Investments Ltd, 1 George Street, Edinburgh EH2 2LL
Tel 0131 245 2700
Fax 0131 245 2710
Web www.standardlife.com
Direct tel 0131 245 2717
Direct fax 0131 240 8272
Email andrew_jackson@standardlife.com

JACKSON, Cliff
Lambert Smith Hampton

Position
Director
Qualifications
MRICS
Career history
1977 Joined Lambert Smith Hampton
Professional memberships
RICS
Interests
Football; golf; motor sports; sport; swimming; tennis
Contact details
Lambert Smith Hampton Ltd, 1st Floor, Brock House, 57 High Street, Maidenhead SL6 1JT
Tel 0162 867 6001
Fax 0162 877 0347
Web www.lsh.co.uk
Mobile 07402 908159
Email cjackson@lsh.co.uk

JACKSON, David
Pilcher Hershman

Position
Partner
Contact details
Pilcher Hershman, 25 Savile Row, London W1S 2ER
Tel 020 7399 8600
Fax 020 7399 8700
Web www.pilcherhershman.co.uk
Email davidjackson@pilcherhershman.co.uk

JACKSON, Graeme
Hampton Trust

Position
Chairman and chief executive
Career history
1996 Acquired control of Southend Property Holdings (now Hampton Trust, following name change). Previously active in property market since 1960s
Interests
Music; opera; sailing
Contact details
Hampton Trust plc, 121 Mount Street, London W1K 3NW
Tel 020 7499 4994
Fax 020 7629 6996
Mobile 07768 155322
Email gjackson@hamptontrust.co.uk

JACKSON, Judith
9 Old Square

Position
QC
Qualifications
LLB; LLM (Lond); QC
Career history
1994 Appointed QC.
1975 Called to Bar
Other roles
Director, Bar Mutual Insurance Fund; founding member, Property Bar Association; bencher of Lincoln's Inn; has served on Supreme Court Procedure Committee and Bar Council; former chairman, Young Barristers' Committee
Professional memberships
Chancery Bar Association; Professional Negligence Bar Association; Property Bar Association
Contact details
9 Old Square (Chambers of Michael Driscoll QC), Ground Floor, London WC2A 3SR
Tel 020 7405 4682
Fax 020 7831 7107
Web www.9oldsquare.co.uk
Email judith.jackson@9oldSquare.co.uk

JACKSON, Ray
Linklaters

Position
Head of environment and planning group
Qualifications
Solicitor
Career history
1985 Joined Linklaters; appointed partner in 1988. Previously in local government
Other roles
Member of BPF planning and environment committee; member of London office review panel of Greater London Authority; founding member of City of London Law Society planning and environment law subcommittee
Professional memberships
BPF; City of London Law Society
Interests
Reading; travel; wine
Contact details
Linklaters, 1 Silk Street, London EC2Y 8HQ
Tel 020 7456 2000
Fax 020 7456 2222

Web www.linklaters.com
Direct tel 020 7456 4884
Email ray.jackson@linklaters.com

JACKSON, William
DTZ Debenham Tie Leung

Position
Head of national office agency and development
Qualifications
MRICS
Career history
1991 Joined Bernard Thorpe (now DTZ Debenham Tie Leung); head of national office agency and development since 1998.
1984-91 Ran own central London development company, Bennick Properties.
1978-84 Anthony Lipton & Co
Professional memberships
RICS
Contact details
DTZ Debenham Tie Leung, One Curzon Street, London W1A 5PZ
Tel 020 7408 1161
Fax 020 7643 6000
Web www.dtz.com
Email william.jackson@dtz.com

JACOBS, Paul
IKEA

Position
Senior acquisitions manager
Contact details
IKEA, 255 North Circular Road, London NW10 0JQ
Tel 020 8233 2300
Web www.ikea.com
Email paul.jacobs@memo.IKEA.com

JACOBSON, Jeff
LaSalle Investment Management

Position
Chief executive officer – Europe
Career history
1997-2000 Managing director, Security Capital Group.
1990-97 Managing director, LaSalle Investment Management, Chicago
Contact details
LaSalle Investment Management, 33 Cavendish Square, London W1A 2NF
Tel 020 7852 4000
Fax 020 7852 4374
Web www.lasalle.com
Direct tel 020 7533 7328
Email jeff.jacobson@lasalle.com

JACOBSON, Nick
Deutsche Bank

Position
Managing director
Qualifications
BComm; LLB
Career history
Since 2002 Managing director and head of European and Asian REIB, Deutsche Bank, London.
2000-02 Managing director (REIB), JP Morgan, London.
1995-2000 Senior vice-president (head of European REIB), ABN AMRO Corporate Finance, Amsterdam/London.
1992-95 UBS, Sydney, Australia
Other roles
Managing board member, European Public Real Estate Association
Professional memberships
European Public Real Estate Association
Interests
Diving/scuba diving; golf; theatre
Contact details
Deutsche Bank AG, Winchester House, 1 Great Winchester Street, London EC2N 2DB
Tel 020 7545 8000
Fax 020 7545 6155
Web www.db.com
Direct tel 020 7545 1167
Direct fax 020 7547 1571
Email nick.jacobson@db.com

JACOVOU, Jack
Wragge & Co

Position
Head of retail and leisure
Qualifications
BA Hons
Career history
1987 Joined Wragge & Co; became partner in 1992.
1983 Admitted to Roll of Solicitors
Professional memberships
British Council of Shopping Centres; British Retail Consortium; Law Society; Leisure Property Forum
Interests
Football; theatre; walking
Contact details
Wragge & Co LLP, 55-73 Colmore Row, Birmingham B3 2AS
Tel 0870 903 1000
Fax 0870 904 1099
Web www.wragge.com
Direct tel 0121 214 1070
Email jack_jacovou@wragge.com

JAFFE, Stephen
Shops etc

Position
Managing director
Contact details
Shops etc, 1 Tenterden Street, London W1S 1TA
Tel 020 7317 3737
Fax 020 7317 3740
Web www.shopsetc.co.uk
Email stephenjaffe@shopsetc.co.uk

JAMES, Nick
British Retail Consortium

Position
Policy executive – property and regeneration
Contact details
British Retail Consortium, 21 Dartmouth Street, London SW1H 9BP
Tel 020 7854 8900
Fax 020 7854 8901
Web www.brc.org.uk
Email nick.james@brc.org.uk

JAMES, Rhys
DTZ Debenham Tie Leung

Position
Director
Qualifications
FRICS
Career history
Since 1983 DTZ Debenham Tie Leung; now director.
1979-83 District Valuer's Office
Other roles
Board member, Business in Focus Enterprise Agency
Interests
Golf (Royal Porthcawl Golf Club)
Contact details
DTZ Debenham Tie Leung, Marchmount House, Dumfries Place, Cardiff CF10 3RJ
Tel 029 2039 8182
Fax 029 2039 5379
Web www.dtz.com
Direct tel 0292 026 2250
Direct fax 0292 037 8870
Mobile 07850 264066
Email rhys.james@dtz.com

JARRETT, Desmond
Henderson Global Investors

Position
Senior portfolio manager – life funds
Qualifications
BA Hons; MURP; P/G Dip Investment & Finance

Career history

1984-97 Fund management and research, DTZ

Professional memberships

Investment Property Forum; Society of Property Researchers

Contact details

Henderson Global Investors Ltd, 4 Broadgate, London EC2M 2DA

Tel 020 7818 1818

Fax 020 7818 1819

Web www.henderson.com

Mobile 07714 415352

Email desmond.jarrett@henderson.com

JARVIS, Sue
Debenhams Retail

Position

Director – property acquisitions

Qualifications

BSc Hons; MRICS

Professional memberships

RICS

Contact details

Debenhams Retail plc, 91 Wimpole Street, London W1M 7DA

Tel 020 7408 4444

Web www.debenhams.com

Direct tel 020 7529 0473

Direct fax 020 7529 0674

Mobile 07710 120473

Email sue.jarvis@debenhams.com

JEANES, Andrew
LaSalle Investment Management

Position

European director

Qualifications

BSc; MRICS

Career history

Since 1984 European director, LaSalle Investment Management.

1980-84 Senior surveyor, British Rail Property Board

Other roles

Director of a number of companies run by LaSalle

Professional memberships

Investment Property Forum

Interests

Fishing; renovation; shooting

Contact details

LaSalle Investment Management, 33 Cavendish Square, London W1A 2NF

Tel 020 7852 4000

Fax 020 7852 4374

Web www.lasalle.com

Direct tel 020 7852 4551

Direct fax 020 7852 4416

Email andrew.jeanes@lasalle.com

JEEPS, Barry
Stephenson Harwood

Position

Partner – head of town and country planning group

Contact details

Stephenson Harwood, 1 St Paul's Churchyard, London EC4M 8SH

Tel 020 7329 4422

Fax 020 7606 0822

Web www.shlegal.com

Direct tel 020 7809 2513

Email barry.jeeps@shlegal.com

JEFFERIES, Thomas
Landmark Chambers

Position

Barrister

Other roles

Contributor to *Halsbury's Laws of England* on mortgages; CEDR accredited mediator

Professional memberships

Chancery Bar Association

Contact details

Landmark Chambers, 4 Breams Buildings, London EC4A 1AQ

Tel 020 7430 1221

Fax 020 7421 1399

Web www.landmarkchambers.co.uk

Email clerks@landmarkchambers.co.uk

JENKIN, Stuart
Frogmore Developments

Position

Director

Qualifications

BSc; FRICS

Career history

1998 Joined Frogmore as director.

1996-98 Head of property, Siemens Group Services.

1982-96 Property manager, Provident Mutual.

1978-82 Surveyor, Abbey Life

Other roles

Director, Frogmore Investments

Professional memberships

Investment Property Forum; RICS

Contact details

Frogmore Developments Ltd, 11-15 Wigmore Street, London W1A 2JZ

Tel 020 7016 6000

Fax 020 7495 5321

Email stuartjenkin@frogmore.co.uk

JENKINS, David
Deloitte

Position

Managing partner – real estate

Contact details

Deloitte, Hill House, 1 Little New Street, London EC4A 3TR

Tel 020 7936 3000

Fax 020 7583 8517

Web www.deloitte.co.uk

Email dajenkins@deloitte.co.uk

JENKINSON, Andrew
Richards Butler

Position

Partner – head of property litigation

Professional memberships

Property Litigation Association

Contact details

Richards Butler, Beaufort House, 15 St Botolph Street, London EC3A 7JJ

Tel 020 7247 6555

Fax 020 7247 5091

Web www.richardsbutler.com

Direct tel 020 7772 5842

Email apj@richardsbutler.com

JENNINGS, Celia
LaSalle Investment Management

Position

Head of global client services group

Contact details

LaSalle Investment Management, 33 Cavendish Square, London W1A 2NF

Tel 020 7852 4000

Fax 020 7852 4374

Web www.lasalle.com

Email celia.jennings@lasalle.com

JENNINGS, Colin
Edward Symmons & Partners

Position

Partner – head of Northern offices

Qualifications

FRICS

Professional memberships

RICS

Contact details

Edward Symmons & Partners, Ground Floor, Cloister House, Riverside, New Bailey Street, Manchester M3 5AG

Tel 0161 216 9197

Fax 0161 216 3123

Web www.edwardsymmons.com

Email colin.jennings@edwardsymmons.com

J

JESSOP, Gareth
Pannone & Partners

Position
Partner
Qualifications
LLB; MCIArb
Career history
1984 Admitted to Roll of Solicitors
Professional memberships
Chartered Institute of Arbitrators; Society of Construction Law
Interests
Antiques; cycling; photography
Contact details
Pannone & Partners, 123 Deansgate, Manchester M3 2BU
Tel 0161 909 3000
Fax 0161 909 4444
Web www.pannone.com
Email gareth.jessop@pannone.co.uk

JEWELL, Russell
Merrill Lynch Global Principal Investments

Position
Managing director – GPI real estate, Europe
Qualifications
MRICS
Career history
Since 1998 Managing director (GPI real estate, Europe), Merrill Lynch Global Principal Investments
Professional memberships
RICS
Contact details
Merrill Lynch Global Principal Investments, 2 King Edward Street, London EC1A 1HQ
Tel 020 7628 1000
Web www.ml.com
Direct tel 020 7996 5202
Direct fax 020 7995 0537
Mobile 07768 556028
Email russell_jewell@ml.com

JOBBURN, Stephen
Hemingway Properties

Position
Chief executive
Contact details
Hemingway Properties Ltd, 21 Devonshire Street, London W1G 6EP
Tel 020 7487 3737
Fax 020 7935 1460
Web www.hemingway.co.uk
Email sj@hemingway.co.uk

JOHN, Gary
Gap

Position
Senior director – real estate and store development, Europe
Qualifications
FRICS
Contact details
Gap, Castle Mound Way, Rugby CV23 0WA
Tel 01788 818300
Web www.gap.com
Email gary_john@gap.com

JOHN, Robert
Canary Wharf Group

Position
Adviser
Career history
1995 Joined Canary Wharf: initially managing director, IPC Advisors; now adviser, Canary Wharf.
1993-95 Partner, KPMG.
1987-92 Deputy chief executive, Olympia & York, Canary Wharf.
1980-87 Executive director, NatWest Investment Bank.
1973-80 Citigroup.
1972-73 Barrister
Other roles
Represents Canary Wharf on London First; Gateway to London board member; London Riverside board member; deputy chair, East London Business Alliance; non-executive chairman, ABROS Enterprise; non-executive director, Simons Group; non-executive director, Symonds Group
Interests
Family; music; rugby
Contact details
Canary Wharf Group plc, 1 Canada Square, London E14 5AB
Tel 020 7418 2000
Fax 020 7418 2222
Web www.canarywharf.com
Direct tel 020 7537 5010
Direct fax 020 7537 5551
Email robert.john@canarywharf.com

JOHNS, Alan
9 Old Square

Position
Barrister
Career history
Since 1994 Barrister, 9 Old Square.
1994 Called to Bar
Contact details
9 Old Square (Chambers of Michael Driscoll QC), Ground Floor, London WC2A 3SR
Tel 020 7405 4682
Fax 020 7831 7107
Web www.9oldsquare.co.uk
Email alan.johns@9oldsquare.co.uk

JOHNS, Michael
Valuation Office Agency

Position
Chief executive
Qualifications
CB; Hon RICS
Career history
1967-97 Inland Revenue: promoted to director of business operations in 1993
Other roles
Board member, Inland Revenue (1997); active in teaching adults
Interests
Skiing
Contact details
Valuation Office Agency, New Court, Carey Street, London WC2A 2JE
Tel 020 7506 1700
Fax 020 7506 1998
Web www.voa.gov.uk
Email michael.a.johns@voa.gsi.gov.uk

JOHNS, Stephen
Cushman & Wakefield Healey & Baker

Position
Partner – City office agency
Contact details
Cushman & Wakefield Healey & Baker, 110 Cannon Street, London EC4N 6EU
Tel 020 7935 5000
Fax 020 7514 2398
Web www.cushwake.com
Direct tel 020 7152 5123
Direct fax 020 7152 5398
Email steve.johns@eur.cushwake.com

JOHNSON, Brian
Aedas AHR Architects

Position
Senior partner – Manchester
Contact details
Aedas AHR Architects Ltd, Sunlight House, Quay Street, Manchester M3 3LF
Tel 0161 828 7900
Fax 0161 828 7930
Web www.aedas.com
Email brian.johnson@ahr.co.uk

JOHNSON, David
Gerald Eve

Position
Partner – head of Newcastle office

Qualifications
BSc; MRICS
Professional memberships
RICS
Contact details
Gerald Eve, Shakespeare House, 18 Shakespeare Street, Newcastle upon Tyne NE1 6AQ
Tel 0191 260 2555
Fax 0191 260 2770
Web www.geraldeve.com
Mobile 07801 019553
Email djohnson@geraldeve.com

JOHNSON, David
Kendall Freeman
Position
Partner – head of construction law
Qualifications
BA, Law; FCIArb
Career history
1987 Joined DJ Freeman (now Kendall Freeman); became partner in 1988.
1979-87 Rowe & Maw
Professional memberships
Adjudication Society; Chartered Institute of Arbitrators; Law Society; Society of Construction Law
Contact details
Kendall Freeman, 43 Fetter Lane, London EC4A 1JU
Tel 020 7583 4055
Fax 020 7353 7377
Web www.kendallfreeman.com
Direct tel 020 7556 4312
Direct fax 020 7716 3670
Email davidjohnson@kendallfreeman.com

JOHNSON, Edwin
9 Old Square
Position
Barrister
Career history
1987 Called to Bar
Professional memberships
Chancery Bar Association; Professional Negligence Bar Association; Property Bar Association
Contact details
9 Old Square (Chambers of Michael Driscoll QC), Ground Floor, London WC2A 3SR
Tel 020 7405 4682
Fax 020 7831 7107
Web www.9oldsquare.co.uk
Email edwin.johnson@9oldsquare.co.uk

JOHNSON, Keith
Glenny
Position
Partner – building consultancy
Qualifications
BSc; FRICS; FBEng; MaPS
Career history
1985 Joined Glenny.
1981-85 Watts & Partners
Professional memberships
Association of Building Engineers; Association of Planning Supervisors; RICS
Contact details
Glenny, Dovetail House, 60 Station Road, London RM14 2TJ
Tel 0170 822 5547
Fax 0170 822 1838
Web www.glenny.co.uk
Mobile 07768 070256
Email k.johnson@glenny.co.uk

JOHNSON, Neville
Land Securities Properties
Position
Director
Contact details
Land Securities Properties Ltd, 5 Strand, London WC2N 5AF
Tel 020 7413 9000
Fax 020 7925 0202
Web www.landsecurities.com
Email neville.johnson@landsecurities.com

JOHNSON, Peter
George Wimpey
Position
Chief executive
Qualifications
MA; BPhil
Career history
1996-2000 Chief executive, Rugby Group.
1973-96 Redland: director from 1988.
1970-73 Unilever
Other roles
Non-executive director and chairman of audit committee, DS Smith; member, Council for Industry & Higher Education
Interests
Cricket; music; tennis
Contact details
George Wimpey plc, Manning House, Carlisle Place, London SW1P 1JA
Tel 020 7802 9888
Web www.georgewimpey.co.uk
Direct tel 020 7963 6350
Direct fax 020 7963 6355
Email pjohnson@georgewimpey.co.uk

JOHNSON, Rupert
Knight Frank
Position
Partner – head of valuations
Qualifications
BSc; MRICS
Career history
1985 Joined Knight Frank
Professional memberships
RICS
Interests
IT; running; sailing; tennis; walking
Contact details
Knight Frank LLP, 20 Hanover Square, London W1S 1HZ
Tel 020 7629 8171
Fax 020 7493 4114
Web www.knightfrank.com
Direct tel 020 7861 1284
Direct fax 020 7495 0556
Email rupert.johnson@knightfrank.com

JOHNSON, Tim
King Sturge
Position
Partner – South East industrial
Qualifications
BSc; MRICS; SIOR
Career history
Since 1984 Surveyor/partner, King Sturge
Other roles
Chairman, Industrial Agents Society (1999-2001)
Professional memberships
100 Property Club; RICS
Contact details
King Sturge, 7 Stratford Place, London W1C 1ST
Tel 020 7493 4933
Fax 020 7409 0469
Web www.kingsturge.com
Direct tel 020 7318 4252
Direct fax 020 7491 7057
Mobile 07889 132957
Email tim.johnson@kingsturge.co.uk

JOHNSTON, Angus
PricewaterhouseCoopers
Position
Partner – head of UK real estate tax
Contact details
PricewaterhouseCoopers, Southwark Towers, 32 London Bridge Street, London SE1 9AE
Tel 020 7583 5000
Web www.pwc.com
Direct tel 020 7804 2722
Direct fax 020 7804 8883
Email angus.i.johnston@uk.pwc.com

J

JOHNSTON, Jim
Arlington Development Services

Position
Managing director
Qualifications
BSc, Est Man; MRICS
Career history
1991 Joined Arlington. Prior to this formed and ran private development company for six years
Professional memberships
British Council for Offices; RICS
Contact details
Arlington Development Services Ltd, Arlington House, 1025 Arlington Business Park, Reading RG7 4SA
Tel 0118 930 4141
Fax 0118 930 4383
Web www.arlington.co.uk
Direct tel 0118 932 7485
Mobile 07966 280117
Email jim.johnston@arlington.co.uk

JOHNSTONE, Laurence
Rogers Chapman

Position
Director – corporate and professional services
Qualifications
FRICS; IRRV
Career history
1985 Joined Rogers Chapman; became managing director in 1996
1968-85 Edwards Bigwood & Bewlay (now part of Chesterton)
Professional memberships
Centre for Effective Dispute Resolution; FIABCI; Institute of Revenues Rating & Valuation; RICS; Worshipful Company of Chartered Surveyors
Contact details
Rogers Chapman plc, Prince Frederick House, 37 Maddox Street, London W1S 2PP
Tel 020 7499 8600
Fax 020 7493 5290
Web www.rogerschapman.co.uk
Email laurence.johnstone@rogerschapman.co.uk

JOHNSTONE, Mark
Kilpatrick Stockton

Position
Head of property, London office
Qualifications
LLB (New Zealand)
Career history
2003 Joined Kilpatrick Stockton.
2002-03 Partner, Altheimer & Gray.
1998-2002 Partner, McGrigor Donald, London.
1989 Admitted to Roll of Solicitors.
1986-98 Joined Reynolds Porter Chamberlain; became partner in 1991.
1983 Qualified as solicitor (New Zealand)
Interests
Sailing; skiing; tennis
Contact details
Kilpatrick Stockton LLP, 68 Pall Mall, London SW1Y 5ES
Tel 020 7321 0477
Fax 020 7930 9733
Web www.kilpatrickstockton.com
Direct tel 020 7786 5783
Mobile 07990 602253
Email majohnstone@kilpatrickstockton.com

JOHNSTONE, Ross
Memery Crystal

Position
Partner – head of commercial property
Contact details
Memery Crystal, 31 Southampton Row, London WC1B 5HT
Tel 020 7242 5905
Fax 020 7242 5908
Web www.memerycrystal.com
Email rjohnstone@memerycrystal.com

JOLLY, Christopher
Commerzbank

Position
General manager and managing director
Qualifications
MA Hons; AIB
Career history
1993-98 Société Générale; deputy chief executive on leaving.
1985-93 Director, SG Warburg.
1981-85 Assistant director, Samuel Montagu
Professional memberships
Association of Property Bankers; Chartered Institute of Bankers
Interests
Art; opera
Contact details
Commerzbank AG, Commerzbank House, 23 Austin Friars, London EC2N 2NB
Tel 020 7638 5895
Web www.commerzbank.com
Direct tel 020 7577 6720
Direct fax 020 7418 4791
Email chris.jolly@commerzbankIB.com

JONES, Alan
Arrowcroft Group

Position
Finance director
Contact details
Arrowcroft Group plc, 110 Park Street, London W1K 6AD
Tel 020 7499 5432
Fax 020 7493 0323
Web www.arrowcroft.com
Email ajones@arrowcroft.com

JONES, Andrew
Pillar Property Group

Position
Director
Qualifications
BSc Hons; MRICS
Career history
1995-98 PillarCaisse.
1995 Joined Pillar Property; appointed to main board in 2002.
1993-95 Burwood House Group.
1991-93 Healey & Baker.
1989-91 Insignia Richard Ellis (St Quintin)
Professional memberships
RICS
Contact details
Pillar Property Group Ltd, Lansdowne House, 57 Berkeley Square, London W1J
Tel 020 7915 8000
Fax 020 7915 8001
Web www.pillarproperty.com
Email andrew.jones@pillarproperty.com

JONES, Chris
GVA Grimley

Position
Partner – global corporate services
Other roles
Managing director, GVA Connect; chair, GVA Worldwide European corporate group; member, Colocation Hosting Association
Contact details
GVA Grimley, 10 Stratton Street, London W1J 8JR
Tel 0870 900 8990
Fax 020 7911 2560
Web www.gvagrimley.co.uk
Direct tel 020 7911 2525
Mobile 07740 510566
Email chris.jones@gvaconnect.com

JONES, Colin
Prudential Property Investment Managers

Position
Director – property development
Professional memberships
RICS
Contact details
Prudential Property Investment Managers Ltd, Princeton House, 271-273 High Holborn, London WC1V 7NE

Tel 020 7548 6600
Fax 020 7548 6999
Web www.prupim.com
Direct tel 020 7548 6837
Direct fax 020 7548 6993
Mobile 07802 249517
Email colin.jones@prupim.com

JONES, Elizabeth
Hewitsons

Position
Partner – head of commercial property
Career history
1984 Joined Hewitson Becke + Shaw as solicitor; became partner in 1988.
1976-78 Macfarlanes.
1976 Admitted to Roll of Solicitors
Professional memberships
Law Society
Contact details
Hewitsons, Shakespeare House, 42 Newmarket Road, Cambridge CB5 8EP
Tel 0122 346 1155
Fax 0122 331 6511
Web www.hewitsons.com
Email elizabethjones@hewitsons.com

JONES, Emrys
Birmingham City Council

Position
Chief planning officer
Qualifications
BA Hons; Dip TP; DMS; MRTPI
Other roles
Chair, West Midlands Regional Planning Officers Group
Professional memberships
Planning Officers Society; RTPI
Interests
Skiing; walking; windsurfing; sailing (Chase Sailing Club)
Contact details
Birmingham City Council, PO Box 28, Alpha Tower, Suffolk Street, Birmingham B1 1TU
Tel 0121 303 3666
Web www.birmingham.gov.uk
Direct tel 0121 303 3163
Direct fax 0121 303 1334
Email emrys.jones@birmingham.gov.uk

JONES, Geraint
Fenners Chambers

Position
Counsel
Qualifications
MA; LLM (Cantab)
Career history
Since 1974 Tenant, Fenners Chambers.
1973-74 Pupil, Temple.
1972 Called to Bar
Other roles
Senior member, Chambers Property Group; chairman, Rent Assessment Committee & Leasehold Valuation Tribunal
Professional memberships
Chancery Bar Association
Interests
Sailing; shooting
Contact details
Fenners Chambers, 3 Madingley Road, Cambridge CB3 0EE
Tel 01223 368761
Fax 01223 313007
Web www.fennerschambers.co.uk
Direct tel 01954 718874
Email geraint.jones@fennerschambers.co.uk

JONES, Howard
AMEC Group

Position
Deputy head of property
Qualifications
FRICS
Career history
1977-85 Estates surveyor, Barclays Bank
Professional memberships
RICS
Interests
Mountaineering; music
Contact details
AMEC Group Ltd, Anchorage 1, Anchorage Quay, Salford M50 3YJ
Tel 0161 877 3400
Fax 0161 848 8742
Web www.amec.com
Direct tel 0161 888 1651
Mobile 07712 137260
Email Howard.Jones@amec.com

JONES, John
GVA Grimley

Position
National head of property management consultancy
Qualifications
BSc; MRICS
Career history
1988 Joined GVA Grimley; appointed head of London property management in 1991 and national head of property management in 1996.
1985-88 Senior surveyor, Morgan Grenfell.
1982-85 Senior surveyor, Greater London Council
Other roles
Member, RICS Football Club
Professional memberships
RICS
Contact details
GVA Grimley, 10 Stratton Street, London W1J 8JR
Tel 0870 900 8990
Fax 020 7911 2560
Web www.gvagrimley.co.uk
Direct tel 020 7911 2144
Direct fax 020 7911 2699
Mobile 07774 995679
Email john.jones@gvagrimley.co.uk

JONES, Keith
DTZ Pieda Consulting

Position
Director
Qualifications
Dip TP; FRTPI; FRICS
Career history
1987 Joined DTZ Debenham Thorpe as director; director of DTZ Pieda Consulting since 1997.
1981-87 Director of development planning, London Borough of Hammersmith & Fulham.
1978-81 Assistant chief planning officer, London Borough of Richmond.
1976-78 Senior lecturer, Polytechnic of Central London.
1971-76 Various local government posts.
1970-71 Hillier Parker
Other roles
Member, RICS management consultancy faculty board; chairman and managing director, Hammersmith & Fulham Business Resources (1982-87); honorary planning adviser, London Planning Advisory Committee (1986-87); chairman of implementation committee, Association of London Borough Planning Officers (1984-87); director, Westminster Enterprise Agency (1987-88); member, RICS planning and development committee (1992-95); chairman, RICS management consultancy practice panel (1995-99); external examiner for BSc in town and country planning, South Bank University (1985-89); external examiner for BSc in estate management, Westminster University (1988-92)
Professional memberships
RICS; RTPI
Interests
Music; photography; rugby; running; travel
Contact details
DTZ Pieda Consulting, Greyfriars Gate, 5 Greyfriars Road, Reading RG1 1NU
Tel 0118 967 2020
Fax 0118 950 3759
Web www.dtz.com

J

Direct tel 0118 901 2054
Email keith.jones@dtz.com

JONES, Martyn
Alder King

Position
Partner
Contact details
Alder King, Pembroke House, 15 Pembroke Road, Bristol BS8 3BA
Tel 0117 317 1000
Fax 0117 317 1001
Web www.alderking.com
Email mjones@alderking.com

JONES, Mike
Drivers Jonas

Position
Partner – West End agency/cultural and heritage sector
Qualifications
MA; FRICS
Career history
Since 1980 Partner, Drivers Jonas.
1978-80 Surveyor, Property Unit Trust.
1976-78 Guardian Royal Exchange
Other roles
Chairman of firm's board
Professional memberships
RICS; Worshipful Company of Chartered Surveyors
Contact details
Drivers Jonas, 6 Grosvenor Street, London W1K 4DJ
Tel 020 7896 8000
Fax 020 7896 8001
Web www.driversjonas.com
Direct tel 020 7896 8160
Email mikejones@driversjonas.com

JONES, Morgan
Ashtenne Holdings

Position
Joint chief executive
Career history
1989 Founder director, Ashtenne.
1986-89 Development executive, Arlington Securities.
1984-86 Management consultant, Touche Ross & Co
Contact details
Ashtenne Holdings plc, 8-9 Northumberland Street, London WC2N 5DA
Tel 020 7930 9425
Fax 020 7930 8469
Email jones.m@ashtenne.co.uk

JONES, Oliver
Carillion

Position
Director – Carillion Business Services
Qualifications
BSc; MBA; FRICS; FBIFM
Career history
1998-2002 Chief executive, Citex Group.
1997-98 Group property and logistics director, Regus.
1989-97 Managing director, Symonds FM.
1981-89 BAA
Other roles
Director, Emrill Services (Dubai); chairman, Babel Language Consulting; UK advisory board member, London Business School
Professional memberships
British Institute of Facilities Management; CoreNet Global UK; International Facilities Management Association; RICS
Interests
Rugby; skiing; tobogganing
Contact details
Carillion plc, Westlink House, 981 Great West Road, Brentford TW8 9DN
Tel 020 8380 5000
Web www.carillionplc.com
Direct tel 020 8380 5554
Mobile 07802 985053
Email oliver.jones@carillionplc.com

JONES, Peter
DTZ Pieda Consulting

Position
Head – retail consultancy
Qualifications
BA, Econ; FRICS
Career history
Since 1980 Director, DTZ Pieda Consulting.
1976-80 Project manager, Unit for Retail Planning Information.
1974-76 Research manager, College of Estate Management.
1969-74 Assistant economist, Donaldson
Other roles
RICS APC assessor; Oxford retail group member, Oxford Institute of Retail Management
Professional memberships
British Council of Shopping Centres; RICS
Contact details
DTZ Pieda Consulting, 1 Curzon Street, London W1A 5PZ
Tel 020 7408 1161
Fax 020 7643 6000
Web www.dtz.com
Direct tel 020 7643 6166
Email peter.m.jones@dtz.com

JONES, Peter
Stiles Harold Williams

Position
Director
Qualifications
FRICS
Contact details
Stiles Harold Williams Ltd, Sterling House, High Street, Crawley RH10 1GE
Tel 0129 344 1300
Fax 0129 344 1334
Web www.shw.co.uk
Direct tel 0129 344 1344
Mobile 07860 334440
Email pjones@shw.co.uk

JONES, Philip
Dunlop Heywood Lorenz

Position
Director – land agency
Contact details
Dunlop Heywood Lorenz Ltd, Abbey House, 32 Booth Street, Manchester M2 4QP
Tel 0161 237 7777
Fax 0161 237 7778
Web www.dhlproperty.co.uk
Email pnj@dhlproperty.co.uk

JONES, Richard
AWG Property Solutions

Position
Director
Qualifications
MBA; BSc Hons; FRICS
Career history
Since 2001 Head of consulting, AWG Property Solutions.
1998-2001 Associate director, Chesterton Consulting.
1996-98 Associate partner, Edmund Kirby.
1990-96 GVA Grimley.
1988-90 Surveyor, British Rail Property Board
Professional memberships
Association of MBAs; CoreNet Global UK; Institute of Value Management; RICS
Interests
Music; travel
Contact details
AWG Property Solutions Ltd, Ambury House, Sovereign Court, Huntingdon PE29 6XU
Tel 01480 410920
Fax 01480 410921
Direct tel 01480 410950
Mobile 07801 674769
Email richard.jones@awgps.com

JONES, Richard
Jones Lang LaSalle

Position
Director
Career history
1979 Joined Jones Lang LaSalle
Contact details
Jones Lang LaSalle Ltd, 22 Hanover Square, London W1A 2BN
Tel 020 7493 6040
Fax 020 7408 0220
Web www.joneslanglasalle.com
Direct tel 020 7399 5864
Direct fax 020 7399 5688
Mobile 07836 293132
Email richard.jones@eu.joneslanglasalle.com

JONES, Richard
Morley Fund Management

Position
Head of life funds
Qualifications
BSc; MRICS
Career history
1986 Joined Norwich Union as asset manager; became fund manager for London office portfolio in 1994, property investment director in 1998, then head of Norwich Union Life Fund in 2000; responsible for all internal life funds since 2001 (investment arm merged with Morley Fund Management in 2000)
Contact details
Morley Fund Management Ltd, 34-36 Lime Street, London EC3M 7JE
Tel 020 7809 6000
Fax 020 7489 7940
Web www.morleyfm.com
Direct tel 020 7809 6840
Email richard.jones@morleyfm.com

JONES, Robert
Knight Frank

Position
Partner
Qualifications
BSc; MRICS
Career history
1986 Joined Knight Frank.
1981-85 Jones Lang Wootton.
1978-81 Greater London Council
Professional memberships
RICS
Interests
Rugby; sailing
Contact details
Knight Frank LLP, Emperor House, Pierhead Street, Cardiff CF10 4PH
Tel 029 2049 2492
Fax 029 2048 5553
Web www.knightfrank.com
Direct tel 029 2044 0128
Mobile 07836 245916
Email rob.jones@knightfrank.com

JONES, Rod
Drivers Jonas

Position
Partner – valuation and European consulting
Qualifications
BSc; FRICS
Career history
1968 Joined Drivers Jonas; appointed partner in 1980; chairman 1995-2000
Other roles
Chairman, Drivers Jonas Charitable Foundation
Professional memberships
RICS
Contact details
Drivers Jonas, 6 Grosvenor Street, London W1K 4DJ
Tel 020 7896 8000
Fax 020 7896 8001
Web www.driversjonas.com
Direct tel +49 69 7593 7144
Mobile 07785 325574
Email rodjones@driversjonas.com

JONES, Ross
GL Hearn

Position
Planning director
Career history
1984 Joined GL Hearn.
1967-84 Healey & Baker.
1962-63 London County Council
Professional memberships
RICS; RTPI
Interests
Architecture; art; cycling
Contact details
GL Hearn Ltd, Leonard House, 5-7 Marshalsea Road, London SE1 1EP
Tel 020 7450 4000
Fax 020 7450 4010
Web www.glhearn.com
Direct tel 020 7450 5125
Mobile 07768 381801
Email ross_jones@glhearn.com

JONES, Rupert
Weil, Gotshal & Manges

Position
Head of real estate group
Qualifications
LLB Hons; Solicitor of the Supreme Court
Career history
2000-02 Partner, Buchanan Ingersoll.
1997-99 Partner, Sonnenschein.
1976-97 Allen & Overy: appointed partner in 1985
Other roles
Member of planning and environmental law subcommittee, City of London Law Society
Professional memberships
British Urban Regeneration Association; City of London Solicitors Company; Law Society; UK Environmental Law Association
Interests
Cinema; gardening; motoring
Contact details
Weil, Gotshal & Manges, One South Place, London EC2M 2WG
Tel 020 7903 1000
Fax 020 7903 0990
Web www.weil.com
Direct tel 020 7903 1537
Email rupert.jones@weil.com

JONES, Selwyn
Collins Stewart

Position
Property analyst
Contact details
Collins Stewart Ltd, 88 Wood Street, London EC2V 7QR
Tel 020 7523 8000
Fax 020 7523 8131
Web www.collins-stewart.com
Email selwynjones@collins-stewart.co.uk

JONES, Simon
Gardiner & Theobald Management Services

Position
Senior partner
Qualifications
LVO; FRICS
Career history
1977 Joined Gardiner & Theobald; became partner in 1989
Other roles
Trustee, Historic Royal Palaces
Professional memberships
RICS
Contact details
Gardiner & Theobald Management Services, 40 Bedford Square, London WC1B 3DP
Tel 020 7209 3333
Fax 020 7209 1850
Web www.gardiner.com
Email anjis@gardiner.com

J

JONES, Steve
Rugby Estates

Position
Finance director
Qualifications
BSc; MSc; FCA
Contact details
Rugby Estates plc, 14 Garrick Street, London WC2E 9SB
Tel 020 7632 2200
Fax 020 7632 2222
Web www.rugbyestates.plc.uk
Direct tel 020 7632 2244
Mobile 07768 681702
Email steve@rugbyestates.plc.uk

JORDAN, Guy
Masons

Position
Partner – head of commercial property, London
Qualifications
BA (Dunelm)
Career history
1983 Joined Masons; partner since 1987.
1981-83 Herbert Smith.
1980 Admitted to Roll of Solicitors.
1978-81 Lawrence Graham
Professional memberships
Law Society
Interests
Farming; field sports; sport
Contact details
Masons, Woodbridge House, 30 Aylesbury Street, London EC1R 0ER
Tel 020 7329 2288
Web www.masons.com
Direct tel 020 7490 6232
Email guy.jordan@masons.com

JORDISON, Donald
Threadneedle Property Investments

Position
Director
Qualifications
BSc Hons; MBA; MRICS
Professional memberships
RICS; Society of Investment Professionals
Interests
Cricket; sport
Contact details
Threadneedle Property Investments, 9-15 Sackville Street, London W1S 3DJ
Tel 020 7437 8000
Fax 020 7464 5811
Direct tel 020 7464 5873
Mobile 07901 513278
Email don.jordison@threadneedle.co.uk

JOSEPH, David
Citib@Se

Position
Joint managing director
Other roles
Director, Freehold Managers; director, Ten Harley Street
Contact details
Citib@Se plc, Vigilant House, 120 Wilton Road, London SW1V 1JZ
Tel 020 7808 7444
Fax 020 7808 7028
Email citibaseplc@citibase.co.uk

JOSLIN, Peter
King Sturge

Position
Partner in charge, City office
Qualifications
FRICS
Career history
Since 1997 Partner in charge (City office), King Sturge.
1983-97 Partner, Bates Richards.
1978-83 Newton Perkins
Professional memberships
RICS
Contact details
King Sturge, Princes Court, 7 Princes Street, London EC2R 8AQ
Tel 020 7796 5454
Fax 020 7796 5450
Web www.kingsturge.com
Direct tel 020 7796 5491
Email peter.joslin@kingsturge.co.uk

JOSS, Norman
5 Paper Buildings

Position
Barrister
Qualifications
BA Hons
Career history
1982 Called to Bar
Contact details
5 Paper Buildings (Chambers of Richard King QC), Ground Floor, London EC4Y 7HB
Tel 020 7815 3200
Fax 020 7815 3201
Web www.5paper.com
Email normanjoss@5paper.com

JOURDAN, Stephen
Falcon Chambers

Position
Barrister
Career history
Since 1990 Barrister, Falcon Chambers.
1989 Called to Bar.
1987 Admitted to Roll of Solicitors.
1985-90 Theodore Goddard
Other roles
Contributor to reissue of *Halsbury's Laws* (vol 27) on landlord and tenant; author, *Adverse Possession* (2002)
Professional memberships
Chancery Bar Association; London Common Law & Commercial Bar Association; Professional Negligence Bar Association
Contact details
Falcon Chambers, Falcon Court, London EC4Y 1AA
Tel 020 7353 2484
Fax 020 7353 1261
Web www.falcon-chambers.com
Email jourdan@falcon-chambers.com

JOYCE, Rory
Drivers Jonas

Position
Partner – planning and development
Qualifications
BA; MSc; FRICS
Career history
1979 Joined Drivers Jonas; managing partner 1998-2001
Other roles
Past president, RICS planning and development division (1996-97)
Contact details
Drivers Jonas, 6 Grosvenor Street, London W1K 4DJ
Tel 020 7896 8000
Fax 020 7896 8001
Web www.driversjonas.com
Direct tel 020 7896 7890
Email roryjoyce@driversjonas.com

JOYCE, Tony
Chapman Swabey

Position
Partner
Qualifications
BSc; FRICS
Career history
Since 1993 Partner, Chapman Swabey.
1990-93 Partner, Lane Fox.
1985-90 Partner, Hampton & Sons.
1979-82 CB Hillier Parker.
1973-78 T&E Homes.
1971-73 Residential management and building surveying, Deanes
Other roles
Governor on estates strategy committee, Kings

College, London; member, Guild of International Bankers; liveryman, Worshipful Company of Chartered Surveyors; chairman, City branch of RICS (2000/01)

Professional memberships

RICS

Interests

Cycling; sailing; shooting; tennis; wine

Contact details

Chapman Swabey Ltd, 1 College Hill, London EC4R 2RA

Tel 020 7236 6363

Fax 020 7236 6464

Web www.chapmanswabey.com

Email tonyjoyce@chapmanswabey.com

JURENKO, Andrew

BAA Lynton

Position

Chairman

Qualifications

Chartered accountant

Career history

1990 Joined BAA as finance director of BAA Lynton; appointed to executive committee in 2000; managing director of BAA Lynton 1999-2000; managing director of World Duty Free (BAA's direct retailing arm) 2000-03; became co-chairman of BAA McArthurGlen (designer outlet business) in 2001; managing director of BAA International and chairman of BAA Lynton since 2003.

1988-90 Trafalgar House.

1982-87 Balfour Beatty

Interests

Opera; sport; theatre

Contact details

BAA Lynton plc, 67-69 New Bond Street, London W1S 1DF

Tel 020 7907 9200

Fax 020 7907 9299

Web www.baa.com

Direct tel 020 7932 6800

Mobile 07785 922826

Email andrew_jurenko@baa.com

JUSTICE, David

Blair Kirkman

Position

Partner

Contact details

Blair Kirkman, St Georges House, 12a St George Street, London W1S 1FQ

Tel 020 7409 0899

Fax 020 7629 8022

Web www.blairkirkman.com

Email davidj@blairkirkman.com

JUSTICE, Martyn

Rollits

Position

Head of property department

Contact details

Rollits, Wilberforce Court, High Street, Hull HU1 1YJ

Tel 01482 323239

Fax 01482 326239

Web www.rollits.co.uk

Email martyn.justice@rollits.com

K

Web www.dhlproperty.co.uk
Email dpk@dhlproperty.co.uk

KAEMPFER, Joseph
McArthurGlen UK

Position
Chairman
Qualifications
MBA
Career history
1993 Founded McArthurGlen alongside partners from Kaempfer Co; now chairman.
1977 Founded Kaempfer Co, Washington, US.
1975-77 Vice-president, Holladay Corp.
1973-75 Vice-president, Glen Investors.
1971-73 Regional manager, Levitt Multi-Housing
Interests
Reading; sailing; skiing
Contact details
McArthurGlen UK Ltd, Seymour Mews House, 26-37 Seymour Mews, London W1H 6BN
Tel 020 7535 2300
Fax 020 7535 2301
Web www.mcarthurglen.com
Direct tel 020 7535 2500
Direct fax 020 7535 2555
Email david.baumunk@b-m-g.com

KAHN, David
Dunlop Heywood Lorenz

Position
Managing director
Career history
1978 Joined Baker Lorenz (now Dunlop Heywood Lorenz) straight from school; became partner in 1989; created investment department; appointed managing director in 2001
Interests
Horse racing; tennis
Contact details
Dunlop Heywood Lorenz Ltd, 10 Queen Anne Street, London W1G 9LH
Tel 020 7636 7000
Fax 020 7636 7002
Web www.dhlproperty.co.uk
Email dpk@dhlproperty.co.uk

KANE, Chris
British Broadcasting Corp

Position
Head of property
Qualifications
MBA; BSc; FRICS; Dip Proj Man
Career history
1984-97 Partner, Jones Lang Wootton
Professional memberships
RICS
Contact details
British Broadcasting Corp, Broadcasting House, 20 Portland Place, London W1A 1AA
Tel 020 7580 4468
Web www.bbc.co.uk
Email chris.kane@bbc.co.uk

KARAS, Jonathan
Wilberforce Chambers

Position
Barrister
Qualifications
MA (Oxon)
Career history
1986 Called to Bar
Other roles
Subject editor, *Hill & Redman's Law of Landlord & Tenant*; co-author, *Unlawful Interference With Land* (2nd edition) (Sweet & Maxwell, 2002); contributing editor, 1996 reissue of compulsory acquisition title of *Halsbury's Laws*; editor, 2000 reissue of distress title of *Halsbury's Laws*; appointee to A panel of junior counsel to the Crown
Professional memberships
Chancery Bar Association; Planning & Environment Bar Association; Property Bar Association
Contact details
Wilberforce Chambers, 8 New Square, London WC2A 3QP
Tel 020 7306 0102
Fax 020 7306 0095
Web www.wilberforce.co.uk
Email jkaras@wilberforce.co.uk

KARIA, Pranai
CMS Cameron McKenna

Position
Lead partner – real estate insolvency
Career history
1989 Admitted to Roll of Solicitors
Professional memberships
Association of Business Recovery Professionals
Interests
Golf; travel
Contact details
CMS Cameron McKenna, Mitre House, 160 Aldersgate Street, London EC1A 4DD
Tel 020 7367 3000
Fax 020 7367 2000
Web www.cmck.com
Direct tel 020 7367 2742
Mobile 07771 674385
Email pranai.karia@cmck.com

KASCH, Peter
Catalyst Capital

Position
Managing partner
Career history
Since 2001 Managing partner, Catalyst Capital.
1993-2001 Managing director, Greenwich Group International.
1990-93 Chief operating officer, Kennedy-Wilson.
1985-90 Partner, Collaborative Companies.
1977-85 Project manager, Barkan Development Co.
1971-77 General manager, Vermont Development Co
Professional memberships
Urban Land Institute
Contact details
Catalyst Capital LLP, 33 Cavendish Square, London W1G 0PW
Tel 020 7290 5100
Fax 020 7290 5115
Web www.catalystcapital.com
Email pkasch@catalystcapital.co.uk

KATKOWSKI, Christopher
Landmark Chambers

Position
Barrister
Qualifications
QC
Career history
1982 Called to Bar
Professional memberships
Administrative Law Bar Association; Planning & Environment Bar Association
Contact details
Landmark Chambers, 4 Breams Buildings, London EC4A 1AQ
Tel 020 7430 1221
Fax 020 7421 1399
Web www.landmarkchambers.co.uk
Email clerks@landmarkchambers.co.uk

KAUFFMAN, Howard
Allsop & Co

Position
Partner – City investments

Contact details
Allsop & Co, 2 London Wall Buildings, London EC2M 5PP
Tel 020 7588 4433
Fax 020 7374 8212
Web www.allsop.co.uk
Mobile 07802 258443
Email howard.kauffman@allsop.co.uk

KAUNTZE, Richard
British Council for Offices

Position
Chief executive

Qualifications
BSc Hons

Career history
Since 1999 Chief executive, British Council for Offices.
1993-99 BPF: director of policy, then deputy director-general from 1996.
1988-93 Parliamentary officer, RICS

Professional memberships
Institute of Directors

Interests
Countryside; food; football; reading; travel; wine

Contact details
British Council for Offices, 3rd Floor, 38 Lombard Street, London EC3V 9BS
Tel 020 7283 4588
Fax 020 7626 2223
Web www.bco.org.uk
Email richard.kauntze@bco.org.uk

KAVANAGH, Anne
Jones Lang LaSalle

Position
International director – European capital markets

Qualifications
BSc; MRICS

Other roles
UK chair, Urban Land Institute

Professional memberships
Investment Property Forum; RICS

Contact details
Jones Lang LaSalle Ltd, 22 Hanover Square, London W1A 2BN
Tel 020 7493 6040
Fax 020 7408 0220
Web www.joneslanglasalle.com
Direct tel 020 7399 5368
Direct fax 020 7399 5470
Email anne.kavanagh@eu.joneslanglasalle.com

KAY, Derek
Exel

Position
Property director – Continental Europe

Qualifications
BSc; Dip Proj Man; FRICS; MAPM

Contact details
Exel plc, 251 Midsummer Boulevard, Milton Keynes MK9 1EQ
Tel 0190 824 4000
Web www.exel.com
Direct tel 0190 824 4022
Direct fax 0190 824 4112
Mobile 07775 840625
Email derek.kay@exel.com

KAY, Mark
Rok Property Solutions

Position
Property director

Contact details
Rok Property Solutions plc, Rok Centre, Guardian Road, Exeter EX1 3PD
Tel 01392 354000
Fax 01392 354101
Email info@rokgroup.com

KAYE, Gerald
Helical Bar

Position
Development director

Qualifications
BSc; FRICS

Career history
Since 1994 Development director, Helical Bar.
1992-94 Chief executive, SPP-LET Europe.
1984-92 Director, London & Edinburgh Trust

Other roles
Management board member, British Council for Offices

Professional memberships
British Council for Offices; Investment Property Forum; RICS

Contact details
Helical Bar plc, 11-15 Farm Street, London W1J 5RS
Tel 020 7629 0113
Fax 020 7408 1666
Web www.helical.co.uk
Direct tel 020 7318 9108
Mobile 07778 418067
Email gak@helical.co.uk

KEANE, Amanda
Investment Property Forum

Position
Executive director

Qualifications
BSc Hons; MRICS; PGCE

Career history
1998 Joined Investment Property Forum.
1995-98 Producer, Television Education Network.
1992-95 Senior lecturer, University of Greenwich.
1989-92 Richard Ellis

Professional memberships
RICS; Urban Land Institute; Institute of Personnel & Development (associate member)

Interests
Judo; skiing; snowboarding

Contact details
Investment Property Forum, 3 Cadogan Gate, London SW1X 0AS
Tel 020 7334 3799
Fax 020 7334 3872
Web www.ipf.org.uk
Direct tel 020 7334 3885
Email amanda.ipf@rics.org.uk

KEATING, Garreth
Marks & Spencer Group

Position
Head of estates management

Qualifications
BSc Hons; MRICS

Professional memberships
British Council of Shopping Centres; Property Managers Association; RICS

Contact details
Marks & Spencer Group plc, Michael House, 37-67 Baker Street, London W1U 8EP
Tel 020 7268 8070
Fax 020 7268 2652
Web www.marksandspencer.com
Direct tel 020 7268 3002
Direct fax 020 7268 2941
Email garreth.keating@marks-and-spencer.com

KEEN, Graeme
Landmark Chambers

Position
Barrister

Professional memberships
Chancery Bar Association; Planning & Environment Bar Association

Contact details
Landmark Chambers, 4 Breams Buildings, London EC4A 1AQ
Tel 020 7430 1221
Fax 020 7421 1399
Web www.landmarkchambers.co.uk
Email clerks@landmarkchambers.co.uk

K

KEEN, Nigel
John David Group

Position
Group property director
Qualifications
BSc Hons; MRICS
Career history
1995 Joined John David Group.
1990-95 Estates surveyor, Burton Group
Professional memberships
RICS
Contact details
John David Group plc, Hollinsbrook Way, Bury BL9 8RR
Tel 0161 767 1044
Fax 0161 767 1040
Direct tel 0161 767 1041
Mobile 07711 535653
Email nigel.keen@thejohndavidgroup.com

KEITH LUCAS, Peter
Wragge & CO

Position
Partner – head of public sector
Qualifications
MA (Oxon)
Career history
Since 1997 Local government partner, Wragge & Co.
1989-97 Director of legal and administrative services, Swansea City Council.
1988-89 Chief executive, Medina Borough Council.
1983-88 Assistant county clerk, West Glamorgan County Council.
1976 Admitted to Roll of Solicitors
Professional memberships
Association of Council Secretaries & Solicitors
Interests
Sailing; tennis
Contact details
Wragge & Co LLP, 55-73 Colmore Row, Birmingham B3 2AS
Tel 0870 903 1000
Fax 0870 904 1099
Web www.wragge.com
Direct tel 0121 214 1084
Email peter_keith_lucas@wragge.com

KELLARD, Michael
Scott Brownrigg & Turner

Position
Chief executive
Qualifications
Dip TP; Dip Arch Hons; RIBA
Professional memberships
Architects Registration Board; RIBA
Interests
Golf; painting; rugby; skiing
Contact details
Scott Brownrigg & Turner Ltd, 77 St Martin's Lane, London WC2N 4RD
Tel 020 7240 7766
Fax 020 7240 2454
Web www.sbt.co.uk
Email architects@sbtlondon.com

KELLY, Crispin
Baylight Properties

Position
Managing director
Other roles
President, Architectural Association (2001-03)
Contact details
Baylight Properties plc, 50 Sullivan Rd, London SW6 3DX
Tel 020 7731 1303
Web www.baylight.co.uk
Email crispin@baylight.co.uk

KELLY, Gordon
FG Burnett

Position
Director
Contact details
FG Burnett, 33 Albyn Place, Aberdeen AB10 1YL
Tel 01224 572661
Fax 01224 593496
Web www.fgburnett.co.uk
Email gsk@fgburnett.co.uk

KEMP, David
Spirit Group

Position
Director of property
Contact details
Spirit Group Ltd, 107 Station Street, Burton upon Trent DE14 1BZ
Tel 01283 545320
Web www.thespiritgroup.com
Email david.kemp@thespiritgroup.com

KEMP, Nick
BDG McColl Scotland

Position
Managing director
Qualifications
BArch Hons
Career history
1989 Joined BDG McColl Scotland.
1984-89 Parr Partnership.
1975-84 Thomas Henney, Architects
Professional memberships
Royal Incorporation of Architects in Scotland
Contact details
BDG McColl Scotland, 124-125 Princes Street, Edinburgh EH2 4AD
Tel 0131 220 3322
Fax 0131 220 4454
Web www.bdg-mccoll.com
Mobile 07768 231261
Email nkemp@bdgmccoll.com

KEMPNER, Nigel
Benchmark Group

Position
Chief executive
Qualifications
BSc, Est Man
Career history
Since 1995 Chief executive, Benchmark Group.
1986-94 Main board property director, Randsworth Trust.
1977-86 Property Investment Consultant, Cooke & Arkwright
Other roles
Vice-chairman, Westminster Property Owners Association; member of court of Worshipful Company of Paviors
Interests
Ballet; food; golf; opera; tennis; travel; wine
Contact details
Benchmark Group plc, 11-14 Grafton Street, London W1S 4EW
Tel 020 7659 0500
Fax 020 7659 0501
Web www.benchmarkgroup.plc.uk
Email nkempner@benchmarkgroup.plc.uk

KEMSLEY, Hugh
Matthews & Goodman

Position
Partner
Qualifications
OBE; MA; FRICS
Career history
1973 Rejoined Kemsley Whiteley & Ferris (in 1997, London office merged with Matthews & Goodman); managing partner 1990-97.
1969-72 Debenham Tewson & Chinnocks.
1966-69 Kemsley Whiteley & Ferris
Other roles
Chairman, RICS disciplinary board; chairman of board of trustees, Winged Fellowship Trust (registered charity); honorary treasurer, RICS (1996-2000); council member, City University
Professional memberships
Arbrix; RICS
Contact details

Matthews & Goodman, Dorland House, 14-16 Regent Street, London SW1Y 4PH
Tel 020 7747 8847
Fax 020 7747 8848
Web www.matthews-goodman.co.uk
Email hkemsley@matthews-goodman.co.uk

KENDALL, Emma
Freshfields Bruckhaus Deringer
Position
Partner – real estate
Career history
1995 Admitted to Roll of Solicitors
Contact details
Freshfields Bruckhaus Deringer, 65 Fleet Street, London EC4Y 1HT
Tel 020 7936 4000
Fax 020 7832 7001
Web www.freshfields.com
Direct tel 020 7832 7516
Email emma.kendall@freshfields.com

KENNEDY, John
Kenmore Property Group
Position
Chief executive
Career history
1986 Formed Kenmore
Professional memberships
RICS
Interests
Sailing; shooting
Contact details
Kenmore Property Group Ltd, 33 Castle Street, Edinburgh EH2 3DN
Web www.kenmore.co.uk
Email jk@kenmore.co.uk

KENNEDY, Lyall
Hartnell Taylor Cook
Position
Partner
Qualifications
MRICS
Professional memberships
RICS
Contact details
Hartnell Taylor Cook, Somerset House, 18 Canynge Road, Bristol BS8 3JX
Tel 0117 923 9234
Fax 0117 923 9237
Web www.htc.uk.com
Direct tel 0117 946 4513
Mobile 07836 365943
Email lyall.kennedy@htc.uk.com

KENNEDY, Dr Paul
INVESCO Real Estate
Position
Head of research – Europe
Qualifications
BSc Hons; PhD
Career history
2001 Joined Parkes & Co (now INVESCO Real Estate).
1998-2001 Henderson Global Investors.
1994-98 Nottingham Trent University
Other roles
Visiting research fellow, University of Reading; committee member, Society of Property Researchers; CPD committee member, Investment Property Forum
Professional memberships
Investment Property Forum; Society of Property Researchers; Urban Land Institute
Interests
Economics; history; skiing; squash
Contact details
INVESCO Real Estate Ltd, 10 Mount Row, London W1K 3SD
Tel 020 7543 3500
Fax 020 7543 3588
Web www.invesco.com
Direct tel 020 7543 3525
Mobile 07753 627768
Email paul_kennedy@ldn.invesco.com

KENNEDY-MCGREGOR, Marilyn
11 Stone Buildings
Position
Barrister
Qualifications
BA (Dunelm)
Career history
1989 Called to Bar
Interests
Football; ornithology; politics; theatre
Contact details
11 Stone Buildings, London WC2A 3TG
Tel 020 7831 6381
Fax 020 7831 2575
Web www.11stonebuildings.com
Email
Kennedy-McGregor@11stonebuildings.com

KENNEY, Michael
Hypo Real Estate Capital
Position
Marketing director, real estate finance
Qualifications
BA Hons
Career history
1995-2000 General manager, Deutsche Hyp.
1993-95 Depfa Bank.
1987-93 Hill Samuel Bank.
1982-87 HM Forces
Professional memberships
Association of Property Bankers; Investment Property Forum
Contact details
Hypo Real Estate Capital Ltd, 110 Cannon Street, London EC4N 6EW
Tel 020 7743 7743
Fax 020 7743 7700
Web www.hypointernational.com
Direct tel 020 7743 7734
Direct fax 020 7743 7737
Mobile 07887 850970
Email michael.kenney@hypointernational.com

KENNINGHAM, David
Dalgleish
Position
Director – head of retail
Contact details
Dalgleish, 80 New Bond Street, London W1S 1DD
Tel 020 7663 5555
Fax 020 7491 0098
Web www.dalgleish.co.uk
Direct tel 020 7663 5510
Mobile 07785 956977
Email dkenningham@dalgleish.co.uk

KENT, Paul
Pinsents
Position
Partner – head of property litigation, Birmingham
Qualifications
LLB Hons
Career history
Since 1993 Partner, Pinsent Curtis (now Pinsents).
1990-93 Associate in commercial litigation department, Keeley Smith & Jobson.
1990 Admitted to Roll of Solicitors.
1975-90 General manager, V Benoist
Professional memberships
Law Society; Property Litigation Association
Interests
Gardening; sailing
Contact details
Pinsents, 3 Colmore Circus, Birmingham B4 6BH
Tel 0121 200 1050
Fax 0121 626 1040
Web www.pinsents.com
Direct tel 0121 626 5755
Email paul.kent@pinsents.com

K

KEOGAN, John
Industrious Asset Management
Position
Managing director
Qualifications
MRICS
Professional memberships
RICS
Contact details
Industrious Asset Management Ltd, Cranford House, Kenilworth Road, Leamington Spa
Tel 01926 426526
Fax 01926 426026
Web www.industrious.co.uk
Email johnk@industrious.co.uk

KERMANI, Kami
PizzaExpress
Position
Head of property
Contact details
PizzaExpress plc, 1 Union Business Park, Uxbridge UB8 2LS
Tel 01895 618618
Fax 01895 618600
Web www.pizzaexpress.co.uk
Direct tel 01895 618722
Direct fax 01895 618603
Email kami.kermani@pizzaexpress.com

KERR, Ian
Reid Architecture
Position
Managing director
Qualifications
MRICS
Professional memberships
RICS; RTPI
Contact details
Reid Architecture, Cochrane House, 29 Cochrane Street, Glasgow G1 1HL
Tel 0141 552 4555
Fax 0141 552 4555
Web www.reidarchitecture.com
Mobile 07831 262434
Email iak@ra-glass.com

KERR, John
Going Places Leisure Travel
Position
Head of retail property
Contact details
Going Places Leisure Travel Ltd, Holiday House, Sandbrook Park, Rochdale OL11 1SA
Tel 01706 742000
Fax 01706 742227
Email john.kerr@airtours.co.uk

KERR, Malcolm
Montagu Evans
Position
Head of planning and development
Career history
1983 Joined Montagu Evans
Contact details
Montagu Evans, 44-48 Dover Street, London W1S 4AZ
Tel 020 7493 4002
Fax 020 7312 7547
Web www.montagu-evans.co.uk
Direct fax 020 7312 7548
Email malcolm.kerr@montagu-evans.co.uk

KERR, Michael
Deloitte
Position
Lead partner, PFI
Contact details
Deloitte, Stonecutter Court, 1 Stonecutter Street, London EC4A 3TR
Tel 020 7936 3000
Fax 020 7583 1198
Web www.deloitte.co.uk
Direct tel 020 7303 6645
Email mkerr@deloitte.co.uk

KERR, Patrick
Allsop & Co
Position
Partner – commercial auctions
Career history
1977 Joined Allsop & Co
Contact details
Allsop & Co, 27 Soho Square, London W1D 3AY
Tel 020 7437 6977
Fax 020 7437 8984
Web www.allsop.co.uk
Direct tel 020 7543 6701
Mobile 07850 976111
Email patrick.kerr@allsop.co.uk

KERSHAW, Chris
Gerald Eve
Position
Head of Birmingham office and business space agency
Qualifications
FRICS
Career history
1993 Joined Gerald Eve.
1975-93 St Quintin
Professional memberships
RICS
Interests
Cycling; rugby; sailing; skiing; yachting
Contact details
Gerald Eve, Bank House, 8 Cherry Street, Birmingham B2 5AQ
Tel 0121 616 4800
Fax 0121 616 4801
Web www.geraldeve.com
Direct tel 0121 616 4803
Mobile 07860 742815
Email ckershaw@geraldeve.com

KERSHAW, Diana
Bristol City Council
Position
Director of planning
Contact details
Bristol City Council, St George's Road, Bristol BS1 5UY
Tel 0117 922 2000
Web www.bristol-city.gov.uk
Email diana_kershaw@bristol-city.gov.uk

KEVILL, John
GVA Saxon Law
Position
Partner
Contact details
GVA Saxon Law, 10 Stratton Street, London W1J 8JR
Tel 0870 900 8990
Fax 020 7911 2560
Email john.kevill@gvagrimley.co.uk

KEYS, James
Slade & Co
Position
Director
Qualifications
BSc
Contact details
Slade & Co, 3 Charles Street, London W1J 5DD
Tel 020 7499 3737
Fax 020 7499 3800
Mobile 07771 997374
Email keysj@slade-co.com

KIBBLE, Ian
Lambert Smith Hampton
Position
Head of office
Qualifications
BSc; MRICS
Career history
1983 Joined Wilson & Partners (became Connell Wilson, then Lambert Smith Hampton in 1996).
1979-83 Surveyor, Milton Keynes Development Corp
Professional memberships

RICS

Contact details

Lambert Smith Hampton Ltd, Fountain Court, 2 Victoria Square, St Albans AL1 3TF
Tel 01442 266691
Fax 01442 245631
Web www.lsh.co.uk
Email ikibble@lsh.co.uk

KIDBY, Robert
Lovells

Position
Partner – head of property
Qualifications
LLB Hons
Career history
1985 Joined Lovells as partner; became head of Lovells property practice in 1995.
1977 Admitted to Roll of Solicitors
Other roles
Lecturer on property finance and corporate outsourcing in UK, Europe and Asia; co-editor of *Property Joint Ventures – Structures & Precedents* (2nd edition) (Sweet & Maxwell, 2001); BPF policy committee member; *Estates Gazette* legal advisory board member; appeal steward of British Boxing Board of Control
Professional memberships
City of London Solicitors Company; Investment Property Forum; Law Society
Interests
Antarctic memorabilia; electric guitar
Contact details
Lovells, Atlantic House, 50 Holborn Viaduct, London EC1A 2FG
Tel 020 7296 2000
Fax 020 7296 2001
Web www.lovells.com
Direct fax 020 7248 4212
Email robert.kidby@lovells.com

KIDD, Martin
B-Serv

Position
Director – asset management
Qualifications
Dip Est Man; FRICS
Career history
1985 Joined Brixton Estate as property manager; now director (asset management), B-Serv.
1980-85 Property manager, AXA Equity & Law.
1976-80 Valuation/rating assistant, King & Co
Professional memberships
RICS
Interests
IT; music; tennis; travel
Contact details
B-Serv Ltd, 50 Berkeley Street, London W1J 8BX
Tel 020 7399 4500
Fax 020 7399 4550
Web www.b-serv.ltd.uk
Direct tel 020 7399 4510
Mobile 07860 654441
Email martinkidd@b-serv.ltd.uk

KIERAN, Peter
Lisney

Position
Director
Qualifications
FIAVI
Contact details
Lisney, 24 St Stephen's Green, Dublin
Tel +353 1 638 2700
Fax +353 1 638 2706
Web www.lisney.com
Email pkieran@lisney.com

KIERSEY, Richard
De Vere Group

Position
Director of property
Qualifications
MRICS
Career history
1996-2000 Greenalls Group: joined as regional property manager; appointed director of acquisitions in 1997.
1989-96 Group property manager, Boddington Group.
1988-89 Estates surveyor, Salford City Council.
1983-88 Estates assistant, Valuation Office
Professional memberships
RICS
Contact details
De Vere Group plc, 2100 Daresbury Park, Warrington WA4 4BP
Tel 01928 712111
Web www.deveregroupplc.co.uk
Mobile 07768 995073
Email richard.kiersey@devere.co.uk

KILDUFF, Christopher
Knight Frank

Position
Partner
Qualifications
FRICS
Career history
1970 Joined Knight Frank as senior assistant, (property management) and became partner in valuation department in 1974; became partner and head of asset management department in 1982; partner in investment department since 1990
Other roles
Knight Frank representative for Investment Property Databank and member of IPD PAS consultative group
Professional memberships
RICS
Interests
Opera; skiing; tennis
Contact details
Knight Frank LLP, 20 Hanover Square, London W1S 1HZ
Tel 020 7629 8171
Fax 020 7493 4114
Web www.knightfrank.com
Direct tel 020 7861 1212
Mobile 07860 674761
Email chris.kilduff@knightfrank.com

KILLEN, Charlie
EA Shaw

Position
Partner
Qualifications
MRICS
Professional memberships
RICS
Contact details
EA Shaw, 9-12 Bow Street, London WC2E 7AB
Tel 020 7240 2255
Fax 020 7831 1012
Web www.eashaw.com
Direct tel 020 7420 3023
Email chk@eashaw.com

KILPATRICK, Michael
Yorkshire Building Society

Position
Property manager
Qualifications
Tech RICS
Career history
Since 1975 Property manager, Yorkshire Building Society.
1972-75 Surveyor (agency/management), Bernard Thorpe & Partners, Leeds and Manchester.
1970-72 Architectural assistant/surveyor, Burtons.
1962-70 Leeds Permanent Building Society
Professional memberships
RICS
Interests
Art; fishing; skiing; walking
Contact details
Yorkshire Building Society, Yorkshire House,

K

Yorkshire Drive, Bradford BD5 8LJ
Tel 01274 740740
Fax 01274 652134
Web www.ybs.co.uk
Direct tel 01274 472286
Direct fax 01274 720067
Email mekilpatrick@ybs.co.uk

KING, Andrew
BAA Lynton

Position
Head of development and marketing
Qualifications
BSc Hons; MRICS
Contact details
BAA Lynton plc, 67-69 New Bond Street, London W1S 1DF
Tel 020 7907 9200
Fax 020 7907 9299
Web www.baa.com
Direct tel 020 7907 9204
Direct fax 020 7907 9388
Email andrew_king@baa.com

KING, Christopher
London & Regional Properties

Position
Deputy managing director
Qualifications
BA, Econ
Career history
1992-2001 Joined Flemings corporate/structured finance team; appointed director/head of real estate finance at Chase Manhattan following merger with Flemings.
1989-92 Graduate trainee (management development programme), Barclays
Professional memberships
Chartered Institute of Bankers
Interests
Golf; music; rugby; theatre
Contact details
London & Regional Properties Ltd, 40 New Bond Street, London W1S 2RX
Tel 020 7499 4060
Fax 020 7499 9922
Email chris.king@lrp.co.uk

KING, Colin
National Australia Bank

Position
Head of corporate services
Qualifications
MRICS; MCIOB; MAPM; MCR
Career history
1991-2000 BUPA: joined as head of project management; appointed group development manager in 1996 and corporate real estate manager in 1998.
1989-91 Property manager, Asheville Construction.
1987-89 Senior quantity surveyor, Berkeley Group
Other roles
Member, RICS forum for corporate occupiers; member, Chartered Institute of Banking panel for property and facilities management
Professional memberships
Association for Project Management; Chartered Institute of Building; Masters of Corporate Real Estate; RICS
Interests
Golf; rugby; tennis
Contact details
National Australia Bank, 88 Wood Street, London EC2V 7QQ
Tel 020 7710 2100
Web www.national.com.au
Direct tel 020 7710 2366
Direct fax 020 7710 1338
Mobile 07740 025580
Email sarah.besant@eu.nabgroup.com

KING, David
Henderson Global Investors

Position
Director – property portfolio management, Europe
Qualifications
BSc; MRICS
Professional memberships
Investment Property Forum; RICS
Contact details
Henderson Global Investors Ltd, 4 Broadgate, London EC2M 2DA
Tel 020 7818 1818
Fax 020 7818 1819
Web www.henderson.com
Direct tel 020 7818 4102
Direct fax 020 7818 4499
Mobile 07714 415442
Email david.king@henderson.com

KING, David
Nelson Bakewell

Position
Chief executive
Qualifications
BSc; FRICS
Career history
1979-85 Portfolio manager, Prudential
Other roles
Contract director, AXA Sun Life Properties; director, Sackville Resource Management; member, RICS commercial property management panel; RICS registered receiver
Professional memberships
Non-Administrative Receivers Association; RICS
Interests
Rowing; tennis
Contact details
Nelson Bakewell Ltd, 25 Sackville Street, London W1S 3HQ
Tel 020 7544 2000
Fax 020 7544 2222
Web www.nelson-bakewell.com
Direct tel 020 7544 2070
Mobile 07721 866484
Email dking@nelson-bakewell.com

KING, Howard
John Lewis Partnership

Position
Property director
Qualifications
FRICS
Other roles
Member of Oxford retail group of the Oxford Institute of Retail Management
Professional memberships
Association of Corporate Real Estate; National Retail Planning Forum; RICS
Contact details
John Lewis Partnership plc, 171 Victoria Street, London SW1E 5NN
Tel 020 7828 1000
Web www.john-lewis-partnership.co.uk
Direct tel 020 7592 6279
Direct fax 020 7592 6479
Email howard_king@johnlewis.co.uk

KING, Malcolm
King Sturge

Position
Senior partner
Qualifications
FRICS; MBA
Career history
1970 Joined King & Co (now King Sturge).
1968-70 MBA programme, University of Western Ontario.
1963-68 Assistant surveyor, Gerald Eve & Co
Other roles
Chairman, King Sturge International; chairman, King Sturge SA; chairman, King Sturge CORFAC International
Professional memberships
RICS
Interests
Aviation; fishing; golf; shooting
Contact details
King Sturge, 7 Stratford Place, London W1C 1ST

K

Tel 020 7493 4933
Fax 020 7409 0469
Web www.kingsturge.com
Direct tel 020 7318 4300
Direct fax 020 7409 0635
Mobile 07802 336356
Email malcolm.king@kingsturge.co.uk

KING, Michael
DTZ Pieda Consulting

Position
Director
Qualifications
MRTPI; MIMC; CMC; BA Hons
Career history
1994 Joined Pieda as associate director; became director in 1996; since 1997 director of DTZ Pieda Consulting.
1986-94 KPMG Peat Marwick: senior management consultant; then head of Northern urban regeneration team from 1988
Professional memberships
Institute of Management Consultants; RTPI
Contact details
DTZ Pieda Consulting, One Marsden Street, Manchester M2 1HW
Tel 0161 236 9595
Fax 0161 834 2055
Web www.dtz.com
Email michael.king@dtz.com

KING, Michael
Dunlop Heywood Lorenz

Position
Director – professional and specialist agency
Qualifications
FRICS
Career history
1988 Dunlop Heywood: joined as senior surveyor in valuation department; appointed associate in 1990 and director in 1996
Other roles
RICS registered property receiver
Professional memberships
Compulsory Purchase Association; Manchester Financial & Professional Forum; RICS
Contact details
Dunlop Heywood Lorenz Ltd, Abbey House, 32 Booth Street, Manchester M2 4QP
Tel 0161 237 7777
Fax 0161 237 7778
Web www.dhlproperty.co.uk
Direct tel 0161 237 7324
Mobile 07970 225024
Email mak@dhlproperty.co.uk

KING, Neil
Landmark Chambers

Position
Barrister
Qualifications
QC; MA (Oxon)
Career history
2000 Appointed QC.
1980 Called to Bar
Professional memberships
Planning & Environment Bar Association
Interests
Golf; music; real tennis
Contact details
Landmark Chambers, 4 Breams Buildings, London EC4A 1AQ
Tel 020 7430 1221
Fax 020 7421 1399
Web www.landmarkchambers.co.uk
Email nking@landmarkchambers.co.uk

KING, Philip
Gerald Eve

Position
Partner
Qualifications
BSc; MRICS; IRRV
Career history
1983 Joined Gerald Eve in Cardiff; moved to Leeds in 1991; became partner in 1996; has headed minerals and waste management department since 2001
Other roles
Member, CBI minerals committee
Professional memberships
CBI; Institute of Revenues Rating & Valuation
Interests
Cars; family
Contact details
Gerald Eve, St James's House, 28 Park Place, Leeds LS1 2SP
Tel 0113 244 0708
Fax 0113 244 0722
Web www.geraldeve.com
Direct tel 0113 218 2090
Email pking@geraldeve.com

KING, Sheila
Hammerson UK Properties

Position
Director – UK retail leasing
Other roles
Board member, British Council of Shopping Centres
Professional memberships
British Council of Shopping Centres; RICS
Contact details
Hammerson UK Properties plc, 100 Park Lane, London W1K 7AR
Tel 020 7887 1000
Fax 020 7887 1090
Web www.hammerson.co.uk
Direct tel 020 7887 1028
Email sking@hammerson.co.uk

KING, Tom
ING Real Estate Investment Management (UK)

Position
Director
Qualifications
FRICS
Career history
Since 1997 Director, ING Real Estate Investment Management (formerly Baring, Houston & Saunders).
1987-97 Director, Rothschild Asset Management
Professional memberships
Investment Property Forum; RICS
Contact details
ING Real Estate Investment Management (UK) Ltd, 9 Devonshire Square, London EC2M 4WX
Tel 020 7398 4310
Fax 020 7398 4311
Web www.ingrealestate.co.uk
Direct tel 020 7398 5553
Email tom.king@ingrealestate.co.uk

KINGSTON, Dick
Slough Estates

Position
Group finance director
Contact details
Slough Estates plc, 234 Bath Road, Slough SL1 4EE
Tel 01753 537171
Fax 01753 820585
Web www.sloughestates.com
Email dick.kingston@sloughestates.co.uk

KINGSTON, Jeremy
Knight Frank

Position
Head of building consultancy
Contact details
Knight Frank LLP, 20 Hanover Square, London W1S 1HZ
Tel 020 7629 8171
Fax 020 7493 4114
Web www.knightfrank.com
Email jeremy.kingston@knightfrank.com

K

KINGSTON, Mark
Tishman Speyer Properties UK

Position
Managing director
Contact details
Tishman Speyer Properties UK Ltd, Millbank Tower, 21-24 Millbank, London SW1P
Tel 020 7333 2400
Fax 020 7333 2500
Web www.tishmanspeyer.com
Email mkingston@tishmanspeyer.com

KINGSTON, Martin
No5 Chambers

Position
Barrister
Qualifications
QC
Other roles
Assistant chairman, Agricultural Lands Tribunal; assistant commissioner, Parliamentary Boundary Commission
Professional memberships
Planning & Environment Bar Association
Interests
Fishing; skiing; travel; walking
Contact details
No5 Chambers, 5 Fountain Court, Birmingham B4 6DR
Tel 0121 606 0500
Web www.no5.com
Email planning@no5.com

KIRBY, Phillip
SecondSite Property Holdings

Position
Managing director
Qualifications
OBE; CE; MIStructE; AMICE
Career history
1992 Joined British Gas Properties (now SecondSite) as construction and environment director; became general manager in 1999 and managing director in 2003.
1989-92 Construction manager, Stanhope
Other roles
General advisory council member, BPF; chair, Contaminated Land Applications in Real Environments; chair, EX-SITE; awarded OBE in 2000 for his contaminated land practitioners team's impact on standards for reclaiming land; past member, Urban Task Force
Professional memberships
British Council for Offices; British Urban Regeneration Association; Institute of Chartered Engineers; Institution of Civil Engineers; Institution of Structural Engineers
Interests
Golf; sailing; walking
Contact details
SecondSite Property Holdings Ltd, Sandpiper House, Wade Road, Basingstoke
Tel 01256 308803
Fax 01256 308799
Direct tel 01256 308648
Direct fax 01256 308804
Email phil.kirby@secondsite-property.com

KIRBY, Richard
ISIS Property Asset Management

Position
Director – property funds
Contact details
ISIS Property Asset Management plc, 100 Wood Street, London EC2V 7AN
Tel 020 7506 1100
Fax 020 7600 4180
Web www.isisam.com
Direct tel 020 7506 1121
Email richard.kirby@isisam.com

KIRBY, Rupert
Ahli United Bank (UK)

Position
Manager – property finance
Career history
Since 2000 Manager (property finance), United Bank of Kuwait (now Ahli United Bank (UK)).
1998-2000 Marketing associate, HVB Real Estate Capital.
1997-98 Healey & Baker.
1993-97 Surveyor, De Groot Collis Finance
Professional memberships
RICS
Interests
Cricket; golf; hockey; tennis
Contact details
Ahli United Bank (UK) plc, 7 Baker Street, London W1U 8EG
Tel 020 7487 6500
Fax 020 7487 6402
Web www.ahliunited.com
Direct tel 020 7487 6992
Direct fax 020 7487 6593
Mobile 07799 343407
Email kirbyr@ahliunited.com

KIRK, Robert
Littman Chambers

Position
Barrister
Qualifications
MA (Cantab); FCIArb
Career history
1972 Called to Bar
Contact details
Littman Chambers (Chambers of Mark Littman QC), 12 Gray's Inn Square, London WC1R 5JP
Tel 020 7404 4866
Fax 020 7404 4812
Web www.littmanchambers.com
Email robert.kirk@btinternet.com

KIRK, Stuart
GL Hearn

Position
Director
Qualifications
BSc, Est Man; FRICS
Career history
1990 Joined GL Hearn as rating valuer; South East regional director from 1996.
1978-90 Senior valuer, Valuation Office
Professional memberships
RICS
Interests
Golf
Contact details
GL Hearn Ltd, Anglo City House, 2-6 Shirley Road, Southampton SO15 3EU
Tel 023 8022 1361
Fax 023 8022 4718
Web www.glhearn.com
Mobile 07831 654905
Email stuart_kirk@glhearn.com

KIRSCHEL, Laurence
Consolidated Developments

Position
Director
Qualifications
FRICS
Other roles
Director, Consolidated Property Corp; director, Consolidated Hotel
Interests
Spirituality and mysticism
Contact details
Consolidated Developments Ltd, 171 Wardour Street, London W1F 8WS
Tel 020 7437 4372
Fax 020 7437 3800
Email laurence@consolidatedgrp.com

KISLINGBURY, Charles
King Sturge

Position
Partner in charge, Exeter
Qualifications
BSc; MRICS
Professional memberships

RICS
Contact details
King Sturge, 37 Southernhay East, Exeter
EX1 1PD
Tel 01392 423696
Fax 01392 423698
Web www.kingsturge.com
Direct tel 01392 429301
Email charles.kislingbury@kingsturge.co.uk

KITCHEN, Ian
Kitchen La Frenais Morgan

Position
Partner
Qualifications
BSc, Est Man; FRICS
Career history
1990 Founding partner, Kitchen La Frenais Morgan.
1979-90 Clive Lewis & Partners: appointed partner in 1987
Professional memberships
British Council of Shopping Centres; RICS; Shop Agents Society
Contact details
Kitchen La Frenais Morgan, 1 Tenterden Street, London W1S 1TA
Tel 020 7317 3700
Fax 020 7317 3701
Web www.klmproperty.co.uk
Direct tel 020 7317 3707
Mobile 07774 940524
Email ikitchen@klmproperty.co.uk

KITCHER, Graham
B&Q

Position
Director – international property
Qualifications
BA; MRTPI
Career history
1997 Joined B&Q; appointed director (international property) in 2002
Professional memberships
RTPI
Interests
Cricket; DIY; football; geography
Contact details
B&Q plc, Portswood House, 1 Hampshire Corporate Park, Chandler's Ford SO53 3YX
Tel 023 8025 6256
Fax 023 8025 7480
Web www.b-and-qproperty.co.uk
Direct tel 023 8062 5026
Direct fax 023 8062 5099
Mobile 07774 169363
Email graham.kitcher@b-and-q.co.uk

KITCHERSIDE, Barry
Frogmore Developments

Position
Planning technical director
Other roles
Director, Frogmore Investments
Contact details
Frogmore Developments Ltd, 11-15 Wigmore Street, London W1A 2JZ
Tel 020 7016 6000
Fax 020 7495 5321
Email barrykitcherside@frogmore.co.uk

KITSON, Tony
CMS Cameron McKenna

Position
Partner – planning
Qualifications
LLB
Career history
1988 Joined CMS Cameron McKenna; appointed partner in 1990.
1975 Admitted to Roll of Solicitors
Other roles
Member, Law Society planning panel
Professional memberships
Law Society
Contact details
CMS Cameron McKenna, Mitre House, 160 Aldersgate Street, London EC1A 4DD
Tel 020 7367 3000
Fax 020 7367 2000
Web www.cmck.com
Direct tel 020 7367 3556
Email tony.kitson@cmck.com

KLEIN, Jonathan
Enterprise Chambers

Position
Barrister
Qualifications
LLB Hons; BCL (Oxon)
Career history
1992 Called to Bar
Professional memberships
Chancery Bar Association; North Eastern Circuit; Northern Chancery Bar Association; Society of Trusts & Estates Practitioners; Solicitors for the Elderly
Contact details
Enterprise Chambers (Chambers of Anthony Mann QC), 38 Park Square North, Leeds LS1 2PA
Tel 0113 246 0391
Fax 0113 242 4802
Web www.enterprisechambers.com
Email jonathanklein@enterprisechambers.com

KLIM, Peter
Russell Jones & Walker

Position
Partner – head of property
Qualifications
LLB
Career history
1994 Joined Russell Jones & Walker; became partner in 1995.
1987-94 Titmuss Sainer & Webb.
1985-87 Waltons & Morse.
1985 Admitted to Roll of Solicitors
Contact details
Russell Jones & Walker, 80-86 Gray's Inn Road, London WC1X 8NH
Tel 020 7837 2808
Web www.rjw.co.uk
Direct tel 020 7399 6516
Email p.e.klim@rjw.co.uk

KLIMT, Peter
Dawnay, Day Property Management

Position
Chief executive
Contact details
Dawnay, Day Property Management Ltd, 15 Grosvenor Gardens, London SW1W 0BD
Tel 020 7834 8060
Fax 020 7931 9854
Web www.dawnayday.co.uk
Email peter.klimt@dawnay-day.co.uk

KNIGHT, Max
Montagu Evans

Position
Partner – investment
Qualifications
BSc Hons; MRICS
Professional memberships
RICS
Contact details
Montagu Evans, 44-48 Dover Street, London W1S 4AZ
Tel 020 7493 4002
Fax 020 7312 7547
Web www.montagu-evans.co.uk
Direct fax 020 7312 7549
Email max.knight@montagu-evans.co.uk

KNIGHT, Simon
United Utilities Facilities & Property Services

Position
Director
Qualifications
BSc; FRICS
Career history

1990-92 Deputy group property director, MAI.
1989-90 Director (out-of-town property), Sinclair Goldsmith.
1984-89 Director (agency and development), Clapshaws

Professional memberships

RICS

Interests

Motor sports; sport; walking

Contact details

United Utilities Facilities & Property Services Ltd, Lingley Mere Business Park, Warrington WA5 3UU
Tel 01925 234000
Direct tel 01925 235800
Mobile 07785 263353
Email simon.knight@uuplc.co.uk

KNIGHT, Simon
Montagu Evans

Position

Partner – agency

Contact details

Montagu Evans, 44-48 Dover Street, London W1S 4AZ
Tel 020 7493 4002
Fax 020 7312 7547
Web www.montagu-evans.co.uk
Email simon.knight@montagu-evans.co.uk

KNIGHTS, Simon
Strutt & Parker

Position

Partner – West End office, London

Qualifications

LLB; BA; MRICS

Professional memberships

RICS

Contact details

Strutt & Parker, 13 Hill Street, London W1J 5LQ
Tel 020 7629 7282
Fax 020 7629 0387
Web www.struttandparker.com
Direct tel 020 7318 5041
Direct fax 020 7499 1269
Mobile 07836 588674
Email sknights@struttandparker.com

KNOTT, James
Edwin Hill

Position

Associate partner – marketing

Career history

1988 Joined Edwin Hill

Professional memberships

Institute of Direct Marketing

Interests

Hockey; hypnotism

Contact details

Edwin Hill, 18 Savile Row, London W1S 3PW
Tel 020 7287 2020
Fax 020 7734 1255
Web www.edwinhill.co.uk
Mobile 07901 712230
Email jamesk@edwinhill.co.uk

KNOWLES, John
DTZ Debenham Tie Leung

Position

Director – head of business space

Qualifications

BSc; MRICS

Career history

Since 1996 Director, DTZ Debenham Tie Leung.
1995-96 Jones Lang LaSalle, Hong Kong and Manila.
1990-95 Debenham Tewson & Chinnocks/ Debenham Thorpe

Professional memberships

RICS

Contact details

DTZ Debenham Tie Leung, One Curzon Street, London W1A 5PZ
Tel 020 7408 1161
Fax 020 7643 6000
Web www.dtz.com
Email John.knowles@dtz.com

KNOX, James
Linklaters

Position

Partner – real estate

Qualifications

LLB Hons

Career history

1987 Joined Linklaters as solicitor (property department); appointed partner in 1999.
1987 Admitted to Roll of Solicitors.
1985-87 Druces & Attlee

Professional memberships

Investment Property Forum

Contact details

Linklaters, 1 Silk Street, London EC2Y 8HQ
Tel 020 7456 2000
Fax 020 7456 2222
Web www.linklaters.com
Direct tel 020 7456 4760
Email james.knox@linklaters.com

KOPEC, Katie
Jones Lang LaSalle

Position

European director – strategic consulting

Qualifications

BSc

Career history

1983 Joined Jones Lang LaSalle; appointed associate in 1987; responsible for setting up and running Docklands office 1987-91; from 1991 based in business space group advising on development opportunities throughout UK; a lead director of strategic consulting since 1994

Professional memberships

RICS

Interests

Family; horse riding; Pilates

Contact details

Jones Lang LaSalle Ltd, 22 Hanover Square, London W1A 2BN
Tel 020 7493 6040
Fax 020 7408 0220
Web www.joneslanglasalle.com
Direct tel 020 7399 5876
Direct fax 020 7399 5688
Email katie.kopec@eu.joneslanglasalle.com

KOSTIC SAMEN, Katrina
Gensler

Position

Vice-president

Contact details

Gensler, Roman House, Wood Street, London EC2Y 5BA
Tel 020 7330 9600
Fax 020 7330 9630
Web www.gensler.com
Email katrina_kostic_samen@gensler.com

KOUNTOURIS, George
Credit Suisse First Boston

Position

European head of real estate capital partners

Qualifications

MBA (Harvard); PhD (MIT)

Career history

1993-2003 Managing director (real estate opportunities group), Deutsche Bank.
1989-93 Assistant director (real estate), Lazard Brothers, London.
1986-89 Vice-president (real estate), Salomon Brothers.
1982-86 Portfolio manager (real estate and venture capital), General Motors Pension Fund

Other roles

Serves on the boards of: Deutsche Logistik Immobilien (chairman of supervisory board); Telereit Holdings (chairman); Amplion Fastighets; Malon Fastighets; EFG Eurobank Properties; REIB International Holdings; REIB Investments Europe

Contact details

Credit Suisse First Boston, One Cabot Square, London E14 4QJ
Tel 020 7888 8888
Fax 020 7883 5819
Web www.csfb.com
Email george.kountouris@csfb.com

KUMAR, Wally
Development Securities

Position
Project director
Qualifications
MA; FRICS
Career history
1996-2000 Consultant to MEPC and LAMP Development Services.
1993-96 Principal, Wilson Centre, Cambridge.
1985-92 Executive director, Greycoat.
1980-85 Development manager, MEPC.
1976-80 Partner, Debenham Tewson & Chinnocks.
1972-75 Development manager, Regional Properties
Other roles
Member, London Office Review Panel; board member, London First
Professional memberships
Cambridge University Land Society; Lambda Alpha; Worshipful Company of Chartered Surveyors
Interests
Architecture; art; cricket; jazz; photography; travel
Contact details
Development Securities plc, Portland House, Stag Place, London SW1E 5DS
Tel 020 7828 4777
Fax 020 7828 4999
Web www.developmentsecurities.com
Direct fax 020 7828 5642
Email wally.kumar@devsecs.com

KUTNER, Michael
Finers Stephens Innocent

Position
Partner – head of property development
Career history
1997-2000 Edward Lewis.
1984-97 Robert Gore & Co/Pritchard Englefield.
1975-84 Kirkwoods.
1973-75 Paisner & Co.
1973 Admitted to Roll of Solicitors
Interests
Cinema; football; keep fit; opera; reading; theatre
Contact details
Finers Stephens Innocent, 179 Great Portland Street, London W1W 5LS
Tel 020 7323 4000
Fax 020 7344 5600
Web www.finersstephensinnocent.com
Direct tel 020 7344 7673
Email mkutner@fsilaw.co.uk

KYRIACOU, George
CIT Group

Position
Development director
Qualifications
BSc; QS; MSc, Construction Law & Arbitration; FRICS; ACIArb
Career history
Since 1998 Director, CIT.
1997-98 Director, Markborough Properties.
1992-97 GK Associates: seconded to Rosehaugh Properties and Markborough.
1988-92 Bowmer & Kirkland (London).
1984-88 Kyle Stewart.
1981-84 Bovis Construction
Professional memberships
Chartered Institute of Arbitrators; RICS
Interests
Football (Arsenal Football Club)
Contact details
CIT Group plc, 8-10 Bourdon Street, London W1K 3PD
Tel 020 7667 7766
Fax 020 7667 7770
Web www.cit.co.uk
Direct fax 020 7667 7763
Email gk@cit.co.uk

LA FRENAIS, Max
Kitchen La Frenais Morgan

Position
Partner
Qualifications
FRICS
Career history
Since 1990 Partner (retail investment and development), Kitchen La Frenais Morgan.
1969-90 Clive Lewis & Partners
Professional memberships
RICS
Contact details
Kitchen La Frenais Morgan, 1 Tenterden Street, London W1S 1TA
Tel 020 7317 3700
Fax 020 7317 3701
Web www.klmproperty.co.uk
Direct tel 020 7317 3711
Mobile 07774 940523
Email mlafrenais@klmproperty.co.uk

LACEY, Chris
CB Richard Ellis

Position
Director – national development
Contact details
CB Richard Ellis, Kingsley House, 1a Wimpole Street, London W1G 0RE
Tel 020 7182 2000
Fax 020 7182 7001
Web www.cbre.com
Email chris.lacey@cbre.com

LACEY, Christopher
Merrill Lynch Investment Managers

Position
Director – real estate division
Qualifications
BSc; MRICS
Career history
1992 Joined Merrill Lynch Investment Managers.
1987-92 Associate partner (investment), Fuller Peiser.
1984-87 Senior investment surveyor, Clive Lewis & Partners.
1982-83 Gerald Eve & Co
Professional memberships
Investment Property Forum; RICS
Interests
Antiques; archaeology; history; rugby; shooting
Contact details
Merrill Lynch Investment Managers, 33 King William Street, London EC4R 9AS
Tel 020 7743 3000
Fax 020 7743 1000
Web www.mlim.co.uk
Email chris_lacey@ml.com

LACEY, Mark
Rogers Chapman

Position
Director – national office agency
Contact details
Rogers Chapman plc, Prince Frederick House, 37 Maddox Street, London W1S 2PP
Tel 020 7499 8600
Fax 020 7493 5290
Web www.rogerschapman.co.uk
Email mark.lacey@rogerschapman.co.uk

LACKEY, Lynette
BDO Stoy Hayward

Position
Partner – property group
Other roles
Awards judging panel member for annual BDO Stoy Hayward property accounts awards
Professional memberships
BPF; Investment Property Forum; Property Valuation Forum
Interests
Cricket; football; rugby; squash
Contact details
BDO Stoy Hayward, 8 Baker Street, London W1U 3LL
Tel 020 7486 5888
Fax 020 7487 3686
Web www.bdo.co.uk
Direct tel 020 7893 2536
Mobile 07836 608768
Email lynette.lackey@bdo.co.uk

LAFFIN, Simon
Safeway

Position
Finance and property director
Career history
1990 Joined Safeway. Previously at BP Oil, Rank Xerox (UK) and Mars Confectionery
Other roles
Member, 100 Group of Finance Directors
Contact details
Safeway plc, 6 Millington Road, Hayes UB3 4AY
Tel 020 8848 8744
Fax 020 8756 1596
Web www.safeway.co.uk
Email simon_laffin@safeway.co.uk

LAHHAM, Aref
Orion Capital Managers (UK)

Position
Managing director
Contact details
Orion Capital Managers (UK) Ltd, 15 rue de Berri, Paris
Tel +33 1 5396 5070
Fax +33 1 5396 5071
Web www.orioncapman.com
Email alahham@orioncapman.com

LAIDLAW, Tom
Scottish Widows Investment Partnership

Position
Head of property
Contact details
Scottish Widows Investment Partnership Ltd, Edinburgh One, 60 Morrison Street, Edinburgh EH3 8BE
Tel 0131 655 8500
Fax 0131 655 3890
Web www.scottishwidows.co.uk
Email tom.laidlaw@swipartnership.com

LAKER, John
Centros Miller

Position
Senior development director
Qualifications
FRICS
Career history
1996 Joined Centros Miller.
1977-96 Wimpey Property Holdings
Professional memberships
British Council of Shopping Centres
Interests
Golf; theatre
Contact details
Centros Miller Ltd, Albemarle House, 1 Albemarle Street, London W1S 4HA
Tel 020 7499 3917
Fax 020 7499 3741
Email john.laker@centros-miller.co.uk

LAMB, Philip
Focus (DIY)

Position
Group property manager
Contact details
Focus (DIY) Ltd, Gawsworth House, Westmere Drive, Crewe CW1 6XB
Tel 01270 501555
Web www.focusdoitall.co.uk
Email philip.lamb@focusdiy.co.uk

LAMBERT, Colin
Lamberts

Position
Director
Qualifications
FRICS
Professional memberships
RICS
Contact details
Lamberts Ltd, 387 City Road, London EC1V 1NA
Tel 020 7278 8191
Fax 020 7837 5790
Web www.lambertsurv.co.uk
Direct tel 020 7520 2309
Email colin@lambertsurv.co.uk

LAMBERT, Nick
DTZ Pieda Consulting

Position
Director – national head of urban renewal
Qualifications
BSc Hons; MRICS
Career history
Since 1997 DTZ Pieda Consulting.
1993-97 DTZ Debenham Tie Leung.
1990-93 Bernard Thorpe
Other roles
Member, RICS regeneration forum
Professional memberships
RICS
Contact details
DTZ Pieda Consulting, 1 Curzon Street, London W1A 5PZ
Tel 020 7408 1161
Fax 020 7643 6000
Web www.dtz.com
Direct tel 020 7643 6185
Direct fax 020 7643 6198
Mobile 07767 890899
Email nick.lambert@dtz.com

LAMOND, Ian
Stephens & Scown

Position
Partner – head of planning unit and environment unit
Other roles
Member of Law Society's planning panel
Professional memberships
Law Society
Contact details
Stephens & Scown Ltd, 3 Cross Lane, St Austell PL25 4AX
Tel 01726 74433
Fax 01726 68623
Web www.stephens-scown.co.uk
Email
commerce.cornwall@stephens-scown.co.uk

LANCASTER, Stafford
Delancey

Position
Director
Contact details
Delancey, 40 Portman Square, London W1H 0AA
Tel 020 7486 6663
Fax 020 7486 6662
Web www.delancey.com
Email stafford.lancaster@delancey.com

LANDAU, Martin
MAB (UK)

Position
Chairman
Qualifications
FCA
Career history
Since 2003 Chairman of UK operations, MAB Groep (a private, pan-European property company).
1993-2002 Founder, Development Securities.
1986-90 Founder and chief executive, City Merchant Developers; became executive deputy chairman in 1998 after merger with Imry International.
1980-86 Managing director, Guinness Peat Properties.
1973-79 Director, Guinness Mahon & Co
Other roles
Director, European Hotels Corp; supervisory board member, MAB Groep; non-executive director, Wilson Connolly Holdings; main sponsor and governor, Landau Forte City Technology College, Derby Special; trustee, Royal London & St Bartholomew's Hospitals Charitable Trust; governor, Ben Gurion University of the Negev, south Israel; member, Council of City Technology Colleges Trust
Professional memberships
Institute of Chartered Accountants in England & Wales
Interests
Bridge; golf; music
Contact details
MAB (UK) Ltd, Carlton House, 30-35 Pall Mall, London SW1Y 5LP
Tel 020 7808 3355
Fax 020 7808 3366
Email mlandau@mab.com

LANDER, Geoffrey
Tricore Equity Partners

Position
Principal
Qualifications
BA Hons
Career history
1976 Admitted to Roll of Solicitors.
1973-2003 Nabarro Nathanson; became partner in 1980
Other roles
Non-executive deputy chairman, Stonemartin; member of executive committee and board, British American Business of New York and London; member, London Headquarters Group; past chairman and founder member, Holborn Business Partnership; past chairman, CoreNet Global in Europe; founder member and past president, British Council for Offices; past chairman of European advisory board, NACORE; past president, NACORE UK; former board member, Central London Partnership
Professional memberships
CoreNet Global UK; Institute of Directors; Law Society
Interests
Ballet; bridge; cricket; football; golf; rugby; sport
Contact details
Tricore Equity Partners LLP, 806 Collingwood House, Dolphin Square, London SW1V
Tel 020 7017 8468
Fax 020 7017 8469
Mobile 07776 172000
Email geoffreylander@tricore-equitypartners.com

LANE, Henry
Dalgleish

Position
Director – head of professional
Qualifications
BSc; FRICS; MCIArb
Professional memberships
Chartered Institute of Arbitrators; RICS
Contact details
Dalgleish, 80 New Bond Street, London W1S 1DD
Tel 020 7663 5555
Fax 020 7491 0098

Web www.dalgleish.co.uk
Direct tel 020 7663 5597
Email hlane@dalgleish.co.uk

LANE, Jonathan
Morgan Stanley

Position
Managing director
Qualifications
BA; MA (Oxon)
Career history
1985-99 Joined SG Warburg & Co as director; became head of global real estate team in 1995 at merged company SBC Warburg Dillon Read.
1981-85 British Petroleum
Other roles
Founding member, European Real Estate Securities Association; frequent speaker and writer on European property
Professional memberships
Investment Property Forum; Securities & Futures Authority
Contact details
Morgan Stanley, 25 Cabot Square, London E14 4QA
Tel 020 7513 8000
Fax 020 7513 8990
Web www.morganstanley.com
Email jonathan.lane@morganstanley.com

LANE, Jonathan
Shaftesbury

Position
Chief executive
Qualifications
MA; FRICS
Career history
1971-86 Managing director, Stock Conversion.
1968-71 Valuer, Inland Revenue
Other roles
Consultant, Theatres Trust of Great Britain; governor, Royal Shakespeare Company; honorary councillor, Lawn Tennis Association; non-executive chairman, Porthminster Hotel Co; non-executive chairman, Tregarthens Hotel (Scilly)
Professional memberships
RICS
Contact details
Shaftesbury plc, Pegasus House, 37-43 Sackville Street, London W1S 3DL
Tel 020 7333 8118
Fax 020 7333 0660
Web www.shaftesbury.co.uk
Email jon.lane@shaftesbury.co.uk

LANE, Phillip
Harvey Ingram Owston

Position
Senior partner
Career history
1974 Admitted to Roll of Solicitors
Interests
Cricket; fishing; football; golf; rugby; skiing
Contact details
Harvey Ingram Owston, 20 New Walk, Leicester LE1 6TX
Tel 0116 254 5454
Fax 0116 255 4559
Web www.hio.co.uk
Direct tel 0116 257 4419
Direct fax 0116 255 3319
Mobile 07767 496018
Email pdl@hio.co.uk

LANG, Tom
Alder King

Position
Partner
Qualifications
FRICS
Other roles
Estates surveyor, Western region of Court Service, DCA; property manager, Bristol International Airport; member of UK reserve forces
Contact details
Alder King, Pembroke House, 15 Pembroke Road, Bristol BS8 3BA
Tel 0117 317 1000
Fax 0117 317 1001
Web www.alderking.com
Direct tel 0117 317 1130
Mobile 07990 891030
Email tlang@alderking.com

LANGHAM, Richard
Landmark Chambers

Position
Barrister
Qualifications
BA (Oxon)
Career history
1986 Called to Bar
Professional memberships
Planning & Environment Bar Association
Contact details
Landmark Chambers, 4 Breams Buildings, London EC4A 1AQ
Tel 020 7430 1221
Fax 020 7421 1399
Web www.landmarkchambers.co.uk
Email clerks@landmarkchambers.co.uk

LANKFER, James
Bidwells Property Consultants

Position
Partner
Qualifications
MRICS
Contact details
Bidwells Property Consultants, Trumpington Road, Cambridge CB2 2LD
Tel 01223 841841
Fax 01223 845150
Web www.bidwells.co.uk
Direct tel 01223 559558
Direct fax 01223 840294
Mobile 07768 935850
Email jlankfer@bidwells.co.uk

LARKIN, Daniel
Squire Sanders & Dempsey

Position
Head of real estate
Other roles
Former vice-chairman of corporate counsel committee, International Bar Association; officer of American Bar Association's section of international law (real estate committee)
Professional memberships
American Bar Association; International Bar Association; International Society of Hospitality Consultants
Contact details
Squire Sanders & Dempsey LLP, 4th Floor, Royex House, Aldermanbury Square, London EC2V 7HR
Tel 020 7776 5200
Fax 020 7776 5233
Web www.ssd.com
Direct tel 020 7776 5254
Email dlarkin@ssd.com

LATHAM, Simon
ING Real Estate Investment Management (UK)

Position
Senior director of fund management
Qualifications
BSc Hons, Val & Est Man; MRICS
Career history
1994 Joined ING Real Estate Investment Management.
1986-94 Assistant partner (investment agency), Cluttons
Other roles
Director, Lionbrook Retirement Rentals (General Partner); director, Lionbrook (General Partner)
Professional memberships
Investment Property Forum; RICS

L

Interests
Cricket; golf
Contact details
ING Real Estate Investment Management (UK) Ltd, 9 Devonshire Square, London EC2M 4WX
Tel 020 7398 4310
Fax 020 7398 4311
Web www.ingrealestate.co.uk
Direct tel 020 7398 5507
Mobile 07778 351772
Email simon.latham@ingrealestate.co.uk

LATHWOOD, David
King Sturge
Position
Partner in charge, North West
Qualifications
BSc Hons; MRICS
Career history
1987 Joined King Sturge.
1984-86 Russell Cash & Co
Professional memberships
British Council for Offices; British North American Business Group; CBI; Industrial Agents Society; RICS
Contact details
King Sturge, 81 Fountain Street, Manchester M2 2EE
Tel 0161 236 8793
Fax 0161 228 7972
Web www.kingsturge.com
Direct tel 0161 238 6220
Mobile 07703 234248
Email david.lathwood@kingsturge.co.uk

LAUDER, Geoffrey
Insight Investment Management
Position
Director – property investment
Qualifications
FRICS
Professional memberships
RICS
Contact details
Insight Investment Management, 33 Old Broad Street, London EC2N 1HZ
Tel 020 7930 5474
Fax 020 7321 1423
Web www.insightinvestment.com
Email geoff.lauder@insightinvestment.com

LAUGHARNE, Richard
GCL Solicitors
Position
Partner
Qualifications
BA; Solicitor
Career history
Since 1994 Partner, GCL Solicitors. Prior to this, head of Ideal Homes legal department and group legal adviser, Rialto Group
Other roles
Marketing partner
Interests
Cricket; keep fit; sport; London Wasps Rugby Club; Tottenham Hotspur
Contact details
GCL Solicitors, Connaught House, Alexandra Terrace, Guildford GU1 3DA
Tel 0148 357 7091
Fax 0148 357 9252
Web www.gcl-solicitors.co.uk
Direct tel 0148 323 0127
Direct fax 0148 323 0154
Mobile 07710 085948
Email Richard.Laugharne@gcl-solicitors.co.uk

LAVER, Michael
Stevens & Bolton
Position
Managing partner and head of commercial property
Qualifications
LLB Hons
Career history
1981 Admitted to Roll of Solicitors.
1979 Joined Stevens & Bolton; became partner in 1986 and managing partner in 1995
Professional memberships
Surrey Law Society
Interests
Music; sailing; travel
Contact details
Stevens & Bolton, The Billings, Guildford GU1 4YD
Tel 01483 302264
Fax 01483 302254
Web www.stevens-bolton.co.uk
Direct tel 01483 734230
Email michael.laver@stevens-bolton.co.uk

LAW, Brian
Association of Planning Supervisors
Position
Chief executive
Qualifications
Dip Arch (Aberdeen); RIBA; RIAS
Professional memberships
Royal Incorporation of Architects in Scotland; RIBA
Contact details
Association of Planning Supervisors Ltd, 16 Rutland Square, Edinburgh EH1 2BB
Tel 0131 221 9959
Fax 0131 221 0061
Web www.aps.org.uk
Email info@aps.org.uk

LAWLEY, Michael
Cooke & Arkwright
Position
Managing director
Qualifications
BSc; FRICS; MCIArb
Career history
1981 Joined Cooke & Arkwright as senior surveyor (valuation, landlord and tenant and residential land works); appointed partner in 1988 and director in 1991; became managing director in 2000.
1977-81 Estates officer, Redditch Newtown Development Corp
Other roles
Board member, RICS in Wales; member, CBI Wales council; governor, University of Glamorgan; past chairman of junior organisation and general practice division, RICS; past chairman, CBI south-east Wales
Professional memberships
Chartered Institute of Arbitrators; CBI; RICS
Interests
Music; sport; walking
Contact details
Cooke & Arkwright, 7-8 Windsor Place, Cardiff CF10 3SX
Tel 029 2034 6346
Fax 029 2034 6300
Web www.coark.co.uk
Direct fax 029 2034 6355
Email michael.lawley@coark.com

LAWRENCE, Roger
King Sturge
Position
Partner
Qualifications
FRICS
Career history
Since 1974 Partner, King Sturge.
1973-74 Chesterton.
1972-73 Knight Frank
Other roles
Past president, Bristol Property Agents Association (1999-2000)
Interests
Sailing
Contact details
King Sturge, 40 Berkeley Square, Bristol BS8 1HU
Tel 0117 927 6691
Fax 0117 929 9669

Web www.kingsturge.com
Direct tel 0117 930 5715
Direct fax 0117 925 3584
Mobile 07836 373519
Email roger.lawrence@kingsturge.co.uk

LAWS, Martin
Deloitte

Position
Lead partner – real estate solutions
Contact details
Deloitte, 180 Strand, London WC2R 1BL
Tel 020 7936 3000
Fax 020 7583 1198
Web www.deloitte.co.uk
Direct tel 020 7007 7919
Direct fax 020 7007 1077
Email mlaws@deloitte.com

LAWSON-MAY, Neil
Eurohypo

Position
Joint chief executive – investment banking
Qualifications
BSc
Contact details
Eurohypo AG, 90 Long Acre, London WC2E 9RA
Tel 020 7759 7600
Fax 020 7759 7672
Web www.eurohypo.com
Direct tel 020 7759 7635
Direct fax 020 7759 7675
Mobile 07767 616029
Email neil.lawson-may@eurohypo.com

LAX, Andrew
GVA Saxon Law

Position
Managing partner
Qualifications
FRICS
Contact details
GVA Saxon Law, 10 Stratton Street, London W1J 8JR
Tel 0870 900 8990
Fax 020 7911 2560
Direct tel 020 7911 2767
Mobile 07831 558815
Email andrew.lax@gvagrimley.co.uk

LAXTON, Bryan
Cushman & Wakefield Healey & Baker

Position
Partner – advisory group
Qualifications
BSc; MRICS
Career history
1981 Joined Cushman & Wakefield Healey & Baker; became partner in 1989 and member of UK management board in 2003
Professional memberships
RICS
Interests
Cars; football; sport
Contact details
Cushman & Wakefield Healey & Baker, 43-45 Portman Square, London W1A 3BG
Tel 020 7935 5000
Fax 020 7152 5360
Web www.cushwake.com
Direct tel 020 7152 5178
Direct fax 020 7152 5363
Email bryan.laxton@eur.cushwake.com

LAXTON, Chris
Morley Fund Management

Position
Head of external funds
Contact details
Morley Fund Management Ltd, 34-36 Lime Street, London EC3M 7JE
Tel 020 7809 6000
Fax 020 7489 7940
Web www.morleyfm.com
Email chris.laxton@morleyfm.com

LE BORGNE, Marc
Royal Bank of Scotland

Position
Head of European real estate portfolio
Qualifications
MBA (Insead)
Career history
1988-99 Associate director (property finance), Société Générale.
1979-87 Project engineer (building and construction), SETEC
Other roles
Co-ordinator, Insead Alumni Network for Property
Interests
Music; sailing
Contact details
Royal Bank of Scotland, 5th Floor, 135 Bishopsgate, London EC2M 3UR
Tel 020 7375 5000
Web www.rbs.co.uk
Direct tel +33 1 4924 1241
Email marc.leborgne@rbos.com

LE GRELLE, Jérôme
Sephora UK

Position
Head of real estate
Contact details
Sephora UK Ltd, Eagle House, Ram Passage, High Street, Kingston upon Thames KT1 1HH
Tel 020 8974 9502
Web www.sephora.com
Email jlegrelle@sephora.fr

LE PARD, Geoff
Freshfields Bruckhaus Deringer

Position
Co-head – global real estate practice
Career history
Since 1987 Partner, Freshfields Bruckhaus Deringer.
1981 Admitted to Roll of Solicitors
Professional memberships
City of London Law Society; Law Society
Contact details
Freshfields Bruckhaus Deringer, 65 Fleet Street, London EC4Y 1HT
Tel 020 7936 4000
Fax 020 7832 7001
Web www.freshfields.com
Direct tel 020 7832 7465
Email geoff.lepard@freshfields.com

LEAFE, Stephen
Mitchells & Butlers

Position
Director – acquisitions
Qualifications
BSc Hons; MRICS
Career history
1997-2001 Operations director, Gala Bingo.
1992-97 Property and development director, Gala Leisure.
1988-92 Director of development, Bass Developments
Contact details
Mitchells & Butlers plc, 27 Fleet Street, Birmingham B3 1JP
Tel 0870 609 3000
Fax 0121 233 2267
Web www.mbplc.com
Direct tel 0121 420 6502
Direct fax 0121 420 6925
Mobile 07808 095157
Email Stephen.Leafe@mbplc.com

LEAHY, Andy
Ballymore Properties

Position
Development director
Qualifications
BSc; ACIOB
Other roles
Managing director, Ballymore Developments;

chairman, Apex Housing Solutions; committee member, London First

Professional memberships

Chartered Institute of Building; Institute of Directors

Interests

Aviation; fishing; rugby

Contact details

Ballymore Properties Ltd, 3 Greenwich View Place, London E14 9NN
Tel 020 7510 9100
Fax 020 7510 9110
Email aleahy@ballymore.co.uk

LEAR, Jeremy
Vail Williams

Position

Consultant – landlord and tenant

Qualifications

FRICS; ACIArb

Career history

1963 Joined LS Vail & Son (now Vail Williams); equity partner since 1973

Other roles

Director, Portsmouth Harbour Events; vice-president, Cutty Sark tall ship organising committee

Professional memberships

Chartered Institute of Arbitrators; RICS

Interests

Rowing (vice-president, Southsea Rowing Club); sailing (Portsmouth Sailing Club; Island Sailing Club; Royal Navy & Royal Albert Yacht Club); shooting; travel

Contact details

Vail Williams, Meridians House, 7 Ocean Way, Southampton SO14 3TJ
Tel 0238 082 0900
Fax 0238 082 0950
Web www.vailwilliams.com
Mobile 07768 724338
Email jlear@vailwilliams.com

LEDGER, Neal
Fortis Bank

Position

Director – head of constuction and real estate

Qualifications

BA Hons, Banking, Insurance & Finance

Career history

Since 1996 Director (head of construction and real estate), London branch, Fortis Bank.
1992-96 Director, Stratford Place Finance.
1989-91 Manager (property department), City Merchants Bank.
1988-89 Manager, Riggs AP Bank.
1984-88 National Westminster Bank

Interests

Diving/scuba diving; mountaineering; rugby; tennis

Contact details

Fortis Bank, Camomile Court, 23 Camomile Street, London EC3A 7PP
Tel 020 7444 8000
Fax 020 7444 8810
Web www.fortisbank.com
Direct tel 020 7444 8738
Direct fax 020 7444 8870
Mobile 07768 155128
Email neal.ledger@fortisbank.com

LEE, Adrian
Big Yellow Group

Position

Operations director

Qualifications

MA; MRICS

Career history

1999 Joined Big Yellow Group.
1995-99 Edge Properties.
1990-95 Lazard Brothers.
1987-90 Knight Frank

Professional memberships

RICS

Contact details

Big Yellow Group plc, 2 The Deans, Bridge Road, Bagshot GU19 5AT
Tel 01276 470190
Fax 01276 470191
Web www.bigyellow.co.uk
Mobile 07774 932792
Email alee@bigyellow.co.uk

LEE, Robert
Davies Arnold Cooper

Position

Partner – head of property

Qualifications

LLB Hons

Career history

1984 Joined Davies Arnold Cooper as solicitor; became partner in 1989

Interests

Keep fit; surfing

Contact details

Davies Arnold Cooper, 6-8 Bouverie Street, London EC4Y 8DD
Tel 020 7936 2222
Fax 020 7936 2020
Web www.dac.co.uk
Direct tel 020 7293 4094
Email rlee@dac.co.uk

LEE, Steve
Brixton Investments

Position

Senior director – customer services

Qualifications

FRICS

Career history

2001 Joined Brixton. Previously managing director of Citex Group; before that, Bucknall Group

Other roles

Managing director, B-Serv (Brixton's asset and customer services company)

Professional memberships

RICS

Contact details

Brixton Investments Ltd, 50 Berkeley Street, London W1J 8BX
Tel 020 7399 4500
Fax 020 7399 4550
Web www.brixton.plc.uk
Direct tel 020 7399 4525
Mobile 07900 407740
Email stevelee@brixton.plc.uk

LEE, Stephen
Orange

Position

Group director – property, environment, health and safety

Career history

1996 Joined Orange; now group director of property, environment, health and safety.
1989-96 Director (facilities, EMEA), American Express.
1986-89 Premises controller, Marks & Spencer Financial Services.
1983-86 Engineering services manager, Beecham Pharmaceuticals.
1976-83 Works officer, NHS.
1968-76 Marine engineer

Interests

Cricket; family; reading; rugby; sport; squash

Contact details

Orange SA, St James Court, Great Park Road, Almondsbury Business Park, Bristol BS32 4QJ
Tel 0870 376 8888
Web www.orange.com
Mobile 07973 820623
Email stephen.lee@orange.co.uk

LEE-DICKSON, Mike
Network Rail Infrastructure

Position

Director of development

Qualifications

BSc; MRICS

L

Professional memberships
RICS
Contact details
Network Rail Infrastructure Ltd, 40 Melton Street, London NW1 2EE
Tel 020 7557 8000
Fax 020 7557 9000
Direct tel 020 7557 8624
Direct fax 020 7557 9090
Mobile 07771 613236
Email michael.lee-dickson@networkrail.co.uk

LEEMING, Ian
St James's Chambers
Position
Barrister
Qualifications
LLB; QC
Other roles
Member, panel of counsel to examine titles for HM Land Registry; barrister, Lamb Chambers, London
Professional memberships
Chancery Bar Association; Society of Construction Law; Technology & Construction Bar Association
Interests
Cars; family; sport
Contact details
St James's Chambers, 68 Quay Street, Manchester M3 3EJ
Tel 0161 834 7000
Fax 0161 834 2341
Web www.stjameschambers.co.uk
Email ian.leeming@stjameschambers.co.uk

LEES, Simon
Edwin Hill
Position
Partner
Qualifications
BSc; MRICS
Professional memberships
RICS
Contact details
Edwin Hill, 18 Savile Row, London W1S 3PW
Tel 020 7287 2020
Fax 020 7734 1255
Web www.edwinhill.co.uk
Email simonl@edwinhill.co.uk

LEFTERIS, Mary
Hemingway Properties
Position
Director
Qualifications
FCCA
Career history
1991 Joined Hemingway Properties.
1983-91 New Cavendish Estates.
1978-83 Gresham House
Interests
Family; music; psychology
Contact details
Hemingway Properties Ltd, 21 Devonshire Street, London W1G 6EP
Tel 020 7487 3737
Fax 020 7935 1460
Web www.hemingway.co.uk
Mobile 07944 648463
Email ml@hemingway.co.uk

LEGGETT, Graeme
Dunlop Heywood Lorenz
Position
Director – agency
Qualifications
MRICS; BSc Hons
Contact details
Dunlop Heywood Lorenz Ltd, 10 Queen Anne Street, London W1G 9LH
Tel 020 7636 7000
Fax 020 7636 7002
Web www.dhlproperty.co.uk
Email gl@dhlproperty.co.uk

LEIBOWITZ, Alan
Dorrington Properties
Position
Managing director
Qualifications
BSc, Building; MSc, Planning
Career history
Since 1986 Managing director, Dorrington Properties.
1977-86 Director, Portmans Property Consultants
Other roles
Joint managing director, Dorrington Holdings; director, Hanover Acceptances; director, Gerber Foods Holdings; director, African Realty Trust; member, design review committee, Commission for Architecture & the Built Environment
Interests
Architecture; RAC
Contact details
Dorrington Properties plc, 16 Hans Road, London SW3 1RT
Tel 020 7581 1477
Fax 020 7225 0989
Web www.dorrington.co.uk
Email alan.leibowitz@dorrington.co.uk

LEON, Caren
Dalgleish
Position
Retail director
Contact details
Dalgleish, 80 New Bond Street, London W1S 1DD
Tel 020 7663 5555
Fax 020 7491 0098
Web www.dalgleish.co.uk
Email cleon@dalgleish.co.uk

LESLAU, Nick
Prestbury Investment Holdings
Position
Chairman and chief executive
Career history
1997 Joined Prestbury (privatised in 2001 and renamed Prestbury Investment) as managing director; now chairman and chief executive.
1982-97 Founding partner and managing director, Burford Group
Interests
Rugby
Contact details
Prestbury Investment Holdings Ltd, 11-12 Wigmore Place, London W1U 2LU
Tel 020 7323 5250
Fax 020 7323 5251
Direct tel 020 7323 7586
Email jemma@prestbury.co.uk

LESLIE, Douglas
Capital Shopping Centres
Position
Managing director
Contact details
Capital Shopping Centres plc, 40 Broadway, London SW1H 0BU
Tel 020 7887 4220
Fax 020 7887 4225
Web www.capital-shopping-centres.co.uk
Email douglas-leslie@capshop.co.uk

LETT, Andrew
Aukett
Position
Executive chairman
Qualifications
Dip Arch
Career history
1976 Joined Aukett; appointed associate in 1979, partner in 1981, principal and board director in 1988, group managing director in 1994 and executive chairman in 2000.
1969-76 Experience with London-based architectural practices on educational and

commercial projects
Professional memberships
ARC UK; Institute of Continuing Professional Development; RIBA; Royal Society of Arts
Interests
Sailing
Contact details
Aukett Ltd, Sterling House, 2 Great Eastern Wharf, London SW11 4TT
Tel 020 7924 4949
Fax 020 7978 6720
Email Andrew@aukett.com

LEVINE, Raymond
Maxwell Batley
Position
Senior partner
Qualifications
MA, Law
Career history
1974 Joined Maxwell Batley.
1972 Admitted to Roll of Solicitors
Professional memberships
Law Society
Interests
Rugby; windsurfing; wine
Contact details
Maxwell Batley, 27 Chancery Lane, London WC2A 1PA
Tel 020 7440 4400
Fax 020 7440 4444
Web www.maxwellbatley.com
Direct tel 020 7440 4441
Email rlevine@maxwellbatley.com

LEVITEN, David
Pannone & Partners
Position
Partner
Career history
1997-2000 Associate, Beachcroft Wansbrough.
1995-97 Partner, Wacks Caller.
1991-95 Assistant/partner, Fox Brooks Marshall.
1989-91 Halliwell Landau.
1987-89 Ashurst Morris Crisp.
1986 Admitted to Roll of Solicitors
Professional memberships
Law Society
Interests
Chess; football; golf; karting
Contact details
Pannone & Partners, 123 Deansgate, Manchester M3 2BU
Tel 0161 909 3000
Fax 0161 909 4444
Web www.pannone.com
Email david.leviten@pannone.co.uk

LEVY, Albert
Ince & Co
Position
Head of property and private client
Qualifications
MA (Cantab)
Career history
Since 1989 Partner, Ince & Co
Interests
Family; sailing (Little Ship Club)
Contact details
Ince & Co Ltd, Knollys House, 11 Byward Street, London EC3R 5EN
Tel 020 7623 2011
Fax 020 7623 3225
Web www.incelaw.com
Email albert.levy@incelaw.com

LEVY, Peter
Shaftesbury
Position
Chairman
Qualifications
OBE; BSc; FRICS
Career history
1986 Joined Shaftesbury.
1964-86 DE&J Levy: partner from 1966
Other roles
Directorships held at: Akiva School, Cystic Fibrosis Trust, CF Merchandising, Haymarket Finance, Snow East Anglian Properties, Institute for Jewish Policy Research, Jewish Chronicle, and Jewish Chronicle Newspaper; chairman, Institute for Jewish Policy Research; vice-chairman, Fordementia (previously Dementia Relief Trust)
Professional memberships
RICS
Contact details
Shaftesbury plc, Pegasus House, 37-43 Sackville Street, London W1S 3DL
Tel 020 7333 8118
Fax 020 7333 0660
Web www.shaftesbury.co.uk
Email peter.levy@shaftesbury.co.uk

LEWIS, Alice
CoreNet Global UK
Position
Executive officer
Contact details
CoreNet Global UK, 6 Rectory Lane, Kettering NN14 4HS
Tel 01832 737909
Fax 01832 735079
Web www.nacore.org.uk
Email alicemlewis@corenetglobal.org.uk

LEWIS, Carl
THI
Position
President
Contact details
THI plc, 22 Grosvenor Square, London W1K 6LF
Tel 020 7493 2288
Fax 020 7493 3168
Email leisure@thi.co.uk

LEWIS, Christine
Hill Dickinson
Position
Partner – head of property development team
Career history
2000 Joined Hill Dickinson.
1996-2000 Partner, Lyons Wilson.
1995-96 Director of legal services, David McLean Homes.
1983-95 Solicitor/partner, Clement Jones.
1980 Admitted to Roll of Solicitors
Professional memberships
Law Society
Contact details
Hill Dickinson, 34 Cuppin Street, Chester CH1 2BN
Tel 01244 896600
Fax 01244 896601
Web www.hilldickinson.com
Direct tel 01244 896620
Email christine.lewis@hilldickinson.com

LEWIS, David
Freshfields Bruckhaus Deringer
Position
Partner – real estate
Career history
Since 1995 Partner, Freshfields Bruckhaus Deringer.
1987 Admitted to Roll of Solicitors
Contact details
Freshfields Bruckhaus Deringer, 65 Fleet Street, London EC4Y 1HT
Tel 020 7936 4000
Fax 020 7832 7001
Web www.freshfields.com
Direct tel 020 7832 7477
Email david.lewis@freshfields.com

LEWIS, Jonathan
Olswang
Position
Partner
Qualifications
BA, Econ
Career history
1978-2003 DJ Freeman

L

Professional memberships
City of London Solicitors Company; Investment Property Forum
Interests
Art; charity; family
Contact details
Olswang, 90 High Holborn, London WC1V 6XX
Tel 020 7067 3000
Fax 020 7067 3999
Web www.olswang.com
Direct tel 020 7067 3577
Mobile 07976 439949
Email jonathan.lewis@olswang.com

LEWIS, Paul
Stanhope
Position
Projects director
Qualifications
Eur Ing; CEng; Dip Industrial Studies; BSc Hons; MICE
Career history
1986 Joined Stanhope.
1978-86 John Laing Group
Other roles
Managing director, Exchequer Partnership; construction committee, BPF
Interests
Cars; family; football; golf; skiing; tennis
Contact details
Stanhope plc, Norfolk House, 31 St James's Square, London SW1Y 4JJ
Tel 020 7170 1700
Fax 020 7170 1701
Web www.stanhopeplc.com
Direct tel 020 7170 1623
Mobile 07980 721322
Email paul.lewis@stanhopeplc.com

LEWIS, Richard
Curzon Global Partners
Position
Chief executive
Other roles
Chief investment officer, Ixis AEW Europe
Contact details
Curzon Global Partners Ltd, 1 Curzon Street, London W1J 5HD
Tel 020 7016 4800
Fax 020 7016 4700
Email rlewis@curzonglobal.com

LEWIS, Robert
11 New Square
Position
Barrister
Qualifications
MA; BCL
Career history
1996 Called to Bar.
1986-96 Solicitor/partner, Freshfields.
1977 Admitted to Roll of Solicitors.
1975-86 Solicitor, local government
Other roles
Member, BPF planning and environmental law subcommittee; planning and environment committee chairman, European Property Federation; joint author, *Tolley's Environmental Law Handbook*, *Environmental Liability* and *Managing the Environmental Challenge*; numerous articles published in legal journals
Professional memberships
BPF; European Property Federation; Planning & Environment Bar Association
Interests
Reading; walking
Contact details
11 New Square (Chambers of Sonia Proudman QC), Ground Floor, London WC2A 3QB
Tel 020 7831 0081
Fax 020 7405 2560
Web www.11newsquare.co.uk
Email lewis.r@btopenworld.com

LEWIS, Roger
Berkeley Group
Position
Chairman
Qualifications
FCA
Career history
1991 Joined Berkeley Group; appointed chairman in 1999.
1983-91 Group chief executive, Crest Nicholson
Professional memberships
Institute of Chartered Accountants in England & Wales
Interests
Cricket; food; skiing; travel
Contact details
Berkeley Group plc, Berkeley House, 19 Portsmouth Road, Cobham KT11 1JG
Tel 0193 286 8555
Fax 0193 286 8667
Email pat.huddleston@berkeleygroup.co.uk

LEWIS, Simon
Lewis Ellis
Position
Partner
Contact details
Lewis Ellis, 11 Albemarle Street, London W1S 4HH
Tel 020 7493 3330
Fax 020 7493 3033
Email slewis@lewisellis.co.uk

LEWIS, Steven
Burford Group
Position
Development director
Contact details
Burford Group Ltd, 20 Thayer Street, London W1U 2DD
Tel 020 7224 2240
Fax 020 7224 1710
Email steven.lewis@burfordgroup.com

LEWIS-PRATT, Andrew
Junction Properties
Position
Chief executive
Qualifications
BSc; MRICS
Career history
1990 Joined Lanham as chief executive; became director of Capital & Regional after its 1997 acquisition of Lanham; now chief executive, Junction Properties.
1985-90 Director, Citygrove
Professional memberships
RICS
Contact details
Junction Properties Ltd, 10 Lower Grosvenor Place, London SW1W 0EN
Tel 020 7932 8000
Fax 020 7802 5600
Web www.thejunction-uk.com
Email andrew.lewis-pratt@thejunction-uk.com

LEWSLEY, Christopher
Landmark Chambers
Position
Barrister
Other roles
Editor and contributor to leading journals and text books on rating and compulsory purchase; member, Land Tribunal users consultative committee
Professional memberships
Planning & Environment Bar Association
Contact details
Landmark Chambers, 4 Breams Buildings, London EC4A 1AQ
Tel 020 7430 1221
Fax 020 7421 1399
Web www.landmarkchambers.co.uk
Email clerks@landmarkchambers.co.uk

LEYBURN, Peter
DTZ Debenham Tie Leung

Position
Director – head of M25 agency
Qualifications
BSc; MRICS
Career history
1988-2002 Director (head of South East office agency), Insignia Richard Ellis
Professional memberships
Office Agents Society; RICS
Interests
Fishing
Contact details
DTZ Debenham Tie Leung, 1 Curzon Street, London W1A 5PZ
Tel 020 7408 1161
Fax 020 7643 6000
Web www.dtz.com
Direct tel 020 7643 6464
Mobile 07785 115108
Email peter.leyburn@dtz.com

LIDDLE, Christopher
HLM Design

Position
Chairman
Contact details
HLM Design Ltd, 1 Old Lodge Place, London TW1 1RQ
Tel 020 8744 1666
Email cliddle@hlm.co.uk

LIEBERMAN, Seth
Hypo Real Estate Investment Banking

Position
Joint managing director
Career history
2003 Joined Hypo Real Estate Investment. Previously executive director, Lehman Brothers (global real estate finance), principal, CSFB Praedium Group and director (Nordic Countries), GE Capital
Contact details
Hypo Real Estate Investment Banking Ltd, 110 Cannon Street, London EC4N 6EW
Tel 020 7743 7743
Fax 020 7743 7700
Direct tel 020 7743 7736
Direct fax 020 7743 7737
Mobile 07810 553040
Email seth.lieberman@hypointernational.com

LIEVEN, Nathalie
Landmark Chambers

Position
Barrister
Career history
1989 Called to Bar
Other roles
Contributor to *Halsbury's Laws of England* on town and country planning
Professional memberships
Planning & Environment Bar Association
Contact details
Landmark Chambers, 4 Breams Buildings, London EC4A 1AQ
Tel 020 7430 1221
Fax 020 7421 1399
Web www.landmarkchambers.co.uk
Email clerks@landmarkchambers.co.uk

LIGHT, Richard
Stephenson Harwood

Position
Partner – head of property and property finance
Qualifications
MA (Cantab)
Career history
1975 Joined Stephenson Harwood; become partner in 1982
Interests
Golf; opera; tennis
Contact details
Stephenson Harwood, 1 St Paul's Churchyard, London EC4M 8SH
Tel 020 7329 4422
Fax 020 7606 0822
Web www.shlegal.com
Direct tel 020 7809 2515
Email richard.light@shlegal.com

LILFORD, Mike
ISG Occupancy

Position
Director – building consultancy
Qualifications
BSc; MRICS; MaPS
Contact details
ISG Occupancy Ltd, 17-19 Maddox Street, London W1S 1QG
Tel 020 7290 3333
Fax 020 7290 3334
Web www.isgplc.com
Email mike.lilford@isgplc.com

LILLIE, Duncan
Shelley Sandzer & Co

Position
Managing director – professional services
Qualifications
BSc; FRICS
Career history
1997-2002 Equity partner, Matthews & Goodman.
1983-97 Kemsley Whiteley & Ferris: appointed equity partner in 1989.
1982-83 Ian Kennard & Co.
1980-82 Kemp & Hawley, London
Other roles
APC assessor for RICS; member of RICS panel of arbitrators and independent experts; member and past chairman, Restaurant Property Advisors Society
Professional memberships
Restaurant Property Advisors Society; RICS
Interests
Keep fit; motor sports; rugby (qualified rugby coach)
Contact details
Shelley Sandzer & Co, 12 Queen Anne Street, London W1G 9AU
Tel 020 7580 3366
Fax 020 7580 3399
Email duncan@shelleysandzer.co.uk

LILLINGTON, Peter
Scottish Widows Investment Partnership

Position
Investment director
Qualifications
BSc; MA
Career history
1990 Joined Scottish Widows.
1983-90 Gooch & Wagstaff
Contact details
Scottish Widows Investment Partnership Ltd, Edinburgh One, 60 Morrison Street, Edinburgh EH3 8BE
Tel 0131 655 8500
Fax 0131 655 3890
Web www.scottishwidows.co.uk
Direct tel 0131 655 8518
Direct fax 0131 662 1553
Email peter.lillington@swipartnership.co.uk

LINDBLOM, Keith
2 Harcourt Buildings

Position
Barrister
Qualifications
QC
Career history
1996 Appointed QC.
1980 Called to Bar
Other roles
Founder member and former committee member, Planning & Environment Bar Association; committee member, Oxford Joint Planning Law Conference; assistant commissioner, Parliamentary Boundary Commission; Crown

L

Court recorder; bench of Gray's Inn

Professional memberships

Anglo-American Real Property Institute; Parliamentary Bar Mess; Planning & Environment Bar Association

Contact details

2 Harcourt Buildings (Chambers of Robin Purchas QC), 2nd Floor, London EC4Y 9DB
Tel 020 7353 8415
Fax 020 7353 7622
Web www.2hblaw.co.uk
Email clerks@2hblaw.co.uk

LINDSAY, David
Royal Bank of Scotland

Position

Director – property finance group

Contact details

Royal Bank of Scotland, 6th Floor, 6-8 George Street, Edinburgh EH2 2SA
Tel 0131 556 8555
Fax 0131 523 5104
Web www.rbs.co.uk
Direct tel 0131 523 5229
Email david.lindsay@rbs.co.uk

LINDSAY, Michael
KPMG Corporate Finance

Position

Head of corporate finance real estate advisory

Qualifications

BSc; MRICS

Career history

1996-2003 Director, Schroder Salomon Smith Barney.
1992-96 Managing director, Marston House.
1986-92 Director, Guinness Mahon & Co.
1982-86 Partner, William H Brown.
1981-82 Fletcher King.
1979-81 Donaldsons

Professional memberships

Investment Property Forum; London Business School Alumni; RICS

Interests

Sailing; skiing; tennis

Contact details

KPMG Corporate Finance, Salisbury Square House, 8 Salisbury Square, London EC4Y 8BB
Tel 020 7311 1000
Fax 020 7311 3311
Web www.kpmg.co.uk
Direct tel 020 7311 4205
Direct fax 020 7311 8806
Mobile 07768 615525
Email michael.lindsay@kpmg.co.uk

LINES, Stephen
King Sturge

Position

Partner – landlord and tenant

Qualifications

FRICS; IRRV; MCIArb

Career history

Since 1988 Partner, King Sturge.
1985-87 Associate, Hillier Parker.
1981-85 Associate, Baker Harris Saunders

Other roles

Member, RICS panel of independent experts and arbitrators; honorary secretary, RICS City of London branch

Professional memberships

Chartered Institute of Arbitrators; Institute of Revenues Rating & Valuation; RICS

Contact details

King Sturge, 7 Stratford Place, London W1C 1ST
Tel 020 7493 4933
Fax 020 7409 0469
Web www.kingsturge.com
Direct tel 0207 529 6875
Direct fax 0207 409 1135
Mobile 07802 656278
Email stephen.lines@kingsturge.co.uk

LING, Graham
Speechly Bircham

Position

Partner – head of property litigation

Qualifications

LLB

Career history

1988 Joined Speechly Bircham; became partner in 1995 and head of property litigation in 1997.
1988 Admitted to Roll of Solicitors.
1986-88 E Edward Son & Noice

Professional memberships

Property Litigation Association

Interests

Cinema; cricket; golf; reading; travel

Contact details

Speechly Bircham, 6 St Andrew Street, London EC4A 3LX
Tel 020 7427 6400
Fax 020 7427 6600
Web www.speechlys.com
Direct tel 020 7427 6416
Mobile 07711 143270
Email graham.ling@speechlys.co.uk

LINKLATER, Lisa
Chancery House Chambers

Position

Barrister

Qualifications

MA (Cantab); Barrister

Career history

Since 1997 Tenant, Chancery House Chambers, Leeds.
1995-96 Pupil barrister, Erskine Chambers, London and 11 New Square, London.
1995 Called to Bar

Other roles

Junior counsel to the Crown (provincial panel); founder and convener of Young Chancery Commercial Group

Professional memberships

Chancery Bar Association; Insolvency Lawyers' Association; North Eastern Circuit; Northern Chancery Bar Association

Interests

Hill walking; languages; travel

Contact details

Chancery House Chambers, 7 Lisbon Square, Leeds LS1 4LY
Tel 0113 244 6691
Fax 0113 244 6766
Web www.chanceryhouse.co.uk
Email lisa.linklater@chanceryhouse.co.uk

LINTOTT, Stephen
Pannone & Partners

Position

Partner

Qualifications

BA Hons (Oxon)

Career history

1995 Admitted to Roll of Solicitors.
1993 Joined Pannone & Partners; became partner in 1999

Professional memberships

Law Society

Interests

Badminton; football; rugby; tennis; walking

Contact details

Pannone & Partners, 123 Deansgate, Manchester M3 2BU
Tel 0161 909 3000
Fax 0161 909 4444
Web www.pannone.com
Email stephen.lintott@pannone.co.uk

LIPMAN, Larry
Safeland

Position

Managing director

Other roles

Chairman, Hercules Property Services; chairman, Bizspace

Contact details

Safeland plc, 94-96 Great North Road, London N2 0NL

Tel 020 8815 1600
Fax 020 8815 1601
Email larry.lipman@safeland.co.uk

LIPMAN, Raymond
Safeland

Position
Chairman
Contact details
Safeland plc, 94-96 Great North Road, London N2 0NL
Tel 020 8815 1600
Fax 020 8815 1601
Email ray.lipman@safeland.co.uk

LIPTON, Sir Stuart
Stanhope

Position
Chief executive
Other roles
Chairman, Commission for Architecture & the Built Environment; special adviser, Network Rail
Contact details
Stanhope plc, Norfolk House, 31 St James's Square, London SW1Y 4JJ
Tel 020 7170 1700
Fax 020 7170 1701
Web www.stanhopeplc.com
Email Stuart.lipton@stanhopeplc.com

LISS, Daniel
Asda Property Holdings

Position
Joint head of central London investment
Qualifications
BSc Hons; MRICS
Career history
1996 Joined Asda Property Holdings
Professional memberships
RICS
Contact details
Asda Property Holdings Ltd, 58 Queen Anne Street, London W1G 8HW
Tel 020 7224 1030
Fax 020 7224 0574
Web www.asda.net
Email dliss@asda.net

LISTER, Michael
Bank of Ireland

Position
Associate director – property lending
Qualifications
BSc; GI Biol; MRICS
Career history
1979-94 Vice-president, Chemical Bank.
1974-79 Hillier Parker
Professional memberships
Association of Property Bankers; British Council for Offices; Chartered Institute of Bankers; RICS
Contact details
Bank of Ireland, 36 Queen Street, London EC4R 1BN
Tel 020 7236 2000
Fax 020 7634 3106
Web www.bankofireland.ie
Direct tel 020 7634 3151
Mobile 07785 920080
Email michael.lister@boiuk.com

LITTLE, Adrian
Insight Investment Management

Position
Director – property investment
Contact details
Insight Investment Management, 33 Old Broad Street, London EC2N 1HZ
Tel 020 7930 5474
Fax 020 7321 1423
Web www.insightinvestment.com
Email adrian.little@insightinvestment.com

LITTON, John
Landmark Chambers

Position
Barrister
Other roles
Contributor to town and country planning titles in both *Halsbury's Laws of England* and *Atkins' Court Forms*
Professional memberships
Administrative Law Bar Association; Chancery Bar Association; Planning & Environment Bar Association
Contact details
Landmark Chambers, 4 Breams Buildings, London EC4A 1AQ
Tel 020 7430 1221
Fax 020 7421 1399
Web www.landmarkchambers.co.uk
Email clerks@landmarkchambers.co.uk

LIVINGSTONE, David
UNITE Group

Position
Group development director
Career history
2000-01 Director and general manager, Unilodge.
1980-2000 Whitbread
Interests
Golf; sailing
Contact details
UNITE Group plc, 103 Temple Street, Bristol BS1 6EN
Tel 0117 907 8100
Fax 0117 907 8101
Web www.unite-group.com
Email david.livingstone@unite-group.co.uk

LIVINGSTONE, Ian
London & Regional Properties

Position
Managing director
Qualifications
BSc; MBCO
Contact details
London & Regional Properties Ltd, 40 New Bond Street, London W1S 2RX
Tel 020 7499 4060
Fax 020 7499 9922
Email Ianl@lrp.co.uk

LIVINGSTONE, Richard
London & Regional Properties

Position
Director
Qualifications
BSc; MRICS
Professional memberships
RICS
Contact details
London & Regional Properties Ltd, 40 New Bond Street, London W1S 2RX
Tel 020 7499 4060
Fax 020 7499 9922
Email rjl@lrp.co.uk

LLEWELYN JONES, Mark
Vail Williams

Position
Partner – landlord and tenant consultancy and valuation
Qualifications
BA Hons; MPhil; MRICS
Career history
2000 Joined Vail Williams.
1986-2000 Gerald Eve
Professional memberships
RICS
Interests
Antiques; cars; motor sports; skiing
Contact details
Vail Williams, Quatro House, Lyon Way, Camberley GU16 7ER
Tel 01276 682501
Fax 01276 684988
Web www.vailwilliams.com
Direct tel 0870 099 3146
Mobile 07768 724348
Email mllewelynjones@vailwilliams.com

LLOYD, Charles
PricewaterhouseCoopers

Position
Partner – PFI consultancy

Contact details
PricewaterhouseCoopers, Southwark Towers, 32 London Bridge Street, London SE1 9AE
Tel 020 7583 5000
Web www.pwc.com
Direct tel 020 7804 5130
Email charles.lloyd@uk.pwcglobal.com

LLOYD, Deborah
Nabarro Nathanson

Position
Partner – real estate finance

Qualifications
LLB

Career history
1987 Joined Nabarro Nathanson

Professional memberships
European Association for Investors in Non-listed Real Estate Vehicles; Investment Property Forum

Interests
Keep fit; skiing; tennis; travel

Contact details
Nabarro Nathanson, Lacon House, Theobald's Road, London WC1X 8RW
Tel 020 7524 6000
Fax 020 7524 6524
Web www.nabarro.com
Direct tel 020 7524 6370
Email d.lloyd@nabarro.com

LLOYD, John
Grosvenor

Position
Tax director

Qualifications
ACA

Other roles
Tax committee member, BPF

Professional memberships
Institute of Chartered Accountants in England & Wales

Contact details
Grosvenor Ltd, 70 Grosvenor Street, London W1K 3JP
Tel 020 7408 0988
Fax 020 7629 9115
Web www.grosvenor.com
Direct tel 020 7312 6303
Direct fax 020 7873 1303
Email john.lloyd@grosvenor.com

LLOYD, Jon
Lawrence Graham

Position
Partner

Career history
1988 Admitted to Roll of Solicitors.
1986 Joined Lawrence Graham; became partner in 1995

Professional memberships
Law Society

Contact details
Lawrence Graham, 190 Strand, London WC2R 1JN
Tel 020 7379 0000
Fax 020 7379 6854
Web www3.lawgram.com
Email jon.lloyd@lawgram.com

LLOYD, Malcolm
Ward Hadaway

Position
Head of commercial property

Career history
1981-2002 Head of commercial property and onetime managing partner, Pinsent Curtis Biddle

Professional memberships
Law Society

Interests
Cinema; shooting; theatre; walking

Contact details
Ward Hadaway, Sandgate House, 102 Quayside, Newcastle upon Tyne NE1 3DX
Tel 0191 204 4000
Fax 0191 204 4001
Web www.wardhadaway.com
Direct tel 0191 204 4186
Email malcolm.lloyd@wardhadaway.com

LLOYD, Martin
Northwest Development Agency

Position
Head of property

Qualifications
FRICS

Other roles
Director, Estuary Management Co

Professional memberships
RICS

Interests
Cinema; music; rugby; sport

Contact details
Northwest Development Agency, Lancaster House, Mercury Court, Liverpool L2 2QP
Tel 0151 236 3663
Web www.nwda.co.uk
Direct tel 0151 242 1064
Email Martin.Lloyd@nwda.co.uk

LLOYD, Simon
DTZ Debenham Tie Leung

Position
Director

Qualifications
BSc; MRICS

Career history
1998 Joined DTZ Debenham Thorpe (now DTZ Debenham Tie Leung) as director (industrial agency); appointed national co-ordinator for agency and development in 1999.
1987-98 Chesterton

Professional memberships
Industrial Agents Society; RICS

Interests
Music; squash; tennis; walking

Contact details
DTZ Debenham Tie Leung, 10 Colmore Row, Birmingham B3 2QD
Tel 0121 200 2050
Fax 0121 200 3022
Web www.dtz.com
Direct tel 0121 697 7392
Mobile 07771 604551
Email simon.f.lloyd@dtz.com

LLOYD HOLT, Suzanne
Wragge & Co

Position
Partner – head of property litigation

Qualifications
BA Hons

Career history
1986 Joined Wragge & Co from Herbert Smith

Other roles
PACT trained arbitrator/expert; law reform subcommittee member, Property Law Association

Professional memberships
Arbrix; Associazione Internazionale Giuristi di Lingua Italiana; Chartered Institute of Arbitrators; International Bar Association; Property Litigation Association; Union Internationale des Avocats

Interests
Cars; singing

Contact details
Wragge & Co LLP, 55-73 Colmore Row, Birmingham B3 2AS
Tel 0870 903 1000
Fax 0870 904 1099
Web www.wragge.com
Direct tel 0121 214 1046
Email suzanne_lloyd_holt@wragge.com

LOBB, Stephen
Chesterton International

Position
Director in charge, Plymouth office

L

Qualifications
BSc; FRICS
Career history
1985 Joined Chesterton: founded Plymouth office in 1985; became equity partner in 1989 and director of Chesterton International on incorporation in 1991.
1981-85 Retail property surveyor, Lalonde Bos & Parham, Bristol.
1979-81 Retail property surveyor, Fifield Glyn, Manchester.
1978-79 Management surveyor, Jones Lang Wootton
Professional memberships
Faculty of Building; RICS
Interests
Art; cars; gardening; golf; IT; music; sailing; skiing; squash; tennis
Contact details
Chesterton International, Princess Court, Princess Street, Plymouth PL1 2EX
Tel 0175 267 1167
Fax 0175 267 1856
Web www.chesterton.co.uk
Direct tel 0175 267 5716
Mobile 07712 868374
Email stephen.lobb@chesterton.co.uk

LOCHHEAD, Elspeth
DTZ Debenham Tie Leung
Position
Director
Contact details
DTZ Debenham Tie Leung, 30 Throgmorton Street, London EC2N 2BL
Tel 020 7710 8000
Fax 020 7710 8080
Web www.dtz.com
Direct tel 020 7710 8135
Email elspeth.lochhead@dtz.com

LOCHRANE, Charles
Strutt & Parker
Position
Investment partner, London
Qualifications
FRICS
Career history
1977 Joined Strutt & Parker.
1974-77 Surveyor, London Transport.
1971-74 Bernard Thorpe
Other roles
Adviser to large construction/development group, various investment vehicles (corporate and private), private individuals and trusts
Professional memberships
RICS
Interests
Conservation; Countryside Alliance; field sports; fishing; golf; shooting
Contact details
Strutt & Parker, 13 Hill Street, London W1J 5LQ
Tel 020 7629 7282
Fax 020 7629 0387
Web www.struttandparker.com
Direct tel 020 7318 5010
Direct fax 020 7355 1385
Mobile 07721 410255
Email clochrane@struttandparker.com

LOCKE, Andrew
Taylor Woodrow Developments
Position
Regional development director – London
Qualifications
BSc Hons; MRICS
Professional memberships
RICS
Contact details
Taylor Woodrow Developments Ltd, 41 Clarendon Road, Watford WD17 1TQ
Tel 01923 478400
Web www.taylorwoodrow.com
Direct tel 020 7264 5338
Direct fax 020 7264 5308
Mobile 07816 515338
Email andrew.locke@uk.taylorwoodrow.com

LOCKE, Duncan
GVA Grimley
Position
Partner – head of landlord and tenant business unit
Qualifications
BSc Hons, Urban Est Surv; FRICS
Career history
1986 Joined GVA Grimley.
1981-86 Conrad Ritblat and Mann & Co Commercial
Other roles
Arbitrator; member, RICS dispute resolution panel
Professional memberships
RICS
Interests
Music; sailing (Frensham Ponds Sailing Club; Hayling Island Sailing Club); skiing (Ski Club of Great Britain); Lansdowne Club
Contact details
GVA Grimley, 10 Stratton Street, London W1J 8JR
Tel 0870 900 8990
Fax 020 7911 2560
Web www.gvagrimley.co.uk
Direct tel 020 7911 2544
Direct fax 020 7911 2548
Mobile 07770 880135
Email duncan.locke@gvagrimley.co.uk

LOCKHART-MUMMERY, Christopher
Landmark Chambers
Position
Barrister
Qualifications
QC
Career history
1986 Appointed QC.
1971 Called to Bar
Professional memberships
Planning & Environment Bar Association
Contact details
Landmark Chambers, 4 Breams Buildings, London EC4A 1AQ
Tel 020 7430 1221
Fax 020 7421 1399
Web www.landmarkchambers.co.uk
Email clerks@landmarkchambers.co.uk

LODGE, Michael
Drivers Jonas
Position
Partner – management
Qualifications
BA; FRICS
Career history
1972 Joined Drivers Jonas
Professional memberships
RICS
Contact details
Drivers Jonas, 6 Grosvenor Street, London W1K 4DJ
Tel 020 7896 8000
Fax 020 7896 8001
Web www.driversjonas.com
Direct tel 020 7896 8060
Mobile 07768 910259
Email mikelodge@driversjonas.com

LOGAN, Michael
Nabarro Nathanson
Position
Partner – real estate
Qualifications
LLB
Career history
1995 Joined Nabarro Nathanson; became partner in 1996.
1994-95 Turner Kenneth Brown
Professional memberships
British Council of Shopping Centres
Interests
Cricket; golf; travel

L

Contact details
Nabarro Nathanson, Lacon House, Theobald's Road, London WC1X 8RW
Tel 020 7524 6000
Fax 020 7524 6524
Web www.nabarro.com
Direct tel 020 7524 6570
Email m.logan@nabarro.com

LOGGIE, Stuart
Cube Real Estate

Position
Founding partner
Qualifications
BSc Hons; MRICS
Career history
1992-2002 Partner, Morgan Loggie.
1988-92 Partner, Blanchflower Morgan.
1984-88 Hillier Parker
Professional memberships
RICS
Interests
Football; golf; keep fit; rugby
Contact details
Cube Real Estate Ltd, 43 Dover Street, London W1S 4NU
Tel 020 7493 5544
Fax 020 7493 5570
Email stuart@cube-re.com

LOMAX, Andrew
Drivers Jonas

Position
Partner – valuation
Qualifications
BSc; MRICS
Career history
1986 Joined Drivers Jonas
Professional memberships
RICS
Contact details
Drivers Jonas, 6 Grosvenor Street, London W1K 4DJ
Tel 020 7896 8000
Fax 020 7896 8001
Web www.driversjonas.com
Direct tel 020 7896 8111
Email andylomax@driversjonas.com

LONG, Jon
Powerhouse Retail

Position
Property director
Qualifications
BA Hons; FRICS
Professional memberships
RICS
Contact details
Powerhouse Retail Ltd, 7-8 Talisman Road, Bicester OX26 6HR
Tel 01869 329329
Fax 01869 322780
Web www.powerhouse.co.uk
Direct tel 01869 329228
Email property@powerhouse.co.uk

LONG, Michael
Briant Champion Long

Position
Equity director
Qualifications
BSc; FRICS
Career history
1985 Joined Briant Champion Long.
1980-85 Surveyor/associate partner, Lambert Smith & Partners.
1976-80 Fresson & Tee
Other roles
Member of RICS president's panel of experts and arbitrators for retail disputes
Professional memberships
Arbrix; RICS
Interests
Football; golf; wine
Contact details
Briant Champion Long Ltd, Nuffield House, 41-46 Piccadilly, London W1J 0DS
Tel 020 7434 7600
Web www.briantchampionlong.com
Direct tel 020 7647 6907
Mobile 07836 687254
Email mlong@bclnet.co.uk

LONG, Roddy
Lambert Smith Hampton

Position
Director
Qualifications
FRICS
Career history
Since 1972 Director, Lambert Smith Hampton
Professional memberships
RICS
Interests
Cricket; golf
Contact details
Lambert Smith Hampton Ltd, 4 Trevone House, Pannells Court, Guildford GU1 4EU
Tel 01483 538181
Fax 01483 532781
Web www.lsh.co.uk
Direct tel 01483 446706
Email rlong@lsh.co.uk

LONGBOTTOM, Stephen
Harvey Spack Field

Position
Development consultant
Contact details
Harvey Spack Field, 33 Bruton Street, London W1J 6QU
Tel 020 7629 9663
Fax 020 7491 1964
Web www.harveyspackfield.co.uk
Direct tel 020 7518 0467
Mobile 07785 275682
Email longbottom@harveyspackfield.co.uk

LOOSEMORE, Mike
CB Richard Ellis

Position
Chairman – asset management
Contact details
CB Richard Ellis, Kingsley House, 1a Wimpole Street, London W1G 0RE
Tel 020 7182 2000
Fax 020 7182 7001
Web www.cbre.com
Email mike.loosemore@cbre.com

LORD, Hugo
Specsavers Optical Superstores

Position
Property director
Contact details
Specsavers Optical Superstores Ltd, Melrose House, 42 Dingwall Road, London CR0 2NE
Tel 020 8760 7400
Web www.specsavers.co.uk
Email hugol@uk.specsavers.com

LORENZ, Anthony
Dunlop Heywood Lorenz

Position
Executive vice-chairman
Career history
1972 Co-founded Baker Lorenz with John Baker; after 2001 merger with Dunlop Heywood became executive vice-chairman and head of professional services at Dunlop Heywood Lorenz.
1966-72 Lewis & Tucker: head of offices department on leaving
Interests
Aviation; field sports; IT; shooting; skiing
Contact details
Dunlop Heywood Lorenz Ltd, 10 Queen Anne Street, London W1G 9LH
Tel 020 7636 7000
Fax 020 7636 7002
Web www.dhlproperty.co.uk

Mobile 07798 583933
Email aml@dhlproperty.co.uk

LOUKES, Ken
Estates & Agency Holdings

Position
Finance director
Contact details
Estates & Agency Holdings plc, 33 Ely Place, London EC1N 6TD
Tel 020 7831 8600
Fax 020 7831 8921
Email nicky.rolls@endeavour-trust.co.uk

LOVATT, Clive
Addleshaw Goddard

Position
Partner – head of construction
Qualifications
MA (Cantab)
Career history
1991 Joined Theodore Goddard (now Addleshaw Goddard).
1982-91 McKenna & Co
Other roles
Member of City of London Law Society construction law subcommittee and its working group on PFI and construction; CSA accredited adjudicator
Professional memberships
Society of Construction Law
Interests
Cricket; rugby; skiing
Contact details
Addleshaw Goddard, 150 Aldersgate Street, London EC1A 4EJ
Tel 020 7606 8855
Fax 020 7606 4390
Web www.addleshawgoddard.com
Direct tel 020 7880 5754
Email clive.lovatt@addleshawgoddard.com

LOVEGROVE, Timothy
Carpetright

Position
Property manager
Professional memberships
Property Managers Association
Contact details
Carpetright plc, Amberley House, New Road, Rainham RM13 8QN
Tel 0170 852 5522
Fax 0170 855 9361
Web www.carpetright.co.uk
Direct tel 0170 852 7755
Direct fax 0170 855 3563
Email tim.lovegrove@carpetright.co.uk

LOVELAND, Roger
Penningtons

Position
Partner – London
Qualifications
LLB Hons
Career history
1969 Joined Penningtons; partner since 1970
Professional memberships
Solicitors' European Group
Contact details
Penningtons, Bucklersbury House, 83 Cannon Street, London EC4N 8PE
Tel 020 7457 3000
Fax 020 7457 3240
Web www.penningtons.co.uk
Email lovelandra@penningtons.co.uk

LOVITT, Arthur
Pinsents

Position
Partner – head of major projects (Leeds)
Career history
1990 Joined Pinsent Curtis (now Pinsents).
1987-90 Linklaters & Paines, London.
1985-87 Daynes, Hill & Perks
Contact details
Pinsents, 1 Park Row, Leeds LS1 5AB
Tel 0113 244 5000
Fax 0113 244 8000
Web www.pinsents.com
Email arthur.lovitt@pinsents.com

LOVITT, Sally
Clifford Chance

Position
Partner
Career history
1994 Joined Clifford Chance; appointed partner in 1999.
1990-93 Barlow Lyde & Gilbert.
1990 Admitted to Roll of Solicitors
Contact details
Clifford Chance, 10 Upper Bank Street, London E14 5JJ
Tel 020 7600 1000
Fax 020 7600 5555
Web www.cliffordchance.com
Direct tel 020 7006 4393
Email sally.lovitt@cliffordchance.com

LOW, Richard
Hermes Property Asset Management

Position
Portfolio manager
Contact details
Hermes Property Asset Management Ltd, Lloyds Chambers, 1 Portsoken Street, London E1 8HZ
Tel 020 7702 0888
Fax 020 7702 9453
Web www.hermes.co.uk
Email r.low@hermes.co.uk

LOWE, Andrew
DTZ Debenham Tie Leung

Position
Head of City
Contact details
DTZ Debenham Tie Leung, 30 Throgmorton Street, London EC2N 2BL
Tel 020 7710 8000
Fax 020 7710 8080
Web www.dtz.com
Email andrew.lowe@dtz.com

LOWE, David
Osmond Tricks

Position
Director
Qualifications
BSc; FRICS; MCIArb
Career history
Since 1992 Director, Osmond Tricks.
1988-92 Director, Pepper Fox.
1979-87 Partner, Osmond Tricks
Professional memberships
Chartered Institute of Arbitrators; RICS
Contact details
Osmond Tricks Ltd, 40 Queen Square, Bristol BS1 4QP
Tel 0117 929 3171
Fax 0117 929 1508
Web www.osmond-tricks.co.uk
Direct tel 0117 929 3172
Mobile 07970 263076
Email dlowe@osmond-tricks.co.uk

LOWE, John
King Sturge

Position
Partner – building consultancy
Qualifications
BSc; MRICS
Professional memberships
RICS
Contact details
King Sturge, 40 Berkeley Square, Bristol BS8 1HU
Tel 0117 927 6691
Fax 0117 929 9669
Web www.kingsturge.com
Direct tel 0117 930 5641
Email john.lowe@kingsturge.co.uk

LOWE, Mark
2-3 Gray's Inn Square

Position
Barrister
Qualifications
QC
Career history
1996 Appointed QC
Other roles
Committee member, Planning & Environment Bar Association; founding committee member, Administrative Law Bar Association
Contact details
2-3 Gray's Inn Square (Chambers of Anthony Scrivener QC), London WC1R 5JH
Tel 020 7242 4986
Fax 020 7405 1166
Web www.2-3graysinnsquare.co.uk
Email mlowe@2-3graysinnsquare.co.uk

LOWE, Peter
Taylor Woodrow Developments

Position
Regional development director – South East
Qualifications
BSc Hons; MRICS
Professional memberships
RICS
Interests
Cycling; golf; rowing
Contact details
Taylor Woodrow Developments Ltd, Peveril Court, Beech Tree Close, Crawley RH10 8JG
Tel 0129 358 3460
Fax 0129 358 3461
Web www.taylorwoodrow.com
Direct tel 020 8671 4983
Mobile 07816 518659
Email peter.lowe@uk.taylorwoodrow.com

LOWN, Roger
Chapman Swabey

Position
Partner – professional and strategic advice
Qualifications
MRICS
Career history
Since 1993 Partner, Chapman Swabey.
1990-93 Partner, Lane Fox.
1986-90 Partner, Hampton & Sons.
1980-86 Associate, Vigers, City.
1978-80 Surveyor, Inland Revenue.
1974-78 Surveyor, Humberside County Council
Professional memberships
RICS
Contact details
Chapman Swabey Ltd, 1 College Hill, London EC4R 2RA
Tel 020 7236 6363
Fax 020 7236 6464
Web www.chapmanswabey.com
Email rogerlown@chapmanswabey.com

LOWNDES, Michael
TP Bennett

Position
Director of urban planning
Qualifications
BA Hons; Dip TP; MSc; Dip Cons; AA
Career history
1999 Joined TP Bennett; director responsible for development planning, urban design, master planning and conservation.
1986-99 Principal conservation and design officer, City of Westminster
Professional memberships
Institute of Historic Building Conservation; Royal Society of Arts; RTPI
Interests
Family; football
Contact details
TP Bennett Ltd, 1 America Street, London SE1 0NE
Tel 020 7208 2000
Fax 020 7208 2020
Web www.tpbennett.co.uk
Direct tel 020 7208 2082
Direct fax 020 7208 2023
Email mlowndes@tpbennett.co.uk

LUCAS, Andrew
DTZ Debenham Tie Leung

Position
Director – head of shopping centre agency
Career history
Since 1998 Head of shopping centre leasing, DTZ Debenham Tie Leung.
1984-98 Director, Churston Heard
Other roles
Chairman elect, Shop Agents Society (2004)
Professional memberships
Shop Agents Society
Interests
Diving/scuba diving; golf; horse riding
Contact details
DTZ Debenham Tie Leung, 1 Curzon Street, London W1A 5PZ
Tel 020 7408 1161
Fax 020 7643 6000
Web www.dtz.com
Direct tel 020 7643 6525
Direct fax 020 7643 6501
Mobile 07771 815153
Email andrew.lucas@dtz.com

LUCAS, Julia
TLT Solicitors

Position
Partner – head of property litigation and leisure team
Qualifications
LLB Hons; LLM Hons, International Law
Career history
1997 Joined TLT; appointed partner in 1999.
1994 Admitted to Roll of Solicitors.
1992-97 Masons, London: seconded for two years to Grand Metropolitan Estates (joint venture between Grand Metropolitan and Courage)
Other roles
Member, Amnesty International lawyers group
Professional memberships
Property Litigation Association; Women in Property
Interests
Golf; IT; literature; theatre; travel; wine
Contact details
TLT Solicitors, 1 Redcliffe Street, Bristol BS99 7JZ
Tel 0117 917 7777
Fax 0117 917 7779
Web www.tltsolicitors.com
Direct tel 0117 917 7957
Direct fax 0117 917 7782
Mobile 07958 350289
Email jlucas@TLTsolicitors.com

LUCAS, Stephen
DTZ Pieda Consulting

Position
Director
Qualifications
BSc; MSc
Career history
Since 1999 Associate director, DTZ Pieda Consulting.
1997-98 Associate, Roger Tym & Partners.
1995-96 Senior consultant, Roger Tym & Partners.
1991-95 Projects and European officer, Development Board for Rural Wales.
1990-91 Policy officer, Water Authority of Western Australia
Interests
Cricket; hill walking; theatre
Contact details
DTZ Pieda Consulting, 1 Marsden Street, Manchester M2 1HW
Tel 0161 236 9595
Fax 0161 834 2055
Web www.dtz.com
Direct tel 0161 235 7637
Email stephen.lucas@dtz.com

LUCK, Ralph
English Partnerships

Position
Director for Thames Gateway Projects
Qualifications
FRICS; DMS; MCMI
Career history
1994 Joined English Partnerships as London and South East regional director; became development director for Greenwich peninsula in 1997 and director for Thames Gateway Projects in 2003.
1991-94 Self-employed development consultant.
1987-91 Senior development surveyor, Taylor Woodrow Property Co.
1985-87 Assistant director of law and administration, London Borough of Harrow.
1984-85 Chief valuer and estates officer, London Borough of Wandsworth
Other roles
Director, British Urban Regeneration Association; member, RICS regeneration panel
Professional memberships
Institute of Management; RICS
Interests
Cricket; rugby; sailing
Contact details
English Partnerships, 110 Buckingham Palace Road, London SW1W 9SA
Tel 020 7881 1600
Fax 020 7730 9162
Web www.englishpartnerships.co.uk
Direct tel 020 7881 1600
Direct fax 020 7730 9162
Mobile 07831 333548
Email ralphluck@englishpartnerships.co.uk

LUCK, Richard
London & Regional Properties

Position
Finance director
Contact details
London & Regional Properties Ltd, 40 New Bond Street, London W1S 2RX
Tel 020 7499 4060
Fax 020 7499 9922
Email richardl@lrp.co.uk

LUCKING, Anne
Aberdeen Property Investors

Position
Director
Contact details
Aberdeen Property Investors, Charles House, 5-11 Regent Street, London SW1Y 4LR
Tel 020 7747 1700
Fax 020 7839 7460
Web www.aberdeenpropertyinvestors.com
Direct tel 020 7747 1706
Direct fax 020 7930 9433
Mobile 07799 131706
Email
anne.lucking@aberdeenpropertyinvestors.com

LUDOLF, Selby
Mason Philips

Position
Director
Qualifications
BSc Hons; MRICS
Career history
1998 Joined Mason Philips as director.
1992-98 Partner, DE&J Levy.
1986-92 Associate, Dunlop Heywood.
1982-86 Investment surveyor, Weatherall Green & Smith.
1979-82 Valuation surveyor, Jones Lang Wooton
Other roles
Company director and trustee, LHP
Professional memberships
RICS
Interests
Golf
Contact details
Mason Philips Ltd, 33 Great Portland Street, London W1W 8QG
Tel 020 7436 1212
Fax 020 7436 1350
Email sludolf@masonphilips.co.uk

LUKER, Edward
CBRE Corporate Finance

Position
Chairman
Qualifications
FRICS
Career history
1973 Joined Insignia Richard Ellis; elected chairman of Insignia Financial Services in 2001; since 2003 chairman of CBRE Corporate Finance and executive director of CB Richard Ellis (following merger with CB Hillier Parker)
Other roles
Past chairman, Investment Property Forum (1997)
Professional memberships
RICS
Interests
Golf; tennis
Contact details
CBRE Corporate Finance Ltd, Kingsley House, 1a Wimpole Street, London W1G 0RE
Tel 020 7182 2000
Fax 020 7182 2001
Web www.cbre.com
Email edward.luker@cbre.com

LUST, Graham
Nabarro Nathanson

Position
Partner – real estate
Career history
1975 Joined Nabarro Nathanson (commercial property department); became partner in 1980
Professional memberships
Investment Property Forum
Contact details
Nabarro Nathanson, Lacon House, Theobald's Road, London WC1X 8RW
Tel 020 7524 6000
Fax 020 7524 6524
Web www.nabarro.com
Direct tel 020 7524 6200
Email g.lust@nabarro.com

LYALL, Ian
McGrigors

Position
Partner
Qualifications
MA; LLB; NP
Career history
1987 Rejoined McGrigor Donald (now McGrigors) as partner.
1985-86 Baker & McKenzie, London.
1980 Admitted to Roll of Solicitors.
1978-85 McGrigor Donald
Other roles
Director and honorary legal adviser to Edinburgh Medical Missionary Society
Professional memberships
Investment Property Forum; Law Society of Scotland
Interests
Cycling; family; literature; sailing
Contact details
McGrigors, Princes Exchange, 1 Earl Grey Street, Edinburgh EH3 9AQ
Tel 0131 777 7000
Fax 0131 777 7003
Web www.mcgrigors.com
Direct tel 0131 777 7033
Mobile 07768 025143
Email ian.lyall@mcgrigors.com

LYNCH, John
Leeds City Council

Position
Director – planning and environment
Qualifications

BA; MRTPI
Professional memberships
RTPI
Contact details
Leeds City Council, Merrion House, 110 Merrion Centre, Leeds LS2 8DR
Tel 0113 247 8000
Web www.leeds.gov.uk
Direct tel 0113 247 8066
Direct fax 0113 247 8178
Email john.lynch@leeds.gov.uk

LYNCH, Susan
Drivers Jonas

Position
Partner – head of planning and development
Qualifications
BSc; MRICS
Career history
1982 Joined Drivers Jonas
Professional memberships
RICS
Contact details
Drivers Jonas, 6 Grosvenor Street, London W1K 4DJ
Tel 020 7896 8000
Fax 020 7896 8001
Web www.driversjonas.com
Direct tel 020 7896 8221
Email susanlynch@driversjonas.com

LYNESS, Scott
Landmark Chambers

Position
Barrister
Qualifications
LLB Hons (Hull)
Career history
2000 Called to Bar of Northern Ireland.
1996 Called to Bar
Other roles
Contributor, *Environmental Law & Practice* (OUP) and planning volume of *Encyclopaedia of Forms and Precedents* (Butterworths); contributor, *Property, Planning & Compensation Reports* (Sweet & Maxwell)
Interests
Hill walking; music; running; travel
Contact details
Landmark Chambers, 4 Breams Buildings, London EC4A 1AQ
Tel 020 7430 1221
Fax 020 7421 1399
Web www.landmarkchambers.co.uk
Email clerks@landmarkchambers.co.uk

LYNN, Bill
storeys:ssp

Position
Director, head of agency and business development
Qualifications
BSc Hons; FRICS
Career history
Since 1980 Director, storeys:ssp (formerly Storey Sons & Parker).
1979-80 Coral Leisure Group.
1975-79 British Rail Property Board
Professional memberships
Accessible Retail; RICS; Royal Society of Arts; Shop Agents Society
Interests
Sport
Contact details
storeys:ssp, Higham House, New Bridge Street West, Newcastle upon Tyne NE1 8AU
Tel 0191 232 6291
Fax 0191 232 4610
Web www.storeys-ssp.com
Direct tel 0191 206 8703
Mobile 07957 823908
Email bill.lynn@storeys-ssp.co.uk

LYON, Stephen
Modus Interiors

Position
Director
Qualifications
MSc; Dip Arch; RIBA; MAPM
Career history
Since 1997 Director, Modus Interiors.
1986-97 Watts & Partners; appointed associate in 1988 and partner in 1995.
1982-86 Senior architect, Wokingham District Council
Professional memberships
Association for Project Management; RIBA
Interests
Golf; keep fit; motor sports; skiing; travel; wine
Contact details
Modus Interiors Ltd, Greencoat House, Francis Street, London SW1P 1DH
Tel 020 7828 9009
Fax 020 7828 0009
Web www.modusinteriors.co.uk
Direct tel 020 7963 1832
Email stephen@modusgroup.com

LYONS, Anthony
Davis Coffer Lyons

Position
Managing director
Contact details
Davis Coffer Lyons Ltd, 52 Portland Place, London W1B 1NH
Tel 020 7299 0700
Fax 020 7299 0710
Web www.daviscofferlyons.co.uk
Email alyons@daviscofferlyons.co.uk

LYTOLLIS, Martyn
storeys:ssp

Position
Managing director
Qualifications
BSc; FRICS
Career history
1978 Joined storeys:ssp (formerly Storey Sons & Parker)
Professional memberships
RICS
Interests
Sport
Contact details
storeys:ssp, Higham House, New Bridge Street West, Newcastle upon Tyne NE1 8AU
Tel 0191 232 6291
Fax 0191 232 4610
Web www.storeys-ssp.com
Direct tel 0191 206 8706
Mobile 07764 159718
Email martyn.lytollis@storeys-ssp.co.uk

MAC DAID, Denis
Taylor Woodrow Developments

Position
Operations director
Qualifications
Eur Ing; BSc; CEng; FICE; FIEI; FRSA
Career history
1965 Joined Taylor Woodrow
Other roles
Chief executive, Bryant Homes; board director, Taylor Woodrow
Professional memberships
Institute of Directors
Interests
Sailing; travel
Contact details
Taylor Woodrow Developments Ltd, 2 Princes Way, Solihull B91 3ES
Tel 0121 600 8000
Fax 0121 600 8001
Web www.taylorwoodrow.com
Direct tel 0121 600 8506
Direct fax 0121 600 8507
Email carole.fogarty@uk.taylorwoodrow.com

MACALPINE, Findlay
Mason Philips

Position
Director
Contact details
Mason Philips Ltd, 33 Great Portland Street, London W1W 8QG
Tel 020 7436 1212
Fax 020 7436 1350
Email fmacalpine@masonphilips.co.uk

MACCOLL, Peter
Knight Frank

Position
Head of investment division
Qualifications
BSc; MRICS
Career history
1981 Joined Knight Frank.
1979-81 Surveyor, Abbey Life Assurance Co
Professional memberships
RICS
Interests
Golf; rugby; tennis
Contact details
Knight Frank LLP, 20 Hanover Square, London W1S 1HZ
Tel 020 7629 8171
Fax 020 7493 4114
Web www.knightfrank.com
Direct tel 020 7861 1211
Direct fax 020 7861 1371
Mobile 07836 718146
Email peter.maccoll@knightfrank.com

MACCUISH, Angus
FG Burnett

Position
Managing director
Qualifications
BSc; FRICS
Career history
1987 Joined FG Burnett.
1983-87 Webster & Co.
1981-83 James Barr.
1978-81 Gerald Eve
Professional memberships
RICS
Interests
Football; golf (Royal Aberdeen Golf Club); historic rallying
Contact details
FG Burnett, 33 Albyn Place, Aberdeen AB10 1YL
Tel 01224 572661
Fax 01224 593496
Web www.fgburnett.co.uk
Mobile 07770 366539
Email amacc@fgburnett.co.uk

MACE, David
Osmond Tricks

Position
Director
Qualifications
BSc; FRICS
Professional memberships
RICS
Contact details
Osmond Tricks Ltd, 40 Queen Square, Bristol BS1 4QP
Tel 0117 929 3171
Fax 0117 929 4508
Web www.osmond-tricks.co.uk
Email dmace@osmond-tricks.co.uk

MACFARLANE, Andrew
Land Securities Group

Position
Group finance director
Contact details
Land Securities Group plc, 5 Strand, London WC2N 5AF
Tel 020 7413 9000
Fax 020 7024 5007
Web www.landsecurities.com
Direct tel 020 7024 5457
Email andrew.macfarlane@landsecurities.com

MACFARLANE, Chris
King Sturge

Position
Partner in charge, Edinburgh
Contact details
King Sturge, Lismore House, 127 George Street, Edinburgh EH2 4JN
Tel 0131 225 4221
Fax 0131 226 3679
Web www.kingsturge.com
Email chris.macfarlane@kingsturge.co.uk

MACFARLANE, Peter
ATIS REAL Weatheralls

Position
Director
Qualifications
BSc; FRICS
Career history
1977 Joined ATIS REAL Weatheralls; worked in New York office 1982-86.
1975-76 Assistant surveyor, Prudential Assurance Co.
1971-73 Assistant premises surveyor, Lloyds Bank
Professional memberships
RICS
Interests
Sailing
Contact details
ATIS REAL Weatheralls Ltd, Norfolk House, 31 St James's Square, London SW1Y 4JR
Tel 020 7338 4200
Web www.atisrealweatheralls.com
Direct tel 020 7338 4216
Email peter.macfarlane@atisrealweatheralls.com

MACGARVIE, Stuart
James Barr

Position
Planning director

Qualifications
BA Hons; MPhil; MBA; MRTPI
Contact details
James Barr, 226 West George Street, Glasgow G2 2LN
Tel 0141 300 8000
Fax 0141 300 8001
Web www.jamesbarr.co.uk
Direct tel 0141 300 8041
Direct fax 0141 300 8090
Email Smacgarvie@jamesbarr.co.uk

MACGREGOR, Robert
Clifford Chance
Position
Partner
Qualifications
LLB Hons
Career history
1990 Joined Clifford Chance; appointed partner in 1992.
1985 Admitted to Roll of Solicitors.
1983-90 Titmuss Sainer & Webb
Professional memberships
Anglo-American Real Property Institute; British Council for Offices; Institute of Directors
Interests
Cars; sailing
Contact details
Clifford Chance, 10 Upper Bank Street, London E14 5JJ
Tel 020 7600 1000
Fax 020 7600 5555
Web www.cliffordchance.com
Email robert.macgregor@cliffordchance.com

MACKANESS, Chris
GVA Grimley
Position
National head of retail
Qualifications
BSc; MRICS
Career history
1994 Joined GVA Grimley; appointed national head of retail in 2000.
1980-94 DTZ
Other roles
Former secretary, Out of Town Retail Agents Society; director, GVA Collyer Coxhead International; director, Development Holdings
Interests
Cooking; cricket (Marylebone Cricket Club); family; gardening; rugby (Richmond Rugby Football Club); shooting; skiing
Contact details
GVA Grimley, 10 Stratton Street, London W1J 8JR
Tel 0870 900 8990
Fax 020 7911 2560
Web www.gvagrimley.co.uk
Direct tel 020 7911 2367
Mobile 07836 210625
Email chris.mackaness@gvagrimley.co.uk

MACKAY, Alasdair
AWG Asset Management
Position
Group director
Contact details
AWG Asset Management Ltd, Atholl House, 49 Melville Street, Edinburgh EH3 7HL
Tel 0131 226 4666
Fax 0131 226 4166
Direct tel 0131 228 4188
Direct fax 0131 200 4480
Email alasdair.mackay@awgdevelopments.com

MACKAY, Andrew
Graves Son & Pilcher
Position
Senior partner, Brighton office
Qualifications
FRICS
Other roles
Accredited independent expert valuer; valuer member, Southern Rent Assessment Panel and Leasehold Valuation Tribunal; past chairman, RICS Sussex branch; and past chairman, RICS Sussex branch of general practice division
Professional memberships
RICS
Interests
Hockey; tennis
Contact details
Graves Son & Pilcher, 51 Old Steyne, Brighton BN1 1HU
Tel 01273 321123
Fax 01273 771070
Web www.gsp.uk.com
Direct tel 01273 267220
Mobile 07714 714220
Email am@gsp.uk.com

MACKAY, Rob
Berkeley Street Properties
Position
Managing director
Qualifications
CEng; MICE; MIHT
Other roles
Director, Bermac Properties
Professional memberships
Institute of Directors
Interests
Food; rugby; sailing; wine
Contact details
Berkeley Street Properties plc, 86a Broomfield Road, Chelmsford CM1 1SS
Tel 01245 496655
Fax 01245 344000
Mobile 07836 729627
Email berkeleystreetproperties@hotmail.com

MACKEAN, Andrew
Bond Pearce
Position
Partner – head of commercial property, South East
Qualifications
LLB Hons
Career history
1983 Admitted to Roll of Solicitors
Contact details
Bond Pearce, Oceana House, Commercial Road, Southampton SO15 1GA
Tel 08701 200 000
Fax 023 8072 0700
Web www.bondpearce.com
Direct tel 023 8020 8330
Email amackean@bondpearce.com

MACKENZIE, Derek
Royal Bank of Scotland
Position
Director – structured property finance, Scotland
Qualifications
MCIBS
Interests
Football; golf; rugby
Contact details
Royal Bank of Scotland, 6th Floor, 6-8 George Street, Edinburgh EH2 2SA
Tel 0131 556 8555
Fax 0131 523 5104
Web www.rbs.co.uk
Direct tel 0131 523 5141
Mobile 07768 424263
Email derek.mackenzie@rbs.co.uk

MACKENZIE, Neil
Safeway
Position
Director of estates
Contact details
Safeway plc, 6 Millington Road, Hayes UB3 4AY
Tel 020 8848 8744
Fax 020 8756 1596
Web www.safeway.co.uk
Email neil_mackenzie@safeway.co.uk

MACKENZIE-GRIEVE, Colin
Stephenson Harwood

Position
Partner – commercial property department
Qualifications
MA (Cantab); Solicitor
Career history
1980 Joined Stephenson Harwood as partner; head of property department 1992-98; member of firm's council (board) since 1997
Professional memberships
BPF; Investment Property Forum; UK Environmental Law Association
Interests
Family; opera; ornithology
Contact details
Stephenson Harwood, 1 St Paul's Churchyard, London EC4M 8SH
Tel 020 7329 4422
Fax 020 7606 0822
Web www.shlegal.com
Direct tel 020 7809 2500
Email colin.mackenzie-grieve@shlegal.com

MACKEY, Paul
HSBC Property Investments

Position
Managing director
Qualifications
BComm Hons; Dip Acc; FCA
Professional memberships
BPF; Institute of Chartered Accountants in Ireland; Investment Property Forum
Interests
Music; sport
Contact details
HSBC Property Investments Ltd, 8-16 Canada Square, London E14 5HQ
Tel 020 7991 8888
Web www.hsbc.com
Mobile 07884 066887
Email paul.e.mackey@hsbcib.com

MACKILLIGIN, Neil
Allsop & Co

Position
Partner – commercial auctions
Qualifications
BSc; FRICS
Career history
1983 Joined Allsop & Co.
1979-83 Conrad Ritblat: rent review/valuation, then auction department from 1982
Professional memberships
RICS
Interests
Cricket; cycling; golf; mountain biking; rugby
Contact details
Allsop & Co, 27 Soho Square, London W1D 3AY
Tel 020 7437 6977
Fax 020 7437 8984
Web www.allsop.co.uk
Direct tel 020 7543 6702
Email neil.mackilligin@allsop.co.uk

MACLACHLAN, Alex
Albury Land

Position
Director
Qualifications
Dip Land Econ; FRICS
Career history
2000-03 JER Real Estate Advisors (UK): managing director, then consultant from 2002.
1998-99 Director, Moorfield Group.
1991-97 Friends Provident life office: chief investment surveyor, then managing director from 1996.
1987-91 Development consultant, Argowan Securities (own company).
1984-87 Director, Pengap Estates.
1973-84 Chartered surveyor, Abbey Life Assurance Co
Professional memberships
RICS
Contact details
Albury Land Ltd, Oak House, 39-41 The Parade, Esher KT10 0PD
Tel 01372 471902
Fax 01372 470970
Mobile 07767 794313
Email alex@alburyland.com

MACLACHLAN, James
King Sturge

Position
Partner – West End investment
Qualifications
MRICS
Career history
1997-2003 Partner (investment), Knight Frank.
1988-97 Investment director (central London), Chesterton.
1984-86 Strutt & Parker
Professional memberships
RICS
Interests
Golf; squash; surfing
Contact details
King Sturge, 7 Stratford Place, London W1C 1ST
Tel 020 7493 4933
Fax 020 7409 0469
Web www.kingsturge.com
Direct tel 020 7529 6715
Direct fax 020 7499 2503
Email james.maclachlan@kingsturge.co.uk

MACLEOD, William
ING Real Estate Investment Management (UK)

Position
Director – UK manager
Qualifications
BSc Hons, Est Man; MRICS
Career history
Since 1990 Fund manager/director, Baring, Houston & Saunders (now ING Real Estate Investment Management (UK)).
1987-90 Investment agent, Walker Son & Packman
Professional memberships
RICS
Interests
Fishing; golf; hockey; tennis; walking
Contact details
ING Real Estate Investment Management (UK) Ltd, 9 Devonshire Square, London EC2M 4WX
Tel 020 7398 4310
Fax 020 7398 4311
Web www.ingrealestate.co.uk
Direct tel 020 7398 5544
Email william.macleod@ingrealestate.co.uk

MACNISH PORTER, Hugh
Royal Bank of Scotland

Position
Director – equity finance
Qualifications
BSc; MRICS
Career history
Since 2001 Director (equity finance), Royal Bank of Scotland. Previously fund manager, Aberdeen Property Investors
Professional memberships
Investment Property Forum; RICS
Contact details
Royal Bank of Scotland, Capital Building, 12-13 St Andrew Square, Edinburgh EH2 2AF
Tel 0131 523 3333
Web www.rbs.co.uk
Direct tel 0131 523 3672
Direct fax 0131 523 4997
Email hugh.macnishporter@rbs.co.uk

MACPHERSON, Ian
Gerald Eve

Position
Partner – head of residential team
Qualifications
MA; FRICS
Professional memberships

M

RICS

Contact details

Gerald Eve, 7 Vere Street, London W1G 0JB
Tel 020 7493 3338
Fax 020 7491 1825
Web www.geraldeve.com
Direct tel 020 7333 6244
Direct fax 020 7333 6404
Email imacpherson@geraldeve.com

MACPHERSON, Peter
ING Real Estate Investment Management (UK)

Position
Director of investor relations
Qualifications
MPhil, Land Man; MRICS
Career history
1990-92 Associate (European team), Healey & Baker.
1988-90 Baring Houston & Saunders.
1985-88 Richard Ellis
Professional memberships
RICS
Contact details
ING Real Estate Investment Management (UK) Ltd, 9 Devonshire Square, London EC2M 4WX
Tel 020 7398 4310
Fax 020 7398 4311
Web www.ingrealestate.co.uk
Direct tel 020 7398 5505
Email peter.macpherson@ingrealestate.co.uk

MADDEN, Michael
Ashurst

Position
Partner – head of property litigation
Qualifications
LLB; FCIArb
Career history
1993 Joined Ashurst Morris Crisp (now Ashurst); became partner in 1995.
1987 Admitted to Roll of Solicitors.
1985-93 Slaughter & May
Professional memberships
Chartered Institute of Arbitrators; Property Litigation Association
Interests
Opera; walking
Contact details
Ashurst, Broadwalk House, 5 Appold Street, London EC2A 2AG
Tel 020 7638 1111
Fax 020 7638 1112
Web www.ashursts.com
Direct tel 020 7859 1539
Email michael.madden@ashursts.com

MADDERN, Kevin
Lambert Smith Hampton

Position
Head of building consultancy
Qualifications
MRICS; MBEng
Career history
1994 Joined Lambert Smith Hampton.
1992-94 Building surveyor, Carter Walker Associates, Nottingham
Professional memberships
Association of Building Engineers; RICS
Interests
Football; golf; rugby
Contact details
Lambert Smith Hampton Ltd, St Giles House, 76 St Giles Street, Northampton NN1 1BG
Tel 01604 233123
Fax 01604 250590
Web www.lsh.co.uk
Mobile 07802 526712
Email kmaddern@lsh.co.uk

MADDOX, Matthew
Churston Heard

Position
Director – retail agency
Qualifications
MRICS
Contact details
Churston Heard Ltd, 7 Hanover Square, London W1S 1HQ
Tel 020 7409 2199
Fax 020 7495 1339
Web www.churstonheard.co.uk
Direct tel 020 7318 7828
Email mmaddox@churstonheard.co.uk

MADDRELL, Geoffrey
UNITE Group

Position
Chairman
Qualifications
MA (Cantab); MBA (Colombia)
Career history
Since 1999 Chairman, UNITE Group.
1994-2002 Chairman/non-executive chairman, Glenmorangie.
1986-91 Chief executive, Tootal Group
Other roles
Chairman, Westbury Group; chairman, Buildstore; chairman, LDV; chairman, Friends Ivory & Sime ISIS Trust; chairman, UNIAID Foundation; chairman, Airborne Forces Charities; civil service commissioner
Interests
Golf; running (Serpentine Running Club)
Contact details
UNITE Group plc, The Tower Building, 11 York Road, London SE1 7NQ
Tel 020 7902 5050
Fax 020 7902 5051
Web www.unite-group.com
Email geoffrey.maddrell@unite-group.co.uk

MADELIN, Roger
Argent Group

Position
Chief executive
Career history
1987 Joined Argent; appointed director in 1989; became chief executive in 1997.
1985-86 Private developer based in Thames Valley.
1979-85 National contractor
Other roles
Flying gliders, balloons and aerobatic biplanes; off-road cycle touring; marathon running
Contact details
Argent Group plc, 5 Albany Courtyard, London W1J 0HF
Tel 020 7734 3721
Fax 020 7734 4474
Web www.argentgroup.plc.uk
Email rogerm@argentgroup.plc.uk

MAGEE, Richard
Lamberts

Position
Managing director – commercial division
Qualifications
FRICS
Professional memberships
RICS
Contact details
Lamberts Ltd, 387 City Road, London EC1V 1NA
Tel 020 7278 8191
Fax 020 7837 5790
Web www.lambertsurv.co.uk
Direct tel 020 7520 2304
Email richardm@lambertsurv.co.uk

MAGILL, Anne
Speechly Bircham

Position
Partner
Career history
2003 Joined Speechly Bircham.
2000-03 Altheimer & Gray. Previously with Slaughter & May
Professional memberships
Law Society
Contact details
Speechly Bircham, 6 St Andrew Street, London

EC4A 3LX
Tel 020 7427 6400
Fax 020 7427 6600
Web www.speechlys.com
Email anne.magill@speechlys.com

MAGUIRE, Andrew
St Philips Chambers

Position
Barrister
Qualifications
LLB
Career history
1988 Called to Bar
Other roles
Founder member, Midland Chancery & Commercial Bar Association
Professional memberships
Midland Chancery & Commercial Bar Association; Property Bar Association
Interests
Cricket; family; football; travel
Contact details
St Philips Chambers (Chambers of John Randall QC), 55 Temple Row, Birmingham B2 5LS
Tel 0121 246 7000
Fax 0121 246 7001
Web www.st-philips.co.uk
Email amaguire@st-philips.co.uk

MAGUIRE, Jim
Drivers Jonas

Position
Partner – head of building
Qualifications
Dip BS; FRICS
Career history
1976 Joined Drivers Jonas
Professional memberships
RICS
Contact details
Drivers Jonas, 6 Grosvenor Street, London W1K 4DJ
Tel 020 7896 8000
Fax 020 7896 8001
Web www.driversjonas.com
Direct tel 020 7896 8320
Email jimmaguire@driversjonas.com

MAGUIRE, John
James Barr

Position
Director – head of building department
Qualifications
Dip BS; MRICS
Professional memberships
RICS
Contact details
James Barr, 226 West George Street, Glasgow G2 2LN
Tel 0141 300 8000
Fax 0141 300 8001
Web www.jamesbarr.co.uk
Email jmaguire@jamesbarr.co.uk

MAHON, Fran
Cluttons

Position
Partner – valuation
Qualifications
MA; MRICS
Professional memberships
RICS
Contact details
Cluttons, Portman House, 2 Portman Street, London W1H 6DU
Tel 020 7408 1010
Fax 020 7629 3263
Web www.cluttons.com
Direct tel 020 7647 7125
Email fmahon@cluttons.com

MAHON, Stephen
Churston Heard

Position
Director – retail agency
Qualifications
BSc Hons; MRICS
Contact details
Churston Heard Ltd, 7 Hanover Square, London W1S 1HQ
Tel 020 7409 2199
Fax 020 7495 1339
Web www.churstonheard.co.uk
Direct tel 020 7318 7806
Mobile 07818 025025
Email smahon@churstonheard.co.uk

MAHONEY, Kevin
FPDSavills

Position
Director – international investment
Qualifications
BSc; MRICS
Career history
Since 2001 Director, FPDSavills.
1982-2001 Director, DTZ Debenham Tie Leung
Professional memberships
RICS
Interests
Rugby
Contact details
FPDSavills Ltd, 20 Grosvenor Hill, London W1K 3HQ
Tel 020 7499 8644
Fax 020 7495 3773
Web www.fpdsavills.co.uk
Direct tel 020 7409 9974
Direct fax 020 7753 0325
Mobile 07967 555449
Email kmahoney@fpdsavills.co.uk

MAIN, Richard
Jones Lang LaSalle

Position
International director – City professional
Qualifications
FRICS
Career history
Since 1997 International director (City professional), Jones Lang LaSalle.
1978-97 Senior partner, Richard Main & Co.
1974-77 Partner, Robert Cutts & Co.
1972-74 Partner, Bloom King Main
Other roles
London regional board member, RICS
Professional memberships
Property Valuation Forum; RICS
Interests
Architecture; cars; cricket; motor sports; music
Contact details
Jones Lang LaSalle Ltd, 9 Queen Victoria Street, London EC4N 4YY
Tel 020 7248 6040
Fax 020 7248 0088
Web www.joneslanglasalle.com
Direct tel 020 7399 5200
Direct fax 020 7399 5222
Mobile 07785 324629
Email richard.main@eu.joneslanglasalle.com

MALCIC, Larry
HOK International

Position
Senior vice-president, director – design
Qualifications
BA; DoE; MArch; AIA
Career history
Since 1989 Director of design, HOK (London office).
1987-89 Visiting professor of architecture, University of Texas.
1984-87 Assistant dean, Olin School of Business, Washington University.
1980-83 Assistant professor of architecture, Washington University
Professional memberships
American Institute of Architects
Interests
History; travel; Philomathean Society of Philadelphia; University Club of St Louis; Penn

M

Club of New York
Contact details
HOK International Ltd, 216 Oxford Street, London W1C 1DB
Tel 020 7636 2006
Fax 020 7636 1987
Web www.hok.com
Email larry.malcic@hok.com

MALE, John
Landmark Chambers
Position
Barrister
Qualifications
QC
Professional memberships
Chancery Bar Association; Planning & Environment Bar Association
Contact details
Landmark Chambers, 4 Breams Buildings, London EC4A 1AQ
Tel 020 7430 1221
Fax 020 7421 1399
Web www.landmarkchambers.co.uk
Email clerks@landmarkchambers.co.uk

MALLEN, Stephen
Knight Frank
Position
Partner – head of global research
Qualifications
BA; MA
Career history
1988 Joined Knight Frank as deputy head of research; appointed partner/head of global research in 1990.
1986-88 Research analyst, Property Market Analysis
Other roles
Member, EG*i* standards advisory board
Professional memberships
Society of Property Researchers
Contact details
Knight Frank LLP, 20 Hanover Square, London W1S 1HZ
Tel 020 7629 8171
Fax 020 7493 4114
Web www.knightfrank.com
Direct tel 020 7861 1235
Direct fax 020 7629 1610
Mobile 07836 292881
Email stephen.mallen@knightfrank.com

MALLOY, Steve
Walker Singleton
Position
Director – head of property management
Contact details
Walker Singleton, Property House, Lister Lane, Halifax HX1 5AS
Tel 01422 430000
Fax 01422 430010
Web www.walker-singleton.co.uk
Email stevem@walker-singleton.co.uk

MALTHOUSE, Timothy
ATIS REAL Weatheralls
Position
Director
Qualifications
BA; MPhil; MRICS
Professional memberships
RICS
Contact details
ATIS REAL Weatheralls Ltd, 22 Chancery Lane, London WC2A 1LT
Tel 020 7338 4000
Fax 020 7430 2628
Web www.atisrealweatheralls.com
Direct tel 020 7338 4010
Direct fax 020 7831 4436
Mobile 07860 553103
Email tim.malthouse@atisrealweatheralls.com

MANCHES, Louis
Manches
Position
Head of property
Interests
Golf; IT; skiing; tennis (Queen's Club); MCC; RAC
Contact details
Manches, Aldwych House, 81 Aldwych, London WC2B 4HN
Tel 020 7404 4433
Fax 020 7430 1133
Web www.manches.com
Direct tel 020 7753 7502
Mobile 07767 678660
Email louis.manches@manches.co.uk

MANLEY, David
Kings Chambers
Position
Barrister
Qualifications
BA Hons
Career history
2002 Appointed QC.
1999 Appointed recorder.
1981 Called to Bar
Professional memberships
Administrative Law Bar Association; Planning & Environment Bar Association; UK Environmental Law Association
Interests
Gardening; military history; swimming; walking
Contact details
Kings Chambers, 40 King Street, Manchester M2 6BA
Tel 0161 832 9082
Fax 0161 835 2139
Web www.kingschambers.com
Direct fax 0161 839 0325
Email dmanley@kingschambers.com

MANN, Anthony
Enterprise Chambers
Position
Head of chambers
Qualifications
QC
Contact details
Enterprise Chambers (Chambers of Anthony Mann QC), 9 Old Square, London WC2A 3SR
Tel 020 7405 9471
Fax 020 7242 1447
Web www.enterprisechambers.com
Email
anthonymann@enterprisechambers.com

MANN, Geoff
RHWL Partnership
Position
Senior partner
Contact details
RHWL Partnership, 77 Endell Street, London WC2H 9AJ
Tel 020 7379 7900
Fax 020 7836 4881
Email gmann@rhwl.co.uk

MANNING, Tim
Boodle Hatfield
Position
Partner
Qualifications
BA
Career history
Since 1978 Partner, including four years as managing partner (1991-94), Boodle Hatfield.
1973 Admitted to Roll of Solicitors
Contact details
Boodle Hatfield, 61 Brook Street, London W1K 4BL
Tel 020 7629 7411
Fax 020 7629 2621
Web www.boodlehatfield.com
Email tmanning@boodlehatfield.com

MANNS, Noel
Europa Capital Partners

Position
Principal
Qualifications
FRICS
Career history
Since 1998 Principal, Europa Capital Partners.
1981-98 Partner/director, Richard Ellis
Other roles
Creation and fund management of pan-European private equity real estate fund, Europa Fund; non-executive director, National Mortgage Bank (wholly owned subsidiary of Bank of England) (1993-2000); chairman, Conservative National Property Advisory Committee; member, Diocese of London property advisory group
Professional memberships
RICS; Worshipful Company of Chartered Surveyors
Interests
Cricket; politics; rugby; shooting
Contact details
Europa Capital Partners Ltd, 136 Sloane Street, London SW1X 9AY
Tel 020 7881 6800
Fax 020 7881 0501
Web www.europafund.com
Direct tel 020 7881 6844
Email noel.manns@europacapitalpartners.com

MANOUSSAKIS, Dimitris
FPDSavills

Position
Director – head of office, Athens
Contact details
FPDSavills Ltd, 79 Kifissias Avenue, Athens
Tel +30 210 699 6311
Fax +30 210 699 6312
Web www.fpdsavills.co.uk
Mobile +30 6932 700715
Email dman@fpdsavills.gr

MANSELL, Michael
Frontier Estates

Position
Director
Qualifications
BSc Hons; MRICS
Career history
Since 2000 Director, Frontier Estates.
1993-2000 Partner, Douglas Duff.
1989-93 William H Brown
Professional memberships
RICS
Interests
Cars; cinema; family; motorcycling; mountain biking; music; shooting
Contact details
Frontier Estates Ltd, Acorn House, Midsummer Boulevard, Milton Keynes MK9 3HP
Tel 01908 238888
Fax 01908 241111
Web www.frontier-estates.com
Mobile 07715 754038
Email michaelmansell@frontier-estates.com

MANSLEY, Nick
Morley Fund Management

Position
Head of property strategy and research
Career history
1997 Joined Norwich Union as property economist, then property strategist; more recently head of strategy with responsibility for strategy, the investment process and all research for all Morley managed property funds.
1987-94 PA Cambridge Economic Consultants: consultant, senior consultant and European development manager
Professional memberships
Society of Property Researchers
Contact details
Morley Fund Management Ltd, 34-36 Lime Street, London EC3M 7JE
Tel 020 7809 6000
Fax 020 7489 7940
Web www.morleyfm.com
Direct tel 020 7809 6810
Email nick.mansley@morleyfm.com

MANT, Trevor
Slough Estates

Position
Group treasurer
Contact details
Slough Estates plc, 234 Bath Road, Slough SL1 4EE
Tel 01753 537171
Fax 01753 820585
Web www.sloughestates.com
Email trevor.mant@sloughestates.co.uk

MARCHINGTON, William
Nelson Bakewell

Position
Director – Edinburgh office
Qualifications
BSc; MRICS
Career history
1994 Joined Nelson Bakewell.
1989-94 Richard Ellis.
1986-89 Lambert Smith Hampton
Professional memberships
CoreNet Global UK; Institute of Directors; RICS
Contact details
Nelson Bakewell Ltd, Hobart House, 80 Hanover Street, Edinburgh EH2 1EL
Tel 0131 240 0960
Fax 0131 240 0969
Web www.nelson-bakewell.com
Direct tel 0131 240 0961
Mobile 07979 700433
Email wmarchington@nelson-bakewell.com

MARCUS, Ian
Credit Suisse First Boston

Position
Managing director – head of real estate investment banking
Qualifcations
MA (Cantab)
Career history
1999 Joined Credit Suisse First Boston.
1998-99 Managing director (real estate investment banking), BT Alex Brown International.
1990-98 NatWest Markets.
1986-90 UBS.
1981-86 Bank of America
Other roles
Non-executive director, Blenheim Bishop; policy committee and conference committee, BPF; chairman, Investment Property Forum; member, *Property Week* advisory board (2003)
Professional memberships
BPF; Investment Property Forum
Interests
Cricket; cycling; football; rugby; squash
Contact details
Credit Suisse First Boston, One Cabot Square, London E14 4QJ
Tel 020 7888 8888
Fax 020 7883 5819
Web www.csfb.com
Direct tel 020 7888 4694
Direct fax 020 7943 2667
Mobile 07747 774290
Email ian.marcus@csfb.com

MARCUS, Jason
Thornfield Properties

Position
Chief executive
Qualifications
BSc Hons; MRICS
Career history
1996 Joined Thornfield Properties; appointed chief executive in 2001.
1994-96 Investment agency, DTZ Debenham Thorpe.

1992-94 Shopping centre management, Bernard Thorpe

Professional memberships

RICS

Contact details

Thornfield Properties plc, 4th Floor, 5-6 Cork Street, London W1S 3NX

Tel 020 7287 6620

Fax 020 7287 6621

Web www.thornfield.co.uk

Email jason.marcus@thornfield-london.co.uk

MARCUS, Tony
Thornfield Properties

Position

Chairman

Contact details

Thornfield Properties plc, 5 St Davids Court, Leeds LS11 5QA

Tel 0113 225 5050

Fax 0113 225 5060

Web www.thornfield.co.uk

Email nova.dean@thornfield-leeds.co.uk

MARCUSE, Paul
AXA Real Estate Investment Managers

Position

Chief executive

Qualifications

MA; MBA, Finance

Career history

Since 2000 Chief executive, AXA Real Estate Investment Managers.

1998-2000 Chief financial officer and managing director (private equity), Rodamco UK.

1997-98 Managing director (real estate advisory and private equity), UBS.

1992-97 Managing director (real estate group and private equity), BZW

Interests

Football; tennis; theatre

Contact details

AXA Real Estate Investment Managers Ltd, 7 Newgate Street, London EC1A 7HD

Tel 020 7003 1000

Fax 020 7575 8585

Web www.axa-im.co.uk

Direct tel 020 7003 1360

Mobile 07977 917286

Email paul.marcuse@axa-im.com

MARKEY, Hugh
Lisney

Position

Director

Qualifications

FSCS; FRICS; MIAVI

Professional memberships

RICS

Contact details

Lisney, 24 St Stephen's Green, Dublin

Tel +353 1 638 2700

Fax +353 1 638 2706

Web www.lisney.com

Email hmarkey@lisney.com

MARKOVITZ, Marke
Landmark Securities

Position

Chairman

Qualifications

Dip Arch (CT); Arch (SA); RIBA; MIA; MIV (SA); IPPSA

Career history

Since 1997 Chairman, Landmark Securities

Other roles

Councillor, Institute of Estate Agents; member, Society of Estate Agents; ministerial nominee on Estate Agents Board

Contact details

Landmark Securities plc, 1 Duchess Street, London W1W 6AN

Tel 020 7255 1666

Fax 020 7255 2322

Email m.markovitz@landmark.globalnet.co.uk

MARKS, Adam
Taylor Wessing

Position

Partner – head of real estate

Career history

1999 Joined Taylor Wessing.

1992-99 Partner, Walsh Lawson.

1987-92 Partner, MS Marks & Co.

1985 Admitted to Roll of Solicitors

Interests

Family; football; golf; tennis

Contact details

Taylor Wessing, Carmelite, 50 Victoria Embankment, London EC4Y 0DX

Tel 020 7300 7000

Fax 020 7300 7100

Web www.taylorwessing.com

Direct tel 020 7300 4619

Email a.marks@taylorwessing.com

MARKS, Christopher
Hammonds

Position

National head of property services

Qualifications

BA Hons; LLM (Cantab)

Career history

1984 Admitted to Roll of Solicitors.

1983 Joined Edge & Ellison (now Hammonds) as associate partner; appointed partner in 1988.

1980-82 Waltons & Morse

Professional memberships

British Urban Regeneration Association

Contact details

Hammonds, 2 Park Lane, Leeds LS3 1ES

Tel 0870 839 0000

Fax 0870 839 7001

Web www.hammonds.com

Direct tel 0113 284 7003

Direct fax 0870 460 3151

Email chris.marks@hammonds.com

MARKS, Peter
Jones Lang LaSalle

Position

European director

Qualifications

BSc, Est Man; MRICS

Career history

Since 1987 European director, Jones Lang LaSalle

Professional memberships

RICS

Interests

Cricket; literature; rugby; theatre

Contact details

Jones Lang LaSalle Ltd, 22 Hanover Square, London W1A 2BN

Tel 020 7493 6040

Fax 020 7408 0220

Web www.joneslanglasalle.com

Direct tel 020 7399 5880

Direct fax 020 7399 5590

Mobile 07831 772188

Email peter.marks@eu.joneslanglasalle.com

MARKWELL, Adam
Shearer Property Group

Position

Director

Contact details

Shearer Property Group Ltd, 31 St George Street, London W1S 2FJ

Tel 020 7290 2390

Fax 020 7290 2399

Email adammarkwell@spglondon.com

MARLEY, Bill
Ryden

Position

Partner

Interests

Football; golf (Empire Golf Society); travel

Contact details

Ryden, 130 St Vincent Street, Glasgow G2 5HF

Tel 0141 204 3838
Fax 0141 204 3554
Web www.ryden.co.uk
Direct tel 0141 270 3145
Mobile 07703 112626
Email bill.marley@ryden.co.uk

MARPLES, Patrick
Workspace Group

Position
Property director
Qualifications
MRICS
Career history
Since 1996 Property director, Workspace Group.
1986-96 Principal, Property Research Services.
1977-86 Associate partner, DE&J Levy
Professional memberships
RICS
Contact details
Workspace Group plc, Magenta House, 85 Whitechapel Road, London E1 1DU
Tel 020 7247 7614
Fax 020 7247 0157
Web www.workspacegroup.co.uk
Email patrick.marples@workspacegroup.co.uk

MARRIS, Ian
Knight Frank

Position
Partner
Qualifications
MRICS
Professional memberships
RICS
Interests
Diving/scuba diving; sailing; shooting; skiing; sport
Contact details
Knight Frank LLP, Granville House, 132-135 Sloane Street, London SW1X 9AX
Tel 020 7598 4000
Fax 020 7598 4001
Web www.knightfrank.com
Direct tel 020 7598 4004
Mobile 07770 856917
Email ian.marris@knightfrank.com

MARSDEN, Philip
King Sturge

Position
Partner – investment
Qualifications
FRICS; BSc Hons, Land Man
Career history
1981 Joined King & Co (Brussels) as letting agent (office and industrial property), Creation Partnerships; investment surveyor/associate, King Sturge from 1983 and partner since 1990
Professional memberships
Investment Surveyors Forum; RICS
Contact details
King Sturge, 7 Stratford Place, London W1C 1ST
Tel 020 7493 4933
Fax 020 7409 0469
Web www.kingsturge.com
Direct tel 020 7318 4215
Direct fax 020 7629 4514
Email philip.marsden@kingsturge.co.uk

MARSH, Geoffrey
London Residential Research

Position
Managing director
Other roles
Managing director, India Property Research; managing director, London Property Research
Contact details
London Residential Research Ltd, 151 Wardour Street, London W1F 8BN
Tel 020 7411 2887
Fax 020 7411 2883
Email geoff.marsh@egi.co.uk

MARSH, Nick
Jones Lang LaSalle Hotels

Position
Chief executive officer – Europe
Qualifications
BSc; MRICS
Career history
1988 Joined Jones Lang LaSalle: since 1990 has worked for Jones Lang LaSalle Hotels, mainly on investment sales in Europe, heading team from 1997; become chief executive of European hotel team in 2003
Professional memberships
RICS
Contact details
Jones Lang LaSalle Hotels, 22 Hanover Square, London W1A 2BN
Tel 020 7493 6040
Fax 020 7399 5694
Web www.joneslanglasallehotels.com
Direct tel 020 7399 5984
Email nick.marsh@eu.joneslanglasalle.com

MARSHALL, Michael
CB Richard Ellis Investors

Position
Chief executive
Qualifications
FRICS
Career history
1978 Joined CB Richard Ellis.
1972-78 Development surveyor, Chesterfield Properties.
1969-72 Assistant estates surveyor, J Sainsbury
Contact details
CB Richard Ellis Investors Ltd, 64 North Row, London W1K 7DA
Tel 020 7399 9600
Fax 020 7399 9601
Web www.cbreinvestors.com
Direct tel 020 7399 9611
Email mmarshall@cbreinvestors.com

MARSHALL, Simon
Edgerley Simpson Howe & Partners

Position
Partner – property management
Qualifications
BSc; MRICS
Career history
1993-94 Asset manager, GKL Management Services.
1990-93 Investment surveyor, Gooch & Wagstaff.
1988-90 Development surveyor, English & Overseas Properties.
1985-88 Gooch & Wagstaff
Professional memberships
RICS
Interests
Food; golf; hockey; wine
Contact details
Edgerley Simpson Howe & Partners, 30 Anyards Road, Cobham KT11 2LA
Tel 01932 860505
Fax 01932 860490
Web www.eshp.com
Email simon@eshp.com

MARTIN, Andrew
Hermes Property Asset Management

Position
Director – retail group
Qualifications
FRICS
Career history
1976 Joined Hermes (formerly Postel).
1973-76 Valuation surveyor, Daniel Watney.
1972-73 Area surveyor, Legal & General
Other roles
Board member, British Council of Shopping Centres; trustee, British Council of Shopping Centres Education Trust; trustee, Hermes Group Pension Scheme; member, Bluewater owner's committee; director, Central Milton Keynes Shopping Management; director, X Leisure Funds

M

Professional memberships

British Council of Shopping Centres; Investment Property Forum; Leisure Property Forum; RICS

Interests

Golf; hill walking; music; running; theatre

Contact details

Hermes Property Asset Management Ltd, Lloyds Chambers, 1 Portsoken Street, London E1 8HZ

Tel 020 7702 0888

Fax 020 7702 9453

Web www.hermes.co.uk

Direct tel 020 7680 2145

Mobile 07711 195383

Email a.martin@hermes.co.uk

MARTIN, Andrew
Strutt & Parker

Position

Partner – investment and business parks, London

Qualifications

BSc; FRICS

Career history

Since 1985 Partner, Strutt & Parker.

1981-85 Richard Ellis.

1971-81 Bernard Thorpe & Partners

Other roles

Property consultancy to major development group; UK board member, Urban Land Institute; member, Investment Property Forum education committee; vice-president, Muscular Dystrophy Campaign

Professional memberships

Investment Property Forum; London Business School Alumni; RICS; Urban Land Institute

Interests

Art; sport; tennis

Contact details

Strutt & Parker, 13 Hill Street, London W1J 5LQ

Tel 020 7629 7282

Fax 020 7629 0387

Web www.struttandparker.com

Direct tel 020 7318 5017

Direct fax 020 7355 1385

Mobile 07768 353832

Email amartin@struttandparker.com

MARTIN, Bert
Lend Lease Real Estate Solutions (UK)

Position

Development director

Contact details

Lend Lease Real Estate Solutions (UK) Ltd, York House, 23 Kingsway, London

Tel 020 7379 0222

Fax 020 7379 0213

Web www.lendlease.com.au

Direct fax 020 7539 7325

Mobile 07801 621762

Email bert.martin@lendlease.com

MARTIN, Bonnie
Masons

Position

Partner – head of property litigation, Bristol

Qualifications

BA Hons

Career history

1988 Joined Masons as partner in London; then moved to set up property litigation department in Bristol.

1986-88 Assistant solicitor (property litigation), Withers Crossman Block.

1985 Admitted to Roll of Solicitors.

1983-86 Lewis Silkin

Professional memberships

Arbrix; Bristol Property Agents' Association; British Council for Offices; BPF; British Urban Regeneration Association; Law Society; Property Litigation Association; Town & Country Planning Association; UK Environmental Law Association

Contact details

Masons, 1-4 Portland Square, Bristol BS2 8RR

Tel 0117 924 5678

Fax 0117 924 6699

Web www.masons.com

Direct tel 0117 970 5204

Mobile 07887 991402

Email bonnie.martin@masons.com

MARTIN, David
Stiles Harold Williams

Position

Director

Qualifications

BSc; FRICS

Contact details

Stiles Harold Williams Ltd, Castle Square House, 9 Castle Square, Brighton BN1 1DZ

Tel 01273 321200

Fax 01273 202436

Web www.shw.co.uk

Email dmartin@shw.co.uk

MARTIN, John
Wilberforce Chambers

Position

Barrister

Qualifications

QC

Professional memberships

Chancery Bar Association

Contact details

Wilberforce Chambers, 8 New Square, London WC2A 3QP

Tel 020 7306 0102

Fax 020 7306 0095

Web www.wilberforce.co.uk

Email jmartin@wilberforce.co.uk

MARTIN, Keith
Donaldsons

Position

Partner

Qualifications

MRICS

Career history

1979 Joined Donaldsons; managing partner 1994-99

Other roles

Director, Surveyors Mutual Assurance Association

Professional memberships

RICS

Interests

Cricket; rugby

Contact details

Donaldsons, 48 Warwick Street, London W1B 5NL

Tel 020 7534 5000

Fax 020 7434 0045

Web www.donaldsons.co.uk

Direct tel 020 7534 8544

Mobile 07808 479221

Email keith.martin@donaldsons.co.uk

MARTIN, Philip
Tuckerman

Position

Director

Qualifications

BEng Hons

Contact details

Tuckerman, 40 Great Smith Street, London SW1P 3BU

Tel 020 7222 5511

Fax 020 7222 0558

Web www.tuckerman.co.uk

Email pmartin@tuckerman.co.uk

MARTIN, Robert
Europa Capital Partners

Position

Associate director – acquisitions

Qualifications

BSc Hons; MRICS; MBA

Career history

1998 Joined Europa Capital Partners.

1996-98 MBA at University of Capetown, Johannesburg.

1993-96 St Quintin.

1990-93 Herring Baker Harris

Professional memberships
RICS
Interests
Cricket; horse riding; tennis
Contact details
Europa Capital Partners Ltd, 136 Sloane Street, London SW1X 9AY
Tel 020 7881 6800
Fax 020 7881 0501
Web www.europafund.com
Direct tel 020 7881 6825
Mobile 07712 134523
Email robert.martin@europacapitalpartners.com

MARTIN, Robert
NFU Mutual Insurance Society
Position
Property investment manager
Qualifications
FRICS
Other roles
Non-executive chairman, Salmon Developments
Professional memberships
RICS
Contact details
NFU Mutual Insurance Society Ltd, Tiddington Road, Stratford-upon-Avon CV37 7BJ
Tel 01789 204211
Fax 01789 298992
Direct tel 01789 202247
Direct fax 01789 202881
Mobile 07967 698059
Email bob_martin@nfumutual.co.uk

MARTIN, Roy
Landmark Chambers
Position
Barrister
Qualifications
QC
Contact details
Landmark Chambers, 4 Breams Buildings, London EC4A 1AQ
Tel 020 7430 1221
Fax 020 7421 1399
Web www.landmarkchambers.co.uk
Email clerks@landmarkchambers.co.uk

MARTIN-JENKINS, James
Henderson Chambers
Position
Barrister
Qualifications
BA Hons (Oxon); Astbury scholar, Middle Temple
Career history
1997 Called to Bar
Interests
Sport
Contact details
Henderson Chambers, Ground Floor, 2 Harcourt Buildings, London EC4Y 9DB
Tel 020 7583 9020
Fax 020 7583 2686
Web www.hendersonchambers.co.uk
Email jjenkins@hendersonchambers.co.uk

MARTINI, Yaser
Fleurets
Position
Director
Qualifications
BSc Hons; MRICS
Career history
1993 Joined Fleurets
Professional memberships
RICS
Interests
Cinema; gadgets; sport
Contact details
Fleurets Ltd, 18 Bloomsbury Square, London WC1A 2NS
Tel 020 7636 8992
Fax 020 7636 7490
Web www.fleurets.com
Mobile 07770 672559
Email yaser.martini@fleurets.com

MARX, Michael
Development Securities
Position
Joint managing director
Contact details
Development Securities plc, Portland House, Stag Place, London SW1E 5DS
Tel 020 7828 4777
Fax 020 7828 4999
Web www.developmentsecurities.com
Email michael.marx@devsecs.com

MASKEY, Michael
Russell-Cooke
Position
Partner – property
Qualifications
LLB
Career history
1969 Admitted to Roll of Solicitors.
1967 Joined Russell-Cooke; partner since 1972
Interests
Reading; sailing; shooting; skiing; theatre
Contact details
Russell-Cooke, 8 Bedford Row, London WC1R 4BU
Tel 020 7405 6566
Fax 020 7831 2565
Web www.russell-cooke.co.uk
Direct fax 020 7405 0115
Email maskeym@russell-cooke.co.uk

MASON, Andrew
Mason & Partners
Position
Director – high-street agency
Career history
1993 Co-founder, Mason & Partners
Contact details
Mason & Partners Ltd, Corn Exchange Building, Fenwick Street, Liverpool L2 7TP
Tel 0151 227 1008
Fax 0151 225 0155
Direct tel 0151 225 0105
Mobile 07774 211230
Email andrewmason@masonpartners.com

MASON, Geoff
Mason & Partners
Position
Director – investment and development
Qualifications
FRICS
Career history
1993 Co-founder, Mason & Partners.
1967-93 Founder and senior partner, Mason Owen & Partners
Contact details
Mason & Partners Ltd, Corn Exchange Building, Fenwick Street, Liverpool L2 7TP
Tel 0151 227 1008
Fax 0151 225 0155
Direct tel 0151 225 0110
Mobile 07836 505126
Email geoffmason@masonpartners.com

MASON, Ian
Merrill Lynch Investment Managers
Position
Managing director – real estate
Other roles
Past chairman, Association of Property Unit Trusts; chair of governors, Columbia Market Nursery School
Contact details
Merrill Lynch Investment Managers, 33 King William Street, London EC4R 9AS
Tel 020 7743 3000
Fax 020 7743 1000
Web www.mlim.co.uk
Direct tel 020 7743 5479
Email ian_mason@ml.com

M

MASON, Nick
Castlemore Securities
Position
Development director
Career history
1995 Joined Castlemore Securities.
1980-95 Guardian Properties
Professional memberships
British Council for Offices
Contact details
Castlemore Securities Ltd, Cedar Court, 221 Hagley Road, Halesowen B63 1ED
Tel 0121 585 4444
Fax 0121 585 4441
Web www.castlemore.co.uk
Direct tel 01225 336277
Direct fax 01225 426264
Email nick@castlemore.co.uk

MASON, Philip
Watson Farley & Williams
Position
Partner – head of property
Contact details
Watson Farley & Williams, 15 Appold Street, London EC2A 2HB
Tel 020 7814 8000
Fax 020 7814 8141
Web www.wfw.com
Email pmason@wfw.com

MASON, Ramsay
Mason Philips
Position
Director
Qualifications
FRICS
Career history
1979 Founding director, Mason Philips.
1968-79 Investment surveyor/associate partner, Richard Ellis
Other roles
Trustee, Investment Property Forum Educational Trust; consultant, Velleman & Co
Professional memberships
Investment Property Forum; RICS
Contact details
Mason Philips Ltd, 33 Great Portland Street, London W1W 8QG
Tel 020 7436 1212
Fax 020 7436 1350
Email rmason@masonphilips.co.uk

MASON, Steve
Edward Symmons & Partners
Position
Partner – machinery and business assets
Qualifications
MRICS
Contact details
Edward Symmons & Partners, 2 Southwark Street, London SE1 1RQ
Tel 020 7955 8454
Fax 020 7407 6423
Web www.edwardsymmons.com
Direct fax 020 7403 1947
Email steve.mason@edwardsymmons.com

MASSEY, John
DFS Furniture Group
Position
Managing director
Contact details
DFS Furniture Group Ltd, Bentley Moor Lane, Doncaster DN6 7BD
Tel 01302 330365
Fax 01302 330880
Web www.dfs-online.co.uk
Email marie.betts@dfs.co.uk

MASTERS, Simon
Aitchison Raffety
Position
Associate
Qualifications
BSc Hons; FRICS; IRRV
Professional memberships
RICS
Contact details
Aitchison Raffety Ltd, Kemp House, Station Road, Reading RG7 5JH
Tel 0118 930 5603
Fax 0118 305 5613
Web www.argroup.co.uk
Email simon.masters@argroup.co.uk

MATHER, Kurt
BASF
Position
Corporate real estate manager
Qualifications
BSc; MRICS
Career history
1996 Joined BASF as property manager; now corporate real estate manager.
1987-96 Associate director (industrial), Lambert Smith Hampton.
1985-87 Edward Rushton Son & Kenyon
Professional memberships
Association of Insurance & Risk Managers; RICS
Interests
Family; food and drink; sport; travel
Contact details
BASF plc, PO Box 4, Earl Road, Cheadle SK8 6QG
Tel 0161 485 6222
Fax 0161 486 0891
Direct tel 0161 488 5424
Mobile 07778 004345
Email kurt.mather@basf-plc.co.uk

MATTHEWS, Christian
Barwood Developments
Position
Director
Qualifications
BSc Hons; MRICS
Professional memberships
RICS
Contact details
Barwood Developments Ltd, The Grange, Warren Office Village, Milton Keynes MK12 5NE
Tel 01908 577600
Fax 01908 312017
Web www.barwood.co.uk
Direct tel 01908 577605
Mobile 07715 577605
Email christian.matthews@barwood.co.uk

MATTHEWS, Peter
CB Richard Ellis
Position
Managing director – asset management
Qualifications
FRICS; MBA; IRRV; FICPD
Career history
1997-99 Head of management, FPDSavills.
1980-97 Partner, Jones Lang Wootton.
1975-80 Valuer, Valuation Office
Other roles
Central London branch representative, RICS general council
Professional memberships
Institute of Continuing Professional Development; Institute of Revenues Rating & Valuation; RICS
Interests
DIY; family; IT; sailing
Contact details
CB Richard Ellis, St Martin's Court, 10 Paternoster Row, London EC4M 7HP
Tel 020 7182 2000
Fax 020 7182 2001
Web www.cbre.com
Direct tel 020 7643 3799
Mobile 07720 349636
Email peter.matthews@cbre.com

MATTHEWS, Philip
Wedlake Bell
Position
Partner – head of banking and commercial

property

Contact details

Wedlake Bell, 16 Bedford Street, London WC2E 9HF

Tel 020 7395 3000
Fax 020 7836 9966
Web www.wedlakebell.co.uk
Email pmatthews@wedlakebell.com

MAUDE, Rupert
Lambert Smith Hampton

Position
Director

Qualifications
FRICS

Career history
1984 Joined Lambert Smith Hampton.
1979-84 Valuation surveyor, Jones Lang Wootton.
1976-79 Anthony Brown Stewart

Other roles
Founding director, Non-Administrative Receivers Association

Professional memberships
RICS

Interests
Cycling; sailing

Contact details
Lambert Smith Hampton Ltd, Regent Arcade House, 19-25 Argyll Street, London W1F

Tel 020 7494 4000
Fax 020 7414 0866
Web www.lsh.co.uk
Direct tel 020 7663 8344
Email rmaude@lsh.co.uk

MAUDSLEY, Charles
AXA Real Estate Investment Managers

Position
Fund manager

Qualifications
MRICS

Career history
1998 Joined AXA Real Estate Investment Managers.
1986-98 DTZ Debenham Thorpe

Professional memberships
Investment Property Forum; RICS

Interests
Golf

Contact details
AXA Real Estate Investment Managers Ltd, 7 Newgate Street, London EC1A 7HD

Tel 020 7003 1000
Fax 020 7575 8585
Web www.axa-im.co.uk
Direct tel 020 7367 8130
Email charles.maudsley@axa-reim.co.uk

MAUGHAN, Richard
Boodle Hatfield

Position
Managing partner and head of property

Career history
1997 Joined Boodle Hatfield as partner; appointed head of property department in 2001.
1988-97 Partner, Rowe & Maw.
1975-88 Joined Bartletts Gluckstein as solicitor; appointed partner in 1977.
1975 Admitted to Roll of Solicitors

Professional memberships
City of Westminster & Holborn Law Society

Interests
Family; fishing; travel

Contact details
Boodle Hatfield, 61 Brook Street, London W1K 4BL

Tel 020 7629 7411
Fax 020 7629 2621
Web www.boodlehatfield.com
Email rmaughan@boodlehatfield.com

MAULEVERER, Bruce
4 Pump Court

Position
Barrister

Qualifications
QC

Contact details
4 Pump Court (Chambers of Christopher Moger QC & David Friedman QC), London EC4Y 7AN

Tel 020 7842 5555
Fax 020 7583 2036
Web www.4pumpcourt.com
Email bmauleverer@4pumpcourt.com

MAWER, Richard
Dreams

Position
Deputy managing director

Qualifications
BSc Hons; MRICS

Career history
1995 Joined Dreams as estates controller; appointed property director in 1997 and deputy managing director in 2001.
1991-95 Surveyor/associate, Duncan & Bailey Kennedy, High Wycombe.
1989-91 Commercial agent, Cluttons, Oxford.
1988-89 Buckell & Ballard Commercial, Oxford.
1986-88 Adkin, Abingdon

Professional memberships
RICS

Interests
Music

Contact details
Dreams plc, Knaves Beech, High Wycombe HP10 9QY

Tel 01628 535353
Fax 01628 535351
Web www.dreamsplc.com
Mobile 07976 823863
Email richardmawer@dreamsplc.com

MAWSON, Peter
Donaldsons

Position
Chief executive

Qualifications
BA; MSc; Dip TP; MRTPI; MRICS

Career history
1989 Joined Donaldsons; became partner of Donaldsons consultancy group in 1991 and regional chairman for Midlands & West in 1997; head of Bristol office 1995-99; elected managing partner in 1999; now chief executive.
1981-89 Principal planner, then chief development surveyor, Telford Development Corp.
1977-81 Planner/statistician, then senior planner, Basildon Development Corp

Professional memberships
RICS; RTPI

Contact details
Donaldsons, 48 Warwick Street, London W1B 5NL

Tel 020 7534 5000
Fax 020 7434 0045
Web www.donaldsons.co.uk
Direct tel 020 7534 5004
Mobile 07808 479232
Email peter.mawson@donaldsons.co.uk

MAX, James
Doughty Hanson & Co

Position
Principal – real estate

Qualifications
BSc Hons; MRICS

Career history
1998-2001 Investment banker (real estate division), Morgan Stanley.
1992-98 Investment director, DTZ Debenham Tie Leung

Other roles
Board member and trustee of Ocean Music Trust, a major music venue in Hackney

Professional memberships
RICS

Interests
Art; current affairs; music; reading; skiing; tennis (Queen's Tennis Club); travel; wine; Carlton Club

Contact details
Doughty Hanson & Co Ltd, Times Place, 45 Pall

M

Mall, London SW1Y 5JG
Tel 020 7663 9300
Fax 020 7747 9342
Web www.doughtyhanson.com
Direct tel 020 7663 0524
Direct fax 020 7663 9375
Email james.max@doughtyhanson.com

MAXFIELD, Jeremy
Bride Hall Group

Position
Finance director
Qualifications
ACA
Career history
1991-93 Finance director, Trinity Estates.
1988-91 Group tax and finance manager, Bredero Properties.
1986-88 Manager, KPMG
Professional memberships
Institute of Chartered Accountants in England & Wales
Contact details
Bride Hall Group Ltd, 49 Hays Mews, London W1J 5QQ
Tel 020 7493 3996
Fax 020 7499 4388
Email jeremy.maxfield@bride-hall.co.uk

MAXTED-JONES, Robert
ISG Occupancy

Position
Director – valuation services
Qualifications
BSc Hons; FRICS
Contact details
ISG Occupancy Ltd, 17-19 Maddox Street, London W1S 1QG
Tel 020 7290 3333
Fax 020 7290 3334
Web www.isgplc.com
Email bob.maxtedjones@isgplc.com

MAY, Diane
Jones Lang LaSalle

Position
European director – strategic consultancy
Contact details
Jones Lang LaSalle Ltd, 22 Hanover Square, London W1A 2BN
Tel 020 7493 6040
Fax 020 7408 0220
Web www.joneslanglasalle.com
Direct tel 020 7399 5331
Direct fax 020 7399 5688
Email diane.may@eu.joneslanglasalle.com

MAY, John
Pemberton Greenish

Position
Partner – head of commercial property group
Qualifications
Solicitor
Career history
1986 Joined Pemberton Greenish; partner since 1988
Other roles
One of the UK's leading ship photographers; author of three books on Mediterranean ferry shipping
Professional memberships
Land Institute; Law Society; Worshipful Company of Paviors
Interests
Photography; shipping
Contact details
Pemberton Greenish, 45 Pont Street, London SW1X 0BX
Tel 020 7591 3333
Fax 020 7591 3300
Web www.pglaw.co.uk
Direct tel 020 7591 3327
Email j.may@pglaw.co.uk

MAYES, Dominic
Knight Frank

Position
Partner – hotels division
Career history
2001 Joined Knight Frank as partner (specialist in sale, acquisition and development of hotel property).
1989-2001 Associate, Druce Hotels & Leisure
Contact details
Knight Frank LLP, 20 Hanover Square, London W1S 1HZ
Tel 020 7629 8171
Fax 020 7493 4114
Web www.knightfrank.com
Direct tel 020 7861 1086
Direct fax 020 7409 7338
Mobile 07769 974820
Email dominic.mayes@knightfrank.com

MAYHEW, John
Homebase

Position
Estates manager
Contact details
Homebase Ltd, Beddington House, Railway Approach, Wallington SM6 0HB
Tel 020 8784 7200
Fax 020 8784 7755
Web www.homebase.co.uk
Direct tel 020 8784 6449
Email john.mayhew@homebase.co.uk

MAYHEW, Luke
John Lewis

Position
Managing director
Career history
1992 Joined John Lewis Partnership; became development director in 1993 and managing director of John Lewis in 2000
Contact details
John Lewis plc, 171 Victoria Street, London SW1E 5NA
Tel 020 7828 1000
Fax 020 7592 6355
Web www.johnlewis.co.uk
Direct tel 020 7592 6256
Email rachael_curtis@johnlewis.co.uk

MAYKELS, Laurence
Maykels

Position
Sole principal
Qualifications
MRICS
Other roles
Franchise and investment consultancy
Professional memberships
RICS
Contact details
Maykels, 78 York Street, London W1H 1DP
Tel 020 7298 6100
Fax 01923 816142
Direct tel 01923 223423
Mobile 07814 274405
Email laurence.maykels@tiscali.co.uk

MCADDEN, Matthew
UNITE London

Position
Regional development director
Qualifications
MA (Cantab)
Career history
2000-02 Director, Domain (joint venture between Bank of Scotland and Moorfield, developing student and key worker accommodation).
1995-2000 Director responsible for North of England, JC Rathbone Associates
Interests
Horse riding; rowing; walking
Contact details
UNITE London Ltd, The Tower Building, 11 York Road, London SE1 7NQ
Tel 020 7902 5050

Fax 020 7902 5051
Email matthew.mcadden@unite-group.co.uk

MCALISTER, Mark
CB Richard Ellis

Position
Senior director
Qualifications
Bsc; FRICS
Career history
1981 Joined Richard Ellis; became associate in 1984 and partner in 1988, specialising in central London agency and development
Other roles
Board director, CB Richard Ellis Gunne, Ireland
Professional memberships
British American Business; Holborn Business Partnership
Interests
History; tennis; travel
Contact details
CB Richard Ellis, St Martin's Court, 10 Paternoster Row, London EC4M 7HP
Tel 020 7182 2000
Fax 020 7182 2001
Web www.cbre.com
Direct tel 020 7643 3747
Email mark.mcalister@cbre.com

MCALLISTER, Ann
Serle Court

Position
Barrister
Other roles
Founder member and current committee member, Property Bar Association
Professional memberships
Property Bar Association
Contact details
Serle Court, 6 New Square, London WC2A 3QS
Tel 020 7242 6105
Fax 020 7405 4004
Web www.serlecourt.co.uk
Email amcallister@serlecourt.co.uk

MCALLISTER, Neil
Ryden

Position
Partner
Qualifications
FRICS
Career history
1984 Joined Ryden; became partner in 1999
Other roles
Vice-president, Industrial Agents Society
Professional memberships
Industrial Agents Society; RICS
Interests
Golf; sailing; skiing; squash
Contact details
Ryden, 46 Castle Street, Edinburgh EH2 3BN
Tel 0131 225 6612
Fax 0131 225 5766
Web www.ryden.co.uk
Direct tel 0131 473 3212
Mobile 07831 610721
Email neil.mcallister@ryden.co.uk

MCARDLE, Ian
AWG Property Solutions

Position
Managing director
Qualifications
MBA; BSc Hons; MRICS
Career history
Since 2001 Managing director, AWG Developments (commercial)/AWG Property Solutions.
1996-2001 Director/managing director, Chesterton Consulting.
1989-96 Portfolio manager, Post Office.
1987-89 Development surveyor, Leeds City Council
Other roles
Director of various subsidiaries and joint-venture companies
Professional memberships
CoreNet Global UK; RICS
Interests
Football; rugby
Contact details
AWG Property Solutions Ltd, Ambury House, Sovereign Court, Huntingdon PE29 6XU
Tel 01480 410920
Fax 01480 410921
Direct tel 01480 410933
Mobile 07802 688414
Email ian.mcardle@awgps.com

MCAULEY, Cliff
Clifford Chance

Position
Partner – global and London head of real estate
Qualifications
BA Hons; BCL
Career history
1987 Admitted to Roll of Solicitors.
1985 Joined Clifford Chance; appointed partner in 1995
Interests
Music
Contact details
Clifford Chance, 10 Upper Bank Street, London E14 5JJ
Tel 020 7600 1000
Fax 020 7600 5555
Web www.cliffordchance.com
Email clifford.mcauley@cliffordchance.com

MCBRIDE, Lee
Wragge & Co

Position
Partner – head of environmental
Career history
1996 Joined Wragge & Co; appointed partner in 2000.
1992 Admitted to Roll of Solicitors
Professional memberships
Law Society; UK Environmental Law Association
Interests
Cycling; golf; squash
Contact details
Wragge & Co LLP, 55-73 Colmore Row, Birmingham B3 2AS
Tel 0870 903 1000
Fax 0870 904 1099
Web www.wragge.com
Direct tel 0121 685 2732
Email lee_mcbride@wragge.com

MCBRYDE, Ian
ISIS Property Asset Management

Position
Director – property funds
Qualifications
FRICS
Career history
1982-2002 Fund manager, Friends Ivory & Sime Property Asset Management.
1979-82 Assistant valuer, Greater London Council.
1976-79 Idris Jones & Partners
Professional memberships
RICS
Contact details
ISIS Property Asset Management plc, 100 Wood Street, London EC2V 7AN
Tel 020 7506 1100
Fax 020 7600 4180
Web www.isisam.com
Direct tel 020 7506 1120
Mobile 07802 972676
Email ian.mcbryde@isisam.com

MCCABE, Kevin
Scarborough Development Group

Position
Chairman
Other roles
Executive chairman, FairBriar; chairman, Scarborough Property Group; chairman, Forsyth

Business Centres; chairman, Sheffield United

Interests

Cricket; football; squash

Contact details

Scarborough Development Group plc, Europa House, 20 Esplanade, Scarborough YO11 2AQ

Tel 01723 500208

Fax 01723 500329

Email enquiries@sdgroup-plc.com

MCCALMONT-WOODS, Nick
GVA Grimley

Position

Partner – City agency

Qualifications

BSc; MRICS

Career history

Since 2000 Partner (City agency), GVA Grimley.
1984-2000 Jones Lang Wootton.
1983-84 Mason Owen & Partners

Other roles

Director, GVA Connect

Professional memberships

RICS

Interests

Classic cars; food; wine; football (Liverpool Football Club)

Contact details

GVA Grimley, 25 Bucklersbury, London EC4N 8DA

Tel 0870 900 8990

Fax 020 7911 2846

Web www.gvagrimley.co.uk

Direct tel 020 7911 2810

Mobile 07775 826626

Email nick.mccalmont-woods@gvagrimley.co.uk

MCCARTHY, Helen
British Property Federation

Position

Director – public relations and membership

Qualifications

BA; Dip Ed

Career history

1983-88 Press and publicity officer, Local Authorities' Management Services & Computer Committee

Interests

Cinema; reading; sailing; travel

Contact details

British Property Federation, 1 Warwick Row, London SW1E 5ER

Tel 020 7828 0111

Fax 020 7834 3442

Web www.bpf.org.uk

Direct tel 020 7802 0106

Email HMcCarthy@BPF.org.uk

MCCLEA, Nigel
Pinsents

Position

National head of property

Qualifications

BA (Cantab)

Career history

1975 Joined Simpson Curtis (now Pinsents); appointed partner in 1978.
1975 Admitted to Roll of Solicitors

Professional memberships

Law Society

Contact details

Pinsents, 1 Park Row, Leeds LS1 5AB

Tel 0113 244 5000

Fax 0113 244 8000

Web www.pinsents.com

Direct tel 0113 294 5282

Mobile 07730 778068

Email nigel.mcclea@pinsents.com

MCCLUSKIE, Mark
ATIS REAL Weatheralls

Position

Director – investment, Glasgow

Qualifications

BSc Hons; Dip LE; MRICS

Other roles

Head of Glasgow office

Interests

Family; football; music

Contact details

ATIS REAL Weatheralls Ltd, Finlay House, 10-14 West Nile Street, Glasgow G1 2PP

Tel 0141 225 5440

Fax 0141 248 6443

Web www.atisrealweatheralls.com

Direct tel 0141 225 5444

Mobile 07717 178285

Email mark.mccluskie@atisrealweatheralls.com

MCCONNELL, Rodger
Glasgow City Council

Position

Director – development and regeneration services

Qualifications

FRICS; MBA

Career history

1995 Glasgow City Council: joined as director (property services); appointed director (development and regeneration services) in 1998.
1992-95 City estates surveyor, Glasgow District Council.
1975-91 Strathclyde Regional Council: assistant head of estates, then deputy director of estates from 1978

Professional memberships

Association of Chief Estates Surveyors & Property Managers; RICS

Contact details

Glasgow City Council, Exchange House, 229 George Street, Glasgow G1 1QU

Tel 0141 287 8555

Fax 0141 287 8444

Web www.glasgow.gov.uk

Direct tel 0141 287 6000

Direct fax 0141 287 6004

Email rodger.mcconnell@drs.glasgow.gov.uk

MCCORMACK, Kenneth
James Barr

Position

Director and head of rating

Qualifications

MRICS

Career history

1989 Joined James Barr & Son.
1978-89 Assessors department, Strathclyde Regional Council

Professional memberships

RICS

Contact details

James Barr, 226 West George Street, Glasgow G2 2LN

Tel 0141 300 8000

Fax 0141 300 8001

Web www.jamesbarr.co.uk

Direct tel 0141 300 8062

Email kmccormack@jamesbarr.co.uk

MCCRACKEN, Robert
2 Harcourt Buildings

Position

Barrister

Qualifications

MA (Oxon); QC

Career history

1973 Called to Bar

Other roles

Chairman, UK Environmental Law Association (1995-97); secretary, Planning & Environmental Bar Association (1994-96)

Interests

Art

Contact details

2 Harcourt Buildings (Chambers of Robin Purchas QC), 2nd Floor, London EC4Y 9DB

Tel 020 7353 8415

Fax 020 7353 7622

Web www.2hblaw.co.uk

Email clerks@2hblaw.co.uk

MCCREADY, John
Ernst & Young

Position
Partner – real estate, hospitality and construction
Qualifications
ACA; MBA
Career history
1997 Joined Blue Circle; chief executive of Blue Circle Properties 1997-99; chairman of disposal group, Blue Circle, 2000-01.
1996 Chief executive, Whitecliff Properties.
1994-95 Chief executive, Bluewater Park
Other roles
Chairman, London & South East Industrial Development Board; chairman, Kent Architecture Centre
Professional memberships
Institute of Chartered Accountants in England & Wales
Interests
Architecture; aviation; history
Contact details
Ernst & Young LLP, 1 More London Place, London SE1 2AF
Tel 020 7951 2000
Fax 020 7951 1345
Web www.ey.com/uk
Direct tel 020 7951 7778
Direct fax 020 7951 3411
Email jmccready1@uk.ey.com

MCCREERY, Paul
Barton Willmore

Position
Partner
Qualifications
BSc; MPhil; FRTPI
Career history
Since 1985 Partner, Barton Willmore, Kent office.
1979-85 Area planning officer, Maidstone Borough Council.
1976-79 Senior planning assistant, Kent County Council
Professional memberships
RTPI
Interests
Sailing; skiing; tennis
Contact details
Barton Willmore, 35 Kings Hill Avenue, West Malling ME19 4BW
Tel 01732 845845
Fax 01732 223808
Web www.bartonwillmore.co.uk
Email paul.mccreery@bartonwillmore.co.uk

MCCULLOCH, Graham
Frogmore Estates

Position
Development director
Other roles
Director, Frogmore Developments; director, Frogmore Investments
Contact details
Frogmore Estates Ltd, 11-15 Wigmore Street, London W1A 2JZ
Tel 020 7016 6000
Fax 020 7495 5321
Web www.frogmore.co.uk
Email grahammcculloch@frogmore.co.uk

MCDERMOTT, Adele
Wilkes Partnership

Position
Partner – head of property
Career history
Since 1994 Partner and head of property, Wilkes Partnership.
1993-94 Group solicitor, Noble Organisation
Other roles
Council member, Birmingham Law Society; former chairman of West Midlands branch, Women in Property
Professional memberships
Women in Property
Interests
Art; design; music
Contact details
Wilkes Partnership Ltd, 41 Church Street, Birmingham B3 2RT
Tel 0121 233 4333
Fax 0121 233 4546
Web www.wilkes.co.uk
Email AdeleM@wilkes.co.uk

MCDONALD, Nigel
Eddisons

Position
Managing director
Qualifications
FRICS
Career history
1975 Joined Eddisons
Professional memberships
RICS
Interests
Fishing; shooting
Contact details
Eddisons, Pennine House, Russell Street, Leeds LS1 5RN
Tel 0113 243 0101
Fax 0113 242 1364
Web www.eddisons.com
Mobile 07767 806369
Email nigel.mcdonald@eddisons.com

MCDOUGALL, Neil
BAA Lynton

Position
Associate director
Qualifications
BSc Hons, Est Man; MRICS
Career history
1991-97 Associate director/director, Revival Properties.
1989-90 Senior agency surveyor, Donaldsons.
1987-89 Commercial agency surveyor, Nationwide Anglia Commercial
Professional memberships
RICS
Interests
Architecture; aviation; conservation; hill walking
Contact details
BAA Lynton plc, 67-69 New Bond Street, London W1S 1DF
Tel 020 7907 9200
Fax 020 7907 9299
Web www.baa.com
Mobile 07767 886636
Email neil_mcdougall@baa.com

MCDOWALL, Robert
DTZ Pieda Consulting

Position
Director
Qualifications
MCIBS
Career history
1999 Joined DTZ Pieda Consulting.
1991-99 Corporate banking, Royal Bank of Scotland: moved from Aberdeen to London in 1997, then to Edinburgh in 1998
Professional memberships
Chartered Institute of Bankers in Scotland
Interests
Football; gardening; golf; running
Contact details
DTZ Pieda Consulting, 28 Drumsheugh Gardens, Edinburgh EH3 7RN
Tel 0131 225 5737
Fax 0131 225 5196
Web www.dtz.com
Direct tel 0131 527 8439
Mobile 07771 933237
Email robert.mcdowall@dtz.com

MCGAHEY, Andrew
Hartnell Taylor Cook

Position
Partner

M

Qualifications
MA (Cantab); MRICS
Professional memberships
Cambridge University Land Society; Investment Property Forum; RICS
Contact details
Hartnell Taylor Cook, 12-13 Conduit Street, London W1S 2XH
Tel 020 7491 7323
Fax 020 7491 3032
Web www.htc.uk.com
Direct tel 020 7409 3710
Mobile 07831 836066
Email andrew.mcgahey@htc.uk.com

MCGARVA, Colin
Lambert Smith Hampton
Position
Director
Qualifications
BSc, Land Econ; MRICS
Career history
1994-98 Estate manager (Scotland), Rail Property.
1989-93 Development and station trading manager, British Rail Property.
1985-89 Estate surveyor, Glasgow City Council
Professional memberships
RICS
Interests
Golf; real tennis; tennis
Contact details
Lambert Smith Hampton Ltd, 176 St Vincent Street, Glasgow G2 5SG
Tel 0141 249 6633
Fax 0141 249 6630
Web www.lsh.co.uk
Mobile 07711 929656
Email cmcgarva@lsh.co.uk

MCGHEE, John
9 Old Square
Position
Barrister
Qualifications
QC; MA (Oxon)
Career history
2003 Appointed QC.
1984 Called to Bar
Other roles
Appointed to supplementary panel of treasury counsel in 1997
Professional memberships
Chancery Bar Association; Property Bar Association
Contact details
9 Old Square (Chambers of Michael Driscoll QC), Ground Floor, London WC2A 3SR
Tel 020 7405 4682
Fax 020 7831 7107
Web www.9oldsquare.co.uk
Email john.mcghee@9oldsquare.co.uk

MCGILL, Ian
Stimpsons
Position
Director
Qualifications
FRICS
Professional memberships
RICS
Interests
Fishing; golf; skiing
Contact details
Stimpsons, Boston House, 64-66 Queensway, Hemel Hempstead HP2 5HA
Tel 01442 240 406
Fax 01442 252 881
Email iwm@stimpsons.co.uk

MCGILLYCUDDY, Patrick
Gazeley Properties
Position
Commercial director
Qualifications
MCIOB; MAPM
Career history
1987 Joined Gazeley as project manager; construction director for 10 years; now commercial director
Other roles
Project manager, Pizza Hut; construction manager, MFI/Allied Carpets
Professional memberships
Association for Project Management; Chartered Institute of Building
Interests
Fishing; golf; shooting
Contact details
Gazeley Properties Ltd, Gazeley House, 26 Rockingham Drive, Milton Keynes MK14 6PD
Tel 01908 838100
Fax 01908 838101
Web www.gazeley.com
Direct tel 01908 838131
Mobile 07801 885445
Email pat_mcgillycuddy@gazeley.co.uk

MCGILP, Niall
Akeler Developments
Position
Director – development partnerships
Qualifications
MA Hons; Dip TP; MRTPI
Career history
Since 2003 Director (development partnerships), Akeler group of companies.
1998-2003 Director (competitive place), Scottish Enterprise.
1992-98 Director of property and environment, Lanarkshire Development Agency.
1987-92 Managing director, Hamilton Enterprise Development Co
Contact details
Akeler Developments Ltd, 7 Clifford Street, London W1S 2WE
Tel 020 7864 1800
Fax 020 7864 1801
Web www.akeler.com
Direct tel 020 7864 1845
Mobile 07711 218208
Email niallm@akeler.com

MCGONIGAL, Gregory
Montagu Evans
Position
Partner – head of management
Qualifications
BSc; MRICS
Career history
1994-2000 NAI Gooch Webster (formerly Gooch & Wagstaff).
1988-94 Cluttons
Professional memberships
RICS
Contact details
Montagu Evans, 44-48 Dover Street, London W1S 4AZ
Tel 020 7493 4002
Fax 020 7312 7547
Web www.montagu-evans.co.uk
Email gregory.mcgonigal@montagu-evans.co.uk

MCGOWAN, Malcolm
Sheppard Robson
Position
Partner
Qualifications
BA; Dip Arch; RIBA
Professional memberships
British Council for Offices; RIBA
Interests
Cricket; rowing
Contact details
Sheppard Robson, 77 Parkway, London NW1 7PU
Tel 020 7504 1700
Fax 020 7504 1701
Web www.sheppardrobson.com
Email malcolm.mcgowan@sheppardrobson.com

MCGRADY, Steven
KPMG

Position
Partner – head of stamp tax
Career history
Since 1998 Partner, KPMG.
1994-97 Rowe & Maw: tax partner 1996-97.
1990 Admitted to Roll of Solicitors.
1987-94 Clifford Chance, London, Amsterdam, Madrid.
1986 Called to Bar
Interests
Cycling
Contact details
KPMG LLP, 1 Canada Square, London E14 5AB
Tel 020 7311 1000
Web www.kpmg.co.uk
Direct fax 020 7311 1700
Email steven.mcgrady@kpmg.co.uk

MCGRATH, Kevin
REIT Asset Management

Position
Partner
Qualifications
BSc, Est Man; Dip Prop Invest; MRICS
Career history
1996 Joined REIT Asset Management.
1989-96 Senior investment surveyor, Hermes Investment Management.
1987-89 Senior surveyor, Westminster Council.
1986-87 Management surveyor, Ealing Council.
1984-86 Valuation surveyor, Greater London Council.
1982-84 National Westminster Bank.
1981-82 Lyons Soft Drinks
Other roles
Director, Queens Park Rangers Football Club; patron, Chaucer Clinic; member of board of governors, GSA Conservatoire
Professional memberships
Investment Property Forum; RICS
Interests
Piano; politics (Labour Party); reading; travel; Hurlingham Club; Royal Horticultural Society
Contact details
REIT Asset Management Ltd, 5 Wigmore Street, London W1U 1PB
Tel 020 7499 2244
Fax 020 7499 7700
Web www.reit.co.uk
Mobile 07768 145757
Email kevinmcgrath@reit.co.uk

MCGREGOR, Andrew
FPDSavills

Position
Director – head of leisure
Contact details
FPDSavills Ltd, 20 Grosvenor Hill, London W1K 3HQ
Tel 020 7499 8644
Fax 020 7495 3773
Web www.fpdsavills.co.uk
Direct tel 020 7409 8861
Mobile 07775 552796
Email amcgregor@fpdsavills.co.uk

MCGUCKIN, Stephen
Land Securities Group

Position
Development director
Qualifications
RIBA; MBA; MSc; MA
Career history
Since 2001 Development director, Land Securities.
1993-2001 Director of consulting, Mace.
1990-93 Associate, Nicholas Grimshaw & Partners.
1988-90 Team leader, Burton Group.
1986-88 Associate director, Fitch RS.
1979-85 Trainee architect, George Wimpey Group
Professional memberships
Association of MBAs; RIBA
Interests
Football; rugby; skiing
Contact details
Land Securities Group plc, 5 Strand, London WC2N 5AF
Tel 020 7413 9000
Fax 020 7024 5007
Web www.landsecurities.com
Direct tel 020 6024 3706
Direct fax 020 7024 3777
Mobile 07770 637655
Email steve.mcguckin@landsecurities.com

MCGUIRE, Martin
Standard Life Investments

Position
Investment director
Qualifications
BLE; MRICS
Career history
1979-85 Jones Lang Wootton, Brussels.
1977-79 Ryden, Edinburgh
Professional memberships
RICS
Contact details
Standard Life Investments Ltd, 1 George Street, Edinburgh EH2 2LL
Tel 0131 245 2700
Fax 0131 245 2710
Web www.standardlife.com
Direct tel 0131 245 2702
Direct fax 0131 240 8307
Email martin_mcguire@standardlife.com

MCINNES, Ken
Ryden

Position
Partner – offices group
Contact details
Ryden, 130 St Vincent Street, Glasgow G2 5HF
Tel 0141 204 3838
Fax 0141 204 3554
Web www.ryden.co.uk
Email ken.mcinnes@ryden.com

MCINTOSH, Dr Angus
King Sturge

Position
Partner and head of research
Qualifications
BA, Econ; MPhil; PhD; FRICS
Career history
Since 2000 Head of research and partner, King Sturge.
1993-2000 Director (European research), Insignia Richard Ellis.
1984-93 Partner/head of research, Healey & Baker.
1982-84 Senior lecturer, Kingston University.
1977-82 Assistant investment surveyor, Provident Mutual Life
Other roles
Chairman, Leisure Property Forum; visiting professor, Oxford Brookes University
Professional memberships
Lambda Alpha; RICS; Urban Land Institute
Interests
Family; running; sailing; skiing; theatre
Contact details
King Sturge, 7 Stratford Place, London W1C 1ST
Tel 020 7493 4933
Fax 020 7409 0469
Web www.kingsturge.com
Direct tel 020 7529 6890
Direct fax 020 7499 0569
Email angus.mcintosh@kingsturge.co.uk

MCKEE, William
Tilfen Land

Position
Non-executive chairman
Qualifications

CBE; BA Hons; MSc, Eng; DIC; Dip TP; Dip TS

Career history

1993-2002 Chief executive, BPF.

1981-92 Chief executive, London Borough of Merton.

1977-81 Director of development, London Borough of Hammersmith

Other roles

Visiting fellow in property, Reading University; chairman, Tilfen Regeneration; chairman, Weber Shandwick Property UK; chief executive, Accessible Retail; property advisory board member, Hotbed Property Investment Fund; principal, WM Consulting; chair, Thurrock Urban Development Corp; governor and trustee, Rambert Dance Company

Professional memberships

BPF (honorary life member); Chartered Institute of Transport in the UK; Institute of Directors; Institute of Highways & Transport; Institute of Logistics & Transport; RICS; RTPI

Interests

Art; ballet; book collecting; cricket; golf (Royal Wimbledon Golf Club); music; reading; theatre; Reform Club

Contact details

Tilfen Land Ltd, Harrow Manor Way, London SE2 9XH
Tel 020 8319 5040
Fax 020 8311 4778
Web www.tilfenland.co.uk
Email william.mckee@btclick.com

MCKELLAR, Rob
Savills

Position

Group finance director

Qualifications

BA Hons; CIMA

Other roles

Chairman, Asia and Australian executive committee

Interests

Fishing; keep fit

Contact details

Savills plc, 25 Finsbury Circus, London EC2M 7EE
Web www.fpdsavills.co.uk
Direct tel 020 7409 8988
Direct fax 020 7409 8989
Mobile 07870 555801
Email rmckellar@fpdsavills.co.uk

MCKENNA, Philip
Strutt & Parker

Position

Partner – head of City agency team

Contact details

Strutt & Parker, 1 Angel Court, London EC2R 7EQ
Tel 020 7600 3456
Fax 020 7600 3330
Web www.struttandparker.com
Email pmckenna@struttandparker.com

MCKIBBIN, Shelagh
Herbert Smith

Position

Partner – real estate

Qualifications

LLB, Law with French (Birmingham); Diplôme d'Études Jurisiques Françaises

Career history

1986 Joined Herbert Smith.

1984-86 Norton Rose.

1984 Admitted to Roll of Solicitors

Professional memberships

Association of Women Solicitors; Investment Property Forum

Interests

Running; tennis

Contact details

Herbert Smith, Exchange House, 10 Primrose Street, London EC2A 2NY
Tel 020 7374 8000
Fax 020 7374 0888
Web www.herbertsmith.com
Direct tel 020 7466 2304
Mobile 07785 254977
Email shelagh.mckibbin@herbertsmith.com

MCKIMM, Daniel
Allen & Overy

Position

Partner – real estate

Qualifications

LLB

Career history

1990 Joined Allen & Overy; partner since 1998

Professional memberships

Law Society

Interests

Cycling; gardening; sailing; theatre; walking

Contact details

Allen & Overy, 1 New Change, London EC4M 9QQ
Tel 020 7330 3000
Fax 020 7330 9999
Web www.allenovery.com
Email daniel.mckimm@allenovery.com

MCKINNEY, Oonagh
Lester Aldridge

Position

Property development partner

Contact details

Lester Aldridge, Russell House, Oxford Road, Bournemouth BH8 8EX
Tel 01202 786161
Fax 01202 786150
Web www.lesteraldridge.com
Direct tel 01202 786159
Email oonagh.mckinney@la-law.com

MCLACHLAN, Lisa
Land Securities Trillium

Position

Asset management director

Qualifications

BSc Hons; MRICS

Professional memberships

RICS

Contact details

Land Securities Trillium Ltd, 140 London Wall, London EC2Y 5DN
Tel 020 7796 5500
Fax 020 7796 5501
Web www.landsecurities.co.uk
Direct tel 020 7796 5522
Direct fax 0845 030 2546
Email lisa.mclachlan@lstrillium.com

MCLEAN, Cathy
RICS in Wales

Position

Director for Wales

Qualifications

BSc; MRICS

Career history

1989-2000 Welsh Development Agency: development executive, then area development manager from 1991.

1985-89 District Valuer's Office, Pontypridd and Port Talbot. Previously in public sector in Liverpool

Other roles

Commissioner, Design Commission for Wales; board member, Artworks Wales: Cywaith Cymru; board member, Rethinking Construction Centre, Wales; executive member, Construction Industry Council, Wales

Professional memberships

Institute of Directors, Wales; RICS

Interests

Badminton; keep fit; sport

Contact details

RICS in Wales, 7 St Andrews Place, Cardiff CF10 3BE
Tel 029 20 224414
Fax 029 20 224416
Web www.rics.org.uk
Email cmclean@rics.org.uk

MCLEAN, Neil
DLA

Position
Location head, real estate (Leeds)
Qualifications
LLB Hons
Career history
Since 1993 Head of property (Leeds), DLA; appointed DLA board member in 1994; national head of property 1995-98.
1979-93 Walker Morris.
1974-79 Atkinson & Sons
Professional memberships
Law Society
Interests
Food; music; sport; travel
Contact details
DLA, Princes Exchange, 2 Princes Square, Leeds LS1 4BY
Tel 08700 111111
Fax 0113 245 0104
Web www.dla.com
Direct tel 0113 369 2800
Email neil.mclean@dla.com

MCMAHON, Patrick
Bidwells Property Consultants

Position
Partner – head of agency
Qualifications
BSc; MRICS
Contact details
Bidwells Property Consultants, Trumpington Road, Cambridge CB2 2LD
Tel 01223 841841
Fax 01223 845150
Web www.bidwells.co.uk
Direct tel 020 7297 6276
Mobile 07831 370404
Email pmcmahon@bidwells.co.uk

MCMEEKING, Veronica
Cisco Systems

Position
Head of property
Contact details
Cisco Systems Ltd, 9 New Square Park, London TW14 8HA
Tel 020 8824 1000
Fax 020 8824 1001
Web www.cisco.com
Email vmcmeeki@cisco.com

MCMULLEN, Stephen
Dalgleish

Position
Retail director
Contact details
Dalgleish, 80 New Bond Street, London W1S 1DD
Tel 020 7663 5555
Fax 020 7491 0098
Web www.dalgleish.co.uk
Direct tel 020 7663 5517
Email smcmullen@dalgleish.co.uk

MCMURRAY, Lindsey
Royal Bank of Scotland

Position
Head – leveraged finance and property securitisation
Contact details
Royal Bank of Scotland, 5th Floor, 135 Bishopsgate, London EC2M 3UR
Tel 020 7375 5000
Web www.rbs.co.uk
Email lindsey.mcmurray@rbos.com

MCNAIR SCOTT, Nigel
Helical Bar

Position
Finance director
Contact details
Helical Bar plc, 11-15 Farm Street, London W1J 5RS
Tel 020 7629 0113
Fax 020 7408 1666
Web www.helical.co.uk
Email nms@helical.co.uk

MCNAMARA, Mike
Ernst & Young

Position
Partner – head of real estate finance
Career history
Since 1997 Partner (head of real estate finance), Ernst & Young
Interests
Golf
Contact details
Ernst & Young LLP, 1 More London Place, London SE1 2AF
Tel 020 7951 2000
Fax 020 7951 1345
Web www.ey.com/uk
Direct tel 020 7951 6351
Direct fax 020 7951 3411
Mobile 07887 847908
Email mmcnamara@uk.ey.com

MCNAMARA, Paul
Lisney

Position
Director
Qualifications
FRICS; FSCS; MCiArb
Career history
1989 Joined Lisney.
1987-89 Group premises department, Midland Bank.
1986-87 Tower Hamlets Borough Council
Professional memberships
RICS
Interests
Golf
Contact details
Lisney, 24 St Stephen's Green, Dublin
Tel +353 1 638 2700
Fax +353 1 638 2706
Web www.lisney.com
Email pmcnamara@lisney.com

MCNAMARA, Dr Paul
Prudential Property Investment Managers

Position
Director – property research
Qualifications
OBE; BSc Hons; PhD; ASIP
Career history
1987 Joined Prudential Property Investment Managers.
1981-87 Senior lecturer, Oxford Polytechnic
Other roles
Visiting professor (department of real estate management), Oxford Brookes University; president and honorary fellow, Society of Property Researchers; chair of Investment Property Forum education strategy committee, member of IPF research committee and IPF representative on ODPM property consultative group; chair, Property Workstream; member of Institutional Investors' Group on Climate Change
Professional memberships
Society of Investment Professionals
Interests
Football; literature; music
Contact details
Prudential Property Investment Managers Ltd, Princeton House, 271-273 High Holborn, London WC1V 7NE
Tel 020 7548 6600
Fax 020 7548 6999
Web www.prupim.com
Direct tel 020 7548 6862
Direct fax 020 7548 6502
Email paul.mcnamara@prupim.com

MCNEE, Andrew
Mason Owen & Partners

Position
Head of valuations

M

Qualifications
FRICS
Professional memberships
RICS
Contact details
Mason Owen & Partners Ltd, Gladstone House, 11 Union Court, Liverpool L2 4UQ
Tel 0151 242 3000
Fax 0151 236 2569
Web www.masonowen.com
Direct tel 0151 242 3072
Mobile 07967 098223
Email andrew.mcnee@masonowen.com

MCNELLIS, David
Lisney
Position
Director – agency
Qualifications
BSc, Est Man; MRICS
Career history
1986 Joined Lisney; appointed director in 1994
Professional memberships
RICS
Contact details
Lisney, Lancashire House, 5 Linenhall Street, Belfast BT2 8AA
Tel 02890 501501
Fax 02890 501500
Web www.lisney.com
Direct tel 02890 501551
Mobile 07887 911077
Email dmcnellis@lisney-belfast.com

MCNULTY, Stephen
Burges Salmon
Position
Partner – head of housing association unit
Qualifications
MA (Oxon)
Contact details
Burges Salmon, Narrow Quay House, Narrow Quay, Bristol BS1 4AH
Tel 0117 939 2000
Fax 0117 902 4400
Web www.burges-salmon.com
Email stephen.mcnulty@burges-salmon.com

MCPARLAND, Andrew
Parlison Properties
Position
Director
Contact details
Parlison Properties Ltd, 94 Mount Street, London W1K 2SZ
Tel 020 7629 0586
Fax 020 7629 1713
Mobile 07768 893223
Email ajm@parlisonproperties.co.uk

MCSHERRY, John
Jones Lang LaSalle
Position
European director
Contact details
Jones Lang LaSalle Ltd, 22 Hanover Square, London W1A 2BN
Tel 020 7493 6040
Fax 020 7408 0220
Web www.joneslanglasalle.com
Direct tel 020 7399 5187
Email john.mcsherry@eu.joneslanglasalle.com

MCSTAY, Adrian
Grenville Smith & Duncan
Position
Chairman
Contact details
Grenville Smith & Duncan Ltd, Waterloo House, 20 Waterloo Street, Birmingham B2 5TB
Tel 0121 631 2277
Fax 0121 665 6565
Web www.g-s-d.co.uk
Email adrian.mcstay@g-s-d.co.uk

MCTAGUE, Peter
Comet Group
Position
Development director
Contact details
Comet Group plc, Meridian North, Leicester LE19 1WR
Tel 01923 710000
Fax 01923 714420
Web www.comet.co.uk
Email peter.mctague@comet.co.uk

MEADE, Karl
Warner Estate Holdings
Position
Property – associate director
Qualifications
MRICS
Contact details
Warner Estate Holdings plc, Nations House, 103 Wigmore Street, London W1U 1AE
Tel 020 7907 5100
Fax 020 7907 5102
Web www.warnerestate.co.uk
Email karlmeade@weh-plc.co.uk

MEADOWS, Russell
Rogers Chapman
Position
Director – national investment and development
Contact details
Rogers Chapman plc, Prince Frederick House, 37 Maddox Street, London W1S 2PP
Tel 020 7499 8600
Fax 020 7493 5290
Web www.rogerschapman.co.uk
Email russell.meadows@rogerschapman.co.uk

MEAGER, Thomas
Associated British Foods
Position
Head of property – Primark and Penneys
Qualifications
BSc Hons; MRICS
Career history
1998-2003 Marks & Spencer: joined as UK development manager; became head of property development in 2001.
1996-98 Property development manager, Lidl UK Assets.
1989-96 Chesterton International: became associate director in 1994
Professional memberships
RICS
Interests
Family; golf; rugby; sport; tennis
Contact details
Associated British Foods plc, 50-51 Russell Square, London WC1B 4JA
Tel 020 7299 3638
Fax 020 7299 3630
Web www.abf.co.uk
Mobile 07771 807533
Email thomasmeager@abfoods.com

MEAKIN, Alan
Crown Estate
Position
Head of Regent Street estate management
Contact details
Crown Estate, 16 Carlton House Terrace, London SW1Y 5AH
Tel 020 7210 4377
Fax 020 7210 4236
Web www.crownestate.co.uk
Email alan.meakin@crownestate.co.uk

MEARES, Nigel
11 Stone Buildings
Position
Barrister
Qualifications
BA (Cantab)

Career history

1975 Called to Bar

Contact details

11 Stone Buildings, London WC2A 3TG
Tel 020 7831 6381
Fax 020 7831 2575
Web www.11stonebuildings.com
Email meares@11stonebuildings.com

MEARS, David
Laytons

Position

Chairman – national property and construction group

Qualifications

BSc; Solicitor

Career history

1988 Joined Laytons; appointed partner in 1990 and national head of commercial property in 2001; chairman of national property and construction group since 2003.
1982-88 Principal, David Mears & Co.
1977-82 Solicitor/partner, Barry & Blott.
1977 Admitted to Roll of Solicitors

Professional memberships

Law Society

Interests

Cycling; hill walking; motorcycling

Contact details

Laytons, St Bartholomews, Lewins Mead, Bristol BS1 2NH
Tel 0117 930 9500
Fax 0117 929 3369
Web www.laytons.com
Email david.mears@laytons.com

MEECH, Martin
Dixons Group Retail Properties

Position

Managing director

Qualifications

BSc Hons; FRICS

Other roles

Group property managing director, Dixons Stores Group; non-executive director, Quintain Estates & Development; non-executive director, Holborn Public Relations

Professional memberships

British Retail Consortium; RICS

Contact details

Dixons Group Retail Properties Ltd, Maylands Avenue, Hemel Hempstead HP2 7TG
Tel 0870 850 3333
Fax 01727 233218
Direct tel 01727 205858
Mobile 07702 684256
Email martin.meech@dixons.co.uk

MEIRE, Tony
Cluttons

Position

Partner – expert witness

Qualifications

FRICS

Career history

1973 Joined Cluttons; London and Canterbury; Maidstone since 2001.
1971-73 Richard Saunders & Partners, London.
1964-71 Richard Ellis & Son, London

Other roles

Member of RICS president's panel acting as arbitrator, independent expert or expert witness in both county court and High Court on valuation and other property-related matters

Contact details

Cluttons, 26-28 Albion Place, Maidstone ME14 5DZ
Tel 01622 756000
Fax 01622 695536
Web www.cluttons.com
Direct tel 01622 607436
Email ameire@cluttons.com

MELLISH, Richard
Compco Holdings

Position

Finance director

Contact details

Compco Holdings plc, De Walden Court, 85 New Cavendish Street, London W1W 6XD
Tel 020 7436 0198
Fax 020 7436 0094
Email rmellish@compco.co.uk

MELLISS, Simon
Hammerson

Position

Group finance director

Qualifications

BA; FCA

Contact details

Hammerson plc, 100 Park Lane, London W1K 7AR
Tel 020 7887 1000
Fax 020 7887 1010
Web www.hammerson.co.uk
Email smelliss@hammerson.co.uk

MENZIES, Alan
Anderson Strathern WS

Position

Chairman and head of commercial property

Qualifications

LLB

Career history

1973 Joined Anderson Strathern WS as commercial property assistant; appointed partner in 1975.
1972 Admitted to Roll of Solicitors

Other roles

Holds personal appointment of Crown Estate Solicitor (Scotland)

Professional memberships

Institute of Directors; Investment Property Forum; Law Society of Scotland; WS Society

Interests

Golf

Contact details

Anderson Strathern WS, 48 Castle Street, Edinburgh EH2 3LX
Tel 0131 220 2345
Fax 0131 226 7788
Web www.andersonstrathern.co.uk
Direct tel 0131 625 7241
Direct fax 0131 225 5994
Mobile 07761 406770
Email alan.menzies@andersonstrathern.co.uk

MERCER, Christopher
Chris Mercer Associates

Position

Principal

Career history

1987-2000 Partner (residential agency), Allsop & Co

Professional memberships

Residential Development Agents Society

Interests

Badminton; fishing; food and drink; squash; wine

Contact details

Chris Mercer Associates, 19 Princes Street, London W1B 2LW
Tel 020 7408 2272
Fax 020 7408 2448
Web www.chrismercer.co.uk
Direct fax 020 7493 4970
Mobile 07860 750641
Email chris@chrismercer.co.uk

MERRY, Simon
King Sturge

Position

Partner – head of investment, Manchester

Qualifications

BSc; MRICS

Professional memberships

RICS

Contact details

King Sturge, 81 Fountain Street, Manchester M2 2EE
Tel 0161 236 8793

M

Fax 0161 228 7972
Web www.kingsturge.com
Email simon.merry@kingsturge.co.uk

MERSH, Kevin
Nelson Bakewell

Position
Director – head of national agency
Qualifications
BSc; FRICS
Career history
Since 2000 Director, Nelson Bakewell.
1993-2000 Director, Leighton Goldhill.
1988-93 Associate director, Pepper Angliss & Yarwood.
1986-88 Lambert Smith Hampton
Other roles
Appointed as LPA receiver on commercial and residential properties for some of UK's largest banks
Professional memberships
RICS
Interests
Football; golf; horse riding; sport; tennis
Contact details
Nelson Bakewell Ltd, 25 Sackville Street, London W1S 3HQ
Tel 020 7544 2000
Fax 020 7544 2222
Web www.nelson-bakewell.com
Direct tel 020 7544 2214
Mobile 07767 887853
Email kmersh@nelson-bakewell.com

METLISS, Cyril
British Land Corp

Position
Executive vice-chairman
Qualifications
FCA
Contact details
British Land Corp Ltd, 10 Cornwall Terrace, London NW1 4QP
Tel 020 7486 4466
Web www.britishland.com
Email cyril.metliss@britishland.com

METLISS, Michael
SJ Berwin

Position
Partner – property litigation
Qualifications
BA Hons
Career history
1987 Joined SJ Berwin & Co; became partner in 1991.
1984 Admitted to Roll of Solicitors
Other roles
Articles published in *Estate Gazette*, *Property Week* and *Property Law Journal*; has lectured to IBC UK and Central Law Training conferences, Property Managers Association and RICS
Interests
Cinema; football; golf; music
Contact details
SJ Berwin, 222 Gray's Inn Road, London WC1X 8HB
Tel 020 7533 2222
Fax 020 7533 2000
Web www.sjberwin.com
Direct tel 020 7533 2235
Email michael.metliss@sjberwin.com

MEW, Steven
McKay Securities

Position
Director
Contact details
McKay Securities plc, 20-30 Greyfriars Road, Reading RG1 1PE
Tel 0118 950 2333
Fax 0118 939 1393
Email steven.mew@mckaysecurities.plc.uk

MEYER, Steven
ProLogis Developments

Position
President and chief operating officer – Europe
Qualifications
BBA; MBA
Career history
1994 Joined ProLogis as managing director (central and Mexico region); now president and chief operating officer for ProLogis European operations.
1979-94 Director of leasing and development, Trammell Crow Co, Dallas industrial division
Professional memberships
National Association of Industrial & Office Properties; Salesmanship Club, Dallas; Society of Industrial & Office Realtors (developer associate)
Contact details
ProLogis Developments Ltd, Capronilaan 25-27, 1119 NP Schiphol-Rijk, Amsterdam, Netherlands
Tel +31 20 655 6666
Fax +31 20 655 6656
Web www.prologis.com
Direct tel +31 20 655 6626
Mobile +31 6 206 23890
Email rwatson@prologis.com

MEYLER, Helen
Campbell Hooper

Position
Partner – head of commercial property
Qualifications
LLB
Career history
1993 Joined Campbell Hooper.
1985-93 Herbert Smith.
1983-85 Jacques & Lewis, London.
1980-83 Rea Grundberg.
1980 Admitted to Roll of Solicitors.
1978-80 Clarkes
Professional memberships
British Council of Shopping Centres
Interests
Sailing; skiing; tennis; walking; RAC; Sub Aqua Club
Contact details
Campbell Hooper, 35 Old Queen Street, London SW1H 9JD
Tel 020 7222 9070
Fax 020 7222 5591
Web www.campbellhooper.com
Direct tel 020 7654 5107
Email helenmeyler@campbellhooper.com

MILES-BROWN, Stephan
Knight Frank

Position
Principal – head of residential development group
Career history
1986 Joined Knight Frank; promoted to associate in 1987, partner in 1988 and principal in 1993
Other roles
Chairman of firm's residential development group
Contact details
Knight Frank LLP, Granville House, 132-135 Sloane Street, London SW1X 9AX
Tel 020 7598 4000
Fax 020 7598 4001
Web www.knightfrank.com
Direct tel 020 7598 4002
Mobile 07836 630836
Email stephan.miles-brown@knightfrank.com

MILLAR, Simon
Enterprise Inns

Position
Head of estates
Contact details
Enterprise Inns plc, Cranmore Avenue, Shirley B90 4LE
Tel 0121 733 7700
Fax 0121 733 6447

Web www.enterpriseinns.com
Direct fax 0121 256 3434
Mobile 07990 550104
Email simon.millar@enterpriseinns.plc.uk

MILLER, Charles
King Sturge

Position
Partner – head of national retail agency
Qualifications
BSc; MRICS
Professional memberships
RICS
Contact details
King Sturge, 7 Stratford Place, London W1C 1ST
Tel 020 7493 4933
Fax 020 7409 0469
Web www.kingsturge.com
Direct tel 020 7318 4316
Direct fax 020 7493 3581
Email charles.miller@kingsturge.co.uk

MILLER, Elspeth
Crown Estate

Position
Head of central London estates
Qualifications
BSc Hons; MRICS
Professional memberships
RICS
Contact details
Crown Estate, 16 Carlton House Terrace, London SW1Y 5AH
Tel 020 7210 4377
Fax 020 7210 4236
Web www.crownestate.co.uk
Direct tel 020 7210 4247
Direct fax 020 7930 8202
Email elspeth.miller@crownestate.co.uk

MILLER, Richard
Harvey Ingram Owston

Position
Partner – head of property
Career history
Since 1979 Harvey Ingram Owston; became partner in 1987.
1978 Admitted to Roll of Solicitors.
1976-78 Owston & Co
Professional memberships
Law Society; Leicestershire Law Society
Interests
Football; golf; Rotary; rugby
Contact details
Harvey Ingram Owston, 20 New Walk, Leicester LE1 6TX
Tel 0116 254 5454
Fax 0116 255 4559
Web www.hio.co.uk
Mobile 07761 959192
Email rfm@hio.co.uk

MILLETT, Paul
Finers Stephens Innocent

Position
Partner – head of corporate and commercial department
Career history
Since 1997 Partner, Finers Stephens Innocent.
1989-97 Mishcon de Reya: became partner in 1991.
1986-89 Speechly Bircham.
1986 Admitted to Roll of Solicitors
Contact details
Finers Stephens Innocent, 179 Great Portland Street, London W1W 5LS
Tel 020 7323 4000
Fax 020 7344 5600
Web www.finersstephensinnocent.com
Direct tel 020 7344 5516
Direct fax 020 7344 5602
Email pmillett@fsilaw.co.uk

MILLS, Ray
PricewaterhouseCoopers

Position
Partner – inward investment
Contact details
PricewaterhouseCoopers, Southwark Towers, 32 London Bridge Street, London SE1 9AE
Tel 020 7583 5000
Web www.pwc.com
Email ray.mills@uk.pwcglobal.com

MILLS, Simon
5 Paper Buildings

Position
Barrister
Qualifications
MA (Cantab)
Career history
1994 Called to Bar
Professional memberships
Property Bar Association
Contact details
5 Paper Buildings (Chambers of Richard King QC), Ground Floor, London EC4Y 7HB
Tel 020 7815 3200
Fax 020 7815 3201
Web www.5paper.com
Mobile 01793 673106
Email simonmills@5paper.com

MILLS, Tracey
Davis Coffer Lyons

Position
Director – agency department
Qualifications
BSc, Est Man; MRICS; MRPAS
Career history
Since 1993 Director, Davis Coffer Lyons.
1984-93 Associate partner, Kemsley Whiteley & Ferris
Professional memberships
RICS
Interests
Wine
Contact details
Davis Coffer Lyons Ltd, 52 Portland Place, London W1B 1NH
Tel 020 7299 0700
Fax 020 7299 0710
Web www.daviscofferlyons.co.uk
Direct tel 020 7299 0744
Mobile 07771 667060
Email tmills@daviscofferlyons.co.uk

MILNE, Julian
Grosvenor

Position
Commercial director (London)
Contact details
Grosvenor Ltd, 70 Grosvenor Street, London W1K 3JP
Tel 020 7408 0988
Fax 020 7629 9115
Web www.grosvenor.com
Email julian.milne@grosvenor.com

MILNER, Michael
Edwin Hill

Position
Partner
Qualifications
BSc; MRICS
Career history
1979 Joined Edwin Hill
Professional memberships
RICS
Contact details
Edwin Hill, 18 Savile Row, London W1S 3PW
Tel 020 7287 2020
Fax 020 7734 1255
Web www.edwinhill.co.uk
Email msm@edwinhill.co.uk

MILNER, Pauline
Groupe Chez Gerard

Position
Development director

Contact details

Groupe Chez Gerard plc, 8 Shelton Street, London WC2H 9JR

Tel 020 7881 8870

Web www.chezgerard.co.uk

Email pauline.m@groupechezgerard.co.uk

MILTON, Claire
Berwin Leighton Paisner

Position

Partner – deputy head of real estate group

Qualifications

LLB Hons

Career history

1986 Joined property department of Berwin Leighton (now Berwin Leighton Paisner); became partner in 1989.

1983-86 Forsyte Kerman.

1983 Admitted to Roll of Solicitors

Professional memberships

British Council of Shopping Centres; Investment Property Forum

Interests

Food; skiing; walking; wine

Contact details

Berwin Leighton Paisner Ltd, Adelaide House, London Bridge, London EC4R 9HA

Tel 020 7760 1000

Fax 020 7760 1111

Web www.berwinleighton.com

Email claire.milton@blplaw.com

MILTON, Neil
Bank of Scotland Corporate Banking

Position

Director – structured property finance

Qualifications

MRICS

Career history

1998-2000 Precis Properties.

1994-98 United Bank of Kuwait.

1986-94 Canadian Imperial Bank of Commerce.

1984-86 Surveyor, County Bank.

1979-83 Surveyor, Abbey Life

Professional memberships

Investment Property Forum; RICS

Interests

Rugby

Contact details

Bank of Scotland Corporate Banking, 155 Bishopsgate, London EC2M 3YB

Tel 020 7012 9400

Direct tel 020 7012 9130

Direct fax 020 7012 9445

Email neil_milton@bankofscotland.co.uk

MILWARD, Jon
Drivers Jonas

Position

Partner – development

Qualifications

BSc Hons; MRICS; MRTPI; Dip TP

Career history

Since 1988 Partner, Drivers Jonas.

1986-87 JR Eve

Professional memberships

RICS; RTPI

Interests

Golf; tennis; travel

Contact details

Drivers Jonas, 6 Grosvenor Street, London W1K 4DJ

Tel 020 7896 8000

Fax 020 7896 8001

Web www.driversjonas.com

Direct tel 020 7896 8223

Mobile 07771 898319

Email jonmilward@driversjonas.com

MINKS, John
Jones Lang LaSalle

Position

Chief executive officer – corporate solutions, Europe

Qualifications

MBA, Finance & Accounting

Other roles

Member of management executive committee and European management board, Jones Lang LaSalle

Professional memberships

CoreNet Global

Interests

Golf; photography; skiing; tennis

Contact details

Jones Lang LaSalle Ltd, 22 Hanover Square London W1A 2BN

Tel 020 7493 6040

Fax 020 7408 0220

Web www.joneslanglasalle.com

Direct tel 020 7399 5699

Direct fax 020 7399 5678

Mobile 07799 658890

Email john.minks@eu.joneslanglasalle.com

MINOGUE, Ann
Linklaters

Position

Partner – real estate

Career history

Since 2001 Partner, Linklaters.

1978-2001 McKenna & Co (now CMS Cameron McKenna); partner from 1985

Professional memberships

Anglo-American Real Property Institute; British Council for Offices; BPF

Interests

Contemporary dance; tennis

Contact details

Linklaters, 1 Silk Street, London EC2Y 8HQ

Tel 020 7456 2000

Fax 020 7456 2222

Web www.linklaters.com

Direct tel 020 7456 4891

Email ann.minogue@linklaters.com

MISSELBROOK, Peter
Tods Murray WS

Position

Chairman

Qualifications

LLB

Career history

Since 1996 Partner, Tods Murray WS.

1987 Admitted to Roll of Solicitors.

1981-96 Partner, J+A Hastie SSC.

1976-81 Maclay Murray & Spens

Other roles

Past chairman, British Association for Shooting & Conservation and legal adviser to BASC (Scotland); former member, Home Office firearms consultative committee; past president, Federation des Associations de Chasseurs de l'UE; member, High Constables and Guard of Honour of Holyroodhouse; executive of council, Royal Zoological Society of Scotland

Interests

Fishing; gardening; golf; hill walking; reading; shooting; tennis

Contact details

Tods Murray WS, 66 Queen Street, Edinburgh EH2 4NE

Tel 0131 226 4771

Fax 0131 225 3676

Web www.todsmurray.com

Direct fax 0131 225 7646

Mobile 07770 472435

Email peter.misselbrook@todsmurray.com

MITCHELL, David
Taylor Woodrow Developments

Position

Development director – Scotland

Qualifications

BSc; MRICS; Dip Prop Inv

Other roles

Director, Southside Capital; director, Strada

Professional memberships

RICS

Contact details

Taylor Woodrow Developments Ltd, 2 Garbett Road, Livingston EH54 7DL
Tel 01506 405700
Fax 01506 405704
Web www.taylorwoodrow.com
Mobile 07816 511012
Email david.mitchell@uk.taylorwoodrow.com

MITCHELL, Kieran
Montagu Evans

Position
Partner and head of department – investment
Qualifications
BSc; MRICS
Career history
1994 Joined Montagu Evans as investment partner; appointed head of investment department in 1998.
1983-94 Gooch & Wagstaff (now Gooch Webster); joined as investment surveyor; became associate partner in 1987 and investment partner in 1989.
1981-83 King & Co
Professional memberships
RICS
Interests
Current affairs; golf; rugby; RAC
Contact details
Montagu Evans, 44-48 Dover Street, London W1S 4AZ
Tel 020 7493 4002
Fax 020 7312 7547
Web www.montagu-evans.co.uk
Direct tel 020 7312 7440
Direct fax 020 7312 7549
Mobile 07818 012440
Email kieran.mitchell@montagu-evans.co.uk

MITCHELL, Paul
Prudential Property Investment Managers

Position
Director – property research
Qualifications
BA Hons, Econ; MSc, Econ
Career history
1987-90 Chief economist, London Chamber of Commerce.
1983-87 Research associate, Technical Change Centre
Professional memberships
Investment Property Forum; Society of Property Researchers
Contact details
Prudential Property Investment Managers Ltd, Princeton House, 271-273 High Holborn, London WC1V 7NE
Tel 020 7548 6600
Fax 020 7548 6999
Web www.prupim.com
Direct tel 020 7548 6863
Direct fax 020 7548 6502
Email paul.mitchell@prupim.com

MITCHELL, Robin
Norton Rose

Position
Partner – head of property department
Career history
1980 Admitted to Roll of Solicitors
Professional memberships
Law Society
Interests
Golf; hockey
Contact details
Norton Rose, Kempson House, Camomile Street, London EC3A 7AN
Tel 020 7283 6000
Fax 020 7283 6500
Web www.nortonrose.com
Email robin.mitchell@nortonrose.com

MITCHELL, Tim
UNITE Group

Position
Regional development director
Qualifications
BSc Hons; MRICS
Career history
1994-2000 Director, Chesterton.
1987-94 Associate partner, Donaldsons
Professional memberships
RICS
Interests
Bee keeping; cycling; mountain biking; sailing; windsurfing
Contact details
UNITE Group plc, Protheroes House, Denmark Street, Bristol BS1 5EJ
Tel 0117 917 2950
Fax 0117 917 2955
Web www.unite-group.com
Mobile 07967 221591
Email tim.mitchell@unite-group.co.uk

MITCHENALL, Neil
Lunson Mitchenall

Position
Senior director
Career history
1969-80 Director, Edward Erdman.
1967-68 Management surveyor, Cluttons
Other roles
Past president, British Council of Shopping Centres (2001-02); member of British Council of Shopping Centres Awards jury (1993-2000), including jury chairman (1998-2000); chairman, International Council of Shopping Centers European Awards jury (1999-2001)
Professional memberships
International Council of Shopping Centers; Urban Land Institute
Interests
Art; rugby; shooting
Contact details
Lunson Mitchenall Ltd, 33 Cork Street, London W1S 3NQ
Tel 020 7478 4950
Fax 020 7491 2344
Web www.lunson-mitchenall.co.uk
Email neilm@lunson-mitchenall.co.uk

MITSOSTERGIOU, Eri
FPDSavills

Position
Associate
Qualifications
BSc Arch; MSc; Dip IPF
Professional memberships
Society of Property Researchers
Contact details
FPDSavills Ltd, 20 Grosvenor Hill, London W1K 3HQ
Tel 020 7499 8644
Fax 020 7495 3773
Web www.fpdsavills.co.uk
Direct tel 020 7409 8791
Direct fax 020 7753 8919
Mobile 07967 555739
Email emitso@fpdsavills.co.uk

MITTON, Chip
Edwin Hill

Position
Partner
Career history
1998 Joined Edwin Hill. Prior to that, Conran Roche, King Sturge and Chesterton
Professional memberships
Industrial Agents Society
Contact details
Edwin Hill, St Johns House, Dartford DA1 2DR
Tel 01322 285588
Fax 01322 285599
Web www.edwinhill.co.uk
Email chip@edwinhill.co.uk

MOBBS, Sir Nigel
Slough Estates

Position
Chairman
Career history

M

1960 Joined Slough Estates (grandfather was a founder); became executive director in 1963, then chairman and chief executive in 1976; executive chairman 1996-99

Other roles

Chairman of trustees, Historic Royal Palaces; non-executive director, Howard De Walden Estates; chairman, Bovis Homes Group; Lord Lieutenant of Buckinghamshire; member, Fifth Advisory Committee on Business & the Environment

Professional memberships

British Council for Offices; BPF; Institute of Directors; Investment Property Forum; RICS (honorary member)

Contact details

Slough Estates plc, 234 Bath Road, Slough SL1 4EE
Tel 01753 537171
Fax 01753 820585
Web www.sloughestates.com
Email anne.baker@sloughestates.co.uk

MOCATTA, Charles
FPDSavills

Position

Director

Contact details

FPDSavills Ltd, 20 Grosvenor Hill, London W1K 3HQ
Tel 020 7499 8644
Fax 020 7495 3773
Web www.fpdsavills.co.uk
Direct tel 020 7409 8726
Mobile 07977 071124
Email cmocatta@fpdsavills.co.uk

MOGRIDGE, Lee
Lambert Smith Hampton

Position

Director

Qualifications

BSc Hons, Land Admin; MRICS

Career history

Since 1997 Director, Lambert Smith Hampton.
1989-97 Associate partner, Alexander & Co

Professional memberships

RICS

Contact details

Lambert Smith Hampton Ltd, Longcross Court, 47 Newport Road, Cardiff CF24 0AD
Tel 029 2049 0499
Fax 029 2045 4235
Web www.lsh.co.uk
Mobile 07768 480934
Email lmogridge@lsh.co.uk

MOGULL, Marc
Doughty Hanson & Co

Position

Managing director – real estate fund

Contact details

Doughty Hanson & Co Ltd, Times Place, 45 Pall Mall, London SW1Y 5JG
Tel 020 7663 9300
Fax 020 7747 9342
Web www.doughtyhanson.com
Email marc.mogull@doughtyhanson.com

MOIR, Duncan
Allsop & Co

Position

Partner – auctioneer

Qualifications

MA

Career history

Since 1986 Auctioneer/partner, Allsop & Co.
1983-86 Storey Sons & Parker, Newcastle upon Tyne

Other roles

Honorary secretary, Select Society of Auctioneers

Contact details

Allsop & Co, 27 Soho Square, London W1D 3AY
Tel 020 7437 6977
Fax 020 7437 8984
Web www.allsop.co.uk
Direct tel 020 7543 6704
Mobile 07836 241306
Email duncan.moir@allsop.co.uk

MOLLOY, Nicholas
Lisney

Position

Director

Qualifications

FSCS; FRICS

Professional memberships

RICS

Contact details

Lisney, 24 St Stephen's Green, Dublin
Tel +353 1 638 2700
Fax +353 1 638 2706
Web www.lisney.com
Direct tel +353 1 638 2754
Email nmolloy@lisney.com

MONCKTON-MILNES, Peter
NAI Fuller Peiser

Position

Partner – head of specialist sector

Contact details

NAI Fuller Peiser, Belgrave House, 47 Bank Street, Sheffield S1 2DR
Tel 0870 700 2233
Fax 0114 275 2565
Web www.nai-fullerpeiser.com
Email pmonckton-milnes@nai-fullerpeiser.com

MONK, Bill
Jones Lang LaSalle

Position

International director – corporate solutions

Qualifications

MRICS

Career history

1972 Joined Jones Lang LaSalle; became partner in 1985; international director (corporate solutions) since 1990

Professional memberships

CoreNet Global UK; RICS

Interests

Golf; music; tennis

Contact details

Jones Lang LaSalle Ltd, 22 Hanover Square, London W1A 2BN
Tel 020 7493 6040
Fax 020 7408 0220
Web www.joneslanglasalle.com
Direct tel 020 7399 5334
Direct fax 020 7493 5536
Mobile 07770 306041
Email bill.monk@eu.joneslanglasalle.com

MONK, Chris
King Sturge

Position

Partner in charge, Birmingham

Qualifications

BSc; FRICS

Other roles

Chairman, Birmingham Forward

Professional memberships

RICS; Society of Industrial & Office Realtors (international affiliate)

Contact details

King Sturge, 1 Cornwall Street, Birmingham B3 2DT
Tel 0121 233 2898
Fax 0121 236 2563
Web www.kingsturge.com
Email chris.monk@kingsturge.co.uk

MONK, Stuart
Jomast Property & Finance Co

Position

Managing director

Contact details

Jomast Property & Finance Co Ltd, Oriel House, Calverts Lane, Stockton-on-Tees TS18 1SW
Tel 0164 267 4203
Email stuart@jomast.co.uk

M

MONTAGUE, Paul
Alder King

Position
Partner
Contact details
Alder King, Pembroke House, 15 Pembroke Road, Bristol BS8 3BA
Tel 0117 317 1000
Fax 0117 317 1001
Web www.alderking.com
Email pmontague@alderking.com

MOODY, James
DTZ Residential

Position
Director – residential
Qualifications
MRICS; BSc Hons
Professional memberships
RICS
Interests
Diving; golf; sailing; snowboarding; tennis
Contact details
DTZ Residential, 1 Curzon Street, London W1A 5PZ
Tel 020 7408 1161
Fax 020 7643 6000
Web www.dtzresidential.co.uk
Direct tel 020 7643 6321
Direct fax 020 7643 6323
Email james.moody@dtz.com

MOODY, Matthew
Lambert Smith Hampton

Position
Chief executive, Bristol
Qualifications
MRICS
Career history
Since 2000 Chief executive (Bristol), Lambert Smith Hampton.
1994-2000 Associate director, DTZ.
1988-94 Hartnell Taylor Cook
Professional memberships
Bristol Property Agents' Association; Shop Agents Society
Interests
Family; football; golf; sport; tennis
Contact details
Lambert Smith Hampton Ltd, 51-55 Whiteladies Road, Bristol BS8 2LY
Tel 0117 926 6666
Fax 0117 925 0527
Web www.lsh.co.uk
Direct tel 0117 914 2138
Mobile 07720 349505
Email mmoody@lsh.co.uk

MOORCROFT, Ian
Ashcroft Estates

Position
Director
Contact details
Ashcroft Estates plc, Ashcroft House, 162-166 Fulham Palace Road, London W6 9PA
Tel 020 8741 7411
Fax 020 8741 7758
Email moorcroft@ashcroft.co.uk

MOORE, Gregory
Chase & Partners

Position
Director
Qualifications
FRICS
Career history
Since 1995 Director, Chase & Partners.
1992-95 Director, Erdman Lewis.
1983-92 Associate, Clive Lewis & Partners
Other roles
Chairman, British Council for Out of Town Retail (2000–01)
Professional memberships
RICS
Interests
Cricket; golf
Contact details
Chase & Partners Ltd, 20 Regent Street, London SW1Y 4PH
Tel 020 7389 9494
Fax 020 7389 9456
Web www.chaseandpartners.com
Email gregory.moore@chaseandpartners.co.uk

MOORE, Martin
Prudential Property Investment Managers

Position
Managing director
Qualifications
MRICS
Career history
1974 Joined Prudential Property Investment Managers
Other roles
Crown Estate commissioner; founding director, New West End Co; junior vice-president, BPF; past chairman, Westminster Property Owners Association; past chairman of management board, Investment Property Form; design review panel member, Commission for Architecture & the Built Environment
Professional memberships
BPF; RICS; Westminster Property Owners Association
Contact details
Prudential Property Investment Managers Ltd, Princeton House, 271-273 High Holborn, London WC1V 7NE
Tel 020 7548 6600
Fax 020 7548 6999
Web www.prupim.com
Direct tel 020 7548 6571
Direct fax 020 7548 6313
Email martin.moore@prupim.com

MOORE, Richard
Warner Estate Holdings

Position
Property director
Qualifications
FRICS
Professional memberships
RICS
Contact details
Warner Estate Holdings plc, Nations House, 103 Wigmore Street, London W1U 1AE
Tel 020 7907 5100
Fax 020 7907 5102
Web www.warnerestate.co.uk
Email richardmoore@weh-plc.co.uk

MOORE, Roger
Eurohypo

Position
Consultant – real estate division
Qualifications
CDip AF; ASIP
Career history
1973-99 Property analyst, Rowe & Pitman/ SG Warburg/SBC Warburg Dillon Read.
1968-73 General analyst, Read Hurst-Brown
Other roles
Non-executive director, Arlington Securities; consultant, Hemingway Properties, Manly International
Professional memberships
Investment Property Forum; Society of Investment Professionals
Contact details
Eurohypo AG, 90 Long Acre, London WC2E 9RA
Tel 020 7759 7600
Fax 020 7759 7672
Web www.eurohypo.com
Direct tel 01707 646663
Email ri.moore@virgin.net

MORAN, Paul
Mason Owen & Partners

Position
Managing partner
Qualifications

MRICS
Career history
1991 Joined Mason Owen.
1989-91 Edmund Kirby, Liverpool.
1975-89 Valuation Office, Inland Revenue
Professional memberships
Compulsory Purchase Association; Rating Surveyors Association; RICS
Interests
Music; photography; reading
Contact details
Mason Owen & Partners Ltd, Gladstone House, 11 Union Court, Liverpool L2 4UQ
Tel 0151 242 3000
Fax 0151 236 2569
Web www.masonowen.com
Direct tel 0151 242 3032
Direct fax 0151 227 1477
Mobile 07767 312443
Email paul.moran@masonowen.com

MORGAN, Charles
Enterprise Chambers
Position
Barrister
Qualifications
MA (Cantab); FCIArb
Career history
Since 1992 Barrister, Enterprise Chambers.
1978-92 Barrister, Trinity Chambers, Newcastle upon Tyne.
1978 Called to Bar
Professional memberships
Bar European Group; Chancery Bar Association; Chartered Institute of Arbitrators; Honourable Society of Middle Temple; Northern Chancery Bar Association; Property Bar Association
Interests
Music
Contact details
Enterprise Chambers (Chambers of Anthony Mann QC), 65 Quayside, Newcastle upon Tyne NE1 3DS
Tel 0191 222 3344
Fax 0191 222 3340
Web www.enterprisechambers.com
Email mail@charlesmorgan.co.uk

MORGAN, Don
Gazeley Properties
Position
Planning and development director
Contact details
Gazeley Properties Ltd, Gazeley House, 26 Rockingham Drive, Milton Keynes MK14 6PD
Tel 01908 838100
Fax 01908 838101
Web www.gazeley.com
Email don_morgan@gazeley.co.uk

MORGAN, Ian
Allsop & Co
Position
Partner – head of commercial valuation department
Qualifications
FRICS
Career history
1973 Joined Allsop & Co; partner since 1980.
1971-73 Surveyor, Greater London Council
Professional memberships
Non-Administrative Receivers Association; RICS
Interests
Skiing
Contact details
Allsop & Co, 27 Soho Square, London W1D 3AY
Tel 020 7437 6977
Fax 020 7437 8984
Web www.allsop.co.uk
Direct tel 020 7543 6733
Email ian.morgan@allsop.co.uk

MORGAN, John
Bucknall Austin
Position
Chief executive
Qualifications
FRICS
Contact details
Bucknall Austin Ltd, Millennium Point, Howe Street, Birmingham B4 7XG
Tel 0121 503 1500
Fax 0121 503 1501
Web www.bucknall.com
Email john.morgan@bucknall.com

MORGAN, Lindsay
Norton Rose
Position
Partner – head of international real estate
Qualifications
LLB Hons
Career history
1982 Admitted to Roll of Solicitors
Professional memberships
City of London Solicitors Company; Law Society; Women in Property
Interests
Cooking; family; walking
Contact details
Norton Rose, Kempson House, Camomile Street, London EC3A 7AN
Tel 020 7283 6000
Fax 020 7283 6500
Web www.nortonrose.com
Email lindsay.morgan@nortonrose.com

MORGAN, Malcolm
Morgan Williams
Position
Partner
Contact details
Morgan Williams, Central House, Central Way, Warrington WA2 7TT
Tel 01925 414909
Fax 01925 637619
Email mmorgan@morganwilliams.biz

MORGAN, Nicholas
Kitchen La Frenais Morgan
Position
Partner
Qualifications
FRICS
Career history
1976-90 Clive Lewis & Partners: progressed to partner and head of shop department.
1971-73 Shop negotiator, Edward Erdman & Co
Professional memberships
FIABCI; RICS; Shop Agents Society
Interests
Football; golf; rugby; sport; squash; tennis
Contact details
Kitchen La Frenais Morgan, 1 Tenterden Street, London W1S 1TA
Tel 020 7317 3700
Fax 020 7317 3701
Web www.klmproperty.co.uk
Email nmorgan@klmproperty.co.uk

MORGAN, Paul
Falcon Chambers
Position
QC
Qualifications
MA (Cantab); QC
Career history
1992 Appointed QC
1975 Called to Bar
Other roles
Deputy chairman, Agricultural Land Tribunal; deputy High Court judge
Professional memberships
Agricultural Law Association; Chancery Bar Association; London Common Law & Commercial Bar Association
Interests
Opera; skiing
Contact details

Falcon Chambers, Falcon Court, London EC4Y 1AA
Tel 020 7353 2484
Fax 020 7353 1261
Web www.falcon-chambers.com
Email morgan@falcon-chambers.com

MORGAN, Richard
Insight Investment Management

Position
Director – property investment
Qualifications
MRICS
Professional memberships
RICS
Contact details
Insight Investment Management, 33 Old Broad Street, London EC2N 1HZ
Tel 020 7930 5474
Fax 020 7321 1423
Web www.insightinvestment.com
Direct tel 020 7321 1025
Direct fax 020 7321 1434
Mobile 07787 152357
Email richard.morgan@insightinvestment.com

MORGAN, Richard
Maitland Chambers

Position
Barrister
Qualifications
LLB; LLM
Career history
1988 Called to Bar
Professional memberships
Chancery Bar Association; Commercial Bar Association
Interests
Cars; rowing; science
Contact details
Maitland Chambers, 7 Stone Buildings, London WC2A 3SZ
Tel 020 7406 1200
Fax 020 7406 1300
Web www.maitlandchambers.com
Email rmorgan@maitlandchambers.com

MORGAN, Roland
GVA Grimley

Position
Partner
Contact details
GVA Grimley, 25 Bucklersbury, London EC4N 8DA
Tel 0870 900 8990
Fax 020 7911 2846
Web www.gvagrimley.co.uk
Direct tel 020 7911 2801
Email roland.morgan@gvagrimley.co.uk

MORGAN, Stephen
Akeler Developments

Position
Director
Professional memberships
British Council for Offices
Contact details
Akeler Developments Ltd, 7 Clifford Street, London W1S 2WE
Tel 020 7864 1800
Fax 020 7864 1801
Web www.akeler.com
Mobile 07771 551482
Email stephenm@akeler.com

MORGAN, Stephen
Landmark Chambers

Position
Barrister
Contact details
Landmark Chambers, 4 Breams Buildings, London EC4A 1AQ
Tel 020 7430 1221
Fax 020 7421 1399
Web www.landmarkchambers.co.uk
Email clerks@landmarkchambers.co.uk

MORIARTY, Steve
M3

Position
Partner
Contact details
M3, 58 Queen Anne Street, London W1G 8HW
Tel 020 7935 3969
Fax 020 7935 4338
Email steve@milnermoffitt.co.uk

MORLEY, Christopher
British Property Federation

Position
Director – planning and construction
Qualifications
BSc Hons
Career history
Since 1999 Director, British Property Federation. Background in trade association work and consultancy
Interests
Classical music; sport
Contact details
British Property Federation, 1 Warwick Row, London SW1E 5ER
Tel 020 7828 0111
Fax 020 7834 3442
Web www.bpf.org.uk
Direct tel 020 7802 0107
Email cmorley@bpf.org.uk

MORLEY, Giles
LaSalle Investment Management

Position
European director
Contact details
LaSalle Investment Management, 33 Cavendish Square, London W1A 2NF
Tel 020 7852 4000
Fax 020 7852 4374
Web www.lasalle.com
Direct tel 020 7533 7562
Direct fax 020 7533 7411
Email giles.morley@lasalle.com

MORLEY, Stuart
GVA Grimley

Position
Research partner
Qualifications
MA; BSc; Dip TP; FRICS
Career history
Since 1989 Head of research, GVA Grimley.
1974-89 Lecturer/course leader/acting head of department, University of Westminster.
1973-74 Sussex University.
1972-73 Land economist/valuer, Hillier Parker.
1969-72 Land economist/valuer, Drivers Jonas
Other roles
External examiner, Kingston University and University of Sheffield
Professional memberships
Investment Property Forum; Leisure Property Forum; RICS; Society of Property Researchers
Interests
Football; motor sports; photography; tennis; travel
Contact details
GVA Grimley, 10 Stratton Street, London W1J 8JR
Tel 0870 900 8990
Fax 020 7911 2560
Web www.gvagrimley.co.uk
Direct tel 020 7911 2427
Mobile 07879 435711
Email stuart.morley@gvagrimley.co.uk

MOROSS, Trevor
Dorrington Holdings

Position
Managing director
Qualifications
BA; BSc, Est Man; FRICS
Career history

M

1975 Joined Dorrington; became managing director in 1987

Professional memberships

RICS; Royal Society of Arts

Contact details

Dorrington Holdings plc, 16 Hans Road, London SW3 1RT

Tel 020 7581 1477

Fax 020 7225 0989

Web www.dorrington.co.uk

Direct tel 020 7590 9421

Mobile 07768 155445

Email trevor.moross@dorrington.co.uk

MORPETH, Iain
Clifford Chance

Position

Partner

Qualifications

LLB Hons (Bristol)

Career history

Since 1988 Partner, Clifford Chance.
1978 Admitted to Roll of Solicitors

Other roles

Contributor to *Joint Ventures in Property; Structures & Precedents* (Sweet & Maxwell); author of various published articles; regularly speaks at real estate investment banking, finance and opportunity fund conferences

Professional memberships

BPF; City of London Solicitors Company; Investment Property Forum; Law Society

Contact details

Clifford Chance, 10 Upper Bank Street, London E14 5JJ

Tel 020 7600 1000

Fax 020 7600 5555

Web www.cliffordchance.com

Direct tel 020 7006 4016

Email iain.morpeth@cliffordchance.com

MORPETH, Tony
GL Hearn

Position

Director – retail

Career history

Since 1998 Retail director, GL Hearn.
1993-98 Catella UK.
1991-92 Stiles Harold Williams.
1989-91 Painter Kelion and Partners

Interests

Sport

Contact details

GL Hearn Ltd, Sutherland House, 5-6 Argyll Street, London W1F 7TE

Tel 020 7287 7800

Fax 020 7287 4867

Web www.glhearn.com

Email tony_morpeth@glhearn.com

MORRELL, Dr Guy
HSBC Specialist Investments

Position

Director of research and indirect investment

Qualifications

PhD; BSc Hons; MRICS

Career history

Since 2004 Director of research and indirect investment, HSBC Specialist Investments.
1996-2004 Henderson/AMP Asset Management (merged in 1998): various roles, then chief investment officer (global property) at Henderson Global Investors from 2001.
1987-96 Assistant director (global policy unit), Prudential Portfolio Managers.
1984-87 Investment surveyor, Healey & Baker

Professional memberships

Investment Property Forum; RICS; Society of Property Researchers

Interests

Cycling; tennis; walking

Contact details

HSBC Specialist Investments Ltd, 8 Canada Square, London E14 5HQ

Tel 020 7991 8888

Fax 020 7991 4310

Email guy.morrell@hsbcib.com

MORRELL, Paul
Davis Langdon & Everest

Position

Senior partner

Other roles

Senior vice-president, British Council for Offices

Contact details

Davis Langdon & Everest, Princes House, 37-39 Kingsway, London WC2B 6TP

Tel 020 7497 9000

Fax 020 7497 8858

Web www.davislangdon.com

Email nick.leggett@davislangdon-uk.com

MORRIS, Antony
Clarks Solicitors

Position

Partner – head of litigation department

Contact details

Clarks Solicitors, 1 Forbury Square, Reading RG1 3EB

Tel 0118 958 5321

Fax 0118 960 4611

Web www.clarkslegal.com

Email antonymorris@clarks-solicitors.co.uk

MORRIS, Chris
Freshfields Bruckhaus Deringer

Position

Partner – real estate

Career history

Since 1991 Partner, Freshfields Bruckhaus Deringer.
1984 Admitted to Roll of Solicitors

Professional memberships

City Property Association; Investment Property Forum

Interests

Food; keep fit; running; swimming; wine

Contact details

Freshfields Bruckhaus Deringer, 65 Fleet Street, London EC4Y 1HT

Tel 020 7936 4000

Fax 020 7832 7001

Web www.freshfields.com

Direct tel 020 7832 7494

Email chris.morris@freshfields.com

MORRIS, Peter
Lewis Silkin

Position

Partner – head of construction

Qualifications

LLB Hons; MSc, Construction Law & Arbitration; FCIArb

Professional memberships

Arbitration Club; Chartered Institute of Arbitrators; Society of Construction Law

Contact details

Lewis Silkin, 12 Gough Square, London EC4A 3DW

Tel 020 7074 8000

Fax 020 7832 1200

Direct tel 020 7074 8018

Direct fax 020 7832 1753

Email peter.morris@lewissilkin.com

MORRIS, Tim
Morgan Stanley

Position

Managing director – investment banking division

Other roles

Chief investment officer, Real Estate Special Situations Funds; chief financial officer, Real Estate Investing Business

Contact details

Morgan Stanley, 1585 Broadway Avenue, New York NY 10036, USA

Tel +1 212 1 761 4000

Fax +1 212 1 761 0086

Web www.morganstanley.com

Direct tel +1 212 761 4575

Email tim.morris@morganstanley.com

MORRIS, Timothy
Monsoon Accessorize

Position
Property director
Qualifications
BSc Hons; MRICS
Career history
Since 2003 Property director, Monsoon Accessorize. Formerly property director for Uniqlo and Starbucks Coffee Co and, prior to that, head of retail property at Arcadia Group
Professional memberships
RICS
Interests
Sport
Contact details
Monsoon Accessorize Ltd, Monsoon Building, 179 Harrow Road, London W2 6NB
Tel 020 7313 4000
Fax 020 7313 4400
Web www.monsoon.co.uk
Email tmorris@monsoon.co.uk

MORRIS, Tricia
Shoosmiths

Position
Partner – head of construction
Career history
1997 Joined Shoosmiths
Contact details
Shoosmiths, Regents Gate, Crown Street, Reading RG1 2SN
Tel 0118 949 8765
Fax 0118 949 8800
Web www.shoosmiths.co.uk
Direct tel 08700 868920
Email patricia.morris@shoosmiths.co.uk

MORRISON, Alastair
Masons

Position
Partner – head of construction and engineering group
Qualifications
LLB Hons; Dip Lp
Career history
Since 1998 Partner, Masons.
1994-98 Partner and head of construction and engineering group, Dundas & Wilson.
1993-94 Associate partner, Dundas & Wilson.
1989-93 McGrigor Donald.
1986-89 Digby Brown
Professional memberships
International Bar Association; Law Society of Scotland
Interests
Rugby; running
Contact details
Masons, 33 Bothwell Street, Glasgow G2 6NL
Tel 0141 248 4858
Fax 0141 248 6655
Web www.masons.com
Direct tel 0141 249 5401
Email alastair.morrison@masons.com

MORRISON, Graham
Allies & Morrison

Position
Partner
Qualifications
MA; Dip Arch; RIBA
Career history
1983 Formed Allies & Morrison (partnership with Bob Allies)
Other roles
Design review panel member, Commission for Architecture & the Built Environment (1999); member of London advisory committee, English Heritage (2001); external examiner, University of Portsmouth (2003); RIBA councillor (1992-95); external examiner, University of Cambridge (1994-97); architecture advisory committee member, Arts Council of England (1997-98); Royal Fine Art Commissioner (1998-99)
Contact details
Allies & Morrison, 85 Southwark Street, London SE1 0HX
Tel 020 7921 0100
Fax 020 7921 0101
Web www.alliesandmorrison.co.uk
Direct tel 020 7921 0241
Email gmorrison@alliesandmorrison.co.uk

MORRISS, David
Comet Group

Position
Head of property
Qualifications
BSc; MRICS
Career history
1991 Joined Comet. Previously worked for B&Q (new store acquisitions) and Abbey Life Investment Services
Professional memberships
Accessible Retail; RICS
Interests
Family; football; skiing; squash
Contact details
Comet Group plc, George House, George Street, Hull HU1 3AU
Tel 01482 320681
Fax 01482 592388
Web www.comet.co.uk
Direct tel 01482 592062
Mobile 07831 823282
Email david.morriss@comet.co.uk

MORSHEAD, Timothy
Landmark Chambers

Position
Barrister
Professional memberships
Chancery Bar Association; Planning & Environment Bar Association
Contact details
Landmark Chambers, 4 Breams Buildings, London EC4A 1AQ
Tel 020 7430 1221
Fax 020 7421 1399
Web www.landmarkchambers.co.uk
Email clerks@landmarkchambers.co.uk

MORTIMER, Richard
Cheetham & Mortimer

Position
Joint senior partner
Interests
Cricket; fishing; rugby; shooting
Contact details
Cheetham & Mortimer, 17 St Ann's Square, Manchester M2 7PW
Tel 0161 832 3375
Fax 0161 832 0453
Mobile 07770 821836
Email rmortimer@cheetham-mortimer.com

MORTON, Christopher
FKI

Position
Group property manager
Qualifications
BSc; FRICS
Professional memberships
RICS
Contact details
FKI plc, Loughborough LE11 1HJ
Tel 01509 617960
Web www.fki.co.uk
Email chris.morton@fkiplc.com

MORTON, Fiona
Ryden

Position
Investment partner and regional managing director, Edinburgh
Qualifications
MA Hons; MRICS
Career history
Since 1989 Ryden, Edinburgh.
1987-89 Drivers Jonas, Aberdeen.
1985-87 Montagu Evans, Glasgow.

1982-85 Ryden, Glasgow
Other roles
Board member, Investment Property Forum; chair, Investment Property Forum in Scotland
Professional memberships
RICS
Interests
Family; reading; skiing
Contact details
Ryden, 46 Castle Street, Edinburgh EH2 3BN
Tel 0131 225 6612
Fax 0131 225 5766
Web www.ryden.co.uk
Direct tel 0131 473 3204
Mobile 07831 476130
Email fiona.morton@ryden.co.uk

MORTON, Jonathan
ATIS REAL Weatheralls
Position
Managing director
Qualifications
BSc; FRICS
Career history
1973 Joined ATIS REAL Weatheralls; became partner in 1988, member of board in 1995 and managing director in 2001
Other roles
Liveryman, Worshipful Company of Chartered Surveyors; freeman, Guild of Air Pilots & Air Navigators
Professional memberships
RICS
Interests
Aviation
Contact details
ATIS REAL Weatheralls Ltd, 22 Chancery Lane, London WC2A 1LT
Tel 020 7338 4000
Fax 020 7430 2628
Web www.atisrealweatheralls.com
Direct tel 020 7338 4051
Email jonathan.morton@atisrealweatheralls.com

MORTON, Neil
Dixon Webb
Position
Partner
Qualifications
FRICS; IRRV
Other roles
Vice-president, and chairman (1982-84), Halton Chamber of Commerce
Professional memberships
Institute of Revenues Rating & Valuation; RICS
Contact details
Dixon Webb, Palmyra Square Chambers, 15 Springfield Street, Warrington WA1 1BJ
Tel 01925 577577
Fax 01925 411116
Web www.dixonwebb.com
Email namorton@dixonwebb.com

MORTSTEDT, Sten
CLS Holdings
Position
Executive chairman
Contact details
CLS Holdings plc, 1 Citadel Place, Tinworth Street, London SE11 5EF
Tel 020 7582 7766
Fax 020 7582 2363
Email CHeathfield@CLSHoldings.com

MOSS, Imogen
Allen & Overy
Position
Partner – real estate
Career history
1989 Joined Allen & Overy; partner since 1999
Professional memberships
Law Society
Interests
Keep fit; tennis
Contact details
Allen & Overy, One New Change, London EC4M 9QQ
Tel 020 7330 3000
Fax 020 7330 9999
Web www.allenovery.com
Email imogen.moss@allenovery.com

MOSS, Joanne
Falcon Chambers
Position
Barrister
Qualifications
MA (Cantab); LLM (Lond); FCIArb
Career history
1992-97 Chairman, Agricultural Law Association.
1976 Called to Bar
Other roles
Founder member and former governor, Anglo-American Real Property Institute; consultant editor, Hill & Redman's *Law of Landlord & Tenant* (Butterworths); editor, Muir Watt & Moss's *Agricultural Holdings* (14th edition, Sweet & Maxwell); admitted as barrister and solicitor of supreme court of state of Victoria, Australia
Professional memberships
Chancery Bar Association; London Common Law & Commercial Bar Association; South Eastern Circuit
Contact details
Falcon Chambers, Falcon Court, London EC4Y 1AA
Tel 020 7353 2484
Fax 020 7353 1261
Web www.falcon-chambers.com
Email clerks@falcon-chambers.com

MOSS, Roger
Grosvenor Securities
Position
Managing director
Qualifications
BSc, Est Man; MRICS; AASA
Career history
1975 Joined Grosvenor Securities; project manager until 1981; appointed managing director in 1982.
1972-74 Project manager, Trafalgar House.
1970-72 Real estate appraiser, Union Bank, San Francisco
Other roles
Chairman, British Car Parks; managing director, Open Storage UK; senior partner, Moss Associates
Professional memberships
ISVA; RICS
Interests
Charity; cycling; opera; skiing; tennis; theatre
Contact details
Grosvenor Securities Ltd, 28 Bolton Street, London W1J 8BP
Tel 020 7629 9933
Fax 020 7493 5561
Mobile 07712 865408
Email susieburbidge@grosvenorsecurities.com

MOSS, Steven
UKAEA Central Property Unit
Position
Head, central property unit
Qualifications
BSc; MIMechE; CEng
Contact details
UKAEA Central Property Unit, Harwell International Business Centre, 392/10 Rutherford Avenue, Didcot OX11 0RA
Tel 01235 861997
Fax 01235 431670
Email steve.moss@ukaea.org.uk

MOSSOP, Guy
Beechcroft Developments
Position
Property director
Contact details
Beechcroft Developments Ltd, 1 Church Lane,

M

Wallingford OX10 0DX
Tel 01491 834975
Fax 01491 825433
Email guymossop@beechcroft.co.uk

MOTT, Nicholas
Denton Wilde Sapte

Position
Partner – commercial property
Qualifications
BSc Hons
Career history
1987 Joined Denton Hall (now Denton Wilde Sapte); appointed partner in 1996.
1984 Admitted to Roll of Solicitors.
1982-87 Kidd Rapinet
Professional memberships
Law Society
Contact details
Denton Wilde Sapte, 5 Chancery Lane, London EC4A 1BU
Tel 020 7242 1212
Fax 020 7404 0087
Web www.dentonwildesapte.com
Direct tel 020 7320 6208
Email neam@dentonwildesapte.com

MOULD, Timothy
Landmark Chambers

Position
Barrister
Career history
1987 Called to Bar
Other roles
Contributor to *Halsbury's Laws of England* on town and country planning; assistant editor of *Encyclopædia of Rating & Local Taxation*
Professional memberships
Administrative Law Bar Association; Chancery Bar Association; Planning & Environment Bar Association
Contact details
Landmark Chambers, 4 Breams Buildings, London EC4A 1AQ
Tel 020 7430 1221
Fax 020 7421 1399
Web www.landmarkchambers.co.uk
Email clerks@landmarkchambers.co.uk

MOYS, Clive
11 New Square

Position
Barrister
Qualifications
LLB (Cardiff); Dip LG Law & Practice
Career history
2000 Joined 11 New Square as barrister.
1988-98 Practised as solicitor
Professional memberships
Administrative Law Bar Association; Chancery Bar Association; Planning & Environment Bar Association
Interests
Sailing; skiing; tennis
Contact details
11 New Square (Chambers of Sonia Proudman QC), Ground Floor, London WC2A 3QB
Tel 020 7831 0081
Fax 020 7405 2560
Web www.11newsquare.co.uk
Direct tel 020 7693 5720
Email cmoys@11newsquare.co.uk

MUCKLOW, Albert
A&J Mucklow & Co

Position
Honorary president
Contact details
A&J Mucklow & Co Ltd, Haden Cross, Haden Cross Drive, Warley B64 7JB
Tel 0121 550 1841
Fax 0121 550 7532
Web www.mucklow.com
Email mucklowaj@mucklow.com

MUCKLOW, Rupert
A&J Mucklow & Co

Position
Chairman
Qualifications
BSc
Career history
Since 1990 A&J Mucklow Group: became managing director in 1996; chair since 2004.
1987-89 Grimley JR Eve, London.
1986-87 Chesshire Gibson, London
Professional memberships
Investment Property Forum
Interests
Golf
Contact details
A&J Mucklow & Co Ltd, Haden Cross, Haden Cross Drive, Warley B64 7JB
Tel 0121 550 1841
Fax 0121 550 7532
Web www.mucklow.com
Email mucklowrj@mucklow.com

MUDIE, Jeremy
Vantage Asset Management

Position
Director
Qualifications
BSc, Est Man; MRICS
Career history
Since 2003 Director, Vantage Asset Management.
2000-03 Investment director, Frogmore.
1993-2000 Manager (property investment), Henderson Investors.
1991-93 UK property director, Heron Corp.
1987-90 Development director, Sheraton Securities.
1983-86 Development surveyor, New England Properties
Professional memberships
Investment Property Forum; RICS
Contact details
Vantage Asset Management Ltd, 63 Grosvenor Street, London W1K 3JG
Tel 020 7499 3555
Email jeremymudie@vantageam.co.uk

MULHOLLAND, Tim
Albert Dock Co

Position
Director
Qualifications
BA Hons; MCIM
Career history
1996 Joined Albert Dock Co as marketing manager; appointed director in 1999.
1987-95 Residential marketing manager, Emerson Group
Professional memberships
Chartered Institute of Marketing; Liverpool Interact
Contact details
Albert Dock Co Ltd, 22 Edward Pavillion, Liverpool L3 4AF
Tel 0151 708 7334
Fax 0151 708 0929
Email tim@albertdock.com

MULLENGER, Stephanie
Urban Splash

Position
Managing director
Qualifications
BSc; FRICS
Professional memberships
RICS
Contact details
Urban Splash Ltd, Timber Wharf, 32 Worsley Street, Manchester M15 4NX
Tel 0161 839 2999
Fax 0161 839 8999
Web www.urbansplash.co.uk
Email stephaniemullenger@urbansplash.co.uk

MULRYAN, Donal
Ballymore Properties

Position
Director

Contact details
Ballymore Properties Ltd, 3 Greenwich View Place, London E14 9NN
Tel 020 7510 9100
Fax 020 7510 9110
Email dmulryan@ballymore.co.uk

MULRYAN, Sean
Ballymore Properties

Position
Chairman – managing director

Contact details
Ballymore Properties Ltd, 3 Greenwich View Place, London E14 9NN
Tel 020 7510 9100
Fax 020 7510 9110
Email info@ballymore.co.uk

MUNDAY, Barry
PRP Management

Position
Chairman

Qualifications
Dip Arch; RIBA

Career history
1973 Joined PRP; became director in 1983 and chairman in 2001

Other roles
Board member, Housing Forum and Design for Homes

Interests
Cinema; golf; music; theatre; Chelsea Football Club; RAC

Contact details
PRP Management Ltd, 10 Lindsey Street, London EC1A 9HP
Tel 020 7653 1200
Fax 020 7653 1201
Web www.prparchitects.co.uk
Direct tel 020 7653 4153
Email barry.munday@prparchitects.co.uk

MUNDEN, Tim
Davis Coffer Lyons

Position
Director – professional department

Career history
1987 Joined Davis Coffer Lyons; appointed director in 1990.
1982-87 Montagu Evans

Professional memberships
Arbrix; Leisure Property Forum; Restaurant Property Advisors Society; RICS

Contact details
Davis Coffer Lyons Ltd, 52 Portland Place, London W1B 1NH
Tel 020 7299 0700
Fax 020 7299 0710
Web www.daviscofferlyons.co.uk
Email tmunden@daviscofferlyons.co.uk

MUNDY, David
Mellersh & Harding

Position
Partner – investment

Qualifications
BSc; MRICS

Career history
1979 Joined Mellersh & Harding

Professional memberships
RICS

Interests
Skiing; tennis; travel

Contact details
Mellersh & Harding, 6 Duke Street, London SW1Y 6BN
Tel 020 7499 0866
Fax 020 7522 8503
Web www.mellersh.co.uk
Direct tel 020 7522 8513
Mobile 07880 740507
Email info@mellersh.co.uk

MUNDY, John
Adval

Position
Director

Qualifications
BSc Hons, Urban Est Surv; FRICS

Career history
2003 Co-founder (with John Slade of Slade & Co), Adval (property investment company).
2000-03 Investment director, CIT Group.
1996-2000 Director (City investment and development), DTZ.
1989-96 Associate/partner (City investment and development), Richard Ellis.
1985-88 Fletcher King

Professional memberships
RICS

Contact details
Adval LLP, 3 Charles Street, London W1J 5DD
Tel 020 7499 6677
Email mundyj@adval-llp.com

MUNDY, Stephen
Legal & General Investment Management

Position
Property director – life fund

Qualifications
MSc; MRICS; CDip AF

Contact details
Legal & General Investment Management Ltd, Bucklersbury House, Walbrook, London EC4N 8EL
Tel 020 7528 6500
Fax 020 7528 6848
Web www.legal-and-general.co.uk
Direct fax 020 7528 6838
Email stephen.mundy@lgim.co.uk

MUNN, Gavin
Stannifer Corovest Fund Management

Position
Director

Contact details
Stannifer Corovest Fund Management Ltd, 213 St Vincent Street, Glasgow G2 5QY
Tel 0141 221 6650
Fax 0141 221 5830
Web www.stannifer.co.uk
Direct tel 0141 227 3401
Email gavinmunn@stannifer.co.uk

MURDOCH, Kirk
McGrigors

Position
Partner – real estate partner

Qualifications
LLB

Career history
1976 Joined McGrigor Donald (now McGrigors); appointed partner in 1982; managing partner 1997-2002

Professional memberships
Common Purpose; Investment Property Forum

Contact details
McGrigors, Pacific House, 70 Wellington Street, Glasgow G2 6SB
Tel 0141 248 6677
Fax 0141 204 1351
Web www.mcgrigors.com
Direct tel 0141 567 9243
Direct fax 0141 221 1390
Mobile 07768 915588
Email kirk.murdoch@mcgrigors.com

MURDOCH, Scott
CWM

Position
Partner

Career history
1992 Co-founded CWM. Previously at Conrad Ritblat, CB Richard Ellis and Hammond Phillips

Interests
Cricket; football; golf; tennis; Wentworth Club

Contact details

CWM, 16 Old Bond Street, London W1S 4PS
Tel 020 7493 5655
Fax 020 7493 5665
Web www.cwm.co.uk
Mobile 07973 734130
Email scott.murdoch@cwm.co.uk

MURPHY, Gary
Allsop & Co

Position
Partner – residential auctions
Qualifications
LLB; FRICS
Career history
1986 Joined Allsop & Co.
1983-86 Partner, Hillyers
Other roles
Member, RICS auctioneering group and RICS residential faculty board; past chairman, RICS agency practice panel; past chairman, ISVA auctioneering committee; director, European Estates
Professional memberships
RICS
Contact details
Allsop & Co, 100 Knightsbridge, London SW1X 7LB
Tel 020 7437 6977
Fax 020 7344 2640
Web www.allsop.co.uk
Direct tel 020 7344 2619
Mobile 07831 433299
Email gary.murphy@allsop.co.uk

MURPHY, Robert
CB Richard Ellis

Position
Senior director – City investment
Qualifications
MRICS
Career history
Since 2003 CB Richard Ellis.
1988-2003 CB Hillier Parker.
1986-88 Weatherall Green & Smith.
1984-86 Healey & Baker
Professional memberships
RICS
Contact details
CB Richard Ellis, St Martin's Court, 10 Paternoster Row, London EC4M 7HP
Tel 020 7182 2000
Fax 020 7182 2001
Web www.cbre.com
Direct tel 020 7182 3449
Direct fax 020 7182 3002
Mobile 07768 487678
Email robert.murphy@cbre.com

MURRAY, Nick
Arlington European Developments

Position
Managing director
Qualifications
BSc; MCIOB
Career history
1990 Joined Arlington Securities.
1985-90 Rosehaugh.
1980-84 George Wimpey
Professional memberships
Chartered Institute of Building
Contact details
Arlington European Developments Ltd, Arlington House, 1025 Arlington Business Park, Reading RG7 4SA
Tel 0118 930 4141
Fax 0118 930 4383
Web www.arlington.co.uk
Email nicholas.murray@arlington.co.uk

MUSGRAVE, Stephen
Grosvenor

Position
Chief executive
Qualifications
MRICS
Professional memberships
RICS
Contact details
Grosvenor Ltd, 70 Grosvenor Street, London W1K 3JP
Tel 020 7408 0988
Fax 020 7629 9115
Web www.grosvenor.com
Direct tel 020 7312 6350
Direct fax 020 7873 1350
Email linda.forth@grosvenor.com

MUSTON, Michael
Harvey Spack Field

Position
Partner
Qualifications
MRICS
Professional memberships
RICS
Contact details
Harvey Spack Field, 33 Bruton Street, London W1J 6QU
Tel 020 7629 9663
Fax 020 7491 1964
Web www.harveyspackfield.co.uk
Direct tel 020 7518 0456
Mobile 07860 598815
Email muston@harveyspackfield.co.uk

MYERS, Martin
Mountgrange Capital

Position
Chairman
Qualifications
FRICS
Other roles
Trustee, Royal Marston Cancer Campaign; project committee chairman and governor, South Bank board
Contact details
Mountgrange Capital plc, Arcade House, 13 Albemarle Street, London W1S 4HJ
Tel 020 7297 4960
Fax 020 7297 4969
Email mtm@mountgrange.net

MYERSON, Brian
Marylebone Warwick Balfour Group

Position
Non-executive chairman
Qualifications
BComm; LLB
Contact details
Marylebone Warwick Balfour Group plc, 1 West Garden Place, London W2 2AQ
Tel 020 7706 2121
Fax 020 7706 8181
Web www.mwb.co.uk

MYLREA, Kathy
Simmons & Simmons

Position
Partner – head of environmental law group
Qualifications
LLB
Career history
1992 Joined Simmons & Simmons. Originally qualified in Canada
Other roles
Co-author of updated *Environmental Compliance Manual* (Gee Publishing) and of environmental law chapter in *Construction Law Handbook* (Thomas Telford); preparing 2nd edition of Sweet & Maxwell's *Environmental Law*
Professional memberships
Law Society
Interests
Cinema; diving/scuba diving; skiing; travel
Contact details
Simmons & Simmons, Citypoint, 1 Ropemaker Street, London EC2Y 9SS
Tel 020 7628 2020
Fax 020 7628 2070
Web www.simmons-simmons.com
Direct tel 020 7825 4022
Email kathryn.mylrea@simmons-simmons.com

N

NABARRO, Rupert
Investment Property Databank

Position
Chairman
Qualifications
MA; MPhil; MRTPI
Career history
1973-85 Partner, Roger Tym & Partners.
1966-71 Economist, Economist Intelligence Unit
Other roles
Author of books and articles on both property and urban economics
Professional memberships
Royal Economic Society; RTPI
Contact details
Investment Property Databank, 7-9 Greenland Place, London NW1 0AP
Tel 020 7482 5149
Fax 020 7267 0208
Web www.ipdindex.co.uk
Direct fax 020 7284 2667
Email rupert.nabarro@ipdindex.co.uk

NACOS, John
Deutsche Bank

Position
Managing director – real estate debt markets
Contact details
Deutsche Bank AG, Winchester House, 1 Great Winchester Street, London EC2N 2DB
Tel 020 7545 8000
Fax 020 7545 6155
Web www.db.com
Direct tel 020 7547 0665
Email john.nacos@db.com

NADDELL, Nicholas
McClure Naismith

Position
Partner – head of retail services group
Qualifications
LLB; Dip LP; NP
Career history
1990 Joined McClure Naismith; appointed partner in 1994.
1987 Admitted to Roll of Solicitors
Other roles
Member of firm's strategy development group
Professional memberships
Law Society of Scotland
Interests
Food; football; France
Contact details
McClure Naismith, 292 St Vincent Street, Glasgow G2 5TQ
Tel 0141 204 2700
Fax 0141 248 3998
Web www.mcclurenaismith.com
Direct tel 0141 303 7737
Mobile 07909 912414
Email nnaddell@mcclurenaismith.com

NADLER, Robert
Western Heritable Investment Co

Position
Non-executive director
Qualifications
MRICS
Career history
1981-2003 Compco Holdings: joined as managing director; became joint chief executive in 1995.
1978-81 Managing director, J Forman/W&F.
1972-78 Jones Lang Wootton
Professional memberships
RICS
Contact details
Western Heritable Investment Co Ltd, 63a South Audley Street, London W1K 2QS
Tel 020 7491 2948
Fax 020 7629 0414
Direct tel 020 7352 1123
Direct fax 020 7352 2123
Mobile 07768 817152
Email rnadler@btopenworld.com

NAHOME, Ezra
Lambert Smith Hampton

Position
National head of investments
Career history
1995-2000 Director, Pepper Angliss & Yarwood.
1986-95 Director, Grant & Partners
Contact details
Lambert Smith Hampton Ltd, Regent Arcade House, 19-25 Argyll Street, London W1F 7TS
Tel 020 7494 4000
Fax 020 7414 0866
Web www.lsh.co.uk
Direct tel 020 7663 8260
Direct fax 020 7414 0838
Mobile 07770 220002
Email enahome@lsh.co.uk

NAIRN, Julian
Jones Lang LaSalle

Position
International director – City investment
Qualifications
MRICS
Career history
Since 1999 International director (City investment), Jones Lang LaSalle.
1989-99 Associate/partner (City investment), Jones Lang Wootton.
1985-89 Associate (City business team), Richard Ellis.
1981-85 Investment and City investment, Vigers
Professional memberships
Investment Property Forum; RICS
Contact details
Jones Lang LaSalle Ltd, 9 Queen Victoria Street, London EC4N 4YY
Tel 020 7248 6040
Fax 020 7248 0088
Web www.joneslanglasalle.com
Direct tel 020 7399 5865
Direct fax 020 7399 5676
Mobile 07771 977692
Email julian.nairn@eu.joneslanglasalle.com

NAISH, Malcolm
DTZ Debenham Tie Leung

Position
Head of fund management
Qualifications
MRICS
Career history
2002-03 Director, Fountain Capital Partners.
1999-2002 Managing director, LaSalle Investment Management.
1981-99 Jones Lang Wootton: lead partner (fund management and advisory) from 1987.
1971-81 GVA Grimley
Professional memberships
Investment Property Forum; RICS
Contact details
DTZ Debenham Tie Leung, 1 Curzon Street, London W1A 5PZ
Tel 020 7408 1161
Fax 020 7643 6000
Web www.dtz.com
Email malcolm.naish@dtz.com

N

NAPIER, David
GL Hearn

Position
Development director
Career history
1982 Joined GL Hearn as associate; became equity partner in 1986, funding partner in 1994 and planning director in 1999; now development director
Professional memberships
RICS
Interests
Motor sports
Contact details
GL Hearn Ltd, Leonard House, 5-7 Marshalsea Road, London SE1 1EP
Tel 020 7450 4000
Fax 020 7450 4010
Web www.glhearn.com
Direct tel 020 7450 5145
Mobile 07768 381830
Email david_napier@glhearn.com

NAPIER, Guy
Knight Frank

Position
Partner – head of City agency
Qualifications
BSc Hons, Est Man; MRICS
Career history
1988 Joined Knight Frank.
1985-88 City agency surveyor, St Quintin
Professional memberships
East India Club; RICS
Interests
Country pursuits; cycling; family
Contact details
Knight Frank LLP, Kings House, 36 King Street, London EC2V 8QQ
Tel 020 7606 0606
Fax 020 7606 5502
Web www.knightfrank.com
Direct tel 020 7861 1315
Mobile 07831 576610
Email guy.napier@knightfrank.com

NEAL, Michael
Insight Investment Management

Position
Director – property investment
Contact details
Insight Investment Management, 33 Old Broad Street, London EC2N 1HZ
Tel 020 7930 5474
Fax 020 7321 1423
Web www.insightinvestment.com
Direct tel 020 7321 1024
Direct fax 020 7321 1434
Mobile 07787 152363
Email michael.neal@insightinvestment.com

NEAL, Morton
St Anselm Development Co

Position
Managing director
Contact details
St Anselm Development Co Ltd, 128 Mount Street, London W1K 3NU
Tel 020 7495 3599
Email paula@st-anselm.co.uk

NEALE, Alan
LCC UK

Position
Managing director
Qualifications
BSc Hons; MRICS
Contact details
LCC UK Ltd, Capital Park, Cambridge CB1 5XE
Tel 01223 883999
Fax 01223 883998
Web www.lcc.com
Direct tel 01223 883930
Mobile 07770 975654
Email alan_neale@lcc.com

NEALE, Robert
Alder King

Position
Partner
Career history
1971 Joined Alder King; now head of agency and leader of corporate client team
Other roles
Past president, Bristol Property Agents Association (1993); director, Juvenile Diabetes Research Foundation; former director, Bristol City Football Club (1993-2001)
Professional memberships
Industrial Agents Society
Interests
Art; cricket (Gloucester County Cricket Club); reading
Contact details
Alder King, Pembroke House, 15 Pembroke Road, Bristol BS8 3BA
Tel 0117 317 1000
Fax 0117 317 1001
Web www.alderking.com
Direct tel 0117 317 1070
Mobile 07990 981033
Email rneale@alderking.com

NEARS, Peter
Peel Holdings

Position
Strategic planning director
Qualifications
BA Hons; MSc; MRTPI
Career history
1988 Joined Peel Group; appointed head of land and planning division in 1991; joined group's executive committee as director of land and planning in 2000; became strategic planning director in 2003.
1984-88 Conservation officer, Macclesfield Borough Council.
1979-84 Design assistant, Durham County Council
Professional memberships
RTPI; Urban Design Group
Contact details
Peel Holdings plc, Peel Dome, The Trafford Centre, Manchester M17 8PL
Tel 0161 629 8200
Fax 0161 629 8333
Web www.peel.co.uk
Mobile 07775 844803
Email pnears@peelholdings.co.uk

NELSON, David
Foster & Partners

Position
Partner
Qualifications
MA; Dip AD
Career history
1976 Joined Foster & Partners
Professional memberships
RIBA (honorary fellow)
Contact details
Foster & Partners, Riverside Three, 22 Hester Road, London SW11 4AN
Tel 020 7738 0455
Fax 020 7738 1107
Web www.fosterandpartners.com
Email dnelson@fosterandpartners.com

NELSON, Phillip
Nelson Bakewell

Position
Chairman
Qualifications
BSc; FRICS
Career history
1982 Co-founded Nelson Bakewell.
1977-82 Gardiner & Theobald
Other roles
Member of management committee, Hermes Property Unit Trust; trustee, Investment Property

N

Forum Education Trust; past chairman, Investment Property Forum; past director, London First

Professional memberships
Investment Property Forum; RICS; Worshipful Company of Chartered Surveyors

Interests
Sailing; tennis

Contact details
Nelson Bakewell Ltd, 25 Sackville Street, London W1S 3HQ
Tel 020 7544 2000
Fax 020 7544 2222
Web www.nelson-bakewell.com
Email pnelson@nelson-bakewell.com

NELSON-SMITH, Daniel
King Sturge

Position
Partner – national head of landlord and tenant

Qualifications
BSc; FRICS

Career history
Since 1978 Partner, King Sturge.
1973-77 Surveyor, Greater London Council

Professional memberships
Arbrix; RICS

Contact details
King Sturge, 7 Stratford Place, London W1C 1ST
Tel 020 7493 4933
Fax 020 7409 0469
Web www.kingsturge.com
Direct tel 020 7318 4378
Direct fax 020 7493 3226
Mobile 07702 064115
Email danielns@kingsturge.co.uk

NETLEY, Jonathan
Tushingham Moore

Position
Partner

Contact details
Tushingham Moore, Acresfield, St Ann's Square, Manchester M2 7HA
Tel 0161 833 1197
Fax 0161 833 1630
Web www.tushinghammoore.co.uk
Email jonathan@tushinghammoore.co.uk

NETTLETON, John
Donaldsons

Position
Senior partner

Qualifications
BSc; FRICS; ACIArb

Other roles
Director, Edward Blake

Professional memberships
Chartered Institute of Arbitrators; RICS

Interests
Gardening; historical buildings; rugby

Contact details
Donaldsons, 48 Warwick Street, London W1B 5NL
Tel 020 7534 5000
Fax 020 7434 0045
Web www.donaldsons.co.uk
Direct tel 020 7534 5002
Mobile 07808 479249
Email john.nettleton@donaldsons.co.uk

NEVETT, Roland
Land Securities Properties

Position
Director – head of retail warehousing and industrial

Qualifications
FRICS

Career history
1981 Joined Land Securities; became director of wholly owned subsidiary Ravenside Investment in 1984, then director of wholly owned subsidiary Ravenseft Industrial Estates in 1986; appointed assistant director of Land Securities Properties in 1988 and director of wholly owned subsidiary LS Leisure in 1996; director of Land Securities Properties since 1999.
1969-81 De Groot Collis: appointed manager of industrial department in 1978

Professional memberships
Accessible Retail; Shopping Park Investors Forum

Contact details
Land Securities Properties Ltd, 5 Strand, London WC2N 5AF
Tel 020 7413 9000
Fax 020 7925 0202
Web www.landsecurities.com
Direct tel 020 7024 5481
Direct fax 020 7024 5008
Mobile 07785 306962
Email roland.nevett@landsecurities.com

NEWALL, David
GVA Grimley

Position
Head of valuation services

Contact details
GVA Grimley, 25 Bucklersbury, London EC4N 8DA
Tel 0870 900 8990
Fax 020 7911 2846
Web www.gvagrimley.co.uk
Direct tel 020 7911 2881
Email david.newall@gvagrimley.co.uk

NEWBERRY, Clive
2 Harcourt Buildings

Position
Barrister

Qualifications
QC

Career history
1993 Appointed QC.
1978 Called to Bar

Other roles
Member of planning committee, RIBA

Professional memberships
Administrative Law Bar Association; Planning & Environment Bar Association; RIBA; Royal Society of Arts

Contact details
2 Harcourt Buildings (Chambers of Robin Purchas QC), 2nd Floor, London EC4Y 9DB
Tel 020 7353 8415
Fax 020 7353 7622
Web www.2hblaw.co.uk
Email clerks@2hblaw.co.uk

NEWBY, Paul
Fleurets

Position
Director

Qualifications
BSc Hons; FRICS; MCIArb

Career history
1990 Joined Fleurets. Previously partner/director at Chesterton International

Professional memberships
Association of Valuers of Licensed Property; Chartered Institute of Arbitrators; RICS

Interests
Family; food; music; reading; sport

Contact details
Fleurets Ltd, 63 St Paul's Square, Birmingham B3 1QS
Tel 0121 236 5252
Fax 0121 236 9400
Web www.fleurets.com
Email birmingham@fleurets.com

NEWENS, Mike
Vodafone

Position
Property director

Contact details
Vodafone Ltd, Vodafone House, The Connection, Newbury RG14 2FN
Tel 01635 33251
Web www.vodafone.co.uk
Email jayne.haw@vodafone.com

NEWISS, Julian
Catalyst Capital

Position
Chairman
Qualifications
FRICS
Professional memberships
RICS
Contact details
Catalyst Capital LLP, 33 Cavendish Square, London W1G 0PW
Tel 020 7290 5100
Fax 020 7290 5115
Web www.catalystcapital.com
Email info@catalystcapital.co.uk

NEWMAN, Andrew
Vail Williams

Position
Partner – business space
Career history
1982 Joined Vail Williams and opened Basingstoke office.
1979-82 Jones Lang Wootton.
1974-79 Edward Erdman & Co.
1972-74 Mann & Co/Gascoigne Pees
Interests
Cricket; fishing; golf; shooting; tennis
Contact details
Vail Williams, 10 Sarum Hill, Basingstoke RG21 8SR
Tel 01256 489800
Fax 01256 489870
Web www.vailwilliams.com
Mobile 07768 724356
Email anewman@vailwilliams.com

NEWSOM, George
Guildhall Chambers

Position
Barrister
Qualifications
MA, Eng & Econ; FCIArb
Career history
Since 1973 Barrister, Guildhall Chambers.
1973 Called to Bar.
1970-71 Civil and mechanical engineer, WS Atkins
Other roles
Chairman, Agricultural Land Tribunal for the South West; author, *Preston & Newsom's Restrictive Covenants Affecting Freehold Land* (9th edition) and *Newsom's Faculty Jurisdiction of the Church of England* (2nd edition)
Professional memberships
Bristol & Cardiff Chancery Bar Association; Chancery Bar Association; Chartered Institute of Arbitrators
Interests
Church; farming; gardening; IT; sailing; tennis
Contact details
Guildhall Chambers (Chambers of Adrian Palmer QC), 23 Broad Street, Bristol BS1 2HG
Tel 0117 927 3366
Fax 0117 930 3800
Web www.guildhallchambers.co.uk
Direct tel 01823 673397
Direct fax 01823 673396
Email george.newsom@guildhallchambers.co.uk

NEWSOM, William
FPDSavills

Position
Director – head of valuation
Qualifications
FRICS
Career history
1983 Joined FPDSavills.
1973-82 Debenham Tewson & Chinnocks
Other roles
Annually presents to property lending bankers a series of seminars on financing property
Interests
Food; genealogy; motorcycling; mountaineering
Contact details
FPDSavills Ltd, 20 Grosvenor Hill, London W1K 3HQ
Tel 020 7499 8644
Fax 020 7495 3773
Web www.fpdsavills.co.uk
Direct tel 020 7409 8780
Mobile 07989 975634
Email wnewsom@fpdsavills.co.uk

NEWSON, Glenn
Credit Suisse Asset Management

Position
Director – head of UK property
Qualifications
BSc Hons, Valuation & Est Man; MRICS
Career history
1989 Joined SLC Langbourn as director of asset management; company then taken over by Credit Suisse; now director and head of UK property.
1986-89 Principal valuation surveyor, Richard Ellis.
1983-86 Group valuer and regional surveyor, National Car Parks
Professional memberships
RICS
Contact details
Credit Suisse Asset Management Ltd, Beaufort House, 15 St Botolph Street, London EC3A 7JJ
Tel 020 7426 2626
Web www.credit-suisse.com
Email glenn.newson@csam.com

NEWSUM, Jeremy
Grosvenor

Position
Group chief executive
Qualifications
BSc; FRICS
Career history
1987 Rejoined Grosvenor Estate; appointed chief executive in 1989 and trustee in 1993.
1984-87 Partner, Bidwells: established London office.
1979-84 Commercial investment department, Savills: became associate in 1983.
1976-79 Grosvenor Estate
Other roles
Trustee, Grosvenor Trusts; director, Sonae Imobiliária; president, BPF (2001/02)
Professional memberships
RICS
Interests
Sport
Contact details
Grosvenor Ltd, 70 Grosvenor Street, London W1K 3JP
Tel 020 7408 0988
Fax 020 7629 9115
Web www.grosvenor.com
Direct tel 020 7312 6164
Direct fax 020 7312 6244
Mobile 07768 600719
Email jeremy.newsum@grosvenor.com

NEWTON, Mark
Dollond & Aitchison

Position
Property manager
Contact details
Dollond & Aitchison Ltd, Dollond & Aitchison Campus, 50 Rocky Lane, Birmingham B6 5RQ
Tel 0121 706 6133
Fax 0121 697 2100
Web www.danda.co.uk
Direct tel 0121 697 2506
Direct fax 0121 697 2525
Email mark.newton@danda.co.uk

NEWTON, Robert
Lambert Smith Hampton

Position
Director – head of Sheffield office
Qualifications
BSc Hons, Urban Land Econ; MRICS
Career history
1997 Joined Lambert Smith Hampton

N

Professional memberships
Office Agents Society; RICS
Contact details
Lambert Smith Hampton Ltd, Fountain Precinct, Sheffield S1 2JA
Tel 0114 275 3752
Fax 0114 273 8963
Web www.lsh.co.uk
Email rnewton@lsh.co.uk

NICHOLAS, Tony
Knight Frank

Position
Joint managing partner, Cardiff
Qualifications
BSc; MRICS
Career history
Since 1998 Joint managing partner, Knight Frank, Cardiff.
1996-98 Director, Saxon Law, London.
1986-96 Partner, Knight Frank, London
Professional memberships
British Council for Offices; Office Agents Society; RICS
Interests
Food; rugby; sport; wine
Contact details
Knight Frank LLP, Emperor House, Pierhead Street, Cardiff CF10 4PH
Tel 029 2049 2492
Fax 029 2048 5553
Web www.knightfrank.com
Mobile 07771 885993
Email tony.nicholas@knightfrank.com

NICHOLL, John
Fleurets

Position
Director
Qualifications
FRICS
Professional memberships
RICS
Contact details
Fleurets Ltd, 18 Bloomsbury Square, London WC1A 2NS
Tel 020 7636 8992
Fax 020 7636 7490
Web www.fleurets.com
Email john.nicholl@fleurets.com

NICHOLLS, Martin
Royal Bank of Scotland

Position
Head of strategy and asset management
Qualifications
FRICS
Career history
1987 Joined Royal Bank of Scotland.
1981-87 Property manager/director, Aberdeen Service Co.
1980-81 Property/development surveyor, Galliford Brindley Properties, Leicester
Professional memberships
RICS
Interests
Travel; walking
Contact details
Royal Bank of Scotland, Drummond House, PO Box 1727, 1 Redheughs Avenue, Edinburgh
Tel 0131 556 8555
Web www.rbs.co.uk
Direct tel 0131 523 7800
Direct fax 0131 317 7964
Mobile 07831 363306
Email martin.nicholls@rbs.co.uk

NICHOLS, Nigel
GL Hearn

Position
Director
Qualifications
FRICS; FCIArb
Professional memberships
RICS
Interests
Skiing
Contact details
GL Hearn Ltd, Sutherland House, 5-6 Argyll Street, London W1F 7TE
Tel 020 7287 7800
Fax 020 7287 4867
Web www.glhearn.com
Email nigel_nichols@glhearn.com

NICHOLSON, David
Lambert Smith Hampton

Position
Director
Qualifications
BSc; MRICS
Career history
2002 Appointed to establish Lambert Smith Hampton in Newcastle. Early career experience with English Estates and Newcastle City Council, followed by 14 years in commercial agency in the North East
Interests
Diving/scuba diving; football (Newcastle United season ticket holder); golf; keep fit
Contact details
Lambert Smith Hampton Ltd, 42-50 Grey Street, Newcastle upon Tyne NE1 6AE
Tel 0191 261 1300
Fax 0191 261 4300
Web www.lsh.co.uk
Direct tel 0191 261 3001
Email dnicholson@lsh.co.uk

NICHOLSON, Greg
CB Richard Ellis

Position
Chairman – capital markets
Qualifications
FRICS
Career history
1980 Joined CB Hillier Parker.
1977-80 Chamberlain & Willows
Contact details
CB Richard Ellis, Kingsley House, 1a Wimpole Street, London W1G 0RE
Tel 020 7182 2000
Fax 020 7182 7001
Web www.cbre.com
Direct tel 020 7182 2775
Direct fax 020 7182 2880
Mobile 07774 824707
Email greg.nicholson@cbre.com

NICHOLSON, Jeremy
4 Pump Court

Position
Barrister
Qualifications
QC
Career history
2000 Appointed QC.
1978 Joined 4 Pump Court.
1977 Called to Bar
Other roles
TECBAR approved adjudicator and trained mediator
Professional memberships
Commercial Bar Association; London Common Law & Commercial Bar Association; Professional Negligence Bar Association; Technology & Construction Bar Association
Interests
Sailing; travel
Contact details
4 Pump Court (Chambers of Christopher Moger QC & David Friedman QC), London EC4Y 7AN
Tel 020 7842 5555
Fax 020 7583 2036
Web www.4pumpcourt.com
Email jnicholson@4pumpcourt.com

NICKLIN, Phil
Deloitte

Position
Tax partner – real estate

Qualifications
BSc; CTA (Fellow); FCA
Career history
Since 2002 Real estate tax partner, Deloitte.
1994-2002 Real estate tax partner, Arthur Andersen
Other roles
BPF tax committee; jazz musician, athlete
Professional memberships
Chartered Institute of Taxation; Institute of Chartered Accountants in England & Wales; Investment Property Forum
Contact details
Deloitte, 180 Strand, London WC2R 1BL
Tel 020 7936 3000
Fax 020 7583 1198
Web www.deloitte.co.uk
Direct tel 020 7007 2984
Direct fax 020 7438 2286
Email pnicklin@deloitte.co.uk

NICOLL, Richard
Richards Butler
Position
Head of property group
Qualifications
LLB
Career history
1973 Admitted to Roll of Solicitors.
1972 Joined Richards Butler; appointed partner in 1981; head of property group for six years; now a board member
Professional memberships
BPF; Business in Sport & Leisure; City Property Association
Interests
Art; cinema; cricket; fishing; rugby; sport
Contact details
Richards Butler, Beaufort House, 15 St Botolph Street, London EC3A 7JJ
Tel 020 7247 6555
Fax 020 7247 5091
Web www.richardsbutler.com
Direct tel 020 7816 3725
Mobile 07768 907903
Email rcn@richardsbutler.com

NIGHTINGALE, Mike
Nightingale Associates
Position
Senior partner
Contact details
Nightingale Associates Ltd, The Cherry Barn, High Street, Harwell OX11 0EY
Tel 01235 820222
Fax 01235 820145
Email harwell@nightingaleassociates.com

NIXON, Richard
Halfords
Position
Head of property
Qualifications
MRICS
Career history
1987 Joined Halfords: various roles in property; head of property since 1994.
1986-87 Real estate surveyor, McDonald's.
1976-86 Property roles in various local authorities
Professional memberships
RICS
Contact details
Halfords Ltd, Icknield Street Drive, Redditch B98 0DE
Tel 01527 517601
Fax 01527 513206
Web www.halfords.co.uk
Direct tel 01527 513001
Direct fax 01527 513203
Mobile 07860 641259
Email richard.nixon@halfords.co.uk

NOBLE, Andrew
Enodis
Position
Group property director
Contact details
Enodis plc, Washington House, 40-41 Conduit Street, London W1S 2YQ
Tel 020 7304 6000
Fax 020 7304 6001
Web www.enodis.com
Email andrew.noble@enodis.com

NOBLE, Ian
Cluttons
Position
Partner – commercial agency
Qualifications
FRICS
Career history
1980-85 Associate, King & Co.
1976-80 Associate, Elliott Son & Boyton.
1971-76 Richard Ellis
Other roles
Management board member of sports facility with charitable status
Professional memberships
British Council for Offices; RICS
Contact details
Cluttons, Portman House, 2 Portman Street, London W1H 6DU
Tel 020 7408 1010
Fax 020 7629 3263
Web www.cluttons.com
Direct tel 020 7647 7161
Direct fax 020 7647 7067
Mobile 07770 568997
Email inoble@cluttons.com

NOCK, Alan
NAI Fuller Peiser
Position
Partner
Contact details
NAI Fuller Peiser, Belgrave House, 47 Bank Street, Sheffield S1 2DR
Tel 0870 700 2233
Fax 0114 275 2565
Web www.nai-fullerpeiser.com
Email anock@nai-fullerpeiser.com

NOCK, Mark
Donaldsons
Position
Partner – office agency and development, Bristol
Contact details
Donaldsons, Beech House, 6 St Paul's Road, Bristol BS8 1LT
Tel 0117 923 9520
Fax 0117 923 9521
Web www.donaldsons.co.uk
Direct tel 0117 933 1801
Email mark.nock@donaldsons.co.uk

NOÉ, Leo
REIT Asset Management
Position
Partner
Contact details
REIT Asset Management Ltd, 5 Wigmore Street, London W1U 1PB
Tel 020 7499 2244
Fax 020 7499 7700
Web www.reit.co.uk
Email leo@reit.co.uk

NOEL, Robert
Great Portland Estates
Position
Property director
Qualifications
BSc; MRICS
Career history
Since 2002 Property director, Great Portland Estates.
1987-2002 Director (investment consulting), Nelson Bakewell
Other roles
Council member, Westminster Property Owners Association

N?

Professional memberships
Investment Property Forum; RICS
Interests
Wine
Contact details
Great Portland Estates plc, 56 Mortimer Street, London W1W 7RT
Tel 020 7580 3040
Fax 020 7631 5169
Web www.gpe.co.uk
Direct tel 020 7612 1443
Direct fax 020 7612 1455
Mobile 07771 512979
Email robert.noel@gpe.co.uk

NOEL, Thomas
Bride Hall Group
Position
Non-executive director
Contact details
Bride Hall Group Ltd, 49 Hays Mews, London W1J 5QQ
Tel 020 7493 3996
Fax 020 7499 4388
Email thomas.noel@bride-hall.co.uk

NOLAN, Brandon
McGrigors
Position
Partner and national head of construction
Contact details
McGrigors, Pacific House, 70 Wellington Street, Glasgow G2 6SB
Tel 0141 248 6677
Fax 0141 204 1351
Web www.mcgrigors.com
Email brandon.nolan@mcgrigors.com

NOLAN, Gerard
FPDSavills
Position
Director – head of hotels
Qualifications
MRICS
Other roles
Board member, Savills Commercial; director, Colliers Erdman Lewis; board director, Christie & Co
Professional memberships
British Association of Hotel Accountants; Institute of Directors; National Association of Estate Agents; RICS
Interests
Cycling; family; golf; sailing; swimming
Contact details
FPDSavills Ltd, 20 Grosvenor Hill, London W1K 3HQ
Tel 020 7499 8644
Fax 020 7495 3773
Web www.fpdsavills.co.uk
Direct tel 020 7409 8771
Mobile 07768 875633
Email gnolan@fpdsavills.co.uk

NORDSTRÖM, Rolf
International Real Estate
Position
Executive chairman
Qualifications
MBA
Career history
1996 Joined International Real Estate (previously Criterion Properties) as executive chairman
Other roles
Executive chairman, Minmet; executive chairman, TripepAB; chairman (since 1996), Realia Fastighets (Swedish company listed on Stockholm stock exchange); chairman, Columna Fastigheter (since 1995); executive chairman, Fastigheter (1995-2000); director of several other property companies
Professional memberships
Institute of Directors
Interests
Aviation
Contact details
International Real Estate plc, 34 St James's Street, London SW1A 1HD
Tel 020 7839 8686
Fax 020 7839 7474
Web www.IREplc.com
Mobile 07776 137400
Email rolf@ireplc.com

NORRIS, Tony
Bevan Ashford
Position
Partner – head of construction
Qualifications
LLB Hons; FCIArb; FFB
Career history
1992 Joined Bevan Ashford; became partner in 1997; specialises in development/project finance.
1991 Admitted to Roll of Solicitors
Professional memberships
Chartered Institute of Arbitrators
Interests
Cricket; golf; rugby; walking
Contact details
Bevan Ashford, 35 Colston Avenue, Bristol BS1 4TT
Tel 0117 923 0111
Fax 0117 929 1865
Web www.bevanashford.co.uk
Direct tel 0117 975 1709
Mobile 07785 598272
Email tony.norris@bevanashford.co.uk

NORTH, Michael
North Rae Sanders
Position
Partner
Qualifications
MRICS
Contact details
North Rae Sanders, Orchard Court, Harry Weston Road, Coventry CV3 2TQ
Tel 024 7663 6888
Fax 024 7663 6114
Web www.northraesanders.co.uk
Email mnorth@northraesanders.co.uk

NORTHCOTT, Michael
Stephens & Scown
Position
Partner and deputy head of property department
Contact details
Stephens & Scown Ltd, 25-28 Southernhay East, Exeter EX1 1RS
Tel 0139 221 0700
Fax 0139 227 4010
Web www.stephens-scown.co.uk
Email property.exeter@stephens-scown.co.uk

NORTON, Richard
Jones Lang LaSalle
Position
Regional director – corporate solutions
Career history
1994 Joined Jones Lang LaSalle
Professional memberships
RICS
Interests
Cricket; DIY; family; performing arts; sailing; tennis
Contact details
Jones Lang LaSalle Ltd, 9 Queen Victoria Street, London EC4N 4YY
Tel 020 7248 6040
Fax 020 7248 0088
Web www.joneslanglasalle.com
Direct tel 020 7399 5627
Direct fax 020 7399 5500
Mobile 07887 625672
Email richard.norton@eu.joneslanglasalle.com

NOYES-LEWIS, Simon
Aitchison Raffety
Position
Associate director – head of commercial agency

Qualifications
BSc Hons; MRICS
Contact details
Aitchison Raffety Ltd, Compass House,
1 Farmoor Court, Oxford OX2 9LU
Tel 01865 865658
Fax 01865 865353
Web www.argroup.co.uk
Email oxford.info@argroup.co.uk

NUGEE, Christopher
Wilberforce Chambers

Position
Barrister
Qualifications
QC
Career history
1998 Appointed QC.
Since 1984 Barrister specialising in property litigation.
1983 Called to Bar
Professional memberships
Chancery Bar Association; Commercial Bar Association
Contact details
Wilberforce Chambers, 8 New Square, London WC2A 3QP
Tel 020 7306 0102
Fax 020 7306 0095
Web www.wilberforce.co.uk
Email cnugee@wilberforce.co.uk

NUTMAN, Bruce
CB Richard Ellis

Position
Director – retail investment
Contact details
CB Richard Ellis, Kingsley House, 1a Wimpole Street, London W1G 0RE
Tel 020 7182 2000
Fax 020 7182 7001
Web www.cbre.com
Email bruce.nutman@cbre.com

O

O'BRIEN, Eugene
Phoenix Beard

Position
Director – Midlands agency

Contact details
Phoenix Beard, The Exchange, 19 Newhall Street, Birmingham B3 3PJ
Tel 0121 200 4500
Fax 0121 200 4599
Web www.phoenix-beard.co.uk
Email eugene@phoenix-beard.co.uk

O'BRIEN, Tom
Glenny

Position
Partner – building consultancy and architecture

Qualifications
BSc Hons; MRICS

Career history
1997 Joined Glenny.
1990-97 Commercial director, Lenister Construction.
1988-90 Senior building surveyor, Glenny.
1987-88 Building surveyor, George Trollope

Professional memberships
RICS

Contact details
Glenny, Dovetail House, 60 Station Road, London RM14 2TJ
Tel 0170 822 5547
Fax 0170 822 1838
Web www.glenny.co.uk
Mobile 07768 068996
Email t.obrien@glenny.co.uk

O'CONNOR, John
Aberdeen Property Investors

Position
Managing director

Contact details
Aberdeen Property Investors, Charles House, 5-11 Regent Street, London SW1Y 4LR
Tel 020 7747 1700
Fax 020 7839 7460
Web www.aberdeenpropertyinvestors.com
Email
john.o'connor@aberdeenpropertyinvestors.com

O'DONNELL, Peter
British Nuclear Fuels

Position
Property manager

Qualifications
BA; MRICS

Professional memberships
RICS

Contact details
British Nuclear Fuels plc, 1100 Daresbury Park, Warrington WA4
Tel 01925 832000
Fax 01925 822711
Web www.bnfl.com
Direct tel 01925 832691
Email peter.o'donnell@bnfl.com

O'HALLORAN, John
BAA Lynton

Position
Managing director

Qualifications
FRICS

Career history
1984 Joined BAA Lynton

Professional memberships
British Council for Offices; Investment Property Forum; RICS

Contact details
BAA Lynton plc, 67-69 New Bond Street, London W1S 1DF
Tel 020 7907 9200
Fax 020 7907 9299
Web www.baa.com
Direct tel 020 7907 9206
Direct fax 020 7907 9321
Mobile 07785 392990
Email john_o'halloran@baa.com

O'HARA, Bill
Montagu Evans

Position
Partner – head of Scotland

Qualifications
FRICS

Professional memberships
RICS

Contact details
Montagu Evans, 302 St Vincent Street, Glasgow G2 5RU
Tel 0141 204 2090
Fax 0141 221 7441
Web www.montagu-evans.co.uk
Email bill.o'hara@montagu-evans.co.uk

O'HOGAN, Aidan
Hamilton Osborne King

Position
Chairman

Qualifications
FRICS; FSCS; FIAVI

Career history
1987 Joined Hamilton Osborne King as retail director; appointed managing director in 1995 and chairman in 2003.
1978-87 Retail director, Osborne King & Megran.
1969-78 Development surveyor, Lisney

Other roles
Council member, Dublin Chamber of Commerce; president, Irish Auctioneers & Valuers Institute; chairman, HOK Residential

Professional memberships
Irish Auctioneers & Valuers Institute; RICS; Society of Chartered Surveyors

Interests
Golf; skiing

Contact details
Hamilton Osborne King, 32 Molesworth Street, Dublin 2
Tel +353 1 618 1300
Fax +353 1 676 7066
Web www.hok.ie
Direct tel +353 1 618 1401
Email aidan.ohogan@cbhok.com

O'KEEFFE, Eugene
Park Nelson

Position
Senior partner and head of commercial property

Qualifications
LLB Hons; Solicitor

Career history
1978 Joined Park Nelson

Other roles
Chair, Governor Bacon's City Technology College; foundation governor, Southwark Diocesan Board of Education; governor, St George's Primary School, Southwark; honorary legal adviser to Franco-British Society

Interests
Cycling; music; reading; swimming; theatre; walking; RAC

Contact details
Park Nelson, 1 Bell Yard, London WC2A 2JP
Tel 020 7539 2000
Fax 020 7405 4266
Web www.parknelson.co.uk

Direct tel 020 7539 2042
Direct fax 020 7539 2972
Email law@parknelson.co.uk

O'KEEFFE, Patrick
GVA Saxon Law

Position
Partner
Qualifications
BSc; MRICS
Career history
2003 Joined GVA Saxon Law/GVA Grimley.
1988-2003 Saxon Law.
1986-88 Chesterton
Contact details
GVA Saxon Law, 10 Stratton Street, London W1J 8JR
Tel 0870 900 8990
Fax 020 7911 2560
Direct tel 020 7911 2768
Direct fax 020 7911 2563
Mobile 07831 558817
Email pok@gvasaxonlaw.com

O'MEARA, Anne
Hammonds

Position
Partner – head of firm's property sector
Qualifications
LLB Hons
Career history
1980 Admitted to Roll of Solicitors.
1978 Joined Hammonds; partner since 1984; now head of property sector and national head of regeneration
Other roles
Director/trustee of City of Birmingham Symphony Orchestra; board member, Sandwell Urban Regeneration Co; member of advisory board, Locate in Birmingham
Professional memberships
Birmingham Law Society; British Urban Regeneration Association; Law Society
Interests
Music; reading
Contact details
Hammonds, Rutland House, 148 Edmund Street, Birmingham B3 2JR
Tel 0870 839 0000
Fax 0870 839 3001
Web www.hammonds.com
Direct tel 0870 839 3249
Direct fax 0870 460 2742
Mobile 07721 865903
Email anne.omeara@hammonds.com

O'NEILL, Anne
Coudert Brothers London

Position
Head of UK real estate
Qualifications
LLB Hons
Career history
Since 1997 Partner, Coudert Brothers.
1988-97 Property partner, Debenham & Co.
1985 Admitted to Roll of Solicitors
Professional memberships
British Council of Shopping Centres; BPF; Law Society; Property Valuation Forum; Women in Property
Contact details
Coudert Brothers London Ltd, 60 Cannon Street, London EC4N 6JP
Tel 020 7248 3000
Fax 020 7248 3001
Web www.coudert.com
Email oneilla@london.coudert.com

O'NEILL, Heather
Henderson Boyd Jackson WS

Position
Partner – head of real estate
Qualifications
LLB; Dip LP; WS; NP
Career history
Since 1993 Partner, Henderson Boyd Jackson.
1991-93 Partner, Boyd Jameson.
1986 Admitted to Roll of Solicitors
Other roles
Director, Edinburgh Business Development (business start-up division of Edinburgh Chamber of Commerce)
Professional memberships
British Council for Offices; Investment Property Forum; Law Society of Scotland
Contact details
Henderson Boyd Jackson WS, Exchange Tower, 19 Canning Street, Edinburgh EH3 8EG
Tel 0131 228 2400
Fax 0131 228 9800
Web www.hbj.co.uk
Direct tel 0131 222 9815
Direct fax 0131 222 9820
Email h.oneill@hbj.co.uk

O'REILLY, Simon
Cushman & Wakefield Healey & Baker

Position
Partner – global corporate services
Qualifications
FRICS
Career history
Since 2000 Partner, Cushman & Wakefield Healey & Baker.
1998-2000 Director (business operations, EMEA), Unisys.
1974-98 Director corporate services, Chesterton
Other roles
Board member, CoreNet Global
Professional memberships
CoreNet Global UK; RICS
Interests
Cricket; gardening; golf; skiing
Contact details
Cushman & Wakefield Healey & Baker, 43-45 Portman Square, London W1A 3BG
Tel 020 7935 5000
Fax 020 7152 5360
Web www.cushwake.com
Direct tel 020 7152 5544
Direct fax 020 7152 5363
Mobile 07879 630121
Email simon.o'reilly@eur.cushwake.com

O'RIORDAN, Michael
AMEC Developments

Position
Chairman – Midlands region
Qualifications
BSc; FRICS; FRSA
Career history
2001 Joined AMEC Developments.
2000-01 Chairman, Faithful & Gould.
1990-2000 Chairman, Silk & Frazier/Silk & Frazier Partnership
Other roles
Chairman, Worcestershire Acute Hospitals Trust
Interests
Football; outdoor pursuits; rugby
Contact details
AMEC Developments Ltd, Bank House, 8 Cherry Street, Birmingham B2 5AQ
Tel 0121 632 4000
Fax 0121 632 5579
Web www.amec.com
Mobile 07815 151011
Email michael.o'riordan@amec.com

O'ROURKE, Terence
Terence O'Rourke

Position
Chairman
Qualifications
MBE; Dip Arch; Dip TP; RIBA; MRTPI; FRSA
Career history
1985 Founded Terence O'Rourke
Other roles
Director, Bournemouth Symphony Orchestra
Professional memberships
RIBA; Royal Society of Arts; RTPI

O

Contact details
Terence O'Rourke, Everdene House, Deansleigh Road, Bournemouth BH7 7DU
Tel 0120 242 1142
Fax 0120 243 0055
Web www.torltd.co.uk
Email maildesk@torltd.co.uk

O'SULLIVAN, Kevin
Maris Interiors
Position
Contracts director (West End)
Qualifications
BSc Arch; Dip Arch
Career history
1992 Joined Maris.
1985-92 Shoralplan
Contact details
Maris Interiors Ltd, The Tower Building, 11 York Road, London SE1 7NQ
Tel 020 7902 1750
Fax 020 7902 1799
Web www.maris-london.co.uk
Mobile 07831 319040
Email kevin.osullivan@maris-westend.co.uk

OAKES, Robert
Manches
Position
Partner – head of construction
Interests
Art; cricket; opera; skiing; sport; theatre
Contact details
Manches, Aldwych House, 81 Aldwych, London WC2B 4HN
Tel 020 7404 4433
Fax 020 7430 1133
Web www.manches.com
Email robert.oakes@manches.co.uk

OAKESHOTT, Matthew
Olim
Position
Joint managing director
Qualifications
MA Hons (Oxon)
Career history
Since 1986 Joint founder and managing director, Olim.
1981-85 Investment manager, Courtaulds Pension Fund.
1976-81 Director, Warburg Investment Management.
1972-76 Special adviser to Rt Hon Roy Jenkins MP
Other roles
Joint managing director, Value & Income Trust; Liberal Democrat treasury and pensions spokesman, House of Lords; House of Lords all-party select committee on economic affairs
Interests
Football; music; politics
Contact details
Olim Ltd, Pollen House, 10-12 Cork Street, London W1S 3NP
Tel 020 7439 4400
Fax 020 7734 1445
Email carolyn_nichols@olim.co.uk

OAKLEY, Mat
FPDSavills
Position
Director
Qualifications
BSc Hons
Career history
Since 1997 Head of commercial research, FPDSavills.
1990-97 Researcher/senior researcher/head of research, Drivers Jonas.
1989-90 Researcher, *Financial Times*
Professional memberships
Society of Property Researchers
Contact details
FPDSavills Ltd, 20 Grosvenor Hill, London W1K 3HQ
Tel 020 7499 8644
Fax 020 7495 3773
Web www.fpdsavills.co.uk
Direct tel 020 7409 8781
Direct fax 020 7753 8919
Mobile 07774 267538
Email moakley@fpdsavills.co.uk

OATES, Jeremy
GVA Grimley
Position
Partner
Contact details
GVA Grimley, 3 Brindleyplace, Birmingham B1 2JB
Tel 0870 900 8990
Fax 0121 609 8314
Web www.gvagrimley.co.uk
Email jeremy.oates@gvagrimley.co.uk

ODOM-HASLETT, Neil
Eurohypo
Position
Director – origination
Career history
Since 2002 Director (origination), Eurohypo, London branch (following merger with Rheinhyp).
2000-02 Senior manager/head of marketing, Rheinhyp.
1999-2000 Assistant director, Société Générale.
1990-99 Manager, Fortis Bank
Other roles
Director, RSM Management
Professional memberships
Association of Property Bankers
Interests
Football; golf
Contact details
Eurohypo AG, 90 Long Acre, London WC2E 9RA
Tel 020 7759 7600
Fax 020 7759 7672
Web www.eurohypo.com
Direct tel 020 7759 7605
Email neil.odom-haslett@eurohypo.com

OGLESBY, Chris
Bruntwood Estates
Position
Managing director
Contact details
Bruntwood Estates Ltd, Manchester Technology Centre, Oxford Road, Manchester M1 7ED
Tel 0161 237 3883
Fax 0161 237 1779
Web www.bruntwood.co.uk
Email chris.oglesby@bruntwood.co.uk

OGLESBY, Michael
Bruntwood Estates
Position
Chairman
Career history
1976 Founded Bruntwood.
1971-74 Director, Lyon Group.
Interests
Rugby; sailing; skiing; theatre; travel
Contact details
Bruntwood Estates Ltd, Manchester Technology Centre, Oxford Road, Manchester M1 7ED
Tel 0161 237 3883
Fax 0161 237 1779
Web www.bruntwood.co.uk
Direct tel 0161 238 7134
Email michael.oglesby@bruntwood.co.uk

OGUNSHAKIN, Nelson
Association of Consulting Engineers
Position
Chief executive
Qualifications
BSc Hons; MSc; MBA; CEng; MICE; MCIM; MCIArb; MIoD
Career history
Since 2003 Association of Consulting Engineers.

2002-03 AEO (Group) UK.
2000-02 WSP North.
1993-2000 High-Point Rendel Group.
1987-93 Rendel Palmer & Tritton.
1982-86 Carillion Construction (formerly Tarmac Construction).
1980-81 Tamworth Borough Council

Professional memberships
Chartered Institute of Arbitrators; Chartered Institute of Marketing; Institute of Directors; Institution of Civil Engineers

Interests
Charity; golf; reading; socialising; squash

Contact details
Association of Consulting Engineers, Alliance House, 12 Alliance House, London SW1H 0QL
Tel 020 7222 6557
Fax 020 7222 0750
Web www.acenet.co.uk
Email nogunshakin@acenet.co.uk

OLDHAM, Robert
Ernst & Young

Position
Partner – corporate real estate advisory services

Qualifications
BEng; MSc; CEng; MICE; MCMI

Career history
Since 1993 Partner, Ernst & Young.
1983-93 Group manager, KPMG

Professional memberships
Chartered Management Institute; Institution of Civil Engineers

Interests
Cycling; sailing

Contact details
Ernst & Young LLP, 1 More London Place, London SE1 2AF
Tel 020 7951 2000
Fax 020 7951 1345
Web www.ey.com/uk
Direct tel 020 7931 3368
Direct fax 020 7951 3411
Mobile 07720 265626
Email roldham@uk.ey.com

OLDRIEVE, Mike
Vickery Holman

Position
Director

Contact details
Vickery Holman Ltd, 26 Lockyer Street, Plymouth PL1 2QW
Tel 01752 261811
Fax 01752 661365
Web www.vickeryholman.com
Email mail@vickeryholman.ltd.uk

OLIVER, Bill
St Modwen Properties

Position
Managing director

Contact details
St Modwen Properties plc, Lyndon House, 62 Hagley Road, Birmingham B16 8PE
Tel 0121 456 2800
Fax 0121 456 1829
Web www.stmodwen.co.uk
Email woliver@stmodwen.co.uk

OLIVER, Christopher
Cube Real Estate

Position
Founding partner

Contact details
Cube Real Estate Ltd, 43 Dover Street, London W1S 4NU
Tel 020 7493 5544
Fax 020 7493 5570
Email chris@cube-re.com

OLIVER, Louise
International Real Estate Federation (FIABCI)

Position
Director of communications – FIABCI UK

Career history
Since 2001 Secretary and director of communications, FIABCI UK

Contact details
International Real Estate Federation (FIABCI), PO Box 1055, Maidenhead SL6 4YA
Tel 01628 680709
Fax 01628 629733
Web www.fiabci.com
Email louise@beryllodge.co.uk

OLIVER, Paul
Teesland

Position
Joint chief executive

Qualifications
BSc, Est Man; FRICS

Career history
Since 2000 Chief executive, Teesland.
1996-2000 Founder, Equity Partnerships.
1991-96 Managing director, Dusco Asset Management and Dusco (UK).
1977-91 Director, GRE Properties (now Guardian Properties)

Professional memberships
British Council of Shopping Centres; BPF; Investment Property Forum; RICS

Interests
Rugby; tennis; travel; wine

Contact details
Teesland plc, 10 Carlos Place, London W1K 3AT
Tel 020 7493 4636
Fax 020 7493 4637
Web www.teesland.com
Email paul.oliver@teesland.com

OLIVER, Taeko
CB Richard Ellis

Position
Executive director – Japanese business

Qualifications
BA; MRICS

Professional memberships
RICS

Interests
Classical music; jazz; opera

Contact details
CB Richard Ellis, St Martin's Court, 10 Paternoster Row, London EC4M 7HP
Tel 020 7182 2000
Fax 020 7182 2001
Web www.cbre.com
Email taeko.oliver@cbre.com

ORR, Robert
Jones Lang LaSalle

Position
European chief executive officer

Qualifications
BSc, Est Man; MRICS

Career history
Since 1998 European chief executive officer, Jones Lang LaSalle.
1986-98 Jones Lang LaSalle, Frankfurt: roles included managing partner (Germany), lead partner (investment, Germany), member of board of Europe.
1983-86 Senior investment and valuation surveyor, Jones Lang Wootton, Paris.
1980-83 Jones Lang Wootton, London

Other roles
Member of global executive committee, Jones Lang LaSalle

Professional memberships
RICS

Interests
Cycling; rugby

Contact details
Jones Lang LaSalle Ltd, 22 Hanover Square, London W1A 2BN
Tel 020 7493 6040
Fax 020 7408 0220
Web www.joneslanglasalle.com
Direct tel 020 7399 5852
Direct fax 020 7399 5271

O

Mobile 07771 921800
Email robert.orr@eu.joneslanglasalle.com

ORRELL, Suzanne
Bank of Scotland Corporate Banking

Position
Director – structured property finance
Career history
Since 2000 Director (structured property finance), Bank of Scotland Corporate Banking.
1993-2000 Manager (property department), Fortis Bank.
1989-93 Aviation group, Long Term Credit Bank of Japan.
1987-89 Commodity and trade finance, Caisse Nationale de Credit.
1986-87 Commercial paper team, Barclays de Zoete Wedd
Professional memberships
Association of Property Bankers; Investment Property Forum
Interests
Cinema; DIY; entertaining; football; singing; socialising; water sports
Contact details
Bank of Scotland Corporate Banking, 155 Bishopsgate, London EC2M 3YB
Tel 020 7012 9400
Direct tel 020 7012 9134
Direct fax 020 7012 9445
Mobile 07748 333104
Email suzanne_orrell@bankofscotland.co.uk

ORRETT, Robert
ATIS REAL Weatheralls

Position
Director
Qualifications
BSc; MRICS
Career history
1989 Joined ATIS REAL Weatheralls; appointed associate within a year and partner within four years; now leads and manages Bristol office.
1979-88 Langley-Taylor: partner on leaving
Professional memberships
RICS
Interests
Cooking; hockey; skiing
Contact details
ATIS REAL Weatheralls Ltd, Broad Quay House, Broad Quay, Bristol BS1 4DJ
Tel 0117 984 8400
Fax 0117 984 8401
Web www.atisrealweatheralls.com
Direct tel 0117 984 8430
Email robert.orrett@atisrealweatheralls.com

ORTON, Melvyn
Finers Stephens Innocent

Position
Partner – head of property investment
Career history
1971 Joined Thornton Lynne & Lawson (merged with Finers Stephens Innocent in 1991); became partner soon after qualification; now head of property investment.
1971 Admitted to Roll of Solicitors
Interests
Cinema; sport; theatre; travel
Contact details
Finers Stephens Innocent, 179 Great Portland Street, London W1W 5LS
Tel 020 7323 4000
Fax 020 7344 5600
Web www.finersstephensinnocent.com
Direct tel 020 7344 5508
Email morton@fsilaw.co.uk

OSBORNE, Andrew
Vail Williams

Position
Partner – business space and development
Qualifications
BSc Hons
Interests
Cycling; golf; mountain biking; squash
Contact details
Vail Williams, 9 The Boulevard, Crawley RH10 1UR
Tel 01293 411111
Fax 01293 411121
Web www.vailwilliams.com
Mobile 07768 724345
Email aosborne@vailwilliams.com

OSBORNE, Terence
Tuckerman

Position
Managing director
Qualifications
FRICS; IRRV
Career history
1976 Joined Tuckerman.
1972-76 Partner, Edward Symmons & Partners.
1970-72 Andrews & Robertson.
1968-70 Weatherall Green & Smith
Other roles
Director, Bartel Property Co; trustee, London Bridge Museum
Professional memberships
Institute of Revenues Rating & Valuation; Investment Property Forum; RICS
Interests
Cinema; golf; local history; skiing; tennis; theatre
Contact details
Tuckerman, 40 Great Smith Street, London SW1P 3BU
Tel 020 7222 5511
Fax 020 7222 0558
Web www.tuckerman.co.uk
Mobile 07768 040404
Email tosborne@tuckerman.co.uk

OSMOND, Christopher
CWM

Position
Partner
Qualifications
MA; FRICS
Career history
1985-2002 CB Hillier Parker.
1984-85 Debenham Tewson & Chinnocks.
1980-84 Hillier Parker
Other roles
RICS arbitrator and independent expert on rent review disputes
Professional memberships
Arbrix; RICS
Interests
Cricket
Contact details
CWM, 16 Old Bond Street, London W1S 4PS
Tel 020 7493 5655
Fax 020 7493 5665
Web www.cwm.co.uk
Direct tel 020 7255 7817
Mobile 07753 826421
Email chris.osmond@cwm.co.uk

OSTRER, Andrew
Stiles Harold Williams

Position
Director
Contact details
Stiles Harold Williams Ltd, 96 Park Lane, London CR9 2NL
Tel 020 8662 2700
Fax 020 8680 3193
Web www.shw.co.uk
Email aostrer@shw.co.uk

OSWALD, Drew
Knight Frank

Position
Managing partner – Scottish commercial practice
Qualifications
BSc; FRICS; ACIArb
Career history
Since 1993 Managing partner (Scottish commercial practice), Knight Frank
Other roles

Member of RICS chairman's panel of arbiters/independent experts for Scottish rent review disputes

Professional memberships
Chartered Institute of Arbitrators; RICS; Scottish Council for Development & Industry

Interests
Art; football; music; travel

Contact details
Knight Frank LLP, Sutherland House, 149 St Vincent Street, Glasgow G2 5NW
Tel 0141 221 9191
Fax 0141 221 2328
Web www.knightfrank.com
Direct tel 0141 566 6024
Mobile 07836 260424
Email drew.oswald@knightfrank.com

OTTER, Mark
Crossland Otter Hunt

Position
Consultant

Qualifications
BSc; MRICS

Professional memberships
RICS

Contact details
Crossland Otter Hunt, PO Box 74, Buxton SK17 8WX
Tel 0870 609 6999
Fax 01298 872896
Web www.c-o-h.com
Email markotter@btopenworld.com

OUTTERSIDE, Andrew
Vail Williams

Position
Partner – landlord and tenant consultancy

Qualifications
BSc; FRICS; MCIArb; IRRV

Career history
1987-89 Prudential Property Services.
1983-87 Parsons Welch & Cowell.
1980-83 Gerald Eve & Co

Professional memberships
Chartered Institute of Arbitrators; Institute of Revenues Rating & Valuation; Rating Surveyors Association; RICS

Interests
Motor sports

Contact details
Vail Williams, 635 Sipson Road, West Drayton UB7 0JE
Tel 020 8564 8300
Fax 020 8759 1599
Web www.vailwilliams.com
Direct tel 020 8283 0618
Mobile 07831 451157
Email aoutterside@vailwilliams.com

OWEN, Adrian
Hamptons International

Position
Director

Contact details
Hamptons International, 168 Brompton Road, London SW3 1HW
Tel 020 7584 2044
Fax 020 7584 2072
Web www.hamptons.co.uk
Email owena@hamptons-int.com

OWEN, Barry
Mason Owen & Partners

Position
Senior partner

Career history
1967 Joined Mason Owen & Partners.
1963-67 Bernard Thorpe & Partners

Other roles
Chairman, Ethel Austin Property Group

Interests
Golf (Royal Liverpool Golf Club); rugby; shooting; Liverpool Artists Club

Contact details
Mason Owen & Partners Ltd, Gladstone House, 11 Union Court, Liverpool L2 4UQ
Tel 0151 242 3000
Fax 0151 236 2569
Web www.masonowen.com
Direct tel 0151 242 3011
Mobile 07836 611822
Email barry.owen@masonowen.com

OWEN, Duncan
Insight Investment Management

Position
Managing director – property

Qualifications
BSc Hons; MRICS

Career history
Since 2003 Managing director (property), Insight Investment Management.
2001-2003 Founding co-director, Gatehouse Investment Management.
1990-2001 Jones Lang LaSalle: appointed associate partner in 1995 and partner in 1997

Professional memberships
Investment Property Forum; RICS

Interests
Rugby; sport

Contact details
Insight Investment Management, City Place House, 55 Basinghall Street, London EC2V 5DL
Tel 020 7930 5474
Web www.insightinvestment.com
Direct tel 020 7321 1677
Email duncan.owen@insightinvestment.com

OWEN, James
Threadneedle Property Investments

Position
Fund manager

Qualifications
BSc Hons; FRICS

Career history
1987-2000 Property fund director, Hill Samuel Asset Management.
1977-87 Associate, George Trollope.
1972-77 Valuation surveyor, Richard Ellis

Professional memberships
RICS

Interests
Reading; shooting; squash

Contact details
Threadneedle Property Investments, 9-15 Sackville Street, London W1S 3DJ
Tel 020 7437 8000
Fax 020 7464 5811
Email james.owen@threadneedle.co.uk

OWEN, Richard
Drivers Jonas

Position
Partner – head of valuation

Qualifications
BA Hons; MRICS; IRRV

Career history
1988 Joined Drivers Jonas

Professional memberships
RICS

Contact details
Drivers Jonas, 6 Grosvenor Street, London W1K 4DJ
Tel 020 7896 8000
Fax 020 7896 8001
Web www.driversjonas.com
Direct tel 020 7896 8110
Email richardowen@driversjonas.com

OWEN, Stephen
Graves Son & Pilcher

Position
Partner

Career history
Since 1972 Graves Son & Pilcher.
1971-72 Habens & Banner

Interests
IT; tennis

Contact details
Graves Son & Pilcher, 51 Old Steyne, Brighton

BN1 1HU
Tel 01273 321123
Fax 01273 771070
Web www.gsp.uk.com
Mobile 07714 714205
Email so@gsp.uk.com

OWEN, Steven
Brixton

Position
Deputy chief executive
Qualifications
LLB; FCA; MCT
Career history
1985 Joined Brixton as financial controller; appointed finance director in 1992 and deputy chief executive in 2000.
1979-85 Peat Marwick Mitchell & Co
Professional memberships
Association of Corporate Treasurers; BPF; Institute of Chartered Accountants in England and Wales
Interests
Cycling; diving/scuba diving; golf; rugby
Contact details
Brixton plc, 50 Berkeley Street, London W1J 8BX
Tel 020 7399 4500
Fax 020 7399 4550
Web www.brixton.plc.uk
Direct tel 020 7399 4532
Mobile 07768 827567
Email stevenowen@brixton.plc.uk

OWEN, Valerie
London First Centre

Position
Director of investor development
Qualifications
BSc; BArch; RIBA; Dip TP; MRTPI; ACIArb; MRICS
Career history
1989-2000 Jones Lang Wootton: joined as associate; became partner in 1994 and director of Jones Lang LaSalle in 1999.
1980-89 Architect/associate/partner, Shenstone & Partners.
1978-79 Architect, Cusdin Burden & Howitt
Professional memberships
RIBA; RICS; Royal Society of Arts; RTPI
Interests
Architecture; conservation; IT; literature; photography; poetry; swimming; theatre
Contact details
London First Centre, 1 Hobhouse Court, Suffolk Street, London SW1Y 4HH
Tel 020 7925 2000
Fax 020 7925 2022
Web www.lfc.co.uk
Email vowen@london-first.co.uk

OXLEY, John
Allsop & Co

Position
Partner – commercial investments
Qualifications
BSc; FRICS
Career history
1968 Joined Allsop & Co.
1966-68 Surveyor, District Valuer's Office and Valuation Office, Walsall
Other roles
Chief executive of European Estates (Spanish company founded by Allsop & Co and Ernst & Young, Spain)
Professional memberships
BSc (Estate Management) Club; Investment Property Forum; RICS
Interests
Fishing; music; opera; tennis; walking
Contact details
Allsop & Co, 27 Soho Square, London W1D 3AY
Tel 020 7437 6977
Fax 020 7437 8984
Web www.allsop.co.uk
Direct tel 020 7543 6719
Mobile 07768 791640
Email john.oxley@allsop.co.uk

P

PAIN, Mike
Rogers Chapman

Position
Director – west London professional services

Qualifications
BSc; FRICS; MCIArb; IRRV

Career history
1988 Joined Rogers Chapman. Prior to that, qualified at Drivers Jonas, then senior surveyor at Property Services Agency

Other roles
Lectures on APC courses at Kingston University and RICS; RICS representative on City University partnership

Professional memberships
Chartered Institute of Arbitrators; Institute of Revenues Rating & Valuation; RICS

Interests
Family; real tennis

Contact details
Rogers Chapman plc, Grantley House, 9 Park Lane, Cranford, Heathrow TW5 9RW
Tel 020 8759 4141
Fax 020 8759 5367
Web www.rogerschapman.co.uk
Direct tel 020 8283 2551
Mobile 07788 188855
Email mike.pain@rogerschapman.co.uk

PAINE, David
Standard Life Investments

Position
Investment director – development, retail, asset management

Qualifications
BLE; MRICS

Professional memberships
RICS

Contact details
Standard Life Investments Ltd, 1 George Street, Edinburgh EH2 2LL
Tel 0131 245 2700
Fax 0131 245 2710
Web www.standardlife.com
Direct tel 0131 245 2801
Direct fax 0131 240 8336
Email david_paine@standardlife.com

PAINE, Oliver
King Sturge

Position
Partner – investment

Qualifications
BSc; MRICS

Contact details
King Sturge, 40 Berkeley Square, Bristol BS8 1HU
Tel 0117 927 6691
Fax 0117 929 9669
Web www.kingsturge.com
Direct tel 0117 930 5718
Email oliver.paine@kingsturge.co.uk

PAINTER, Robert
Laura Ashley

Position
Shop development manager

Contact details
Laura Ashley Ltd, 27 Bagleys Lane, London SW6 2AR
Tel 020 7880 5100
Fax 020 7880 5200
Web www.lauraashley.com
Email robert.painter@lauraashley.com

PAINTING, Iain
Barton Willmore

Position
Partner

Qualifications
BSc Hons; Dip TP

Career history
1996 Joined Barton Willmore as senior planner; became partner in 2002.
1989-96 Planning officer, Westminster Council

Professional memberships
RTPI

Interests
Cinema; football; golf

Contact details
Barton Willmore, Venture House,
27-29 Glasshouse Street, London W1B 5BW
Tel 020 7446 6888
Fax 020 7446 6889
Web www.bartonwillmore.co.uk
Email iain.painting@bartonwillmore.co.uk

PALMER, Charles
Speechly Bircham

Position
Partner – head of property

Contact details
Speechly Bircham, 6 St Andrew Street, London EC4A 3LX
Tel 020 7427 6400
Fax 020 7427 6600
Web www.speechlys.com
Email charles.palmer@speechlys.co.uk

PALMER, Ray
Palmer Capital Partners

Position
Chairman

Career history
Since 1992 Chairman, Palmer Capital Partners.
1969-91 Joined Lambert Smith & Partners; appointed managing director in 1970.
1968-69 Allsop & Co.
1967-68 Edward Erdman & Co

Other roles
Chairman, Wrenbridge Land and associated companies; chairman, Frontier Estates and associated companies; senior partner, R Palmer & Co; chairman, Opus Land and associated companies; chairman, Danescroft Commercial Developments and associated companies; chairman, Thistle Land and associated companies; chairman, Ediston Properties and associated companies

Interests
Fishing; skiing; wine

Contact details
Palmer Capital Partners Ltd, 17 Clifford Street, London W1S 3RQ
Tel 020 7437 9444
Fax 020 7437 9555
Web www.palmercapital.co.uk
Direct tel 020 7479 7121
Email sue.curran@palmercapital.co.uk

PALMI, Richard
Midlands Co-operative Society

Position
General manager – property

Contact details
Midlands Co-operative Society Ltd, Central House, Hermes Road, Lichfield WS13
Tel 01543 414140
Email richard.palmi@midlandsco-op.com

PANTON, Nigel
Briant Champion Long

Position
Equity director

P

Career history
Since 1999 Equity director, Briant Champion Long (professional department undertaking high-street rent reviews for landlords).
1990-99 Salaried partner, Cushman & Wakefield Healey & Baker, West End head office.
1984-90 Local director, Whitman Porter/Barnard Marcus
Professional memberships
RICS
Interests
Rowing
Contact details
Briant Champion Long Ltd, Nuffield House, 41-46 Piccadilly, London W1J 0DS
Tel 020 7434 7600
Web www.briantchampionlong.com
Direct tel 020 7647 6911
Mobile 07788 457632
Email npanton@bclnet.co.uk

PARK, David
Valuation Office Agency
Position
Deputy chief executive
Qualifications
MA (Cantab); FRICS
Career history
Since 1971 Various public-sector roles, including district valuer for Reigate and district valuer for City of London, within the Valuation Office
Other roles
RICS valuation vaculty board member (2003/04)
Interests
Architecture; gardening; walking
Contact details
Valuation Office Agency, New Court, Carey Street, London WC2A 2JE
Tel 020 7506 1700
Fax 020 7506 1998
Web www.voa.gov.uk
Direct tel 020 7506 1787
Direct fax 020 7506 1991
Email david.park@voa.gsi.gov.uk

PARKER, Alistair
Cushman & Wakefield Healey & Baker
Position
Partner – development consultancy
Qualifications
MRICS; MRTPI
Career history
1984 Joined Cushman & Wakefield Healey & Baker
Professional memberships
Association of Town Centre Management; British Council of Shopping Centres; British Urban Regeneration Association; RICS; RTPI; Urban Villages Forum
Interests
History; IT; opera; skiing
Contact details
Cushman & Wakefield Healey & Baker, 43-45 Portman Square, London W1A 3BG
Tel 020 7935 5000
Fax 020 7152 5360
Web www.cushwake.com
Direct tel 020 7152 5203
Direct fax 020 7152 5383
Email alistair.parker@eur.cushwake.com

PARKER, Andrew
Folkes Properties
Position
Director
Qualifications
MRICS
Contact details
Folkes Properties Ltd, Forge House, Dudley Road, Lye DY9 8EL
Tel 01384 424242
Fax 01384 424455
Web www.folkesproperties.co.uk
Email a.s.parker@folkesproperties.ltd.uk

PARKER, Bob
Esso UK
Position
Regional manager – global real estate
Contact details
Esso UK Ltd, St Catherine's House, PO Box 397, 2 Kingsway, London WC2B 6WJ
Tel 020 7412 4000
Fax 020 7412 2506
Web www.esso.com
Email bob.parker@exxonmobil.com

PARKER, Guy
Taylor Woodrow Developments
Position
UK commercial property development director
Qualifications
BSc Hons; MRICS
Professional memberships
RICS
Contact details
Taylor Woodrow Developments Ltd, Genesis Centre, Science Park South, Warrington WA1 7SP
Tel 01925 250250
Fax 01925 250251
Web www.taylorwoodrow.com
Mobile 07816 517035
Email guy.parker@uk.taylorwoodrow.com

PARKES, Gerald
INVESCO Real Estate
Position
Chief executive
Qualifications
MA; FRICS; SFA
Career history
Since 2001 Chief executive, INVESCO Real Estate.
1996-2001 Founder and chief executive, Parkes & Co.
1993-95 Head of European investment management services, Lend Lease.
1989-93 Founder and partner, Yarmouth Group.
1977-88 Investment surveyor, Richard Ellis, City office
Other roles
Trustee of Urban Land Institute and member of ULI executive committee; global partner, AMVESCAP; non-executive director, Stannifer Group; investment adviser, Teachers Insurance, Real Estate Opportunities
Professional memberships
British Council of Shopping Centres; International Council of Shopping Centers; Investment Property Forum; Lambda Alpha; RICS; Society of Property Researchers; Urban Land Institute
Contact details
INVESCO Real Estate Ltd, 10 Mount Row, London W1K 3SD
Tel 020 7543 3500
Fax 020 7543 3588
Web www.invesco.com
Direct fax 020 7543 3555
Email gerald_parkes@ldn.invesco.com

PARLING, John
Insight Investment Management
Position
Director – property investment
Qualifications
BSc; FRICS
Career history
Since 2001 Director (property investment), Insight Investment.
1990-2001 Senior investment manager, Hill Samuel Asset Management.
1984-90 Senior development manager, 3i
Professional memberships
Investment Property Forum; RICS
Interests
Cricket; golf; rugby
Contact details
Insight Investment Management, City Place House, 55 Basinghall Street, London EC2V
Tel 020 7930 5474
Web www.insightinvestment.com

Direct tel 020 7321 1254
Direct fax 020 7321 1434
Mobile 07876 396478
Email john.parling@insightinvestment.com

PARNELL, Lawrence
Taylor Woodrow Developments

Position
Projects director
Qualifications
Dip Proj Man; FRICS
Professional memberships
RICS
Contact details
Taylor Woodrow Developments Ltd, 41 Clarendon Road, Watford WD17 1TQ
Tel 01923 478400
Web www.taylorwoodrow.com
Direct tel 020 7488 0555
Direct fax 020 7493 1066
Mobile 07816 518723
Email lawrence.parnell@uk.taylorwoodrow.com

PARRY, Deborah
Nabarro Nathanson

Position
Partner – real estate
Career history
1987 Joined Nabarro Nathanson; appointed partner in 1990
Professional memberships
Law Society
Contact details
Nabarro Nathanson, Lacon House, Theobald's Road, London WC1X 8RW
Tel 020 7524 6000
Fax 020 7524 6524
Web www.nabarro.com
Direct tel 020 7524 6317
Email d.parry@nabarro.com

PARRY, Emrys
Bond Pearce

Position
Partner – commercial property
Qualifications
BSc Hons, Econ
Career history
1993 Joined Cartwrights as partner and head of property department (Cartwrights merged with Bond Pearce in 2001); now heads public sector department.
1982-93 DJ Freeman, London.
1977-82 Legal adviser, Land Authority for Wales
Other roles
Former board member and chairman of Surrey Heath Housing Association; legal associate, RTPI; vice-chairman, Compulsory Purchase Association
Professional memberships
Institute of Management
Interests
Golf
Contact details
Bond Pearce, Bristol Bridge House, Redcliff Street, Bristol BS1 6BJ
Tel 0117 929 9197
Fax 0117 929 9198
Web www.bondpearce.com
Direct tel 0117 929 3601
Email eparry@bondpearce.com

PARRY, John
Glenny

Position
Partner
Qualifications
FRICS; IRRV
Career history
1987 Joined Glenny.
1973-87 Valuation Office, Inland Revenue
Professional memberships
RICS
Interests
Rowing; running
Contact details
Glenny, Glenny House, Southfields Business Park, Fenton Way, Basildon SS15 6TD
Tel 01268 540771
Fax 01268 540772
Web www.glenny.co.uk
Mobile 07768 070247
Email j.parry@glenny.co.uk

PARSONS, Scott
Land Securities Group

Position
Business development director
Career history
2003 Joined Land Securities. Previously head of new business at GE Real Estate
Interests
Family; sailing; skiing
Contact details
Land Securities Group plc, 5 Strand, London WC2N 5AF
Tel 020 7413 9000
Fax 020 7024 5007
Web www.landsecurities.com
Direct tel 020 7024 5473
Direct fax 020 7024 5012
Email scott.parsons@landsecurities.com

PARTINGTON, David
Chancery House Chambers

Position
Barrister
Contact details
Chancery House Chambers, 7 Lisbon Square, Leeds LS1 4LY
Tel 0113 244 6691
Fax 0113 244 6766
Web www.chanceryhouse.co.uk
Email david.partington@chanceryhouse.co.uk

PARTON, David
Shoosmiths

Position
Partner – head of direct conveyancing
Qualifications
LLB Hons
Career history
1991 Joined Shoosmiths; partner since 1997.
1991 Admitted to Roll of Solicitors.
1989-91 Edge & Ellison
Other roles
Director, Direct Conveyancing Association
Interests
Football; music; running
Contact details
Shoosmiths, The Lakes, Bedford Road, Northampton NN4 7SH
Tel 08700 868788
Fax 08700 863001
Web www.shoosmiths.co.uk
Direct tel 08700 862105
Direct fax 08700 862169
Mobile 07808 811872
Email david.parton@shoosmiths.co.uk

PARTRIDGE, David
Argent Group

Position
Deputy chief executive
Qualifications
MA (Cantab); Dip Arch; RIBA
Career history
1990 Joined Argent Group.
1981-90 Founding partner and managing director, Gebler Tooth
Professional memberships
RIBA
Interests
Art; literature; mathematics; philosophy; science; sport
Contact details
Argent Group plc, 5 Albany Courtyard, London W1J 0HF
Tel 020 7734 3721
Fax 020 7734 4474

Web www.argentgroup.plc.uk
Email davidp@argentgroup.plc.uk

PARTRIDGE, John
FPDSavills

Position
Director
Contact details
FPDSavills Ltd, 20 Grosvenor Hill, London W1K 3HQ
Tel 020 7499 8644
Fax 020 7495 3773
Web www.fpdsavills.co.uk
Direct tel 020 7409 5904
Mobile 07815 877574
Email jpartridge@fpdsavills.co.uk

PARTRIDGE, Philip
Wilks Head & Eve

Position
Head – national agency team
Qualifications
BSc; MRICS
Professional memberships
RICS
Interests
Golf; running
Contact details
Wilks Head & Eve, 9 Harley Street, London W1G 9AL
Tel 020 7637 8471
Fax 020 7631 0536
Web www.wilks-head.co.uk
Email ppartridge@wilks-head.co.uk

PASS, Michael
Granwood Holdings

Position
Director
Contact details
Granwood Holdings, Stubben Edge Hall, Stubben Edge, Chesterfield S45 0EU
Tel 01246 590543
Fax 01246 590449

PATEL, Hitesh
AXA Real Estate Investment Managers

Position
Fund manager
Contact details
AXA Real Estate Investment Managers Ltd, 7 Newgate Street, London EC1A 7HD
Tel 020 7003 1000
Fax 020 7575 8585
Web www.axa-im.co.uk
Direct tel 020 7367 8150
Email hitesh.patel@axa-reim.co.uk

PATEL, Kiran
AXA Real Estate Investment Managers

Position
Global head of research and strategy
Qualifications
BSc Hons
Professional memberships
Investment Property Forum; Society of Business Economists; Society of Property Researchers
Contact details
AXA Real Estate Investment Managers Ltd, 7 Newgate Street, London EC1A 7HD
Tel 020 7003 1000
Fax 020 7575 8585
Web www.axa-im.co.uk
Direct tel 020 7003 1364
Email kiran.patel@axa-im.com

PATERSON, Christopher
Morley Fund Management

Position
Fund manager – in-town retail
Qualifications
BSc; Dip Prop Inv; FRICS
Other roles
Co-opted board member, British Council of Shopping Centres
Professional memberships
Investment Property Forum; RICS
Contact details
Morley Fund Management Ltd, 34-36 Lime Street, London EC3M 7JE
Tel 020 7809 6000
Fax 020 7489 7940
Web www.morleyfm.com
Direct tel 020 7809 6831
Direct fax 020 7332 9143
Mobile 07771 988909
Email chris.paterson@morleyfm.com

PATON, Ewan
Guildhall Chambers

Position
Barrister
Qualifications
BCL; MA (Oxon)
Career history
1996 Called to Bar.
1993-95 Lecturer in law, University of Nottingham.
1991-92 Research assistant, Law Commission
Other roles
Tutor in property law, University of Bristol
Professional memberships
Chancery Bar Association
Interests
Football; golf; music
Contact details
Guildhall Chambers (Chambers of Adrian Palmer QC), 23 Broad Street, Bristol BS1 2HG
Tel 0117 927 3366
Fax 0117 930 3800
Web www.guildhallchambers.co.uk
Email ewan.paton@guildhallchambers.co.uk

PATTEN, Alan
Harbottle & Lewis

Position
Partner – head of property group
Contact details
Harbottle & Lewis Ltd, Hanover House, 14 Hanover Square, London W1S 1HP
Tel 020 7667 5000
Fax 020 7667 5100
Web www.harbottle.com
Email alan.patten@harbottle.com

PATTERSON, Alan
HSBC Bank

Position
European property analyst
Qualifications
MSc; FRICS; SIAFF
Professional memberships
Investment Property Forum; RICS; Securities Institute; Society of Property Researchers
Contact details
HSBC Bank plc, 8 Canada Square, London E14 5HQ
Tel 020 7991 8888
Fax 020 7992 4880
Web www.hsbc.com
Direct tel 020 7991 6796
Direct fax 020 7992 4862
Email alan.patterson@hsbcib.com

PATTERSON, Frances
Kings Chambers

Position
Barrister
Qualifications
QC
Career history
1977 Called to Bar
Other roles
Has written various papers for a number of planning law conferences, including RTPI, Bar Council, Law Society and RICS; various articles published in *Journal of Planning Law*
Professional memberships
Administrative Law Bar Association; Planning & Environment Bar Association
Contact details
Kings Chambers, 40 King Street, Manchester

P

M2 6BA
Tel 0161 832 9082
Fax 0161 835 2139
Web www.kingschambers.com
Email fpatterson@kingschambers.com

PATTERSON, Tony
Forsters
Position
Partner
Qualifications
LLB
Career history
Since 1998 Partner, Forsters.
1975 Admitted to Roll of Solicitors.
1973-98 Frere Cholmeley Bischoff: became partner in 1980 and head of property department in 1994
Professional memberships
100 Property Club; Investment Property Forum; Law Society
Contact details
Forsters, 67 Grosvenor Street, London W1K 3JN
Tel 020 7863 8333
Fax 020 7863 8444
Web www.forsters.co.uk
Direct tel 020 7863 8460
Mobile 07774 746413
Email AJPatterson@forsters.co.uk

PATTISON, Mark
Beachcroft Wansbroughs
Position
Partner – head of commercial property, Manchester
Career history
1982 Admitted to Roll of Solicitors.
1980 Joined Vaudreys; became partner in 1983 and head of property in 1984; Vaudreys merged with Wansborough Willey Hargrave in 1998 and Beachcroft Stanley in 1999 to form Beachcroft Wansbroughs
Professional memberships
Law Society
Interests
Fly fishing; food; music; running; shooting; skiing; swimming; walking; wine
Contact details
Beachcroft Wansbroughs, St Ann's House, St Ann Street, Manchester M2 7LP
Tel 0161 934 3000
Fax 0161 934 3288
Web www.bwlaw.co.uk
Direct tel 0161 934 3130
Email mpattison@bwlaw.co.uk

PAYNE, Jeremy
DTZ Debenham Tie Leung
Position
Managing director – UK
Qualifications
BSc; MRICS
Career history
Since 2003 Managing director (UK), DTZ Debenham Tie Leung.
1993-2003 Director, then from 1997 regional managing director, DTZ.
1990-93 Director, Debenham Tewson Chesshire.
1981-90 Chesshire Gibson & Co: became associate partner in 1987
Interests
Cricket; golf
Contact details
DTZ Debenham Tie Leung, 1 Curzon Street, London W1A 5PZ
Tel 020 7408 1161
Fax 020 7643 6000
Web www.dtz.com
Direct tel 020 7643 6388
Direct fax 020 7643 6060
Mobile 07771 604531
Email jeremy.payne@dtz.com

PAYNE, John
King Sturge
Position
Partner – investment
Qualifications
BSc; FRICS; SIOR
Career history
1976 Joined JP Sturge & Sons (now King Sturge); appointed partner in 1986
Professional memberships
BSc (Estate Management) Club; RICS
Contact details
King Sturge, 40 Berkeley Square, Bristol BS8 1HU
Tel 0117 927 6691
Fax 0117 929 9669
Web www.kingsturge.com
Direct tel 0117 930 5716
Mobile 07836 373413
Email john.payne@kingsturge.co.uk

PAYNE, Richard
Barclays Bank
Position
Head of structured finance – property team
Qualifications
ACIB
Professional memberships
Association of Property Bankers
Interests
Archery; hill walking; rugby
Contact details
Barclays Bank plc, 54 Lombard Street, London EC3P 3AH
Tel 020 7699 5000
Web www.barclays.com
Direct tel 020 7699 4183
Mobile 07775 545587
Email richard.payne@barclays.co.uk

PAYNTER, Mark
Chase & Partners
Position
Director
Qualifications
MRICS
Career history
Since 1995 Director, Chase & Partners.
1993-95 Director, Colliers Erdman Lewis.
1988-93 Associate, Clive Lewis & Partners.
1986-88 Healey & Baker.
1982-86 Bernard Thorpe & Partners
Professional memberships
RICS
Interests
Golf; sailing; skiing
Contact details
Chase & Partners Ltd, 20 Regent Street, London SW1Y 4PH
Tel 020 7389 9494
Fax 020 7389 9456
Web www.chaseandpartners.com
Email mark.paynter@chaseandpartners.co.uk

PEACE, Liz
British Property Federation
Position
Chief executive
Qualifications
BA Hons
Career history
2002 Joined British Property Federation as director-general; title then changed to chief executive.
1989-2002 Director of corporate affairs/company secretary, Defence Evaluation & Reserve Agency (later QinetiQ).
1974-89 Administrator, MOD
Other roles
Chairman of managing committee of European Property Federation; non-executive director, Planning Inspectorate
Professional memberships
Institute of Public Relations; Royal Society of Arts
Interests
Conservation; gardening; keep fit; opera; reading; shopping

P

Contact details
British Property Federation, 1 Warwick Row, London SW1E 5ER
Tel 020 7828 0111
Fax 020 7834 3442
Web www.bpf.org.uk
Email lpeace@bpf.org.uk

PEACH, Bill
Cushman & Wakefield Healey & Baker

Position
Chairman – City office
Qualifications
FRICS
Career history
2000 Joined Cushman & Wakefield Healey & Baker; chairman of City office since 2002.
1997-2000 Director, Richard Ellis St Quintin.
1995-96 Director, Lambert Smith Hampton.
1984-95 Director, Herring Baker Harris
Professional memberships
RICS
Interests
Golf; motor sports; skiing
Contact details
Cushman & Wakefield Healey & Baker, 110 Cannon Street, London EC4N 6EU
Tel 020 7935 5000
Fax 020 7514 2398
Web www.cushwake.com
Direct tel 020 7152 5373
Direct fax 020 7152 5398
Mobile 0776 4398373
Email bill.peach@eur.cushwake.com

PEACHEY, Adrian
Churston Heard

Position
Investment director
Qualifications
BSc, Est Man; MRICS
Career history
1991 Joined Churston Heard as associate investment surveyor; appointed director in 1994.
1981-91 Investment surveyor, Bernard Thorpe & Partners
Professional memberships
RICS
Contact details
Churston Heard Ltd, 7 Hanover Square, London W1S 1HQ
Tel 020 7409 2199
Fax 020 7495 1339
Web www.churstonheard.co.uk
Direct tel 020 7318 7810
Mobile 07976 423253
Email apeachey@churstonheard.co.uk

PEACOCK, Andrew
Morley Fund Management

Position
Fund manager – central London office portfolio
Contact details
Morley Fund Management Ltd, 34-36 Lime Street, London EC3M 7JE
Tel 020 7809 6000
Fax 020 7489 7940
Web www.morleyfm.com
Direct tel 020 7809 6845
Email andrew.peacock@morleyfm.com

PEACOCK, Nick
Maitland Chambers

Position
Barrister
Contact details
Maitland Chambers, 7 Stone Buildings, London WC2A 3SZ
Tel 020 7406 1200
Fax 020 7406 1300
Web www.maitlandchambers.com
Email npeacock@maitlandchambers.com

PEARCE, Amanda
Cushman & Wakefield Healey & Baker

Position
Partner – retail rent review
Contact details
Cushman & Wakefield Healey & Baker, 43-45 Portman Square, London W1A 3BG
Tel 020 7935 5000
Fax 020 7152 5360
Web www.cushwake.com
Direct tel 020 7152 5067
Direct fax 020 7152 5393
Email amanda.pearce@eur.cushwake.com

PEARCE, Ian
ING Real Estate Development UK

Position
Chief executive
Contact details
ING Real Estate Development UK Ltd, 33 Cavendish Square, London W1G 0BO
Tel 020 7659 9620
Fax 020 7659 9621
Email ian.pearce@ingrealestate.co.uk

PEARCE, Philip
FPDSavills

Position
Director – investment, central London
Qualifications
MA (Cantab); MRICS
Career history
1988 Joined FPDSavills
Interests
Family; fishing; shooting
Contact details
FPDSavills Ltd, 25 Finsbury Circus, London EC2M 7EE
Tel 020 7499 8644
Fax 020 7588 7323
Web www.fpdsavills.co.uk
Direct tel 020 7409 8917
Mobile 07870 555727
Email ppearce@fpdsavills.co.uk

PEAREY, Jeff
Chesterton International

Position
Director in charge, Leeds office
Qualifications
BSc; MRICS
Career history
Since 2000 Director in charge, Chesterton, Leeds.
1998-2000 Director (agency), Insignia Richard Ellis.
1988-98 Partner (agency), St Quintin
Other roles
Chairman, North East branch of Office Agents Society
Professional memberships
Office Agents Society; RICS
Interests
Architecture; mountain biking; running; skiing
Contact details
Chesterton International, Minerva House, 29 East Parade, Leeds LS1 5PS
Tel 0113 242 0044
Fax 0113 234 0235
Web www.chesterton.co.uk
Mobile 07712 868572
Email jeff.pearey@chesterton.co.uk

PEARL, David
Structadene

Position
Chief executive
Contact details
Structadene Ltd, Angel House, 9 White Lion Street, London N1 9PD
Tel 020 7843 3788

PEARSE, Raymond
Development Securities (Projects)

Position
Managing director
Qualifications
FRICS
Career history

1990-94 Head of development, Natwest EM&D.
1985-90 Director, City Merchant Developers/Imry Merchant Developers.
1980-85 Chief building surveyor, St Martins Property Corp

Professional memberships
Freeman of the City of London; RICS

Interests
Cricket; football; motor sports; shooting; skiing

Contact details
Development Securities (Projects) Ltd, Portland House, Stag Place, London
Tel 020 7828 4777
Fax 020 7828 4999
Email ray.pearse@devsecs.co.uk

PEARSON, Christopher
Chesterton International

Position
Director in charge, Newcastle office

Qualifications
BSc Hons, Urban Land Econ; MRICS; MBA

Career history
1992 Joined Chesterton, London, as director; moved to Newcastle office in 1999; appointed regional director in 2002.
1988-92 Associate partner, De Groot Collis.
1988 Jones Lang Wootton.
1986-88 De Groot Collis

Professional memberships
RICS

Interests
Family; sport

Contact details
Chesterton International, New England House, Ridley Place, Newcastle upon Tyne NE1 8JW
Tel 0191 232 8127
Fax 0191 221 0126
Web www.chesterton.co.uk
Direct tel 0191 227 5706
Mobile 07712 868388
Email chris.pearson@chesterton.co.uk

PEARSON, Martyn
Autoglass

Position
National property manager

Contact details
Autoglass Ltd, 1 Priory Business Park, Bedford MK44 3US
Tel 01234 273636
Email martyn.pearson@autoglass.co.uk

PECK, Ian
Bidwells Property Consultants

Position
Partner – head of corporate consultancy and valuation

Qualifications
MA; Dip Prop Invest; MRICS

Contact details
Bidwells Property Consultants, Trumpington Road, Cambridge CB2 2LD
Tel 01223 841841
Fax 01223 845150
Web www.bidwells.co.uk
Direct tel 01223 559534
Direct fax 01223 840294
Mobile 07774 700605
Email ipeck@bidwells.co.uk

PEDDAR, Michael
Michael Peddar & Co

Position
Director

Qualifications
FRICS

Career history
Since 1984 Director, Michael Pedder & Co, buying and selling shops throughout UK.
1978-84 Associate partner, Ian Scott & Co.
1971-78 Healey & Baker

Professional memberships
RICS

Interests
History; music; philately; reading; squash; tennis

Contact details
Michael Peddar & Co, 12 John Princes Street, London W1G 0NY
Tel 020 7629 3004
Fax 020 7491 3314
Web www.michaelpeddar.co.uk
Email mpeddar@michaelpeddar.co.uk

PEDDER, John
Field Fisher Waterhouse

Position
Property partner

Career history
1996 Joined Field Fisher Waterhouse.
1973-96 Partner, Bischoff & Co/Frere Cholmely Bischoff

Contact details
Field Fisher Waterhouse, 35 Vine Street, London EC3N 2AA
Tel 020 7861 4000
Fax 020 7488 0084
Web www.ffwlaw.com
Email John.Pedder@ffw.com

PEET, Tim
C2G Property Solutions

Position
Director

Qualifications
FILT; FCIT

Career history
Since 2003 Director, C2G Property Solutions.
1992-2003 Deputy managing director/ development director, P&O Trans European

Other roles
Managing director, C2G Consulting

Professional memberships
Institute of Logistics & Transport

Interests
Rugby

Contact details
C2G Property Solutions Ltd, 58 Queen Anne Street, London W1G 8HW
Tel 0845 230 6700
Web www.c2gworld.com
Direct tel 01473 289000
Direct fax 01473 289009
Mobile 07702 600060
Email timpeet@c2gworld.com

PELLOW, Mark
Vickery Holman

Position
Director

Contact details
Vickery Holman Ltd, 24 Southernhay West, Exeter EX1 1PR
Tel 01392 203010
Fax 01392 203005
Web www.vickeryholman.com
Email mpellow@vickeryholman.com

PELMORE, Alec
Merrill Lynch Global Principal Investments

Position
Property analyst

Contact details
Merrill Lynch Global Principal Investments, 2 King Edward Street, London EC1A 1HQ
Tel 020 7628 1000
Web www.ml.com
Email alec_pelmore@ml.com

PEMBERTON, Giles
Pemberton Greenish

Position
Managing partner

Qualifications
LLB

Career history
1978 Admitted to Roll of Solicitors.
1976 Joined Pemberton Greenish (formerly Lee & Pembertons)

Professional memberships

P

Law Society
Interests
Cricket; football; golf; opera; real tennis; tennis; theatre
Contact details
Pemberton Greenish, 45 Pont Street, London SW1X 0BX
Tel 020 7591 3333
Fax 020 7591 3300
Web www.pglaw.co.uk
Direct tel 020 7591 3320
Email g.pemberton@pglaw.co.uk

PEMBERTON, Michael
Air Products
Position
European real estate manager
Qualifications
BSc; FRICS; IRRV
Other roles
General council member, Machinery Users Association
Professional memberships
CoreNet Global UK; Institute of Revenues Rating & Valuation; RICS
Contact details
Air Products plc, Hersham Place, Molesey Road, Walton on Thames KT12 4RZ
Tel 01932 249200
Fax 01932 249565
Direct tel 01932 249800
Direct fax 01932 258194
Email pembermh@apci.com

PENFOLD, Adrian
British Land Corp
Position
Head of planning and environment
Qualifications
BA Hons; MRTPI
Career history
1996 Joined British Land.
1990-96 Chief planner, Dartford Borough Council.
1988-90 London Docklands Development Corp.
1976-88 London Borough of Hammersmith & Fulham
Professional memberships
RTPI
Contact details
British Land Corp Ltd, 10 Cornwall Terrace, London NW1 4QP
Tel 020 7486 4466
Web www.britishland.com
Email adrian.penfold@britishland.com

PENFOLD, Julia
T&S Stores
Position
Property director
Qualifications
BSc; MRICS
Contact details
T&S Stores plc, Apex Road, Walsall WS8 7TS
Tel 01543 363000
Fax 01543 363628
Direct tel 01543 363083
Direct fax 01543 363102
Email julia_penfold@tands.co.uk

PENMAN, Catherine
Knight Frank
Position
Partner – head of UK research
Qualifications
MRICS
Career history
Since 2000 Partner (head of UK research), Knight Frank.
1999-2000 Senior analyst, CB Hillier Parker.
1997-99 Analyst, St Quintin.
1994-97 Analyst, Investment Property Databank
Professional memberships
RICS
Contact details
Knight Frank LLP, 20 Hanover Square, London W1S 1HZ
Tel 020 7629 8171
Fax 020 7493 4114
Web www.knightfrank.com
Direct tel 020 7861 1236
Direct fax 020 7629 1610
Mobile 07799 347200
Email catherine.penman@knightfrank.com

PENNELL, Martin
CMS Cameron McKenna
Position
Partner – real estate
Qualifications
BA Hons, Law
Career history
1988 Joined McKenna & Co (now CMS Cameron McKenna): appointed partner in 1997.
1988 Admitted to Roll of Solicitors
Professional memberships
Law Society
Contact details
CMS Cameron McKenna, Mitre House, 160 Aldersgate Street, London EC1A 4DD
Tel 020 7367 3000
Fax 020 7367 2000
Web www.cmck.com
Direct tel 020 7367 2195
Email martin.pennell@cmck.com

PENNELS, Simon
Alder King
Position
Partner
Qualifications
BSc; MRICS
Career history
1988 Joined Alder King; partner since 1991. Previously at Chesterton
Contact details
Alder King, Brunswick House, Gloucester Business Park, Gloucester GL3 4AA
Tel 01452 384333
Fax 01452 528680
Web www.alderking.com
Mobile 07798 588412
Email spennels@alderking.com

PENNY, Andrew
JP Morgan
Position
Head of global real estate equity research
Qualifications
BSc; MRICS
Career history
1999 Joined JP Morgan.
1996-99 Real estate analyst, HSBC Securities.
1994-96 Associate (investment agency), Gerald Eve.
1987-94 Associate (investment agency), Knight Frank
Professional memberships
RICS
Interests
Sailing; tennis
Contact details
JP Morgan plc, 10 Aldermanbury, London EC2V 7RF
Tel 020 7642 4000
Web www.jpmorgan.com
Direct tel 020 7325 0770
Direct fax 020 7325 8550
Mobile 07788 184127
Email andrew.s.penny@jpmorgan.com

PENTECOST, Geoffrey
Jones Lang LaSalle
Position
European director
Qualifications
MA; FRICS
Other roles
Surveyor to Worshipful Company of Barbers
Contact details

Jones Lang LaSalle Ltd, 9 Queen Victoria Street, London EC4N 4YY
Tel 020 7248 6040
Fax 020 7248 0088
Web www.joneslanglasalle.com
Direct tel 020 7399 5390
Email
geoffrey.pentecost@eu.joneslanglasalle.com

PEREIRA GRAY, Peter
Wellcome Trust

Position
Head of property investment
Qualifications
MRICS
Career history
Since 2001 Property investment manager, Wellcome Trust. Formerly director of fund management, Prudential Property
Professional memberships
RICS
Interests
Church; family; tennis
Contact details
Wellcome Trust Ltd, 1 Park Square West, London NW1 4LJ
Tel 020 7611 8888
Fax 020 7611 8545
Web www.wellcome.ac.uk
Direct tel 020 7611 8621
Direct fax 020 7611 8795
Email p.pereiragray@wellcome.ac.uk

PERKINS, Chris
Prudential Property Investment Managers

Position
Director – fund management
Qualifications
BSc Hons; FRICS
Contact details
Prudential Property Investment Managers Ltd, Princeton House, 271-273 High Holborn, London WC1V 7NE
Tel 020 7548 6600
Fax 020 7548 6999
Web www.prupim.com
Direct tel 020 7548 6583
Direct fax 020 7548 6502
Email chris.perkins@prupim.com

PERKINS, Michael
Lambert Smith Hampton

Position
Director – national head of retail
Qualifications
BSc; FRICS
Career history
Since 2002 Director (national head of retail), Lambert Smith Hampton.
1992-2001 Partner, Hartnell Taylor Cook.
1987-92 Director, Pepper Fox.
1986-87 Retail negotiator, Hillier Parker.
1983-86 Asset manager, Richard Ellis
Professional memberships
RICS
Interests
Football; RAC; sport
Contact details
Lambert Smith Hampton Ltd, Regent Arcade House, 19-25 Argyll Street, London W1F 7TS
Tel 020 7494 4000
Fax 020 7414 0866
Web www.lsh.co.uk
Direct tel 020 7663 8270
Direct fax 020 7663 8203
Mobile 07768 150792
Email mperkins@lsh.co.uk

PERKINS, Simon
McKay Securities

Position
Managing director
Contact details
McKay Securities plc, 20-30 Greyfriars Road, Reading RG1 1PE
Tel 0118 950 2333
Fax 0118 939 1393
Email simon.perkins@mckaysecurities.plc.uk

PERL, Leigh
Fairacre Properties

Position
Director
Qualifications
BSc; MRICS
Career history
1996-2002 Director, Capital & Regional Property Investments.
1993-96 Portfolio manager, Manny Davidson Family Trust.
1990-93 Investment surveyor, Houston Lawrence.
1988-90 Investment surveyor, Anthony Lipton & Co.
1986-88 Investment surveyor, Allsop & Co.
1984-86 Barrington Laurence
Professional memberships
RICS
Interests
Football; golf; tennis; theatre
Contact details
Fairacre Properties Ltd, 32 Wigmore Street, London W1U 2RP
Tel 020 7486 9400
Fax 020 7486 9697
Web www.fairacreproperty.co.uk
Email leigh@fairacreproperty.co.uk

PERLOFF, Andrew
Panther Securities

Position
Joint managing director
Other roles
Managing director, Eurocity Properties
Contact details
Panther Securities plc, Panther House, 38 Mount Pleasant, London WC1X 0AP
Tel 020 7278 8011
Fax 020 7278 3608
Email kerryhoward@btopenworld.com

PEROWNE, Mark
King Sturge

Position
Joint managing partner
Qualifications
BSc; FRICS
Career history
1975 Joined King Sturge.
1974-75 Town & City Properties
Professional memberships
British Council for Offices; RICS
Contact details
King Sturge, 7 Stratford Place, London W1C 1ST
Tel 020 7493 4933
Fax 020 7409 0469
Web www.kingsturge.com
Direct tel 020 7318 4250
Email mark.perowne@kingsturge.co.uk

PERRETT, Stephen
Cheetham & Mortimer

Position
Partner
Qualifications
BSc Hons; MRICS
Career history
1988 Joined Cheetham & Mortimer; working in retail warehouse/out-of-town retail sector since 1993
Interests
Golf (RICS Golfing Society)
Contact details
Cheetham & Mortimer, 17 St Ann's Square, Manchester M2 7PW
Tel 0161 832 3375
Fax 0161 832 0453
Email sperrett@cheetham-mortimer.com

P

PERRIN, Neil
Hartnell Taylor Cook

Position
Partner – out-of-town retail and leisure agency
Qualifications
FRICS
Career history
Since 1992 Partner (out-of-town retail agency/development), Hartnell Taylor Cook.
1991-92 Associate partner (retail department), Pepper Fox.
1984-91 Associate partner (retail department), Chesterton
Professional memberships
Accessible Retail; Leisure Property Forum; RICS
Interests
Golf; skiing; travel
Contact details
Hartnell Taylor Cook, 12-13 Conduit Street, London W1S 2XH
Tel 020 7491 7323
Fax 020 7491 3032
Web www.htc.uk.com
Direct tel 020 7409 3707
Mobile 07831 350810
Email neil.perrin@htc.uk.com

PERRY, Chris
Vail Williams

Position
Partner – landlord and tenant consultancy and Valuation
Qualifications
BSc; FRICS; ACIArb; IRRV
Professional memberships
Chartered Institute of Arbitrators; Institute of Revenues Rating & Valuation; RICS
Interests
Badminton; cycling; football; reading; sport
Contact details
Vail Williams, Thames Valley Office, 130 Wharfedale Road, Winnersh RG41 5RB
Tel 0118 933 5600
Fax 0118 933 5634
Web www.vailwilliams.com
Mobile 07774 982555
Email cperry@vailwilliams.com

PERRY, Keith
Lend Lease Europe

Position
Chief operating officer
Qualifications
ACA
Career history
1999 Joined Lend Lease. Formerly at PricewaterhouseCoopers and Oriental Steam Navigation Co
Professional memberships
Institute of Chartered Accountants in England & Wales
Contact details
Lend Lease Europe Ltd, York House, 23 Kingsway, London WC2B 6UJ
Tel 020 7379 0222
Fax 020 7379 0213
Web www.lendlease.com.au
Direct tel 020 7395 7317
Direct fax 020 7395 7496
Email keith_perry@lendlease.com

PERRY, Lyn
Wine Cellar

Position
Property director
Qualifications
MRICS
Professional memberships
RICS
Contact details
Wine Cellar Ltd, PO Box 476 Loushers Lane, Warrington WA4 6RR
Tel 01925 454545
Fax 01925 240266
Web www.winecellar.co.uk
Email lyn.perry@winecellar.co.uk

PESKIN, Richard
Great Portland Estates

Position
Chairman
Qualifications
MA; LLM; FRSA; CIMgt
Career history
1967 Joined Great Portland Estates; appointed managing director in 1985; executive chairman and managing director 1986-2000; chairman since 2000
Other roles
Director, Royal & Sun Alliance Insurance Group, London region; member of general council of BPF; member of estates committee of MCC
Professional memberships
Institute of Management Consultants; Royal Society of Arts
Interests
Golf; wine
Contact details
Great Portland Estates plc, 56 Mortimer Street, London W1W 7RT
Tel 020 7580 3040
Fax 020 7631 5169
Web www.gpe.co.uk
Email sally.mclaren@gpe.co.uk

PETERS, Roy
Aerion Fund Management

Position
Chief executive
Qualifications
BA, Econ
Career history
1989 Joined Aerion Fund Management (formerly British Gas Pension Funds Management).
1980-89 Director, County Bank.
1966-80 Head of investment research, Hoare Govett
Other roles
Director, Blue Circle Pension Trustees; director, John Lewis Pension Trustees; director, JP Morgan Fleming Emerging Markets International Trust
Professional memberships
Royal Society of Arts
Interests
Cricket; golf; military history; rugby
Contact details
Aerion Fund Management Ltd, Heron House, 322 High Holborn, London WC1V 7PW
Tel 020 7242 5005
Direct tel 020 7269 4951
Direct fax 020 7269 4963
Email roy.peters@aerionfm.com

PETO, Robert
DTZ Debenham Tie Leung

Position
Chairman
Qualifications
BA, Land Econ; MA (Cantab); FRICS
Career history
1971 Joined Debenham Chewson & Chinnocks; became equity partner in 1981; chairman of DTZ Debenham Tie Leung since 1999
Other roles
Property adviser to British Museum; chairman, RICS appraisals and valuations standards board; member of RICS working party on valuation of owner-occupied premises; member of BPF general council; surveyor to Worshipful Company of Armourers & Brasiers; chairman, RICS/Investment Property Forum working party on calculation of investment worth
Professional memberships
FIABCI; RICS
Interests
Diving/scuba diving; rugby; sailing; tennis
Contact details
DTZ Debenham Tie Leung, 1 Curzon Street, London W1A 5PZ
Tel 020 7408 1161
Fax 020 7643 6000
Web www.dtz.com

P

Direct tel 020 7643 6127
Direct fax 020 7643 6120
Mobile 07768 003677
Email robert.peto@dtz.com

PETTIT, Stephen
Catalyst Capital

Position
Director – investment underwriting
Career history
Since 2001 Catalyst Capital.
1998-2001 Hatfield Philips
Interests
Cricket; football; skiing
Contact details
Catalyst Capital LLP, 33 Cavendish Square, London W1G 0PW
Tel 020 7290 5100
Fax 020 7290 5115
Web www.catalystcapital.com
Email spettit@catalystcapital.com

PHILIPSON, Sue
Dixons Group Retail Properties

Position
Property director
Qualifications
BSc Hons; FRICS
Career history
Since 2000 Property director, Dixons Group Retail Properties. Formerly at Carter Commercial Developments, Somerfield Stores and Halfords
Other roles
Director, British Council of Shopping Centres, director, Accessible Retail
Professional memberships
RICS
Interests
Badminton; music; reading; swimming; tennis
Contact details
Dixons Group Retail Properties Ltd, Maylands Avenue, Hemel Hempstead HP2 7TG
Tel 0870 850 3333
Fax 01727 233218
Direct tel 0172 720 3990
Direct fax 0172 720 4758
Mobile 07831 204758
Email sue.philipson@dixons.co.uk

PHILLIPS, Christopher
Cushman & Wakefield Healey & Baker

Position
Partner – retail
Qualifications
BSc, Est Man; FRICS; ACIArb; MEWI
Career history
1970 Joined Cushman & Wakefield Healey & Baker
Other roles
Also acts as independent expert appointed by president of RICS
Professional memberships
Chartered Institute of Arbitrators; Expert Witness Institute; RICS
Interests
Gardening; golf; skiing
Contact details
Cushman & Wakefield Healey & Baker, 43-45 Portman Square, London W1A 3BG
Tel 020 7935 5000
Fax 020 7152 5360
Web www.cushwake.com
Direct tel 020 7152 5035
Direct fax 020 7152 5880
Email chris.phillips@eur.cushwake.com

PHILLIPS, David
199 Strand

Position
Barrister
Qualifications
QC; MA (Oxon)
Career history
Since 1990 Tenant at 199 Strand.
1978-90 Tenant at 3 New Square, Lincoln's Inn.
1976 Called to Bar (Arden, Atkin, Mould & Reid prizewinner)
Other roles
Deputy high court judge; recorder; treasurer, Barristers' Benevolent Association; trustee, Disability Law Service
Professional memberships
Association of Regulatory & Disciplinary Lawyers; Association of Road Transport Lawyers; Chancery Bar Association; Professional Negligence Bar Association; Wales Commercial Law Association
Contact details
199 Strand (Chambers of David Phillips QC), London WC2R 1DR
Tel 020 7520 4000
Fax 020 7379 9481
Web www.199strand.co.uk
Direct tel 020 7520 4050
Direct fax 020 7520 4070
Email dphillipsqc@199strand.co.uk

PHILLIPS, David
Chelsfield

Position
Director – investment
Contact details
Chelsfield plc, 17 Grosvenor Street, London W1K 4QG
Tel 020 7493 3977
Web www.chelsfield.com
Direct tel 020 7255 7911
Direct fax 020 7629 9923
Email dphillips@chelsfield.com

PHILLIPS, Gary
Matthews & Goodman

Position
Partner
Contact details
Matthews & Goodman, Dorland House, 14-16 Regent Street, London SW1Y 4PH
Tel 020 7747 8847
Fax 020 7747 8848
Web www.matthews-goodman.co.uk
Email gphillips@matthews-goodman.co.uk

PHILLIPS, Graham
Foster & Partners

Position
Partner and managing director
Qualifications
BArch Hons (Liverpool)
Career history
Since 1975 Foster & Partners
Professional memberships
Hong Kong Institute of Architecture; RIBA
Interests
Golf; sailing
Contact details
Foster & Partners, Riverside Three, 22 Hester Road, London SW11 4AN
Tel 020 7738 0455
Fax 020 7738 1107
Web www.fosterandpartners.com
Email gphillips@fosterandpartners.com

PHILLIPS, Ian
Prudential Property Investment Managers

Position
Investment management director – shopping centres
Qualifications
FRICS
Other roles
Co-opted board member, British Council of Shopping Centres
Professional memberships
British Council of Shopping Centres; RICS
Contact details
Prudential Property Investment Managers Ltd, Princeton House, 271-273 High Holborn, London WC1V 7NE
Tel 020 7548 6600
Fax 020 7548 6999
Web www.prupim.com

Direct tel 020 7548 6686
Direct fax 020 7548 6624
Email ian.phillips@prupim.com

PHILLIPS, Jonathan
Dunlop Heywood Lorenz

Position
Director
Career history
1977 Set up own practice, which merged in 1990 with Dunlop Heywood (now Dunlop Heywood Lorenz).
1971-75 Development company in Benelux.
1968-71 Jones Lang Wootton
Professional memberships
Anglo-German Association; Non-Administrative Receivers Association; RICS
Interests
Golf (Richmond Golf Club); horse racing; shooting
Contact details
Dunlop Heywood Lorenz Ltd, 38 Bow Lane, London EC4M 9AY
Tel 020 7489 1400
Fax 020 7248 4053
Web www.dhlproperty.co.uk
Email jlp@dhlproperty.co.uk

PHILLIPS, Nicolas
Navatar

Position
Managing director
Qualifications
FRICS
Career history
2001 Joined Navatar.
1986-2001 Managing director (property), Lloyd's of London (now Lloyd's).
1976-86 Development/special projects surveyor, Midland Bank.
1973-76 Jones Lang Wootton
Other roles
Chairman, Trafalgar Computer Solutions; facilities management advisory board member, College of Estate Management
Professional memberships
CoreNet Global UK; RICS
Contact details
Navatar Ltd, 22 Ashleigh Road, Horsham RH12 2LF
Tel 01403 253955
Mobile 07732 662014
Email nickphillips@onetel.net.uk

PHILLIPS, Richard
2 Harcourt Buildings

Position
Barrister
Qualifications
QC
Career history
1990 Appointed QC.
1970 Called to Bar
Other roles
Assistant commissioner, Parliamentary Boundary Commission
Professional memberships
Planning & Environment Bar Association
Contact details
2 Harcourt Buildings (Chambers of Robin Purchas QC), 2nd Floor, London EC4Y 9DB
Tel 020 7353 8415
Fax 020 7353 7622
Web www.2hblaw.co.uk
Email clerks@2hblaw.co.uk

PHILLIPS, Richard
Jones Lang LaSalle

Position
European director – property management
Contact details
Jones Lang LaSalle Ltd, 22 Hanover Square, London W1A 2BN
Tel 020 7493 6040
Fax 020 7408 0220
Web www.joneslanglasalle.com
Direct tel 020 7399 5948
Direct fax 020 7399 5180
Mobile 07768 311052
Email richard.phillips@eu.joneslanglasalle.com

PHILLIPS, Trevor
Churston Heard

Position
Chairman
Qualifications
FRICS
Professional memberships
RICS
Interests
Sailing; skiing
Contact details
Churston Heard Ltd, 7 Hanover Square, London W1S 1HQ
Tel 020 7409 2199
Fax 020 7495 1339
Web www.churstonheard.co.uk
Direct tel 020 7318 7804
Mobile 07976 393875
Email tphillips@churstonheard.co.uk

PHILLIPSON, Mark
Briant Champion Long

Position
Managing director
Qualifications
BSc; MRICS
Career history
1990 Joined Briant Champion Long; appointed retail director in 1997 and managing director in 1999.
1988-90 Retail agent, Oliver Liggins.
1986-88 Retail agent, Montagu Evans
Other roles
Past chairman, Shop Agents Society (2000-02); retained agent for a number of retailers, including Carphone Warehouse, Pret A Manger and Pizza Hut
Professional memberships
RICS
Interests
Fishing; rugby; shooting; snowboarding
Contact details
Briant Champion Long Ltd, Nuffield House, 41-46 Piccadilly, London W1J 0DS
Tel 020 7434 7600
Web www.briantchampionlong.com
Direct tel 020 7434 7101
Mobile 07850 828007
Email mphillipson@bclnet.co.uk

PHILPOT, David
Pinsents

Position
Partner – property
Qualifications
LLB Hons
Career history
1988 Joined Pinsents.
1987 Admitted to Roll of Solicitors.
1983-88 Denton Hall
Interests
History; reading
Contact details
Pinsents, 3 Colmore Circus, Birmingham B4 6BH
Tel 0121 200 1050
Fax 0121 626 1040
Web www.pinsents.com
Direct tel 0121 625 3068
Email david.philpot@pinsents.com

PHILPOTT, Gary
Veale Wasbrough

Position
Partner – head of property services
Qualifications
MA (Cantab)
Career history
1985 Admitted to Roll of Solicitors.
1983 Joined Stanley Wasbrough (now Veale Wasbrough); became partner in 1994
Other roles

Joint author, *Managing Business Tenants* (Estates Gazette, 1994); joint author, *Lending on Commercial Property* (1995); articles on commercial property; editor of property section, *Public Private Partnerships & PFI*

Professional memberships

Chartered Institute of Arbitrators; Institute of Indirect Taxation

Interests

IT; motorcycling

Contact details

Veale Wasbrough, Orchard Court, Orchard Lane, Bristol BS1 5DS
Tel 0117 925 2020
Fax 0117 925 2025
Web www.vwl.co.uk
Email gphilpott@vwl.co.uk

PHOENIX, Mike
Brown & Lee

Position

Partner

Contact details

Brown & Lee, Elopak House, Meadway Technology Park, Stevenage SG1 2EF
Tel 01438 316655
Fax 01438 315377
Web www.brownandlee.co.uk
Direct tel 01438 794589
Email mike.phoenix@brownandlee.co.uk

PIANI, Olivier
GE Capital

Position

President – Europe

Contact details

GE Capital Ltd, 24 rue Cambacérès, Paris
Tel +33 1 4312 1800
Fax +33 1 431894
Web www.gecapital.com
Direct tel +33 1 4312 1780
Direct fax +33 1 4312 1705
Email olivier.piani@gecapital.com

PIATT, Andrew
Halliwell Landau

Position

Head of planning

Qualifications

Solicitor; LLB Hons

Career history

Since 2002 Head of planning, Halliwell Landau.
1996-2002 Head of planning, DLA, Manchester.
1987-96 Solicitor, South Ribble Borough Council and St Helens Metropolitan Borough Council

Interests

Church, family; gardening

Contact details

Halliwell Landau, St James Court, 30 Brown Street, Manchester M2 2LD
Tel 0161 835 3003
Fax 0161 835 2994
Web www.halliwells.co.uk
Direct tel 0161 831 2740
Direct fax 0161 831 2836
Mobile 07802 663593
Email apiatt@halliwells.co.uk

PICKETT, Andrew
Burger King

Position

Development director

Qualifications

MRICS

Contact details

Burger King, Charter Place, Vine Street, Uxbridge UB8 1BZ
Tel 01895 206000
Fax 01895 206026
Web www.burgerking.co.uk
Direct tel 01895 206065
Direct fax 01895 206036
Email apickett@whopper.com

PICKSTON, John
Clifford Chance

Position

Partner

Career history

1990 Joined Clifford Chance; appointed partner in 1996.
1986 Admitted to Roll of Solicitors

Contact details

Clifford Chance, 10 Upper Bank Street, London E14 5JJ
Tel 020 7600 1000
Fax 020 7600 5555
Web www.cliffordchance.com
Direct tel 020 7006 8724
Email john.pickston@cliffordchance.com

PICKUP, Bryan
SJ Berwin

Position

Partner – head of real estate department

Qualifications

MA Hons

Career history

Since 1988 Partner, SJ Berwin.
1981 Admitted to Roll of Solicitors

Professional memberships

BPF

Interests

Golf

Contact details

SJ Berwin, 222 Gray's Inn Road, London WC1X 8HB
Tel 020 7533 2222
Fax 020 7533 2000
Web www.sjberwin.com
Direct tel 020 7533 2468
Email bryan.pickup@sjberwin.com

PIKE, Beverley
Masons

Position

Partner – property, planning and environment group

Qualifications

LLB

Career history

Since 1994 Partner, Masons.
1986-94 Herbert Smith: partner from 1990.
1984-86 BICC.
1982-84 Warmingtons & Hasties.
1982 Admitted to Roll of Solicitors.
1980-82 Hancock & Willis

Professional memberships

Law Society

Interests

Rugby; skiing; tennis

Contact details

Masons, 1-4 Portland Square, Bristol BS2 8RR
Tel 0117 924 5678
Fax 0117 924 6699
Web www.masons.com
Direct tel 0117 970 5210
Mobile 07899 993625
Email beverley.pike@masons.com

PIKE, Chad
Blackstone Group

Position

Senior managing director – real estate group

Career history

1995 Joined Blackstone Group.
1993-95 Morgan Stanley Real Estate Fund

Contact details

Blackstone Group Ltd, Stirling Square, 5-7 Carlton Gardens, London SW1Y 5AD
Tel 020 7451 4000
Fax 020 7451 4034
Web www.blackstone.com
Email pike@blackstone.com

PIKE, John
Network Rail Infrastructure

Position

Head of commercial property

Qualifications

BSc; FRICS; MBIFM

Professional memberships

RICS

Contact details

Network Rail Infrastructure Ltd, Euston Square, 40 Melton Street, London NW1 2EE

Tel 020 7557 8000

Fax 020 7557 9000

Email john.pike@networkrail.co.uk

PILCHER, James
Caxtons

Position

Director

Qualifications

BSc Hons; FRICS

Career history

1990 Joined Caxtons

Professional memberships

RICS

Interests

Golf; guitar; hockey; tennis

Contact details

Caxtons, 49-50 Windmill Street, Gravesend DA12 1BG

Tel 01474 537733

Fax 01474 537039

Web www.caxtons.com

Email jpilcher@caxtons.com

PILLOW, Michael
FPDSavills

Position

Director – head of building construction

Contact details

FPDSavills Ltd, 25 Finsbury Circus, London EC2M 7EE

Tel 020 7499 8644

Fax 020 7588 7323

Web www.fpdsavills.co.uk

Direct tel 020 7409 8985

Mobile 07968 550348

Email mpillow@fpdsavills.co.uk

PINCOTT, David
Edward Symmons & Partners

Position

Partner – national head of construction

Qualifications

MA (Oxon); MRICS

Career history

1997 Joined Edward Symmons & Partners; promoted to partner in 2000; also national head of building consultancy. Previously with Mellersh & Harding, Drivers Jonas and Gross Fine

Other roles

Author of publications in *Estates Gazette*, *Facilities Management Journal* and other professional journals

Professional memberships

RICS

Interests

Golf; hill walking; music; skiing

Contact details

Edward Symmons & Partners, Nuffield House, 41-46 Piccadilly, London W1J 0DS

Tel 020 7344 4500

Fax 020 7344 4555

Web www.edwardsymmons.com

Direct tel 020 7344 4520

Mobile 07979 541231

Email david.pincott@edwardsymmons.com

PINNER, Julian
Knight Frank

Position

Partner – head of corporate real estate

Career history

2000 Joined Knight Frank.

1988-2000 DTZ Debenham Thorpe: director from 1997

Other roles

Committee member, CoreNet UK

Professional memberships

RICS

Interests

Athletics; cooking; walking

Contact details

Knight Frank LLP, 20 Hanover Square, London W1S 1HZ

Tel 020 7629 8171

Fax 020 7493 4114

Web www.knightfrank.com

Direct tel 020 7861 1160

Direct fax 020 7409 7825

Email julian.pinner@knightfrank.com

PITCHER, Derek
Cyril Sweett

Position

UK managing director

Qualifications

BSc; FRICS; Dip Proj Man

Career history

1978 Joined Cyril Sweett & Partners; became associate in 1986 and partner in 1989; appointed deputy managing director in 1993 and managing director in 1996

Other roles

Honorary treasurer, British Council of Shopping Centres

Professional memberships

RICS

Interests

Golf; theatre; travel

Contact details

Cyril Sweett Ltd, 60 Gray's Inn Road, London WC1X 8AQ

Tel 020 7061 9000

Fax 020 7430 0603

Web www.cyrilsweett.co.uk

Email derek.pitcher@cyrilsweett.com

PLANT, Patrick
Linklaters

Position

Partner – head of real estate

Qualifications

LLB Hons

Career history

1990 Joined Linklaters; became partner in 1994 and partner and head of real estate in 2003.

1989-90 Mallesons Stephen Jacques, Sydney.

1986-89 Linklaters

Contact details

Linklaters, 1 Silk Street, London EC2Y 8HQ

Tel 020 7456 2000

Fax 020 7456 2222

Web www.linklaters.com

Direct tel 020 7456 4718

Email patrick.plant@linklaters.com

PLANT, Richard
Stiles Harold Williams

Position

Director

Qualifications

BSc Hons; MRICS

Professional memberships

RICS

Contact details

Stiles Harold Williams Ltd, 96 Park Lane, London CR9 2NL

Tel 020 8662 2700

Fax 020 8680 3193

Web www.shw.co.uk

Email rplant@shw.co.uk

PLASCOW, Ronald
Mills & Reeve

Position

Partner – head of construction and projects department

Qualifications

LLB Hons

Professional memberships

Chartered Institute of Arbitrators; Society of Construction Law; Technology & Construction Solicitors Association

Contact details

Mills & Reeve, Francis House, 112 Hills Road, Cambridge CB2 1PH

Tel 01223 364422
Fax 01223 355848
Web www.mills-reeve.com
Direct tel 01223 222261
Direct fax 01223 222258
Email ronald.plascow@mills-reeve.com

PLATT, Harry
Workspace Group

Position
Chief executive
Qualifications
MA; MRTPI
Career history
1991 Joined Workspace Group as managing director; appointed chief executive in 1999.
1989-91 Operations director, Dixons Commercial Properties.
1982-89 Chief executive, Harlow District Council
Professional memberships
RTPI; Society of Local Authority Chief Executives
Interests
Cinema; football; rugby
Contact details
Workspace Group plc, Magenta House, 85 Whitechapel Road, London E1 1DU
Tel 020 7247 7614
Fax 020 7247 0157
Web www.workspacegroup.co.uk
Mobile 07860 863569
Email harry.platt@workspacegroup.co.uk

PLEASS, Kevin
Tesco Stores

Position
Programme director
Contact details
Tesco Stores Ltd, Cirrus B, Shire Park, Welwyn Garden City AL7 1AB
Tel 01992 632222
Fax 01707 634937
Web www.tesco.com
Direct tel 01707 395150
Direct fax 01707 634486
Email kevin.pleass@uk.tesco.com

PLEETH, Chris
C&J Clark Properties

Position
Director
Qualifications
BSc; FRICS
Career history
1992 Joined C&J Clark Properties.
1984-92 Director, Churston Heard.
1982-84 Edward Erdman
Other roles
Director, Street Estates
Professional memberships
Property Managers Association; RICS
Interests
Family; football; golf; sailing; skiing; tennis; travel
Contact details
C&J Clark Properties Ltd, 40 High Street, Street BA16 0EQ
Tel 01458 442131
Fax 01458 446504
Mobile 07836 590805
Email chris.pleeth@clarks.com

PLUMMER, Richard
PRICOA Investment Management

Position
Chairman
Qualifications
Dip Est Man; FRICS
Career history
1982-93 Managing director, MIM Property Services.
1979-82 Property investment director, Samuel Montagu.
1973-79 Investment surveyor, Knight Frank
Professional memberships
RICS
Contact details
PRICOA Investment Management Ltd, 166 Sloane Street, London SW1X 9QF
Tel 020 7761 3300
Fax 020 7761 3400
Email richard.plummer@prudential.com

PODD, Henrietta
Royal Bank of Canada Trust Corp

Position
Head of institutional debt placement
Career history
Since 1992 Director and head of institutional debt placement, Hambro – RBC DS Global Markets.
1991-92 Director (fixed income), NatWest Markets.
1987-91 Assistant director (fixed income), BZW
Professional memberships
Securities Institute
Contact details
Royal Bank of Canada Trust Corp Ltd, 71 Queen Victoria Street, London EC4V 4DE
Tel 020 7489 1188
Fax 020 7248 3065
Direct tel 020 7653 4876
Mobile 07050 286421
Email henrietta.podd@rbccm.com

POLISANO, Lee
Kohn Pedersen Fox Associates

Position
President
Qualifications
FAIA; RIBA; Dipl Ing
Career history
Since 1993 Founding partner of Kohn Pedersen Fox International (London); worldwide president of Kohn Pedersen Fox Associates since 2003
Other roles
Has lectured in architecture and is frequently invited to address academic and professional symposia; has published several articles on a range of subjects; member, British Council for Offices tall buildings committee; member, Commission for Architecture & the Built Environment; co-chairman of Urban Land Institute's European office and mixed-use development council
Professional memberships
American Institute of Architects; Association of Consultant Architects; British American Chamber of Commerce; British Council for Offices; City Property Association; Commission for Architecture & the Built Environment; RIBA; Urban Design Group; Urban Land Institute; Westminster Property Owners Association
Interests
Architecture; music; skiing
Contact details
Kohn Pedersen Fox Associates, 13 Langley Street, London WC2H 9JG
Tel 020 7836 6668
Fax 020 7497 1175
Web www.kpf.com
Direct tel 020 7596 4304
Email lpolisano@kpf.co.uk

POLLARD, Paul
Salmon Developments

Position
Finance director and company secretary
Contact details
Salmon Developments plc, 46 Mount Street, London W1K 2HH
Tel 020 7499 4378
Fax 020 7499 1317
Web www.salmondevelopments.com
Email p.pollard@salmondevelopments.com

POLLARD, Remi
Stiles Harold Williams

Position
Director
Qualifications
BA Hons; MIMgt (Finance)

Contact details
Stiles Harold Williams Ltd, Castle Square House, 9 Castle Square, Brighton BN1 1DZ
Tel 01273 321200
Fax 01273 202436
Web www.shw.co.uk
Email rpollard@shw.co.uk

POLLARD, Tracey
Markham Vaughan Gillingham

Position
Director
Contact details
Markham Vaughan Gillingham, Clifton Heights, Bristol BS8 1EJ
Tel 0117 909 9000
Fax 0117 915 9764
Web www.mvgretail.com
Email tpollard@mvgretail.com

POOLE, Martin
Greycoat Estates

Position
Finance director
Qualifications
MA; FCA
Career history
1986 Joined Greycoat as financial controller; finance director since 1994; also director of all group's companies.
1974-85 Ernst & Young
Professional memberships
Institute of Chartered Accountants in England & Wales
Contact details
Greycoat Estates Ltd, Brettenham House, 9 Savoy Street, London WC2E 7EG
Tel 020 7379 1000
Fax 020 7379 8744
Email mpoole@greycoat.co.uk

POPE, Nigel
Akeler Developments

Position
Finance director
Qualifications
BSc; ACA
Career history
1998-2000 Head of finance, Security Capital European Realty.
1996-98 Head of financial control, Etam.
1990-96 Financial controller, SPP Investment Management
Professional memberships
Institute of Chartered Accountants in England & Wales
Contact details
Akeler Developments Ltd, 7 Clifford Street, London W1S 2WE
Tel 020 7864 1800
Fax 020 7864 1801
Web www.akeler.com
Direct tel 020 7864 1849
Direct fax 020 7864 1805
Email nigelp@akeler.com

POPE, Shelagh
Reed Elsevier (UK)

Position
Group property manager
Qualifications
MRICS; BSc Hons, Est Man
Career history
1989 Joined Reed Elsevier (UK) as estates surveyor; appointed property manager in 1996
Professional memberships
RICS; Women in Property
Interests
Art; golf; IT; karting; skiing; sport; walking; wine
Contact details
Reed Elsevier (UK) Ltd, Quadrant House, The Quadrant, Sutton SM2 5AS
Tel 020 8652 3555
Web www.reed-elsevier.com
Direct tel 020 8653 8343
Direct fax 020 8652 3947
Mobile 07770 267878
Email shelagh.pope@reedelsevier.co.uk

PORTEN, Anthony
2-3 Gray's Inn Square

Position
Barrister
Qualifications
QC
Career history
1988 Appointed QC.
1969 Called to Bar
Other roles
Master of the Bench, Inner Temple; assistant boundary commissioner, Parliamentary Boundary Commission
Professional memberships
Administrative Law Bar Association; Planning & Environment Bar Association; Society of Advanced Legal Studies; UK Environmental Law Association
Contact details
2-3 Gray's Inn Square (Chambers of Anthony Scrivener QC), London WC1R 5JH
Tel 020 7242 4986
Fax 020 7405 1166
Web www.2-3graysinnsquare.co.uk
Email aporten@2-3graysinnsquare.co.uk

PORTER, Nicholas
UNITE Group

Position
Chief executive
Career history
1991 Founder, UNITE Group
Other roles
Trustee, UNIAID Foundation
Interests
Antiques; art; golf; sailing
Contact details
UNITE Group, 103 Temple Street, Bristol BS1 6EN
Tel 0117 907 8100
Fax 0117 907 8101
Web www.unite-group.com
Direct tel 0117 907 8112
Direct fax 0117 907 8151
Email nicholas.porter@unite-group.co.uk

PORTER, Robert
Clifford Chance

Position
Partner – property
Career history
Since 2000 Partner, Clifford Chance.
1989-2000 McKenna & Co (now CMS Cameron McKenna); partner from 1993
Other roles
Co-head of Clifford Chance's real estate funds and investment banking group
Contact details
Clifford Chance, 10 Upper Bank Street, London E14 5JJ
Tel 020 7600 1000
Fax 020 7600 5555
Web www.cliffordchance.com
Direct tel 020 7006 4389
Email robert.porter@cliffordchance.com

POTTER, Carl
GVA Grimley

Position
Partner – national head of business parks
Contact details
GVA Grimley, 3 Brindleyplace, Birmingham B1 2JB
Tel 0870 900 8990
Fax 0121 609 8314
Web www.gvagrimley.co.uk
Direct tel 0121 609 8388
Email carl.potter@gvagrimley.co.uk

POTTER, Richard
Edwin Hill

Position
Partner – head of Manchester and Birmingham

P

office
Qualifications
BSc; MRICS
Career history
1993 Joined Edwin Hill in West End office; appointed associate partner in 1995 in Heathrow office before opening Manchester and Birmingham offices in 1995 and 2003 respectively; partner since 1997
Professional memberships
RICS
Interests
Sailing; rugby (Northampton Rugby Club)
Contact details
Edwin Hill, Olympic Court, The Village, Manchester M17 1AP
Tel 0161 877 6622
Fax 0161 877 9876
Web www.edwinhill.co.uk
Email rgcp@edwinhill.co.uk

POTTS, Andrew
Hammonds
Position
Partner – head of licensing unit
Qualifications
LLB Hons
Contact details
Hammonds, Rutland House, 148 Edmund Street, Birmingham B3 2JR
Tel 0870 839 0000
Fax 0870 839 3001
Web www.hammonds.com
Direct tel 0121 222 3206
Email andrew.potts@hammonds.com

POWELL, Adrian
Donaldsons
Position
Partner
Qualifications
BSc Hons; MRICS
Career history
1994 Joined Donaldsons; elected equity partner in 1997.
1982-94 Goadsby & Harding
Professional memberships
RICS
Contact details
Donaldsons, 48 Warwick Street, London W1B 5NL
Tel 020 7534 5000
Fax 020 7434 0045
Web www.donaldsons.co.uk
Direct tel 020 7534 8452
Mobile 07808 479251
Email adrian.powell@donaldsons.co.uk

POWELL, Chris
Churston Heard
Position
Chief executive
Qualifications
BSc Hons, Est Man; MRICS
Professional memberships
Investment Property Forum; RICS
Interests
Golf; tennis
Contact details
Churston Heard Ltd, 7 Hanover Square, London W1S 1HQ
Tel 020 7409 2199
Fax 020 7495 1339
Web www.churstonheard.co.uk
Mobile 07976 393880
Email cpowell@churstonheard.co.uk

POWELL, William
CFGB
Position
Property director
Contact details
CFGB Ltd, The Grange, 1 Central Road, London SM4 5PQ
Tel 020 8640 3322
Fax 020 8528 7505
Email bpowell@courts.plc.uk

POWER, Mary
FPDSavills
Position
Director – head of planning
Contact details
FPDSavills Ltd, 20 Grosvenor Hill, London W1K 3HQ
Tel 020 7499 8644
Fax 020 7495 3773
Web www.fpdsavills.co.uk
Direct tel 020 7409 5919
Mobile 07870 555804
Email mpower@fpdsavills.co.uk

POWER, Nick
GVA Grimley
Position
Partner
Contact details
GVA Grimley, 3 Brindleyplace, Birmingham B1 2JB
Tel 0870 900 8990
Fax 0121 609 8314
Web www.gvagrimley.co.uk
Email nick.power@gvagrimley.co.uk

POWER, Patrick
Castlemore Securities
Position
Planning director
Qualifications
BA; Dip TP; MRTPI
Career history
1994 Joined Castlemore.
1988-94 Planning consultant, Mason Richards Planning.
1975-88 Planning department, Avon County Council.
1969-75 Planning department, Surrey County Council
Professional memberships
RTPI
Interests
Cricket; literature; opera
Contact details
Castlemore Securities Ltd, Cedar Court, 221 Hagley Road, Halesowen B63 1ED
Tel 0121 585 4444
Fax 0121 585 4441
Web www.castlemore.co.uk
Direct fax 0121 585 4442
Mobile 07774 780144
Email patrick@castlemore.co.uk

POWERS, Richard
Goldman Sachs International
Position
Managing director – real estate
Qualifications
BA
Career history
Since 1999 Managing director, Goldman Sachs International, London (responsible for Whitehall funds).
1998-99 Director, New Europe Properties Advisory.
1991-97 GE Capital: joined as operations leader; became managing director in 1993
Contact details
Goldman Sachs International, Peterborough Court, 133 Fleet Street, London EC4A 2PP
Tel 020 7774 1000
Fax 020 7774 4477
Email richard.powers@gs.com

POWLESLAND, Nicholas
Knight Frank
Position
Partner – head of European valuation services
Qualifications
BSc Hons; FRICS
Career history
1985 Joined Knight Frank; appointed to head of

P

European valuation services in 2000.
1983-85 Estates manager, Lloyds Bank.
1980-83 John D Wood

Other roles

Member of RICS Valuation Forum

Professional memberships

RICS

Interests

Badminton; cycling; theatre

Contact details

Knight Frank LLP, 20 Hanover Square, London W1S 1HZ
Tel 020 7629 8171
Fax 020 7493 4114
Web www.knightfrank.com
Direct tel 020 7861 1283
Direct fax 020 7495 0556
Email nick.powlesland@knightfrank.com

POYNTON, Roger
Phoenix Beard

Position

Managing director

Contact details

Phoenix Beard, The Exchange, 19 Newhall Street, Birmingham B3 3PJ
Tel 0121 200 4500
Fax 0121 200 4599
Web www.phoenix-beard.co.uk
Email roger.poynton@phoenix-beard.co.uk

PREEDY, Keith
Associated British Foods

Position

Group property manager

Qualifications

FRICS

Contact details

Associated British Foods plc, 50-51 Russell Square, London WC1B 4JA
Tel 020 7299 3638
Fax 020 7299 3630
Web www.abf.co.uk
Email keithpreedy@abfoods.com

PRENTICE, Graham
Freshfields Bruckhaus Deringer

Position

Partner – real estate

Career history

1981 Joined Freshfields Bruckhaus Deringer; partner since 1986.
1980 Admitted to Roll of Solicitors

Interests

Photography; skiing; travel

Contact details

Freshfields Bruckhaus Deringer, 65 Fleet Street, London EC4Y 1HT
Tel 020 7936 4000
Fax 020 7832 7001
Web www.freshfields.com
Direct tel 020 7832 7464
Email graham.prentice@freshfields.com

PRENTICE, Mike
CB Richard Ellis

Position

Managing director – retail

Career history

1977 Joined Hillier Parker (now CB Richard Ellis); appointed partner in 1993 and director in 1998.
1973-76 Development surveyor, Argyle Securities.
1970-73 Healey & Baker

Contact details

CB Richard Ellis, Kingsley House, 1a Wimpole Street, London W1G 0RE
Tel 020 7182 2000
Fax 020 7182 7001
Web www.cbre.com
Direct tel 020 7182 2039
Direct fax 020 7182 2980
Mobile 07831 280259
Email mike.prentice@cbre.com

PRESCOTT, Henry
Mason Owen & Partners

Position

Partner – out-of-town retail

Qualifications

BSc; FRICS

Other roles

Chairman, Accessible Retail (2002/03)

Professional memberships

Accessible Retail; RICS

Contact details

Mason Owen & Partners Ltd, Gladstone House, 11 Union Court, Liverpool L2 4UQ
Tel 0151 242 3000
Fax 0151 236 2569
Web www.masonowen.com
Direct tel 0151 242 3017
Mobile 07798 576810
Email henry.prescott@masonowen.com

PRESSMAN, Stephen
Dunlop Heywood Lorenz

Position

Director

Contact details

Dunlop Heywood Lorenz Ltd, Abbey House, 32 Booth Street, Manchester M2 4QP
Tel 0161 237 7777
Fax 0161 237 7778
Web www.dhlproperty.co.uk
Email sgp@dhlproperty.co.uk

PRESTON, Sara-Jane
NAI Fuller Peiser

Position

Equity partner

Career history

Since 2002 Partner, Fuller Peiser.
1987-2002 Director (industrial agency), Chesterton.
1982-87 Industrial negotiator, Dunlop Heywood

Professional memberships

Industrial Agents Society

Interests

Photography; swimming

Contact details

NAI Fuller Peiser, 4th Floor, Northern Assurance Building, Albert Square, Manchester M2 4DN
Tel 0870 700 2233
Fax 0161 835 2005
Web www.nai-fullerpeiser.com
Direct tel 0161 214 5023
Mobile 07919 044979
Email sjpreston@nai-fullerpeiser.com

PREVEZER, Sue
Essex Court Chambers

Position

Barrister

Qualifications

QC

Career history

2000 Appointed QC.
1998 Joined Essex Court Chambers.
1991-98 At 3-4 South Square (insolvency set)

Other roles

Recorder; member of Bar pro bono management committee; contributor to *Lightman & Moss on Receivers*; past chairman of Space Studios; patron, Tate Gallery

Professional memberships

Chancery Bar Association; Commercial Bar Association

Contact details

Essex Court Chambers, 24-26 Lincoln's Inn Fields, London WC2A 9LZ
Tel 020 7813 8000
Fax 020 7813 8080
Web www.essexcourt-chambers.law.co.uk
Email clerksroom@essexcourt-chambers.co.uk

PREW, Mike
Citigroup Smith Barney

Position

Property research analyst

Contact details
Citigroup Smith Barney, 33 Canada Square, London E14 5LB
Tel 020 7986 4000
Web www.citigroup.com
Email michael.prew@citigroup.com

PRICE, Alan
Cosnett Price
Position
Partner
Qualifications
BSc; MRICS
Career history
1984-87 Agency manager, Nattrass Giles.
1981-84 Industrial negotiator, Grimley
Professional memberships
Industrial Agents Society; RICS
Interests
Music; sailing; skiing; tennis
Contact details
Cosnett Price, Kings Court, 17 School Road, Birmingham B28 8JG
Tel 0121 244 1804
Fax 0121 244 1801
Mobile 07973 632324
Email aprice@cosnettprice.co.uk

PRICE, Christopher
Edward Symmons & Partners
Position
Partner
Contact details
Edward Symmons & Partners, Harford House, Frogmore Street, Bristol BS1 5LZ
Tel 0117 927 3454
Fax 0117 927 2006
Web www.edwardsymmons.com
Email chris.price@edwardsymmons.com

PRICE, Guy
Cushman & Wakefield Healey & Baker
Position
Partner – retail warehouses and leisure
Qualifications
BSc, Valuation & Est Man; MRICS
Professional memberships
RICS
Interests
Amateur dramatics; football (qualified football referee); golf; rugby; travel
Contact details
Cushman & Wakefield Healey & Baker, 43-45 Portman Square, London W1A 3BG
Tel 020 7935 5000
Fax 020 7152 5360
Web www.cushwake.com
Direct tel 020 7152 5208
Direct fax 020 7152 5367
Email guy.price@eur.cushwake.com

PRICE, Humphrey
Pillar Property
Position
Finance director
Qualifications
FCA
Career history
1983-93 Finance director, Arlington Securities
Professional memberships
Institute of Chartered Accountants in England & Wales
Contact details
Pillar Property plc, Lansdowne House, Berkeley Square, London W1J 6HQ
Tel 020 7915 8000
Fax 020 7915 8001
Web www.pillarproperty.com
Direct fax 020 7915 8022
Email humphrey.price@pillarproperty.com

PRICE, Richard
Pannone & Partners
Position
Partner – litigation (head of property litigation)
Qualifications
MA, Law (Cantab)
Career history
1992 Admitted to Roll of Solicitors.
1990 Joined Pannone & Partners
Other roles
Northern group committee member, Property Litigation Association
Professional memberships
Law Society; Property Litigation Association
Interests
Rugby; skiing
Contact details
Pannone & Partners, 123 Deansgate, Manchester M3 2BU
Tel 0161 909 3000
Fax 0161 909 4444
Web www.pannone.com
Email richard.price@pannone.co.uk

PRICE, Simon
Alder King
Position
Partner – head of office agency
Qualifications
BSc Hons; MRICS
Career history
1988 Joined Alder King at Bristol head office; appointed head of office agency in 1997
Professional memberships
Office Agents Society
Interests
Cricket; hockey
Contact details
Alder King, Pembroke House, 15 Pembroke Road, Bristol BS8 3BA
Tel 0117 317 1000
Fax 0117 317 1001
Web www.alderking.com
Direct tel 0117 317 1084
Mobile 07990 891021
Email sprice@alderking.com

PRICHARD, Simon
Gerald Eve
Position
Partner – head of offices
Qualifications
BA; MRICS
Career history
1998 Joined Gerald Eve.
1991-98 Wright Oliphant.
1987-91 Herring, Son & Daw
Professional memberships
RICS
Contact details
Gerald Eve, Royex House, 5 Aldermanbury Square, London EC2V 7HR
Tel 020 7489 8900
Fax 020 7489 8800
Web www.geraldeve.com
Email sprichard@geraldeve.com

PRIME, Neil
Knight Frank
Position
Partner
Qualifications
BSc Hons; MRICS
Professional memberships
RICS
Contact details
Knight Frank LLP, Kings House, 36 King Street, London EC2V 8QQ
Tel 020 7606 0606
Fax 020 7606 5502
Web www.knightfrank.com
Mobile 07979 530454
Email neil.prime@knightfrank.com

PRIMETT, Peter
Watts & Partners
Position
Chairman
Qualifications
FRICS

P

Career history
1972 Joined Watts & Partners; chairman since 1999
Professional memberships
RICS
Interests
Sport; travel
Contact details
Watts & Partners, 11 Haymarket, London SW1Y 4BP
Tel 020 7533 4800
Fax 020 7839 4740
Web www.wattsandpartners.com
Email peter.primett@watts.co.uk

PRINCE, Edwin
Falcon Chambers
Position
Barrister
Qualifications
BA Hons (Oxon)
Career history
1955 Called to Bar
Other roles
Elected bencher of Inner Temple (1991)
Professional memberships
Chancery Bar Association; London Common Law & Commercial Bar Association
Contact details
Falcon Chambers, Falcon Court, London EC4Y 1AA
Tel 020 7353 2484
Fax 020 7353 1261
Web www.falcon-chambers.com
Email prince@falcon-chambers.com

PRINCE, Neil
Matthews & Goodman
Position
Partner – West End offices
Qualifications
BSc; MRICS
Career history
1986-91 Director, DTZ Debenham Thorpe.
1983-86 Parnis Bird.
1982-83 Sinclair Goldsmith.
1980-82 Healey & Baker
Professional memberships
RICS
Interests
Cycling; diving/scuba diving; photography; rugby; swimming; wine
Contact details
Matthews & Goodman, Dorland House, 14-16 Regent Street, London SW1Y 4PH
Tel 020 7747 8847
Fax 020 7747 8848
Web www.matthews-goodman.co.uk
Direct tel 020 7747 3170
Mobile 07778 911061
Email nprince@matthews-goodman.co.uk

PRINCE, Philip
ISG Occupancy
Position
Director
Qualifications
BSc; MRICS
Career history
Since 2002 Director (head of corporate real estate and professional services), ISG Occupancy.
1987-2002 Director, Colliers CRE (formerly Conrad Ritblat)
Contact details
ISG Occupancy Ltd, 17-19 Maddox Street, London W1S 1QG
Tel 020 7290 3333
Fax 020 7290 3334
Web www.isgplc.com
Email philip.prince@isgplc.com

PRIOR, Stuart
Matthews & Goodman
Position
Partner
Qualifications
BSc Hons; MRICS
Career history
1995 Joined Matthews & Goodman as investment surveyor.
1987-94 Investment surveyor, Morgan Grenfell Laurie/Michael Laurie Partnership
Professional memberships
BSc (Estate Management) Club; RICS
Contact details
Matthews & Goodman, Dorland House, 14-16 Regent Street, London SW1Y 4PH
Tel 020 7747 8847
Fax 020 7747 8848
Web www.matthews-goodman.co.uk
Email sprior@matthews-goodman.co.uk

PRIOR, Vincent
Jones Lang LaSalle
Position
European director
Contact details
Jones Lang LaSalle Ltd, 22 Hanover Square, London W1A 2BN
Tel 020 7493 6040
Fax 020 7408 0220
Web www.joneslanglasalle.com
Email vince.prior@joneslanglasalle.com

PRISK, Graham
C2G Property Solutions
Position
Director
Qualifications
BSc Hons; MSc, Project Management; MRICS
Career history
2003 Established C2G World (niche supply chain and property consultancy) with Charles Binks and Tim Peet.
1989-2003 Fuller Peiser: became partner in 1997 and head of logistics discipline in 2001.
1987-89 Baxter Payne & Lepper, London SW1.
1987 Qualified as chartered building surveyor
Contact details
C2G Property Solutions Ltd, 58 Queen Anne Street, London W1G 8HW
Tel 0845 230 6700
Web www.c2gworld.com
Direct tel 020 7486 5591
Direct fax 01473 289009
Mobile 07793 441912
Email grahamprisk@c2gworld.com

PRITCHARD, Ian
Crown Estate
Position
Head of Scotland office
Contact details
Crown Estate, 6 Bells Brae, Edinburgh EH4 3BJ
Tel 0131 260 6070
Fax 0131 260 6090
Web www.crownestate.co.uk
Email ian.pritchard@crownestate.co.uk

PRITCHARD, Neville
King Sturge
Position
Partner – investment
Qualifications
BSc; MRICS
Professional memberships
RICS
Contact details
King Sturge, 7 Stratford Place, London W1C 1ST
Tel 020 7493 4933
Fax 020 7409 0469
Web www.kingsturge.com
Direct tel 020 7318 4213
Email neville.pritchard@kingsturge.co.uk

PRITCHARD, Nick
TLT Solicitors
Position
Partner – commercial property
Career history

1972 Joined Bristol & Trumps (now TLT Solicitors, following merger); became partner in 1974.
1970 Admitted to Roll of Solicitors

Professional memberships
Law Society

Interests
Golf; sailing; tennis; windsurfing

Contact details
TLT Solicitors, 1 Redcliffe Street, Bristol BS99 7JZ
Tel 0117 917 7777
Fax 0117 917 7779
Web www.tltsolicitors.com
Direct tel 0117 917 7947
Email npritchard@TLTsolicitors.com

PRITCHARD, Stephen
Associated British Ports

Position
Regional property manager, South Wales

Qualifications
Dip Est Man; FRICS; FFB

Career history
1987-89 Chief executive, D'Arcy Developments.
1981-87 English Estates: various positions; development executive of Chatham Maritime from 1986

Professional memberships
Faculty of Building; RICS

Interests
Rugby; travel

Contact details
Associated British Ports, Queen Alexandra House, Cargo Road, Cardiff CF10 4LY
Tel 029 20 835030
Fax 029 20 835003
Web www.abports.co.uk
Email spritchard@abports.co.uk

PRITCHETT, Stephen
Kings Chambers

Position
Barrister

Qualifications
LLB Hons

Career history
1997 Joined Kings Chambers.
1989 Called to Bar.
1989-97 Barrister, 20 North John Street, Liverpool

Professional memberships
Chancery Bar Association; Honourable Society of Lincoln's Inn; Northern Chancery Bar Association

Contact details
Kings Chambers, 40 King Street, Manchester M2 6BA
Tel 0161 832 9082
Fax 0161 835 2139
Web www.kingschambers.com
Email spritchett@kingschambers.com

PROBERT, John
Slough Estates

Position
Group company secretary

Qualifications
FCIS

Career history
1996 Joined Slough Estates

Contact details
Slough Estates plc, 234 Bath Road, Slough SL1 4EE
Tel 01753 537171
Fax 01753 820585
Web www.sloughestates.com
Direct fax 01753 693369
Email john.probert@sloughestates.co.uk

PROBERT, Michael
Moorevale

Position
Director

Qualifications
BSc Hons; MRICS

Career history
Since 2003 Founding director, Moorevale.
1998-2003 Chief executive, Merivale Moore.
1995-98 Weatherall Green & Smith: joined as associate in investment department.
1989-95 Hillier Parker

Professional memberships
RICS

Interests
Golf; sailing; shooting; skiing

Contact details
Moorevale Ltd, 53-54 Brook's Mews, London W1K 4EF
Tel 020 7399 2300
Fax 020 7399 2309
Web www.moorevale.com
Mobile 07775 566325
Email mikeprobert@moorevale.com

PROBYN, Alex
Edwin Hill

Position
Partner

Qualifications
BSc; MRICS

Professional memberships
RICS

Contact details
Edwin Hill, Warlies Park House, Horseshoe Hill, Waltham Abbey EN9 3SL
Tel 01992 700710
Fax 01992 700720
Web www.edwinhill.co.uk
Email alexp@edwinhill.co.uk

PROCTOR, John
Prudential Property Investment Managers

Position
Investment management director

Qualifications
BSc Hons; FRICS

Other roles
Director, New West End Co; director, Association of Town Centre Management

Professional memberships
Association of Town Centre Management; RICS

Contact details
Prudential Property Investment Managers Ltd, Princeton House, 271-273 High Holborn, London WC1V 7NE
Tel 020 7548 6600
Fax 020 7548 6999
Web www.prupim.com
Direct tel 020 7548 6789
Direct fax 020 7548 6701
Email john.proctor@prupim.com

PROCTOR, Neil
Hodnett Martin Smith

Position
Partner

Contact details
Hodnett Martin Smith Ltd, Charles House, 5-11 Regent Street, London SW1Y 4LR
Tel 020 7839 8181
Fax 020 7839 8069
Web www.hodnettmartinsmith.com
Email neilproctor@hodms.co.uk

PROCTOR, Paul
Edward Symmons & Partners

Position
Senior partner

Qualifications
BSc; MRICS

Career history
1983 Joined Edward Symmons & Partners; appointed partner in 1988, full equity partner in 1999 and senior partner in 2003.
1981-83 Healey & Baker.
1980-81 District Valuer's Office, Dorset

Contact details
Edward Symmons & Partners, 2 Southwark Street, London SE1 1RQ
Tel 020 7955 8454
Fax 020 7407 6423

P

Web www.edwardsymmons.com
Mobile 07979 541255
Email paul.proctor@edwardsymmons.com

PROSSER, Mike
Stiles Harold Williams

Position
Director – head of London office
Qualifications
BSc; MRICS
Professional memberships
RICS
Contact details
Stiles Harold Williams Ltd, 6 Babmaes Street, London SW1Y 6HD
Tel 020 7389 1500
Fax 020 7389 1515
Web www.shw.co.uk
Direct tel 020 7389 1512
Direct fax 020 7389 1529
Mobile 07702 240211
Email mprosser@shw.co.uk

PROTHERO, Graham
Ernst & Young

Position
Partner – real estate, hospitality and construction
Contact details
Ernst & Young LLP, 1 More London Place, London SE1 2AF
Tel 020 7951 2000
Fax 020 7951 1345
Web www.ey.com/uk
Direct tel 020 7951 3774
Email gprothero@uk.ey.com

PROWER, Jim
Argent Group

Position
Finance director
Qualifications
BTech; ACA
Career history
1998 Joined Argent Group.
1995-97 NOBO Group.
1989-95 Co-ordinated Land & Estates/Creston Land & Estates.
1987-89 Minty.
1985-87 Medi Cine International.
1976-85 Peat Marwick Mitchell & Co, London and Sydney
Professional memberships
Institute of Chartered Accountants in England & Wales
Interests
Cycling; family; history; sailing (Newport Boat Club, Royal Lymington Yacht Club, Royal Ocean Racing Club, Weir Wood Sailing Club)
Contact details
Argent Group plc, 5 Albany Courtyard, London W1J 0HF
Tel 020 7734 3721
Fax 020 7734 4474
Web www.argentgroup.plc.uk
Email jimp@argentgroup.plc.uk

PUDNEY, Michael
DTZ Debenham Tie Leung

Position
Director – retail agency and development
Qualifications
BSc Hons; FRICS
Career history
Since 1998 Director of retail agency and development, DTZ Debenham Tie Leung.
1983-98 St Quintin: joined Leeds office; became associate in charge of retail department in 1989 and partner in 1996
Other roles
National co-ordinator, Out-of-Town Retail & Leisure
Professional memberships
Accessible Retail; RICS
Interests
Cycling; golf; sport; walking
Contact details
DTZ Debenham Tie Leung, The Embankment, 2 Sovereign Street, Leeds LS1 4BP
Tel 0113 254 3000
Fax 0113 254 3030
Web www.dtz.com
Direct tel 0113 254 3055
Mobile 07747 008449
Email michael.pudney@dtz.com

PUGH, Charles
Old Square Chambers

Position
Barrister
Qualifications
BSc, Econ
Professional memberships
UK Environmental Law Association
Contact details
Old Square Chambers (Chambers of John Hendy QC), 1 Verulam Buildings, London WC1R 5LQ
Tel 020 7269 0300
Fax 020 7405 1387
Web www.oldsquarechambers.co.uk
Email pugh@oldsquarechambers.co.uk

PUGH, David
Aitchison Raffety

Position
Director
Qualifications
FRICS
Professional memberships
RICS
Contact details
Aitchison Raffety Ltd, 20 Waterloo Street, Birmingham B2 5TD
Tel 0121 643 8181
Fax 0121 633 0663
Web www.argroup.co.uk
Email david.pugh@argroup.co.uk

PUGH, Timothy
Berwin Leighton Paisner

Position
Partner – joint head of planning and environment
Qualifications
LLB Hons; Solicitor
Career history
1984 Joined Berwin Leighton Paisner; appointed partner in 1990.
1984 Admitted to Roll of Solicitors
Other roles
Member, City of London Law Society planning and environmental law committee; member of international environmental law committee, International Bar Association; member, BPF planning and environment committee; associate of Society of Advanced Legal Studies and member of SALS working party on reform of planning and environmental law
Professional memberships
City of London Law Society; International Bar Association; Society for Advance Legal Studies; UK Environmental Law Association
Interests
Cycling; skiing
Contact details
Berwin Leighton Paisner Ltd, Adelaide House, London Bridge, London EC4R 9HA
Tel 020 7760 1000
Fax 020 7760 1111
Web www.berwinleighton.com
Email timothy.pugh@blplaw.com

PULLEN, Matthew
CB Richard Ellis

Position
Executive director – head of corporate advisory
Qualifications
MRICS
Career history
1990 Joined Insignia Richard Ellis; appointed executive director (head of corporate advisory services) in 2001
Other roles
Young Property Person of the Year 2001 (UK

P

Property Industry Awards)

Professional memberships

RICS

Interests

Aviation; hockey

Contact details

CB Richard Ellis, Kingsley House, 1a Wimpole Street, London W1G 0RE

Tel 020 7182 2000

Fax 020 7182 7001

Web www.cbre.com

Direct tel 020 7182 2317

Email matthew.pullen@cbre.com

PULLEN, Richard
Austin-Smith:Lord

Position

Managing partner

Career history

1987 Joined Austin-Smith:Lord.

1978-87 Fitch & Co.

1974-78 Lane Crawford.

1969-74 Hille International.

1964-69 Conran Design Group.

Other roles

Director, Wren Insurance

Professional memberships

Chartered Society of Designers; Royal Society of Arts

Contact details

Austin-Smith:Lord, 17 Bowling Green Lane, London EC1R 0QA

Tel 020 7251 6161

Fax 020 7608 3409

Web www.austinsmithlord.com

Email london@austinsmithlord.com

PULLEN, Xavier
Capital & Regional

Position

Deputy chief executive

Contact details

Capital & Regional plc, 10 Lower Grosvenor Place, London SW1W 0EN

Tel 020 7932 8000

Fax 020 7802 5600

Web www.capreg.com

Email xavier.pullen@capreg.com

PULSFORD, Jeffrey
Arlington Securities

Position

Finance director

Qualifications

ACMA; MCT

Career history

1991-96 Treasurer (operations and corporate finance), British Aerospace.

1990-91 US treasurer, BAe

Professional memberships

Association of Corporate Treasurers; Chartered Institute of Management Accountants

Interests

Cricket; golf; rugby

Contact details

Arlington Securities plc, Arlington House, 1025 Arlington Business Park, Reading RG7 4SA

Tel 0118 930 4141

Fax 0118 930 4383

Web www.arlington.co.uk

Mobile 07966 280141

Email jeff.pulsford@arlington.co.uk

PURCHAS, Robin
2 Harcourt Buildings

Position

Barrister

Qualifications

QC

Career history

1987 Appointed QC.

1968 Called to Bar

Other roles

Vice-chairman, Planning & Environmental Bar Association

Professional memberships

Administrative Law Bar Association; Bar European Group; Planning & Environment Bar Association

Contact details

2 Harcourt Buildings (Chambers of Robin Purchas QC), 2nd Floor, London EC4Y 9DB

Tel 020 7353 8415

Fax 020 7353 7622

Web www.2hblaw.co.uk

Email clerks@2hblaw.co.uk

PYE, James
Budgens Stores

Position

Property director

Interests

Rugby

Contact details

Budgens Stores Ltd, Stonefield Way, Ruislip HA4 0JR

Tel 020 8422 9511

Fax 020 8864 2800

Web www.budgens.com

Direct tel 020 8966 6158

Direct fax 020 8864 6382

Mobile 07977 019116

Email james.pye@budgens.co.uk

PYLE, Robyn
Land Securities Development

Position

Director

Qualifications

FRICS

Professional memberships

RICS

Contact details

Land Securities Development Ltd, 5 Strand, London WC2N 5AF

Tel 020 7413 9000

Web www.landsecurities.com

Email robyn.pyle@landsecurities.com

PYMONT, Christopher
Maitland Chambers

Position

Barrister

Qualifications

MA (Oxon); QC

Career history

1996 Appointed QC.

1979 Called to Bar

Professional memberships

Chancery Bar Association; Commercial Bar Association; Property Bar Association

Contact details

Maitland Chambers, 7 Stone Buildings, London WC2A 3SZ

Tel 020 7406 1200

Fax 020 7406 1300

Web www.maitlandchambers.com

Email cpymont@maitlandchambers.com

PYNE, Stephen
ING Real Estate Investment Management (UK)

Position

Director – segregated accounts

Qualifications

FRICS

Professional memberships

RICS

Contact details

ING Real Estate Investment Management (UK) Ltd, 9 Devonshire Square, London EC2M 4WX

Tel 020 7398 4310

Fax 020 7398 4311

Web www.ingrealestate.co.uk

Email stephen.pyne@ingrealestate.co.uk

QUAYLE, Simon
Shaftesbury

Position
Executive director
Qualifications
BSc; MRICS
Career history
1987 Joined Shaftesbury; prior to that worked with Richard Ellis, Stock Conversion and St Martins Property Corp
Professional memberships
RICS
Contact details
Shaftesbury plc, Pegasus House, 37-43 Sackville Street, London W1S 3DL
Tel 020 7333 8118
Fax 020 7333 0660
Web www.shaftesbury.co.uk
Mobile 07721 450168
Email simon.quayle@shaftesbury.co.uk

QUAYLE, Sophie
Herbert Smith

Position
Partner – head of planning
Qualifications
LLB (Soton)
Career history
1991 Admitted to Roll of Solicitors.
1989 Joined Herbert Smith
Other roles
Vice-chairman of planning and environmental subcommittee, City of London Law Society
Professional memberships
City of London Law Society; Law Society
Interests
Cinema; diving/scuba diving; sailing; skiing; travel
Contact details
Herbert Smith, Exchange House, 10 Primrose Street, London EC2A 2NY
Tel 020 7374 8000
Fax 020 7374 0888
Web www.herbertsmith.com
Direct tel 020 7466 2087
Email sophie.quayle@herbertsmith.com

QUICKE, Martin
Denton Wilde Sapte

Position
Partner – head of real estate
Career history
1982 Admitted to Roll of Solicitors.
1980 Joined Oppenheimers (merged with Denton Hall, now Denton Wilde Sapte); appointed partner in 1989 and head of London real estate in 2001; became head of real estate and retail sector firmwide in 2003
Other roles
Rhythm guitarist for DWS house band "Big Bill & the Write-offs"
Professional memberships
Anglo-American Real Property Institute; British Chamber of Commerce Hong Kong; British Council for Offices; Law Society of Hong Kong; Law Society
Interests
Guitar; music
Contact details
Denton Wilde Sapte, 5 Chancery Lane, London EC4A 1BU
Tel 020 7242 1212
Fax 020 7404 0087
Web www.dentonwildesapte.com
Direct tel 020 7320 6252
Direct fax 020 7246 7777
Email mwq@dentonwildesapte.com

QUILLE, Jim
Lend Lease Global Investment

Position
Chairman and chief executive – Lend Lease Global Properties
Contact details
Lend Lease Global Investment plc, Level 7, 23 Kingsway, London WC2B 6UJ
Tel 020 7379 0222
Fax 020 7379 0213
Web www.lendlease.com.au
Direct tel 020 7395 7685
Email james_quille@lendlease.co.uk

QUINLAN, Michael
Deloitte

Position
Lead partner, stamp duty
Contact details
Deloitte, Stonecutter Court, 1 Stonecutter Street, London EC4A 3TR
Tel 020 7936 3000
Fax 020 7583 1198
Web www.deloitte.co.uk
Direct tel 020 7007 0889
Email mquinlan@deloitte.co.uk

RACE, David
Nicholson Graham & Jones

Position
Partner – head of construction and engineering
Qualifications
LLB Hons; ACIArb
Career history
1987 Joined Nicholson Graham & Jones as partner.
1982-86 Chief solicitor, Blue Circle Industries.
1978-82 Legal adviser to Hong Kong Mass Transit Railway Corp
Professional memberships
Chartered Institute of Arbitrators; Law Society; Society of Construction Law; Technology & Construction Solicitors Association
Interests
Fishing
Contact details
Nicholson Graham & Jones, 110 Cannon Street, London EC4N 6AR
Tel 020 7648 9000
Fax 020 7648 9001
Web www.ngj.co.uk
Direct tel 020 7360 8106
Email david.race@ngj.co.uk

RADEVSKY, Anthony
Falcon Chambers

Position
Barrister
Qualifications
LLB Hons
Career history
1978 Called to Bar
Other roles
Co-author, *Tenants' Right of First Refusal* (Butterworths, 2001) and *Hague on Leasehold Enfranchisement* (4th edition, 2003); author, *Drafting Pleadings* (1995) and *Service of Documents* (1989)
Professional memberships
Chancery Bar Association; Property Bar Association
Contact details
Falcon Chambers, Falcon Court, London EC4Y 1AA
Tel 020 7353 2484
Fax 020 7353 1261
Web www.falcon-chambers.com
Email radevsky@falcon-chambers.com

RADFORD, Hugh
CB Richard Ellis

Position
Senior director – shopping centre leasing
Other roles
Board member, British Council of Shopping Centres
Contact details
CB Richard Ellis, Kingsley House, 1a Wimpole Street, London W1G 0RE
Tel 020 7182 2000
Fax 020 7182 7001
Web www.cbre.com
Email hugh.radford@cbre.com

RADFORD, Simon
CB Richard Ellis Investors

Position
Director
Contact details
CB Richard Ellis Investors Ltd, 64 North Row, London W1K 7DA
Tel 020 7399 9600
Fax 020 7399 9601
Web www.cbreinvestors.com
Email sradford@cbreinvestors.com

RADKIEWICZ, Andrew
NM Rothschild & Sons

Position
Executive director – head of real estate finance
Qualifications
BA Hons, Econ
Interests
Interior design; skiing; tennis
Contact details
NM Rothschild & Sons Ltd, New Court, St Swithin's Lane, London EC4P 4DU
Tel 020 7280 5000
Fax 020 7280 5560
Web www.rothschild.com
Direct tel 020 7280 5745
Direct fax 020 7280 1918
Mobile 07780 700443
Email andrew.radkiewicz@rothschild.co.uk

RADLEY, Bob
Prudential Property Investment Managers

Position
Investment management director
Qualifications
MRICS
Career history
Since 1992 Investment management director, Prudential Property Investment Managers; previously London regional property director and before that property development director
Other roles
Director, New West End Co; director, Foundry Properties; director, GreenPark (Reading)
Professional memberships
British Council for Offices; Institute of Directors; RICS
Contact details
Prudential Property Investment Managers Ltd, Princeton House, 271-273 High Holborn, London WC1V 7NE
Tel 020 7548 6600
Fax 020 7548 6999
Web www.prupim.com
Direct tel 020 7548 6842
Email bob.radley@prupim.com

RAE, Robert
North Rae Sanders

Position
Partner
Contact details
North Rae Sanders, Orchard Court, Harry Weston Road, Coventry CV3 2TQ
Tel 024 7663 6888
Fax 024 7663 6114
Web www.northraesanders.co.uk
Email rrae@northraesanders.co.uk

RAEBURN, Ian
Delancey

Position
Retail director
Qualifications
BSc; MRICS
Career history
1986-98 Healey & Baker
Professional memberships
RICS
Interests
Golf; sport
Contact details
Delancey, 40 Portman Square, London W1H 0AA
Tel 020 7486 6663
Fax 020 7486 6662
Web www.delancey.com

R

Mobile 07774 235083
Email ian.raeburn@delancey.com

RAFFERTY, Owen
Rosling King

Position
Senior partner
Qualifications
MA (Oxon)
Career history
1980 Joined Rosling King.
1976-80 Titmuss Sainer Webb.
1976 Admitted to Roll of Solicitors
Interests
Golf; horse racing; rugby; skiing
Contact details
Rosling King, 2-3 Hind Court, Fleet Street, London EC4A 3DL
Tel 020 7353 2353
Fax 020 7583 2035
Web www.roslingking.co.uk
Email owen.rafferty@roslingking.co.uk

RAGGETT, Dr Brian
CB Richard Ellis

Position
Senior director – public-sector consultancy
Qualifications
PhD; MRTPI; MRICS; FRSA
Career history
1979 Joined Hillier Parker (now CB Richard Ellis); became associate in 1983 and equity partner in 1987
Other roles
President, Urban Design Alliance (2000); president, RTPI (1999-2000); director, RTPI Services; chair, British Council of Shopping Centres urban task force (2001); Commission for Architecture & the Built Environment enabler (2001)
Contact details
CB Richard Ellis, Kingsley House, 1a Wimpole Street, London W1G 0RE
Tel 020 7182 2000
Fax 020 7182 7001
Web www.cbre.com
Direct tel 020 7182 2120
Direct fax 020 7182 2021
Mobile 07785 381774
Email brian.raggett@cbre.com

RAICHURA, Naren
British Land Co

Position
Group chief accountant
Qualifications
FCCA
Contact details
British Land Co plc, 10 Cornwall Terrace, London NW1 4QP
Tel 020 7486 4466
Fax 020 7935 5552
Web www.britishland.com
Direct tel 020 7467 2846
Email naren.raichura@britishland.com

RAINFORD, Ben
ING Real Estate Development UK

Position
Managing director
Contact details
ING Real Estate Development UK Ltd, 33 Cavendish Square, London W1G 0BQ
Tel 020 7659 9620
Fax 020 7659 6221
Email ben.rainford@ingrealestate.co.uk

RAMSAY, Alasdair
Drivers Jonas

Position
Partner – head of Scottish offices
Qualifications
MRICS
Career history
1987 Joined Drivers Jonas
Professional memberships
RICS
Contact details
Drivers Jonas, Delta House, 50 West Nile Street, Glasgow G1 2NP
Tel 0141 226 4200
Fax 0141 226 4212
Web www.driversjonas.com
Direct tel 0141 240 1211
Mobile 07768 604632
Email alasdairramsay@driversjonas.com

RAMSAY, Patrick
Knight Frank

Position
Partner – head of country business
Qualifications
FRICS
Career history
1976 Joined Knight Frank as negotiator in country house department; became partner in 1988.
1974-76 Assistant land agent, Strutt & Parker.
1969-70 Assistant (private clients department), James Capel
Professional memberships
RICS
Contact details
Knight Frank LLP, 20 Hanover Square, London W1S 1HZ
Tel 020 7629 8171
Fax 020 7493 4114
Web www.knightfrank.com
Direct fax 020 7491 0854
Email patrick.ramsay@knightfrank.com

RANDALL, John
St Philips Chambers

Position
QC – head of chambers
Qualifications
MA (Cantab); QC
Career history
Since 2001 Head of chambers, St Philips Chambers.
2001 Called to Bar (Western Australia).
1979 Called to Bar (New South Wales).
1978 Called to Bar (Lincoln's Inn)
Other roles
Recorder; deputy high court judge (since 2000); bencher of Lincoln's Inn (since 2003); past chairman, Midland Chancery & Commercial Bar Association
Professional memberships
Chancery Bar Association; International Bar Association; Midland Chancery & Commercial Bar Association; Midland Circuit
Contact details
St Philips Chambers (Chambers of John Randall QC), 55 Temple Row, Birmingham B2 5LS
Tel 0121 246 7000
Fax 0121 246 7001
Web www.st-philips.co.uk
Email jrandall@st-philips.co.uk

RANDLE, Simon
11 New Square

Position
Barrister
Career history
1982 Called to Bar, Inner Temple
Other roles
Acted for DETR throughout inquiry into BAA's application for fifth terminal at Heathrow Airport
Contact details
11 New Square (Chambers of Sonia Proudman QC), Ground Floor, London WC2A 3QB
Tel 020 7831 0081
Fax 020 7405 2560
Web www.11newsquare.co.uk
Email clerks@11newsquare.co.uk

RANGECROFT, Pippa
Threadneedle Property Investments

Position
Property asset manager

Contact details
Threadneedle Property Investments, 9-15 Sackville Street, London W1S 3DJ
Tel 020 7437 8000
Fax 020 7464 5811
Direct tel 020 7464 5890
Direct fax 020 7464 5812
Email pippa.rangecroft@threadneedle.co.uk

RAPP, Michael
Westcity Holdings

Position
Chairman
Other roles
Non-executive director – Liberty International
Interests
Golf
Contact details
Westcity Holdings plc, 3 Prince Albert Road, London NW1 7SN
Tel 020 7424 6700
Fax 020 7267 4771
Direct tel 020 7584 4203
Direct fax 020 7591 0570
Mobile 0778 5291824
Email michael@westcity.co.uk

RATCLIFF, Peter
Blair Kirkman

Position
Partner
Qualifications
BSc; FRICS
Professional memberships
RICS
Contact details
Blair Kirkman, St Georges House, 12a St George Street, London W1S 1FQ
Tel 020 7409 0899
Fax 020 7629 8022
Web www.blairkirkman.com
Email peterr@blairkirkman.com

RAVEN, Tony
Moto Hospitality

Position
Property and estates director
Career history
1974 Joined Granada (now Moto Hospitality).
1963-74 Local government
Professional memberships
Faculty of Building
Interests
Golf; rugby; travel; wine
Contact details
Moto Hospitality Ltd, PO Box 218, Toddington, Dunstable LU5 6QG
Tel 0870 191 1900
Web www.moto-way.com
Direct tel 01525 878305
Direct fax 01525 878231
Mobile 07836 752607
Email tony.raven@moto-way.co.uk

RAVENHILL, Stanley
ep2

Position
Head of professional department
Qualifications
DipArb; FRICS; FCIArb
Career history
Since 1995 Head of professional, ep2 (formerly ep2 Elliott Partnership).
1973-95 Partner, WT Gunson & Son; responsible for agency and subsequently professional work.
1969-73 Property developers: Lyon Group, Deacon Group, Mount St Bernard
Other roles
Past chairman, RICS Manchester branch (elected 1997)
Professional memberships
Arbitration Club; Arbrix; Chartered Institute of Arbitrators; Non-Administrative Receivers Association; RICS; Valuation Forum
Interests
Cycling; rugby
Contact details
ep2, Brazennose House West, Brazennose Street, Manchester M2 5EP
Tel 0161 834 0011
Fax 0161 834 0146
Web www.ep2.co.uk
Direct tel 0161 934 2104
Email stan.ravenhill@ep2.co.uk

RAWNSLEY, Jonathan
Freeport

Position
Chief executive
Contact details
Freeport plc, 9-13 George Street, London W1U 3FL
Tel 020 7299 9360
Fax 020 7299 9388
Web www.freeportplc.com
Email jonathanrawnsley@freeportleisure.com

RAWSTRON, Mark
GVA Grimley

Position
Partner – head of investment, Manchester
Qualifications
MRICS
Professional memberships
RICS
Interests
Antiques; architecture; art; sport
Contact details
GVA Grimley, 81 Fountain Street, Manchester M2 2EE
Tel 0870 900 8990
Fax 0161 956 4009
Web www.gvagrimley.co.uk
Direct tel 0161 956 4100
Mobile 07831 820633
Email mark.rawstron@gvagrimley.co.uk

RAYNE, Robert
London Merchant Securities

Position
Chief executive
Other roles
Trustee, Rayne Foundation (since 1970)
Professional memberships
Institute of Directors; Institute of Management; Royal Society of Arts
Interests
Art; sailing
Contact details
London Merchant Securities plc, Carlton House, 33 Robert Adam Street, London W1U 3HR
Tel 020 7935 3555
Fax 020 7935 3737
Web www.lms-plc.com
Email rrayne@lms-plc.com

RAYNOR, James
Royal Bank of Scotland

Position
Senior director – European real estate
Qualifications
BA Hons
Contact details
Royal Bank of Scotland, 8 Rue Lavoisier, Paris
Tel +33 1 4924 1244
Web www.rbs.co.uk
Email james.raynor@rbos.com

READ, Graham
Devereux Chambers

Position
Barrister
Qualifications
QC
Career history
2003 Appointed QC
Contact details
Devereux Chambers (Chambers of Jeffrey Burke QC), Devereux Court, London WC2R 3JH
Tel 020 7353 7534

Fax 020 7353 1724
Web www.devchambers.co.uk
Email read@devchambers.co.uk

READ, Ian
citib@se

Position
Joint managing director
Other roles
Director, Freehold Managers; director, Ten Harley Street
Contact details
citib@se plc, Vigilant House, 120 Wilton Road, London SW1V 1JZ
Tel 020 7808 7444
Fax 020 7808 7028
Email citibaseplc@citibase.co.uk

READ, Lionel
Landmark Chambers

Position
Head of chambers
Qualifications
QC
Contact details
Landmark Chambers, 4 Breams Buildings, London EC4A 1AQ
Tel 020 7430 1221
Fax 020 7421 1399
Web www.landmarkchambers.co.uk
Email clerks@landmarkchambers.co.uk

READMAN, John
Bhs

Position
Property director
Other roles
Group property director, Arcadia Group
Contact details
Bhs Ltd, 129-137 Marylebone Road, London NW1 5QD
Tel 020 7339 4013
Fax 020 7339 4169
Web www.bhs.co.uk
Direct tel 020 7927 3765
Direct fax 020 7927 3778
Email penny.gibbon@arcadiagroup.co.uk

REDFERN, Gary
NAI Fuller Peiser

Position
Equity partner – head of Manchester office
Qualifications
MRICS
Career history
1996 Joined NAI Fuller Peiser.
1991-96 Valuation Office Agency mineral valuers, Leeds.
1978-91 NCB/British Coal, South Yorkshire
Professional memberships
Rating Surveyors Association; RICS
Interests
Golf; motor sports
Contact details
NAI Fuller Peiser, 4th Floor, Northern Assurance Building, Albert Square, Manchester M2 4DN
Tel 0870 700 2233
Fax 0161 835 2005
Web www.nai-fullerpeiser.com
Email gredfern@nai-fullerpeiser.com

REDMAN, Colin
Grosvenor

Position
Director of trusts
Qualifications
FRICS
Career history
1982 Joined Grosvenor as chief building surveyor at Grosvenor Estate Holdings; became managing director of Grosvenor Restorations in 1987; appointed Grosvenor's London estate director in 1992 and director of trusts in 2000.
1977-82 Partner, Cluttons.
1973-77 Sole principal, Redman & Co
Other roles
Chairman, Westminster Property Owners Association; director, Central London Partnership; chairman of planning and heritage, Estates Business Group; committee member, Urban Villages Forum
Professional memberships
Institute of Historic Building Conservation; RICS
Interests
Gardening; music; walking; wine
Contact details
Grosvenor Ltd, 70 Grosvenor Street, London W1K 3JP
Tel 020 7408 0988
Fax 020 7629 9115
Web www.grosvenor.com
Direct tel 020 7312 6173
Direct fax 020 7312 6244
Email colin.redman@grosvenor.com

REDMAN, Philip
CB Richard Ellis

Position
Managing director – business space consultancy
Qualifications
FRICS; IRRV
Career history
1987 Joined Hillier Parker.
1974-87 District Valuer's Office/Valuation Office.
1971-74 Executive officer, Inland Revenue
Contact details
CB Richard Ellis, Kingsley House, 1a Wimpole Street, London W1G 0RE
Tel 020 7182 2000
Fax 020 7182 7001
Web www.cbre.com
Direct tel 020 7882 8314
Direct fax 020 7882 8721
Mobile 07774 824712
Email philip.redman@cbre.com

REDMAN, Simon
Aberdeen Asset Management

Position
Associate director
Contact details
Aberdeen Asset Management plc, Charles House, 5-11 Regent Street, London SW1Y 4LR
Tel 020 7747 1700
Web www.aberdeen-asset.com
Direct tel 020 7747 1713
Direct fax 020 7930 9433
Email
simon.redman@aberdeenpropertyinvestors.com

REDMOND, John
Osborne Clarke

Position
Partner – head of construction law
Qualifications
BA; FCIArb
Career history
1978-2000 Laytons.
1976-78 Assistant solicitor, Clyde & Co.
1976 Admitted to Roll of Solicitors.
1974-76 Cobbetts
Professional memberships
Chartered Institute of Arbitrators; Law Society; Society of Construction Law
Interests
Sailing
Contact details
Osborne Clarke, 2 Temple Back East, Bristol BS1 6EG
Tel 0117 917 3000
Fax 0117 917 3005
Web www.osborneclarke.com
Direct tel 0117 917 3458
Email john.redmond@osborneclarke.com

REED, Adrian
Aberdeen Property Investors

Position
Director – office and industrial
Contact details
Aberdeen Property Investors, Charles House,

5-11 Regent Street, London SW1Y 4LR
Tel 020 7747 1700
Fax 020 7839 7460
Web www.aberdeenpropertyinvestors.com
Direct tel 020 7747 1703
Mobile 07799 131703
Email
adrian.reed@aberdeenpropertyinvestors.com

REED, Philip
ING Real Estate Investment Management (UK)

Position
Director – property accounts
Qualifications
BSc, Econ
Career history
1992 Joined Baring, Houston & Saunders (now ING Real Estate Investment Management (UK)).
1991-92 Olympia & York.
1985-91 Edward Erdman.
1983-85 DE&J Levy.
1981-83 Jones Lang Wootton
Contact details
ING Real Estate Investment Management (UK) Ltd, 9 Devonshire Square, London EC2M 4WX
Tel 020 7398 4310
Fax 020 7398 4311
Web www.ingrealestate.co.uk
Direct tel 020 7398 5545
Email philip.reed@ingrealestate.co.uk

REES, Brian
Matthews & Goodman

Position
Partner
Qualifications
MRICS; BSc
Contact details
Matthews & Goodman, 23 Ironmonger Lane, London EC2V 8EY
Tel 020 7367 5533
Fax 020 7367 5535
Web www.matthews-goodman.co.uk
Direct tel 020 7367 5538
Email brees@matthews-goodman.co.uk

REES, Peter
Norton Rose

Position
Partner – head of global dispute resolution
Qualifications
MA; MBA; FCIArb
Career history
1979 Joined Norton Rose; became partner in 1987 and head of dispute resolution in 1996
Other roles
Chairman, Technology & Construction Solicitor's Association; solicitor representative, Technology & Construction Court users' committee; past chair of international construction projects committee, International Bar Association council, and member of IBA business law section; TeCSA accredited adjudicator
Professional memberships
Chartered Institute of Arbitrators; International Bar Association; Technology & Construction Solicitors Association
Interests
Diving/scuba diving; football; gardening; golf
Contact details
Norton Rose, Kempson House, Camomile Street, London EC3A 7AN
Tel 020 7283 6000
Fax 020 7283 6500
Web www.nortonrose.com
Email peter.rees@nortonrose.com

REES, Simon
Gerald Eve

Position
Partner – head of Cardiff office
Qualifications
BSc; FRICS
Career history
1987 Joined Gerald Eve; partner in charge of Cardiff office since 1994
Professional memberships
RICS
Interests
Golf; rugby; skiing
Contact details
Gerald Eve, 32 Windsor Place, Cardiff CF10 3BZ
Tel 029 2038 8044
Fax 029 2034 4177
Web www.geraldeve.com
Email srees@geraldeve.com

REES, Stephen
UBS

Position
Director – head of real estate advisory
Contact details
UBS AG, 1 Curzon Street, London W1J 5HD
Tel 020 7568 7025
Web www.ubs.com
Direct tel 020 7567 5552
Direct fax 020 7567 5630
Email stephen.rees@ubs.com

REEVE, Christopher
Lambert Smith Hampton

Position
Director
Qualifications
BSc Hons; MRICS
Career history
1993 Joined Connell Wilson (now Lambert Smith Hampton); now director of office agency, disposals and acquisitions
Professional memberships
RICS
Contact details
Lambert Smith Hampton Ltd, Holybrook House, 63 Castle Street, Reading RG1 7SN
Tel 0118 959 8855
Fax 0118 950 3363
Web www.lsh.co.uk
Mobile 07836 749368
Email creeve@lsh.co.uk

REEVES, Suzanne
Wedlake Bell

Position
Partner – head of construction group
Contact details
Wedlake Bell, 16 Bedford Street, London WC2E 9HF
Tel 020 7395 3000
Fax 020 7836 9966
Web www.wedlakebell.co.uk
Email sreeves@wedlakebell.com

REEVEY, Michael
Addleshaw Goddard

Position
Partner – national head of commercial property
Qualifications
MA
Career history
1980 Joined Addleshaw Booth & Co (now Addleshaw Goddard); became partner in 1988 and board member in 1997
Professional memberships
Law Society
Interests
Golf
Contact details
Addleshaw Goddard, Sovereign House, Sovereign Street, Leeds LS1 1HQ
Tel 0113 209 2000
Fax 0113 209 2060
Web www.addleshawgoddard.com
Direct tel 0113 209 2409
Email michael.reevey@addleshawgoddard.com

REGAN, Michael
Mayer, Brown, Rowe & Maw

Position
Partner
Contact details

Mayer, Brown, Rowe & Maw LLP, 11 Pilgrim Street, London EC4V 6RW
Tel 020 7248 4282
Fax 020 7248 2009
Web www.mayerbrownrowe.com
Direct tel 020 7782 8899
Email mregan@mayerbrownrowe.com

REICHMANN, Paul
Canary Wharf Group

Position
Chairman
Other roles
Chief executive, Reichmann Group of Companies, Toronto, Canada
Contact details
Canary Wharf Group plc, One Canada Square, London E14 5AB
Tel 020 7418 2000
Fax 020 7418 2222
Web www.canarywharf.com
Direct tel 020 7418 2223
Direct fax 020 7418 2085
Email paul.reichmann@canarywharf.com

REICHWALD, Iain
ISIS Property Asset Management

Position
Director – property finance and operations
Qualifications
BSc, Econ; FCA
Career history
1988-92 Finance director, Amos Brooke Associates.
1984-88 Development and overseas accountant, Debenham Tewson & Chinnocks.
1982-84 Supervising manager, Binder Hamlyn
Professional memberships
Institute of Chartered Accountants in England & Wales
Contact details
ISIS Property Asset Management plc, Park Lodge, London Road, Dorking RH4 1QP
Tel 01306 651800
Fax 01306 651802
Web www.isisam.com
Direct tel 01306 651837
Email iain.reichwald@isisam.com

REID, David
Montagu Evans

Position
Partner – planning and development
Qualifications
MRICS
Professional memberships
RICS; RTPI
Contact details
Montagu Evans, 44-48 Dover Street, London W1S 4AZ
Tel 020 7493 4002
Fax 020 7312 7547
Web www.montagu-evans.co.uk
Direct tel 020 7312 7415
Direct fax 020 7312 7548
Email david.reid@montagu-evans.co.uk

REID, Martin
Thomas & Adamson

Position
Senior partner
Qualifications
FRICS; FCIOB
Career history
1977 Joined Thomas & Adamson.
1970-77 Davis Langdon & Everest.
1965-70 J Nairne Campbell & Sons, Perth
Professional memberships
Chartered Institute of Building; RICS
Contact details
Thomas & Adamson, 10 Wemyss Place, Edinburgh EH3 6DL
Tel 0131 225 4072
Fax 0131 225 5514
Web www.thomasandadamson.com
Direct tel 0131 260 2606
Mobile 07798 926333
Email martin.reid@thomasandadamson.com

REID, Philip
CB Richard Ellis

Position
Managing director – Scotland
Contact details
CB Richard Ellis, Pacific House, 70 Wellington Street, Glasgow G2 6UA
Tel 0141 204 7666
Fax 0141 306 0141
Web www.cbre.com
Direct tel 0141 204 7713
Email philip.reid@cbre.com

REID, Sandy
Biggart Baillie

Position
Partner
Qualifications
LLB WS NP
Career history
Since 2001 Partner, Biggart Baillie.
1980-2001 Steedman Ramage: became chairman in 1993.
1977 Admitted to Roll of Solicitors
Professional memberships
British Council of Shopping Centres; International Bar Association; Law Society of Scotland; Union Internationale des Avocats
Interests
Family; football; music; sport
Contact details
Biggart Baillie, 11 Castle Street, Edinburgh EH2 3AP
Tel 0131 226 5541
Fax 0131 226 2278
Web www.biggartbaillie.co.uk
Direct tel 0131 260 6630
Email sreid@biggartbaillie.co.uk

REILLY, Andrew
Chesterton International

Position
Director in charge, Edinburgh offices
Other roles
Director, GIA Business Properties
Professional memberships
Institute of Revenues Rating & Valuation; RICS
Interests
Golf (past captain, Balbirnie Park Golf Club, Marchinch, Fife); Glenrothes Rotary Club
Contact details
Chesterton International, 36 Castle Street, Edinburgh EH2 3HT
Tel 0131 226 4791
Fax 0131 225 3451
Web www.chesterton.co.uk
Mobile 07712 868350
Email andrew.reilly@chesterton.co.uk

REILLY, Dominic
Kingfisher Property Finance

Position
Director
Qualifications
MA Cantab; FRICS
Career history
Since 1988 Director, Kingfisher Property Finance and Kingfisher Property Partnerships.
1986-88 JLW Financial Services.
1985-86 JLW travelling scholarship.
1981-85 King & Co.
1978-81 Weatherall Green & Smith
Other roles
External tutor for RICS Diploma in Property Investment, College of Estate Management; editorial board member, *Briefings in Real Estate Finance*; member of faculty board for Investment Property Forum advanced education programme
Professional memberships
Investment Property Forum; RICS
Interests
Golf; skiing; tennis

Contact details
Kingfisher Property Finance Ltd, 41-43 Maddox Street, London W1S 2PD
Tel 020 7491 0380
Fax 020 7491 9202
Web www.kingfisherpropertyfinance.co.uk
Mobile 07968 307775
Email
dominic.reilly@kingfisherpropertyfinance.co.uk

REILLY, Peter
JP Morgan

Position
Managing director – JP Morgan Partners
Qualifications
MBA
Career history
Since 2001 Managing director, JP Morgan Partners.
1998-2000 Vice-president, JP Morgan.
1984-97 Principal, O'Connor Group
Professional memberships
International Council of Shopping Centers; Real Estate Investment Advisory Council; Urban Land Institute
Contact details
JP Morgan plc, 125 London Wall, London EC2Y 5AJ
Tel 020 7777 2000
Web www.jpmorgan.com
Direct tel 020 7777 0410
Direct fax 020 7777 0998
Email peter.m.reilly@jpmorganpartners.com

REVELL, Geoffrey
Express Park Development Co

Position
Marketing director
Career history
Since 2002 Marketing director, Express Park Development Co.
1993-2002 Partner, Alder King Taunton
Contact details
Express Park Development Co Ltd, Bristol Road, Bridgwater TA6 4RN
Tel 01278 459292
Fax 01278 453109
Web www.expresspark.co.uk
Email geoff@expresspark.co.uk

REYNOLDS, John
Big Food Group

Position
Group property director
Qualifications
BSc; MRICS
Career history
Since 2003 Group property director, Big Food Group.
1988-2003 McDonald's Restaurants: appointed regional property manager in 1993 and head of property in 1997.
1985-88 Acquisition surveyor, Kwik Save supermarkets
Professional memberships
RICS
Interests
Motor sports; sailing; travel
Contact details
Big Food Group plc, Second Avenue, Deeside CH5 2NW
Tel 01244 830100
Fax 01244 814531
Web www.bigfoodgroup.co.uk
Direct tel 01244 842331
Direct fax 01244 843905
Mobile 07985 889774
Email john.reynolds@thebigfoodgroup.co.uk

REYNOLDS, Kirk
Falcon Chambers

Position
Barrister
Qualifications
QC
Career history
Since 1975 Member of chambers at 11 King's Bench Walk (now Falcon Chambers).
1974 Called to Bar
Other roles
Co-author, *The Handbook of Rent Review* (loose-leaf edition, 1981 to date); joint editor, *Renewal of Business Tenancies* (2nd edition, 2002); joint editor, *Dilapidations: The Modern Law & Practice* (2nd edition, 2000)
Professional memberships
Arbrix (honorary member); RICS (honorary member)
Contact details
Falcon Chambers, Falcon Court, London EC4Y 1AA
Tel 020 7353 2484
Fax 020 7353 1261
Web www.falcon-chambers.com
Email reynolds@falcon-chambers.com

REYNOLDS, Simon
GVA Grimley

Position
Partner – head of corporate occupier services
Qualifications
BA; MBIFM
Career history
1984 Joined Grimley, Manchester.
1979-84 Agency surveyor, Lambert Smith Hampton (then WH Robinson)
Other roles
Former director, North West Regional Development Organisation
Professional memberships
British Council for Offices; British Institute of Facilities Management; CoreNet Global UK; Office Agents Society
Interests
Sailing (Royal Thames Yacht Club); skiing
Contact details
GVA Grimley, 10 Stratton Street, London W1J 8JR
Tel 0870 900 8990
Fax 020 7911 2560
Web www.gvagrimley.co.uk
Direct tel 020 7911 2173
Mobile 07831 820692
Email simon.reynolds@gvagrimley.co.uk

RICE, Stephen
Frontier Estates

Position
Head of project management
Career history
Since 1999 Development associate/head of project management, Frontier Estates.
1994-99 Associate director, Fletcher King Howard.
1979-93 Contracts manager, various top-50 building contractors
Interests
Cycling; running; triathlon
Contact details
Frontier Estates Ltd, Acorn House, Midsummer Boulevard, Milton Keynes MK9 3HP
Tel 01908 238888
Fax 01908 241111
Web www.frontier-estates.com
Mobile 07764 784374
Email steverice@frontier-estates.com

RICH, Peter
Rich Investments

Position
Managing director
Other roles
Chairman, Cherwell Capital; chairman, Jeroboams; chairman, Laytons Wine Merchants
Contact details
Rich Investments Ltd, 43 Portland Road, London W11 4LJ
Tel 020 7985 1560
Fax 020 7229 1085
Email pcr@richgroup.co.uk

R

RICHARDS, Howard
Drivers Jonas

Position
Partner – head of investment
Qualifications
BSc; FRICS
Career history
1986 Joined Drivers Jonas.
1979-86 Associate, Wright & Partners.
1976-79 Debenham Tewson & Chinnocks
Professional memberships
Investment Property Forum; RICS; Securities Institute
Contact details
Drivers Jonas, 6 Grosvenor Street, London W1K 4DJ
Tel 020 7896 8000
Fax 020 7896 8001
Web www.driversjonas.com
Direct tel 020 7896 8271
Mobile 07771 898957
Email howardrichards@driversjonas.com

RICHARDS, Jeremy
King Sturge

Position
Partner in charge, Bristol
Qualifications
BA; BSc; MRICS
Career history
Since 2003 Partner (head of Bristol office), King Sturge.
1988-2003 Office agent, King Sturge.
1984-88 Stephen & Co
Other roles
Chairman, Bristol Property Forum
Professional memberships
RICS
Interests
Food and drink; golf; tennis
Contact details
King Sturge, 40 Berkeley Square, Bristol BS8 1HU
Tel 0117 927 6691
Fax 0117 929 9669
Web www.kingsturge.com
Direct tel 0117 930 5745
Mobile 07770 567903
Email jeremy.richards@kingsturge.co.uk

RICHARDS, John
Hammerson

Position
Chief executive
Qualifications
BSc; FRICS
Career history
1981 Joined Hammerson; appointed director of the UK business in 1987, plc director in 1990 and managing director (UK) in 1993; became international managing director in 1998 and chief executive in 1999.
1978-81 Investment surveyor, Edward Erdman & Co
Other roles
President, British Council of Shopping Centres (2003-04)
Professional memberships
British Council of Shopping Centres; RICS
Contact details
Hammerson plc, 100 Park Lane, London W1K 7AR
Tel 020 7887 1000
Fax 020 7887 1010
Web www.hammerson.co.uk
Direct tel 020 7887 1054
Direct fax 020 7887 1100
Email jrichards@hammerson.co.uk

RICHARDS, Peter
Atkinson Richards

Position
Director
Career history
Since 1995 Director, Atkinson Richards.
1982-95 Partner, Pilgrim Miller & Partners.
1978-82 Office management, Crown Life Insurance
Professional memberships
100 Property Club; Industrial Agents Society; Office Agents Society
Interests
Cycling; golf; motor sports
Contact details
Atkinson Richards, 11 Kings Road, Fleet GU51 3AA
Tel 01252 816061
Fax 01252 816062
Web www.atkinsonrichards.com
Mobile 07803 078011
Email peter@atkinsonrichards.com

RICHARDS, Peter
King Sturge

Position
Partner – national head of office agency
Career history
1980 Joint founding partner of City of London practice, Bates Richards (merged with King Sturge in 1996); became head of City office agency after merger; appointed head of national office agency in 1999.
1976-80 City agency, Hampton & Son
Interests
Motorcycling; sailing; squash; walking
Contact details
King Sturge, 7 Stratford Place, London W1C 1ST
Tel 020 7493 4933
Fax 020 7409 0469
Web www.kingsturge.com
Direct tel 020 7529 6510
Direct fax 020 7409 1135
Mobile 07710 887758
Email peter.richards@kingsturge.co.uk

RICHARDS, Tim
Hewitsons

Position
Partner – head of property/construction and PFI
Qualifications
LLB
Career history
Since 1996 Partner (head of property/construction and PFI), Hewitson Becke + Shaw (now Hewitsons).
1985-96 Linklaters & Paines.
1985 Admitted to Roll of Solicitors
Other roles
Member, Cambridge Forum for Construction Industry
Professional memberships
Society of Construction Law
Interests
Golf; rugby; skiing
Contact details
Hewitsons, Shakespeare House, 42 Newmarket Road, Cambridge CB5 8EP
Tel 0122 346 1155
Fax 0122 331 6511
Web www.hewitsons.com
Direct tel 01223 532727
Mobile 07081 081106
Email timrichards@hewitsons.com

RICHARDS, Windsor
Arlington Developments

Position
Managing director
Other roles
Construction director, Arlington Property Developments
Contact details
Arlington Developments Ltd, Arlington House, 1025 Arlington Business Park, Reading RG7 4SA
Tel 0118 930 4141
Fax 0118 930 4383
Web www.arlington.co.uk
Direct tel 0118 932 7483
Email windsor.richards@arlington.co.uk

RICHARDSON, Clive
Stiles Harold Williams

Position
Director
Qualifications
BSc Hons; TechRICS
Career history
1987 Joined Stiles Harold Williams as property manager; appointed associate in 1990 and director in 2001
Professional memberships
RICS
Interests
Cycling
Contact details
Stiles Harold Williams Ltd, Sterling House, High Street, Crawley RH10 1GE
Tel 0129 344 1300
Fax 0129 344 1334
Web www.shw.co.uk
Email crichardson@shw.co.uk

RICHARDSON, David
Phoenix Beard

Position
Director – building consultancy
Qualifications
FRICS; FBEng; FFB
Career history
1990 Joined Phoenix Beard as associate director; appointed director in 1998 and equity director in 2000.
1986-90 Assistant director (estate management), University of Birmingham
Professional memberships
Association of Building Engineers; Faculty of Building; RICS
Interests
Motor sports; sport; swimming; travel
Contact details
Phoenix Beard, The Exchange, 19 Newhall Street, Birmingham B3 3PJ
Tel 0121 200 4500
Fax 0121 200 4599
Web www.phoenix-beard.co.uk
Direct tel 0121 200 4549
Mobile 07808 784790
Email david.richardson@phoenix-beard.co.uk

RICHARDSON, Neil
Land Securities Trillium

Position
Asset management director
Qualifications
BSc Hons; MRICS; Dip Prop Inv
Professional memberships
Investment Property Forum; RICS
Contact details
Land Securities Trillium Ltd, 140 London Wall, London EC2Y 5DN
Tel 020 7796 5500
Fax 020 7796 5501
Web www.landsecurities.co.uk
Direct tel 020 7796 5716
Direct fax 0845 090 2613
Email neil.richardson@lstrillium.com

RICHARDSON, Stephen
ATIS REAL Weatheralls

Position
Director – hotels
Qualifications
MA; FRICS
Career history
1978 Joined ATIS REAL Weatheralls.
1973-78 Valuation office
Professional memberships
Arbrix; Business in Sport & Leisure; Entertainment & Leisure Forum; Hotel Property Network; RICS; Worshipful Company of Paviors
Interests
Gardening; rugby; sailing
Contact details
ATIS REAL Weatheralls Ltd, Norfolk House, 31 St James's Square, London SW1Y 4JR
Tel 020 7338 4200
Fax 020 7493 0746
Web www.atisrealweatheralls.com
Direct tel 020 7338 4360
Email
stephen.richardson@atisrealweatheralls.com

RICHES, John
Withers

Position
Principal – head of entrepreneurs group
Qualifications
LLB (Birmingham)
Career history
1996 Joined Withers as a principal.
1990-96 Pinsent Curtis.
1985-90 Two major regional firms.
1982-85 Mills & Reeves
Other roles
Council member of Society of Trust & Estate Practitioners, serving on technical and education committees
Interests
Skiing; walking
Contact details
Withers LLP, 16 Old Bailey, London EC4M 7EG
Tel 020 7597 6000
Fax 020 7597 6543
Web www.withersworldwide.com
Direct tel 020 7597 6109
Email john.riches@withersworldwide.com

RICHMOND, Stephen
Edwin Hill

Position
Partner
Qualifications
BSc Hons; MRICS
Professional memberships
RICS
Interests
Rugby
Contact details
Edwin Hill, St Johns House, Dartford DA1 2DR
Tel 01322 285588
Fax 01322 285599
Web www.edwinhill.co.uk
Email stephenr@edwinhill.co.uk

RICHMOND-WATSON, Stuart
LaSalle Investment Management

Position
European director
Qualifications
FRICS
Contact details
LaSalle Investment Management, 33 Cavendish Square, London W1A 2NF
Tel 020 7852 4000
Fax 020 7852 4374
Web www.lasalle.com
Email stuart.richmond-watson@lasalle.com

RICKARD, Steven
British Land Properties

Position
Director
Qualifications
BSc; MRICS
Professional memberships
RICS
Contact details
British Land Properties Ltd, 10 Cornwall Terrace, London NW1 4QP
Tel 020 7486 4466
Fax 020 7935 5552
Web www.britishland.com
Email steven.rickard@britishland.com

RICKARDS, Michael
Vebnet (Holdings)

Position
Joint managing director
Contact details
Vebnet (Holdings) plc, The Courtyard, New

Lodge, Drift Road, Windsor SL4 4RR
Tel 01344 884662
Fax 01344 884878
Email stockb@stockbourne.co.uk

RIDGWELL, Ben
Fletcher King
Position
Director – head of property asset management
Qualifications
Dip Prop Inv; MRICS
Professional memberships
RICS
Contact details
Fletcher King plc, Stratton House, 1 Stratton Street, London W1J 8LA
Tel 020 7493 8400
Fax 020 7491 2100
Web www.fletcherking.co.uk
Email benr@fletcherking.co.uk

RIDING, Clive
Montagu Evans
Position
Partner – head of professional services
Qualifications
FRICS
Professional memberships
RICS
Contact details
Montagu Evans, 44-48 Dover Street, London W1S 4AZ
Tel 020 7493 4002
Fax 020 7312 7547
Web www.montagu-evans.co.uk
Email clive.riding@montagu-evans.co.uk

RIDLER, Andrew
Alder King
Position
Partner
Contact details
Alder King, Pembroke House, 15 Pembroke Road, Bristol BS8 3BA
Tel 0117 317 1000
Fax 0117 317 1001
Web www.alderking.com
Email aridler@alderking.com

RIDLEY, Mark
FPDSavills
Position
Director – head of office, Manchester
Qualifications
BSc Hons; MRICS
Professional memberships
RICS
Contact details
FPDSavills Ltd, Fountain Court, 68 Fountain Street, Manchester M2 2FB
Tel 0161 236 8644
Fax 0161 228 0544
Web www.fpdsavills.co.uk
Direct tel 0161 277 7210
Mobile 07870 555771
Email mridley@fpdsavills.co.uk

RIDSDALE, Tim
Gamestation
Position
Property director
Contact details
Gamestation, 10-11 Stirling Park, York YO30 4WU
Tel 01904 692224
Web www.gamestation.co.uk

RIEDEL, Frank
H&M
Position
Property manager
Contact details
H&M, Holden House, 2nd Floor, 57 Rathbone Place, London W1T 1NP
Tel 020 7323 2211
Web www.hm.com
Direct tel 020 7290 0338
Email frank.riedel@hm.com

RIGBY, Mark
Lambert Smith Hampton
Position
Chief executive officer
Qualifications
BA Hons; MRICS
Other roles
Group board director, Lambert Smith Hampton; president, RICS RFC; former director, Loftis Road; former playing captain, Wasps
Professional memberships
RICS; Institute of Directors
Contact details
Lambert Smith Hampton Ltd, Regent Arcade House, 19-25 Argyll Street, London W1F 7TS
Tel 020 7494 4000
Fax 020 7414 0866
Direct tel 0207 663 8347
Mobile 07702 801766
Email marigby@lsh.co.uk

RIGBY, Russell
Innes England
Position
Director
Career history
1986 Joined Innes England. Previously with Dacre Son & Hartley in Ottley and Leeds
Other roles
Chairman of ProHelp, southern Derbyshire
Interests
Football; golf; wine
Contact details
Innes England Ltd, Wilmot House, St James Court, Derby DE1 1BT
Tel 01332 362244
Fax 01332 360436
Web www.innes-england.com
Mobile 07974 663063
Email rrigby@innes-england.com

RIGG, John
FPDSavills
Position
Director – head of international investment
Qualifications
BSc Hons; FRICS
Career history
Since 2001 Director, FPDSavills.
1976-2001 Director, DTZ Debenham Tie Leung.
1974-76 Gerald Eve.
1973-74 Greater London Council
Professional memberships
RICS
Interests
Football; opera; rugby; walking
Contact details
FPDSavills Ltd, 20 Grosvenor Hill, London W1K 3HQ
Tel 020 7499 8644
Fax 020 7495 3773
Web www.fpdsavills.co.uk
Direct tel 020 7409 4949
Mobile 07870 555784
Email jrigg@fpdsavills.co.uk

RILEY, Michael
Castlemore Securities
Position
Director
Qualifications
BSc Hons; MRICS
Career history
Since 2002 Director, Castlemore Securities.
2001-02 Chief executive, Quintain Estates & Development.
1997-2001 Joint managing director, HVB Real Estate Capital.
1989-97 Managing director, Chesterton Financial/De Groot Collis.

1986-89 CB Hillier Parker

Professional memberships

Investment Property Forum; RICS

Interests

Fishing; IT; keep fit; running; sailing

Contact details

Castlemore Securities Ltd, Morley House, 11-12 Hanover Street, London W1S 1YF

Tel 020 7187 4444

Web www.castlemore.co.uk

Email mikeriley@castlemore.co.uk

RINTOUL, David
Clarks Solicitors

Position

Partner – head of construction team

Qualifications

Solicitor

Professional memberships

Adjudication Society; Chartered Institute of Arbitrators; Law Society; Society of Construction Law

Contact details

Clarks Solicitors, 1 Forbury Square, Reading RG1 3EB

Tel 0118 958 5321

Fax 0118 960 4611

Web www.clarkslegal.com

Email davidrintoul@clarks-solicitors.co.uk

RIORDAN, Michael
Gerald Eve

Position

Partner

Qualifications

BSc; MRICS

Career history

2001 Joined Gerald Eve.

1995-2001 Colliers CRE.

1991-95 Wright Oliphant

Contact details

Gerald Eve, Royex House, 5 Aldermanbury Square, London EC2V 7HR

Tel 020 7489 8900

Fax 020 7489 8800

Web www.geraldeve.com

Direct tel 020 7776 8828

Email mriordan@geraldeve.com

RITBLAT, Jamie
Delancey

Position

Chairman and chief executive

Career history

2003 Joined Delancey Real Estate Asset Management.

1998-2003 Delancey Estates.

1995-98 Freehold Portfolio Estates.

1990-95 British Land Co.

1986-90 Morgan Grenfell

Other roles

Trustee, Gordon Russell Trust

Interests

Gardening; real tennis; skiing; tennis

Contact details

Delancey, 40 Portman Square, London W1H 0AA

Tel 020 7486 6663

Fax 020 7486 6662

Web www.delancey.com

Email jamie.ritblat@delancey.com

RITBLAT, John
British Land Co

Position

Chairman

Qualifications

FRICS; CIMgt

Other roles

Fellow and companion, Institute of Management; honorary fellow, member board of governors and deputy chairman, Royal Academy of Music; chairman, Colliers Conrad Ritblat Erdman; deputy chairman of governors, Hall School; honorary fellow and governors' board member, London Business School; board member, British Library; president, British Ski Federation; honorary surveyor, King George's Fund for Sailors; member of board of governors, Weizmann Institute; patron, Investment Property Forum Educational Trust

Professional memberships

FIABCI; RICS; Royal Society of Arts

Interests

Art; ballet; golf; literature; opera; real tennis; skiing; squash; tennis

Contact details

British Land Co plc, 10 Cornwall Terrace, London NW1 4QP

Tel 020 7486 4466

Fax 020 7935 5552

Web www.britishland.com

Direct fax 020 7467 2990

Email john.ritblat@britishland.com

RITBLAT, Nicholas
British Land Co

Position

Director

Contact details

British Land Co plc, 10 Cornwall Terrace, London NW1 4QP

Tel 020 7486 4466

Fax 020 7935 5552

Web www.britishland.com

Email nicholas.ritblat@britishland.com

RITCHIE, James
Association of Planning Supervisors

Position

President

Contact details

Association of Planning Supervisors Ltd, 16 Rutland Square, Edinburgh EH1 2BB

Tel 0131 221 9959

Fax 0131 221 0061

Web www.aps.org.uk

Email info@aps.org.uk

RIVLIN, Paul
Eurohypo

Position

Joint chief executive – European real estate investment

Qualifications

Barrister; FCMA; MCT

Career history

Since 2002 Joint chief executive (European real estate investment banking), Eurohypo.

1995-2002 Deutsche Bank Group.

1988-95 Rosehaugh/Broadgate Properties.

1985-88 County Bank

Contact details

Eurohypo AG, 90 Long Acre, London WC2E 9RA

Tel 020 7759 7600

Fax 020 7759 7672

Web www.eurohypo.com

Direct tel 020 7759 7634

Direct fax 020 7759 7675

Mobile 07976 274398

Email paul.rivlin@eurohypo.com

ROBERTS, Ben
Travelodge

Position

Development director

Qualifications

BSc; MRICS

Career history

1989-97 Director (asset management), Fletcher King.

1987-89 Estates surveyor, Trafalgar House

Professional memberships

RICS

Contact details

Travelodge Ltd, Oxford House, Oxford Road, Thame OX9 2AH

Tel 0121 521 6000

Web www.travelodge.com

Direct tel 0121 521 6613

Direct fax 0121 521 6682

Mobile 07770 651466
Email ben.roberts@travelodge.co.uk

ROBERTS, Christopher
Lamberts

Position
Chairman
Qualifications
MRICS
Professional memberships
RICS
Contact details
Lamberts Ltd, 387 City Road, London EC1V 1NA
Tel 020 7278 8191
Fax 020 7837 5790
Web www.lambertsurv.co.uk
Direct tel 020 7520 2306
Direct fax 020 7837 0898
Email chris.roberts@lambertsurv.co.uk

ROBERTS, David
Jones Day

Position
Partner – head of real estate
Qualifications
LLB Hons
Career history
1989 Admitted to Roll of Solicitors.
1987 Joined Gouldens; became partner in 1996 and head of property in 2002
Professional memberships
Law Society
Contact details
Jones Day, 21 Tudor Street, London EC4Y 0DJ
Tel 020 7039 5959
Fax 020 7039 5999
Web www.jonesday.com
Direct tel 020 7842 6263
Email daroberts@jonesday.com

ROBERTS, James
Littman Chambers

Position
Barrister
Contact details
Littman Chambers (Chambers of Mark Littman QC), 12 Gray's Inn Square, London WC1R 5JP
Tel 020 7404 4866
Fax 020 7404 4812
Web www.littmanchambers.com
Email jamesroberts@littmanchambers.com

ROBERTS, John
LSM Partners

Position
Director – investment and business space leasing
Qualifications
FRICS
Career history
Since 1992 Director, LSM Partners.
1990-92 John Roberts & Co.
1989-90 De Morgan Group.
1985-89 Jones Lang LaSalle
Professional memberships
Institute of Directors; RICS
Interests
Family; sport
Contact details
LSM Partners, 25 James Street, London W1U 1DU
Tel 020 7616 0100
Fax 020 7616 0101
Web www.lsmpartners.co.uk
Email jroberts@lsmpartners.co.uk

ROBERTS, Martin
CIT Group

Position
Deputy chief executive and property director
Qualifications
BSc Hons, Urban Est & Surv; MRICS
Career history
1993-98 Partner (City investment and development), Knight Frank.
1989-93 Associate (City investment and development), Richard Ellis
Professional memberships
RICS
Contact details
CIT Group plc, 8-10 Bourdon Street, London W1K 3PD
Tel 020 7667 7766
Fax 020 7667 7770
Web www.cit.co.uk
Direct fax 020 7667 7759
Email mr@cit.co.uk

ROBERTS, Mike
Gerald Eve

Position
Partner – head of Leeds office
Qualifications
BSc; MRICS
Career history
1984 Joined Gerald Eve in Liverpool; moved to Leeds office in 1992.
1979-84 Deputy valuation officer, Kensington & Chelsea Valuation Office.
1975-79 District Valuer's Office, Liverpool
Professional memberships
RICS
Interests
Golf; wildlife photography in Falkland Islands
Contact details
Gerald Eve, St James's House, 28 Park Place, Leeds LS1 2SP
Tel 0113 244 0708
Fax 0113 244 0722
Web www.geraldeve.com
Direct tel 0113 218 2082
Email mroberts@geraldeve.com

ROBERTS, Nigel
Jones Lang LaSalle

Position
European director – head of European research
Qualifications
BA Hons; Dip TP; MRTPI
Career history
1983 Joined Jones Lang LaSalle; appointed European director/head of European research in 1999.
1980-83 Freelance consultant.
1979-80 Research associate, University of East Anglia.
1978-79 Planner, Mid Glamorgan County Council.
1974-78 Planner, Norfolk County Council
Other roles
Co-chair, Jones Lang LaSalle global research board
Professional memberships
Investment Property Forum; RTPI; Society of Business Economists; Society of Property Researchers
Interests
Current affairs; family; sport; squash; tennis
Contact details
Jones Lang LaSalle Ltd, 22 Hanover Square, London W1A 2BN
Tel 020 7493 6040
Fax 020 7408 0220
Web www.joneslanglasalle.com
Direct tel 020 7399 5319
Direct fax 020 7399 5470
Mobile 07785 932662
Email nigel.roberts@eu.joneslanglasalle.com

ROBERTS, Paul
Forsters

Position
Managing partner
Qualifications
BA, Law (Oxon)
Career history
Since 1998 Managing partner, Forsters.
1981 Admitted to Roll of Solicitors.
1979-98 Joined Frere Cholmeley Bischoff; became partner in 1988
Professional memberships
Law Society

Interests
Golf; rugby; tennis
Contact details
Forsters, 67 Grosvenor Street, London W1K 3JN
Tel 020 7863 8333
Fax 020 7863 8444
Web www.forsters.co.uk
Direct tel 020 7863 8480
Mobile 07957 361709
Email paroberts@forsters.co.uk

ROBERTS, Richard
Edwin Hill
Position
Partner
Qualifications
BSc; MRICS
Professional memberships
RICS
Contact details
Edwin Hill, Olympic Court, The Village, Manchester M17 1AP
Tel 0161 877 6622
Fax 0161 877 9876
Web www.edwinhill.co.uk
Email richardr@edwinhill.co.uk

ROBERTS, Timothy
British Land Corp
Position
Joint head of asset management – JV and retail
Qualifications
BSc Hons; MRICS
Professional memberships
Investment Property Forum; RICS
Contact details
British Land Corp Ltd, 10 Cornwall Terrace, London NW1 4QP
Tel 020 7486 4466
Web www.britishland.com
Direct tel 020 7467 2977
Direct fax 020 7467 2964
Email tim.roberts@britishland.com

ROBERTSON, Bob
Lester Aldridge
Position
Partner – head of business property team
Contact details
Lester Aldridge, Russell House, Oxford Road, Bournemouth BH8 8EX
Tel 01202 786161
Fax 01202 786150
Web www.lesteraldridge.com
Email bob.robertson@la-law.com

ROBERTSON, Douglas
Memery Crystal
Position
Partner
Qualifications
MA (Oxon); Solicitor
Career history
Since 1992 Partner, Memery Crystal.
1981-92 Partner, Turner Kenneth Brown.
1977 Admitted to Roll of Solicitors
Other roles
Director, Redab and subsidiaries
Professional memberships
Law Society
Interests
Sport
Contact details
Memery Crystal, 31 Southampton Row, London WC1B 5HT
Tel 020 7242 5905
Fax 020 7242 5908
Web www.memerycrystal.com
Direct tel 020 7400 3246
Direct fax 020 7242 2058
Email drobertson@memerycrystal.com

ROBERTSON, Ian
Wilson Bowden
Position
Chief executive
Qualifications
CA; FCMI
Career history
1994 Joined Wilson Bowden as finance director; appointed deputy chief executive in 2001 and chief executive in 2003.
1987-94 Northern Foods: finance director (dairy division), then group financial controller from 1992
Other roles
Senior vice-president, Institute of Chartered Accountants of Scotland
Professional memberships
Chartered Management Institute; Institute of Chartered Accountants of Scotland
Interests
Music; reading
Contact details
Wilson Bowden plc, Wilson Bowden House, Leicester Road, Ibstock LE67 6WB
Tel 01530 260777
Fax 01530 262805
Web www.wilsonbowden.plc.uk
Direct tel 01530 265248
Email IRobertson@wilsonbowden.plc.uk

ROBERTSON, Dr Mark
Ryden
Position
Partner and head of consulting
Qualifications
BSc; PhD
Career history
1995 Joined Ryden as research associate; became head of research and information in 1997; appointed partner in 1998
Professional memberships
Investment Property Forum; Society of Property Researchers
Interests
Outdoor pursuits; sport; theatre
Contact details
Ryden, 46 Castle Street, Edinburgh EH2 3BN
Tel 0131 225 6612
Fax 0131 225 5766
Web www.ryden.co.uk
Direct tel 0131 473 3293
Email mark.robertson@ryden.co.uk

ROBERTSON, Neil
Oddbins
Position
Head of property
Contact details
Oddbins Ltd, 31-33 Weir Road, London SW19 8UG
Tel 020 8944 4400
Web www.oddbins.com
Direct tel 020 8944 4543
Direct fax 020 8944 4412
Email neil_robertson@oddbins.com

ROBIN, Philip
King Sturge
Position
Partner – national head of planning
Qualifications
BA; MPhil; MRTPI
Career history
1996 Joined King Sturge as head of planning and development.
1984-96 Partner, Healey & Baker: head of planning department 1991-96.
1983-84 Berwin Leighton
Professional memberships
RTPI
Interests
Sailing
Contact details
King Sturge, 7 Stratford Place, London W1C 1ST
Tel 020 7493 4933
Fax 020 7409 0469
Web www.kingsturge.com

Direct tel 020 7318 4340
Direct fax 020 7493 3226
Mobile 07785 727603
Email philip.robin@kingsturge.co.uk

ROBINSON, Alice
Landmark Chambers
Position
Barrister
Qualifications
LLB
Career history
1983 Called to Bar
Other roles
Contributor to *Halsbury's Laws of England* on town and country planning
Professional memberships
Planning & Environment Bar Association
Contact details
Landmark Chambers, 4 Breams Buildings, London EC4A 1AQ
Tel 020 7430 1221
Fax 020 7421 1399
Web www.landmarkchambers.co.uk
Email clerks@landmarkchambers.co.uk

ROBINSON, Mark
Hammonds
Position
Partner – construction, engineering and projects
Contact details
Hammonds, Rutland House, 148 Edmund Street, Birmingham B3 2JR
Tel 0870 839 0000
Fax 0870 839 3001
Web www.hammonds.com
Email mark.robinson@hammonds.com

ROBINSON, Patrick
Herbert Smith
Position
Partner – real estate
Qualifications
LLB (Nottingham)
Career history
1980 Admitted to Roll of Solicitors.
1978 Joined Herbert Smith
Other roles
Joint editor, *Blundell & Dobry: Planning Applications & Appeals* (5th edition); member, Law Society's specialist planning panel
Professional memberships
Law Society
Interests
Family; France; jazz; music; reading; sport; travel
Contact details
Herbert Smith, Exchange House, 10 Primrose Street, London EC2A 2NY
Tel 020 7374 8000
Fax 020 7374 0888
Web www.herbertsmith.com
Email patrick.robinson@herbertsmith.com

ROBINSON, Paul
CB Richard Ellis
Position
Senior director – investment agency
Contact details
CB Richard Ellis, Kingsley House, 1a Wimpole Street, London W1G 0RE
Tel 020 7182 2000
Fax 020 7182 7001
Web www.cbre.com
Email paul.robinson@cbre.com

ROBINSON, Ronnie
Quintain Estates & Development
Position
Head of development – special projects
Career history
1997-2003 Grosvenor Estates: retail projects director (responsible for business activities in Ireland)
Contact details
Quintain Estates & Development plc, 58 Davies Street, London W1K 5JF
Tel 020 7495 8968
Fax 020 7499 5583
Web www.quintain-estates.com
Email ronnie.robinson@quintain-estates.com

ROBINSON, Stephen
GVA Grimley
Position
Regional senior partner, London
Qualifications
MA; FRICS; MRTPI
Career history
1969 Joined JR Eve (now GVA Grimley, following 1988 merger)
Other roles
Chairman, Planning Surveyors Club; chairman, RICS London policy group; London regional council member, CBI; BPF planning and environment committee member
Professional memberships
RICS; RTPI
Interests
Ballet; foreign culture
Contact details
GVA Grimley, 10 Stratton Street, London W1J 8JR
Tel 0870 900 8990
Fax 020 7911 2560
Web www.gvagrimley.co.uk
Direct tel 020 7911 2345
Mobile 07774 622746
Email stephen.robinson@gvagrimley.co.uk

ROBINSON, Stuart
CB Richard Ellis
Position
Senior director – planning
Qualifications
Dip TP; MRTPI
Career history
1982 Joined Hillier Parker; partner since 1990; senior director of CB Hillier Parker since 1998.
1981-82 Planner, Healey & Baker.
1978-81 Nathaniel Lichfield & Partners
Other roles
Council member and chairman of planning committee, Westminster Property Owners Association; member, London Office Review Panel (mayor of London's advisory group)
Professional memberships
RTPI
Interests
Cricket (MCC); football; golf; sailing; RAC
Contact details
CB Richard Ellis, Kingsley House, 1a Wimpole Street, London W1G 0RE
Tel 020 7182 2000
Fax 020 7182 7001
Web www.cbre.com
Direct tel 020 7182 2700
Direct fax 020 7182 2050
Mobile 07774 824715
Email stuart.robinson@cbre.com

ROBINSON, Tim
Knight Frank
Position
Partner – head of West End offices
Qualifications
BSc; MRICS
Career history
1994 Joined Knight Frank; appointed partner in 1999 and head of West End offices in 2003
Other roles
Past chairman of Office Agents Society, West End
Professional memberships
RICS
Interests
Fishing; shooting
Contact details
Knight Frank LLP, 20 Hanover Square, London W1S 1HZ
Tel 020 7629 8171
Fax 020 7493 4114
Web www.knightfrank.com

Direct tel 020 7861 1194
Direct fax 020 7861 1358
Mobile 07836 264424
Email tim.robinson@knightfrank.co.uk

ROBINSON, Tony
Rank Group

Position
Director of property
Qualifications
Dip Est Man; MRICS
Career history
1989 Joined Rank Group
Contact details
Rank Group plc, Stafferton Way, Maidenhead SL6 1AY
Tel 01628 504000
Direct fax 01628 504196
Email tony_robinson@rank.com

ROBSON, Chris
McDonald's Restaurants

Position
Head of property
Qualifications
BSc Hons; FRICS
Other roles
Management board member, British Council of Shopping Centres; property policy advisory group member, British Retail Consortium; chair, British Retail Consortium business improvement districts working group
Professional memberships
Institute of Revenues Rating & Valuation; RICS
Contact details
McDonald's Restaurants Ltd, 11-59 High Road, London N2 8AW
Tel 020 8700 7000
Fax 020 8700 7053
Web www.mcdonalds.co.uk
Direct tel 020 8700 7198
Mobile 07702 449113
Email crobson@uk.mcd.com

ROBSON, Jonathan
Legal & General Property

Position
Fund manager
Contact details
Legal & General Property Ltd, Bucklersbury House, 3 Queen Victoria Street, London EC4N 8NH
Tel 020 7528 6500
Fax 020 7528 6848
Web www.legal-and-general.co.uk
Email jonathan.robson@lgim.co.uk

ROBSON, Neil
Ward Hadaway

Position
Head of property
Qualifications
BA
Career history
1977 Admitted to Roll of Solicitors.
1975 Joined Ward Hadaway
Professional memberships
Law Society
Interests
Horse riding; tennis
Contact details
Ward Hadaway, Sandgate House, 102 Quayside, Newcastle upon Tyne NE1 3DX
Tel 0191 204 4000
Fax 0191 204 4001
Web www.wardhadaway.com
Direct tel 0191 204 4124
Email neil.robson@wardhadaway.com

ROCHE, Susan
Legal & General Investment Management

Position
Property management services director
Contact details
Legal & General Investment Management Ltd, Bucklersbury House, Walbrook, London EC4N 8EL
Tel 020 7528 6500
Fax 020 7528 6848
Web www.legal-and-general.co.uk
Email susan.roche@lgim.co.uk

RODGER, Andrew
GVA Grimley

Position
Regional senior partner – North East region
Qualifications
BSc; MRICS
Career history
1987 Joined Grimley.
1984-87 Minerals surveyor, ARC Western
Professional memberships
Association of Business Recovery Professionals; Leeds Financial Services Initiative; RICS; Non-Administrative Receivers Association
Interests
Golf; lacrosse
Contact details
GVA Grimley, Gresham House, 5-7 St Pauls Street, Leeds LS1 2JG
Tel 0870 900 8990
Fax 0113 244 8153
Web www.gvagrimley.co.uk
Direct tel 0113 280 8023
Mobile 07336 785699
Email andrew.rodger@gvagrimley.co.uk

RODGER, Martin
Falcon Chambers

Position
Barrister
Qualifications
BA (Oxon)
Career history
1986 Called to Bar
Other roles
Editor, *Woodfall: Landlord & Tenant*; deputy chairman, Agricultural Land Tribunal
Contact details
Falcon Chambers, Falcon Court, London EC4Y 1AA
Tel 020 7353 2484
Fax 020 7353 1261
Web www.falcon-chambers.com
Email rodger@falcon-chambers.com

RODGER, Phillip
Jones Lang LaSalle

Position
European director
Qualifications
BSc; FRICS
Career history
Since 2000 European director, Jones Lang LaSalle.
1999-2000 Director, LaSalle Investment Management.
1989-99 Jones Lang Wootton Fund Management: associate, then partner from 1993
Professional memberships
RICS
Contact details
Jones Lang LaSalle Ltd, 22 Hanover Square, London W1A 2BN
Tel 020 7493 6040
Fax 020 7408 0220
Web www.joneslanglasalle.com
Direct tel 020 7852 4877
Direct fax 020 7399 5590
Mobile 07831 240190
Email phillip.rodger@eu.joneslanglasalle.com

RODHAM, Ian
UKAEA Central Property Unit

Position
Commercial manager
Career history
Since 1995 Commercial manager, UKAEA.
1993-95 Estate manager, Harwell International Business Centre.
1990-93 Assistant company secretary, Fusion

Directorate

Professional memberships

Institution of Occupational Safety & Health

Interests

Cycling; mountaineering; walking

Contact details

UKAEA Central Property Unit, Harwell International Business Centre, 392/10 Rutherford Avenue, Didcot OX11 0RA

Tel 01235 861997

Fax 01235 431670

Direct tel 01235 431573

Email ian.rodham@ukaea.org.uk

ROE, Mark
Masons

Position

Head of international construction and engineering

Career history

1981 Joined Masons; partner since 1985. 1981 Admitted to Roll of Solicitors

Other roles

Member of Lord Chancellor's IT advisory committee; committee member, Technology & Construction Solicitors Association

Professional memberships

American Bar Association; International Bar Association; Law Society; Society for Computers & Law; Society of Construction Law; Technology & Construction Solicitors Association

Interests

Cycling; rugby; skiing; tennis

Contact details

Masons, Woodbridge House, 30 Aylesbury Street, London EC1R 0ER

Tel 020 7329 2288

Fax 020 7490 2545

Web www.masons.com

Direct tel 020 7490 6212

Email mark.roe@masons.com

ROE, Martyn
UNITE Group

Position

Regional development director

Qualifications

BSc; MBA; Dip Proj Man; MRICS

Contact details

UNITE Group plc, 27 James Craig Walk, Edinburgh EH1 3BA

Tel 0131 550 1300

Fax 0131 558 7879

Web www.unite-group.com

Mobile 07967 221612

Email martyn.roe@unite-group.co.uk

ROGERS, Martin
Knight Frank

Position

Partner

Qualifications

MRICS

Career history

Since 1994 Partner, Knight Frank. 1980-94 Director, Waycotts

Professional memberships

RICS

Interests

Cricket; sailing; squash

Contact details

Knight Frank LLP, 19 Southernhay East, Exeter EX1 1QD

Tel 01392 433033

Fax 01392 277944

Web www.knightfrank.com

Direct tel 01392 493101

Direct fax 01392 499815

Mobile 07836 248959

Email martin.rogers@knightfrank.com

ROGERS, Nan
Bridgewell Securities

Position

Consultant

Qualifications

MRICS

Career history

2002 Joined Bridgewell Securities. 2000-02 Director, ING Barings/Charterhouse. 1994-2000 Assistant director, Charterhouse. 1986-94 Analyst, James Capel

Professional memberships

RICS

Contact details

Bridgewell Securities, Old Change House, 128 Queen Victoria Street, London EC4V 4BJ

Tel 020 7003 3000

Direct tel 020 7003 3503

Direct fax 020 7003 3398

Mobile 07785 538181

Email nanr@hillcroft18.freeserve.co.uk

ROGERS, Peter
Stanhope

Position

Director

Qualifications

Eur Ing; BSc; CEng; MICE; FRSA; Hon FRIBA

Career history

1984 Joined Stanhope Properties; co-founded Stanhope plc in 1995 as a result of management buyout

Other roles

Chairman, Strategic Forum for Construction; chairman, Constructing Excellence; non-executive director of internet portal Asite; trustee, V&A; adviser to Royal Shakespeare Company, Serpentine Gallery, and Channel 4 steering group for Castleford regeneration project

Professional memberships

Royal Society of Arts

Contact details

Stanhope plc, Norfolk House, 31 St James's Square, London SW1Y 4JJ

Tel 020 7170 1700

Fax 020 7170 1701

Web www.stanhopeplc.com

Email peter.rogers@stanhopeplc.com

ROGERS, Lord Richard
Richard Rogers Partnership

Position

Chairman

Qualifications

AA Dipl; MArch (Yale); RIBA; RA Hon; FAIA Hon; Dr RCA Hon; BDA Hon

Other roles

Chairman, Richard Rogers Partnership, Richard Rogers Architects, London, Richard Rogers Japan, Tokyo, Richard Rogers, Spain; mayor's chief adviser on architecture and urbanism and member of the mayor of London's advisory cabinet; adviser to the mayor, Barcelona Urban Strategies Council; chairman, National Tenants Resource Centre; trustee, Médecins du Monde, UK board; patron, Society of Black Architects; academician, International Academy of Architecture; member, UN architects' committee; member, RIBA council and policy committees (1984-87); honorary fellow, Royal Academy of Art, The Hague (1979); honorary fellow, Cardiff University, Wales (1999); life baron of the UK (1996); Royal Gold Medal for Architecture (1985); knighthood (1991); Chevalier, l'Ordre National de la Légion d'Honneur (1986); Officier de L'Ordre des Arts et des Lettres, France (1995); Praemium Imperiale architecture laureate (2000); Friend of Barcelona (1997); Thomas Jefferson Memorial Foundation Medal in Architecture (1999); Royal Academician, London (1984); American Academy & Institute of Arts & Letters: Arnold W Brunner Memorial Prize (1989)

Professional memberships

Bund Deutscher Architekten (honorary member); Academie d'Architecture; American Institute of Architects; Royal Institute of Architects in Scotland

Contact details

Richard Rogers Partnership, Thames Wharf, Rainville Road, London W6 9HA

Tel 020 7385 1235

Fax 020 7385 8409
Web www.richardrogers.co.uk
Email enquiries@rrp.co.uk

ROGERS, Steven
London & Regional Properties

Position
Director
Career history
Since 1999 Director, London & Regional Properties.
1990-99 Development executive, Arlington Securities
Contact details
London & Regional Properties Ltd, 40 New Bond Street, London W1S 2RX
Tel 020 7499 4060
Fax 020 7499 9922
Email srogers@lrp.co.uk

ROGERSON, Malcolm
Barlow Lyde & Gilbert

Position
Partner – head of commercial property dept
Qualifications
MA, Law
Career history
1987 Joined Barlow Lyde & Gilbert; appointed partner in 1990.
1983-87 Wedlake Bell.
1982-83 Slaughter & May.
1981-82 Rosling King.
1981 Admitted to Roll of Solicitors.
1979-81 Druces & Attlee
Professional memberships
Law Society
Interests
Cricket; fishing; football; golf; horse racing; rugby
Contact details
Barlow Lyde & Gilbert Ltd, Beaufort House, 15 St Botolph Street, London EC3A 7JJ
Tel 020 7247 2277
Fax 020 7071 9000
Web www.blg.co.uk
Direct tel 020 7782 8581
Direct fax 020 7071 9715
Email mrogerson@blg.co.uk

ROLES, Anthony
SHM Smith Hodgkinson

Position
Senior partner, London
Career history
Since 2003 Senior partner, SHM Smith Hodgkinson.
1962-2003 Edward Symmons & Partners: became associate partner in 1970, partner in 1973, equity partner in 1975 and chief executive in 1994
Other roles
Executive board member, Friends of Guys Hospital
Professional memberships
National Association of Estate Agents; Royal Society of Arts
Interests
Cricket; horse racing; motor sports; rugby; travel
Contact details
SHM Smith Hodgkinson, 40 Lime Street, London EC3M 5BS
Tel 020 7626 7300
Fax 020 7626 7330
Web www.shm-group.com
Mobile 07717 366525
Email anthony.roles@shm-group.com

ROLFE, Kevin
Aitchison Raffety

Position
Director – land and development
Qualifications
BSc; MRICS
Professional memberships
RICS
Contact details
Aitchison Raffety Ltd, 154-158 High Street, Berkhamsted HP4 3AT
Tel 01442 864713
Fax 01442 862405
Web www.argroup.co.uk
Direct tel 01442 875509
Email kevin.rolfe@argroup.co.uk

ROLLS, Michael
Prudential Property Investment Managers

Position
Director – property development
Qualifications
FRICS
Other roles
Board member, Thames Valley Economic Partnership
Interests
Football; music; reading; walking
Contact details
Prudential Property Investment Managers Ltd, Princeton House, 271-273 High Holborn, London WC1V 7NE
Tel 020 7548 6600
Fax 020 7548 6999
Web www.prupim.com
Direct tel 020 7548 6844
Direct fax 020 7548 6701
Email mike.rolls@prupim.com

ROMNEY, Charles
CMS Cameron McKenna

Position
Partner – real estate
Career history
1973 Admitted to Roll of Solicitors
Professional memberships
Association of Town Centre Management; British Council of Shopping Centres; FIABCI; Town & Country Planning Association
Contact details
CMS Cameron Mckenna, Mitre House, 160 Aldersgate Street, London EC1A 4DD
Tel 020 7367 3000
Fax 020 7367 2000
Web www.cmck.com
Email charles.romney@cmck.com

RONSON, Gerald
Heron International

Position
Chief executive
Contact details
Heron International, Heron House, 19 Marylebone Road, London NW1 5JP
Tel 020 7486 4477
Fax 020 7486 3349
Web www.heron-international.com
Email gmronson@heron.co.uk

RONSON, Lisa
Heron International

Position
Marketing director
Qualifications
BSc, Management Sciences
Interests
Skiing; tennis; water sports
Contact details
Heron International, Heron House, 19 Marylebone Road, London NW1 5JP
Tel 020 7486 4477
Fax 020 7486 3349
Web www.heron-international.com
Direct fax 020 7299 9771
Email lronson@heron.co.uk

ROOCROFT, Mike
Gerald Eve

Position
Partner – head of Liverpool office
Qualifications
BSc; MRICS
Career history
1990 Joined Gerald Eve
Professional memberships
RICS

R

Contact details
Gerald Eve, Charleston House, 12 Rumford Place, Liverpool L3 9DG
Tel 0151 236 3009
Fax 0151 236 5041
Web www.geraldeve.com
Direct tel 0151 236 3009
Email mroocroft@geraldeve.com

ROOK, John
Greggs
Position
Property director
Qualifications
FRICS
Career history
Since 1984 Property director, Greggs
Professional memberships
Property Managers Association; RICS
Contact details
Greggs plc, 59 Clayton Road, Newcastle upon Tyne NE2 1TL
Tel 0191 212 7611
Fax 0191 281 1444
Web www.greggs.co.uk
Email property.dept@greggs.plc.uk

ROOM, David
GVA Grimley
Position
Partner – head of national rating business unit
Qualifications
BA; FRICS
Career history
1982 Joined JR Eve (now GVA Grimley, following mergers); appointed partner in 1987.
1975-82 Valuation Office
Other roles
Non-executive chairman of board/director, GVA Holdings and other GVA subsidiaries; member, CBI rating and valuation panel; member, CBI property group; member, RICS rating and local taxation policy panel
Professional memberships
Rating Surveyors Association; RICS
Contact details
GVA Grimley, 10 Stratton Street, London W1J 8JR
Tel 0870 900 8990
Fax 020 7911 2560
Web www.gvagrimley.co.uk
Direct tel 020 7911 2545
Direct fax 020 7911 2548
Mobile 07831 391408
Email david.room@gvagrimley.co.uk

ROONEY, Paul
Arun Estate Agencies
Position
Director
Contact details
Arun Estate Agencies Ltd, St Leonards House, North Street, Horsham RH12 1RJ
Tel 0140 328 2400
Fax 0140 325 5237
Web www.arunestates.co.uk
Email paul.rooney@arunestates.co.uk

ROONEY, Philip
DLA
Position
Partner – real estate
Qualifications
BA, Jurisprudence (Oxon)
Career history
1980 Joined DLA: appointed partner (property department) in 1984 and location head (real estate) in 1992; group head of real estate since 1998
Professional memberships
Law Society
Contact details
DLA, India Buildings, Water Street, Liverpool L2 0NH
Tel 0870 011 1111
Web www.dla.com
Direct tel 0151 237 4730
Direct fax 0151 237 4891
Email philip.rooney@dla.com

ROOTS, Guy
2 Mitre Court Buildings
Position
Barrister – head of chambers
Qualifications
QC
Career history
1989 Appointed QC.
1968 Called to Bar
Other roles
Chairman, Planning & Environment Bar Association; bencher of Middle Temple; general editor, *Butterworths' Compulsory Purchase & Compensation Service;* general editor, *Ryde on Rating*; member, ODPM compulsory purchase policy review advisory group
Professional memberships
Administrative Law Bar Association; Planning & Environment Bar Association
Contact details
2 Mitre Court Buildings (Chambers of Guy Roots QC), 2nd Floor, London EC4Y 7BX
Tel 020 7583 1380
Fax 020 7353 7772
Web www.2mcb.co.uk
Email guy.roots@2mcb.co.uk

ROSCOE, James
Fyfe Ireland WS
Position
Partner – head of commercial property department
Qualifications
MA (Oxon); LLB; NP; WS
Career history
1994 Admitted to Roll of Solicitors.
1989 Joined Fyfe Ireland; appointed partner in 1992; mainly practising in property finance and investment property.
1987 Admitted to Roll of Solicitors in Scotland
Interests
Cycling; rugby; squash
Contact details
Fyfe Ireland WS, Orchard Brae House, 30 Queensferry Road, Edinburgh EH4 2HG
Tel 0131 343 2500
Fax 0131 343 3166
Web www.fyfeireland.com
Direct tel 0131 315 8155
Email jroscoe@fyfeireland.com

ROSCOE, Tony
James Smith Estates
Position
Chief executive
Qualifications
FRICS
Professional memberships
RICS
Contact details
James Smith Estates plc, 22-23 Princes Street, London W1B 2LU
Tel 020 7408 1515
Fax 020 7408 1919
Web www.jse.co.uk
Email adr@jse.co.uk

ROSCROW, Peter
Close Property Management
Position
Managing director
Qualifications
ACA
Career history
1991 Joined Close Property Management as director; appointed managing director in 1996.
1988-91 Corporate finance manager, Chancery Corporate Finance.
1980-88 KMG Hungerfords, Australia
Professional memberships

BPF; Institute of Chartered Accountants in England & Wales; Investment Property Forum

Interests

Architecture; DIY; gardening; music; travel

Contact details

Close Property Management, 10 Crown Place, London EC2A 4FT

Tel 020 7426 4174

Fax 020 7426 4763

Web www.cbil.com

Email proscrow@cbil.com

ROSE, Jonathan
Asda Property Holdings

Position

Director

Qualifications

BSc Hons; MRICS

Career history

2001 Joined Asda Property Holdings from Davidson Family Property Co

Professional memberships

RICS

Contact details

Asda Property Holdings Ltd, 58 Queen Anne Street, London W1G 8HW

Tel 020 7224 1030

Fax 020 7224 0574

Web www.asda.net

Email jrose@asda.net

ROSE, Nick
Gerald Eve

Position

Partner – head of Belfast office

Qualifications

BSc; MRICS

Career history

2000 Joined Gerald Eve, Belfast.

1996-2000 Kenneth Crothers Deane & Curry, Belfast.

1987-96 Gerald Eve, London and Birmingham offices.

1984-87 Reading University

Professional memberships

RICS

Interests

Family; golf

Contact details

Gerald Eve, 38 Hill Street, Belfast BT1 2LB

Tel 028 9043 4300

Fax 028 9043 4330

Web www.geraldeve.com

Direct tel 028 9031 6745

Mobile 07968 797160

Email nrose@geraldeve.com

ROSE, Phillip
ABN AMRO Corporate Finance

Position

European head of real estate

Qualifications

MA (Cantab); ASIA; MSI

Career history

Since 2001 European head of real estate, ABN AMRO.

1999-2000 Chief operating officer (responsible for UK, France, Germany, Italy, Spain, Greece and central Europe), TrizecHahn Europe.

1992-99 Lend Lease Corp: joined as executive manager of General Property Trust in Australia; transferred to London in 1994 to become managing director of Lend Lease Global Investment

Other roles

Member of management committee, Hermes Property Unit Trust

Professional memberships

Investment Property Forum; Securities Institute of Australia; Securities Institute

Contact details

ABN AMRO Corporate Finance Ltd, 250 Bishopsgate, London EC2M 4AA

Tel 020 7678 8000

Fax 020 7256 8500

Web www.abnamro.com

Direct tel 020 7678 2601

Email phillip.rose@uk.abnamro.com

ROSE, Zoe
Hamptons International

Position

Lettings director – country lettings

Contact details

Hamptons International, 5 Jubilee Place, London SW3 3TD

Tel 020 7808 9001

Fax 020 7808 9000

Web www.hamptons.co.uk

Email rosez@hamptons-int.com

ROSEFIELD, John
Estates & Agency Holdings

Position

Chairman

Qualifications

BA (Oxon); MBA (Harvard)

Contact details

Estates & Agency Holdings plc, 33 Ely Place, London EC1N 6TD

Tel 020 7831 8600

Fax 020 7831 8921

Email John.Rosefield@estatesandagency.co.uk

ROSEMAN, Eric
Frogmore Investments

Position

Director

Career history

1979 Joined Frogmore; previously with HQ Business Centres, Hirshfields and Conrad Ritblat

Interests

Cinema; literature; music; opera; theatre; walking

Contact details

Frogmore Investments Ltd, 11-15 Wigmore Street, London W1A 2JZ

Tel 020 7016 6000

Fax 020 7495 5321

Direct fax 020 7016 6065

Email ericroseman@frogmore.co.uk

ROSEN, David
Pilcher Hershman

Position

Partner

Qualifications

Hon FRIBA

Contact details

Pilcher Hershman, 25 Savile Row, London W1S 2ER

Tel 020 7399 8600

Fax 020 7399 8700

Web www.pilcherhershman.co.uk

Email davidrosen@pilcherhershman.co.uk

ROSEN, Jeffrey
Ockway Estates

Position

Director of estates

Qualifications

BSc; FRICS; ACIArb

Career history

Since 2002 Director of estates, Ockway Estates.

1995-2002 Director of property services, JC Property Holdings.

1984-95 Director of development and strategic planning, Grosvenor Square Properties Developments.

1982-84 Keith Cardale Groves

Other roles

Development consultant, JC Holdings Property Holdings; consultant, Cordell Marks Chartered Development & Planning Surveyors; editor, *Guidance Notes for Consultants in Business Space Design & Construction*; member, Board of Deputies working party on new synagogue siting, development and design

Professional memberships

Chartered Institute of Arbitrators; RICS; Land Society

Interests

Golf; photography; swimming; walking

Contact details

Ockway Estates Ltd, Ockway House,
41 Stamford Hill, London N16 5SR
Tel 020 8800 6699
Fax 020 8800 6543
Mobile 07721 429774
Email jeffrey@ockwayestates.co.uk

ROSINA, Lionello
FPDSavills

Position

Director – head of office, Milan

Contact details

FPDSavills Ltd, Via Cusani 10, Milan, Italy
Tel +39 02 365 6931
Fax +39 02 365 6928
Web www.fpdsavills.co.uk
Direct tel +39 02 3656 8322
Mobile +39 335 6324212
Email lrosina@fpdsavills.gr

ROSS, Jonathan
Forsters

Position

Head of property litigation

Other roles

Writer of weekly column, *Property Week*; regular lecturer on property litigation issues

Contact details

Forsters, 67 Grosvenor Street, London W1K 3JN
Tel 020 7863 8333
Fax 020 7863 8444
Web www.forsters.co.uk
Email jmross@forsters.co.uk

ROSS, Ken
Burness

Position

Partner – commercial property

Contact details

Burness, 50 Lothian Road, Edinburgh EH3 9WJ
Tel 0131 473 6000
Fax 0131 473 6006
Web www.burness.co.uk
Email kar@burness.co.uk

ROSS, Kenneth
Bishops

Position

Partner – head of commercial property

Qualifications

LLB Hons

Career history

1984 Joined Bishop & Robertson Chalmers (now Bishops) as partner.
1982-84 McLure Naismith Brodie.
1982 Admitted to Roll of Solicitors.
1980-82 Moncrieff Warren Paterson

Other roles

Convenor of Scottish committee, UK Environmental Law Association

Professional memberships

Law Society of Scotland; UK Environmental Law Association

Contact details

Bishops, 2 Blythswood Square, Glasgow G2 4AD
Tel 0141 248 4672
Fax 0141 221 9270
Web www.bishopslaw.biz
Email kenneth.ross@bishopslaw.biz

ROSS, Rod
Aberdeen Property Investors UK

Position

Director

Contact details

Aberdeen Property Investors UK Ltd,
123 St Vincent Street, Glasgow G2 5EA
Tel 0141 306 7600
Fax 0141 306 7706
Web www.aberdeenpropertyinvestors.com
Direct tel 0141 306 7581
Email rod.ross@aberdeenpropertyinvestors.com

ROSS, Dr Sidney
11 Stone Buildings

Position

Barrister

Qualifications

BSc; LLB; MSc; PhD; FCIArb

Career history

1984 Joined 11 Stone Buildings.
1983 Called to Bar.
1958-82 Chemistry department, Chelsea College, University of London: senior lecturer from 1975

Other roles

Author, *Inheritance Act Claims – Law and Practice* (2nd edition, Sweet & Maxwell, 2000); regular contributor of articles to legal journals on family provision, wills and trusts

Professional memberships

Chancery Bar Association; Chartered Institute of Arbitrators; Midlands & Oxford Circuit; Society of Trusts & Estates Practitioners

Interests

Chess; cricket; rugby; singing

Contact details

11 Stone Buildings, London WC2A 3TG
Tel 020 7831 6381
Fax 020 7831 2575
Web www.11stonebuildings.com
Email ross@11stonebuildings.com

ROSSINGTON, Roz
Brixton Investments

Position

Director – portfolio management

Qualifications

MA; MRICS

Contact details

Brixton Investments Ltd, 50 Berkeley Street, London W1J 8BX
Tel 020 7399 4500
Fax 020 7399 4550
Web www.brixton.plc.uk
Direct tel 020 7399 4513
Mobile 07909 925083
Email rozrossington@b-serv.ltd.uk

ROSSITER, Tom
Penningtons

Position

Head of commercial property, Newbury

Qualifications

Solicitor

Career history

Since 1984 Partner, Penningtons.
1981-84 Simmons & Simmons.
1979 Admitted to Roll of Solicitors.
1977-81 Rowe & Maw

Professional memberships

Business Network International; Federation of Small Businesses; Law Society

Interests

Opera; rugby; sailing

Contact details

Penningtons, Phoenix House, 9 London Road, Newbury RG14 1DH
Tel 01635 571000
Fax 01635 523444
Web www.penningtons.co.uk
Mobile 07798 815872
Email rossitertw@penningtons.co.uk

ROTHERY, Andrew
Deloitte

Position

Lead partner – real estate transactions

Qualifications

ACA

Career history

Since 2001 Real estate industry leader, Andersen/Deloitte (Deloitte acquired Andersen's business in the UK in 2002)

Contact details

Deloitte, 180 Strand, London WC2R 1BL
Tel 020 7936 3000
Fax 020 7583 1198
Web www.deloitte.co.uk
Direct tel 020 7007 1847

Mobile 07836 742004
Email arothery@deloitte.co.uk

ROTHWELL, Mark
Alder King

Position
Partner – investment
Qualifications
MRICS
Interests
Rugby; sailing
Contact details
Alder King, Pembroke House, 15 Pembroke Road, Bristol BS8 3BA
Tel 0117 317 1000
Fax 0117 317 1001
Web www.alderking.com
Direct tel 0117 317 1101
Direct fax 0117 317 1005
Mobile 07990 891014
Email mrothwell@alderking.com

ROUGHT-WHITTAR, Stephen
Blacks Outdoor Leisure

Position
Property director
Contact details
Blacks Outdoor Leisure, Mansard Close, Northampton NN5 5DL
Tel 01604 441111
Web www.blacks.co.uk
Email
stephen.rought-whitta@theoutdoorgroup.co.uk

ROUSE, Jon
Commission for Architecture & the Built Environment

Position
Chief executive
Qualifications
LLB; MA; Hon RIBA; MBA; Hon RTPI
Interests
Cinema; music; tennis
Contact details
Commission for Architecture & the Built Environment, The Tower Building, 11 York Road, London SE1 7NQ
Tel 020 7960 2402
Web www.cabe.org.uk
Mobile 07900 498725
Email jrouse@cabe.org.uk

ROUTLEDGE, James
Matthews & Goodman

Position
Partner
Qualifications
BSc Hons; MRICS
Contact details
Matthews & Goodman, Dorland House, 14-16 Regent Street, London SW1Y 4PH
Tel 020 7747 8847
Fax 020 7747 8848
Web www.matthews-goodman.co.uk
Direct tel 020 7747 3189
Mobile 07776 227639
Email jroutledge@matthews-goodman.co.uk

ROWAN, John
Anglo Irish Bank Corp

Position
Managing director
Other roles
Member of main board
Interests
Golf (Richmond Golf Club); rugby (London Irish Amateur Rugby Club); skiing
Contact details
Anglo Irish Bank Corp plc, 10 Old Jewry, London EC2R
Tel 020 7710 7000
Fax 020 7710 7050
Direct tel 020 7710 7011
Email johnrowan@angloirishbank.co.uk

ROWAN, Peter
Lambert Smith Hampton

Position
Chief executive – Dublin
Contact details
Lambert Smith Hampton Ltd, 115 Lower Baggot Street, Dublin
Tel +353 1 676 0331
Fax +353 1 662 4805
Web www.lsh.co.uk
Email prowan@lsh.ie

ROWBOTHAM, Tony
Montagu Evans

Position
Partner – professional services
Contact details
Montagu Evans, 44-48 Dover Street, London W1S 4AZ
Tel 020 7493 4002
Fax 020 7312 7547
Web www.montagu-evans.co.uk
Email tony.rowbotham@montagu-evans.co.uk

ROWE, Nigel
ATIS REAL Weatheralls

Position
Director
Qualifications
BSc; MRICS
Career history
Since 2001 Head of UK industrial team, ATIS REAL Weatheralls. Previously with Insignia Richard Ellis and King Sturge in London, specialising in industrial sector for 15 years
Other roles
Vice-chairman, Industrial Agents Society
Professional memberships
Industrial Agents Society; RICS
Contact details
ATIS REAL Weatheralls Ltd, Norfolk House, 31 St James's Square, London SW1Y 4JR
Tel 020 7338 4200
Fax 020 7493 0746
Web www.atisrealweatheralls.com
Direct tel 020 7338 4263
Direct fax 020 7839 4962
Email nigel.rowe@atisrealweatheralls.com

ROWLAND, Jim
King Sturge

Position
Partner – national head of building consultancy
Qualifications
BEng; Dip Proj Man; FRICS; ACIArb
Contact details
King Sturge, 7 Stratford Place, London W1C 1ST
Tel 020 7493 4933
Fax 020 7409 0469
Web www.kingsturge.com
Direct tel 020 7318 4330
Email jim.rowland@kingsturge.co.uk

ROWLEY, Ed
One NorthEast

Position
Head of subregional partnership (South)
Contact details
One NorthEast, Cavendish House, Teesdale Business Park, Stockton-on-Tees TS17 6QY
Tel 01642 853600
Fax 01642 853601
Web www.onenortheast.co.uk
Email ed.rowley@onenortheast.co.uk

ROWSON, Peter
Panther Securities

Position
Company secretary
Contact details
Panther Securities plc, Panther House, 38 Mount Pleasant, London WC1X 0AP
Tel 020 7278 8011
Fax 020 7278 3608
Email kerryhoward@btconnect.com

ROWSON, William
ING Real Estate Investment Management (UK)

Position
Director – European fund management
Career history
1987-2003 Strutt & Parker; appointed partner in charge of international department in 1999.
1985-87 King & Co
Other roles
Elected member of Business & Industrial Agents Society national committee (1989-99)
Professional memberships
RICS; Urban Land Institute
Interests
Football; history; local history; reading; rugby; snowboarding; tennis
Contact details
ING Real Estate Investment Management (UK) Ltd, 9 Devonshire Square, London EC2M 4WX
Tel 020 7398 4310
Fax 020 7398 4311
Web www.ingrealestate.co.uk
Direct tel 020 7398 5549
Email will.rowson@ingrealestate.co.uk

ROWTON-LEE, Charles
Lambert Smith Hampton

Position
Director – head of office agency
Career history
1994 Joined Lambert Smith Hampton; became director in 1997.
1992-94 Campsie & Co.
1990-92 Hodgson & Co
Professional memberships
Office Agents Society
Interests
Fishing; sailing; shooting
Contact details
Lambert Smith Hampton Ltd, Burlington Court, 1 Burlington Road, Slough SL1 2JS
Tel 01753 511567
Fax 01753 694880
Web www.lsh.co.uk
Mobile 07885 185230
Email crowtonLee@lsh.co.uk

ROY, Alasdair
James Barr

Position
Director – property management
Qualifications
BSc; MRICS
Professional memberships
RICS
Contact details
James Barr, 226 West George Street, Glasgow G2 2LN
Tel 0141 300 8000
Fax 0141 300 8001
Web www.jamesbarr.co.uk
Email aroy@jamesbarr.co.uk

ROYCE, David
Ernst & Young

Position
Partner – real estate, hospitality and construction
Qualifications
BA; FCA
Career history
1982 Joined Ernst & Young; partner since 1997
Professional memberships
Institute of Internal Auditors
Contact details
Ernst & Young LLP, 1 More London Place, London SE1 2AF
Tel 020 7951 2000
Fax 020 7951 1345
Web www.ey.com/uk
Direct tel 020 7951 4253
Direct fax 020 7951 3411
Mobile 07771 936989
Email droyce@uk.ey.com

RUANE, Erik
Europa Projects

Position
Development director
Qualifications
MA Hons; MRICS
Career history
1994-2001 Development director, Development Securities (Projects).
1990-94 Senior executive, Emarel Services.
1987-90 Development executive, City Merchant Developers/Imry Merchant Developers.
1982-87 Weatherall Green & Smith
Professional memberships
RICS
Contact details
Europa Projects Ltd, 136 Sloane Street, London SW1X 9AY
Tel 020 7881 6800
Fax 020 7881 0501
Web www.europafund.com
Direct tel 020 7881 6835
Email erik.ruane@europafund.com

RUBACK, Jonathan
Allsop & Co

Position
Partner – City investments
Qualifications
BSc; MRICS
Career history
Since 1987 City agency and investment partner, Allsop & Co.
1978-87 Management, then valuation surveyor, Jones Lang Wootton
Professional memberships
RICS
Contact details
Allsop & Co, 2 London Wall Buildings, London EC2M 5PP
Tel 020 7588 4433
Fax 020 7374 8212
Web www.allsop.co.uk
Mobile 07802 258445
Email jonathan.ruback@allsop.co.uk

RUDGE, Alan
Barwood Developments

Position
Chairman
Contact details
Barwood Developments Ltd, The Grange, Warren Office Village, Milton Keynes MK12 5NE
Tel 01908 577600
Fax 01908 312017
Web www.barwood.co.uk
Direct tel 01908 577601
Mobile 07715 577601
Email alan.rudge@barwood.co.uk

RUDGE, Martin
Credit Lyonnais

Position
Managing director – head of property and hotel finance
Qualifications
BA Hons, Econ; ACIB
Career history
1999-2000 Director (international investors division), Westdeutsche Immobilien Bank.
1996-99 Director (specialist property finance team), Barclays Bank.
1991-95 Assistant director (structured finance division), Barclays de Zoete Wedd
Other roles
Association of Property Bankers (president 1997-98)
Professional memberships
Association of Property Bankers; Investment Property Forum
Contact details
Credit Lyonnais, Broadwalk House, 5 Appold Street, London EC2A 2DA
Tel 020 7588 4000
Fax 020 7214 7070
Web www.creditlyonnais.com

Direct tel 020 7214 7077
Direct fax 020 7214 7159
Email martin.rudge@creditlyonnais.co.uk

RUDLAND, Ian
Vail Williams

Position
Chief executive and partner
Career history
1980 Joined Vail Williams (formerly Pearson Williams) as chief executive; now responsible for overall leadership, business strategy, planning and development for the firm
Other roles
Spent three years involved in research at Henley Management College, resulting in publication of *Inspiring Leadership – Staying Afloat in Turbulent Times*; committee member, CoreNet Global UK
Professional memberships
CoreNet Global UK
Interests
Rugby; sailing; skiing
Contact details
Vail Williams, Thames Valley Office, 130 Wharfedale Road, Winnersh RG41 5RB
Tel 0118 933 5600
Fax 0118 933 5634
Web www.vailwilliams.com
Mobile 07831 474997
Email irudland@vailwilliams.com

RUDOLF, Peter
Berwin Leighton Paisner

Position
Partner – real estate
Career history
1975 Admitted to Roll of Solicitors.
1973 Joined Berwin Leighton (now Berwin Leighton Paisner)
Interests
Squash; triathlon
Contact details
Berwin Leighton Paisner Ltd, Adelaide House, London Bridge, London EC4R 9HA
Tel 020 7760 1000
Fax 020 7760 1111
Web www.berwinleighton.com
Email peter.rudolf@blplaw.com

RUGG, David
Christie & Co

Position
Chairman
Contact details
Christie & Co, 50 Victoria Street, London SW1H 0NW
Tel 020 7227 0700
Fax 020 7220 0702
Web www.christie.com
Email david.rugg@christie.com

RUMSEY, Christopher
Baffin Property

Position
Managing director
Qualifications
MSc; FRICS
Career history
Since 2001 Managing director, Baffin.
1995-2001 Managing director, Dusco.
1986-94 Director, Burton Property Trust
Professional memberships
British Council of Shopping Centres; Investment Property Forum; RICS
Contact details
Baffin Property Ltd, 33 St James's Square, London SW1Y 4JS
Tel 020 7661 9360
Fax 020 7661 9455
Email crumsey@baffin.co.uk

RUNCORN, Rebecca
Gerald Eve

Position
Partner – head of loan security valuation
Qualifications
BSc; MRICS
Career history
1985-97 Chesterton.
1984-85 Leslie Lintot
Other roles
Involved with Sparkle (organisation which raises money for children's hospice)
Professional memberships
RICS
Interests
Animal welfare; drama; horse riding; literature
Contact details
Gerald Eve, 7 Vere Street, London W1G 0JB
Tel 020 7493 3338
Fax 020 7491 1825
Web www.geraldeve.com
Direct tel 020 7333 6421
Direct fax 020 7333 6409
Email rruncorn@geraldeve.com

RUSHMORE, Gillian
DTZ Corporate Finance

Position
Director
Qualifications
BSc, Est Man; FRICS
Career history
1982 Joined DTZ, London; appointed director in valuation department of investment division in 1994, then national skills head for valuation in 1998; director/joint head (UK valuation) since 1999
Other roles
Past chairman and current committee member, Property Valuation Forum; committee member, Investment Property Forum working party; member, Appraisal & Valuation Standards Board; member of Red Book editorial board, including responsibility for rewriting the Red Book
Interests
Art; food and drink; gardening; music; travel
Contact details
DTZ Corporate Finance Ltd, 1 Curzon Street, London W1A 5PZ
Tel 020 7408 1161
Fax 020 7643 6000
Web www.dtz.com
Direct tel 020 7643 6262
Direct fax 020 7643 6303
Email gillian.rushmore@dtz.com

RUSHTON, John
Mayer, Brown, Rowe & Maw

Position
Partner
Career history
1980 Joined Mayer, Brown, Rowe & Maw: appointed partner in 1991.
1975 Admitted to Roll of Solicitors.
1973-80 Freshfields
Contact details
Mayer, Brown, Rowe & Maw LLP, 11 Pilgrim Street, London EC4V 6RW
Tel 020 7248 4282
Fax 020 7248 2009
Web www.mayerbrownrowe.com
Direct tel 020 7782 8917
Direct fax 020 7782 8913
Email jrushton@mayerbrownrowe.com

RUSSELL, Alistair
Jones Lang LaSalle

Position
European director – head of Leeds office
Qualifications
BSc; FRICS
Career history
1985 Joined Jones Lang LaSalle; appointed director in 1988; opened Leeds office in 1994.
1979-85 Associate partner, Bernard Thorpe.
1977-79 Jones Lang LaSalle
Other roles
Director, Leeds Financial Services Initiative; member, English management committee of Jones Lang LaSalle

Professional memberships
RICS
Interests
Golf; reading; travel; walking; wine
Contact details
Jones Lang LaSalle Ltd, St Paul's House, Park Square, Leeds LS1 2ND
Tel 0113 244 6440
Fax 0113 245 4664
Web www.joneslanglasalle.com
Direct tel 0113 261 6233
Mobile 07836 546740
Email alistair.russell@eu.joneslanglasalle.com

RUSSELL, Gary
Freeport
Position
Commercial director
Contact details
Freeport plc, 9-13 George Street, London W1U 3FL
Tel 020 7299 9360
Fax 020 7299 9388
Web www.freeportplc.com
Email garyrussell@freeportleisure.com

RUSSELL, Simon
ATIS REAL Weatheralls
Position
Director
Qualifications
MA; MRICS
Career history
1984 Joined ATIS REAL Weatheralls; appointed partner in 1994; resident partner in Birmingham office responsible for valuation and strategic consultancy services in West and East Midlands. 1981-84 Hillier Parker
Professional memberships
RICS
Interests
Photography; rugby
Contact details
ATIS REAL Weatheralls Ltd, Bank House, 8 Cherry Street, Birmingham B2 5AQ
Tel 0121 696 8000
Fax 0121 696 1234
Web www.atisrealweatheralls.com
Direct tel 0121 6968008
Email simon.russell@atisrealweatheralls.com

RUSSELL-SMITH, Charles
Alder King
Position
Partner
Contact details
Alder King, Pembroke House, 15 Pembroke Road, Bristol BS8 3BA
Tel 0117 317 1000
Fax 0117 317 1001
Web www.alderking.com
Email crussellsmith@alderking.com

RUTHERFORD, Anthony
James Smith Estates
Position
Director
Qualifications
BSc; MRICS
Professional memberships
RICS
Contact details
James Smith Estates plc, 22-23 Princes Street, London W1B 2LU
Tel 020 7408 1515
Fax 020 7408 1919
Web www.jse.co.uk
Email arr@jse.co.uk

RUTHERFORD, Hugh
Montagu Evans
Position
Partner – office agency/development
Qualifications
BSc Hons; Dip LE; MRICS
Career history
2001 Joined Montagu Evans as equity partner. 1984-2001 Ryden: on leaving, partner and head of offices and industrial group
Other roles
Corporate member, British Council for Offices; former external examiner for RICS in Scotland; chairman of Scottish Property Industry's charity, SPIFOX
Professional memberships
British Council for Offices; CoreNet Global UK; Office Agents Society; RICS
Interests
Family; fishing; food; golf; shooting; sport; walking; wine
Contact details
Montagu Evans, 37 Melville Street, Edinburgh EH3 7JF
Tel 0131 225 9541
Fax 0131 225 3677
Web www.montagu-evans.co.uk
Direct tel 0131 240 5422
Mobile 07730 001748
Email hugh.rutherford@montagu-evans.co.uk

RUTHERFORD, Russell
Ryden
Position
Partner
Qualifications
BSc; FRICS
Career history
1978 Joined Ryden; appointed associate in 1983 and partner in 1985
Professional memberships
RICS
Interests
DIY; gardening; motor sports; music; sport
Contact details
Ryden, 130 St Vincent Street, Glasgow G2 5HF
Tel 0141 204 3838
Fax 0141 204 3554
Web www.ryden.co.uk
Direct tel 0141 270 3128
Mobile 07831 467169
Email russell.rutherford@ryden.co.uk

RUTHVEN, James
NAI Fuller Peiser
Position
Partner – national head of rating
Contact details
NAI Fuller Peiser, 16 St George Street, London W1S 1LX
Tel 0870 700 2233
Fax 020 7491 1961
Web www.nai-fullerpeiser.com
Email jruthven@nai-fullerpeiser.com

RYLAND, Jane
Cripps Harries Hall
Position
Partner – head of construction
Career history
2001 Joined Cripps Harries Hall as partner. 1989-2001 Laytons: partner from 1999
Other roles
Qualified construction adjudicator
Professional memberships
Chartered Institute of Arbitrators; Women in Property
Contact details
Cripps Harries Hall, Seymour House, 11-13 Mount Ephraim Road, Tunbridge Wells TN1 1EG
Tel 01892 515121
Fax 01892 544878
Web www.e-cripps.co.uk
Direct tel 01892 506354
Direct fax 01892 506060
Email hjr@crippslaw.com

SABBERTON, David
Hewitsons

Position
Partner – head of residential property, Cambridge

Qualifications
MA (Cantab)

Career history
1966 Joined Wild Hewitson & Shaw (now Hewitsons); became partner in 1971

Professional memberships
Cambridgeshire & District Law Society; Law Society

Interests
Family; golf; tennis; travel

Contact details
Hewitsons, Shakespeare House, 42 Newmarket Road, Cambridge CB5 8EP
Tel 0122 346 1155
Fax 0122 331 6511
Web www.hewitsons.com
Email davidsabberton@hewitsons.com

SADLER, Jonathan
South East England Development Agency

Position
Projects director

Contact details
South East England Development Agency, The Observatory, Brunel, Chatham ME4 4NT
Tel 01634 899900
Fax 01634 899901
Web www.seeda.co.uk
Email jonathansadler@seeda.co.uk

SADLER, Keith
Sea Space – Hastings & Bexhill Renaissance

Position
Deputy project director

Contact details
Sea Space – Hastings & Bexhill Renaissance Ltd, Queensbury House, Havelock Road, Hastings TN34 1BP
Tel 01424 781735
Fax 01424 781490
Web www.seaspace.org.uk
Email keithsadler@seeda.co.uk

SADLER, Stephen
South East England Development Agency

Position
Projects director

Qualifications
FRICS

Contact details
South East England Development Agency, The Observatory, Brunel, Chatham ME4 4NT
Tel 01634 899900
Fax 01634 899901
Web www.seeda.co.uk
Email stephensadler@seeda.co.uk

SAGGERS, John
Capital & Counties

Position
Managing director

Qualifications
FRICS

Other roles
Executive director, Liberty International; policy committee, BPF; committee member, London Development Agency; policy committee member, Investment Property Forum

Professional memberships
BPF; Investment Property Forum; Westminster Property Owners Association

Contact details
Capital & Counties, 40 Broadway, London SW1H 0BU
Tel 020 7887 7000
Fax 020 7887 0003
Web www.capitalandcounties.com
Direct tel 020 7887 7041
Email john-saggers@capcount.com

SAHONTE, Rajinder
Guildhall Chambers

Position
Barrister

Qualifications
LLB Hons

Professional memberships
Chancery Bar Association

Interests
Cooking; travel; wine

Contact details
Guildhall Chambers (Chambers of Adrian Palmer QC), 23 Broad Street, Bristol BS1 2HG
Tel 0117 927 3366
Fax 0117 930 3800
Web www.guildhallchambers.co.uk
Direct fax 0117 930 3803
Email raj@guildhallchambers.co.uk

SALES, Michael
Henderson Global Investors

Position
Director of property, portfolio management – Europe

Qualifications
BA Hons; MPhil; MRICS

Career history
1994 Joined Hendersons as fund manager; appointed portfolio director in 1996, director of UK property funds in 1999 and director of property, portfolio management (Europe) in 2002.
1991-94 Associate director, Michael Laurie Partnership.
1989-91 Development surveyor, Morgan Grenfell Laurie

Professional memberships
RICS

Interests
Football; golf; literature; music; reading

Contact details
Henderson Global Investors Ltd, 4 Broadgate, London EC2M 2DA
Tel 020 7818 1818
Fax 020 7818 1819
Web www.henderson.com
Direct tel 020 7818 4376
Email michael.sales@henderson.com

SALISBURY, Nick
Barclays Bank

Position
Director – head of PFI and structured project finance

Qualifications
BA Hons; ACIB

Career history
1978 Joined Barclays

Other roles
School governor

Interests
Music; walking

Contact details
Barclays Bank plc, 54 Lombard Street, London EC3P 3AH
Tel 020 7699 5000
Web www.barclays.com
Direct tel 020 7699 2797

Mobile 07775 550716
Email nick.salisbury@barclays.co.uk

SALMON, James
Aberdeen Property Investors

Position
Director – retail
Qualifications
BSc; MRICS
Career history
Since 1998 Director, Aberdeen Property Investors.
1993-98 Capital & Regional Properties.
1992-93 St Quintin
Professional memberships
Accessible Retail; British Council of Shopping Centres; Investment Property Forum; RICS
Contact details
Aberdeen Property Investors, Charles House, 5-11 Regent Street, London SW1Y 4LR
Tel 020 7747 1700
Fax 020 7839 7460
Web www.aberdeenpropertyinvestors.com
Direct tel 020 7747 1736
Mobile 07799 131736
Email
james.salmon@aberdeenpropertyinvestors.com

SALOMON, Judith
London First Centre

Position
Director of property and planning
Career history
1994 Joined London First.
1991-94 Jones Lang LaSalle
Other roles
Consultant director to CB Richard Ellis planning department
Interests
Rugby
Contact details
London First Centre, 1 Hobhouse Court, Suffolk Street, London SW1Y 4HH
Tel 020 7925 2000
Fax 020 7925 2022
Web www.lfc.co.uk
Email jsalomon@london-first.co.uk

SALTER, Jeremy
Matthews & Goodman

Position
Partner
Interests
Family; football; rugby
Contact details
Matthews & Goodman, Dorland House, 14-16 Regent Street, London SW1Y 4PH
Tel 020 7747 8847
Fax 020 7747 8848
Web www.matthews-goodman.co.uk
Direct tel 020 7747 3181
Mobile 07770 742385
Email jsalter@matthews-goodman.co.uk

SALTER, Neil
Wake Smith

Position
Head of property
Career history
1995 Joined Wake Smith as partner; became head of property in 1997.
1989-95 Associate, Dibb Lupton Broomhead.
1988 Admitted to Roll of Solicitors.
1987-89 Hammond Suddards
Professional memberships
Law Society
Interests
Family; food; football; music; squash; wine
Contact details
Wake Smith, 68 Clarkehouse Road, Sheffield S10 2LJ
Tel 0114 266 6660
Fax 0114 267 1253
Web www.wake-smith.co.uk
Mobile 07798 678574
Email neil.salter@wake-smith.com

SALVESEN, Duncan
Dorrington Investment

Position
Executive director
Qualifications
MRICS
Other roles
Board member, Kensington Housing Trust; member of residential leasehold reform committee/working party, BPF; member, RICS private rented sector working party
Professional memberships
RICS
Contact details
Dorrington Investment plc, 16 Hans Road, London SW3 1RT
Tel 020 7581 1477
Fax 020 7753 7613
Web www.dorrington.co.uk
Email duncan.salvesen@dorrington.co.uk

SALWAY, Francis
Land Securities Group

Position
Chief operating officer
Qualifications
MA; FRICS
Career history
2000 Joined Land Securities Group.
1986-2000 Standard Life.
1982-85 Abacus Developments.
1979-82 Richard Ellis
Other roles
Author of book *Depreciation of Commercial Property* (CALUS, 1986); member, Investment Property Databank Index consultative group; editorial advisory board member, *Property Week*
Professional memberships
Cambridge University Land Society; RICS
Contact details
Land Securities Group plc, 5 Strand, London WC2N 5AF
Tel 020 7413 9000
Fax 020 7024 5007
Web www.landsecurities.com
Direct tel 020 7024 3737
Direct fax 020 7024 3777
Email francis.salway@landsecurities.com

SAMSON, Alan
Gibson Dunn & Crutcher

Position
Partner – head of European real estate
Career history
2000 Joined Gibson Dunn & Crutcher as partner and head of European real estate.
1989-2000 Partner, Nabarro Nathanson
Professional memberships
American Bar Association; Law Society; New York Bar Association; New York University Real Estate Round Table; Urban Land Institute
Contact details
Gibson Dunn & Crutcher, Telephone House, 2-4 Temple Avenue, London EC4Y 0HB
Tel 020 7071 4000
Fax 020 7071 4244
Web www.gdclaw.com
Direct tel 020 7071 4222
Direct fax 020 7070 9222
Email asamson@gibsondunn.com

SAMUEL-CAMPS, Matthew
Vail Williams

Position
Partner – valuation and bank consultancy
Qualifications
MRICS; ACIArb
Professional memberships
Chartered Institute of Arbitrators; RICS; Non-Administrative Receivers Association
Interests
Cycling; mountain biking; travel
Contact details
Vail Williams, Meridians House, 7 Ocean Way,

Southampton SO14 3TJ
Tel 0238 082 0900
Fax 0238 082 0950
Web www.vailwilliams.com
Direct tel 023 8082 0923
Mobile 07836 774298
Email msamuel-camps@vailwilliams.com

SAMUELS, Michael
Kleinwort Benson Private Bank

Position
Head of real estate advisory service
Contact details
Kleinwort Benson Private Bank Ltd, 9 Grosvenor Square, London W1K 5AE
Tel 020 7475 6600
Web www.kbpb.co.uk
Email mike.samuels@kbpb.co.uk

SAMWORTH, Martin
CB Richard Ellis

Position
Joint UK managing director
Qualifications
BSc; MRICS
Professional memberships
RICS
Contact details
CB Richard Ellis, Kingsley House, 1a Wimpole Street, London W1G 0RE
Tel 020 7182 2000
Fax 020 7182 7001
Web www.cbre.com
Email martin.samworth@cbre.com

SANDBACH, Julian
King Sturge

Position
Partner – landlord and tenant
Career history
Since 1994 Partner (landlord and tenant), King Sturge
Contact details
King Sturge, 81 Fountain Street, Manchester M2 2EE
Tel 0161 236 8793
Fax 0161 228 7972
Web www.kingsturge.com
Direct tel 0161 238 6235
Mobile 07889 896871
Email julian.sandbach@kingsturge.co.uk

SANDERS, Bill
North Rae Sanders

Position
Partner
Contact details
North Rae Sanders, Orchard Court, Harry Weston Road, Coventry CV3 2TQ
Tel 024 7663 6888
Fax 024 7663 6114
Web www.northraesanders.co.uk
Email sue@northraesanders.co.uk

SANDERS, Peter
Gardiner & Theobald

Position
Managing partner
Qualifications
FRICS
Other roles
Chairman, Chartered Surveyors Training Trust
Professional memberships
RICS
Contact details
Gardiner & Theobald, 32 Bedford Square, London WC1B 3JT
Tel 020 7209 3000
Fax 020 7209 1840
Web www.gardiner.com
Direct fax 020 7209 1852
Email p.sanders@gardiner.com

SANDERSON, Andrew
Thornfield Properties

Position
Managing director
Qualifications
BSc; MRICS
Professional memberships
RICS
Interests
Fly fishing; football; golf
Contact details
Thornfield Properties plc, 5 St Davids Court, Leeds LS11 5QA
Tel 0113 225 5050
Fax 0113 225 5060
Web www.thornfield.co.uk
Direct tel 0113 225 5055
Email andrew.sanderson@thornfield-leeds.co.uk

SANDERSON, Charles
FPDSavills

Position
Director – City agency
Qualifications
FRICS
Career history
1976 Joined Savills
Professional memberships
FIABCI; RICS
Interests
Boating; skiing
Contact details
FPDSavills Ltd, 25 Finsbury Circus, London EC2M 7EE
Tel 020 7499 8644
Fax 020 7588 7323
Web www.fpdsavills.co.uk
Direct tel 020 7409 8925
Mobile 07741 040487
Email csanderson@fpdsavills.co.uk

SANGSTER, James
Land Securities Trillium

Position
National asset management director
Qualifications
MRICS; AAPI
Professional memberships
Australian Property Institute; RICS
Contact details
Land Securities Trillium Ltd, 140 London Wall, London EC2Y 5DN
Tel 020 7796 5500
Fax 020 7796 5501
Web www.landsecurities.co.uk
Direct tel 020 7796 5540
Direct fax 0845 090 2545
Email james.sangster@lstrillium.com

SASSON, Eric
Carlyle Group

Position
Managing director
Qualifications
MBA (Insead); MS (MIT); ESTP
Career history
2001 Joined Carlyle Group.
1995-2001 Managing director, LaSalle Investment Management.
1991-94 Asset manager, Sinvim – Paribas.
1988-91 Air Products
Contact details
Carlyle Group Ltd, 112 Avenue Kléber, Paris, France
Tel +33 1 5370 3520
Fax +33 1 5370 3530
Web www.thecarlylegroup.com
Direct tel +33 1 5370 3516
Email christiane.rakoto@carlyle.com

SATCHELL, Susan
Withers

Position
Partner – head of property litigation
Professional memberships
Property Litigation Association
Contact details
Withers LLP, 16 Old Bailey, London EC4M 7EG

Tel 020 7597 6000
Fax 020 7597 6543
Web www.withersworldwide.com
Email susan.satchell@withersworldwide.com

SAUER, Ole
FPDSavills

Position
Director – head of office, Berlin
Contact details
FPDSavills Ltd, Carree Am Gendarmenmarkt, Berlin 10117, Germany
Tel +49 30 726 165165
Fax +49 30 726 165166
Web www.fpdsavills.co.uk
Direct tel +49 30 726 165185
Mobile +49 172 773 1232
Email osauer@fpdsavills.de

SAULL, David
Dalgleish

Position
Investment director
Qualifications
FRICS
Career history
1987 Joined Dalgleish.
1984-87 Debenham Tewson & Chinnocks.
1979-84 Prudential Assurance Co
Other roles
Chairman, RICS RFC; vice-president, Woodford RFC
Professional memberships
RICS
Interests
Golf (Chigwell Golf Club); rugby
Contact details
Dalgleish, 80 New Bond Street, London W1S 1DD
Tel 020 7663 5555
Fax 020 7491 0098
Web www.dalgleish.co.uk
Direct tel 020 7663 5592
Direct fax 020 7663 5502
Email dsaull@dalgleish.co.uk

SAUVAIN, Stephen
Kings Chambers

Position
Barrister
Qualifications
QC
Career history
1995 Appointed QC.
1977 Called to Bar.
1971-78 Law lecturer, Manchester University
Other roles
Member of 2 Mitre Court Chambers, London; assistant boundary commissioner, Parliamentary Boundary Commission; editor, *Encyclopedia of Highway Law & Practice*; author, *Highway Law* (2nd edition)
Professional memberships
Planning & Environment Bar Association; UK Environmental Law Association
Interests
Gardening; music
Contact details
Kings Chambers, 40 King Street, Manchester M2 6BA
Tel 0161 832 9082
Fax 0161 835 2139
Web www.kingschambers.com
Direct tel 0161 819 8252
Email ssauvain@kingschambers.com

SAVAGE, Hugh
Lambert Smith Hampton

Position
Director
Qualifications
BSc; FRICS
Professional memberships
RICS
Contact details
Lambert Smith Hampton Ltd, 51-55 Whiteladies Road, Bristol BS8 2LY
Tel 0117 926 6666
Fax 0117 925 0527
Web www.lsh.co.uk
Email hsavage@lsh.co.uk

SAXON, Jonathan
Knight Frank

Position
Partner
Qualifications
MRICS
Professional memberships
RICS
Contact details
Knight Frank LLP, 18 Cabot Square, London E14 4QW
Tel 020 7512 9966
Fax 020 7512 9977
Web www.knightfrank.com
Direct tel 020 7715 9453
Email jonathan.saxon@knightfrank.com

SAXON, Richard
Building Design Partnership

Position
Director of strategic marketing
Qualifications
CBE; BArch; MCD; RIBA; MCIM; FRSA
Career history
1966 Joined BDP; appointed partner in 1977; chairman of London office 1993-99; national chair 1996-2002; now director of strategic marketing
Other roles
Chairman, Be (cross-industry think tank and collaboration centre on the built environment); vice-president for practice, RIBA; member, RIBA professional services board; past president, British Council for Offices
Professional memberships
Architectural Association; Friends of the Earth; Institute of Directors; RIBA; Urban Design Group
Interests
Food; photography; politics; travel
Contact details
Building Design Partnership Ltd, 16 Brewhouse Yard, London EC1V 4LJ
Tel 020 7812 8000
Fax 020 7812 8399
Web www.bdp.co.uk
Direct tel 020 7462 8002
Direct fax 020 7462 6348
Email RG-SAXON@bdp.co.uk

SAYER, David
Edmund Kirby

Position
Partner
Qualifications
FRICS
Other roles
Board member, Parkhaven Trust; director, Vesta Property Developments
Professional memberships
RICS
Interests
Golf; sailing; skiing
Contact details
Edmund Kirby, India Buildings, Water Street, Liverpool L2 0TZ
Tel 0151 236 4552
Fax 0151 236 4024
Web www.edmundkirby.co.uk
Mobile 07860 778409
Email davidsayer@edmundkirby.co.uk

SCAMMELL, Martin
Ernst & Young

Position
Partner – real estate, hospitality and construction
Career history
1986 Joined Ernst & Young (previously Arthur Young); became VAT partner in 1996.
1980-86 HM Customs & Excise
Other roles

S

VAT committee member, BPF; co-author, *Tolley's VAT on Construction, Land & Property*

Contact details

Ernst & Young LLP, 1 More London Place, London SE1 2AF
Tel 020 7951 2000
Fax 020 7951 1345
Web www.ey.com/uk
Direct tel 020 7951 3577
Direct fax 020 7928 0468
Email mscammell@uk.ey.com

SCHOFIELD, Andrew
Henderson Global Investors

Position
Director and head of global property research

Contact details
Henderson Global Investors Ltd, 4 Broadgate, London EC2M 2DA
Tel 020 7818 1818
Fax 020 7818 1819
Web www.henderson.com
Email andrew.schofield@henderson.com

SCHREINER, Klaus
Westdeutsche Immobilienbank

Position
Head of London branch

Qualifications
Dipl-Kfm

Career history
Since 2000 Director (UK real estate) and head of London branch, Westdeutsche ImmobilienBank.
1986-2000 Helaba: became general manager in 1994.
1984-86 Manager, Saudi International Bank.
1980-84 Manager, Hessische Landesbank

Other roles
Past president, Association of Property Bankers (1999-2002); past chairman, Association of International Savings Banks in London (1999-2001)

Interests
Golf; music; theatre; travel; RAC

Contact details
Westdeutsche Immobilienbank, 42 Moorgate, London EC2R 6EL
Tel 020 7330 0988
Web www.westimmobank.com
Direct tel 020 7330 0970
Direct fax 020 7330 0992
Email klaus.schreiner@westimmobank.com

SCHROEDER, Jürgen
Aareal Bank

Position
Managing director

Qualifications
Industrial engineer

Career history
Since 2000 Managing director, Aareal Bank.
1997-2000 Senior vice-president, Deutsche Interhotel (Aareal Bank/Deutsche Bank).
1993-97 Assistant manager, Deutsche Immobilien Anlage Ges (Deutsche Bank).
1990-93 Account officer, DG Immobilien Leasing (DZ Bank)

Interests
Marathon running

Contact details
Aareal Bank AG, Postfach 2125, Paulinenstrasse 15, 65011 Wiesbaden, Germany
Tel +49 611 348 2363
Fax +49 611 348 3587
Web www.aareal-bank.com
Direct tel +49 611 348 2488
Direct fax +49 611 348 72488
Email juergen.schroeder@aareal-bank.com

SCHUWER, Roderik
FPDSavills Nederland

Position
Director – head of office, Amsterdam

Contact details
FPDSavills Nederland BV, Gabriël Metsustraat 13, Amsterdam, Netherlands
Tel +31 20 672 2211
Fax +31 20 672 1400
Mobile +31 06 5314 7187
Email r.schuwer@fpdsavills.nl

SCHWER, Chris
Birketts

Position
Partner – commercial property

Career history
Since 2000 Partner, Birketts.
1998-2000 Bell Gully Biddle Weir, Auckland, New Zealand.
1989-97 DJ Freeman: became partner in 1996.
1986-88 Birketts

Professional memberships
Law Society

Interests
Family; golf

Contact details
Birketts, 24-26 Museum Street, Ipswich IP1 1HZ
Tel 0147 323 2300
Fax 0147 323 0524
Web www.birketts.co.uk
Direct tel 0147 340 6274
Direct fax 0147 340 6385
Email chris-schwer@birketts.co.uk

SCOTT, George
Ward Hadaway

Position
Consultant

Career history
1964 Joined Wheldon Houlsby & Scott (now Ward Hadaway, following merger).
1964 Admitted to Roll of Solicitors

Other roles
Director, Jarrow 700 AD (Bede's World)

Professional memberships
Law Society

Contact details
Ward Hadaway, Sandgate House, 102 Quayside, Newcastle upon Tyne NE1 3DX
Tel 0191 204 4000
Fax 0191 204 4001
Web www.wardhadaway.com
Direct tel 0191 204 4119
Email george.scott@wardhadaway.com

SCOTT, Giles
Chesterton International

Position
Director in charge, Manchester office

Qualifications
BSc Hons; MRICS

Career history
1998 Joined Chesterton.
1992-98 Director, Booker.
1988-90 Berry Bros

Professional memberships
RICS

Interests
Football; golf; skiing

Contact details
Chesterton International, Lombard Chambers, 1 St James's Square, Manchester M2 6DN
Tel 0161 835 3434
Fax 0161 835 3883
Web www.chesterton.co.uk
Direct tel 0161 955 6711
Mobile 07712 868307
Email giles.scott@chesterton.co.uk

SCOTT, Keith
Catalyst Capital

Position
Finance director

Contact details
Catalyst Capital LLP, 33 Cavendish Square, London W1G 0PW
Tel 020 7290 5100
Fax 020 7290 5115
Web www.catalystcapital.com
Email kscott@catalystcapital.co.uk

S

SCOTT, Paul
British Airways Pension Fund

Position
Deputy property manager
Qualifications
BSc Hons; MRICS
Career history
Since 2001 Deputy property manager, British Airways Pension Investment Management.
1994-2001 Divisional director (retail), Henderson Global Investors.
1989-94 Conrad Ritblat & Co
Professional memberships
RICS
Contact details
British Airways Pension Fund, Alton House, 177 High Holborn, London WC1V 7AA
Tel 020 7845 4900
Web www.britishairways.com
Direct tel 020 7845 4960
Mobile 07776 200294
Email paul.scott@bapensions.co.uk

SCOTT, Peter
Bevan Ashford

Position
Partner – head of real estate
Qualifications
MA (Cantab)
Career history
Since 1975 Partner, Bevan Ashford.
1972-75 Boodle Hatfield.
1972 Admitted to Roll of Solicitors
Contact details
Bevan Ashford, 35 Colston Avenue, Bristol BS1 4TT
Tel 0117 923 0111
Fax 0117 929 1865
Web www.bevanashford.co.uk
Email peter.scott@bevanashford.co.uk

SCOTT, Peter
Keppie Design

Position
Chairman
Contact details
Keppie Design Ltd, 160 West Regent Street, Glasgow G2 4RL
Tel 0141 204 0066
Fax 0141 226 4571
Web www.keppiedesign.co.uk
Email glasgow@keppiedesign.co.uk

SCOTT, Peter
Peel Holdings

Position
Group managing director
Qualifications
FCCA
Career history
1977 Joined Peel Holdings as company secretary; became financial director in 1982 and group managing director in 1985.
1975-77 Financial accountant, Crane Fruehauf Trailers.
1962-75 Financial accountant, Fothergill & Harvey
Professional memberships
Association of Chartered Certified Accountants
Interests
Skiing; tennis
Contact details
Peel Holdings plc, Peel Dome, The Trafford Centre, Manchester M17 8PL
Tel 0161 629 8200
Fax 0161 629 8333
Web www.peel.co.uk
Email pscott@peelholdings.co.uk

SCOTT, Richard
Mellersh & Harding

Position
Partner
Qualifications
BSc; FRICS
Career history
1976 Joined Mellersh & Harding
Other roles
Member, RICS panel of independent experts for office rent review and valuation work
Professional memberships
RICS
Interests
Antiques; horse riding; music; sport
Contact details
Mellersh & Harding, 6 Duke Street, London SW1Y 6BN
Tel 020 7499 0866
Fax 020 7522 8503
Web www.mellersh.co.uk
Direct tel 020 7522 8516
Mobile 07880 740508
Email rscott@mellersh.co.uk

SCRUTTON, Anne
Scrutton Estates

Position
Company secretary
Contact details
Scrutton Estates Ltd, 1 Cambus Road, London E16 4AY
Tel 020 7476 1215
Fax 020 7511 8721
Email barry@scruttonestates.co.uk

SCRUTTON, Charles
Scrutton Estates

Position
Managing director
Qualifications
MRICS
Contact details
Scrutton Estates Ltd, 1 Cambus Road, London E16 4AY
Tel 020 7476 1215
Fax 020 7511 8721
Email barry@scruttonestates.co.uk

SEABORN, Hugh
Portman Estate

Position
Chief executive
Qualifications
BSc; FRICS
Career history
Since 2000 Chief executive, Portman Estate.
1991-2000 Insignia Richard Ellis; director (investment management department) on leaving.
1988-91 Richard Ellis Fleetwood Bird, Botswana
Other roles
Council member, Westminster Property Owners Association
Professional memberships
RICS
Interests
Golf; running; skiing; squash; Oriental Club
Contact details
Portman Estate, 38 Seymour Street, London W1H 7BP
Tel 020 7563 1400
Fax 020 7563 1401
Web www.portmanestate.co.uk
Email hugh.seaborn@portmanestate.co.uk

SEAGER, Nicola
Masons

Position
Partner – property litigation
Career history
1996 Joined Masons; became partner in 2001.
1991 Admitted to Roll of Solicitors.
1989-96 Stephenson Harwood
Other roles
South West and south Wales group chair, Property Litigation Association
Professional memberships
Law Society; Property Litigation Association
Contact details
Masons, 1-4 Portland Square, Bristol BS2 8RR
Tel 0117 924 5678
Fax 0117 924 6699

Web www.masons.com
Direct tel 0117 970 5206
Mobile 07831 827660
Email nicola.seager@masons.com

SEAL, Jonathan
Hamptons International

Position
Managing director – London residential development and investment
Other roles
Joint managing director, Vecchia (joint venture company owned by CB Hillier Parker and Hamptons International)
Contact details
Hamptons International, 7 Lower Sloane Street, London SW1W 8AY
Tel 020 7824 8822
Fax 020 7730 5331
Web www.hamptons.co.uk
Email sealj@hamptons-int.com

SEARLE, Geoffrey
Geoffrey Searle Planning & Property Solicitors

Position
Principal
Career history
1998-2000 Consultant/head of planning, Olswang.
1994-98 Geoffrey Searle Planning Solicitor.
1973-94 Denton Hall: including managing partner 1988-1992.
1969-73 Brentwood Council.
1968 Admitted to Roll of Solicitors
Professional memberships
FIABCI
Contact details
Geoffrey Searle Planning & Property Solicitors, 26 Priestgate, Peterborough PE1 1WG
Tel 01733 865051
Fax 01733 865052
Email gjs@geoffreysearle.com

SEARY, Nick
King Sturge

Position
Partner – development
Qualifications
BSc; FRICS
Career history
1983 Joined JP Sturge (now King Sturge); appointed partner in 1990
Professional memberships
Accessible Retail; RICS
Contact details
King Sturge, 40 Berkeley Square, Bristol BS8 1HU
Tel 0117 927 6691
Fax 0117 929 9669
Web www.kingsturge.com
Direct tel 0117 930 5731
Email nick.seary@kingsturge.co.uk

SEATON, Graham
Matalan Retail

Position
Director of estates
Qualifications
BSc; FRICS
Career history
1986-95 Development manager, B&Q.
1984-86 Regional site acquisition manager, Gateway Foodmarket.
1981-84 Senior management surveyor, Bristol City Council
Professional memberships
RICS
Contact details
Matalan Retail Ltd, Gillibrands Road, Skelmersdale WN8 9TB
Tel 01695 552400
Fax 01695 552401
Web www.matalan.co.uk
Direct tel 01695 552524
Direct fax 01695 554399
Mobile 07770 565726
Email seaton_g@matalan.co.uk

SEATON, Roger
Clarke Willmott

Position
Head of commercial property
Qualifications
MA (Oxon)
Career history
1983 Joined Clarke Willmott & Clarke; became partner in 1987.
1981 Admitted to Roll of Solicitors.
1979-83 Clarks, Reading
Other roles
Management board member
Professional memberships
Law Society
Contact details
Clarke Willmott, Blackbrook Gate, Blackbrook Park Avenue, Taunton TA1 2PG
Tel 0182 344 2266
Fax 0182 344 5800
Web www.clarkewillmott.com
Direct tel 0182 344 5205
Direct fax 0182 344 5803
Email rseaton@clarkewillmott.com

SECKINGTON, Jonathan
Land Securities Trillium

Position
Acquisitions director – corporate real estate group
Qualifications
FRICS
Career history
1998 Joined Land Securities Trillium.
1993-97 Senior property manager, Ex-Lands Properties.
1984-93 Associate, Richard Ellis.
1980-84 Estate surveyor, GRE Properties
Professional memberships
RICS
Contact details
Land Securities Trillium Ltd, 140 London Wall, London EC2Y 5DN
Tel 020 7796 5500
Fax 020 7796 5501
Web www.landsecurities.co.uk
Direct tel 020 7796 5660
Direct fax 0845 090 2562
Email jonathan.seckington@lstrillium.com

SEDDON, David
Jones Lang LaSalle

Position
International director
Contact details
Jones Lang LaSalle Ltd, 22 Hanover Square, London W1A 2BN
Tel 020 7493 6040
Fax 020 7408 0220
Web www.joneslanglasalle.com
Direct tel 020 7399 5351
Direct fax 020 7399 5470
Email david.seddon@eu.joneslanglasalle.com

SEDDON, Tim
Land Securities Properties

Position
Director
Qualifications
BSc Hons; MRICS
Career history
1994 Joined Land Securities.
1986-94 Edward Erdman
Other roles
Director, Ravenseft Properties
Professional memberships
RICS
Interests
Cricket; golf; wine
Contact details
Land Securities Properties Ltd, 5 Strand, London WC2N 5AF
Tel 020 7413 9000

S

Fax 020 7925 0202
Web www.landsecurities.com
Direct tel 020 7024 3734
Direct fax 020 7024 3770
Mobile 07768 598787
Email tim.seddon@landsecurities.com

SEFTON, Mark
Falcon Chambers

Position
Barrister
Contact details
Falcon Chambers, Falcon Court, London
EC4Y 1AA
Tel 020 7353 2484
Fax 020 7353 1261
Web www.falcon-chambers.com
Email sefton@falcon-chambers.com

SEIFERT, Anne
Landmark Chambers

Position
Barrister
Other roles
Part-time chairman of rent assessment committees and rent tribunals
Professional memberships
Chancery Bar Association; Chartered Institute of Arbitrators
Contact details
Landmark Chambers, 4 Breams Buildings, London EC4A 1AQ
Tel 020 7430 1221
Fax 020 7421 1399
Web www.landmarkchambers.co.uk
Email clerks@landmarkchambers.co.uk

SEITLER, Jonathan
Wilberforce Chambers

Position
Barrister
Qualifications
QC
Career history
2003 Appointed QC.
1985 Called to Bar
Other roles
Co-author, *Property Finance Negligence: Claims Against Solicitors & Valuers* (FT Law & Tax, 1996) and new, loose-leaf *Commercial Property Disputes* (Sweet & Maxwell, 1999)
Professional memberships
Chancery Bar Association; Professional Negligence Bar Association; Property Bar Association
Contact details
Wilberforce Chambers, 8 New Square, London WC2A 3QP
Tel 020 7306 0102
Fax 020 7306 0095
Web www.wilberforce.co.uk
Email jseitler@wilberforce.co.uk

SELIGMAN, Mark
Credit Suisse First Boston

Position
Chairman – UK investment banking
Other roles
Deputy chairman, CSFB Europe
Contact details
Credit Suisse First Boston, 1 Cabot Square, London E14 4QJ
Tel 020 7888 8888
Fax 020 7883 5819
Web www.csfb.com
Direct tel 020 7888 6061
Email mark.seligman@csfb.com

SELLAR, Irvine
Sellar Property Group

Position
Chairman
Contact details
Sellar Property Group, 103 Park Street, London W1K 7JN
Tel 020 7493 5311
Fax 020 7408 2343
Email sellarprop@aol.com

SELLERS, Justin
Lear House Properties

Position
Director
Qualifications
MA; FRICS
Other roles
Consultant, ING Real Estate Investment Management
Contact details
Lear House Properties Ltd, 13 High Street, Aylesbury HP22 4NW
Tel 01296 640524
Fax 01296 640525
Mobile 07770 777221
Email sellers@learhouse.fsnet.co.uk

SELLERS, Tim
Turbervilles

Position
Partner – commercial and residential development
Qualifications
LLB
Career history
1983 Admitted to Roll of Solicitors.
1981 Joined Turbervilles
Professional memberships
Institute of Directors
Interests
Golf
Contact details
Turbervilles, 118 High Street, Uxbridge UB8 1JT
Tel 01895 201700
Fax 01895 273519
Web www.turbervilles.co.uk
Email tim.sellers@turbervilles.co.uk

SELWYN, Ray
Lamberts

Position
Director – commercial valuation
Qualifications
MRICS
Professional memberships
RICS
Contact details
Lamberts Ltd, 387 City Road, London EC1V 1NA
Tel 020 7278 8191
Fax 020 7837 5790
Web www.lambertsurv.co.uk
Direct tel 020 7520 2308
Email ray.selwyn@lambertsurv.co.uk

SEMPLE, Jeff
James Barr

Position
Director
Qualifications
FRICS
Career history
1978 Joined James Barr
Professional memberships
Industrial Agents Society; RICS
Interests
Fishing; golf; skiing
Contact details
James Barr, 226 West George Street, Glasgow G2 2LN
Tel 0141 300 8000
Fax 0141 300 8001
Web www.jamesbarr.co.uk
Mobile 07836 656180
Email jeffsemple@jamesbarr.co.uk

SENIOR, Graham
Edwin Hill

Position
Partner
Qualifications
BSc; MRICS

Career history
1992 Joined Edwin Hill.
1991-92 Estates surveyor, Runnymede Borough Council
Professional memberships
RICS
Interests
Football; rugby; skiing; tennis
Contact details
Edwin Hill, Highbridge House, Padbury Oaks, London UB7 0EH
Tel 01753 689000
Fax 01753 689191
Web www.edwinhill.co.uk
Email grahams@edwinhill.co.uk

SENIOR, Robert
Hodnett Martin Smith
Position
Partner
Contact details
Hodnett Martin Smith Ltd, Charles House, 5-11 Regent Street, London SW1Y 4LR
Tel 020 7839 8181
Fax 020 7839 8069
Web www.hodnettmartinsmith.com
Email robertsenior@hodms.co.uk

SERGINSON, Roger
Angermann Goddard & Loyd
Position
Director – local authority
Contact details
Angermann Goddard & Loyd Ltd, 26 Mount Row, London W1K 3SQ
Tel 020 7409 7303
Fax 020 7493 1029
Direct tel 020 7465 5102
Email roger.serginson@agl-london.co.uk

SEXTON, Bill
Citigroup Alternative Investments
Position
Vice-president, European real estate
Qualifications
BSc; MRICS; SIAff
Career history
2002 Joined Citigroup Alternative Investments.
2001-02 Director of international investment, FPDSavills.
1990-2001 Director of international investment, Debenham Tie Leung
Professional memberships
RICS; Securities Institute (affiliate)
Interests
Cricket; golf; hockey
Contact details
Citigroup Alternative Investments, 41 Berkeley Square, London W1J 5AN
Tel 020 7508 8000
Fax 020 7508 8932
Web www.citigroup.com
Direct tel 020 7508 8755
Email william.sexton@citigroup.com

SHADAREVIAN, Paul
2 Mitre Court Buildings
Position
Barrister
Career history
1984 Called to Bar
Other roles
Original joint author and now consultant editor, *Butterworths' Planning Law Service*
Professional memberships
Planning & Environment Bar Association
Interests
Sailing
Contact details
2 Mitre Court Buildings (Chambers of Guy Roots QC), 2nd Floor, London EC4Y 7BX
Tel 020 7583 1380
Fax 020 7353 7772
Web www.2mcb.co.uk
Email clerks@2mcb.co.uk

SHAH, Rajesh
Land Securities Trillium
Position
Investment strategy director
Qualifications
MSc; BSc
Contact details
Land Securities Trillium Ltd, 140 London Wall, London EC2Y 5DN
Tel 020 7796 5500
Fax 020 7796 5501
Web www.landsecurities.co.uk
Email rajesh.shah@lstrillium.com

SHANKLAND, Jim
Ryden
Position
Managing partner
Qualifications
BSc, Land Econ; FRICS; Dip TP
Career history
Since 1998 Managing partner, Ryden.
1995-98 Managing director, Ryden, South Africa.
1989-95 Partner in charge, Ryden, Glasgow.
1977-89 Partner, Speirs Gumley
Other roles
Chairman RICS Scotland; executive committee member, Scottish Council for Development & Industry
Professional memberships
RICS
Interests
Fishing; golf; sailing; walking
Contact details
Ryden, 130 St Vincent Street, Glasgow G2 5HF
Tel 0141 204 3838
Fax 0141 204 3554
Web www.ryden.co.uk
Direct tel 0141 270 3141
Mobile 07836 661373
Email jim.shankland@ryden.co.uk

SHARP, Cate
Mayer, Brown, Rowe & Maw
Position
Partner – head of environment group, London
Qualifications
BSc Hons (Lond)
Career history
1991 Joined Mayer, Brown, Rowe & Maw; member of environment group since 1993 and partner and head of London group since 2000
Contact details
Mayer, Brown, Rowe & Maw LLP, 11 Pilgrim Street, London EC4V 6RW
Tel 020 7248 4282
Fax 020 7248 2009
Web www.mayerbrownrowe.com
Direct tel 020 7782 8891
Email csharp@mayerbrownrowe.com

SHARP, Colin
GVA Grimley
Position
Partner
Qualifications
MBA; FRICS
Career history
1996 Joined GVA Grimley; set up telecoms department.
1987-96 Telecoms industry.
1984-87 Valuation Office Agency.
1980-84 Mann & Co Commercial
Professional memberships
Rating Surveyors Association; RICS
Interests
Motor sports; skiing; squash; travel
Contact details
GVA Grimley, 10 Stratton Street, London W1J 8JR
Tel 0870 900 8990
Fax 020 7911 2560
Web www.gvagrimley.co.uk
Direct tel 020 7911 2223

Mobile 07770 846826
Email colin.sharp@gvagrimley.co.uk

SHARP, Michael
Gerald Eve

Position
Partner – head of retail
Contact details
Gerald Eve, 7 Vere Street, London W1G 0JB
Tel 020 7493 3338
Fax 020 7491 1825
Web www.geraldeve.com
Direct tel 020 7333 6330
Mobile 07831 149961
Email msharp@geraldeve.com

SHARPE, Andrew
Grattan

Position
Associate director – facilities and property
Qualifications
BSc Hons; CEng; MIMechE; MBIFM
Career history
1995 Joined Grattan (part of Otto Versand)
Professional memberships
British Institute of Facilities Management; Institution of Mechanical Engineers
Interests
Football; music
Contact details
Grattan plc, Anchor House, Ingleby Road, Bradford BD99 2XG
Tel 01274 575511
Fax 01274 625591
Web www.grattanplc.com
Direct tel 01274 624219
Mobile 07808 729620
Email andrew.sharpe@grattan.co.uk

SHARPE, Darren
Tops Estates

Position
Director
Contact details
Tops Estates plc, 77 South Audley Street, London W1K 1EE
Tel 020 7355 3000
Fax 020 7355 2222
Email darren.sharpe@topsestates.co.uk

SHARPE-NEALE, Michael
Hamptons International

Position
Director – valuation and survey
Qualifications
FRICS
Career history
1994 Joined Hamptons; became associate director in 1997 and director in 2000
Professional memberships
RICS
Contact details
Hamptons International, 168 Brompton Road, London SW3 1HW
Tel 020 7584 2044
Fax 020 7584 2072
Web www.hamptons.co.uk
Email Sharpenealm@hamptons-int.com

SHASHOU, Joe
Marylebone Warwick Balfour Group

Position
Main board director
Other roles
Various directorships of Marylebone Warwick Balfour subsidiary companies
Interests
Golf; skiing; tennis
Contact details
Marylebone Warwick Balfour Group plc, 1 West Garden Place, London W2 2AQ
Tel 020 7706 2121
Fax 020 7706 8181
Web www.mwb.co.uk
Direct tel 020 7479 2904
Mobile 07768 100091
Email jshashou@mwb.co.uk

SHATTOCK, Nick
Quintain Estates & Development

Position
Property director
Qualifications
BA Hons, Law
Career history
Since 1995 Main board director, Quintain Estates & Development.
1990-95 Partner, SJ Berwin & Co
Professional memberships
Investment Property Forum; Law Society
Interests
Football; theatre
Contact details
Quintain Estates & Development plc, 58 Davies Street, London W1K 5JF
Tel 020 7495 8968
Fax 020 7499 5583
Web www.quintain-estates.com
Email nick.shattock@quintain-estates.com

SHAW, Alistair
Bride Hall Group

Position
Joint managing director
Contact details
Bride Hall Group Ltd, 49 Hays Mews, London W1J 5QQ
Tel 020 7493 3996
Fax 020 7499 4388
Email alistair.shaw@bride-hall.co.uk

SHAW, David
Crown Estate

Position
Head of Regent Street strategy and development
Qualifications
FRICS
Career history
1999-2002 Nomura.
1992-99 Burton Group/Arcadia.
1984-92 Shearwater
Other roles
Director, New West End Co; director, Westminster CCTV Trust
Professional memberships
RICS
Contact details
Crown Estate, 16 Carlton House Terrace, London SW1Y 5AH
Tel 020 7210 4377
Fax 020 7210 4236
Web www.crownestate.co.uk
Direct tel 020 7210 4253
Direct fax 020 7930 8202
Mobile 07900 901135
Email david.shaw@crownestate.co.uk

SHAW, Donald
Dundas & Wilson

Position
Partner – real estate industry leader
Qualifications
LLB; NP; WS; FSALS
Career history
1979 Joined Dundas & Wilson: partner from 1985; became head of commercial property group in 1995 and of real estate industry in 2000.
1979 Admitted to Roll of Solicitors
Other roles
Former head of Andersen Legal Real Estate for Europe, Middle East, India and Africa (1998-2000)
Professional memberships
British Council for Offices; Investment Property Forum; Law Society of Scotland; Society for Advanced Legal Studies; Urban Land Institute
Interests
History; music; travel; walking; wine
Contact details
Dundas & Wilson, Bush House, 9th Floor,

Aldwych, London WC2B 4EZ
Tel 020 7240 2401
Fax 020 7240 2448
Web www.dundas-wilson.com
Direct tel 020 7759 3559
Mobile 07887 626474
Email donald.shaw@dundas-wilson.com

SHAW, John
Donaldsons

Position
Partner
Qualifications
Dip BS; FRICS; MaPS
Career history
Since 1995 Head of building and project consultancy, Donaldsons.
1979-95 Head of building surveying, Bayleys.
1974-79 Architects department, Gloucestershire County Council
Professional memberships
Association of Planning Supervisors; RICS
Interests
Cricket; golf; water sports
Contact details
Donaldsons, Beech House, 6 St Paul's Road, Bristol BS8 1LT
Tel 0117 923 9520
Fax 0117 923 9521
Web www.donaldsons.co.uk
Mobile 07973 822251
Email cjohn.shaw@donaldsons.co.uk

SHAW, John
Stannifer Group Holdings

Position
Managing director
Contact details
Stannifer Group Holdings Ltd, Ryon Hill House, Ryon Hill Park, Stratford-upon-Avon CV37 0UX
Tel 01789 415565
Fax 01789 415262
Web www.stannifer.co.uk
Direct tel 01789 207002
Direct fax 01789 207025
Email johnshaw@stannifer.co.uk

SHAW, Ken
Ryden

Position
Partner – investment and finance group
Qualifications
BSc; MRICS
Career history
1991 Joined Ryden, Aberdeen.
1988-90 Herring Son & Daw, London.
1986-88 Chesterton, Glasgow
Interests
Golf; music; travel
Contact details
Ryden, 1 Albyn Terrace, Aberdeen AB10 1YP
Tel 01224 637300
Fax 01224 642349
Web www.ryden.co.uk
Email ken.shaw@ryden.co.uk

SHAW, Michael
Cobbetts

Position
Managing partner
Career history
1981 Admitted to Roll of Solicitors.
1979 Joined Cobbetts
Professional memberships
Law Society
Contact details
Cobbetts, Ship Canal House, King Street, Manchester M2 4WB
Tel 0161 833 3333
Fax 0161 833 3030
Web www.cobbetts.co.uk
Email michael.shaw@cobbetts.co.uk

SHAW, Peter
GVA Saxon Law

Position
Partner
Contact details
GVA Saxon Law, 10 Stratton Street, London W1J 8JR
Tel 0870 900 8990
Fax 020 7911 2560
Email peter.shaw@gvagrimley.co.uk

SHAW, Peter
RHWL Partnership

Position
Partner
Qualifications
MA; Dip Arch (Cantab); RIBA
Professional memberships
Architektenkammer Berlin; Architektenkammer Hessen; RIBA
Contact details
RHWL Partnership, 77 Endell Street, London WC2H 9AJ
Tel 020 7379 7900
Fax 020 7836 4881
Email pshaw@rhwl.co.uk

SHAW, Stephen
Lamb Chambers

Position
Barrister
Qualifications
LLB; MCIArb
Career history
1975 Called to Bar
Other roles
Part-time lawyer chairman of London Rent Assessment Panel and Leasehold Valuation Tribunal; CEDR accredited mediator
Professional memberships
Chancery Bar Association; Chartered Institute of Arbitrators; London Common Law & Commercial Bar Association; Professional Negligence Bar Association; Property Bar Association
Interests
Cycling; gardening; jazz
Contact details
Lamb Chambers, Lamb Building, London EC4Y 7AS
Tel 020 7797 8300
Fax 020 7797 8308
Web www.lambchambers.co.uk
Email stephenshaw@lambchambers.co.uk

SHEARER, Eric
Chesterton International

Position
Director in charge, Aberdeen office
Qualifications
FRICS
Professional memberships
RICS
Contact details
Chesterton International, 3 Rubislaw Terrace, Aberdeen AB10 1XE
Tel 0122 464 4272
Fax 0122 463 9277
Web www.chesterton.co.uk
Email eric.shearer@chesterton.co.uk

SHEARER, Guy
Shearer Property Group

Position
Managing director
Contact details
Shearer Property Group Ltd, 31 St George Street, London W1S 2FJ
Tel 020 7290 2390
Fax 020 7290 2399
Email guyshearer@spglondon.com

SHEAVILLS, Ernest
Royal Bank of Scotland

Position
Director – property development and asset management
Qualifications
FRICS; ACIArb

Career history
1990-92 Chief executive, Hunting Gate Group.
1989-90 Chief executive, Citygrove.
1972-89 Managing director, Ladbroke Group Properties
Other roles
Scottish regional chairman, CoreNet Global UK; vice-chairman, Edinburgh City Centre Management Co; member, CBI property board
Professional memberships
British Council for Offices; Chartered Institute of Arbitrators; CoreNet Global UK; RICS
Interests
Art; rugby; tennis; theatre
Contact details
Royal Bank of Scotland, Drummond House, PO Box 1727, 1 Redheughs Avenue, Edinburgh EH12 9JN
Tel 0131 556 8555
Web www.rbs.co.uk
Direct tel 0131 523 7025
Direct fax 0131 523 7022
Email ernest.sheavills@rbs.co.uk

SHEEDY, Chris
Brixton Investments
Position
Senior director – project management
Qualifications
MRICS
Professional memberships
RICS
Contact details
Brixton Investments Ltd, 50 Berkeley Street, London W1J 8BX
Tel 020 7399 4500
Fax 020 7399 4550
Web www.brixton.plc.uk
Direct tel 020 7399 4530
Email chrissheedy@brixton.plc.uk

SHELLARD, Julian
CB Richard Ellis
Position
Chairman – regional business
Qualifications
MRICS
Career history
1975 Joined Insignia Richard Ellis (now CB Richard Ellis); moved from London to Birmingham in 1993.
1972-75 Dunster & Morton, Reading
Other roles
Member, Birmingham City 2000
Professional memberships
British American Chamber of Commerce; RICS
Interests
Music; sport; travel; MCC
Contact details
CB Richard Ellis, 85-89 Colmore Row, Birmingham B3 2BB
Tel 0121 233 9070
Fax 0121 233 3986
Web www.cbre.com
Direct tel 0121 627 5525
Mobile 07778 600411
Email julian.shellard@cbre.com

SHEPHERD, Michael
Martineau Johnson
Position
Partner
Qualifications
MA (Oxon)
Career history
Since 1987 Partner (commercial property department), Martineau Johnson.
1966 Admitted to Roll of Solicitors
Other roles
Member of CBI Birmingham business group; council member and past president (1997/98), Birmingham Law Society
Professional memberships
Association of Partnership Practitioners; Birmingham Law Society; CBI
Interests
Art; gardening; sport; travel; wine
Contact details
Martineau Johnson Ltd, St Philips House, St Philips Place, Birmingham B3 2PP
Tel 0121 200 3300
Fax 0121 200 3330
Web www.martineau-johnson.co.uk
Direct tel 0121 678 1587
Direct fax 0121 606 0150
Mobile 07831 160757
Email michael.shepherd@martjohn.com

SHEPHERD, Nicholas
Drivers Jonas
Position
Managing partner
Qualifications
MA; FRICS
Career history
1982 Joined Drivers Jonas as partner.
1980-82 Winkworth & Co
Other roles
Council member, BPF
Professional memberships
BPF; RICS; Worshipful Company of Masons
Contact details
Drivers Jonas, 6 Grosvenor Street, London W1K 4DJ
Tel 020 7896 8000
Fax 020 7896 8001
Web www.driversjonas.com
Direct tel 020 7896 8396
Email nickshepherd@driversjonas.com

SHEPPARD, Dr Stephen
DTZ Pieda Consulting
Position
Director
Qualifications
PhD, Econ Dev
Career history
1989-96 Senior project manager, Segal Quince Wicksteed, Cambridge and Hong Kong.
1987-89 Head of economic consultancy and research, GVA Grimley, London and Birmingham.
1986-87 Assistant head of research, Chesterton, London.
1984-86 Freelance consultant, PA Cambridge Economic Consultants.
1980-82 Economic analyst, Open University, Milton Keynes.
1976-79 Assistant area surveyor, Grand Metropolitan Group
Contact details
DTZ Pieda Consulting, 1 Marsden Street, Manchester M2 1HW
Tel 0161 236 9595
Fax 0161 834 2055
Web www.dtz.com
Direct tel 0161 235 7641
Mobile 07879 481474
Email steve.sheppard@dtz.com

SHERIDAN, Niall
EA Shaw
Position
Senior partner
Qualifications
FRICS; ACIArb
Career history
1974 Joined EA Shaw
Other roles
Acts as arbitrator and independent expert
Professional memberships
Chartered Institute of Arbitrators; RICS
Interests
Golf (West Sussex Golf Club); sailing; skiing; RAC
Contact details
EA Shaw, 9-12 Bow Street, London WC2E 7AB
Tel 020 7240 2255
Fax 020 7831 1012
Web www.eashaw.com
Direct tel 020 7420 3028
Mobile 07976 281247
Email nms@eashaw.com

SHERIDAN, Paul
CMS Cameron McKenna

Position
Partner – head of environment law group
Professional memberships
Chartered Insurance Institute; Institute of Petroleum; Institute of Waste Management; International Bar Association; Law Society; UK Environmental Law Association
Contact details
CMS Cameron McKenna, Mitre House, 160 Aldersgate Street, London EC1A 4DD
Tel 020 7367 3000
Fax 020 7367 2000
Web www.cmck.com
Direct tel 020 7367 2186
Email paul.sheridan@cmck.com

SHERLEY-DALE, Michael
City North Group

Position
Managing director
Contact details
City North Group plc, 1 Udall Street, London SW1P 2PP
Tel 020 7932 0421
Fax 020 7932 0446
Email msd@citynorth.com

SHERWOOD, Mark
Vail Williams

Position
Equity partner – investment
Qualifications
BSc Hons; Dip LE; MRICS
Career history
1997 Joined Vail Williams.
1994-97 St Quintin
Professional memberships
RICS
Interests
Golf; rugby; sailing; shooting; windsurfing
Contact details
Vail Williams, Thames Valley Office, 130 Wharfedale Road, Winnersh RG41 5RB
Tel 0118 933 5600
Fax 0118 933 5634
Web www.vailwilliams.com
Email msherwood@vailwilliams.com

SHIELLS, Keith
BTWShiells

Position
Chief executive
Qualifications
BSc, Est Man; FRICS
Career history
Since 2003 Chief executive, BTWShiells.
1988-2003 Lambert Smith Hampton: joined as director; appointed regional chief executive in 1998.
1981-88 Partner, Milhench Crothers.
1979-81 Morton Commercial
Professional memberships
RICS
Interests
Cycling; golf; rugby; walking
Contact details
BTWShiells, 4-10 May Street, Belfast BT1 4NJ
Tel 02890 327954
Fax 02890 244057
Web www.info@btwshiells.co.uk
Direct tel 02890 269201
Mobile 07767 846286
Email kshiells@btwshiells.co.uk

SHINE, Ross
Brabners Chaffe Street

Position
Partner – head of department, Preston
Career history
1994 Joined Brabner Holden Banks Wilson (now Brabners Chaffe Street) as partner
Professional memberships
Preston Incorporated Law Society
Interests
Bridge; football; sport
Contact details
Brabners Chaffe Street, 7-8 Chapel Street, Preston PR1 8AN
Tel 01772 823921
Fax 01772 201918
Web www.brabnerschaffestreet.com
Email ross.shine@brabnerscs1.com

SHIPMAN, Mark
Michael Elliott

Position
Director
Contact details
Michael Elliott, 53 Brooks Mews, London W1K 4ED
Tel 020 7493 8184
Fax 020 7409 2985
Email markshipman@michaelelliott.co.uk

SHORT, Grahame
White & Bowker

Position
Partner – head of commercial property
Qualifications
MA (Cantab)
Career history
Since 1982 Partner, White & Bowker.
1979-82 White Brooks & Gilman.
1979 Admitted to Roll of Solicitors
Contact details
White & Bowker, Turnpike House, Tollgate, Eastleigh SO53 3TG
Tel 01962 844440
Fax 023 8032 2277
Web www.wandb.co.uk
Direct tel 01962 830106
Email grahame.short@wandb.co.uk

SHORT, John
Haslams

Position
Partner
Qualifications
BSc, Est Man; FRICS
Career history
1969 Joined Haslams as valuer; appointed partner in 1972.
1967-69 Valuer, District Valuation Office
Professional memberships
RICS
Interests
Golf; opera; rugby; sailing
Contact details
Haslams, 156 Friar Street, Reading RG1 1HH
Tel 0118 960 1010
Fax 0118 960 1022
Web www.haslams-online.co.uk
Direct tel 0118 960 1031
Email js@haslams-surveyors.co.uk

SHORT, Jonathan
PRICOA Property Private Equity

Position
Chief executive
Qualifications
BSc, Banking & Finance; ACIB
Career history
1999 Joined PRICOA.
1998-99 Executive director (corporate finance), Lazard Brothers & Co.
1991-98 Director, Baring Brothers.
1986-91 Manager, SG Warburg
Other roles
SFA registered representative
Professional memberships
Chartered Institute of Bankers; Property & Finance Club; Securities & Futures Authority
Interests
Rugby; theatre; travel
Contact details
PRICOA Property Private Equity Ltd, 166 Sloane Street, London SW1X 9QF
Tel 020 7661 3300
Email jonathan.short@prudential.com

SHORT, Mark
Aitchison Raffety

Position
Associate director
Qualifications
BSc Hons; MRICS
Contact details
Aitchison Raffety Ltd, Clifford House, 15 Clifford Street, London W1S 4JY
Tel 020 7851 6950
Fax 020 7851 6953
Web www.argroup.co.uk
Email mark.short@argroup.co.uk

SHUTTLEWORTH, Craig
Jones Day

Position
Partner – head of construction
Qualifications
MA (Oxon); MSc, Construction Law & Arbitration
Career history
1989 Admitted to Roll of Solicitors.
1987 Joined Gouldens (now Jones Day)
Professional memberships
Chartered Institute of Arbitrators
Interests
Golf; triathlon
Contact details
Jones Day, 21 Tudor Street, London EC4Y 0DJ
Tel 020 7039 5959
Fax 020 7039 5999
Web www.jonesday.com
Direct tel 020 7039 5117
Email ccshuttleworth@jonesday.com

SIBLEY, Vince
Game

Position
Head of property
Qualifications
BSc; MRICS; ACIArb
Career history
1995-97 Regional estates manager, Woolworths.
1989-95 Estates manager, Martin Retail Group (now TM Retail)
Professional memberships
Chartered Institute of Arbitrators; RICS
Interests
DIY; rugby; skiing; squash
Contact details
Game, Link House, Ellesfield Avenue, Bracknell RG12 8TB
Tel 01344 464000
Web www.game.uk.com
Direct tel 01344 464055
Mobile 07767 766606
Email vince.sibley@game.net

SIDDALL, Stephen
Campbell Hooper

Position
Partner – joint head of commercial property
Qualifications
LLB
Professional memberships
Law Society
Interests
Cycling; gardening; running; skiing
Contact details
Campbell Hooper, 35 Old Queen Street, London SW1H 9JD
Tel 020 7222 9070
Fax 020 7222 5591
Web www.campbellhooper.com
Direct tel 020 7654 5165
Mobile 07970 857872
Email stephensiddall@campbellhooper.com

SIDWELL, Andrew
GVA Grimley

Position
Partner – national healthcare business unit
Qualifications
MA (Cantab); FRICS
Career history
1993 Joined GVA Grimley
Professional memberships
Non-Administrative Receivers Association; RICS
Interests
Family; sport
Contact details
GVA Grimley, 3 Brindleyplace, Birmingham B1 2JB
Tel 0870 900 8990
Web www.gvagrimley.co.uk
Direct tel 0121 609 8410
Email andrew.sidwell@gvagrimley.co.uk

SIEGLE, Bill
Cluttons

Position
Partner – head of consultancy
Qualifications
FRICS
Professional memberships
RICS
Interests
Cricket; fishing; golf
Contact details
Cluttons, Portman House, 2 Portman Street, London W1H 6DU
Tel 020 7408 1010
Fax 020 7629 3263
Web www.cluttons.com
Email bsiegle@cluttons.com

SIERACKI, Dr Karen
KASPAR Associates

Position
Director
Qualifications
BA; MA; PhD; MRICS
Career history
1986-96 Director (property research), ESN Property Investments
Other roles
Research consultant, BH2; director, Investment Property Forum; council member, Urban Land Institute; editorial board member, *Briefings in Real Estate Finance*, *Journal of Property Finance & Investment* and *Journal of Property Research*
Professional memberships
American Real Estate Society; European Real Estate Society; Investment Property Forum; RICS; Society of Property Researchers; Urban Land Institute
Contact details
KASPAR Associates Ltd, 2 Ashbourne Court, Bretland Road, Tunbridge Wells TN4 8PF
Tel 01892 534293
Fax 01892 547399
Email kaspar@dial.pipex.com

SIERRA, Borja
FPDSavills

Position
Director – head of office, Madrid
Qualifications
MBA, International Business Studies
Professional memberships
Club Financiero Madrid; International Association of Facilities Management
Contact details
FPDSavills Ltd, Torres de Colon 2-19, Plaza de Colon, Madrid, Spain
Tel +34 91 310 1016
Fax +34 91 310 1024
Web www.fpdsavills.co.uk
Direct tel +34 91 310 1016
Mobile +34 61 052 1229
Email bsierra@fpdsavills.es

SIGRE, Sess
Turbervilles

Position
Senior partner
Qualifications
BA
Career history
1981 Admitted to Roll of Solicitors.
1975 Joined Turbervilles
Other roles
Life governor, Cancer Research

Professional memberships
Law Society
Interests
Art; food; martial arts; rugby; travel
Contact details
Turbervilles, 118 High Street, Uxbridge UB8 1JT
Tel 01895 201700
Fax 01895 273519
Web www.turbervilles.co.uk
Direct tel 01895 201731
Email sess.sigre@turbervilles.co.uk

SILBY, Philip
Matthews & Goodman
Position
Partner – head of agency division
Qualifications
BSc; MRICS
Career history
1982 Joined Matthews & Goodman.
1979-82 Conrad Ritblat
Professional memberships
Office Agents Society; RICS
Interests
Cycling; family; golf; music; rugby; running; squash
Contact details
Matthews & Goodman, Dorland House, 14-16 Regent Street, London SW1Y 4PH
Tel 020 7747 8847
Fax 020 7747 8848
Web www.matthews-goodman.co.uk
Direct tel 020 7747 3179
Mobile 07850 242145
Email psilby@matthews-goodman.co.uk

SILK, Phillip
ProLogis Developments
Position
First vice-president – development
Qualifications
MRICS
Interests
Field sports; rugby; wine
Contact details
ProLogis Developments Ltd, ProLogis House, 1 Monkspath Hall Road, Solihull B90 4FY
Tel 0121 224 8700
Fax 0121 224 8904
Web www.prologis.com
Email psilk@prologis.com

SILL, David
Aberdeen Property Investors
Position
Associate director
Qualifications
MRICS; Dip Est Man
Career history
1995 Joined Celexa Real Estate Investment Management (now Aberdeen Property Investors following 2001 acquisition).
1993-94 Investment property co-ordinator, SPP-LET International.
1985-93 Group estates manager, London & Edinburgh Trust.
1979-84 Senior management surveyor, Fletcher King.
1977-79 Farebrother Ellis.
1975-77 Student, Kingston Polytechnic College.
1972-75 Gooch & Wagstaff
Professional memberships
RICS
Contact details
Aberdeen Property Investors, Charles House, 5-11 Regent Street, London SW1Y 4LR
Tel 020 7747 1700
Fax 020 7839 7460
Web www.aberdeenpropertyinvestors.com
Direct tel 020 7747 1749
Mobile 07876 331749
Email david.sill@aberdeenpropertyinvestors.com

SILLERY, Steve
Bidwells Property Consultants
Position
Partner – head of planning
Qualifications
MA; MRTPI
Career history
Since 1987 Head of planning, Bidwells Property Consultants.
1974-87 Deputy planning officer, South Cambridgeshire District Council.
1968-74 Assistant planning officer, Cambridgeshire County Council
Other roles
Past chairman and current council member, Cambridge Forum for the Construction Industry
Contact details
Bidwells Property Consultants, Trumpington Road, Cambridge CB2 2LD
Tel 01223 841841
Fax 01223 845150
Web www.bidwells.co.uk
Email ssillery@bidwells.co.uk

SILVA, David
IBB Solicitors
Position
Partner – commercial property group
Qualifications
LLB
Career history
1996 Joined IBB; appointed partner in 1998.
1988-96 Frere Cholmeley Bischoff
Professional memberships
Law Society
Interests
Football
Contact details
IBB Solicitors, Lovell House, 271 High Street, London UB8 1LQ
Tel 01895 230941
Fax 01895 811926
Web www.ibblaw.co.uk
Direct tel 01895 207801
Email david.silva@ibblaw.co.uk

SILVER, Simon
Derwent Valley Holdings
Position
Property director
Professional memberships
Royal Academy of Arts; RIBA
Interests
Golf
Contact details
Derwent Valley Holdings plc, 25 Savile Row, London W1S 2ER
Tel 020 7659 3000
Fax 020 7659 3100
Web www.derwentvalley.co.uk
Direct fax 020 7659 3080
Email simon.silver@derwentvalley.co.uk

SILVER, Trevor
Akeler Developments
Position
Chief executive officer
Qualifications
CEng; MICE; MCIWEM
Career history
1988 Founding director, Akeler Developments; appointed managing director, then chief executive from 2001.
1987-88 Development executive, Baltic Developments, London.
1980-87 Associate partner, Mander & Marshall.
1974-80 Consulting civil engineer
Professional memberships
Chartered Institution of Water & Environmental Management; Institution of Civil Engineers
Interests
Sailing; shooting
Contact details
Akeler Developments Ltd, 7 Clifford Street, London W1S 2WE
Tel 020 7864 1800
Fax 020 7864 1801
Web www.akeler.com
Email trevors@akeler.com

S

SIMKIN, Richard
Kier Property

Position
Managing director
Contact details
Kier Property Ltd, Berkeley Square House, Berkeley Square, London W1J 6BD
Tel 020 7887 6200
Fax 020 7887 6299
Web www.kier.co.uk
Direct tel 020 7887 6276
Mobile 07831 680441
Email richard.simkin@kier.co.uk

SIMMONDS, Brigid
Business in Sport & Leisure

Position
Chief executive
Career history
Since 1992 Chief executive, Business in Sport & Leisure.
1986-91 Director of PR and marketing, Sargent & Potiriatis (architects).
1978-86 Officer, Women's Royal Army Corps
Other roles
Member of main board, Sport England; director, Central Council of Physical Recreation
Interests
Sport
Contact details
Business in Sport & Leisure, 17a Chartfield Avenue, London SW15 6DX
Tel 020 8780 2377
Fax 020 8788 2277
Web www.bisl.org
Mobile 07710 485119
Email brigid.simmonds@btconnect.com

SIMMONS, Elliot
Edwin Hill

Position
Partner
Qualifications
BSc Hons; MRICS
Contact details
Edwin Hill, St Johns House, Dartford DA1 2DR
Tel 01322 285588
Fax 01322 285599
Web www.edwinhill.co.uk
Email elliots@edwinhill.co.uk

SIMON, Lloyd
Dunlop Heywood Lorenz

Position
Head of national agency
Career history
1983 Joined Baker Lorenz (now Dunlop Heywood Lorenz); became full partner in 1994; head of agency since 2001
Interests
Architecture; art; horse racing; travel
Contact details
Dunlop Heywood Lorenz Ltd, 10 Queen Anne Street, London W1G 9LH
Tel 020 7636 7000
Fax 020 7636 7002
Web www.dhlproperty.co.uk
Direct tel 020 7299 7241
Mobile 07881 625629
Email ls@dhlproperty.co.uk

SIMPKIN, Andrew
Pannone & Partners

Position
Head of commercial property
Career history
Since 1978 Partner, Pannone & Partners.
1973-78 Partner, Ogden & Simpkin.
1972 Admitted to Roll of Solicitors
Other roles
Member, Council of City College, Manchester; board member, Arawak Housing Association
Professional memberships
Law Society
Interests
Diving/scuba diving; mountaineering; sailing
Contact details
Pannone & Partners, 123 Deansgate, Manchester M3 2BU
Tel 0161 909 3000
Fax 0161 909 4444
Web www.pannone.com
Direct tel 0161 909 4004
Direct fax 0161 909 4001
Email andrew.simpkin@pannone.co.uk

SIMPSON, Andrew
Dron & Wright

Position
Partner – investment agency
Qualifications
FRICS
Professional memberships
RICS
Contact details
Dron & Wright, 54 Conduit Street, London W1S 2YY
Tel 020 7891 2345
Fax 020 7543 0290
Web www.dronwright.co.uk
Direct tel 020 7534 0295
Mobile 07803 726242
Email andrewsimpson@dronwright.co.uk

SIMPSON, David
Caxtons

Position
Director
Qualifications
BSc; MRICS
Career history
1990 Founder member, Caxtons.
1984-1990 Cobbs/GA Commercial
Professional memberships
RICS
Contact details
Caxtons, 6 White Oak Square, Swanley BR8 7AG
Tel 01322 614771
Fax 01332 614382
Web www.caxtons.com
Email dsimpson@caxtons.com

SIMPSON, James
Edgerley Simpson Howe & Partners

Position
Partner
Contact details
Edgerley Simpson Howe & Partners, 39 Dover Street, London W1S 4NN
Tel 020 7499 6000
Fax 020 7499 9433
Web www.eshp.com
Email james@eshp.com

SIMPSON, Jeremy
Tushingham Moore

Position
Partner
Qualifications
BSc; FRICS; MBA
Professional memberships
RICS
Interests
Golf; mountaineering; rugby; tennis
Contact details
Tushingham Moore, Acresfield, St Ann's Square, Manchester M2 7HA
Tel 0161 833 1197
Fax 0161 833 1630
Web www.tushinghammoore.co.uk
Mobile 07768 857687
Email jeremy@tushinghammoore.co.uk

SIMS, John
iOG

Position
Chief executive
Career history
1986 Founded Industrial Ownership (now iOG) (a wholly owned subsidiary of Property Fund Management); responsible for extending

company's operations into areas where client investor demand has been established

Other roles

Chief executive, Property Fund Management

Interests

Gardening; photography; sailing; shooting

Contact details

iOG, Heron Place, 3 George Street, London W1U 3QG

Tel 020 7535 1818
Fax 020 7535 1819
Web www.iog.co.uk
Email johns@iog.co.uk

SINCLAIR, Chris
Chesterton International

Position

Director in charge, Birmingham office

Qualifications

FRICS

Career history

1990 Joined Chesterton in Birmingham office; became director in charge of Nottingham office in 1992 and of Birmingham office in 1997.
1989-90 Associate director, Richard Ellis, Sydney.
1975-89 Partner, Hallam Bracket, Nottingham

Contact details

Chesterton International, 84 Colmore Row, Birmingham B3 2HG

Tel 0121 200 3111
Fax 0121 200 2425
Web www.chesterton.co.uk
Direct tel 0121 606 2496
Mobile 07712 868426
Email chris.sinclair@chesterton.co.uk

SINCLAIR, Graham
East Anglian Chambers

Position

Barrister

Qualifications

LLB

Career history

1981 Joined East Anglian Chambers.
1979 Called to Bar

Other roles

Part-time chairman, Eastern Rent Assessment Panel and Leasehold Valuation Tribunal; director, Adroit Dispute Resolution, Norwich; director, Mediators in East Anglia; practises as general or commercial mediator; co-author, *Neighbours & the Law* (3rd edition, Sweet & Maxwell, 2001) and has devised and, with co-author William Upton, maintains online supplement to *Neighbours & the Law*

Interests

Subscribing member, British Film Institute and CAMRA; occasional hill-walker and Munro-bagger

Professional memberships

Academy of Experts; Professional Negligence Bar Association; Society for Computers & Law

Contact details

East Anglian Chambers, 15 The Close, Norwich NR1 4DZ

Tel 01603 617351
Fax 01603 751400
Web www.ealaw.co.uk
Email gks@adroit-adr.com

SINGH, Jag
Marylebone Warwick Balfour Group

Position

Main board director

Contact details

Marylebone Warwick Balfour Group plc, 1 West Garden Place, London W2 2AQ

Tel 020 7706 2121
Fax 020 7706 8181
Web www.mwb.co.uk
Email jsingh@mwb.co.uk

SINGLETON, Peter
Edward Rushton International

Position

Director – Edward Rushton

Qualifications

BA; MRICS; SIOR

Contact details

Edward Rushton International, 81 Fountain Street, Manchester M2 2EE

Tel 0161 834 1814
Fax 0161 839 0152
Web www.edwardrushton.com
Direct tel 0161 238 6264
Direct fax 0161 834 7348
Email peter.singleton@kingsturge.co.uk

SISKIND, Ed
Goldman Sachs International

Position

Head of European real estate

Contact details

Goldman Sachs International, Peterborough Court, 133 Fleet Street, London EC4A 2PP

Tel 020 7774 1000
Fax 020 7774 4477
Email ed.siskind@gs.com

SIVEWRIGHT, David
Grosvenor

Position

Senior development manager

Qualifications

MRICS

Career history

1999-2002 Director, Aberdeen Property Asset Management.
1986-99 Fund manager, Royal London Asset Management

Professional memberships

RICS

Contact details

Grosvenor Ltd, 22 Alva Street, Edinburgh EH2 4PY

Tel 0131 225 5775
Fax 0131 225 1955
Web www.grosvenor.com
Email david.sivewright@grosvenor.com

SKELSTON, Rob
Brixton Investments

Position

Director – development and lettings

Qualifications

BSc; MRICS

Professional memberships

RICS

Interests

Golf; skiing; travel

Contact details

Brixton Investments Ltd, 50 Berkeley Street, London W1J 8BX

Tel 020 7399 4500
Fax 020 7399 4550
Web www.brixton.plc.uk
Direct tel 020 7399 4516
Mobile 07884 116402
Email robskelston@brixton.plc.uk

SKELTON, Peter
Lambert Smith Hampton

Position

Director – head of national agency

Qualifications

BSc; MRICS

Career history

1982 Joined Lambert Smith Hampton.
1979-82 Joshua Bury Earle & Co

Professional memberships

British Council for Offices; Office Agents Society; RICS

Interests

Art; gardening; golf

Contact details

Lambert Smith Hampton Ltd, 79 Mosley Street, Manchester M2 3LQ

Tel 0161 228 6411
Fax 0161 228 7354
Web www.lsh.co.uk

Mobile 07702 883824
Email pskelton@lsh.co.uk

SKETCHLEY, Timothy
Cushman & Wakefield Healey & Baker

Position
Partner – head of investment
Qualifications
MA (Cantab); FRICS
Career history
1973 Joined Cushman & Wakefield Healey & Baker; Cushman & Wakefield Healey & Baker VOF in Amsterdam 1974-87
Other roles
Member of firm's international board
Professional memberships
British Council for Offices; Investment Property Forum; RICS
Interests
Rugby; sailing; swimming; tennis
Contact details
Cushman & Wakefield Healey & Baker, 43-45 Portman Square, London W1A 3BG
Tel 020 7935 5000
Fax 020 7152 5360
Web www.cushwake.com
Direct tel 020 7152 5177
Direct fax 020 7152 5382
Mobile 07764 398177
Email tim.sketchley@eur.cushwake.com

SKINNER, Stephen
Edward Symmons & Partners

Position
Partner
Qualifications
BSc Hons; MRICS
Career history
Since 1992 Partner, Edward Symmons & Partners.
1990-92 Director/shareholder, Hutchinson Commercial.
1984-90 LS Vail & Son: associate from 1989
Professional memberships
Non-Administrative Receivers Association; RICS
Interests
Cycling; rugby; wine
Contact details
Edward Symmons & Partners, Park House, Franconia Drive, Southampton SO16 0YW
Tel 023 8074 1212
Fax 023 8074 1454
Web www.edwardsymmons.com
Mobile 07979 541229
Email steve.skinner@edwardsymmons.com

SLADE, David
Westfield Shoppingtowns

Position
Director of leasing
Other roles
Director (leasing, new projects), Australia
Contact details
Westfield Shoppingtowns Ltd, MidCity Place, 58-71 High Holborn, London WC1R 4TP
Tel 020 7734 2121
Fax 020 7734 6545
Web www.westfield.com
Email david.slade@westfield-uk.com

SLADE, John
Slade & Co

Position
Director
Qualifications
BSc Hons, Est Man; FRICS
Career history
2002 Founded Slade & Co (led management buyout of Hamptons Commercial).
1997-2002 Managing director, Hamptons Commercial.
1988-97 Richard Ellis: partner/director, head of Japanese business from 1991, then chief executive (City office) from 1992.
1984-88 Director (investment), Fletcher King.
1983-84 Associate (investment), J Trevor & Sons.
1979-83 Investment surveyor, Richard Ellis
Other roles
Board director, Reading Real Estate Foundation
Professional memberships
Broad St Ward Club; Freeman of the City of London; Investment Property Forum; RICS
Interests
Family; golf; rugby; skiing; squash; tennis; travel
Contact details
Slade & Co, 3 Charles Street, London W1J 5DD
Tel 020 7499 3737
Fax 020 7499 3800
Email sladej@slade-co.com

SLADE, Michael
Helical Bar

Position
Managing director
Qualifications
BSc, Est Man; FRICS; FSVA
Contact details
Helical Bar plc, 11-15 Farm Street, London W1J 5RS
Tel 020 7629 0113
Fax 020 7408 1666
Web www.helical.co.uk
Email slade@helical.co.uk

SLATER, John
Crown Office Chambers

Position
Barrister
Qualifications
QC
Contact details
Crown Office Chambers, 2 Crown Office Row, London EC4Y 7HJ
Tel 020 7797 8100
Fax 020 7797 8101
Web www.crownofficechambers.com
Direct tel 020 7797 6245
Direct fax 020 7583 5014
Mobile 07770 998018
Email jslaterqc@crownofficechambers.com

SLOGGETT, Brian
GL Hearn

Position
Managing director
Qualifications
BA, Econ; MRICS
Career history
1987 Joined GL Hearn.
1986-87 Drivers Jonas, West End.
1985-86 London Borough of Camden.
1981-85 London City & Westcliffe
Professional memberships
RICS
Interests
Football; golf; tennis; travel
Contact details
GL Hearn Ltd, Leonard House, 5-7 Marshalsea Road, London SE1 1EP
Tel 020 7450 4000
Fax 020 7450 4010
Web www.glhearn.com
Mobile 07768 381815
Email brian_sloggett@glhearn.com

SMALL, Jonathan
Falcon Chambers

Position
Barrister
Contact details
Falcon Chambers, Falcon Court, London EC4Y 1AA
Tel 020 7353 2484
Fax 020 7353 1261
Web www.falcon-chambers.com
Email small@falcon-chambers.com

SMALLWOOD, Madeleine
Denton Wilde Sapte

Position
Partner – commercial property

Career history
Since 1998 Partner, Denton Wilde Sapte, London.
1991-98 Fox & Gibbons: partner from 1994 and head of property department from 1996.
1989-91 Practised in the City with niche property firm.
1988 Admitted to Roll of Solicitors
Other roles
Member of firm's development sector group, Middle Eastern group and energy and infrastructure sector group
Professional memberships
Law Society; Women in Property
Interests
Aviation; sport; travel
Contact details
Denton Wilde Sapte, 1 Fleet Place, London EC4M 7WS
Tel 020 7246 7000
Fax 020 7246 7777
Web www.dentonwildesapte.com
Direct tel 020 7320 7719
Email mas@dentonwildesapte.com

SMALLWOOD, Peter
Matthews & Goodman
Position
Chairman
Qualifications
FRICS
Career history
1971 Joined Matthews & Goodman.
1969-71 Deputy divisional estates surveyor, Bass Charrington.
1963-69 GH Bayley & Sons, Cheltenham
Professional memberships
RICS
Contact details
Matthews & Goodman, Dorland House, 14-16 Regent Street, London SW1Y 4PH
Tel 020 7747 8847
Fax 020 7747 8848
Web www.matthews-goodman.co.uk
Direct tel 020 7747 3118
Email psmallwood@matthews-goodman.co.uk

SMEE, Richard
Ernst & Young
Position
Head of real estate, hospitality and construction
Qualifications
ACA
Other roles
Trustee, Civic Trust
Professional memberships
Institute of Chartered Accountants in England & Wales
Contact details
Ernst & Young LLP, 1 More London Place, London SE1 2AF
Tel 020 7951 2000
Fax 020 7951 1345
Web www.ey.com/uk
Direct tel 020 7951 4646
Direct fax 020 7951 3411
Mobile 07774 646821
Email rsmee@uk.ey.com

SMIDDY, Chris
Aitchison Raffety
Position
Associate director
Career history
2000 Aitchison Raffety: appointed as associate to manage Watford commercial office.
1993-2000 Lambert Smith Hampton.
1985-93 Gardner Smiddy & Co, Watford (own company).
1978-85 Gordon Hudson & Co: became associate in charge of Hemel Hempstead commercial office in 1983
Professional memberships
Property Consultants Society
Interests
Motor sports; motorcycling
Contact details
Aitchison Raffety Ltd, 131 The Parade, Watford WD17 1NA
Tel 01923 210733
Fax 01923 698216
Web www.argroup.co.uk
Direct tel 01923 698212
Email chris.smiddy@argroup.co.uk

SMITH, Andrew
Aberdeen Property Investors
Position
Director – head of investment strategy
Qualifications
BA Hons, Dip Surv; ACII; AMSI
Career history
1998-2002 Director (European property research), Henderson Global Investors.
1991-98 Property research manager, AMP Asset Management.
1986-91 Pearl Assurance
Other roles
Member, Bank of England property forum; member, National Retail Planning Forum research group; committee member, Society of Property Researchers; editorial board member, *Journal of Property Investment & Finance*
Professional memberships
Chartered Insurance Institute; Investment Property Forum; RICS; Securities Institute; Society of Property Researchers
Contact details
Aberdeen Property Investors, Charles House, 5-11 Regent Street, London SW1Y 4LR
Tel 020 7747 1700
Fax 020 7839 7460
Web www.aberdeenpropertyinvestors.com
Direct tel 020 7747 1733
Email
andrew.smith@aberdeenpropertyinvestors.com

SMITH, Andrew
LSM Partners
Position
Managing director
Qualifications
FRICS
Career history
1989-91 Teacher Marks Deal.
1987-89 Bidwells.
1971-87 Valuation Office, Inland Revenue
Professional memberships
Institute of Directors; RICS
Contact details
LSM Partners, 25 James Street, London W1U 1DU
Tel 020 7616 0100
Fax 020 7616 0101
Web www.lsmpartners.co.uk
Email asmith@lsmpartners.co.uk

SMITH, Brian
Adams Childrenswear
Position
Head of property
Interests
Cinema; travel
Contact details
Adams Childrenswear Ltd, Attleborough House, Townsend Drive, Nuneaton CV11 6RU
Tel 024 7635 1000
Fax 024 7634 5583
Web www.adams.co.uk
Email brian.smith@adams.co.uk

SMITH, Brian
Browne Jacobson
Position
Managing partner
Qualifications
LLB
Career history
1997 Joined Browne Jacobson as partner and head of property; managing partner since 2001.
1991-97 Partner and head of commercial

property, Wilde Sapte.
1989-91 Head of legal (property division), Costain Group.
1977 Admitted to Roll of Solicitors

Other roles
Member, Law Society's planning panel

Professional memberships
Land Institute; Law Society; RTPI; UK Environmental Law Association

Interests
Cycling; golf; sailing

Contact details
Browne Jacobson, 44 Castle Gate, Nottingham NG1 7BJ
Tel 0115 976 6000
Fax 0115 947 5246
Web www.brownejacobson.com
Direct tel 0115 976 6268
Mobile 07979 536991
Email Bsmith@brownej.co.uk

SMITH, Catriona
Penningtons

Position
Partner, head of property, London

Qualifications
BA (Cantab)

Career history
1975 Joined Penningtons; made partner in 1982 and appointed head of property department in 2000.
1970-74 BAA

Professional memberships
Clarity

Interests
Food; reading; wine

Contact details
Penningtons, Bucklersbury House, 83 Cannon Street, London EC4N 8PE
Tel 020 7457 3000
Fax 020 7457 3240
Web www.penningtons.co.uk
Email smithch@penningtons.co.uk

SMITH, Christopher
Hammerson

Position
Director of corporate affairs

Contact details
Hammerson plc, 100 Park Lane, London W1K 7AR
Tel 020 7887 1000
Fax 020 7887 1010
Web www.hammerson.co.uk
Direct fax 020 7887 1850
Email csmith@hammerson.co.uk

SMITH, David
Landmark Chambers

Position
Barrister

Professional memberships
Planning & Environment Bar Association

Contact details
Landmark Chambers, 4 Breams Buildings, London EC4A 1AQ
Tel 020 7430 1221
Fax 020 7421 1399
Web www.landmarkchambers.co.uk
Email clerks@landmarkchambers.co.uk

SMITH, Donald
GVA Grimley

Position
Finance director

Qualifications
BSc Hons; CA

Career history
1997 Joined GVA Grimley.
1994-97 British Rail privatisation team.
1981-94 Price Waterhouse

Contact details
GVA Grimley, 10 Stratton Street, London W1J 8JR
Tel 0870 900 8990
Fax 020 7911 2560
Web www.gvagrimley.co.uk
Direct tel 020 7911 2364
Direct fax 020 7911 2438
Email donald.smith@gvagrimley.co.uk

SMITH, Douglas
CB Richard Ellis

Position
Chairman – Scotland

Career history
1981 Joined Insignia Richard Ellis (now CB Richard Ellis).
1977-81 James Barr & Son

Contact details
CB Richard Ellis, Pacific House, 70 Wellington Street, Glasgow G2 6UA
Tel 0141 204 7666
Fax 0141 306 0141
Web www.cbre.com
Email douglas.smith@cbre.com

SMITH, Douglas
TP Bennett

Position
Partner

Career history
1988 Joined TP Bennett as partner; managing partner since 1999

Professional memberships
Institute of Directors; RIBA

Interests
Family; football; pets; skiing; travel

Contact details
TP Bennett Ltd, 1 America Street, London SE1 0NE
Tel 020 7208 2000
Fax 020 7208 2020
Web www.tpbennett.co.uk
Direct tel 020 7208 2451
Direct fax 020 7208 2022
Email dougsmith@tpbennett.co.uk

SMITH, Geoffrey
Edmund Kirby

Position
Partner

Qualifications
FRICS

Contact details
Edmund Kirby, India Buildings, Water Street, Liverpool L2 0TZ
Tel 0151 236 4552
Fax 0151 236 4024
Web www.edmundkirby.co.uk
Email geoffreysmith@edmundkirby.co.uk

SMITH, Grahame
Arcadia Group

Position
Head of property

Qualifications
BA; MRICS

Professional memberships
RICS

Contact details
Arcadia Group Ltd, Colegrave House, 68-70 Berners Street, London W1T 3NL
Tel 020 7636 8040
Web www.arcadia.co.uk
Direct fax 020 7927 3777
Mobile 07711 797207
Email grahame.smith@arcadiagroup.co.uk

SMITH, Ken
Castlemore Securities

Position
Finance director

Qualifications
FCA

Contact details
Castlemore Securities Ltd, Cedar Court, 221 Hagley Road, Halesowen B63 1ED
Tel 0121 585 4444
Fax 0121 585 4441
Web www.castlemore.co.uk

Direct tel 0121 585 4404
Direct fax 0121 585 4442
Mobile 0774 8776109
Email ken@castlemore.co.uk

SMITH, Malcolm
GVA Grimley

Position
Partner
Contact details
GVA Grimley, 3 Brindleyplace, Birmingham B1 2JB
Tel 0870 900 8990
Fax 0121 609 8314
Web www.gvagrimley.co.uk
Email malcolm.smith@gvagrimley.co.uk

SMITH, Martin
Finers Stephens Innocent

Position
Partner – head of property finance
Career history
2001 Joined Finers Stephens Innocent.
1999-2001 Head of property department, Wildes.
1997-99 Cameron McKenna.
1992 Admitted to Roll of Solicitors.
1990-97 Gouldens
Contact details
Finers Stephens Innocent, 179 Great Portland Street, London W1W 5LS
Tel 020 7323 4000
Fax 020 7344 5600
Web www.finersstephensinnocent.com
Direct tel 020 7344 5596
Direct fax 020 7580 7069
Mobile 07971 206957
Email msmith@fsilaw.co.uk

SMITH, Michael
Baker & McKenzie

Position
Head of property
Qualifications
LLB
Contact details
Baker & McKenzie, 100 New Bridge Street, London EC4V 6JA
Tel 0207 919 1000
Fax 020 7919 1999
Web www.bakernet.com
Email michael.smith@bakernet.com

SMITH, Murray
Dunphys

Position
Managing director – property valuation
Contact details
Dunphys, York House, Montague Road, London TW3 1JZ
Tel 020 8577 5172
Fax 020 8577 2219
Web www.dunphys.cpd.co.uk
Email murray.smith@dunphys.co.uk

SMITH, Paul
Hodnett Martin Smith

Position
Partner
Qualifications
BSc Hons; FRICS; ACIArb
Career history
Since 1987 Partner, Hodnett Martin Smith.
1982-87 Surveyor/associate, John D Wood
Professional memberships
Chartered Institute of Arbitrators; RICS
Contact details
Hodnett Martin Smith Ltd, Charles House, 5-11 Regent Street, London SW1Y 4LR
Tel 020 7839 8181
Fax 020 7839 8069
Web www.hodnettmartinsmith.com
Email paulsmith@hodms.co.uk

SMITH, Peter
Lamb & Edge

Position
Senior partner
Qualifications
BSc, Est Man; FRICS
Career history
1971 Joined Lamb & Edge
Other roles
Member of Crown Estate's valuation committee; member, RICS panel for arbitration and independent expert role in North of England; Crown agent for marine estates in North East
Professional memberships
RICS
Contact details
Lamb & Edge, Yorkshire Chambers, 112-118 Pilgrim Street, Newcastle upon Tyne NE1 6LL
Tel 0191 261 2361
Fax 0191 232 6374
Web www.lambedge.co.uk
Direct tel 0191 269 0503
Email peter.s@lambedge.co.uk

SMITH, Richard
Nicholson Graham & Jones

Position
Partner
Qualifications
BA (Cantab)
Career history
1983 Joined Nicholson Graham & Jones; promoted to partner in 1985.
1980-83 Lane & Partners.
1976 Admitted to Roll of Solicitors.
1974-80 Durant Piesse
Professional memberships
BPF; City Property Owners Association; Law Society; Westminster Property Owners Association
Contact details
Nicholson Graham & Jones, 110 Cannon Street, London EC4N 6AR
Tel 020 7648 9000
Fax 020 7648 9001
Web www.ngj.co.uk
Direct tel 020 7360 8200
Email richard.smith@ngj.co.uk

SMITH, Richard
Walker Singleton

Position
Director – head of commercial
Contact details
Walker Singleton, Property House, Lister Lane, Halifax HX1 5AS
Tel 01422 430000
Fax 01422 430010
Web www.walker-singleton.co.uk
Email richards@walker-singleton.co.uk

SMITH, Rob
Davis Langdon & Everest

Position
Senior partner
Qualifications
MRICS; Dip Building Econ
Career history
1975 Joined Davis Langdon & Everest; became London managing partner in 1997 and Southern region managing partner in 2001; now senior partner
Other roles
Director of RIBA professional services board; external examiner for Architectural Association and Brighton University
Professional memberships
RICS
Interests
Keep fit; sailing; skiing; sport
Contact details
Davis Langdon & Everest, MidCity Place, 58-71 High Holborn, Red Lion Street, London WC1R 4TP
Tel 020 7497 9000
Web www.davislangdon.com

S

Direct tel 020 7061 7000
Direct fax 020 7061 7003
Email rob.smith@davislangdon-uk.com

SMITH, Stephen
AXA Real Estate Investment Managers

Position
Managing director
Contact details
AXA Real Estate Investment Managers Ltd, 7 Newgate Street, London EC1A 7HD
Tel 020 7003 1000
Fax 020 7575 8585
Web www.axa-im.co.uk
Direct tel 020 7367 8100
Email stephen.smith@axa-reim.co.uk

SMITH, Steven
Haslams

Position
Senior partner
Qualifications
BSc, Est Man; FRICS; FCIArb; FBEng
Career history
1981 Joined Haslams; became equity partner in 1986 and senior partner in 1999.
1979-81 Senior valuer, Reading Borough Council.
1976-79 Valuer, Leicestershire County Council
Other roles
Past member, RICS practice panel, RICS working parties and RICS Berkshire, Bedfordshire and Oxfordshire branch committee; registered mediator with CEDR and RICS
Professional memberships
Arbitration Club; Centre for Effective Dispute Resolution; Chartered Institute of Arbitrators; Non-Administrative Receivers Association; Property Peoples Network; Rating Surveyors Association; RICS
Interests
Antiques; music; reading; sport
Contact details
Haslams, 156 Friar Street, Reading RG1 1HH
Tel 0118 960 1010
Fax 0118 960 1022
Web www.haslams-online.co.uk
Direct tel 0118 960 1027
Email ss@haslams-surveyors.co.uk

SMITHER, Warwick
Cheetham & Mortimer

Position
Partner – head of in-town retail
Other roles
Vice-president and first team manager, Ben Rhydding Hockey Club
Interests
Hockey
Contact details
Cheetham & Mortimer, 17 St Ann's Square, Manchester M2 7PW
Tel 0161 832 3375
Fax 0161 832 0453
Mobile 07990 576966
Email wsmither@cheetham-mortimer.com

SMYLIE, Chris
Maclay Murray & Spens

Position
Partner – head of environmental and planning
Contact details
Maclay Murray & Spens, 3 Glenfinlas Street, Edinburgh EH3 6AQ
Tel 0131 226 5196
Fax 0131 226 3174
Web www.mms.co.uk
Email chris.smylie@mms.co.uk

SMYTH, Robert
Burges Salmon

Position
Partner – chair of environmental unit
Qualifications
BSc Hons, Econ
Career history
1983 Joined Burges Salmon; previously practised for four years in commercial property and town and country planning with DJ Freeman & Co in London.
1978 Admitted to Roll of Solicitors
Other roles
Steering group member, Western Partnership for Sustainable Development; co-opted member of Country Land & Business Association legal and parliamentary committee; Law Society's representative on British Standards Institute technical committee E/S2, contributing to new international standard BS ISO 140015; business representative in Bristol's Local Agenda 21 strategy process; director, Circomedia (Bristol circus school); director, Cycle West
Professional memberships
Society for Advanced Legal Studies
Contact details
Burges Salmon, Narrow Quay House, Narrow Quay, Bristol BS1 4AH
Tel 0117 939 2000
Fax 0117 902 4400
Web www.burges-salmon.com
Direct tel 0117 939 2224
Email bob.smyth@burges-salmon.com

SNELLING, Tony
Dunlop Heywood Lorenz

Position
Director
Contact details
Dunlop Heywood Lorenz Ltd, 38 Bow Lane, London EC4M 9AY
Tel 020 7489 1400
Fax 020 7248 4053
Web www.dhlproperty.co.uk
Email anps@dhlproperty.co.uk

SNOW, John
Knight Frank

Position
Partner – head of central London offices
Career history
1980 Joined Knight Frank; appointed associate partner in 1985, partner in 1986, head of West End offices in 1992 and head of central London offices in 1999.
1977-80 Davis & Co
Other roles
Partner responsible for Knight Frank's strategic alliance with Grubb & Ellis (2000)
Interests
Classic cars; golf; tennis
Contact details
Knight Frank LLP, 20 Hanover Square, London W1S 1HZ
Tel 020 7629 8171
Fax 020 7493 4114
Web www.knightfrank.com
Direct tel 020 7861 1190
Direct fax 020 7861 1358
Mobile 07770 965661
Email john.snow@knightfrank.com

SOBER, Phillip
Liberty International

Position
Consultant
Qualifications
FCA; FRSA
Career history
1985-90 Senior partner, Stoy Hayward
Other roles
Former non-executive director, Liberty International; trustee of Royal Opera House Trust (1985-91); Crown Estate commissioner (1983-94); chairman of accounting standards committee, BPF (1976-83)
Professional memberships
Institute of Chartered Accountants in England & Wales; Royal Society of Arts
Interests
Art; golf; opera

Contact details
Liberty International plc, 40 Broadway, London SW1H 0BT
Tel 020 7960 1200
Fax 020 7960 1333
Direct tel 020 7937 8217
Mobile 07836 761270
Email viviphil@aol.com

SOLLEY, Ian
Dunedin Property

Position
Director
Qualifications
BSc; MRICS
Career history
Since 2001 Director, Dunedin Property Asset Management.
1999-2001 Founder director, Retail Success Asset Management.
1998-99 Director, Colliers Erdman Lewis.
1997-98 Asset manager, Dusco Asset Management.
1995-97 Partner (management), Strutt & Parker.
1987-95 Director (shopping centre management), Nelson Bakewell.
1985-87 Hillier Parker
Professional memberships
British Council of Shopping Centres; RICS
Contact details
Dunedin Property Ltd, 27 Dover Street, London W1S 4DY
Tel 020 7495 1011
Fax 020 7495 1044
Web www.dunedinproperty.co.uk
Email isolley@dunedinproperty.co.uk

SOLOMON, Jonathan
Clifford Chance

Position
Partner
Career history
Since 2000 Partner, Clifford Chance.
1995-2000 Partner, Norton Rose
Contact details
Clifford Chance, 10 Upper Bank Street, London E14 5JJ
Tel 020 7600 1000
Fax 020 7600 5555
Web www.cliffordchance.com
Direct tel 020 7006 4024
Email jonathan.solomon@cliffordchance.com

SOLOMONS, Alan
Lambert Smith Hampton

Position
Regional chief executive – North
Qualifications
FRICS
Professional memberships
RICS
Contact details
Lambert Smith Hampton Ltd, 79 Mosley Street, Manchester M2 3LQ
Tel 0161 228 6411
Fax 0161 228 7354
Web www.lsh.co.uk
Email asolomons@lsh.co.uk

SOMMERVILLE, Tom
Rogers Chapman

Position
Divisional director – airport property services
Qualifications
FRICS
Career history
Since 1995 Rogers Chapman.
1973-95 Aviation property, BOAC
Other roles
Supports Heathrow airline operators committee in property matters including regulatory issues
Interests
Theatre; travel
Contact details
Rogers Chapman plc, Grantley House, 9 Park Lane, Cranford, Heathrow TW5 9RW
Tel 020 8759 4141
Fax 020 8759 5367
Web www.rogerschapman.co.uk
Direct tel 020 8283 2563
Mobile 07788 188868
Email tom.sommerville@rogerschapman.co.uk

SONDEN, Erik
Fountain Capital Partners

Position
Partner
Qualifications
DHS (Stockholm School of Economics)
Career history
2000-02 Managing director (head of real estate investment banking – advisory, Europe), Deutsche Bank, Paris & London.
1995-2000 European director/head of investment department/member of European investment board, Jones Lang LaSalle, Paris.
1989-95 Founder and chief executive, Nordic Property Brussels.
1989-95 Managing director, Swedish International Property Association, Brussels & Paris.
1985-89 Head of real estate financing, PK Banken Frankfurt/M&PK Banke, Luxembourg
Contact details
Fountain Capital Partners, Claridge House, 32 Davies Street, London W1K 4ND
Tel 020 7647 2777
Fax 020 7647 2799
Web www.fountaincapitalpartners.com
Email erik.sonden@fountaincp.com

SORENSEN, Philip
CIT Group

Position
Legal director
Qualifications
BA Hons; MSc, Construction Law & Arbitration
Career history
1986-99 Macfarlanes.
1984-86 Sears, Tooth & Co
Contact details
CIT Group plc, 8-10 Bourdon Street, London W1K 3PD
Tel 020 7667 7766
Fax 020 7667 7770
Web www.cit.co.uk
Direct fax 020 7667 7759
Email ps@cit.co.uk

SOUTHAM, Roger
Chainbow Holdings

Position
Managing director
Qualifications
BSc Hons; FRICS
Career history
1989 Founded Chainbow.
1987-89 Senior development executive, London Shop.
1984-87 Estates surveyor, Speciality Shops
Other roles
RICS national junior organisation chairman (1993-94); RICS general council member (1990-95); RICS access committee chairman (1993-95); member, BPF stamp duty committee (2002)
Professional memberships
British Council of Shopping Centres; BPF; Investment Property Forum; RICS; Worshipful Company of Chartered Surveyors
Interests
Cinema; cooking; golf; rugby; skiing
Contact details
Chainbow Holdings plc, Hope House, 45 Great Peter Street, London SW1P 3LT
Tel 020 7222 0220
Fax 020 7976 7252
Web www.chainbow.co.uk
Mobile 07919 444968
Email rogersoutham@chainbow.co.uk

SOUTHORN, Liz
Richards Butler

Position
Partner – head of licensing unit
Qualifications
MA, Jurisprudence
Career history
Since 1993 Partner and head of licensing unit, Richards Butler.
1988-93 Partner and head of licensing, Penningtons
Contact details
Richards Butler, Beaufort House, 15 St Botolph Street, London EC3A 7JJ
Tel 020 7247 6555
Fax 020 7247 5091
Web www.richardsbutler.com
Email es@richardsbutler.com

SPACK, Harvey
Harvey Spack Field

Position
Consultant
Contact details
Harvey Spack Field, 33 Bruton Street, London W1J 6QU
Tel 020 7629 9663
Fax 020 7491 1964
Web www.harveyspackfield.co.uk
Email harris-taylor@harveyspackfield.co.uk

SPANSWICK, John
Bovis Lend Lease

Position
Chairman and chief executive
Contact details
Bovis Lend Lease Ltd, Bovis House, 142 Northolt Road, Harrow HA2 0EE
Tel 020 8271 8000
Fax 020 8271 8018
Web www.bovislendlease.com
Direct tel 020 8271 8281
Direct fax 020 8271 8109
Mobile 07702 285649
Email john.spanswick@eu.bovislendlease.com

SPEAIGHT, Anthony
4 Pump Court

Position
Barrister
Qualifications
QC
Contact details
4 Pump Court (Chambers of Christopher Moger QC & David Friedman QC), London EC4Y 7AN
Tel 020 7842 5555
Fax 020 7583 2036
Web www.4pumpcourt.com
Email aspeaight@4pumpcourt.com

SPEEDIE, Andrew
Aberdeen Property Investors International

Position
Finance director
Qualifications
BAdmin; CA
Professional memberships
Institute of Chartered Accountants of Scotland
Contact details
Aberdeen Property Investors International Ltd, Charles House, 5-11 Regent Street, London SW1Y 4LR
Tel 020 7747 1700
Web www.aberdeenpropertyinvestors.com
Direct tel 0141 306 7439
Mobile 07775 792046
Email
andy.speedie@aberdeenpropertyinvestors.com

SPEIRS, Simon
Osborne Clarke

Position
Partner
Qualifications
MA
Career history
1984-86 Solicitor, Imperial Group.
1982-84 Stanley Wasbrough, Bristol.
1982 Admitted to Roll of Solicitors.
1980-82 Veale Benson, Bristol
Other roles
Main board director, James Smith Estates
Professional memberships
Bristol Law Society; Law Society
Interests
Sailing; tennis; walking
Contact details
Osborne Clarke, 2 Temple Back East, Bristol BS1 6EG
Tel 0117 917 3000
Fax 0117 917 3005
Web www.osborneclarke.com
Direct tel 0117 917 3222
Direct fax 0117 917 3223
Mobile 07831 192418
Email simon.speirs@osborneclarke.com

SPENCER, Antony
Anthony Green & Spencer

Position
Partner
Qualifications
BSc, Est Man; MRICS
Professional memberships
RICS
Contact details
Anthony Green & Spencer Ltd, 7 Manchester Square, London W1U 3PG
Tel 020 7935 2335
Fax 020 7935 3586
Email ais@ags.uk.com

SPENCER, David
King Sturge

Position
Partner in charge, Swindon
Qualifications
FRICS
Professional memberships
RICS
Interests
Cricket; golf
Contact details
King Sturge, Berkeley House, 9 Milton Road, Swindon SN1 5JE
Tel 01793 533155
Fax 01793 618873
Web www.kingsturge.com
Mobile 07970 610207
Email david.spencer@kingsturge.co.uk

SPENCER, Irene
Vail Williams

Position
Partner – business space
Professional memberships
Institute of Directors
Interests
Reading; running
Contact details
Vail Williams, Meridians House, 7 Ocean Way, Southampton SO14 3TJ
Tel 0238 082 0900
Fax 0238 082 0950
Web www.vailwilliams.com
Mobile 07768 722104
Email ispencer@vailwilliams.com

SPENCER, Lloyd
Lambert Smith Hampton

Position
Director – head of Luton office
Contact details
Lambert Smith Hampton Ltd, 26-28 Stuart Street, Luton LU1 2SW
Tel 01582 450444
Fax 01582 400362
Web www.lsh.co.uk
Email lspencer@lsh.co.uk

SPENCER, Mike
Pizza Hut

Position
Head of equity acquisitions
Contact details
Pizza Hut, 1 Imperial Place, Elstree Way, Borehamwood WD6 1JN
Tel 020 8732 9000
Fax 020 8732 9001
Web www.pizzahut.co.uk
Direct tel 020 8732 9373
Direct fax 020 8953 1909
Mobile 07773 326582
Email mike.spencer@pizzahut.co.uk

SPICE, John
Bidwells Property Consultants

Position
Partner – head of business space agency
Qualifications
BSc; MRICS
Contact details
Bidwells Property Consultants, Trumpington Road, Cambridge CB2 2LD
Tel 01223 841841
Fax 01223 845150
Web www.bidwells.co.uk
Direct tel 01473 617714
Mobile 07850 136409
Email jspice@bidwells.co.uk

SPIES, Michael
Tishman Speyer Properties UK

Position
Senior managing director – Europe
Career history
1989 Joined Tishman Speyer Properties. Previously executive vice-president, New York City Public Development Corp
Other roles
Chairman, Tishman Speyer's investment committee
Contact details
Tishman Speyer Properties UK Ltd, Millbank Tower, 21-24 Millbank, London SW1P
Tel 020 7333 2400
Fax 020 7333 2500
Web www.tishmanspeyer.com
Email mspies@tishmanspeyer.com

SPILLER, Geoff
Glenny

Position
Managing partner
Qualifications
BSc; FRICS
Career history
1981-82 Associate, Edward Symmons & Partners.
1974-81 Edwards Bigwood & Bewley (now part of Chestertons).
1973-74 Donaldsons.
1971-72 Greater London Council
Professional memberships
RICS
Interests
Food; sport; travel
Contact details
Glenny, Glenny House, Southfields Business Park, Fenton Way, Basildon SS15 6TD
Tel 01268 540771
Fax 01268 540772
Web www.glenny.co.uk
Mobile 07768 070250
Email g.spiller@glenny.co.uk

SPINNEY, Ronald
Hammerson

Position
Non-executive chairman
Qualifications
FRICS
Career history
1993-99 Joined Hammerson as chief executive; non-executive chairman since 1999.
1976-92 Joint managing director and deputy chairman, Greycoat.
1970-76 Executive director, Sterling Land.
1966-70 Manager (property department), Canada Life Assurance Co
Other roles
Chairman, Hanover Property Unit Trust; chairman, London First; chairman, European Public Real Estate Association; non-executive director, Rentokil Initial; non-executive director, Fuller Smith & Turner; non-executive director, Homestyle Group; past president, BPF; Crown Estate commissioner; chairman, Unicorn Children's Centre; patron, National Youth Ballet
Professional memberships
BPF; RICS
Interests
Architecture; music; sport
Contact details
Hammerson plc, 100 Park Lane, London W1K 7AR
Tel 020 7887 1000
Fax 020 7887 1010
Web www.hammerson.co.uk
Email bknight@hammerson.co.uk

SPOONER, Stephen
British Land Corp

Position
Director
Qualifications
BSc; FRICS
Professional memberships
RICS
Contact details
British Land Corp Ltd, 10 Cornwall Terrace, London NW1 4QP
Tel 020 7486 4466
Web www.britishland.com
Email stephen.spooner@britishland.com

SPRAY, Richard
Lafarge Cement UK

Position
Group head of property
Qualifications
FRICS
Career history
2001-02 Started own consultancy, advising on real estate matters.
1990-2001 Blue Circle: group lands director, then head of group property.
1985-90 Lands director, ARC.
1980-85 Regional estate manager, ARC SE
Other roles
Founder member and chairman, Brownlands Group
Professional memberships
Association of Corporate Real Estate; CoreNet Global UK; RICS
Interests
Fishing; reading; rugby; sailing
Contact details
Lafarge Cement UK Ltd, The Manor Estate Building, Manor Court, Didcot OX11 0RN
Tel 01235 448400
Fax 01235 448410
Direct tel 01235 448628
Direct fax 01235 765124
Mobile 07802 203108
Email richard.spray@lafarge.com

SPRINGALL, Paul
Howard Kennedy

Position
Head of property department
Qualifications
LLB
Career history
1984 Admitted to Roll of Solicitors
Professional memberships
Law Society
Interests
Family; golf; travel; RAC
Contact details
Howard Kennedy, Harcourt House, 19 Cavendish Square, London W1G 0AJ

Tel 020 7636 1616
Fax 020 7491 2899
Web www.howardkennedy.com
Direct tel 020 7546 8896
Direct fax 020 7664 4496
Mobile 07970 612000
Email P.Springall@howardkennedy.com

SPRINGETT, Alan
Sumitomo Mitsui Banking Corp Europe

Position
Head of property finance
Contact details
Sumitomo Mitsui Banking Corp Europe Ltd, Temple Court, 11 Queen Victoria Street, London EC4N 4TA
Tel 020 7786 1000
Web www.smbc.co.jp
Direct tel 020 7786 1164
Direct fax 020 7786 1328
Email alan_springett@gb.smbcgroup.com

SPROUL, David
Deloitte

Position
Country managing partner, consulting and advisory
Contact details
Deloitte, Stonecutter Court, 1 Stonecutter Street, London EC4A 3TR
Tel 020 7936 3000
Fax 020 7583 1198
Web www.deloitte.co.uk
Direct tel 020 7303 6641
Email dsproul@deloitte.co.uk

SQUIRE, Roger
Roger Squire

Position
Commercial property consultant
Qualifications
MA; FRICS
Career history
1991-98 Joint chief executive, London Docklands Development Corp.
1972-91 Director, MEPC
Other roles
Director, Development Securities (Projects); director and former chairman of Joint Contracts Tribunal; property adviser to University of Cambridge; holds a number of consultancy positions
Professional memberships
RICS; Royal Society of Arts
Interests
Sailing
Contact details
Roger Squire Ltd, Fourth Floor, 3 Cromwell Place, London SW7 2JE
Tel 020 7589 6314
Fax 020 7681 2644
Web www.rogersquire.com
Mobile 07884 432356
Email rms@rogersquire.com

STACEY, Andrew
FPDSavills

Position
Director – head of office, Paris
Qualifications
BSc Hons; MRICS
Interests
Family; food; rugby; travel; wine; Queen's Club
Contact details
FPDSavills Ltd, 55 boulevard Haussman, Paris
Tel +33 1 4451 7300
Fax +33 1 4451 7301
Web www.fpdsavills.co.uk
Direct tel +33 1 4451 7317
Mobile +33 6 11 361486
Email astacey@fpdsavills.fr

STACEY, Martin
Lawrence Graham

Position
Partner
Qualifications
LLB Hons
Career history
1989 Joined Lawrence Graham; became partner in 1997.
1989 Admitted to Roll of Solicitors.
1987-89 Turner Kenneth Brown
Professional memberships
British Council for Offices; Law Society; Society of Construction Law
Interests
Football; golf; opera; wine
Contact details
Lawrence Graham, 190 Strand, London WC2R 1JN
Tel 020 7379 0000
Fax 020 7379 6854
Web www3.lawgram.com
Email martin.stacey@lawgram.com

STAITE, Simon
Nabarro Nathanson

Position
Partner – real estate
Qualifications
BA (Oxon); MSc
Career history
1995 Joined Nabarro Nathanson.
1986-95 Turner Kenneth Brown.
1983-86 Herbert Smith
Professional memberships
British Council of Shopping Centres; British Council for Offices; Investment Property Databank
Interests
Family; golf; sport; tennis; walking
Contact details
Nabarro Nathanson, Lacon House, Theobald's Road, London WC1X 8RW
Tel 020 7524 6000
Fax 020 7524 6524
Web www.nabarro.com
Direct tel 020 7524 6278
Email s.staite@nabarro.com

STANCOMBE, Michael
Lovells

Position
Partner
Qualifications
LLB Hons
Career history
1979 Admitted to Roll of Solicitors.
1977 Joined Lovells; became partner in 1982
Other roles
Lovells' representative member of City Property Owners' Association and Westminster Property Owners' Association
Professional memberships
British Council for Offices; BPF; Global Real Estate Institute; Investment Property Forum; Urban Land Institute
Contact details
Lovells, Atlantic House, 50 Holborn Viaduct, London EC1A 2FG
Tel 020 7296 2000
Fax 020 7296 2001
Web www.lovells.com
Direct tel 020 7296 5253
Mobile 07710 620428
Email michael.stancombe@lovells.com

STANFORD, David
REID Architecture

Position
Managing director
Qualifications
BA; BArch; RIBA
Professional memberships
RIBA
Contact details
REID Architecture, West End House, 11 Hills Place, London W1F 7SE
Tel 020 7297 5600
Fax 020 7297 5601

Web www.reidarchitecture.com
Email david.stanford@ra-lond.com

STANLEY, Graham
Moorfield Group

Position
Director
Career history
1996 Joined Moorfield.
1994-96 Goldman Sachs.
1989-94 NatWest Markets.
1989 Hoare Govett.
1987-89 Provident Mutual.
1985-87 Chesterton
Interests
Golf; skiing; travel
Contact details
Moorfield Group Ltd, Premier House, 44-48 Dover Street, London W1S 4NX
Tel 020 7399 1900
Fax 020 7499 2114
Email graham.stanley@moorfield.com

STANLEY, John
Matthews & Goodman

Position
Partner
Contact details
Matthews & Goodman, 23 Ironmonger Lane, London EC2V 8EY
Tel 020 7367 5533
Fax 020 7367 5535
Web www.matthews-goodman.co.uk
Direct tel 020 7367 5530
Mobile 07771 941360
Email jstanley@matthews-goodman.co.uk

STANLEY, Paul
Taylor Woodrow Developments

Position
Business development director
Qualifications
BSc, Val & Est Dev; MRICS
Professional memberships
RICS
Contact details
Taylor Woodrow Developments Ltd, Century Way, Leeds LS15 8ZB
Tel 0113 232 1400
Fax 0113 232 1401
Web www.taylorwoodrow.com
Direct tel 0113 232 1409
Direct fax 0113 232 1485
Mobile 07816 511060
Email paul.stanley@uk.taylorwoodrow.com

STANSFIELD, Mike
David Wilson Homes

Position
Chief executive
Qualifications
MRICS
Other roles
Board member, Housing Forum; chairman, National Customer Satisfaction Survey
Professional memberships
RICS
Contact details
David Wilson Homes Ltd, Wilson Bowden House, Leicester Road, Ibstock LE67 6WB
Tel 01530 276700
Fax 01530 260193
Web www.dwh.co.uk
Email mstansfield@wilsonbowden.plc.uk

STAPLETON, Peter
Lisney

Position
Managing director
Qualifications
FSCS; FRICS; MIAVI
Other roles
Director, Clanmil Housing Association Ireland
Professional memberships
Irish Auctioneers & Valuers Institute; RICS; Society of Chartered Surveyors
Contact details
Lisney, 24 St Stephen's Green, Dublin 2
Tel +353 1 638 2700
Fax +353 1 638 2706
Web www.lisney.com
Direct tel +353 1 638 2740
Direct fax +353 1 661 5086
Mobile +353 1 86 2527470
Email pstapleton@lisney.com

STAPLETON, Richard
Stiles Harold Williams

Position
Chairman
Qualifications
FRICS
Career history
1978 Joined Stiles Harold Williams; managing partner during 1980s; now chairman
Other roles
Surveyor to Whitgift Foundation
Interests
Sailing
Contact details
Stiles Harold Williams Ltd, Castle Square House, 9 Castle Square, Brighton BN1 1DZ
Tel 01273 321200
Fax 01273 202436
Web www.shw.co.uk
Direct tel 01273 231245
Direct fax 01273 730547
Email rstapleton@shw.co.uk

STAPLETON, Timothy
King Sturge

Position
Partner – head of public sector
Qualifications
MPhil; BSc; FRICS
Career history
1973 Joined JP Sturge (now King Sturge) as consultant; appointed partner in 1988.
1971-88 Principal lecturer, Bristol Polytechnic.
1969-71 Weatherall Green & Smith
Other roles
Board member, College of Estate Management; member, RICS compliance panel
Professional memberships
RICS
Interests
Gardening; sailing
Contact details
King Sturge, 40 Berkeley Square, Bristol BS8 1HU
Tel 0117 927 6691
Fax 0117 929 9669
Web www.kingsturge.com
Direct tel 0117 930 5830
Direct fax 0117 927 3886
Mobile 07802 665720
Email tim.stapleton@kingsturge.co.uk

STEADMAN, Tim
Clifford Chance

Position
Partner – head of construction
Qualifications
BA, Jurisprudence
Career history
1997 Joined Clifford Chance.
1982-97 Baker & McKenzie; partner from 1985.
1978 Admitted to Roll of Solicitors.
1976-82 Lovell White & King
Contact details
Clifford Chance, 10 Upper Bank Street, London E14 5JJ
Tel 020 7600 1000
Fax 020 7600 5555
Web www.cliffordchance.com
Direct fax 020 7282 6692
Email tim.steadman@cliffordchance.com

S

STEBBING, Hugh
Lloyds TSB Bank

Position
Head of group property support
Qualifications
BSc, Est Man; FRICS; FBIFM; FRSA; FICPD
Career history
1970 Joined Lloyds Bank; became estates manager for Northern region in 1977, senior estates manager for Midlands region in 1980, chief estates manager in 1988, then head of premises division; appointed managing director of Lloyds Commercial Properties in 1990, head of central property services in 1994, then head of group property support in 1996
Professional memberships
British Institute of Facilities Management; Institute of Continuing Professional Development; RICS; Royal Society of Arts; Strategic Planning Institute; Worshipful Company of Chartered Surveyors
Contact details
Lloyds TSB Bank plc, PO Box 112, Canons House, Canons Way, Bristol BS99 7LB
Tel 0117 943 3433
Fax 0117 905 5855
Web www.lloydstsb.co.uk
Direct tel 0117 943 4400
Direct fax 0117 943 4133
Email hugh.stebbing@lloyds.co.uk

STEDMAN, Julian
Cardiff County Council

Position
Strategic planning manager
Qualifications
BSc; Dip Arch; MA; MRTPI
Contact details
Cardiff County Council, County Hall, Atlantic Wharf, Cardiff CF10 5UW
Tel 029 2087 2000
Web www.cardiff.gov.uk
Direct tel 029 2087 3191
Direct fax 029 2087 2060
Email j.stedman@cardiff.gov.uk

STEDMAN, Steven
Dalgleish

Position
Retail director
Contact details
Dalgleish, 80 New Bond Street, London W1S 1DD
Tel 020 7663 5555
Fax 020 7491 0098
Web www.dalgleish.co.uk
Direct tel 020 7663 5512
Email sstedman@dalgleish.co.uk

STEEL, Amanda
Odeon

Position
Property director
Qualifications
BSc Hons; MRICS
Career history
Since 2000 Property director, Odeon.
1998-2000 Head of estates, Rank Leisure.
1991-98 Allied Domecq
Professional memberships
RICS
Interests
Cycling; golf; music; skiing; tennis
Contact details
Odeon Ltd, 54 Whitcomb Street, London WC2H 7DN
Tel 020 7321 6224
Fax 020 7839 5802
Email ASteel@odeonuk.com

STEEL, Andrew
Eddisons

Position
Director
Qualifications
MRICS
Career history
1988 Joined Eddisons
Professional memberships
Industrial Agents Society; RICS
Contact details
Eddisons, Pennine House, Russell Street, Leeds LS1 5RN
Tel 0113 243 0101
Fax 0113 242 1364
Web www.eddisons.com
Email andrew.steel@eddisons.com

STEELE, David
William Hill Organization

Position
Property director
Contact details
William Hill Organization Ltd, Greenside House, 50 Station Road, London N22 7TP
Tel 020 8918 3600
Email dsteele@williamhill.co.uk

STEPHEN, John
Jones Lang LaSalle

Position
Director – central London investment
Qualifications
BSc, Est Man; FRICS
Career history
Since 1984 Director (central London investment), Jones Lang LaSalle.
1980-84 Commercial director, Jones Lang Wootton, Hong Kong and Tokyo
Other roles
Hon treasurer, Westminster Property Owners Association; honorary treasurer, BPF
Professional memberships
BPF; Investment Property Forum; RICS; Westminster Property Owners Association
Interests
Cycling; family; theatre; wine
Contact details
Jones Lang LaSalle Ltd, 22 Hanover Square, London W1A 2BN
Tel 020 7493 6040
Fax 020 7408 0220
Web www.joneslanglasalle.com
Direct tel 020 7399 5306
Direct fax 020 7399 5653
Email john.stephen@eu.joneslanglasalle.com

STEPHENS, Huw
AXA Real Estate Investment Managers

Position
Fund manager – Sun Life Assurance Long Term Fund
Career history
1994 Joined AXA Real Estate Investment Managers.
1988-94 Trafalgar House.
1987-88 CB Hillier Parker.
1983-87 Legal & General Property
Contact details
AXA Real Estate Investment Managers Ltd, 7 Newgate Street, London EC1A 7HD
Tel 020 7003 1000
Fax 020 7575 8585
Web www.axa-im.co.uk
Direct tel 020 7367 8110
Mobile 07977 917214
Email huw.stephens@axa-reim.co.uk

STEPHENS, Stephen
Lawrence Graham

Position
Partner – head of real estate
Career history
1998 Joined Lawrence Graham, London, as partner; appointed head of property in 2002.
1994-98 Partner, Forsyte Saunders Kerman, London.
1984 Admitted to Roll of Solicitors.
1983-94 Saunders Sobell Leigh & Dobin, London.
1981-83 Turner Peacock, London.
1977-80 Flower & Hart, Brisbane
Interests

Family; music; walking

Contact details

Lawrence Graham, 190 Strand, London WC2R 1JN
Tel 020 7379 0000
Fax 020 7379 6854
Web www3.lawgram.com
Direct tel 020 7759 6710
Direct fax 020 7173 8710
Mobile 07802 967330
Email stephen.stephens@lawgram.com

STEPHENSON, Peter
Able UK

Position

Managing director

Contact details

Able UK Ltd, Able House, Haverton Hill Road, Billingham TS23 1PX
Tel 01642 806080
Email info@ableuk.com

STEPHENSON, Peter
Mytravel Group

Position

Chief operating officer and managing director

Contact details

Mytravel Group plc, Parkway Business Centre, 300 Princess Road, Manchester M14 7QU
Tel 0161 232 2700
Fax 0161 232 2801
Web www.mytravelgroup.com
Email peter.stephenson@mytravel.com

STEPIEN, Kaz
Stepien Lake Gilbert & Paling

Position

Partner – sales, acquisitions, property finance

Qualifications

MA (Oxon)

Career history

1991 Joined Stepien Lake Gilbert & Paling.
1981-91 Birkbeck Montagu's.
1973-81 Freshfields

Professional memberships

Law Society

Contact details

Stepien Lake Gilbert & Paling, 8-14 Vine Hill, London EC1R 5DX
Tel 020 7812 0900
Fax 020 7812 0999
Email kjs@slgp.co.uk

STEVENS, Alex
GVA Grimley

Position

Partner – business rates

Qualifications

BSC; FRICS

Career history

1988 Joined Vigers (now GVA Grimley). Previously qualified with Gerald Eve & Co, then spent five years with Hillier Parker

Interests

Squash; tennis

Contact details

GVA Grimley, 10 Stratton Street, London W1J 8JR
Tel 0870 900 8990
Fax 020 7911 2560
Web www.gvagrimley.co.uk
Direct tel 020 7911 2383
Direct fax 020 7911 2548
Email alex.stevens@gvagrimley.co.uk

STEVENS, Mark
Glenny

Position

Partner

Qualifications

BSc

Career history

1981 Joined Glenny; became associate partner in 1986 and equity partner in 1989.
1980-81 Knight Frank & Rutley

Other roles

Director of a number of charities including Barnabas Trust and Prospect Training; governor of Mayflower County High School

Contact details

Glenny, Dovetail House, 60 Station Road, London RM14 2TJ
Tel 0170 822 5547
Fax 0170 822 1838
Web www.glenny.co.uk
Mobile 07778 476545
Email m.stevens@glenny.co.uk

STEVENS, Michael
Cripps Harries Hall

Position

Partner – head of commercial property

Qualifications

LLB

Career history

1986 Joined Cripps Harries Hall.
1977-85 Herbert Smith.
1975-77 Radcliffes & Co.
1975 Admitted to Roll of Solicitors

Professional memberships

CBI

Contact details

Cripps Harries Hall, Seymour House, 11-13 Mount Ephraim Road, Tunbridge Wells TN1 1EG
Tel 01892 515121
Fax 01892 544878
Web www.e-cripps.co.uk
Direct tel 01892 506094
Email mfs@crippslaw.com

STEVENS, Michael
London & Associated Properties

Position

Director and company secretary

Qualifications

FCA

Career history

1983-85 Finance director/secretary, R Woolfe.
1971-83 Finance director/company secretary, Dataday

Other roles

Company secretary, Bisichi Mining; director/secretary, Dragon Retail Properties

Professional memberships

Institute of Chartered Accountants in England and Wales

Contact details

London & Associated Properties plc, 8-10 New Fetter Lane, London EC4A 1NQ
Tel 020 7415 5000
Fax 020 7353 3500
Web www.laprops.co.uk
Email m.stevens@laprops.co.uk

STEVENS, Michael
Warner Estate Holdings

Position

Associate director – property

Qualifications

BSc, Est Man; FRICS

Career history

1994-2000 Asset manager, SPP Investment Management/Celexa.
1991-94 Associate (business space), Grimley JR Eve.
1987-91 City of London agency, St Quintin

Professional memberships

RICS

Contact details

Warner Estate Holdings plc, Nations House, 103 Wigmore Street, London W1U 1AE
Tel 020 7907 5100
Fax 020 7907 5102
Web www.warnerestate.co.uk
Email mikestevens@weh-plc.co.uk

STEVENS, Paul
Investec Bank (UK)

Position

Head of property

S

Qualifications
ACIB
Career history
1978 Joined Investec Bank (UK); has focused mainly on structured finance and direct real estate activities
Interests
Cricket; golf
Contact details
Investec Bank (UK) Ltd, 2 Gresham Street, London EC2V 7PB
Tel 020 7597 4000
Fax 020 7597 4070
Web www.investec.com/uk
Direct tel 020 7597 4435
Direct fax 020 7597 4441
Email pstevens@investec.co.uk

STEVENSON, Bob
Donaldsons
Position
Partner – asset management Europe
Qualifications
BA; FRICS; MBIFM
Career history
1983-86 Estates surveyor, PSA Estates.
1981-83 Rating assessor, Lothian region.
1979-81 Valuer, Inland Revenue
Other roles
Managing director, Estatius; director, Environmental Services
Professional memberships
British Institute of Facilities Management; RICS
Interests
Golf; reading; travel; wine
Contact details
Donaldsons, 48 Warwick Street, London W1B 5NL
Tel 020 7534 5000
Fax 020 7434 0045
Web www.donaldsons.co.uk
Mobile 07808 479218
Email bob.stevenson@donaldsons.co.uk

STEVENSON, Huw
Dalgleish
Position
Director – head of out-of-town
Other roles
Deputy chairman, Accessible Retail
Contact details
Dalgleish, 80 New Bond Street, London W1S 1DD
Tel 020 7663 5555
Fax 020 7491 0098
Web www.dalgleish.co.uk
Direct tel 020 7663 5522
Email hstevenson@dalgleish.co.uk

STEWART, Doug
Salmon Developments
Position
Development director
Qualifications
FRICS
Career history
1983-93 Development director, Bride Hall.
1979-83 Investment surveyor, Richard Ellis
Professional memberships
100 Property Club; RICS
Interests
Cars; shooting
Contact details
Salmon Developments plc, 46 Mount Street, London W1K 2HH
Tel 020 7499 4378
Fax 020 7499 1317
Web www.salmondevelopments.com
Direct tel 020 7409 1503
Mobile 07778 355739
Email dstewart@salmondevelopments.com

STEWART SMITH, Rodney
New Square Chambers
Position
Barrister
Contact details
New Square Chambers (Chambers of Charles Purle QC), 12 New Square, London WC2A 3SW
Tel 020 7419 8000
Fax 020 7419 8050
Web www.newsquarechambers.co.uk
Email
rodney.stewartsmith@newsquarechambers.co.uk

STILEMAN, Richard
City Estates
Position
Director
Qualifications
BSc, Urban Land Econ; FRICS
Career history
2001-03 London regional development director, UNITE Group.
1996-2001 Group property director, Hartwell.
1988-96 Development manager, B&Q.
1986-88 Manager (commercial agency), Morris Dibben
Professional memberships
RICS
Interests
Music; squash; tennis; windsurfing
Contact details
City Estates Ltd, Brunswick House, Brunswick Place, Southampton SO15 2AP
Tel 023 8021 2060
Fax 023 8021 2007
Mobile 07734 704282
Email richard.stileman@rokgroup.com

STILES, Robert
Stiles Harold Williams
Position
Executive chairman
Qualifications
BSc, Est Man; FRICS
Career history
1972 Joined Stiles Harold Williams.
1970-72 Investment department, Healey & Baker.
1968-70 King & Co
Other roles
Chairman, Brighton & Hove Enterprise Agency
Professional memberships
RICS
Interests
Sailing
Contact details
Stiles Harold Williams Ltd, Castle Square House, 9 Castle Square, Brighton BN1 1DZ
Tel 01273 321200
Fax 01273 202436
Web www.shw.co.uk
Direct tel 01273 231221
Direct fax 01273 203600
Email rstiles@shw.co.uk

STIMPSON, Kevin
Nabarro Nathanson
Position
Partner – real estate
Qualifications
LLB
Career history
1980 Joined Nabarro Nathanson
Professional memberships
Law Society
Interests
Food; music; skiing
Contact details
Nabarro Nathanson, Lacon House, Theobald's Road, London WC1X 8RW
Tel 020 7524 6000
Fax 020 7524 6524
Web www.nabarro.com
Direct tel 020 7524 6273
Email k.stimpson@nabarro.com

STIRLING, Mark
Pillar Property Group

Position
Managing director – Pillar Retail Parks

Qualifications
FRICS

Contact details
Pillar Property Group Ltd, Lansdowne House, 57 Berkeley Square, London W1J 6HQ
Tel 020 7915 8000
Fax 020 7915 8001
Web www.pillarproperty.com
Direct fax 020 7915 8026
Email mark.stirling@pillarproperty.com

STOCKDALE, Peter
Masons

Position
Partner

Qualifications
LLB Hons

Career history
1979 Joined Masons; specialises in property and planning law and property development.
1974 Admitted to Roll of Solicitors

Professional memberships
Law Society; Society of Construction Law

Interests
Cricket; rugby; sailing; skiing; tennis; theatre

Contact details
Masons, Woodbridge House, 30 Aylesbury Street, London EC1R 0ER
Tel 020 7329 2288
Fax 020 7490 2545
Web www.masons.com
Direct tel 020 7490 6233
Direct fax 020 7490 6448
Mobile 07831 462877
Email peter.stockdale@masons.com

STOCKLEY, Grahame
GL Hearn

Position
Director – North West

Qualifications
FRICS; BSc, Est Man

Career history
1983 Joined GL Hearn; became partner/director in 1992

Professional memberships
RICS

Interests
Cricket; football

Contact details
GL Hearn Ltd, St George Court, 230 Cygnet Court, Warrington WA1 1PD
Tel 01925 897000
Fax 01925 897010
Web www.glhearn.com
Email grahame_stockley@glhearn.com

STOCKLEY, Ruth
Kings Chambers

Position
Barrister

Qualifications
LLB; Barrister

Career history
1988 Joined Kings Chambers.
1988 Called to Bar

Other roles
Assistant editor, *Encyclopaedia of Highway Law & Practice* (Sweet & Maxwell); has delivered papers to various planning and highway law conferences; president of Manchester Law Library

Professional memberships
Administrative Law Bar Association; Planning & Environment Bar Association

Contact details
Kings Chambers, 40 King Street, Manchester M2 6BA
Tel 0161 832 9082
Fax 0161 835 2139
Web www.kingschambers.com
Email rstockley@kingschambers.com

STOCKS, Jo
Watts & Partners

Position
Managing partner

Qualifications
FRICS; MAPM

Career history
1978 Joined Watts & Partners; became partner in 1985; opened City of London office in 1999; elected managing partner in 2002

Other roles
Past chairman, Bureau of European Building Consultants & Experts and Association of Consultant Building Surveyors; regularly presents papers on development-related topics; has provided expert evidence on construction defects and contract disputes

Professional memberships
RICS

Contact details
Watts & Partners, 1 Great Tower Street, London EC3R 5AA
Tel 020 7090 7820
Fax 020 7623 4450
Web www.wattsandpartners.com
Email jo.stocks@watts.co.uk

STOCKS, Julian
Jones Lang LaSalle

Position
European director – West End investment

Qualifications
BSc; MRICS

Career history
1988 Joined Jones Lang LaSalle; became associate in 1994 and director in 1998

Professional memberships
RICS

Interests
Cricket; football; golf; hockey; wine

Contact details
Jones Lang LaSalle Ltd, 22 Hanover Square, London W1A 2BN
Tel 020 7493 6040
Fax 020 7408 0220
Web www.joneslanglasalle.com
Direct tel 020 7399 5915
Direct fax 020 7399 5653
Mobile 07770 880157
Email julian.stocks@eu.joneslanglasalle.com

STOLL, Peter
Blackstone Group

Position
Executive director

Career history
Since 2002 Executive director, Blackstone Group.
2001-02 Associate director, Carlyle Group.
1999-2002 Morgan Stanley Real Estate Fund.
1994-99 LaSalle Investment Management

Contact details
Blackstone Group Ltd, Stirling Square, 5-7 Carlton Gardens, London SW1Y 5AD
Tel 020 7451 4000
Fax 020 7451 4034
Web www.blackstone.com
Direct tel 020 7451 4288
Direct fax 020 7451 4036
Email stoll@blackstone.com

STONE, Keith
Land Securities Properties

Position
Retail leasing director

Qualifications
BA Hons; FRICS; MRTPI

Career history
2004 Joined Land Securities Properties.
1994-2004 Lend Lease.
1992-94 BPT & White Rose.
1980-92 Bredero Properties

Professional memberships
RICS; RTPI

Contact details

Land Securities Properties Ltd, 5 Strand, London WC2N 5AF
Tel 020 7413 9000
Fax 020 7925 0202
Email keith.stone@landsecurities.com

STONE, Matthew
Cushman & Wakefield Healey & Baker

Position
Partner – advisory group
Qualifications
TD; BSc; MCR; MRICS
Career history
Since 2004 Partner (advisory group), Cushman & Wakefield Healey & Baker.
1991-2004 Nelson Bakewell: became divisional director in 1996 and director in 1998.
1989-91 Knight Frank & Rutley
Professional memberships
CoreNet Global UK; Institute of Directors; RICS
Interests
Hill walking; IT; music; rugby; sailing; Territorial Army; walking
Contact details
Cushman & Wakefield Healey & Baker, 43-45 Portman Square, London W1A 3BG
Tel 020 7935 5000
Fax 020 7152 5360
Web www.cushwake.com
Direct tel 020 7152 5678
Mobile 07973 909518
Email matthew.stone@eur.cushwake.com

STONE, Peter
Cobbetts

Position
Head of property litigation/property management
Qualifications
LLB; NP
Career history
1976 Admitted to Roll of Solicitors.
1974 Joined Cobbetts; appointed partner in 1979 and became head of property litigation in 1986
Professional memberships
Law Society; Notaries' Society
Interests
Cycling; mountain biking; mountaineering
Contact details
Cobbetts, Ship Canal House, King Street, Manchester M2 4WB
Tel 0161 833 3333
Fax 0161 833 3030
Web www.cobbetts.co.uk
Direct tel 0161 833 5246
Direct fax 0161 830 2786
Email peter.stone@cobbetts.co.uk

STONE, Stephen
Crest Nicholson Residential

Position
Managing director
Contact details
Crest Nicholson Residential plc, 39 Thames Street, Weybridge KT13 8JL
Tel 01932 847272
Email sstone@crestnicholson.com

STONES, Patrick
Tesco Stores

Position
Regional director – acquisitions
Qualifications
BSc Hons; MRICS
Professional memberships
RICS
Contact details
Tesco Stores Ltd, Cirrus B, Shire Park, Welwyn Garden City AL7 1AB
Tel 01992 632222
Fax 01707 634937
Web www.tesco.com
Direct tel 01707 634289
Email patrick.stones@uk.tesco.com

STOODLEY, Paul
Salmon Developments

Position
Development director
Qualifications
BA Hons; MRICS
Professional memberships
100 Property Club; RICS
Interests
Motor sports; sailing; shooting
Contact details
Salmon Developments plc, 46 Mount Street, London W1K 2HH
Tel 020 7499 4378
Fax 020 7499 1317
Web www.salmondevelopments.com
Email pstoodley@salmondevelopments.com

STOREY, Kevin
Cushman & Wakefield Healey & Baker

Position
Partner – head of industrial, London
Qualifications
FRICS
Professional memberships
RICS
Contact details
Cushman & Wakefield Healey & Baker, 43-45 Portman Square, London W1A 3BG
Tel 020 7935 5000
Fax 020 7152 5360
Web www.cushwake.com
Direct tel 020 7152 5217
Direct fax 020 7152 5395
Mobile 07818 406404
Email kevin.storey@eur.cushwake.com

STORY, James
BPT

Position
Property director
Contact details
BPT Ltd, St Johns House, Barrington Road, Altrincham WA14 1TJ
Tel 0161 929 0044
Fax 0161 929 0077
Direct tel 01829 730456
Mobile 07976 417168
Email jstory@graingertrust.co.uk

STOUGHTON-HARRIS, Peter
DTZ Debenham Tie Leung

Position
Managing director – European valuations
Qualifications
MRICS
Career history
1986 Joined Debenham Tewson Chinnocks; became associate director in 1987 and full director in 1989, then managing director of investment division in 1995; appointed managing director of DTZ Debenham Tie Leung (the primary subsidiary of DTZ Holdings) in 2000 then managing director (European valuations) in 2003
Professional memberships
RICS
Contact details
DTZ Debenham Tie Leung, 1 Curzon Street, London W1A 5PZ
Tel 020 7408 1161
Fax 020 7643 6000
Web www.dtz.com
Email peter.stoughton-harris@dtz.com

STRACHAN, John
Cushman & Wakefield Healey & Baker

Position
International managing partner
Qualifications
BSc, Est Man; FRICS
Other roles
Head of retail and leisure for Cushman & Wakefield Healey & Baker; management board member, British Council of Shopping Centres
Professional memberships
British Council of Shopping Centres; International

Council of Shopping Centers; RICS
Contact details
Cushman & Wakefield Healey & Baker,
43-45 Portman Square, London W1A 3BG
Tel 020 7935 5000
Fax 020 7152 5360
Web www.cushwake.com
Direct tel 020 7152 5090
Direct fax 020 7152 5310
Email john.strachan@eur.cushwake.com

STRANG, Andrew
Threadneedle Property Investments

Position
Managing director
Qualifications
BSc; FRICS
Career history
1991-94 Managing director, Allied Dunbar Property Fund Managers.
1988-91 Managing director, Schroder Properties.
1982-88 Director, Hill Samuel Property Services
Other roles
Director, Threadneedle Investment Holdings; Director, BPF
Professional memberships
Investment Property Forum; RICS
Contact details
Threadneedle Property Investments,
9-15 Sackville Street, London W1S 3DJ
Tel 020 7437 8000
Fax 020 7464 5811
Direct tel 020 7464 5824
Email andrew.strang@threadneedle.co.uk

STRANGE, Alf
Land Securities Properties

Position
Portfolio director – head of property management
Qualifications
FRICS
Career history
1974 Joined Land Securities Properties.
1970-74 J Sainsbury
Other roles
Director, Broadmead Company, Bristol; board member, Cardiff Initiative; executive board member, Association of Town Centre Management; director, Ealing Centre Partnership; advisory board member, British Council of Shopping Centres Diploma in Shopping Centre Management
Professional memberships
Association of Town Centre Management; British Council of Shopping Centres; British Council for Offices; International Council of Shopping Centers; RICS
Interests
Eating out; football; music; reading; theatre; walking
Contact details
Land Securities Properties Ltd, 5 Strand, London WC2N 5AF
Tel 020 7413 9000
Fax 020 7925 0202
Web www.landsecurities.com
Direct tel 020 7024 5430
Direct fax 020 7024 5006
Mobile 07768 936338
Email alf.strange@landsecurities.com

STREET, David
Whitbread

Position
Property director
Qualifications
FRICS
Career history
1980 Joined Whitbread; appointed estates manager in 1984, disposals director in 1989 and acquisitions director in 1993; became property director of Whitbread Property in 2000
Professional memberships
RICS
Contact details
Whitbread plc, Whitbread Court, Houghton Hall Park, Dunstable LU5 5XE
Tel 01582 499499
Fax 01582 844855
Web www.whitbread.co.uk
Direct tel 01582 844817
Direct fax 01582 844844
Email david.street@whitbread.com

STREET, John
Brabners Chaffe Street

Position
Partner – head of department, Manchester
Qualifications
MA
Career history
Since 1987 Partner, Brabners Chaffe Street.
1980 Admitted to Roll of Solicitors.
1978-87 Leak Almond & Parkinson: partner on leaving
Professional memberships
Law Society
Interests
Cricket; football; golf
Contact details
Brabners Chaffe Street, Brook House,
77 Fountain Street, Manchester M2 2EE
Tel 0161 236 5800
Fax 0161 228 6862
Web www.brabnerschaffestreet.com
Email john.street@brabnerscs2.com

STRICKLAND, Christopher
Greycoat Estates

Position
Development director
Qualifications
BTech Hons; CEng; MICE
Career history
1982 Joined Greycoat as construction director; became development director in 1992.
1974-82 Project manager, Taylor Woodrow
Other roles
Past president, British Council for Offices; governor, Peabody Trust
Professional memberships
British Council for Offices; BPF; Institution of Civil Engineers
Interests
Fishing; golf; skiing
Contact details
Greycoat Estates Ltd, Brettenham House,
9 Savoy Street, London WC2E 7EG
Tel 020 7379 1000
Fax 020 7379 8744
Email cstrickland@greycoat.co.uk

STRINGER, Clive
Chesterton International

Position
Head – Chesterton Property Asset Management
Qualifications
BA Hons; MRICS
Career history
Since 2002 Managing director, Chesterton Property Asset Management.
1998-2001 Senior director (commercial management), CB Hillier Parker.
1995-98 Salaried partner, director (property management), Hillier Parker.
1991-95 Associate/salaried partner (fund management), Hillier Parker.
1981-91 Hillier Parker May & Rowden.
1978-81 Donaldsons
Professional memberships
RICS
Contact details
Chesterton International, Lily Hill House, Lily Hill Road, Bracknell RG12 2SJ
Tel 01344 645866
Fax 01344 457208
Web www.chesterton.co.uk
Direct tel 01344 448730
Direct fax 01344 307496
Mobile 07712 868430
Email clive.stringer@chesterton.co.uk

STRINGER, Ian
GVA Grimley

Position
Partner
Qualifications
BSc; FRICS
Career history
1983 Joined Grimley & Son (now GVA Grimley); appointed partner in 1989 and head of agency in Birmingham in 1995; national head of offices (UK) from 2001
Professional memberships
British Council for Offices; Office Agents Society; RICS
Interests
Cars; keep fit; motor sports
Contact details
GVA Grimley, 3 Brindleyplace, Birmingham B1 2JB
Tel 0870 900 8990
Fax 0121 609 8314
Web www.gvagrimley.co.uk
Direct tel 0121 609 8308
Mobile 07831 820648
Email ian.stringer@gvagrimley.co.uk

STRONG, Christopher
Citigroup

Position
Vice-president real estate – central and eastern EMEA
Qualifications
MRICS
Career history
1989-2000 Vice-president (real estate, EMEA), American Express.
1984-89 Principal estate surveyor, overseas estate department, Foreign & Commonwealth Office.
1981-84 Valuation Office, Government Republic of Zambia
Other roles
Member, RICS corporate occupiers group
Professional memberships
CoreNet Global UK; RICS
Interests
Hockey; running; squash
Contact details
Citigroup Ltd, Citigroup Centre, 33 Canada Square, London E14 5LB
Fax 020 7500 2852
Web www.citigroup.com
Direct tel 020 7986 2818
Direct fax 020 7658 7776
Mobile 0774 810 6148
Email chris.strong@citigroup.com

STRONG, Michael
CB Richard Ellis

Position
European chairman
Qualifications
FRICS
Career history
1972 Joined Insignia Richard Ellis; made partner/director in 1977 and appointed chairman in 2001.
1967-72 Healey & Baker.
1964-67 Surveyor, Prudential Assurance Co
Other roles
Board member, Insignia Europe; chairman designate, CBRE European Business
Professional memberships
BPF; CBI; RICS
Interests
Gardening; golf; music; theatre; travel
Contact details
CB Richard Ellis, Kingsley House, 1a Wimpole Street, London W1G 0RE
Tel 020 7182 2000
Fax 020 7182 7001
Web www.cbre.com
Direct fax 020 7495 7527
Mobile 07785 114787
Email mike.strong@cbre.com

STRUCKETT, Mark
DTZ Holdings

Position
Group chief executive
Qualifications
MA; MBA; FRICS
Career history
1979 Joined DTZ; on secondment to Olympia & York (Canary Wharf) in 1988 as senior vice-president; became London investment division chairman in 1990; appointed London managing director in 1993; now group chief executive, DTZ Holdings
Other roles
Member of advisory board for College of Estate Management investment diploma; director, Surveyors Mutual Insurance Society
Professional memberships
RICS
Interests
Sailing
Contact details
DTZ Holdings plc, 1 Curzon Street, London W1A 5PZ
Tel 020 7408 1161
Fax 020 7643 6000
Web www.dtz.com
Direct tel 020 7643 6050
Mobile 07767 613527
Email mark.struckett@dtz.com

STUART, Henry
Withers

Position
Principal – head of residential property
Qualifications
LLB
Career history
1987 Joined Withers; became partner in 1992.
1986-87 Jacques & Lewis.
1982-86 May May & Merrimans
Professional memberships
Agricultural Law Association; UK Environmental Law Association
Contact details
Withers LLP, 16 Old Bailey, London EC4M 7EG
Tel 020 7597 6000
Fax 020 7597 6543
Web www.withersworldwide.com
Direct tel 020 7597 6031
Email henry.stuart@withersworldwide.com

STUBBS, Colin
British Land Corp

Position
Director
Contact details
British Land Corp Ltd, 10 Cornwall Terrace, London NW1 4QP
Tel 020 7486 4466
Web www.britishland.com
Email colin.stubbs@britishland.com

STUPPLES, Mark
King Sturge

Position
Partner – national head of asset management
Qualifications
BSc; MRICS
Career history
1984 Joined JP Sturge & Sons (now King Sturge); appointed partner in 1991
Other roles
Director, Edward Rushton Son & Kenyon; director, King Sturge Management; senior vice-president, Bristol Property Agents Association; surveyor, Trustees of the Temple Ecclesiastical Charity; surveyor, Trustees of Bishop Monks Horfield Trust
Professional memberships
Bristol Property Agents' Association; Non-Administrative Receivers Association; RICS
Interests
Hockey
Contact details

King Sturge, 7 Stratford Place, London W1C 1ST
Tel 020 7493 4933
Fax 020 7409 0469
Web www.kingsturge.com
Direct tel 020 7529 6965
Mobile 07801 505282
Email mark.stupples@kingsturge.co.uk

STYLES, Paul
Rapleys

Position
Managing partner
Qualifications
FRICS
Career history
Since 1997 Managing partner, Rapleys.
1989-96 Managing partner (London office), Rapleys.
1981-88 Partner, Rapleys.
1980-81 Investment associate, Rapleys.
1977-80 Senior shops negotiator, Michael Laurie & Partners.
1973-77 Professional services department manager, Bairstow Eves
Other roles
Director, Frontier Joint Venture (development company jointly owned by Frontier Estates and Chubb Common Investment Fund)
Professional memberships
Investment Property Forum; RICS
Interests
Fishing
Contact details
Rapleys, Maddox House, 1 Maddox Street, London W1S 2PZ
Tel 0870 777 6292
Fax 020 7439 7678
Web www.rapleys.co.uk
Email prs@rapleys.co.uk

SUDELL, Peter
ATIS REAL Weatheralls

Position
Director
Qualifications
MA; MRICS
Career history
1985 Joined ATIS REAL Weatheralls; appointed partner in 1997 and now jointly heads investment consulting team
Professional memberships
RICS
Interests
Cricket; gardening; golf; hockey
Contact details
ATIS REAL Weatheralls Ltd, Norfolk House, 31 St James's Square, London SW1Y 4JR
Tel 020 7338 4200
Fax 020 7493 0746
Web www.atisrealweatheralls.com
Direct tel 020 7338 4277
Email peter.sudell@atisrealweatheralls.com

SULLIVAN, Peter
Underwoods

Position
Partner – retail
Qualifications
FRICS
Career history
1988 Joined Underwoods. Previous posts included property manager with Next
Professional memberships
RICS
Contact details
Underwoods, Shire House, Pyramid Close, Northampton NN3 8PH
Tel 01604 404060
Fax 01604 404099
Web www.underwoods.co.uk
Direct tel 01604 783006
Mobile 07710 911159
Email pjs@underwoods.co.uk

SUMMERSGILL, Andrew
King Sturge

Position
Partner – investment
Qualifications
BSc; MRICS
Professional memberships
RICS
Contact details
King Sturge, Capitol House, Russell Street, Leeds LS1 5SP
Tel 0113 244 1441
Fax 0113 242 1404
Web www.kingsturge.com
Direct tel 0113 235 5209
Email andrew.summersgill@kingsturge.co.uk

SUMNER, Damian
Churston Heard

Position
Director – retail agency
Qualifications
BSc Hons; MRICS
Career history
Since 1996 Director of North East retail, Churston Heard.
1995-96 Disposal surveyor, Sears Group Props.
1992-95 Graduate surveyor/acquisition surveyor, Mason Owen & Partners
Professional memberships
RICS
Interests
Football; golf; sport
Contact details
Churston Heard Ltd, 7 Hanover Square, London W1S 1HQ
Tel 020 7409 2199
Fax 020 7495 1339
Web www.churstonheard.co.uk
Direct tel 020 7318 7835
Direct fax 020 7318 7835
Mobile 07974 085738
Email dsumner@churstonheard.co.uk

SUMNER, Patrick
Henderson Global Investors

Position
Divisional director – European property
Qualifications
MA (Oxon); MSc (Lond)
Professional memberships
RICS
Contact details
Henderson Global Investors Ltd, 4 Broadgate, London EC2M 2DA
Tel 020 7818 1818
Fax 020 7818 1819
Web www.henderson.com
Direct tel 020 7818 4291
Direct fax 020 7410 4446
Mobile 07714 415265
Email patrick.sumner@henderson.com

SUNNUCKS, William
Capital & Regional

Position
Group finance director
Qualifications
MA; ACA; MBA
Career history
2000-01 Finance director, Partnerships UK.
1996-2000 Chief financial officer, English Welsh & Scottish Railways.
1992-96 Finance director, Securum International
Other roles
Chairman, Land Management
Interests
Sailing
Contact details
Capital & Regional plc, 10 Lower Grosvenor Place, London SW1W 0EN
Tel 020 7932 8000
Fax 020 7802 5600
Web www.capreg.com
Email william.sunnucks@capreg.com

S

SUNTER, Graeme
DLA

Position
Location head, real estate, Scotland
Qualifications
LLB
Career history
1985 Joined Bird Semple (merged with DLA in 2000); became partner in 1987.
1977-85 Walker & Laird: partner from 1980.
1977 Admitted to Roll of Solicitors
Other roles
Member, Law Society of Scotland's environmental law committee
Professional memberships
British Council of Shopping Centres; Investment Property Forum; Law Society of Scotland
Interests
Art; cricket; football; running; sport
Contact details
DLA, 249 West George Street, Glasgow G2 4RB
Tel 08700 111111
Fax 0141 204 1902
Web www.dla.com
Direct tel 0141 305 5308
Direct fax 0141 305 5308
Email graeme.sunter@dla.com

SUPPLE, Martin
FPDSavills

Position
Director – head of out-of-town retail
Qualifications
MRICS; MRTPI
Career history
1998 Joined FPDSavills.
1989-98 Fuller Peiser.
1987-89 Anthony Bowhill & Associates
Professional memberships
Accessible Retail; RICS; RTPI
Interests
Cricket; football; golf
Contact details
FPDSavills Ltd, 20 Grosvenor Hill, London W1K 3HQ
Tel 020 7499 8644
Fax 020 7495 3773
Web www.fpdsavills.co.uk
Direct tel 020 7409 9909
Mobile 07870 555770
Email msupple@fpdsavills.co.uk

SUTTON, Laura
FPDSavills

Position
Director, head of department
Contact details
FPDSavills Ltd, 20 Grosvenor Hill, London W1K 3HQ
Tel 020 7499 8644
Fax 020 7495 3773
Web www.fpdsavills.co.uk
Direct tel 020 7409 8708
Mobile 07870 555746
Email lsutton@fpdsavills.co.uk

SWABEY, Nicholas
Chapman Swabey

Position
Senior partner
Qualifications
FRICS
Professional memberships
RICS
Interests
Golf; skiing; tennis
Contact details
Chapman Swabey Ltd, 1 College Hill, London EC4R 2RA
Tel 020 7236 6363
Fax 020 7236 6464
Web www.chapmanswabey.com
Mobile 07801 393351
Email alexjacobs@chapmanswabey.com

SWAFFIELD, David
Hill Dickinson

Position
Partner – head of commercial property
Qualifications
MA (Cantab)
Career history
1979 Admitted to Roll of Solicitors
Other roles
President, Liverpool Law Society (1999-2000); Mersey Partnership ambassador for Merseyside; governor, Birkenhead School; board member, Professional Liverpool
Professional memberships
Law Society; Liverpool Law Society
Contact details
Hill Dickinson, Pearl Assurance House, 2 Derby Square, Liverpool L2 9XL
Tel 0151 236 5400
Fax 0151 236 2175
Web www.hilldickinson.com
Email david.swaffield@hilldickinson.com

SWALLOW, Mark
Knight Frank

Position
Managing partner – Birmingham
Qualifications
BSc; MRICS
Career history
Since 1994 Partner (head of office), Knight Frank.
1992-94 Associate director, Storey Sons & Parker.
1986-91 Director, Colliers Stewart Newiss
Other roles
Past treasurer, Northumberland & Durham junior organisation, RICS; member, Northern Counties Club; govenor, Mowden Hall School
Professional memberships
RICS
Interests
Golf; horse racing; skiing; tennis
Contact details
Knight Frank LLP, 85-89 Colmore Row, Birmingham B3 2BB
Tel 0121 200 2220
Fax 0121 200 2381
Web www.knightfrank.com
Mobile 07831 343642
Email mark.swallow@knightfrank.com

SWANSON, Ford
Ryden

Position
Partner – investment
Qualifications
BSc Hons, Est Man; MRICS
Professional memberships
RICS
Contact details
Ryden, 46 Castle Street, Edinburgh EH2 3BN
Tel 0131 225 6612
Fax 0131 225 5766
Web www.ryden.co.uk
Email ford.swanson@ryden.co.uk

SWEENEY, Fiona
Hermes Property Asset Management

Position
Director – strategy
Qualifications
BSc, Surv; MLitt; Dip E Econ
Contact details
Hermes Property Asset Management Ltd, Lloyds Chambers, 1 Portsoken Street, London E1 8HZ
Tel 020 7702 0888
Fax 020 7702 9453
Web www.hermes.co.uk
Email f.sweeney@hermes.co.uk

SWEENEY, Tony
Milln Gate Properties

Position
Managing director
Qualifications

BA Hons; Dip TP; MSc; MRTPI; MRICS

Career history

Since 1997 Managing director, Milln Gate Properties.

1993-97 Team leader, British Gas Properties.

1988-93 Development executive/consultant, Berisford International.

1986-88 Senior development surveyor, Cluttons.

1985-86 Senior surveyor/planner, GL Hearn & Partners.

1983-85 Investment surveyor, Hillier Parker

Professional memberships

RICS; RTPI

Interests

Badminton; fishing; football; golf; sailing; windsurfing

Contact details

Milln Gate Properties Ltd, 12 St James's Square, London SW1Y 4LB

Tel 020 8433 6588

Fax 020 8433 7088

Web www.millngate.com

Direct tel 0142 565 0856

Direct fax 0142 565 7120

Mobile 07970 471770

Email t.sweeney@millngate.com

SYKES, Jonathan
King Sturge

Position

Partner in charge, Newcastle

Qualifications

BSc Hons, Land Man; MRICS

Career history

1991 Joined King Sturge, London; partner in charge of Newcastle office from 2001.

1989-91 Fletcher King, London.

1988-89 Edward Erdman, London

Professional memberships

Accessible Retail; British Council for Offices; Leisure Property Forum

Contact details

King Sturge, 51 Grey Street, Newcastle upon Tyne NE1 6EE

Tel 0191 230 2033

Fax 0191 230 2031

Web www.kingsturge.com

Email jonathan.sykes@kingsturge.co.uk

SYMONS, Nicholas
Blair Kirkman

Position

Partner

Qualifications

BSc; MRICS

Career history

1993 Joined Blair Kirkman.

1991-93 London retail team, Gerald Eve (included seven-month secondment to Marks & Spencer estates team)

Professional memberships

RICS; Shop Agents Society

Interests

Golf; rugby; sailing; travel

Contact details

Blair Kirkman, St Georges House, 12a St George Street, London W1S 1FQ

Tel 020 7409 0899

Fax 020 7629 8022

Web www.blairkirkman.com

Mobile 07977 998825

Email nicks@blairkirkman.com

T

TABOR, Christopher
ING Real Estate Investment Management (UK)

Position
Director – head of corporate real estate
Qualifications
BSc Hons, Land Man; MRICS
Career history
1987 Joined Baring, Houston & Saunders (now ING Real Estate Investment Management (UK)).
1984-87 Gerald Eve
Interests
Art; cooking; interior design; squash; tennis; theatre
Contact details
ING Real Estate Investment Management (UK) Ltd, 9 Devonshire Square, London EC2M 4WX
Tel 020 7398 4310
Fax 020 7398 4311
Web www.ingrealestate.co.uk
Direct tel 020 7398 5536
Email Christopher.tabor@ingrealestate.co.uk

TAGER, Romie
Selborne Chambers

Position
Head of chambers
Qualifications
QC
Career history
2002 Established Selborne Chambers as specialist set specialising in property and commercial work.
1995 Appointed QC.
1971 Called to Bar
Other roles
Chairman, Greenquest Group; chairman of trustees, Hampstead Dyslexia Trust
Professional memberships
Chancery Bar Association; London Common Law & Commercial Bar Association; Professional Negligence Bar Association; Property Bar Association
Interests
Opera; theatre; travel
Contact details
Selborne Chambers, 10 Essex Street, London WC2R 3AA
Tel 020 7420 9501
Fax 020 7420 9555
Web www.selbornechambers.co.uk
Direct tel 020 7420 9500
Direct fax 020 7420 9518
Mobile 07968 030524
Email romie.tager@selbornechambers.co.uk

TAGGART, Nicholas
Landmark Chambers

Position
Barrister
Qualifications
LLB (London); BCL (Oxon)
Career history
1991 Called to Bar
Other roles
Editor, *Hill & Redman's Law of Landlord & Tenant*; contributor, *Bullen & Leake & Jacob's Precedents of Pleading*
Professional memberships
Chancery Bar Association; Property Litigation Association
Contact details
Landmark Chambers, 4 Breams Buildings, London EC4A 1AQ
Tel 020 7430 1221
Fax 020 7421 1399
Web www.landmarkchambers.co.uk
Direct tel 020 7421 1324
Email ntaggart@landmarkchambers.co.uk

TALBOT, Richard
Nicholson Graham & Jones

Position
Partner and head of company department
Career history
1988 Joined Nicholson Graham & Jones.
Previously at Slaughter & May and Richards Butler
Other roles
General editor, *Practical Lending & Security Precedents* (Sweet & Maxwell)
Contact details
Nicholson Graham & Jones, 110 Cannon Street, London EC4N 6AR
Tel 020 7648 9000
Fax 020 7648 9001
Web www.ngj.co.uk
Direct tel 020 7360 8110
Direct fax 020 7360 6305
Email richard.talbot@ngj.co.uk

TALJAARD, Desmond
J Sainsbury

Position
Property director
Qualifications
ACA; BSc, Econ
Career history
2003 Joined J Sainsbury as property director.
1991-2003 Ladbroke Group (now Hilton Group): joined as finance director of Ladbroke Group Properties; became president and chief executive of Ladbroke Group Properties US division in 1992, then senior vice-president (real estate) and board director of Hilton International in 1995.
1982-91 Ernst & Young
Professional memberships
Institute of Chartered Accountants in England & Wales
Interests
Rugby; tennis
Contact details
J Sainsbury plc, 33 Holborn, London EC1N 2HT
Tel 020 7695 6000
Fax 020 7695 7610
Web www.j-sainsbury.co.uk
Email diayn.sherman@sainsburys.co.uk

TANDY, Didier
Scarborough Development Group

Position
Managing director
Other roles
Director, Scarborough Property Holdings; director, Ancient Mariner Properties
Contact details
Scarborough Development Group plc, 10 Carlos Place, London W1K 3AT
Tel 020 7493 4636
Fax 020 7491 4991
Email didier.tandy@sdgroup-plc.com

TANNER, Ian
Dron & Wright

Position
Partner – rating
Qualifications
MRICS
Professional memberships
RICS
Contact details
Dron & Wright, Bankside House, 107-112 Leadenhall Street, London EC3A 4AQ

Tel 020 7891 2345
Fax 020 7891 2300
Web www.dronwright.co.uk
Direct tel 020 7891 2303
Mobile 07867 982548
Email iantanner@dronwright.co.uk

TANNEY, Anthony
Falcon Chambers

Position
Barrister
Other roles
Contributor, *Fisher & Lightwood's Law of Mortgage* (11th edition, 2001)
Contact details
Falcon Chambers, Falcon Court, London EC4Y 1AA
Tel 020 7353 2484
Fax 020 7353 1261
Web www.falcon-chambers.com
Email clerks@falcon-chambers.com

TASKIS, Catherine
Falcon Chambers

Position
Barrister
Qualifications
BA (Oxon); BCL
Career history
1995 Called to Bar
Other roles
Assistant editor, *Muir Watt & Moss on Agricultural Holdings* (14th edition, Sweet & Maxwell, 1998); contributor, *Local Law Property Update Service* (Sweet & Maxwell)
Professional memberships
Agricultural Law Association; Chancery Bar Association; London Common Law & Commercial Bar Association; Property Bar Association
Interests
Ballet; rowing
Contact details
Falcon Chambers, Falcon Court, London EC4Y 1AA
Tel 020 7353 2484
Fax 020 7353 1261
Web www.falcon-chambers.com
Email taskis@falcon-chambers.com

TATES, Nico
Aberdeen Property Investors Continental Europe

Position
Chief executive officer
Qualifications
BA; MSc
Career history
Since 2001 Chief executive officer of Aberdeen Property Investors Continental Europe and board member of Aberdeen Property Investors International in London.
1998-2001 Managing director, Celexa Real Estate Investment Management, Amsterdam.
1994-98 Chief investment officer, SPP Real Estate (Continental Europe), Amsterdam.
1990-94 Vice-president, AEGON real estate department, The Hague.
1987-90 Marketing manager, ABN Real Estate investment and management department, Amsterdam.
1984-87 Research manager, EMPEO (property division of Bredero), Utrecht.
1980-83 Assistant lecturer, Institute of Economic Geography, University of Amsterdam
Other roles
Board member of SBV real estate school, University of Amsterdam; founder, fund-raiser and manager of CELOGIX Property Fund; non-executive board member, AZL Vastgoed Winkels; board member, IVBN (Dutch association of institutional real estate investors); non-executive board member, AZL Vastgoed Woningen; visiting lecturer at University of Amsterdam and for postgraduate MRE course at University of Rotterdam and University of Maastricht (1993-98); member of municipal council, City of Zaanstad (1982-86)
Professional memberships
European Institute of Business Administration (Insead)
Interests
Golf; jazz; opera; tennis
Contact details
Aberdeen Property Investors Continental Europe BV, De Lairessestraat 180, Amsterdam 1075 HM, Netherlands
Tel +31 20 577 7666
Fax +31 20 671 7476
Direct tel +31 20 577 7605
Mobile +31 6 534 10611
Email nico.tates@aberdeenpropertyinvestors.com

TATTERSALL, Steven
iOG

Position
Managing director
Career history
1995 Joined Industrial Ownership (now iOG) (a wholly owned subsidiary of Property Fund Management) as estates director; appointed managing director in 2001
Interests
Golf; IT; sailing
Contact details
iOG, Heron Place, 3 George Street, London W1U 3QG
Tel 020 7535 1818
Fax 020 7535 1819
Web www.iog.co.uk
Email steven.tattersall@iog.co.uk

TATTRIE, Robert
Alfred McAlpine Developments

Position
Managing director
Qualifications
BSc; MRICS; MACostE; ACIArb
Interests
Diving/scuba diving (Mercian Divers' Club)
Contact details
Alfred McAlpine Developments Ltd, Venture Court, Wolverhampton WV10 6TB
Tel 01902 394000
Fax 01902 394001
Web www.mcalpineplc.com
Mobile 07767 818164
Email bob.tattrie@mcalpineplc.com

TAVENER, Chris
Herbert Smith

Position
Partner
Career history
1973 Admitted to Roll of Solicitors.
1970 Joined Herbert Smith; appointed partner in 1982
Interests
Family; golf; music; skiing
Contact details
Herbert Smith, Exchange House, 10 Primrose Street, London EC2A 2NY
Tel 020 7374 8000
Fax 020 7374 0888
Web www.herbertsmith.com
Email chris.tavener@herbertsmith.com

TAYLOR, Christopher
Prudential Property Investment Managers

Position
Director – fund management
Qualifications
MRICS; BSc Hons, Est Man
Career history
1987 Joined Prudential
Professional memberships
RICS
Interests
Cricket; football; golf; history; reading; rugby; swimming; travel
Contact details

Prudential Property Investment Managers Ltd, Princeton House, 271-273 High Holborn, London WC1V 7NE
Tel 020 7548 6600
Fax 020 7548 6999
Web www.prupim.com
Direct fax 020 7548 6832
Email chris.taylor@prupim.com

TAYLOR, Colin
Energis Communications

Position
Group property and facilities director
Career history
1993 Joined Energis.
1983-93 Construction director for leading fit-out company.
1978-83 Partner in family residential development company
Professional memberships
British Institute of Facilities Management
Interests
Golf; travel
Contact details
Energis Communications Ltd, 185 Park Street, London SE1 9DY
Tel 020 7206 5555
Fax 020 7206 6539
Web www.energis.co.uk
Direct tel 020 7206 6515
Direct fax 020 7206 6050
Email ctaylor@energis.co.uk

TAYLOR, David
Chesterton International

Position
Managing director of residential
Career history
2003 Rejoined Chesterton.
2000-03 Cendant.
2000 HomeDirectory.
1989-99 Chesterton
Professional memberships
National Association of Estate Agents
Interests
Family
Contact details
Chesterton International, 40 Connaught Street, London W2 2AA
Tel 020 7262 5060
Fax 020 7724 4432
Web www.chesterton.co.uk
Direct tel 020 7298 5917
Mobile 07764 755132
Email david.taylor@chesterton.co.uk

TAYLOR, Frank
Bennett Urban Planning

Position
Consultant
Qualifications
BSc; Dip TP; MRTPI
Other roles
Consultant, TP Bennett
Professional memberships
RTPI
Interests
Family; gardening; opera; singing; travel
Contact details
Bennett Urban Planning Ltd, 1 America Street, London SE1 0NE
Tel 020 7208 2002
Fax 020 7208 2023
Web www.bennettup.co.uk
Direct tel 020 7208 2424
Email ftaylor@tpbennett.co.uk

TAYLOR, Graeme
Skipton Building Society

Position
Head of commercial lending
Qualifications
ACIB
Career history
1993 Joined Skipton Building Society; responsible for commercial arrears 1993-96; responsible for development and expansion of commercial lending book since 1996.
1971-92 Various appointments to senior manager level, TSB
Professional memberships
Chartered Institute of Bankers
Interests
Cricket; football; golf
Contact details
Skipton Building Society, The Bailey, Skipton BD23 1DN
Tel 01756 705000
Fax 01756 705700
Web www.skipton.co.uk
Email pthornton@skipton.co.uk

TAYLOR, Guy
Cushman & Wakefield Healey & Baker

Position
Partner – head of West End office agency
Qualifications
BSc; MRICS
Career history
Since 2000 Partner, Cushman & Wakefield Healey & Baker.
1994-2000 Associate partner, Jones Lang LaSalle.
1987-94 Weatherall Green & Smith
Professional memberships
RICS
Contact details
Cushman & Wakefield Healey & Baker, 43-45 Portman Square, London W1A 3BG
Tel 020 7935 5000
Fax 020 7152 5360
Web www.cushwake.com
Direct tel 020 7152 5236
Direct fax 020 7152 5385
Mobile 07769 976614
Email guy.taylor@eur.cushwake.com

TAYLOR, John
Hartnell Taylor Cook

Position
Partner – professional
Qualifications
FRICS
Professional memberships
RICS
Contact details
Hartnell Taylor Cook, Somerset House, 18 Canynge Road, Bristol BS8 3JX
Tel 0117 923 9234
Fax 0117 923 9237
Web www.htc.uk.com
Direct tel 0117 946 4508
Mobile 07836 520239
Email john.taylor@htc.uk.com

TAYLOR, Justin
Cushman & Wakefield Healey & Baker

Position
Partner – head of national retail
Qualifications
MRICS
Career history
1981 Joined Cushman & Wakefield Healey & Baker
Professional memberships
RICS
Contact details
Cushman & Wakefield Healey & Baker, 43-45 Portman Square, London W1A 3BG
Tel 020 7935 5000
Fax 020 7152 5360
Web www.cushwake.com
Direct tel 020 7152 5198
Direct fax 020 7152 5383
Email justin.taylor@eur.cushwake.com

TAYLOR, Kenneth
Aedas AHR Architects

Position
Joint managing director

Qualifications
MSc; Dip Arch; RIBA
Contact details
Aedas AHR Architects Ltd, St Mary's Court, 21 St Mary's Street, Shrewsbury SY1 1ED
Tel 0174 328 3000
Fax 0174 323 2717
Web www.aedas.com
Mobile 07710 576784
Email ken.taylor@ahr.co.uk

TAYLOR, Mark
Workspace Group
Position
Finance director
Qualifications
BSc; FCA
Career history
Since 1995 Finance director, Workspace Group.
1994-95 Finance director, Crown Housing Trust, (MOD).
1978-94 John Laing; latterly as joint managing director of John Laing Developments and director of group investments
Professional memberships
Institute of Chartered Accountants in England & Wales
Contact details
Workspace Group plc, Magenta House, 85 Whitechapel Road, London E1 1DU
Tel 020 7247 7614
Fax 020 7247 0157
Web www.workspacegroup.co.uk
Email mark.taylor@workspacegroup.co.uk

TAYLOR, Michael
King Sturge
Position
Partner, national head of out-of-town retail
Qualifications
BSc, Urban Land Econ; MRICS
Career history
1979 Joined King Sturge
Professional memberships
Accessible Retail; RICS
Contact details
King Sturge, 7 Stratford Place, London W1C 1ST
Tel 020 7493 4933
Fax 020 7409 0469
Web www.kingsturge.com
Direct tel 020 7318 4310
Email michael.taylor@kingsturge.co.uk

TAYLOR, Michael
Tuffin Ferraby & Taylor
Position
Joint senior partner
Qualifications
FRICS; MAPM
Professional memberships
RICS
Contact details
Tuffin Ferraby & Taylor, Friary Court, 13-21 High Street, Guildford GU1 3DG
Tel 020 8549 8763
Fax 020 8546 1589
Web www.tftsurveyors.co.uk
Email mtaylor@tftkingston.com

TAYLOR, Neal
Rugby Estates
Position
Director
Qualifications
BSc Hons; MRICS
Career history
Since 1992 Property director (investment and development), Rugby Estates.
1989-92 Fund manager, CB Hillier Parker
Professional memberships
RICS
Contact details
Rugby Estates plc, 14 Garrick Street, London WC2E 9SB
Tel 020 7632 2200
Fax 020 7632 2222
Web www.rugbyestates.plc.uk
Mobile 07768 681703
Email neal@rugbyestates.plc.uk

TAYLOR, Paul
Berrymans Lace Mawer
Position
National senior partner
Qualifications
LLB
Career history
1970 Joined Berrymans (now Berrymans Lace Mawer); became partner in 1973, senior partner in 1991 and national senior partner of merged firm in 1997.
1969 Admitted to Roll of Solicitors
Other roles
Author of many articles for legal, construction and insurance journals; regularly addresses conferences and seminars in UK and overseas
Professional memberships
City of London Solicitors Company; International Association of Defence Lawyers; International Federation of Consulting Engineers; Society of Construction Law; Technology & Construction Solicitors Association
Contact details
Berrymans Lace Mawer, Salisbury House, London Wall, London EC2M 5QN
Tel 020 7638 2811
Fax 020 7920 0361
Web www.blm-law.com
Email paul.taylor@blm-law.com

TAYLOR, Paul
Rotch Property Group
Position
Group chief executive
Career history
1999 Joined Rotch. Previously headed structured finance team at NatWest Bank; spent 17 years at the bank
Interests
Chelsea Football Club
Contact details
Rotch Property Group, 18 Upper Grosvenor Street, London W1K 7PW
Tel 020 7550 3800
Direct tel 020 7550 3899
Mobile 07818 421964
Email pvt@rotch.com

TAYLOR, Peter
Hewitsons
Position
Partner
Career history
1986 Joined Hewitson Becke + Shaw (now Hewitsons); appointed partner in 1989.
1985-86 Shacklocks
Other roles
Legal associate, RTPI; member, Law Society's specialist planning panel
Professional memberships
Law Society
Interests
Running
Contact details
Hewitsons, 7 Spencer Parade, Northampton NN1 5AB
Tel 01604 233233
Fax 01604 627941
Web www.hewitsons.com
Email petertaylor@hewitsons.com

TAYLOR, Peter
John Laing Partnership
Position
Managing director
Qualifications
BSc Hons, Construction
Other roles
Chairman, John Laing Training; housing forum steering group committee, RICS residential policy group

T

Professional memberships
RICS
Contact details
John Laing Partnership Ltd, The Waterfront, Elstree Road, Borehamwood WD6 3BS
Tel 020 8236 3700
Fax 020 8236 8756
Web www.laingpartnership.co.uk
Email peter.taylor@jlaingpartnership.co.uk

TAYLOR, Roger
Taylor Woodrow Developments

Position
Property director
Qualifications
FRICS
Professional memberships
RICS
Contact details
Taylor Woodrow Developments Ltd, 41 Clarendon Road, Watford WD17 1TQ
Tel 01923 478400
Web www.taylorwoodrow.com
Direct tel 020 7264 5232
Direct fax 020 7481 4515
Mobile 07816 515232
Email Roger.Taylor@uk.taylorwoodrow.com

TAYLOR, Simon
Workspace Group

Position
Divisional director
Career history
1988-96 Director (asset management), Phoenix Beard
Professional memberships
RICS
Contact details
Workspace Group plc, Magenta House, 85 Whitechapel Road, London E1 1DU
Tel 020 7247 7614
Fax 020 7247 0157
Web www.workspacegroup.co.uk
Direct tel 020 7369 2329
Mobile 07811 450950
Email simon.taylor@workspacegroup.co.uk

TCHENGUIZ, Robert
R20

Position
Chairman
Qualifications
BA
Career history
Since 1982 Chairman, Rotch Group
Interests
Shooting; skiing; tennis
Contact details
R20 Ltd, Leconfield House, Curzon Street, London W1J 5JA
Tel 020 7550 3860
Fax 020 7491 0410
Web www.r20.co.uk
Direct fax 020 7629 5544
Email robert@rotch.com

TCHENGUIZ, Vincent
Rotch Group

Position
Chairman
Other roles
Founder and chairman, Consensus (property company)
Contact details
Rotch Group, Leconfield House, Curzon Street, London W1J 5JA
Tel 020 7409 1055
Fax 020 7409 2304
Direct tel 020 7550 3862
Mobile 07802 308607
Email vincent@rotch.com

TEASDALE, Robert
Wincanton Group

Position
Group property manager
Qualifications
FRICS
Career history
1988 Joined Wincanton
Contact details
Wincanton Group Ltd, Cale House, Station Road, Wincanton BA9 9AD
Tel 0196 382 8282
Fax 0196 382 8288
Direct tel 0196 382 8370
Direct fax 0196 382 8375
Email bob.teasdale@wincanton.co.uk

TECKS, Jonathan
Littman Chambers

Position
Barrister
Qualifications
MA Hons (Cantab); FCIArb
Career history
Since 1995 Barrister/arbitrator/mediator, Littman Chambers.
1989-95 Barrister/arbitrator/mediator, 3 Paper Buildings, Temple.
1980-89 Barrister, 10 King's Bench Walk, Temple.
1978 Called to Bar
Other roles
Director of advocacy and dispute resolution, University of the West of England; chartered arbitrator and panel member of Chartered Institute of Arbitrators; co-author, *The Arbitration Act 1996 – A Commentary* (Blackwell Science, 1996, 2nd edition 2000); directs and lectures on Chartered Institute of Arbitrators training courses; founder member, City Disputes Panel
Professional memberships
Chartered Institute of Arbitrators
Interests
Cycling; horse riding
Contact details
Littman Chambers (Chambers of Mark Littman QC), 12 Gray's Inn Square, London WC1R 5JP
Tel 020 7404 4866
Fax 020 7404 4812
Web www.littmanchambers.com
Email jotecks@littmanchambers.com

TEMPERTON, Andrew
Bermac Properties

Position
Managing director
Qualifications
BSc Hons; MRICS
Career history
1997 Joined Bermac Properties as director; appointed managing director in 2003.
1988-97 Land and development director, Countryside Properties
Professional memberships
RICS
Interests
Family; golf; rugby; sailing
Contact details
Bermac Properties plc, 86a Broomfield Road, Chelmsford CM1 1SS
Tel 01245 344444
Fax 01245 344000
Web www.bermacproperties.co.uk
Mobile 07798 771721
Email andrewt@bermacproperties.co.uk

TEMPLEMAN, Chris
J Sainsbury

Position
Head – asset development
Contact details
J Sainsbury plc, 33 Holborn, London EC1N 2HT
Tel 020 7695 6000
Fax 020 7695 7610
Web www.j-sainsbury.co.uk
Email chris.templeman@sainsburys.co.uk

TERRAFRANCA, Raymond
Northridge Capital

Position
Managing director
Qualifications
MBA
Career history
2000-02 Vice-president, Credit Suisse First Boston.
1997-99 Terranet Capital Partners.
1994-97 Managing director, Rimco.
1992-94 Property director, Al Baraka Investment Co.
1990-92 Vice-president, Bankers Trust Co
Contact details
Northridge Capital Ltd, 72 New Bond Street, London W1S 1RR
Tel 020 7629 5131
Fax 020 7629 6283
Email rterrafranca@nridge.com

THAKER, Harin
Hypo Real Estate International

Position
Chief executive
Qualifications
MBA
Career history
Since 2003 Chief executive, Hypo Real Estate International.
1989-2003 Hypo-und Vereinsbank Group
Other roles
Chief executive, Hypo Real Estate Investment Banking
Professional memberships
Institute of Directors
Contact details
Hypo Real Estate International, 110 Cannon Street, London EC4N 6EW
Tel 020 7743 7743
Fax 020 7743 7700
Web www.hypointernational.com
Direct tel 020 7743 7600
Direct fax 020 7743 7606
Mobile 07774 443598
Email harin.thaker@hypointernational.com

THATCHER, Michael
Lambert Smith Hampton

Position
Director – head of investment
Qualifications
BSc Hons; MRICS
Career history
1989 Joined Lambert Smith Hampton
Other roles
South area board member, Lambert Smith Hampton
Professional memberships
RICS
Interests
Cricket; fishing; sailing; shooting; tennis
Contact details
Lambert Smith Hampton Ltd, Regent Arcade House, 19-25 Argyll Street, London W1F 7TS
Tel 020 7494 4000
Fax 020 7414 0866
Web www.lsh.co.uk
Direct tel 020 7663 8296
Direct fax 020 7414 0838
Mobile 07768 094019
Email mthatcher@lsh.co.uk

THEAKSTON, Tim
Allsop & Co

Position
Partner – residential investments
Career history
Since 1981 Partner (residential investments), Allsop & Co.
1978-81 Residential negotiator, Sturgis & Co
Contact details
Allsop & Co, 100 Knightsbridge, London SW1X 7LB
Tel 020 7437 6977
Fax 020 7344 2640
Web www.allsop.co.uk
Direct fax 020 7344 2630
Email tim.theakston@allsop.co.uk

THERON, Nicola
PricewaterhouseCoopers

Position
Director – real estate
Qualifications
MRICS
Career history
1991 Joined management consultancy team, PricewaterhouseCoopers; has worked with a number of occupational property clients in exploiting the value of their occupational portfolios
Professional memberships
Investment Property Forum
Interests
Church; family; sport
Contact details
PricewaterhouseCoopers, Plumtree Court, London EC4A 4HT
Tel 020 7583 5000
Fax 020 7862 4652
Web www.pwc.com
Direct tel 020 7212 6140
Direct fax 020 7212 6666
Mobile 07710 737709
Email nicola.a.theron@uk.pwcglobal.com

THEYER, Nigel
Bond Pearce

Position
Senior partner
Qualifications
MA (Cantab)
Career history
1977 Admitted to Roll of Solicitors.
1975 Joined Bond Pearce; became partner in 1982 and senior partner in 1996
Professional memberships
Law Society
Interests
Cricket; golf; tennis
Contact details
Bond Pearce, Bristol Bridge House, Redcliff Street, Bristol BS1 6BJ
Tel 0117 929 9197
Fax 0117 929 9198
Web www.bondpearce.com
Direct tel 0117 917 1461
Mobile 07831 464402
Email ntheyer@bondpearce.com

THOM, James
New Square Chambers

Position
Barrister
Qualifications
QC; MA; BCL; Barrister
Career history
2003 Appointed QC.
1997 Called to Bar (St Vincent and the Grenadines).
1974 Called to Bar
Other roles
Recorder
Professional memberships
Chancery Bar Association; Professional Negligence Bar Association
Contact details
New Square Chambers (Chambers of Charles Purle QC), 12 New Square, London WC2A 3SW
Tel 020 7419 8000
Fax 020 7419 8050
Web www.newsquarechambers.co.uk
Mobile 07860 214669
Email james.thom@NewSquareChambers.co.uk

THOMAS, Dorrien
AXA Real Estate Investment Managers

Position
Asset manager
Qualifications

T

MRICS
Professional memberships
RICS
Contact details
AXA Real Estate Investment Managers Ltd, 7 Newgate Street, London EC1A 7HD
Tel 020 7003 1000
Fax 020 7575 8585
Web www.axa-im.co.uk
Email Dorrien.Thomas@axa-reim.co.uk

THOMAS, Geoff
DTZ Debenham Tie Leung
Position
Regional chairman – Midlands and South West
Qualifications
BSc; FRICS
Career history
Since 1972 Regional chairman (Midlands & South West), DTZ Debenham Tie Leung.
1971-72 Articled accountant, Tansley Witt & Co
Other roles
Deputy bailiff and governor, King Edward VI Schools Foundation; board member, Locate in Birmingham; board member, Birmingham Forward transport committee
Professional memberships
Arbrix; Birmingham Forward; British Council for Offices; BPF; Locate in Birmingham; Office Agents Society; RICS
Interests
Antiques; architecture; field sports; fishing; food and drink; golf; history; IT; local history; photography; shooting; wine
Contact details
DTZ Debenham Tie Leung, 10 Colmore Row, Birmingham B3 2QD
Tel 0121 200 2050
Fax 0121 200 3022
Web www.dtz.com
Direct tel 0121 697 7235
Mobile 07771 604548
Email geoff.thomas@dtz.com

THOMAS, Ian
DTZ Debenham Tie Leung
Position
Director
Qualifications
BSc; MRICS
Career history
1985 Joined Debenham Tewson & Chinnocks (became DTZ Debenham Thorpe, then DTZ Debenham Tie Leung)
Other roles
Regional co-ordinator for disaster recovery, British Council for Offices
Professional memberships
British Council for Offices
Interests
Golf
Contact details
DTZ Debenham Tie Leung, Marchmount House, Dumfries Place, Cardiff CF10 3RJ
Tel 029 2039 8182
Fax 029 2039 5379
Web www.dtz.com
Direct tel 029 2026 2261
Direct fax 029 2038 7780
Email ian.thomas@dtz.com

THOMAS, Martin
City & West End Developments
Position
Construction director
Contact details
City & West End Developments Ltd, 34 Jermyn Street, London SW1Y 6HS
Tel 020 7292 6100
Fax 020 7292 6111
Email martin.thomas@cwe.co.uk

THOMAS, Pat
SJ Berwin
Position
Partner – head of planning and environment
Qualifications
OBE; MA (Oxon); LARTPI
Career history
Since 1988 Partner, SJ Berwin.
1979-88 Denton Hall: partner from 1981.
1975-79 Greater London Council and London Borough of Southwark
Other roles
Member of planning and environmental law committee and specialist planning panel, Law Society; member, CBI property group; planning and environment committee member, BPF; committee member, Law Society Bar council; involved in RICS Oxford annual joint planning law conference; planning and environment committee member, City of London Solicitors' Company; member, CBI property management forum; involved in ODPM quinquennial review of the planning inspectorate; principal author and editor, *Planning Factbook* (Gee); contributor of planning law chapter in *Surveyors' Factbook* (Gee)
Professional memberships
City of London Law Society; International Bar Association
Interests
Fly fishing; theatre; travel
Contact details
SJ Berwin, 222 Gray's Inn Road, London WC1X 8HB
Tel 020 7533 2222
Fax 020 7533 2000
Web www.sjberwin.com
Direct tel 020 7533 2450
Email pat.thomas@sjberwin.com

THOMAS, Richard
Montagu Evans
Position
Managing partner
Qualifications
MA; BSc; MRICS
Professional memberships
RICS
Contact details
Montagu Evans, 44-48 Dover Street, London W1S 4AZ
Tel 020 7493 4002
Fax 020 7312 7547
Web www.montagu-evans.co.uk
Email richard.thomas@montagu-evans.co.uk

THOMAS, Rod
Vail Williams
Position
Partner – rating
Qualifications
FRICS
Career history
1997 Partner and head of rating, Vail Williams.
1982-97 Head of rating, Fuller Peiser.
1967-82 Valuation Office, Portsmouth, Southampton, Westminster
Professional memberships
Rating Surveyors Association; RICS
Interests
Aviation; sailing; tennis
Contact details
Vail Williams, Thames Valley Office, 130 Wharfedale Road, Winnersh RG41 5RB
Tel 0118 933 5600
Fax 0118 933 5634
Web www.vailwilliams.com
Direct tel 0118 933 5624
Mobile 07881 516567
Email rthomas@vailwilliams.com

THOMAS, Roger
Cooke & Arkwright
Position
Chairman
Qualifications
FRICS
Career history
1972 Joined Cooke & Arkwright; moved to London office in 1978 as associate partner;

returned to Cardiff in 1980; became chairman in 2001

Other roles

Committee member, British Council for Offices; committee member, Office Agents Society

Professional memberships

British Council for Offices; Office Agents Society; RICS

Interests

Cars; field sports

Contact details

Cooke & Arkwright, 7-8 Windsor Place, Cardiff CF10 3SX

Tel 029 2034 6346

Fax 029 2034 6300

Web www.coark.co.uk

Direct fax 029 2034 6350

Email roger.thomas@coark.com

THOMAS, Stephen
Montagu Evans

Position

Partner – head of department (rating)

Qualifications

BSc, Est Man; FRICS

Career history

Since 1993 Partner, Montagu Evans.
1978-93 Director, Herring Son & Daw.
1975-78 Valuation Office of Inland Revenue

Professional memberships

RICS

Interests

Cricket

Contact details

Montagu Evans, 44-48 Dover Street, London W1S 4AZ

Tel 020 7493 4002

Fax 020 7312 7547

Web www.montagu-evans.co.uk

Direct fax 020 7312 7535

Email steve.thomas@montagu-evans.co.uk

THOMLINSON, Nick
Knight Frank

Position

Senior partner

Qualifications

MA (Oxon); FRICS

Career history

1974 Joined Knight Frank

Professional memberships

RICS

Contact details

Knight Frank LLP, 20 Hanover Square, London W1S 1HZ

Tel 020 7629 8171

Fax 020 7493 4114

Web www.knightfrank.com

Direct tel 020 7861 1001

Email nick.thomlinson@knightfrank.com

THOMPSON, Brian
Chesterton International

Position

Managing director, Chesterton Strategic Services

Qualifications

BSc; MBA; MRICS

Career history

1993 Joined Chesterton as director of Chesterton Consulting; became director of Chesterton Strategic Services in 1999 and managing director of Chesterton Strategic Services in 2002.
1990-93 Manager, Price Waterhouse

Professional memberships

RICS

Interests

Food; motor sports; wine

Contact details

Chesterton International, Swan House, 37-39 High Holborn, London WC1V 6AA

Tel 020 7242 0333

Fax 020 7242 1058

Web www.chesterton.co.uk

Direct tel 020 7242 9494

Direct fax 020 7242 9898

Mobile 07712 868675

Email brian.thompson@chesterton.co.uk

THOMPSON, Christopher
Beechcroft Developments

Position

Chief executive

Contact details

Beechcroft Developments Ltd, 1 Church Lane, Wallingford OX10 0DX

Tel 01491 834975

Fax 01491 825433

Email christopherthompson@beechcroft.co.uk

THOMPSON, David
AYH

Position

Chairman

Qualifications

FRICS

Career history

1977 Joined Axtell Yates Hallett (now AYH); became partner in 1984; appointed chairman of AYH in 1999

Professional memberships

British Council for Offices; RICS; Worshipful Company of Chartered Surveyors

Interests

Architecture; fishing; reading; sailing; shooting

Contact details

AYH plc, 1 East Harding Street, London EC4A 3AH

Tel 020 7216 1000

Fax 020 7216 1001

Web www.ayh.com

Direct tel 020 7418 1283

Mobile 07885 321293

Email david.thompson@ayh.co.uk

THOMPSON, Ian
Hartnell Taylor Cook

Position

Partner

Qualifications

FRICS

Career history

1976 Joined Hartnell Taylor Cook.
1975-76 Surveyor, Ladbroke Group Properties

Other roles

Director of project management company

Professional memberships

British Council of Shopping Centres; Bristol Property Agents' Association; RICS; Shop Agents Society

Interests

Golf

Contact details

Hartnell Taylor Cook, Somerset House, 18 Canynge Road, Bristol BS8 3JX

Tel 0117 923 9234

Fax 0117 923 9237

Web www.htc.uk.com

Direct tel 0117 946 4506

Mobile 07836 599904

Email Ian.thompson@htc.uk.com

THOMPSON, Jonathan
KPMG

Position

Partner – UK head of real estate and construction

Professional memberships

BPF; Institute of Chartered Accountants in England & Wales

Contact details

KPMG LLP, 1 Canada Square, London E14 5AB

Tel 020 7311 1000

Web www.kpmg.co.uk

Direct tel 020 7311 4183

Direct fax 020 7311 4122

Email jonathan.thompson@kpmg.co.uk

THOMPSON, Neville
Austin Adams

Position

Director

Qualifications
BSc; MRICS
Career history
Since 1991 Co-founder and director, Austin Adams.
1983-91 Austin & Wyatt, Southampton.
1980-83 Winchester District Valuer's Office
Other roles
Commercial property consultant, legal and taxation committee of Chamber of Commerce; member, National Committee on Health and Hospital Rating (national consortium representing health and hospital occupiers)
Professional memberships
RICS
Interests
Cycling; yachting
Contact details
Austin Adams, 10 Cumberland Place, Southampton SO15 2BH
Tel 023 8033 8811
Fax 023 8023 6588
Web www.austinadams.co.uk
Email NJT@austinadams.co.uk

THOMPSON, Nicholas
Fitzroy Robinson
Position
Managing director
Qualifications
BSc Hons; MBA; ACMA
Career history
1994 Joined Fitzroy Robinson.
1990-93 Deputy group finance director, DTZ Debenham Thorpe.
1987-90 Finance director, Elsworth Sykes
Other roles
Non-executive chairman, Thompson & Newman
Professional memberships
Chartered Institute of Management Accountants
Interests
Golf; opera; rugby; walking
Contact details
Fitzroy Robinson, 14 Devonshire Street, London W1G 7AE
Tel 020 7636 8033
Fax 020 7580 3996
Web www.fitzroyrobinson.com
Direct fax 020 7636 6418
Email nicholas.t@fitzroyrobinson.com

THOMPSON, Nicholas
Prudential Property Investment Managers
Position
Director – head of fund and investment management
Qualifications
FRICS
Career history
1967 Joined Prudential; became divisional director (fund management) in 1990 and chairman of divisional investment panel in 1993; became chief property investment officer at PPM in 1996 and director/head of fund and investment management at PPIM in 1999; expected to retire around Easter 2004
Other roles
Member, Bank of England property forum; member, ODPM property industry forum
Professional memberships
Association of British Insurers; Association of Foreign Investors in Real Estate; Investment Property Forum; RICS; Worshipful Company of Chartered Surveyors
Contact details
Prudential Property Investment Managers Ltd, Princeton House, 271-273 High Holborn, London WC1V 7NE
Tel 020 7548 6600
Fax 020 7548 6999
Web www.prupim.com
Direct tel 020 7548 6572
Direct fax 020 7548 6502
Email nick.thompson@prupim.com

THOMPSON, Sir Nigel
Arup Group
Position
Deputy chairman – Ove Arup & Partners
Qualifications
KCMG; CBE; CEng; FICE; FIStructE
Career history
1960 Joined Ove Arup & Partners
Interests
Conservation; cricket; farming; rugby
Contact details
Arup Group Ltd, 13-17 Fitzroy Street, London W1T 4BS
Tel 020 7636 1531
Web www.arup.com
Direct tel 020 7755 3186
Direct fax 020 7755 3666
Email nigel.thompson@arup.com

THOMPSON, Sarah
Wragge & Co
Position
Partner
Qualifications
LLB
Career history
1986-91 Wilde Sapte.
1984-86 Towers & Hamlin.
1984 Admitted to Roll of Solicitors
Professional memberships
Property Litigation Association
Interests
Theatre; travel
Contact details
Wragge & Co LLP, 55-73 Colmore Row, Birmingham B3 2AS
Tel 0870 903 1000
Fax 0870 904 1099
Web www.wragge.com
Direct tel 0121 214 1089
Email sarah_thompson@wragge.com

THOMSON, Andrew
Aberdeen Property Investors
Position
Director – new business
Qualifications
BSc; MRICS
Career history
Since 1993 Director, Aberdeen Celexa Property Investors (now Aberdeen Property Investors).
1984-93 Associate, Richard Ellis
Professional memberships
Investment Property Forum; RICS
Contact details
Aberdeen Property Investors, Charles House, 5-11 Regent Street, London SW1Y 4LR
Tel 020 7747 1700
Fax 020 7839 7460
Web www.aberdeenpropertyinvestors.com
Direct tel 020 7747 1707
Direct fax 020 7930 9433
Mobile 07799 131707
Email
andrew.thomson@aberdeenpropertyinvestors.com

THOMSON, David
Ryden
Position
Partner – property management
Qualifications
FRICS
Professional memberships
RICS
Contact details
Ryden, 130 St Vincent Street, Glasgow G2 5HF
Tel 0141 204 3838
Fax 0141 204 3554
Web www.ryden.co.uk
Email david.thomson@ryden.co.uk

THOMSON, Ron
Royal Bank of Scotland
Position
Head of property finance group
Contact details

Royal Bank of Scotland, 6th Floor, 6-8 George Street, Edinburgh EH2 2SA
Tel 0131 556 8555
Fax 0131 523 5104
Web www.rbs.co.uk
Direct tel 0131 523 5242
Email ron.thomson@rbs.co.uk

THORNILEY-WALKER, Michael
RadcliffesLeBrasseur

Position
Partner – head of property, Leeds
Career history
Since 1995 Partner/head of property, Le Brasseur J Tickle in Leeds (now RadcliffesLeBrasseur, following merger with Radcliffes).
1974-95 Partner, Sugden & Spencer.
1971-73 Boodle Hatfield.
1971 Admitted to Roll of Solicitors
Other roles
Danish vice-consul for Bradford and Leeds
Professional memberships
Law Society
Interests
Bridge; gardening; rugby; tennis; walking
Contact details
RadcliffesLeBrasseur, 6-7 Park Place, Leeds LS1 2RU
Tel 0113 234 1220
Fax 0113 234 1573
Web www.rlb-law.com
Direct tel 0113 261 5511
Direct fax 0113 245 7329
Email michael.thorniley-walker@rlb-law.com

THORNLEY, Dave
Wilkinson Hardware Stores

Position
Group estates surveyor
Contact details
Wilkinson Hardware Stores Ltd, JK House, PO Box 20 Roebuck Way, Worksop S80 3YY
Tel 01909 505505
Web www.wilko.co.uk
Email dave.thornley@wilko.co.uk

THORNTON, Peter
Greycoat Estates

Position
Chief executive
Qualifications
BSc; FRICS; FICE
Career history
1979 Joined Greycoat (name changed to Greycoat Estates in 1999 following management buyout).
1975-79 Commercial manager, subsidiary property company of Sears Holdings
Professional memberships
Institution of Civil Engineers; RICS
Interests
Cars; motor sports; tennis
Contact details
Greycoat Estates Ltd, Brettenham House, 9 Savoy Street, London WC2E 7EG
Tel 020 7379 1000
Fax 020 7379 8744
Direct fax 020 7836 3865
Mobile 07768 152584
Email pthornton@greycoat.co.uk

THORNTON, Roger
RadcliffesLeBrasseur

Position
Partner – head of property department
Qualifications
MA (Cantab)
Career history
2000 Joined Radcliffes (now RadcliffesLeBrasseur following merger of Le Brasseur J Tickle and Radcliffes); appointed partner same year.
1995-99 Norton Rose.
1993-95 Ashurst Morris Crisp.
1990 Admitted to Roll of Solicitors.
1988-93 Norton Rose
Professional memberships
City of Westminster & Holborn Law Society; Law Society
Interests
Travel; walking
Contact details
RadcliffesLeBrasseur, 5 Great College Street, London SW1P 3SJ
Tel 020 7222 7040
Fax 020 7222 6208
Web www.rlb-law.com
Email roger.thornton@rlb-law.com

THURTELL, Ken
Gerald Eve

Position
Partner – head of Glasgow office
Qualifications
FRICS; ACIArb
Career history
1995 Joined Gerald Eve; partner since 1998.
1992-95 Strathclyde Regional Council.
1990-92 Roy Slater.
1988-90 Speirs Parnie Residential.
1985-88 Slater Hogg & Howison.
1983-85 Broseley Estates
Professional memberships
RICS
Interests
Rugby; skiing; travel
Contact details
Gerald Eve, Caithness House, 127 St Vincent Street, Glasgow G2 5JF
Tel 0141 221 6397
Fax 0141 204 2226
Web www.geraldeve.com
Direct tel 0141 227 2371
Email kthurtell@geraldeve.com

THWAITES, Paul
Ashwell Property Group

Position
Chief executive
Career history
1981 Set up TP Associates; multi-million pound contract secured with US government in 1998 to build homes for servicemen and their families in Lakenheath area led to creation of Ashwell Property Group
Other roles
Member, Great Eastern Investment Forum; driving force behind SOFAST (Stride Out For Addenbrooke's And Sargent Together), which raises money for Sargent Cancer Care for Children and Addenbrooke's Hospital Children's Services
Professional memberships
Chartered Institute of Building; Institute of Directors; Professional Cricketers Association; RICS
Interests
Cricket (Bunbury Cricket Club, Cambridge Youth Cricket, Essex County Cricket Club, MCC); supports and sponsors local cricket clubs and has own charity cricket side, Ashwell
Contact details
Ashwell Property Group plc, Botanic House, 100 Hills Road, Cambridge CB2 1JZ
Tel 01223 443340
Fax 01223 443371
Web www.ashwellproperty.co.uk
Email info@ashwellproperty.co.uk

TICE, Martin
Vail Williams

Position
Equity partner
Qualifications
BSc; FRICS
Career history
1983 Joined LS Vail & Son (now Vail Williams)
Professional memberships
RICS
Interests
Motorbikes; sailing; tennis; theatre; walking
Contact details
Vail Williams, 1 The Quarterdeck, Portsmouth

PO6 4TP
Tel 023 9220 3200
Fax 023 9221 9990
Web www.vailwilliams.com
Email mtice@vailwilliams.com

TIESI, Doug
Credit Suisse First Boston

Position
Director – head of European real estate
Qualifications
BS, Accounting (Lehigh University)
Career history
2000 Joined Credit Suisse First Boston (as result of merger with DLJ): head of European real estate securitisation and finance group
Other roles
Certified public accountant
Contact details
Credit Suisse First Boston, 1 Cabot Square, London E14 4QJ
Tel 020 7888 8888
Fax 020 7883 5819
Web www.csfb.com
Direct tel 020 7888 6199
Email Doug.Tiesi@csfb.com

TILLSON, Mark
Edward Symmons & Partners

Position
Partner – head of agency & investment
Qualifications
MRICS
Career history
Since 2000 Partner, Edward Symmons & Partners.
1994-2000 Director, Lambert Smith Hampton.
1992-94 Partner, Conrad Ritblat.
1981-92 Surveyor/partner, De Morgan & Co
Professional memberships
RICS
Interests
Cricket; cycling; swimming
Contact details
Edward Symmons & Partners, Nuffield House, 41-46 Piccadilly, London W1J 0DS
Tel 020 7344 4500
Fax 020 7344 4555
Web www.edwardsymmons.com
Direct tel 020 7344 4601
Mobile 07979 541220
Email mark.tillson@edwardsymmons.com

TINDLEY, George
FPDSavills

Position
Director – fund management
Contact details
FPDSavills Ltd, 20 Grosvenor Hill, London W1K 3HQ
Tel 020 7499 8644
Fax 020 7495 3773
Web www.fpdsavills.co.uk
Direct tel 020 7409 8722
Mobile 07764 608657
Email gtindley@fpdsavills.co.uk

TIPLADY, Michael
Jones Lang LaSalle

Position
European director – project and development services
Qualifications
BSc; FRICS
Career history
1986 Joined Jones Lang LaSalle as partner (development and project management); became director (building surveying) in 1992 and European director (project and development services) in 2001
Other roles
Lead director (building surveying) for England, Jones Lang LaSalle
Professional memberships
RICS
Interests
Field sports; gardening; motor sports
Contact details
Jones Lang LaSalle Ltd, 22 Hanover Square, London W1A 2BN
Tel 020 7493 6040
Fax 020 7408 0220
Web www.joneslanglasalle.com
Direct tel 020 7399 5908
Direct fax 020 7399 5784
Email michael.tiplady@eu.joneslanglasalle.com

TIPPLES, Amanda
Maitland Chambers

Position
Barrister
Qualifications
MA (Cantab)
Career history
1991 Called to Bar
Other roles
Elected member of Bar Council (1995-97); past chairman, Young Barristers' Committee
Professional memberships
Chancery Bar Association; Commercial Bar Association; Property Bar Association
Contact details
Maitland Chambers, 7 Stone Buildings, London WC2A 3SZ
Tel 020 7406 1200
Fax 020 7406 1300
Web www.maitlandchambers.com
Email atipples@maitlandchambers.com

TITCHEN, Jeremy
Grosvenor

Position
Commercial director
Qualifications
MRICS
Other roles
Member, Grosvenor's UK and Ireland statutory board
Professional memberships
RICS
Contact details
Grosvenor Ltd, 70 Grosvenor Street, London W1K 3JP
Tel 020 7408 0988
Fax 020 7629 9115
Web www.grosvenor.com
Direct tel 020 7312 6354
Direct fax 020 7873 1354
Mobile 07768 217895
Email jeremy.titchen@grosvenor.com

TITCOMB, Mark
Eurohypo

Position
Managing director – origination
Qualifications
BSc; MRICS
Career history
1995-2002 General manager, Rheinische Hypothekenbank.
1992-95 Assistant director, Savills Finance.
1987-92 Associate, Savills Commercial.
1984-87 Richard Ellis
Professional memberships
Association of Property Bankers; Investment Property Forum; RICS
Interests
Fishing; golf; shooting; sport
Contact details
Eurohypo AG, 90 Long Acre, London WC2E 9RA
Tel 020 7759 7600
Fax 020 7759 7672
Web www.eurohypo.com
Direct tel 020 7759 7607
Mobile 07802 769319
Email mark.titcomb@eurohypo.com

TITHERIDGE, Tim
City Estates

Position
Director

Career history
1974-86 Partner, Mason Owen & Partners.
1970-74 Clive Lewis & Partners
Other roles
Director, Southampton City Radio; vice-chairman, Wessex Cancer Trust; chairman, Hampshire Sporting Club
Interests
Golf; rugby; sport
Contact details
City Estates Ltd, Brunswick House, Brunswick Place, Southampton SO15 2AP
Tel 023 8021 2060
Fax 023 8021 2007
Mobile 07702 089009
Email tim.titheridge@rokgroup.com

TITMUS MATHER, Marc
ABN AMRO Corporate Finance

Position
Assistant director – real estate
Qualifications
BSc Hons; MSc; ACIOB
Career history
Since 2001 Assistant director, ABN AMRO Real Estate Investment Banking Group.
2001 European development analyst, Tishman Speyer Properties.
2000 Investment analyst, TrizecHahn.
1996-2000 Senior consultant, Arthur Andersen.
1993-96 EC Harris Project Management
Professional memberships
Securities & Futures Authority
Interests
Cycling; fishing; horse riding; shooting
Contact details
ABN AMRO Corporate Finance Ltd, 250 Bishopsgate, London EC2M 4AA
Tel 020 7678 8000
Fax 020 7256 8500
Web www.abnamro.com
Direct tel 020 7678 2838
Direct fax 020 7678 1370
Mobile 07810 555653
Email marc.titmus@uk.abnamro.com

TIZZARD, Robert
Edwin Hill

Position
Partner – head of professional services and rating
Qualifications
BSc; MRICS; IRRV
Career history
Since 1986 Partner, Edwin Hill.
1978-86 Board director/head of rating, Sinclair Goldsmith.
1976-78 Valuation Office
Professional memberships
Institute of Revenues Rating & Valuation; RICS
Interests
Sport
Contact details
Edwin Hill, 18 Savile Row, London W1S 3PW
Tel 020 7287 2020
Fax 020 7734 1255
Web www.edwinhill.co.uk
Email rgt@edwinhill.co.uk

TOBIN, Benjamin
Strettons

Position
Director
Qualifications
BSc; FRICS
Career history
1978-79 Surveyor, Portman Estates.
1977-78 Sweby Cowen
Other roles
Practising tutor for Masters course in property valuation, City University Business School; APC assessor, RICS; registered property receiver; member of RICS property auctioneering and insolvency groups; co-author of RICS/ISVA/NAEA *Guidance Notes for Auctioneers*
Professional memberships
RICS
Interests
Charity; classical music; IT; jazz; reading; walking
Contact details
Strettons Ltd, Central House, 189-203 Hoe Street, London E17 3SZ
Tel 020 8520 9911
Fax 020 8520 8022
Web www.strettons.co.uk
Mobile 07989 395650
Email btobin@strettons.co.uk

TOBIN, Peter
Strettons

Position
Director
Qualifications
BSc; MPhil; FRICS; FCIArb
Career history
Since 1967 Strettons.
1965-67 Weatherall Green & Smith
Other roles
Board member, Bnei Brith JBG Housing Association; member, Chartered Institute of Arbitrators panel of arbitrators assigned to determine disputes between RICS members and the public; member, RICS president's panel of independent experts; member, RICS disciplinary and appeals board
Professional memberships
Chartered Institute of Arbitrators; Expert Witness Institute; RICS
Interests
Gardening; IT; walking
Contact details
Strettons Ltd, Central House, 189-203 Hoe Street, London E17 3SZ
Tel 020 8520 9911
Fax 020 8520 8022
Web www.strettons.co.uk
Email petertobin@strettons.co.uk

TOBIN, Philip
Strettons

Position
Director
Qualifications
FRICS; MCIArb
Career history
1980 Became principal at Strettons Hackney office; principal at Spitalfields and City Office since 1987
Other roles
External tutor, City University Business School; valuer-member, Residential Property Tribunal Service; member, RICS president's panels of arbitrators; RICS assessor for testing professional competence of newly qualified surveyors; listed in Law Society *Directory of Expert Witnesses*
Professional memberships
Chartered Institute of Arbitrators; RICS
Interests
Art; family; IT; literature; theatre; travel
Contact details
Strettons Ltd, 41 Artillery Lane, London E1 7LP
Tel 020 7375 1801
Fax 020 7375 1010
Web www.strettons.co.uk
Direct tel 020 7422 0987
Email philip.tobin@strettons.co.uk

TODD, David
Strutt & Parker

Position
Head of City professional department
Qualifications
BSc, Econ; FRICS; FCIArb
Contact details
Strutt & Parker, 1 Angel Court, London EC2R 7EQ
Tel 020 7600 3456
Fax 020 7600 3330
Web www.struttandparker.com
Email dtodd@struttandparker.com

T

TOLLAST, Cris
CB Richard Ellis

Position
Managing director
Qualifications
MRICS; IRRV
Career history
Since 1975 CB Richard Ellis.
1973-74 Investment surveyor, Pepper Angliss & Yarwood
Professional memberships
Institute of Revenues Rating & Valuation; RICS
Contact details
CB Richard Ellis, Kingsley House, 1a Wimpole Street, London W1G 0RE
Tel 020 7182 2000
Fax 020 7182 7001
Web www.cbre.com
Direct tel 020 7182 2292
Email cris.tollast@cbre.com

TOLLEY, Michael
Cluttons

Position
Partner – building surveying
Qualifications
BSc; CEng; FRICS; PPCSI; MIStructE
Career history
1976-82 Associate partner (building surveying department), Matthews & Goodman.
1974-76 Senior building surveyor, Gooch & Wagstaff.
1970-74 Acting assistant district surveyor, Greater London Council District Surveyors Service, Lambeth
Professional memberships
RICS
Contact details
Cluttons, Portman House, 2 Portman Street, London W1H 6DU
Tel 020 7408 1010
Fax 020 7629 3263
Web www.cluttons.com
Direct tel 020 7647 7356
Mobile 07775 618511
Email mfa.tolley@cluttons.com

TOMALIN, Phillip
CNP

Position
Managing director
Qualifications
BSc Hons; MRICS
Career history
Since 1998 Director, CNP.
1995-98 Partner, King Sturge & Co.
1989-95 Colliers Erdman Lewis.
1986-87 Keith Snell & Partners
Professional memberships
RICS
Contact details
CNP Ltd, 75 Devonshire Avenue, Leeds LS8 1AU
Tel 0113 266 0011
Fax 0113 266 0022
Email philtomalin@cnpltd.co.uk

TOMKINS, Glenn
CIT Group

Position
Chief financial officer
Qualifications
BComm; ACA
Career history
1991-96 Finance director, International Fiscal Services.
1986-91 Chief accountant, Prasidial Anstalt Group
Professional memberships
Institute of Chartered Accountants in England & Wales
Contact details
CIT Group plc, 8-10 Bourdon Street, London W1K 3PD
Tel 020 7667 7766
Fax 020 7667 7770
Web www.cit.co.uk
Direct fax 020 7667 7759
Email gt@cit.co.uk

TOMKINSON, Mike
Carisbrooke Alliance

Position
Director
Contact details
Carisbrooke Alliance Ltd, 22 Grosvenor Square, London W1K 6DT
Tel 020 7493 6774
Fax 020 7493 2454
Email mtomkinson@carisbrookealliance.co.uk

TOMNAY, Gerard
Manches

Position
Partner – head of corporate real estate
Career history
2002 Joined Manches.
1987-2002 Nabarro Nathanson.
1987 Admitted to Roll of Solicitors
Other roles
Member, RICS corporate real estate group; member, RICS examinations board; member, RICS telecoms forum
Professional memberships
British Council for Offices; Institute of Directors
Interests
Football (keen Arsenal fan and qualified Football Association coach and referee); golf; skiing
Contact details
Manches, Aldwych House, 81 Aldwych, London WC2B 4HN
Tel 020 7404 4433
Fax 020 7430 1133
Web www.manches.com
Direct tel 020 7753 7507
Mobile 07831 146799
Email gerard.tomnay@manches.co.uk

TÖPEL, Sven
Hammerson

Position
Director – acquisitions and development
Qualifications
BSc Hons, Econ; MRICS; MSc, Est Man
Career history
1996 Joined Hammerson.
1989-96 Investment surveyor, Jones Lang LaSalle
Professional memberships
RICS
Contact details
Hammerson plc, 100 Park Lane, London W1K 7AR
Tel 020 7887 1000
Fax 020 7887 1010
Web www.hammerson.co.uk
Email stopel@hammerson.co.uk

TOUGH, Andrew
Hamilton Osborne King

Position
Director, Belfast office
Qualifications
BSc; MRICS; ACIArb
Career history
Since 2001 Director (Belfast office), Hamilton Osborne King.
1988-2001 Director (professional services), Lisney.
1985-88 Edward Erdman.
1984-85 Richard Ellis.
1983-84 Jones Lang Wootton
Professional memberships
Chartered Institute of Arbitrators; RICS
Contact details
Hamilton Osborne King, Rose Building, 16 Howard Street, Belfast BT1 6PA
Tel 028 9026 7820
Fax 028 9026 7829
Web www.hok.ie
Direct tel 028 9026 7822
Email andrew.tough@hok.ie

TOUGH, David
Ryden

Position
Partner and head of planning, consulting group
Qualifications
FRICS; Dip TP; MRTPI
Career history
1989 Joined Ryden.
1975-89 Principal planner, Kyle & Carrick District Council
Other roles
External examiner, University of Paisley
Professional memberships
RICS; RTPI
Interests
Golf; music; travel
Contact details
Ryden, 46 Castle Street, Edinburgh EH2 3BN
Tel 0131 225 6612
Fax 0131 225 5766
Web www.ryden.co.uk
Direct tel 0131 473 3292
Mobile 07774 127086
Email david.tough@ryden.co.uk

TOWNSEND, John
Cushman & Wakefield Healey & Baker

Position
Partner and auctioneer
Qualifications
BSc; FRICS
Career history
Since 1996 Partner and auctioneer, Cushman & Wakefield Healey & Baker.
1983-95 Director and head of auctions, Colliers Erdman Lewis.
1981-83 West End office agency, Debenham Tewson & Chinnocks
Other roles
Member, RICS auctioneering skills panel; member and former chairman, ISVA auctioneering committee; member and former chairman, ISVA central London branch committee
Professional memberships
RICS
Contact details
Cushman & Wakefield Healey & Baker, 43-45 Portman Square, London W1A 3BG
Tel 020 7935 5000
Fax 020 7152 5360
Web www.cushwake.com
Direct tel 020 7152 5025
Direct fax 020 7152 5394
Email john.townsend@eur.cushwake.com

TOWNSEND, Kevin
ISG Occupancy

Position
Director – London property management
Qualifications
MRICS
Contact details
ISG Occupancy Ltd, 17-19 Maddox Street, London W1S 1QG
Tel 020 7290 3333
Fax 020 7290 3334
Web www.isgplc.com
Direct tel 020 7290 3321
Email kevin.townsend@isgplc.com

TOZER, Stephanie
9 Old Square

Position
Barrister
Contact details
9 Old Square (Chambers of Michael Driscoll QC), Ground Floor, London WC2A 3SR
Tel 020 7405 4682
Fax 020 7831 7107
Web www.9oldsquare.co.uk
Email stephanie.tozer@9oldsquare.co.uk

TRACE, Anthony
Maitland Chambers

Position
Barrister
Qualifications
MA (Cantab); QC
Career history
1981 Called to Bar
Other roles
Contributed to *Butterworths' Practical Insolvency*; deputy managing editor, *Receivers Administrators & Liquidators Quarterly*; vice-chairman, Chancery Bar Association
Professional memberships
Bar Sports Law Group; Chancery Bar Association; Commercial Bar Association
Contact details
Maitland Chambers, 7 Stone Buildings, London WC2A 3SZ
Tel 020 7406 1200
Fax 020 7406 1300
Web www.maitlandchambers.com
Email atrace@maitlandchambers.com

TRAVERS, John
Cushman & Wakefield Healey & Baker

Position
Chairman and senior partner
Qualifications
BSc; FRICS
Career history
1975 Joined Cushman & Wakefield Healey & Baker.
1973-75 Laing Development Corp
Professional memberships
RICS
Contact details
Cushman & Wakefield Healey & Baker, 43-45 Portman Square, London W1A 3BG
Tel 020 7935 5000
Fax 020 7152 5360
Web www.cushwake.com
Direct tel 020 7152 5004
Direct fax 020 7152 5350
Email john.travers@eur.cushwake.com

TREHEARNE, Ian
Berwin Leighton Paisner

Position
Partner – planning and environment
Qualifications
BA; MRTPI
Career history
1985 Joined Berwin Leighton. Background in local government (London boroughs of Islington and Camden, City of Westminster).
1980 Called to Bar
Other roles
Member of London First urban regeneration task force; council member, British Urban Regeneration Association steering group
Professional memberships
British Council for Offices; British Urban Regeneration Association; RTPI
Interests
Opera; sailing; theatre
Contact details
Berwin Leighton Paisner Ltd, Adelaide House, London Bridge, London EC4R 9HA
Tel 020 7760 1000
Fax 020 7760 1111
Web www.berwinleighton.com
Direct tel 020 7760 4259
Email ian.trehearne@blplaw.com

TRELOAR, Alan
Vickery Holman

Position
Associate director
Contact details
Vickery Holman Ltd, Walsingham House, Newham Road, Truro TR1 2DP
Tel 01872 271033
Fax 01872 222791
Web www.vickeryholman.com
Email mail@vickeryholman.ltd.uk

T

TRIBE, Nicholas
Catalyst Capital

Position
Partner, director – asset management
Qualifications
BSc Hons; MRICS
Career history
1989-98 Fund manager, Royal & Sun Alliance Property Investments.
1988-89 Pepper Fox
Professional memberships
Investment Property Forum; RICS
Contact details
Catalyst Capital LLP, 33 Cavendish Square, London W1G 0PW
Tel 020 7290 5100
Fax 020 7290 5115
Web www.catalystcapital.com
Email ntribe@catalystcapital.com

TRICKEY, Henry
Starbucks Coffee Co

Position
Director – real estate
Contact details
Starbucks Coffee Co Ltd, 11 Heathmans Road, London SW6 4TJ
Tel 020 7878 4900
Web starbucks.co.uk/en-us
Direct tel 020 7878 4951
Email HTrickey@starbucks.com

TRINDER, Peter
Nelson Bakewell

Position
Director – investment consulting
Qualifications
BSc Hons; MRICS
Career history
Since 1999 Board director, Nelson Bakewell.
1989-99 St Quintin: became associate in 1995 and partner in 1998.
1986-89 General management surveyor, Crown Estate
Professional memberships
RICS
Interests
Football; hockey
Contact details
Nelson Bakewell Ltd, 25 Sackville Street, London W1S 3HQ
Tel 020 7544 2000
Fax 020 7544 2222
Web www.nelson-bakewell.com
Direct tel 020 7544 2254
Mobile 07831 396542
Email ptrinder@nelson-bakewell.com

TRIPP, Alan
Insight Investment Management

Position
Director – property investments
Qualifications
BSc; MRICS
Career history
1989-91 Investment division, Carroll Group.
1985-89 Senior investment surveyor, ESN.
1981-85 Estates surveyor, Telford Development Corp
Professional memberships
RICS
Interests
Fishing; golf
Contact details
Insight Investment Management, 33 Old Broad Street, London EC2N 1HZ
Tel 020 7930 5474
Fax 020 7321 1423
Web www.insightinvestment.com
Direct tel 020 7321 1019
Direct fax 020 7321 1434
Email alan.tripp@insightinvestment.com

TROLLOPE, Denise
GVA Grimley

Position
Partner – rating
Qualifications
BA; FRICS; Dip Rating; IRRV
Career history
Since 1987 Partner (rating), GVA Grimley.
1979-87 Valuation Office Agency
Other roles
Past president, Rating Surveyors Association
Professional memberships
Institute of Revenues Rating & Valuation; Rating Surveyors Association; RICS
Interests
Geography; sailing; travel; walking; yachting; yoga
Contact details
GVA Grimley, 10 Stratton Street, London W1J 8JR
Tel 0870 900 8990
Fax 020 7911 2560
Web www.gvagrimley.co.uk
Direct tel 020 7911 2860
Direct fax 020 7911 2848
Email denise.trollope@gvagrimley.co.uk

TROMANS, Prof Stephen
39 Essex Street

Position
Barrister
Qualifications
MA (Cantab)
Career history
1999-2000 Barrister, 11 King's Bench Walk Chambers.
1999 Called to Bar.
1990-99 Partner/head of environmental law, Simmons & Simmons.
1981-90 Lecturer, University of Cambridge.
1981 Admitted to Roll of Solicitors
Professional memberships
Chartered Institution of Water & Environmental Management
Contact details
39 Essex Street, London WC2R 3AT
Tel 020 7832 1111
Fax 020 7353 3978
Web www.39essex.com
Email stephen.tromans@39essex.com

TROTT, Fiona
Society of Property Researchers

Position
Membership secretary
Qualifications
BA Hons; MCLIP
Contact details
Society of Property Researchers, St Marys, Gandish Road, East Bergholt CO7 6UR
Tel 01206 298205
Fax 01206 298683
Web www.sprweb.co.uk
Email ftrott@sprweb.com

TSANG, Anthony
CIT Group

Position
Finance director
Qualifications
BSc Hons; ACA; FSI
Career history
1995-2000 Assistant director, Lazard Brothers.
1991-95 Associate director, European Capital.
1990-91 Senior analyst (corporate finance), Wallace, Smith Trust Co.
1986-90 Ernst & Young
Professional memberships
Institute of Chartered Accountants in England & Wales; Securities Institute
Contact details
CIT Group plc, 8-10 Bourdon Street, London W1K 3PD
Tel 020 7667 7766
Fax 020 7667 7770
Web www.cit.co.uk
Email at@cit.co.uk

T

TUCKER, Christopher
ATIS REAL Weatheralls

Position
Director – building consultancy and project management

Qualifications
BSc Hons; Dip Bldg Cons; MRICS

Career history
1981 Joined Weatherall Green and Smith; became chartered building surveyor in 1984; now director with overall responsibility for building consultancy and project management departments in London

Professional memberships
RICS

Interests
Cycling; football

Contact details
ATIS REAL Weatheralls Ltd, 22 Chancery Lane, London WC2A 1LT
Tel 020 7338 4000
Fax 020 7430 2628
Web www.atisrealweatheralls.com
Direct tel 020 7338 4016
Direct fax 020 7404 2319
Mobile 07770 854978
Email chris.tucker@atisrealweatheralls.com

TUCKER, Paul
Kings Chambers

Position
Barrister

Qualifications
MA (Cantab); Barrister

Career history
Since 1990 Member of Kings Chambers.
1990 Called to Bar

Other roles
Undertakes occasional supervisory work of students on pro-bono basis for Manchester University law department's legal advice centre

Professional memberships
Administrative Law Bar Association; Planning & Environment Bar Association

Interests
Cinema; football (supports Scarborough FC); rugby

Contact details
Kings Chambers, 40 King Street, Manchester M2 6BA
Tel 0161 832 9082
Fax 0161 835 2139
Web www.kingschambers.com
Direct fax 01254 762423
Mobile 07968 770197
Email ptucker@kingschambers.com

TUCKEY, James
James Tuckey

Position
Consultant

Qualifications
FRICS

Other roles
Director, English Partnerships; chief executive, Butterfield Land; chairman, World Golf Systems; investment adviser, BP Pension Fund

Professional memberships
RICS

Interests
Architecture; IT; tennis; walking

Contact details
James Tuckey, 95 Elgin Crescent, London W11 2JF
Tel 020 7565 2868
Fax 020 7565 2801
Email jltuckey@msn.com

TUDOR, Andy
Donaldsons

Position
Partner – head of investment agency, London

Contact details
Donaldsons, 48 Warwick Street, London W1B 5NL
Tel 020 7534 5000
Fax 020 7434 0045
Web www.donaldsons.co.uk
Direct tel 020 7534 8400
Email andy.tudor@donaldsons.co.uk

TUDOR, Paul
Underwoods

Position
Senior partner

Qualifications
BSc Hons; FRICS

Career history
1985 Joined Underwoods as partner; appointed senior partner in 2001.
1984-85 Assistant manager (industry), Milton Keynes Development Corp.
1978-84 Senior estate surveyor, Northampton Development Corp.
1976-78 Assistant surveyor and valuer, Gloucester City Council

Other roles
Director, Property Agents International; member, Northamptonshire ProHelp Group

Interests
Golf; rugby (Northampton Saints)

Contact details
Underwoods, Shire House, Pyramid Close, Northampton NN3 8PH
Tel 01604 404060
Fax 01604 404099
Web www.underwoods.co.uk
Direct tel 01604 783007
Mobile 07710 911156
Email pt@underwoods.co.uk

TUFFIN, David
Tuffin Ferraby & Taylor

Position
Joint senior partner

Qualifications
FRICS; FBEng; MCIArb; FICPD

Career history
Since 1973 Joint senior partner, Tuffin Ferraby & Taylor

Other roles
Freeman of the City of London; chairman, RICS South East regional board; chairman, RICS Awards working party

Professional memberships
100 Property Club; Association of Building Engineers; Association of Consultant Building Surveyors; British Council for Offices; British Institute of Facilities Management; Chartered Institute of Arbitrators; Institute of Continuing Professional Development; Worshipful Company of Chartered Surveyors

Interests
Diving; rugby; shooting; skiing; windsurfing

Contact details
Tuffin Ferraby & Taylor, The Tower Building, 11 York Road, London SE1 7NQ
Tel 020 7928 7998
Fax 020 7928 2779
Web www.tftsurveyors.co.uk
Mobile 07768 648266
Email dtuffin@tftkingston.com

TULLEY, Graeme
Donaldsons

Position
Partner – head of planning and compensation team

Career history
2002 Joined Donaldsons.
2001-2002 Chesterton.
1987-2001 Drivers Jonas.
1983-87 City of Westminster Council.
1979-83 Greater London Council

Other roles
Member, English Historic Towns Forum

Professional memberships
British Council of Shopping Centres; RTPI

Contact details
Donaldsons, 48 Warwick Street, London W1B 5NL

Tel 020 7534 5000
Fax 020 7434 0045
Web www.donaldsons.co.uk
Direct tel 020 7534 5053
Email graeme.tulley@donaldsons.co.uk

TULLOCH, Michael
Boodle Hatfield

Position
Partner
Qualifications
LLB
Career history
1974 Joined Boodle Hatfield; appointed partner in 1976.
1970-73 Cooke, Matheson & Co.
1970 Admitted to Roll of Solicitors
Other roles
Specialist member, Law Society's housing law committee
Professional memberships
City of Westminster & Holborn Law Society; Solicitors Family Law Association
Interests
Cycling; music; walking
Contact details
Boodle Hatfield, 61 Brook Street, London W1K 4BL
Tel 020 7629 7411
Fax 020 7629 2621
Web www.boodlehatfield.com
Direct tel 020 7318 8184
Direct fax 020 7318 8203
Email mtulloch@boodlehatfield.com

TUNKEL, Alan
3 Stone Buildings

Position
Barrister
Qualifications
BA (Oxon)
Professional memberships
Association of Contentious Trust & Probate Specialists; Chancery Bar Association
Contact details
3 Stone Buildings (Chambers of Geoffrey Vos QC), Ground Floor, London WC2A 3XL
Tel 020 7242 4937
Fax 020 7405 3896
Web www.3stonebuildings.com
Email atunkel@3sb.law.co.uk

TUNNICLIFFE, Roger
Lambert Smith Hampton

Position
Regional chief executive
Contact details
Lambert Smith Hampton Ltd, Saddlers House, Gutter Lane, London EC2V 6HS
Tel 020 7796 4000
Fax 020 7600 1398
Web www.lsh.co.uk
Email rtunniclif@lsh.co.uk

TURLEY, Rob
Turley Associates

Position
Chairman
Career history
1983 Formed Robert Turley Associates (now Turley Associates)
Contact details
Turley Associates, The Chancery, 56-58 Spring Gardens, Manchester M2 1EW
Tel 0161 831 1300
Fax 0161 831 1301
Email rturley@rta.co.uk

TURNBULL, Patrick
TK Maxx

Position
Director – property development
Career history
1983-93 Associate director, Edward Erdman
Contact details
TK Maxx, 50 Clarendon Road, Watford WD17 1TX
Tel 01923 473736
Fax 01923 473506
Web www.tkmaxx.com
Mobile 07831 550833
Email patrick_turnbull@tkmaxx.com

TURNER, Christopher
TR Property Investment Trust

Position
Fund manager
Career history
1995 Joined Henderson Global Investors as head of indirect property investment and fund manager of TR Property Investment Trust.
1988-95 Director of equities and head of property share research department, Barclays de Zoete Wedd.
1977-88 Laing & Cruickshank: property share analyst, then director of international equities from 1984
Contact details
TR Property Investment Trust plc, 4 Broadgate, London EC2M 2DA
Tel 020 7818 1818
Direct tel 020 7818 4348
Direct fax 020 7818 4446
Email chris.turner@henderson.com

TURNER, David
Aberdeen Property Investors UK

Position
Associate director
Qualifications
BSc Hons; MRICS
Career history
2001 Joined Aberdeen Property Asset Managers.
1999-2001 Celexa Real Estate Investment Management.
1996-99 CB Hillier Parker
Professional memberships
RICS
Contact details
Aberdeen Property Investors UK Ltd, 5-11 Regent Street, London SW1Y 4LR
Tel 020 7447 1700
Web www.aberdeenpropertyinvestors.com
Direct tel 020 7747 1756
Mobile 07876 331756
Email
david.turner@aberdeenpropertyinvestors.com

TURNER, David
LA Fitness Group

Position
Property director
Contact details
LA Fitness Group, 60 Commercial Road, London E1 1LP
Tel 020 7366 8080
Fax 020 7366 8081
Direct tel 020 7366 8015
Direct fax 020 7366 8042
Mobile 07768 910170
Email david.turner@lafitness.co.uk

TURNER, David
Regent Inns

Position
Property director
Contact details
Regent Inns plc, 77 Muswell Hill, London N10 3PJ
Tel 020 8375 3000
Web www.regentinns.co.uk
Email david.turner@regent-inns.plc.uk

TURNER, David
Thames Water

Position
Managing director – property worldwide
Qualifications
MRICS
Other roles
Member of property board, Network Rail
Professional memberships

T?

RICS

Contact details

Thames Water plc, Business Centre, Vastern Road, Reading RG1 8DB

Tel 0118 373 8000

Web www.thames-water.com

Direct tel 0118 373 8001

Direct fax 0118 373 8008

Email David.Turner@rwethameswater.com

TURNER, John
Ballymore Properties

Position

Head of planning

Career history

Since 1998 Head of planning, Ballymore Properties.

1993-98 Estates planning manager, NHS Estates North Thames region.

1984-93 ABA Group: managing director of ABA Town Planning, then town planning consultant from 1991.

1977-84 Headquarters divisional planning officer, London Borough of Barnet

Professional memberships

RICS; RTPI

Interests

Cinema; cricket; football; reading; travel

Contact details

Ballymore Properties Ltd, 3 Greenwich View Place, London E14 9NN

Tel 020 7510 9100

Fax 020 7510 9110

Direct tel 020 7510 9118

Email jeturner@ballymore.co.uk

TURNER, Mark
Thresher Group

Position

Managing director – property and new concepts

Qualifications

BSc; MRICS

Professional memberships

RICS

Contact details

Thresher Group, Enjoyment Hall, Bessemer Road, Welwyn Garden City AL7 1BL

Tel 0170 738 7453

Fax 0170 738 7272

Direct tel 0170 738 7247

Email mark.turner@threshergroup.com

TURNER, Nigel
Kier Property

Position

Director – industrial

Qualifications

BSc Hons, Urban Est Surv; MRICS

Career history

1988-97 Surveyor/associate, Gerald Eve

Professional memberships

RICS

Interests

Sport; yachting

Contact details

Kier Property Ltd, Berkeley Square House, Berkeley Square, London W1J 6BD

Tel 020 7887 6200

Fax 020 7887 6299

Web www.kier.co.uk

Direct tel 020 7887 6294

Mobile 07836 729626

Email nigel.turner@kier.co.uk

TURNER, Paul
Folkes Properties

Position

Acting managing director

Career history

1991 Joined Folkes Group; appointed finance director in 1996 and acting managing director of Folkes Properties in 2001.

1989-91 Group accountant, EIP Group

Other roles

Director, Multi Triumph

Interests

Cricket; cycling; football; mountain biking

Contact details

Folkes Properties Ltd, Forge House, Dudley Road, Lye DY9 8EL

Tel 01384 424242

Fax 01384 424455

Web www.folkesproperties.co.uk

Mobile 07778 498672

Email p.turner@folkesproperties.ltd.uk

TURNER, Peter
Stiles Harold Williams

Position

Director

Qualifications

BSc; FRICS; IRRV Rating Diploma

Career history

1981 Joined Harold Williams Bennett (now Stiles Harold Williams) in Croydon office; moved to London office in 1983; became equity partner; transferred to Crawley office in 1994.

1976-81 Tunbridge Wells Valuation Office.

1971-76 Gerald Eve, London

Contact details

Stiles Harold Williams Ltd, Sterling House, High Street, Crawley RH10 1GE

Tel 0129 344 1300

Fax 0129 344 1334

Web www.shw.co.uk

Direct tel 01293 441310

Mobile 07711 685655

Email pturner@shw.co.uk

TUSTIN, Peter
GCL Solicitors

Position

Partner

Career history

2002 Joined GCL Solicitors (formerly Gellhorn Cooney Laugharne).

1997-2002 Partner (commercial property), Nelson Cuff.

1991-97 Merriman White, Guildford.

1988-90 Clifton Ingram, Wokingham.

1986 Admitted to Roll of Solicitors.

1983-88 Ideal Homes, Trafalgar House Commercial Property and Trafalgar House Developments

Professional memberships

Law Society; Surrey Law Society

Interests

Classic cars

Contact details

GCL Solicitors, Connaught House, Alexandra Terrace, Guildford GU1 3DA

Tel 0148 357 7091

Fax 0148 357 9252

Web www.gcl-solicitors.co.uk

Direct tel 01483 230130

Email Peter.Tustin@gcl-solicitors.co.uk

TWEDDLE, John
Bidwells Property Consultants

Position

Chairman – commercial

Qualifications

FRICS

Career history

1969 Joined Bidwells; appointed partner in 1982; senior partner 1989-99; chairman of commercial division since 2000

Other roles

Governor, Long Road Sixth Form College, Cambridge; member, Cambridge Branch of ProHelp; trustee, Vivat Trust; member, Prince's Trust development committee, Cambridgeshire

Professional memberships

RICS

Interests

Art; ballet; dingy sailing

Contact details

Bidwells Property Consultants, Trumpington Road, Cambridge CB2 2LD

Tel 01223 841841

Fax 01223 845150

Web www.bidwells.co.uk
Direct tel 01223 559550
Direct fax 01223 559335
Mobile 07774 146052
Email jtweddle@bidwells.co.uk

TWEEDDALE-TYE, David
Rugby Estates

Position
Chairman
Qualifications
BSc; FRICS
Career history
1980 Joined Rugby Securities as managing director; became chairman of Rugby Estates in 1991.
1979-80 Investment surveyor, Druce & Co.
1978-79 Norwich Union
Other roles
Chairman, M4 Estates; non-executive chairman, Prodat Systems; trustee, Babes in Arms (researching into cot death); trustee, Oxfordshire Community Foundation; trustee, River & Rowing Museum, Henley on Thames
Professional memberships
RICS
Interests
Cricket; golf; RAC; shooting; tennis
Contact details
Rugby Estates plc, 14 Garrick Street, London WC2E 9SB
Tel 020 7632 2200
Fax 020 7632 2222
Web www.rugbyestates.plc.uk
Mobile 07768 681700
Email david@rugbyestates.plc.uk

TYLER, Scott
FPDSavills

Position
Director – head of investment sales
Qualifications
BSc Hons; MRICS
Career history
1990 Joined FPDSavills; joined provincial office agency team in 1991 and set up investment sales department in 1993; head of investment sales since 2001
Professional memberships
Investment Property Forum; RICS
Interests
Cars; golf; tennis
Contact details
FPDSavills Ltd, 20 Grosvenor Hill, London W1K 3HQ
Tel 020 7499 8644
Fax 020 7495 3773
Web www.fpdsavills.co.uk
Direct tel 020 7409 8825
Direct fax 020 7409 2635
Mobile 07787 501732
Email styler@fpdsavills.co.uk

TYRRELL, Nick
Deutsche Bank

Position
Head of European research – DB Real Estate
Qualifications
MA
Career history
2000 Joined DB Real Estate.
1994-99 Director of forecasting, BAK Basel.
1987-94 Senior European economist, Oxford Economic Forecasting
Professional memberships
Investment Property Forum; Society of Property Researchers
Contact details
Deutsche Bank AG, 1 Appold Street, London EC2A 2HE
Tel 020 7545 8000
Fax 020 7545 4444
Web www.db.com
Direct tel 020 7547 4742
Mobile 0790 151 8732
Email nick.tyrrell@db.com

UNDERHILL, Simon
Strutt & Parker

Position
Partner – head of national office agency
Career history
1981 Joined Strutt & Parker
Professional memberships
Office Agents Society
Interests
Cricket; tennis; travel
Contact details
Strutt & Parker, 13 Hill Street, London W1J 5LQ
Tel 020 7629 7282
Fax 020 7629 0387
Web www.struttandparker.com
Direct tel 020 7318 5064
Direct fax 020 7493 7334
Mobile 07831 308924
Email sunderhill@struttandparker.com

UNDERHILL, Tony
Henderson Global Investors

Position
Manager – property portfolios
Contact details
Henderson Global Investors Ltd, 4 Broadgate, London EC2M 2DA
Tel 020 7818 1818
Fax 020 7818 1819
Web www.henderson.com
Email tony.underhill@henderson.com

UPTON, David
Association of Consulting Engineers

Position
Chairman
Qualifications
BSc, Eng; ACGI; CEng; FICE; FIHT; MIWEM; FConsE
Career history
1981 Co-founder, Upton McGougan.
1975-81 Roughton.
1966-74 Sir Alexander Gibb & Partners
Professional memberships
Chartered Institution of Water & Environmental Management; Institute of Highways & Transport; Institution of Civil Engineers
Interests
Windsurfing
Contact details
Association of Consulting Engineers, Alliance House, 12 Alliance House, London SW1H 0QL
Tel 020 7222 6557
Fax 020 7222 0750
Web www.acenet.co.uk
Email consult@acenet.co.uk

UPTON, Richard
Cathedral Group

Position
Chief executive
Career history
1997 Established Cathedral Group; now chief executive.
1991-97 Established Mount Anvil Group.
1989-91 Land buyer, McInerney UK
Interests
Sport
Contact details
Cathedral Group plc, Foxbury Manor, Kemnal Road, Chislehurst BR7 6LY
Tel 020 8295 8660
Fax 020 8467 9838
Web www.cathedralgroup.com
Direct tel 020 8295 8668
Mobile 07961 339667
Email richard@cathedral-plc.com

UPTON, Robert
Royal Town Planning Institute

Position
Secretary-general
Qualifications
MA (Cantab)
Career history
Since 1996 Secretary-general, Royal Town Planning Institute.
1992-96 Chief executive, Rushmoor Borough Council.
1989-91 Director of planning, Hong Kong government
Contact details
Royal Town Planning Institute, 41-42 Botolph Lane, London EC3R 8DL
Tel 020 7929 9494
Fax 020 7929 9490
Email robert.upton@rtpi.org.uk

V

VAGO, Derek
Nomura International

Position
Managing director/co-head of real estate finance group

Contact details
Nomura International plc, Nomura House, 1 St Martin's-le-grand, London EC1A 4AS
Tel 020 7521 2000
Fax 020 7521 3565
Web www.nomura.com
Direct tel 020 7521 2864
Direct fax 020 7521 1663
Email derek.vago@uk.nomura.com

VALE, David
GVA Grimley

Position
Partner in charge, Bristol and Cardiff

Contact details
GVA Grimley, University Gate, Park Row, Bristol BS1 5UB
Tel 0870 900 8990
Fax 0117 926 0607
Web www.gvagrimley.co.uk
Email david.vale@gvagrimley.co.uk

VALENTE, Joe
DTZ Debenham Tie Leung

Position
Director – UK research and development

Qualifications
MLitt; BSc

Career history
1984 Joined DTZ in research department; appointed director in 1998 and director of UK research and development in 2002.
1981-84 Research manager, Ecotec Research & Consulting

Other roles
Advisory panel member, CPD Foundation

Professional memberships
Society of Property Researchers; Strategic Planning Society

Contact details
DTZ Debenham Tie Leung, 3-5 Swallow Place, London W1A 4NA
Tel 020 7408 1161
Fax 020 7493 0937
Web www.dtz.com
Email joe.valente@dtz.com

VALLANCE, Tim
Churston Heard

Position
Director – investment department

Qualifications
BSc Hons; MRICS

Career history
Since 1996 Investment director, Churston Heard.
1992-96 Hillier Parker.
1989-92 Healey & Baker

Professional memberships
RICS

Interests
Golf; skiing; squash

Contact details
Churston Heard Ltd, 7 Hanover Square, London W1S 1HQ
Tel 020 7409 2199
Fax 020 7495 1339
Web www.churstonheard.co.uk
Direct tel 020 7318 7838
Mobile 07976 424190
Email tvallance@churstonheard.co.uk

VAN BOMMEL, Victor
Goldman Sachs International

Position
Executive director – specialist sales real estate

Career history
2000 Joined Goldman Sachs.
1997-2000 ABN Amro.
1996-97 MPMA Pension Fund

Interests
Golf; shopping; windsurfing; football (Chelsea Football Club)

Contact details
Goldman Sachs International, Peterborough Court, 133 Fleet Street, London EC4A 2PP
Tel 020 7774 1000
Fax 020 7774 4477
Direct tel 020 7552 3703
Direct fax 020 7552 8218
Mobile 07796 307530
Email victor.vanbommel@gs.com

VAN ROMUNDE, Paul
PropertyMall.com

Position
Director

Qualifications
MBA (Stanford); master of law degree

Career history
Since 1995 Founder/director, PropertyMall.com.
1980-95 Rodamco: various management positions, including member of the board of directors; managing director of Haslemere Estates (subsidiary of Rodamco) from 1986

Contact details
PropertyMall.com, 36 Great Queen Street, London WC2B 5AA
Tel 020 7611 5040
Fax 020 7611 5041
Web www.propertymall.com
Email paul@propertymall.com

VANDERMOLEN, Jonathan
Blenheim Bishop

Position
Managing director

Career history
1991 Formed Blenheim Bishop after seven years in residential sales

Other roles
Barker of Variety Club of Great Britain

Interests
Football; keep fit; running

Contact details
Blenheim Bishop Ltd, 55 South Audley Street, London W1K 2BL
Tel 020 7290 2800
Fax 020 7290 2801
Direct tel 020 7290 2828
Direct fax 020 7290 2802
Mobile 07831 509965
Email
jonathan.vandermolen@blenheimbishop.com

VARNHAM, Neil
Henderson Global Investors

Position
Director of retail (Europe)

Contact details
Henderson Global Investors Ltd, 4 Broadgate, London EC2M 2DA
Tel 020 7818 1818
Fax 020 7818 1819
Web www.henderson.com
Direct tel 020 7818 5634
Direct fax 020 7818 5670
Email neil.varnham@henderson.com

VAUGHAN, Patrick
Pillar Property

Position
Chief executive

Career history
Since 1994 Chief executive, Pillar Property Investments.
1976-94 Arlington: chief executive of Arlington Securities from 1987

Interests
Golf; photography; golf (New Zealand Golf Club, Valderrama Golf Club); Turf Club; White's

Contact details
Pillar Property plc, Lansdowne House, Berkeley Square, London W1J 6HQ
Tel 020 7915 8000
Fax 020 7915 8001
Web www.pillarproperty.com
Direct fax 020 7915 8024
Email jayne.hollings@pillarproperty.com

VAUGHAN, Robin
Architects Registration Board

Position
Chief executive and registrar

Qualifications
BA Hons

Career history
Since 2000 Architects Registration Board. Previously at Council of Legal Education and Institute of Chartered Accountants in England & Wales

Other roles
Board member, Quality Assurance Agency for Higher Education (2004-07)

Contact details
Architects Registration Board, 8 Weymouth Street, London W1W 5BU
Tel 020 7580 5861
Fax 020 7436 5269
Web www.arb.org.uk
Email info@arb.org.uk

VEITCH, Giles
Dwyer

Position
Property director

Qualifications
BSc Hons; MRICS

Career history
Since 1992 Property director, Dwyer

Interests
Motor sports; sailing; shooting

Contact details
Dwyer plc, 40 Park Street, London W1K 2JG
Tel 020 7629 6666
Fax 020 7493 5096
Direct tel 020 7514 5230
Mobile 07831 182288
Email giles.veitch@dwyer.co.uk

VENEIK, Vinay
Berwin Leighton Paisner

Position
Partner – real estate

Qualifications
MSc; LLB

Career history
1996 Joined Berwin Leighton (now Berwin Leighton Paisner); joined commercial property department; became partner in 1998. Previously with Penningtons.
1988 Admitted to Roll of Solicitors

Interests
Food; reading; rugby

Contact details
Berwin Leighton Paisner Ltd, Adelaide House, London Bridge, London EC4R 9HA
Tel 020 7760 1000
Fax 020 7760 1111
Web www.berwinleighton.com
Email vinay.veneik@blplaw.com

VERDUYN, Anthony
St Philips Chambers

Position
Barrister

Qualifications
BA Hons; DPhil (Oxon)

Career history
1998 Joined St Philips Chambers.
1993-98 Priory Chambers.
1993 Called to Bar

Other roles
Has an academic interest in all things historical and has contributed to various journals and *New Dictionary of National Biography*

Professional memberships
Midland Chancery & Commercial Bar Association; Property Bar Association

Interests
History; walking

Contact details
St Philips Chambers (Chambers of John Randall QC), 55 Temple Row, Birmingham B2 5LS
Tel 0121 246 7000
Fax 0121 246 7001
Web www.st-philips.co.uk
Email averduyn@st-philips.co.uk

VERE, Hugo
Insight Investment Management

Position
Director – property investment

Qualifications
BSc Hons; MRICS

Career history
Since 2001 Director (property investment), Insight Investment.
1997-2001 Associate director (property investment), Clerical Medical Investment Management.
1995-97 Dunlop Heywood

Professional memberships
Investment Property Forum; RICS

Interests
Field sports; hockey; rugby; sailing; shooting; skiing; tennis; yachting

Contact details
Insight Investment Management, City Place House, 55 Basinghall Street, London EC2V 5DL
Tel 020 7930 5474
Web www.insightinvestment.com
Direct tel 020 7321 1027
Direct fax 020 7321 1434
Mobile 07867 908647
Email hugo.vere@insightinvestment.com

VERNON, Peter
Eddisons

Position
Director

Qualifications
BSc Hons; MRICS

Career history
Since 1999 Director, Eddisons.
1995-99 Associate director and head of industrial agency, Elliott Partnership.
1988-95 Senior agency surveyor, Dunlop Heywood

Other roles
RICS education and membership committee member (since 2001); external examiner, College of Estate Management (1993-96); external examiner, Sheffield Hallam University (from 2000); Northern branch committee member, Industrial Agents Society; board member, RICS Surveying Courses (1992-2000); member, RICS partnership and accreditation board (2000-01)

Professional memberships
Industrial Agents Society; RICS

Interests
Fishing; golf; rugby; walking

Contact details
Eddisons, Ridgefield House, 14 John Dalton Street, Manchester M2 6JR
Tel 0161 831 9444
Fax 0161 839 6633
Web www.eddisons.com
Mobile 07702 415772
Email peter.vernon@eddisons.com

V

VERNON, Stephen
Green Property

Position
Chairman

Contact details
Green Property Ltd, Styne House, Hatch Street Upper, Dublin
Tel +353 1 241 8400
Fax +353 1 241 8484
Email svernon@greenpropertyplc.com

VERSCHOYLE, Andrew
EA Shaw

Position
Investment partner
Qualifications
MA; MRICS
Professional memberships
RICS
Contact details
EA Shaw, 9-12 Bow Street, London WC2E 7AB
Tel 020 7240 2255
Fax 020 7831 1012
Web www.eashaw.com
Direct tel 020 7420 3048
Mobile 07973 642335
Email ajv@eashaw.com

VETCH, Nicholas
Big Yellow Group

Position
Chief executive
Qualifications
MRICS
Career history
1998 Joined Big Yellow Group.
1989-98 Edge Properties: joined as director; joint chief executive from 1996.
1986-89 Development surveyor, Citygrove.
1985-86 King & Co
Professional memberships
RICS
Contact details
Big Yellow Group plc, 2, The Deans, Bridge Road, Bagshot GU19 5AT
Tel 01276 470190
Fax 01276 470191
Web www.bigyellow.co.uk
Email nvetch@thebigyellow.co.uk

VIGRASS, Christopher
Ashurst

Position
Partner – head of construction
Qualifications
MA (Cantab); FCIArb
Career history
1986 Joined Ashurst Morris Crisp; became partner in 1988.
1980 Admitted to Roll of Solicitors.
1978-86 Linklaters & Paines
Professional memberships
Chartered Institute of Arbitrators
Interests
Badminton; real tennis; squash; walking
Contact details
Ashurst, Broadwalk House, 5 Appold Street, London EC2A 2AG
Tel 020 7638 1111
Fax 020 7638 1112
Web www.ashursts.com
Direct tel 020 7859 1569
Email chris.vigrass@ashursts.com

VINCENT, Patrick
12 King's Bench Walk Chambers

Position
Barrister
Contact details
12 King's Bench Walk Chambers, 12 King's Bench Walk, London EC4Y 7EL
Tel 020 7583 0811
Fax 020 7583 7228
Web www.12kbw.co.uk
Email vincent@12kbw.co.uk

VINES, Tony
De La Rue

Position
Group property manager
Qualifications
MRICS; Dip FM (CEM)
Career history
Since 1990 Group property manager, De La Rue.
1986-90 Director of development, Arundell House Securities.
1984-86 Director of development, Sherfield Investments.
1972-84 Chief estates surveyor, Basingstoke & Deane Borough Council
Professional memberships
RICS
Interests
Golf; music; rugby; sailing
Contact details
De La Rue plc, Jays Close, Basingstoke RG22 4BS
Tel 01256 329122
Fax 01256 467106
Web www.delarue.com
Direct tel 01256 605006
Direct fax 01256 605330
Email tony.vines@uk.delarue.com

VINEY, Richard
12 King's Bench Walk Chambers

Position
Barrister
Contact details
12 King's Bench Walk Chambers, 12 King's Bench Walk, London EC4Y 7EL
Tel 020 7583 0811
Fax 020 7583 7228
Web www.12kbw.co.uk
Email viney@12kbw.co.uk

VIRGO, John
Guildhall Chambers

Position
Barrister
Qualifications
MA (Oxon)
Career history
1983 Called to Bar
Other roles
Author, *Surveyors' Liability, Law & Practice* (Jordans, 1998)
Professional memberships
Honourable Society of the Inner Temple
Interests
Family; opera
Contact details
Guildhall Chambers (Chambers of Adrian Palmer QC), 23 Broad Street, Bristol BS1 2HG
Tel 0117 927 3366
Fax 0117 930 3800
Web www.guildhallchambers.co.uk
Email john.virgo@guildhallchambers.co.uk

VIVIAN, Nick
Glenny

Position
Partner – head of asset management division
Qualifications
BSc; FRICS
Career history
1985 Joined Glenny; appointed partner in 1990 and equity partner in 1992.
1980-85 Bairstow Eves: regional associate from 1984
Professional memberships
RICS
Interests
Sailing; squash
Contact details
Glenny, 56 Longbridge Road, Barking IG11 8RT
Tel 020 8591 6671
Fax 020 8594 1315
Web www.glenny.co.uk
Direct tel 020 8532 6816
Email n.vivian@glenny.co.uk

VON BRADSKY, Andy
PRP Management

Position

Managing director

Contact details

PRP Management Ltd, 10 Lindsey Street,
London EC1A 9HP

Tel 020 7653 1200

Fax 020 7653 1201

Web www.prparchitects.co.uk

Email lon.prp@prparchitects.co.uk

W

WADSLEY, Peter
St John's Chambers

Position
Barrister
Qualifications
MA; LLM
Career history
1984 Called to Bar.
1974 Admitted to Roll of Solicitors
Professional memberships
Planning & Environment Bar Association
Contact details
St John's Chambers, Small Street, Bristol BS1 1DW
Tel 0117 921 3456
Fax 0117 929 4821
Email clerks@stjohnschambers.co.uk

WAGHORN, Mark
Berwin Leighton Paisner

Position
Partner – head of property finance
Qualifications
LLB Hons
Career history
1992 Admitted to Roll of Solicitors.
1990 Joined Berwin Leighton (now Berwin Leighton Paisner); became partner in 1997; head of property finance from 1999
Professional memberships
Association of Business Recovery Professionals; Law Society; Non-Administrative Receivers Association; Society for Computers & Law
Interests
Cars; football; travel; walking
Contact details
Berwin Leighton Paisner Ltd, Adelaide House, London Bridge, London EC4R 9HA
Tel 020 7760 1000
Fax 020 7760 1111
Web www.berwinleighton.com
Mobile 07767 790904
Email mark.waghorn@blplaw.com

WAGMAN, Colin
Delancey

Position
Deputy chairman
Qualifications
FCA
Career history
Since 1995 Deputy chairman, Delancey Estates.
1991-2000 Consultant, British Land Co.
1971-92 Senior partner, Casson Beckman.
1970 Admitted to Roll of Solicitors
Other roles
Non-executive director, GET; non-executive director, Fitzhardinge; trustee, ChildLine; trustee, Muswell Hill Charitable Trust
Professional memberships
Institute of Chartered Accountants in England & Wales
Contact details
Delancey, 40 Portman Square, London W1H 0AA
Tel 020 7486 6663
Fax 020 7486 6662
Web www.delancey.com
Direct tel 020 7467 5555
Direct fax 020 7486 2993
Email colin.wagman@delancey.com

WAINSCOTT, Paul
Peel Holdings

Position
Finance director
Contact details
Peel Holdings plc, Peel Dome, The Trafford Centre, Manchester M17 8PL
Tel 0161 629 8200
Fax 0161 629 8333
Web www.peel.co.uk
Email pwainscott@peelholdings.co.uk

WAIT, Steven
Stephenson Harwood

Position
Partner – head of construction and engineering group
Qualifications
BA Hons (Dunelm)
Career history
1986 Joined Stephenson Harwood; appointed partner in 1991.
1982-86 Bischoff & Co
Contact details
Stephenson Harwood, 1 St Paul's Churchyard, London EC4M 8SH
Tel 020 7329 4422
Fax 020 7606 0822
Web www.shlegal.com
Direct tel 020 7809 2343
Email steven.wait@shlegal.com

WAITE, Philip
Aitchison Raffety

Position
Director
Qualifications
BSc; MRICS; IRRV
Career history
1998 Joined Aitchison Raffety.
1995-98 Valuation Office specialist rating unit.
1990-95 Valuation Office Agency, Oxford.
1989-90 Valuation Office Agency, Salisbury
Professional memberships
RICS
Interests
Music; sailing
Contact details
Aitchison Raffety Ltd, Compass House, 1 Farmoor Court, Oxford OX2 9LU
Tel 01865 865658
Fax 01865 865353
Web www.argroup.co.uk
Email philip.waite@argroup.co.uk

WAKEFIELD, Simon
RadcliffesLeBrasseur

Position
Partner – property department
Contact details
RadcliffesLeBrasseur, 5 Great College Street, London SW1P 3SJ
Tel 020 7222 7040
Fax 020 7222 6208
Web www.rlb-law.com
Direct tel 020 7227 7461
Email simon.wakefield@rlb-law.com

WAKEFORD, Carol
Cripps Harries Hall

Position
Partner – head of property dispute resolution
Qualifications
LLB Hons
Career history
1996 Joined Cripps Harries Hall as partner.
1985-96 Nabarro Nathanson; appointed partner in 1990.
1985 Admitted to Roll of Solicitors
Professional memberships
Property Litigation Association; Women in Property
Interests
Entertaining; horse riding; reading; sailing

Contact details
Cripps Harries Hall, Seymour House,
11-13 Mount Ephraim Road, Tunbridge Wells
TN1 1EG
Tel 01892 515121
Fax 01892 544878
Web www.e-cripps.co.uk
Direct tel 01892 506116
Email caw@crippslaw.com

WALDEN, Robert
USS

Position
Fund surveyor
Qualifications
BSc; FRICS
Career history
1977-88 Legal & General.
1975-77 Trent Polytechnic.
1974-75 Norwich City Council.
1973-74 Norwich Union
Other roles
Governor, Cambridge International Land Institute; director, Stockley Park Management
Professional memberships
British Council of Shopping Centres; Investment Property Forum
Interests
Family; local history; walking
Contact details
USS Ltd, 99 Bishopsgate, London EC2M 3XD
Tel 020 7972 0300
Fax 020 7628 0662
Web www.usshq.co.uk
Direct tel 020 7972 6394
Email rwalden@uss.co.uk

WALDER, John
Lamb & Edge

Position
Partner
Qualifications
FRICS
Career history
Since 1966 Associate partner, then partner from 1971, Lamb & Edge
Professional memberships
RICS
Interests
Cricket; rugby; sport
Contact details
Lamb & Edge, Yorkshire Chambers,
112-118 Pilgrim Street, Newcastle upon Tyne
NE1 6LL
Tel 0191 261 2361
Fax 0191 232 6374
Web www.lambedge.co.uk
Direct tel 0191 269 0504
Mobile 07831 256284
Email john.w@lambedge.co.uk

WALES, Matthew
Guildhall Chambers

Position
Barrister
Qualifications
BA Hons
Career history
1993 Called to Bar
Other roles
Honorary secretary to Bristol & Cardiff Chancery Bar Association
Professional memberships
Chancery Bar Association
Interests
Rugby
Contact details
Guildhall Chambers (Chambers of Adrian Palmer QC), 5-8 Broad Street, Bristol BS1 2HW
Tel 0117 927 3366
Fax 0117 930 3837
Web www.guildhallchambers.co.uk
Email matthew.wales@guildhallchambers.co.uk

WALICKNOWSKI, Peter
Majid Al Futtaim Investments

Position
Chief executive officer
Qualifications
BArch Hons; BSc, Arch
Career history
Since 2002 Chief executive officer, Majid Al Futtaim Investments.
2000-02 Director, Land Securities.
1990-2000 Chief executive officer, Lend Lease Europe.
1980-90 Lend Lease Retail, Australia: development manager, then development director from 1985
Professional memberships
British Council of Shopping Centres; Institute of Directors
Contact details
Majid Al Futtaim Investments LLC, PO Box 60811, Dubai, United Arab Emirates
Tel +971 4 209 3422
Fax +971 4 294 5290
Web www.ameinfo.com
Email peterw@mafgroup.co.ae

WALKER, Andrew
9 Old Square

Position
Barrister
Career history
1991 Called to Bar
Professional memberships
Chancery Bar Association; Professional Negligence Bar Association; Property Bar Association
Contact details
9 Old Square (Chambers of Michael Driscoll QC), Ground Floor, London WC2A 3SR
Tel 020 7405 4682
Fax 020 7831 7107
Web www.9oldsquare.co.uk
Email andrew.walker@9oldsquare.co.uk

WALKER, Andrew
CMS Cameron McKenna

Position
Partner – head of real estate disputes
Career history
Since 1993 Partner, CMS Cameron McKenna.
1986 Admitted to Roll of Solicitors
Professional memberships
City Property Association; Property Litigation Association
Interests
Cars; gardening; walking
Contact details
CMS Cameron Mckenna, Mitre House,
160 Aldersgate Street, London EC1A 4DD
Tel 020 7367 3000
Fax 020 7367 2000
Web www.cmck.com
Direct tel 020 7367 2710
Email andrew.walker@cmck.com

WALKER, Andrew
Pret A Manger

Position
Construction director
Qualifications
BSc Hons, Business Studies
Other roles
IT director
Contact details
Pret A Manger, 16 Palace Street, London
SW1E 5PT
Tel 020 7827 8000
Fax 020 7827 8787
Web www.pret.co.uk
Email andrew.walker@pret.com

WALKER, Chris
Fairview New Homes

Position
Land-buying director
Contact details
Fairview New Homes Ltd, 50 Lancaster Road,

Enfield EN2 0BY
Tel 020 8366 1271
Fax 020 8366 0189
Web www.fairview.co.uk
Email chris.walker@fnhltd.co.uk

WALKER, John
English Partnerships

Position
Director
Career history
1994 Joined English Partnerships; appointed finance and administration director in 1999 and finance and commercial director in 2002.
1990-94 Management consultant, local government
Other roles
Director, Priority Sites and Network Space; project board chairman, Central Milton Keynes Partnership; board member of Tees Valley and Sunderland urban regeneration companies; board member, English Cities Fund; board member, Housing Corporation
Professional memberships
Chartered Institute of Public Finance & Accountancy
Contact details
English Partnerships, St Georges House, Kingsway, Gateshead NE11 0NA
Tel 0191 487 6565
Fax 0191 487 5690
Web www.englishpartnerships.co.uk
Direct tel 0191 497 7577
Direct fax 0191 487 1705
Email johnwalker@englishpartnerships.co.uk

WALKER, Julian
Vail Williams

Position
Equity partner – investment
Qualifications
TD; BSc; MRICS
Professional memberships
RICS
Interests
Running; sailing
Contact details
Vail Williams, Meridians House, 7 Ocean Way, Southampton SO14 3TJ
Tel 0238 082 0900
Fax 0238 082 0950
Web www.vailwilliams.com
Direct tel 0238 082 0905
Mobile 07836 744406
Email jwalker@vailwilliams.com

WALKER, Philip
King Sturge

Position
Partner in charge, Scotland
Qualifications
FRICS
Professional memberships
RICS
Contact details
King Sturge, 10-14 West Nile Street, Glasgow G1 2PP
Tel 0141 204 2221
Fax 0141 204 2201
Web www.kingsturge.com
Mobile 07702 616004
Email philip.walker@kingsturge.co.uk

WALKER, Ronald
12 King's Bench Walk Chambers

Position
Barrister
Qualifications
QC
Contact details
12 King's Bench Walk Chambers, London EC4Y 7EL
Tel 020 7583 0811
Fax 020 7583 7228
Web www.12kbw.co.uk
Email walker@12kbw.co.uk

WALKER-ARNOTT, Tim
NHP

Position
Director – asset management
Qualifications
BSc, Est Man; FRICS
Contact details
NHP plc, Dukes Court, Duke Street, Woking GU21 5BH
Tel 01483 754760
Fax 01483 727509
Direct tel 01483 754772
Mobile 07850 797481
Email TimWA@nhprops.co.uk

WALLACE, John
Royal Bank of Scotland

Position
Head of property development
Qualifications
BSc; MRICS
Professional memberships
RICS
Contact details
Royal Bank of Scotland, 5-10 Great Tower Street, London EC3P 3HX
Tel 020 7833 2121
Web www.rbs.co.uk
Direct tel 020 7615 5153
Direct fax 020 7615 5160
Email john.wallace@rbs.co.uk

WALLACE, Martin
Jones Lang LaSalle

Position
European director – head of City agency
Qualifications
BSc; MRICS
Career history
Since 1994 European director (head of City agency), Jones Lang LaSalle.
1988-94 Associate (City agency), St Quintin.
1986-88 Surveyor in City surveyor's department, Corporation of London
Other roles
Non-executive director, WTA; freeman of City of London;
Professional memberships
City Agents Club; RICS
Interests
Beer; golf; rugby; wine
Contact details
Jones Lang LaSalle Ltd, 9 Queen Victoria Street, London EC4N 4YY
Tel 020 7248 6040
Fax 020 7248 0088
Web www.joneslanglasalle.com
Direct tel 020 7399 5233
Direct fax 020 7399 5500
Mobile 07836 531005
Email martin.wallace@eu.joneslanglasalle.com

WALLEY, John
Drivers Jonas

Position
Partner – head of Manchester office
Qualifications
FRICS; Dip Proj Man
Career history
Since 1993 Partner, Drivers Jonas.
1990-93 Partner, John Walley & Co.
1972-90 Dunlop Heywood; joined as partner; became director in 1987
Professional memberships
RICS
Interests
Music; sport
Contact details
Drivers Jonas, 60 Fountain Street, Manchester M2 2FE
Tel 0161 839 9731
Fax 0161 834 3690
Web www.driversjonas.com

Direct tel 0161 827 7308
Mobile 07990 527354
Email johnwalley@driversjonas.com

WALLIS, Guy
DWF Solicitors

Position
Partner
Career history
Since 1977 Partner, Davies Wallis Foyster.
1973 Admitted to Roll of Solicitors.
1971-77 Assistant solicitor and partner, Bullivant & Co.
1966-71 Layton & Co
Professional memberships
Law Society; Liverpool Law Society; Manchester Law Society
Interests
Architecture; golf; IT; photography; skiing
Contact details
DWF Solicitors, 5 Castle Street, Liverpool L2 4XE
Tel 0151 907 3000
Fax 0151 236 3088
Web www.dwf.co.uk
Email guy.wallis@dwf.co.uk

WALSH, Kevin
Debenhams Retail

Position
Director – head of property management
Qualifications
BSc; FRICS
Career history
Since 1986 Various roles within Burton Group and merged company of Debenhams; becoming head of property management at Debenham Retail in 1998.
1976-85 Midland Bank
Professional memberships
RICS
Contact details
Debenhams Retail plc, Estates Property Management Department, The Moor, Sheffield S1 3LR
Tel 0114 273 1168
Fax 0114 275 1164
Web www.debenhams.com
Email kevin.walsh@debenhams.com

WALSH, Matthew
Land Securities Trillium

Position
Asset management director
Qualifications
BA Hons; MRICS
Career history
1998 Joined Trillium (now Land Securities Trillium).
1995-98 Asset manager, Hemingway Properties.
1992-95 Investment surveyor, Pepper Angliss & Yarwood
Professional memberships
RICS
Interests
Football
Contact details
Land Securities Trillium Ltd, 140 London Wall, London EC2Y 5DN
Tel 020 7796 5500
Fax 020 7796 5501
Web www.landsecurities.co.uk
Direct tel 020 7796 5670
Mobile 07711 732774
Email matthew.walsh@lstrillium.com

WALSH, Tim
Guildhall Chambers

Position
Barrister
Contact details
Guildhall Chambers (Chambers of Adrian Palmer QC), 23 Broad Street, Bristol BS1 2HG
Tel 0117 927 3366
Fax 0117 930 3800
Web www.guildhallchambers.co.uk
Email tim.walsh@guildhallchambers.co.uk

WALTERS, Jayne
Pinder Fry & Benjamin

Position
Director
Qualifications
MA Hons (Cantab)
Career history
1998-2002 Director and head of legal services, Akeler.
1984-98 Solicitor/partner, Macfarlanes
Professional memberships
Law Society
Interests
Skiing; tennis; theatre
Contact details
Pinder Fry & Benjamin Ltd, 7 Cavendish Square, London W1G 0PE
Tel 020 7612 7650
Fax 020 7612 7660
Web www.p-f-b.com
Direct tel 020 7612 7667
Email j.walters@p-f-b.com

WARD, Daniel
Threadneedle Property Investments

Position
Property director
Qualifications
BSc; MRICS
Contact details
Threadneedle Property Investments, 9-15 Sackville Street, London W1A 2JP
Tel 020 7437 8000
Fax 020 7464 5811
Email daniel.ward@threadneedle.co.uk

WARD, Peter
Insinger De Beaufort (Corporate Finance)

Position
Director
Qualifications
FCA
Career history
1987-97 Corporate finance executive, Banque Paribas.
1982-87 Corporate finance executive, Quilter Goodison
Professional memberships
Institute of Chartered Accountants in England & Wales
Interests
Golf; theatre
Contact details
Insinger De Beaufort (Corporate Finance) Ltd, 12a Charterhouse Square, London EC1M 6AX
Tel 020 7377 6161
Web www.insinger.com
Email pward@insinger.com

WARD, Simon
Deutsche Bank

Position
Head of corporate real estate and services, EMEA
Qualifications
MRICS
Career history
2000-01 Director (real estate and workplace resources EMEA), Cisco.
1988-2000 European director, Jones Lang LaSalle.
1987-88 Director, Sinclair Goldsmith.
1978-87 Partner, Gooch & Wagstaff
Other roles
Junior vice-president and chairman of occupiers group, British Council for Offices; co-chair of European team, Corporate Real Estate 2010 (research and leadership development initiative of CoreNet Global, aimed at defining the corporate business environment in the future)
Professional memberships
RICS
Interests
Cricket; golf; music; opera; rugby; theatre

Contact details
Deutsche Bank AG, 6-8 Bishopsgate, London EC2N 2DB
Tel 020 7545 8000
Fax 020 7545 7130
Web www.db.com
Direct tel 020 7545 3949
Direct fax 0113 336 1707
Mobile 07769 934785
Email simon.ward@db.com

WARD, Simon
Vail Williams
Position
Head of research and consultancy
Qualifications
BSc; MRICS
Other roles
Chairman, research and information group of Hampshire Economic Partnership
Professional memberships
RICS; Society of Property Researchers
Interests
Cricket; golf; skiing; sport
Contact details
Vail Williams, Meridians House, 7 Ocean Way, Southampton SO14 3TJ
Tel 0238 082 0900
Fax 0238 082 0950
Web www.vailwilliams.com
Email sward@vailwilliams.com

WARNER, David
New Square Chambers
Position
Barrister
Qualifications
LLB Hons
Professional memberships
Chancery Bar Association; Property Bar Association
Contact details
New Square Chambers (Chambers of Charles Purle QC), 12 New Square, London WC2A 3SW
Tel 020 7419 8000
Fax 020 7419 8050
Web www.newsquarechambers.co.uk
Email david.warner@newsquarechambers.co.uk

WARNER, Malcolm
Guildhall Chambers
Position
Barrister
Contact details
Guildhall Chambers (Chambers of Adrian Palmer QC), 23 Broad Street, Bristol BS1 2HG
Tel 0117 927 3366
Fax 0117 930 3800
Web www.guildhallchambers.co.uk
Email
malcolm.warner@clerks@guildfordbarristers.com

WARNER, Matthew
Lambert Smith Hampton
Position
Head of West End office agency and development
Qualifications
BA; Dip PVL; MRICS
Career history
1989 Joined Connell Collier Madge (now Lambert Smith Hampton, following merger); now head of West End office agency and development and also national office agency division board member
Professional memberships
RICS
Interests
Ballet; fencing; horse riding; opera; theatre
Contact details
Lambert Smith Hampton Ltd, Regent Arcade House, 19-25 Argyll Street, London W1F 7TS
Tel 020 7494 4000
Fax 020 7414 0866
Web www.lsh.co.uk
Direct tel 020 7663 8276
Mobile 07885 778845
Email mwarner@lsh.co.uk

WARNER, Mike
CB Richard Ellis
Position
EMEA chairman – building consultancy
Qualifications
MSc Arch; FRICS
Career history
1978 Joined CB Richard Ellis.
1970-78 JA Warner & Partners.
1968-70 Drivers Jonas.
1965-68 Richard Ellis
Interests
Motorcycling (leader of El Beardos Wierdos motorcycle club)
Contact details
CB Richard Ellis, Kingsley House, 1a Wimpole Street, London W1G 0RE
Tel 020 7182 2000
Fax 020 7182 7001
Web www.cbre.com
Direct tel 020 7182 2503
Mobile 07904 017336
Email mike.warner@cbre.com

WARNER, Philip
Warner Estate Holdings
Position
Chairman
Contact details
Warner Estate Holdings plc, Nations House, 103 Wigmore Street, London W1U 1AE
Tel 020 7907 5100
Fax 020 7907 5102
Web www.warnerestate.co.uk
Email warner.estate@weh-plc.co.uk

WARREN, Chris
Cushman & Wakefield Healey & Baker
Position
Partner – retail warehouses and leisure
Qualifications
BSc; MRICS
Career history
1985 Joined Cushman & Wakefield Healey & Baker; has worked in valuation, West End shops and retail warehouse and leisure department since 1991; now heads European factory outlet team
Professional memberships
RICS
Interests
Golf; keep fit
Contact details
Cushman & Wakefield Healey & Baker, 43-45 Portman Square, London W1A 3BG
Tel 020 7935 5000
Fax 020 7152 5360
Web www.cushwake.com
Direct tel 020 7152 5209
Direct fax 020 7152 5367
Mobile 07764 398209
Email chris.warren@eur.cushwake.com

WASSELL, Richard
CWM
Position
Partner
Qualifications
BSc; MRICS
Career history
1990 Formed Carter Wassell (now CWM).
1986-90 Nelson Bakewell.
1984-86 Jones Lang Wootton
Other roles
Former chairman, Shop Agents Society
Professional memberships
British Council of Shopping Centres; Shop Agents Society
Contact details
CWM, 16 Old Bond Street, London W1S 4PS
Tel 020 7493 5655

Fax 020 7493 5665
Web www.cwm.co.uk
Direct tel 020 7255 7801
Mobile 07971 556041
Email richard.wassell@cwm.co.uk

WATERFIELD, Philip
Strettons

Position
Director
Qualifications
BSc; FRICS
Career history
Since 1987 Director, Strettons.
1984-87 General surveyor (Eastern region) and surveyor (station trading), British Rail Property Board.
1982-84 Norfolk County Council
Other roles
Director, Hackney Business Centre; member, South Leytonstone Community Partnership; chairman, RICS London junior branch (1987-88)
Professional memberships
RICS
Interests
Family; gardening
Contact details
Strettons Ltd, Central House, 189-203 Hoe Street, London E17 3SZ
Tel 020 8520 9911
Fax 020 8520 8022
Web www.strettons.co.uk
Email philip.waterfield@strettons.co.uk

WATERWORTH, David
Aberdeen Property Investors

Position
Associate director
Contact details
Aberdeen Property Investors, Charles House, 5-11 Regent Street, London SW1Y 4LR
Tel 020 7747 1700
Fax 020 7839 7460
Web www.aberdeenpropertyinvestors.com
Email
david.waterworth@aberdeenpropertyinvestors.com

WATKINS, Mark
Jones Lang LaSalle

Position
National director – retail and leisure agency
Contact details
Jones Lang LaSalle Ltd, 22 Hanover Square, London W1A 2BN
Tel 020 7493 6040
Fax 020 7408 0220
Web www.joneslanglasalle.com
Direct tel 020 7399 5326
Direct fax 020 7399 5667
Email mark.watkins@eu.joneslanglasalle.com

WATKINS, Paul
Sheppard Robson

Position
Partner
Qualifications
BA; BArch; RIBA
Career history
1974 Joined Sheppard Robson; became partner in 1988.
Professional memberships
RIBA
Interests
Badminton; cinema; football; photography; running; travel
Contact details
Sheppard Robson, 77 Parkway, London NW1 7PU
Tel 020 7504 1700
Fax 020 7504 1701
Web www.sheppardrobson.com
Email paul.watkins@sheppardrobson.com

WATKINS, Timothy
Montagu Evans

Position
Partner – head of City agency
Qualifications
BSc; FRICS
Career history
Since 1994 Equity partner, Montagu Evans.
1992-94 Equity partner, Daniel Watney.
1978-92 Holdings board director, Herring Son & Daw
Professional memberships
RICS
Interests
Art; rugby; running; tennis; wine
Contact details
Montagu Evans, 27-32 Old Jewry, London EC2R 8DQ
Tel 020 7606 1336
Fax 020 7606 1356
Web www.montagu-evans.co.uk
Email tim.watkins@montagu-evans.co.uk

WATSON, Adrian
DLA

Position
Location head – real estate, Birmingham
Qualifications
BA Hons, Law
Career history
1999 Joined DLA.
1995-99 Head of commercial property, Garretts.
1986-95 Head of commercial property, Anthony Collins Solicitors.
1982-86 Partner, Pinsent & Co.
1978-82 Bannister King & Rigbeys, Stourbridge.
1978 Admitted to Roll of Solicitors
Professional memberships
Law Society
Interests
Golf; music; skiing; sport
Contact details
DLA, Victoria Square House, Victoria Square, Birmingham B2 4DL
Tel 08700 111111
Fax 0121 262 5795
Web www.dla.com
Direct tel 0121 262 5875
Mobile 07971 142390
Email adrian.watson@dla.com

WATSON, Andrew
Alder King

Position
Partner
Qualifications
BSc; FRICS
Career history
1988 Joined Alder King; now senior professional services partner specialising in investment and development valuations, landlord and tenant, and asset management
Contact details
Alder King, Pembroke House, 15 Pembroke Road, Bristol BS8 3BA
Tel 0117 317 1000
Fax 0117 317 1001
Web www.alderking.com
Direct tel 0117 317 1111
Mobile 07990 891026
Email awatson@alderking.com

WATSON, Andy
Barclays Bank

Position
Manager – structured finance
Contact details
Barclays Bank plc, 54 Lombard Street, London EC3P 3AH
Tel 020 7699 5000
Web www.barclays.com
Email andy.watson@barclays.co.uk

WATSON, Brian
Guildhall Chambers

Position
Barrister
Professional memberships

Professional Negligence Bar Association

Contact details

Guildhall Chambers (Chambers of Adrian Palmer QC), 23 Broad Street, Bristol BS1 2HG

Tel 0117 927 3366

Fax 0117 930 3800

Web www.guildhallchambers.co.uk

Email brian.watson@guildhallchambers.co.uk

WATSON, Grant
Alder King

Position

Chairman

Qualifications

FRICS

Career history

1957 Joined Alder King

Other roles

Chairman, South West regional board of RICS; board director, Broadmead; chairman, Coombe Dingle Sports Trust; past president, Bristol Property Agents Association; past president, Bristol Rotary Club; president, Clifton RFC; past master, Guild of Guardians; presidents group, Bristol Chamber of Commerce

Professional memberships

Non-Administrative Receivers Association; RICS

Interests

Rugby; skiing; tennis; walking

Contact details

Alder King, Pembroke House, 15 Pembroke Road, Bristol BS8 3BA

Tel 0117 317 1000

Fax 0117 317 1001

Web www.alderking.com

Mobile 07990 891035

Email gwatson@alderking.com

WATSON, Ian
Ashtenne Holdings

Position

Joint chief executive

Career history

1989 Founder director, Ashtenne.

1986-89 Development executive, Arlington Securities.

1982-86 Solicitor, Gouldens

Professional memberships

Law Society

Contact details

Ashtenne Holdings plc, 8-9 Northumberland Street, London WC2N 5DA

Tel 020 7930 9425

Fax 020 7930 8469

Email hughes.p@ashtenne.co.uk

WATSON, Paul
GVA Grimley

Position

Partner

Career history

1991 Joined GVA Grimley; partner since 1987, leading project management/procurement consultancy assignments; now national head of strategic property consultancy.

1978-91 Vigers.

1973-77 Higgs & Hill

Professional memberships

Association for Project Management; Chartered Institute of Building; RICS

Interests

Sailing; skiing; tennis; 1894 Club; Hurlingham Club; Norfolk Punt

Contact details

GVA Grimley, 10 Stratton Street, London W1J 8JR

Tel 0870 900 8990

Fax 020 7911 2560

Web www.gvagrimley.co.uk

Direct tel 020 7911 2290

Direct fax 020 7911 2438

Email paul.watson@gvagrimley.co.uk

WATSON, Trevor
Davis Coffer Lyons

Position

Director – special projects

Qualifications

BSc; MBA; FRICS

Career history

Since 1996 Director, Davis Coffer Lyons.

1994-96 Associate director, Christie & Co.

1986-94 Senior surveyor/associate partner, Kemsley Whiteley & Ferris.

1984-86 Biscoe & Stanton

Other roles

Member, RICS trade-related valuation panel

Professional memberships

Entertainment & Leisure Forum; Leisure Property Forum; Restaurant Property Advisors Society; RICS

Interests

Opera; sailing

Contact details

Davis Coffer Lyons Ltd, 52 Portland Place, London W1B 1NH

Tel 020 7299 0700

Fax 020 7299 0710

Web www.daviscofferlyons.co.uk

Direct tel 020 7299 0699

Mobile 07958 235166

Email trevorw@daviscofferlyons.co.uk

WATT, Alexander
Standard Life Investments

Position

Managing director – property investments

Qualifications

FRICS

Career history

1982 Joined Standard Life; became assistant property investment manager in 1983 and property investment manager in 1988; managing director (property investments) since 1998

Professional memberships

RICS

Contact details

Standard Life Investments Ltd, 1 George Street, Edinburgh EH2 2LL

Tel 0131 245 2700

Fax 0131 245 2710

Web www.standardlife.com

Direct tel 0131 245 2701

Direct fax 0131 240 8475

Email alex_watt@standardlife.com

WATT, Duncan
Invesco Real Estate

Position

Chief investment officer (UK and Ireland)

Contact details

Invesco Real Estate Ltd, 10 Mount Row, London W1K 3SD

Tel 020 7543 3500

Fax 020 7543 3588

Web www.invesco.com

Direct tel 020 7543 3585

Direct fax 020 7543 3547

Email duncan_watt@ldn.invesco.com

WATT, Ian
Old Mutual Properties

Position

Managing director

Career history

1969 Joined Old Mutual Properties; appointed regional property manager for Johannesburgh in 1983; became national property investment manager in 1989 and and managing director in 1998

Other roles

Member of International Council of Shopping Centers worldwide commission for retail trends; councillor, South African Property Owners Association; director, Old Mutual Properties (UK); governor, Global Real Estate Institute

Professional memberships

Institute of Estate Agents; Institute of Marketing Management; Institute Property Practitioners of South Africa

Interests
Ornithology; reading; swimming
Contact details
Old Mutual Properties Pty Ltd, Property Factory, PO Box 327, Howard Place, Cape Town, South Africa
Tel +27 21 530 4500
Fax +27 21 531 3003
Web www.properties.oldmutual.co.za
Direct tel +27 21 530 4582
Email iwatt@oldmutual.com

WATTIE, Ian
Burness
Position
Partner – commercial property
Qualifications
LLB
Career history
1988 Admitted to Roll of Solicitors.
1987 Joined Burness; became partner in 1992.
1985-87 J&F Anderson
Professional memberships
WS Society
Interests
Cinema; skiing
Contact details
Burness, 50 Lothian Road, Edinburgh EH3 9WJ
Tel 0131 473 6000
Fax 0131 473 6006
Web www.burness.co.uk
Direct tel 0131 473 6159
Email jiw@burness.co.uk

WATTS, Bill
Jones Lang LaSalle
Position
European director – retail
Career history
Since 1996 European director (retail), Jones Lang LaSalle
Professional memberships
British Council of Shopping Centres
Interests
Motor sports, motorcycling, sailing, shooting
Contact details
Jones Lang LaSalle Ltd, 22 Hanover Square, London W1A 2BN
Tel 020 7493 6040
Fax 020 7408 0220
Web www.joneslanglasalle.com
Direct tel 020 7399 5396
Direct fax 020 7399 5667
Mobile 07768 353943
Email bill.watts@eu.joneslanglasalle.com

WAUGH, Simon
Montagu Evans
Position
Partner – head of department (retail)
Qualifications
BSc; MRICS
Professional memberships
Accessible Retail; RICS; Worshipful Company of Chartered Surveyors
Contact details
Montagu Evans, 44-48 Dover Street, London W1S 4AZ
Tel 020 7493 4002
Fax 020 7312 7547
Web www.montagu-evans.co.uk
Direct tel 020 7312 7425
Direct fax 020 7312 7549
Mobile 07818 012425
Email simon.waugh@montagu-evans.co.uk

WEATHERHEAD, Peter
DTZ Pieda Consulting
Position
Director – head of planning
Qualifications
BA Hons; MRTPI; FRICS
Career history
Since 1989 Director, DTZ Pieda Consulting.
1987-89 Associate, Lawson-Price.
1978-87 Assistant borough planning officer, London Borough of Greenwich
Other roles
Member, RICS planning and environment policy panel; author of numerous articles on planning and regeneration in technical press
Interests
Walking
Contact details
DTZ Pieda Consulting, 1 Curzon Street, London W1A 5PZ
Tel 020 7408 1161
Fax 020 7643 6000
Web www.dtz.com
Direct tel 020 7643 6171
Direct fax 020 7643 6199
Mobile 07771 604566
Email peter.weatherhead@dtz.com

WEAVER, Francis
Kingsley Napley
Position
Partner – head of commercial property
Qualifications
Solicitor
Contact details
Kingsley Napley, Knights Quarter, 14 St Johns Lane, London EC1M 4AJ
Tel 020 7814 1200
Fax 020 7490 2288
Web www.kingsleynapley.co.uk
Email fweaver@kingsleynapley.co.uk

WEBB, Matthew
Edwin Hill
Position
Partner
Qualifications
BSc; MRICS
Professional memberships
RICS
Contact details
Edwin Hill, Highbridge House, Padbury Oaks, London UB7 0EH
Tel 01753 689000
Fax 01753 689191
Web www.edwinhill.co.uk
Email matthew@edwinhill.co.uk

WEBB, Nigel
British Land Corp
Position
Director – head of developments
Qualifications
BSc Hons; MRICS
Career history
1992 Joined British Land Corp.
1988-92 Development executive, Greycoat.
1985-88 Investment surveyor, Edward Erdman
Professional memberships
British Council for Offices; Investment Property Forum; RICS
Interests
Golf; rugby
Contact details
British Land Corp Ltd, 10 Cornwall Terrace, London NW1 4QP
Tel 020 7486 4466
Web www.britishland.com
Direct tel 020 7467 2860
Direct fax 020 7467 2996
Email nigel.webb@britishland.com

WEBB, Peter
Travis Perkins
Position
Group estates manager
Qualifications
FRIC; ACIArb
Career history
Since 1994 Group estates manager, Travis Perkins.
1990-94 Associate, Chesterton.
1986-90 Principal investment surveyor, Prudential Investment Services.

1982-86 Knight Frank.
1979-82 Abbey Life
Professional memberships
Chartered Institute of Arbitrators; RICS
Interests
Badminton; golf; Rotary; rugby
Contact details
Travis Perkins plc, Ryehill House, Ryehill Close, Northampton NN5 7UA
Tel 01604 752424
Web www.travisperkins.co.uk
Direct fax 01604 683156
Email peter.webb@travisperkins.co.uk

WEBER, James
Commerzbank
Position
Director – UK property group
Contact details
Commerzbank AG, Commerzbank House, 23 Austin Friars, London EC2N 2NB
Tel 020 7638 5895
Web www.commerzbank.com
Email james.weber@commerzbank.co.uk

WEBSTER, Dean
Cyril Sweett
Position
Joint managing director
Qualifications
MBS; BSc; MRICS; MAPM
Career history
2003 Joined Cyril Sweett
Professional memberships
Association for Project Management; RICS
Contact details
Cyril Sweett Ltd, 60 Gray's Inn Road, London WC1X 8AQ
Tel 020 7061 9000
Fax 020 7430 0603
Web www.cyrilsweett.co.uk
Direct tel 020 7061 9333
Mobile 07770 852273
Email dean.webster@cyrilsweett.com

WEBSTER, Mark
Knight Frank
Position
Partner
Qualifications
BSc Hons; MRICS
Career history
Since 1995 Associate/partner, Knight Frank.
1994-95 Weatherall Green & Smith.
1989-94 Montagu Evans
Other roles
National committee member, Industrial Agents Society
Professional memberships
Industrial Agents Society; RICS
Interests
Rugby; sport; wine
Contact details
Knight Frank LLP, 20 Hanover Square, London W1S 1HZ
Tel 020 7629 8171
Fax 020 7493 4114
Web www.knightfrank.com
Direct tel 020 7861 1146
Direct fax 020 7495 0925
Mobile 07721 935202
Email mark.webster@knightfrank.com

WEBSTER, Ted
Chesterton International
Position
Chief executive and head of commercial
Qualifications
FRICS
Career history
Since 2003 Group chief executive, Chesterton.
1975-2002 Partner/director, Insignia Richard Ellis.
1972-75 Jones Lang Wootton
Other roles
Non-executive director, Dunfermline Building Society; chairman, Gune MacKenzie (Dublin)
Professional memberships
RICS
Interests
Cricket; fishing; golf
Contact details
Chesterton International, 54 Brook Street, London W1A 2BU
Tel 020 7499 0404
Fax 020 7629 7804
Web www.chesterton.co.uk
Email ted.webster@chesterton.co.uk

WEBSTER, Tina
Thomas Eggar
Position
Partner – head of commercial property, Chichester
Career history
1983 Joined Thomas Eggar; appointed partner in 1989
Professional memberships
House Builders Federation
Interests
Art; golf; sailing
Contact details
Thomas Eggar, The Corn Exchange, Baffins Lane, Chichester PO19 1GE
Tel 01243 786111
Fax 01243 775640
Web www.thomaseggar.com
Email tina.webster@thomaseggar.com

WEIGHTMAN, Anita
DLA
Position
Location head – real estate, Manchester
Qualifications
LLB Hons
Career history
1991 Joined DLA; appointed partner in 1997 and location head (real estate) for Manchester in 2002.
1987-91 Halliwell Landau
Professional memberships
Law Society
Contact details
DLA, 101 Barbirolli Square, Manchester M2 3DL
Tel 08700 111111
Web www.dla.com
Direct tel 0161 235 4037
Direct fax 0161 235 4125
Email anita.weightman@dla.com

WEINER, Matthew
Development Securities
Position
Investment director
Qualifications
BSc Hons; MRICS
Professional memberships
RICS
Contact details
Development Securities plc, Portland House, Stag Place, London SW1E 5DS
Tel 020 7828 4777
Fax 020 7828 4999
Web www.developmentsecurities.com
Direct tel 020 7802 9931
Email matthew.weiner@devsecs.com

WELBORN, Peter
Knight Frank
Position
Head of corporate finance
Qualifications
BSc; FRICS; MSI
Career history
1976 Joined Knight Frank
Other roles
Managing director, Knight Frank Corporate Finance; partner, Knight Frank (Nigeria); director, Paramount Homes; director, Mayfair Fund
Professional memberships
RICS; Securities Institute

W

Contact details
Knight Frank LLP, 20 Hanover Square, London W1S 1HZ
Tel 020 7629 8171
Fax 020 7493 4114
Web www.knightfrank.com
Direct tel 020 7861 1200
Direct fax 020 7495 0436
Email peter.welborn@knightfrank.com

WELLINGS, Chris
Graves Son & Pilcher
Position
Partner
Qualifications
FRICS
Career history
1961 Joined Graves Son & Pilcher
Professional memberships
RICS
Interests
Golf; music
Contact details
Graves Son & Pilcher, 51 Old Steyne, Brighton BN1 1HU
Tel 01273 321123
Fax 01273 771070
Web www.gsp.uk.com
Mobile 07714 714230
Email cw@gsp.uk.com

WELLS, Yvonne
Land Securities Trillium
Position
Account director – BBC
Career history
1997 Joined Land Securities Trillium as Northern regional director; became Southern regional director in 1999; account director for BBC since 2001
Contact details
Land Securities Trillium Ltd, 140 London Wall, London EC2Y 5DN
Tel 020 7796 5500
Fax 020 7796 5501
Web www.landsecurities.co.uk
Direct tel 020 7796 5757
Direct fax 0845 090 2839
Mobile 07802 686548
Email yvonne.wells@lstrillium.com

WELSH, Alan
Antler Property Corp
Position
Managing director
Qualifications
BSc; MRICS
Career history
1993 Joined Antler.
1991-93 Director, Larkmont Investments.
1986-91 Associate director, Rugby Estates
Professional memberships
Investment Property Forum
Interests
Cycling; family
Contact details
Antler Property Corp plc, The Old Warehouse, 37 Church Street, Weybridge KT13 8DG
Tel 01932 870140
Fax 01932 870141
Email alanwelsh@antler-property.co.uk

WELTON, Michael
Balfour Beatty
Position
Chief executive
Career history
1978 Joined Balfour Beatty Group; became director in 1996 and chief executive in 1999
Professional memberships
Institution of Civil Engineers
Contact details
Balfour Beatty plc, 130 Wilton Road, London SW1V 1LQ
Tel 020 7216 6800
Web www.balfourbeatty.com
Email gill.locke@balfourbeatty.com

WELTON, Thomas
Shaftesbury
Position
Executive director
Qualifications
MRICS
Professional memberships
RICS
Contact details
Shaftesbury plc, Pegasus House, 37-43 Sackville Street, London W1S 3DL
Tel 020 7333 8118
Fax 020 7333 0660
Web www.shaftesbury.co.uk
Email tom.welton@shaftesbury.co.uk

WEST, Lawrence
Henderson Chambers
Position
Barrister
Qualifications
QC; BA; LLB; LLM
Contact details
Henderson Chambers, Ground Floor, 2 Harcourt Buildings, London EC4Y 9DB
Tel 020 7583 9020
Fax 020 7583 2686
Web www.hendersonchambers.co.uk
Email lwest@hendersonchambers.co.uk

WEST, Mark
Lamb Chambers
Position
Barrister
Qualifications
Barrister; LLB
Career history
Since 1973 In private practice, specialising in property law advice and litigation, including related professional negligence.
1973 Called to Bar, Inner Temple
Other roles
Editor and co-author of land division of *Butterworths' Law of Limitation*; recorder (1999)
Professional memberships
Professional Negligence Bar Association; Property Bar Association; Society of Construction Law; Technology & Construction Bar Association
Interests
Skiing; walking
Contact details
Lamb Chambers, Lamb Building, London EC4Y 7AS
Tel 020 7797 8300
Fax 020 7797 8308
Web www.lambchambers.co.uk
Email markwest@lambchambers.co.uk

WEST, Nichola
Denton Wilde Sapte
Position
Partner – commercial property
Career history
1988 Joined Denton Hall (now Denton Wilde Sapte); appointed partner in 1996.
1985 Admitted to Roll of Solicitors.
1983-88 Clifford Turner/Clifford Chance
Professional memberships
BPF; City of London Solicitors Company; Law Society
Other roles
Freeman of the City of London
Interests
Bridge; family; gardening; opera; swimming; tennis
Contact details
Denton Wilde Sapte, 5 Chancery Lane, London EC4A 1BU
Tel 020 7242 1212
Fax 020 7404 0087
Web www.dentonwildesapte.com
Direct tel 020 7320 6217
Email nbhw@dentonwildesapte.com

W

WEST, Nicholas
Land Securities Development

Position
Development director
Qualifications
BSc; MSc; CEng
Contact details
Land Securities Development Ltd, 5 Strand, London WC2N 5AF
Tel 020 7413 9000
Web www.landsecurities.com
Email nick.west@landsecurities.com

WEST, Richard
Lamberts

Position
Director – administration and professional
Qualifications
FRICS
Professional memberships
British Institute of Facilities Management; RICS
Contact details
Lamberts Ltd, 387 City Road, London EC1V 1NA
Tel 020 7278 8191
Fax 020 7837 5790
Web www.lambertsurv.co.uk
Email rw@lambertsurv.co.uk

WESTHEAD, Tim
Olswang

Position
Partner – head of property
Qualifications
LLB Hons
Career history
1996 Joined Olswang; partner/head of property since 1999.
1985-96 Stones Porter: partner from 1986.
1982 Admitted to Roll of Solicitors.
1980-85 Stafford Clark
Interests
Cycling; mountain biking; rugby
Contact details
Olswang, 90 High Holborn, London WC1V 6XX
Tel 020 7067 3000
Fax 020 7067 3999
Web www.olswang.com
Direct tel 020 7067 3627
Email tim.westhead@olswang.com

WESTLAKE, Edward
Edwin Hill

Position
Partner
Qualifications
BSc; FRICS
Career history
1972 Joined Edwin Hill
Professional memberships
RICS
Contact details
Edwin Hill, 18 Savile Row, London W1S 3PW
Tel 020 7287 2020
Fax 020 7734 1255
Web www.edwinhill.co.uk
Email tedw@edwinhill.co.uk

WESTON, Paul
ProLogis Developments

Position
Vice-president – development
Qualifications
BA Hons; MRICS
Career history
2003 Joined ProLogis.
2002-03 Brixton.
1998-2002 Gazeley Properties.
1990-98 Jones Lang Wootton
Professional memberships
RICS
Contact details
ProLogis Developments Ltd, ProLogis House, 1 Monkspath Hall Road, Solihull B90 4FY
Tel 0121 224 8700
Fax 0121 224 8904
Web www.prologis.com
Email pweston@prologis.com

WESTON SMITH, John
British Land Co

Position
Director and chief operating officer
Qualifications
MA; FCIS; ACII; ACIB
Other roles
Managing director of British Land Corp; chairman of British Land Developments and of Broadgate Estates; chairman, St Christopher's School (Hampstead)
Contact details
British Land Co plc, 10 Cornwall Terrace, London NW1 4QP
Tel 020 7486 4466
Fax 020 7935 5552
Web www.britishland.com
Direct tel 020 7467 2899
Direct fax 020 7467 2959
Email john.westonsmith@britishland.com

WHALE, Keith
Gooch Cunliffe Whale

Position
Director
Qualifications
BSc; FRICS; ACIArb
Career history
Since 1989 Director, Gooch Cunliffe Whale.
1980-89 Partner, Healey & Baker
Professional memberships
Chartered Institute of Arbitrators; RICS
Interests
Rugby; skiing; squash
Contact details
Gooch Cunliffe Whale Ltd, Allan House, 10 John Princes Street, London W1G 0JW
Tel 020 7408 0030
Fax 020 7495 4248
Web www.gcw.co.uk
Direct tel 020 7647 4800
Mobile 07977 416944
Email keith.whale@gcw.co.uk

WHATELEY, Grahame
Castlemore Securities

Position
Chairman
Career history
1970 Founded Castlemore.
1966 Founded Riley Whateley & Co.
1963-66 John Howell & Co
Other roles
Director, Castlemore Securities; director, Castlemore Estates; director, Castlemore Properties; director, Castlemore (Huddersfield); director, Castlemore (Maidenhead); director, Castlemore (Temple Quay); director, Castlemore Holdings; director, Cedar Investments; director, Cedar Investment (Holdings); director, Cedar Investments (Bournemouth); director, Provident Securities; director, Britten Investments; director, Valley Park Properties; director, Great Northern Retail Park; director, Cofton Land & Property (Taunton); director, Hampshire Centre
Interests
Golf; IT; Italy; rugby; shooting; skiing; theatre
Contact details
Castlemore Securities Ltd, Cedar Court, 221 Hagley Road, Halesowen B63 1ED
Tel 0121 585 4444
Fax 0121 585 4441
Web www.castlemore.co.uk
Direct tel 0121 585 4401
Direct fax 0121 585 4436
Mobile 07836 510623
Email grahame@castlemore.co.uk

WHATSON, Andy
UNITE Group

Position
Regional development director

Contact details
UNITE Group plc, 2 Acton Square, Salford M5 4NY
Tel 0161 736 7812
Fax 0161 736 7749
Web www.unite-group.com
Email andy.whatson@unite-group.co.uk

WHEELER, John
Centros Miller

Position
Chairman
Contact details
Centros Miller Ltd, Albemarle House, 1 Albemarle Street, London W1S 4HA
Tel 020 7499 3917
Fax 020 7499 3741
Email john.ac.rwheeler@centros-miller.co.uk

WHEELER, John
Media Business Centre

Position
Development director
Career history
Since 1997 Director, Media Business Centre.
1992-97 Self-employed property consultant.
1984-92 European development director with Reinhold; during this time founded Regus.
1971-84 Project manager, Morrison Son & Jones
Other roles
Founder, Regus Serviced Offices; director, Reinhold Group; director, Sheraton Skyline Hotel (1986-96)
Interests
Field sports; golf; sport
Contact details
Media Business Centre Ltd, The Media Centre, 131-151 Great Titchfield Street, London W1W 5BB
Tel 020 7665 8200
Fax 020 7665 8201
Web www.themediacentre.co.uk
Direct tel 020 7665 8217
Direct fax 01438 232575
Mobile 07970 830345
Email wheeler@estatesgazette.net

WHEELER, Martin
GMAC Commercial Mortgage Europe

Position
Director – real estate finance
Qualifications
BSc Hons; MRICS
Career history
1998-2002 Structured property finance, HBOS.
1997-98 Property finance, HSBC.
1990-97 Legal & General Investment Management
Professional memberships
RICS
Interests
Rugby; windsurfing
Contact details
GMAC Commercial Mortgage Europe, Buchanan House, 3 St James's Square, London SW1Y 4JU
Tel 020 7393 6200
Fax 020 7393 6286
Email martin_wheeler@gmaccm.com

WHEELER, Nigel
Nelson Bakewell

Position
Director – head of property management
Qualifications
BSc; MRICS
Career history
1984 Joined Nelson Bakewell; became director in 1989.
1981-84 Weatherall Green & Smith
Other roles
Director, Sackville Resource Management; director, Nelson Bakewell Management; director, Nelson Bakewell Professional
Professional memberships
British Council for Offices; Non-Administrative Receivers Association; RICS
Interests
Golf; sailing; skiing; squash; tennis
Contact details
Nelson Bakewell Ltd, 25 Sackville Street, London W1S 3HQ
Tel 020 7544 2000
Fax 020 7544 2222
Web www.nelson-bakewell.com
Direct tel 020 7544 2060
Mobile 07775 676435
Email nwheeler@nelson-bakewell.com

WHEELER, Tim
Brixton

Position
Chief executive
Qualifications
BSc; FRICS
Career history
1985 Joined Brixton; appointed assistant director (acquisitions) in 1988, property director in 1997 and chief executive in 2000.
1984-85 Development surveyor, Townsend Thoresen Properties.
1983-84 Development surveyor, Crouch Group.
1980-83 Gooch & Wagstaff
Professional memberships
RICS
Interests
Sport
Contact details
Brixton plc, 50 Berkeley Street, London W1J 8BX
Tel 020 7399 4500
Fax 020 7399 4550
Web www.brixton.plc.uk
Direct tel 020 7399 4526
Email timwheeler@brixton.plc.uk

WHEELHOUSE, Mark
Freshfields Bruckhaus Deringer

Position
Partner – real estate
Career history
Since 1996 Partner, Freshfields Bruckhaus Deringer.
1987 Admitted to Roll of Solicitors
Professional memberships
City of London Solicitors Co; Law Society
Interests
Entertaining; reading; sport
Contact details
Freshfields Bruckhaus Deringer, 65 Fleet Street, London EC4Y 1HT
Tel 020 7936 4000
Fax 020 7832 7001
Web www.freshfields.com
Direct tel 020 7832 7272
Email mark.wheelhouse@freshfields.com

WHETSTONE, Malcolm
GVA Grimley

Position
Partner – building, project management and consultancy
Qualifications
BSc; FRICS; Dip Proj Man
Career history
1978 Established building surveying division at Grimley & Son (now GVA Grimley).
1976-78 Richard Ellis
Other roles
Committee member, Project Management Diploma Association; director, GVA Europe; director, GVA Global; director, GVA Grimley (Construction Services); director, GVA Software; director, REAL Products Software
Interests
Gardening
Contact details
GVA Grimley, 10 Stratton Street, London W1J 8JR
Tel 0870 900 8990
Fax 020 7911 2560
Web www.gvagrimley.co.uk

W

Direct tel 020 7911 2408
Direct fax 020 7911 2438
Email malcolm.whetstone@gvagrimley.co.uk

WHIPP, Nick
GVA Grimley

Position
Partner
Qualifications
FRICS; Dip Est Man
Career history
1979 Joined Grimley to open agency in Manchester; became partner in 1982. Previously head of offices team/business space; head of agency since 1995
Other roles
Director, GVA Worldwide; director, GVA Connect; director, GVA Collyer Coxhead International; director, GVA Grimley, Australia; racing sailboats for 30 years: former national champion
Professional memberships
British Council for Offices; Office Agents Society; RICS
Interests
Sailing
Contact details
GVA Grimley, 81 Fountain Street, Manchester M2 2EE
Tel 0870 900 8990
Fax 0161 956 4009
Web www.gvagrimley.co.uk
Direct tel 0161 956 4113
Direct fax 0161 956 4446
Mobile 07836 244302
Email nick.whipp@gvagrimley.co.uk

WHITAKER, Steven
199 Strand

Position
Barrister
Qualifications
MA (Cantab)
Career history
Since 1990 Barrister, 199 Strand.
1974-90 At 3 Paper Buildings, Temple.
1973 Called to Bar
Professional memberships
Chancery Bar Association; Professional Negligence Bar Association; Property Bar Association
Interests
Horse riding; IT; literature; music; opera; theatre
Contact details
199 Strand (Chambers of David Phillips QC), London WC2R 1DR
Tel 020 7520 4000
Fax 020 7379 9481
Web www.199strand.co.uk
Mobile 07970 201375
Email rcroke@199strand.co.uk

WHITE, Colin
Edward Symmons & Partners

Position
Partner – hotel and leisure
Professional memberships
Business in Sport & Leisure; Leisure Property Forum
Interests
Football; golf; music; skiing
Contact details
Edward Symmons & Partners, Nuffield House, 41-46 Piccadilly, London W1J 0DS
Tel 020 7344 4500
Fax 020 7344 4555
Web www.edwardsymmons.com
Mobile 07785 500326
Email colin.white@edwardsymmons.com

WHITE, Malcolm
BW Investor Services

Position
Director
Qualifications
BA, Econ
Professional memberships
Society of Property Researchers
Contact details
BW Investor Services Ltd, 3rd Floor, 4 Gees Court, London W1U 1JD
Tel 020 7629 8383
Fax 020 7495 2977
Email malcolm@barberwhite.co.uk

WHITE, Martin
Pinsents

Position
Consultant – head of planning and environmental unit
Qualifications
MA (Cantab)
Career history
1981 Joined Pinsent & Co (now Pinsents); became partner in 1987.
1979 Admitted to Roll of Solicitors.
1977-81 Solihull Metropolitan Borough Council
Professional memberships
Law Society; RTPI
Interests
Music; theatre; travel
Contact details
Pinsents, 3 Colmore Circus, Birmingham B4 6BH
Tel 0121 200 1050
Fax 0121 626 1040
Web www.pinsents.com
Mobile 07771 915236
Email martin.white@pinsents.com

WHITE, Paul
Frogmore Estates

Position
Managing director
Other roles
Director, Frogmore Developments; director, Frogmore Investments
Professional memberships
BPF; Investment Property Forum
Interests
Golf; skiing
Contact details
Frogmore Estates Ltd, 11-15 Wigmore Street, London W1A 2JZ
Tel 020 7016 6000
Fax 020 7495 5321
Web www.frogmore.co.uk
Email paulwhite@frogmore.co.uk

WHITE, Richard
Ernst & Young

Position
Partner – real estate, hospitality and construction
Contact details
Ernst & Young LLP, 1 More London Place, London SE1 2AF
Tel 020 7951 2000
Fax 020 7951 1345
Web www.ey.com/uk
Direct tel 020 7951 4699
Direct fax 020 7951 3411
Mobile 07711 425977
Email richard.white@uk.ey.com

WHITE, Richard
Thomas Cook

Position
Property director – UK and Ireland
Career history
1998 Joined Thomas Cook as head of UK property; property director since 2003.
1996-98 Property manager, Scottish Power Retail.
1993-96 Facilities and administration manager, Samsung UK.
1990-93 Facilities manager, Smith & Nephew
Other roles
President, Property Managers Association (2003/04)
Professional memberships
British Institute of Facilities Management; Property Managers Association

Contact details
Thomas Cook, PO Box 701, 15-16 Coningsby Road, Peterborough PE3 8AB
Tel 01733 417401
Web www.thomascook.co.uk
Direct tel 01733 417234
Direct fax 01733 417455
Email richard.white@thomascook.com

WHITE, Stephen
Cobbetts
Position
Senior partner
Career history
1974 Admitted to Roll of Solicitors.
1972 Joined Cobbetts (formerly Leak Almond & Parkinson); became partner in 1977 and senior partner in 1999; managing partner 1990-96
Professional memberships
American Bar Association; Law Society
Interests
Photography; tennis
Contact details
Cobbetts, Ship Canal House, King Street, Manchester M2 4WB
Tel 0161 833 3333
Fax 0161 833 3030
Web www.cobbetts.co.uk
Direct tel 0161 833 5222
Mobile 07712 661945
Email stephen.white@cobbetts.co.uk

WHITEHEAD, John
Deloitte
Position
Partner, head of real estate tax group
Qualifications
ACA; CTA
Career history
2003 Joined Deloitte.
1998-2002 Arthur Andersen
Contact details
Deloitte, Stonecutter Court, 1 Stonecutter Street, London EC4A 3TR
Tel 020 7936 3000
Fax 020 7583 1198
Web www.deloitte.co.uk
Direct tel 020 7007 2978
Direct fax 020 7007 2258
Email jgwhitehead@deloitte.co.uk

WHITEHEAD, Oliver
Alfred McAlpine
Position
Chairman
Contact details
Alfred McAlpine plc, Kinnaird House, 1 Pall Mall East, London SW1Y 5AZ
Tel 020 7930 6255
Fax 020 7839 6902
Web www.alfred-mcalpine.com
Email nancy.betterton@mcalpineplc.com

WHITEHURST, John
Prestbury Investment Holdings
Position
Managing director
Contact details
Prestbury Investment Holdings Ltd, 11-12 Wigmore Place, London W1U 2LU
Tel 020 7323 5250
Fax 020 7323 5251
Email john@prestbury.co.uk

WHITELAW, Alan
NAI Fuller Peiser
Position
Equity partner – head of Scottish office
Qualifications
MRICS; IRRV
Career history
1997 Joined Fuller Peiser; now head of office responsible for all services provided from Scotland
Professional memberships
Rating Surveyors Association
Contact details
NAI Fuller Peiser, Hanover Buildings, 66 Rose Street, Edinburgh EH2 2NN
Tel 0870 700 2233
Fax 0131 225 5126
Web www.nai-fullerpeiser.com
Email awhitelaw@nai-fullerpeiser.com

WHITELAW, Colin
Antler Property Investments
Position
Director
Qualifications
BSc, Land Econ; MRICS
Career history
Since 2000 Director, Antler Property Investments.
1996-99 Group property director, USC Group.
1990-96 Partner, Whitelaw Baikie & Co.
1984-90 Watson Neave; progressed to director/shareholder
Other roles
Non-executive director, Broom Estates; non-executive property director, USC Group
Professional memberships
RICS
Interests
Football; golf; sailing; shooting
Contact details
Antler Property Investments plc, 75 Bothwell Street, Glasgow G2 6TS
Tel 0141 222 1080
Fax 0141 222 1081
Mobile 07900 911406
Email Colin@whitelawconsulting.co.uk

WHITELEY, John
Great Portland Estates
Position
Finance director
Qualifications
FCA; BA, Econ
Career history
1992 Joined Great Portland Estates; appointed director in 1995.
1983-92 Ernst & Young.
1980-83 Spicer & Pegler
Professional memberships
Institute of Chartered Accountants in England & Wales
Contact details
Great Portland Estates plc, 56 Mortimer Street, London W1W 7RT
Tel 020 7580 3040
Fax 020 7631 5169
Web www.gpe.co.uk
Email john.whiteley@gpe.co.uk

WHITNEY, Sarah
DTZ Pieda Consulting
Position
Managing director
Qualifications
BSc; ACA
Career history
Since 2003 Managing director, DTZ Pieda Consulting. Previously partner at PricewaterhouseCoopers and held corporate finance roles at Barings and Kleinwort
Contact details
DTZ Pieda Consulting, 1 Curzon Street, London W1A 5PZ
Tel 020 7408 1161
Fax 020 7643 6000
Web www.dtz.com
Direct tel 020 7757 6619
Direct fax 020 7643 6198
Email sarah.whitney@dtz.com

WHITTAKER, John
Peel Holdings
Position
Chairman
Contact details
Peel Holdings plc, Peel Dome, The Trafford

W

Centre, Manchester M17 8PL
Tel 0161 629 8200
Fax 0161 629 8333
Web www.peel.co.uk
Email hseddon@peel.co.uk

WHITTAKER, Shaun
Thames Valley Economic Partnership
Position
Chief executive
Contact details
Thames Valley Economic Partnership, 100 Longwater Avenue, Reading RG2 6GP
Tel 0118 945 0040
Fax 0118 945 0037
Email info@thamesvalley.co.uk

WHITTINGHAM, Mike
Stiles Harold Williams
Position
Director
Qualifications
BSc; MRICS
Professional memberships
RICS
Contact details
Stiles Harold Williams Ltd, 6 Babmaes Street, London SW1Y 6HD
Tel 020 7389 1500
Fax 020 7389 1515
Web www.shw.co.uk
Email mwhittingham@shw.co.uk

WHITTLE, Robert
Fleurets
Position
Director
Qualifications
FAVLP; ABII
Career history
1979 Joined Fleurets.
1971-79 Worked in brewing industry: transport management at Scottish & Newcastle Breweries; estates management at Tollemache & Cobbold Breweries
Other roles
Honorary secretary, Association of Valuers of Licensed Property
Professional memberships
Association of Valuers of Licensed Property; British Institute of Innkeeping (affiliate)
Interests
Cycling; food and drink; music
Contact details
Fleurets Ltd, Wellesley House, 96 East Street, Sudbury CO10 2TP
Tel 01787 378050
Fax 01787 880292
Web www.fleurets.com
Mobile 07836 680490
Email bob.whittle@fleurets.com

WHYBROW, Christopher
Landmark Chambers
Position
Barrister
Qualifications
LLB; QC
Career history
1992 Appointed QC.
1965 Called to Bar
Other roles
Deputy Social Security Commissioner
Professional memberships
London Common Law & Commercial Bar Association; Parliamentary Bar Mess; Planning & Environment Bar Association
Contact details
Landmark Chambers, 4 Breams Buildings, London EC4A 1AQ
Tel 020 7430 1221
Fax 020 7421 1399
Web www.landmarkchambers.co.uk
Email clerks@landmarkchambers.co.uk

WILBY, Tony
Taylor Woodrow Developments
Position
Operations director – North
Qualifications
MRICS
Professional memberships
RICS
Contact details
Taylor Woodrow Developments Ltd, 2 Princes Way, Solihull B91 3ES
Tel 0121 600 8000
Fax 0121 600 8001
Web www.taylorwoodrow.com
Direct tel 0121 600 8510
Direct fax 0121 600 8525
Email tony.wilby@uk.taylorwoodrow.com

WILCOCK, Marion
DMH
Position
Partner – head of commercial property group
Contact details
DMH, 100 Queens Road, Brighton BN1 3YB
Tel 01273 329833
Fax 01273 747500
Web www.dmh.co.uk
Email marion.wilcock@dmh.co.uk

WILDEN, Nicky
Topland Group of Companies
Position
Group finance director
Career history
1996-2001 Director, Jones Lang LaSalle Corporate Finance.
1990-96 Director, DTZ Debenham Thorpe.
1987-90 Group financial controller, Imry Merchant Developers.
1984-87 Assistant manager, KPMG
Other roles
RICS taxation policy panel member
Professional memberships
Institute of Chartered Accountants in England & Wales; Investment Property Forum
Contact details
Topland Group of Companies, Nations House, 103 Wigmore Street, London W1U 1QS
Tel 020 7493 3373
Fax 020 7493 4055
Web www.topland.co.uk
Email nickyw@topland.co.uk

WILDER, Gary
Nomura International
Position
Managing director – co-head real estate finance group
Contact details
Nomura International plc, Nomura House, 1 St Martin's-le-grand, London EC1A 4AS
Tel 020 7521 2000
Fax 020 7521 3565
Web www.nomura.com
Email gary.wilder@uk.nomura.com

WILKES, Simon
Legal & General Property
Position
Head of property development team
Qualifications
BSc Hons; MRICS
Career history
1988 Joined Legal & General
Professional memberships
RICS
Interests
Mountaineering; photography; tennis
Contact details
Legal & General Property Ltd, Bucklersbury House, 3 Queen Victoria Street, London EC4N 8NH
Tel 020 7528 6500
Fax 020 7528 6848
Web www.legal-and-general.co.uk
Direct tel 020 7528 6877

Mobile 07796 442829
Email simon.wilkes@lgim.co.uk

WILKINS, Christopher
11 Stone Buildings

Position
Barrister
Qualifications
MA (Oxon)
Career history
1993 Called to Bar
Professional memberships
Chancery Bar Association; Property Bar Association
Contact details
11 Stone Buildings, London WC2A 3TG
Tel 020 7831 6381
Fax 020 7831 2575
Web www.11stonebuildings.com
Email wilkins@11stonebuildings.com

WILKINSON, Chris
MFI Properties

Position
Property director
Contact details
MFI Properties Ltd, 333 Edgware Road, London NW9 6TD
Tel 020 8913 5164
Email chris.wilkinson@mfi.co.uk

WILKINSON, Jonathan
GVA Grimley

Position
National head of residential
Career history
1988 Joined GVA Grimley; appointed national head of residential in 1998.
1980-88 Local government and NHS
Contact details
GVA Grimley, 81 Fountain Street, Manchester M2 2EE
Tel 0870 900 8990
Fax 0161 956 4009
Web www.gvagrimley.co.uk
Direct tel 0161 956 4114
Mobile 07831 555250
Email jonathan.wilkinson@gvagrimley.co.uk

WILKINSON, Paul
Wilkinson Williams

Position
Director
Qualifications
BSc; MRICS
Career history
1991 Joint founder, Wilkinson Williams.
1987-91 Associate investment surveyor, Vigers.
1984-86 Management surveyor, CIN Properties
Professional memberships
Accessible Retail; Investment Agents Society; RICS
Interests
Football; skiing
Contact details
Wilkinson Williams Ltd, Meadows House, 20-22 Queen Street, London W1J 5PR
Tel 020 7495 4321
Fax 020 7495 5432
Web www.wilkinsonwilliams.co.uk
Mobile 07770 585313
Email p.wilkinson@wwprop.co.uk

WILKINSON, Peter
Aitchison Raffety

Position
Director
Qualifications
FRICS
Professional memberships
RICS
Contact details
Aitchison Raffety Ltd, 8 High Street, High Wycombe HP11 2AZ
Tel 01494 538800
Fax 01494 436362
Web www.argroup.co.uk
Email peter.wilkinson@argroup.co.uk

WILKINSON, Simon
Bradford & Bingley

Position
Director of property finance
Career history
1989 Joined Bradford & Bingley as development manager of corporate lending; appointed director of commercial property finance in 1998.
1972-89 Midland Bank
Professional memberships
Association of Property Bankers
Contact details
Bradford & Bingley plc, PO Box 88, Crossflatts, Bingley BD16 2UA
Web www.bbg.co.uk
Direct tel 01274 554189
Mobile 07721 978159
Email simon.wilkinson@bbg.co.uk

WILLIAMS, Anne
Landmark Chambers

Position
Barrister
Qualifications
BA Hons, Econ; MPhil; MRTPI
Career history
1980 Called to Bar
Other roles
Co-editor, *Blundell & Dobry on Planning Applications & Appeals*; contributor to *Halsbury's Laws of England* on town and country planning; treasurer, Planning & Environment Bar Association; lecturer in town and country planning, University College, London
Professional memberships
Planning & Environment Bar Association
Interests
Ice skating; IT; literature; skiing; tennis
Contact details
Landmark Chambers, 4 Breams Buildings, London EC4A 1AQ
Tel 020 7430 1221
Fax 020 7421 1399
Web www.landmarkchambers.co.uk
Email clerks@landmarkchambers.co.uk

WILLIAMS, Bryn
DTZ Debenham Tie Leung

Position
Director
Qualifications
BSc Hons; MRICS
Career history
1986 Joined DTZ (formerly Bernard Thorpe); appointed director in 1990 and national valuation co-ordinator in 1999.
1982-86 Edward Erdman
Other roles
RICS registered fixed-charge receiver
Professional memberships
Investment Property Forum; Non-Administrative Receivers Association; Property Valuation Forum; RICS
Interests
Cricket; football; golf; rugby; tennis
Contact details
DTZ Debenham Tie Leung, 1 Curzon Street, London W1A 5PZ
Tel 020 7408 1161
Fax 020 7643 6000
Web www.dtz.com
Direct tel 020 7643 6243
Mobile 07774 449265
Email bryn.williams@dtz.com

WILLIAMS, Chris
Carisbrooke Suon Limited Partnership

Position
Director – asset management
Contact details
Carisbrooke Suon Limited Partnership, D11 Point 2, Treforest Industrial Estate,

W

Pontypridd CF37 5UR
Tel 01443 841558
Email cwilliams@carisbrookesuon.co.uk

WILLIAMS, Christopher
Marks & Spencer Group

Position
Director of property
Qualifications
BSc Hons; FRICS
Career history
1990 Joined Marks & Spencer as acquisition surveyor; became estate manager in 1994 and executive (UK estates) in 1998.
1986-90 Development executive, Tesco
Other roles
Board member, British Council of Shopping Centres
Professional memberships
British Council of Shopping Centres; BPF; RICS
Interests
Family; music; running; travel
Contact details
Marks & Spencer Group plc, Michael House, 37-67 Baker Street, London W1U 8EP
Tel 020 7268 8070
Fax 020 7268 2652
Web www.marksandspencer.com
Mobile 07831 829851
Email
christopher.williams@marks-and-spencer.com

WILLIAMS, David
Allen & Overy

Position
Partner – real estate
Career history
1982 Joined Allen & Overy; appointed partner in 1988
Professional memberships
Law Society; UK Environmental Law Association
Interests
Cycling; photography; swimming
Contact details
Allen & Overy, 1 New Change, London EC4M 9QQ
Tel 020 7330 3000
Fax 020 7330 9999
Web www.allenovery.com
Direct tel 020 7330 4806
Email david.williams@allenovery.com

WILLIAMS, David
Dalgleish

Position
Director – head of client liaison
Contact details
Dalgleish, 80 New Bond Street, London W1S 1DD
Tel 020 7663 5555
Fax 020 7491 0098
Web www.dalgleish.co.uk
Direct tel 020 7663 5537
Email dwilliams@dalgleish.co.uk

WILLIAMS, David
FPDSavills

Position
Director – head of commercial agency
Interests
Farming; field sports; fishing; gardening; shooting
Contact details
FPDSavills Ltd, 20 Grosvenor Hill, London W1K 3HQ
Tel 020 7499 8644
Fax 020 7495 3773
Web www.fpdsavills.co.uk
Direct tel 020 7409 8709
Mobile 07879 402559
Email dwilliams@fpdsavills.co.uk

WILLIAMS, David
Vebnet (Holdings)

Position
Joint managing director
Contact details
Vebnet (Holdings) plc, The Courtyard, New Lodge, Drift Road, Windsor SL4 4RR
Tel 01344 884662
Fax 01344 884878
Email stockb@stockbourne.co.uk

WILLIAMS, James
Drivers Jonas

Position
Partner – public sector planning
Qualifications
MA; FRICS; FRTPI; Dip TP
Career history
1972 Joined Drivers Jonas.
1970-72 Planning assistant, Royal Borough of Kensington & Chelsea.
1966-68 Planning assistant, Norfolk County Council
Professional memberships
RICS; Royal Society of Arts; RTPI
Contact details
Drivers Jonas, 6 Grosvenor Street, London W1K 4DJ
Tel 020 7896 8000
Fax 020 7896 8001
Web www.driversjonas.com
Direct tel 020 7896 8080
Email jameswilliams@driversjonas.com

WILLIAMS, John
Lambert Smith Hampton

Position
Head of office
Qualifications
FRICS
Career history
1991 Joined Lambert Smith Hampton.
1975-91 Partner, Giddy & Giddy Commercial
Professional memberships
RICS
Interests
Golf; rugby
Contact details
Lambert Smith Hampton Ltd, First Floor, Brock House, 57 High Street, Maidenhead SL6 1JT
Tel 0162 867 6001
Fax 0162 877 0347
Web www.lsh.co.uk
Email jwilliams@lsh.co.uk

WILLIAMS, John
Old Square Chambers

Position
Barrister
Qualifications
QC
Other roles
Non-executive chairman, Claim Room.Com (online dispute resolution company)
Contact details
Old Square Chambers (Chambers of John Hendy QC), 1 Verulam Buildings, London WC1R 5LQ
Tel 020 7269 0300
Fax 020 7405 1387
Web www.oldsquarechambers.co.uk
Email williamsqc@oldsquarechambers.co.uk

WILLIAMS, Ken
Vail Williams

Position
Partner – business space and development and investment
Qualifications
FRICS
Other roles
Chairman, Blackwater Valley Business Association
Professional memberships
RICS
Interests
Golf; shooting
Contact details
Vail Williams, Quatro House, Lyon Way, Camberley GU16 7ER
Tel 01276 682501
Fax 01276 684988

Web www.vailwilliams.com
Direct tel 0870 099 3152
Mobile 07768 724346
Email kwilliams@vailwilliams.com

WILLIAMS, Mark
DTZ Debenham Tie Leung

Position
Director – head of retail
Qualifications
MBA; BSc Hons
Career history
1982 Joined DTZ; became associate in 1989, director in 1994 and head of UK retail in 1997
Other roles
Board member, British Council of Shopping Centres; chairman, DTZ European Retail & Leisure Group
Professional memberships
British Council of Shopping Centres; International Council of Shopping Centers; Leisure Property Forum; RICS; Strategic Management Society
Interests
Family; golf; horse riding; skiing
Contact details
DTZ Debenham Tie Leung, 1 Curzon Street, London W1A 5PZ
Tel 020 7408 1161
Fax 020 7643 6000
Web www.dtz.com
Direct tel 020 7643 6520
Mobile 07771 807428
Email mark.williams@dtz.com

WILLIAMS, Mark
Lambert Smith Hampton

Position
Director – head of Manchester office
Qualifications
BSc Hons; MRICS
Career history
1988 Joined Lambert Smith Hampton.
1986-88 Surveyor, English Estates.
1985-86 Graduate surveyor, Inland Revenue
Professional memberships
RICS
Interests
Golf
Contact details
Lambert Smith Hampton Ltd, 79 Mosley Street, Manchester M2 3LQ
Tel 0161 228 6411
Fax 0161 228 7354
Web www.lsh.co.uk
Direct tel 0161 242 7074
Email mwilliams2@lsh.co.uk

WILLIAMS, Martyn
Cushman & Wakefield Healey & Baker

Position
Partner – investment
Qualifications
FRICS
Career history
1973 Joined Cushman & Wakefield Healey & Baker
Professional memberships
RICS
Contact details
Cushman & Wakefield Healey & Baker, 43-45 Portman Square, London W1A 3BG
Tel 020 7935 5000
Fax 020 7152 5360
Web www.cushwake.com
Direct tel 020 7152 5011
Email martyn.williams@eur.cushwake.com

WILLIAMS, Mike
Morgan Williams

Position
Partner
Qualifications
FRICS
Professional memberships
RICS
Contact details
Morgan Williams, Central House, Central Way, Warrington WA2 7TT
Tel 01925 414909
Fax 01925 637619
Email mwilliams@morganwilliams.biz

WILLIAMS, Paul
Derwent Valley Holdings

Position
Director
Qualifications
FRICS
Professional memberships
RICS
Contact details
Derwent Valley Holdings plc, 25 Savile Row, London W1S 2ER
Tel 020 7659 3000
Fax 020 7659 3100
Web www.derwentvalley.co.uk
Email paul.williams@derwentvalley.co.uk

WILLIAMS, Paul
DTZ Pieda Consulting

Position
Director – European research and development
Qualifications
MA Hons; MSc; MCS
Career history
1999 Joined DTZ Pieda Consulting's economic consulting team; appointed head of international research and development in 2001
Professional memberships
Society of Property Researchers
Interests
Literature; sailing
Contact details
DTZ Pieda Consulting, 1 Curzon Street, London W1A 5PZ
Tel 020 7408 1161
Fax 020 7643 6000
Web www.dtz.com
Direct tel 020 7757 6628
Direct fax 020 7493 6198
Email paul.williams@dtz.com

WILLIAMS, Paul
King Sturge

Position
Partner, national head of investment
Qualifications
FRICS
Professional memberships
RICS
Contact details
King Sturge, 7 Stratford Place, London W1C 1ST
Tel 020 7493 4933
Fax 020 7409 0469
Web www.kingsturge.com
Direct tel 020 7318 4120
Email paul.williams@kingsturge.co.uk

WILLIAMS, Peter
Lambert Smith Hampton

Position
Director
Qualifications
BSc; FRICS; ACIArb
Career history
Since 1988 Director in charge of Peterborough office, Lambert Smith Hampton (formerly Connell Wilson).
1980-86 Senior commercial surveyor, Norman Wright & Hodgkinson
Other roles
RICS panel arbitrator; RICS panel independent expert
Professional memberships
Chartered Institute of Arbitrators; RICS
Interests
Beer; fishing; football; music; sailing; wine
Contact details
Lambert Smith Hampton Ltd, 2-6 Priestgate, Peterborough PE1 1JQ
Tel 01733 563921

W

Fax 01733 342201
Web www.lsh.co.uk
Direct tel 01733 564670
Mobile 07885 778901
Email pwilliams@lsh.co.uk

WILLIAMS, Peter
Selfridges

Position
Chief executive
Qualifications
ACA; BSc
Other roles
Chairman, London Retail Consortium
Professional memberships
Institute of Chartered Accountants in England & Wales
Interests
Shopping; skiing; tennis
Contact details
Selfridges, 400 Oxford Street, London W1A 1AB
Tel 08708 377377
Fax 020 7495 8321
Web www.selfridges.co.uk
Direct tel 020 7318 3000
Direct fax 020 7318 3002
Email peter.williams@selfridges.co.uk

WILLIAMS, Phillip
Associated British Ports

Position
Group property director
Qualifications
FRICS
Career history
Since 2002 Group property director for Associated British Ports holdings, with overall responsibility for all aspects of the company's property portfolio, including US-based seaports business AMPORTS.
1994-2002 Grosvenor Waterside Group (ABP's then-property subsidiary): initially development manager; promoted to estates director in 1998; managing director from 2001.
1987-94 Development director, Govan Davies Group and Port of Pembroke
Other roles
External professional adviser to National Assembly for Wales debating chamber board
Professional memberships
RICS; UK Environmental Law Association
Interests
Gardening; motor sports
Contact details
Associated British Ports, 150 Holborn, London EC1N 2LR
Tel 020 7430 1177
Web www.abports.co.uk
Direct fax 020 7405 6188
Email pwilliams@abports.co.uk

WILLIAMS, Ray
Grosvenor

Position
Property finance director
Contact details
Grosvenor Ltd, 70 Grosvenor Street, London W1K 3JP
Tel 020 7408 0988
Fax 020 7629 9115
Web www.grosvenor.com
Email ray.williams@grosvenor.com

WILLIAMS, Richard
Nelson Bakewell

Position
Director – portfolio management
Qualifications
BSc; MRICS
Career history
1989 Joined Nelson Bakewell.
1986-89 Richard Ellis
Other roles
Director, Sackville Resource Management
Professional memberships
RICS
Contact details
Nelson Bakewell Ltd, 25 Sackville Street, London W1S 3HQ
Tel 020 7544 2000
Fax 020 7544 2222
Web www.nelson-bakewell.com
Direct tel 020 7544 2065
Mobile 07887 825694
Email rwilliams@nelson-bakewell.com

WILLIAMS, Robert
Wilkinson Williams

Position
Joint senior partner
Qualifications
BSc, Econ; Dip LE; MRICS
Contact details
Wilkinson Williams Ltd, Meadows House, 20-22 Queen Street, London W1J 5PR
Tel 020 7495 4321
Fax 020 7495 5432
Web www.wilkinsonwilliams.co.uk
Email r.williams@wwprop.co.uk

WILLIAMS, Simon
Lamb Chambers

Position
Barrister
Qualifications
LLB
Career history
1984 Called to Bar
Other roles
Recent seminars given on various aspects of law of forfeiture, distress and commonhold
Professional memberships
Chancery Bar Association; London Common Law & Commercial Bar Association; Property Bar Association
Interests
Cricket; football; photography; travel
Contact details
Lamb Chambers, Lamb Building, London EC4Y 7AS
Tel 020 7797 8300
Fax 020 7797 8308
Web www.lambchambers.co.uk
Email simonwilliams@lambchambers.co.uk

WILLIAMS, Timothy
Nelson Bakewell

Position
Head of City office and agency
Qualifications
BSc Hons, Land Man; MRICS
Career history
Since 2000 Head of City office and agency, Nelson Bakewell.
1990-2000 Partner, Knight Frank.
1989-90 Lambert Smith Hampton.
1986-88 Vigers
Professional memberships
RICS
Interests
Geography; skiing; theatre; travel; water sports
Contact details
Nelson Bakewell Ltd, 14 Nicholas Lane, London EC4N 7BN
Tel 020 7544 2000
Fax 020 7544 2222
Web www.nelson-bakewell.com
Direct tel 020 7544 2273
Mobile 07050 049154
Email tgwilliams@nelson-bakewell.com

WILLIAMSON, Andrew
Pannone & Partners

Position
Partner
Qualifications
LLB; MSc, Construction Law & Arbitration; MCIArb
Career history
1998 Joined Pannone & Partners; appointed partner in 1999.

1996-98 Glaisyers.
1993 Admitted to Roll of Solicitors
Professional memberships
Adjudication Society; Chartered Institute of Arbitrators; Law Society; Society of Construction Law
Interests
Football
Contact details
Pannone & Partners, 123 Deansgate, Manchester M3 2BU
Tel 0161 909 3000
Fax 0161 909 4444
Web www.pannone.com
Email andrew.williamson@pannone.co.uk

WILLIAMSON, Anthony
Frontier Estates
Position
Associate director
Qualifications
BSc Hons, Est Man; MRICS
Career history
1991-2000 Associate director, Jones Lang LaSalle
Professional memberships
RICS
Interests
Golf; walking
Contact details
Frontier Estates Ltd, Acorn House, Midsummer Boulevard, Milton Keynes MK9 3HP
Tel 01908 238888
Fax 01908 241111
Web www.frontier-estates.com
Mobile 07713 412894
Email anthonywilliamson@frontier-estates.com

WILLIAMSON, Hazel
Maitland Chambers
Position
Barrister
Qualifications
QC; MA (Oxon); FCIArb
Career history
1988 Appointed QC.
1972 Called to Bar
Other roles
Co-author, *The Law & Valuation of Leisure Property*; recorder; deputy High Court judge; acting deemster of Isle of Man; qualified mediator
Professional memberships
Chancery Bar Association; Chartered Institute of Arbitrators; Commercial Bar Association; Property Bar Association
Contact details
Maitland Chambers, 7 Stone Buildings, London WC2A 3SZ
Tel 020 7406 1200
Fax 020 7406 1300
Web www.maitlandchambers.com
Email hwilliamson@maitlandchambers.com

WILLINGHAM, Steve
Merrill Lynch International
Position
Director – debt markets, real estate finance
Qualifications
FCIB; MBA
Career history
2003 Joined Merrill Lynch.
1990-2003 Nationwide Building Society.
1987-90 TSB Bank
Professional memberships
Association of Property Bankers; Investment Property Forum
Interests
Rugby; theatre
Contact details
Merrill Lynch International, 2 King Edward Street, London EC1A 1HQ
Tel 020 7628 1000
Web www.mlim.co.uk
Direct tel 020 7995 2616
Mobile 07860 891588
Email steve_willingham@ml.com

WILLIS, Martin
Fleurets
Position
Director
Qualifications
FRICS; FAVLP
Career history
1980-84 Bass.
1974-80 Inland Revenue Valuation Office
Professional memberships
RICS
Interests
Boating; football; sailing
Contact details
Fleurets Ltd, 18 Bloomsbury Square, London WC1A 2NS
Tel 020 7636 8992
Fax 020 7636 7490
Web www.fleurets.com
Email martin.willis@fleurets.com

WILLS-WILLIAMS, Mark
ATIS REAL Weatheralls
Position
Director – head of retail and leisure
Qualifications
MRICS
Career history
1993-2002 Director, Colliers CRE
Professional memberships
British Council of Shopping Centres; Gold & Silver Wyre Drawers Livery Company; RICS; Shop Agents Society
Interests
Cooking; cycling; entertaining; family; food and drink; football; golf; horse racing; outdoor pursuits
Contact details
ATIS REAL Weatheralls Ltd, Norfolk House, 31 St James's Square, London SW1Y 4JR
Tel 020 7338 4200
Fax 020 7493 0746
Web www.atisrealweatheralls.com
Direct tel 020 7338 4351
Direct fax 020 7925 0340
Mobile 07721 892959
Email
mark.wills-williams@atisrealweatheralls.com

WILLSON, Stephen
SJ Berwin
Position
Partner – real estate
Career history
Since 1982 Partner, SJ Berwin.
1971 Admitted to Roll of Solicitors.
1967-82 Burton & Ramsden: partner from 1972
Professional memberships
Law Society
Interests
Squash; tennis; RAC
Contact details
SJ Berwin, 222 Gray's Inn Road, London WC1X 8HB
Tel 020 7533 2222
Fax 020 7533 2000
Web www.sjberwin.com
Direct tel 020 7533 2255
Email stephen.willson@sjberwin.com

WILMOT, David
Frogmore Estates
Position
Finance director
Qualifications
FCA
Other roles
Director, Frogmore Developments; director, Frogmore Investments
Contact details
Frogmore Estates Ltd, 11-15 Wigmore Street, London W1A 2JZ
Tel 020 7016 6000
Fax 020 7495 5321

Web www.frogmore.co.uk
Email davidwilmot@frogmore.co.uk

WILSON, Alex
Legal & General Investment Management

Position
Director – external clients property funds
Contact details
Legal & General Investment Management Ltd, Bucklersbury House, Walbrook, London EC4N 8EL
Tel 020 7528 6500
Fax 020 7528 6848
Web www.legal-and-general.co.uk
Email alex.wilson@lgim.co.uk

WILSON, Alistair
Fyfe Ireland WS

Position
Senior partner
Qualifications
LLB; WS; NP
Career history
1968 Joined Fyfe Ireland WS; appointed partner in 1971 and senior partner in 2000
Interests
Fishing; hill walking
Contact details
Fyfe Ireland WS, Orchard Brae House, 30 Queensferry Road, Edinburgh EH4 2HG
Tel 0131 343 2500
Fax 0131 343 3166
Web www.fyfeireland.com
Direct tel 0131 315 8158
Email awilson@fyfeireland.com

WILSON, Andrew
Rugby Estates

Position
Managing director
Qualifications
BSc, Est Man; FRICS
Career history
Since 1987 Managing director, Rugby Estates.
1983-87 Chief surveyor, Royal Insurance.
1978-83 Associate/partner, James Abbot Partnership
Professional memberships
RICS
Contact details
Rugby Estates plc, 14 Garrick Street, London WC2E 9SB
Tel 020 7632 2200
Fax 020 7632 2222
Web www.rugbyestates.plc.uk
Email andrew@rugbyestates.plc.uk

WILSON, Christopher
9 Gough Square

Position
Barrister
Qualifications
LLB
Career history
1980 Called to Bar
Other roles
Recorder (2003)
Professional memberships
London Common Law & Commercial Bar Association
Interests
Photography; wine
Contact details
9 Gough Square (Chambers of John Foy QC), London EC4A 3DE
Tel 020 7832 0500
Fax 020 7353 1344
Web www.9goughsquare.co.uk
Email cwilson@9goughsquare.co.uk

WILSON, Christopher
GE Capital

Position
Director – business development
Qualifications
CFA; MBA, Finance; BSc, Business & Econ; CPA
Career history
1996 Joined GE Capital Markets Services as vice-president (securitisation); became director of debt products and capital markets at GE Capital Real Estate Europe in 1998; appointed director (business development) of GE Capital in 2000.
1993-96 Manager (risk management consulting), Ernst & Young
Professional memberships
American Institute of Certified Public Accountants; Association of Investment Management & Research; New York Society of Securities Analysts
Contact details
GE Capital Ltd, Clarges House, 6-12 Clarges Street, London W1J 8DH
Tel 020 7302 6000
Fax 020 7302 6830
Web www.gecapital.com
Direct tel 020 7302 6255
Mobile 07901 510430
Email christopher.wilson@gecapital.com

WILSON, Colin
DTZ Debenham Tie Leung

Position
Director
Contact details
DTZ Debenham Tie Leung, 1 Curzon Street, London W1A 5PZ
Tel 020 7408 1161
Fax 020 7643 6000
Web www.dtz.com
Email colin.wilson@dtz.com

WILSON, David
Wilson Bowden

Position
Chairman
Contact details
Wilson Bowden plc, Wilson Bowden House, Leicester Road, Ibstock LE67 6WB
Tel 01530 260777
Fax 01530 262805
Web www.wilsonbowden.plc.uk
Email cpheasant@wilsonbowden.plc.uk

WILSON, Guy
Catalyst Capital

Position
Director – acquisitions
Qualifications
MRICS
Career history
Since 1998 Senior asset manager, Greenwich Group (now Catalyst Capital).
1994-98 Insignia Richard Ellis.
1994 Negotiator, Churston Heard
Professional memberships
RICS
Interests
Cricket; rugby; sport; tennis; windsurfing
Contact details
Catalyst Capital LLP, 33 Cavendish Square, London W1G 0PW
Tel 020 7290 5100
Fax 020 7290 5115
Web www.catalystcapital.com
Email gwilson@catalystcapital.co.uk

WILSON, Jeremy
GVA Grimley

Position
Partner
Qualifications
MA; MSc; FRICS; MRTPI
Career history
1983 Joined GVA Grimley as planning and development consultancy surveyor; appointed partner in 1987 and equity partner in 1991; now partner in charge of advisory services to education sector
Professional memberships
RICS; RTPI
Contact details

GVA Grimley, 10 Stratton Street, London W1J 8JR
Tel 0870 900 8990
Fax 020 7911 2560
Web www.gvagrimley.co.uk
Direct tel 020 7911 2422
Mobile 07774 483353
Email jeremy.wilson@gvagrimley.co.uk

WILSON, John
Britannic Asset Management
Position
Head of property
Qualifications
BSc; MRICS
Career history
Since 1991 Head of property, Britannic Asset Management.
1984-91 Scottish Amicable Investment Managers: investment surveyor, then fund manager from 1989.
1981-84 Estates surveyor, Strathclyde Regional Council
Professional memberships
Investment Property Forum; RICS
Interests
Golf; tennis
Contact details
Britannic Asset Management Ltd, Britannic Court, 50 Bothwell Street, Glasgow G2 6HR
Tel 0141 222 8000
Web www.britannicasset.com
Direct tel 0141 222 8015
Direct fax 0141 222 8315
Email jwilson@britannicasset.com

WILSON, Mickola
Teesland
Position
Joint chief executive
Qualifications
BSc Hons, Est Man; FRICS
Career history
Since 2002 Joint chief executive, Teesland.
2000-02 Managing director (fund management division), MWB.
1977-2000 Guardian Properties: director from 1989 and managing director from 1997.
1975-76 District Valuer/Valuation Office, Southwark
Professional memberships
BPF; Investment Property Forum; RICS; Worshipful Company of Chartered Surveyors
Interests
Cooking; horse riding; reading; skiing; tennis
Contact details
Teesland plc, 10 Carlos Place, London W1K 3AT
Tel 020 7493 4636
Fax 020 7493 4637
Web www.teesland.com
Email mickola.wilson@teesland.com

WILSON, Nigel
Maxwell Batley
Position
Partner – property and construction
Qualifications
BA Hons, Business Law
Career history
1982 Joined Maxwell Batley; appointed partner in 1984 and head of property and construction group in 1999.
1976-82 Richards Butler.
1976 Admitted to Roll of Solicitors
Professional memberships
British Council of Shopping Centres; BPF; City of London Solicitors Company; Investment Property Forum; Law Society
Contact details
Maxwell Batley, 27 Chancery Lane, London WC2A 1PA
Tel 020 7440 4400
Fax 020 7440 4444
Web www.maxwellbatley.com
Email nwilson@maxwellbatley.com

WILSON, Peter
Helaba (Landesbank Hessen-Thüringen)
Position
Director – property finance
Career history
1998-2000 Head of commercial property finance, Halifax.
1985-98 Senior manager (property finance), Hongkong Bank.
1979-85 Manager (property lending), Johnson Matthey.
1976-79 Barclays Bank
Contact details
Helaba (Landesbank Hessen-Thüringen), 11 Ironmonger Lane, London EC2V 8JN
Tel 020 7334 4500
Fax 020 7334 4534
Web www.helaba.de
Direct tel 020 7334 4556
Email peter.wilson@helaba.de

WILSON, Robert
HBSV
Position
Director
Qualifications
FRICS; IRRV
Other roles
Trustee, Incorporated Association for the General Welfare of the Blind
Professional memberships
Institute of Revenues Rating & Valuation; RICS
Interests
Sailing
Contact details
HBSV, Portland House, 4 Great Portland Street, London W1W 8QJ
Tel 020 7907 4500
Fax 020 7907 4501
Mobile 07774 417231
Email robert.wilson@hbsv.com

WILSON, Simon
Dalgleish
Position
Out-of-town director
Contact details
Dalgleish, 80 New Bond Street, London W1S 1DD
Tel 020 7663 5555
Fax 020 7491 0098
Web www.dalgleish.co.uk
Direct tel 020 7663 5525
Direct fax 020 7663 5502
Email swilson@dalgleish.co.uk

WINDSOR, Emily
Falcon Chambers
Position
Barrister
Qualifications
MA (Oxon); MA; DSU, European Law
Career history
Since 1997 Barrister, Falcon Chambers.
1995 Called to Bar
Professional memberships
Agricultural Law Association; Chancery Bar Association; London Common Law & Commercial Bar Association; Property Bar Association
Contact details
Falcon Chambers, Falcon Court, London EC4Y 1AA
Tel 020 7353 2484
Fax 020 7353 1261
Web www.falcon-chambers.com
Email windsor@falcon-chambers.com

WINSLOW, Simon
Aberdeen Property Investors
Position
Director – asset management
Contact details
Aberdeen Property Investors, Charles House, 5-11 Regent Street, London SW1Y 4LR
Tel 020 7747 1700

W

Fax 020 7839 7460
Web www.aberdeenpropertyinvestors.com
Email simon.winslow@aberdeenpropertyinvestors.com

WINTER, Jeremy
Baker & McKenzie

Position
Partner and manager of construction department
Contact details
Baker & McKenzie, 100 New Bridge Street, London EC4V 6JA
Tel 0207 919 1000
Fax 020 7919 1999
Web www.bakernet.com
Email jeremy.winter@bakernet.com

WISE, David
Morley Fund Management

Position
Property investment director
Qualifications
BSc Hons ; MRICS
Career history
1986 Joined Commercial Union; following merger of Norwich Union and CGU, appointed head of the Commercial Union and General Accident life funds; now property investment director, Morley Fund Management
Other roles
Member, BPF/ODPM working party on commercial property lease code; director of numerous Morley-owned companies
Contact details
Morley Fund Management Ltd, 34-36 Lime Street, London EC3M 7JE
Tel 020 7809 6000
Fax 020 7489 7940
Web www.morleyfm.com
Email david.wise@morleyfm.com

WOLFE, Stephen
Strutt & Parker

Position
Partner – head of landlord and tenant, London
Qualifications
BSc; MRICS; IRRV
Career history
1989 Joined Strutt & Parker.
1986-89 Black Horse Agencies
Other roles
Seconded as group property director to United Business Media (1996-2002)
Professional memberships
Institute of Revenues Rating & Valuation; RICS
Interests
Cars; golf; tennis; travel
Contact details
Strutt & Parker, 13 Hill Street, London W1J 5LQ
Tel 020 7629 7282
Fax 020 7629 0387
Web www.struttandparker.com
Direct tel 020 7318 5081
Direct fax 020 7499 7341
Mobile 07831 470983
Email swolfe@struttandparker.com

WOLLENBERG, Richard
Cardiff Property

Position
Chairman
Career history
1980 Joined Cardiff Property; has been actively involved in corporate acquisitions, mergers and capital reorganisations of public and private companies
Other roles
Non-executive director, Celltalk Group and General Industries; investment consultant, Brown Shipley Stockbroking (1981-96)
Contact details
Cardiff Property plc, 56 Station Road, Egham TW20 9LF
Tel 01784 437444
Fax 01784 439157
Web www.cardiff-property.com
Email webmaster@cardiff-property.com

WOMACK, Ian
Morley Fund Management

Position
Managing director – property
Qualifications
BSc Hons; FRICS
Career history
1993 Joined Norwich Union Investment Management as property management director; appointed property director in 1998; managing director (property), Morley Fund Management since 2000
Other roles
Board member, Investment Property Forum; board member, British Council for Offices; general council member, BPF
Professional memberships
British Council of Shopping Centres; RICS
Interests
Aviation (private pilot); family; sailing; skiing
Contact details
Morley Fund Management Ltd, 34-36 Lime Street, London EC3M 7JE
Tel 020 7809 6000
Fax 020 7489 7940
Web www.morleyfm.com
Direct tel 020 7809 6800
Direct fax 020 7332 9104
Mobile 07860 208942
Email ian.womack@morleyfm.com

WONNACOTT, Mark
Maitland Chambers

Position
Barrister
Qualifications
LLB (Lond); Barrister
Career history
1989 Called to Bar
Professional memberships
Chancery Bar Association; Professional Negligence Bar Association
Contact details
Maitland Chambers, 7 Stone Buildings, London WC2A 3SZ
Tel 020 7406 1200
Fax 020 7406 1300
Web www.maitlandchambers.com
Email mwonnacott@maitlandchambers.com

WONNACOTT, Peter
Dron & Wright

Position
Senior partner
Qualifications
FRICS
Career history
1987 Joined Dron & Wright.
1979-87 Robert Fleming & Co.
1973-79 Friends Provident Life Office
Professional memberships
RICS; Worshipful Company of Chartered Surveyors
Contact details
Dron & Wright, Bankside House, 107-112 Leadenhall Street, London EC3A 4AQ
Tel 020 7891 2345
Fax 020 7891 2300
Web www.dronwright.co.uk
Direct tel 020 7891 2301
Mobile 07867 982540
Email peterwonnacott@dronwright.co.uk

WOOD, Christopher
Edward Symmons & Partners

Position
Partner
Career history
1976 Joined Edward Symmons & Partners.
1974-76 Gerald Eve
Professional memberships

Non-Administrative Receivers Association; RICS
Interests
Outdoor pursuits; rugby; sailing
Contact details
Edward Symmons & Partners, 2 Southwark Street, London SE1 1RQ
Tel 020 7955 8454
Fax 020 7407 6423
Web www.edwardsymmons.com
Email christopher.wood@edwardsymmons.com

WOOD, David
Bevan Ashford
Position
Partner – regulatory department
Career history
Since 1988 Partner, Bevan Ashford.
1976-88 Partner, Harris & Harris.
1969-76 Hatten Jewers & Mepham
Interests
Cricket; music; theatre; walking
Contact details
Bevan Ashford, 35 Colston Avenue, Bristol BS1 4TT
Tel 0117 923 0111
Fax 0117 929 1865
Web www.bevanashford.co.uk
Email david.wood@bevanashford.co.uk

WOOD, Gordon
Dexter Wood & Partners
Position
Managing director
Qualifications
MA (Cantab); FRICS
Career history
1995-2003 Investment director, Catella UK.
1993-95 Director in charge of in-house funds, Colliers Erdman Lewis.
1977-92 Investment partner, Clive Lewis & Partners
Other roles
Chairman of National Surveyors Rugby Sevens committee
Professional memberships
Investment Property Forum; RICS
Interests
Cricket; golf; rugby; skiing; tennis
Contact details
Dexter Wood & Partners, 15 Berkeley Street, London W1J 8DY
Tel 020 7355 0950
Fax 020 7355 0955
Direct tel 020 7355 0940
Email gordon.wood@dexterwood.co.uk

WOOD, Graeme
Knight Frank
Position
Partner
Qualifications
BSc Hons; MRICS
Career history
Since 1999 Partner, Knight Frank.
1993-99 Partner, King Sturge & Co.
1988-93 Associate/partner, Chesterton
Professional memberships
British Council for Offices; Office Agents Society; RICS
Interests
Football; golf
Contact details
Knight Frank LLP, 86 King Street, Manchester M2 4WQ
Tel 0161 833 0023
Fax 0161 832 1478
Web www.knightfrank.com
Email graeme.wood@knightfrank.com

WOOD, Graham
Virgin Retail
Position
Head of property
Contact details
Virgin Retail Ltd, The School House, 50 Brook Green, London W6 7RR
Tel 020 8752 9000
Web www.virgin.com
Email graham.wood@virginmega.co.uk

WOOD, John
Cluttons
Position
Partner – telecoms, infrastructure and utilities
Qualifications
BSc (Hons); MRICS
Career history
1996 Joined Daniel Smith (merged with Cluttons in 1997); appointed partner in 2000.
1992-96 Healey & Baker.
1991-92 Valuation Office Agency.
1989-90 Gerald Eve
Other roles
Member of Cluttons' CEO working party on rating of telecommunications sites
Professional memberships
RICS
Interests
Golf; history; theatre
Contact details
Cluttons, Portman House, 2 Portman Street, London W1H 6DU
Tel 020 7408 1010
Fax 020 7629 3263
Web www.cluttons.com
Direct tel 020 7647 7232
Mobile 07919 926095
Email jwood@cluttons.com

WOOD, Philip
Harvey Spack Field
Position
Partner – head of professional department
Qualifications
BA Hons; FRICS; ACIArb
Professional memberships
Chartered Institute of Arbitrators; RICS
Contact details
Harvey Spack Field, 33 Bruton Street, London W1J 6QU
Tel 020 7629 9663
Fax 020 7491 1964
Web www.harveyspackfield.co.uk
Direct tel 020 7518 0471
Mobile 07774 703526
Email wood@harveyspackfield.co.uk

WOOD, Ralph
AXA Real Estate Investment Managers
Position
Strategic manager
Contact details
AXA Real Estate Investment Managers Ltd, 7 Newgate Street, London EC1A 7HD
Tel 020 7003 1000
Fax 020 7575 8585
Web www.axa-im.co.uk
Direct tel 020 7367 8122
Email ralph.wood@axa-reim.co.uk

WOOD, Simon
Premier Hotels
Position
Group property director
Contact details
Premier Hotels Ltd, Station House, 4-8 High Street, London UB7 7DJ
Tel 0870 444 5545
Email SimonWood@PremierHotels.co.uk

WOODBURN, Andy
Edwin Hill
Position
Partner
Qualifications
BSc; FRICS; MCIArb; MEWI
Professional memberships
Chartered Institute of Arbitrators; Expert Witness Institute; RICS
Interests

Golf

Contact details

Edwin Hill, 18 Savile Row, London W1S 3PW
Tel 020 7287 2020
Fax 020 7734 1255
Web www.edwinhill.co.uk
Email aw@edwinhill.co.uk

WOODBURN, James
Edwin Hill

Position
Managing partner
Qualifications
BSc; FRICS; IRRV
Career history
Since 1987 Partner/managing partner, Edwin Hill.
1982-86 Associate partner, Richard Ellis.
1975-82 Senior valuer, Inland Revenue Valuation Office
Professional memberships
RICS
Contact details
Edwin Hill, 18 Savile Row, London W1S 3PW
Tel 020 7287 2020
Fax 020 7734 1255
Web www.edwinhill.co.uk
Email jw@edwinhill.co.uk

WOODS, Andrew
Commercial Estates Management

Position
Investment director
Career history
1988-91 Nelson Bakewell.
1985-88 Conrad Ritblat
Contact details
Commercial Estates Management Ltd, Plaza 535, Kings Road, London SW10 0SZ
Tel 020 7376 4601
Fax 020 7823 3246
Mobile 07774 483905
Email andy@c-e-m.co.uk

WOODS, Ian
Kier Property

Position
Finance director
Qualifications
FCA
Career history
1992 Joined Kier Property
Professional memberships
Institute of Chartered Accountants in England & Wales
Contact details
Kier Property Ltd, Berkeley Square House, Berkeley Square, London W1J 6BD
Tel 020 7887 6200
Fax 020 7887 6299
Web www.kier.co.uk
Direct tel 020 7887 6275
Mobile 07776 226385
Email ian.woods@kier.co.uk

WOOKEY, Paul
Locate in Kent

Position
Chief executive
Contact details
Locate in Kent, 2 Kings Hill Avenue, West Malling ME19 4AQ
Tel 01732 520700
Fax 01732 520701
Direct tel 01732 520706
Mobile 07860 937386
Email paulw@locateinkent.com

WOOLF, David
Citygrove Leisure

Position
Executive chairman
Qualifications
FCA
Career history
1971-90 Chairman and chief executive, Citygrove.
1969-71 Corob Holdings
Other roles
Co-chair, British ORT
Professional memberships
Institute of Chartered Accountants in England & Wales
Interests
Opera; sailing; tennis
Contact details
Citygrove Leisure Ltd, Mill House, 216 Chiswick High Road, London W4 1PD
Tel 08700 601123
Fax 08700 601124
Web www.citygrove.com
Email davidwoolf@uk.citygrove.com

WOOLLARD, Grant
GL Hearn

Position
Director – head of retail
Qualifications
MRICS; BSc Hons, Land Admin
Career history
1987 Joined GL Hearn; became associate partner in 1992 and retail director in 1999; director (head of retail) since 2002
Professional memberships
RICS
Interests
Fishing; golf; travel
Contact details
GL Hearn Ltd, Sutherland House, 5-6 Argyll Street, London W1F 7TE
Tel 020 7287 7800
Fax 020 7287 4867
Web www.glhearn.com
Mobile 07901 517941
Email grant_woollard@glhearn.com

WOOLLASTON, Howard
Knight Frank

Position
Partner – head of professional services group
Qualifications
BSc; FRICS
Career history
1975 Joined Knight Frank
Professional memberships
RICS; Worshipful Company of Chartered Surveyors
Contact details
Knight Frank LLP, 20 Hanover Square, London W1S 1HZ
Tel 020 7629 8171
Fax 020 7493 4114
Web www.knightfrank.com
Direct tel 020 7861 1140
Direct fax 020 7409 7134
Mobile 07836 718100
Email howard.woollaston@knightfrank.com

WOOLLER, Simon
Land Securities Trillium

Position
Managing director – corporate real estate group
Qualifications
MRICS; BSc Hons; Dip Arb
Professional memberships
RICS
Contact details
Land Securities Trillium Ltd, 140 London Wall, London EC2Y 5DN
Tel 020 7796 5500
Fax 020 7796 5501
Web www.landsecurities.co.uk
Direct tel 020 7796 5660
Direct fax 0845 090 2392
Email simon.wooller@lstrillium.com

WOOLLEY, David
Landmark Chambers

Position
Barrister
Qualifications

QC

Career history

1980 Appointed QC.
1962 Called to Bar

Other roles

Author of numerous articles for professional journals; holds lectures and seminars; visiting scholar at Wolfson College, Cambridge, while also giving lectures at the university (1985-90); author, *The Town Hall & the Property Owner* (Methuen, 1967); co-author (with other members of chambers), *Environmental Law* (Oxford University Press, 2001)

Interests

Horse riding; IT; literature; opera

Contact details

Landmark Chambers, 4 Breams Buildings, London EC4A 1AQ
Tel 020 7430 1221
Fax 020 7421 1399
Web www.landmarkchambers.co.uk
Email clerks@landmarkchambers.co.uk

WOOLLEY, Peter
Freeport

Position

Finance director

Contact details

Freeport plc, 9-13 George Street, London W1U 3FL
Tel 020 7299 9360
Fax 020 7299 9388
Web www.freeportplc.com
Email peterwoolley@freeportleisure.com

WOOLLEY, Roger
Lester Aldridge

Position

Managing partner

Qualifications

LLB Hons

Other roles

President, Dorset Chamber of Commerce & Industry

Contact details

Lester Aldridge, Russell House, Oxford Road, Bournemouth BH8 8EX
Tel 01202 786161
Fax 01202 786150
Web www.lesteraldridge.com
Direct tel 01202 786158
Email Roger.Woolley@la-law.com

WOOLNER, Nigel
Chapman Taylor

Position

Board director

Qualifications

Dip Arch; RIBA; FRSA

Other roles

British Council of Shopping Centres urban task force committee member and chairman of BCSC Awards panel; council member of Royal Society of Arts and chairman of RSA House panel; examiner in professional practice, Architectural Association; chairman of estates committee, Royal College of Music; governor, Latymer Upper School

Professional memberships

RIBA

Interests

Opera; painting; theatre

Contact details

Chapman Taylor LLP, MacMillan House, 96 Kensington High Street, London W8 4SG
Tel 020 7371 3000
Fax 020 7371 1949
Web www.chapmantaylor.com
Email nwoolner@chapmantaylor.com

WORBOYS, Ian
Gazeley Properties

Position

Director-general, France and Belgium

Qualifications

FRICS

Career history

1978-97 Strutt & Parker: divisional partner (national office agency) from 1981.
1977-78 Idris Jones & Partners

Other roles

Development of Gazeley's European expansion

Professional memberships

Industrial Agents Society; RICS

Interests

Family; football; golf; rugby; sailing; skiing

Contact details

Gazeley Properties Ltd, Gazeley House, 26 Rockingham Drive, Milton Keynes MK14 6PD
Tel 01908 838100
Fax 01908 838101
Web www.gazeley.com
Direct tel 01908 838161
Mobile 07710 006470
Email ian_worboys@gazeley.com

WORLEY, Mike
Bayerische Landesbank

Position

Head of property finance

Qualifications

BSc

Career history

Since 1999 Head of property finance, Bayerische Landesbank.
1998-99 Marketing director, Eurohypo.
1995-97 Assistant general manager, Sumitomo Trust & Banking Co.
1993-94 Managing director, Yelrow.
1986-92 Assistant general manager, Sumitomo Trust & Banking Co

Professional memberships

Association of Property Bankers

Interests

Rowing

Contact details

Bayerische Landesbank, Bavaria House, 13-14 Appold Street, London EC2A 2NB
Tel 020 7247 0056
Direct tel 020 7955 5701
Direct fax 020 7955 5700
Mobile 07956 322076
Email mike.worley@bayernlb.co.uk

WORTHINGTON, Rebecca
Quintain Estates & Development

Position

Finance director

Contact details

Quintain Estates & Development plc, 58 Davies Street, London W1K 5JF
Tel 020 7495 8968
Fax 020 7499 5583
Web www.quintain-estates.com
Email
rebecca.worthington@quintain-estates.com

WORTHINGTON, Robin
Cadbury Schweppes

Position

Head of group property

Qualifications

FRICS

Career history

1997-2000 Head of estates, Marston's Brewery, Burton-on-Trent.
1993-97 Self-employed consultant, trading as Appreciating Property Matters, London.
1986-92 Director, Grand Metropolitan Estates.
1984-86 Regional director, Carter Commercial Developments.
1977-84 Estate manager, Bass Charrington, London.
1970-77 Charles F Jones & Son, Rhyl and later London

Other roles

Member, CBI property group

Professional memberships

Association of Corporate Real Estate

Interests

Music; squash

Contact details

Cadbury Schweppes plc, 25 Berkeley Square, London W1J 6HB
Tel 020 7409 1313
Fax 020 7830 5200
Web www.cadburyschweppes.com
Email robin.worthington@csplc.com

WORTHINGTON, Stephen
12 King's Bench Walk Chambers

Position
Barrister

Contact details
12 King's Bench Walk Chambers, 12 King's Bench Walk, London EC4Y 7EL
Tel 020 7583 0811
Fax 020 7583 7228
Web www.12kbw.co.uk
Email worthington@12kbw.co.uk

WRATHER, Stephen
Mason Owen & Partners

Position
Partner – retail agency

Qualifications
BSc Hons; MRICS

Career history
1999-2001 Retail consultant, Ian Scott & Co.
1992-99 Associate partner, Mason Owen & Partners.
1990-92 Savills Commercial

Professional memberships
RICS

Interests
Diving/scuba diving; golf; sailing; yachting

Contact details
Mason Owen & Partners Ltd, 46 James Street, London W1U 1EZ
Tel 020 7224 4141
Fax 020 7224 4121
Web www.masonowen.com
Mobile 07770 855813
Email stephen.wrather@masonowen.com

WRAY, Paul
Hermes Property Asset Management

Position
Portfolio manager – retail

Qualifications
MRICS

Contact details
Hermes Property Asset Management Ltd, Lloyds Chambers, 1 Portsoken Street, London E1 8HZ
Tel 020 7702 0888
Fax 020 7702 9453
Web www.hermes.co.uk
Direct tel 020 7680 2226
Direct fax 020 7680 2577
Email p.wray@hermes.co.uk

WRAY, Stephen
Bristol City Council

Position
Director of environment, transport and leisure

Contact details
Bristol City Council, St George's Road, Bristol BS1 5UY
Tel 0117 922 2000
Web www.bristol-city.gov.uk
Direct tel 0117 922 2632
Email stephen_wray@bristol-city.gov.uk

WRAY, Tim
Turner & Townsend Group

Position
Group chairman

Contact details
Turner & Townsend Group Ltd, Low Hall, Caverley Lane, Leeds LS18 4GH
Tel 0113 258 4400
Fax 0113 258 2911
Web www.turnerandtownsend.com
Email twray@turntown.co.uk

WRIGHT, Carol
Property Market Analysis

Position
Senior partner

Qualifications
BSc Hons

Professional memberships
British Council of Shopping Centres; Royal Society of Arts; Society of Property Researchers

Contact details
Property Market Analysis LLP, 2 Lygon Place, London SW1W 0JR
Tel 020 7881 0300
Fax 020 7881 0400
Web www.pma.co.uk
Direct tel 020 7881 0345
Email carol.wright@pma.co.uk

WRIGHT, Geoffrey
Hammerson UK Properties

Position
Director – project management

Contact details
Hammerson UK Properties plc, 100 Park Lane, London W1K 7AR
Tel 020 7887 1000
Fax 020 7887 1090
Web www.hammerson.co.uk
Email gwright@hammerson.co.uk

WRIGHT, Liz
Majestic Wine Warehouse

Position
Property director

Contact details
Majestic Wine Warehouse, Majestic House, Otterspool Way, Watford WD25 8WW
Tel 01923 298200
Web www.majestic.co.uk
Direct tel 01923 298230
Mobile 07901 856736
Email lwright@majestic.co.uk

WRIGHT, Mark
British Land Developments

Position
Head of London development

Contact details
British Land Developments Ltd, 10 Cornwall Terrace, London NW1 4QP
Tel 020 7486 4466
Fax 020 7935 5552
Web www.britishland.com
Email mark.wright@britishland.com

WRIGHT, Simon
Virgin Retail

Position
Finance and property director

Contact details
Virgin Retail Ltd, 120 Campden Hill Road, London W8 7AR
Tel 020 7229 1282
Web www.virgin.com
Email simon.wright@virginmega.co.uk

WRIGHT, Tom
WS Atkins

Position
Design director

Qualifications
BA Hons; Dip Arch; RIBA

Professional memberships
RIBA

Contact details
WS Atkins plc, Woodcote Grove, Ashley Road, Epsom KT18 5BW
Tel 01372 726140
Fax 01372 740055
Web www.wsatkins.com
Direct tel 01372 752064
Email tom.wright@atkinsglobal.com

WRIGLEY, William
Dunlop Heywood Lorenz

Position
Director

Qualifications
FRICS; MCIArb
Career history
1972 Joined Dunlop Heywood (now Dunlop Heywood Lorenz).
1970-72 Rural estates surveyor, Manchester City Council.
1965-70 Cordingleys
Other roles
External examiner, Liverpool John Moores University
Professional memberships
Arbrix; Chartered Institute of Arbitrators; Manchester Society of Land Agents & Surveyors; Non-Administrative Receivers Association; RICS
Interests
Golf
Contact details
Dunlop Heywood Lorenz Ltd, Abbey House, 32 Booth Street, Manchester M2 4QP
Tel 0161 237 7777
Fax 0161 237 7778
Web www.dhlproperty.co.uk
Email wsw@dhlproperty.co.uk

WYATT, Adrian
Quintain Estates & Development
Position
Chairman and chief executive
Qualifications
FRICS; ASIP
Career history
1971-92 Partner, Jones Lang Wootton.
1969-71 MEPC
Professional memberships
RICS; Society of Investment Professionals
Contact details
Quintain Estates & Development plc, 58 Davies Street, London W1K 5JF
Tel 020 7495 8968
Fax 020 7499 5583
Web www.quintain-estates.com
Email kathleen.finnegan@quintain-estates.com

WYATT, Colin
Gardiner & Theobald
Position
Senior partner
Qualifications
FRICS
Career history
1968 Joined Gardiner & Theobald.
1966-68 MK Boyden & Co.
1963-65 VJ Mendoza.
1959-63 Brown & Biddis
Professional memberships
Major Projects Association; RICS
Interests
Boating; photography; rugby; sailing; tennis; theatre; water sports; windsurfing
Contact details
Gardiner & Theobald, 32 Bedford Square, London WC1B 3JT
Tel 020 7209 3000
Fax 020 7209 1840
Web www.gardiner.com
Direct fax 020 7209 1843
Email c.wyatt@gardiner.com

WYLIE, Matthew
EDS International
Position
EMEA strategy and real estate manager
Qualifications
MBA; BSc Hons
Professional memberships
Association of MBAs; RICS
Contact details
EDS International, 4 Roundwood Avenue, London UB11 1BQ
Tel 020 8848 8989
Fax 020 8756 0130
Direct fax 020 535 3006
Mobile 07790 490814
Email matthew.wylie@eds.com

WYMER, Patrick
Laura Ashley
Position
Head of property and facilities
Contact details
Laura Ashley Ltd, 27 Bagleys Lane, London SW6 2AR
Tel 020 7880 5100
Fax 020 7880 5200
Web www.lauraashley.com
Email patrick.wymer@lauraashley.com

WYTHE, John
Prudential Property Investment Managers
Position
Director – fund management
Qualifications
BSc Hons; FRICS
Career history
1978 Joined Prudential; now director of fund management and head of internal funds
Professional memberships
Investment Property Forum; RICS
Contact details
Prudential Property Investment Managers Ltd, Princeton House, 271-273 High Holborn, London WC1V 7NE
Tel 020 7548 6600
Fax 020 7548 6999
Web www.prupim.com
Direct tel 020 7548 6574
Direct fax 020 7548 6502
Email john.wythe@prupim.com

Y

YARDLEY, Gary
King Sturge Financial Services

Position
Managing director
Qualifications
BSc; MBA; MRICS
Contact details
King Sturge Financial Services Ltd, 7 Stratford Place, London W1C 1ST
Tel 020 7493 4933
Fax 020 7409 0469
Web www.kingsturge.com
Direct tel 020 7318 4227
Email garyyardley@kingsturge.co.uk

YARNOLD, Stephen
Harvey Spack Field

Position
Partner
Qualifications
BSc, Est Man; FRICS
Contact details
Harvey Spack Field, 33 Bruton Street, London W1J 6QU
Tel 020 7629 9663
Fax 020 7491 1964
Web www.harveyspackfield.co.uk
Direct tel 020 7518 0458
Mobile 07774 188262
Email yarnold@harveyspackfield.co.uk

YATES, Stephen
AXA Real Estate Investment Managers

Position
Asset manager
Contact details
AXA Real Estate Investment Managers Ltd, 7 Newgate Street, London EC1A 7HD
Tel 020 7003 1000
Fax 020 7575 8585
Web www.axa-im.co.uk
Direct tel 020 7367 8123
Email stephen.yates@axa-reim.co.uk

YATES, Tim
Cooltrader

Position
Group property director
Contact details
Cooltrader Ltd, 5 Castle Street, Liverpool L2 4XE

YEANDLE, Andrew
Strutt & Parker

Position
Central London investment partner, London
Qualifications
BSc; MRICS
Professional memberships
RICS
Contact details
Strutt & Parker, 13 Hill Street, London W1J 5LQ
Tel 020 7629 7282
Fax 020 7629 0387
Web www.struttandparker.com
Direct tel 020 7318 5016
Direct fax 020 7499 1269
Mobile 07768 361925
Email ayeandle@struttandparker.com

YEARLEY, Paul
Jones Lang LaSalle

Position
Managing director – corporate property services
Contact details
Jones Lang LaSalle Ltd, 22 Hanover Square, London W1A 2BN
Tel 020 7493 6040
Fax 020 7408 0220
Web www.joneslanglasalle.com
Direct tel 020 7399 5356
Direct fax 020 7399 5776
Email paul.yearley@eu.joneslanglasalle.com

YEWMAN, Steve
Minerva

Position
Director – acquisitions
Contact details
Minerva plc, 42 Wigmore Street, London W1U 2RY
Tel 020 7535 1000
Fax 020 7535 1001
Email syewman@minervaplc.co.uk

YIANNAKIS, Anthony
Catalyst Capital

Position
Investment director
Qualifications
MRICS
Career history
Since 1994 Investment director, Catalyst Capital.
1988-94 Associate director, Colliers Stewart Newiss.
1985-88 Property Services Agency
Professional memberships
RICS
Interests
Aviation; skiing
Contact details
Catalyst Capital LLP, 33 Cavendish Square, London W1G 0PW
Tel 020 7290 5100
Fax 020 7290 5115
Web www.catalystcapital.com
Email ayiannakis@catalystcapital.co.uk

YOUNG, Anthony
Transport Development Group

Position
Group property adviser
Qualifications
FRICS
Career history
1977-82 Regional surveyor, Grand Metropolitan.
1975-77 WH Smith.
1972-75 Grimley
Professional memberships
RICS;
Contact details
Transport Development Group Ltd, 25 Victoria Street, London SW1H 0EX
Tel 020 7222 7411
Fax 020 7222 2806
Web www.tdg.com
Email youngt2@tdg.co.uk

YOUNG, Richard
Donaldsons

Position
Partner – head of corporate, Birmingham
Qualifications
MRICS
Career history
Since 1984 Partner, Donaldsons.
1978-84 Senior surveyor, Leeds City Council
Professional memberships
RICS
Contact details
Donaldsons, 120 Edmund Street, Birmingham B3 2ED
Tel 0121 212 1090
Fax 0121 212 1099
Web www.donaldsons.co.uk
Direct tel 0121 710 5621

Mobile 07808 479262
Email richard.young@donaldsons.co.uk

YOUNG, Rupert
CB Richard Ellis

Position
Managing director – Birmingham
Qualifications
MRICS
Career history
1987 Joined Hillier Parker (now CB Richard Ellis); became director in charge of Birmingham office and head of investment properties in 2001; managing director in charge of Birmingham office and dealing with invesment and development since 2003.
1986-87 Office development, Donaldsons, London
Professional memberships
RICS;
Interests
Music; reading; rugby; sailing
Contact details
CB Richard Ellis, Embassy House, 60 Church Street, Birmingham B3 2DJ
Tel 0121 609 7666
Fax 0121 609 0121
Web www.cbre.com
Direct tel 0121 609 3378
Mobile 07831 775914
Email rupert.young@cbre.com

YOUNG, Simon
King Sturge

Position
Partner – asset management
Qualifications
MA; MBA; FRICS
Career history
1981 Joined King Sturge
Professional memberships
RICS
Contact details
King Sturge, 7 Stratford Place, London W1C 1ST
Tel 020 7493 4933
Fax 020 7409 0469
Web www.kingsturge.com
Direct tel 020 7318 4234
Direct fax 020 7493 6409
Email simon.young@kingsturge.co.uk

YOUNG, Tim
NAI Fuller Peiser

Position
Head of office agency and development
Qualifications
BA Hons; MRICS
Other roles
Past chairman – office agents society
Professional memberships
RICS
Contact details
NAI Fuller Peiser, 16 St George Street, London W1S 1LX
Tel 0870 700 2233
Fax 020 7491 1961
Web www.nai-fullerpeiser.com
Email tyoung@nai-fullerpeiser.com

Z

ZAKAY, Eddie
Topland Group of Companies

Position
Managing director

Contact details
Topland Group of Companies, Nations House, 103 Wigmore Street, London W1U 1QS
Tel 020 7493 3373
Fax 020 7493 4055
Web www.topland.co.uk
Email eddiez@topland.co.uk

ZAKAY, Sol
Topland Group of Companies

Position
Chairman and chief executive

Contact details
Topland Group of Companies, Nations House, 103 Wigmore Street, London W1U 1QS
Tel 020 7493 3373
Fax 020 7493 4055
Web www.topland.co.uk
Email solz@topland.co.uk

ZEHNER, Jon
JP Morgan

Position
Managing director and global head of real estate

Career history
1981 Joined JP Morgan

Other roles
National Realty committee member (real estate round table operating out of New York); Wharton Real Estate Centre executive committee member

Professional memberships
Association of Foreign Investors in Real Estate; International Council of Shopping Centers; Urban Land Institute

Contact details
JP Morgan plc, 10 Aldermanbury, London EC2V 7RF
Tel 020 7642 4000
Web www.jpmorgan.com
Direct tel 020 7325 9398
Direct fax 020 7325 0580
Email jon.zehner@jpmorgan.com

ZIFF, Arnold
Town Centre Securities

Position
Chairman

Contact details
Town Centre Securities plc, Town Centre House, Merrion Centre, Leeds LS2 8LY
Tel 0113 222 1234
Fax 0113 242 1026
Direct fax 0113 234 0442
Email arnold.ziff@tcs-plc.co.uk

ZIFF, Edward
Town Centre Securities

Position
Chief executive

Career history
1981 Joined Town Centre Securities (family firm); appointed to board in 1985 and served as managing director since 1993; appointed chief executive in 2001

Other roles
Governor of Leeds Grammar School and chairman of school fund-raising group; vice-president of Leeds Jewish Welfare board and chairman of fund-raising committee; trustee of Moor Allerton Golf Club

Interests
Antiques; art; football; golf

Contact details
Town Centre Securities plc, Town Centre House, Merrion Centre, Leeds LS2 8LY
Tel 0113 222 1234
Fax 0113 242 1026
Direct fax 0113 234 0442
Email edward.ziff@tcs-plc.co.uk

ZWART, Christiaan
39 Essex Street

Position
Barrister

Career history
Since 2002 At 39 Essex Street.
1997 Called to Bar

Other roles
Author of built environment chapter, *Civic Appeals* (Emis); case editor, *Environmental Due Diligence & Risk Management* (Emis)

Professional memberships
Environmental Law Foundation; Planning & Environment Bar Association; RIBA

Interests
Architecture; art; cinema; history; swimming

Contact details
39 Essex Street, London WC2R 3AT
Tel 020 7832 1111
Fax 020 7353 3978
Web www.39essex.com
Direct tel 020 7832 1113
Email christiaan.zwart@39essex.com

Index

Company index

Company index

Company index

Company index

Company index

Company index

Company index

Company index

Company index

Company index

Company index

Company index

Company index

Company index

Company index

Company index

Nick Shattock
Rebecca Worthington
Adrian Wyatt

R20
Mark Grunnell
Michael Ingham
Robert Tchenguiz

RADCLIFFESLEBRASSEUR
Colin Dixon
Charles Farrer
Michael Thorniley-Walker
Roger Thornton
Simon Wakefield

RANK GROUP
Gary Dooley
Tony Robinson

RAPLEYS
James Banks
Paul Styles

RAVEN GROUP
Anton John Godfrey Bilton

REALM
Colin Brooks

REDROW COMMERCIAL DEVELOPMENTS
Simon Isherwood

REED ELSEVIER (UK)
Shelagh Pope

REGENT INNS
David Turner

REGUS
Mark Dixon

REID ARCHITECTURE
Ian Kerr
David Stanford

REIT ASSET MANAGEMENT
Kevin McGrath
Leo Noé

REUTERS GROUP
Peter Copley

REYNOLDS PORTER CHAMBERLAIN
David Haywood

RHWL PARTNERSHIP
Geoff Mann
Peter Shaw

RICH INVESTMENTS
Peter Rich

RICHARD ROGERS PARTNERSHIP
Lord Richard Rogers

RICHARDS BUTLER
Andrew Jenkinson
Richard Nicoll
Liz Southorn

RICKERBYS
Robin Beckley

RICS FOUNDATION
Stephen Brown

RICS IN WALES
Cathy McLean

RIVER ISLAND CLOTHING CO
Richard Gee

ROBERT ADAM ARCHITECTS
Robert Adam

ROBERT HITCHINS
David Herbert

ROCK CAPITAL GROUP
Michael Birch

ROGER SQUIRE
Roger Squire

ROGERS CHAPMAN
Philip Daniels
Simon Howell
John Izett
Laurence Johnstone
Mark Lacey
Russell Meadows
Mike Pain
Tom Sommerville

ROK PROPERTY SOLUTIONS
Mark Kay

ROLFE JUDD
Geoffrey Adams

ROLLITS
Martyn Justice

ROSLING KING
Owen Rafferty

ROTCH GROUP
Vincent Tchenguiz

ROTCH PROPERTY GROUP
Paul Taylor

ROYAL BANK OF CANADA TRUST CORP
Henrietta Podd

ROYAL BANK OF SCOTLAND
Suzanne Avery
Kevin Biggs
Joss Brushfield
David Cockerton
Lawrence Cole
Alan Dickinson
Peter Fletcher
Alison Fyfe
Roy Harris
Simon Hersom
Marc Le Borgne
David Lindsay
Derek MacKenzie
Hugh MacNish Porter
Lindsey McMurray
Martin Nicholls
James Raynor
Ernest Sheavills
Ron Thomson
John Wallace

ROYAL INSTITUTION OF CHARTERED SURVEYORS
John 'Louis' Armstrong

ROYAL TOWN PLANNING INSTITUTE
Robert Upton

RUGBY ESTATES
Steve Jones
Neal Taylor
David Tweeddale-Tye
Andrew Wilson

RUSSELL JONES & WALKER
Peter Klim

RUSSELL-COOKE
Stephen Clarke
Peter Dawson
Jim Fairclough
Jason Hunter
Michael Maskey

RUTLAND INVESTMENT MANAGEMENT
Peter Farnfield

RYDEN
Tim Bunker
Ewan Cameron
Ian Dougherty
Bill Duguid
Roy Durie
Matthew Edwards
Charles Guest
William Henderson
Bill Marley
Neil McAllister
Ken McInnes
Fiona Morton
Dr Mark Robertson
Russell Rutherford
Jim Shankland
Ken Shaw
Ford Swanson
David Thomson
David Tough

RYDERHKS
Paul Hyett

SAFELAND
Raymond Lipman
Larry Lipman

SAFEWAY
Fernando Garcia-Valencia
Simon Laffin
Neil Mackenzie

SALMON DEVELOPMENTS
Rorie Henderson
Paul Pollard
Doug Stewart
Paul Stoodley

SANDERSON WEATHERALL
Tim Catterall
John Craig
David Cuthbert

SAVILLS
Rob McKellar

SCARBOROUGH DEVELOPMENT GROUP
Kevin McCabe
Didier Tandy

SCHRODER PROPERTY INVESTMENT MANAGEMENT
Neil Gardiner
William Hill

SCOTT BROWNRIGG & TURNER
Michael Kellard

SCOTTISH & NEWCASTLE
Rodger Crichton
Gordon Izatt

SCOTTISH EXECUTIVE
Anthony Andrew

SCOTTISH POWER
Steven Dickson

SCOTTISH WIDOWS INVESTMENT PARTNERSHIP
Michael Ewing
Gerry Ferguson
Tom Laidlaw
Peter Lillington

SCRUTTON ESTATES
Charles Scrutton
Anne Scrutton

SEA SPACE – HASTINGS & BEXHILL RENAISSANCE
Keith Sadler

SECONDSITE PROPERTY HOLDINGS
Phillip Kirby

SELBORNE CHAMBERS
Romie Tager

SELFRIDGES
Martin Illingworth
Peter Williams

SELLAR PROPERTY GROUP
Irvine Sellar

SEMPLE FRASER
Elspeth Carson

SEPHORA UK
Pierre Fayard
Jérôme Le Grelle

SERLE COURT
Michael Briggs
Ann McAllister

SHAFTESBURY
Brian Bickell
Jonathan Lane
Peter Levy
Simon Quayle
Thomas Welton

SHEARER PROPERTY GROUP
Adam Markwell
Guy Shearer

SHELLEY SANDZER & CO
Duncan Lillie

SHEPHERD + WEDDERBURN
Colin Innes

SHEPPARD ROBSON
Mark Dillon
Tim Evans
Graham Francis
Anthony Furlong
Malcolm McGowan
Paul Watkins

Company index

Company index

Company index